Oxford University Press
Digital Learning
Resources

Patterns of World History with Sources

Volume Two from 1400

FOURTH EDITION

Peter von Sivers
Charles A. Desnoyers
George B. Stow

Carefully scratch off the silver coating to see your personal redemption code.

This code can be redeemed only once.

Once the code has been revealed, this access card cannot be returned to the publisher.

Access can also be purchased online during the registration process.

The code on this card is valid for two years from the date of first purchase. Oxford University Press reserves the right to retire resources following publication of a new edition of this textbook. The access code above will no longer be valid should resources be superseded by a new edition. Complete terms and conditions are available at learninglink.oup.com

Access Length: 180 days from redemption of the code.

Directions for accessing your

Oxford Insight Study Guide and Additional Digital Course Materials

Patterns of World History comes with a wealth of powerful tools to help you succeed in your course.

Follow these steps to access your resources:

Visit oup.com/he/vonsivers4e

Select the edition you are using, then select student resources for that edition

Follow the on-screen instructions, entering your personal redemption code when prompted

For assistance with code redemption or registration, please contact customer support at **learninglinkdirect.support@oup.com**.
or 855-281-8749.

About the Cover

The Canadian photographer Edward Burtynsky's color photographs document the ramifications of human industry on the natural world. Burtynsky intends his work to spark "a second look at what we call progress," which has won him acclaim as an environmental champion as well as an artist. The photograph on the cover, "Salinas #2," shows an aerial view of saltpans near Cadíz, in southern Spain. Salt pans are large flat areas where seawater is pumped and slowly evaporated in man-made basins of increasing salinity to produce sea salt. The interlacing of the estuary with the salt pans powerfully demonstrates patterns of interaction between humans and nature.

Patterns of World History

Patterns of World History

VOLUME TWO from 1400

Fourth Edition

Peter von Sivers
University of Utah

Charles A. Desnoyers
La Salle University

George B. Stow
La Salle University

New York Oxford
OXFORD UNIVERSITY PRESS

Oxford University Press is a department of the University of Oxford.
It furthers the University's objective of excellence in research, scholarship,
and education by publishing worldwide. Oxford is a registered trade mark of
Oxford University Press in the UK and certain other countries.

Published in the United States of America by Oxford University Press
198 Madison Avenue, New York, NY 10016, United States of America.

For titles covered by Section 112 of the US Higher Education
Opportunity Act, please visit www.oup.com/us/he for the latest
information about pricing and alternate formats.

Library of Congress Control Number: 2020030201

Printing number: 9 8 7 6 5 4 3 2 1
Printed in Mexico by Quad/Mexico

Coniugi Judithae dilectissimae

—PETER VON SIVERS

To all my students over the years,
who have taught me at least as much as I've taught them;
and most of all to my wife, Jacki, beloved in all things,
but especially in her infinite patience and fortitude
in seeing me through the writing of this book.

—CHARLES A. DESNOYERS

For Susan and our children, Meredith and Jonathan.

—GEORGE B. STOW

—I hear and I forget; I see and I remember; I do and I understand
(Chinese proverb) 我听见我忘记;我看见我记住;我做我了解

Brief Contents

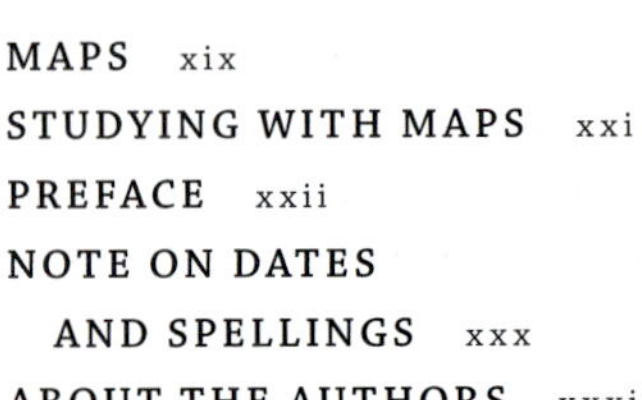

MAPS xix
STUDYING WITH MAPS xxi
PREFACE xxii
NOTE ON DATES AND SPELLINGS xxx
ABOUT THE AUTHORS xxxi

WORLD PERIOD THREE

The Formation of Religious Civilizations

600–1450 CE 350

15. The Rise of Empires in the Americas, 600–1550 CE 350

WORLD PERIOD FOUR

Interactions across the Globe

1450–1750 370

16. Western Christian Overseas Expansion and the Ottoman–Habsburg Struggle, 1450–1650 370

17. The Renaissance, New Sciences, and Religious Wars in Europe, 1450–1750 394

18. New Patterns in New Worlds: Colonialism and Indigenous Responses in the Americas, 1500–1800 422

19. African Kingdoms, the Atlantic Slave Trade, and the Origins of Black America, 1450–1800 450

20. The Mughal Empire: Muslim Rulers and Hindu Subjects, 1400–1750 476

21. Regulating the "Inner" and "Outer" Domains: China and Japan, 1500–1800 498

WORLD PERIOD FIVE

The Origins of Modernity

1750–1900 522

22. Patterns of Nation-States and Culture in the Atlantic World, 1750–1871 522

23. Creoles and Caudillos: Latin America in the Nineteenth Century, 1790–1917 550

24. The Challenge of Modernity: East Asia, 1750–1900 576

25. Adaptation and Resistance: The Ottoman and Russian Empires, 1683–1908 600

26. Industrialization and Its Discontents, 1750–1914 624

27. The New Imperialism in the Nineteenth Century, 1750–1914 650

WORLD PERIOD SIX

From Three Modernities to One

1914–Present 676

28. World Wars and Competing Visions of Modernity, 1900–1945 676

29. Reconstruction, Cold War, and Decolonization, 1945–1962 706

30. The End of the Cold War, Western Social Transformation, and the Developing World, 1963–1991 736

31. A Fragile Capitalist-Democratic World Order, 1991–2020 764

FURTHER RESOURCES R-1

CREDITS C-1

SOURCE INDEX SI-1

SUBJECT INDEX I-1

Contents

MAPS xix
STUDYING WITH MAPS xxi
PREFACE xxii
NOTE ON DATES AND SPELLINGS xxx
ABOUT THE AUTHORS xxxi

WORLD PERIOD THREE
The Formation of Religious Civilizations
600–1450 CE

Chapter 15
600–1550 CE
The Rise of Empires in the Americas 350

The Legacy of Teotihuacán and the Toltecs in Mesoamerica 352
Militarism in the Mexican Basin 352
Late Maya States in Yucatán 354

The Legacy of Tiwanaku and Wari in the Andes 355
The Expanding State of Tiwanaku 355
The Expanding City-State of Wari 357

American Empires: Aztec and Inca Origins and Dominance 358
The Aztec Empire of Mesoamerica 358
The Inca Empire of the Andes 360

Imperial Society and Culture 363
Imperial Capitals: Tenochtitlán and Cuzco 364
Power and Its Cultural Expressions 365

Putting It All Together 367

PATTERNS OF EVIDENCE: Sources for Chapter 15
15.1—Skeletons in a Wari royal tomb site, El Castillo de Huarmey, Peru • 15.2—Ahuitzotl, Eighth King (*Tlatloani*) of the Aztec Empire • 15.3—Bernal Díaz, *The Conquest of New Spain* • 15.4—Pedro Cieza de León on Incan roads

Features:
Patterns Up Close: Human Sacrifice 366
Against the Grain: Amazon Rain-Forest Civilizations 369

WORLD PERIOD FOUR
Interactions across the Globe
1450–1750

Chapter 16
1450–1650
Western Christian Overseas Expansion and the Ottoman–Habsburg Struggle 370

The Muslim–Christian Competition in the East and West, 1450–1600 372
Iberian Christian Expansion, 1415–1498 372
Rise of the Ottomans and Struggle with the Habsburgs for Dominance, 1300–1609 376

The Centralizing State: Origins and Interactions 384
State Transformation, Money, and Firearms 384

Imperial Courts, Urban Festivities, and the Arts 387
The Ottoman Empire: Palaces, Festivities, and the Arts 387
The Spanish Habsburg Empire: Popular Festivities and the Arts 389

Putting It All Together 391

PATTERNS OF EVIDENCE: Sources for Chapter 16
16.1—Columbus reports on his first voyage, 1493 • 16.2—Christopher Columbus, *The Book of Prophecies* • 16.3—Thomas the Eparch and Joshua Diplovatatzes, "The Fall of Constantinople" • 16.4—Evliya Çelebi, "A Procession of Artisans at Istanbul" • 16.5—Ogier Ghiselin de Busbecq, "The Court of Suleiman the Magnificent" • 16.6—Janissary musket

Features:
Patterns Up Close: Shipbuilding 378
Against the Grain: Tilting at Windmills 392

Chapter 17 1450–1750 The Renaissance, New Sciences, and Religious Wars in Europe 394

Cultural Transformations: Renaissance, Baroque, and New Sciences 396
The Renaissance and Baroque Arts 396
The New Sciences 398
The New Sciences and Their Social Impact 401
The New Sciences: Philosophical Interpretations 404

Centralizing States and Religious Upheavals 405
The Rise of Centralized Kingdoms 405
The Protestant Reformation, State Churches, and Independent Congregations 407
Religious Wars and Political Restoration 411

Putting It All Together 419

PATTERNS OF EVIDENCE: Sources for Chapter 17
17.1—Examination of Lady Jane Grey, London • 17.2—Emilie du Châtelet, *Discourse on Happiness* • 17.3—Sebastian Castellio, *Concerning Whether Heretics Should Be Persecuted* • 17.4—Duc de Saint-Simon, "The Daily Habits of Louis XIV at Versailles" • 17.5—Giorgio Vasari, *The Life of Michelangelo Buonarroti* • 17.6—Galileo Galilei, Letter to the Grand Duchess Christina de' Medici

Features:
Patterns Up Close: Mapping the World 406
Against the Grain: The Digger Movement 420

Chapter 18 1500–1800 New Patterns in New Worlds: Colonialism and Indigenous Responses in the Americas 422

The Colonial Americas: Europe's Warm-Weather Extension 424
The Conquest of Mexico and Peru 424
The Establishment of Colonial Institutions 428

The Making of American Societies: Origins and Transformations 438
Exploitation of Mineral and Tropical Resources 438
Social Strata, Castes, and Ethnic Groups 440

The Adaptation of the Americas to European Culture 443

Features:

Patterns Up Close: The Columbian Exchange 436

Against the Grain: Juana Inés de la Cruz 448

Putting It All Together 446

PATTERNS OF EVIDENCE: **Sources for Chapter 18**

18.1—Scandal at the Church: José de Álfaro accuses Doña Theresa Bravo and others of insulting and beating his Castiza wife, Joséfa Cadena • 18.2—Marina de San Miguel's confessions before the Inquisition, Mexico City • 18.3—Nahuatl Land Sale Documents, Mexico • 18.4—*The Jesuit Relations,* French North America

WORLD PERIOD FOUR

Interactions across the Globe

1450–1750

Chapter 19 1450–1800

African Kingdoms, the Atlantic Slave Trade, and the Origins of Black America 450

African States and the Slave Trade 452

The End of Empires in the North and the Rise of States in the Center 453

Portugal's Explorations along the African Coast and Contacts with Ethiopia 455

Coastal Africa and the Atlantic Slave Trade 457

American Plantation Slavery and Atlantic Mercantilism 459

The Special Case of Plantation Slavery in the Americas 460

Slavery in British North America 463

The Fatal Triangle: The Economic Patterns of the Atlantic Slave Trade 465

Culture and Identity in the African Diaspora 468

A New Society: Creolization of the Early Atlantic World 468

Features:

Patterns Up Close: Voodoo and Other New World Slave Religions 468

Against the Grain: Oglethorpe's Free Colony 474

Putting It All Together 472

PATTERNS OF EVIDENCE: **Sources for Chapter 19**

19.1—Abd al-Rahman al-Saadi on the scholars of Timbuktu • 19.2—Letter of Nzinga Mbemba (Afonso I) of Kongo to the King of Portugal • 19.3—Documents concerning the slave ship *Sally*, Rhode Island • 19.4—*The Interesting Narrative of the Life of Olaudah Equiano* • 19.5—Casta painting, Mexico

Chapter 20 1400–1750

The Mughal Empire: Muslim Rulers and Hindu Subjects 476

History and Political Life of the Mughals 478

From Samarkand to Hindustan 478

The Summer and Autumn of Empire 482

Administration, Society, and Economy 487

Mansabdars and Bureaucracy 487

The Mughals and Their Early Modern Economy 488

Society, Family, and Gender 490

Science, Religion, and the Arts 491
Science and Technology 491
Religion: In Search of Balance 492
Literature and Art 493

Putting It All Together 494

PATTERNS OF EVIDENCE: Sources for Chapter 20
20.1—Babur, *The Baburnama* • 20.2—Muhammad Dara Shikuh, *The Mingling of Two Oceans* • 20.3—Edicts of Aurangzeb • 20.4—Mughal emerald box

Features:
Patterns Up Close:
Akbar's Attempt at Religious Synthesis 484
Against the Grain:
Sikhism in Transition 496

Chapter 21
1500–1800
Regulating the "Inner" and "Outer" Domains: China and Japan 498

Late Ming and Qing China to 1750 500
From Expansion to Exclusion 500
The Spring and Summer of Power: The Qing to 1750 503
Village and Family Life 508
Science, Culture, and Intellectual Life 509

The Long War and Longer Peace: Japan, 1450–1750 512
The Struggle for Unification 512
The Tokugawa *Bakufu* to 1750 514
Growth and Stagnation: Economy and Society 515
Hothousing "Japaneseness": Culture, Science, and Intellectual Life 518

Putting It All Together 519

PATTERNS OF EVIDENCE: Sources for Chapter 21
21.1—Matteo Ricci, *China in the Sixteenth Century* • 21.2—Macartney's observations on China and possibilities for British commerce (excerpts) • 21.3—Emperor Qianlong's Imperial Edict to King George III • 21.4—Honda Toshiaki, "Secret Plan for Managing the Country"

Features:
Patterns Up Close:
The "China" Trade 504
Against the Grain:
Seclusion's Exceptions 520

WORLD PERIOD FIVE
The Origins of Modernity
1750–1900

Chapter 22
1750–1871
Patterns of Nation-States and Culture in the Atlantic World 522

Origins of the Nation-State, 1750–1815 524
The American, French, and Haitian Revolutions 524

Enlightenment Culture: Radicalism and Moderation 533
The Enlightenment and Its Many Expressions 533

The Other Enlightenment: The Ideology of Ethnic Nationalism 535

The Growth of the Nation-State, 1815–1871 536
Restoration Monarchies, 1815–1848 536
Nation-State Building in Anglo-America, 1783–1900 540

Features:
Patterns Up Close: The Guillotine 530
Against the Grain: Defying the Third Republic 548

Romanticism and Realism: Philosophical and Artistic Expression to 1850 544
Romanticism 544
Realism 545

Putting It All Together 546

PATTERNS OF EVIDENCE: Sources for Chapter 22
22.1—*Declaration of the Rights of Man and of the Citizen* • 22.2—Olympe de Gouges, *The Declaration of the Rights of Woman* • 22.3—Voltaire, "Torture," from the *Philosophical Dictionary* • 22.4—Edmund Burke, *Reflections on the Revolution in France* • 22.5—Thomas Paine, *Rights of Man* • 22.6—Clemens von Metternich, Secret Memorandum to Tsar Alexander I

Chapter 23 1790–1917
Creoles and Caudillos : Latin America in the Nineteenth Century 550

Independence, Constitutionalism, and Landed Elites 552
Independence in the Southern Cone: State Formation in Argentina 552
Brazil: From Kingdom to Republic 554
Independence and State Formation in Western and Northern South America 556
Independence and Political Development in the North: Mexico 558

Latin American Society and Economy in the Nineteenth Century 564
Rebuilding Societies and Economies 565
Export-Led Growth 568
Culture, Family, and the Status of Women 572

Putting It All Together 573

PATTERNS OF EVIDENCE: Sources for Chapter 23
23.1— Josefina Bachellery, "The Education of Women" • 23.2—Domingo Faustino Sarmiento, *Travels in the United States in 1847* • 23.3—Amulet containing passages from the Qur'an, worn by Muslim slaves who rioted in Bahia, Brazil • 23.4—Photograph of a Chinese coolie, Peru

Features:
Patterns Up Close: Slave Rebellions in Cuba and Brazil 566
Against the Grain: Resistance in Brazil's Backcountry 574

Chapter 24 1750– 1900
The Challenge of Modernity: East Asia 576

China and Japan in the Age of Imperialism 578
China and Maritime Trade, 1750–1839 578
The Opium Wars and the Treaty Port Era 580
Toward Revolution: Reform and Reaction to 1900 585
In Search of Security through Empire: Japan in the Meiji Era 588

Economy and Society in Late Qing China 591
The Seeds of Modernity and the New Economic Order 591
Culture, Arts, and Science 592

Zaibatsu and Political Parties: Economy and Society in Meiji Japan 593
Commerce and Cartels 593
"Civilization and Enlightenment": Science, Culture, and the Arts 596

Features:
Patterns Up Close: Interaction and Adaptation: "Self-Strengthening" and "Western Science and Eastern Ethics" 584
Against the Grain: Reacting to Modernity 599

Putting It All Together 597

PATTERNS OF EVIDENCE: **Sources for Chapter 24**

24.1—Lin Zexu's letter to Queen Victoria of Great Britain • 24.2—Supression of the opium trade • 24.3—The Meiji Constitution of the Empire of Japan • 24.4—Natsume Soseki, *Kokoro*

Chapter 25 1683–1908

Adaptation and Resistance: The Ottoman and Russian Empires 600

Decentralization and Reforms in the Ottoman Empire 602

Ottoman Imperialism in the 1600s and 1700s 602

The Western Challenge and Ottoman Responses 603

Iran's Effort to Cope with the Western Challenge 609

Westernization, Reforms, and Industrialization in Russia 612

Russia and Westernization 613

Russia in the Early Nineteenth Century 614

The Great Reforms 616

Russian Industrialization 618

The Abortive Russian Revolution of 1905 620

Features:

Patterns Up Close: Sunni and Shiite Islam 610

Against the Grain: A Precursor to Lenin 623

Putting It All Together 621

PATTERNS OF EVIDENCE: **Sources for Chapter 25**

25.1—Lady Mary Wortley Montagu, *Letters from the Levant* • 25.2—Imperial Edict of the Rose Garden • 25.3—Tsar Alexander II's abolition of serfdom • 25.4—Female workers' strike at the Gal'pern matchbox factory in Pinsk

Chapter 26 1750–1914

Industrialization and Its Discontents 624

Origins and Growth of Industrialism, 1750–1914 625

Early Industrialism, 1750–1870 626

The Spread of Early Industrialism 628

Later Industrialism, 1871–1914 628

The Social and Economic Impact of Industrialism, 1750–1914 635

Demographic Changes 635

Industrial Society 637

Critics of Industrialism 639

Improved Standards of Living 641

Improved Urban Living 641

Big Business 642

Intellectual and Cultural Responses to Industrialism 643

Scientific and Intellectual Developments 644

Toward Modernity in Philosophy and Religion 646

Toward Modernity in Literature and the Arts 646

Features:

Patterns Up Close: "The Age of Steam" 632

Against the Grain: The Luddites 648

Putting It All Together 647

PATTERNS OF EVIDENCE: **Sources for Chapter 26**

26.1—Charles Dickens, *Hard Times* • 26.2—The death of William Huskisson, first casualty of a railroad accident • 26.3—Young miners testify to the Ashley Commission • 26.4—Karl Marx, "Wage Labour and Capital" • 26.5—Charles Darwin, *On the Origin of Species* • 26.6—Emmeline Pankhurst, *My Own Story*

Chapter 27
1750–1914

The New Imperialism in the Nineteenth Century 650

The British Colonies of India and Australia 652
- The British East India Company 652
- Direct British Rule 656
- British Settler Colonies: Australia 658

European Imperialism in the Middle East and Africa 660
- The Rising Appeal of Imperialism in the West 660
- The Scramble for Africa 663

Western Imperialism and Colonialism in Southeast Asia 667
- The Dutch in Indonesia 667
- Spain in the Philippines 668
- The French in Vietnam 671

Putting It All Together 673

PATTERNS OF EVIDENCE: **Sources for Chapter 27**

27.1—The Indian Revolt • 27.2—Ismail ibn 'Abd al-Qadir, *The Life of the Sudanese Mahdi* • 27.3—Rudyard Kipling, "The White Man's Burden" • 27.4—Mark Twain, "To the Person Sitting in Darkness"

Features:

Patterns Up Close: Military Transformations and the New Imperialism 658

Against the Grain: An Anti-Imperial Perspective 674

WORLD PERIOD SIX

From Three Modernities to One

Chapter 28
1900–1945

World Wars and Competing Visions of Modernity 676

The Great War and Its Aftermath 678
- A Savage War and a Flawed Peace 678
- America First: The Beginnings of a Consumer Culture and the Great Depression 681
- Great Britain and France: Slow Recovery and Troubled Empires 685
- Latin America: Independent Democracies and Authoritarian Regimes 690

New Variations on Modernity: The Soviet Union and Communism 691
- The Communist Party and Regime in the Soviet Union 691
- The Collectivization of Agriculture and Industrialization 692

New Variations on Modernity: Supremacist Nationalism in Italy, Germany, and Japan 693
- From Fascism in Italy to Nazism in the Third Reich 693
- Japan's "Greater East Asia Co-Prosperity Sphere" and China's Struggle for Unity 698

Putting It All Together 702

Features:

Patterns Up Close: The Harlem Renaissance and the African Diaspora 686

Against the Grain: Righteous among the Nations 704

PATTERNS OF EVIDENCE: **Sources for Chapter 28**

28.1—ANZAC troops at Gallipoli • 28.2—Vera Brittain, *Testament of Youth* • 28.3—Benito Mussolini and Giovanni Gentile, "Foundations and Doctrine of Fascism" • 28.4—Adolf Hitler, *Mein Kampf* • 28.5—Franklin D. Roosevelt, undelivered address planned for Jefferson Day • 28.6—*Hiroshima Diary*

Chapter 29 1945–1962

Reconstruction, Cold War, and Decolonization 706

Superpower Confrontation: Capitalist Democracy and Communism 708
- The Cold War Era, 1945–1962 708
- Society and Culture in Postwar North America, Europe, and Japan 715

Populism and Industrialization in Latin America 717
- Slow Social Change 717
- Populist-Guided Democracy 718

The End of Colonialism and the Rise of New Nations 719
- "China Has Stood Up" 719
- Decolonization, Israel, and Arab Nationalism in the Middle East 721
- Decolonization and Cold War in Asia 724
- Decolonization and Cold War in Africa 730

Putting It All Together 732

Features:
Patterns Up Close: Bandung and the Origins of the Non-Aligned Movement (NAM) 726
Against the Grain: Postwar Counterculture 734

PATTERNS OF EVIDENCE: **Sources for Chapter 29**

29.1—The Universal Declaration of Human Rights • 29.2—Winston Churchill, "The Iron Curtain Speech" • 29.3—Letters on the Cuban Missile Crisis between Fidel Castro and Nikita Khrushchev • 29.4—Ho Chi Minh, "The Path Which Led Me to Leninism" • 29.5—Indira Gandhi, "What Educated Women Can Do" • 29.6—Kwame Nkrumah, "I Speak of Freedom"

Chapter 30 1963–1991

The End of the Cold War, Western Social Transformation, and the Developing World 736

The Climax of the Cold War 738
- The Soviet Superpower in Slow Decline 738

Transforming the West 743
- Civil Rights Movements 744

From "Underdeveloped" to "Developing" World, 1963–1991 748
- China: Cultural Revolution to Four Modernizations 748
- Vietnam and Cambodia: War and Communist Rule 750
- The Middle East 752
- Africa: From Independence to Development 756
- Latin America: Proxy Wars 759

Putting It All Together 760

Features:
Patterns Up Close: From Women's Liberation to Feminism 746
Against the Grain: The African National Congress 762

PATTERNS OF EVIDENCE: **Sources for Chapter 30**

30.1—Mikhail Gorbachev, *Perestroika: New Thinking for Our Country and the World* • 30.2—Martin Luther King, Jr., "I Have a Dream" • 30.3—Simone de Beauvoir, *The Second Sex* • 30.4—Coverage of the Tiananmen Square protests • 30.5—Salvador Allende, "Last Words to the Nation" • 30.6—Nelson Mandela's inauguration speech

Chapter 31
1991–2020

Features:

Patterns Up Close:
Social Networking 786

Against the Grain:
North Korea: Lone Holdout against the World 792

A Fragile Capitalist-Democratic World Order 764

Capitalist Democracy: The Dominant Pattern of Modernity 766

A Decade of Global Expansion: The United States and the World in the 1990s 766

Two Communist Holdouts: China and Vietnam 774

Pluralist Democracy under Strain 775

The Environmental Limits of Modernity 788

Putting It All Together 790

PATTERNS OF EVIDENCE: **Sources for Chapter 31**

31.1— Osama bin Laden, "Declaration of War against the Americans Occupying the Land of the Two Holy Places" • 31.2—Vladimir Putin, Address to the Duma concerning the annexation of Crimea • 31.3—Remarks by President Obama in Address to European Youth, March 26, 2014 • 31.4—United Nations Framework Convention on Climate Change, Paris

FURTHER RESOURCES R-1

CREDITS C-1

SOURCE INDEX SI-1

SUBJECT INDEX I-1

Maps

Map 15.1 North America and Mesoamerica, ca. 1100 353
Map 15.2 Tiwanaku and Wari, ca. 1000 357
Map 15.3 The Aztec Empire, ca. 1520 359
Map 15.4 The Inca Empire, ca. 1525 361
Map 15.5 Tenochtitlán and the Mexican Basin 365
Map 16.1 Africa, the Mediterranean, and the Indian Ocean, 1415–1498 373
Map 16.2 The Ottoman Empire, 1307–1683 380
Map 16.3 Europe and the Mediterranean, ca. 1560 381
Map 16.4 Ottoman–Portuguese Competition in the Indian Ocean, 1536–1580 383
Map 17.1 Centers of Learning in Europe, 1500–1770 402
Map 17.2 European Warfare, 1450–1750 408
Map 17.3 The Protestant Reformation, ca. 1580 410
Map 17.4 Europe in 1648 415
Map 17.5 The Expansion of Russia, 1462–1795 417
Map 18.1 The European Exploration of the Americas, 1519–1542 427
Map 18.2 The Colonization of Central and South America to 1750 430
Map 18.3 The Colonization of North America to 1763 434
Map 18.4 The Columbian Exchange 437
Map 19.1 Peoples and Kingdoms in Sub-Saharan Africa, 1450–1750 454
Map 19.2 Regions from which Captured Africans Were Brought to the Americas, 1501–1867 461
Map 19.3 Regions in which Enslaved Africans Landed, 1501–1867 463
Map 19.4 The North Atlantic System, ca. 1750 466
Map 19.5 Slave Revolts in the Americas, 1500–1850 472
Map 20.1 Area Subjugated by Timur-i Lang, 1360–1405 479
Map 20.2 The Conquests of Babur 480
Map 20.3 Mughal India under Akbar 481
Map 20.4 European Trading Ports in India and Southeast Asia, ca. 1690 489
Map 21.1 China in 1600 501
Map 21.2 World Trade Networks, ca. 1770 502
Map 21.3 Silver Flows and Centers of Porcelain Production 504
Map 21.4 China during the Reign of Qianlong 506
Map 21.5 The Campaigns of Hideyoshi 513
Map 21.6 Urban Population and Major Transport Routes in Japan, ca. 1800 516
Map 22.1 British North America in 1763 525
Map 22.2 Napoleonic Europe, 1796–1815 529
Map 22.3 Europe after the Congress of Vienna 537
Map 22.4 Europe in 1871 541
Map 22.5 The Expanding United States in 1900 542
Map 23.1 The New Nation-States of Latin America and the Caribbean, 1831 560
Map 23.2 Mexico's Loss of Territory to the United States, 1824–1854 561
Map 23.3 The Economy of Latin America and the Caribbean, ca. 1900 565
Map 23.4 Non-Western Migrations in the Nineteenth Century 571
Map 24.1 The Opium Trade: Origins, Interactions, Adaptations 580
Map 24.2 Treaty Ports and Foreign Spheres of Influence in China, 1842–1907 582
Map 24.3 The Taiping Rebellion, 1851–1864 583
Map 24.4 Japanese Territorial Expansion, 1870–1905 590
Map 24.5 The Modernization of Japan to 1910 595
Map 25.1 The Decline of the Ottoman Empire, 1683–1923 604
Map 25.2 The Territorial Expansion of the Russian Empire, 1795–1914 615
Map 26.1 Industrializing Britain in 1850 629
Map 26.2 The Industrialization of Europe by 1914 630
Map 26.3 World Population Growth, 1700–1900 636
Map 26.4 European Population Movements, 1750–1914 638
Map 27.1 The Expansion of British Power in India, 1756–1805 654
Map 27.2 The British Empire in India, 1858–1914 657
Map 27.3 Competitive Imperialism: The World in 1914 661
Map 27.4 The Scramble for Africa 664
Map 27.5 Western Imperialism in Southeast Asia, 1870–1914 669
Map 28.1 Europe, the Middle East, and North America in 1914 and 1923 682
Map 28.2 European Empires, 1936 688
Map 28.3 World War II in Europe, 1939–1945 699
Map 28.4 World War II in the Pacific, 1937–1945 703
Map 29.1 The Cold War, 1947–1991 710
Map 29.2 The Cuban Missile Crisis 715
Map 29.3 Urbanization and Population Growth in Latin America and the Caribbean, ca. 1950 718
Map 29.4 Decolonization in Africa, the Middle East, and Asia since 1945 722
Map 29.5 The Palestine Conflict, 1947–1949 723
Map 30.1 Communist Eastern Europe, 1945–1989 740
Map 30.2 The Fall of Communism in Eastern Europe and the Soviet Union 743
Map 30.3 Governmental Participation by Women 746
Map 30.4 The Vietnam War 751
Map 30.5 The Arab–Israeli Wars, 1967 and 1973 753
Map 31.1 The Global Distribution of Wealth, 2012 767
Map 31.2 The Global Balance of Trade, 2008 768
Map 31.3 US Security Commitments since 1945 772
Map 31.4 World Map of Climate Change Performance 790

Studying with Maps

MAPS

World history cannot be fully understood without a clear comprehension of the chronologies and parameters within which different empires, states, and peoples have changed over time. Maps facilitate this understanding by illuminating the significance of time, space, and geography in shaping the patterns of world history.

Global Locator

Many of the maps in *Patterns of World History* include *global locators* that show the area being depicted in a larger context.

Projection

A map *projection* portrays all or part of the earth, which is spherical, on a flat surface. All maps, therefore, include some distortion. The projections in *Patterns of World History* show the earth at global, continental, regional, and local scales.

Topography

Many maps in *Patterns of World History* show *relief*—the contours of the land. Topography is an important element in studying maps because the physical terrain has played a critical role in shaping human history.

Scale Bar

Every map in *Patterns of World History* includes a *scale* that shows distances in both miles and kilometers, and in some instances in feet as well.

Map Key

Maps use symbols to show the location of features and to convey information. Each symbol is explained in the map's *key*.

Preface

The response to the first three editions of *Patterns of World History* has been extraordinarily gratifying to those of us involved in its development. The diversity of schools that have adopted the book—community colleges as well as state universities; small liberal arts schools as well as large private universities—suggests to us that its central premise of exploring *patterns* in world history is both adaptable to a variety of pedagogical environments and congenial to a wide body of instructors. Indeed, from the responses to the book we have received thus far, we expect that the level of writing, timeliness and completeness of the material, and analytical approach will serve it well as the discipline of world history continues to mature. These key strengths are enhanced in the fourth edition of *Patterns* by constructive, dynamic suggestions from the broad range of students and instructors who are using the book.

It is widely agreed that world history is more than simply the sum of all national histories. Likewise, *Patterns of World History*, Fourth Edition, is more than an unbroken sequence of dates, battles, rulers, and their activities, and it is more than the study of isolated stories of change over time. Rather, in this textbook we endeavor to present in a clear and engaging way how world history "works." Instead of merely offering a narrative history of the appearance of this or that innovation, we present an analysis of the process by which an innovation in one part of the world is diffused and carried to the rest of the globe. Instead of focusing on the memorization of people, places, and events, we strive to present important facts in context and draw meaningful connections, analyzing whatever patterns we find and drawing conclusions where we can. In short, we seek to examine the interlocking mechanisms and animating forces of world history, without neglecting the human agency behind them.

The *Patterns* Approach

Our approach in this book is, as the title suggests, to look for patterns in world history. We should say at the outset that we do not mean to select certain categories into which we attempt to stuff the historical events we choose to emphasize, nor do we claim that all world history is reducible to such patterns, nor do we mean to suggest that the nature of the patterns determines the outcome of historical events. We see them instead as broad, flexible organizational frameworks around which to build the structure of a world history in such a way that the enormous sweep and content of the past can be viewed in a comprehensible narrative, with sound analysis and ample scope for debate and discussion. In this sense, we view them much like the armatures in clay sculptures, giving support and structure to the final figure but not necessarily preordaining its ultimate shape.

From its origins, human culture grew through interactions and adaptations on all the continents except Antarctica. A voluminous scholarship on all regions of the world has been accumulated, which those working in the field have to attempt to master if their explanations and arguments are to sound even remotely persuasive. The sheer volume and complexity of the sources, however, mean that even the knowledge and expertise of the best scholars are going to be incomplete. Moreover, the humility with which all historians must approach their material contains within it the realization that no historical explanation is ever fully satisfactory or final; as a driving force in the historical process, creative human agency moves events in directions that are never fully predictable, even if they follow broad patterns. Learning to discern patterns in this process not only helps novice historians to appreciate the complex challenges (and rewards) of historical inquiry; it also develops critical thinking abilities in all students.

As we move into the third decade of the twenty-first century, world historians have long since left behind the "West plus the rest" approach that marked the field's early years, together with economic and geographical reductionism, in the search for a new balance between comprehensive cultural and institutional examinations on the one hand and those highlighting human agency on the other. All too often, however, this is reflected in texts that seek broad coverage at the expense of analysis, thus resulting in a kind of "world history lite." Our aim is to simplify the study of the world—to make it accessible to the student—without making world history itself simplistic.

Patterns of World History, Fourth Edition, proposes the teaching of world history from the perspective of the relationship between continuity and change. What we advocate in this book is a distinct intellectual framework for this relationship and the role of innovation and historical change through patterns of origins, interactions, and adaptations. Each small or large technical or cultural innovation originated in one geographical center or independently in several different centers. As people in the centers interacted with their neighbors, the neighbors adapted to, and in many cases were transformed by, the innovations. For us, "adaptation" includes the entire spectrum of human responses, ranging from outright rejection to creative borrowing and, at times, forced acceptance.

Small technical innovations often went through the pattern of origin, interaction, and adaptation across the world without arousing much attention, even though they had major consequences. For example, the horse collar, which originated in the last centuries BCE in China and allowed for the replacement of oxen with stronger horses, gradually improved the productivity of agriculture in eleventh-century western Europe. More sweeping intellectual–cultural innovations, by contrast, such as the spread of universal religions like Buddhism, Christianity, and Islam and the rise of science, have obviously had profound consequences—in some cases leading to conflicts lasting centuries—and affect us even today.

Sometimes change was effected by commodities that to us seem rather ordinary. Take sugar, for example. It originated in Southeast Asia and was traded and grown in the Mediterranean, where its cultivation on plantations created the model for expansion into the vast slave system of the Atlantic basin from the fifteenth through the nineteenth centuries, forever altering the histories of four continents. What would our diets look like today without sugar? Its history continues to unfold as we debate its merits and health risks and it supports huge multinational agribusinesses.

Or take a less ordinary commodity: opium. Opium had been used medicinally for centuries in regions all over the world. But the advent of tobacco traded from the Americas to the Philippines to China, and the encouragement of Dutch traders in the region, created an environment in which the drug was smoked for the first time. Enterprising rogue British merchants, eager to find a way to crack closed Chinese markets for other goods, began to smuggle it in from India. The market grew, the price went down, addiction spread, and Britain and China ultimately went to war over China's attempts to eliminate the traffic. Here, we have an example of an item generating interactions on a worldwide scale, with impacts on everything from politics to economics, culture, and even the environment. The legacies of the trade still weigh heavily on two of the rising powers of the recent decades: China and India. And opium and its derivatives, like morphine and heroin, continue to bring relief as well as suffering on a colossal scale to hundreds of millions of people.

What, then, do we gain by studying world history through the use of such patterns? First, if we consider innovation to be a driving force of history, it helps to satisfy an intrinsic human curiosity about origins—our own and others'. Perhaps more importantly, seeing patterns of various kinds in historical development brings to light connections and linkages among peoples, cultures, and regions—as in the aforementioned examples—that might not otherwise present themselves.

Second, such patterns can also reveal similarities and differences among cultures that other approaches to world history tend to neglect. For example, the differences between the civilizations of the Eastern and Western Hemispheres are generally highlighted in world history texts, but the broad commonalities of human groups creating agriculturally based cities and states in widely separated areas also show deep parallels in their patterns of origins, interactions, and adaptations. Such comparisons are at the center of our approach.

Third, this kind of analysis offers insights into how an individual innovation was subsequently developed and diffused across space and time—that is, the patterns by which the new eventually becomes a necessity in our daily lives. Through all of this we gain a deeper appreciation of the unfolding of global history from its origins in small, isolated areas to the vast networks of global interconnectedness in our present world.

Finally, our use of a broad-based understanding of continuity, change, and innovation allows us to restore culture in all its individual and institutionalized aspects—spiritual, artistic, intellectual, scientific—to its rightful place alongside technology, environment, politics, and socioeconomic conditions. That is, understanding innovation in this way allows this text to help illuminate the full range of human ingenuity over time and space in a comprehensive, even-handed, and open-ended fashion.

Options for Teaching with *Patterns of World History*, Fourth Edition

Patterns of World History is available in two versions designed to offer instructors flexible teaching options:

1) *Patterns of World History with Sources,* which includes approximately four textual and visual sources after every chapter. This section, called "Patterns of Evidence," enhances student engagement with key chapter patterns through contemporaneous voices and perspectives. Each source is accompanied by a concise introduction to provide chronological and geographical context; "Working with Sources" questions after each selection prompt students to make critical connections between the source and the main chapter narrative.
2) *Patterns of World History, Brief Edition,* which provides the same organization and narrative as *Patterns of World History with Sources,* but does not include source material at the end of each chapter.

For the convenience of instructors teaching a course over two 15-week semesters, both versions of *Patterns* are limited to 31 chapters. For the sake of continuity and to accommodate the many different ways schools divide the midpoint of their world history sequence, Chapters 15–18 overlap in both volumes; in Volume 2, Chapter 15 is given as a "prelude" to Part Four. Those using a trimester system will also find divisions made in convenient places, with Chapter 10 coming at the beginning of Part Two and Chapter 22 at the beginning of Part Five.

Patterns of Change and Six Periods of World History

Similarly, *Patterns* is adaptable to both chronological and thematic styles of instruction. We divide the history of the world into six major time periods and recognize for each period one or two main patterns of innovation, their spread through interaction, and their adoption by others. Obviously, lesser patterns are identified as well, many of which are of more limited regional interactive and adaptive impact. We wish to stress again that these are broad categories of analysis and that there is nothing reductive or deterministic in our aims or choices. Nevertheless, we believe the patterns we have chosen help to make the historical process more intelligible, providing a series of lenses that can help to focus the otherwise confusing facts and disparate details that comprise world history.

World Period One (Prehistory–600 BCE): Origins of human civilization—tool making and symbol creating—in Africa as well as the origins of agriculture, urbanism, and state formation in the three agrarian centers of the Middle East, India, and China.

World Period Two (600 BCE–600 CE): Emergence of the Axial Age thinkers and their visions of a transcendent god or first principle in Eurasia; elevation of these visions to the status of state religions in empires and kingdoms, in the process forming multiethnic and multilinguistic polities.

World Period Three (600–1450): Disintegration of classical empires and formation of religious civilizations in Eurasia, with the emergence of religiously unified regions divided by commonwealths of multiple states.

World Period Four (1450–1750): Rise of new empires; interaction, both hostile and peaceful, among the religious civilizations and new empires across all continents of the world. Origins of the New Science in Europe, based on the use of mathematics for the investigation of nature.

World Period Five (1750–1900): Origins of scientific–industrial "modernity," simultaneous with the emergence of constitutional and ethnic nation-states, in the West (Europe and North America); interaction of the West with Asia and Africa, resulting in complex adaptations, both coerced and voluntary, on the part of the latter.

World Period Six (1900–Present): Division of early Western modernity into three competing visions: communism, supremacist nationalism, and capitalism. After two horrific world wars and the triumph of nation-state formation across the world, capitalism remains as the last surviving version of modernity. Capitalism is then reinvigorated by the increasing use of social networking tools, which popularizes both "traditional" religious and cultural ideas and constitutionalism in authoritarian states.

Chapter Organization and Structure

Each world period addresses the role of change and innovation on a broad scale in a particular time and/or region, and each chapter contains different levels of exploration to examine the principal features of particular cultural or national areas and how each affects, and is affected by, the patterns of origins, interactions, and adaptations:

- *Geography and the Environment*: The relationship between human beings and the geography and environment of the places they inhabit is among the most basic factors in understanding human societies. In this chapter segment, therefore, the topics under investigation involve the natural environment of a particular region and the general conditions affecting change and innovation. Climatic conditions, earthquakes, tsunamis, volcanic eruptions, outbreaks of disease, and so forth all have obvious effects on how humans react to the challenge of survival. The initial portions of chapters introducing new regions for study therefore include environmental and geographical overviews, which are revisited and expanded in later chapters as necessary. The larger issues of how decisive the impact of geography on the development of human societies is—as in the commonly asked question "Is geography destiny?"—are also examined here.
- *Political Developments:* In this segment, we ponder such questions as how rulers and their supporters wield political and military power. How do different political traditions develop in different areas? How do states expand, and why? How do different political arrangements attempt to strike a balance between the rulers and the ruled? How and why are political innovations transmitted to other societies? Why do societies accept or reject such innovations from the outside? Are there discernible patterns in the development of kingdoms or empires or nation-states?
- *Economic and Social Developments*: The relationship between economics and the structures and workings of societies has long been regarded as crucial by historians and social scientists. But what patterns, if any, emerge in how these relationships develop and function among different cultures? This segment explores such questions as the following: What role does economics play in the dynamics of change and continuity? What, for example, happens in agrarian societies when merchant classes develop? How does the accumulation of wealth lead to social hierarchy? What forms do these hierarchies take? How do societies formally and informally try to regulate wealth and poverty? How are economic conditions reflected in family life and gender relations? Are there patterns that reflect the varying social positions of men and women that are characteristic of certain economic and social institutions? How are these in turn affected by different cultural practices?
- *Intellectual, Religious, and Cultural Aspects*: Finally, we consider it vital to include an examination dealing in some depth with the way people understood their existence and life during each period. Clearly, intellectual innovation—the generation of new ideas—lies at the heart of the changes we have singled out as pivotal in the patterns of origins, interactions, and adaptations that form the heart of this text. Beyond this, those areas concerned with the search for and construction of meaning—particularly religion, the arts, philosophy, and science—not only reflect shifting perspectives but also, in many cases, play a leading role in determining the course of events within each form of society. All of these facets of intellectual life are in turn manifested in new perspectives and representations in the cultural life of a society.

Features

- **Seeing Patterns/Thinking Through Patterns:** "Seeing Patterns" and "Thinking Through Patterns" use a question–discussion format in each chapter to pose several broad questions ("Seeing Patterns") as advance organizers for key themes, which are then matched up with short essays at the end ("Thinking Through Patterns") that examine these same questions in a sophisticated yet student-friendly fashion.

- **Patterns Up Close:** Since students frequently apprehend macro-level patterns better when they see their contours brought into sharper relief, "Patterns Up Close" essays in each chapter highlight a particular innovation that demonstrates origins, interactions, and adaptations in action. Spanning technological, social, political, intellectual, economic, and environmental developments, the "Patterns Up Close" essays combine text, visuals, and graphics to consider everything from the pepper trade to the guillotine.
- **Against the Grain:** These brief essays consider counterpoints to the main patterns examined in each chapter. Topics range from visionaries who challenged dominant religious patterns, to women who resisted various forms of patriarchy, to agitators who fought for social and economic justice.
- **Marginal Glossary:** To avoid the necessity of having to flip pages back and forth, definitions of key terms are set directly in the margin at the point where they are first introduced.

Today, more than ever, students and instructors are confronted by a vast welter of information on every conceivable subject. Beyond the ever-expanding print media, the Internet and the Web have opened hitherto unimaginable amounts of data to us. Despite such unprecedented access, however, all of us are too frequently overwhelmed by this undifferentiated—and too often indigestible—mass. Nowhere is this truer than in world history, by definition the field within the historical profession with the broadest scope. Therefore, we think that an effort at synthesis—narrative and analysis structured around a clear, accessible, widely applicable theme—is needed, an effort that seeks to explain critical patterns of the world's past behind the billions of bits of information accessible at the stroke of a key on a computer keyboard. We hope this text, in tracing the lines of transformative ideas and things that left their patterns deeply imprinted into the canvas of world history, will provide such a synthesis.

Changes to the Fourth Edition

- **New Feature: Integrated World Period and Chapter Overviews** We have eliminated the separate world period introductions in favor of including their key points on the opening left-hand page of each chapter, with their relationship to specific origins, interactions, and adaptations highlighted, as well as the uniqueness and similarities these share with the other chapters in that World Period. We believe this specificity and recursiveness will enhance the pedagogical possibilities of the text.
- We have continued to tighten the narrative, focusing even more on key concepts and (with the guidance of reviewers) discarding inessential historical details. We are profoundly grateful to the reviewers who pointed out errors and conceptual shortcomings.
- **Updated scholarship** All chapters were revised and updated in accordance with recent developments and new scholarship. Here is a chapter-by-chapter overview that highlights the changes we made in the fourth edition:
- **World Period One** Chapter 1 was largely rewritten to reflect the results of recent research on early hominins, Neanderthals, cave paintings, and the settling of the Americas. Chapter 2 contains new paragraphs on the collapse of the Bronze Age and Sea People, as well as the Göbekli archaeological site, incorporating new information. Chapter 3 updates the material on ancient India and Harappans and employs the latest scholarship on the interaction of Indo-Europeans with peoples of northern India. Chapter 4 includes updated material on the Tarim Basin mummies, and Chapter 5 contains new sections on the weather/climate phenomena El Niño and Younger Dryas.
- **World Period Two** In Chapter 6, the account of Aksum, Himyar, and Yemen in the sixth century CE was rewritten, as was the feature "Against the Grain" on the Nasca lines in ancient South America. Chapter 7 begins with a new vignette on Queen Shirin (ca. 575–628) in the Sasanid Persian Empire, followed by added segments concerning the status of women in Greek and Roman society and Aristotle's role in Greek philosophy, along with

a rewritten "Patters Up Close Essay" on the Plague of Justinian. Chapter 8 contains a revised section on Jainism and additional material on Buddhism, and Chapter 9 adds a survey of the contemporary debate about the "Han Synthesis."

- **World Period Three** In Chapter 10 the text has been shortened, streamlining the discussion of Islamic theology and law. Chapter 11 conveys references to St. Hilda, abbess of the monastery of Whitby, along with a revised segment on feudalism. Chapter 12 has been renamed "Contrasting Patterns in Eurasia" to better reflect the full range of material contained within it; it focuses more strongly on the Mongol interval and adds specificity to the discussion of Neo-Confucian philosophy. The coverage of the Mongols has been increased in Chapter 13, and the new chapter title, "Religious Civilizations Interacting," reflects these changes.
- **World Period Four** In Chapter 15, the feature "Patterns Up Close" was rewritten to reflect the recent archaeological discovery of the Templo Mayor skull racks. The account in Chapter 16 of the Ottoman conquest of 1453 has been rewritten, along with revised segments concerning Apocalyptic Expectations and Charles V.
- **World Period Five** In Chapter 22 the discussion of the Haitian Revolution has been revised. Chapter 23 has a new "Patterns Up Close" feature on the uprising of the town of Canudos in Brazil, 1895–1898. Chapter 25 offers revised discussions of Abdülhamit II's accession to the throne of the Ottoman Empire in 1876 and of serfdom in Russia. A new section on agriculture in Russia during the first half of the nineteenth century has been added to enhance the understanding of the empire's economy and society in the early part of the century. Chapter 26 has new discussions of the weapons revolution and modernism in music.
- **World Period Six** Chapter 28 includes rewritten discussions of the founding of the Weimar Republic, along with a relocated section on the republican revolution in China. In Chapter 29 several segments, including Cold War origins, postwar Eastern Europe, and partition on the Indian subcontinent, have been rewritten. In Chapter 30 we revised the discussion of "To Get Rich is Glorious": China's Four Modernizations; Zimbabwe and Angola: The Revolution Continued; and South Africa: From Apartheid to "Rainbow Nation," including reference to the Soweto uprising. Chapter 31 updates world events to the beginning of 2020.

Ensuring Learning Success

Oxford University Press offers instructors and students a comprehensive ancillary package for qualified adopters.

Enhanced eBook

Every new copy of the fourth edition comes with an access code that provides students with resources designed to enhance their engagement with world history, including an eBook enhanced with these learning tools:

- "Closer Look" videos that analyze selected artworks, accompanied by narration and self-assessment
- interactive maps
- interactive timelines
- flashcards
- chapter quizzes
- matching activities
- primary sources
- note-taking guides

Oxford Insight Study Guide

The Oxford Insight Study Guide increases student understanding of core course material by engaging students in the process of actively reading, validating their understanding, and delivering tailored practice. The study guide delivers a custom-built adaptive practice session based on the student's demonstrated performance within each learning objective. In-depth data on student performance powers a rich suite of reporting tools that inform instructors on their students' proficiency across learning objectives.

Oxford Learning Link

Instructors who adopt the Fourth Edition have access to an instructor's resource manual, a computerized test-item file, videos from the Oxford University Press World History Video and Image Libraries, and PowerPoint slides of all the images, maps, charts, and figures in the text. All of these items, and much more, are available to adopters at the Oxford Learning Link.

For those instructors who wish to integrate Oxford's instructor and student learning resources directly into their campus learning management system, an interoperable course cartridge can be installed. Contact your OUP representative to learn more about the interoperable course cartridge for *Patterns of World History.*

Additional Learning Resources

Uncovering World History

Make history meaningful and memorable for students by teaching them the skills to "Do History." Oxford University Press is proud to develop and support innovative learning experiences for today's students. "Uncovering World History" offers students and instructors a rich and rewarding learning experience in their World History course. Embracing this model of "uncovering," and focusing on major transcultural and transnational events and experiences, the units develop student's historical thinking skills. To learn more about "Uncovering World History," please go to https://www.oxfordpresents.com/ms/getz/.

- ***Mapping Patterns of World History,* Volume 1: To 1600:** Includes approximately 50 full-color maps, each accompanied by a brief headnote, as well as blank outline maps and Concept Map exercises.
- ***Mapping Patterns of World History,* Volume 2: Since 1400:** Includes approximately 50 full-color maps, each accompanied by a brief headnote, as well as blank outline maps and Concept Map exercises.

FORMATS

Offering choices for both students and instructors, Oxford University Press makes *Patterns of World History* available in different formats:

- paperback
- eBook (available from several vendors, including RedShelf, Vital Source, and Chegg)
- loose-leaf
- inclusive access

Packaging Options

Patterns of World History can be bundled at a significant discount with any of the titles in the popular Very Short Introductions, World in a Life, or Oxford World's Classics series, as well as other titles from the Higher Education division world history catalog (www.oup.com/us/catalog/he). Please contact your OUP representative for details.

Acknowledgments

Throughout the course of writing, revising, and preparing *Patterns of World History* for publication we have benefited from the guidance and professionalism accorded us by all levels of the staff at Oxford University Press. John Challice, vice president and publisher, had faith in the inherent worth of our project from the outset and provided the initial impetus to move forward. Katie Tunkavige carried out the thankless task of assembling the manuscript and did so with generosity and good cheer, helping us with many details in the final manuscript. Keith Faivre steered us through the intricacies of production with the stoicism of a saint.

Most of all, we owe a special debt of gratitude to Charles Cavaliere, our editor. Charles took on the daunting task of directing this literary enterprise at a critical point in the book's career. He pushed this project to its successful completion, accelerated its schedule, and used a combination of flattery and hard-nosed tactics to make sure we stayed the course. His greatest contribution, however, is in the way he refined our original vision for the book with several important adjustments that clarified its latent possibilities. From the maps to the photos to the special features, Charles's high standards and concern for detail are evident on every page.

Developing a book like *Patterns of World History* is an ambitious project, a collaborative venture in which authors and editors benefit from the feedback provided by a team of outside readers and consultants. We gratefully acknowledge the advice that the many reviewers, focus group participants, and class testers (including their students) shared with us along the way. We tried to implement all of their excellent suggestions. We owe a special debt of thanks to Evan R. Ward, who provided invaluable guidance for the revision of the coverage of Latin America and the Caribbean in World Period Five. Of course, any errors of fact or interpretation that remain are solely our own.

Reviewers of the Fourth Edition

Beau Bowers, Central Piedmont Community College

Mark Z. Christensen, Brigham Young University

James S. Day, University of Montevallo

Caroline Hasenyager, Virginia State University

Randi Howell, Central Piedmont Community College

Andrey Ivanov, University of Wisconsin at Platteville

Sean Kane, Central Piedmont Community College

Rose Mary Sheldon, Virginia Military Institute

Joshua Shiver, Auburn University

Arlene Sindelar, University of British Columbia

Jean Skidmore-Hess, Georgia Southern University

Ryan H. Wilkinson, Ambrose University

Please let us know your experiences with *Patterns of World History* so that we may improve it in future editions. We welcome your comments and suggestions.

Peter von Sivers
pv4910@xmission.com

Charles A. Desnoyers
desnoyer@lasalle.edu

George B. Stow
gbsgeorge@aol.com

Note on Dates and Spellings

In keeping with widespread practice among world historians, we use "BCE" and "CE" to date events and the phrase "years ago" to describe developments from the remote past.

The transliteration of Middle Eastern words has been adjusted as much as possible to the English alphabet. Therefore, long vowels are not marked. The consonants specific to Arabic (alif, dhal, ha, sad, dad, ta, za, `ayn, ghayn, and qaf) are either not indicated or rendered with common English letters. A similar procedure is followed for Farsi. Turkish words follow the alphabet reform of 1929, which adds the following letters to the Western alphabet or modifies their pronunciation: *c* (pronounced "j"), *ç* (pronounced "tsh"), *ğ* (not pronounced but lengthening the preceding vowel), *ı* ("i" without dot, pronunciation close to short e), *i/İ* ("i" with dot, including in caps), ö (no English equivalent), *ş* ("sh"), and *ü* (no English equivalent). The spelling of common contemporary Middle Eastern and Islamic terms follows daily press usage (which, however, is not completely uniform). Examples are "al-Qaeda," "Quran," and "Sharia."

The system used in rendering the sounds of Mandarin Chinese—the northern Chinese dialect that has become in effect the national spoken language in China and Taiwan—into English in this book is *hanyu pinyin,* usually given as simply pinyin. This is the official romanization system of the People's Republic of China and has also become the standard outside of Taiwan (the Republic of China). Most syllables are pronounced as they would be in English, with the exception of the letter *q,* which has a palatal "ch" sound (pronounced at the very front of the mouth); ch itself has a non-palatal "ch" sound (pronounced further back, as in English). *Zh* is a non-palatal "j" and *j* a palatal "j." Some syllables also are pronounced—particularly in the regions around Beijing—with a retroflex r so that the syllable *shi,* for example, carries a pronunciation closer to "shir." Finally, the letter *r* in the *pinyin* system has no direct English equivalent, but an approximation may be had by combining the sounds of "r" and "j."

Japanese terms have been romanized according to a modification of the Hepburn system. The letter *g* is always hard; vowels are handled as they are in Italian—*e,* for example, carries a sound like "ay." We have not, however, included diacritical markings to indicate long vowel sounds for *u* or *o.* Where necessary, these have been indicated in the pronunciation guides.

For Korean terms, we have used a variation of the McCune-Reischauer system, which remains the standard romanization scheme for Korean words used in English academic writing, but eliminated any diacritical markings. Here again, the vowel sounds are pronounced more or less like those of Italian and the consonants like those of English.

For Vietnamese words, we have used standard renditions based on the modern Quoc Ngu ("national language") system in use in Vietnam today. The system was developed by Jesuit missionaries and is partly based on the Portuguese alphabet. Once more, we have avoided diacritical marks, and the reader should follow the pronunciation guides for approximations of Vietnamese terms.

Latin American terms (Spanish, Nahuatl, or Quechua) generally follow local usage, including accents, except where they are Anglicized, per the *Oxford English Dictionary.* The now commonly used form "Tiwanaku" is preferred to the traditional Spanish spelling "Tiahuanaco."

We use the terms "Native American" and "Indian" interchangeably to refer to the peoples of the Americas in the pre-Columbian period and "Amerindian" in our coverage of Latin America since independence.

In keeping with widely recognized practice among paleontologists and other scholars of the deep past, we use the term "hominins" in Chapter 1 to emphasize their greater remoteness from apes and proximity to modern humans.

Phonetic spellings often follow the first appearance of a non-English word whose pronunciation may be unclear to the reader. We have followed the rules for capitalization per *The Chicago Manual of Style.*

About the Authors

Peter von Sivers is associate professor emeritus of Middle Eastern history at the University of Utah. He has previously taught at UCLA, Northwestern University, the University of Paris VII (Vincennes), and the University of Munich. He has also served as chair of the Joint Committee of the Near and Middle East, Social Science Research Council, New York, 1982–1985; editor of the *International Journal of Middle East Studies*, 1985–1989; member of the board of directors of the Middle East Studies Association of North America, 1987–1990; and chair of the SAT II World History Test Development Community of the Educational Testing Service, Princeton, NJ, 1991–1994. His publications include *Caliphate, Kingdom, and Decline: The Political Theory of Ibn Khaldun* (1968), several edited books, and three dozen peer-reviewed chapters and articles on Middle Eastern and North African history, as well as world history. He received his Dr. phil. from the University of Munich.

Charles A. Desnoyers is professor of history at La Salle University in Philadelphia. He has previously taught at Temple University, Villanova University, and Pennsylvania State University. In addition to serving as History Department chair from 1999 to 2007, he was a founder and long-time director of the Greater Philadelphia Asian Studies Consortium, and president (2011–2012) of the Mid-Atlantic Region Association for Asian Studies. He has served as a reader, table leader, and question writer for the AP European and World History exams. He served as co-editor of the World History Association's *Bulletin* from 1995 to 2001. In addition to numerous articles in peer-reviewed and general publications, his work includes *Patterns of East Asian History* (2019, Oxford University Press), *Patterns of Modern Chinese History* (2016, Oxford University Press), and *A Journey to the East: Li Gui's "A New Account of a Trip Around the Globe"* (2004, University of Michigan Press). He received his PhD from Temple University.

George B. Stow is professor of ancient and medieval history and director of the graduate program in history at La Salle University, Philadelphia. His teaching experience embraces a variety of undergraduate and graduate courses in ancient Greece and Rome, medieval England, and world history, and he has been awarded the Lindback Distinguished Teaching Award. Professor Stow is a member of the Medieval Academy of America and a Fellow of the Royal Historical Society. He is the recipient of a National Defense Education Act Title IV Fellowship, a Woodrow Wilson Foundation Fellowship, and research grants from the American Philosophical Society and La Salle University. His publications include a critical edition of a fourteenth-century monastic chronicle, *Historia Vitae et Regni Ricardi Secundi* (University of Pennsylvania Press, 1977), as well as numerous articles and reviews in scholarly journals including *Speculum*, *The English Historical Review*, the *Journal of Medieval History*, the *American Historical Review*, and several others. He received his PhD from the University of Illinois.

Patterns of World History

World Period Three

Religious Civilizations, 600–1450 CE

The rise of religious civilizations on the continents of Asia, Europe, and Africa is a striking phenomenon that unifies the period of 600–1450 in world history. It can be considered as a continuation of the intellectual and institutional transformations that began with the emphasis on monotheism and monism by the visionaries of the mid-first millennium BCE as ways to understand the world in which they lived.

The religious civilizations were not monolithic and displayed many regional variations. Internal diversity notwithstanding, they shared a number of common characteristics:

- Religious civilizations formed in regions which were larger than any single state within them: They superseded empires as the largest units of human unification.
- The civilizations were *scriptural*—that is, based on canonical (commonly agreed on) texts inherited in most cases from earlier periods. Members of educated elites (clergy, scholars, sages) taught and interpreted the scriptures to the laypeople.
- Despite hostilities among the religious civilizations, merchants, missionaries, pilgrims, and travelers visited each other's areas. They fostered a lively exchange of technical and cultural innovations from one end of Eurasia and Africa to the other.

Chapter 15

The Rise of Empires in the Americas

600–1550 CE

CHAPTER FIFTEEN PATTERNS

Origins, Interactions, Adaptations In the three agrarian–urban zones of the Americas, state building continued unabated in the period after 600 CE. In the south, it moved from the Andean coast to inland valleys and highlands. Here, the states of Wari and Tiwanaku, based on corn and potatoes, respectively, dominated until around 1050. In Mesoamerica, the Maya were able to overcome a severe drought and survive until ca. 1200 in the climatically different Chichén Itzá city-state. In the Mexican basin and adjacent obsidian-carrying mountains, the Toltecs dominated (900–1200). State-building in the Americas peaked with the creation of the Aztec (1427–1521) and Inca (1438–1533) empires, both of which were cut short by the Spanish conquest.

Uniqueness and Similarities The agrarian–urban states of the Americas, evolving into empires parallel to those in Eurasia and Africa, were sophisticated organizations. They all had to reckon with the technical limitations (no work animals, plows, and wheeled transportation) prevalent in the Americas. Nevertheless, the Aztecs and the Incas created remarkably large-sized states with impressive military and administrative structures.

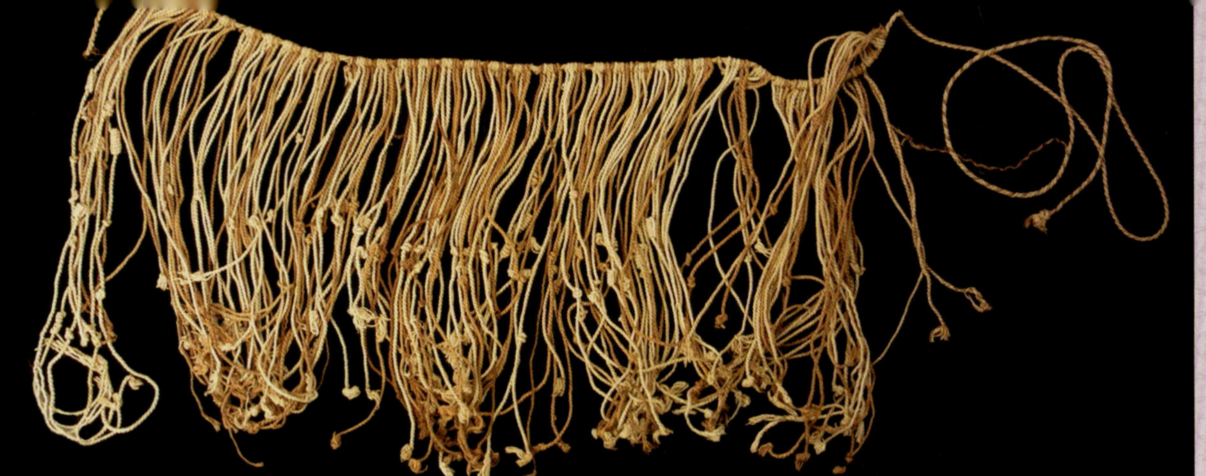

Just outside Lima lies the shantytown of Túpac Amaru, named after the last Inca ruler, who died in 1572. People fleeing the Maoist Shining Path guerillas southeast of Lima settled here during the 1980s. Archaeologists knew that the site was an ancient burial place called Puruchuco (Quechua, "Feathered Helmet") but could not prevent the influx of settlers. By the late 1990s, the temporary shantytown had become an established settlement. However, residents realized that archaeologists had to be consulted before the shantytown could be officially recognized.

During excavations from 1999 to 2001, archaeologists unearthed one of the most astounding treasures in the history of American archaeology. The team discovered some 2,200 mummies, most of them bundled up in blankets and perfectly preserved. Many bundles also contained burial gifts of food and jewelry.

Scholars hope that when all of the mummies have been unwrapped, more will be learned about the social characteristics of the buried people, as so much about the Inca Empire that ruled the Andes from 1438 to 1533 remains unknown.

The Inca Empire and the Aztec Empire (1427–1521) grew from patterns that began to form around 600 CE in Mesoamerica and the Andes (see Chapter 5). After 600, kingdom formation spread across Mesoamerica and arose for the first time in the Andes. These kingdoms were states with military ruling classes that could conquer larger territories than was possible prior to the 600s. Military competition prepared the way for the origin of empires. Even though empires arrived later in the Americas than in Eurasia, they demonstrate that humans, once they had adopted agriculture, followed similar patterns of social and political formation across the world.

CHAPTER OUTLINE

The Legacy of Teotihuacán and the Toltecs in Mesoamerica

The Legacy of Tiwanaku and Wari in the Andes

American Empires: Aztec and Inca Origins and Dominance

Imperial Society and Culture

Putting It All Together

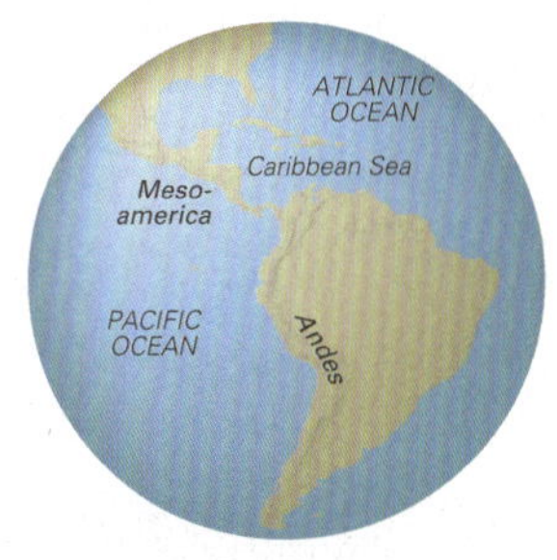

ABOVE: This kind of knotted string assembly (a *quipu*) was used in the Andes from ca. 2500 BCE onward for the recording of taxes, population figures, calendar dates, troop numbers, and other data.

Seeing Patterns

> Within the patterns of state formation basic to the Americas, which types of states emerged in Mesoamerica and the Andes during the period 600–1550? What characterized these states?

> Why did the Tiwanaku and Wari states have ruling classes but no dynasties and central bureaucracies? How were these patterns expressed in the territorial organization of these states?

> What patterns of urban life characterized the cities of Tenochtitlán and Cuzco, the capitals of the Aztec and Inca Empires? In which ways were these cities similar to those of Eurasia and Africa?

The Legacy of Teotihuacán and the Toltecs in Mesoamerica

The city-state of Teotihuacán had dominated northern Mesoamerica from 200 BCE to the late 500s CE (see Chapter 6). After its collapse, the surrounding towns and villages perpetuated the cultural legacy of Teotihuacán. Employing this legacy, the conquering state of the Toltecs unified part of the region from 900 to 1180. At the same time, after an internal crisis, the southern Maya kingdoms on the Yucatán Peninsula reached their late flowering, together with the northern state of Chichén Itzá.

Militarism in the Mexican Basin

After the ruling class of Teotihuacán disintegrated at the end of the sixth century, the newly independent small successor states of Mesoamerica continued Teotihuacán's cultural heritage. The Toltecs, migrants from the north, militarized the Teotihuacán legacy and transformed it into a program of conquest.

Ceremonial Centers and Chiefdoms In the three centuries after the end of Teotihuacán, the local population declined from some 200,000 to about 30,000. However, other places around the Mexican Basin and beyond rose in importance. The region to the northwest of the valley had an extensive mining industry that produced a variety of gemstones. Independent after 600, inhabitants built small states and traded their gemstones to their neighbors.

To the north were the Pueblo cultures in today's southwestern United States. These cultures, which flourished between 700 and 1500, were based on irrigated farming systems and are known for their painted pottery styles. These cultures might have been in contact with the Mississippi cultures, of which the city of Cahokia (650–1400) near modern St. Louis is the best-known site (see Map 15.1).

To the south, in western Mesoamerica, chiefdoms flourished on the basis of metallurgy (especially copper), which arrived with Ecuadoran seaborne merchants ca. 600–800. Copper, too soft for agricultural implements or military weapons, was used mostly in household objects and as jewelry.

The Toltec Conquering State Soon after the collapse of Teotihuacán, craftspeople and farmers migrated north to Tula. They founded a ceremonial center and town with workshops known for tools fabricated from the local Pachuca obsidian. Around 900, new migrants arrived from northwest Mexico as well as the Gulf Coast. The northerners spoke Nahuatl [NAH-wat], the language of the later Aztecs, and after taking possession of Tula, they made it their ancestral city.

The integration of the new arrivals resulted in the abandonment of the temple and the departure of a defeated party of Tulans.

The new Tula of 900 developed quickly into a large city with a new temple. It later became the capital of the conquering state of the Toltecs, whose warrior culture influenced Mesoamerica from around 900 to 1180 (see Map 15.1).

The Toltecs introduced two innovations in weaponry that improved the effectiveness of hand-to-hand combat: a short sword made of hardwood with inlaid obsidian edges that could slash as well as crush, and obsidian daggers with wooden

North America and Mesoamerica, ca. 1100 CE

Pueblo cultures
Mississippian cultures
Movement of trade goods north from Mesoamerica
Sea route from Mesoamerica to Mississippi River valley
Mayan trade route
Toltec conquests
Chontal Peoples
UTAH Modern-day state

MAP 15.1 North America and Mesoamerica, ca. 1100

handles worn inside a band on the left arm. Traditional dart throwers and slings for stone projectiles completed the offensive armament of the warriors.

The Toltec army was sufficiently large to engage in battles of conquest within four days' march from Tula. Any target beyond this range was beyond their capabilities, given the logistics—and, of course, Toltecs did not have the benefit of

600 End of city-state of Teotihuacán in Mexican Basin

600–1100 Conquering state of Tiwanaku in Andes (southern Peru/Bolivia)

600–900 Late Maya kingdoms in Yucatán Peninsula

700–1000 Conquering state of Wari in Andes (central Bolivia)

850–1000 City-state of Chichén Itzá in northern Yucatán Peninsula

900–1170 Toltec conquering state, north of Mexican Basin

1427–1521 Aztec Empire in Mesoamerica

1438–1533 Inca Empire in Andes

wheeled vehicles. Thus, the only way of projecting power beyond the four-day range was to establish colonies and to have troops accompany traders. As a result, the Toltec state projected its power through the prestige of its large military, rather than through an administrative imposition of governors, tributes, and taxes.

Trade The Toltecs established a large trade network based on Tula's obsidian. Merchants moved southward into the cacao, vanilla, and bird-feather production centers of Chiapas and Guatemala, to the north into gemstone mining regions, and westward into centers of metal mining. Metallurgy advanced around 1200 with the development of the technology of bronze casting. Bronze was preferable to copper for axes and bells; both were prized by the elites in Tula.

The Late Toltec Era Toltec military power declined in the twelfth century when the taxable grain yield around the city diminished. Sometime around 1180, foraging peoples from the northwest invaded, attacking Toltec communication lines. The disruptions caused an internal revolt, which brought down the ceremonial center and its palaces. By 1200, Mesoamerica relapsed into a period of small-state coexistence.

Late Maya States in Yucatán

Teotihuacán's demise at the end of the sixth century was paralleled by a realignment of the balance of power among the Maya kingdoms in the southern Yucatán lowlands of Mesoamerica. This realignment was resolved by around 650. A period of late flowering spanned the next two centuries, followed by a shift of power from the southern to the northern part of the peninsula.

The Southern Kingdoms At its height during the fourth and fifth centuries, Teotihuacán had interjected itself into the balance of power among the Maya kingdoms of southern Yucatán. Alliances shifted, and wars racked the lowlands, destroying several older states. A dozen new kingdoms emerged and established a new balance of power among themselves. After a lengthy hiatus, Maya culture entered its final period (650–900).

The final period in the southern, rain forest–covered lowlands and adjacent highlands was marked by agricultural expansion and ceremonial monument construction. The rain forest on hillsides was cut down and terraces were built for soil retention. The largest kingdoms grew to 50,000–60,000 inhabitants and reached astounding rural population densities of about 1,000 persons per square mile. They were administratively the most centralized polities ever created in indigenous American history.

The late Maya states did not last long. Torrential downpours washed the topsoil from the newly built hillside terraces. Malnutrition resulting from the shrinking agricultural surface began to reduce the labor force. In the end, even the ruling classes suffered, with members killing each other for what remained of agricultural surpluses. By about 900, the Maya kingdoms in southern Yucatán had shriveled.

Chichén Itzá in the North A few small Maya states on the periphery survived. The most prominent among them was Chichén Itzá [chee-CHEN eet-SAH], which flourished from about 850 to 1000. The region would appear to be inhospitable, as the climate was very dry and the surface was rocky or covered with thin topsoil. There were no rivers, but many sinkholes in the porous limestone underneath the soil held water. Cisterns to hold additional amounts of water for year-round use were cut into the limestone; this water, carried in jars to the surface, supported a productive garden agriculture.

Chichén Itzá was founded during the phase of renewed urbanization in 650. The population was composed of local Maya as well as the Maya-speaking Chontal from the Gulf Coast farther west. Groups among these people engaged in long-distance trade, both overland and in boats along the coast. Since trade in the most lucrative goods required contact with people outside even the farthest political reach of either Teotihuacán or Tula, merchants traveled in armed caravans.

Chontal traders adopted Toltec culture, and in Chichén Itzá around 850 they superimposed their adopted culture over that of the original Maya. At the very end of the period of Teotihuacán, Maya, and Toltec cultural expansion, the three cultures finally merged on the Yucatán Peninsula. This merger did not last long: Already around 1000 the ruling-class factions left the city-state for unknown reasons, and it diminished in size and power.

Chacmool (Offering Table) at the Entrance to the Temple of Warriors, Chichén Itzá. Chacmools originated here and spread to numerous places in Mesoamerica, as far north as Tenochtitlán and Tula. Offerings to the gods included food, tobacco, feathers, and incense. Offerings might have included also human sacrifices. The table in the form of a prostrate human figure is in itself symbolic of sacrifice.

The Legacy of Tiwanaku and Wari in the Andes

Mesoamerica and the Andes shared the tradition of regional temple pilgrimages. In the Andes, the chiefdoms remained mostly coastal. Around 600 CE, the two conquering states of Tiwanaku in the highlands of what are today southern Peru and Bolivia and Wari in central Peru emerged. Both states represented a major step in the formation of larger, militarily organized polities.

The Expanding State of Tiwanaku

Tiwanaku was a political and cultural power in the south-central Andes during the period 600–1100. It began as a ceremonial center and developed into a state dominating the region around Lake Titicaca. At its apogee it planted colonies in regions far from the lake and conveyed its culture through trade to peoples even farther away.

Agriculture on the High Plain The Andes consist of two parallel mountain chains along the west coast of South America. In southeastern Peru and western Bolivia, an intermountain plain, 12,500 feet above sea level, extends as wide as 125 miles. At its northern end lies Lake Titicaca, which has one outlet at its southern

Tiwanaku, Kalassaya Gate. Within the Temple of the Sun, this gate is aligned with the sun's equinoxes and was used for festive rituals. Note the precise stonework, which the Incas later developed further.

end, a river flowing into Lake Poopó [po-PO], a salt lake 150 miles south. The Lake Titicaca region receives winter rains sufficient for agriculture and grazing.

The region around Lake Titicaca offered nearly everything necessary for an advanced urbanization process. The lake's freshwater supported fish and resources such as reeds from the swamps, which served for the construction of boats and roofs. The food staples were potatoes and quinoa. The grasslands of the upper hills served as pastures for llama and alpaca herds. Llamas were used as transportation animals, and alpacas provided wool; the meat of both animals was a major protein source.

Farmers grew their crops on hillside terraces or on raised fields close to the lake. The raised-field system, which farmers adopted from peoples of the Maya lowlands, consisted of a grid of narrow strips of earth, separated from each other by channels. Mud from the channels, heaped onto the strips, replenished their fertility. By 700, the city of Tiwanaku had 20,000 inhabitants.

Ceremonial feasts brought together elite lineages and clients, or ordinary craftspeople and villagers. Elites and clients cohered through **reciprocity**—that is, communal labor by clients rewarded by the elites with feasting. Forced labor through conscription or taxation did not appear until shortly before the collapse of the state.

Reciprocity: In its basic form, an informal agreement among people according to which a gift or an invitation has to be returned after a reasonable amount of time; in the pre-Columbian Americas, an arrangement of feasts instead of taxes shared by ruling classes and subjects in a state.

Expansion and Colonization The region around southern Lake Titicaca housed related but competing elite–client hierarchies. Ruling clans and ordinary farmers comprised a state capable of imposing military power beyond the center. Counterbalancing clans at the head of similar hierarchies prevented the rise of permanent, unified central administrations and military forces.

The hallmark of Tiwanaku authority was the prestige of its ceremonial center rather than military might. Tiwanaku feasting ceremonies could be considered expressions of Tiwanaku authority—and pilgrims who partook in the feasts came into its orbit.

Yet military force did play a role in the western valleys of the Andes. Merchants accompanied by warriors traveled hundreds of miles. Settler colonies were additional forms of power projection, especially those established in the Moquegua [mow-KAY-gwah] valley to the west. Here, Tiwanaku emigrants established villages, which sent some of their corn or beer to the capital in return for salt and obsidian tools. Although overall less militarily inclined than the Mesoamerican states of the same time period, Tiwanaku wielded a visible influence over southern Peru (see Map 15.2).

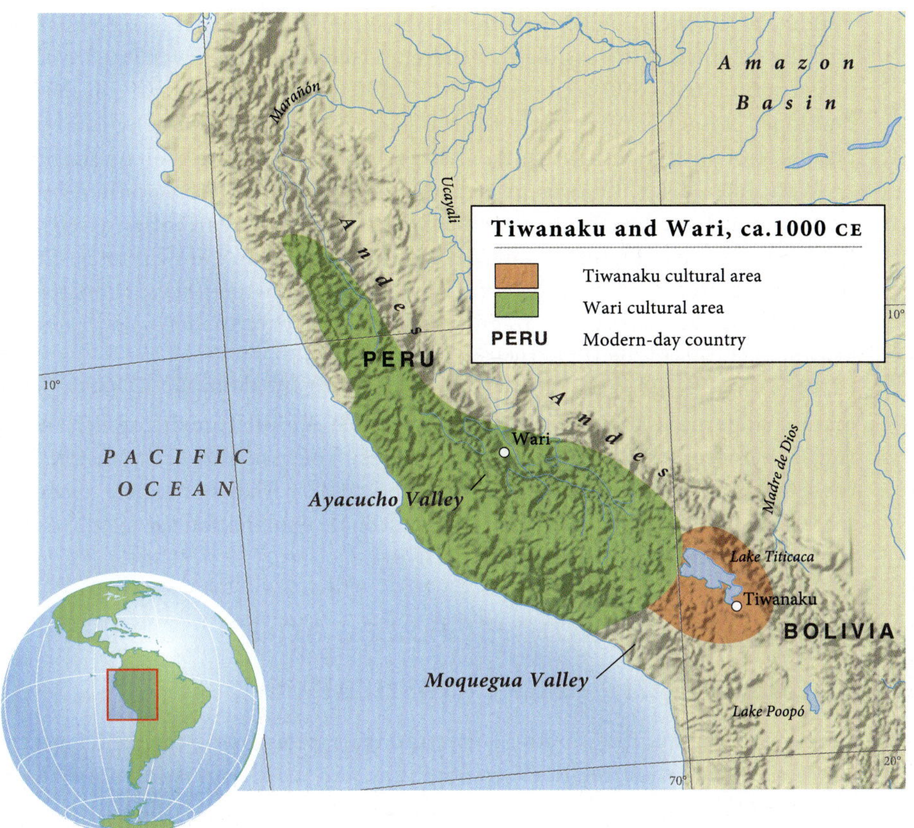

MAP 15.2 **Tiwanaku and Wari, ca. 1000**

The Expanding City-State of Wari

Little is known about early settlements in central Peru. The state of Wari emerged around 600, and expansion to the south put Wari into direct contact with Tiwanaku. The two states came to some form of mutual accommodation, and it appears that neither embarked on an outright conquest of the other. Their military postures remained limited to their regional spheres of influence.

Origins and Expansion Wari was centered on the Ayacucho valley, a narrow 9,000-foot-high plain in northern Peru. The land is mountainous, interspersed with valleys and rivers. Farmers grew potatoes, corn and cotton. In the seventh century, Wari grew to 30,000 inhabitants and brought neighboring cities under its control. It also expanded terrace farming. Like Tiwanaku, Wari became the center of a developed urbanism and a diversified agriculture.

In addition to maintaining control over the cities in its vicinity, Wari constructed new towns with plazas, housing for laborers, and halls for feasting. Outside the core area, Wari elites established colonies. It appears that Wari exercised much stronger political control over the chiefs of its core region than Tiwanaku and was more active in founding colonies.

The Wari–Tiwanaku Frontier Wari established a colony upstream in the Moquegua valley with extensive terraces, canals, and protective walls. This building activity coincided with the establishment by Tiwanaku of downstream farming colonies. It is possible that there was tension with Tiwanaku during the initial period (650–800), but during 800–1000 the two agricultural communities developed closer ties. Very likely, the Moquegua valley was politically so far on the periphery of both states that neither had the means to impose itself on the other.

Wari, like Tiwanaku, was an expanding state. Both were governed by elite clans which benefited from reciprocal patron–client organizations. However, there is evidence of increased internal tension after 950 in the two states. Groups defaced sculptures, destroyed portals, and burned down edifices. Scholars have argued that it was perhaps the fragility of power based on an increasingly unequal sharing that caused the rift between elites and subjects.

Why would elites allow reciprocity to be weakened? Some suggest that climatic change made large feasts no longer possible. A more convincing explanation suggests environmental degradation as the result of agricultural expansion. As in the late Maya kingdoms, the exhausted land could perhaps no longer sustain an increasing population. Unfortunately, an ultimate explanation for the disintegration of Tiwanaku and Wari remains elusive.

American Empires: Aztec and Inca Origins and Dominance

Building on the traditions of the Toltec and Wari states, in the early fifteenth century centralized multireligious, multiethnic, and multilinguistic polities arose. They were the empires of the Aztecs and Incas.

The Aztec Empire of Mesoamerica

The ancestors of the Aztecs (also called Mexica [me-SHEE-ka]) left Tula and arrived at the Mexican Basin at an unknown time. They eventually conquered the Mexican Basin, the site of today's Mexico City. In the fifteenth century, they conquered an empire that encompassed Mesoamerica from the Pacific to the Gulf of Mexico and from the middle of modern northern Mexico to the Isthmus of Panama.

Settlement in the Mexican Valley According to the Aztecs' founding myth, the first Aztec was born on an island in a lake or in a mountain cave northwest of the Mexican Basin. This Aztec ancestor and his descendants migrated south, guided by their hunter–warrior patron god Huitzilopochtli [weet-see-lo-POCHT-lee] to a land of plenty. When the ancestors arrived at the Mexican Basin, an eagle perched on a cactus commanded the Aztecs to settle and build a temple to their god. In this temple they were to sacrifice to the god the blood of humans captured in war.

The historical record in the Mexican Basin becomes clearer in the fourteenth century, during which the Aztecs appeared as clients of two Toltec-descended overlords in city-states on the southwestern shore. Here they created two islands, founded a city with a ceremonial center, and rendered military service to their overlords. Aztec leaders married into the elites of the neighboring city-states and gained the right to have their own ruler presiding over a council of the elite and priests.

The Rise of the Empire After the successful rebellion in 1428 of a triple alliance among the Aztec city-state and two other vassal states against the reigning city-state in the Mexican Basin, the Aztec leader Itzcóatl [its-CO-at(l)] (r. 1428–1440) emerged as the dominant figure. Tenochtitlán, the Aztec city on one of the islands, became the capital of an empire that consisted of a set of six "inner provinces" in the Mexican Basin. Local elites were required to attend ceremonies in Tenochtitlán, bring and receive gifts, leave their sons as hostages, and intermarry with the elites of the triple alliance. Farmers had to provide tribute, making the imperial core self-sufficient.

After further conquests by the middle of the fifteenth century, the triple alliance created an imperial polity from the Pacific to the Gulf (see Map 15.3). This state was more centralized than the Teotihuacán and Toltec city-states. In this empire, local ruling families were generally left in place, but commoners had to produce tributes of foodstuffs and manufactures. In some provinces, Aztec governors replaced the rulers; in others, Aztec tribute collectors (supported by troops) held local rulers in check and supervised the transportation of the tributes. Although reciprocity

MAP 15.3 The Aztec Empire, ca. 1520

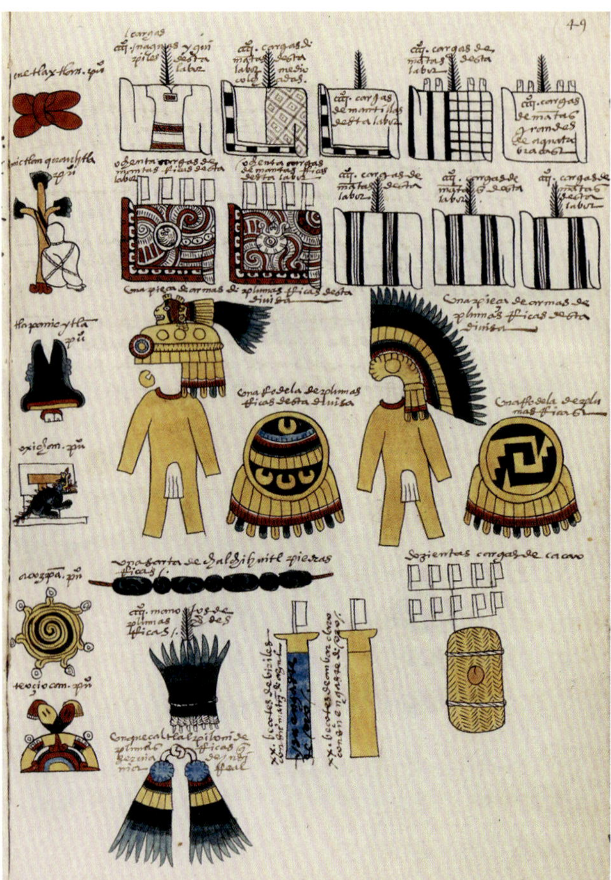

List of Tributes Owed to the Aztecs. The list includes quantities of cotton and wool textiles, clothes, headgear with feathers, and basketry. The Aztecs did not continue the complex syllabic script of the Maya, but used instead images, including persons with speech bubbles, for communication. Spanish administrators and monks who copied the Aztec manuscripts added their own explanations to keep track of Native American tributes.

continued, it was now clearly subordinate to military considerations. The resulting multiethnic, multireligious, and multilinguistic empire was still developing in the early sixteenth century when the Spanish arrived. The state of Tlaxcala [tlash-KAH-la], held out in opposition, together with enemy states on the periphery. Although the triple alliance did everything to expand, pockets of anti-Aztec states survived and eventually became allies of the Spanish. The key policy of continued expansion of Aztec central control was the threat of warfare. This fear-inducing tactic was an integral innovation in the imperialism of the Aztecs.

The Military Forces The triple alliance ruled 1.5 million inhabitants in the Mexican Basin. This number yielded up to a quarter of a million potential soldiers. Initially, the army was recruited from among the elite of the Aztecs and their allies. But toward the middle of the fifteenth century, Aztec rulers set up separate military school systems for the sons of the elite as well as the commoners. After graduation, soldiers rose in the army hierarchy on the basis of merit, particularly their success in the capture of enemies for future sacrifice.

The Aztecs inherited the weaponry and armor of the Toltecs, including the bow and arrow, as well as the obsidian-spiked broadsword, derived from the Toltec short sword. Clubs, maces, and axes functioned as secondary weapons. Body armor, consisting of quilted, sleeveless cotton shirts, thick cotton helmets, and round wooden or cane shields, was also adopted from the Toltecs. With the arrival of the Aztecs, the Americas had acquired the heaviest infantry weaponry in their history.

The Inca Empire of the Andes

The southern Peruvian city-state of Cuzco, with its Inca elite, emerged in the early fifteenth century at the head of a militaristic conquering polity. Within another century, the Incas had established an empire, called Tawantinsuyu [ta-wan-tin-SOO-yoo] (Quechua, "Four Regions"), symbolizing its geographical expanse. It stretched from Ecuador in the north to central Chile in the south, with extensions into the upper Amazon and western Argentina (see Map 15.4).

The Incas, like the Aztecs, had a founding myth. In one version, the creator god Viracocha [vee-ra-KO-cha] summoned four brothers and four sisters, pairing them as couples and promising them a land of plenty. They would find this land when a golden rod would get stuck in the soil. Alternatively, the sun god Inti [IN-tee] did the pairing of the couples before sending them with the golden rod to their promised land. In Cuzco, where the rod plunged into fertile soil, the Incas drove out the existing farmers.

MAP 15.4 The Inca Empire, ca. 1525

In the fourteenth century, Cuzco became a serious contender in the regional city-state competition. Eight rulers are said to have succeeded each other in the consolidation of Cuzco as a local power, although little is known about them. Firm historical terrain is reached with the ninth ruler, Pachacuti (r. 1438–1471). The history of the Incas from 1438 onward is known much better, primarily because of the records of the Spanish conquerors.

Imperial Expansion The system of reciprocity that characterized earlier Mesoamerican and Andean history continued under the Incas. *Ayllu* [AY-yoo], the Quechua term for a household with an ancestral lineage, implied mutual

Aztec Weapons. Aztec weapons were well-crafted hardwood implements with serrated obsidian edges, capable of cutting through metal, including iron. As slashing weapons they were highly effective in close combat.

obligations among groups of households, neighborhoods, villages, and city-states. The most important social expression of reciprocity remained the feast. In the Incan Empire, the state collected more from the *ayllus* than Tiwanaku and Wari had done, but whether it returned comparable amounts through feasts and celebrations was a matter of contention, often leading to armed rebellion.

The earliest conquests under Pachacuti were around Lake Titicaca, as well as the north of the former Wari state. The Incas then expanded 1,300 miles northward to southern Ecuador and 1,500 miles southward to Chile. The final provinces, added in the early sixteenth century, were in northern Ecuador as well as on the eastern slopes of the Andes. The capital, Cuzco, with some 100,000 inhabitants in the early sixteenth century, was laid out in a grid of four streets. Symbolically, the capital reached out to the four regions of the empire—coast, north, south, and Amazon rain forest.

Administration Ethnic Inca governors administered the four regions, which were subdivided into provinces, each with an Inca subgovernor. Most provinces were composites of former city-states, which remained under their local elites. A system of population organization was imposed by the Inca rulers. According to this system, members of the local elites commanded 10,000, 1,000, 100, and 10 household heads for the ***mit'a*** [MIT-ah] (Quechua, "turn," in reference to service obligations rotating among the subject lineages). The services were owed by subjects to the empire as a form of taxes.

***Mit'a*:** Innovation of the Incas in which subjects were obligated to deliver a portion of their harvests, animal products, and domestically produced goods to nearby storehouses for use by Inca officials and troops. The *mit'a* also provided laborers for construction projects as well as workers on state farms or mines.

The *mit'a* was an important innovation the Incas contributed to the history of the Americas. In contrast to the Aztecs, who shipped taxes in kind to their capital by boat, the Incas had no efficient means of transportation for long distances. The only way to make use of the taxes in kind was to store them locally. The Incas built storehouses and required subjects to deliver a portion of their goods and harvests under *mit'a* obligations to the nearest storehouse. These supplies enabled the Incas to conduct military campaigns far from Cuzco. In addition, it was through the *mit'a* that laborers were assembled for construction projects, often far from the urban center. Finally, *mit'a* provided laborers for mines, quarries, farms, and colonies.

To keep track of *mit'a* obligations, officials used bundles of knotted cord (***quipu***, or *khipu* [KEE-poo], "knot"). The numbers of knots on each cord in the bundles contained information on population figures and service obligations. The use of quipus was widespread in the Andes long before the Inca. Although some 700 have been preserved, attempts to decipher them have so far failed (see Chapter 5).

***Quipu*:** Knotted string assembly, used in the Andes from ca. 2500 BCE onward for the recording of taxes, population figures, calendar dates, troop numbers, and other data.

Military Organization Under the *mit'a* system of the Inca Empire, men were required to serve in the military. As in the Aztec Empire, administrators made sure that enough laborers remained in the villages to take care of their other obligations of farming, herding, transporting, and manufacturing. Intermediate commanders came from the local and regional elites, and the top commanders were members of the two upper and lower Inca ruling elites.

Inca weaponry was comparable to that of the Aztecs, consisting of bows and arrows, dart throwers, slings, clubs with spiked bronze heads, wooden

Inca Roads. Inca roads were paths reserved for runners and the military. They were built on beds of rocks and rubble and connected strategic points in the most direct line possible.

broadswords, bronze axes, and bronze-tipped javelins. The Incas also used a snare to entangle the enemy's legs. Protective armor consisted of quilted cotton shirts, copper breastplates, wooden helmets, and shields.

During the second half of the fifteenth century, the Incas turned from conquest to consolidation. Faced with rebellions, they deemphasized the draft and recruited longer-serving troops from a smaller number of trusted peoples. These troops garrisoned forts throughout the empire and were part of the settler colonies in rebellious provinces and border regions. Personal guards recruited from non-Inca populations accompanied leading ruling-class members. The professionalization of the Inca army, however, lagged behind that of the Aztecs, since the Incas did not have military academies open to their subjects.

Communications The Incas created an excellent imperial communication and logistics structure. They improved on the road network that they inherited from Tiwanaku, Wari, and other states. Roads extended from Cuzco nearly the entire length of the empire. The roads often required extensive grounding, paving, staircasing, and tunneling. In many places, the 25,000-mile road network still exists today.

The roads were reserved for troops, officials, and runners carrying messages. For their convenience, every 15 miles, or at the end of a slow one-day journey, an inn provided accommodation. Armies stopped at barracks or pitched tents. Despite the fact that they did not have wheeled transport, the Incas were aware of how crucial paved and well-supplied roads were for infantry soldiers.

Imperial Society and Culture

As Mesoamerica and the Andes entered their imperial age, cosmopolitan capitals with monumental ceremonial centers and palaces emerged. Ceremonies and rituals impressed on enemies and subjects alike the irresistible might of the empires.

Aqueduct from the Western Hills to Tenochtitlán. This aqueduct, still standing today, provided fresh water to the palace and mansions of the center of the island, to be used as drinking water and for washing.

Imperial Capitals: Tenochtitlán and Cuzco

In the fifteenth century, the Aztec and Inca capitals were among the largest cities of the world, encompassing between 100,000 and 200,000 inhabitants. Although their monumental architecture followed different artistic traditions, both emphasized platforms and sanctuaries atop large pyramid-like structures as symbols of elevated power as well as closeness to the gods.

Tenochtitlán as an Urban Metropolis

More than half of the approximately 1.5 million people living during the fifteenth century in the Mexican Basin were urban dwellers. Such an extraordinary concentration of urban citizens was unique in the agrarian world prior to the industrialization of Europe, when cities usually held no more than 10 percent of the total population (see Map 15.5).

The center of Tenochtitlán, on the southern island, was a large platform. In an enclosure on this platform were the main pyramid, with temples to the Aztec gods on top, and smaller ceremonial centers. Also on the platform were a food market, palaces of the ruling elite, courts of law, workshops, a prison, and councils for teachers and the military. Aztecs and visitors assembled each day to pay respect to the ruler and to trade in the market.

In 1473, the southern island was merged with the northern island. At the center of the northern island was the principal market of the combined islands, which attracted as many as 40,000 people each day. The sophistication of the market was comparable to that of any market in Eurasia during the fifteenth century.

Causeways linked the capital with the lakeshore, and people traveled inside the city on a system of canals. Dikes with sluices regulated both the water level and the salinity of the lake. Potable water arrived from the shore via an aqueduct on one of the western causeways. Professional water carriers took fresh water from the aqueduct to commoners in the city; professional waste removers collected human waste from urban residences and took it to farmers for fertilizer.

The two city centers—the pyramid and palaces in the south and the market in the north—were surrounded by residential quarters, many of which were inhabited by craftspeople of a shared profession. The rooms of the houses surrounded a central patio—an architectural preference common to Mesoamerica and the Andes, as well as the Middle East and Mediterranean.

Residents of quarters farther away from the center were farmers. Here, a grid of canals encased small, rectangular islands devoted to housing compounds and/or farming. A raised-field system prevailed, whereby farmers dredged the canals and heaped the fertile mud on top of the rectangular islands, called ***chinampas***. In contrast to the luxurious palaces of the elite, housing for farmers consisted of humble plastered huts. As in all agrarian societies, farmers—subject to high taxes or rents—were among the poorest folk.

Chinampas: Small, artificial islands in Lake Texcoco created by farmers for raising agricultural crops.

On the surface of the *chinampas*, farmers grew seed plants as well as maguey [mag-AY], a large succulent agave. This evergreen plant has a large root system, which stabilizes the ground, and produces fiber for weaving and pulp for making pulque [POOL-kay], a fermented drink.

Ownership of the *chinampas* was vested in clans, which, under neighborhood leaders, were responsible for the allocation of land and adjudication of disputes as well as the payment of taxes in kind to the elite. There were also members of the elite who possessed estates and employed managers to collect rents from the farmers. Whether there was a trend from taxes to rents is unknown.

MAP 15.5 **Tenochtitlán and the Mexican Basin**

Cuzco as a Ceremonial-Administrative City The site of the Inca city of Cuzco was a triangle formed by the confluence of two rivers. At one end was a hill on which were built the imperial armory and a temple dedicated to the sun god. Enormous stone walls followed the contours of the hill.

Below, the city was laid out in a grid pattern. The residents of the city, all belonging to the Inca ruling class, lived in adobe houses arranged in a block-and-courtyard pattern similar to that of Wari. Squares and temples served as ceremonial centers. The Coricancha [ko-ri-KAHN-cha], the city's main temple, stood near the confluence of the rivers. This temple was a walled compound set around a courtyard. Each year, priests of the empire's ceremonial centers sent a sacred object to the Coricancha to demonstrate their obedience to the central Inca temple.

Across the rivers were settlements for commoners with markets and storehouses. In the fields, interspersed stone pillars and shrines were aligned on sight lines radiating from the Coricancha, tying the countryside closely to the urban center. They bore a similarity to the Nasca lines in southern Peru (see Chapter 5). Farther away were imperial estates with unfree laborers from outside the *mit'a* system. In contrast to the Aztec elite, which allowed meritorious generals to rise in the hierarchy, the Inca elite remained exclusionary, allowing no commoners to reside in Cuzco.

Power and Its Cultural Expressions

Ruling elites emphasized the display of power during the period 600–1500. This was particularly true with the Aztecs and Incas during the fifteenth century.

Inca Ruling-Class Gender Relations The greatest honor for Inca girls in Cuzco and provincial colonies was to enter at age 10–12 into the service of a

Patterns Up Close

Human Sacrifice

In the first millennium CE, Mesoamerica and the Andes evolved from their early nature spirituality to polytheism. The earlier heritage, however, remained a strong undercurrent, as seen in human as well as animal and agricultural sacrifices. Rulers appeased the gods also through a form of self-sacrifice, the piercing of tongue and penis. The feathered serpent god Quetzalcóatl was the Mesoamerican deity of self-sacrifice, revered in the city-states of Teotihuacán (200 BCE–570 CE) and Tula (ca. 900 CE). Under the Toltecs and the Aztecs, this god receded in favor of warrior gods such as Tezcatlipoca and Huitzilopochtli. The survival of traditional blood rituals and human sacrifices within polytheism was a pattern that distinguished the early American empires from their contemporary Eurasian counterparts.

In 2015, Mexican archaeologists discovered the remnants of what once was the huge skull rack (*tzompantli*) in front of the main temple. Here, expert sacrificers first cut out the hearts of the victims, most of whom were captured warriors. Then they

Human Sacrifice. Human sacrifice among the pre-Columbian Mesoamericans and Andeans was based on the concept of a shared life spirit or mind, symbolized by the life substance of blood. In the American spiritual-polytheistic conceptualization, the gods sacrificed their blood, or themselves altogether, during creation; rulers pierced their earlobes, tongues, or penises for blood sacrifices; and war captives lost their lives when their hearts were sacrificed to sustain the gods.

"House of Chosen Women." An inspector from Cuzco visited villages to select attractive young girls for the service. These houses had female instructors who provided the girls with an education in cooking, beer making, weaving, and officiating in the ceremonies of the Inca religion. After their graduation, the young women became virgin temple priestesses, were given in marriage to non-Incas honored for service to the ruler, or became servants or concubines of the Inca elite. The collection of this girl tribute was separate from the reciprocity system.

The form of agriculture in Mesoamerica and the Andes gave males fewer opportunities to accumulate wealth and power than plow agriculture did in Eurasia. Nevertheless, the gradual agrarian–urban diversification of society, even if it was slower in the Americas than in Eurasia, proceeded along similar paths of increasing male power concentration. An emphasis on gender differences, therefore, should be viewed as a characteristic phenomenon arising in imperial contexts.

Inca Mummy Veneration Other houses in Cuzco were ghostly residences in which servants catered to the needs of deceased, mummified Inca emperors and their principal wives. During the mummification process, attendants removed the cadaver's internal organs, placed them in special containers, and desiccated the bodies until they were completely mummified. Servants dressed the mummies in their finest clothing and placed them back into their residences amid their possessions, as if they had never died. The mummies received daily meals and were carried around by their retinues for visits to their mummified relatives. On special occasions, mummies were lined up according to rank on Cuzco's main plaza to participate in ceremonies and processions. In this way, they remained fully integrated in the daily life of the elite.

severed the heads, cleaned them of their flesh, cut holes into the temples, and lined up the skulls on the bars of a rack 118 feet long and 16 feet high. Years later, the remains were taken off and cemented into two five-foot-high towers in front of the rack. The number of skulls is estimated to be in the thousands.

It is possible that the *tzompantli* was a heritage from earlier American societies. A few skulls with holes in the temples were found, for example, in Chichén Itzá. But it was Aztec society where the divine blood ritual reached its apogee in importance—evidently in conjunction with their empire being the most populated and expansive.

Questions

- In examining the question of whether empires such as the Inca and the Aztec employed human sacrifice for prestige purposes, can this practice be considered an adaptation that evolved out of earlier rituals, such as royal bloodletting?
- If the Aztec and the Inca did indeed employ human sacrifice for prestige purposes, what does this say about the ability of these two empires to use cultural and religious practices to consolidate their power?

In Andean society, mummies were crucial ingredients in the religious heritage, in which strong nature-spiritual elements survived underneath the polytheistic overlay of astral gods. In the spiritual tradition, a dead person's spirit, while no longer in the body, remains nearby and needs daily nourishment in order not to be driven away. Hence, even though non-Incan Andean societies removed the dead from their daily living spaces, descendants had to visit tombs regularly with food and beer. The tradition survives today in the Catholic Días de Muertos customs on November 1 and 2.

The expenses for the upkeep of the mummy households were the responsibility of the deceased emperor's bloodline, headed by a surviving brother. As heirs of the emperor's estate, the members of the bloodline formed a powerful clan within the ruling class. The new emperor was excluded from this estate and had to acquire his own new one in the course of his rule. In the early sixteenth century, however, this mechanism of keeping the upper and lower rungs of the ruling class united became counterproductive. Emperors lacking resources had to contend with brothers richly endowed with inherited wealth and ready to engage in dynastic warfare—as actually occurred shortly before the arrival of the Spanish (1529–1532).

Putting It All Together

The Aztec and Inca Empires unleashed extraordinary creative energies. Sculptors, painters, and (after the arrival of the Spanish) writers recorded the traditions as well as the innovations of the fifteenth century. Aztec painters produced codices, or illustrated manuscripts, that present the cultural and administrative activities of their societies in exquisite detail. Today, a handful of these codices survive, preserved in Mexican and European libraries.

The Aztec and Inca Empires were polities that illustrate how humans not in contact with the rest of the world developed patterns of innovation that were remarkably similar. On the basis of an agriculture that produced ample surpluses, humans made the same choices as their cousins in Eurasia and Africa. Specifically, in the period 600–1500, they created temple-centered city-states, just like their Sumerian and Hindu counterparts. Their military states were not unlike the Chinese warring states. And, finally, their empires were comparable to those of the New Kingdom Egyptians or the Assyrians. The Americas had their own unique variations of these larger historical patterns, but they nevertheless displayed the same humanity as found elsewhere.

Review and Relate

Thinking Through Patterns

Examine the ways historians approach the big questions of this chapter.

Within the patterns of state formation basic to the Americas, which types of states emerged in Mesoamerica and the Andes during the period 600–1550? What characterized these states?

The basic pattern of state formation in the Americas was similar to that of Eurasia and Africa. Historically, it began with the transition from foraging to agriculture and settled village life. As the population increased, villages became chiefdoms, which in turn became city-states. American city-states often became conquering states, beginning with the Maya kingdoms and Teotihuacán. Military states in which ruling classes sought to expand territories, such as Tula and Tiwanaku and Wari, were characteristic of the early part of the period 600–1550. Their successors—the Aztec and Inca Empires—were multiethnic, multilinguistic, and multireligious polities that dominated Mesoamerica and the Andes before the Spanish conquest brought them to a premature end.

Why did the Tiwanaku and Wari states have ruling classes but no dynasties and central bureaucracies? How were these patterns expressed in the territorial organization of these states?

The states of Tiwanaku and Wari had cohesive ruling classes but no dynasties or centralized bureaucracies. These ruling classes and their subjects were integrated through systems of reciprocity. Over time, tensions arose, either between stronger and weaker branches of the ruling classes or between rulers and subjects over questions of obligations and justice. When these tensions erupted into internal warfare, the states disintegrated, often in conjunction with environmental degradation and climate change.

What patterns of urban life characterized the cities of Tenochtitlán and Cuzco, the capitals of the Aztec and Inca Empires? In which ways were these cities similar to those of Eurasia and Africa?

Tenochtitlán and Cuzco, the capitals of the Aztec and Inca Empires, were urban centers organized around temples and associated residences of the ruling dynasties and their priestly classes. They also contained quarters inhabited by craftspeople, and large central markets. Armed caravans of merchants and porters transported luxury goods across hundreds of miles. Tenochtitlán had an aqueduct for the supply of drinking water, and Cuzco was traversed by a river. Both capitals had agricultural suburbs in which farmers used irrigation for their crops.

Against the Grain

Consider this as a counterpoint to the main patterns examined in this chapter.

Amazon Rain-Forest Civilizations

For years, scholarly opinion held that the Amazonian river basin, covered by rain forest, was too inhospitable to allow for more than small numbers of widely dispersed foragers. Even farmers, living in populated villages, could not possibly have founded complex societies. Slash-and-burn agriculture prevented the advance of urban life: After exhausting the soil, whole villages had to pack up and move.

However, scholars now realize that this belief was erroneous. Modern farmers, encroaching on the rain forest, noticed two hitherto neglected features. First, these farmers found in stretches of forest and savanna a black soil so fertile that it did not require fertilizers. Second, as they slashed and burned the rain forest and savanna with their modern tools, the farmers exposed monumental earthworks that had previously escaped attention. The two features were connected. The black soil was the result of centuries of soil enrichment by indigenous people who also built the earthworks. Instead of slashing and burning, these people had engaged in "slashing and charring"—that is, turning the trees into nutrient-rich charcoal rather than quickly depleted ash.

Scholars have now documented large-scale settlements in areas along the southern tributaries to the Amazon. In the Purus region, for example, researchers employing aerial photography revealed a huge area home to perhaps 60,000 inhabitants during a period around the late thirteenth century. This area is adjacent to the farthest northeastern extension of the Inca Empire into the Amazon. Thus, when the Incas expanded into the rain forest, they clearly did so to incorporate advanced societies into their empire. Thanks to scholars who challenged the orthodoxy of the "empty rain forest," we are rediscovering the Amazonian past.

- Which is more important: to save the rain forest or uncover its archaeological past? Can the two objectives be combined?
- Compare the Amazonian earthworks to those of Benin in Africa during the same period (Chapter 14). Which similarities and differences can you discover?

Key Terms

Chinampas 364
Mit'a 362
Quipu 362
Reciprocity 356

Learn more with this chapter's digital tools, including the Oxford Insight Study Guide, at http://www.oup.com/he/vonsivers4e. Please see the Further Resources section at the back of the book for additional readings and suggested websites.

PATTERNS OF EVIDENCE |

Sources for Chapter 15

SOURCE 15.1 Skeletons in a Wari royal tomb site, El Castillo de Huarmey, Peru

ca. 600–1000 CE

In 2013, 63 skeletons were discovered in a tomb at El Castillo de Huarmey, about 175 miles north of Lima, in what would seem to be the first imperial tomb of the Wari culture discovered in modern times. Most of the bodies were female, and wrapped in bundles in the seated position typical of Wari burials. Three of the women appear to have been Wari queens, as they were buried with gold and silver jewelry and brilliantly painted ceramics.

Source: REUTERS/Enrique Castro-Mendivil.

However, six of the skeletons were not wrapped in the textiles, but instead positioned on top of the burials. Archaeologists have concluded that these people may have been sacrificed for the benefit of the others.

▶ **Working with Sources**

1. **How do the burial practices of Wari culture compare with those of other civilizations in Mesoamerica and the Andes?**
2. **What might this tomb suggest about the roles and expectations of women in Wari culture?**

SOURCE 15.2

Ahuitzotl, Eighth King (*Tlatloani*) of the Aztec Empire

Ruled 1486–1502

Ahuitzotl was a celebrated military leader, whose fame rested on his successes in war. The Spanish chronicler Fray Diego Durán collected a number of orations from the time of his reign, among which three are reproduced below in English translation. The first is a prayer by the women of the Aztec Empire for Ahuitzotl's victory in the war against the province of Tecuantepec, the second is Ahuitzotl's victory address to the Aztecs' patron god Huitzilopochtli, and the third is the funerary speech by the king of one of the Aztecs' allies at the occasion of Ahuizotl's unexpected death.

Prayer of the Aztec Women during the War of the Triple Alliance (Aztecs, Tezcoco, and Tlacopán) under Ahuitzotl against Tecuantepec

Oh great Lord of All Created Things, remember your servant who has gone to exalt your honor and the greatness of your name. He has gone to offer his blood in that sacrifice which is war, to serve you. Behold, Lord, that he did not go out to work for me or for his children! Nor did he go to his usual labors to support his home, with tumpline on his head, or with a digging stick in his hand. He went for your sake, in your name, to obtain glory for you. Therefore, oh Lord, let your pious heart have pity on him who with great labor and affliction now goes through the mountains and valleys, hills and precipices, offering you the moisture, the sweat, from his brow. Grant him victory in this war so that he may return to rest in his home, and so my children and I may see his countenance again, may feel his presence.

Ahuitzotl: Victory Address to the Patron God Huitzilopochtli

Oh almighty, powerful Lord of All Created Things, You for whom we live, whose vassals and slaves we are, Lord of the Day and of the Night, of the Wind and the Water, whose strength keeps us alive! I offer You thanks for the help You

Source: Adapted from Fray Diego Durán, *The History of New Spain*, trans. Doris Heyden (Norman, OK: University of Oklahoma Press, 1994), 351, 357, and 384.

have given me, for having brought me back to Your city with the victory You granted me. I have returned to this great city of Mexico-Tenochtitlán where our ancestors, the Chichimecs and Aztecs, with great pains and the sweat of their brows discovered the blissful eagle seated upon the prickly pear cactus. There the eagle ate and rested, next to the springs of blue and red waters, which were filled with flying fish and with white snakes and white frogs. This wondrous thing appeared because You wanted to show us the greatness of Your power and Your will. You made us masters of the wealth we now possess, and I give You infinite thanks, Oh Lord, for not frowning upon my extreme youth—for I am still a boy—or my lack of strength or the weakness of my chest.

You have subjected those remote and barbarous nations to my power, to my control. You have won all these things, all is Yours! All has been won to give You honor and praise! Therefore, Oh powerful and heroic Huitzilopochtli, in order to honor You and to be successful in war, You have brought us to this place that was only water before, which our ancestors filled in and upon it built our city under Your orders. In thanks for these favors I offer You part of the spoils that have been won by the strength of our chests and arms and aided by You, Oh Lord!

Death of Ahuitzotl: Funerary Address by Nezahualpilli, King of Tezcoco and Member of the Triple Alliance (Aztecs, Texcoco, and Tlacopan)

Oh my son, valorous youth, lord and powerful king, be at ease, let rest and tranquility be with you. Now, Lord, you have left the difficult task of ruling Mexico-Tenochtitlán and the hardship of that work, where you were obliged to receive and attend all those who came before the grandeur of the god Huitzilopochtli and this illustrious city. You have left as unprotected orphans the lords and great men in your kingdom, you have left the old men, the old women, the widows and orphans and all the poor people who looked to you to remedy their poverty. You have gone to rest with your fathers and grandfathers but you have abandoned the loved ones who helped you bear the work of governing this world: they are your brothers, your cousins, your uncles, your close relatives. Your sons and daughters have become orphans, your wives are forsaken.

This city has been steeped in darkness since the sun has gone down, the sun has been hiding since your death. The royal seat is without light because your majesty and grandeur illuminated it, threw light upon it. The place, the chamber, of the omnipotent god is now full of dust, of refuse, the chamber that you ordered swept and kept clean, for you were the image of this god and you governed his state, pulling out the weeds and thorns that appeared in it. Now you have been freed from performing this servile and confining task. The ties with which you were bound have now been broken, those ties that held you to them with the care and sense of responsibility that you always exercised in making decisions about this, about that. Rest then, my son, rest in peace. Here I bring you these creatures of God, your servants, so they will go before you and serve you there in the place of rest.

Working with Sources

1. What do the sources say about the role of war in the Aztec Empire? How was war justified?

2. Who was Ahuitzotl? Describe his personality, both in terms of his own self-view and those of the Aztec women and Nezahualpilli.

SOURCE 15.3

Bernal Díaz, *The Conquest of New Spain*

ca. 1568

In the course of the fifteenth century, the Aztecs established an empire centered in the Mexican Basin (surrounding present-day Mexico City, after the drainage of most of the valley) but encompassing Mesoamerica from the Pacific to the Gulf of Mexico. The resulting state, far more centralized than the preceding Teotihuacán and Toltec city-states, commanded a large extent of territory and thrived on the trade in raw materials that were brought in from both coasts of their empire. Bernal Díaz, born in 1492 in Spain, would join the Spaniards in the conquest of Mexico, but he also left behind vivid eyewitness accounts of occupied Aztec society in the sixteenth century. Among them is this description of the market in Tlatelolco, one of the central cities at the heart of Aztec imperial power.

Caciques: Nobles.

Our Captain and those of us who had horses went to Tlatelolco mounted, and the majority of our men were fully equipped. On reaching the market-place, escorted by the many ***Caciques*** whom Montezuma had assigned to us, we were astounded at the great number of people and the quantities of merchandise, and at the orderliness and good arrangements that prevailed, for we had never seen such a thing before. The chieftains who accompanied us pointed everything out. Every kind of merchandise was kept separate and had its fixed place marked for it.

Let us begin with the dealers in gold, silver, and precious stones, feathers, cloaks, and embroidered goods, and male and female slaves who are also sold there. They bring as many slaves to be sold in that market as the Portuguese bring Negroes from Guinea. Some are brought there attached to long poles by means of collars round their necks to prevent them from escaping, but others are left loose. Next there were those who sold coarser cloth, and cotton goods and fabrics made of twisted thread, and there were chocolate merchants with their chocolate. In this way you could see every kind of merchandise to be found anywhere in New Spain, laid out in the same way as goods are laid out in my own district of Medina del Campo, a centre for fairs, where each line of stalls has its own particular sort. So it was in this great market. There were those who sold sisal cloth and ropes and the sandals they wear on their feet, which are made from the same plant. All these were kept in one part of the market, in the place assigned to them, and in another part were skins of tigers and lions, otters, jackals, and deer, badgers, mountain cats, and other wild animals, some tanned and some untanned, and other classes of merchandise.

. . .

Then there were the sellers of pitch-pine for torches, and other things of that kind, and I must also mention, with all apologies, that they sold many canoe-loads of human excrement, which they keep in the creeks near the market. This was for the manufacture of salt and the curing of skins, which they say cannot be done without it. I know that many gentlemen will laugh at this, but I assure them it is true. I may add that on all the roads they have shelters made of reeds or straw

---

Source: Bernal Díaz del Castillo, *The Conquest of New Spain*, trans. J. M. Cohen (Baltimore: Penguin, 1963), 232–234.

or grass so that they can retire when they wish to do so, and purge their bowels unseen by passers-by, and also in order that their excrement shall not be lost.

But why waste so many words on the goods in their great market? If I describe everything in detail I shall never be done. Paper, which in Mexico they call *amal*, and some reeds that smell of liquid amber, and are full of tobacco, and yellow ointments and other such things, are sold in a separate part. Much cochineal is for sale too, under the arcades of that market, and there are many sellers of herbs and other such things. They have a building there also in which three judges sit, and there are officials like constables who examine the merchandise. I am forgetting the sellers of salt and the makers of flint knives, and how they split them off the stone itself, and the fisherwomen and the men who sell small cakes made from a sort of weed which they get out of the great lake, which curdles and forms a kind of bread which tastes rather like cheese. They sell axes too, made of bronze and copper and tin, and gourds and brightly painted wooden jars.

Cue: Temple.

We went on to the great **cue**, and as we approached its wide courts, before leaving the market-place itself, we saw many more merchants who, so I was told, brought gold to sell in grains, just as they extract it from the mines. This gold is placed in the thin quills of the large geese of that country, which are so white as to be transparent. They used to reckon their accounts with one another by the length and thickness of these little quills, how much so many cloaks or so many gourds of chocolate or so many slaves were worth, or anything else they were bartering.

Working with Sources

1. **How and why does Díaz use comparisons from other markets while describing the one in Tlatelolco?**
2. **What do the specific elements of this market suggest about the importance of trade and commerce in pre-Columbian Mexico?**

SOURCE 15.4

Pedro Cieza de León on Incan roads

1541–1547

The Incas created an imperial communications and logistics infrastructure that was unparalleled in the Americas, with two highways extending to the north and south from Cuzco nearly the entire length of the empire. The roads, which were up to 12 feet wide, crossed the terrain as directly as possible, which clearly required a tremendous labor force to create. In many places, even today, the 25,000-mile road network still exists. Pedro Cieza de León was born in Spain in 1520 and undoubtedly traveled along the extensive, and still functional, Roman road system of his native land as a child. When he arrived in the New World at the age of 13, he was captivated and impressed by the civilizations that the Spanish were supplanting. In 1541, he began writing his account of the Incas, tracing their heritage and government for the benefit of those who would never see the territory he did—or travel the roads that made his observations possible.

Source: Pedro Cieza de León, *The Incas*, trans. Harriet de Onis, ed. Victor Wolfgang von Hagen (Norman: University of Oklahoma Press, 1959), 135–137.

CHAPTER 42 (ii.xv)

Of how the buildings for the Lord-Incas were constructed, and the highways to travel through the kingdom [of Peru].

One of the things that most took my attention when I was observing and setting down the things of this kingdom was how and in what way the great, splendid highways we see throughout it could be built, and the number of men that must have been required, and what tools and instruments they used to level the mountains and cut through the rock to make them as broad and good as they are. For it seems to me that if the Emperor were to desire another highway built like the one from Quito to Cuzco, or that which goes from Cuzco to Chile, truly I do not believe he could do it, with all his power and the men at his disposal, unless he followed the method the Incas employed. For if it were a question of a road fifty leagues long, or a hundred, or two hundred, we can assume that, however rough the land, it would not be too difficult, working hard, to do it. But these were so long, one of them more than 1100 leagues, over mountains so rough and dismaying that in certain places one could not see bottom, and some of the sierras so sheer and barren that the road had to be cut through the living rock to keep it level and the right width. All this they did with fire and picks.

. . .

When a Lord-Inca had decided on the building of one of these famous highways, no great provisioning or levies or anything else was needed except for the Lord-Inca to say, let this be done. The inspectors then went through the provinces, laying out the route and assigning Indians from one end to the other to the building of the road. In this way, from one boundary of the province to the other, at its expense and with its Indians, it was built as laid out, in a short time; and the others did the same, and, if necessary, a great stretch of the road was built at the same time, or all of it. When they came to the barren places, the Indians of the lands nearest by came with victuals and tools to do the work, and all was done with little effort and joyfully, because they were not oppressed in any way, nor did the Incas put overseers to watch them.

Aside from these, great fine highways were built, like that which runs through the valley of Xaquixahuana, and comes out of the city of Cuzco and goes by the town of Muhina. There were many of these highways all over the kingdom, both in the highlands and the plains. Of all, four are considered the main highways, and they are those which start from the city of Cuzco, at the square, like a crossroads, and go to the different provinces of the kingdom. As these monarchs held such a high opinion of themselves, when they set out on one of these roads, the royal person with the necessary guard took one [road], and the rest of the people another. So great was their pride that when one of them died, his heir, if he had to travel to a distant place, built his road larger and broader than that of his predecessor, but this was only if this Lord-Inca set out on some conquest, or [performed] some act so noteworthy that it could be said the road built for him was longer.

▶ Working with Sources

1. **How were the Incas' roads a manifestation of royal power, at least in Cieza de León's estimation?**
2. **What technical challenges faced the Incan road builders, and how did they overcome them?**

World Period Four

Interactions across the Globe, 1450–1750

The fifteenth century saw a renewal of the imperial impulse in the religious civilizations of the world. A forerunner had been the Mongol empire, which however did not last long; in less than 100 years it was replaced in China by the Ming. The founders of the subsequent new empires were the Mughals in India; the Ottomans, Safavids, and Songhay in the Middle East and Islamic Africa; the Habsburgs in Europe; and the seaborne empires of Portugal and Spain. One byproduct of this new imperial impulse was the discovery of the Americas, which in turn inspired the formulation of the heliocentric universe. The rediscovery of Greek literature in Europe had already set into motion the Renaissance, a broad new approach to understanding the world that provided the spark for the New Science.

China and India, by far the wealthiest and most populous agrarian–urban empires, enjoyed leading positions in the world because they produced everything they needed and wanted. Europe, however, acquired warm-weather crops and minerals through overseas colonial expansion, which would help it to challenge the traditional order.

Chapter 16

Western Christian Overseas Expansion and the Ottoman–Habsburg Struggle

1450–1650

CHAPTER SIXTEEN PATTERNS

Origins, Interactions, Adaptations In 600 CE, Western Christian civilization was the poorest and least diversified religious civilization in Eurasia. In contrast to the other religious civilizations, which continued to undergo refinements instead of diversification, Western Christianity acculturated through interaction and adaptation by absorbing outside stimuli from its Islamic and Eastern Christian neighbors. This process of absorption resulted in a heterogeneous rather than uniform culture by the time of the Renaissance in Europe (ca. 1450).

Uniqueness and Similarities Western Christian civilization is unique among the religious civilizations for its high degree of political, social, and cultural diversity. Islamic civilization, heir of deep and differentiated traditions, continued to undergo adaptations under the Ottoman Empire, but it did not break with the past. By contrast, Western Christianity evolved with often increasing internal tensions that were political (competing monarchies), social (religious divisions), and cultural (New Science and Enlightenment). Out of these tensions, the West eventually broke with its agrarian–urban past through what we call "modernity"—a decisive break that presented a unique challenge for the world's peoples.

Al-Hasan ibn Muhammad al-Wazzan

Al-Hasan ibn Muhammad al-Wazzan (ca. 1494–1550) was born in Muslim Granada soon after the Christian conquest of this kingdom in southern Iberia in 1492. Unwilling to convert to Christianity, Hasan's family emigrated to Muslim Morocco around 1499–1500. Here, Hasan received a good education and entered the administration of the Moroccan sultan, traveling to sub-Saharan Africa and the Middle East on diplomatic missions.

In 1517, as he was returning home from a mission to Constantinople, Christian **corsairs** kidnapped him. Like their Muslim counterparts, these corsairs roamed the Mediterranean to capture travelers, whom they then held for ransom or sold into slavery. For a handsome sum of money, they turned Hasan over to Pope Leo X (1513–1521), who ordered Hasan to convert to Christianity and baptized him with his own family name, Giovanni Leone di Medici. Hasan became known in Rome as Leo Africanus ("Leo the African"). He stayed for 10 years in Italy, initially at the papal court and later as a scholar in Rome. During this time, he taught Arabic to Roman clergymen and compiled an Arabic–Hebrew–Latin dictionary. His most enduring work was a travelogue, *Description of Africa*, which was for years the sole source of information about sub-Saharan Africa in the Western Christian world.

In 1527 Charles V (r. 1516–1558), king of Spain and emperor of the Holy Roman Empire of Germany, invaded Italy and sacked Rome. Hasan survived but probably departed for Tunis sometime after 1531, seeking a better life in Muslim North Africa. Unfortunately, all traces of Hasan after his departure from Rome are lost. It is possible that he perished in 1535 when Charles V attacked and occupied Tunis (1535–1574), although it is generally assumed that he lived there until around 1550.

CHAPTER OUTLINE

The Muslim–Christian Competition in the East and West, 1450–1600

The Centralizing State: Origins and Interactions

Imperial Courts, Urban Festivities, and the Arts

Putting It All Together

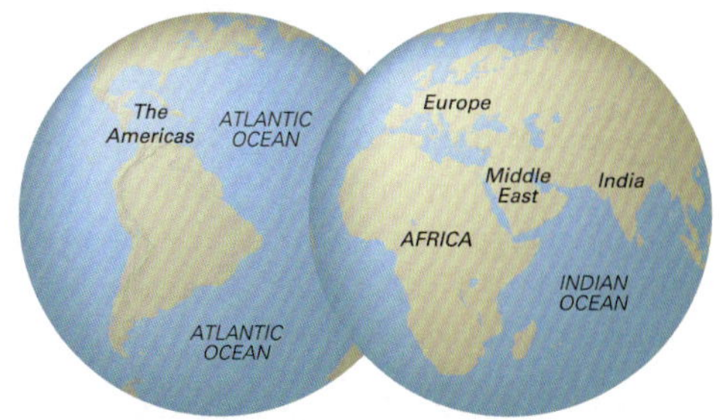

ABOVE: This 1630 map by João Teixeira Albernaz the Elder (late 1500s–ca. 1662), member of a prominent family of Portuguese mapmakers, shows Arabia, India, and China.

Seeing Patterns

➤ What patterns characterized Christian and Muslim competition in the period 1300–1600? Which elements distinguished them from each other, and which elements were similar? How did the pattern change over time?

➤ How did centralizing states in the Middle East and Europe function in the period 1450–1600? How did economics, military power, and imperial objectives interact to create the centralizing state?

➤ Which patterns did cultural expressions follow in the Habsburg and Ottoman Empires? Why did the ruling classes of these empires sponsor these expressions?

The world in which Hasan lived was a Muslim–Christian world composed of the Middle East, North Africa, and Europe. Although Muslims and Christians traveled with relative freedom in much of this world, the two religious civilizations were locked in a pattern of fierce competition.

By the fifteenth century, the Christians sought to rebuild the crusader kingdom of Jerusalem, which had been lost to the Muslims in 1291. Searching for a route that would take them around Africa, they hoped to defeat the Muslims in Jerusalem with an attack from the east. In the process, the Christians discovered the Americas. For their part, the Muslims under the Ottoman sultans conquered eastern and central Europe while defending North Africa and driving the Portuguese out of the Indian Ocean.

The Muslim–Christian Competition in the East and West, 1450–1600

In the second half of the fifteenth century, the Western Christian kings resumed the *Reconquista* of Iberia. During the same period, the Muslim principality of the Ottomans conquered lands in both Anatolia and the Balkans. After the Muslim conquest of Constantinople in 1453 and the Western Christian conquest of Granada in 1492, the Ottoman and Habsburg Empires emerged and evolved into the main Muslim-Christian rivals of the seventeenth century.

Iberian Christian Expansion, 1415–1498

Portugal resumed its *Reconquista* policies by expanding to North Africa in 1415. Looking to circumnavigate the Muslims, collect West African gold, and reach the Indian spice coast, the Portuguese established fortified harbors along the African coastline. Castile and Aragon conquered Granada in 1492, occupied ports in North Africa, and sent Columbus to discover an alternate route to India. Columbus's discovery of America instead delivered the prospect of a new continent to the rulers of Castile and Aragon (see Map 16.1).

Corsairs: In the context of this chapter, Muslim or Christian pirates who boarded ships, confiscated the cargoes, and held the crews and travelers for ransom; they were nominally under the authority of the Ottoman sultan or the pope in Rome, but operated independently.

Maritime Explorations In 1277–1281, mariners of the Italian city-state of Genoa resumed commerce by sea between the Mediterranean and the economically emerging northwestern Europe. In Lisbon, Portuguese shipwrights and their Genoese teachers developed ships suited for Atlantic seas. In the early fifteenth century they developed the caravel, a ship with upward-extending fore and aft sides, a stern rudder, and square as well as triangular lateen sails. The Portuguese became important traders between Mediterranean, Flemish, and English ports. The sea trade stimulated an exploration of the eastern Atlantic. By the early fifteenth century, the Portuguese had discovered the Azores and Madeira, while the Castilians began a conquest of the Canary Islands. Here, the indigenous inhabitants, the Guanches, put up a fierce resistance. But settlers carved out colonies on conquered parcels of land, enslaving the Guanches to work in sugarcane plantations. They thus introduced the sugarcane plantation system from the eastern Mediterranean, where it had Byzantine and Crusader roots on the island of Cyprus, to the Atlantic.

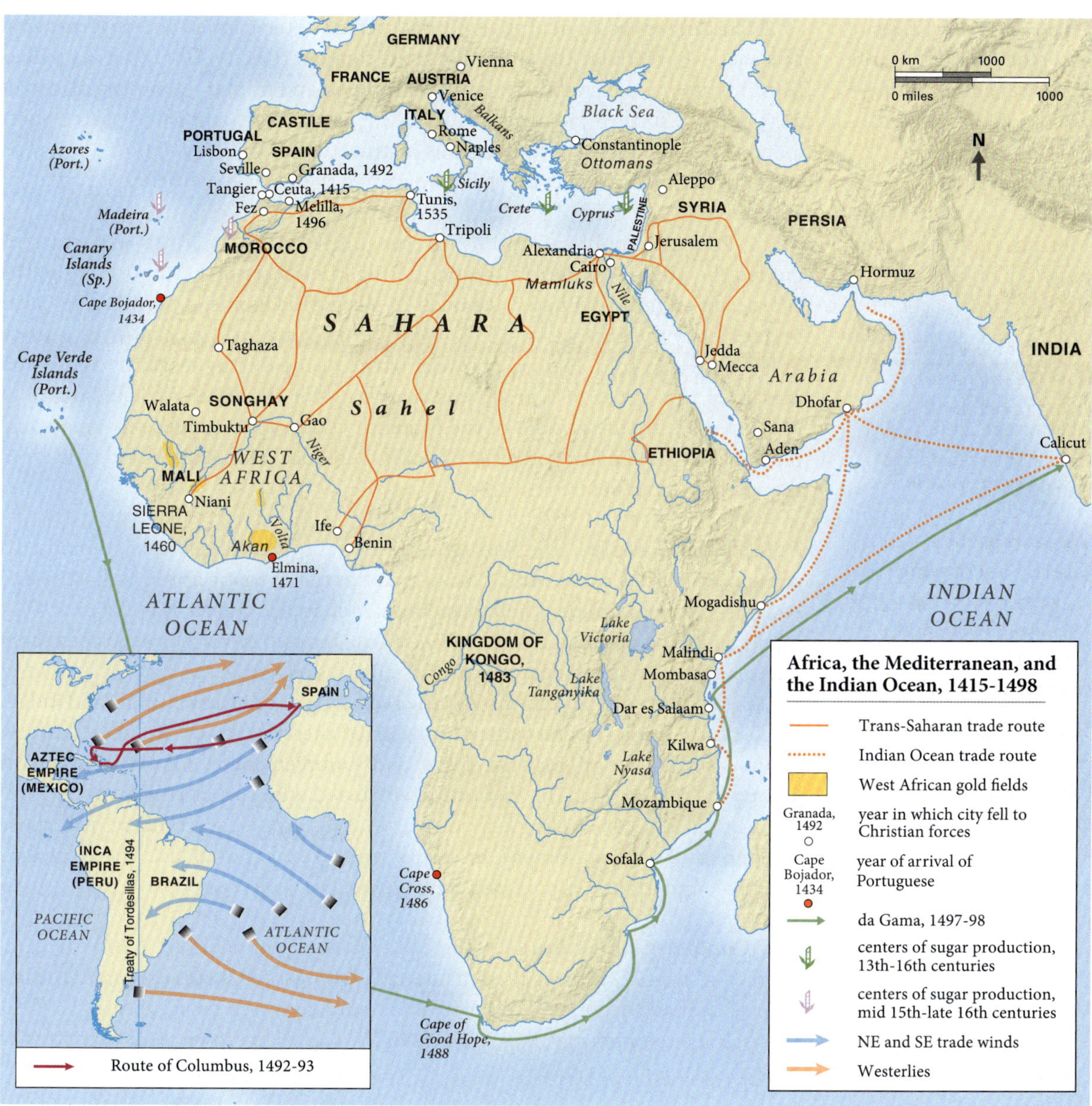

MAP 16.1 **Africa, the Mediterranean, and the Indian Ocean, 1415–1498**

Apocalyptic Expectations The loss of the crusader kingdom in Palestine to the Muslim Mamluks in 1291 had stirred deep feelings of guilt among Western Christians. Efforts to reconquer Jerusalem failed, in part because rulers in Europe were warring against each other for territorial gain. The failure did not dampen periodic spiritual revivals, however, especially in the Franciscan and **military orders** of Iberia. These monks, often well connected with the Iberian royal courts, were believers in apocalypse—that is, the imminent end of the world and the Second Coming of Christ.

Military orders: Ever since the early 1100s, the papacy encouraged the formation of monastic fighting orders, such as the Hospitalers and Templars, to combat the Muslims in the crusader kingdom of Jerusalem; similar *Reconquista* orders, such as the Order of Christ (successor of the Templars) and Order of Santiago, emerged in Iberia to eliminate Muslim rule.

Apocalypse: In Greek, "uncovering" or "revelation"—that is, the unveiling of events at the end of history, before God's judgment; during the 1400s, expectation of the imminence of Christ's Second Coming, with precursors paving the way.

According to the **Apocalypse**, Christ's return could happen only in Jerusalem. This made it urgent for the Christians to reconquer the city. Christians as well as Muslims saw no contradiction between religion and military conquest. A providential God, so they believed, justified the conquest of lands and the enslavement of the conquered. The religious justification of military action, therefore, was a declaration by believers that God was on their side to help them to conquer and convert.

In Portugal, political claims in the guise of apocalyptic expectations guided the military orders in "reconquering" Ceuta, a northern port city of the Moroccan sultans that had once been in Visigothic hands. Accordingly, a fleet under Henry the Navigator (1394–1460) took Ceuta in 1415, capturing a stock of West African gold. Henry, a brother of the ruling Portuguese king and grand master of the Order of Christ, was searching for the West African source of Muslim gold. By the middle of the fifteenth century, Portuguese mariners had reached the "gold coast" of West Africa, where local rulers imported gold from the interior Akan fields.

Reforms in Castile The Portuguese renewal of the *Reconquista* stimulated a similar revival in Castile, which occurred after the dynastic union of Castile and Aragon–Catalonia under their respective monarchs, Queen Isabella (r. 1474–1504) and King Ferdinand II (r. 1479–1516). The two monarchs used the reconquest ideology to speed up political and religious reforms.

Among the political reforms was the recruitment of urban militias and judges to check the military and judicial powers of the aristocracy. Religious reform focused on education for the clergy and enforcement of Christian doctrine among the population. The institution entrusted with the latter was the Spanish Inquisition, a body of clergy appointed in 1481 to discover and punish those deemed to be in violation of Christian theology and church law. These reforms laid the foundations for increased state power.

The Conquest of Granada The *Reconquista* culminated in a 10-year campaign (1482–1492) that resulted in Granada falling into Christian hands. The last emir of Granada negotiated terms for an honorable surrender. According to these terms, Muslims who stayed as subjects of the Castilian crown were permitted to worship in their mosques.

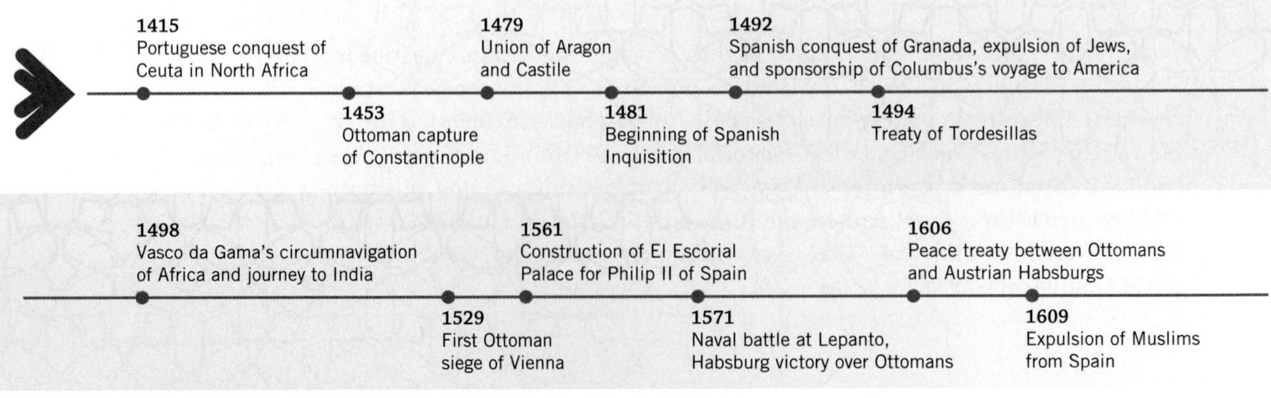

The treaty did not apply to the Jews of Granada, however, who were forced to either convert to Christianity or emigrate. Many emigrated in 1492 to Portugal and the Ottoman Empire. Portugal adopted its own expulsion decree in 1497. This ended the nearly millennium-and-a-half-long Jewish presence in Sefarad, as Spain was called in Hebrew.

After the expulsion of the Jews, it did not take long for the Christians to violate the Muslim treaty of surrender. The church forced conversions, burned Arabic books, and transformed mosques into churches. In 1499 the Muslims of Granada rebelled. Christian troops crushed the uprising, and Isabella and Ferdinand abrogated the treaty of surrender. During the early sixteenth century, Muslims were forced to convert, disperse to other provinces, or emigrate.

Columbus's Journey to the Caribbean In early 1492, Isabella and Ferdinand authorized the mariner Christopher Columbus (1451–1506) to build two caravels and a larger carrack and sail across the Atlantic. Columbus promised to reach India ahead of the Portuguese. Money for the construction of ships came from Castilian and Aragonese crusade levies on the Muslims.

In September, Columbus and his mariners departed from the Castilian Canary Islands, catching the favorable South Atlantic easterlies. After a voyage of a little over a month, Columbus landed on one of the Bahaman islands, mistakenly assuming that he was close to the Indian subcontinent. After three months, he left a colony of settlers behind and returned to Iberia with seven captured Caribbean islanders and some gold.

Although disappointed by the meager returns of Columbus's first and subsequent voyages, Isabella and Ferdinand were delighted to have acquired new islands in the Caribbean, in addition to the Canaries. In one blow they had drawn even with Portugal.

Christopher Columbus. Because there is no known contemporary portrait of Columbus, considerable conjecture attends his real appearance. Apart from scattered descriptions presented by a few who knew him, scholars consider this portrait painted by Lorenzo Lotto in 1512 as perhaps the most accurate depiction.

Vasco da Gama's Journey to India Portugal continued to search for a way to India around Africa. In 1498, the king appointed a member of the crusading Order of Santiago, Vasco da Gama (ca. 1469–1524), to command four caravels for the journey to India. After six months, the ships arrived in Calicut, the main spice trade center on the Indian west coast.

The first Portuguese mariner sent ashore by da Gama in Calicut encountered two North African Muslims, who addressed him in Castilian Spanish and Genoese Italian: "The Devil take you! What brought you here?" The mariner replied: "We came to seek Christians and spices." The Muslim and Hindu merchants were uninterested in the goods designed for the African market offered by da Gama and demanded gold or silver, which the Portuguese had only in small amounts. As rumors spread about a Muslim and Hindu plot against him, da Gama prudently sailed home.

However, Portugal soon mastered the India trade. The Portuguese crown organized regular journeys around Africa, and when Portuguese mariners ventured in the other direction to northeast Brazil, they claimed it for their expanding commercial network. During the early sixteenth century, as the Portuguese India fleets brought considerable amounts of spices from India back to Portugal, the project of retaking Jerusalem receded into the background.

Rise of the Ottomans and Struggle with the Habsburgs for Dominance, 1300–1609

While Muslim rule was disappearing from the Iberian Peninsula in the late fifteenth century, the opposite was happening in the Balkans. Here, the Ottoman Turks expanded Islamic rule over Christians. By the late sixteenth century, when conflict between the Habsburgs and Ottomans reached its peak, entire generations of Croats, Germans, and Italians feared a Muslim conquest of all of Western Christian Europe.

Late Byzantium and Ottoman Origins The rise of the Ottomans was related to the decline of Byzantium. The emperors of Byzantium had reclaimed their "empire" in 1261 from its Latin rulers and Venetian troops. This empire was a midsize kingdom with modest agricultural resources. But it was still a valuable trading hub, given Constantinople's strategic position. Thanks to its commercial wealth, Byzantium experienced a cultural revival that influenced the Western Renaissance in Italy.

Both Balkan Slavs and Anatolian Turks appropriated Byzantine provinces in the late thirteenth century, further reducing the empire. One of the lost provinces was Bithynia, where, in 1299, the Turkish warlord Osman (1299–1326) declared himself an independent ruler. Osman and other Turkish lords in the region were nominally subject to the Seljuks, the Turkish dynasty that had conquered Anatolia from the Byzantines two centuries earlier but by the early 1300s was disintegrating.

During the first half of the fourteenth century, Osman and his successors conquered further Anatolian provinces from Byzantium. In 1354, the Ottomans gained their first European foothold on a peninsula about 100 miles southwest of Constantinople. Thereafter, it seemed only a matter of time before the Ottomans would conquer Constantinople.

Through skillful mixture of defense and diplomacy, however, the Byzantine emperors salvaged their rule for another century. They were also helped by Timur the Great (also known as Tamerlane; r. 1370–1405), a Turkish-descended ruler from central Asia who sought to rebuild the Mongol Empire. He defeated the Ottomans in 1402. Timur and his successors were unsuccessful with their dream of Mongol world rule; the Ottomans needed nearly two decades (1402–1421) to reconstitute their empire in the Balkans and Anatolia. Under Mehmet II, "the Conqueror" (r. 1451–1481), they finally laid siege to the Byzantine capital.

From Constantinople to the Adriatic Sea Mehmet's siege and conquest of Constantinople (April 5–May 29, 1453) is one of the stirring events of world history. Using their superiority in troop strength, the Ottomans bombarded Constantinople's walls with heavy cannons. Unable to cut the heavy chain blocking the entrance to the harbor in the Golden Horn, Mehmet circumvented it by having troops drag ships on rollers over the Galata hill on the opposite side into the harbor. The soldiers massed on these ships assaulted the harbor walls with the help of ladders. When cannon fire succeeded in breaching a relatively weak wall section in the north, the Ottoman besiegers stormed the city. The last Byzantine emperor, Constantine XI, perished in the massacre that followed the Ottoman occupation of the city.

Mehmet repopulated Constantinople and appointed a new patriarch at the head of the Eastern Christians, to whom he promised full protection as his subjects. He ordered the construction of the Topkapı Palace (1459), the transfer of the administration to the city, and the resumption of expansion in the Balkans, where he forced the majority of rulers into submitting to vassal status.

Mehmet's Balkan conquests brought him to the Adriatic Sea, from where the Ottomans were poised to launch a full-scale invasion of Italy. When the sultan died unexpectedly, his successor turned back, preferring instead to consolidate the Ottoman Empire in the Balkans.

Imperial Apogee In 1514, they defeated the Persian Safavids in Iran, who had risen in 1501 to form a rival Shiite empire in opposition to the Sunni Ottomans. In the southern Middle East, tensions between the Ottomans and the Mamluk Turks erupted in war in 1517. The Ottomans defeated the Mamluks and took control of western Arabia, including the holy pilgrimage city of Mecca. A year later, in 1518, the future Sultan Süleyman I, "the Magnificent" (r. 1520–1566), drove the Spanish from much of North Africa, which the latter had conquered in the name of the *Reconquista* in the 1490s and early 1500s.

In the Balkans, the Ottomans completed their conquests of Serbia and Hungary with the annexation of Belgrade and Buda (now part of Budapest) as well as a brief siege of Vienna in 1529. By the second half of the sixteenth century, the Ottoman Empire was a vast multiethnic and multireligious state of some 15 million inhabitants extending from Algeria in the Maghreb to Yemen in Arabia and from Upper Egypt to the Balkans and the northern shores of the Black Sea (see Map 16.2).

Morocco and Persia In the period 1450–1600, the Ottomans and Indian Mughals dominated Islamic civilization. Two smaller realms existed in Morocco and Persia, ruled by the Saadid (1509–1659) and Safavid (1501–1722) dynasties, respectively. The Saadid sultans defended themselves successfully against the Ottoman expansion and liberated themselves from the Portuguese occupation of Morocco's Atlantic ports. In 1591, the Saadids sent an army to West Africa in an unsuccessful attempt to revive the gold trade. Moroccan army officers assumed power in Timbuktu, and their descendants, the Ruma, became provincial lords independent of Morocco. Without West African gold, the Saadids in Morocco split into provincial realms and were succeeded in 1659 by the Alaouite dynasty which is still in power today.

The Safavids grew in the mid-1400s from a mixed Kurdish-Turkish mystical brotherhood in northwestern Iran into a Shiite warrior organization that carried out raids against Christians in the Caucasus. In 1501, the leadership of the brotherhood put forward a 14-year-old boy named Ismail as the Hidden Twelfth Imam. According to Shiite doctrine, the Hidden Imam, or Messiah, was expected to arrive and establish a Muslim apocalyptic realm of justice at the end of time, before God's Last Judgment. This realm would replace the "unjust" Sunni

Patterns Up Close

Shipbuilding

With the appearance of empires during the Iron Age, four regional but interconnected shipbuilding traditions—Mediterranean, North Sea, Indian Ocean, and China Sea—emerged.

In the Mediterranean, around 500 BCE, shipwrights began to use nailed planks for their war galleys as well as for cargo transports. In the Roman Empire (ca. 200 BCE–500 CE), nailed planking allowed the development of the roundship (image *a*), a large vessel 120 feet in length with a capacity of 400 tons of cargo for the transport of grain from Egypt to Italy. The roundship and its variations had double planking, multiple masts, and multiple square sails. After 100 BCE, the originally Egyptian triangular (lateen) sail allowed for tacking (zigzagging) against the wind, greatly expanding shipping during the summer sailing season.

The Celtic North Sea tradition adapted to the Mediterranean patterns of the Romans. Shipwrights in Celtic regions shifted to frame-first construction for small boats in the 300s. At the same time, Norsemen, or Vikings, innovated by introducing overlapping (clinkered) plank joining for their seagoing boats. The North Sea innovations, arriving as they did at the end of the western Roman Empire, remained local for nearly half a millennium.

China made major contributions to ship construction. In the Han period (206 BCE–220 CE) there is evidence from clay models for the use of nailed planks in riverboats. One model, dating to the first century CE, shows a central steering rudder at the end of the boat. At the same time, similar stern rudders appeared in the Roman Empire. Who adopted what from whom, if there was any borrowing at all, is still an unanswered question.

Patterns of Shipbuilding. Left to right: (a) Hellenistic-Roman roundship, (b) Chinese junk, (c) Indian Ocean dhow

Ottoman Empire. The Ottomans, however, crushed the Safavid challenge in 1514 at the Battle of Chaldiran, as mentioned above. Ismail dropped his claim to messianic status, and his successors assumed the more modest title of king (Persian *shah*) as the head of state.

The Safavids recruited a standing infantry from among young Christians on lands conquered in the Caucasus. They held fast to Shiism, thereby continuing their opposition to the Sunni Ottomans, and made this form of Islam dominant

Shipbuilding innovations continued after 600 CE. In Tang China, junks with multiple bulkheads (watertight compartments) and layers of planks appeared. The average junk was 140 feet long, had a cargo capacity of 600 tons, and could carry on its three or four decks several hundred mariners and passengers (see image *b*). Junks had multiple masts, and their trapezoidal (lug) and square sails made of matted fibers were strengthened (battened) with poles sewed to the surface. The Middle Eastern, eastern African, and Indian dhow was built with sewed or nailed planks and rigged with lateen and square sails, traveling as far as southern China (see image *c*).

In western Europe, the patterns of Mediterranean and North Sea shipbuilding merged during the thirteenth century. At that time, northern shipwrights developed the cog, a ship of some 60 feet in length and 30 tons in cargo capacity, with square sails and flush planking below and clinkered planking above the waterline. Northern European crusaders traveled during 1150–1300 on cogs via the Atlantic to the Mediterranean. Builders adapted the cog's clinker technique to the roundship tradition that Muslims as well as Eastern and Western Christians had modified in the previous centuries. Genoese clinkered roundships pioneered the Mediterranean–North Sea trade in the early fourteenth century (see image *d*).

Lisbon shipwrights in Portugal developed the caravel around 1430. The caravel was a 60-foot-long ship with a 50-ton freight capacity, a stern rudder, square and lateen sails, and a magnetic compass (of Chinese origin). The caravel and, after 1500, the similarly built but much larger galleon were the main vessels the Portuguese, Spanish, Dutch, and English used during their oceanic voyages from the mid-fifteenth to mid-eighteenth centuries (see image *e*).

(d)

(e)

Patterns of Shipbuilding (*continued*). From top: (d) Baltic cog, (e) Iberian caravel. These ships illustrate the varieties of shipbuilding traditions that developed over thousands of years.

Questions

- How does the history of shipbuilding demonstrate the ways in which innovations spread from one place to another?
- Do the adaptations in shipbuilding that flowed between cultures that were nominally in conflict with each other provide a different perspective on the way these cultures interacted?

in Iran. They moved the capital from Tabriz to the centrally located Isfahan in 1590, and built a palace, administration, and mosque complex in the city. They also held the monopoly in the production of Caspian Sea silk, a high-quality export product.

Not everyone accepted Shiism, however. An attempt to force the Shiite doctrines on the Afghanis backfired badly when enraged Sunni tribes formed a coalition, defeated the Safavids, and ended their regime in 1722.

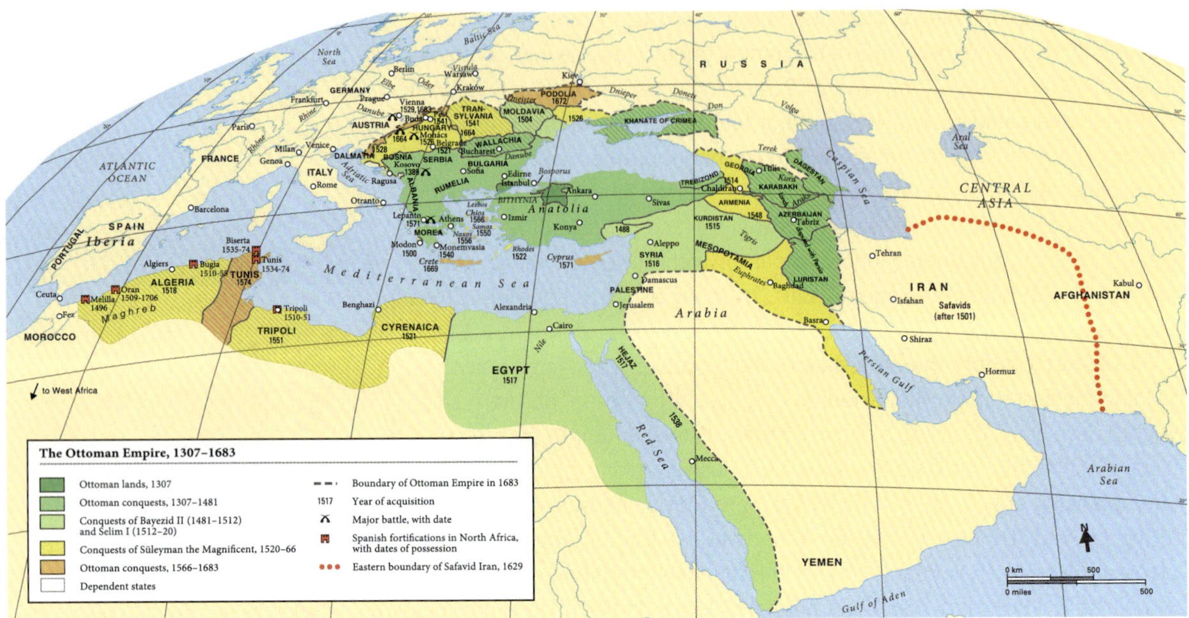

MAP 16.2 The Ottoman Empire, 1307–1683

Rise of the Habsburgs On the Iberian Peninsula, Castile-Aragon evolved into the center of a vast empire. A daughter of Isabella and Ferdinand married a member of the Habsburg dynastic family, which ruled Flanders, Burgundy, Naples, Sicily, as well as the "Holy Roman Empire of the German Nation," as the collection of German principalities was called. Their son, Charles V, not only inherited Castile–Aragon, now merged and called Spain, and the first four of the above Habsburg territories but also became the ruler of the Aztec and Inca empires in the Americas. In both Austria and the western Mediterranean the Habsburgs were direct neighbors of the Ottomans (see Map 16.3).

In addition, in 1519 the princely and ecclesiastic electors of the Holy Roman Empire elevated Charles to the position of German king and Roman emperor. They did so after having received lavish sums of money from Charles to prevent them from electing the French or English king to the imperial position. In his new role he was now the direct counterpart of Sultan Süleyman in the struggle for dominance in the Christian–Muslim world of Europe, the Middle East, and northern Africa. Both the Habsburgs and the Ottomans renewed the traditional Islamic–Christian imperialism which had characterized the period 629–950 and which had been replaced by the Muslim and Christian commonwealths of 950–1450.

Habsburg Distractions Charles V faced a daunting task in his effort to prevent the Ottomans from advancing against the Christians in the Balkans and the Mediterranean. Problems in his European territories diverted his attention from what Christians in most parts of Europe perceived as a pervasive Ottoman–Muslim threat. During the first three decades of the sixteenth century, revolts in

MAP 16.3 Europe and the Mediterranean, ca. 1560

Iberia, the Protestant Reformation in the German states, and renewed war with France commanded Charles's attention.

The emperor's distractions increased further in 1534 when, in an attempt to drive the Habsburgs out of Italy, France forged an alliance with the Ottomans. While this alliance horrified western Europe, it demonstrated that the Ottomans had become crucial players in European politics.

Habsburg and Ottoman Losses The multiple engagements strained Habsburg resources against the Ottomans, who pressed ahead on the two fronts of the Balkans and North Africa. Although Charles V deputized his younger brother Ferdinand

I to shore up the Balkan defenses, he was unable to send him enough troops. After a series of defeats, Austria had to pay the Ottomans tribute and, eventually, sign a humiliating truce (1562). On the western Mediterranean front, by 1556, at the end of Charles V's reign, only two of eight Habsburg garrisons had survived Ottoman onslaught.

A third frontier of the Muslim–Christian struggle for dominance was the Indian Ocean. After Vasco da Gama had returned from India in 1498, the Portuguese kings sought to break into the Muslim-dominated Indian Ocean trade. In response, the Ottomans protected existing Muslim commercial interests in the Indian Ocean. They blocked Portuguese military support for Ethiopia and strengthened their ally, the sultan of Aceh (AH-chay) on the Indonesian island of Sumatra, by providing him with troops and weapons. War on land and on sea raged in the Indian Ocean through most of the sixteenth century.

In the long run, the Portuguese were successful in destroying the Ottoman fleets sent against them, but smaller convoys of Ottoman galleys continued to harass Portuguese shipping interests. By 1570 the Muslims traded as much via the Red Sea route to the Mediterranean as the Portuguese did by circumnavigating Africa. In addition, the Ottomans now benefited from the trade of coffee, newly produced in Ethiopia and Yemen. Both Portugal and the Ottomans reduced their by now unsustainable military presence in the Indian Ocean, which allowed the Netherlands in the early seventeenth century to overtake both Portugal and the Ottoman Empire in the Indian Ocean spice trade (see Map 16.4).

Habsburg–Ottoman Balance In the 1550s, Charles V decided to ensure the continuation of Habsburg power through a division of his western and eastern territories. Accordingly, he bestowed Spain, Naples, the Netherlands, and the Americas on his son Philip II (r. 1556–1598). The Habsburg possessions of Austria, Bohemia, and the remnant of Hungary not lost to the Ottomans, as well as the Holy Roman Empire (Germany), went to his brother Ferdinand I (r. 1558–1564). Charles hoped that his son and brother would cooperate and help each other militarily against the Ottomans.

When Philip took over the Spanish throne, he realized that most of the Habsburg military was stationed outside Spain, leaving that country vulnerable to attack—especially as the Ottomans had recently conquered Spanish strongholds in North Africa. Fearful of **Morisco** support for an Ottoman invasion of Spain, Philip's administration and the Inquisition renewed their decrees of conversion.

Moriscos: From Latin *maurus* ("Moor"; in medieval usage, also "dark-skinned"); Castilian term referring to North Africans and to Muslims under Spanish rule.

This sparked a revolt among the Moriscos of Granada in 1568–1570, which Philip was able to suppress only after recourse to troops and firearms from Italy. To break up the large concentrations of Granadan Moriscos in the south of Spain, Philip ordered them to be dispersed throughout the peninsula. At the same time, to alleviate the Ottoman naval threat, Philip, the pope, Venice, and Genoa formed a Holy Christian League. The fleet succeeded in 1571 in destroying the entire Ottoman navy at Lepanto (now Nafpaktos), in Ottoman Greece.

The Ottomans, however, rebuilt their navy and captured the strategic port city of Tunis in 1574 from the Spaniards. After this date, Venice was the only naval enemy of the Ottomans. The Ottomans turned their attention to the rival Safavid

MAP 16.4 Ottoman–Portuguese Competition in the Indian Ocean, 1536–1580

Empire, where they exploited a period of dynastic instability for the conquest of territories in the Caucasus (1578–1590). The Catholic Philip II, for his part, was faced with the Protestant war of independence in the Netherlands. This war was so expensive that Philip II had to declare bankruptcy and sue for peace with the Ottomans (1580).

The Limits of Ottoman Power After their victory over the Safavids, the Ottomans looked again to the west, where a long peace with Ferdinand I in Austria (since 1562) was ready to collapse. A series of raids and counter-raids at the Austrian and Transylvanian borders had inflamed tempers, and in 1593 the Ottomans went on the attack.

Eventually, the Ottomans were not able to defeat the Austrians on the battlefield. In 1606, the Ottomans and Austrian Habsburgs made peace again. With minor modifications in favor of the Austrians, the two sides returned to their earlier borders. The Austrians made one more tribute payment and then let their obligation lapse. Officially, the Ottomans conceded nothing, but in practical terms Austria was no longer a vassal state.

Paolo Veronese, *Battle of Lepanto*, altar painting with four saints beseeching the Virgin Mary to grant victory to the Christians (ca. 1572). In the sixteenth century, the entire Mediterranean, from Gibraltar to Cyprus, was a naval battleground between Christians and Muslims. The Christians won the Battle of Lepanto thanks to superior naval tactics. At the end of the battle "the sea was entirely covered, not just with masts, spars, oars, and broken wood, but with an innumerable quantity of blood that turned the water as red as blood."

Expulsion of the Moriscos Although the peace between the Ottomans and Spanish Habsburgs held, Philip and his successors were aware of the possibility of renewed Ottoman aid to the Moriscos, who continued to resist conversion. The church advocated the expulsion of the Moriscos, arguing that the allegedly high Muslim birthrate was a serious threat.

Fierce resistance against the proposed expulsion, however, rose among the Christian landowners in the southeastern province of Valencia. These landowners benefited from the skills of their Morisco tenant farmers. Weighing the potential Ottoman threat against the possibility of economic damage, the government decided in 1580 in favor of expulsion.

It took until 1609, however, before a compensation deal with the landowners in Valencia was worked out. In the following five years, some 300,000 Moriscos were forcibly expelled from Spain, under often appalling circumstances. As in the case of the Jews a century earlier, Spain's loss was the Ottoman Empire's gain, this time mostly in the form of skilled irrigation farmers.

The Centralizing State: Origins and Interactions

The major technological change in the Middle East and Europe during 1250–1350 was the appearance of firearms. It took until the mid-1400s, however, before cannons and muskets were effective enough to make a difference in warfare. At this time, a pattern emerged whereby rulers created centralized states to finance their shift to firearm-bearing infantries. Consequently, they resumed the policy of conquest and imperialism. Both the Ottomans and the Habsburgs raised immense amounts of silver and gold to spend on cannons, muskets, and ships for achieving world rule.

State Transformation, Money, and Firearms

In the early stages of their realms, the kings of Iberia (1150–1400) and the Ottoman sultans (1300–1400) compensated military commanders for their service with land grants. Once the Iberian and Ottoman rulers had conquered cities and gained control over long-distance trade, however, patterns changed. Rulers began collecting taxes in cash, with which they paid regiments of personal guards to supplement the army of land-grant officers. This centralizing state was the forerunner of the absolutist state of the early seventeenth century.

The Land-Grant System In the 1300s, Ottoman military lords created personal domains on lands they had conquered and took rents in kind from villagers to finance their dynastic households. Members of their clan or adherents (many of whom were holy warriors and/or adventurers), received other conquered lands, from which they collected rents. As the Ottomans conquered Byzantine cities, they enjoyed the benefits of a **money economy**. They collected taxes in coins from the markets and tollbooths at city gates, as well as from the Christians and Jews subject to the head tax.

Money economy: Form of economic organization in which mutual obligations are settled through monetary exchanges; in contrast, a system of land grants obliges the landholders to provide military service, without payment, to the grantee (sultan or king).

After the conquest of the southern Balkans by the Ottoman Empire in the fifteenth and sixteenth centuries, both the land-grant system and the money economy expanded. A military ruling class of grant holders emerged, cavalrymen who lived with their households of retainers in the interior of Anatolia and the Balkans. Most of the time, they were away on campaign with the sultans, leaving managers in charge of the collection of rents. By the early years of the sixteenth century, the landed ruling class of cavalrymen constituted a reserve of warriors for the mobilization of troops each summer.

The Janissaries The military institution of the **Janissaries**—troops who received salaries from the central treasury—is first documented in 1395. It was based on a practice (called ***devşirme*** [DEV-shirm]) of conscripting young boys from the empire's Christian population. Boys between the ages of 6 and 16 were sent to Constantinople, where they were converted to Islam and trained as future soldiers and administrators. The youth then entered the system of manumitted palace slaves under the orders of the sultan and his ministers.

Janissaries: Infantry soldiers recruited among the Christian population of the Ottoman Empire and paid from the central treasury; from Turkish *yeniçeri*, "new troops."

The practice of *devşirme* contradicted Islamic law, which forbade the enslavement of "peoples of the Book" (Jews, Christians, and Zoroastrians). Its existence, therefore, documents the extent to which the sultans reasserted the Roman–Sasanid–Arab imperial traditions of the ruler making doctrine and law.

Devşirme: The levy on boys in the Ottoman Empire; that is, the obligation of the Christian population to contribute adolescent males to the military and administrative classes.

Toward the first half of the fifteenth century, the sultans equipped their Janissaries with cannons and matchlock muskets. By this point, firearms had undergone some 150 years of development in the Middle East and North Africa. By the mid-1400s, gigantic siege cannons and slow but reliable matchlock muskets were the standard equipment of Ottoman and other armies, and the sultans relied on indigenous, rather than European, gunsmiths.

Revenues and Money The maintenance of a salaried standing army and a central administration would have been impossible without precious metals. Therefore, the Ottoman imperial expansion was driven by the need to acquire mineral deposits. During the fifteenth century the Ottomans captured the silver, lead, and iron mines of Serbia and Bosnia. Together with Anatolian copper, iron, and silver mines, the Balkan mines made the Ottomans the owners of the largest precious metal production centers prior to the Habsburg acquisition of the Mexican and Andean mines in the mid-1500s.

The sultans left the Balkan mining and smelting operations in the hands of preconquest Christian entrepreneurs, who were integrated into the Ottoman imperial money economy as tax farmers. **Tax farming** was the preferred method of producing cash revenues for the central administration. The holders of tax farms delivered the profits from the production of minerals to the state, minus the commission they were entitled to subtract for themselves. Thus, tax farmers were crucial members of the ruling class.

Tax farming: Governmental auction of the right to collect taxes in a district. The tax farmer advanced these taxes to the treasury and retained a commission.

The right to mint silver was part of the tax-farm regime, as were the market, city gate, and port duties. The tax-farm regime was dependent on a strong sultan

Boy Levy (*devşirme*) in a Christian Village. This miniature graphically depicts the trauma of conscription, including the wailing of the village women and the assembly of boys waiting to be taken away by implacable representatives of the sultan.

or chief minister, the grand vizier. Without close supervision, this regime could easily become decentralized, which indeed eventually happened in the Ottoman Empire.

Süleyman's Centralizing State The Ottoman state reached its apogee under Sultan Süleyman I, "the Magnificent." The sultan financed a massive expansion of the military and bureaucracy and formed a centralized state, the purpose of which was to project power and cultural splendor toward its subjects as well as Christian enemies outside the empire.

The bureaucrats were recruited from two population groups. Most top ministers and officers in the fifteenth and sixteenth centuries came from the *devşirme* among the Christians. The empire's other recruits came from colleges to which the Muslim population of the empire had access. Ambitious villagers far from urban centers could gain upward mobility through the colleges. Muslims of Christian parentage made up the top layer of the elite, while Muslims of Islamic descent occupied the middle ranks.

Under Süleyman, the Janissaries comprised musket-equipped troopers, a cavalry, and artillery regiments. Most were stationed in Constantinople, while others served in provincial cities and border fortresses.

Typical military campaigns required sophisticated logistics. Wages, gunpowder, weapons, and foodstuffs were carried on wagons and barges, since soldiers were not permitted to provision themselves from villagers, whether friend or foe. Although the state collected heavy taxes, it had a strong interest in not destroying village productivity.

Charles V's Centralizing State The centralizing state began in Iberia with the reforms of Isabella and Ferdinand and reached its mature phase under Charles V. From the late fifteenth century onward, Castile and Aragon shared fiscal characteristics with the Ottomans, such as tax farming. In addition, Muslims paid head taxes in cash. Most of the money taxes were also enforced in Flanders, Burgundy, Naples, Sicily, and Austria, after Iberia's incorporation into the Habsburg domain in 1516. These taxes were more substantial than those of Spain.

From 1521 to 1536, the Spanish crown enlarged its money income from looted Aztec and Inca gold and silver. Under Charles V, Habsburg imperial revenues doubled, reaching about the same level as those of the Ottomans. At the height of their struggle for dominance in the Muslim–Christian world, the Habsburgs and the Ottomans expended similar resources in wars with each other.

In one significant respect, however, the two empires differed. The cavalry ruling class of the Ottoman Empire was nonhereditary. By contrast, the Iberian landholder cavalry possessed a legal right to inheritance. When Isabella and Ferdinand embarked on state centralization, they had to wrestle with a powerful, landed aristocracy that had taken over royal jurisdiction and tax prerogatives on their vast lands. The two monarchs took back much of the jurisdiction but were unable to do much about the taxes.

The Habsburgs sought to overcome their lack of power over the aristocracy and the weakness of their Spanish tax base by exploiting the Italian and Flemish cities and the American colonies. But in the long run their finances remained precarious. Spanish aristocrats seldom fulfilled their obligation to unpaid military service. As a result, the kings hired as many Italians, Flemings, and Germans as possible, and at times they deployed these mercenaries to Spain in order to maintain peace there.

Although the Ottoman and Habsburg patterns of centralized state formation bore similarities to patterns in the earlier Roman and Arab Empires, the centralizing states of the period after 1450 were much more potent enterprises because of firearms. They were established polities, evolving into absolutist and eventually national states.

Ottoman Siege of a Christian Fortress. By the middle of the fifteenth century, cannons had revolutionized warfare. Niccolò Machiavelli, ever attuned to new developments, noted in 1519 that "no wall exists, however thick, that artillery cannot destroy in a few days." Machiavelli could have been commenting on the Ottomans, who were masters of siege warfare. Sultan Mehmet II, the conqueror of Constantinople in 1453, founded the Imperial Cannon Foundry shortly thereafter; it would go on to make some of the biggest cannons of the period.

Imperial Courts, Urban Festivities, and the Arts

Ottoman and Habsburg rulers projected the splendor of their states to subjects at home as well as enemies abroad. Although Christian and Muslim artists and artisans belonged to different religious and cultural traditions, their artistic achievements were inspired by the same impulse: to glorify their states through religious expression.

The Ottoman Empire: Palaces, Festivities, and the Arts

The Ottomans built palaces and celebrated public feasts to demonstrate their imperial power and wealth. Many mosques were built during the sixteenth century. Painting and illustration were found only inside the privacy of the Ottoman palace and wealthy households. Theater and music were enjoyed on the popular level, in defiance of religious restrictions.

The Topkapı Palace When the Ottoman sultans conquered the Byzantine capital Constantinople in 1453, it was dilapidated and depopulated. The sultans initiated large construction projects and populated the city with craftspeople and traders from across their empire. By 1600 the city was again an imposing metropolis, easily the largest city in Europe at that time.

One of the construction projects was a new palace for the sultans, the Topkapı Sarayı, or "Palace of the Gun Gate," begun in 1459. (It was originally called the "Imperial New Palace," receiving its current name in the nineteenth century.) The Topkapı complex included the main administrative school, military barracks, an armory, a hospital, and living quarters, or harem, for the ruling family.

The institution of the harem arose during the reign of Süleyman. At that time, sultans no longer pursued marriage alliances with neighboring Islamic rulers. Instead, they chose slave concubines (often Christian) for the procreation of children. A concubine who bore a son to the reigning sultan acquired privileges.

The head eunuch of the harem guard evolved into a powerful intermediary for diplomatic and military decisions between the sultan's mother, who was confined to the harem, and those she sought to influence. In addition, the sultan's mother arranged marriages of her daughters to high-ranking officials. In the face of the strong patriarchal order of the Ottoman Empire, such women exercised considerable power.

Public Festivities As in Habsburg Spain, feasts and celebrations were events that displayed the state's largesse. Typical festivities commemorated Muslim holidays. Other feasts were connected with the birthday of the Prophet Muhammad and his journey to heaven and hell. Processions and communal meals commemorated the birthdays of local Muslim saints in many cities. As in Christian Spain, these feasts attracted large crowds.

Wrestlers, ram handlers, and horsemen performed in the Hippodrome, the stadium for public festivities. At the harbor of the Golden Horn, tightrope artists performed high above the water. Court painters recorded the procession and performance scenes in picture albums. The sultans incorporated these albums into their libraries, together with history books recording their military victories against the Habsburgs.

Imperial Hall, Topkapı Palace. The Ottomans never forgot their nomadic roots. Topkapı Palace, completed in 1479 and expanded and redecorated several times, resembles in many ways a vast encampment, with a series of enclosed courtyards. At the center of the palace complex were the harem and the private apartments of the sultan, which included the Imperial Hall, where the sultan would receive members of his family and closest advisors.

Popular Theater The evenings of the fasting month of Ramadan were filled with festive meals and a special form of entertainment, the Karagöz ("Black Eye") shadow theater. This form of theater came from Egypt, although it probably had Javanese–Chinese roots. For boys, a performance of the Karagöz theater accompanied the ritual of circumcision, a rite of passage from the ancient Near East adopted by Islamic civilization. Circumcision signified the passage from the nurturing care of the mother to the educational discipline of the father.

Mosque Architecture During the sixteenth century, the architect Sinan (ca. 1492–1588) filled Constantinople and the earlier Ottoman capital Edirne with imperial mosques, defined by their slender minarets. Sultan Süleyman, wealthy officials, and private donors provided the funds. Sinan was able to hire as many as 25,000 laborers, enabling him to build each of his mosques in six years or less.

Sinan's most original contribution to architecture was the replacement of the highly visible and massive four exterior buttresses, which marked the square ground plan of the Hagia Sophia, with up to eight slender pillars as hidden internal supports of the dome. His intention was not massive monumentality but elegant spaciousness.

The Spanish Habsburg Empire: Popular Festivities and the Arts

The culture of the Habsburg Empire was strongly religious, and both state-sponsored spectacles and popular festivities displayed devotion to the Catholic faith. Secular tendencies, however, emerged also as a result of the Renaissance. Originating in Italy and the Netherlands, the Renaissance emphasized pre-Christian Greek and Roman heritages.

Faith, Capital and Palace Catholicism was the majority religion by the sixteenth century and a powerful unifying force, in spite of the strong linguistic differences among the provinces of the Iberian Peninsula. Charles V resided for a while in a palace in Granada next door to the formerly Muslim Alhambra palace—but Granada was too Moorish and, geographically too far away from the north for many Spanish subjects to be properly awed.

Only a few places in Spain were suited for the location of a central palace and administration. Philip II eventually found such a place near the city of Madrid, which had once been a Muslim provincial capital. There, royal architect Juan Bautista de Toledo (ca. 1515–1567) built the Renaissance-style palace and monastery complex of El Escorial (1563–1584). As a result, Madrid became the seat of the administration and later of the court.

Christian State Festivities Given the close association between the state and the church, the Spanish crown expressed its glory through the observance of feast days of the Christian calendar. These feasts were the occasion for processions and **passion plays**, during which urban residents affirmed their Catholic faith. During Holy Week, the week preceding Easter, Catholics marched through the streets, carrying heavy crosses or shouldering wooden platforms with statues of Jesus and Mary. The physical rigors of the Holy Week processions were collective reenactments of Jesus's suffering on the Cross.

Passion play: Dramatic representation of the trial, suffering, and death of Jesus Christ; passion plays are still an integral part of Holy Week in many Catholic countries today.

By contrast, the processions that took place several weeks after Easter were joyous celebrations. Costumed marchers participated in jostling and pushing contests, played music, performed dances, and enacted scenes from the Bible.

The Auto-da-Fé The investigation or proceeding of faith (Portuguese *auto-da-fé*, "act of faith") was a show trial in which the state, through the Spanish Inquisition, judged a person's commitment to Catholicism. The Inquisition employed thousands of state-appointed church officials to investigate anonymous denunciations of individuals failing to conform to the Catholic faith.

Suspected offenders, such as Jewish or Muslim converts to Catholicism or perceived deviants from Catholicism, had to appear before a tribunal. In secret trials, officials determined the offense and the appropriate punishment. These trials often employed torture. However, scholarship has emphasized that in the great majority of cases the punishments were minor, or the investigations did not lead to convictions.

Popular Festivities Jousts (mock combats between contestants mounted on horseback) were secular, primarily aristocratic events. Contestants rode their horses into the city square and led their horses through a complex series of movements. At the height of the spectacle, contestants galloped past each other, hurling their javelins at one another while protecting themselves with their shields. The joust evolved eventually into exhibitions of dressage ("training"), cultivated by the Austrian Habsburgs, who in 1572 founded the Spanish Court Riding School in Vienna.

Bullfights often followed the jousts. During the Middle Ages, bullfights were aristocratic pastimes that drew spectators from local estates. Bullfighters, armed with detachable metal points on three-foot-long spears, tackled several bulls in a town square. The bullfighter who stuck the largest number of points into the shoulders of the bull was the winner.

Theater, Literature, and Painting The dramatic enactments of biblical scenes in the passion plays and religious processions were the origin of secular theater in Italy and Spain. Stationary theaters appeared in the main cities of Spain during the sixteenth century. A performance typically began with a musical prelude and a prologue describing the piece, followed by the three acts of a drama or comedy. Many were hugely successful, enjoying the attendance or even sponsorship of courtiers, magistrates, and merchants.

An important writer of the period was Miguel de Cervantes (1547–1616). His masterpiece, *Don Quixote*, describes the adventures of a poverty-stricken knight and his attendant, the peasant Sancho Panza, as they wander around Spain

Auto-da-Fé, Madrid. This detail from a 1683 painting by the Italian-born painter Francisco Rizi shows a huge assembly in the Plaza Mayor of Madrid. It captures the solemn spectacle of the trial: in the center, below a raised platform, the accused stand in the docket waiting for their convictions to be pronounced; ecclesiastical and civil authorities follow the proceedings from grandstands. On the left, an altar is visible: The celebration of mass, often lasting for hours, was a common feature of the auto-da-fé.

searching for the life of bygone *Reconquista* chivalry. *Don Quixote* is an example of a new literary form: the novel.

The outstanding painter of Spain during Philip II's reign was El Greco (Domenikos Theotokopoulos, ca. 1546–1614), a native of the island of Crete. El Greco's works reflect Spanish Catholicism, with its emphasis on strict obedience to traditional faith and fervent personal piety. His characteristic style represents a variation of Mannerism (with its perspective exaggerations), which succeeded the Renaissance style in Venice during the later sixteenth century.

Putting It All Together

The Ottoman–Habsburg struggle can be seen as another chapter in the long history of competition that began when the Achaemenid Persian Empire expanded into the Mediterranean and was resisted by the Greeks in the middle of the first millennium BCE. There were obvious religious and cultural differences between the Islamic and Western Christian civilizations as they encountered each other during the Ottoman–Habsburg period. But their commonalities are equally interesting. Both were representatives of the return to imperialism, and in the pursuit of their imperial goals, both adopted the policy of the centralizing state with its firearm infantries and urban money economy. Both found it crucial to project their glory to the population and to sponsor artistic expression. In the long run, however, the imperial ambitions of the Ottomans and Habsburgs exceeded their ability to raise cash. Although firearms and a monetized urban economy made them different from previous empires, they were as unstable as all their imperial predecessors. Eventually, around 1600, they reached the limits of their conquests.

Review and Relate

Thinking Through Patterns

Examine the ways historians approach the big questions of this chapter.

In 1300, the Ottomans renewed the Arab-Islamic tradition of jihad against the Eastern Christian empire of Byzantium, defeating the empire with the conquest of Constantinople in 1453. They also carried the war into the western Mediterranean and Indian Ocean. In Western Christian Iberia, the rekindling of the reconquest was more successful. Invigorated by a merging of the concepts of the Crusade and the *Reconquista*, the Iberians expanded overseas to circumvent the Muslims and trade for Indian spices directly. The so-called Age of Exploration is rooted in the Western traditions of war against Islamic civilization.

What patterns characterized the Christian and Muslim imperial competition in the period 1300–1600? Which elements distinguished them from each other, and which elements were similar? How did the pattern change over time?

➤ How did the centralizing state in the Middle East and Europe function in the period 1450–1600? How did economics, military power, and imperial objectives interact to create the centralizing state?

➤ Which patterns did cultural expressions follow in the Habsburg and Ottoman Empires? Why did the ruling classes of these empires sponsor these expressions?

In the mid-1400s, the Middle East and Europe returned to the pattern of imperial state formation after a lull during which states had competed against each other within their respective commonwealths. The element which fueled this return was gunpowder weaponry. The use of cannons and handheld firearms became widespread during this time but required major financial outlays on the part of the states. The two empires became states based on a money economy: bureaucracies maintained centralized departments that regulated the collection of taxes and the payroll of soldiers.

The rulers of these empires were concerned to portray themselves, their military, and their bureaucracies as highly successful and just. The state had to be as visible and benevolent as possible. Rulers, therefore, were builders of palaces, churches, or mosques. They celebrated religious and secular festivities with great pomp and encouraged ministers and the nobility to do likewise. In the imperial capitals, they patronized architects, artists, and writers, resulting in an explosion of intellectual and artistic creativity. In this regard, the Ottomans and the Habsburgs followed similar patterns of cultural expression.

Against the Grain

Consider this as a counterpoint to the main patterns examined in this chapter.

Tilting at Windmills

- What explains the lasting literary success of Don Quixote?
- Why has the phrase "tilting at windmills" undergone a change of meaning from the original "fighting imaginary foes" to "taking on a situation against all seeming evidence" in our own time?

Cervantes's *The Ingenious Gentleman Don Quixote of La Mancha* contributed to the rise of the novel as a characteristic European form of literary expression. Cervantes composed his novel in opposition to the dominant literary conventions of his time—as he wrote, to "ridicule the absurdity of those books of chivalry, which have, as it were, fascinated the eyes and judgement of the world, and in particular of the vulgar."

Every episode in this novel parodies one or another absurdity in society. The frame is provided by the fictional figure of Cide Hamete Benengeli, a purportedly perfidious Muslim historian who might have been lying when he chronicled the lives of the knight Don Quixote and his squire Sancho Panza. Don Quixote's joust, or "tilting," against windmills has become a powerful metaphor for rebelling against the overpowering conventions of society.

Don Quixote is today acclaimed as the second-most-printed text after the Bible. Over the past four centuries, each generation has interpreted the text anew. Revolutionary France saw Don Quixote as a doomed visionary; German Romantics, as a hero destined to fail; Communists, as an anti-capitalist rebel before his time; and secular progressives, as an unconventional hero at the dawn of modern free society. For Karl Marx, Don Quixote was the hidalgo who yearned for a return to the feudal aristocracy of the past. Sigmund Freud saw the knight-errant as "tragic in his helplessness while the plot is unraveled." In our own time, Don Quixote has become the quintessential postmodern figure; in the words of Michel Foucault, his "truth is not in the relation of the words to the world but in that slender and constant relation woven between themselves as verbal signs." As a tragic or comic figure, Don Quixote continues to be an irresistible symbol of opposition.

Key Terms

Apocalypse 374
Corsairs 372
Devşirme 385
Janissaries 385
Military orders 373
Money economy 385
Moriscos 382
Passion play 389
Tax farming 385

Learn more with this chapter's digital tools, including the Oxford Insight Study Guide, at http://www.oup.com/he/vonsivers4e. Please see the Further Resources section at the back of the book for additional readings and suggested websites.

PATTERNS OF EVIDENCE |

Sources for Chapter 16

SOURCE 16.1 Columbus reports on his first voyage, 1493

Born in Genoa, Italy, Christopher Columbus (1451–1506) spent his early years in maritime ventures and later sailed with the Portuguese fleet. In his desire to acquire wealth and fame, and inspired by Portuguese attempts to gain access to the Spice Islands, Columbus studied several global maps which indicated that it was possible to reach Asia by sailing westward across the Atlantic. Confident that he could fulfill his ambition, Columbus sought funding from the Portuguese king, John II, who denied his request. Columbus then turned to Ferdinand and Isabella, rulers of Spain, who were determined to best Portugal in the race to reach the riches of the Indies. After initially turning him down, Ferdinand and Isabella finally granted Columbus the financial backing to undertake his expedition. After a five-week voyage from the Canary Islands, Columbus landed in the Bahamas, thinking that he had successfully reached Asia. After returning to Spain early in 1493, Columbus penned a letter to Ferdinand and Isabella in which he described his discoveries, along with the proclamation that the Caribbean Islands were now in the possession of Spain.

On the thirty-third day after leaving Cadiz I came into the Indian Sea, where I discovered many islands inhabited by numerous people. I took possession of all of them for our most fortunate King by making public proclamation and unfurling his standard, no one making any resistance. To the first of them I have given the name of our blessed Saviour, whose aid I have reached this and all the rest; but the Indians call it Guanahani. To each of the others also I gave a new name, ordering one to be called Sancta Maria de Concepcion, another Fernandina, another Isabella, another Juana; and so with all the rest. As soon as we reached the island which I have just said was called Juana, I sailed along its coast some considerable distance towards the West, and found it to be so

Source: © 2012 The Gilder Lehrman Institute of American History, www.gilderlehrman.org

large, without any apparent end, that I believed it was not an island, but a continent, a province of Cathay.

. . .

In the island, which I have said before was called Hispana, there are very lofty and beautiful mountains, great farms, groves and fields, most fertile both for cultivation and for pasturage, and well adapted for constructing buildings. The convenience of the harbors in this island, and the excellence of the rivers, in volume and salubrity, surpass human belief, unless one should see them. In it the trees, pasture-lands and fruits different much from those of Juana. Besides, this Hispana abounds in various kinds of species, gold and metals. The inhabitants of both sexes of this and of all the other islands I have seen, or of which I have any knowledge, always go as naked as they came into the world, except that some of the women cover their private parts with leaves or branches, or a veil of cotton, which they prepare themselves for this purpose. They are all, as I said before, unprovided with any sort of iron, and they are destitute of arms, which are entirely unknown to them, and for which they are not adapted; not on account of any bodily deformity, for they are well made, but because they are timid and full of terror. They carry, however, canes dried in the sun in place of weapons, upon whose roots they fix a wooded shaft, dried and sharpened to a point. But they never dare to make use of these; for it has often happened, when I have sent two or three of my men to some of their villages to speak with the inhabitants, that a crowd of Indians has sallied forth; but when they saw our men approaching, they speedily took to flight, parents abandoning children, and children their parents. This happened not because any loss or injury had been inflicted upon any of them. On the contrary I gave whatever I had, cloth and many other things, to whomsoever I approached, or with whom I could get speech, without any return being made to me; but they are by nature fearful and timid. But when they see that they are safe, and all fear is banished, they are very guileless and honest, and very liberal of all they have

. . .

They do not practice idolatry; on the contrary, they believe that all strength, all power, in short all blessings, are from Heaven, and I have come down from there with these ships and sailors; and in this spirit was I received everywhere, after they had got over their fear. They are neither lazy nor awkward; but, on the contrary, are of an excellent and acute understanding. Those who have sailed these seas give excellent accounts of everything; but they have never seen men wearing clothes, or ships like ours.

I saw no monsters, neither did I hear accounts of any such except in an island called Charis, the second as one crosses over from Spain to India, which is inhabited by a certain race regarded by their neighbors as very ferocious. They eat human flesh, and make use of several kinds of boats by which they cross over to all the Indian islands, and plunder and carry off whatever they can. But they differ in no respect from the others except in wearing their hair long after the fashion of women. They make use of bows and arrows made of reeds, having pointed shafts fastened to the thicker portion, as we have before described. For this reason they are considered to be ferocious, and the other Indians consequently are terribly afraid of them; but I consider them of no more account than the others. They have intercourse with certain women who dwell alone upon the island of Mateurin, the first as one crosses from Spain to India. These women follow none of the usual occupations of their sex; but they use bows and arrows like those of their husbands, which I have described, and protect themselves with plates of copper, which is found in the greatest abundance among them.

Finally, to sum up in a few words the chief results and advantages of our departure and speedy return, I make this promise to our most invincible Sovereigns, that, if I am supported by some little assistance from them, I will give them as much gold as they have need of, and in addition spices, cotton and mastic, which is found only in Chios, and as much aloes-wood, and as many heathen slaves as their majesties may choose to demand; besides these, rhubarb and other kinds of drugs, which I think the men I left in the fort before alluded to, have already discovered, or will do so; as I have delayed nowhere longer than the winds compelled me, except while I was providing for the construction of a fort in the city of Nativity, and for making all things safe. . . .

Therefore let King and Queen and Princes, and their most fortunate realms, and all other Christian provinces, let us all return thanks to our Lord and Saviour Jesus Christ, who has bestowed so great a victory and reward upon us; let there be processions and solemn sacrifices prepared; let the churches be decked with festal boughs; let Christ rejoice upon Earth as he rejoices in Heaven, as he foresees that so many souls of so many people heretofore lost are to be saved; and let us be glad not only for the exaltation of our faith, but also for the increase of temporal prosperity, in which not only Spain but all Christendom is about to share. As these things have been accomplished so have they been briefly narrated. Farewell.

Christopher Colom,
Admiral of the Ocean Fleet
Lisbon, March 14th.

Working with Sources

1. **How does Columbus describe differences between the "Indians" and Europeans?**
2. **Why did Columbus dash this letter off to Ferdinand and Isabella soon after he returned from his voyage to the Caribbean?**

SOURCE 16.2

Christopher Columbus, *The Book of Prophecies*

1501–1502

Although he is more famous for his voyages—and for the richly detailed accounts he made of them—Columbus also composed a book of prophetic revelations toward the end of his life, entitled *El Libro de las Profecías*. Written after his third voyage to the Americas, the book traces the development of God's plans for the end of the world, which could be hastened along, particularly by a swift and decisive move to reclaim Jerusalem from Muslim control. When Jerusalem was once more restored to Christian sovereignty, Columbus predicted, Jesus could return to earth, and all of the events foreseen in the Book of Revelation (and in various medieval revelations, as well) could unfold. It is helpful to place the plans for Columbus's original voyage in 1492 against the backdrop of his religious beliefs, as he encourages Ferdinand and Isabella to take their rightful place in God's mystical plan—as well as in Columbus's own cartographic charts.

Letter from the Admiral to the King and Queen [Ferdinand and Isabella]

. . .

Most exalted rulers: At a very early age I began sailing the sea and have continued until now. This profession creates a curiosity about the secrets of the world. I have been a sailor for forty years, and I have personally sailed to all the known regions. I have had commerce and conversation with knowledgeable people of the clergy and the laity. Latins and Greeks, Jews and Moors, and with many others of different religions. Our Lord has favored my occupation and has given me an intelligent mind. He has endowed me with a great talent for seamanship; sufficient ability in astrology, geometry, and arithmetic; and the mental and physical dexterity required to draw spherical maps of cities, rivers and mountains, islands and ports, with everything in its proper place.

During this time I have studied all kinds of texts: cosmography, histories, chronicles, philosophy, and other disciplines. Through these writings, the hand of Our Lord opened my mind to the possibility of sailing to the Indies and gave me the will to attempt the voyage. With this burning ambition I came to your Highnesses. Everyone who heard about my enterprise rejected it with laughter and ridicule. Neither all the sciences that I mentioned previously nor citations drawn from them were of any help to me. Only Your Highnesses had faith and perseverance. Who could doubt that this flash of understanding was the work

Source: Christopher Columbus, *The Book of Prophecies*, ed. Roberto Rusconi, trans. Blair Sullivan, vol. 3 (Berkeley: University of California Press, 1997), 67–69, 75–77.

of the Holy Spirit, as well as my own? The Holy Spirit illuminated his holy and sacred Scripture, encouraging me in a very strong and clear voice from the forty-four books of the Old Testament, the four evangelists, and twenty-three epistles from the blessed apostles, urging me to proceed. Continually, without ceasing a moment, they insisted that I go on. Our Lord wished to make something clearly miraculous of this voyage to the Indies in order to encourage me and others about the holy temple.

. . .

Most of the prophecies of holy Scripture have already been fulfilled. The Scriptures say this and the Holy Church loudly and unceasingly is saying it, and no other witness is necessary. I will, however, speak of one prophecy in particular because it bears on my argument and gives me support and happiness whenever I think about it.

I have greatly sinned. Yet, every time that I have asked, I have been covered by the mercy and compassion of Our Lord. I have found the sweetest consolation in throwing off all my cares in order to contemplate his marvelous presence.

I have already said that for the voyage to the Indies neither intelligence nor mathematics nor world maps were of any use to me; it was the fulfillment of Isaiah's prophecy. This is what I want to record here in order to remind Your Highnesses and so that you can take pleasure from the things I am going to tell you about Jerusalem on the basis of the same authority. If you have faith in this enterprise, you will certainly have the victory.

. . .

I said above that much that has been prophesied remains to be fulfilled, and I say that these are the world's great events, and I say that a sign of this is the acceleration of Our Lord's activities in this world. I know this from the recent preaching of the gospel in so many lands.

The Calabrian abbot Joachim said that whoever was to rebuild the temple on Mount Zion would come from Spain.

The cardinal Pierre d'Ailly wrote at length about the end of the religion of Mohammed and the coming of the Antichrist in his treatise *De concordia astronomicae veritatis et narrationis historicae* [*On the agreement between astronomical truth and historical narrative*]; he discusses, particularly in the last nine chapters, what many astronomers have said about the ten revolutions of Saturn.

▸ Working with Sources

1. **How does Columbus appeal to the "crusading" goals of Ferdinand and Isabella, and why?**
2. **Would this appeal have found favor with the monarchs, given their other actions in Spain in 1492?**

SOURCE 16.3

Thomas the Eparch and Joshua Diplovatatzes, "The Fall of Constantinople"

1453

The siege and conquest of Constantinople by the Ottoman Turks under Mehmet II (r. 1451–1481) was one of the turning points of world history. Unfolding over two months between April 5 and May 29, 1453, the siege exposed the inability of the Byzantine emperor Constantine XI to withstand a sustained and massive attack. Outnumbering the defenders 11 to 1, the Ottomans battered Constantinople's walls with heavy cannons and took advantage of the natural weaknesses of the city's geography. This account, told by two survivors and (self-proclaimed) eyewitnesses to the siege and its aftermath, details some of the specific stages of the defeat—and the suffering for Christians that came as a result.

When the Turk then drew near to Pera in the fortified zone, he seized all the boats he could find and bound them to each other so as to form a bridge which permitted the combatants to fight on the water just as they did on land. The Turks had with them thousands of ladders which they placed against the walls, right at the place which they had fired [their cannon] and breached the wall, just as they did at the cemetery of St. Sebold. The Genoese handled this breach; they wanted to protect it with their ships because they had so many. In the army of the Turk the order had been given fifteen days before the attack that each soldier would carry a ladder, whether he was fighting on land or sea. There also arrived galleys full of armed men: it seemed that they were Genoese and that they had come to aid the besieged, but in fact they were Turks and they were slipping into the gates. Just as this was becoming less worrisome and the city seemed secure, there arrived under the flag of the Genoese several ships which repelled the Turks with great losses.

At dawn on Monday, 29 May, they began an attack that lasted all night until Tuesday evening and they conquered the city. The commander of the Genoese, who was leading the defense of the breach, pretended to be wounded and abandoned his battle station, taking with him all his people. When the Turks realized this, they slipped in through the breach. When the emperor of the Greeks saw this, he exclaimed in a loud voice: "My God, I have been betrayed!" and he suddenly appeared with his people, exhorting the others to stand firm and defend themselves. But then the gate was opened and the crush of people

---

Source: trans. William L. North from the Italian version in A. Pertusi, ed., *La Caduta di Constantinopoli: Le testimonianze dei contemporanei* (Milan: Mondadori, 1976), 234–239, available online at https://d31kydh6n6r5j5.cloudfront.net/uploads/sites/83/2019/06/Thomas_the_Eparch_and_Joshua_Diplovatatzes_for_MARS_website.pdf became such that the emperor himself and his [men] were killed by the Turks and the traitors.

Then the Turks ran to the Hagia Sophia, and all those whom they had imprisoned there, they killed in the first heat of rage. Those whom they found later, they bound with a cord around their neck and their hands tied behind their backs and led them out of the city. When the Turk learned that the emperor had been killed in Constantinople, he captured the Grand Duke who was governing in the emperor's stead and had the Grand Duke's son beheaded and then the Grand Duke himself. Then he seized one of the Grand Duke's daughters who was quite beautiful and made her lie on the great altar of Hagia Sophia with a crucifix under her head and then raped her. Then the most brutish of the Turks seized the finest noble women, virgins, and nuns of the city and violated them in the presence of the Greeks and in sacrilege of Christianity. Then they destroyed all the sacred objects and the bodies of the saints and burned everything they found, save for the cross, the nail, and the clothing of Christ: no one knows where these relics ended up, no one has found them. They also wanted to desecrate the image of the Virgin of St. Luke by stabbing six hundred people in front of it, one after another, like madmen. Then they took prisoner those who fell into their hands, tied them with a rope around the neck and calculated the value of each one. Women had to redeem themselves with their own bodies, men by fornicating with their hands or some other means. Whoever was able to pay the assessed amount could remain in his faith and whoever refused had to die. The Turk who had become governor of Constantinople, named Suleiman in German, occupied the temple of Hagia Sophia to practice his faith there. For three days the Turks sacked and pillaged the city, and each kept whatever he found—people and goods—and did with them whatever he wished.

. . .

All this was made known by Thomas the Eparch, a count of Constantinople, and Joshua Diplovatatzes. Thutros of Constantinople translated their Greek into "welisch" and Dumita Exswinnilwacz and Matheus Hack of Utrecht translated their welisch into German.

Working with Sources

1. **What does this account suggest about the preparedness of the Turks for the sack of Constantinople—and the lack of preparation on the part of the Byzantine defenders?**
2. **What details indicate that the taking of Constantinople was seen as a "religious" war on the Ottoman side?**

SOURCE 16.4

Evliya Çelebi, "A Procession of Artisans at Istanbul"

ca. 1638

Born on the Golden Horn and raised in the sultan's palace in Istanbul, Çelebi traveled throughout Ottoman domains between 1640 and 1680. He published an account of his travels and experiences as the *Seyahatname*, or *Book of Travels*. In the first of his 10 books in the document, Çelebi provides a lengthy description of Istanbul around the year 1638, including a panoramic view of 1,100 artisan and craft guilds. The numbers and diversity of trades represented underscore the extent of Ottoman commerce—as well as the pride of place each of the city's working people claimed as their due.

The numbers in brackets refer to the order of listing in this chapter.

I: Ship-captains [7] vs. Saddlers [30]

Following the bakers [6], the saddlers wished to pass, but the ship-captains and sea-merchants raised a great fuss. When Sultan Murad got wind of the matter, he consulted with the ulema and the guild shaikhs. They all agreed that it made sense for the ship-captains to proceed after the bakers, because it was they who transported the wheat, and the bakers were dependent on them, and also because Noah was their patron saint.

Comment: the saddlers do not reappear until much later, between the tanners [29] and the shoemakers [31].

. . .

III: Egyptian Merchants [9] vs. Butchers [10]

Following the procession of these Mediterranean Sea captains, the butchers were supposed to pass, according to imperial decree. But all the great Egyptian merchants, including the dealers in rice, hemp, Egyptian reed mats, coffee and sugar gathered together and began quarreling with the butchers. Finally they went before the sultan and said: "My padishah, our galleons are charged with transporting rice, lentils, coffee and hemp. They cannot do without us, nor we without them. Why should these bloody and tricky butchers come between us? Plagues have arisen from cities where they shed their blood, and for fear of this their stalls and shambles in other countries are outside of the city walls.

Source: Robert Dankoff, *An Ottoman Mentality: The World of Evliya Çelebi*, 2nd ed. (Leiden, the Netherlands: Brill, 2006), 86–89.

They are a bloody and filthy band of ill-omen. We, on the other hand, always make Istanbul plentiful and cheap with grains of all sorts."

Now the butchers' eyes went bloodshot. "My padishah," they said, "Our patron saint is Butcher Cömerd and our occupation is with sheep, an animal which the Creator has made the object of mercy, and whose flesh He has made lawful food for the strengthening of His servants' bodies. Bread and meat are mentioned as the foremost of God's gifts to mankind: with a small portion of meat, a poor man can subsist for five or six days. We make our living with such a lawful trade, and are known for our generosity (*cömerdlik*). It is we who make Istanbul plentiful and cheap. As for these merchants and dealers and profiteers: concerning them the Koran says (2:275), 'God has made selling lawful and profiteering unlawful'. They are such a despised group that after bringing their goods from Egypt they store it in magazines in order to create a shortage, thus causing public harm through their hoarding.

. . .

"Egyptian sugar? But in the Koran the rivers of paradise are praised as being made 'of pure honey' (47:15). Now we have honey from Turkey, Athens, Wallachia, Moldavia, each with seventy distinct qualities. Furthermore, if my padishah wished, thousands of quintals of sugar could be produced in Alanya, Antalya, Silifke, Tarsus, Adana, Payas, Antakya, Aleppo, Damascus, Sidon, Beyrut, Tripoli and other such provinces—enough to make it plentiful and cheap throughout the world—so why do we need your sugar?

"As for coffee: it is an innovation; it prevents sleep; it dulls the generative powers; and coffee houses are dens of sedition. When roasted it is burnt; and in the legal compilations known as *Bezzaziye* and *Tatarhaniye* we have the dictum that 'Whatever is carbonized is absolutely forbidden'—this holds even for burnt bread. Spiced sherbet, pure milk, tea, fennel, salep, and almond-cream—all these are more wholesome than coffee."

. . .

To these objections of the butchers, the Egyptian merchants replied:

. . . "It is true that Turkey has no need of sugar and hemp, and that European sugar is also very fine. But tell us this, O band of butchers: what benefit and return do you offer to the public treasury?"

The butchers had nothing to say to this, and the Egyptian merchants continued: "My padishah, the goods arriving in our galleons provide the public treasury an annual revenue of 11,000 purses from customs dues. As a matter of justice (*'adalet ederseñiz*) we ought to have precedence in the Muhammadan procession, and the butchers ought to come after us." The *şeyhülislam* Yahya Efendi and Mu'id Ahmed Efendi cited the hadith, "The best of men is he who is useful to mankind," and the sultan gave the Egyptian merchants a noble rescript authorizing them to go first, and the butchers to go second.

▶ Working with Sources

1. **Why did the order in which they appeared in the procession matter so much to these particular groups?**
2. **How did appeals to the Quran accentuate or diminish their case to be placed ahead in the procession?**

SOURCE 16.5

Ogier Ghiselin de Busbecq, "The Court of Suleiman the Magnificent"

1581

Ghiselin (1522–1592) was a Flemish ambassador who represented the Austrian Habsburgs at the court of Süleyman, "the Magnificent" (1520–1566) in Istanbul. In 1581, he published an account of his time among the Ottomans as *Itinera Constantinopolitanum et Amasianum* (*Travels in Constantinople and Asia Minor*). In this segment of his travel narrative, he draws attention to the personal habits and behaviors of a contemporary emperor—one who saw himself as the heir to the Romans as well as to the other monarchs who had held Constantinople.

The Sultan was seated on a very low ottoman, not more than a foot from the ground, which was covered with a quantity of costly rugs and cushions of exquisite workmanship; near him lay his bow and arrows. His air, as I said, was by no means gracious, and his face wore a stern, though dignified, expression. On entering we were separately conducted into the royal presence by the chamberlains, who grasped our arms. . . . After having gone through a pretense of kissing his hand, we were conducted backwards to the wall opposite his seat, care being taken that we should never turn our backs on him. The Sultan then listened to what I had to say; but the language I held was not at all to his taste, for the demands of his Majesty breathed a spirit of independence and dignity . . . and so he made no answer beyond saying in a tetchy way, "Giusel, giusel," i.e. well, well . . .

. . .

I was greatly struck with the silence and order that prevailed in this great crowd. There were no cries, no hum of voices, the usual accompaniments of a motley gathering, neither was there any jostling; without the slightest disturbance each man took his proper place according to his rank. The Agas, as they call their chiefs, were seated, to wit, generals, colonels (*bimbashi*), and captains (*soubashi*). Men of a lower position stood. The most interesting sight in this assembly was a body of several thousand Janissaries, who were

Source: Wayne S. Vucinich, *The Ottoman Empire: Its Record and Legacy* (Princeton, NJ: Van Nostrand, 1965), 127–129.

drawn up in a long line apart from the rest; their array was so steady and motionless that, being at a little distance, it was some time before I could make up my mind as to whether they were human beings or statues; at last I received a hint to salute them, and saw all their heads bending at the same moment to return my bow.

. . .

When the cavalry had ridden past, they were followed by a long procession of Janissaries, but few of whom carried any arms except their regular weapon, the musket. They were dressed in uniforms of almost the same shape and colour, so that you might recognize them to be the slaves. . . . There is only one thing in which they are extravagant, viz., plumes, head-dresses, etc., and veterans who formed the rear guard were specially distinguished by ornaments of this kind. The plumes which they insert in their frontlets might well be mistaken for a walking forest.

Working with Sources

1. **Why were order and discipline apparently so important at Suleiman's court?**
2. **Why might Ghiselin have found the Janissaries so particularly impressive?**

SOURCE 16.6 Janissary Musket

ca. 1750–1800

The Janissaries constitute the most famous and centralized of the Ottomans' military institutions. A feared and respected military force, the Janissaries were Christian-born males who had been seized from their homes as boys, converted to Islam, and then trained as future soldiers and administrators for the Turks. Under the direct orders of the sultan and his viziers, the Janissaries were equipped with the latest military innovations. These units received cannons and matchlock (later flintlock, below) muskets. The muskets continued their evolution in the Janissaries' hands, becoming standard equipment for Ottoman and other armies.

Source: © INTERFOTO/Alamy.

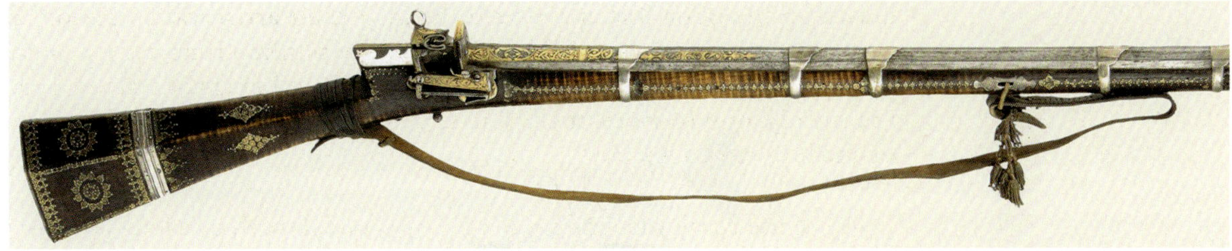

Working with Sources

1. What does the elaborate decoration of this musket suggest about its psychological as well as its practical effects?
2. Was this firearm likely to have been produced by indigenous, rather than European, gunsmiths? Why or why not?

World Period Four

Interactions across the Globe, 1450–1750

The fifteenth century saw a renewal of the imperial impulse in the religious civilizations of the world. A forerunner had been the Mongol empire, which however did not last long; in less than 100 years it was replaced in China by the Ming. The founders of the subsequent new empires were the Mughals in India; the Ottomans, Safavids, and Songhay in the Middle East and Islamic Africa; the Habsburgs in Europe; and the seaborne empires of Portugal and Spain. One byproduct of this new imperial impulse was the discovery of the Americas, which in turn inspired the formulation of the heliocentric universe. The rediscovery of Greek literature in Europe had already set into motion the Renaissance, a broad new approach to understanding the world that provided the spark for the New Science.

China and India, by far the wealthiest and most populous agrarian–urban empires, enjoyed leading positions in the world because they produced everything they needed and wanted. Europe, however, acquired warm-weather crops and minerals through overseas colonial expansion, which would help it to challenge the traditional order.

Chapter 17

The Renaissance, New Sciences, and Religious Wars in Europe

1450–1750

CHAPTER SEVENTEEN PATTERNS

Origins, Interactions, Adaptations During the Middle Ages, a relatively coherent Western Christian religious civilization emerged in Europe. By the middle of the fifteenth century, interactions with Eastern Christianity put in motion the Renaissance, which made European culture highly heterogeneous, with many conflicting political, religious, and social trends. In contrast, the other, more homogeneous religious civilizations in the world rested on deep internal roots and received far fewer outside stimuli for their transformation.

Uniqueness and Similarities The Renaissance, New Science, and Enlightenment are phenomena that helped Europe chart its unique path in world history. These phenomena are not the result of some special genius among Europeans, but rather due to the much humbler historical trajectory of a poor and largely uncultured region that began on the periphery of the Eurasian continent and acculturated itself to the level of a sophisticated, fully diversified religious civilization only thanks to interaction with and adaptation to outside stimuli. Eventually, the tables would turn: for the last few hundred years, Asia, Africa, and Latin America have adapted to the modern stimulus of Western scientific–industrial civilization.

One of the most remarkable scientific minds of the seventeenth century was Maria Cunitz (ca. 1607–1664). Under the tutorship of her father, a physician, she became accomplished in six languages, the humanities, and the sciences. During the Thirty Years' War (1618–1648), as Cunitz and her Protestant family sought refuge in a Cistercian monastery, she wrote *Urania propitia* (*Companion to Urania*), in praise of the Greek muse and patron of astronomy. When the family returned home, Cunitz continued to devote her life to science through her careful astronomical observations.

Cunitz's book is a popularization of the astronomical tables of Johannes Kepler (1571–1630), who discovered the elliptical trajectories of the planets. Cunitz's book, published privately in 1650, makes corrections in Kepler's tables and offers simplified calculations of star positions. It was generally well received, although there were a few detractors who found it hard to believe that a woman could succeed in the sciences.

Cunitz lived in a time when Western Christianity had entered the age of early global interaction, from 1450 until 1750. Europe remained institutionally similar to the other parts of the world, especially the Middle East, India, China, and Japan: Rulers throughout Eurasia governed by divine grace; all large states followed patterns of political centralization; and their economies depended on the productivity of agriculture.

Culturally, however, northwestern Europe began to move in a different direction from Islamic, Hindu, Neo-Confucian, and Buddhist civilizations after 1500. New developments in the sciences and philosophy in Europe initiated new cultural patterns. As significant as these patterns were, these new mathematized sciences remained limited to a relatively few educated persons, largely outside the ruling classes. Their ideas diverged substantially from those represented by the Catholic and Protestant ruling classes

CHAPTER OUTLINE

Cultural Transformations: Renaissance, Baroque, and New Sciences

Centralizing States and Religious Upheavals

Putting It All Together

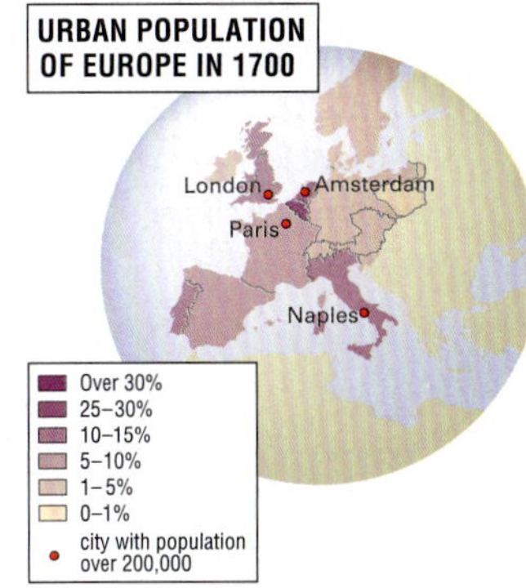

ABOVE: In his *Principia Mathematica*, first published in 1687, Isaac Newton (1643–1727) unified physics and astronomy into a single mathematical system.

Seeing Patterns

> What were the reasons for the cultural change that began in Europe with the Renaissance around 1400? In which ways were the subsequent patterns of cultural change different from those in the other religious civilizations of Eurasia?

> When and how did the mathematization of the sciences begin, and how did it gain popularity in northwestern Europe? Why is the popularization of the sciences important for understanding the period 1500–1750?

> What were the patterns of centralized state formation and transformation in the period 1400–1750? How did the Protestant Reformation and religious wars modify these patterns?

Renaissance: "Rebirth" of culture based on new publications and translations of Greek, Hellenistic, and Roman authors whose writings were previously unknown in Western Christianity.

New Sciences: Mathematized sciences, such as physics, introduced in the 1500s.

and resulted in tensions or even repression of scientists by the authorities. The new scientific and intellectual culture broadened after 1750 and eventually led to the Industrial Revolution.

The European Renaissance, Baroque, and New Sciences began with the appropriation of the Greek and Roman cultural heritage, allegedly absent from the Middle Ages, by an educated elite. However, this elite overestimated the extent of their break from the Middle Ages. Scholars today understand this break as far less radical, with much in culture remaining unchanged. Similarly, the political and social changes of the period 1400–1750 have to be balanced against inherited continuities. While the seeds of a departure of Western Christianity from the general patterns of agrarian–urban society were planted around 1500, the "great divergence" from the agrarian–urban patterns of Islamic, Hindu, and Chinese civilizations began only after 1750.

Cultural Transformations: Renaissance, Baroque, and New Sciences

The **Renaissance** was a period of cultural transformation in the fifteenth century that followed the scholastic Middle Ages in Western Christianity. Its thinkers and artists considered their period a time of "rebirth" (which is the literal meaning of "renaissance" in French). They were powerfully influenced by the writings of Greek and Hellenistic-Roman authors who had been unknown during the scholastic age. In the sixteenth century, the Renaissance gave way to the Baroque in the arts and the **New Sciences**.

The Renaissance and Baroque Arts

An outpouring of learning, scholarship, and art began around 1400 in Italy and spread through northwestern Europe. Thinkers and artists benefited from Greek and Hellenistic-Roman texts that scholars had discovered in Byzantium. The emerging cultures of the Renaissance and Baroque were creative adaptations of those Greek and Hellenistic-Roman writings to the cultural heritage of Western Christianity. This vibrant mixture led to the movement of **Humanism**.

New Manuscripts and Printing Eastern Christian Byzantium experienced a cultural revival between 1261 and the 1453 Muslim Ottoman conquest of Constantinople. Italian scholars, aware of how much of Greek literature was still absent from Western Christianity, invited Eastern Christian scholars to bring manuscripts to Italy for teaching and translation. Their students became fluent in Greek and translated Hesiod and Homer, Greek plays, Plato and the Neo-Platonists, the still missing works of Aristotle, Hellenistic scientific texts, and the Greek church fathers.

The dissemination of these works was helped by the development of paper. Experimentation in the 1430s with movable metal typeface led to the printing press. A half century later, a printing revolution had taken place in Europe.

Humanism: Intellectual movement focusing on human culture, in such fields as philosophy, philology, and literature, and based on the corpus of Greek and Roman texts.

Philology and Political Theory This examination of manuscripts encouraged the study of Greek, Latin, and Hebrew philology. The best-known philologist was the Dutchman Desiderius Erasmus (1466–1536), who published an edition of the Greek and Latin New Testaments in 1516.

Another approach emerged as a central element in political thought. In *The Prince*, Niccolò Machiavelli (1469–1527) argued that what Italy needed was a unifier who possessed what Aristotle discussed in Book 5 of his *Politics:* a person of indomitable spirit (Italian *virtù*) to take the proper steps when political success was to be achieved. Many Renaissance scholars preferred Plato, but Machiavelli remained faithful to Aristotle—an Aristotle later esteemed by the American founding fathers.

The Renaissance Arts In Italy, a new artistic way of looking at the Roman past and the natural world emerged. The first artists to adopt this perspective were the sculptor Donatello (ca. 1386–1466) and the architect Filippo Brunelleschi (1377–1446), who received their inspiration from Roman imperial statues and ruins. The artistic triumvirate of the high Italian Renaissance was composed of Leonardo da Vinci (1452–1519), Michelangelo (1475–1564), and Raphael (1483–1520). Inspired by the Italian creative outburst, the Renaissance flourished also in Germany, the Netherlands, and France.

For musical composers of the Renaissance, the difficulty was that the music of the Greeks and Romans was completely unknown. A partial solution for this difficulty was found through emphasizing the relationship between the word—that is, rhetoric—and music. In the sixteenth century this emphasis coincided with the Protestant and Catholic demand for liturgical music, such as hymns and masses.

The theater was a relatively late expression of the Renaissance. The popular mystery, passion, and morality plays from the centuries prior to 1400 continued in Catholic countries. In Italy, in the course of the fifteenth century, the *commedia dell'arte* (a secular popular theater) emerged. In England during the sixteenth century, theater troupes were stationary and professional. Sponsored by the aristocracy and the Elizabethan court, the best-known playwright was William Shakespeare (1564–1616).

The Baroque Arts The Renaissance gave way around 1600 to the Baroque, which dominated the arts until about 1750. Two factors influenced its emergence. First, the Protestant Reformation, Catholic Reformation, and religious wars changed the nature of patronage, on which artists depended. Many Protestant

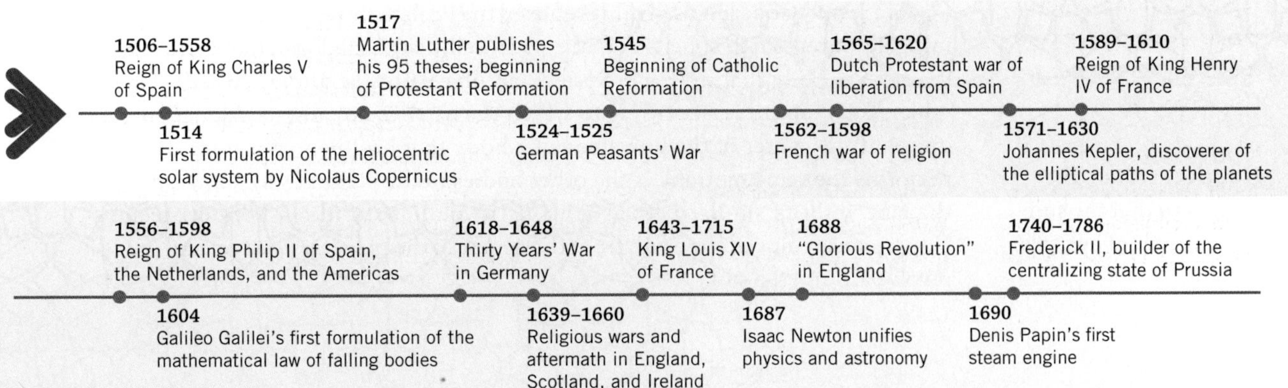

churches, opposed to imagery as incompatible with their view of early Christianity, did not sponsor artists for the adornment of their buildings with religious art.

Second, the predilection for Renaissance balance and restraint gave way to greater spontaneity and dramatic effect. Church and palace architecture shifted to the "baroque" voluptuousness of forms and decorations seen in Bavarian and Austrian Catholic churches, the Versailles Palace, and St. Paul's Cathedral in London, all completed between 1670 and 1750. Baroque composers, as exemplified by the Italian Antonio Vivaldi (1678–1741) and the German Johann Sebastian Bach (1685–1750), benefited from ample church and palace patronage.

The New Sciences

Italian Renaissance scholars were divided between those who continued to adhere to the scholastic Aristotelian scientific method and those (such as Copernicus) who were more interested in newly translated Hellenistic mathematical, astronomical, and geographical texts. In the 1600s, two scientists—Galileo and Newton—abandoned much of the *qualitative* scientific method of Aristotelian scholasticism in favor of the *mathematized* science of physics. In the eighteenth century, Newton's science of a mechanical, deterministic universe became the foundation of modern scientific–industrial society.

Copernicus's Incipient New Science Nicolaus Copernicus (1473–1543) was born in Toruń, a German-founded city under Polish rule. He studied at the University of Kraków, the only eastern European school to offer courses in astronomy. During the years 1495–1504, he continued his studies at Italian universities. In 1500 he taught mathematics in Rome and perhaps read Greek astronomical texts translated from Arabic. After he graduated with a degree in canon law, Copernicus took an administrative position at the cathedral of Toruń, which allowed him time to pursue astronomical research. One text that Copernicus read, the *Geography* written by the Hellenistic cosmographer Ptolemy, proposed the geographical concept of Earth as a globe composed of a single sphere of intermingled earth and water. This text contradicted the medieval floating theory, according to which the Eurasian-African land mass was one compact body floating on a large surrounding ocean.

Between 1507 and 1514, Copernicus realized that the discovery of the Americas in 1492 provided empirical proof for the theory of the world as a single earth-water sphere, where earth and water were more or less evenly distributed across the surface. It is likely that he saw the new world map by the German cartographer Martin Waldseemüller (ca. 1470–1520), which made him aware of the Americas as hitherto unknown inhabited lands on the other side of the world.

As a result, Copernicus firmly espoused the Ptolemaic theory of the single intermingled water–earth sphere. A globe with well-distributed water and landmasses is a perfect body that moves in perfect circular paths, he argued further. He formulated a hypothesis, according to which the earth is not an exceptional physical object at the center of the universe but a body that has the same appearance and performs the same motions as the other bodies in the planetary system, especially the sun with its similar path. With this revolutionary idea—**heliocentrism**—Copernicus removed the earth from the center of the planetary system and made it revolve around the sun.

Heliocentrism: The discovery that the sun is the center of our solar system.

Renaissance Art. Brunelleschi's cupola for the cathedral of Florence, completed in 1436, was one of the greatest achievements of the early Renaissance (a). Raphael's School of Athens (1509–1510) depicts some 50 philosophers and scientists, with Plato (in red tunic) and Aristotle (blue) in the center of the painting (b).

Galileo's Mathematical Physics In the decades between the births of Copernicus and Galileo Galilei (1564–1642), mathematics expanded considerably. Euclid's *Elements* was retranslated correctly from the original Greek in 1543. A translation in 1544 of a text on floating and descending bodies by the Hellenistic scholar Archimedes (287–212 BCE) also attracted intense scholarly attention.

In 1604, Galileo combined geometry, algebra, and Archimedean physics to formulate his mathematical "law of falling bodies." While earlier scholars reflected on the logical and/or geometric properties of motion only "according to imagination," Galileo systematically combined imagination with empirical research and experimentation. He thereby established what we now call the (mathematized) "New Sciences."

Running Afoul of the Church Galileo was one of the first astronomers to use a telescope, which had been recently invented in Flanders. On the basis of his astronomical work, in 1610 he became chief mathematician and philosopher at the court of the Medici, the ruling family of Florence. But his increasing fame also attracted the enmity of the Catholic Church.

As a proponent of Copernican heliocentrism, Galileo seemed to contradict the passage in the Hebrew Bible where God recognized the motion of the sun around the earth. (In Joshua 10:12–13, God stopped the sun's revolution for a day so that the Israelites could win a battle.) In contrast to the more tolerant pope at the time of Copernicus, the Roman Inquisition favored a strictly literal interpretation of this passage. In 1633 Galileo was condemned to house arrest and forced to make a public repudiation of heliocentrism.

The condemnation of Galileo had a chilling effect on scientists in countries where the Catholic Reformation was dominant, such as Italy, Spain, and Portugal. During the seventeenth century, interest in the New Sciences shifted to France,

Waldseemüller's 1507 World Map. The German mapmaker Martin Waldseemüller was the first western Christian to draw a world map which included the newly discovered Americas. He gave them the name "America" after the Italian explorer Amerigo Vespucci (1454–1512), who was the first to state that the Americas were a separate landmass, unconnected to Asia. The single copy of Waldseemüller's map still extant is among the holdings of the US Library of Congress.

Germany, the Netherlands, and England. In these countries, no single church authority was sufficiently dominant to enforce the literal understanding of scripture. As a result, these countries produced mathematicians, astronomers, physicists, and inventors, Catholic as well as Protestant. It was this relative intellectual freedom, not sympathy on the part of religious authorities for the New Sciences, which allowed the latter to flourish, especially in the Netherlands and England.

Iberian Natural Sciences Southern European countries were still well situated to make substantial scientific contributions, even if not in the New Sciences. Botanists, geographers, ethnographers, physicians, and metallurgists fanned out across the new colonies to research the new plants, diseases, peoples, and mineral resources of the New World, Africa, and Asia. They used the traditional methods of the natural sciences and accumulated a voluminous amount of knowledge. For long periods, the Habsburg monarch kept these discoveries hidden, fearful that colonial competitors would benefit from them. It is only recently that the Iberian contributions to the sciences in the 1500s and 1600s have become more widely known.

Isaac Newton's Mechanics In the middle of the English struggles between the Protestants and the Catholic/Philo-Catholic Stuart monarchs, Isaac Newton (1643–1727) brought the New Sciences of Copernicus and Galileo to their culmination. As a professor at the University of Cambridge, his primary early contribution was calculus, which he developed at the same time as the German philosopher Gottfried Wilhelm Leibniz (1646–1716). Later in his career, Newton unified the fields of physics and astronomy, establishing the so-called Newtonian synthesis. His *Mathematical Principles of Natural Philosophy*, published in 1687, established a deterministic universe following mathematical rules and formed the basis of science until the early twentieth century, when quantum physics with its conclusion of indeterminacy superseded Newtonianism.

The New Sciences and Their Social Impact

Scientists in the seventeenth century met each other in scientific societies or residential salons. Popularizers introduced the public to the New Sciences. Scientific instruments such as telescopes, microscopes, thermometers, and barometers were constantly improving. Experimentation with barometers, vacuum chambers, and cylinders operating with condensing steam culminated with the invention of the steam engine in England in 1712.

New Science Societies When the Catholic Reformation drove the New Sciences to northwestern Europe, chartered scientific societies, such as the Royal Society of London (1660) and the Paris Academy of Sciences (1666), were established. These societies co-opted scientists as fellows, held regular meetings, challenged their fellows to answer scientific questions, awarded prizes, and organized expeditions. They also published their findings. Some societies attracted thousands of members representing an important cross section of seventeenth-century urban society in northwest Europe (see Map 17.1).

The New Science triumphed in northwestern Europe in a large, scientifically and technically interested public of experimenters, engineers, instrument makers, artisans, businesspeople, and lay folk. Popularizers lectured to audiences of middle-class amateurs, instrument makers, and craftspeople, especially in England and the Netherlands. Coffeehouses allowed the literate urban public to meet, hear lectures, read the daily newspapers (first appearing in the early seventeenth century), and exchange ideas. Wealthy businessmen endowed public lectures and supported elaborate experiments and expensive laboratory equipment. Male urban literacy is estimated to have exceeded 50 percent in England and the Netherlands during this period, although it remained considerably lower in France, Germany, and Italy.

Women, Social Salons, and the New Science Women were part of this scientifically inclined public. In the fields of mathematics and astronomy, Sophie Brahe (1556–1643), sister of the Danish astronomer Tycho Brahe (1546–1601), and Maria Cunitz (see the Vignette at the beginning of the chapter) made contributions to the new astronomy of Copernicus and Kepler. According to some estimates, in the second half of the seventeenth century about 14 percent of German astronomers were women. A dozen prominent female astronomers practiced their science privately in Germany, Poland, the Netherlands, France, and England.

Another institution that helped in the popularization of the New Sciences was the salon. As the elegant living room of an urban residence, the salon was a meeting place for the urban social elite to engage in conversations, presentations, and experiments. The culture of the salon emerged first in Paris. Since the Catholic French universities were hostile to many new ideas, educated urban aristocrats and middle-class professionals turned to the salons as places to learn about new scientific developments. Furthermore, French universities and scientific

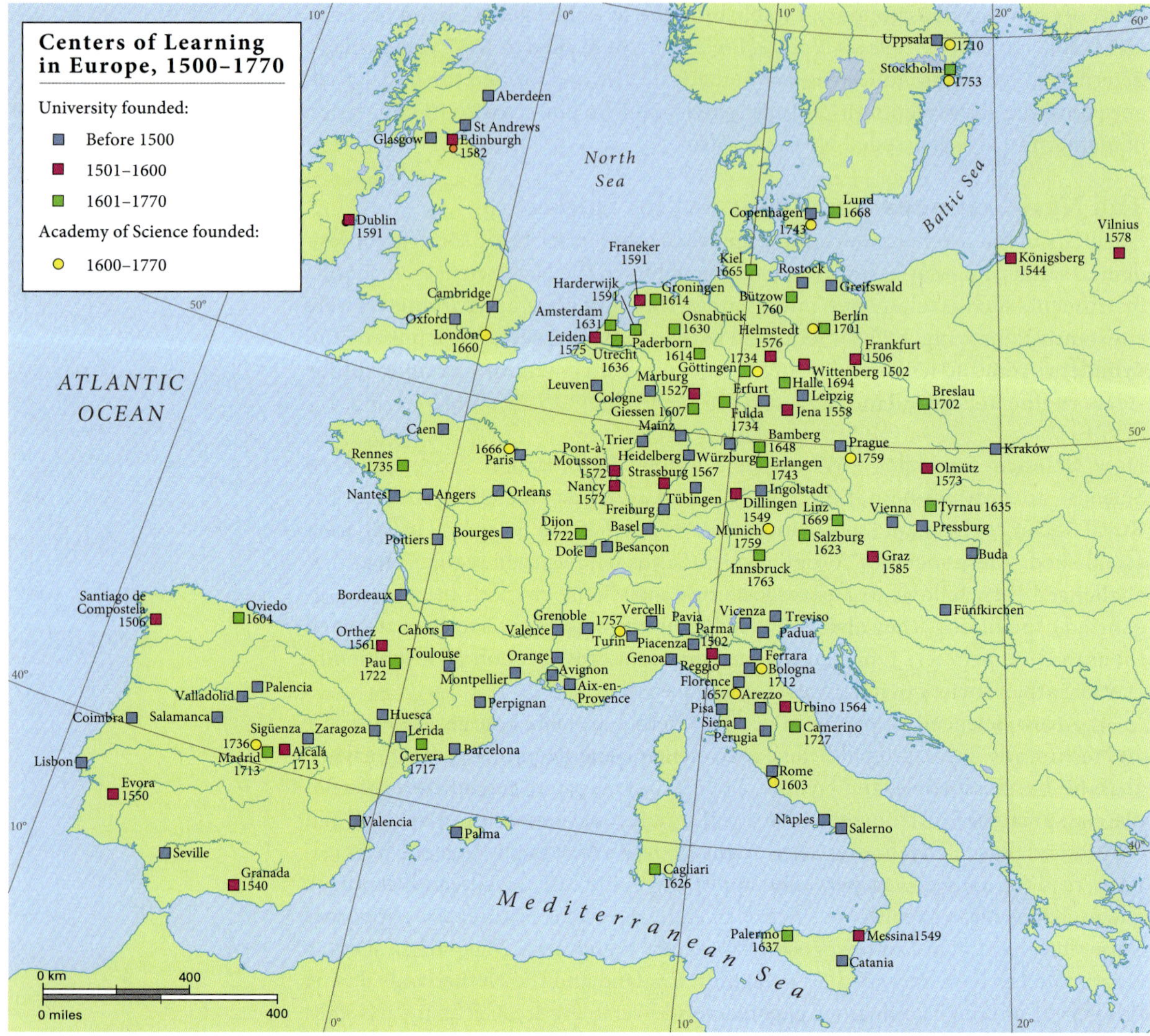

MAP 17.1 Centers of Learning in Europe, 1500–1770

academies refused to admit women, in contrast to Italian and German institutions. The French salon, therefore, became a bastion of female scholars.

One example of a French woman scientist was Émilie du Châtelet (1706–1749). In a Paris salon she met François-Marie Arouet, known as Voltaire (1694–1778), a writer, skeptic, satirist, and amateur Newtonian. Although Voltaire published prolifically, Châtelet eventually outstripped him in both research and scientific understanding. Her lasting achievement was the translation of Newton's *Mathematical Principles* into French, published in 1759.

Discovery of the Vacuum Of all the new scientific instruments available at the time, it was the barometer that would prove crucial for the exploration of the properties of the vacuum and condensing steam, eventually leading to the invention of the steam engine. The scientist who laid the groundwork for the barometer was Evangelista Torricelli (1608–1647), an assistant of Galileo. He experimented with mercury-filled glass tubes, demonstrating that atmospheric pressure produced a vacuum inside these tubes.

A few years later, the French mathematician and philosopher Blaise Pascal (1623–1662) used a mercury barometer to demonstrate lower air pressures at higher altitudes. Soon thereafter, scientists discovered the connection between changing atmospheric pressures and the weather. The discovery of the vacuum was an important step toward the practical application of the New Sciences to mechanical engineering in the eighteenth century.

The Steam Engine The French Huguenot scientist and engineer Denis Papin (ca. 1647–1712) made the first step from the vacuum chamber to the steam engine. In 1690, Papin constructed a cylinder with a piston. Weights, via a cord and two pulleys, held the piston at the top of the cylinder. When heated, water in the bottom of the cylinder turned into steam. When subsequently cooled through the injection of water, the steam condensed, forcing the piston down and lifting the weights up. The Royal Society of London held discussions of his papers, thereby alerting engineers, craftspeople, and entrepreneurs in England to the steam engine as a labor-saving machine. In 1712, the mechanic Thomas Newcomen built the first practical steam engine to pump water from coal mine shafts.

Altogether, it took a little over a century for Europeans to apply the New Sciences to engineering—that is, to the construction of the steam engine. Prior to 1600, mechanical inventions—such as the wheel, the compass, the stern rudder, and the firearm—had been constructed by anonymous tinkerers. By 1700, engineers needed at least a basic understanding of mathematics and such abstract physical phenomena as inertia, gravity, vacuums, and condensing steam in order to build a steam engine or other complex machinery.

Vacuum Power. In 1672, the mayor of Magdeburg, the New Scientist Otto von Guericke, demonstrated the experiment that made him a pioneer in the understanding of the physical properties of the vacuum. In the presence of German emperor Ferdinand III, two teams of horses were unable to pull the two sealed hemispheres apart. Guericke had created a vacuum by pumping out the air from the two sealed copper spheres.

The New Sciences: Philosophical Interpretations

The New Sciences engendered a pattern of radically new intellectual, religious, and political thinking. This thought evolved into a powerful instrument of critique of Christian doctrine and the constitutional order of the absolutist states. Through the new concept of the social contract, these ideas became a potent political force in the course of the 1700s.

Descartes's New Philosophy The first major New Scientist who started a radical reconsideration of philosophy was the Frenchman René Descartes (1596–1650). In the service of the Dutch and Bavarian courts, he bore witness to the atrocities committed in the name of religious doctrines during the Thirty Years' War. He spent two decades in the Netherlands, studying and teaching the New Sciences. His principal innovation in mathematics was the discovery that geometry could be converted, through algebra, into analytic geometry.

Descartes was shocked by the condemnation of Galileo and decided to abandon all traditional propositions and doctrines of the church. Realizing that the five senses of seeing, hearing, touching, smelling, and tasting were unreliable, he determined that the only reliable body of knowledge was thought, especially mathematical thought. As a person capable of thought, he concluded—bypassing his unreliable senses—that he existed: "I think, therefore I am" (*cogito ergo sum*). A further conclusion from this argument was that he was composed of two radically different substances, a material substance consisting of his body (that is, his senses) and another, immaterial substance consisting of his thinking mind.

Variations on Descartes's New Philosophy Descartes's radical distinction between body and mind stimulated a lively debate. Was this distinction only conceptual, while reality was experienced as a unified whole? If the dualism was real as well as conceptual, which substance was more fundamental, sensual bodily experience or mental activity, as the creator of the concepts of experience? The answers of three philosophers—Baruch Spinoza, Thomas Hobbes, and John Locke—set the course for two major directions of philosophy during the so-called Enlightenment of the 1700s (see Chapter 23), one Continental European and the other Anglo-American.

For Baruch Spinoza (1632–1677), Descartes's distinction between body and mind was to be understood only in a conceptual sense. He therefore abandoned Descartes's distinction and developed a philosophical system that sought to integrate Galilean nature, the ideas of God, the Good in ethics, and the Just in politics into a unified whole. The Jewish community of Amsterdam, into which he had been born, excommunicated him for heresy, since he seemed to make God immanent in the world.

Both Thomas Hobbes (1588–1679) and John Locke (1632–1704) not only accepted Descartes's radical distinction; they made the body the fundamental reality and the mind a dependent function. Consequently, they focused on the bodily passions, not reason, as the principal human character trait. Hobbes speculated that individuals in the primordial state of nature were engaged in a "war of all against all." To survive, they forged a **social contract** in which they transferred

Social contract: An implicit agreement among the members of a society to cooperate for mutually shared benefits.

all power to a sovereign. Hobbes's book *Leviathan* (1651) can be read as a political theory of absolute rule, but his ideas of a social contract and transfer of power nevertheless move also toward constitutionalism.

Locke focused on the more benign bodily passion of acquisitiveness. Primordial individuals, so he argued, engaged as equals in a social contract for the purpose of erecting a government that protected their properties and established a civil society governed by law. With Hobbes and Locke a line of new thought came to its conclusion, leading from Descartes's two substances to the ideas of absolutism as well as democratic constitutionalism.

Centralizing States and Religious Upheavals

The pattern of the centralizing state transforming the institutional structures of society was characteristic not only of the Ottoman and Habsburg Empires during 1450–1750, but also of other countries of Europe, the Middle East, and India. The financial requirements for such a state required a reorganization of the relationship between rulers, ruling classes, and regional forces. Although the Protestant Reformation and religious wars slowed the pattern of central state formation, two types of states eventually emerged: the French, Russian, and Prussian landed centralizing state and the Dutch and English naval centralizing state.

The Rise of Centralized Kingdoms

The shift from feudal knights to firearm-equipped professional infantries led to states whose rulers sought to strengthen their administrations. Rulers centralized state power, collected taxes, and curbed the decentralizing forces of the nobility, cities, and local institutions. Not all city-states, city-leagues, and religious orders dating to the previous period (600–1450) survived the race to centralization. A winnowing process during 1450–1550 left only a few kingdoms in control of European politics.

The Demographic Curve Following the demographic disaster of the Black Death, the population of the European states expanded again after 1470 and continued to grow until about 1600, when it entered a half century of stagnation during the coldest and wettest period in recorded history, the Little Ice Age (1550–1750). During 1650–1750, the population rose slowly at a moderate rate from 105 to 140 million. The overall population figures for Europe demonstrate that Western Christianity had risen by 1750 to demographic equivalence to the two leading religious civilizations of India (155 million) and China (225 million).

A Heritage of Decentralization Bracketed between the two empires of the Ottomans and Habsburgs, Western Christian Europe during the second half of the fifteenth century was comprised of independent or autonomous units,

...terns Up Close

Mapping the World

In 1400, no accurate map of the world existed anywhere. Prior to the first Portuguese sailing expeditions down the west coast of Africa in the 1420s and 1430s, mariners relied upon local knowledge of winds, waves, and stars to navigate. The Portuguese were the first to use science to sail, adapting scholarship in trigonometry, astronomy, and solar timekeeping developed by Jewish and Muslim scientists in Iberia.

Crucial to this approach was latitude, which required precise calculations of the daily changes in the path of the sun relative to the earth and determination of the exact height of the sun. The invention of the nautical astrolabe in 1497 by the Jewish scientist Abraham Zacuto aided this process. To determine longitude, Jewish scientists in Portugal adapted a method based on the work of the Islamic astronomer al-Biruni (973–1048).

The new maps of the fifteenth century also drew upon an innovation from another part of the world: the compass. Originating in China, the compass was used as a navigational instrument by Muslim sailors during the twelfth century. In the thirteenth century, mapmakers in the Mediterranean began to include compasses on portolans, or nautical charts, enabling sailors to follow their direction on a map.

including the centralizing kingdoms of France and England; the Hanseatic League of trading cities; the Baltic territory ruled by the Catholic crusading order of Teutonic Knights; and the small kingdoms of Denmark, Sweden, Norway, Poland–Lithuania, Bohemia, and Hungary. It furthermore comprised the principalities and cities of Germany, the duchy of Burgundy, the republic of Switzerland, and the city-states of Italy. At the northeastern periphery was the Grand Duchy of Moscow, representing Eastern Christianity after the fall of Byzantium to the Ottomans in 1453. Many of these units competed with each other.

Military and Administrative Capacities In the course of the sixteenth century, some kingdoms turned their mercenary troops into standing armies and stationed them in star-shaped forts capable of withstanding artillery fire. Habsburg as well as Dutch troops introduced the line infantry in the course of the sixteenth century. Since the line formation required peacetime drills and maneuvers, the regimental system came into use. Soldiers formed permanent regiments and wore standardized multicolored uniforms.

The French-invented flintlock gradually replaced the matchlock musket during 1620–1630. Similarly, during 1660–1700 the French introduced and improved the bayonet. By 1750, armies in the larger European countries were more uniform in their armaments and increased to tens of thousands of soldiers (see Map 17.2).

The military forces were expensive, and taxes expanded during the period 1450–1550. But rulers could not raise taxes without the assent of the ruling classes and cities. Villagers simply moved when taxes became too oppressive. The taxation limits were reached in most European countries in the mid-sixteenth century,

With an accurate science for fixing latitude and improved knowledge for longitude, the science of cartography was transformed in the fifteenth and sixteenth centuries. Any place on earth could be mapped mathematically in relation to any other place, and the direction in which one place lay in relation to another could be plotted using compass lines. By 1500 mapmakers could locate any newly discovered place in the world on a map.

Portolan by Pedro Reinel. Drawn in 1504 by the great Portuguese cartographer Pedro Reinel (ca. 1462–ca. 1542), this nautical chart (portolan) shows compass lines and is the earliest known map to include lines of latitude.

Questions

- How were adaptations from various cultural traditions essential to the transformation of cartography in the fifteenth and sixteenth centuries?
- How are developments in cartography in this time period an example of the shift from descriptive science to mathematical science?

and for the next two centuries rulers could raise finances only to the detriment of their central powers, such as by borrowing from merchants and selling offices. The Netherlands was an exception. Only there did the urban population rise from 10 to 40 percent, willing to pay higher taxes on expanded urban manufactures and commercial suburban farming. The Dutch government also derived revenues from charters granted to overseas trading companies. Given the severe limits on revenue-raising measures in most of Europe, the eighteenth century saw a general deterioration of state finances, which eventually contributed to the American and French Revolutions.

The Protestant Reformation, State Churches, and Independent Congregations

Parallel to the centralism of the kings, the popes restored the central role of the Vatican in the church hierarchy. The popes undertook expensive Vatican construction projects that aroused criticism, especially in Germany, where the leading clergy was strongly identified with Rome. Growing literacy and lay religiosity nurtured a profound theological dissatisfaction, leading to the **Protestant Reformation**. The Reformation began as a movement in the early sixteenth century that demanded a return to the simplicity of early Christianity. The movement quickly engulfed the kingdoms and resulted in religious wars. The divisions mark the culture of Europe even today.

Protestant Reformation: Broad movement to reform the Roman Catholic Church, the beginnings of which are usually associated with Martin Luther.

Background to the Reformation Religious and political changes in the fifteenth century led to the Protestant Reformation. One religious shift was the growth of popular theology, a consequence of the introduction of the printing

MAP 17.2 **European Warfare, 1450–1750**

press (1454/1455). Devotional tracts catered to the spiritual interests of ordinary people. Many Christians attended Mass daily. Wealthy Christians endowed saint cults and charitable institutions; poor people studied scripture on their own (provided they could read).

Indulgence: Partial remission of sins after payment of a fine or presentation of a donation. Remission would mean the forgiveness of sins by the Church, but the sinner still remained responsible for his or her sins before God.

A key political change was an increasing inability of the popes to appoint archbishops and bishops outside Italy. The kings of France, Spain, England, and Sweden were transforming their kingdoms into centralized states, reducing the influence of the popes. (The popes' influence remained strong in the politically splintered Germany.) What remained to the popes was the right to collect dues, which they used to finance their expensive administration in Rome. One of the dues was the sale of **indulgences**, which, in popular understanding, were tickets to heaven. Those disturbed by the discrepancy between declining papal power and the remaining financial privileges demanded reforms.

Luther's Reformation One such observer was the German monk, priest, and professor Martin Luther (1483–1546). Influenced in part by the Bohemian reformer John Huss (see Chapter 11), Luther wrote his archbishop a letter in 1517 conveying 95 theses in which he condemned the indulgences and other matters as contrary to scripture. What was to become the Protestant Reformation had begun.

News of Luther's protest traveled across Europe. Sales of indulgences fell off sharply. In a series of writings, Luther spelled out further reforms. One was the elevation of original New Testament scripture over canon law and papal decisions. Another reform was the declaration of the priesthood of all Christians, doing away with the privileged position of the clergy. A third reform was a call to German princes to begin church reform through their power over clerical appointments, even if the Habsburg emperor was opposed. Finally, by translating the Bible into German, Luther made the text available to all who could read.

Reaction to Luther's Demands Both the emperor and the pope failed to arrest Luther and suppress his call for church reform. Emperor Charles V, a devout Catholic, was distracted by the Ottoman-led Islamic threat in eastern Europe and the western Mediterranean. In addition, his rivalry with the French king precluded the formation of a common Catholic front against Luther. People in Germany exploited Charles's divided attention and abandoned both Catholicism and secular obedience. A savage civil war, called the Peasants' War, engulfed Germany from 1524 to 1525.

Luther and other reformers were horrified by the war. They drew up church ordinances that regulated preaching and other church matters. In Saxony, the duke endorsed this order in 1528, creating the model of Lutheran Protestantism as a state religion with the rulers as protectors and supervisors of the churches in their territories.

Other German princes and the kings of Denmark and Sweden followed suit. In England, Protestants gained strength when Henry VIII (r. 1509–1547) broke with Rome and took over church leadership in his kingdom. Although remaining Catholic, he proclaimed an Anglican state church that combined elements of Catholicism and Protestantism. Switzerland and Scotland also adopted reforms. Thus, most of northern Europe followed a pattern of alliances between Protestant reformers and the state (see Map 17.3).

Calvinism in Geneva and France In France, King Francis I controlled all church appointments but did not create an independent state church. Since he competed with Charles V of the Habsburg Empire for dominance over the papacy in Italy, he had to appear especially loyal and devout. When Protestants in France demanded church reform, Francis I gave them the choice of exile or burning at the stake.

One reformer who chose exile was John Calvin (Jean Cauvin, 1509–1564). During his exile in Geneva, he began a stormy career as the city's religious reformer. Geneva, under the nominal authority of Savoy, a fief of the Holy Roman Empire and thus theoretically subject to the Habsburgs, was unsure about which path of reform to embrace. It was not until the 1550s that Calvin's form of Protestantism prevailed in the city.

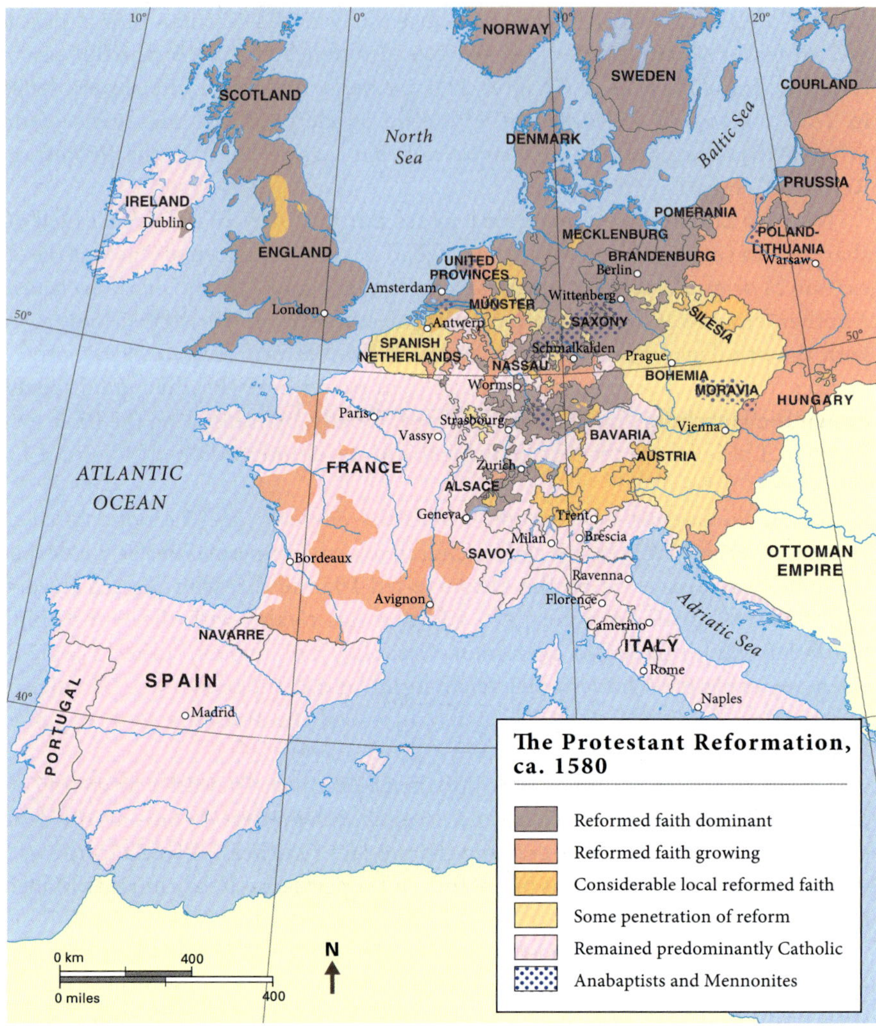

MAP 17.3 The Protestant Reformation, ca. 1580

A crucial doctrine of Calvin's was *predestination*. According to this doctrine, God has "predestined" each human prior to birth for heaven or hell. Believers could only hope, through faith alone, that they would receive a glimpse of their fate. In contrast to Luther, however, Calvin made the enforcement of a moral code by local authorities part of his version of Protestantism.

Interestingly, this code did not prohibit the taking of interest on loans. While Luther as well as the Catholic Church, in accordance with scripture, condemned all interest as usury, Calvin placed moneylending into the increasingly urban context of the 1500s. Acquiring wealth with the help of money and thereby perhaps gaining a glimpse of one's fate became a hallmark of Calvinism. Wealth began to become respectable in Christian society.

Calvinist preachers went to France and the Netherlands in the mid-1500s. Under the protection of local magistrates, they organized the first independent Calvinist congregations. Calvinist religious self-organization by independent congregations became an alternative to Lutheran state religion.

The Catholic Reformation The rivalry between Spain and France made it difficult for the popes to address Catholic reforms in order to meet the Protestant challenge. Finally, at the Council of Trent (1545–1563), they abolished payment for indulgences and phased out other church practices considered to be corrupt. These actions launched the **Catholic Reformation**, an effort to gain back dissenting Catholics. Supported by the kings of Spain and France, however, the popes made no changes to the traditional doctrines of faith together with good works, priestly mediation between believer and God, and monasticism. They even revived the papal Inquisition and promulgated a new Index of Prohibited Books.

Catholic Reformation: Also known as Counter-Reformation. Reaffirmation of Catholic papal supremacy and the doctrine of faith together with works as preparatory to salvation. Such practices as absenteeism (bishops in Rome instead of their bishoprics) and pluralism (bishops and abbots holding multiple appointments) were abolished.

The popes also furthered the work of the priest Ignatius Loyola (1491–1556). At the head of the Jesuits, Loyola devoted himself to the education of the clergy, the establishment of a network of Catholic schools and colleges, and the conversion of Protestants as well as non-Christians by missionaries to the Americas and eastern Asia. Thanks to Jesuit discipline, Catholics regained self-assurance against the Protestants.

Religious Wars and Political Restoration

The growth of Calvinism led to a civil war in France and a war of liberation from Spanish Catholic rule in the Netherlands in the later sixteenth century. In England, the slow pace of reform in the Anglican Church erupted in the early seventeenth century into a civil war. In Germany, the Catholic–Protestant struggle turned into the Thirty Years' War (1618–1648). The centralizing states evolved into polities based on absolutism, tempered by provincial and local administrative practices.

Civil War in France During the mid-1500s, Calvinism in France grew mostly in the western cities, where literate merchants and craftspeople were receptive to Protestant publications. Calvinism was an urban denomination; peasants, rooted more deeply in traditional ways of life, did not join in large numbers. Some 10 percent of the population were Huguenots, as the Protestants were called in France. The Huguenots posed a formidable challenge to French Catholicism; and although the government persecuted them, it was impossible to imprison or execute them all.

In many cities, relations between Huguenots and Catholics were uneasy. From time to time, groups of agitators crashed each other's church services. Hostilities escalated after 1560, when the government weakened under a child king and was unable to deal with the increasingly powerful Huguenots. In four western cities, the Huguenots achieved self-government and full freedom of religious practice from the crown. Concerned to find a compromise, in 1572 the now reigning king married his sister to the leader of the Huguenots, King Henry III of Navarre (later King Henry IV of France, 1589–1610), a Protestant of the Bourbon family in southwestern France. Henry detested the fanaticism that surrounded him.

Only six days after the wedding, on St. Bartholomew's Day (August 24, 1572), outraged members of the Catholic aristocracy perpetrated a wholesale slaughter of thousands of Huguenots. This massacre, in response to the assassination of a French admiral, occurred with the apparent connivance of the court. For over a decade and a half, civil war raged, in which Spain aided the Catholics and Henry enrolled German and Swiss Protestant mercenaries. A turning point came only when Henry of Navarre became King Henry IV in 1589. It was nine years before he was able to calm the religious fanaticism of the French people. With the Edict of Nantes in 1598, he decreed freedom of religion for Protestants. However, Catholic adherents were deeply offended by the edict as well as by the alleged antipapal policies of Henry IV, and the king was assassinated in 1610. In 1685, King Louis XIV revoked the edict and triggered the emigration of Huguenots to the Netherlands, Germany, England, and North America. At last, France was Catholic again.

The Dutch War of Independence In the Netherlands, the Spanish overlords were determined to keep the country Catholic. When Charles V resigned in 1556 (effective 1558), his son Philip II (r. 1556–1598) became king of Spain and the Netherlands. Like his father, Philip supported the Catholic Reformation. He asked the Jesuits and the Inquisition to aggressively persecute the Calvinists. Philip also subdivided the bishoprics into smaller units and recruited clergymen in place of members of the nobility.

In response, in 1565 the nobility and Calvinist congregations rose in revolt, triggering what was to become a Protestant war of Dutch liberation from Catholic Spanish overlordship (1565–1620). Philip suppressed the liberation movement, re-imposed Catholicism, and executed thousands of rebels, many of them members of the Dutch aristocracy.

In 1579, rebels renewed the war of liberation. Spain kept fighting the rebellion until acute Spanish financial difficulties prompted the truce of 1609–1621. Although drawn into fighting again during the Thirty Years' War, the Netherlands gained its full independence eventually in 1648.

Civil War in England The prevalent form of Protestantism in England was Calvinism. During the sixteenth century, the majority of people in England, including Calvinists, belonged to the Anglican Church. English Catholics were a small minority. The percentage of Calvinists was the same as in France before 1685, but the partially reformed Anglican Church under the tolerant queen Elizabeth I (1533–1603) was able to hold them in check.

The Calvinists encompassed moderate and radical tendencies that neutralized each other. Among the radicals were the Puritans, who demanded the abolition of the Anglican clerical hierarchy and a new church order of independent congregations. When Anglican Church reform slowed with the arrival of the Stuart monarchs on the throne of England (1603–1685), unfortunately the balance among the religious tendencies unraveled. As rulers of England, the Stuarts were officially heads of the Anglican state church, but except for the first king, the three successors were either Catholics or Catholic sympathizers. Since they were furthermore rulers of what was called the England of the Three Kingdoms they found it impossible to maneuver among the demands of the English Puritans, Scottish Presbyterians (self-governing regional Calvinists), and Catholic Irish. The issue of how little or how far the Anglican Church had been reformed away from Catholicism and how dominant it should be in the three realms became more and more divisive (see Source 17.1).

In addition, the Stuarts were intent on building a centralized state, highlighting the supremacy of royal over parliamentary power. They collected taxes without the approval of Parliament. Many members of Parliament resented being bypassed. A slight majority in the House of Commons was Puritan, and what they considered the stalled church reform added to their resentment. Eventually, when all tax resources were exhausted, the king had to call Parliament back together. The two sides were unable to come to an agreement, however, and civil war broke out. Since this war was also a conflict among the Three Kingdoms, it had both religious and regional aspects (1639–1651).

Because of widespread pillage and destruction, the indirect effects of the war for the rural population were severe. The **New Model Army**, a professional body of 22,000 troops raised by the Puritan-dominated English Parliament against the royal forces, caused further upheavals by cleansing villages of their "frivolous" local traditions. In the end, Charles was beheaded in 1649 and the monarchy was replaced with a republican theocracy, the "Commonwealth of England."

New Model Army: Army founded by the English parliament in 1645. Infused with Puritan zeal, it was equipped with standardized weapons and professionally trained.

Republic, Restoration, and Revolution The ruler of this theocracy, Oliver Cromwell (r. 1649–1658), was a Puritan member of the lower nobility and a commander in the New Model Army. After dissolving Parliament, Cromwell handpicked a new parliament but ruled mostly without its consent. Since both Scotland and Ireland were opposed to the English Puritans, Cromwell waged a savage war of submission against the two. The Dutch and Spanish, also opponents of the Puritans, were defeated in naval wars that increased English power in the Atlantic. But fear in Parliament of a permanent centralized state led to a refusal of financial subsidies for the military. After Cromwell's death in 1658, it took just three years to restore the Stuart monarchy and the Anglican state church.

The recalled Stuart kings, however, resumed the policies of centralization. As before, the kings rarely called Parliament together and raised funds without its authorization. But their standing army was intended more to intimidate the parliamentarians than to subjugate them. In the "Glorious Revolution" of 1688, a defiant Parliament deposed the king and made his daughter and her Dutch husband the new co-regents.

The Thirty Years' War in Germany Continuing religious tensions in Germany erupted into the Thirty Years' War. Rulers of the German principalities had made either Catholicism or Protestantism their state religion, though most tolerated minorities or even admitted them to offices. The Jesuit-educated Ferdinand II (r. 1619–1637), ruler of the Holy Roman Empire, however, refused to appoint Protestants in majority-Protestant Bohemia. In response, Protestant leaders in 1618 renounced Ferdinand's authority and made the Calvinist prince of the Palatinate in the Rhineland their new king.

In a first round of war (1619–1630), Ferdinand and the Catholic princes suppressed the rebellion and advanced toward northern Germany, capturing Lutheran territories for reconversion to Catholicism and defeating Denmark. In 1630, however, the Lutheran king Gustavus II Adolphus (r. 1611–1632) of Sweden intervened. By aiding the German Lutherans, he hoped to consolidate his predominance in the region. Louis XIII (r. 1610–1643) of France granted Sweden financial subsidies, since he was concerned that Ferdinand's victories would further strengthen the Habsburg grip around France. With the politically motivated alliance between Sweden and France, the German Catholic–Protestant war turned into a war for state dominance in Europe.

The Swedes were initially successful but withdrew when Gustavus II Adolphus fell. Ferdinand compromised with the Protestant princes of Germany, by reestablishing the prewar divisions, in order to keep the French out of the war. But Louis XIII entered anyway and occupied Habsburg Alsace. Swedish armies, exploiting the French successes against the Habsburgs, fought their way back into Germany. In 1648, the exhausted Austrian–German Habsburgs agreed to the Peace of Westphalia.

The agreement provided for religious freedom in Germany and ceded Habsburg territories in Alsace to France and the southern side of the Baltic Sea to Sweden. It granted territorial integrity to all European powers. The Spanish

Versailles. Built between 1676 and 1708 on the outskirts of Paris, Versailles emphatically demonstrated the new centralized power of the French monarchy. The main building is a former hunting lodge that Louis XIV decorated with mythological scenes that showed him as the "Sun King." The outer wings housed government offices. Behind the palace, elaborate entertainments were held in the gardens.

Habsburgs continued their war against France until their defeat in 1659, which accelerated the decline of Spain's overseas power. France emerged as the strongest country in Europe, and the Spanish-dominated Caribbean became an area of open rivalry (see Map 17.4).

Absolutism in France? During its period of greatest political dominance, France came under the rule of its longest-reigning monarch, King Louis XIV (r. 1643–1715). He made Versailles—a gigantic palace and gardens near Paris, populated with 10,000 courtiers, attendants, and servants—into a site of almost continuous feasting, entertainment, and intrigue. It was here that Louis, the "Sun King," exercised his "absolute" divine mandate upon his aristocracy and commoners alike.

In practice, the **absolutism** of Louis XIV, as well as absolutism in other European countries, was a mixture of centralized and decentralized forces. On one hand, after the end of the religious wars in 1648, mercenary armies under

Absolutism: Theory of the state in which the unlimited power of the king, ruling under God's divine mandate, was emphasized. In practice, it was neutralized by the nobility and provincial and local communities.

MAP 17.4 Europe in 1648

autonomous dukes and counts were replaced by permanent armies or navies under the central command of royal relatives or favorites. The kings no longer called assemblies together to have new taxes approved (in France from 1614 to 1789), and thus many of the nobility's tax privileges disappeared.

On the other hand, kings were aware that true absolutism was possible only if the taxes were collected by centrally salaried employees. However, a centrally paid bureaucracy would have required a central bank with provincial branches, using a credit and debit system. The failed experiment with such a bank in Paris from 1714 to 1720 demonstrated that absolute central control was beyond the powers of the kings.

Instead, the kings had to rely on subcontracting out the collection of taxes to the highest bidders, who then helped themselves to the collection of their incomes. Under Louis XIV anyone who had money or borrowed it from financiers was encouraged to buy an office. The government often forced these officers to grant additional loans to the crown. To retain their loyalty, the government rewarded them with first picks for retaining their offices within the family. They were also privileged to buy landed estates or acquire titles of nobility. By selling offices and titles, the king sought to bind the financial interests of the two nobilities to those of his own.

Louis XIV sent salaried *intendants* to the provinces to ensure that collecting taxes, rendering justice, and policing functioned properly. About half of the provinces had *parlements*—appointed assemblies for the ratification of decrees from Paris—whose officeholders, drawn from the local noble, clerical, and commoner classes, frequently resisted the intendants.

In later years, when Louis XIV was less successful in his wars against the rival Habsburgs and Protestant Dutch, the crown overspent and had to borrow heavily. Louis's successors in the second half of the eighteenth century were saddled with crippling debts, in part brought on by themselves.

The Rise of Russia The ideological embodiment of absolutism in the Versailles of Louis XIV spawned adaptations across Europe. These adaptations were most visible in eastern Europe, which had far fewer towns and cities. Without a large population of urban commoners to aid them in building the centralized state, rulers there had to make do with the landowning aristocracy. As a result, rulers and aristocracy connived to finance state centralization through an increased exploitation of farmers. In the 1600s, the legal status of farmers deteriorated, their tax liabilities increased, and they became serfs.

Tsar (also spelled czar): Derived from Caesar, title used by the Russian rulers to emphasize their imperial ambitions.

In Russia, **Tsar** Peter I the Great (r. 1682–1725), of the Eastern Christian Romanov dynasty, sought to establish the French-type centralized state. Peter invited western European soldiers, mariners, administrators, craftspeople, scholars, and artists into his service. He built ports on the Baltic Sea and established the new capital of St. Petersburg, with beautiful palaces and official buildings.

The Russian military was completely reorganized by the tsar. Peter made the inherited firearm regiments part of a new army recruited from the traditional Russian landed nobility. Soldiers received education at military schools and academies and were required to provide lifelong service. A census was taken to facilitate the shift from the inherited household tax on the villagers to a new capitation tax collected by military officers. In the process, many farmers now found themselves classified and taxed as serfs, unfree to leave their villages. The result of Peter's reforms was a powerful, expansionary centralizing state (see Map 17.5).

The Rise of Prussia Like Russia, the principality of Prussia-Brandenburg was underurbanized. When the Lutheran Hohenzollern rulers embarked on the construction of a centralized state in the later seventeenth century, they first broke the tax privileges of the landowning aristocracy and raised taxes themselves through agents. As in Russia, farmers who worked on estates held by landlords were serfs. Since there were few urban middle-class merchants and professionals, the kings enrolled members of the landlord aristocracy in the army and civilian administration.

The Hohenzollern monarchs enlarged the army, employing it during peacetime for drainage and canal projects as well as palace construction in Berlin, the capital. Under Frederick II the Great (r. 1740–1786), Prussia pursued an aggressive foreign policy, seizing Silesia from the Habsburgs in 1742. Frederick also

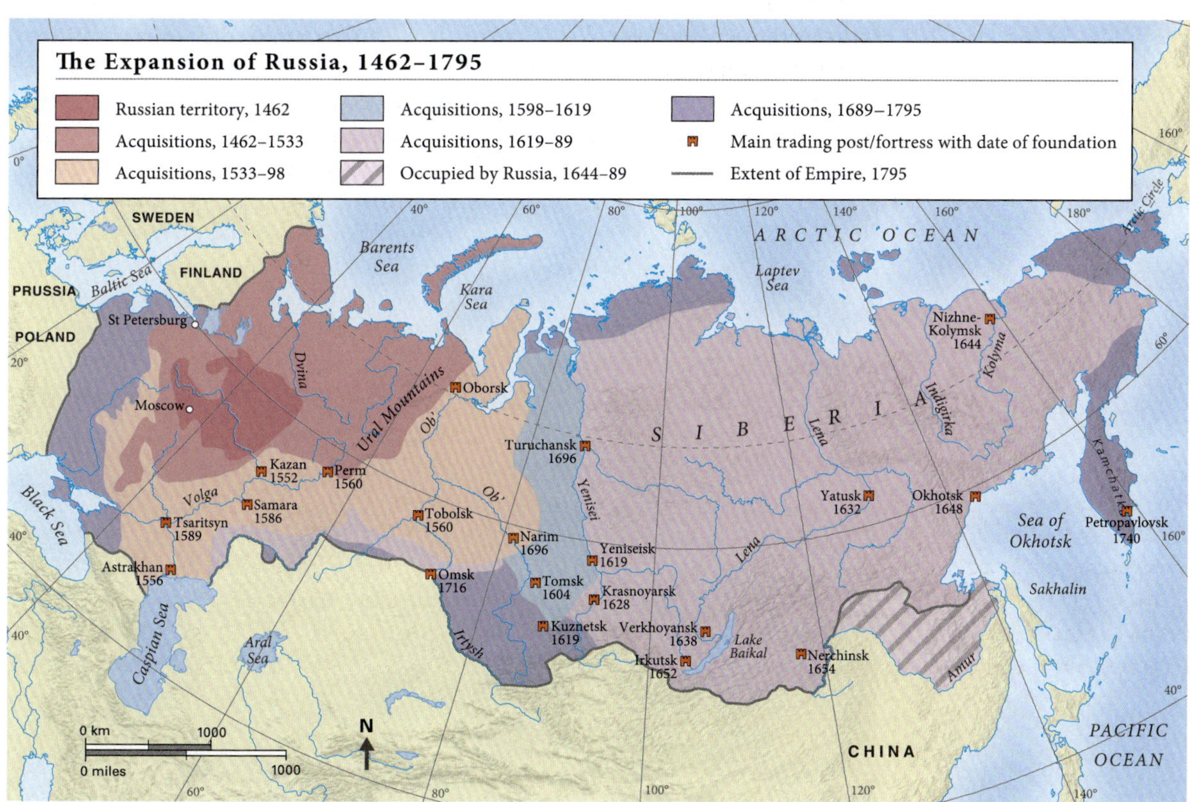

MAP 17.5 **The Expansion of Russia, 1462–1795**

sought to attract immigrants, intensify agriculture, and establish manufacturing. Prussia emerged as a serious competitor of the Habsburgs in the Holy Roman Empire of Germany.

English Constitutionalism In contrast to Prussia, France, Spain, Austria, and other European states, England had since 1450 a political system ruled by a king or a queen, with a parliament composed of the aristocracy as well as representatives of towns and cities. Only in England did the interests of the nobility and the urban merchants gradually converge: younger sons, unable to inherit the family estate, sought their fortunes in London. English cities allied with the aristocracy in resisting indirect tax increases and forcing the throne to use the revenues of its royal estates to pay soldiers. The efforts of the Stuart kings to create a centralized state based on firearm infantries failed. Instead, the ruling class preferred to build a centralized naval state. After the Glorious Revolution of 1688, England became the world's dominant naval power.

After its victory over the Stuart kings, Parliament consolidated its financial powers through the creation of the Bank of England in 1694. When Mary and William died without children, England continued in 1714 with a king from the principality of Hannover in Germany who was distantly related to the previous royals. Around the same time, England and Scotland united, creating the United Kingdom. Parliament collected taxes and, through its bank, was able to keep its debt service low during the early 1700s. The navy grew twice as large as that of France and was staffed by a well-salaried, disciplined military, while the few land troops were mostly low-paid Hessian-German mercenaries. A two-party system of two aristocracy–merchant alliances emerged. The two

Prussian Military Discipline. The Prussian line infantry made full use in the mid-1700s of flintlock muskets, bayonets, and drilling.

parties were known as the Tories and the Whigs, with the Whigs in power for most of the first half of the eighteenth century.

Putting It All Together

Prior to 1500, all religious civilizations possessed mathematics and qualitative sciences. Trigonometry-based astronomy existed in the Islamic, Hindu, and Christian religious civilizations and was practiced also in China. Physics became the second mathematical science in the early 1500s, but only in Western Christianity. This transformation of the sciences had no practical consequences prior to the invention of the steam engine in the 1700s. Furthermore, the mathematization of physics did little to influence the continued prevalence of qualitative description as the methodology of the other sciences. Most importantly, the rise of the New Sciences should not be confused with the vast changes, called "modernity" after 1800, which propelled the West to world dominance. Although the West began to acquire its scientific and philosophical identity with the introduction of the mathematical sciences in the century between Copernicus and Galileo (1514–1604), the impact of these sciences on the world was felt only after 1800, when they were applied to industry. Once this application gathered momentum in the nineteenth century, Asia and Africa had no choice but to adapt to modern science and industrialization.

Review and Relate

Thinking Through Patterns

Examine the ways historians approach the big questions of this chapter.

What were the reasons for the cultural change that began in Europe with the Renaissance around 1400? In which ways were the subsequent patterns of cultural change different from those in the other religious civilizations of Eurasia?

Located far from the traditional agrarian–urban centers of Eurasia, Western Christianity adapted its culture in response to outside stimuli coming from Islamic and Eastern Christian civilizations. Without these stimuli, the Renaissance, Baroque, New Science, and Enlightenment would not have developed. In contrast, the Middle East, Byzantium, India, and China, originating within the traditional agrarian–urban centers, received far fewer outside stimuli prior to the scientific– industrial age. Scholars and thinkers in these religious civilizations did not feel the same pressure to change their cultural heritage and adapt as their colleagues in Western Christianity did.

When and how did the New Sciences begin, and how did they gain popularity in

The discovery of the two new continents of the Americas prompted Nicolaus Copernicus to posit a sun-centered planetary system. Copernicus's new approach to science continued with Galileo Galilei's discovery of the mathematical law of falling bodies in physics and was completed when Isaac Newton unified physics and

northwestern European society? Why is the popularization of the New Sciences important for understanding the period 1450–1750?

astronomy. The New Sciences became popular in educated urban circles in northwestern Europe, where Catholic and Protestant church authorities were largely divided. In southern Europe, where the Catholic Reformation was powerful and rejected Galileo, the adoption of the New Sciences occurred more slowly. Scientists in northwestern Europe discovered the practical applicability of the New Sciences as they experimented with steam engines, a catalyst for the launching of the scientific–industrial age.

➤ What were the patterns of centralized state formation and transformation in the period 1450–1750? How did the Protestant Reformation and religious wars modify these patterns?

European kingdoms expanded their powers of taxation to the detriment of the nobility. With these funds, they hired and salaried mercenary infantries equipped with firearms, using them to conquer land from their neighbors. The religious wars of the 1500s and 1600s strengthened centralization efforts and hastened the demise of the nobility as an obstacle to the centralized state. In England, Parliament blocked the Stuart kings from building a landed central state and instead pursued the construction of a naval state.

Against the Grain

Consider this as a counterpoint to the main patterns examined in this chapter.

The Digger Movement

- Was Winstanley hopelessly utopian in his efforts to establish farmer communities on common land in England?
- How have other figures in world history sympathized with the lot of poor and landless farmers and attempted reform (or revolution) on their behalf?

In April 1649, toward the end of the English Civil War and just three months after the execution of King Charles I, a group of farmers and day laborers occupied "common" (public) land south of London to establish a colony. As the farmers and laborers dug up the soil, they came to be called the "Diggers."

Driven off by small landowners who benefited from the use of common land for grazing sheep and cutting timber, a smaller group of Diggers moved on to common land in nearby Cobham in August 1649. This time it was the gentry with their manor rights to the common land who destroyed the Diggers' cottages and fields in the winter of 1650. The Diggers made a much-publicized statement that public land was "the treasure of all people" and should not be reserved for the benefit of anyone—a bold demand that ran counter to the rapidly increasing privatization of land and commercialization of agriculture.

The leader of the group was Gerrard Winstanley (1609–1670), a former cloth merchant in London who had had to abandon his trade in 1643 after he became insolvent. He struggled to regain his solvency in the countryside of Surrey, at one point working as a grazier of cattle. Parts of Surrey had suffered substantial hardship during the Civil War, having been forced to provision and quarter troops. In pamphlets between 1648 and 1650, Winstanley explained the motives and goals of the Diggers, making these affairs relevant, in the religious idiom of Protestantism, for England as a whole. He was the first to identify the problem of the rising numbers of rural landless laborers victimized by the increasing commercialization of agriculture in England—a labor force that continued to increase until the industrializing cities of the later 1700s eventually absorbed them.

Key Terms

Absolutism 415
Catholic Reformation 411
Heliocentrism 398
Humanism 396
Indulgence 408
New Model Army 413
New Sciences 396
Protestant Reformation 407
Renaissance 396
Social contract 402
Tsar 416

Learn more with this chapter's digital tools, including the Oxford Insight Study Guide, at http://www.oup.com/he/vonsivers4e. Please see the Further Resources section at the back of the book for additional readings and suggested websites.

PATTERNS OF EVIDENCE |

Sources for Chapter 17

SOURCE 17.1 Examination of Lady Jane Grey, London

1554

Jane Grey, the granddaughter of Henry VIII's sister Mary, was born in 1537, the same year as Edward VI, the only surviving son of the king who had sought a male heir so desperately. Jane, who like Edward was raised in the Protestant religion Henry had introduced to England, proved a diligent and intellectually gifted teenager. In spite of her youth and gender, Jane corresponded with Protestant authorities on the Continent, but fast-moving events in England precluded further study. When Edward died without an heir in 1553, the throne passed, by prearranged agreement, to his fiercely Catholic half-sister Mary.

However, in order to forestall a Catholic successor—and the dramatic rollback of the Protestant reforms instituted by Henry's and Edward's Church of England—Jane's relatives proclaimed her queen. Her rule lasted a mere nine days. She was imprisoned in the Tower of London by Mary, who was then forced to consider whether Jane's execution was warranted. Shortly before Jane's death, at age 16, Queen Mary sent her own chaplain, Master Feckenham (sometimes rendered as "Fecknam") to try to reconcile Jane to the Catholic faith. The results of this attempt were triumphantly recorded in John Foxe's *Acts and Monuments*, published after the Protestant Queen Elizabeth had triumphed over Mary and the Catholics. Although the conversation recorded here is not a trial transcript—and is a highly partisan account—it does distill some of the central issues that divided Catholics and Protestants in an extremely chaotic and violent period.

FECKNAM: "I am here come to you at this present, sent from the queen [Mary] and her council, to instruct you in the true doctrine of the right faith: although I have so great confidence in you, that I shall have, I trust, little need to travail with you much therein."

Source: "The Examination of Lady Jane Grey (1554)," from Denis R. Janz, ed., *A Reformation Reader: Primary Texts with Introductions*, 2nd ed. (Minneapolis, MN: Fortress Press, 2008), 360–362, taken from *The Acts and Monuments of John Foxe* (London: Seeleys, 1859), 415–417.

JANE: "Forsooth, I heartily thank the queen's highness, which is not unmindful of her humble subject: and I hope, likewise, that you no less will do your duty therein both truly and faithfully, according to that you were sent for."

. . .

FECKNAM: "How many sacraments are there?"

JANE: "Two: the one the sacrament of baptism, and the other the sacrament of the Lord's Supper."

FECKNAM: "No, there are seven."

JANE: "By what Scripture find you that?"

FECKNAM: "Well, we will talk of that hereafter. But what is signified by your two sacraments?"

JANE: "By the sacrament of baptism I am washed with water and regenerated by the Spirit, and that washing is a token to me that I am the child of God. The sacrament of the Lord's Supper, offered unto me, is a sure seal and testimony that I am, by the blood of Christ, which he shed for me on the cross, made partaker of the everlasting kingdom."

FECKNAM: "Why? What do you receive in that sacrament? Do you not receive the very body and blood of Christ?"

JANE: "No, surely, I do not so believe. I think that at the supper I neither receive flesh nor blood, but bread and wine: which bread when it is broken, and the wine when it is drunken, put me in remembrance how that for my sins the body of Christ was broken, and his blood shed on the cross; and with that bread and wine I receive the benefits that come by the breaking of his body, and shedding of his blood, for our sins on the cross."

FECKNAM: "Why, doth not Christ speak these words, 'Take, eat, this is my body?' Require you any plainer words? Doth he not say, it is his body?"

JANE: "I grant, he saith so; and so he saith, 'I am the vine, I am the door'; but he is never the more for that, the door or the vine. Doth not St. Paul say, 'He calleth things that are not, as though they were?' God forbid that I should say, that I eat the very natural body and blood of Christ: for then either I should pluck away my redemption, or else there were two bodies, or two Christs. One body was tormented on the cross, and if they did eat another body, then had he two bodies: or if his body were eaten, then was it not broken upon the cross; or if it were broken upon the cross, it was not eaten of his disciples."

. . .

With these and like such persuasions he would have had her lean to the [Catholic] church, but it would not be. There were many more things whereof they reasoned, but these were the chiefest.

After this, Fecknam took his leave, saying, that he was sorry for her: "For I am sure," quoth he, "that we two shall never meet."

JANE: "True it is," said she, "that we shall never meet, except God turn your heart; for I am assured, unless you repent and turn to God, you are in an evil case. And I pray God, in the bowels of his mercy, to send you his Holy Spirit; for he hath given you his great gift of utterance, if it please him also to open the eyes of your heart."

Working with Sources

1. **What does this source reveal about the religious education of young people in the extended royal household during the final years of Henry VIII and the reign of Edward VI?**
2. **How does the literal interpretation of the Bible enter into this discussion, and why?**

SOURCE 17.2

Emilie du Châtelet, *Discourse on Happiness*

1748

During the Age of Enlightenment, Emilie du Châtelet (1706-1749) was known among philosophes primarily for her translation of Newton's *Mathematical Principles.* A well-educated polymath, she is also remembered for her interest in philosophy; her life-long friend Voltaire remarked that "Her dominant taste was for mathematics and philosophy." Du Châtelet's interest in philosophy is manifested in her *Discourse on Happiness* (*Discours sur le bonheur*), a topic of wide interest discussed in several works of leading male philosophes. What renders Du Châtelet's essay unique, however, are its occasional references to her personal life, its subtle expression of male dominance in the intellectual world, as well as its interests in "illusions" and the value of reason over obeisance to religion.

Would we have a moment of pleasure at the theater if we did not lend ourselves to the illusion that makes us see famous individuals that we know have been dead for a long time, speaking in Alexandrine verse? Truly, what pleasure would one have at any other spectacle where all is illusion if one was not able to abandon oneself to it? Surely there would be much to lose, and those at the opera who only have the pleasure of the music and the dances have a very meager pleasure, one well below that which this enchanting spectacle viewed as a whole provides. I have cited spectacles, because illusion is easier to perceive there. It is, however, involved in all the pleasures of our life, and provides the polish, the gloss of life. Some will perhaps say that illusion does not depend on

Source: Emilie Du Châtelet, *Selected Philosophical and Scientific Writings*, ed. and trans. by Isabelle Bour and Judith P. Zinsser (University of Chicago Press, 2009), 354–364.

us, and that is only too true, up to a point. We cannot give ourselves illusions any more than we can give ourselves tastes, or passions; but we can keep the illusions that we have; we can seek not to destroy them. We can choose not to go behind the set, to see the wheels that make flight, and the other machines of theatrical productions. Such is the artifice that we can use, and that artifice is neither useless nor unproductive.

These are the great machines of happiness, so to speak; but there are yet other, lesser skills that can contribute to our happiness. The first is to be resolute about what one wants to be and about what one wants to do. This is lacking in almost all men; it is, however, the pre-requisite without which there is no happiness at all. Without it, one swims forever in a sea of uncertainties, one destroys in the morning what one made in the evening; life is spent doing stupid things, putting them right, repenting of them. This feeling of repentance is one of the most useless and most disagreeable that our soul can experience. One of the great secrets is to know how to guard against it. As no two things in life are alike, it is almost always useless to see one's errors, or at least to pause a long time to consider them and to reproach oneself with them. In so doing we cover ourselves with confusion in our own eyes for no gain. One must start from where one is, use all one's sagacity to make amends and to find the means to make amends, but there is no point in looking back, and one must always brush from one's mind the memory of one's errors. The ability to benefit from an initial examination, dismiss sad ideas and substitute agreeable ideas, is one of the mainsprings of happiness, and we have this in our power, at least up to a point. . .

One must have passions to be happy; but they must be made to serve our happiness, and there are some that must absolutely be prevented from entering our soul. I am not speaking here of the passions that are vices, like hatred, vengeance, rage; but ambition, for example, is a passion that I believe one must defend one's soul against, if one wants to be happy. This is not because it does not give enjoyment, for I believe this passion can provide that; it is not because ambition can never be satisfied—that is surely a great good. Rather, it is because ambition, of all the passions, makes our happiness dependent on others. Now the less our happiness depends on others the easier it is for us to be happy. Let us not be afraid to reduce our dependence on others too much, or happiness will always depend on others quite enough. If we value independence, the love of study is, of all the passions, the one that contributes most to our happiness. This love of study holds within it a passion from which a superior soul is never entirely exempt, that of glory. For half the world, glory can only be obtained in this manner, and it is precisely this half whose education made glory inaccessible and made a taste for it impossible.

Undeniably, the love of study is much less necessary to the happiness of men than it is to that of women. Men have infinite resources for their happiness that women lack. They have many means to attain glory, and it is quite certain that the ambition to make their talents useful to their country and to serve their fellow citizens, perhaps by their competency in the art of war, or by their talents for government, or negotiation, is superior to that which one can gain for oneself by study. But women are excluded by definition, from every kind of glory, and when, by chance, one is born with a rather superior soul, only study remains to console her for all the exclusions and all the dependencies to which she finds herself condemned by her place in society... I have said that the love of study is the passion most necessary to our happiness. It is an unfailing resource against misfortunes, it is an inexhaustible source of pleasures, and Cicero is right to say: The pleasures of the senses and those of the heart are, without doubt, above those of study; study is not necessary for happiness: but we may need to feel that we have within us this resource and this support. One may love study and spend whole years, perhaps one's whole life, without studying. Happy is he who spends it thus: for only more lively pleasures cause one to sacrifice a pleasure that one is sure to find and that can be made lively enough to compensate for the loss of others.

I have said that the more our happiness depends on us, the more assured it is; yet the passion that can give us the greatest pleasures and make us happiest, places our happiness entirely in the hands of others. You have already gathered that I am speaking of love. This passion is perhaps the only one that can make us wish to live, and bring us to thank the author of nature, whoever he is, for giving us life... The best thing we can do is to persuade ourselves that this happiness is not impossible. However, I do not know if love has ever brought together two people who are so made for each other that they have never known the satiety of delight, nor the cooling of passion caused by a sense of security, nor the indolence and the tedium that arise from the ease and the continuity of a relationship, and whose power of illusion never wanes (for where is illusion more important than in love?); and, last, whose ardor remains the same whether in the enjoyment or in the deprivation of the other's presence, and equally tolerates both unhappiness and pleasure...

I have been endowed by God, it is true, with one of these loving and steadfast souls that know neither how to disguise nor how to moderate its passions, that know neither their diminution nor disgust with them, and whose tenacity can resist everything, even the certainty of being no longer loved. But I was happy for ten years because of the love of the man who had completely seduced my soul; and these ten years I spent tête-à-tête with him without a single moment of distaste or hint of melancholy. When age, illness, as well as perhaps the ease of pleasure made his inclination less, for a long time I did not perceive it; I was loving for two, I spent all my time with him, and my heart, free from suspicion, delighted in the pleasure of loving and in the illusion of believing myself loved. True, I have lost this happy state, and this has cost me many tears. Terrible shocks are needed to break such chains. The wound to my heart bled for a long time; I had grounds to complain, and I have pardoned all. I was fair enough to accept that in the whole world, perhaps only my heart possessed the steadfastness that annihilates the power of time; that if age and illness had not entirely extinguished his desire, it would perhaps still have been for me, and that love would have restored him to me; lastly, that his heart, incapable of love, felt for me the most tender affection, and caused him to dedicate his life to me. The certainty that a return of his inclination and his passion was impossible—I know well that such a return is not in nature—imperceptibly led my heart to the peaceful feeling of deep affection; and this sentiment, together with the passion for study, made me happy enough...

The great secret for preventing love from making us unhappy is to try never to appear in the wrong with your lover, never to display eagerness when his love is cooling, and always to be a degree cooler than he. This will not bring him back, but nothing could bring him back; there is nothing for us to do then but to forget someone who ceases to love us. If he still loves you, nothing can revive his love and make it as fiery as it was at first, except the fear of losing you and of being less loved. I know that for the susceptible and sincere this secret is difficult to put into practice; however, no effort will be too great, all the more so as it is much more necessary for the susceptible and sincere than for others. Nothing degrades as much as the steps one takes to regain a cold or inconstant heart. This demeans us in the eyes of the one we seek to keep, and in those of other men who might take an interest in us. But, and this is even worse, it makes us unhappy and uselessly torments us. So we must follow this maxim with unwavering courage and never surrender to our own heart on this point. We must attempt, before surrendering to our inclination, to become acquainted with the character of the person to whom we are becoming attached. Reason must be heard when we take counsel with ourselves; not the reason that condemns all types of commitment as contrary to happiness, but that which, in agreeing that one cannot be very happy without loving, wants one to love only in order to be happy, and to conquer an attraction by which it is obvious that one would only suffer unhappiness.

Discussion Questions

1. **What are du Châtelet's recommendations for attaining happiness?**
2. **How does du Châtelet explain differences between male and female quests for happiness; and how does she describe her personal experiences with love?**

SOURCE 17.3 Sebastian Castellio, *Concerning Whether Heretics Should Be Persecuted*

1554

In October 1553, the extraordinarily gifted Spanish scientist Michael Servetus was executed with the approval and the strong support of John Calvin and his followers in Geneva. The charge was heresy, specifically for denying the existence of the Trinity and the divinity of Christ, and the method of execution—burning at the stake—elicited commentary and protest from across Europe. One of the fullest and most sophisticated protests against this execution was issued by Sebastian Castellio, a professor of Greek language and New Testament theology in the Swiss city of Basel. His book

Source: Sebastian Castellio, *Concerning Heretics, Whether They Are to Be Persecuted and How They Are to Be Treated, A Collection of the Opinions of Learned Men Both Ancient and Modern*, trans. Roland H. Bainton (New York: Octagon, 1965), 132–134.

De Haereticis is a collection of opinions, drawn from Christian writers, from both before and after the Protestant Reformation and across 15 centuries. It is more than an academic exercise, however, as this dedication of the Latin work to a German noble demonstrates.

From the Dedication of the book to Duke Christoph of Württemberg:

Turks: Muslims.

. . . And just as the **Turks** disagree with the Christians as to the person of Christ, and the Jews with both the Turks and the Christians, and the one condemns the other and holds him for a heretic, so Christians disagree with Christians on many points with regard to the teaching of Christ, and condemn one another and hold each other for heretics. Great controversies and debates occur as to baptism, the Lord's Supper, the invocation of the saints, justification, free will, and other obscure questions, so that Catholics, Lutherans, Zwinglians, Anabaptists, monks, and others condemn and persecute one another more cruelly than the Turks do the Christians. These dissensions arise solely from ignorance of the truth, for if these matters were so obvious and evident as that there is but one God, all Christians would agree among themselves on these points as readily as all nations confess that God is one.

What, then is to be done in such great contentions? We should follow the counsel of Paul, "Let not him that eateth despise him that eateth not . . . To his own master he standeth or falleth" [Romans 14:3–4]. Let not the Jews or Turks condemn the Christians, nor let the Christians condemn the Jews or Turks, but rather teach and win them by true religion and justice, and let us, who are Christians, not condemn one another, but, if we are wiser than they, let us also be better and more merciful. This is certain that the better a man knows the truth, the less is he inclined to condemn, as appears in the case of Christ and the apostles. But he who lightly condemns others shows thereby that he knows nothing precisely, because he cannot bear others, for to know is to know how to put into practice. He who does not know how to act mercifully and kindly does not know the nature of mercy and kindness, just as he who cannot blush does not know the nature of shame.

If we were to conduct ourselves in this fashion we should be able to dwell together in concord. Even though in some matters we disagreed, yet should we consent together and forbear one another in love, which is the bond of peace, until we arrive at the unity of the faith [Ephesians 4:2–3]. But now, when we strive with hate and persecutions we go from bad to worse. Nor are we mindful of our office, since we are wholly taken up with condemnation, and the Gospel because of us is made a reproach unto the heathen [Ezekiel 22:4], for when they see us attacking one another with the fury of beasts, and the weak oppressed by the strong, these heathen feel horror and detestation for the Gospel, as if it made men such, and they abominate even Christ himself, as if he commanded men to do such things. We rather degenerate into Turks and Jews than convert them into Christians. Who would wish to be a Christian, when he saw that those who confessed the name of Christ were destroyed by Christians themselves with fire, water, and the sword without mercy and more cruelly treated than brigands and murderers? Who would

Moloch: A Phoenician deity who, according to the Bible, demanded the sacrifice of human children.
Phalaris: Tyrant in pre-Christian Sicily who burned victims alive in a giant bronze bull.

not think Christ a **Moloch**, or some such god, if he wished that men should be immolated to him and burned alive? Who would wish to serve Christ on condition that a difference of opinion on a controversial point with those in authority would be punished by burning alive at the command of Christ himself more cruelly than in the bull of **Phalaris**, even though from the midst of the flames he should call with a loud voice upon Christ, and should cry out that he believed in Him? Imagine Christ, the judge of all, present. Imagine Him pronouncing the sentence and applying the torch. Who would not hold Christ for a Satan? What more could Satan do than burn those who call upon the name of Christ?

Working with Sources

1. **Was Castellio minimizing the significant theological disputes that had arisen as a result of the Reformation? Were his objections directly applicable to the Servetus case?**
2. **What did Castellio see as the practical, as well as the theological, consequences of burning those perceived to be "heretics"? Is he convincing on this point?**

SOURCE 17.4

Duc de Saint-Simon, "The Daily Habits of Louis XIV at Versailles"

ca. 1715

A noble at Louis XIV's court at Versailles, Louis de Rouvroy, the duc de Saint-Simon (1675–1755), would achieve lasting fame after his death with the publication of his copious, frank, and witty observations of the court. While resident at Versailles for brief periods after 1702 until the king's death in 1715, Saint-Simon paid particular attention to the maneuverings of his fellow aristocrats. He managed to garner the resentment of many of them, especially the king's illegitimate children, "the Bastards," who held a prominent place at court. His accounts of the daily routine of life at Versailles, and the central position of the king who had famously declared "L'état, c'est moi!" are often applied today to spectacles that can also be described as at once grand and a little absurd.

Source: *Memoirs of the Duc de Saint-Simon*, trans. Bayle St. John, ed. W. H. Lewis (New York: Macmillan, 1964), 140–141, 144–145.

At eight o'clock the chief valet de chambre on duty, who alone had slept in the royal chamber, and who had dressed himself, awoke the King. The chief physician, the chief surgeon, and the nurse (as long as she lived), entered at the same time. The latter kissed the King; the others rubbed and often changed his shirt, because he was in the habit of sweating a great deal. At the quarter [hour], the grand chamberlain was called (or, in his absence, the first gentleman of the chamber), and those who had, what was called the *grandes entrées*. The chamberlain (or chief gentleman) drew back the curtains which had been closed again, and presented the holy water from the vase, at the head of the bed. These gentlemen stayed but a moment, and that was the time to speak to the King, if any one had anything to ask of him; in which case the rest stood aside. When, contrary to custom, nobody had aught to say, they were there but for a few moments. He who had opened the curtains and presented the holy water, presented also a prayer-book. Then all passed into the cabinet of the council. A very short religious service being over, the King called, they re-entered. The same officer gave him his dressing-gown; immediately after, other privileged courtiers entered, and then everybody, in time to find the King putting on his shoes and stockings, for he did almost everything himself and with address and grace. Every other day we saw him shave himself; and he had a little short wig in which he always appeared, even in bed, and on medicine days. He often spoke of the chase, and sometimes said a word to somebody. No toilette table was near him; he had simply a mirror held before him.

As soon as he was dressed, he prayed to God, at the side of his bed, where all the clergy present knelt, the cardinals without cushions, all the laity remaining standing; and the captain of the guards came to the balustrade during the prayer, after which the King passed into his cabinet.

He found there, or was followed by all who had the entrée, a very numerous company, for it included everybody in any office. He gave orders to each for the day; thus within half a quarter of an hour it was known what he meant to do; and then all this crowd left directly. The bastards, a few favourites, and the valets alone were left. It was then a good opportunity for talking with the King; for example, about plans of gardens and buildings; and conversation lasted more or less according to the person engaged in it.

. . .

At ten o'clock his supper was served. The captain of the guard announced this to him. A quarter of an hour after the King came to supper, and from the ante-chamber of Madame de Maintenon [his principal mistress] to the table again, any one spoke to him who wished. This supper was always on a grand scale, the royal household (that is, the sons and daughters of France), at table, and a large number of courtiers and ladies present, sitting or standing, and on the evening before the journey to Marly all those ladies who wished to take part in it. That was called presenting yourself for Marly. Men asked in the morning, simply saying to the King, "Sire, Marly." In later years, the King grew tired of this, and a valet wrote up in the gallery the names of those who asked. The ladies continued to present themselves.

. . .

Ruelle: The "little path" between a bed and the wall.

The King, wishing to retire, went and fed his dogs; then said good night, passed into his chamber to the **ruelle** of his bed, where he said his prayers, as in the morning, then undressed. He said good night with an inclination of the head, and whilst everybody was leaving the room stood at the corner of the mantelpiece, where he gave the order to the colonel of the guards alone. Then commenced what was called the *petit coucher,* at which only the specially privileged remained. That was short. They did not leave until he got into bed. It was a moment to speak to him.

▸ Working with Sources

1. **Why does Saint-Simon pay particular attention to moments of the day during which a courtier could speak directly with the king?**
2. **What does the combination of religious and secular pursuits in the king's daily habits suggest about life at his court?**

SOURCE 17.5

Giorgio Vasari, *The Life of Michelangelo Buonarroti*

1550

Trained as a painter, architect, and goldsmith, Giorgio Vasari (1511–1574) practiced various artistic trades, but is most renowned today as the first art historian. His *Lives of the Most Eminent Painters, Sculptors, and Architects*, first published in 1550, is the principal source of information about the most prominent artists of the European Renaissance. Having studied under the great artist Michelangelo Buonarroti (1475–1564), Vasari was particularly keen to tell his story. In these scenes from his biography of Michelangelo, Vasari draws attention to his master's early training, as well as the prominent roles Lorenzo "il Magnifico" de' Medici and ancient sculpture played in his artistic development.

Source: Giorgio Vasari, *The Lives of the Artists*, trans. Julia Conaway Bondanella and Peter Bondanella (Oxford and New York: Oxford University Press, 1998), 418–420; 427–428.

In those days Lorenzo de' Medici the Magnificent kept Bertoldo the sculptor in his garden near Piazza San Marco, not so much as the custodian or guardian of the many beautiful antiquities he had collected and assembled there at great expense, but rather because he wished above all else to create a school for excellent painters and sculptors . . . Thus, Domenico [Ghirlandaio] gave him some of his best young men, including among others Michelangelo and Francesco Granacci; and when they went to the garden, they found that Torrigiani, a young man of the Torrigiani family, was there working on some clay figures in the round that Bertoldo had given him to do.

After Michelangelo saw these figures, he made some himself to rival those of Torrigiani, so that Lorenzo, seeing his high spirit, always had great expectations for him, and, encouraged after only a few days, Michelangelo began copying with a piece of marble the antique head of an old and wrinkled faun with a damaged nose and a laughing mouth, which he found there. Although Michelangelo had never before touched marble or chisels, the imitation turned out so well that Lorenzo was astonished, and when Lorenzo saw that Michelangelo, following his own fantasy rather than the antique head, had carved its mouth open to give it a tongue and to make all its teeth visible, this lord, laughing with pleasure as was his custom, said to him: "But you should have known that old men never have all their teeth and that some of them are always missing." In that simplicity of his, it seemed to Michelangelo, who loved and feared this lord, that Lorenzo was correct; and as soon as Lorenzo left, he immediately broke a tooth on the head and dug out the gum in such a way that it seemed the tooth had fallen out, and anxiously awaited Lorenzo's return, who, after coming back and seeing Michelangelo's simplicity and excellence, laughed about it on more than one occasion, recounting it to his friends as if it were miraculous. . . .

. . .

Around this time it happened that Piero Soderini saw the statue [the *David*, finished in 1504], and it pleased him greatly, but while Michelangelo was giving it the finishing touches, he told Michelangelo that he thought the nose of the figure was too large. Michelangelo, realizing that the Gonfaloniere [a civic official in Florence] was standing under the giant and that his viewpoint did not allow him to see it properly, climbed up the scaffolding to satisfy Soderini (who was behind him nearby), and having quickly grabbed the chisel in his left hand along with a little marble dust that he found on the planks in the scaffolding, Michelangelo began to tap lightly with the chisel, allowing the dust to fall little by little without retouching the nose from the way it was. Then, looking down at the Gonfaloniere who stood there watching, he ordered:

"Look at it now."

"I like it better," replied the Gonfaloniere: "you've made it come alive."

Thus Michelangelo climbed down, and, having contented this lord, he laughed to himself, feeling compassion for those who, in order to make it appear that they understand, do not realize what they are saying; and when the statue was finished and set in its foundation, he uncovered it, and to tell the truth, this work eclipsed all other statues, both modern and ancient, whether Greek or Roman; and it can be said that neither the Marforio in Rome, nor the Tiber and the Nile of the Belvedere, nor the colossal statues of Monte Cavallo can be compared to this David, which Michelangelo completed with so much measure and beauty, and so much skill.

▶ **Working with Sources**

1. **How do these anecdotes illustrate the relationship between artists and their patrons (and funders) during the Renaissance?**
2. **How did Michelangelo deal with the legacy of artists from Greco-Roman antiquity?**

SOURCE 17.6

Galileo Galilei, Letter to the Grand Duchess Christina de' Medici

1615

This famous letter is often cited as an early sign of Galileo's inevitable conflict with church authorities over the Copernican system of planetary motion—and the theory's theological, as well as its scientific, ramifications. Galileo (1564–1642) would be condemned to house arrest in 1632 and forced to make a public repudiation of the heliocentric theory first advanced by Copernicus in the sixteenth century. However, Galileo's connection to the renowned Medici family of Florence was also cause for comment—and caution—from 1610, when he received an appointment and their implicit endorsement.

Constructing a telescope in 1609 (which he proudly claimed could "magnify objects more than 60 times"), Galileo trained it on the moons of Jupiter, which he tracked over several days in 1610. Having named these objects for the Medici family, he rushed these and many other astronomical observations into print in the *Sidereus Nuncius* (*The Starry Messenger*). Inviting other scientists to "apply themselves to examine and determine" these planetary motions, Galileo demonstrated a preference for the Copernican theory and elicited sharp responses, particularly from church officials. In

---

Source: Galileo Galilei, *The Essential Galileo*, ed. and trans. Maurice A. Finocchiaro (Indianapolis: Hackett, 2008), §4.2.5—4.2.6, 140–144.

1615, the dowager Grand Duchess Christina, mother of his patron, Cosimo II, expressed her own reservations about the implications of the Copernican theory for a passage in the Old Testament. Galileo's response attempts, or seems to attempt, to reconcile experimental science and received religion.

Thus let these people apply themselves to refuting the arguments of Copernicus and of the others, and let them leave its condemnation as erroneous and heretical to the proper authorities; but let them not hope that the very cautious and very wise Fathers and the Infallible One with his absolute wisdom are about to make rash decisions like those into which they would be rushed by their special interests and feelings. For in regard to these and other similar propositions which do not directly involve the faith, no one can doubt that the Supreme Pontiff always has the absolute power of permitting or condemning them; however, no creature has the power of making them be true or false, contrary to what they happen to be by nature and de facto. So it seems more advisable to first become sure about the necessary and immutable truth of the matter, over which no one has control, than to condemn one side when such certainty is lacking; this would imply a loss of freedom of decision and of choice insofar as it would give necessity to things which are presently indifferent, free, and dependent on the will of the supreme authority. In short, if it is inconceivable that a proposition should be declared heretical when one thinks that it may be true, it should be futile for someone to try to bring about the condemnation of the earth's motion and sun's rest unless he first shows it to be impossible and false.

There remains one last thing for us to examine: to what extent it is true that the Joshua passage [Joshua 10:12–13] can be taken without altering the literal meaning of the words, and how it can be that, when the sun obeyed Joshua's order to stop, from this it followed that the day was prolonged by a large amount.

. . .

I think therefore, if I am not mistaken, that one can clearly see that, given the Ptolemaic system, it is necessary to interpret the words in a way different from their literal meaning. Guided by St. Augustine's very useful prescriptions, I should say that the best nonliteral interpretation is not necessarily this, if anyone can find another which is perhaps better and more suitable. So now I want to examine whether the same miracle could be understood in a way more in accordance with what we read in Joshua, if to the Copernican system we add another discovery which I recently made about the solar body. However, I continue to speak with the same reservations—to the effect that I am not so enamored with my own opinions as to want to place them ahead of those of others; nor do I believe it is impossible to put forth interpretations which are better and more in accordance with the Holy Writ.

Let us first assume in accordance with the opinion of the above-mentioned authors, that in the Joshua miracle the whole system of heavenly motions was stopped, so that the stopping of only one would not introduce unnecessarily universal confusion and great turmoil in the whole order of nature.

. . .

Furthermore, what deserves special appreciation, if I am not mistaken, is that with the Copernican system one can very clearly and very easily give a literal meaning to another detail which one reads about the same miracle; that is, that the sun stopped in the middle of heaven. Serious theologians have raised a difficulty about this passage: it seems very probable that, when Joshua asked for the prolongation of the day, the sun was close to setting and not at the meridian; for it was then about the time of the summer solstice, and consequently the days were very long, so that if the sun had been at the meridian then it does not seem likely that it would have been necessary to pray for a lengthening of the day in order to win a battle, since the still remaining time of seven hours or more could very well have been sufficient.

. . .

We can remove this and every other implausibility, if I am not mistaken, by placing the sun, as the Copernican system does and as it is most necessary to do, in the middle, namely, at the center of the heavenly orbs and of the planetary revolutions; for at any hour of the day, whether at noon or in the afternoon, the day would not have been lengthened and all heavenly turnings stopped by the sun stopping in the middle of the heavens, namely, at the center of the heavens, where it is located. Furthermore, this interpretation agrees all the more with the literal meaning inasmuch as, if one wanted to claim that the sun's stopping occurred at the noon hour, then the proper expression to use would have been to say that it "stood still at the meridian point," or "at the meridian circle," and not "in the middle of the heaven"; in fact, for a spherical body such as heaven, the middle is really and only the center.

▶ Working with Sources

1. **How does Galileo deal with the apparently irreconcilable conclusions of science and the Bible?**
2. **How would you characterize Galileo's tone in his analysis of the verses from the Book of Joshua?**

World Period Four

Interactions across the Globe, 1450–1750

The fifteenth century saw a renewal of the imperial impulse in the religious civilizations of the world. A forerunner had been the Mongol empire, which however did not last long; in less than 100 years it was replaced in China by the Ming. The founders of the subsequent new empires were the Mughals in India; the Ottomans, Safavids, and Songhay in the Middle East and Islamic Africa; the Habsburgs in Europe; and the seaborne empires of Portugal and Spain. One byproduct of this new imperial impulse was the discovery of the Americas, which in turn inspired the formulation of the heliocentric universe. The rediscovery of Greek literature in Europe had already set into motion the Renaissance, a broad new approach to understanding the world that provided the spark for the New Science.

China and India, by far the wealthiest and most populous agrarian–urban empires, enjoyed leading positions in the world because they produced everything they needed and wanted. Europe, however, acquired warm-weather crops and minerals through overseas colonial expansion, which would help it to challenge the traditional order.

Chapter 18

New Patterns in New Worlds

COLONIALISM AND INDIGENOUS RESPONSES IN THE AMERICAS, 1500–1800

CHAPTER EIGHTEEN PATTERNS

Origins, Interactions, Adaptations The Americas had just reached their agrarian–urban peak with the Aztec and Inca empires when Spanish *conquistadors* arrived from across the Atlantic. After destroying the empires, the Iberians turned the double continent into the colonial warm-weather extension they had previously lacked. A still sparsely populated Iberia, however, could not spare many settlers and, as a result, small minorities governed large labor forces of indigenous Amerindians and slaves imported from Africa to work on sugar, coffee, and cotton plantations, as well as in mines. In North America, Europeans displaced the Amerindian population and drove it into the interior. Over time, urban colonial societies of Hispanics and Anglo-Americans emerged, with their own *creole* culture that distinguished them from Europe.

Uniqueness and Similarities The Spanish and Portuguese colonies evolved along distinct paths, depending on the proportions of settlers, Amerindians, and African slaves in each country. Argentina and Chile had few Amerindians and slaves, but Brazil and many Caribbean islands had huge numbers of African slaves, and large numbers of Amerindians lived in Mexico. Nevertheless, however distinct the colonies were, by 1750 they were all firmly dependent extensions of Europe.

CHAPTER OUTLINE

The Colonial Americas: Europe's Warm-Weather Extension

The Making of American Societies: Origins and Transformations

Putting It All Together

Alonso Ortiz fled from his creditors in Spain in the early 1570s to find a new life in the Americas. In Mexico City, he set up shop as a tanner. Eight Native American employees did the actual labor of stomping the hides in the vats filled with tanning acids. A black slave was the supervisor. Ortiz concentrated on giving instructions and hustling his flourishing business.

Ortiz's situation in Mexico City was not entirely legal, however. He had left his wife and children in Spain, though the law required that families should be united. The authorities rarely enforced this law, but that was no guarantee for Ortiz. Furthermore, he had not yet sent his family any remittances. And then there was still the debt. Ortiz had reasons to be afraid of the law.

To avoid prosecution, Ortiz wrote a letter to his wife. In this letter, he described the comfortable position he had achieved. He announced that his business partner was sending her a sum of money sufficient to begin preparations for her departure from Spain. To his creditors, Ortiz promised to send 100 tanned hides within a year. Evidently aware of her reluctance to join him in Mexico, Ortiz closed his letter with a request to grant him four more years abroad and to do so with a notarized document from her hand. Unfortunately, we do not know her answer.

The Ortiz family drama gives a human face to European colonialism and emigration to the "New World" of the Americas. Like Alonso Ortiz, some 300,000 other Spaniards left the "Old World" (Europe, contiguous with Asia and Africa) between 1500 and 1800. A few hundred letters by emigrants exist, giving us glimpses of their lives in the parts of the Americas conquered by the Spanish and Portuguese in the sixteenth century. These relatively privileged immigrants hoped to build successful enterprises using the labor of Native Americans as well as black slaves imported from Africa. The example of Ortiz shows that even in the socially not very prestigious

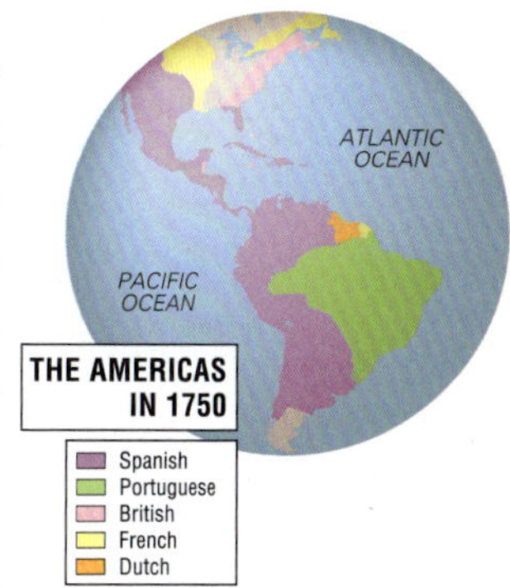

ABOVE: In his monumental *Historia de la conquista de México*, written more than 150 years after the events described, Antonio de Solís (1610–1686) depicted the meeting of Moctezuma and Cortés.

craft of tanning, a man could achieve a measure of comfort by having people of even lower status working for him.

Seeing Patterns

> What is the significance of western Europeans acquiring the Americas as a warm-weather extension of their northern continent?

> What was the main pattern of social development in colonial America during the period 1500–1800?

> Why and how did European settlers in South and North America strive for self-government, and how successful were they in achieving their goals?

Beginning in the sixteenth century, the Americas became an extension of Europe. European settlers extracted mineral and agricultural resources from these new lands. A pattern emerged in which gold and silver, as well as agricultural products, were intensively exploited. In this role, the Americas became a crucial factor in Europe's changing position in the world. First, Europe acquired precious metals, which its two largest competitors, India and China, lacked. Second, with agricultural commodities pouring in from the Americas, Europe rose to a position of agrarian autonomy similar to that of India and China.

The Colonial Americas: Europe's Warm-Weather Extension

The European extension into the Americas followed Columbus's pursuit of a sea route to India that would circumvent the Muslim dominance of the trade with India and China. The Spaniards financed their imperial expansion as well as their wars against Ottoman and European rivals with American gold and silver, leaving little for domestic investment. A pattern evolved in which Iberian settlers transformed the Americas into mineral-extracting and agrarian colonies based on either cheap or forced labor.

The Conquest of Mexico and Peru

The Spanish conquerors of the Aztec and Inca Empires exploited internal weaknesses in the empires. They eliminated the top of the power structures, paralyzing the decision-making apparatuses long enough for their conquests to succeed. Soon after the conquests, the Old World disease of smallpox ravaged the Native American population and dramatically reduced the indigenous labor force. To make up for this reduction, colonial authorities imported black slaves from Africa. A three-tiered society of European immigrants, Native Americans, and black slaves emerged in the Spanish and Portuguese Americas.

Land-labor grant (*encomienda*): Land grant by the government to an entrepreneur, entitling him to use forced indigenous or imported slave labor on that land for the exploitation of agricultural and mineral resources.

From Trading Posts to Conquest Columbus had discovered the Caribbean islands under a royal commission which entitled him to build fortified posts and to trade with the indigenous Taínos. Trade relations with the Taínos, however, deteriorated into exploitation, with the Spaniards usurping the traditional entitlements of the Taíno chiefs to the labor of their fellow men. With the help of **land-labor grants** (Spanish *encomiendas*), the Spanish took over from the Taíno chiefs and, through forced labor, amassed quantities of gold. What had begun as trade-post settlement turned into full-blown conquest of land.

The Spaniards conquered the Caribbean islands not only through force. Much more severe in its consequences was the indirect conquest through disease. Smallpox wiped out an estimated 250,000 to 1 million Taínos as well as the Caribs. Isolated from the rest of humankind, Native Americans possessed no immunity against smallpox and other introduced diseases.

Protests, mostly among some members of the clergy, arose against both the labor exploitation and the helplessness of the Taínos against disease. The land-labor grant system finally came to an end after 1542 with the introduction of the *repartimiento* system (see p. 429).

Cultural Intermediary. The Tabascans gave Malinche, or Doña Marina, to Hernán Cortés as a form of tribute after they were defeated by the Spanish. Malinche served Cortés as a translator and mistress, playing a central role in Cortés's eventual victory over the Aztecs. She was in many respects the principal face of the Spanish and is always depicted center stage in Native American visual accounts of the conquest.

First Mainland Conquests Hernán Cortés (1485–1547), upon arriving on Hispaniola in 1504, advanced from governmental scribe in Hispaniola to mayor of Santiago in Cuba. Thanks to labor grants, he became rich. When the Cuban governor asked him in 1518 to lead an expedition for trade and exploration to the Yucatán Peninsula in Mexico, Cortés enthusiastically agreed. He assembled 300 men, considerably exceeding his contract. The governor tried to stop him, but Cortés departed quickly for the American mainland.

As the Cuban governor had feared, Cortés did not bother with trading posts in Yucatán. The Spanish had learned of the existence of the Aztec Empire, with its immense silver and gold treasures. In a first encounter, Cortés's small Spanish force defeated a much larger indigenous force at Tabasco. The Spaniards' steel weapons and armor proved superior in hand-to-hand combat against the defenders.

Among the gifts presented by the defeated Native Americans in Tabasco was Malinche, an enslaved Nahuatl [NAH-wat(l)]-speaking woman. Malinche quickly learned Spanish and became the consort of Cortés. As a translator, Malinche was nearly as decisive as Cortés in shaping events, given that the latter was ignorant of indigenous affairs. With Tabasco conquered, Cortés quickly moved on; he was afraid that the Cuban governor would otherwise force him to return to Cuba.

Conquest of the Aztec Empire On the southeast coast of Mexico, Cortés founded the city of Veracruz. He had his followers elect a town council, which made Cortés their head and chief justice, allowing Cortés to claim legitimacy for his march inland. Marching inland, the Spaniards ran into resistance from indigenous people, suffering their first losses of horses and men. They pressed onward with thousands of Native American allies, most notably the Tlaxcalans [tlash-KAH-lans], traditional enemies of the Aztecs. The support from these indigenous peoples proved essential when Cortés and his army reached the court of the Aztecs.

1492
Christopher Columbus lands in the Caribbean

1500
Pedro Álvares Cabral claims Brazil for Portugal

1516–1556
Reign of Charles V, Habsburg king of Spain and the Americas

1519–1521
Reign of Cuauhtémoc, last ruler of the Aztec Empire

1521
Spanish conquest of the Aztec Empire in Mexico

1532–1533
Reign of Atahualpa, last ruler of the Inca Empire

1533
Spanish conquest of the Inca Empire in Peru

1545
Founding of silver mine of Potosí

1607
Jamestown, Virginia, first permanent English settlement

1608
Quebec City, first permanent French settlement

1690
Gold discovered in Brazil

When Cortés arrived at the city of Tenochtitlán on November 2, 1519, the emperor Moctezuma II (r. 1502–1519) was unsure of how to react to the invaders. To gain time, Moctezuma greeted the Spaniard in person and invited him to his palace. Cortés and his company, now numbering some 600 Spaniards, took up quarters in the palace precincts. After a week of deteriorating discussions, Cortés suddenly put the incredulous emperor under house arrest and made him swear allegiance to Charles V.

However, Cortés was diverted by the need to march back east, where troops from Cuba had arrived to arrest him. After defeating these troops, he pressed the remnants into his own service and returned to Tenochtitlán. During his absence, the Spaniards who had remained in Moctezuma's palace had massacred Aztec nobles. As an infuriated crowd of Tenochtitlán's inhabitants invaded the palace, Moctezuma and some 200 Spaniards died. The rest of the Spanish retreated east to their Tlaxcalan allies. There, after his return, Cortés devised a new plan for capturing Tenochtitlán.

After 10 months of preparations, the Spaniards returned to the Aztec capital. In command now of about 2,000 Spanish soldiers and assisted by some 50,000 Native American troops, Cortés laid siege to the city. After nearly three months, much of the city was in ruins, water and food became scarce, and smallpox began to decimate the population. On August 21, 1521, the Spaniards and their allies stormed the city and looted its gold treasury. They captured the last emperor, Cuauhtémoc [kwaw-TAY-mok] and executed him in 1525, thus ending the Aztec Empire (see Map 18.1).

Conquest by Surprise. The Spanish conqueror Francisco Pizarro captured Emperor Atahualpa in an ambush. Atahualpa promised a roomful of gold in return for his release, but the Spaniards collected the gold and murdered Atahualpa before generals of the Inca army could organize an armed resistance.

Conquest of the Inca Empire A relative of Cortés, Francisco Pizarro (ca. 1475–1541), planned to conquer the Andean empire of the Incas. Pizarro, like Cortés born in Spain but uneducated, had arrived in Hispaniola as part of an expedition in 1513 that went on to discover Panama and the Pacific. He became mayor of Panama City, acquired some wealth, and heard rumors about an empire of gold and silver to the south. After a failed initial expedition, he captured some precious metal from an oceangoing Inca sailing raft. Upon receiving a permit from Charles V to establish a trading post, Pizarro and a team departed in late December 1530.

In the years before Pizarro's expedition, smallpox had ravaged the Inca Empire, killing the emperor and his heir apparent and leading to a protracted war of succession between two surviving sons. When Pizarro entered the Inca Empire, one of those sons, Atahualpa, was encamped with an army of 40,000 men near the town of Cajamarca.

Arriving at Cajamarca, Pizarro arranged an unarmed audience with Atahualpa. On November 16, 1532, Atahualpa came to this audience, surrounded by several thousand unarmed retainers, while Pizarro's soldiers hid nearby. At a signal, these soldiers rushed forward, capturing Atahualpa and massacring his retainers. Not one Spanish soldier was killed.

The ambush paralyzed the Inca Empire at the very top. Atahualpa offered his captors a room full of gold and silver as ransom. In the following two months, Inca administrators delivered immense quantities of precious metals to Pizarro. But

MAP 18.1 **The European Exploration of the Americas, 1519–1542**

Spanish officers executed Atahualpa anyway on July 26, 1533, hoping to keep the Incas disorganized.

The Spaniards then captured the Incan capital, Cuzco, massacring the inhabitants and stripping the city of its immense gold and silver treasures. In 1535 Pizarro founded a new capital, Lima, which was more conveniently located on the coast. Although Incas in the south rebuilt a kingdom, the Spanish eventually gained full control of the Inca Empire in 1572.

The Portuguese Conquest of Brazil Navigators from both Spain and Portugal had first sighted the Brazilian coast in 1499–1500, and the Portuguese quickly claimed it for themselves. The majority of Brazil's indigenous population at that time lived in villages based on agriculture, fishing, and hunting.

The Portuguese were interested initially in trade with villagers, mostly for brazilwood, which was used to make a red dye and for which the country of Brazil was named. When French traders appeared, ignoring the Portuguese commercial treaties with the tribes, the Portuguese crown shifted to trading-post settlements. Land grants were made with the obligation to build fortified coastal villages for settlers and to engage in agriculture and friendly trade. By the mid-sixteenth century, inhabitants of some of these villages intermarried with local indigenous chieftain families and established sugarcane plantations.

Explanations for the Spanish Success The stupendous victories of handfuls of Spaniards over huge empires defies easy explanation. Four factors invite consideration. First, the conquistadors went straight to the top of the imperial pyramid. The emperors expected diplomatic deference, but confronted instead with arrogance and brutality, they were thrown off balance by the Spaniards. Second, in both the Aztec and Inca Empires, individuals and groups contested the hierarchical power structure. The conquistadors either found allies among the subject populations or encountered a divided leadership. Third, European-introduced diseases took a devastating toll. In both empires, smallpox hit at critical moments during or right before the Spanish invasions. Finally, thanks to horses and European steel weapons and armor, small numbers of Spaniards were able to hold large numbers of attacking Aztecs and Incas at bay in hand-to-hand combat. Cannons and matchlock muskets were less important, since they were useless in close encounters.

The Establishment of Colonial Institutions

The Spanish crown established administrative hierarchies in the Americas, with governors at the top and lower ranks of functionaries. Some settler autonomy was permitted through town and city councils, but the crown was determined to make the Americas a territorial extension of the European pattern of centralized state formation. Several hundred thousand settlers found a new life in the Americas. By the early seventeenth century, an elite of Spaniards who had been born in America, called **Creoles** (Spanish *criollos*), first assisted and later replaced most of the administrators sent from Spain (see Map 18.2).

Creoles: American-born descendants of European, primarily Spanish, immigrants.

From Conquest to Colonialism The riches of Cortés and Pizarro inspired further expeditions into Central and North America, Chile, and the Amazon. These expeditions, however, yielded only modest amounts of gold and earned more from selling captured Native Americans into slavery. In the north, expeditions penetrated as far as Arizona, New Mexico, Texas, Oklahoma, Kansas, and Florida, but encountered only relatively poor villagers and Pueblo towns. No new golden kingdoms beyond the Aztec and Inca Empires were discovered in the Americas.

In the mid-sixteenth century, the conquistadors shifted from looting to the exploitation of Native American labor in mines and in agriculture. Explorers discovered silver in Bolivia (1545) and northern Mexico (1556), gold in Chile (1552), and mercury in Peru (1563).

Indigenous peoples occasionally resisted incorporation into the Spanish colonies. Notably, the Mapuche in southern Chile repulsed all attempts by the Spanish to subdue them. Initially, in 1550–1553 the Spanish succeeded in establishing forts and opening a gold mine, but they failed to gain more than a border strip with an adjacent no-man's-land. In 1612 they agreed to a temporary peace that left the majority of the Mapuche independent.

Another Native American people who successfully resisted the Spanish conquest were the Asháninka in the Peruvian rain forest. The Asháninka exploited hillside salt veins in their region and were traders of goods between the Andes and the rain forest. It was only in 1737 that the Spanish finally succeeded in building a fort in the region—a first step toward projecting colonial power into the rain forest.

Brazil in 1519. This early map is fairly accurate for the northern coast, but increasingly less accurate as one moves south. First explorations of the south by both Portuguese and Spanish mariners date to 1513–1516. Ferdinand Magellan passed through several places along the southern coast on his journey around the world in 1520–1521. The scenes on the map depict Native Americans cutting and collecting brazilwood, the source of a red dye much in demand by the Portuguese during the early period of colonization.

Bureaucratic Efficiency During the first two generations after the conquest, Spain maintained an efficient colonial administration to deliver revenues to Spain. In addition, the viceroyalty of New Spain in Mexico remitted another 25 percent of its revenues to the Philippines, the Pacific province for which it was administratively responsible from 1571 onward. Settlers in New Spain had to pay up to 40 different taxes and dues. The only income tax was the tithe to the church, which the administration collected and, at times, used for its own budgetary purposes. Altogether, however, for the settlers the tax level was lower in the New World than in Spain, and the same was true for the English and French colonists in North America.

In the 1540s the government introduced rotating **labor assignments** (*repartimientos*) to phase out the *encomiendas*. This institution of rotating labor assignments was a continuation of the *mit'a* system, which the Incas had devised as a form of taxation (see Chapter 15). Rotating labor assignments meant that a percentage of villagers had to provide labor to the state. Private entrepreneurs could also contract for indigenous labor assignments, especially in mining regions.

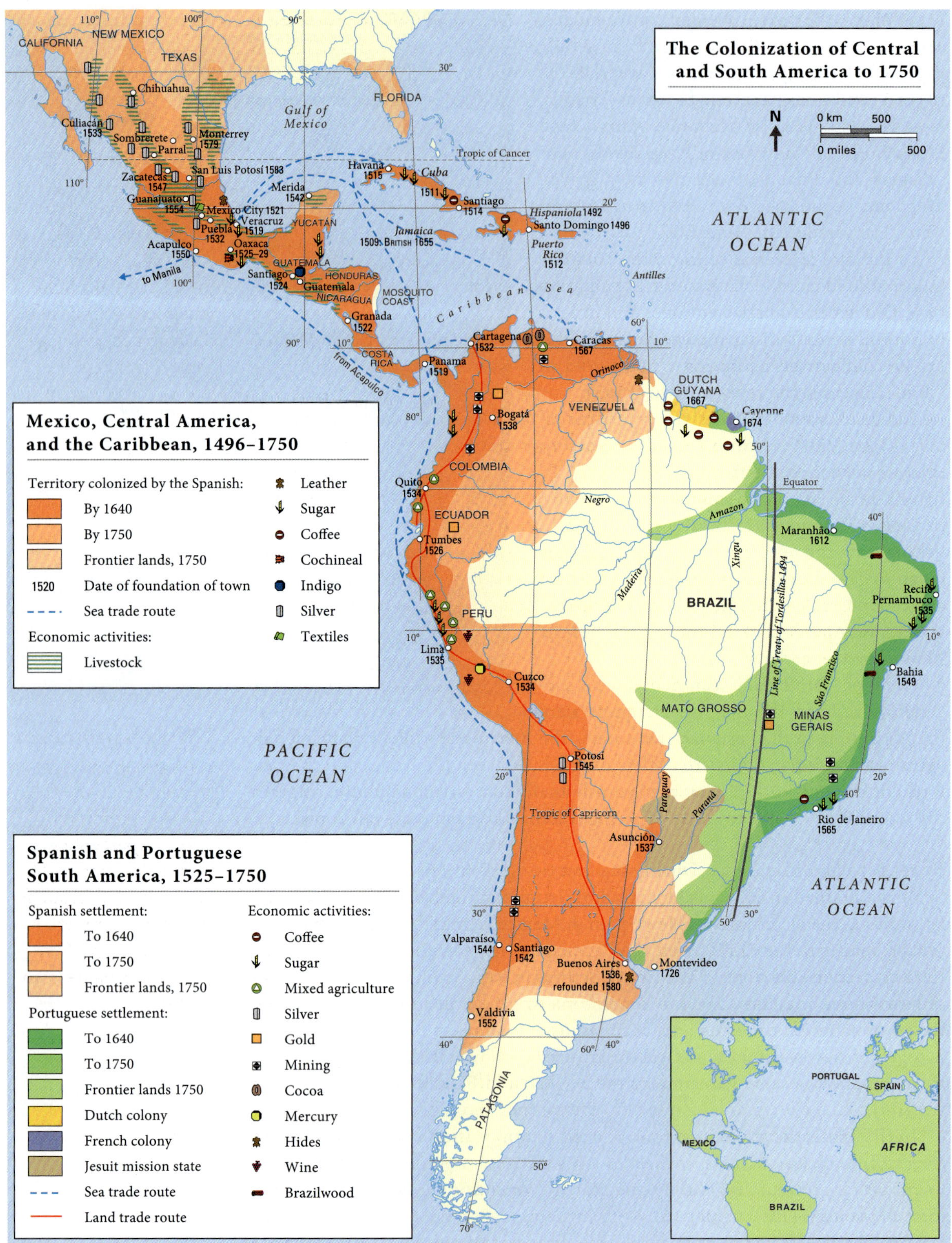

MAP 18.2 **The Colonization of Central and South America to 1750**

In Mexico the *repartimiento* fell out of use in the first half of the seventeenth century due to the toll of smallpox on the Native American population. The replacement for the lost workers was wage labor. In highland Peru, where the effects of smallpox were less severe, the assignment system lasted to the end of the colonial period. Wage labor expanded there as well. Wages for Native Americans and blacks remained everywhere lower than those for Creoles.

Labor assignment (*repartimiento*)**:** Obligation by villagers to send stipulated numbers of people as laborers to a contractor, who had the right to exploit a mine or other labor-intensive enterprise; the contractors paid the laborers minimal wages and bound them through debt peonage (repayment of money advances) to their businesses.

The Rise of the Creoles Administrative and fiscal efficiency did not last very long. The wars of the Spanish Habsburg Empire cost more than the crown was able to collect in revenues. In order to make up the financial deficit, the crown began to sell offices in the Americas to the highest bidders. By the end of the century, Creoles had purchased life appointments in city councils as well as other important sinecures that allowed them to collect fees and rents. Local oligarchies emerged, effectively ending participatory politics in Spanish colonial America.

The effects of the change from recruitment by merit to recruitment by wealth on the functioning of the bureaucracy were far-reaching. Creoles advanced on a broad front in the administrative positions, while fewer Spaniards found it attractive to buy positions from abroad. The only opportunities which European Spaniards still found enticing were positions that gave their owners the right to subject the Native Americans to forced purchases of goods, yielding huge profits. By 1700, the consequences of the Spanish crown selling most of its American administrative offices were a decline in the competence of officeholders, the emergence of a Creole elite able to bend the Spanish administration to its will, and a decentralization of the decision-making processes.

Northwest European Interference As Spain's administrative grip on the Americas weakened during the seventeenth century, the need to defend the continents militarily against European interlopers arose. European **privateers**, holding royal charters, harassed Spanish silver shipments and ports in the Caribbean. In the early seventeenth century, the French, English, and Dutch governments occupied the smaller Caribbean islands not claimed by Spain. Privateer and contraband traders stationed on these islands further damaged Spain's monopoly of shipping between Europe and the Caribbean.

Privateers: Individuals or ships granted permission to attack enemy shipping and to keep a percentage of the prize money the captured ships brought at auction; in practice, privateers were often indistinguishable from pirates.

Conquests of Spanish islands followed in the second half of the century. England captured Jamaica in 1655, and France colonized western Hispaniola (Saint-Domingue) in 1665. Along the Pacific coast, the galleons of the annual Acapulco–Manila fleet were the targets of English privateers. Over the course of the seventeenth century, Spain allocated one-half to two-thirds of its American revenues to the defense of its annual treasure fleets and Caribbean possessions.

Bourbon Reforms After the death of the last, childless Habsburg king of Spain in 1700, the new French-descended dynasty of the Bourbons made major efforts to regain control over their American possessions. Fortunately, population increases among the settlers as well as the Native Americans offered opportunities to Spanish manufacturers and merchants. By the middle of the eighteenth century, the Bourbon reform program began to show results.

The reforms aimed to improve naval connections and administrative control between the mother country and the colonies. The monopolistic annual armed silver fleet was reduced. Instead, the government authorized more frequent single sailings. Newly formed Spanish companies, receiving exclusive rights at specific ports, reduced contraband trade. Elections took place again for municipal councils. Spanish-born salaried officials replaced many Creole tax and office farmers. The original two viceroyalties were subdivided into four, to improve administrative control. The sale of tobacco and brandy became state monopolies. Silver mining and cotton textile manufacturing were expanded. By the second half of the eighteenth century, Spain had regained a measure of control over its colonies.

As a result, government revenues rose substantially. In the end, however, the reforms remained incomplete. Since the Spanish economy was not also reformed, the changes did not much diminish the English and French dominance of the import market. Spain failed to produce goods at competitive prices for the colonies; thus the level of English and French exports to the Americas remained high.

Early Portuguese Colonialism In contrast to the Spanish Americas, the Portuguese overseas province of Brazil developed only slowly during the sixteenth century. The first governor-general arrived in 1549. He and his successors (after 1640 called viceroys, as in the Spanish colonies) were members of the high aristocracy, but their positions were salaried and subject to term limits. As the colony grew, the crown created a council in the capital of Lisbon for all Brazilian appointments and established a high court for all judicial affairs in Bahia in northern Brazil. In the early seventeenth century, offices became as open to purchase as in the Spanish colonies, although not on the city council level, where an electoral process survived.

Jesuits converted the Native Americans, whom they transported to Jesuit-administered villages. Colonial cities and Jesuits repeatedly clashed over the slave raids of the "pioneers" (*bandeirantes*) in village territories. Although the Portuguese crown and church had, like the Spanish, forbidden the enslavement of Native Americans, the *bandeirantes* exploited a loophole. The law was interpreted as allowing the enslavement of Native Americans who resisted conversion to Christianity. For a long time, Lisbon and the Jesuits were powerless against this interpretation.

Expansion into the Interior In the middle of the seventeenth century, the Jesuits and Native Americans pushed many *bandeirantes* west and north, where the latter switched from slave raiding to prospecting for gold. In the far north, however, the raids continued until 1680, when the Portuguese administration finally ended Native American slavery, almost a century and a half after Spain.

As a result of gold discoveries in Minas Gerais in 1690 by *bandeirantes*, the European immigrant population increased rapidly. Brazilians imported slaves from Africa, to work at first in the sugar plantations and, after 1690, in the mines, where their numbers increased to two-thirds of the labor force. The peak of the gold boom came in the 1750s, when the importance of gold was second only to that of sugar among Brazilian exports to Europe.

Early in the gold boom, the crown created the new Ministry of the Navy and Overseas Territories, which greatly expanded the administrative structure in Brazil, and moved the capital from Bahia to Rio de Janeiro in 1736. The ministry in Lisbon ended the sale of offices, increased the efficiency of tax collection, and encouraged Brazilian textile manufacturing to render the province more independent from English imports. By the mid-1700s, Brazil was a flourishing overseas colony of Portugal.

North American Settlements Efforts at settlement in North America in the sixteenth century were unsuccessful. Only in the early part of the seventeenth century did French, English, and Dutch merchant investors succeed in establishing small communities of settlers on the coast: Jamestown (founded in 1607 in today's Virginia), Quebec (1608, Canada), Plymouth and Boston (1620 and 1630, respectively, in today's Massachusetts), and New Amsterdam (1625, today's New York). Subsistence agriculture and fur, however, were not enough for growth. The settlements struggled through the seventeenth century, sustained either by Catholic missionary efforts or by the Puritans who had escaped persecution in England. Southern places like Jamestown survived because they adopted tobacco as a cash crop for export to Europe. In contrast to Mexico and Peru, the North American settlements were not followed—at least, not at first—by territorial conquests (see Map 18.3).

Native Americans European arrivals in North America soon began supplementing agriculture with trade, exchanging metal and glass wares, beads, and seashells for furs with the Native American groups of the interior. As a result, smallpox, already a menace during the 1500s in North America, became devastating as contacts intensified.

The introduction of guns contributed an additional lethal factor to trading arrangements, as traders provided Native American trading partners with flintlocks in order to increase the yield of furs. As a result, during the 1600s the Iroquois in the northeast were able to organize themselves into an armed federation, capable of inflicting heavy losses on rival groups as well as on European traders and settlers.

Mine Workers. The discovery of gold and diamonds in Minas Gerais led to a boom but did little to contribute to the long-term health of the Brazilian economy. With the Native American population decimated by disease, African slaves performed the backbreaking work.

Farther south, in Virginia, the Jamestown settlers encountered the Powhatan confederacy. These Native Americans dominated the region between the Chesapeake Bay and the Appalachian Mountains. Initially, the Powhatan supplied Jamestown with foodstuffs and sought to integrate the settlement into their confederation. When this attempt failed, however, the confederacy raided Jamestown twice. But the settlers defeated the Powhatan in 1646, thereafter

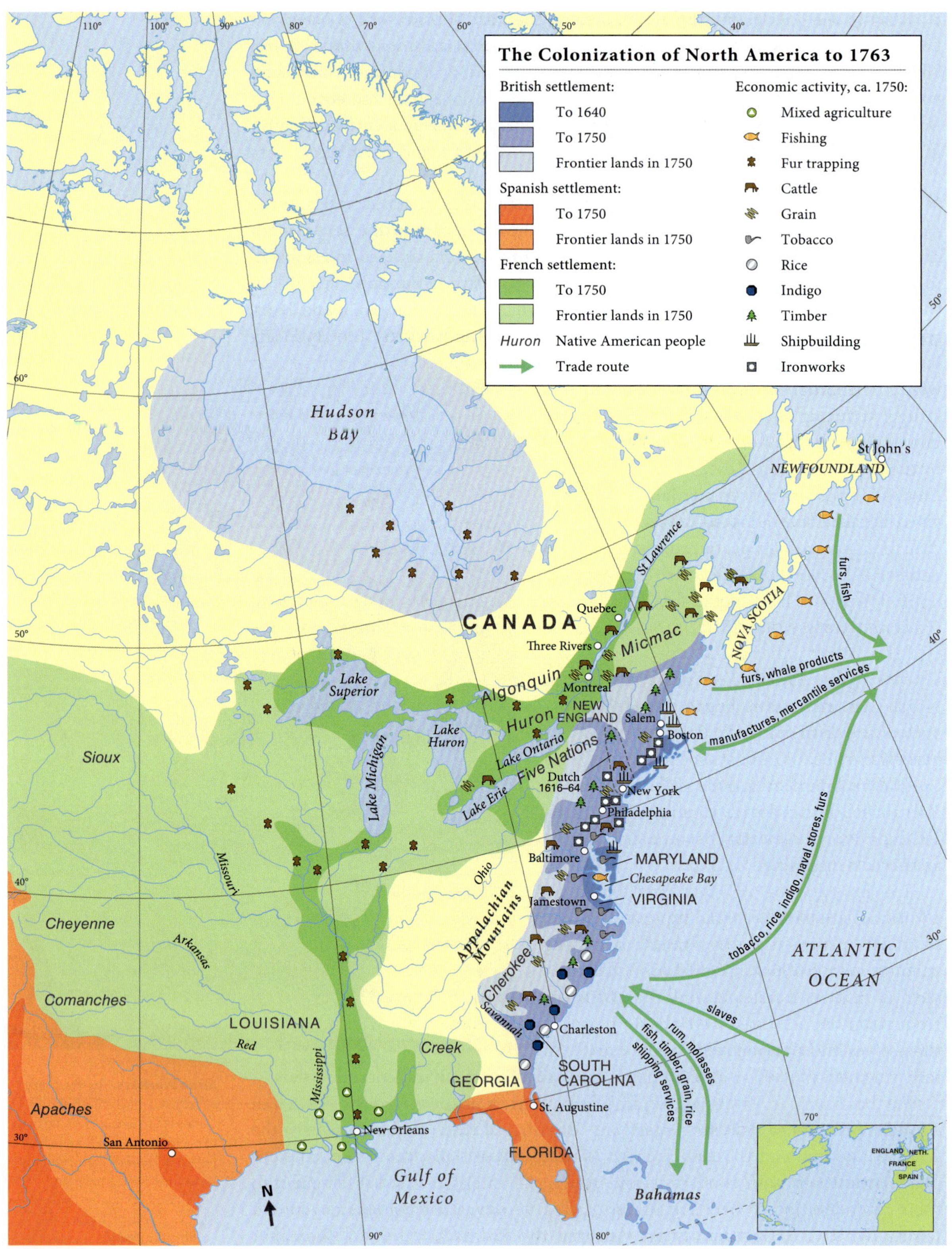

MAP 18.3 The Colonization of North America to 1763

occupying their lands. The decline of the Powhatan in the later 1600s allowed the English settlers of Virginia to move westward, in contrast to the Puritans in New England, where the Iroquois, although allied with the English against the French, blocked any western expansion.

The Iroquois were determined to maintain their dominance of the fur trade, driving smaller Native American groups westward into the Great Lakes region and Mississippi plains, where these groups settled as refugees. French officials and Jesuit missionaries sought to create an alliance with the refugee peoples, to counterbalance the powerful Iroquois to the east. Many Native Americans converted to Christianity, creating a Creole Christianity similar to that of the Africans of Kongo and the Mexicans after the Spanish conquest of the Aztecs.

Major population movements also occurred further west on the Great Plains, where the Apaches arrived from the Great Basin in the Rockies. They had captured horses that had escaped during the Pueblo uprising of 1680–1695 against Spain. The Comanches, who arrived from the west on horses at the same time, had, in addition, acquired firearms and around 1725 began their expansion at the expense of the Apaches. The Sioux from the northern forests and the Cheyenne from the Great Basin added to the mix of federations on the Great Plains in the early 1700s. Smallpox epidemics did not reach the Plains until the mid-1700s, while in the east the ravages of this epidemic had weakened the Iroquois so much that they concluded a peace with the French in 1701.

French Canada The involvement of the French in the Great Lakes region with refugees fleeing from the Iroquois was part of a program of expansion into the center of North America, begun in 1663. The governor of Quebec had dispatched explorers, fur traders, and missionaries into the Great Lakes region and the Mississippi valley. The French government then sent farmers, craftspeople, and single women from France to establish settlements. The most successful settlement, called *la Louisiane*" (Louisiana in English, after which the later state was named) in honor of Louis XIV, was at the mouth of the Mississippi, where settlers with African slaves founded sugar plantations. Because immigration was restricted to French subjects and excluded Protestants, Louisiana had far fewer settlers than English North America.

Colonial Assemblies As immigration to New England picked up, the merchant companies in Europe, which had financed the journeys of the settlers, were initially responsible for the administration of settlement colonies. The first settlers to demand participation in the colonial administration were Virginian tobacco growers, who in 1619 created an early popular assembly. The other English colonies soon followed suit, creating their own assemblies. In contrast to Spain and Portugal, England was initially uninvolved in the governance of the overseas territories.

When England eventually took the governance of the colonies away from the charter merchants and companies in the second half of the seventeenth century, it faced entrenched settler assemblies. Many governors were deputies of aristocrats who never traveled to America. These governors were powerless to prevent the assemblies from appropriating rights to levy taxes and making appointments. The assemblies thus modeled themselves after Parliament in London. As in England,

Patterns Up Close

The Columbian Exchange

Few of us can imagine an Italian kitchen without tomatoes or an Irish meal without potatoes or Chinese or Indian cuisine without chilies, but until fairly recently each of these foods was unknown to the Old World. Likewise, for millennia apples, as well as many other common fruits, were absent from the New World. It was not until the sixteenth century that new patterns of ecology and biology changed the course of millions of years of divergent evolution.

When considering the long list of life forms that moved across the oceans in the Columbian Exchange, the impact of European weeds and grasses on American grasslands, which made it possible for the North American prairie and the South American pampas to support livestock, should not be overlooked. By binding the soil together with their long, tough roots, the "empire of the dandelion" provided the conditions for the grazing of sheep, cattle, and horses, as well as the planting of crops like wheat.

The other silent invader that accompanied the conquistadors was disease. Thousands of years of mutual isolation between the Americas and Afro-Eurasia rendered the immune systems of Native Americans vulnerable to the scourges that European colonists unwittingly brought with them. By some estimates, the native populations of Mesoamerica and the Andes plummeted by 90 percent in the period 1500–1700. In comparison, the contagions the New World reciprocated upon the Old World—syphilis and tuberculosis—did not unleash nearly the same devastation, and the New World origin of these diseases is still debated.

Therefore, the big winner in the Columbian Exchange was western Europe, though the effects of the New World bounty took centuries to be fully discerned. While Asia and Africa also benefited from the Columbian Exchange, the Europeans got a continent endowed with a warm climate in which they could create new and improved versions of their homelands. The Native Americans were nearly wiped out by disease, their lands appropriated, and the survivors either enslaved or marginalized. The precipitous drop in the population of Native Americans, combined with the tropical and semitropical climate of much of the Americas, created the necessary

these assemblies excluded poorer settlers who did not meet the property requirements to vote or stand for elections.

Territorial Expansion Steady immigration encouraged land speculators in the British colonies to cast their sights beyond the Appalachian Mountains. In 1749, the Ohio Company of Virginia received a royal permit to develop land, together with a protective fort, south of the Ohio River. The French, however, also claimed the Ohio valley. Tensions over the valley soon erupted into open hostility. Initially, the local encounters went badly for the Virginian militia and British army. In 1755, he British and French broadened their clash into a worldwide war for dominance in the colonies and Europe, the Seven Years' War of 1756–1763.

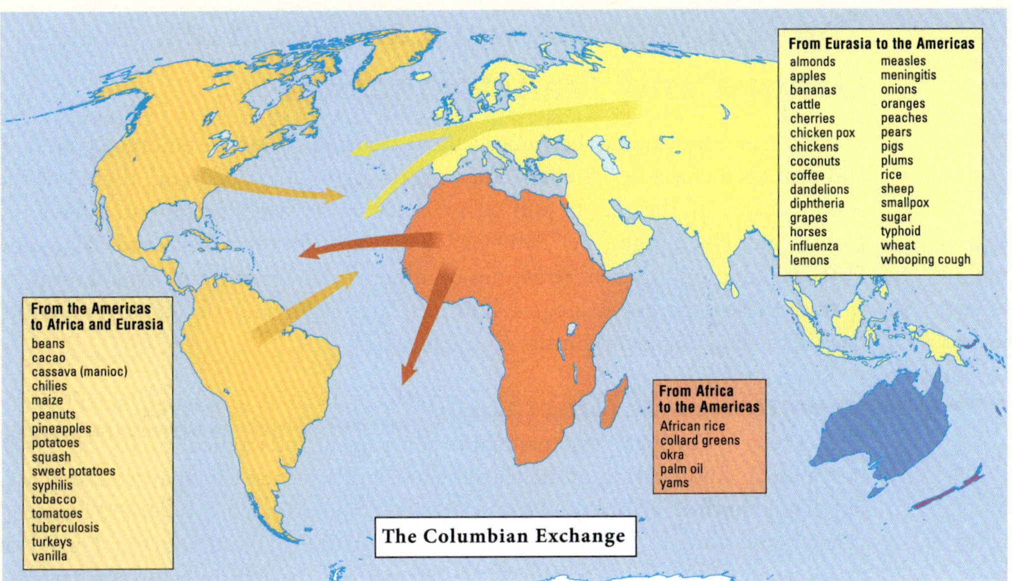

MAP 18.4 The Columbian Exchange

conditions for the Atlantic slave trade. The population losses from this trade were monumental.

Questions

- Can the Columbian Exchange be considered one of the origins of the modern world? How? Why? How does the Columbian Exchange demonstrate the origins, interactions, and adaptations model that is used throughout this book?
- Weigh the positive and negative outcomes of the Columbian Exchange. Is it possible to determine whether the overall effects of the Columbian Exchange on human society and the natural environment were for the better or for the worse?

The Seven Years' War Both France and Great Britain borrowed heavily to finance the war. England had the superior navy and France the superior army. Since the British navy succeeded in choking off French supplies to its increasingly isolated land troops, Britain won the war overseas. In Europe, Britain's failure to supply the troops of its ally Prussia against the Austrian–French alliance caused the war on that front to end in a draw. Overseas, the British gained most of the French holdings in India, several islands in the Caribbean, all of Canada, and all the land east of the Mississippi. The costs, however, proved to be unmanageable for all concerned. The unpaid debts became the root cause of the American, French, and Haitian constitutional revolutions that began 13 years later.

The Making of American Societies: Origins and Transformations

Columbian Exchange: Exchange of plants, animals, and diseases between the Americas and the rest of the world.

The patterns which made the Americas an extension of Europe emerged gradually and displayed characteristics specific to each region. On one hand, there was the slow transfer of the plants and animals native to each continent, called the **Columbian Exchange** (see "Patterns Up Close"). On the other hand, Spain and Portugal adopted different strategies of mineral and agricultural exploitation. In spite of these different strategies, however, the settler societies of the two countries in the end displayed similar characteristics.

Exploitation of Mineral and Tropical Resources

The pattern of European expansion into subtropical and tropical lands began with the Spanish colonization of the Caribbean islands. When the Spanish crown ran out of gold in the Caribbean, it exported silver from Mexico and Peru to finance a centralizing state. By contrast, Portugal's colony of Brazil did not at first mine for precious metals, and consequently the Portuguese crown pioneered the growing of sugar on plantations. The North American colonies of England and France had, in comparison, little native industry at first. When they moved farther south, however, they adopted the plantation system for indigo and rice.

Silver Mines

Two main mining centers emerged in the Spanish colonies: Potosí in southeastern Peru (today Bolivia) and Zacatecas and Guanajuato in northern Mexico. During the eighteenth century, gold mining in Colombia and Chile rose to importance as well.

Innovations such as the "patio" method (named for the enclosure where the process was carried out), which facilitated the extraction of silver through the use of mercury, and the unrestrained exploitation of indigenous labor made American silver highly competitive in the world market. Conditions among the Native Americans and blacks employed as labor were abominable. Few laborers lasted through more than two forced recruitment (*repartimiento*) cycles before they were incapacitated or dead.

Since the exploitation of the mines was of central importance, for the first century and a half of New World colonization, the Spanish crown organized its other provinces around the needs of the mining centers. The main function of Hispaniola and Cuba in the Caribbean was to feed and protect Havana, the collection point for Mexican and Peruvian silver and the port from where the annual Spanish fleet shipped the American silver across the Atlantic.

A second region, Argentina and Paraguay, was colonized as a bulwark to prevent the Portuguese and Dutch from accessing Peruvian silver. Once established, the two colonies produced goods and foodstuffs to supply the miners in Potosí.

A third colonial region, Venezuela, began as a grain and cattle supply base for Cartagena, the port for the shipment of Colombian gold, and Panama City (on the south coast of Panama) and Portobelo (on the north coast), ports for the transshipment of Peruvian silver from the Pacific to Havana. Thus, three major regions of the Spanish overseas empire in the Americas were mostly peripheral as agricultural producers during the sixteenth century. Only after the middle of the century did they begin to specialize in tropical agricultural goods, and they were exporters only in the eighteenth century.

Wheat Farming and Cattle Ranching To support the mining centers and administrative cities, the Spanish colonial government encouraged the development of agricultural estates (*haciendas*). Native American tenant farmers were forced to grow wheat and raise livestock for the conquerors, who were now agricultural entrepreneurs. In the latter part of the sixteenth century, the land grants gave way to rotating forced labor as well as wage labor. A landowner class emerged.

Like the conquistadors before, a majority of landowners produced wheat and animals for sale to urban and mining centers. As the Native American population declined in the seventeenth century and the church helped in consolidating the remaining population in large villages, additional land became available for the establishment of estates. From 1631 onward, authorities granted Spanish settler families the right to maintain their estates undivided from generation to generation. Secular and clerical landowning interests supported a powerful upper social stratum of Creoles from the eighteenth century onward.

Plantations and Gold Mining in Brazil Brazil's economic activities began with brazilwood, followed by sugar plantations, before gold mining rose to prominence in the eighteenth century.

These gold-mining operations were less capital-intensive than the silver mines in Spanish America. Most miners were relatively small operators with a few black slaves as unskilled laborers. Many entrepreneurs were indebted for their slaves to absentee capitalists, with whom they shared the profits. Since prospecting took place on the land of Native Americans, bloody encounters were frequent. Brazil's gold production was a welcome bonanza for Portugal at a time of low agricultural prices.

The Silver Mountain of Potosí. Note the patios in the left foreground and the water-driven crushing mill in the center, which ground the silver-bearing ore into a fine sand that then was moistened, caked, amalgamated with mercury, and dried on the patio. The mine workers' insect-like shapes reinforce the dehumanizing effects of their labor.

Plantations in Spanish and English America The expansion of plantation farming in the Spanish colonies was a result of the Bourbon reforms. Although sugar, tobacco, and rice had been introduced early into the Caribbean and southern Mexico, it was only in the plantation system of the eighteenth century that these and other crops were produced for export to Europe. The owners of plantations invested in African slave labor, with the result that the slave trade hit full stride beginning around 1750.

English northeast American settlements in Virginia and Carolina exported tobacco and rice beginning in the 1660s. Georgia joined southern Carolina as a major plantation colony in 1750. In the eighteenth century, New England exported timber for shipbuilding and charcoal production in Great Britain. These timber exports illustrate the importance of the Americas as a replacement for dwindling fuel resources across much of northern Europe. Altogether, it was thanks to the Americas that mostly cold and rainy Europe rose into the ranks of the wealthy Indian and Chinese empires.

Social Strata, Castes, and Ethnic Groups

Given the small settler population of the Americas, the temptation to develop a system of forced labor in agriculture and mining was irresistible. Since the Native Americans and African slaves pressed into labor were ethnically so different from the Europeans, however, a social system evolved in which the latter two not only were economically underprivileged but also made up the ethnically nonintegrated lowest rungs of the social ladder. A pattern of legal and customary discrimination evolved which prevented the integration of American ethnicities into settler society.

The Social Elite The heirs of the Spanish conquistadors and estate owners maintained city residences and employed managers on their agricultural properties. In Brazil, cities emerged more slowly. During the seventeenth century, estate owners intermarried with the Madrid- and Lisbon-appointed administrators, creating the top tier of settler society known as Creoles. They formed a relatively closed society in which descent, intermarriage, landed property, and a government position counted more than money and education.

In the seventeenth and eighteenth centuries, the estate owners farmed predominantly with Native American forced labor. In contrast to the black slave plantation estates of the Caribbean and coastal regions of Spanish and Portuguese America, these farming estates did not export their goods to Europe.

As local producers with little competition, farming and ranching estate owners did not feel market pressures. They exploited their estates with minimal investments and usually drew profits of less than 5 percent of annual revenues. As a result, they were often heavily indebted.

Lower Creoles The second tier of Creole society consisted of privileged European settlers who, as craftspeople and traders, theoretically worked with their hands. In practice, many of them were owner-operators who employed Native Americans and/or black slaves. Many strove to rise into the ranks of the landowning Creoles.

Wealthy weavers ran textile manufactures mostly concentrated in the cities of Mexico, Peru, Paraguay, and Argentina. On a smaller scale, manufactures also existed for pottery and leather goods. On the whole, the urban manufacturing activities of the popular people, serving the poor in local markets, remained vibrant until well into the nineteenth century, in spite of massive European imports. Prior to the arrival of railroads, the transportation of imports into the interior of the Americas was prohibitively expensive.

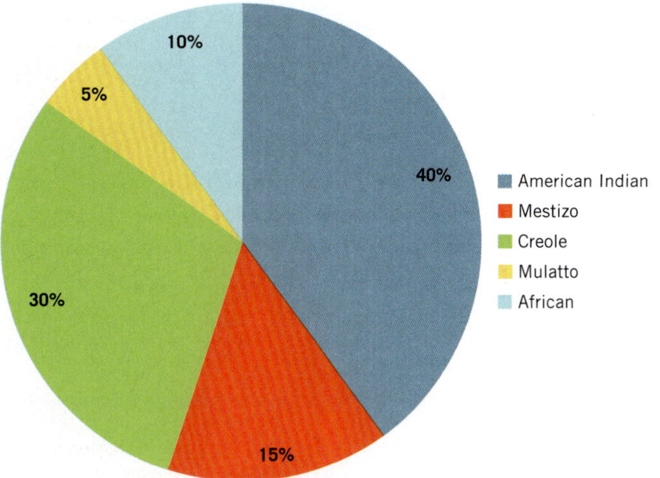

Figure 18.1 Ethnic Composition of Latin America, ca. 1800

Mestizos and Mulattoes The mixed European–Native American and European–African population had the collective name of "caste" (*casta*), something like an ethnic group. The two most important castes were the *mestizos* (Spanish), or *mestiços* (Portuguese), who had Iberian fathers and Native American mothers, and *mulatos*, who had Iberian fathers and black mothers. By 1800 the *castas* as a whole formed the third largest population category in Latin America. In both Spanish and Portuguese America, there were also a small percentage of people descended from Native American and black unions. These intermediate population groups played important neutralizing roles in colonial society, as they had one foot in both the Creole and subordinate social strata (see Figure 18.1).

Mestizos and **mulattoes** filled the lower levels of the bureaucracy and the lay hierarchy in the church. They held skilled and supervisory positions in mines and on estates. In addition, in the armed forces mulattoes dominated the ranks of enlisted men; in the defense militias, they even held officer ranks. In Brazil, many mulattoes and black freedmen were farmers. Much of the craft production was in their hands. Many laws kept mestizos and mulattoes in their intermediate social and political positions.

Mestizo: The offspring of a Spanish or Portuguese father and a Native American mother.

Mulatto: The offspring of a Spanish or Portuguese father and an African mother.

Women The roles played by women depended on their social position. Elite Creole households followed the Mediterranean tradition of secluding women from men. Within the household, Creole women were the owners of substantial dowries and legally stipulated grooms' gifts. Often, they actively managed the investment of their assets. Outside the household, however, even elite women lost all protection. Husbands and fathers could banish daughters or wives to convents for alleged lapses in chastity, or even kill them without punishment. Thus, even elite women were bound by limits set by a patriarchal society.

On the lower rungs of society, gender separation was much less prevalent. Men, women, and children shared labor in the fields and workshops. Girls or wives took in clothes to wash or went out to work as domestics in wealthy households. Older women dominated retail in market stalls. Working families with few assets suffered abandonment by males. Women headed one-third of all households in Mexico City, according to an 1811 census. Among black slaves in the region of São Paulo, 70 percent of women were without formal ties to the men who fathered their children. The most pronounced division in colonial society was that of a patriarchy among the Creoles and a slave society dominated by women, with frequently absent men.

Amerindians (Native Americans) In the immediate aftermath of the conquest, Amerindians could be found at all social levels. Social distinctions, however, disappeared during the first 150 years of Spanish colonialism as disease

Illustration from an Indian Land Record. The Spaniards almost completely wiped out the Aztec archives after the conquest of Mexico; surviving examples of Indian manuscripts are thus extremely rare. Although the example shown here, made from the bark of a fig tree, claims to date from the early 1500s, it is part of the so-called Techialoyan land records created in the seventeenth century to substantiate native land claims. These "*títulos primordiales*," as they were called, were essentially municipal histories that documented in text and pictures local accounts of important events and territorial boundaries.

reduced the Amerindian population by nearly 80 percent. It was only in the twentieth century that population figures reached the preconquest level again in most parts of Latin America.

Apart from European diseases, the Amerindians in the Amazon, Orinoco, and Maracaibo rain forests were the least affected by European colonials during the period 1500–1800. Not only were their lands economically the least promising, but they also defended those lands successfully. In many arid or semiarid regions, such as Patagonia, southern Chile, the Argentine grasslands (pampas), the Paraguayan salt marshes and deserts, and northern Mexican mountains and steppes, the seminomadic Amerindians quickly adopted the European horse and became highly mobile warrior peoples in defense of their mostly independent territories.

The villagers of Mexico, Yucatán, Guatemala, Colombia, Ecuador, and Peru had fewer choices. When smallpox reduced their numbers in the second half of the sixteenth century, authorities razed villages and concentrated the survivors in *pueblos de indios*. Initially, the Amerindians put up strong resistance against these resettlements. From the middle of the seventeenth century, however, the pueblos were self-administering units, with councils (*cabildos*), churches, schools, communal lands, and family parcels.

The councils were important institutions of legal training and social mobility for Amerindians. Initially, the traditional "noble" chiefly families descending from the preconquest Aztec and Inca ruling classes were in control as administrators. The many village functions, however, for which the *cabildos* were responsible allowed commoners to move up into auxiliary roles.

Amerindian villages were closed to settlers, and the only outsiders admitted were Catholic priests. Contact with the Spanish world remained minimal, and acculturation went little beyond official conversion to Catholicism. Thus, even in the heartlands of Spanish America, Amerindian adaptation to the rulers remained limited.

Unfortunately, however, tremendous demographic losses made the Amerindians in the pueblos vulnerable to the loss of their land. Estate owners expanded their holdings, and when the population rebounded, many estates had grown to immense sizes. Villages began to run out of land for their inhabitants. Increasing numbers of Amerindians had to rent land from estate owners or find work on estates as farmhands. They became estranged from their villages, fell into debt peonage, and entered the ranks of the working poor.

New England Society In the early modern period, the small family farm remained the norm for the majority of New England's population. An acute lack of money and cheap means of transportation hampered the development of market networks in the interior well into the 1770s. The situation was better in the agriculturally more favored colonies in the Mid-Atlantic, especially in Pennsylvania. The number of plantations in the south rose steadily, demanding a substantial increase in numbers of slaves, although world market fluctuations left planters vulnerable. Except for boom periods in the plantation sector, the rural areas remained largely poor.

Real changes occurred during the early eighteenth century in the urban regions of New England. Large port cities emerged which shipped in goods from Europe in return for timber. A wealthy merchant class formed, spawning urban strata of professionals. Primary school education was provided by municipal public schools as well as by some churches, and evening schools for craftspeople also existed. By the middle of the eighteenth century, a majority of men could read and write. Finally, in contrast to Latin America, social ranks in New England were less elaborate.

The Adaptation of the Americas to European Culture

European settlers brought two distinct cultures to the Americas. In the Mid-Atlantic, the Caribbean, and Central and South America, they brought with them the Catholic Reformation, a culture that resisted the New Science and the Enlightenment until the late eighteenth century. In the northeast, colonists implanted dissident Protestantism as well as the Anglicanism of Great Britain and the Presbyterianism of Scotland.

Catholic Missionary Work Spanish and Portuguese monarchs relied on the Catholic Church for their rule in the new American provinces. A strong motive driving many in the church and society was the belief in the imminent Second Coming of Jesus. This belief was one inspiration for the original Atlantic expansion (see Chapter 16). When the Aztec and Inca Empires fell, members of the Franciscan order, the main proponents of the belief in the imminence of the Second Coming, interpreted it as a sign of the urgent duty to convert the Amerindians to Christianity.

Spanish Cruelty to Incas. Felipe Guamán Poma de Ayala, a Peruvian claiming noble Inca descent, was a colonial administrator, well educated and an ardent Christian. He is remembered today as a biting critic of the colonial administration and the clergy, whom he accused of mistreating and exploiting the Andean population, as in this colored woodcut print.

Thousands of preaching monks, later followed by the Jesuits, fanned out among the Amerindians. They baptized them, introduced the sacraments, and taught them basic theological concepts. The missionaries learned native languages, translated the catechism and New Testament into those languages, and taught the children of the ruling native families how to read and write.

The role and function of saints formed one element of Catholic Christianity to which Amerindians acculturated early. Good works as God-pleasing human efforts to gain salvation in the afterlife formed another. The veneration of images of the Virgin Mary and pilgrimages to the chapels and churches where they were kept constituted a third element. On the other hand, the Spanish Inquisition also operated in the Spanish and Portuguese colonies, seeking to limit the degree to which Catholicism and traditional religion mingled.

Education and the Arts The Catholic Reformation also influenced the organization of education. The Franciscans and Dominicans had offered education to the children of settlers early on and, in colleges, trained graduates for missionary work. New World universities taught theology, church law, and Native American languages. Under the impact of the Jesuits, universities broadened the curriculum. Although the universities did not teach the New Sciences and Enlightenment of northwestern Europe, there was nevertheless scientific research on tropical diseases, plants, and animals. The extent of this research was long kept secret by the Spanish and Portuguese monarchs from their European competitors.

Furthermore, missionary monks collected and recorded Native American manuscripts and oral traditions, such as the Aztec *Anales de Tula* and the Maya *Popol Vuh*. Others wrote histories and ethnographies of the indigenous peoples.

A number of Amerindian and mestizo chroniclers, historians, and commentators on the early modern state and society are similarly noteworthy. Felipe Guamán Poma de Ayala (ca. 1535–1616), a native Peruvian, is of particular interest. He accompanied his 800-page manuscript, entitled (in English translation) *The First New Chronicle and Good Government*, with some 400 drawings of daily-life activities in the Peruvian villages. Unfortunately, King Philip II of Spain forbade in 1577 the publication of all manuscripts dealing with what he called idolatry and superstition. Many manuscripts lay hidden in archives until modern times.

Protestantism in New England Religious diversity was a defining cultural trait of English settlements in North America. The spectrum of Christian denominations ranged from English and continental European versions of Protestantism to Anglicanism and a minority of Catholics. Dissenters frequently split from the existing denominations, moved into new territory, and founded new settlements.

An early example of religious splintering was the rise of an antinomian ("opposed to the law") group within Puritan-dominated Massachusetts. The preachers and settlers represented in the General Court, as their assembly was called, were committed to the Calvinist balance between "inner" personal grace obtained from God and "outer" works according to the moral law mandated by the Ten Commandments. The antinomian (or Free Grace) group, however, advocated an exclusive commitment to inner grace through spiritual perfection.

Their leader was Anne Hutchinson, an early proponent of women's rights and an inspiring preacher. She was accused of arguing that she could recognize those believers in Calvinist Protestantism who were predestined for salvation and that these believers would be saved even if they had sinned. After a power struggle, the General Court prevailed and forced the antinomians to move to Rhode Island in 1638.

Witch Trial. In the course of the 1600s, in the relatively autonomous English colonies of Northeast America, more persons were accused, tried, and convicted of witchcraft than anywhere else. Of the 140 persons coming to trial between 1620 and 1725, 86 percent were women. Three witch panics are recorded: Bermuda, 1651; Hartford, Connecticut, 1652–1665; and Salem, Massachusetts, 1692–1693. This anonymous American woodcut of the early 1600s shows one method used to try someone for witchcraft: The accused would swim or float, if guilty—or sink, if innocent.

The example of Hutchinson is noteworthy in part because it led to the founding of Harvard College in 1636 by the General Court as an institution combating antinomianism. Harvard was the first institution of higher learning in North America.

New Sciences Research As discussed in Chapter 17, the New Sciences had their most hospitable home in northwestern Europe, where the rivalry between Protestantism and Catholicism had left enough of an authority-free space for the New Sciences to flourish. Under similar circumstances—intense rivalry among denominations—English North America also proved hospitable to the New Sciences. An early practitioner was Benjamin Franklin (1706–1790), who began his career as a printer, journalist, and newspaper editor. Franklin founded the University of Pennsylvania (1740), the first secular university in North America, and the American Philosophical Society (1743), the first scientific society. This hospitality for the New Sciences in North America was in contrast to Latin America, where a uniform Catholic Reformation prevented its rise.

Witch Hunts In the last decade of the seventeenth century, religious intensity was at the root of a witchcraft frenzy that seized New England. Witches, male and female, were believed to be persons exerting a negative influence, or black magic, on their victims. In medieval Europe, the church had kept witchcraft hidden, but in the wake of challenges to church authority, it had become more visible. In the North American colonies, with no overarching religious authority, the visibility of witchcraft was particularly high.

This sensitivity erupted into hysteria in Salem, Massachusetts, in 1692. Tituba, a Native American slave from Barbados, worked in the household of a pastor. She practiced voodoo, the West African–originated, part-African and part-Christian religious practice of influencing others. When young girls in the pastor's household suffered from convulsions, mass hysteria broke out, in which 14 women and five men accused of being witches or accomplices were executed. (Tituba, ironically, survived.) A new governor finally restored order.

Revivalism Religious fervor expressed itself also in periodic Protestant renewal movements, such as the "Great Awakening" of the 1730s and 1740s. The main impulse for this revivalist movement came from the brothers John and Charles Wesley, two Methodist preachers in England who toured Georgia in 1735, and their friend George Whitefield (WHIT-field), who traveled to North America in 1739 and preached a series of sensational and popular revival sermons. Preachers from other denominations joined, all exhorting Protestants to literally "start anew" in their relationship with God. Thus, revivalism, recurring with great regularity to the present, became a potent force in Protestant America, at opposing purposes with secular founding-father constitutionalism.

Putting It All Together

During the period 1500–1800, the contours of a new pattern in which the Americas formed a resource-rich extension of Europe took shape. During this time, China and India continued to be the most populous and wealthiest agrarian–urban regions of the world. In 1500, Europe was struggling to defend itself against the push of the Ottoman Empire into eastern Europe and the western Mediterranean. But its successful conquest of Iberia from the Muslims led to the discovery of the Americas. Possession of the Americas made Europe similar to China and India in that it now encompassed, in addition to its northerly cold climates, subtropical and tropical regions that produced cash crops as well as precious metals. Over the next 300 years, Europe narrowed the gap between itself and China and India.

However, because of fierce competition both with the Ottoman Empire and internally, much of the wealth Europe gained in the Americas was wasted on warfare. The centralizing state, created in part to support war, ran into insurmountable budgetary barriers. Even mercantilism, a logical extension of the centralizing state, had limited effects. Its centerpiece, state support for the export of manufactures to the American colonies, functioned unevenly. The Spanish and Portuguese governments, with weak urban infrastructures and low manufacturing capabilities, were unable to enforce this state-supported trade until the eighteenth century and even then only in very limited ways. France and England practiced mercantilism more successfully but were able to do so in the Americas only from the late seventeenth century onward, when their plantation systems began to take shape. Although the American extension of Europe had the potential of making Europe self-sufficient, this potential was realized only partially during the colonial period.

Debate continues over the question of the degree of wealth the Americas added to Europe. On one hand, research has established that the British slave trade for sugar plantations added at best 1 percent to the British gross domestic product (GDP). The profits from the production of sugar on the English island of Jamaica may have added another 4 percent to the British GDP. Without doubt, private slave-trading and sugar-producing enterprises were immensely profitable to individuals and groups. However, these profits were smaller if one takes into account the immense waste of revenues on military ventures—hence the doubts raised by scholars today about large gains made by Europe through its American colonial acquisitions.

On the other hand, the European extension to the Americas was clearly a momentous event in world history. It might have produced dubious overall profits for Europe, but it definitely encouraged the parting of ways between Europe on one hand and Asia and Africa on the other, once a new scientific–industrial society began to emerge around 1800.

Review and Relate

Thinking Through Patterns

Examine the ways historians approach the big questions of this chapter.

What is the significance of western Europeans acquiring the Americas as a warm-weather extension of their northern continent?

In their role as subtropical and tropical extensions of Europe, the Americas had a considerable impact on Europe's changing position in the world. First, Europe acquired large quantities of precious metals, which its two largest competitors, India and China, lacked. Second, with its new access to warm-weather agricultural products, Europe rose to a position of agrarian autonomy similar to that of India and China. In terms of resources, compared with the principal religious civilizations of India and China, Europe grew between 1550 and 1800 from a position of inferiority to one of near parity.

What was the main pattern of social development in colonial America during the period 1500–1800?

Because the numbers of Europeans who emigrated to the Americas was low for most of the colonial period, they never exceeded the numbers of Native Americans or African slaves. The result was a privileged settler society that held superior positions on the top rung of the social hierarchy. In principle, given an initially large indigenous population, labor was cheap but should have become more expensive as diseases reduced the Native Americans. In fact, labor always remained cheap, in part because of forced labor and in part because of racial prejudice.

Why and how did European settlers in South and North America strive for self-government, and how successful were they in achieving their goals?

Two contrasting patterns characterized the way in which European colonies were governed. The Spanish and Portuguese crowns, interested in extracting minerals and warm-weather products from the colonies, were motivated to exercise centralized control over their possessions in the Americas. In contrast, the British crown granted self-government to the Northeast American colonies from the start, in part because the colonies were far less important economically and in part because of a long tradition of self-rule at home. Nevertheless, even though Latin American settlers achieved only partial self-rule in their towns and cities, they destroyed central rule indirectly through the purchase of offices. After financial reforms, Spain and Portugal reestablished a degree of central rule through the appointment of officers from the home countries.

Against the Grain

Consider this as a counterpoint to the main patterns examined in this chapter.

Juana Inés de la Cruz

- Why were the Latin American colonies more socially conservative than Europe?
- Was de la Cruz right to stop her correspondence with the Mexican clergy in 1693?

In the wake of the Protestant and Catholic Reformations of the 1500s, it was no longer unusual for European women to pursue higher education. In the more conservative Latin American colonies of Spain, Juana Inés de la Cruz (1651–1695) was less fortunate, even though her fame as the intellectually most brilliant figure of the seventeenth century in the colonies endured.

De la Cruz was the illegitimate child of a Spanish immigrant father and a Creole mother. She grew up on the hacienda of her maternal grandfather, in whose library she secretly studied Latin, Greek, and Nahuatl, and also composed her first poems. Unable, as a woman, to be admitted to the university in Mexico City, de la Cruz was fortunate to receive further education from the wife of the vice regent of New Spain. In order to continue her studies, she entered a convent in 1668. Here, she continued to study and write hundreds of poems, comedies, religious dramas, and theological texts. Her seminars with courtiers and scholarly visitors were a major attraction.

In 1688, however, she lost her protection at court with the departure of her vice regal supporters for Spain. Her superior, the archbishop of Mexico, was an open misogynist. A crisis came in 1690 when the bishop of Puebla published de la Cruz's critique of a famous sermon of 1650 by the Portuguese Jesuit António Vieira on Jesus's act of washing his disciples' feet, together with his own critique of de la Cruz. De la Cruz viewed Vieira's interpretation as more hierarchical/male and her own interpretation as humbler/female.

A year later, in 1691, de la Cruz wrote a spirited riposte to the bishop's apparently well-meaning advice to her in his critique to be more conscious of her status as a woman. Her message was clear: even though women had to be silent in church, as St. Paul had taught, neither study nor writing was prohibited for women. Before the church could censor her, in 1693 Juana Inés de la Cruz stopped writing. She died two years later.

Key Terms

Columbian Exchange 438
Creoles 428
Labor assignment (*repartimiento*) 429
Land-labor grant (*encomienda*) 424
Mestizo 441
Mulatto 441
Privateers 431

Learn more with this chapter's digital tools, including the Oxford Insight Study Guide, at http://www.oup.com/he/vonsivers4e. Please see the Further Resources section at the back of the book for additional readings and suggested websites.

PATTERNS OF EVIDENCE | Sources for Chapter 18

SOURCE 18.1 Scandal at the church: José de Álfaro accuses Doña Theresa Bravo and others of insulting and beating his castiza wife, Joséfa Cadena

1782

In all agrarian–urban societies, honor codes of varying degrees of severity regulated social relations. Precolonial Latin America was no different; with the Creoles at the top of the social hierarchy, this code demanded severe retribution against anyone besmirching the honor of its members, but members of lower-level strata were no less vigilant in the protection of their members. What happened when the honor codes of people from different social strata clashed? The following court case occurred in a Mexican city in 1782. Unfortunately, no settlement of the case is recorded.

The Court Case

17.1 Alcalde Mayor Don Thomás Velasco Receives the Criminal Complaint
Criminal proceedings as a result of the denunciation by José de Álfaro against doña Teresa Bravo, her daughter Teresa, and her sisters Francisca, as well as a woman deposited in their home, and don Diego Fernández, the husband of doña Teresa, for the mistreatment of his wife, Joséfa Cadena. All are *vecinos* [residents] of this town. The presiding judge in this jurisdiction is don Thomas de Velasco, alcalde mayor and commissioner. . .

In the town and *cabecera* [municipality] of San Juan Teotihuacán, on October 16, 1782, before me, Captain don Tomás de Velasco, *alcalde mayor* [regional magistrate] of this jurisdiction for His Majesty, may God protect him, this petition and its contents are presented, in the presence of witnesses and in the absence of a notary.

17.2 The Petition and Criminal Complaint of José de Álfaro
I, José de Álfaro, resident of this town . . . say that on Sunday the thirteenth of this month, my wife, Joséfa Cadena, was coming [out of church] after mass and

Source: Excerpted and adapted from Sonya Lipsett Rivera, "Scandal at the Church: José de Álfaro Accuses Doña Theresa Bravo and Others of Insulting and Beating His Castiza Wife, Joséfa Cadena (Mexico, 1782)," in Richard Boyer and Geoffrey Spurling, eds., *Colonial Lives: Documents in Latin American History, 1550–1850* (Oxford and New York: Oxford University Press, 2000), 216–223, http://chnm.gmu.edu/wwh/p/232.html

passed close to doña Teresa Bravo, the wife of don Diego Fernández, *cobrador de las rentas de alcabalas y pulques* [official in charge of the collection of sales taxes and taxes on pulque]. Doña Teresa, using the pretext that my wife had brushed against her, which was not true, sprung forward, saying to her, "Oh, you black whore, you dare to brush against me." And throwing her to the ground, not only doña Teresa, but also her daughter, her sister, and the woman who was deposited with them and was in their company, hit her [Joséfa] many times. Although don Diego was present, instead of trying to calm them, he said, "Give it to that black whore again." In this way, my wife came out of this attack with marks on her face and a big scratch. She has bruises all over her body because of the beating, and since she is pregnant and now she is bleeding, we are worried about the unfortunate consequences of this encounter and that she might lose not only the baby's life but her own.

In the above related events, doña Teresa and her husband, as well as the other accomplices, insulted my wife and me in a very grave manner, and in all the ways imaginable. To a married woman, no insult is greater than to call her a black whore, since this offends her fidelity and her *calidad* [here: race]. Her honor is publicly known, and she is not a black but rather a *castiza* [three-quarters white, one-quarter Amerindian]. In regards to actions, none is worse than to have hit her all over her body and to have marked her face. What makes all this much worse is that the insults occurred in public and in the presence of a numerous crowd who were leaving mass. Don Diego is a participant in this crime, not only because he did not prevent it as he should have and as would have been easy for him due to the power vested in him as a husband, but also because he encouraged his wife and the others who insulted my wife, to consummate the humiliation. . .

[José de Álfaro] does not know how to sign.

Signed by Licentiate Manuel Cordero

17. 3 [The Alcalde Mayor orders that information on the petition be collected and that two surgeons examine Joséfa Cadena.] *17.4–17. 5* [Two surgeons examined Joséfa Cadena and testified that she had a scar running from her right eyebrow to her hairline apparently caused by fingernails, and while six months' pregnant had suffered injuries to her hips, thighs, and groin and had been hemorrhaging through her vagina since the previous Sunday and so was at risk of miscarriage]. *17.6 [The Alcalde Mayor Orders José de Álfaro to Present His Witnesses.]*

17.7 Testimony of Don Manuel Delfin

On October 18, 1782 . . . José de Álfaro presented as a witness a man from whom I took the oath that he made to God and the holy cross in accordance with the law. He said that his name is Manuel Delfin, that he is married, of Spanish *calidad*, and forty years of age, and is a resident of this *cabecera*. He knows the person who presents him as a witness. And it is true that on Sunday, the thirteenth of the present month, he was leaving early mass in the company of don Diego Fernández . . . they heard shouts and turned around to see that Joséfa Cadena was seated on the ground, in the company of her sister, and that doña Teresa Bravo and her daughter Teresa and her aunt Francisca, as well as a woman deposited with them and many other women who he does not remember, were mistreating her with words. Joséfa Cadena got up and tried to hit them, and the young Teresa threw her onto the ground. He saw this because he went there to separate them, which he was able to do. But the others continued to mistreat her with very indecorous words and indecent expressions. And Chepa's [a nickname for Joséfa] brother arrived and tried to defend her with indecorous words, and it was then that don Diego Fernández answered them with the same impurity and without stopping. And then near the house of don Diego, the witness revealed that Joséfa had said to doña Teresa that she was a whore and that no one had found a friend under her [Joséfa's] bed. It was then that the fight began. All who participated were hit and scratched, but there was no use of arms . . .

[Ratifies and signs].

Working with Sources

1. **What appears to us as a simple legal case of assault actually involves the view of honor on different social levels. Which levels are involved and what are the distinctive definitions of honor on each level?**
2. **Compare premodern and modern definitions of honor with each other. What are the main differences?**

SOURCE 18.2 Marina de San Miguel's Confessions before the Inquisition, Mexico City

1598–1599

The Inquisition was well established in Spain at the time of Cortés's conquest in the 1520s. A tribunal of the Holy Office of the Inquisition came in the conquistadors' wake, ultimately established at Mexico City in 1571 with authority to regulate Catholic morality throughout "New Spain." Most of the Inquisition trials concerned petty breaches of religious conduct, but others dealt with the much more serious crime of heresy. In November 1598, the Inquisition became alarmed about the rise of a group who believed that the Day of Judgment was at hand. Among the group denounced to the Holy Office was Marina de San Miguel, a Spanish-born woman who held a high status due to her mystical visions. Her confessions reveal the degree to which admissions of "deviance" could be extorted from a victim.

Source: Jacqueline Holler, "The Spiritual and Physical Ecstasies of a Sixteenth-Century Beata: Marina de San Miguel Confesses Before the Mexican Inquisition," in Richard Boyer and Geoffrey Spurling, eds., *Colonial Lives: Documents on Latin American History, 1550–1850* (Oxford and New York: Oxford University Press, 2000), 79–98.

In March 1601, Marina was stripped naked to the waist and paraded upon a mule. Forced to confess her errors, she was sentenced to 100 lashes with a whip. Confined to a plague hospital, she died some time later.

First Confession

In the city of Mexico, Friday, November 20, 1598. The Lord Inquisitor *licenciado* don Alonso de Peralta in his morning audience ordered that a woman be brought before him from one of the secret prisons of this Holy Office. Being present, she swore an oath *en forma devida de derecho* under which she promised to tell the truth here in this audience and in all the others that might be held until the determination of her case, and to keep secret everything that she might see or believe or that might be talked about with her or that might happen concerning this her case.

. . .

She was asked if she knows, presumes, or suspects the cause for her arrest and imprisonment in the prisons of the Holy Office. . .. The inquisitor said that with her illness she must have imagined it. And she says that she wants to go over her memory so that she can tell the truth about everything that she might remember.

With this the audience ceased, because it was past eleven. The above was read and she approved it and signed it. And she was ordered to return to her cell, very admonished to examine her memory as she was offered to do.

. . .

Third Confession

In the city of Mexico, Tuesday, November 24, 1598. . ..

She said that what she has remembered is that in the course of her life some spiritual things have happened to her, which she has talked about to some people. And she believes that they have been the cause of her imprisonment, because they were scandalized by what she told them.

. . .

And then she opened her eyes and began to shake and get up from the bench on which she was seated, saying, "My love, help me God, how strongly you have given me this." And among these words she said to the Lord Inquisitor that when she is given these trances, she should be shaken vigorously to awaken her from her deep dream. Then she returned to being as though sleeping. The inquisitor called her by her name and she did not respond, nor the second time. And the third time she opened her eyes and made faces, and made signs with her hands to her mouth.

. . .

Sixth Confession

In the city of Mexico, Monday, January 25, 1599. . . .

She said that it's like this. . . . She has been condemned to hell, because for fifteen years she has had a sensual temptation of the flesh, which makes her perform dishonest acts with her own hands on her shameful parts. She came to pollution [orgasm] saying dishonest words that provoke lust, calling by their dishonest names many dirty and lascivious things. She was tempted to this by the devil, who appeared to her internally in the form of an Angel of Light, who told her that she should do these things, because they were no sin. This was to make her abandon her scruples. And the devil appeared to her in the form of Christ our Redeemer, in such a way that she might uncover her breasts and have carnal union with him. And thus, for fifteen years, she has had carnal union occasionally from month to month, or every two months. And if it had been more she would accuse herself of that too, because she is only trying to save her soul, with no regard to honor or the world. And the carnal act that the devil as Angel of Light and in the form of Christ had with her was the same as if she had had it with a man. And he kissed her, and she enjoyed it, and she felt a great ardor in her whole body, with particular delight and pleasure.

. . .

Eighth Confession

In the city of Mexico, Wednesday, January 27, 1599. . . .

But all the times she had the copulation with the devil in the form of Christ she doubted whether it was the devil or not, from which doubts one can infer that she did not believe as firmly as she ought to have that such things could not possibly be from Christ. In this she should urgently discharge her conscience. . . .

. . .

[After the *Ninth Confession*:]

In the city of Mexico, Tuesday, Day of the Purification of our Lady, February 2, 1599, the Lord Inquisitor in his afternoon audience ordered Marina de San Miguel brought before him. And once present she was told that if she has remembered anything in her case she should say it, and the truth, under the oath that she has made.

She said no. . . .

▸ Working with Sources

1. **What does this document indicate about the working methods of the Inquisition (and their "successes") in Mexico in the 1590s?**
2. **Does the Inquisition seem to have been more concerned about Marina's sexuality than her mystical experiences?**

SOURCE 18.3 Nahuatl Land Sale Documents, Mexico

ca. 1610

After the conquest of the Aztec imperial capital of Tenochtitlán, Spaniards turned their attention to the productive farmland in the surrounding countryside, which was inhabited by Nahuatl-speaking native people. By the late sixteenth century, Spaniards began to expand rapidly into this territory. They acquired estates in a variety of ways, from royal grants to open seizure of property. Nevertheless, the purchase of plots of land from individual Nahuas was also common—although sometimes the sellers came to regret the transaction and petitioned higher authorities for redress of their grievances.

Altepetl: City-state.

Teopixqui: Priest, in Nahuatl.

Tlaxilacalli: Subunit of an *altepetl*

Teniente: Lieutenant.

Here in the ***altepetl*** Santo Domingo Mixcoac, Marquesado del Valle, on the first day of July of the year 1612, I, Joaquín de San Francisco, and my wife, Juana Feliciana, citizens here in the *altepetl* of Santa María Purificación Tlilhuacan, sell to Dr. Diego de León Plaza, ***teopixqui***, one field and house that we have in the ***tlaxilacalli*** Tlilhuacan next to the house of Juan Bautista, Spaniard. Where we are is right in the middle of [in between] their houses. And now we receive [the money] in person. The reason we sell it is that we have no children to whom it might belong. For there is another land and house, but [the land] here we can no longer [work] because it is really in the middle of [land belonging to] Spaniards. [The land] is not *tributario*, for my father, named Juan Altamirano, and my mother, María Catalina, really left it to me. And now I give it to [the doctor] very voluntarily. And now he is personally giving me 130 pesos. Both my wife and I receive it in person before the witnesses. And the tribute will be remedied with [the price]; it will pay it. The land [upon which tribute is owed] is at Colonanco. It is adjacent to the land of Miguel de Santiago and Lucas Pérez. And the witnesses [are] Antonio de Fuentes and señora Inés de Vera and Juana de Vera, Spanish women (and the Nahuas) Juan Josef, Gabriel Francisco, María, Mariana, and Sebastián Juan. And because we do not know how to write, I, Joaquín [de San] Francisco, and my wife asked a witness to set down [a signature] on our behalf [along with the notary?] Juan Vázquez, Spaniard. Witnesses, Antonio de Fuentes, [etc.] Before me, Matías Valeriano, notary. And both of them, he and his wife [Joaquín de San Francisco and Juana Feliciana], received the 140 pesos each three months, [presumably paid in installments?] before the witnesses who were mentioned. Before me, Matías Valeriano, notary.

. . .

Source: Rebecca Horn, "Spaniards in the Nahua Countryside: Dr. Diego de León Plaza and Nahuatl Land Sale Documents (Mexico, Early Seventeenth Century)," in Richard Boyer and Geoffrey Spurling, eds., *Colonial Lives: Documents on Latin American History, 1550–1850* (Oxford and New York: Oxford University Press, 2000), 102–103, 108–109.

[Letter of complaint to the authorities of Santo Domino Mixcoac, on the behalf of a group of Nahuas, undated:]

We are citizens here in Santo Domingo Mixcoac. We state that we found out that Paula and Juana and María and Catalina and Inés and Anastacia complain about the **teniente** before you [the *corregidor, gobernador, regidores,* etc.]. It is Antonio de Fuentes whom they are accusing because they say he mistreats them. [They say] he robs [people's land].

. . .

And now [the] Spaniard Napolles disputes with the *teniente.* And Napolles goes around to each house exerting pressure on, forcing many people [to say "get rid of the *teniente*"]. [He says:] "Let there be no officer of the justice. I will help you expel the *teniente* because we will be happy if there is no officer of the law on your land." Napolles, Spaniard, keeps a woman at his house and he is forcing her. For this reason [the authorities] arrested him for concubinage. They gave him a fine about which he became very angry and they arrested him. He stole four pigs, the property of a person named Francisco Hernández, Spaniard, and because of that they arrested him. He was scorched [burned] for their relatives accuse them.

. . .

And so now with great concern and with bowing down we implore you [the *corregidor, gobernador,* and *regidores,* etc.] and we ask for justice. Everyone knows how [the blacks and *mestizos*] mistreat us. They don't go to confession. They are already a little afraid and are already living a little better. And we ask for justice. Let them be punished. We who ask it are Juan Joseph, Francisco de San Juan, and Francisco Juan.

Working with Sources

1. **Why do the documents incorporate Nahuatl terms at some times but not at others?**
2. **How do the documents illustrate the various levels of justice available to native people and to "Spaniards"?**

SOURCE 18.4 *The Jesuit Relations,* French North America

1649

The Jesuit Relations are the most important documents attesting to the encounter between Europeans and native North Americans or Amerindians in the seventeenth century. These annual reports of French missionaries from the Society of Jesus document the conversions—or attempted conversions—of the various indigenous peoples in what is today the St. Lawrence River basin and the Great Lakes region. When they arrived on the banks of the St. Lawrence in 1625, French Jesuits were entering a continent still very much under control of First Nations peoples, who were divided by their own ethnic and linguistic differences. Even the catchall terms "Huron" and "Iroquois" masked their nature as confederacies, composed of several distinct nations, who had joined together prior to the arrival of Europeans.

When the Jesuits made headway with one group, they usually lost initiative with the group's rivals—and sometimes found themselves in the midst of a conflict that they could barely understand or appreciate. This section of the *Relations* concerns the torture and murder of Jean Brébeuf, who had lived among the Hurons at various points from the 1620s through the 1640s, observing their culture and systematically attempting to convert them to Catholicism. However, when an Iroquois raiding party invaded his settlement, the depth of the Hurons' Christian commitment—and his own—would be tested.

The sixteenth day of March in the present year, 1649, marked the beginning of our misfortunes—if an event, which no doubt has been the salvation of many of God's elect, can be called a misfortune.

The Iroquois, enemies of the Hurons, arrived by night at the frontier of this country. They numbered about a thousand men, well furnished with weapons, most of them carrying firearms obtained from their allies, the Dutch. We had no knowledge of their approach, although they had started from their country in the autumn, hunting in the forests throughout the winter, and had made a difficult journey of nearly two hundred leagues over the snow in order to take us by surprise. By night, they reconnoitered the condition of the first place upon which they had designs. It was surrounded by a pine stockade fifteen or sixteen feet in height, and a deep ditch with which nature had strongly fortified this place on three sides. There remained only a small space that was weaker than the others.

Source: Paul Ragueneau, "Relation of 1648–49," in Allan Greer, ed., *The Jesuit Relations: Natives and Missionaries in Seventeenth-Century North America* (Boston: Bedford/St. Martin's, 2000), 112–115.

It was at this weak point that the enemy made a breach at daybreak, but so secretly and promptly that he was master of the place before anyone could mount a defense. All were then sleeping deeply, and they had no time to recognize the danger. Thus this village was taken, almost without striking a blow and with only ten Iroquois killed. Part of the Hurons—men, women, and children—were massacred then and there, while the others were made captives and were reserved for cruelties more terrible than death.

. . .

The enemy did not stop there, but followed up his victory, and before sunrise he appeared in arms to attack the town of St. Louis, which was fortified with a fairly good stockade. Most of the women and the children had just gone from it upon hearing the news which had arrived regarding the approach of the Iroquois. The people of greatest courage, about eighty persons, being resolved to defend themselves well, courageously repulsed the first and the second assaults, killing about thirty of the enemy's boldest men, in addition to many wounded. But finally, the larger number prevailed, as the Iroquois used their hatchets to undermine the palisade of stakes and opened a passage for themselves through some considerable breaches.

About nine o'clock in the morning, we perceived from our house at St. Marie the fire which was consuming the cabins of that town, where the enemy, after entering victoriously, had reduced everything to desolation. They cast into the flames the old, the sick, the children who had not been able to escape, and all those who, being too severely wounded, could not have followed them into captivity. At the sight of those flames, and by the color of the smoke which issued from them, we understood sufficiently what was happening, for this town of St. Louis was no more than a league distant from us. Two Christians who escaped the fire arrived about this time and confirmed this.

In this town of St. Louis were at that time two of our fathers, Father Jean de Brébeuf and Father Gabriel Lalemant, who had charge of a cluster of five towns. These formed but one of the eleven missions of which we have spoken above, and we call it the mission of St. Ignace.

Some Christians had begged the fathers to preserve their lives for the glory of God, which would have been as easy for them as for the more than five hundred persons who went away at the first alarm, for there was more than enough time to reach a place of safety. But their zeal could not permit such a thing, and the salvation of their flock was dearer to them than the love of their own lives. They employed the moments left to them as the most precious which they had ever had in the world, and through the heat of the battle their hearts were on fire for the salvation of souls. One was at the breach, baptizing the **catechumens**, and the other was giving absolution to the **neophytes**. Both of them urged the Christians to die in the sentiments of piety with which they consoled them in their miseries. Never was their faith more alive, nor their love for their good fathers and pastors more keenly felt.

Catechumens: Native converts who had not yet been baptized.

Neophytes: Recently baptized Christians.

An infidel, seeing the desperate situation, spoke of taking flight, but a Christian named Etienne Annaotaha, the most esteemed in the country for his courage and his exploits against the enemy, would never allow it. "What!" he said. "Could we ever abandon these two good fathers, who have exposed their lives for us? Their love for our salvation will be the cause of their death, for there is no longer time for them to flee across the snows. Let us then die with them, and we shall go together to heaven." This man had made a general confession a few days previously, having had a presentiment of the danger awaiting him and saying that he wished that death should find him disposed for Heaven. And indeed he, as well as many other Christians, had abandoned themselves to fervor in a manner so extraordinary that we shall never be sufficiently able to bless the guidance of God over so many predestinated souls. His divine providence continues lovingly to guide them in death as in life.

▶ Working with Sources

1. **How well do the Jesuits seem to have understood the conflicts among native peoples in this region?**
2. **How was Ragueneau's reporting of the battle designed to highlight the "success" of the mission, despite an apparent setback?**

World Period Four

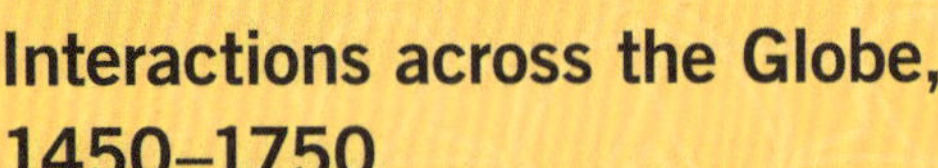

Interactions across the Globe, 1450–1750

The fifteenth century saw a renewal of the imperial impulse in the religious civilizations of the world. A forerunner had been the Mongol empire, which however did not last long; in less than 100 years it was replaced in China by the Ming. The founders of the subsequent new empires were the Mughals in India; the Ottomans, Safavids, and Songhay in the Middle East and Islamic Africa; the Habsburgs in Europe; and the seaborne empires of Portugal and Spain. One byproduct of this new imperial impulse was the discovery of the Americas, which in turn inspired the formulation of the heliocentric universe. The rediscovery of Greek literature in Europe had already set into motion the Renaissance, a broad new approach to under-standing the world that provided the spark for the New Science.

China and India, by far the wealthiest and most populous agrarian–urban empires, enjoyed leading positions in the world because they produced everything they needed and wanted. Europe, however, acquired warm-weather crops and minerals through overseas colonial expansion, which would help it to challenge the traditional order.

Chapter 19

African Kingdoms, the Atlantic Slave Trade, and the Origins of Black America

1450–1800

CHAPTER NINETEEN PATTERNS

Origins, Interactions, Adaptations In Africa, the agrarian–urban trend peaked with the Islamic empire of Songhay. When Morocco destroyed it, small kingdoms took its place in West and Central Africa. Portuguese mariners and merchants encountered these kingdoms as they explored and expanded their trading activities along the Atlantic coast. Kongo, the most important of the kingdoms that the Portuguese encountered, converted to Christianity and became a major trading partner. At the same time, European merchants built up the slave trade with the Americas: African merchants, kings, or chieftains collaborated to capture victims for what became one of the largest forced human movements, with consequences that still reverberate.

Uniqueness and Similarities The Atlantic slave trade set into motion a unique European-dominated triangular trade. European merchants traveled to Africa, sold textiles and firearms for slaves, and transported the slaves to the Americas. There they traded the slaves for sugar, coffee, and rum for shipment to Europe. Unable to produce these expensive luxury goods at home, the Europeans made this triangular trade the backbone of colonialism. Over the centuries, the Muslim slave trade across the Sahara reached similar proportions as the Atlantic slave trade, although here it was for the purpose of domestic slavery.

It was a claim the Catholic Capuchin monks of the kingdom of Kongo denounced as a heretical abomination: that Dona Beatriz Kimpa Vita (1684–1706) had been reborn as St. Anthony of Padua. For many subjects of the kingdom, this claim was perfectly reasonable as part of an African Christian spirituality in which a gifted person could enter other people's minds and assume their identity. But the monks prevailed. The king of Kongo had Dona Beatriz condemned after a trial and burned at the stake.

Dona Beatriz had been intellectually precocious. In her childhood, her family had her initiated as a *nganga marinda* (*nganga* "medium" is derived from a Kikongo word meaning "knowledge" or "skill"; a *nganga marinda* addressed social problems). In her initiation ceremony, Dona Beatriz was put into a trance that enabled her to recognize and repel troubling forces that might disturb a person or the community.

The people in Kongo were aware, however, that not all *ngangas* were benevolent. Some *ngangas* were thought to engage in witchcraft. For the missionary Capuchin monks, preaching the Catholic Reformation in the 1500s and 1600s, all *ngangas* were seen as witches. Whether the young Doa Beatriz was intimidated by the monks' denunciations or not, she renounced her initiation, married, and pursued the domestic life of any other young woman in Kongo society.

But Dona Beatriz's spiritual path did not end here. In 1704, she underwent another religious transformation; she "died," only to be reborn as St. Anthony of Padua (1195–1231), one of the patron saints of Portugal. In her new saintly and male identity, more powerful than her earlier one as a *nganga*, Dona Beatriz preached that she had arrived to restore the Catholic faith and reunify the kingdom of Kongo, after nearly half a century of dynastic disunity and civil war (1665–1709).

CHAPTER OUTLINE

African States and the Slave Trade

American Plantation Slavery and Atlantic Mercantilism

Culture and Identity in the African Diaspora

Putting It All Together

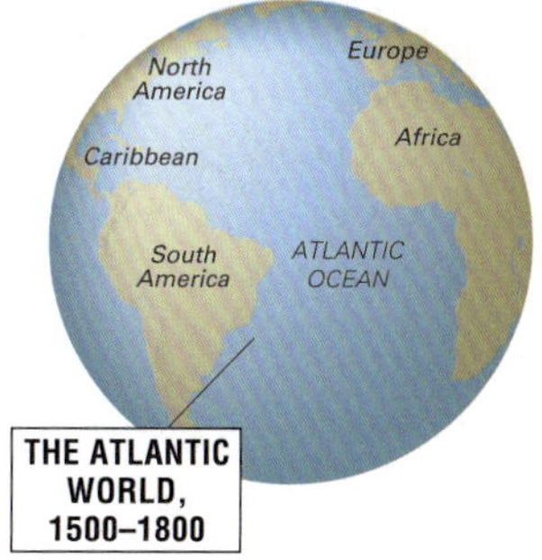

ABOVE: In this watercolor by Capuchin monk Antonio Cavazzi (1621–1678), a European monk and Kongo natives participate in a religious procession.

Seeing Patterns

> What was the pattern of kingdom and empire formation in Africa during the period 1450–1800?

> How did patterns of plantation slavery evolve in the Atlantic and the Americas?

> What are the historic roots from which modern racism evolved?

After her spiritual rebirth, Dona Beatriz went to Pedro IV, king of Kongo (r. 1695–1718), and his Capuchin ally, the chief missionary Bernardo da Gallo, and accused them of failing to restore the faith and unity of the kingdom. Bernardo angrily interrogated Dona Beatriz, and she responded with an attack on the Catholic cornerstone of the sacraments. Like Martin Luther (although unbeknownst to her) it was intention or faith alone, she argued, not the sacraments of the church, that would bring salvation. She derived her convictions from her *nganga* initiation: it was her good intentions that distinguished her from a malevolent witch.

Undecided how to respond to this assertion of a religious doctrine, the king and Bernardo let Beatriz go. She promptly led a crowd of followers to the ruined capital of Kongo, M'banza (called São Salvador by the Portuguese). There she trained "little Anthonies" as missionaries to convert the Kongolese to her new Antonian-African Christianity. Beatriz was at the pinnacle of her spiritual power when everything unraveled. Though already married, she gave birth to a child conceived with one of her followers. Allies of King Pedro arrested the lovers and brought them before the king. After a state trial—the church stayed out of the proceedings—Beatriz, her companion, and the baby were executed by burning at the stake.

The story of Dona Beatriz illustrates a pattern discussed in this chapter, the process by which Africans adapted their religious heritage to the challenge of European Christianity. Europeans arrived on the western coast of Africa in the late fifteenth century as missionaries and merchants—and also as slave traders and slave raiders. Africans responded with gold, goods, and their own adaptive forms of Christianity, as well as efforts to limit the slave trade in some of the coastal kingdoms.

African States and the Slave Trade

In the north of sub-Saharan Africa, the pattern of Islamic and Christian dynastic state formation continued to dominate herder and village societies in the period 1500–1800. An invasion by Muslim forces from Morocco during the sixteenth century, however, ended the trend toward empire building in West Africa and strengthened the forces of decentralization. By contrast, in the savanna and Great Lakes regions of central Africa, improved agricultural wealth and intensified regional trade helped perpetuate the kingdom formation already under way. Slavery existed in the chiefdoms and states of Africa, though it was far different from the chattel slavery that would characterize the Americas. The implications of the new trade provided both enormous opportunities and horrific challenges for African traders and local leaders. While the growing Atlantic slave trade appealed to some West African rulers as a path to enhanced wealth and power, more often, rulers tried to resist what ultimately became the greatest forced migration in human history.

The End of Empires in the North and the Rise of States in the Center

Mali (1240–1460), which united peoples of many different religions, languages, and ethnic affiliations, was the first African empire that was similar to the empires of Eurasia in this respect. Mali's successor state, the focus of this section, was the even larger Songhay Empire (1460–1591). Though vast, it lasted only a short time.

Origins of the Songhay Songhay was initially a tributary state of Mali. It was centered on the city of Gao, downstream on the Niger River from Jenné-jeno and Timbuktu. Gao's origins dated to 850, when it emerged as the end point of the eastern trans-Saharan route from Tunisia and Algeria. Gao was located at the northern end of the Songhay Empire and was inhabited by the Songhay, an ethnic grouping composed of herders, villagers, and fishermen.

At the end of the eleventh century, the leading families of the Songhay, profiting from the trans-Saharan trade, converted to Islam. Two centuries later, the warriors among them assumed positions of leadership as vassals of the *mansa*, or emperor, of Mali.

The Songhay Empire The Songhay began their imperial expansion in the mid-1400s. Mali lost its northern outpost, Timbuktu, to the Songhay in 1469. In the following decades, Mali slowly retreated, eventually becoming a minor vassal of the Songhay. At its height, the Songhay Empire stretched from Hausaland in the savanna southeast of Gao all the way westward to the Atlantic coast (see Map 19.1).

The factor that elevated the Songhay emperors above their vassals was their taxation of the gold trade. The gold fields of the Upper Niger, Senegal, and Black Volta Rivers were outside the empire, but merchant clans transported the gold to Timbuktu and Gao. Here, North African merchants exchanged their Mediterranean manufactures and salt for gold and slaves. Agents of the emperors in these cities collected market taxes in the form of gold. Agricultural taxes and tributes supported kingdoms; long-distance trade was needed for an empire to come into being.

Songhay's Sudden End After the initial conquests, the Songhay Empire had little time to consolidate its territory. After just over a century, the Songhay Empire

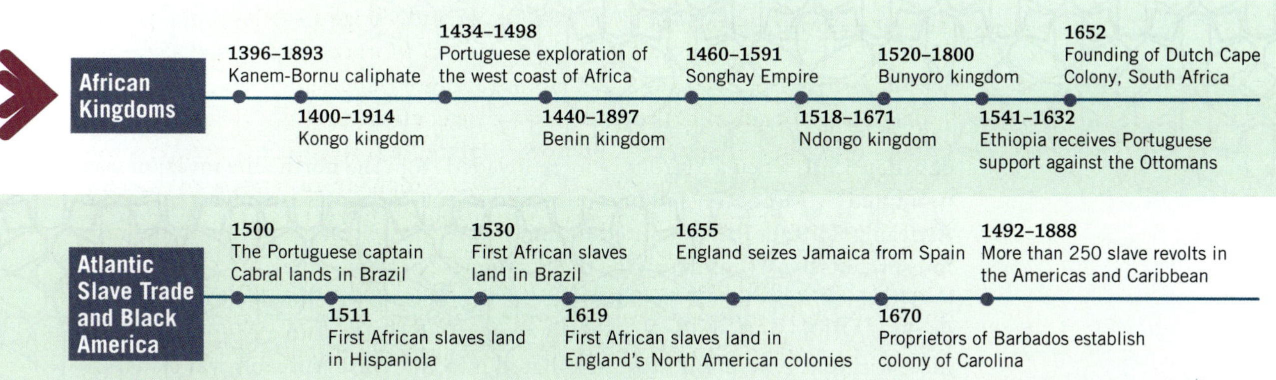

MAP 19.1 Peoples and Kingdoms in Sub-Saharan Africa, 1450–1750

ended in 1591, when a Moroccan force invaded from the north. The invasion was prompted by Moroccan sultans concerned about Portuguese involvement in the African gold trade. They wanted to find the West African gold fields in the rain forest themselves, thus depriving the Portuguese of their supply.

However, after defeating Songhay, the Moroccans were unable to march any farther. Although the officers initially turned the region into a Moroccan province, within a generation they assimilated into the West African royal clans. As a result, imperial politics in West Africa disintegrated, together with much of the trans-Saharan gold trade.

The Eastern Sahel and Savanna The area between Songhay in the west and Ethiopia in the northeastern highlands also was home to Islamic regimes. Kanem-Bornu (1396–1893) was a long-lived Islamic realm, calling itself a caliphate, but with a majority of subjects following African religious traditions. It was based on a slave and ivory trade with the Mediterranean and on agriculture and fishing for its internal organization on the south side of Lake Chad. Kanem-Bornu waged wars with the neighboring kingdoms of Hausaland.

The Hausa kingdoms had formed during the height of the Mali-dominated trans-Saharan trade. During the period 1500–1800, many of the ruling clans converted to Islam. They maintained cavalry forces for both military and trade purposes. The Hausa kings collected taxes on traders and dues from the villagers. Craftspeople manufactured a range of goods, and miners and smiths smelted and forged copper, iron, and steel.

Farther east, between Lake Chad and the Nile, the Fur and the Funj, cattle-breeding clan-lineage federations, converted fully to Islam. In contrast, in West Africa, only the dynasties and merchants became Muslim. Their leaders adopted the title "sultan" and became increasingly Arabized in the period 1500–1800, while Christianity along the Upper Nile disappeared.

South Central Africa On the southern side of the rain forest, the eastern part of the southern savanna and the Great Lakes area in central Africa remained outside the reach of the slave trade to the Americas. Farmer and cattle herder groups, organized in chiefdoms, inhabited these regions. In the eastern savanna, the kingdom of Luba emerged before 1500, while others followed thereafter.

An increase in regional trade enabled chieftain clans to enlarge their holdings into kingdoms. Living in enclosures and surrounded by dense ruling-class settlements, kings maintained agricultural domains worked by slaves. Villages delivered tribute of foodstuffs. From the mid-seventeenth century onward, the American-origin staples corn and cassava were cultivated. Tributaries at some distance delivered prestige goods. At times, the kings mobilized thousands of workers for construction projects around their courts.

In the Great Lakes region, to the north, south, and west of Lake Victoria, agriculture, cattle breeding, and trade supported political competition. Small agricultural–mercantile kingdoms shared the region, but sometime in the sixteenth century the Luo, who were cattle breeders, arrived from the north and shook up the existing political and social structures. Pronounced disparities in cattle ownership emerged. Cattle lords, bolstered by their wealth and status, rose as competitors of the kings.

North of Lake Victoria, the Bunyoro kingdom held the cattle lords at bay, while on the south side of the lake, the cattle lords created new small kingdoms. After a while, dominant cattle breeders and inferior farmers settled into relations of mutual dependence. Under the colonial system in the nineteenth century, these unequal relations froze into a caste system in which the dominant but minority Tutsi cattle breeders were continually at odds with the majority Hutu farmers.

Portugal's Explorations along the African Coast and Contacts with Ethiopia

The Portuguese expansion into North Africa and the exploration of the West African coast were outgrowths of both the *Reconquista* and religious crusading impulses (see Chapter 16). Mixed in with these religious motives was the necessity of financing the exploration through trade. The combination of the two guided Portugal within a single century around the African continent to India. Along the coast, the Portuguese established forts to protect their merchants. In East Africa they protected the Ethiopian Christian kingdom against the Ottomans in Yemen.

Chartered Explorations in West Africa Henry the Navigator (1394–1460), brother of the ruling king, occupied the Moroccan port of Ceuta in 1415 under the pretext that Ceuta was once Christian. He also wished to renew crusading for the reconquest of Jerusalem. But the Lisbon court was wary of military expenditures. During the fifteenth century, campaigns for the military occupation of other cities of Morocco alternated with voyages financed by Portuguese merchants and aristocrats for commerce along the West African coast.

Between 1434 and 1472, Portuguese mariners explored the West African coast as far east as the Bight of Benin. They traded European woolens and linens for gold, cottons, and Guinea pepper. Some African slaves were traded, mostly through purchases from chieftains and kings. The Portuguese used slaves to establish sugar plantations on islands off the African coast and shipped other slaves to Europe for domestic employment.

Portugal and Ethiopia In the second half of the fifteenth century, the military wing of the Portuguese court revived crusading. From 1483 through 1486 the king organized state expeditions for further expansion from the Bight of Benin south to the Congo River. Here, mariners sailed upstream and encountered the ruler of the kingdom of Kongo, who converted to Christianity and established close relations with Portugal.

A few years later, the Portuguese crown continued the search for a way to Ethiopia or India. Eventually, Vasco da Gama circumnavigated the southern tip of Africa, established trade outposts in the Swahili city-states of East Africa, and reached India in 1498. From this point, Portuguese development of the Indian spice trade grew in importance.

The Portuguese discovered in the early sixteenth century that the Ethiopian kingdom was weak in the face of the Muslim sultanate of Adal, on the Red Sea to the east. Until the end of the fifteenth century, Ethiopia had been a powerful Coptic Christian kingdom. Its people practiced a productive agriculture, and its kings controlled a trade of gold, ivory, animal skins, and slaves. Ethiopia and Adal struggled to possess a Red Sea port for this trade during the first half of the sixteenth century.

A Christian incursion into Muslim territory in 1529 triggered a destructive Muslim holy war by Adal. Ethiopia would have been destroyed had a Portuguese fleet with artillery and musketeers not arrived in 1541. For its part, Adal received Ottoman Muslim support, but the Christians eventually prevailed.

Ethiopia paid a high price for its victory, however. Adal Muslim power was destroyed, but in its place the Ottomans took over the entire west coast of the Red Sea. Non-Christian cattle breeders from the southwest occupied the Rift Valley, which separated the northern and southern Ethiopian highlands, and Christians in the southern highlands were left to their own devices. Small numbers of Portuguese stayed in Ethiopia, with Jesuit missionaries threatening to dominate the Ethiopian church. In 1632 the Ethiopian king expelled the Jesuits and consolidated the kingdom.

From about 1700 Ethiopia decentralized into provincial lordships. Only in the mid-nineteenth century did the kings take back their power from the provincial lords.

Coastal Africa and the Atlantic Slave Trade

Portuguese mariners initially focused on developing their spice trade with India. Gradually, however, they also built their Atlantic slave trade. To understand the pattern underlying the slave trade from 1500–1800, it is crucial to be aware of the importance of slavery within the African historical context. In many places, a form of slavery existed in the place of land ownership. The more slaves a householder, clan leader, chief, or king owned, the wealthier he was. This form of **household slavery** was the most common variety.

... administrators, soldiers, domestics, craftspeople, and farmers; many among these were slaves, acquired through raids and wars but also as a form of punishment for infractions of royal, chiefly, or clan law.

Trade Forts

In the 1440s, Portuguese mariners raided the West African coast for slaves. But they suffered losses, since their muskets were not yet superior to the poisoned arrows of the Africans. Furthermore, West African warriors paddled along the coast and picked off the mariners from their caravels with their arrows if they approached the coast in a hostile manner. The Portuguese thus took a different approach, developing a lucrative coastal fort trade in a variety of items, including slaves.

Through treaties with local African leaders, Portugal acquired the right to build forts from which to trade. Africans involved in this trade produced items such as cloth and metal that were soon to be in demand in Europe. In particular, Africans smelted iron and forged steel that was of higher quality than that of iron-poor Portugal.

Trade was for luxury goods, not ordinary articles of daily life. Merchants had to be able to achieve high profits while carrying comparatively little to weigh down their ships. African rulers purchased luxuries in order to enhance their status and cement power relations. They sold slaves to the Europeans in a similar fashion, as luxuries in return for luxuries.

Outer defensive walls of Elmina. This town in present-day Ghana was, along with the village of São Jorge da Mina, the first Portuguese fortified trading post on the African coast, from 1482 until it passed to the Dutch in 1637. Merchants used it for storing the goods they traded and for protection in case of conflicts with Africans. It was staffed by a governor and 20–60 soldiers along with a priest, surgeon, apothecary, and a variety of craftspeople. Throughout the first half of the sixteenth century, Elmina was also the center of Portuguese slaving activities.

African Slavery

Sub-Saharan Africa offered enormous hurdles to a shift in patterns from local self-sufficiency to exchange agriculture and urbanization. Inland exchanges of food for manufactured goods over long distances were prohibitively expensive. Because of the tsetse fly (see Chapter 6), human portage or animal transport were limited to highly valuable merchandise. Everything else was manufactured within self-sufficient households.

Such self-sufficiency required large households. In villages with limited outside trade, the polygamous household with the largest number of people employed at home and in the fields was the wealthiest. To increase his wealth further, a household master often raided neighboring villages and acquired captives, to be enslaved and put to work inside and outside the household. Slave raiding and household slavery were common in sub-Saharan African societies. The more

Portuguese Traders. This brass plaque, from about the middle of the sixteenth century, decorated the palace of the Benin *obo* and shows two Portuguese traders. The fact that they are holding hands suggests they could be father and son.

stratified slaveholding societies were, the more slaves rose into positions of responsibility and, frequently, autonomy. Thus, as in many societies outside of Africa, the varieties of slavery in sub-Saharan Africa tended to be highly complex in structure and function.

Limited Slave Trade from Benin When Portugal began the slave trade, African chiefs and kings had to evaluate the comparative value of slaves for their households or for sale. The kingdom of Benin west of the Niger delta was an example of this calculation. The ruler Ewuare (r. 1440–1473) was the first to rise to dominance over chiefs and assume the title of king. Through conquests, Ewuare acquired slaves who were employed in his army and for the construction of earthworks protecting the capital, Benin City.

Early trade contacts between Portuguese mariners and Benin intensified when the successor of Ewuare granted permission to build a fort on the coast in 1487. But the king closely controlled the exchange of goods and slaves. A generation later, when the kings prohibited the sale of male slaves, the Portuguese abandoned their fort. A compromise was reached whereby a limited number of slaves were traded in return for firearms. The kingdom admitted missionaries and members of the dynasty acculturated to the Portuguese. Benin became economically diversified and culturally complex.

Slave exports remained restricted while Benin was a strong, centralized state. Under weak kings and during times of civil war, more slaves were sold as more weapons were purchased. But overall, compared to the slave trade farther west on the West African coast, the large centralized kingdom of Benin with its high internal demand for slave labor remained a modest exporter of slaves and thus retained a considerable degree of autonomy and agency.

The Kingdom of Kongo Farther south, on the central West African coast, the Portuguese established trade relations with the Kongo and Ndongo kingdoms. Kongo, the oldest and most centralized kingdom in the region, emerged about 1400. By the sixteenth century, its capital, M'banza (São Salvador) was comparable in size to London, Amsterdam, Moscow, and Rome. M'banza also contained a large palace population and a royal domain farmed by slaves.

To defend their rule, the kings relied on a standing army of 5,000 troops. They appointed members of the royal family as governors, who were entitled to rents but were also obliged to deliver taxes in kind to the palace. In addition, the kings collected a head tax. This region of direct rule was marked by a unified law and administration. Vassal kings, called dukes (Portuguese *duque*), governed and sent tribute or gifts to the capital. They sometimes rebelled and broke away; thus, the territory of Kongo, like that of Songhay, shifted constantly in size.

The kings of Kongo converted to Christianity early and sent members of the ruling family to Portugal for their education. Portuguese missionaries converted the court and a number of provincial chiefs. Among the ruling class, many read and wrote Portuguese and Latin fluently. Kongolese royalty wore Portuguese dress, listened to church music and hymns, and drank wine imported from Madeira. Lay assistants converted many commoners to Catholicism, and schoolmasters instructed children at churches and chapels. The result was an African Creole culture, in which the veneration of territorial and ancestral spirits was combined with Catholicism.

Kongo began to sell slaves to Portuguese traders as early as 1502. By the mid-1500s, the kings permitted the export of a few thousand slaves a year. But Portugal wanted more slaves, and in 1571 the crusader king Sebastião I (r. 1557–1578) chartered a member of the aristocracy to create a colony in the adjacent kingdom of Ndongo for the mining of salt and silver by slaves. At first, this holder of the charter assisted the king of Ndongo in defeating rebels, but when his colonial aims became clear, the king turned against him, and a full-scale Portuguese war of conquest and for slaves erupted.

Kongolese Cross of St. Anthony. Considered an emblem of spiritual authority and power, the Christian cross was integrated into Kongo ancestral cults and burial rituals and was believed to contain magical protective properties. In Antonianism, the religious reform movement launched by Dona Beatriz Kimpa Vita, in 1704, St. Anthony of Padua, a thirteenth-century Portuguese-born saint, became known as Toni Malau, or "Anthony of Good Fortune," and was the patron of the movement. His image was widely incorporated into religious objects and personal items, such as this cross.

In this war (1579–1657), the Portuguese allied themselves with the Ibangala, fierce warriors from the eastern outreaches of Kongo and Ndongo into central Africa. Together, a few hundred Portuguese musketeers and tens of thousands of Ibangalas raided the kingdoms of Ndongo and Kongo for slaves, often capturing as many as 15,000 a year.

Portuguese and allied Ibangala troops also exploited a long civil war (1665–1709) in Kongo. That war expanded further when the Dutch West India Company mistakenly assumed that the small numbers of Portuguese troops would be unable to defend the coastal forts. Thanks to Brazilian help, however, Portugal was able to drive out the Dutch. The latter decided to return to a more peaceful trade for slaves from different fortified strongholds on the African west coast.

The Dutch in South Africa In 1652, the Dutch built a fort on the South African coast to supply ships traveling around the Cape of Good Hope. Employees of the company grew wheat and bought cattle from the Khoi, local cattle breeders. A few wealthy landowners imported the first black slaves in 1658 to convert the original Dutch smallholdings into larger plantations. Gradually, a culturally Dutch settler society emerged.

The majority of these settlers were urban craftspeople and traders, while most of the actual farmers employed slaves. Around 1750, there were about 10,000 Boers (Dutch for "farmer") in the Cape Colony, easily outnumbered by slaves. Through expansion into the interior, ranchers destroyed the Khoi, forcing their absorption into other local groups. The Boers governed themselves, and their descendants, who called themselves Afrikaners, would one day create the system of apartheid in South Africa.

American Plantation Slavery and Atlantic Mercantilism

While European slave traders exploited existing African slave systems, the American plantation slave system had its roots in the Eastern Christian religious civilization of Byzantium. There, the Roman institution of agricultural estate slavery had survived. Byzantine estates on the Mediterranean islands of Cyprus and

Crete employed Muslim prisoners as well as captives as slaves for the cultivation of labor-intensive crops. After 1191, crusader landlords and Venetian and Genoese merchants expanded into sugar production, which had been introduced from Iran to the eastern Mediterranean by the Muslims.

The Special Case of Plantation Slavery in the Americas

Plantation slavery: Economic system in which slave labor was used to grow cash crops such as sugarcane, tobacco, and cotton on large estates.

In examining the patterns of American **plantation slavery**, a number of questions arise. How many Africans were forcibly taken from Africa to the Americas? Who were they, and who were the people who exploited their labor? What institutions were created to capture, transport, supply, and work slaves? What did the labor of the African slaves help to build? Why did this system develop the way it did—and last so long?

Numbers The enslavement of Africans for labor in the Western Hemisphere constituted the largest human migration in world history before the late nineteenth century. While the figures have been debated, estimates put the numbers of Africans shipped out of Africa at around 12.5 million. An estimated 1.4 million, or 12 percent, may have died between their initial capture and transfer to the African coast, or at sea. Nearly half of the surviving slaves, 5.8 million, were sent to Brazil. These figures exclude the numbers killed in the African slave raids and wars themselves, which will never be precisely known (see Map 19.2).

Chattel: Literally, an item of moveable personal property (from Latin *capitale* "holdings"); chattel slavery is the reduction of the status of the slave to an item of personal property of the owner, to dispose of as he or she sees fit.

Presentism: A bias toward present-day attitudes, especially in the interpretation of history.

Chattel Slavery In legal terms, African slaves in the New World were reduced to the status of **chattel**. A significant difference between chattel slavery and earlier kinds of enslavement was what came to be known as the "color line." By the eighteenth century, color was the determining factor in American slavery. The equation of blackness with chattel slavery created the basis for the modern phenomenon of racism, an attitude that has plagued all societies touched by the institution of African slavery to this day.

Historians debate the role of present-day sensibilities and issues in the study of the past. The practice of looking at the past through the lens of the present is called **presentism**. Historians try to distance themselves from their biases while attempting to empathetically enter the past. Nowhere is this problem more evident than in considering the origins of the plantation system and African slavery. While those origins are distant in time, what they led to remains repellent to our present sensibilities.

Caribbean Plantations Following the first European voyages to the Americas, indigenous populations were decimated by smallpox. To replenish the labor force, as early as 1511, the Spanish crown authorized the importation of 50 African slaves for gold mining on the island of Hispaniola. In the following decades thousands more followed for work on newly established sugar plantations. By the late sixteenth century, African slaves outnumbered Europeans on the Spanish-controlled islands and in Mexico and Peru, where they were primarily involved in mining.

Apart from mining, plantation work for sugar production is among the most arduous forms of labor. The average slave field hand on a sugar plantation

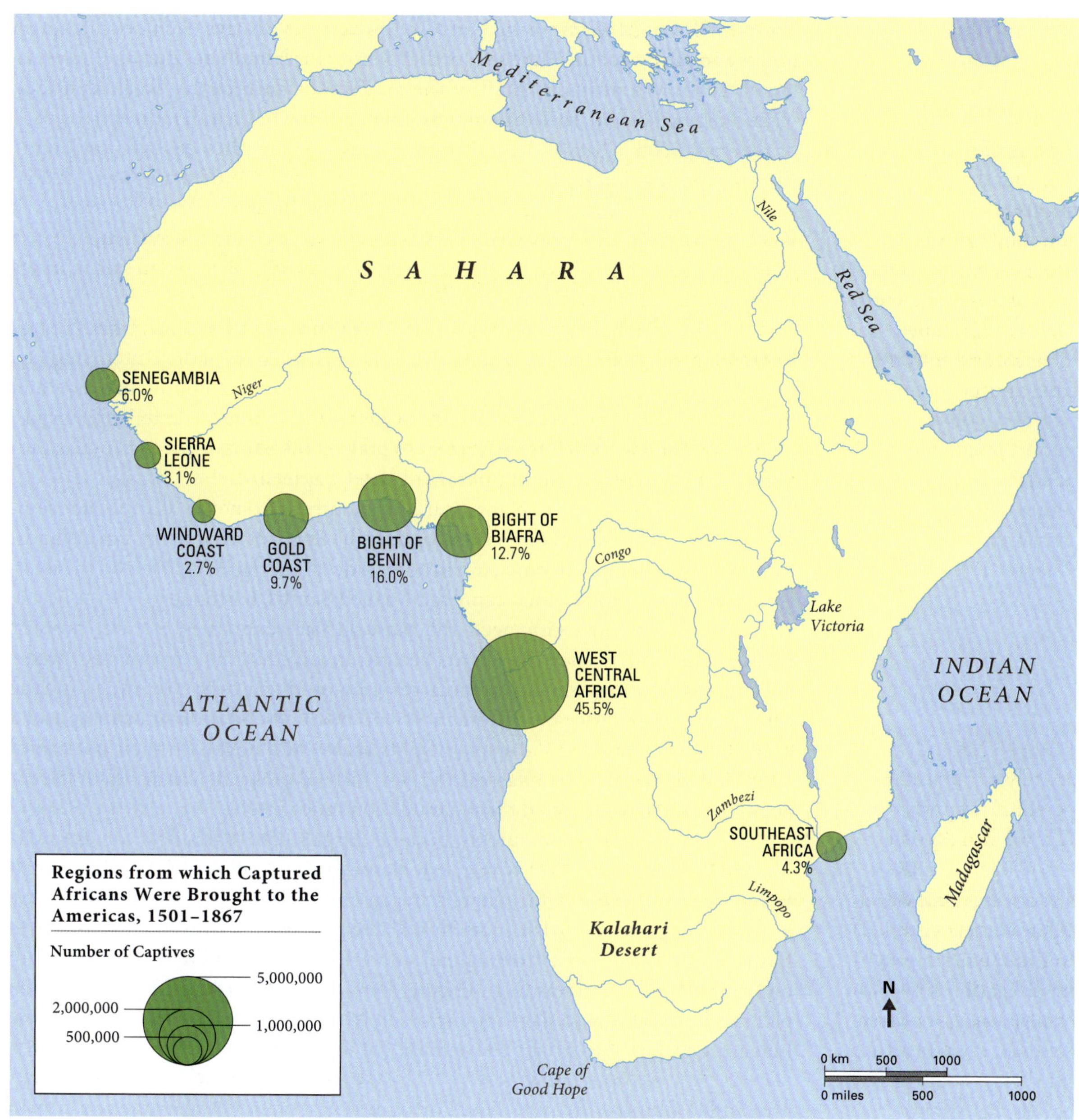

MAP 19.2 Regions from which Captured Africans Were Brought to the Americas, 1501–1867

was estimated to live just five or six years. Early on, the workforce was largely male, which meant that there were relatively few children to replenish the slave population. With the price of slaves low and the mortality rate high, it was economically more desirable to literally work slaves to death and buy more than to make the investments necessary to cultivate families. Not surprisingly, revolts, work slowdowns, and sabotage were frequent, with punishments being severe and public.

Mercantilism: Political theory according to which the wealth derived from the mining of silver and gold and the production of agricultural commodities should be restricted to each country's market, with as little as possible expended on imports from another country. In addition, colonies should import manufactured goods only from their respective European overlords (see Chapter 18).

Mercantilism in Action in the Caribbean With the decline of Spanish power and the rise of the English North Atlantic maritime states during the seventeenth century, a profound shift of the political balance in the Caribbean took place. Portugal, Spain, the Netherlands, England, and France all followed the path of **mercantilism**—that is, belief that the wealth of the state depends on having the maximum amount of gold and silver in its treasury. Thus, states should keep their economies blocked off from competitors and import as little and export as much as possible. Colonies were seen as vital to this economic system, because they supplied raw materials to the European homeland and provided safe markets for goods manufactured in the home country.

One way to enhance riches was to capture those of rivals. Thus, from the late sixteenth through the early eighteenth centuries, the navies of the Dutch, English, French, Spanish, and Portuguese all attacked each other's shipping interests and maritime colonies. Moreover, all of these governments issued "letters of marque" allowing warships owned by privateers to prey on the shipping of rival powers for a share in the prize money they obtained (see Chapter 18).

The lucrative trade in plantation commodities from the Caribbean compelled Spain's European competitors to oust the Spanish from their sugar islands. England seized Jamaica from Spain in 1655; a decade later, France seized the western part of Hispaniola, which came to be called Saint-Domingue.

Two developments enhanced the mercantilist economies of both powers. First, English and French merchants became involved in the African slave trade. Second, the growing demand for molasses (a by-product of sugar refining) and the even greater popularity of its fermented and distilled end product, rum, pushed both sugar planting and slavery to heights that would not reach their peak until after 1750. Sugar, slaves, molasses, and rum formed the principal driver of the triangular trade that sustained the Atlantic economic system.

Indentured laborers: Poor workers enrolled in European states with an obligation to work in the Americas for three to seven years in return for their prepaid passage across the Atlantic.

The demand for labor quickly became gargantuan. Barbados, for example, was settled initially in 1627 by English planters who employed English and Irish **indentured laborers**. After planters began cultivating sugarcane around 1640, however, English and Irish indentured laborers proved so unwilling to go to Barbados that law courts in England and Ireland resorted to convicting them on trumped-up charges and sentencing them to "transportation." But even then planters had to resort to slave imports from Africa, at the rate of two slaves to one indentured laborer, to satisfy the demand for workers.

The Sugar Empire: Brazil The Portuguese first planted sugarcane as a crop in Brazil in the 1530s. Also, in the 1530s, the Portuguese trading network on the central African coast began to supply the colony with African slaves. By the end of the century, a dramatic rise in demand for sugar in Europe increased the importation of African slaves. The insatiable demand of the sugar industry for slaves received a further boost in 1680 when enslavement of Indians was finally abolished, and in 1690 the discovery of gold in Minas Gerais further increased demand for labor. Brazil ultimately went on to be the largest slave state in the world, with about two-fifths of its entire population consisting of people of African descent. It was also the last country in the Americas to give up the institution of slavery, in 1888 (see Map 19.3).

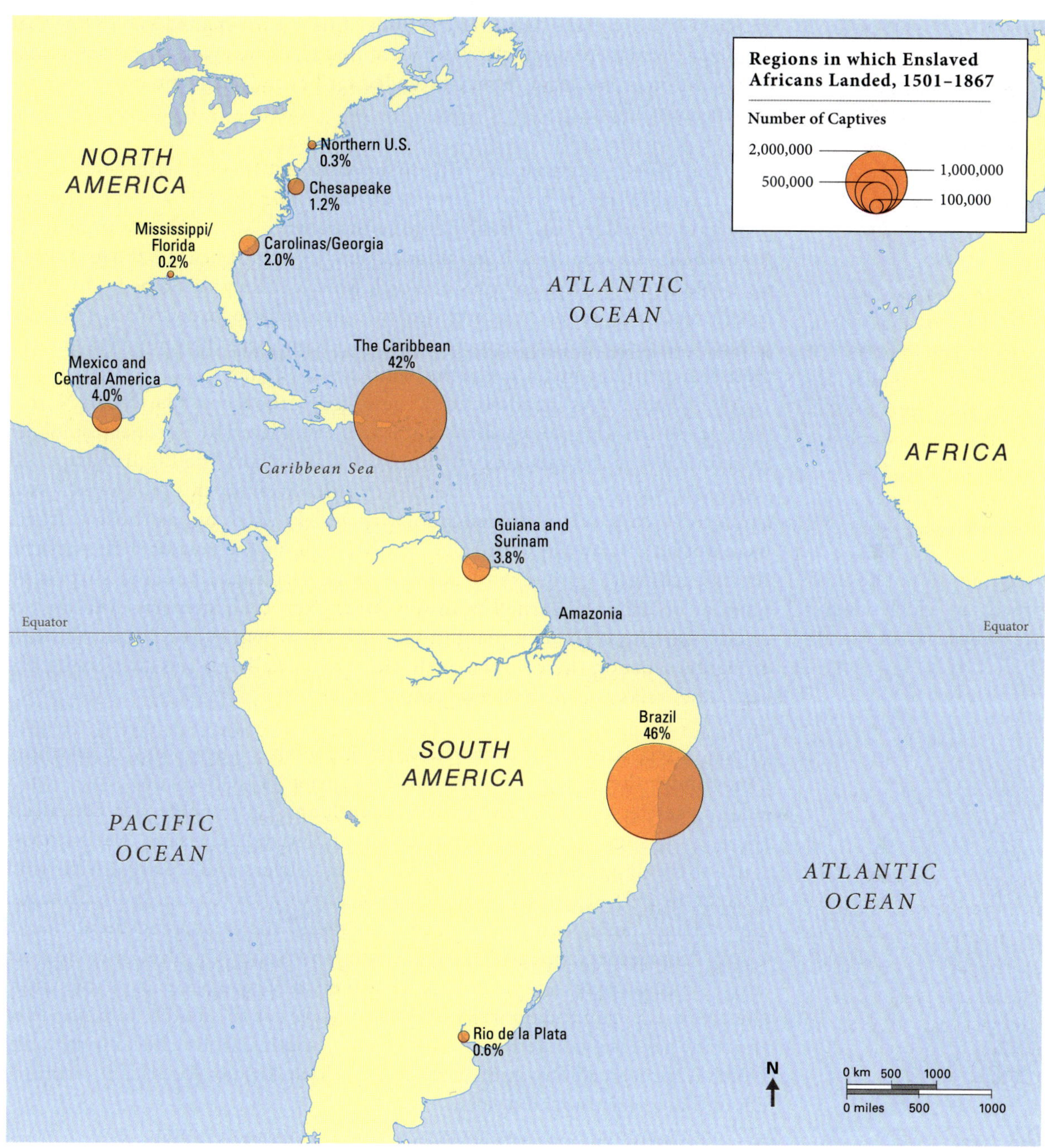

MAP 19.3 Regions in which Enslaved Africans Landed, 1501–1867

Slavery in British North America

In 1750, a plantation zone extended unbroken from Chesapeake Bay in England's North American colonies to Brazil, embracing the entire Caribbean. This zone represented a pattern unprecedented in world history. It created the largest demand for human labor yet seen, which after 1700 was satisfied almost exclusively through the African slave trade. This in turn created a color line that defined a permanent underclass and identified blackness with slavery and inferiority. At one time, legal slavery extended far beyond the plantation zone into what is now Canada.

The "Sot-Weed" Enterprise The first permanent English settlements in the Americas were the for-profit enterprise at Jamestown in 1607 and the religious "errand in the wilderness" of the initial settlements in Massachusetts from 1620. Both would soon count Africans among them. In August of 1619, the first slaves were sold in the English colonies of North America. They would be far from the last. Though only about 3–5 percent of the slaves shipped from Africa ended up in North America, through procreation on the continent their numbers grew to more than 4 million by the eve of the American Civil War.

Their labor was needed for a new crop, tobacco. The local Native Americans already grew tobacco, but it was considered by European smokers to be inferior to the varieties grown in the Caribbean. The English acquired some of the Caribbean plants and began cultivation of this "sot-weed," as it came to be called. Indentured labor was widely used, but as those workers were bound to stay only until they had worked off the cost of their passage, slaves became the preferred labor source in Virginia. Though a surprising number of Africans earned **manumission** from their owners, even on occasion starting their own plantations with their own slaves during the seventeenth century, the colonial authorities eventually passed laws fixing the slave underclass as one based on color.

Manumission: The process by which slaves are given legal freedom.

Sugar, Rice, and Indigo in the Lower South The colony of Carolina came under the purview of the Lords Proprietors in Barbados, who began sending settlers in 1670. In the seventeenth and early eighteenth centuries, these settlers enslaved tens of thousands of Native Americans. Native resistance to slaving resulted in war between the settlers and a Native American alliance in 1715–1717 that almost lost the colony for the Lords Proprietors. The settlers, angry with what they considered the mismanagement of the Lords Proprietors, appealed to the crown, and South Carolina was split off in 1719 and set up as a royal colony. Deprived of Native Americans for slaves, the colonies began to import West African slaves as the Dutch dominance of the trade gave way to the British. Ultimately, South Carolina became the only North American colony, and later state, in which African Americans outnumbered those of European descent.

South Carolina produced many of the same plantation commodities as Brazil and the Caribbean (such as sugarcane, molasses, and rice), along with indigo, which was destined to become the colony's most important cash crop until the cotton boom of the nineteenth century. The indigo plant was used to produce a dark blue dye popular in Europe. The need for labor in planting indigo, stripping the leaves, fermenting, cleaning, draining, scraping, and molding the residue into balls or blocks drove the slave trade even further.

The last new English possession in southern North America prior to 1750 was Georgia. The southern regions of what was to become the colony of Georgia had been claimed by the Spanish as early as 1526. Attempts by the French to found a colony near present-day Jacksonville in the 1560s failed. With the expansion of the English presence in the seventeenth century and the French concentrating on their vast claims in Canada and the Mississippi valley, the territory between Carolina and the Spanish fort at St. Augustine became increasingly disputed.

Into this situation stepped James Oglethorpe (1696–1785), whose vision was to set up a colony for England's poor, debtors, and dispossessed. He obtained a royal charter and in 1733 arrived at the site of the modern city of Savannah. After buying land from the local Native Americans, he began to develop the colony as a free area in which slavery was banned. The Spanish attempted to claim Georgia in 1742 but were repulsed. Pressed by settlers bringing their slaves in from South Carolina, Georgia's ban on slave labor was soon rescinded. By the end of Oglethorpe's life, Georgia had developed its own slave-based plantation economy, which included cotton—the commodity that would ensure slavery's survival in the United States until 1865.

Advertisement for a Slave Auction. In this notice from 1766, potential slave buyers in Charleston, South Carolina, are informed of the time and place for the sale of a "choice cargo" of recently arrived Africans. As Charleston was undergoing a smallpox epidemic at the time, potential customers are reassured that the captives are healthy and likely to be immune to the disease.

The Fatal Triangle: The Economic Patterns of the Atlantic Slave Trade

The European countries that dominated the transportation of slaves from the West African coast developed in a pattern that paralleled their naval and merchant marine power. During the fifteenth and sixteenth centuries, Portugal had an effective monopoly on the trade from African outposts, including Elmina. The success of Dutch and English privateers encouraged the seizure by the Dutch of Elmina in 1637. Now it was the Dutch who became the principal slave carriers, part of a pattern of aggressive colonizing that made the Netherlands the world's richest country through much of the seventeenth century. The rise of England's naval power at the expense of the Dutch and the fading of the Spanish and Portuguese naval presence next allowed the English to dominate the slave trade. By the mid-eighteenth century, the slave trade had become the base of the world's most lucrative economic triangle (see Map 19.4).

Rum, Guns, and Slaves England's colonies in the Americas were by the eighteenth century producing valuable crops for export to the Old World. Tobacco was raised mainly in England's North American colonies, along with some cotton for export to England. So profitable were these exports that, in keeping with the policy of mercantilism, the government passed the Navigation Acts in 1651 and 1660. These acts required that all goods imported to England from American colonies had to be transported only on English ships, thereby guaranteeing a virtual monopoly on transatlantic trade.

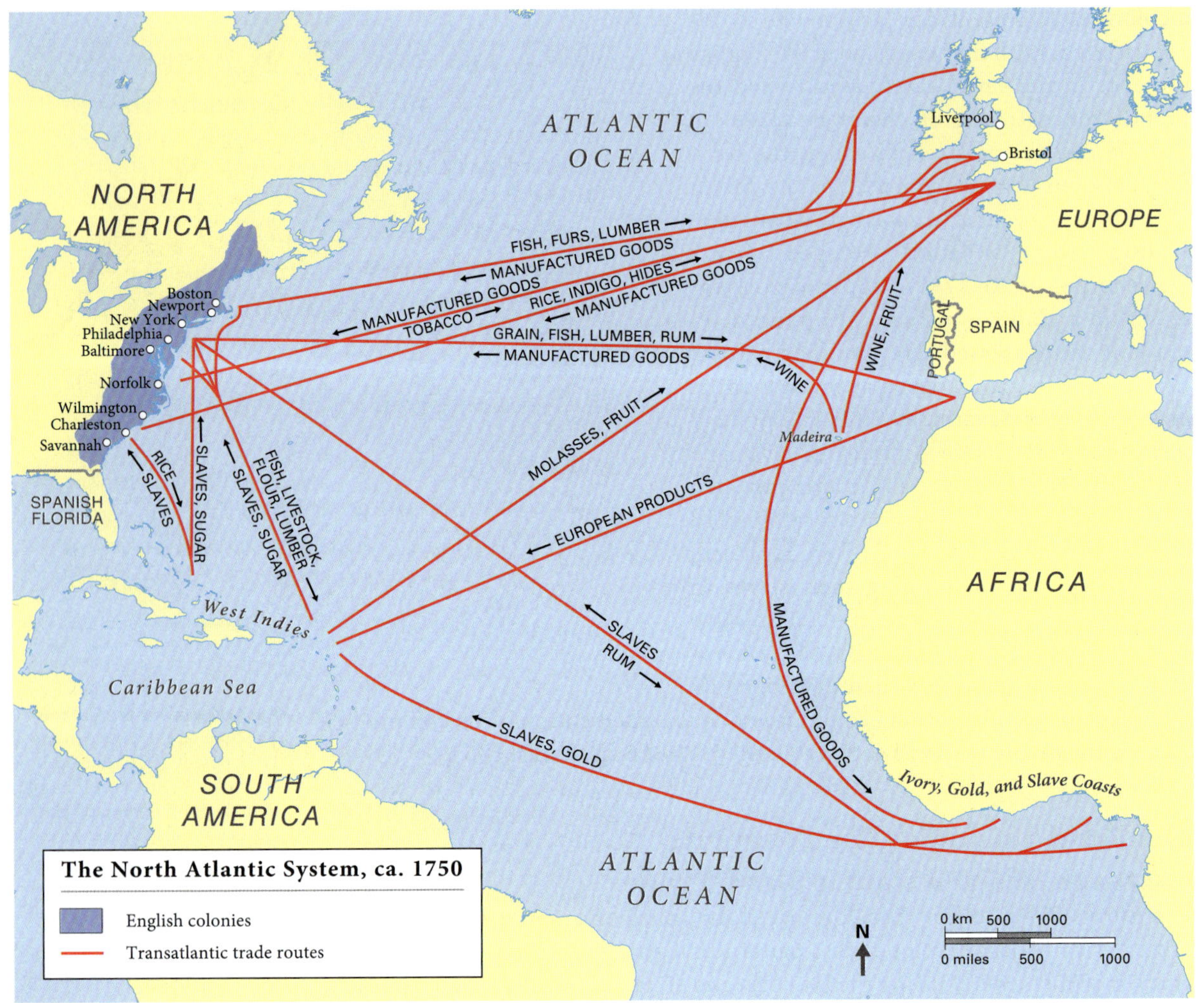

MAP 19.4 The North Atlantic System, ca. 1750

Atlantic system: Economic system in which European ships would exchange goods for slaves in West Africa and slaves would then be brought to America and exchanged for goods that would be carried back to the home port.

English merchants acquired enormous profits through their colonial trading practices, particularly with the Atlantic colonies. An analysis of the **Atlantic system**, or the "triangular trade," illustrates how this system worked. In general terms, English ships would leave home ports in either their North American colonies or England with trade goods, then travel to ports along the western coast of Africa, where these goods would be exchanged for African slaves; these ships would then cross the Atlantic, where slaves would be exchanged for goods produced in western Atlantic colonies; and finally, these goods would be carried back to the home port.

In one common pattern, an English ship loaded with rum would sail from Europe to the western coast of Africa, where the rum would be exchanged for slaves; laden with slaves, the ship would cross the Atlantic to sugar colonies in the Caribbean, where the slaves would be exchanged for molasses; the ship would then sail to New England, where the molasses would be processed into rum.

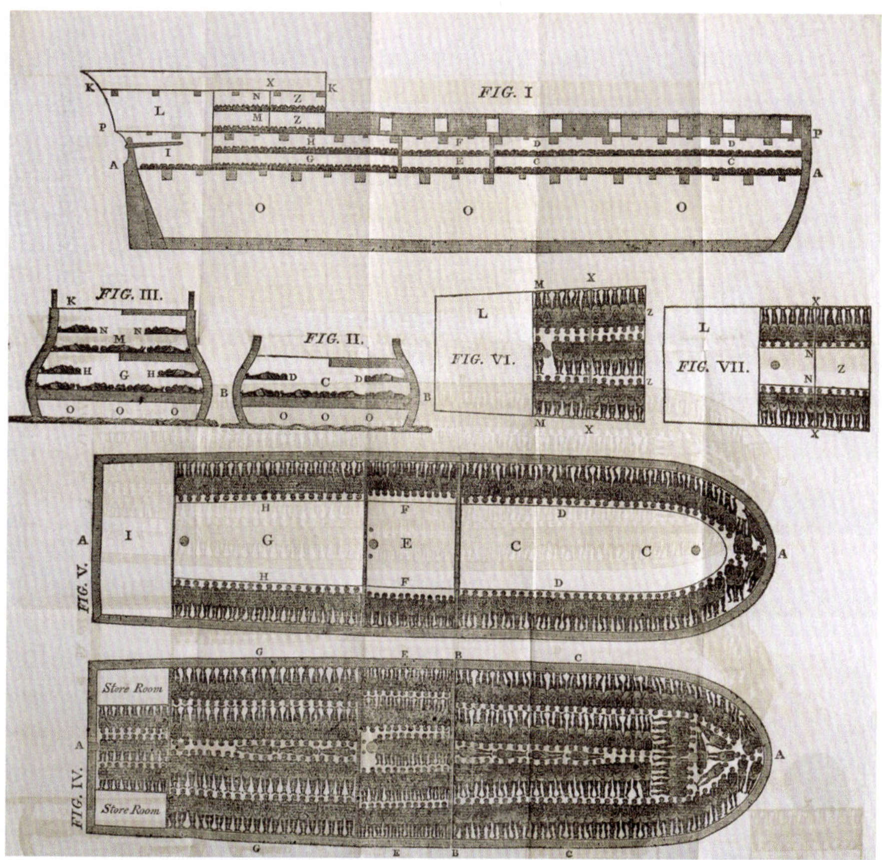

Plan of a Slave Ship, 1789. This image, based on the *Brooks*, a Liverpool slave ship, was one of the first to document the horrors of the slave trade. It shows the captives laid out like sardines below deck. In such conditions, slaves perished at the rate of 10–30 percent during the Middle Passage. The engraving was widely distributed by British abolitionists, who eventually succeeded in banning the trade in 1807.

The Middle Passage Following capture in Africa, prisoners were usually marched to slave markets and embarkation ports. Slave lots were then wholesaled to middlemen or auctioned directly to foreign factors. From this point they would be imprisoned until the next ship bound for their sale destination arrived. But it was on the voyage from Africa to the Americas, the infamous "Middle Passage," that the full horror of the slave's condition was most vividly demonstrated.

Because the profits involved in transportation were so high, mariners constantly experimented with ways to pack the maximum number of human beings into the holds of their ships. Because a certain percentage of mortality was expected during the long voyage, some ship captains favored "tight packing"—deliberate overcrowding on the assumption that a few more captives might survive than on a ship with fewer captives but a higher rate of survival. On the other hand, some captains favored the "loose pack" method, with the assumption that a higher number would survive if given marginally more room.

Patterns Up Close | Voodoo and Other New World Slave Religions

Altar and Shrine from the Interior of the Historic Voodoo Museum in New Orleans

One prominent pattern of world history is the way indigenous elements shape the identity of imported religions. Buddhism in China and Japan, for example, adopted elements from Daoism and Chinese folk beliefs as well as spirits and demons from Shinto. Christianity added Roman and Germanic elements to its calendar of holidays, architecture, and cult of saints. Islam in Iran and India and Christianity in Africa underwent similar processes. This trend of interaction continues today, when we find the African Christian churches among the fastest growing in the world.

In the Americas, three main strains of interaction and adaptation of imported and indigenous traditions developed: Santeria, which is found primarily in Cuba, among the Spanish-speaking Africans of the Caribbean, and in cities of North America with communities of Caribbean immigrants; *vodoun*, usually called "voodoo" in English, which developed in Haiti and old Saint-Domingue and is widely practiced among African-descended French speakers around the

Fearing slave mutiny, the holds of slave ships were locked and barred, and slaves chained in tiers configured to maximize the space of the hold. Food was minimal and sanitation nonexistent. The dead, sick, and resistant were thrown overboard. The ship and crew were also well armed to fight off mutineers and attacks by competitors or pirates. On landing at their destination, the slaves were imprisoned, cleaned up, and given better meals pending their auction to individual buyers. Between 10 and 30 percent of them died en route.

Culture and Identity in the African Diaspora

The term "diaspora" is used by scholars for the wide dispersal by forced or voluntary migration of any large group. In the case of the **African diaspora**, in which Africans moved to nearly all parts of the Americas primarily through the slave trade, the story is far too complex for us to do more than note some general patterns related to culture and identity.

African diaspora: Dispersal of African peoples throughout the world, particularly the Americas, as part of the transatlantic slave trade.

A New Society: Creolization of the Early Atlantic World

An effect of the Portuguese trade forts and colonies in coastal Africa was the adaptation of African societies to Western Christianity and Portuguese culture.

Caribbean and in areas of Louisiana; and Candomblé, which is found mostly in Brazil.

All three are syncretic religions composed of elements which practitioners see as part of an integrated whole. They intermingle Roman Catholic saints with West African natural and ancestral spirits and gods, see spiritual power as resident in natural things, and incorporate images of objects to represent a person or thing whose power the believer wants to tap or disperse (as in the use of so-called voodoo dolls). They also hold that ritual and sacrifices by priests and priestesses can tune in to the spirits of the natural world. Such innovations allowed slaves to create a religious and cultural space in which they carved out autonomy from their masters—indeed, in which they *were* the masters. They also provided alternate beliefs that could be invoked alongside more mainstream Christian practices. In a real sense, they provided a precious degree of freedom for people who had almost no other form of it.

Mami Wata. Both a protector and a seducer, Mami Wata is an important spirit figure throughout much of Africa and the African Atlantic. She is usually portrayed as a mermaid, a snake charmer, or a combination of both. She embodies the essential, sacred nature of water, across which so many African Americans traveled in their diaspora.

Questions

- How do black Christianity and voodoo religion show the new patterns of origins, interaction, and adoption that emerged after 1500?
- Can you think of more recent examples of syncretic religions? If so, which ones? Why are they syncretic?

Clan- or lineage-based societies welcomed trade with outsiders; others were militarily oriented and saw the new arrivals as unwelcome competitors; still others were kingdoms, some of which cooperated intermittently or permanently with the Portuguese and other Europeans. In the interactions of these societies with Portuguese Christianity, African Creole cultures of different characters emerged.

While earlier scholarship described this creolization as the uneasy grafting of an alien, colonizing culture onto "genuine" Africanness, Creole culture is now understood as an "authentic" phenomenon in its own right. This is similarly true for black Creole cultures in the Americas, where Africans arrived with either their own local spiritual traditions or as Christians and Muslims. African slaves adapted to plantation life through creolization or, as African Christian or Muslim Creoles, through further creolization, a process that expressed itself in distinct languages or dialects as well as synthetic (or hybrid) religious customs. Adaptation was a creative transformation of cultural elements to fit a life of forced labor abroad.

A key element in the development of culture and identity of Africans in the Americas lay in the influence of the central African creoles from Kongo and Ndongo up to the middle of the seventeenth century. The Christianity of some believers and its later variants helped to nurture this religion among Africans in the new lands, especially when it was reinforced by the religious practices of the slave owners. The mix of language and terms similarly gave the early arrivals a degree of agency in navigating the institutions of slavery as they were being established.

An example of a creole language that has survived for centuries is Gullah, used by the isolated slave communities along the coastal islands of South Carolina and Georgia and still spoken by their descendants today. In Haiti, Creole (*Kreyòl*) is not only the daily spoken language but one used in the media and in literary works. Creole cultures thus typically involve not only adaptation but also multiple identities—in language, religion, and culture.

Music and Food The roots of most popular music in the Americas are African. African slaves brought with them musical instruments, songs, and chants, all of which contributed to shaping the musical tastes of their owners and society at large. The widespread use of drumming and dance in African celebrations, funerals, and even coded communications was the basis for Brazilian samba, Cuban and Dominican rumba and merengue, and American jazz, blues, rock and roll, soul, and hip-hop. American country-and-western music and bluegrass feature the banjo, descended from a West African stringed instrument. The chants of field hands, rhyming contests, and gospel music also contributed to these genres.

Like music, cuisine passed easily across institutional barriers. Many dishes that most Americans consider "Southern" have African roots. The first rice brought to the Carolinas was a variety native to West Africa. Africans brought with them the knowledge of setting up an entire rice-based food system, which was established in the Carolina lowlands and Gulf Coast. The yam, the staple of West African diets, also made its way to the Americas. The heart of Louisiana creole cooking, including gumbos, "dirty rice," and jambalaya, relies on the African vegetable okra and a mixture of African, American, and Asian spices along with rice.

Plantation Life and Resistance Although nineteenth-century apologists for slavery frequently portrayed life under it as tranquil, the system was in fact one of constant violence.

Most slaves navigated their condition as best they could but were constantly reminded of their status. Those who endured the Middle Passage had violence thrust upon them immediately upon capture. Even those born into slavery lived in squalid shacks or cabins, ate inadequate rations, and spent most of their waking hours at labor.

House servants had a somewhat easier life than field hands. In some cases, they were the primary guardians, midwives, wet nurses, and even confidants of their masters' families. Often, there was affection between the household slaves and the master's family. But this was tempered by the knowledge that they or their family members could be sold at any time, and that infractions would be severely punished.

Field hands led a far harder and shorter life. The price of slavery for the master was eternal vigilance; his nightmare was slave revolt. A variety of methods kept

Slave Culture. This ca. 1790 painting from Beaufort, South Carolina, shows the vibrancy of African American culture in the face of great hardship. Note the banjo, whose origins lie in West Africa and which would have a great impact on the development of American music.

slaves in line and at their work. Overseers ran the work schedules and supervised punishments; drivers kept slaves at their work with a bullwhip to beat the slow. Slaves leaving plantations on errands had to carry passes, and precautions were taken to discourage escape or even unauthorized visits to neighboring plantations. Runaways were relentlessly pursued and flogged, branded, maimed, or castrated when returned.

Given these conditions, slaves tried to manage their work on their own terms or to get back at their owners. Slaves staged work slowdowns, feigned illnesses, sabotaged tools and equipment, or pretended not to understand how to perform certain tasks. Despite the risks, runaways were common. Later, in the United States in the 1850s, enforcement of the Fugitive Slave Act would be a prime factor driving the country toward civil war.

Slave owners faced the constant prospect of slave insurrection. The most famous of these revolts in the United States was that of Nat Turner in Virginia in 1831. In 2016 a feature-length drama titled *Birth of a Nation* about Turner's rebellion was released—its title meant to counter the racist sentiments of the famous film of that name released a century before. In some cases, these rebellions were successful enough for the slaves to create their own settlements where they could, for a time, live in freedom. These escapees were called Maroons. Three of the more successful Maroon settlements existed in Jamaica, Colombia, and Surinam. Map 19.5 lists some of the larger slave insurrections from 1500 to 1850.

MAP 19.5 Slave Revolts in the Americas, 1500–1850

Putting It All Together

Portugal, the Netherlands, England, France, and Spain built up a pattern of trading for plantation slaves on the Atlantic coast of Africa in the course of the sixteenth and seventeenth centuries. The trade took off toward the end of the sixteenth century, and by 1700 it had reached 80,000 annually, where it stayed until the early nineteenth century, when the slave trade was abolished. As for the patterns of state formation in Africa, the more powerful a kingdom was, the fewer slaves it sold, given its own labor requirements. Conversely, the more conducive the circumstances were to the collapse of chiefly or royal rule and the emergence of raider societies, the more damaging the impact was on a given population. The period marked a profound transformation for Africa, with many areas depopulated by the slave trade, some enhanced through the trade and the introduction of new food crops, and others undergoing creolization.

The interaction and adaptation patterns of Europeans and Africans in Africa and Europeans, Africans, and Native Americans in the Caribbean and Americas during the period 1500–1800 created not just a new world system of trade but a new kind of society as well. The Atlantic slave trade was the foundation of the mass production of cash crops and commodities, the first world pattern of its kind. This economic sphere was the richest of its kind in the world, but with it came the creation of an enduring social underclass and the emergence of modern racism.

Yet even as early as the 1750s, one finds the origins of the abolition movement—the international movement to end first the slave trade and ultimately slavery itself. Among the leaders of Europe's Enlightenment, thinkers were already calling for the end of the trade and institution. Elsewhere, it would take a revolution, as in Haiti, or a civil war, as in the United States, for abolition to occur. In the Atlantic world, slavery finally ended in Brazil in 1888. But it persists informally in India, Africa, and the Middle East even today.

Review and Relate

Thinking Through Patterns

Examine the ways historians approach the big questions of this chapter.

What was the pattern of kingdom and empire formation in Africa during the period 1450–1800?

Africa during these 300 years continued its pattern of kingdom and empire formation at an accelerated pace, on the basis of increased intra-African trade. In the interior of Africa, the pattern continued in spite of the demographic effects of the Atlantic slave trade on the coasts.

The pattern of plantation production was transplanted to the islands of the Atlantic and the Caribbean as well as the Americas. It was a system for growing labor-intensive cash crops—indigo, sugar, tobacco—that relied increasingly on African slave labor. By 1800, the demand for plantation commodities by Europeans and the guns, textiles, rum, and other manufactured goods that Africans took in trade for slaves swelled the system to huge proportions. In turn, the mercantilist economics of western Europe regulated the trade within an efficient triangular system.

How did the patterns of slave trade and plantation slavery evolve in the Atlantic and the Americas?

The domination of African slavery in the Americas and Caribbean over other kinds of servitude created a pattern of racism, in which blackness was permanently associated with slavery. As the economics of slavery became entrenched, the participants in the system answered the criticism of slavery on moral grounds by claiming that black Africans were inherently inferior. The argument was essentially circular: They were enslaved because they were inferior, and they were inferior because they were slaves.

What are the historic roots from which modern racism evolved?

In North America, long after slavery was abolished, these attitudes were preserved in law and custom and reinforced during the colonization of Africa in the nineteenth century and in the practice of segregation in the United States. In Latin America—although racism is no less pervasive—racial views are more subtle. People describing themselves as *mulato*, *sambo*, or *pardo* have had a better chance to be recognized as members of their own distinct ethnic groups than in the United States, where until recently the census classified people simply as either Black or Caucasian. The 2010 census form, however, expanded its choices to 14 racial categories and allowed people to check multiple boxes. Clearly, the complexities of race and ethnicity in the Americas are continuing to evolve.

Against the Grain

Consider this as a counterpoint to the main patterns examined in this chapter.

Oglethorpe's Free Colony

- How did the patterns of slave trade and plantation slavery evolve in the Americas?
- What are the historical roots from which racism evolved?

Set against the backdrop of both expanding colonial slavery and the hardening of the so-called color line, James Oglethorpe's dream of a colony of Georgia in which both slavery and rum were to be banned, and where the colonists were to consist of the "worthy poor" freed from the threat of debtor's prison, would appear to defy the patterns of the times. Oglethorpe, as a young member of the House of Commons, was appalled by the practice of imprisoning debtors and forcing them to pay for their own upkeep while incarcerated. Appointed to a parliamentary committee investigating the situation, he developed a scheme to address problems plaguing English society: indebtedness on the part of the working poor and the jobless, alcoholism fueled by cheap rum and gin, and migration to cities by the landless.

His solution was to found a colony for those afflicted by these ills. He bought land at fair prices from the Creek people, ensured that skilled craftsmen and laborers were among the initial settlers, and laid out what became the city of Savannah in a design that included farms outside the city for self-sufficiency and common areas to create close-knit neighborhoods. To ensure that the labor of the immigrants would be valued, slavery was forbidden, as was the slave-produced product of rum. While scholars differ on whether he was a true abolitionist, he did declare slavery to be "immoral" and felt that it violated English law.

As we saw in this chapter, however, his visionary aims were ultimately defeated by the colony's position on the border with Spanish Florida. With Oglethorpe's retirement to England in 1750, his fellow trustees returned control of the colony to the British crown, and the ban on slavery was rescinded. Soon, cotton would become the most valuable export in the world and the bulwark of the US economy. And as cotton became king, the slave state of Georgia would be at the epicenter of its expansion. Oglethorpe himself became the only founder of an English colony to see it become a state in the new United States, dying in 1785.

Key Terms

African diaspora 468
Atlantic system 466
Chattel 460
Household slavery 457
Indentured laborers 462
Manumission 464
Mercantilism 462
Plantation slavery 460
Presentism 460

Learn more with this chapter's digital tools, including the Oxford Insight Study Guide, at http://www.oup.com/he/vonsivers4e. Please see the Further Resources section at the back of the book for additional readings and suggested websites.

PATTERNS OF EVIDENCE |

Sources for Chapter 19

SOURCE 19.1

Abd al-Rahman al-Saadi on the scholars of Timbuktu

ca. 1655

Born in Timbuktu in 1596, Abd al-Rahman al-Saadi wrote, in Arabic, a chronicle titled *Tarikh al-Sudan* (*History of the Sudan*). The document addresses the political, cultural, and religious history of the Songhay state in the fifteenth and sixteenth centuries, and it also offers detailed accounts of various states in the Niger River valley into al-Saadi's own day. Al-Saadi was particularly interested in the impact of Islamic thought and culture on the African kingdoms, as the following excerpt demonstrates. The document was discovered by a German explorer in the 1850s during his visit to Timbuktu.

This is an account of some of the scholars and holymen who dwelt in Timbuktu generation after generation—may God Most High have mercy on them, and be pleased with them, and bring us the benefit of their *baraka* in both abodes—and of some of their virtues and noteworthy accomplishments. In this regard, it is sufficient to repeat what the trustworthy shaykhs have said, on the authority of the righteous and virtuous Friend of God, locus of manifestations of divine grace and wondrous acts, the jurist *Qāḍī* Muhammad al-Kābarī—may God Most High have mercy on him. He said: "I was the contemporary of righteous folk of Sankore, who were equaled in their righteousness only by the Companions of the Messenger of God—may God bless him and grant him peace and be pleased with all of them."

Among them were (1) the jurist al-Ḥājj, grandfather of *Qāḍī* ʿAbd al-Raḥmān b. Abī Bakr b. al-Ḥājj. He held the post of *qāḍī* during the last days of Malian rule, and was the first person to institute recitation of half a **hizb** of the Qur'ān for teaching purposes in the Sankore mosque after both the mid-afternoon and the evening worship. He and his brother Sayyid Ibrāhīm the jurist left Bīru to settle in Bangu. His tomb there is a well-known shrine, and it is said he is a **badal**. The following account is related on the authority of our virtuous and ascetic shaykh, the jurist al-Amīn b. Ahmad, who said, "In his day the Sultan of Mossi came campaigning as far as Bangu, and people went out to fight him. It so happened that a group of people were sitting with al-Ḥājj at

Hizb: Segment.

Badal: Elevated rank of saints in the Sufi hierarchy.

Source: Abd al-Rahman al-Saadi, *Timbuktu and the Songhay Empire*, trans. John Hunwick (Leiden, the Netherlands, and Boston: Brill, 2003), 38–40.

that moment, and he uttered something over [a dish of] millet and told them to eat it. They all did so except for one man, who was his son-in-law, and he declined to do so because of their relationship by marriage. Then the holyman said to them, "Go off and fight. Their arrows will do you no harm." All of them escaped harm except for the man who did not eat, and he was killed in that battle. The Sultan of Mossi and his army were defeated and driven off, having gained nothing from the people of Bangu, thanks to the *baraka* of that sayyid.

From him is descended the Friend of God the Most High the jurist Ibrāhīm, son of the Friend of God Most High, the jurist *Qādī* ʻUmar who lived in Yindubu'u, both of whom were righteous servants of God. It was Askiya *al-hājj* Muhammad who appointed ʻUmar *qādī* of that place. From time to time one of his sister's sons used to visit Timbuktu, and the jurist *Qādī* Mahmūd complained to Askiya *al-hājj* Muhammad that this man was slandering them to the people of Yindubu'u. When the Askiya visited Tila the jurist *Qādī* ʻUmar came with a group of men from Yindubu'u to pay him a courtesy call. The Askiya inquired after his sister's son, so ʻUmar presented him to him. The Askiya said, "You are the one who has been sowing discord between the jurist Mahmūd and your maternal uncle." The *qādī* was annoyed, and retorted, "You, who appointed one *qādī* in Timbuktu and another in Yindubu'u, are the one sowing discord." Then he got up angrily and went off to the waterfront, saying to his companions, "Let us go off and cross the river and be on our way." When they got there, he wanted to cross it, but they said, "It is not yet time for the ferry. Be patient until it comes." He replied, "What if it does not come?" They realised that he was prepared to cross the river without a boat. So they restrained him and sat him down until the ferry came, and they all crossed over together—may God have mercy on them and bring us benefit through them. Amen!

Working with Sources

1. **Why did the scholars and holy men of Timbuktu draw a visitor's attention?**
2. **Are there indications in this document of a culture that was still fusing Islamic and non-Islamic traditions together?**

SOURCE 19.2

Letter of Nzinga Mbemba (Afonso I) of Kongo to the King of Portugal

1526

A Portuguese sailor came into contact with the Kingdom of Kongo, which occupied a vast territory along the Congo River in central Africa, in 1483. When he returned in 1491, he was accompanied by Portuguese priests and Portuguese products, and in the same year the Kongolese king

Source: Basil Davidson, ed., *The African Past: Chronicles from Antiquity to Modern Times* (London: Longmans, 1964), 191–194. Also: https://genius.com/Nzinga-mbemba-afonso-i-letters-to-the-king-of-portugal-1526-annotated and his son were baptized as Catholics. When the son succeeded his father in 1506, he took the Christian name Afonso and promoted the introduction of European culture and religion within his kingdom. His son Henrique was educated in Portugal and became a Catholic bishop. However, Afonso's kingdom began to deteriorate in subsequent decades, as the Portuguese made further inroads into his territory, pursuing ruthless commercial practices and trading in slaves captured in his dominions. In 1526, the king sent desperate letters to King João III of Portugal, urging him to control his own subjects and to respect the alliance—and the common Catholic faith—that bound the Europeans and the Africans.

Sir, Your Highness should know how our Kingdom is being lost in so many ways that it is convenient to provide for the necessary remedy, since this is caused by the excessive freedom given by your agents and officials to the men and merchants who are allowed to come to this Kingdom to set up shops with goods and many things which have been prohibited by us, and which they spread throughout our Kingdoms and Domains in such an abundance that many of our vassals, whom we had in obedience, do not comply because they have the things in greater abundance than we ourselves; and it was with these things that we had them content and subjected under our vassalage and jurisdiction, so it is doing a great harm not only to the service of God, but the security and peace of our Kingdoms and State as well.

And we cannot reckon how great the damage is, since the mentioned merchants are taking every day our natives, sons of the land and the sons of our noblemen and vassals and our relatives, because the thieves and men of bad conscience grab them wishing to have the things and wares of this Kingdom which they are ambitious of; they grab them and get them to be sold; and so great, Sir, is the corruption and licentiousness that our country is being completely depopulated, and Your Highness should not agree with this nor accept it as in your service. And to avoid it we need from those (your) Kingdoms no more than some priests and a few people to teach in schools, and no other goods except wine and flour for the holy sacrament. That is why we beg of Your Highness to help and assist us in this matter, commanding your factors that they should not send here either merchants or wares, because it is our will that in these Kingdoms there should not be any trade of slaves nor outlet for them. Concerning what is referred [to] above, again we beg of Your Highness to agree with it, since otherwise we cannot remedy such an obvious damage. Pray Our Lord in His mercy to have Your Highness under His guard and let you do forever the things of His service. I kiss your hands many times. . . .

(At our town of Kongo, written on the sixth day of July in 1526.)

Moreover, Sir, in our Kingdoms there is another great inconvenience which is of little service to God, and this is that many of our people, keenly desirous as they are of the wares and things of your Kingdoms, which are brought here by your people, and in order to satisfy their voracious appetite, seize many of our people, freed and exempt men, and very often it happens that they kidnap even noblemen and the sons of noblemen, and our relatives, and take them to be sold to the white men who are in our Kingdoms; and for this purpose they have concealed them; and others are brought during the night so that they might not be recognized.

And as soon as they are taken by the white men they are immediately ironed and branded with fire, and when they are carried to be embarked, if they are caught by our guards' men the whites allege that they have bought them but they cannot say from whom, so that it is our duty to do justice and to restore to the freemen their freedom, but it cannot be done if your subjects feel offended, as they claim to be.

And to avoid such a great evil we passed a law so that any white man living in our Kingdoms and wanting to purchase goods in any way should first inform three of our noblemen and officials of our court whom we rely upon in this matter, and these are Dom Pedro Manipanza and Dom Manuel Manissaba, our chief usher, and Goncalo Pires our chief freighter, who should investigate if the mentioned goods are captives or free men, and if cleared by them there will be no further doubt nor embargo for them to be taken and embarked. But if the white men do not comply with it they will lose the aforementioned goods. And if we do them this favor and concession it is for the part Your Highness has in it, since we know that it is in your service too that these goods are taken from our Kingdom, otherwise we should not consent to this. . ..

(date of letter, October 18, 1526)

▸ Working with Sources

1. **What do these documents indicate about the intersections of international commerce and the slave trade?**
2. **In what terms does King Afonso issue his protest to the Portuguese king, and why?**

SOURCE 19.3

Documents concerning the slave ship *Sally*, Rhode Island

1765

Rhode Islanders were the principal American slave traders during the eighteenth century, during which a total of approximately 1,000 slave-trading voyages set out from the colony to Africa. The "triangular trade" among the Atlantic seaboard, the Caribbean, and West Africa was the main source of great wealth for many families in this small British settlement. Among these families was that of John Brown, whose donation to a struggling college in Providence would lead to the renaming of the institution in his honor. Aware of their university's explicit connection to the profitable and lethal slave trade, archivists at Brown University have attempted to tell the

Source: John Carter Brown Library: http://cds.library.brown.edu/projects/sally/documents.html

full story of voyages like that of the *Sally*. In the excerpts that follow, lines from the ship's log are annotated with details of the events they describe; italicized text is transcribed directly from the log.

December 11, 1764: At James Fort, on the River Gambia
By early December, the Sally had arrived at James Fort, the primary British slave "factory" on Africa's Windward Coast. Located fifteen miles from the mouth of the Gambia River, James Fort was the collection point for slaves coming down from the interior, and British and North American ships routinely stopped there to acquire provisions and slaves. On December 11, Hopkins purchased thirteen Africans from Governor Debatt, the British official who ran the fort, in exchange for 1,200 gallons of rum and sundry stores.

June 8, 1765: "Woman Slave hanged her Self between Decks"
While most slave ships worked their way along the coast, the Sally appears to have remained largely in one place, apparently at a small British slave "factory" near the mouth of the River Grande, in what is today Guinea-Bissau. Hopkins traded rum with passing slave ships, acquiring manufactured goods like cloth, iron bars, and guns, which he then used to acquire slaves. On June 8, 1765, he purchased his 108th captive. That same day, an enslaved woman committed suicide. She was the second captive to die on the ship.

Newport July 17, 1765
Sir
Having heard by Capt Morris that you had Lost all your Hands in the River Basa I came down here, last Evening on purpose to Take Some method to suply the misfortune as much as Possable, by the Two Vessels Just about sailing from

this place Capt Briggs & Capt Moor but Receiving your Letter of ye 15th May this morning which giving us Such favourable accounts of your Circumstance from what we had heard Quite aleviates our Misfortune and prevents dewing any thing further than Writing you by these opertunitys principaly to Inform you that (Notwithstanding our first orders to you & our Letter to Barbadoes of ye 4th Ultimo advising you to go to South Carolina,) that the market there is Surprise-ingly Glutted with Slaves So that it will not by any means do to go there Therefore Recomend if you Can get £20 Sterling for your Well Slaves Land at Barbadoes to sell there . . . and Lay out ye Neet proceed in 30 hogshead Rum 8 or 10 hogshead Sugar & 3 or 4 Baggs of Cotton the remainder in full Weight money or Good Bills but money full Weight is 5 percent better for us than bills and proceed home, without giving yourself any further trouble about Loading with Salt But if your Slaves Should be in good order and you Cannot get that proceed to Jamaica and there Dispose of them for ye same of pay & proceed home, but Notwithstanding what we here advise if you think any other port in the Westindes will Do better Considering all ye Risque, you are At full Liberty to go and Inshort do by Vessel & Cargo in that Respect as if She wass your own all friends and particularly your family is Well
M

2
Burroughs is this morning gone to Providence in order to Carry your Letter to Mrs Hopkins. you may depend. . . . Friends nor money shall not be Wanting to make the Insurance you Wish for to your Wife whose Letter Mr Burrows opend in order to Relieve the aprehentions of his father & family from ye Maloncholy Tale Brought by Capt Morris
I am for Self & Co. your Assured Frend
MB
Copy Letter
to Capt Esek
Hopkins July
1765

July 17, 1765: The Browns receive word from Hopkins
In June, 1765, after months with no news from the Sally, the Browns received reports that the ship and crew had been lost. Those rumors were contradicted on July 17, when a letter belatedly arrived from Hopkins, safe on the River Grande. Though Hopkins reported the loss of one crewman and substantial loss of his cargo through leakage, the Browns were elated. Your letter "Quite Aleviates our Misfortune," they wrote.

August 20, 1765: The Sally embarks for the Americas
On August 20, 1765, more than nine months after his arrival on the African coast, Hopkins acquired his 196th and final captive. Nineteen Africans had already died on the ship. A twentieth captive, a "woman all Most dead," was left behind as a present for Anthony, the ship's "Linguister," or translator. At least twenty-one Africans had been sold to other slave traders on the coast, bringing the Sally's "cargo" to about 155 people.

August 28, 1765: "Slaves Rose on us was obliged fire on them and Destroyed 8"

Four more Africans died in the first week of the Sally's return voyage. On August 28, desperate captives staged an insurrection, which Hopkins and the crew violently suppressed. Eight Africans died immediately, and two others later succumbed to their wounds. According to Hopkins, the captives were "so Desperited" after the failed insurrection that "Some Drowned them Selves Some Starved and Others Sickened & Dyed."

October, 1765: The Sally arrives in the West Indies

The Sally reached the West Indies in early October, 1765, after a transatlantic passage of about seven weeks. After a brief layover in Barbados, the ship proceeded to Antigua, where Hopkins wrote to the Browns, alerting them to the scope of the disaster. Sixty-eight Africans had perished during the passage, and twenty more died in the days immediately following the ship's arrival, bringing the death toll to 108. A 109th captive would later die en route to Providence.

November 16, 1765: "Sales of Negroes at Public Vendue"

When they dispatched the Sally, the Brown brothers instructed Hopkins to return to Providence with four or five "likely lads" for the family's use. The rest of the Sally survivors were auctioned in Antigua. Sickly and emaciated, they commanded extremely low prices at auction. The last two dozen survivors were auctioned in Antigua on November 16, selling, in one case, for less than £5, scarcely a tenth of the value of a "prime slave."

Working with Sources

1. **How do these documents illuminate the economic and market forces that were bound up in the transatlantic slave trade?**
2. **What were the practical consequences of viewing human slaves as a commercial product?**

SOURCE 19.4 *The Interesting Narrative of the Life of Olaudah Equiano*

1789

This autobiography of a slave who would emerge as a leading voice in the abolitionist cause has been enormously significant for understanding Atlantic slavery. Equiano said he was born a prince among the Igbo people of modern Nigeria around 1745, kidnapped as a child, and transported across the ocean to the West Indies and Virginia. Named by his first (of several) masters after the sixteenth-century King Gustav I of Sweden, "Gustavus

---

Source: Henry Louis Gates, Jr., ed., *The Classic Slave Narratives* (New York: Mentor, 1987), 99–100, 102–103.

Vas[s]a" would travel throughout the southern American colonies and the Caribbean, always longing to achieve his freedom. Shaming his Quaker master into honoring a promise, Equiano was freed in 1765, but he continued to suffer the indignities and risks attending a free black man living in a slave society. His published memoir was designed to galvanize antislavery forces, and his work elicited sufficient sympathy and respect to contribute to the abolition of the British slave trade (though not slavery itself) in 1807.

We set sail once more for Montserrat, and arrived there safe; but much out of humour with our friend, the silversmith. When we had unladen the vessel, and I had sold my venture, finding myself master of about forty-seven pounds, I consulted my true friend, the Captain, how I should proceed in offering my master the money for my freedom. He told me to come on a certain morning, when he and my master would be at breakfast together. Accordingly, on that morning I went, and met the Captain there, as he had appointed. When I went in I made my obeisance to my master, and with my money in my hand, and many fears in my heart, I prayed him to be as good as his offer to me, when he was pleased to promise me my freedom as soon as I could purchase it. This speech seemed to confound him; he began to recoil; and my heart that instant sunk within me. "What," said he, "give you your freedom? Why, where did you get the money? Have you got forty pounds sterling?" "Yes, sir," I answered. "How did you get it?" replied he. I told him, "very honestly." The Captain then said he knew I got the money very honestly and with much industry, and that I was particularly careful. On which my master replied, I got money much faster than he did; and said he would not have made me the promise which he did, had he thought I should have got the money so soon. "Come, come," said my worthy Captain, clapping my master on the back. "Come, Robert, (which was his name) I think you must let him have his freedom. You have laid your money out very well; you have received good interest for it all this time, and here is now the principal at last. I know Gustavus has earned you more than a hundred a year, and he will still save you money, as he will not leave you. Come, Robert, take the money." My master then said, he would not be worse than his promise; and, taking the money, told me to go to the Secretary at the Register Office, and get my manumission drawn up.

These words of my master were like a voice from heaven to me: in an instant all my trepidation was turned into unutterable bliss, and I most reverently bowed myself with gratitude, unable to express my feelings, but by the overflowing of my eyes, and a heart replete with thanks to God; while my true and worthy friend, the Captain, congratulated us both with a peculiar degree of heartfelt pleasure.

. . .

During our stay at this place [Savannah, Georgia], one evening a slave belonging to Mr. Read, a merchant of Savannah, came near our vessel, and began to use me very ill. I entreated him, with all the patience of which I was master, to desist, as I knew there was little or no law for a free negro here. But the fellow, instead of taking my advice, persevered in his insults, and even struck me. At this I lost all temper, and fell on him, and beat him soundly. The next morning his master came to our vessel, as we lay alongside the wharf, and desired me to come ashore that he might have me flogged all round the town, for beating his negro slave! I told him he had insulted me, and had given the provocation by first striking me. I had also told my Captain the whole affair that morning, and desired him to go along with me to Mr. Read, to prevent bad consequences; but he said that it did not signify, and if Mr. Read said any thing he would make matters up, and desired me to go to work, which I accordingly did.

The Captain being on board when Mr. Read came and applied to him to deliver me up, he said he knew nothing of the matter, I was a free man. I was astonished and frightened at this, and thought I had better keep where I was, than go ashore and be flogged round the town, without judge or jury. I therefore refused to stir; and Mr. Read went away, swearing he would bring all the constables in the town, for he would have me out of the vessel. When he was gone, I thought his threat might prove too true to my sorrow; and I was confirmed in this belief, as well by the many instances I had seen of the treatment of free negroes, as from a fact that had happened within my own knowledge here a short time before.

There was a free black man, a carpenter, that I knew, who for asking a gentleman that he had worked for, for the money he had earned, was put into gaol; and afterwards this oppressed man was sent from Georgia, with false accusations, of an intention to set the gentleman's house on fire, and run away with his slaves. I was therefore much embarrassed, and very apprehensive of a flogging at least. I dreaded, of all things, the thoughts of being stripped, as I never in my life had the marks of any violence of that kind. At that instant a rage seized my soul, and for a little I determined to resist the first man that should attempt to lay violent hands on me, or basely use me without a trial; for I would sooner die like a free man, than suffer myself to be scourged, by the hands of ruffians, and my blood drawn like a slave.

Working with Sources

1. **What did being free mean to Equiano? Was he disappointed in his change of status?**
2. **What role does the captain play in the narrative at this point?**

SOURCE 19.5

Casta painting, Mexico

Eighteenth century

Some of the most remarkable visual records of colonial Mexico are the series of paintings called "casta" paintings, illustrating every racial combination of Spanish, mestizo, black, Native American, and other types thought possible in the New Spain of the eighteenth and early nineteenth centuries.

Source: De Espanol y Negra, Mulato (From Spaniard and Black, Mulatto), attributed to Jose de Alcibar, ca. 1760. Denver Art Museum: Collection of Frederick and Jan Mayer. Photo © James O. Milmoe

Casta paintings were always created in a series, and each picture usually contains a male–female couple and at least one child. Occasionally more than one child and even other animal or human figures are depicted. This painting from about 1765 shows a Spanish man whose cigarette is being lit by a brazier held by a mulatto child. In the background, a black woman prepares a chocolate beverage. The man wears a morning coat adorned in a floral pattern of Asian origin.

▸ Working with Sources

1. Look at the arrangement of the three figures in the painting. Which person dominates the scene? What does this say about social relations in colonial Mexico?
2. Examine the man's morning coat. Considering that its design is of Asian origin, what does this say about the fashion consciousness of Mexico's colonial elite?

World Period Four

Interactions across the Globe, 1450–1750

The fifteenth century saw a renewal of the imperial impulse in the religious civilizations of the world. A forerunner had been the Mongol empire, which however did not last long; in less than 100 years it was replaced in China by the Ming. The founders of the subsequent new empires were the Mughals in India; the Ottomans, Safavids, and Songhay in the Middle East and Islamic Africa; the Habsburgs in Europe; and the seaborne empires of Portugal and Spain. One byproduct of this new imperial impulse was the discovery of the Americas, which in turn inspired the formulation of the heliocentric universe. The rediscovery of Greek literature in Europe had already set into motion the Renaissance, a broad new approach to under-standing the world that provided the spark for the New Science.

China and India, by far the wealthiest and most populous agrarian–urban empires, enjoyed leading positions in the world because they produced everything they needed and wanted. Europe, however, acquired warm-weather crops and minerals through overseas colonial expansion, which would help it to challenge the traditional order.

Chapter 20

The Mughal Empire

Muslim Rulers and Hindu Subjects, 1400–1750

CHAPTER TWENTY PATTERNS

Origins, Interactions, and Adaptations The breakup of the Mongol super-empire in the 1400s had spurred attempts at reunion by Tamerlane, whose putative descendent, Babur, would successfully invade India and set up a new Islamic dynasty, the Mughals, in 1526. At the peak of its power in the mid- to late seventeenth century, it would be surpassed in wealth and power only by Qing China. Its adaptations by its emperors to governing a vast and populous realm created a degree of stability. The attempts at religious harmony by an Islamic minority were less successful. These legacies continue today.

Uniqueness and Similarities While Mughal India shared a number of characteristics with the Islamic regimes of the Ottomans and Safavids, it faced a number of unique challenges. Foremost among these was the position of the rulers as Turkic Muslims governing a large Hindu population. Both the Ottomans and Safavids had considerable non-Muslim populations. But nowhere else was the difference between the faith of the rulers and the vast majority of their subjects so stark.

All three empires, like the developing European states, had come to power through the advancing technology of firearms. Moreover, along with China, the three empires collectively held the bulk of the wealth of the world as well as the majority of its trade until the world trading and colonial systems created by the expanding European maritime states began to shift the balance.

When Mumtaz Mahal, the wife of the Mughal emperor Shah Jahan, died in childbirth in 1631, the royal family was plunged into mourning.

Inconsolable for months, Shah Jahan finally resolved to build a magnificent tomb complex for Mumtaz Mahal over her burial site along the Jumna (or Yamuna) River near the fortress at Agra. This tomb, with its balance of deceptively simple lines, harmony of proportion, and technical skill, would become the most recognized symbol of India throughout the world: the Taj Mahal.

The Taj Mahal illustrates in many respects the circumstances of Mughal rule in India, particularly the attempted syncretism of Muslim rulers and Hindu subjects. Like their predecessors, the Mughals discovered the difficulties of being an ethnic and religious minority ruling a diverse population. By Shah Jahan's time, moreover, religious revival was sweeping Islamic India, and earlier Mughal rulers were subject to criticism about their laxity in ruling according to Islamic law. Shah Jahan devoted himself to a study of the Quran and resolved to rule according to Islamic precepts. The resulting policy changes would raise tensions between Hindus and Muslims.

CHAPTER OUTLINE

History and Political Life of the Mughals

Administration, Society, and Economy

Science, Religion, and the Arts

Putting It All Together

Shah Jahan's architectural masterpiece is at the center of a much larger complex that serves as an **allegory** of Allah's judgment in paradise on the day of the resurrection. In the end, Mughal ambition to create an empire as the earthly expression of this vision lent itself to that empire's ultimate decline. The drive to bring the remaining independent Indian states under Mughal control strained imperial resources. Dynastic succession almost always resulted in internal wars. By the eighteenth century, rebellion and the growing influence of the European powers would send the dynasty into a downward spiral from which it never recovered.

Because the Mughals represent the most concerted attempt at creating a unified empire from radically different religious and social traditions, their attempt embodies an important pattern of world history. Moreover, their position as a

ABOVE: The Taj Mahal (1631–1653), a magnificent architectural synthesis of Hindu and Muslim influences and Persian classicism.

Seeing Patterns

> **What were the strengths and weaknesses of Mughal rule?**

> **What was the Mughal policy toward religious accommodation? How did it change over time?**

> **What factors account for the Mughal decline during the eighteenth century?**

minority attempting to rule a vast and diverse majority represents an important pattern as well. Thus, the Mughal experience merits a somewhat closer examination than might otherwise be the case.

History and Political Life of the Mughals

Relations between Muslims and India's other religions were *syncretic*, coexisting on occasionally difficult or hostile terms, but remaining largely separate from the other traditions. Yet the political and social systems created by the Mughals were in many respects a successful *synthesis*. That is, the Mughals brought with them a tradition that blended the practices of conquest and plunder with several centuries of ruling more settled areas by peaceful means. This legacy would guide them as they struggled to create an empire centered on one religion. The Mughals created a flexible bureaucracy with a hierarchy of ranks and separation of powers but with ultimate power concentrated in the hands of the emperors. Like those of the Chinese and Ottomans, the system was easily expanded into newly conquered areas, gave free rein to the ambitious, and weathered major political storms until its decline during the eighteenth century.

From Samarkand to Hindustan

When the Mongol Empire fell apart, the Central Asian heartland of the Turkic peoples evolved into a patchwork of smaller states, many of whose rulers claimed descent from Genghis Khan. With the ousting of the Mongol Yuan dynasty from China in 1368, the eastern regions of this territory were thrown into further disarray, which set the stage for another movement toward consolidation.

The Empire of Timur Islam, by the fourteenth century, was the dominant religion among the Central Asian Turkic peoples. In the interior of Central Asia, the memory of the accomplishments of the Mongol Empire among the inhabitants of Chagatai—the area given to Genghis Khan's son of that name—was still fresh. Their desire for a new Mongol Empire, now coupled with Islam, created opportunities for military action to unite the settled and nomadic tribes of Chagatai. The result was the stunning rise of Temur Gurgan (r. 1370–1405), more widely known by the Persian rendering of his name, Timur-i Lang ("Timur the Lame"), or Tamerlane.

Though Timur came close to matching the conquests of Genghis Khan, his forebears were not direct descendants of the conqueror. He therefore devised genealogies connecting him to the dominant Mongol lines to give him legitimacy as a ruler, and he even found a direct descendant of Genghis Khan to use as a figurehead for his regime.

From 1382, when he secured the region of his homeland around the capital, the Silk Road trading center of Samarkand, until his death in 1405, Timur ranged through western Central Asia, Afghanistan, northern India, Iran, Anatolia, and the eastern Mediterranean (see Map 20.1). Like his model, Genghis Khan, he proved surprisingly liberal in his treatment of certain cities that surrendered peacefully. Many more times, however, he reduced cities to rubble, slaughtered the inhabitants, and erected pyramids of skulls as a warning to others to submit.

MAP 20.1 **Area Subjugated by Timur-i Lang, 1360–1405**

Shortly after his death in 1405, Timur's empire, like that of Genghis Khan, fell apart. The Chagatai peoples resumed their feuds, once again leaving the way open for a strong military force to impose order.

Babur and the Timurid Line in India By the beginning of the sixteenth century, the region from Samarkand south into the Punjab in northern India had become the province of feuding Turkic tribes and clans of Afghan fighters. Into this volatile environment was born Zahir ud-Din Muhammad Babur (1483–1530, r. 1526–1530), more commonly known as simply Babur. His claims to legitimate rule were considerable: His father was a direct descendant of Timur, while his mother claimed the lineage of Genghis Khan.

In 1504, Babur moved into Afghanistan, captured Kabul, and went on to raid points farther south over the following decade. By 1519, he raided northern India with a view to subjugating and ruling it. After seven more years of campaigning, this goal was achieved. In 1526, Babur's army met the forces of Sultan Ibrahim Lodi at Panipat, near Delhi. Though the sultan's forces were much larger, Babur's forces employed the new technologies of matchlock muskets and field cannon to devastating effect. In the end, the Lodi sultan was killed, and Babur's way was now clear to consolidate his new Indian territories.

Victory at Panipat was followed by conquest of the Lodi capital of Agra and further success over the Hindu Rajputs in 1528. At his death in 1530, Babur controlled territory extending from Samarkand in the north to Gwalior in India in the south (see Map 20.2). For Babur and his successors, their ruling family would always be the "House of Timur." Because of their claims to the legacy of Genghis Khan, however, they would be better known to the world as the Mughals (Urdu *mughal* from Persian *mughul* "Mongol").

Loss and Recovery of Empire Babur's son, Humayun (r. 1530–1556) was now faced with the problem of consolidating, organizing, and administering this vast domain. However, Humayun was more interested in literature (and, at times, wine and opium) than leadership.

1336–1405 Timur (Tamerlane), founder of Timurid line of rulers

1483–1530 Babur, founder of Timurid line in India—the Mughals

1542–1605 Akbar, most innovative of Mughal rulers

1627–1657 Shah Jahan, builder of the Taj Mahal

1618–1707 Aurangzeb, last powerful Mughal ruler

1707–1858 Ebbing of Mughal power in India; rise of British influence

1739 Invasion by Persians; looting of Delhi; taking of Peacock Throne

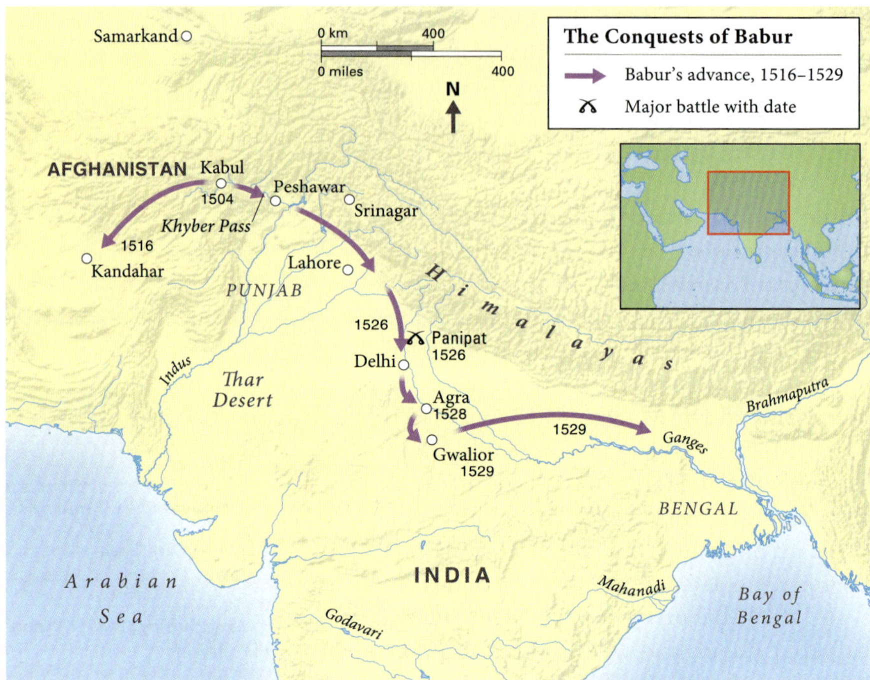

MAP 20.2 **The Conquests of Babur**

Institutionalization: The creation of a regular system for previously improvised or ad hoc activities or things, such as law codes to replace local customs.

Portrait of Babur. This imagined portrait of Babur was done about 60 years after his death. He is shown receiving representatives of the Uzbeks of Central Asia and the Rajputs of India in an audience dated December 18, 1528.

A chronic problem was the **institutionalization** of traditional nomadic succession practices among the Mughal rulers. Though only one son was designated as the ruler's successor, the others were given territories within the empire, which led to conflict. Humayun also faced hostile military forces in unconquered areas of northern India and Afghanistan. When the Afghan leader Sher Khan Suri invaded the extreme eastern region of Bengal, Humayun, twice routed, fled to Persia, where he was forced to convert to Shia Islam as the price for aid. As distasteful as this was for him as a Sunni Muslim, he now at least had Persian backing, and he proceeded to move into Afghanistan and, ultimately, to Delhi. By 1555, the dynasty was restored. For Humayun, however, the peace brought only a brief respite. In a final irony for this scholarly man, as he was descending the stairs from the roof terrace of his palace library with a pile of books in his arms, he heard the sound of the muezzin's call to prayer. As he went to kneel on the staircase, he tripped on his robe and fell. After several days, he died of his injuries in January 1556.

Consolidation and Expansion Humayun's death was kept secret while the court worked out plans for a **regency** for the emperor's son, 14-year-old Jalal ud-Din Akbar (r. 1556–1605). His military education began quickly, however, as Humayun's old enemy, Sher Khan, sent an army to attack Delhi in 1557. The Mughal forces triumphed, and went on to secure the eastern, southern, and western flanks of their lands, once again anchoring Islam in the former areas of its influence—"Hindustan."

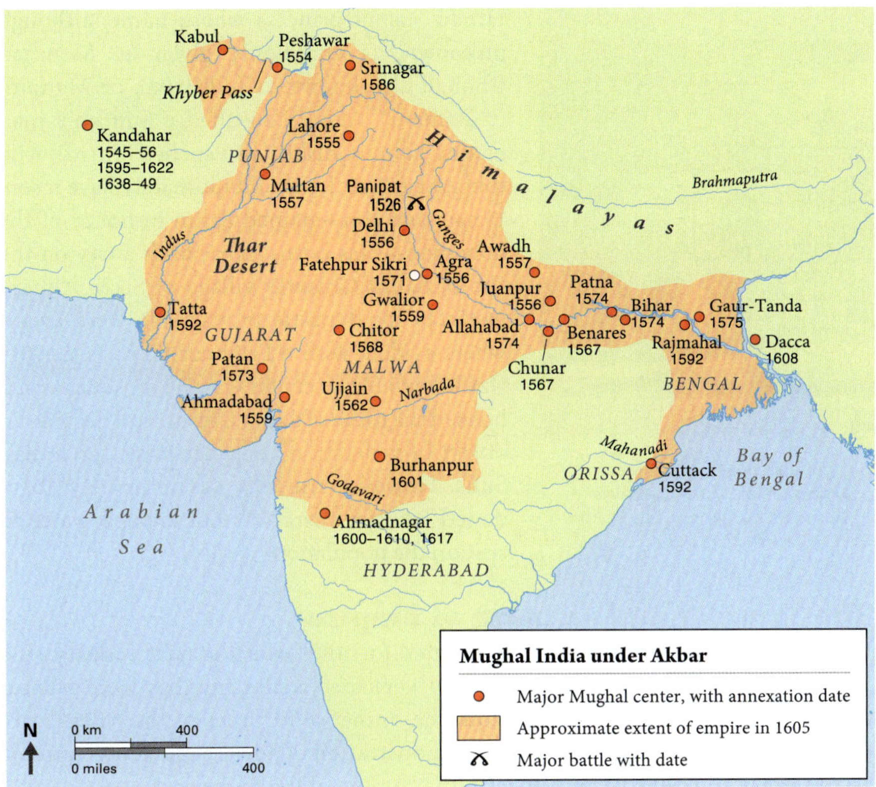

MAP 20.3 **Mughal India under Akbar**

Akbar plunged into renewed campaigning in quest of more territory. Although determined to master all India by any military means necessary, Akbar, who abhorred religious violence, worked to reconcile the different religious traditions of his empire. But his attempts would prove futile, earning him the enmity of many of his fellow Muslims, who felt he had become an unbeliever.

As a warrior Akbar was far more successful. Through the 1560s, Mughal armies continued to push the boundaries of the empire west, south, and east. This string of victories continued into the next decade, with the long-sought conquest of Gujarat taking place in 1573. Turning eastward, Akbar set his sights on Bengal, which, along with the neighboring regions of Bihar and Orissa, fell to the Mughals by the mid-1570s. They remained, however, volatile and hostile to Mughal occupation. Both Muslim and Hindu princes in the region continued their resistance into the following decades (see Map 20.3).

Resistance and rebellion plagued other areas of the empire. In order to keep the old Islamic heartland of northern India—Hindustan—under Mughal control, the Mughals built fortresses throughout their inner domains as well as along the frontier. Among the most important of these were at Allahabad, Lahore (in modern Pakistan), Ajmer (the Amber Fort in Jaipur), and the Red Fort in Delhi.

The New City In addition to fielding large armies and maintaining forts, the immense revenues of the Mughal lands allowed for other monumental projects. In an effort to show solidarity with his non-Muslim subjects, Akbar had married a

Humayun's Tomb Complex. Humayun's difficult reign and tragic end are commemorated today in his extensive tomb complex in Delhi. It was commissioned by his first wife, Bega Begum, in 1569 and shows the Persian influence that marked Mughal architecture and reached its highest expression in the Taj Mahal.

Hindu Rajput princess whose name, although unknown, is commonly given as Manmati (though also known as Jodha Bai, or Mariam-uz-Zamani). Akbar consulted a Sufi holy man named Salim Chishti (also spelled Chisti), who told Akbar that he would ultimately have a son. When that son—named Salim in honor of the holy man—was born, Akbar built a city on the site of Salim Chishti's village of Sikri. Akbar's instincts for dynastic propaganda were everywhere evident within Fatehpur Sikri, as the city was known. At its center was the mosque, which housed the tomb of Salim Chishti and became an object of veneration and pilgrimage for Indian Sufis. However, the city was ultimately abandoned because there was not enough water to sustain the population.

The Summer and Autumn of Empire

The saga of Fatehpur Sikri reflects Mughal fortunes over the next century. The military accomplishments of the dynasty were spectacular, but they were eventually worn down by internal rebellion; the immense fortunes of the rulers were depleted by the needs of defense and demonstration of power; and new economic and military competitors arrived with the coming of the Europeans.

The Revolt of the Sons In 1585, Akbar left Fatehpur Sikri with his army for Lahore, which he made his temporary capital. Once again, the Afghan princes were chafing under Mughal domination and intriguing with the Uzbeks and Safavid Persians to wrest local control for themselves. For Akbar, it was vital to maintain a hold over these areas because of their connection to the peoples of Chagatai and the need to keep control of the essential Silk Road trade. Now the key city of Kandahar, in modern Afghanistan, was in Safavid Persian hands, disrupting Mughal control of the trade. For the next 13 years, Akbar and his generals fought to subdue the Afghans and roll back the Safavids. In the end, the Mughals acquired Sind and Kashmir, subdued for a time the region of Swat, and, with the defection of a Safavid commander, occupied Kandahar. By 1598, the regions in question were secure enough for Akbar to move back to Agra.

In 1600, Akbar embarked on his last great campaign against the remaining free Muslim sultanates of central India. These were reduced within a year, but Akbar was now faced with a domestic crisis. His son Salim launched a coup and occupied the fort at Agra. Salim declared himself emperor and raised his own army. In the end, one of Akbar's wives and a group of court women were able to reconcile Akbar and Salim, and upon Akbar's death on October 25, 1605, Salim acceded to the throne as Jahangir (r. 1605–1627).

Renewed Expansion of the "War State" Jahangir continued the tradition of conquest and expansion. This now meant pushing south into the Deccan and periodically resecuring Afghanistan and its adjacent regions. A move into Bengal, however, foreshadowed a major clash with a very different kind of enemy: the Shan people of

Southeast Asia called the Ahoms. Though they had converted to Hinduism, the Ahoms had no caste system and drew upon a legacy of self-confident expansion. With little fixed territory to defend because of their mobility, the Ahoms proved the most stubborn enemies the empire had yet encountered. Though both sides employed troops armed with matchlocks and cannon, neither side could obtain a clear tactical edge, and their wars dragged on for decades.

A different threat to the Mughals was posed by the empire to their west, Safavid Persia. Both sides periodically went to war, and there was also intense religious rivalry, with the predominantly Sunni Mughals and Shiite Safavid Persians each denouncing the other as heretical unbelievers. For the Mughals, it was particularly galling that they owed the survival of their dynasty in part to the Persian shah Tahmasp, who had forced Humayun to convert to Shiism.

In addition, many Persians and Shiites within the Mughal elites felt that the Persian culture, language, and literature were superior to those of the Turks and Muslim India as a whole. In some respects, both Persians and "Persianized" Indians saw Muslim India as a kind of cultural colonial outpost. This made for complex relations between the two empires, with both vying for power in religious and cultural terms as much as in the political and military realm.

Visions of Akbar. A depiction of Akbar from ca. 1630 shows him in all of his religious glory: surrounded by a luminous halo, surmounted by angels glorifying him and holding his crown, and graced with the holiness to make the lion lie down with the heifer.

New Directions in Religious Politics

After Jahangir died in October 1627, his eldest son, Khurram, reigned as Shah Jahan (r. 1627–1657). His rule coincided with the high point of Mughal cultural power and prestige, as reflected in the Taj Mahal. However,

Salim Chishti's Tomb at Fatehpur Sikri. The tomb of the Sufi mystic Salim Chishti shows the sense of restrained flamboyance that marks the mature Mughal architectural style. The Chishtis had long been revered by India's Sufis, and Salim's simple, elegant tomb, with its domed sarcophagus, multihued marble, and Quranic inscriptions, quickly became a favorite pilgrimage site. Surrounding it is one of the red sandstone courtyards of Akbar's Fatehpur Sikri.

Patterns Up Close | Akbar's Attempt at Religious Synthesis

The Mughals as Muslim rulers in India were faced with an array of diverse religious and cultural traditions. Akbar's innovation within the world-historical pattern of religious civilizations was to create a new religion that would encompass these traditions and bind his followers directly to him as emperor and religious leader: an Indian "religious synthesis."

Akbar was resistant to the strictures of Sunni Islam or any other organized religion. He developed an extraordinary memory for literature and poetry, and his tastes within Islam centered on Sufi mysticism, which had a long tradition of tolerance and eclecticism. This openness encouraged him to study the mystical traditions of the Hindus, Parsis (Zoroastrian immigrants from Persia), and Christians. After establishing himself at Fatehpur Sikri, he sponsored regular theological debates, mostly among Muslim scholars but gradually including Hindus, Parsis, and in 1578 Catholic missionaries. He honored many of the cultural traditions of India's various religions as well: He wore his hair long under his turban like the Sikhs and some Hindus, coined emblems of the sun to honor the Parsis, and kept paintings of the Virgin Mary as a nod to the Christians.

Akbar Presiding Over a Religious Debate. Akbar's distaste for religious orthodoxy manifested itself most dramatically in his conducting regular debates among theologians from many of India's faiths. Here, a discussion is taking place with two Jesuit missionaries, Fathers Rudolph Aquaviva and Francis Henriquez (dressed in black) in 1578. Interestingly, the priests had unfettered access to Akbar, were free to preach, and even gave instruction to members of Akbar's family at his request.

his record is less spectacular in political and military terms. The Mughal obsession with controlling the northern trade routes coincided with the need to take back the fort at Kandahar, once again in Persian hands. Thus, Shah Jahan spent much of his reign on the ultimately fruitless drive to finally subdue the northwest.

The reigns of Akbar and of Jahangir were marked by extraordinary religious tolerance. The attraction of both men to the Sufi school of Salim Chishti created a favorable emotional environment for religious pluralism. It also made some Muslims, for whom strict adherence to Sunni doctrine was necessary to guard against Persian Shia influence, apprehensive. Others noted that Hindus incorporated the beliefs of other faiths into their own, and so feared that the ruling Muslim minority might ultimately be assimilated into the Hindu majority.

With Shah Jahan, however, we see a turn toward a more legalistic tradition. Under the influence of Sunni theologians, Shah Jahan began to block the construction and repair of non-Muslim religious buildings, instituted more state support for Islamic festivals, and furnished subsidies for Muslim pilgrims to Mecca. The ideal of a unified Muslim world governed by Quranic law gained ground at the Mughal court and would see its greatest champion in Shah Jahan's son Aurangzeb.

During a lavish and bloody hunting party in 1578, he had a sudden, intense mystical experience. Like Ashoka so long before him—of whom Akbar was completely unaware—he was now appalled by the destruction and waste in which he had participated. He developed a personal philosophy he called *sulh-i kull*—"peace with all." While this did not end his military campaigns, which he saw as ordained by God, it did push him to develop a new religion he called *din-i ilahi* (divine faith). Akbar directed the movement at those aspiring to gain favor from the regime. He devised rituals in which adherents swore loyalty to him not only as emperor but as the enlightened religious master of the new sect. Borrowing from Sufi mysticism, Persian court protocols, Zoroastrian sun and fire veneration, and even Christian-influenced spiritualism, he sought to at once limit the power of Sunni Islamic clerics and draw followers of other religions to what he taught was a "higher" realm, one that embraced all religions and provided the elect with secret insights into their ultimate truths.

In the end, however, despite its merging of the needs of state and religion to overcome religious and cultural divisions, Akbar's attempt must be considered a failure. While some Hindu and Muslim courtiers embraced *din-i ilahi* for its perceived religious truths, many did so for opportunistic reasons, and it was condemned by most Sunni theologians. Akbar's successors not only repudiated it but swung increasingly in the direction of stricter Sunni Islam.

Questions

- How does Akbar's attempt at religious syncretism demonstrate the pattern of origins–innovations–adaptations that informs the approach of this book?
- Why was Akbar's attempt to create a new divine faith doomed to failure?

The Pinnacle of Power The ascendancy of Aurangzeb (r. 1658–1707) was marked by the familiar pattern of princely infighting. In this case, it was brought on by the extended illness of Shah Jahan in 1657. A four-way struggle broke out among his sons. By 1661 three had been killed, leaving Aurangzeb in control of the empire. Shah Jahan lived on in captivity until 1666.

Aurangzeb's long rule seemed to begin auspiciously when his armies fought the Ahoms to a standstill in the early 1660s and made them Mughal clients. When Mughal control of the area around Kabul and the Khyber Pass was threatened by local tribesmen, Aurangzeb fought to retain control of the region and bought off other troublesome groups with gifts.

With these campaigns, the political power of the Mughals reached perhaps its greatest extent. But the period also marked a watershed in several respects. First, it launched decades of wars with the Hindu Marathas in which the empire's cohesion was eroded. In addition, European trading companies expanded their own fortified outposts in Indian ports outside Mughal domains. As Mughal power was sapped by the revolts of the eighteenth century, the companies' armed forces became important players in regional politics.

The other watershed was Aurangzeb's bid for a more effective "Islamification" of Mughal India ruled by Islamic Sharia law. As the ruler of an Islamic state, connected to the larger commonwealth of Islamic states, he believed that Mughal rule should be primarily for the benefit of Muslims. This was an almost complete repudiation of his great-grandfather Akbar's vision of religious synthesis. While Aurangzeb stopped short of forcible conversion, elites who converted to Islam were given gifts and preferential assignments, while those who did not convert found themselves isolated. Muslim judges prompted protests from Hindus regarding their rulings. Aurangzeb further ordered the demolition of Hindu temples. Finally, he reinstated the *jizya* tax on unbelievers, which had been abolished by Akbar.

The new religious policies created problems with self-governing, non-Muslim groups within the empire. The distrust of the Mughals among the Sikhs was inflamed by Aurangzeb's attempts to intervene in the selection of a new Sikh religious leader and by the destruction of some Sikh temples. These conditions would soon lead to a full-blown Sikh revolt.

Maratha: Warrior group from the Deccan Plateau in central India that was in conflict with the Mughals and controlled much of the Indian subcontinent in the eighteenth century.

The Maratha Revolt Aurangzeb conquered areas that had long eluded Mughal efforts: Bijapur, Golconda, and much of the **Maratha** lands of south central India. Yet here, too, the preconditions were already in place for a rebellion.

The Hindu Marathas had evolved working relationships with the old Muslim sultanates that, over time, had been annexed by the Timurids. For the earlier Mughal rulers, it was often enough for these small states to remit tribute and supply troops in order to retain their autonomy. For Aurangzeb, however, commitment to a more legalistic Islam also meant political expansion of the Mughal state. Hence, Aurangzeb spent many years campaigning to bring central India under his sway.

Despite the tenacity of Maratha resistance, Aurangzeb's strategy—supporting pro-Mughal factions among the Maratha leaders, lavishing money and gifts on Maratha converts and deserters, and fielding large armies to attack Maratha fortifications—was successful. Yet prolonged fighting also led to problems at court and in the interior of the empire.

The demands of constant campaigning reduced the flow of money and goods across central India. Moreover, by the early eighteenth century, the Maratha frontier was actually expanding into Mughal areas. The Marathas had set up their own administrative system and encouraged raids on Mughal caravans and pack trains. Persia exploited the weakening of the Mughal interior, sacking Delhi in 1739 and carrying off Shah Jahan's fabled Peacock Throne—associated ever since with the monarchs of Persia and Iran, rather than with India and the Mughals.

The East India Companies Soon after Vasco da Gama's first voyage to India in 1498, armed Portuguese merchant ships seized the port of Goa (1510). Other European maritime countries began to imitate Portugal's spice trade, building their own fortified bases from which to conduct business. For the English, Dutch, and French, these enterprises were conducted by royally chartered companies, which were given a monopoly over their country's trade within a certain region. These companies acted much like independent states. They maintained fortified warehouses, their armed merchant ships functioned as naval forces, and they assembled their own mercenary armies.

Throughout the seventeenth century English, French, and Dutch enterprises largely supplanted Portuguese influence in the region, while the location of their trading ports outside Mughal lands allowed them considerable freedom. As the companies grew richer and more powerful, they increasingly found themselves involved in local politics. For the English, the acquisition of Bombay (now Mumbai) from Portugal in the 1660s gave the company a superb harbor. In 1690, British traders began building a trading station called Calcutta (today's Kolkata), not to be confused with the port of Calicut, on the west coast of India. By 1750, the power of the Dutch in India had been eclipsed by that of the British and French East India Companies. With the victory of the British East India Company over French forces in 1757 came British domination of Bengal and, by century's end, much of northern India.

Administration, Society, and Economy

A characteristic pattern of the period under consideration in this section was a trend toward **centralization**. The creation of states and empires required power at the center to hold the state together, ensure consistent governance, provide for revenues, and maintain defense. What is noteworthy, however, is that in widely separate regions throughout Eurasia a variety of states concurrently reached a point where their governments, with armies now aided by firearms, made concerted efforts to focus more power than ever at the center. As part of this effort, some form of enforcement of approved religion or belief system legitimating the rulers was also present. For Mughal India, the system that attempted to coordinate and balance so many disparate and often hostile elements of society is sometimes called "autocratic centralism." Its policies and demands influenced the lives of its inhabitants in often unexpected ways.

Centralization: The process by which power or legal authority is exerted or controlled by a political leader to which smaller units are considered subject.

Mansabdars and Bureaucracy

Babur and his successors attempted to govern a largely settled society whose traditions, habits, and (for the majority) religious affiliations were different from their own. The nomadic Timurids initially felt more comfortable in adapting their own institutions and then grafting them onto the existing political and social structures. The result was hybrid institutions that, given the tensions within Indian society, worked well when the empire was guided by tolerant rulers but became increasingly problematic under more dogmatic ones.

Political Structure The Timurids sought to create a uniform administrative structure that did not rely on a single, charismatic ruler. Thus, Akbar created four principal ministries: one for army and military matters, one for taxation and revenue, one for legal and religious affairs, and one for the royal household.

Under the broad central powers of these ministries, provincial governors held political and military power and were responsible directly to the emperor. In order to prevent their having too much power, however, the fiscal responsibility for the provinces was in the hands of officers who reported to the finance minister. Thus, arbitrary or rebellious behavior could, in theory at least, be checked by the separation of financial control.

Administrative Personnel One key problem faced by the Mughals was how to impose a centralized administrative system on a state whose nobles were used to wielding power themselves. For the Mughals, India's diversity and patchwork of small states meant that competition among the ambitious for imperial favor was intense. The Timurid rulers were careful to avoid overt favoritism toward particular groups, and though most of their recruited nobility were Sunni Muslims, Hindus and even Shiite Muslims were also represented.

Mansabdars: Administrative officials of the Mughal Empire, whose positions were first introduced by Akbar.

The primary criteria were military and administrative skills. A system of official ranks was created in which the recipients, called **mansabdars**, were awarded grants of land and the revenues those working the land generated. In turn, the mansabdars were responsible for remitting taxes and, above a certain rank, for furnishing men and materiel for the army. The positions in the provincial governments and state ministries were filled by candidates from this new mansabdar elite chosen by the court. Thus, although the nobles retained considerable power in their own regions, they had no hope of political advancement if they did not get court preferment.

The Mughals and Their Early Modern Economy

Mughal India had a vigorous trade and manufacturing economy, and Hindu, Muslim, Buddhist, and Jain traditions reserved an honored place for commerce and those who conducted it. Thus, Mughal economic interests sought to promote the flow of goods moving around the empire while maintaining import and export trade and safeguarding access to the Silk Road routes.

Agriculture and Rural Life The basic administrative unit of rural India at the time of the Mughals was the pargana, a unit comprising a town and up to 100 villages. It was in the pargana that the lowest levels of officialdom had met the network of clan and caste leaders of the villages under both the Hindu rajas and the Muslim sultans before the Timurids, and this pattern continued over the coming centuries, with village life going on much as it had before the conquest. Thus, the duties of the local chiefs and headmen were to channel the local clans, castes, and ethnic and religious groups into activities the Mughals considered productive, such as clearing forests for farmland, harvesting tropical products for market, and driving off bands of foragers from the forests and hills.

Agricultural expansion required systematic integration of the rural and urban economies. One enormous obstacle facing the Mughals was efficiency and equity in rural taxation. Agricultural commodities provided the bulk of Indian tax revenues, but differences in regional soil conditions, climate, and productivity made uniform tax rates difficult to enforce. During Akbar's reign, surveys of local conditions were conducted to monitor harvests and grain prices. These data were used by local officials to calculate expected harvests and tax obligations. Imperial and local officials would sign agreements as to grain amounts to meet tax obligations over a set period. These obligations would then be paid in silver or copper coin.

The net effect of rural economic expansion in Mughal India allowed for a population increase from about 150 million in 1600 to 200 million in 1800. Moreover, the acreage under cultivation increased by perhaps as much as one-third over this same period. Preferential tax rates on coveted trade items meant that their supply would be secure. India began a burgeoning silk industry during this time as well.

Revenues more than doubled between Akbar's and Aurangzeb's reigns, while the increase in population meant that the per capita tax burden actually went down.

International Trade The intense and growing competition among the English, Dutch, and French East India Companies meant that Indian commodities were now being shipped globally, while imports of American silver and food and cash crops were growing annually. By the mid-seventeenth century, the Dutch and English dominated maritime trade in Indian spices. An often added bonus was Indian saltpeter, a vital component of gunpowder, used as ships' ballast (see Map 20.4).

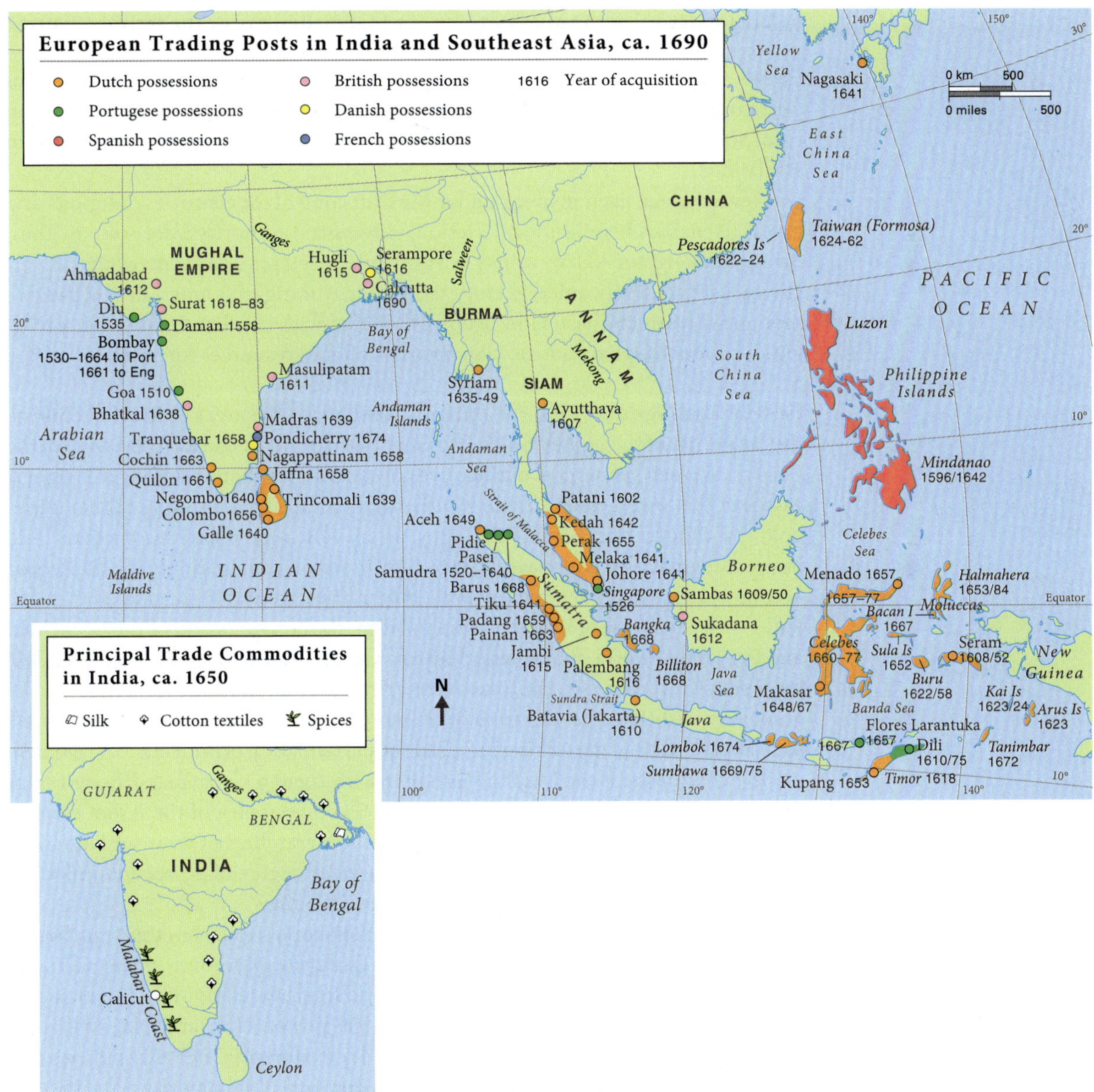

MAP 20.4 European Trading Ports in India and Southeast Asia, ca. 1690

Perhaps of even more long-term importance, however, was the growth of India's textile trade, especially the rapid rise of Indian cotton exports. Lighter and more comfortable than wool or linen, Indian cotton calicoes (named for the Indian port of Calicut) proved popular for underwear and summer clothing.

Society, Family, and Gender

Though much of this chapter describes the activities of the Muslim Timurids in India, it must be kept in mind that the majority of people in India were Hindus rather than Muslims. Thus, although the laws and customs of the areas controlled by the Mughals had an effect on Indian society, most of the everyday lives of Indians at the pargana, village, clan, and family levels went on much as it had before the arrival of the Mughals—or, for that matter, before the arrival of Islam.

Caste, Clan, and Village The ties of family, clan, and caste were the most important for the majority of Indians (most of whom were Hindu), particularly in rural society. Indeed, many new converts to Islam retained their caste and clan affiliations.

Nevertheless, even in areas under Muslim control for centuries, religious and cultural tensions as well as local friction with central authority were present. Thus, during the reign of Akbar, whose tolerant rule eased tensions somewhat, clan archives were relatively quiet; in contrast, during Aurangzeb's long rule and periods of internal conflict, these same archives bristled with conflict. In areas only marginally under Mughal control, clan councils offered resources for potential rebels.

Family and Gender For the Indian elites outside the areas of Mughal control, the family life of the higher castes also went on largely as it had from the time of the Guptas. Women spent most of their lives in seclusion. Whether among the highest castes or the lowest, their primary duties still included the running of the household and childrearing. Among the elites, where education in literature, poetry, and basic mathematics was also available to certain women, maintaining the household accounts, supervising servants, as well as education were also considered part of a wife's proper knowledge. In all cases, however, the "inner" world of the household and the "outer" world of business, politics, warfare, and so on were clearly defined by gender. In rural areas, the lives and work of peasant families, though generally guided by traditional gender roles, were more flexible in that large collective tasks such as planting and harvesting required the participation of both men and women.

The conquests of the Mughals brought with them a somewhat different temperament among their elites. The nomadic Turkic peoples of the Asian steppes had not developed the class, caste, and gender hierarchies of their settled neighbors. Women could, and often did, enjoy a greater degree of power and influence than among the Hindu, Sikh, or Muslim elites in India.

Even after the conversion of these nomadic peoples to Islam, this tradition of female independence continued among the Timurids. Moreover, since marriages played a vital role in cementing diplomatic and internal relations, women wielded influence in terms of the extension of imperial power. Nur Jahan (d. 1645), the Persian princess married to Jahangir, played a leading role in court politics and in mediation during the succession wars at the end of Jahangir's reign. Indeed, Jahangir occasionally turned the running of the empire over to her.

As the Mughals assimilated local Muslim elites, the court set up the harem as an institution of seclusion and protection for court women. Within the harem, women constructed their own hierarchies and celebrated their own holidays and ceremonies largely insulated from the influence of men. It was a kind of alternative women's society, in which distinct values were instilled in daughters and women newly married into the household. For these women, navigating the harem's social relationships was of critical importance, since the inner harmony of the court depended on it.

Jahangir's Influential Wife, the Former Persian Princess Nur Jahan, in Her Silk Gauze Inner-Court Dress

Science, Religion, and the Arts

Mughal India achieved noteworthy developments in weaponry, mathematics, and astronomy. In terms of religion, the great theological differences between Hindus and Muslims persisted—and with the reign of Aurangzeb increased. However, the tendency of Hinduism to assimilate other traditions and the compatibility of Islamic Sufi practices with other mystical traditions did sometimes decrease tensions. Finally, the attempts of language, literature, art, and architecture to reconcile religions left a brilliant legacy of cultural synthesis.

Science and Technology

Muslim scholars in India continued to draw upon the rich scientific history of the subcontinent, merging it with their efforts at preserving the ancient Greco-Roman and Persian achievements. Among the most important developments in this regard was the spreading of the Indian decimal number system and the use of zero as a placeholder in mathematical computations. Among the developments that fostered the rise of Muslim empires, the most important was the use of gunpowder weapons.

New Directions in Firearms in the Gunpowder Empires By the beginning of the sixteenth century, the armies of the major European kingdoms, Ming China, Ottoman Turkey, and Persia had all become accustomed to employing cannons and explosive charges for besieging fortresses. They were developing more convenient small arms for their infantries and were beginning to employ portable cannons as field guns for pitched battles. The use and effect of these weapons became so important that scholars often refer to the states of the Mughals, Persians, and Ottomans as the **gunpowder empires**.

Gunpowder empires: Muslim-ruled empires of the Ottomans, Safavids, and Mughals that used cannons and small arms in their military campaigns, 1450–1750.

Mathematics and Astronomy A century before Akbar, Indian mathematicians had pushed their calculations of the value of pi to nine decimal places and expanded their facility with trigonometry to the point where some of the fundamental concepts of infinite series and calculus had been worked out.

Dependent on an accurate calendar for the yearly agricultural and ceremonial cycle, Mughal rulers had a vital interest in knowing when unusual celestial phenomena such as comets, eclipses, and meteor showers were due. Using extremely fine calculations and careful observation, the astronomers of the Kerala school had calculated elliptical orbits for the visible planets a century in advance of Johannes Kepler and suggested systems of planetary orbits similar to those of both Tycho Brahe and Copernicus (Chapter 17).

Religion: In Search of Balance

Indian Islam went through relatively open, inclusive, and Sufi-oriented cycles, and phases in which a more rigorous attention to orthodox Sunni practices and the desire to connect with Muslim communities beyond India prevailed. These latter periods played an important role in mandating which forms of Islam would be most influential in Mughal India and the relations of the Mughals with the Muslims of other regions.

The Position of Non-Muslims in Mughal India As we have seen, despite profound theological differences between the monotheism of Islam and the polytheism of Hindu religious traditions, there was a degree of attraction between the adherents of the two religions. The mystical and devotional sects of both saw a commonality in their ways of encountering the profound mysteries of faith. Thus, Akbar's grounding in Islamic Sufi mysticism made him interested in, and receptive to, Hindu mystical traditions. For their part, in addition to the mystical elements of Islam, Hindus of the lower castes were attracted to the equality before God of all Islamic believers. Thus, like Buddhism before it, Islam promised emancipation from the restrictions of the caste system.

More generally, however, the religious divisions remained difficult to reconcile. From the first occupation of territories by Muslim armies in the seventh century, nonbelievers had been granted the legal status of protected peoples (Chapter 10). There were also inducements and penalties aimed at conversion to Islam. For their part, Hindus considered Muslims to be ritually unclean, and upper-caste members underwent purification rites after contact with them.

Yet the presence of a vastly larger Hindu population also meant that rulers had to make accommodations in order to run the empire effectively. In addition, the financial skills of Hindus and Jains were increasingly sought by the court, and their status rose further when Akbar made a Hindu his finance minister and employed Hindu court astrologers. Perhaps of even more symbolic and political importance was the habit of Mughal rulers of occasionally marrying Hindu women.

The position of Christians was similar. They, along with Jews, were protected but were still subject to the same taxes and impediments as before the reign of Akbar. While the position of Christian missionaries in Mughal lands was often precarious, the reverence with which Muslims regarded the biblical prophets and Jesus also helped to smooth diplomatic relations at court. As we have seen, Akbar even invited Jesuits to his debates.

After Akbar, the pendulum soon began to swing back toward less openness. Mughal receptiveness of Islamic mysticism and other religions offended more orthodox Sunni Muslims, whose influence was felt at court during the reigns of Jahangir and Shah Jahan, reaching its zenith during Aurangzeb's reign. Aurangzeb reimposed the taxes on unbelievers and purged many Hindus from his court.

Islamic Developments While the majority of India's Muslims remained adherents of the Sunni branch of Islam, there was an influential Shiite presence in India. For centuries, Shiites had migrated into Hindu areas of southern India, where they generally escaped the discrimination at the hands of Sunnis characteristic of the north. In addition, Mughal relations with Safavid Persia, where Shia Islam was the official state religion, meant that a certain influence on the Mughal court was unavoidable. Hence, Akbar studied mystical elements of Shiism, while Jahangir married the Safavid princess Nur Jahan.

Literature and Art

During the Mughal period, India's rich multicultural environment fostered arrestingly synthetic works of literature, art, and architecture.

New Literary Directions Arabic and Persian were the principal literary languages of Islamic India. The use of both, however, was enlivened by the introduction of Turkic terms by the Chagatai–Turkic Mughals. Chagatai itself remained in use among the elites until the nineteenth century, while many of its loan words, along with Persian and Arabic vocabulary, were grafted onto the base of Sanskrit to form the modern languages Hindi and Urdu. Regional languages, such as Kashmiri and Bengali, were also in literary and general use.

Ironically, the catalysts for the explosion of literary work from the mid-sixteenth to the mid-seventeenth centuries came from the Mughals' most humiliating period. The exile of Humayun to Persia in the 1540s coincided with the Persian Shah Tahmasp embarking on reforms in response to criticism about the worldliness of his court. Writers, painters, and poets who suddenly found themselves out of favor at the Persian court followed Humayun to India. Their classical Arab and Persian verse forms were ultimately adopted into Urdu.

Sufi scholarship proliferated under Akbar, borrowing concepts and terminology from non-Islamic sources. By Aurangzeb's reign, the pendulum had swung back to the more legalistic-centered strain in Indian Islam. Thus, the works tended to be more often treatises on Islamic law, interpretation of hadith—the traditions of the Prophet—and Sunni works on theology and philosophy.

Art and Painting One of the more interesting aspects of Islam as practiced by the Mughals—as well as the Safavid Persians and Ottomans—was that the injunctions against depicting human beings in art were often ignored in the private rooms of the court.

Akbar had a direct hand in the creation of what is considered to be the first painting in the "Mughal style"—a combination of the delicacy of Persian miniature work with the vibrant colors and bold themes of Hindu painters. Akbar inherited two of the master painters who accompanied Humayun from Persia, and the contact they acquired with Hindu works under Akbar's patronage resulted in hundreds of Mughal **gouache** works, including the colossal illustrated *Hamzanama* of 1570. Mughal artists often passed their skills on within their families and

Gouache: Watercolors with a gum base.

represented an important subset of members at the imperial court and among the entourages of regional elites.

By the end of the sixteenth century, the realistic approach of European artists and their use of perspective began to influence painters at the courts of Akbar and Jahangir. One prominent female artist, Nadira Banu (1618-1659), specialized in producing Flemish-style works. The period of Akbar's religious experiments also prompted Mughal painters to try their hand at representing Christian religious figures. A picture of the Virgin Mary even appears in a portrait of Jahangir.

Architecture Nowhere was the Mughal style more in evidence than in the construction of tombs and mausoleums. The ethereal lightness of the Taj Mahal and the perfection of its layout make it the most distinctive construction of its kind. The chief architect, Ustad Ahmad Lahori (d. 1649), also designed the famous Red Fort of Shah Jahan's city, Shahjahanabad, now one of Delhi's "Seven Cities."

Mosques were among the empire's most important constructions. Once again, a distinctive style emerged in which the basic form of the dome and the minaret interacted with Central Asian, Persian, and even Hindu architectural influences. The largest Mughal mosques, like the Jama Masjid (the Friday mosque) in Shahjahanabad (Old Delhi) and Aurangzeb's huge Badshahi Mosque in Lahore, contain immense courtyards surrounded by cloisters leading to small rooms for intimate gatherings, separate domed areas for men and women, and distinctive minarets with fluted columns and bell-shaped roofs. Like some cathedrals in Europe, many of the largest mosques were built adjacent to government buildings in order to demonstrate the seamless connections of these religious civilizations.

The *Hamzanama* (Book of Hamza). Akbar so enjoyed the *Hamzanama*, a heroic romance about the legendary adventures of the Prophet Mohammad's uncle Amir Hamza, that he commissioned an illustrated version in 1562. This painting from Akbar's version shows the prophet Elijah rescuing Hamza's nephew.

Putting It All Together

The rise of the Turkic Central Asian peoples to prominence and power, from the borders of successive Chinese dynasties to Anatolia and the domains of the Ottomans, including the rise of the Timurids—the Mughals—in India, is one of the most dramatic sagas of world history. In India, these outside conquerors grappled with the question of how to create a viable state out of so many long-standing religious traditions. With the arrival of Islam, a new religion that stood in opposition to the older Hindu pattern of assimilation of gods and favored instead the conquest and conversion of opponents, a divide was created, which persists to this day. The later development of Sikhism, an attempt at a syncretic bridge across India's religious divide, sometimes added to efforts for greater tolerance and at other times contributed to religious tensions.

Against this backdrop, the accomplishments of the Mughals must be weighed as significant in terms of statecraft and artistic and cultural achievement, and perhaps less so in religious areas. At its height, Mughal India was the most populous, wealthy, politically powerful, and economically vibrant empire in the world next to China. Yet, for all its wealth and power, the Mughal dynasty was plagued by problems that ultimately proved insoluble. The old nomadic succession practices of the Timurids repeatedly led to palace revolts by potential heirs. These wars in turn encouraged conflict with internal and external enemies who sensed weakness at the core of the regime. Protracted conflicts in Afghanistan, with Safavid Persia, and in Bengal also bled this centralized state of resources. Finally, the Maratha wars slowly wore down even the semblance of unity among the rulers following Aurangzeb.

But perhaps an equally important factor in the ultimate dissolution of the empire was that of Hindu–Muslim syncretism. Despite the flexibility of the early rulers in trying to deemphasize the more oppressive elements of Islamic rule in Hindu India, the attempt at a stricter orthodoxy under Aurangzeb hardened Hindu–Muslim and Sikh divisions for centuries to come.

Throughout the period, one other factor loomed as the dynasty went into decline. The well-financed and well-armed trading companies of the Europeans gradually moved into positions of regional power. By 1750, they were on the cusp of changing the political situation completely.

Review and Relate

Thinking Through Patterns

Examine the ways historians approach the big questions of this chapter.

What were the strengths and weaknesses of Mughal rule?

Two weaknesses are immediately apparent: first, the position of the Mughals as an ethnic and religious minority ruling a larger majority population, and second, the conflict-prone succession practices of the older Central Asian Turkic leaders. The minority position of the Mughals aggravated tensions between Hindu subjects and Muslim rulers in India, of which the Mughals were to be the last line. Central Asian Turkic succession practices almost always guaranteed conflict when it was time for a new ruler to accede to the throne. Nearly every Mughal successor during this period ended up having to fight factions and family to gain the empire.

What was the Mughal policy toward religious accommodation? How did it change over time?

In some respects, the strengths of Mughal rule developed in reaction to these problems. Babur and Akbar, in particular, were extraordinarily tolerant rulers in terms of religion. When later rulers like Aurangzeb returned to strict Sunni Islamic policies, they met with resistance, especially among Hindus. Also, while Mughal rulers were never able to completely free themselves from succession struggles, they succeeded in setting up a well-run fiscal–military state, largely undercutting old local and regional loyalties and tying the new loyalty to the state.

Mughal rulers faced the problem confronted by nearly all religious civilizations: religious orthodoxy was seen as an element of loyalty to the state. But for the Mughals, the desire for strict adherence to Muslim law was always tempered by the problem of Islam being a minority religion in India. Early Mughal rulers upheld Sunni Islam as the approved state religion but refrained from forcing Muslim practices on other religious groups. Akbar went so far as to create a new religion and met with leaders of other religions to find ways to satisfy the desires of all. Shah Jahan, however, enforced stricter practices, which peaked during the long reign of Aurangzeb. By the end of Aurangzeb's reign, the Sikhs were near revolt and the long Hindu Maratha revolt was in full swing. But even during this period, local religious customs remained largely intact and, indeed, often thrived.

➤ What factors account for the Mughal decline during the eighteenth century?

At the beginning and for much of the eighteenth century, Mughal India was the second richest and most prosperous empire in the world, after China. But by 1750 it was already in pronounced decline. A large part of this was due to rebellions by the Sikhs, the Rajputs, and especially the Marathas. By the 1750s, the European trading companies were becoming locally powerful. Here, the great milestone would take place during the Seven Years' War (1756–1763), when the British East India Company eliminated its French competitors and in essence took over the rule of Bengal from its headquarters in Calcutta. Within 100 years it would take over all of India.

Against the Grain

Consider this as a counterpoint to the main patterns examined in this chapter.

Sikhism in Transition

- Why would both Hindus and Muslims express hostility toward a religion that claims to want to transcend the differences between them? Did the Sikhs appear to have any alternatives to becoming a fighting faith in order to ensure their survival?
- Why does it seem that, on the whole, what we have termed "religious civilizations" have difficulty

As we saw in Chapter 13, Zen Buddhism affords an example of a pacifistic religious tradition that was taken up by warrior classes. In some respects, Sikhism underwent a similar transformation, although one that took place for very different reasons. The Sikhs had started from an avowedly peaceful premise: that the conflict between Hindus and Muslims must somehow be transcended. Influenced by poets and mystics and drawing upon the emotional connections experienced by Muslim Sufis and Hindu Bhakti devotees, the Sikhs had emerged during the sixteenth century as an entirely new religious movement.

Yet, far from providing a model for the two contending religions to emulate, Sikhs were viewed with suspicion by both. Although they attracted enough of a following to remain vital to the present day, their attempts at transcendence were viewed in much the same light as Akbar's attempts at a new religious synthesis were. Though they were awarded the city of Amritsar, the Golden Temple of which became their religious center,

Mughal repression of the Sikhs under Aurangzeb in the seventeenth century turned them into a fierce fighting faith in self-defense. The Sikhs established control of most of the Punjab region during the eighteenth-century decline of the Mughals. During the days of British control, the reputation of the Sikhs as fighters prompted the British to employ them as colonial troops and policemen throughout their empire. Even after independence, smoldering disputes between the government and Sikhs urging local autonomy for Punjab led to the assassination of Indian Prime Minister Indira Gandhi in 1984, in retaliation for a government operation to forcibly remove a Sikh splinter group from the Golden Temple.

tolerating different religious traditions within their domains? Does loyalty to a state require loyalty to its approved religion(s) as well? Why?

Key Terms

Centralization 487
Gouache 493
Gunpowder empires 491
Institutionalization 480
Mansabdars 488
Maratha 487

Learn more with this chapter's digital tools, including the Oxford Insight Study Guide, at http://www.oup.com/he/vonsivers4e. Please see the Further Resources section at the back of the book for additional readings and suggested websites.

PATTERNS OF EVIDENCE

Sources for Chapter 20

SOURCE 20.1

Babur, *The Baburnama*

ca. 1528

Zahiruddin Muhammad Babur (1483–1530) was born a prince of Fergana in Transoxiana (modern Uzbekistan and Tajikistan), a region that had been conquered (briefly) by the army of Alexander the Great in the 320s BCE and more recently by Babur's ancestor Timur-i Lang, or Tamerlane (r. 1370–1405). Driven from his homeland, Babur conquered neighboring kingdoms and moved south into Afghanistan, capturing Kabul in 1504. By 1519, he stepped up his raids into northern India, and his highly mobile, if vastly outnumbered, army defeated Sultan Ibrahim Lodi at Panipat in 1526. Victory at Panipat was followed by the conquest of the Lodi capital of Agra and further defeats of Hindu leaders in northern India. Babur's dynasty would become known as the Mughals (from "Mongols"), but his legacy can also be gauged from the success of his memoirs, the *Baburnama*. Composed and reworked throughout his life, the *Baburnama* is the first true autobiography in Islamic literature, and it can be read for insights into his own character as well as the military tactics he employed on the battlefield.

On Wednesday afternoon the twenty-eighth of Rajab [May 10], I entered Agra and camped in Sultan Ibrahim's quarters.

Begs: Subordinate rulers.

Ghari: Measure of time, about 24 minutes.

From the year 910 [1504–05], when Kabul was conquered, until this date I had craved Hindustan. Sometimes because my **begs** had poor opinions, and sometimes because my brothers lacked cooperation, the Hindustan campaign had not been possible and the realm had not been conquered. Finally all such impediments had been removed. None of my little begs and officers were able any longer to speak out in opposition to my purpose. In 925 [1519] we led the army and took Bajaur by force in two or three **gharis**, massacred the people, and came to Bhera. The people of Bhera paid ransom to keep their property from being plundered and pillaged, and we took four hundred thousand shahrukhis worth of cash and goods, distributed it to the army according to the number of liege men, and returned to Kabul.

From that date until 932 [1525–26], we led the army to Hindustan five times within seven or eight years. The fifth time, God through his great grace vanquished and reduced a foe like Sultan Ibrahim and made possible for us a realm like Hindustan. From the time of the Apostle until this date only three padishahs gained dominion over and ruled the realm of Hindustan. The first was Sultan Mahmud

---

Source: *The Baburnama: Memoirs of Babur, Prince and Emperor*, trans. and ed. Wheeler M. Thackston (London and New York: Oxford University Press, 1996), 328–329, 330, 331.

Ghazi, who, with his sons, occupied the throne of Hindustan for a long time. The second was Sultan Shihabuddin Ghuri and his slaves and followers, who ruled this kingdom for many years. I am the third. My accomplishment, however, is beyond comparison with theirs, for when Sultan Mahmud subdued Hindustan, the throne of Khurasan was under his control, the rulers of Khwarazm and the marches were obedient to him, and the padishah of Samarkand was his underling. If his army was not two hundred thousand strong, it must have been at least one hundred thousand. Moreover, his opponents were rajahs. There was not a single padishah in all of Hindustan. Every rajah ruled independently in a different region.

. . .

Hindustan is a vast and populous kingdom and a productive realm. To the east and south, in fact to the west too, it ends at the ocean. To the north is a mountain range that connects the mountains of the Hindu Kush, Kafiristan, and Kashmir. To the northwest are Kabul, Ghazni, and Kandahar. The capital of all Hindustan is Delhi. After Sultan Shihabuddin Ghuri's reign until the end of Sultan Firozshah's, most of Hindustan was under the control of the Delhi sultans. Up to the time that I conquered Hindustan, five Muslim padishahs and two infidels had ruled there. Although the mountains and jungles are held by many petty rays and rajahs, the important and independent rulers were the following five.

. . .

Of the infidels, the greater in domain and army is the rajah of Vijayanagar. The other is Rana Sanga, who had recently grown so great by his audacity and sword. His original province was Chitor. When the sultans of Mandu grew weak, he seized many provinces belonging to Mandu, such as Ranthambhor, Sarangpur, Bhilsan, and Chanderi. Chanderi had been in the **daru'l-harb** for some years and held by Sanga's highest-ranking officer, Medini Rao, with four or five thousand infidels, but in 934 [1528], through the grace of God, I took it by force within a ghari or two, massacred the infidels, and brought it into the bosom of Islam, as will be mentioned.

***Daru'l-harb*:** "Abode of war," Islamic term for non-Islamicized countries.

All around Hindustan are many rays and rajahs. Some are obedient to Islam, while others, because they are so far away and their places impregnable, do not render obedience to Muslim rulers.

▸ Working with Sources

1. **Why was it important for Babur to display his knowledge of the history and geography of Hindustan?**
2. **Was he driven by a "crusading" goal to liberate Hindustan from control by the "infidels" and convert its inhabitants to Islam?**

SOURCE 20.2

Muhammad Dara Shikuh, *The Mingling of Two Oceans*

ca. 1650s

The eldest son of Shah Jahan, the fifth Mughal emperor, Dara Shikuh was defeated by his younger brother in a struggle for power in 1658. The victorious brother, Muhiuddin, ruled as the Emperor Aurangzeb, and he

Source: Muhammad Dara Shikuh, *The Mingling of Two Oceans*, trans. and ed. M. Mafuz ul-Haq (Calcutta: Asiatic Society of Bengal, 1929), 50–53.

had Dara declared, by a court of nobles and clergy, an apostate from Islam and assassinated in 1659. Dara left behind a remarkable series of writings, advocating an enlightened program of harmonizing the various, bitterly opposed religions of the subcontinent. He had developed friendships with Sikhs, followed a Persian mystic, and completed a translation of 50 Upanishads from their original Sanskrit into Persian in 1657. His most famous work, the *Majma-ul-Bahrain* (*The Mingling of Two Oceans*), addressed the overlapping ideas of Hindu and Muslim mysticism. His attempt to combine the traditions into a coherent whole may have been rejected by his fervently Muslim brother, but he also represents a strain of ecumenical thought within the Mughal Empire.

x. Discourse on the vision of god (*rūyat*).

The Indian monotheists call the Vision of God, *Sāchātkār*, that is, to see God with the (ordinary) eyes of the forehead. Know that the Vision of God, either by the Prophets, may peace be on them, or by the perfect divines, may their souls be sanctified, whether in this or the next world and whether with the outer or the inner eyes, cannot be doubted or disputed; and the "men of the Book" (*ahl-i-kitāb*), the perfect divines and the seers of all religions—whether they are believers in the Kur'ān, the Vedas, the Book of David or the Old and the New Testaments—have a (common) faith in this respect. Now, one who disbelieves the beholding of God is a thoughtless and sightless member of his community, the reason being: if the Holy Self is Omnipotent, how can He not have the potency to manifest himself? This matter has been explained very clearly by the *'Ulamā* of the Sunnī Sect. But, if it is said, that (even) the Pure Self (*dhāt-i-baht*) can be beheld, it is an impossibility; for the Pure Self is elegant and undetermined, and, as He cannot be determined, He is manifest in the veil of elegance only, and as such cannot be beheld, and such beholding is an impossibility. And the suggestion that He can be beheld in the next and not in this world, is groundless, for if He is Omnipotent, He is potent to manifest Himself in any manner, anywhere and at any time He likes. (I hold) that one who cannot behold Him here (i.e., in this world) will hardly behold Him there (i.e. in the next world); as He has said in the Holy verse: "And whoever is blind in this, he shall (also) be blind in the hereafter" [Qur'an 17:72].

The *Mu'tazila* and the *Shī'a* doctors, who are opposed to *rūyat* (Beholding), have committed a great blunder in this matter, for had they only denied the capability of beholding the Pure Self, there would have been some justification, but their denial of all forms of *rūyat* is a great mistake; the reason being that most of the Prophets and perfect divines have beheld God with their ordinary eyes and have heard His Holy words without any intermediary and, now, when they are, by all means, capable of hearing the words of God, why should they not be capable of beholding Him? Verily, they must be so; and, just as it is obligatory to have faith in God, the Angels, the (revealed) Books, the Prophets, the Destiny, the Good and the Evil, and the Holy Places, etc., so it is obligatory and incumbent to have faith in *rūyat*.

. . .

Now, the beholding of God is of five kinds: first, in dream with the eyes of heart; secondly, beholding Him with the ordinary eyes; thirdly, beholding Him in an intermediate state of sleep and wakefulness, which is a special kind of Selflessness; fourthly, (beholding Him) in (a stage of) special determination;

fifthly, beholding the One Self in the multitudinous determinations of the internal and external worlds. In such a way beheld our Prophet, may peace be on him, whose "self" had disappeared from the midst and the beholder and the beheld had merged in one and his sleep, wakefulness and selflessness looked as one and his internal and the external eyes had become one unified whole—such is the state of perfect *rūyat,* which is not confined either to this or the next world and is possible everywhere and at every period.

XI. Discourse on the Names of God, the Most High *(Asmāi Allāh Ta'ālā).*

Know that the names of God, the Most High, are numberless and beyond comprehension. In the language of the Indian divines, the Absolute, the Pure, the Hidden of the hidden and the Necessary Self is known as *asan, tirgun, nirankār, niranjan, sat* and *chit.* If knowledge is attributed to Him, the Indian divines designate Him as *chitan,* while the Muslims call Him *'Alīm* (Knowing).

▸ Working with Sources

1. **To what extent, and in what specific ways, did Dara Shikuh represent an ecumenical spirit with respect to Islam and other religions?**
2. **How does Dara Shikuh anticipate and address the objections of others within the Muslim community?**

SOURCE 20.3

Edicts of Aurangzeb

1666–1679

When he became emperor in 1658, Aurangzeb attempted a radical "Islamification" of Mughal India, imposing a strict interpretation of Sharia law and implementing reforms that he thought would benefit Muslims more than adherents of other religions. Repudiating his great-grandfather Akbar's vision of religious transcendence and harmony but stopping short of forcible conversion, Aurangzeb offered incentives to non-Muslims to convert, destroyed many of their temples, and reimposed the hated *jizya* tax. This tax on Hindus had been abolished by Akbar in 1564, and its reinstatement by Aurangzeb in 1679 triggered mass protests and violent reactions from authorities in many cities. Revolts among Sikhs and among Hindus left the Mughal Empire weakened and in decline by the time of Aurangzeb's death in 1707. An excerpt from his proscriptions is offered below.

Exhibit No. 6: Keshava Rai Temple. "Even to look at a temple is a sin for a Musalman," Aurangzeb. Umurat-i-Hazur Kishwar-Kashai Julus (R.Yr.) 9, Rabi II 24 / 13 October 1666.

'It was reported to the Emperor (Aurangzeb) that in the temple of Keshava Rai at Mathura, there is a stone railing presented by Bishukoh (one without

---

Source: V.S. Bhatnagar, *Emperor Aurangzeb and Destruction of Temples, Conversions, and Jizya (A study largely based on his Court Bulletins or AkhbÁrÁt DarbÁr Mu'alla)* (Jaipur, India: Literary Circle, 2017), http://www.aurangzeb.info/2008/06/exhibit-no_7171.html

dignity i.e. Prince Dara, Aurangzeb's elder brother). On hearing of it, the Emperor observed, "In the religion of the Musalmans it is improper even to look at a temple and this Bishukoh has installed this kathra (barrier railing). Such an act is totally unbecoming of a Musalman. This railing should be removed (forthwith)." His Majesty ordered Abdun Nabi Khan to go and remove the kathra, which is in the middle of the temple. The Khan went and removed it. After doing it he had audience. He informed that the idol of Keshava Rai is in the inner chamber. The railing presented by Dara was in front of the chamber and, formerly, it was of wood. Inside the kathra used to stand the sevakas of the shrine (pujaris etc.) and outside it stood the people (khalq)'.

Exhibit No. 7: Demolition of Kalka's Temple - I. Siyah Waqa'i-Darbar Regnal Year 10, Rabi I, 23 / 3 September 1667.

'The asylum of Shariat (Shariat Panah) Qazi Abdul Muqaram has sent this arzi to the sublime Court: a man known to him told him that the Hindus gather in large numbers at Kalka's temple near Barahapule (near Delhi); a large crowd of the Hindus is seen here. Likewise, large crowds are seen at (the mazars) of Khwaja Muinuddin, Shah Madar and Salar Masud Ghazi. This amounts to bid'at (heresy) and deserves consideration. Whatever orders are required should be issued.

Saiyid Faulad Khan was thereupon ordered (by the Emperor) to send one hundred beldars to demolish the Kalka temple and other temples in its neighbourhood which were in the Faujdari of the Khan himself; these men were to reach there post haste, and finish the work without a halt'.

Exhibit No. 8: Demolition of Kalka Temple II. Siyah Akhbarat-i-Darbar-i-Mu'alla Julus 10, Rabi II 3 / 12 September 1667.

'Saiyad Faulad Khan reported that in compliance with the orders, beldars were sent to demolish the Kalka temple which task they have done. During the course of the demolition, a Brahmin drew out a sword, killed a bystander and then turned back and attacked the Saiyad also. The Brahmin was arrested'.

Exhibit No. 16: Reimposition of Jizyah by Aurangzeb. (2nd April 1679)

'As all the aims of the religious Emperor were directed to the spreading of the law of Islam and the overthrow of the practices of the infidels, he issued orders to the high diwani officers that from Wednesday, the 2nd April 1679 / 1st Rabi I, in obedience to the Quranic injunction, "till they pay commutation money (Jizyah) with the hand in humility," and in agreement with the canonical tradition, Jizyah should be collected from the infidels (zimmis) of the capital and the provinces. Many of the honest scholars of the time were appointed to discharge the work (of collecting Jizyah). May God actuate him (Emperor Aurangzeb) to do that which He loves and is pleased with, and make his future life better than the present'.

Working with Sources

1. **How did the legacy of Akbar's and Dara's ecumenism influence Aurangzeb's policies?**
2. **What was the stated purpose of the reimposition of financial penalties on non-Muslims? Was this policy likely to have the effect he intended?**

SOURCE 20.4

Mughal emerald box

ca. 1635

As one of the most opulent courts in the world, the Mughals had direct access to fabulous gemstones, pearls, and precious metals, but emeralds were difficult to obtain since Old World sources were scarce. However, beginning in the late sixteenth century, emeralds from Spain's American colony of New Granada (present-day Colombia) began to enter the world market. Mined in the Andes, the emeralds were sold to Spanish and Portuguese merchants with ties to Goa, Portugal's most important trading post in India. From there, the emeralds made their way inland to artisans who worked for the Mughal court where they were fashioned into exquisite luxury items such as this spectacular box crafted around 1635. Set with 103 emeralds, each stone is meticulously carved in shallow relief with a floral design. Narrow bands of gold hold the stones in place, and a diamond sits at the apex of the box's lid. The precious materials and the high quality of the craftsmanship suggest that the box was made at the highest level of Mughal court patronage.

Working with Sources

1. **How does this precious object demonstrate patterns of trade and interaction in the period 1450–1750?**
2. **By commissioning emeralds for the design of this box, what message did the owner wish to convey?**

Source: The Nasser D. Khalili Collection of Islamic Art.

World Period Four

Interactions across the Globe, 1450–1750

The fifteenth century saw a renewal of the imperial impulse in the religious civilizations of the world. A forerunner had been the Mongol empire, which however did not last long; in less than 100 years it was replaced in China by the Ming. The founders of the subsequent new empires were the Mughals in India; the Ottomans, Safavids, and Songhay in the Middle East and Islamic Africa; the Habsburgs in Europe; and the seaborne empires of Portugal and Spain. One byproduct of this new imperial impulse was the discovery of the Americas, which in turn inspired the formulation of the heliocentric universe. The rediscovery of Greek literature in Europe had already set into motion the Renaissance, a broad new approach to under-standing the world that provided the spark for the New Science.

China and India, by far the wealthiest and most populous agrarian–urban empires, enjoyed leading positions in the world because they produced everything they needed and wanted. Europe, however, acquired warm-weather crops and minerals through overseas colonial expansion, which would help it to challenge the traditional order.

Chapter 21

Regulating the "Inner" and "Outer" Domains

China and Japan, 1500–1800

CHAPTER TWENTY-ONE PATTERNS

Origins, Interactions, and Adaptations While their commonalities were apparent, by 1500 China and Japan were on different historical tracks. Yet, along with Korea, they both sought to preserve themselves from turmoil by regulating their respective societies. Japan, wracked by civil war for much of the sixteenth century, achieved unification by force. The factional conflict that followed ended with the rule of the Tokugawa Shogunate, which lasted until 1867.

For China, the end of the weakened Ming Dynasty came about at the hands of the Manchus, whose new dynasty, the Qing, would prove to be China's last. Along the way, China's rulers, like those of Japan, interacted with Europeans. The Qing elevated Neo-Confucianism as strict orthodoxy and, like Japan, it sought to regulate behavior.

Uniqueness and Similarities Unlike the Mughals, whose internal conflicts allowed Europeans to gain a substantial foothold, or the Ottomans with their continual warfare with the Habsburgs, China and Japan were able to regulate their respective states to avoid and control foreign intruders. Like other agrarian empires, China and Japan faced similar challenges. European traders and missionaries sought commerce and converts in both countries. Japan's position as an island empire, however, and China's situation as a well-governed and powerful state, allowed both to enforce restrictions on foreign contact in ways that were unique to themselves but also strikingly similar.

CHAPTER OUTLINE

Late Ming and Qing China to 1750

The Long War and Longer Peace: Japan, 1450–1750

Putting It All Together

The time seemed right for a letter home. In only two weeks the Japanese invasion force had captured the Korean capital of Seoul, and the skill and firepower of the Japanese warriors seemed to let them brush their opponents aside at will. The Japanese commander, Toyotomi Hideyoshi, was a battle-hardened commoner who had embarked on an audacious campaign to extend his power to the Asian mainland. Six years before, he had written his mother that he contemplated nothing less than the conquest of China. Now seemed like a good time to inform her that his goal might actually be within his grasp.

However, the Japanese soon faced a massive Chinese and Korean counterattack and became mired in a bloody stalemate, their guns and tactics barely enough to compensate for the determination and numbers of their enemies. After four more years of negotiation punctuated by bitter fighting, Hideyoshi finally withdrew to Japan. One final invasion attempt of Korea in 1597 collapsed when his death the following year set off a bloody struggle for succession, which ultimately placed in power the Tokugawa family, who would go on to rule Japan for more than 250 years.

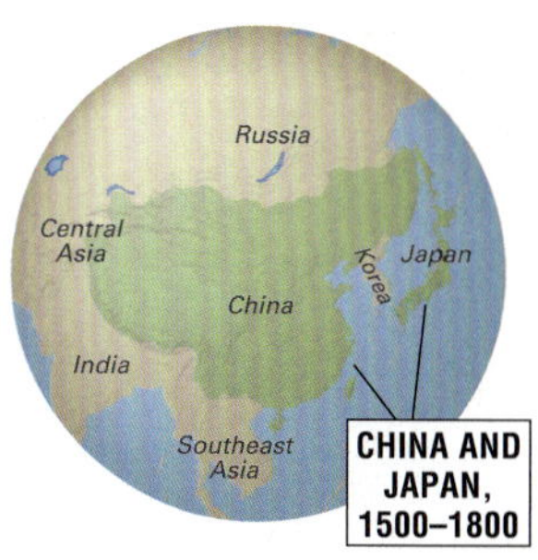

The rise of Japanese power represents a vitally important pattern of world history, which we have seen in other areas, such as the Mediterranean and the expanding kingdoms of Europe: A state on the periphery absorbs innovation from a cultural center, in this case China, and then becomes a vital center itself. And like the other states in the region, Japan had absorbed the structures of "religious civilizations," as we have termed them—in this case, the Chinese philosophical system of Neo-Confucianism.

Hideyoshi's invasion was made possible in part by the appearance in the sixteenth century of the first Europeans in the region. By the middle of the nineteenth century, their presence would create a crisis of power and acculturation for all of East Asia. European intrusions provided powerful incentives for both China and Japan to turn inward to safeguard their own security and stability.

ABOVE: This painting shows the island of Deshima, near the port of Nagasaki in southern Japan. By 1640, all European missionaries and traders had been expelled from Japan, with the exception of the Dutch, who were restricted to Deshima and forbidden to leave the island.

Seeing Patterns

> **Why did late Ming and early Qing China look inward after such a successful period of overseas exploration?**

> **How do the goals of social stability drive the policies of agrarian states? How does the history of China and Japan in this period show these policies in action?**

> **In what ways did contact with the maritime states of Europe alter the patterns of trade and politics in eastern Asia?**

> **How did Neo-Confucianism in China differ from that of Tokugawa Japan?**

Late Ming and Qing China to 1750

Proclaimed as a new dynasty in 1368, the Ming at first followed the pattern of the "dynastic cycle" of previous dynasties. Having driven out the Mongol remnant, the Hongwu emperor and his immediate successors consolidated their rule, elevated the Confucian bureaucracy to its former place, and set up an administrative structure more focused on the person of the emperor than in previous dynasties. In 1382, the Grand Secretariat was created as the top governmental board below the emperor. Under the Grand Secretariat were the six boards, the governors and governors-general of the provinces, and lower-level officials down to the district magistrate.

In this section we will also take up the question of China's retreat from its greatest period of maritime expansion in the early 1400s—and sudden withdrawal to concentrate on domestic matters. Why such an abrupt change in policy? What factors led to the ultimate decline of the Ming dynasty and the rise to power of the Manchus? By what means did the Manchus create a state that endured into the twentieth century? Finally, what hints of the dynasty's problems appeared during the mid-eighteenth century?

From Expansion to Exclusion

During the late fourteenth and early fifteenth centuries, while China was rebuilding from the war to drive out the Mongols, the problems of land distribution and tenancy had abated somewhat. The depopulation of some areas from fighting, banditry, and the Black Death had raised the value of labor, depressed the price of land, and increased the amount of money in circulation. In addition, the Columbian Exchange introduced new food that had a substantial impact on the world's agricultural productivity, including China's (see Chapter 18).

New Food Crops In addition to new, higher-yielding rice strains from Southeast Asia, the Chinese began to cultivate crops that came from Africa and the Americas by way of the Spanish in the Philippines and the Portuguese at Macau. Corn and potatoes swiftly became staples, while peanuts, sugarcane, indigo, and tobacco established themselves as important cash crops.

Aided by the productivity of these new crops, China's population more than doubled between the beginning of the Ming period and 1600. Urbanism increased as market towns multiplied. The efficiency of Chinese agriculture, the incorporation of marginal lands into production, and the empire's internal trade all contributed to another doubling of the population, to perhaps 300 million, by 1800. This accelerating growth began China's movement toward what some historical demographers have argued was a *high-level equilibrium trap*—a condition in which the land was approaching its maximum potential for feeding an increasing population but the economy had not reached a point of disequilibrium that could only be corrected by a technological and/or institutional change. In this schema, for example, the unbalanced nature of England's economy in the mid-eighteenth century created an environment favorable to the innovations in the textile industry that began the Industrial Revolution. China, which continued to have abundant labor, no large pool of capital in search of investment, and no obvious need for more efficient agriculture or labor-saving machinery, would go

MAP 21.1 **China in 1600**

through the nineteenth century in a "balanced" state but one in which the growing population was slowly squeezed into impoverishment (see Map 21.1). Though the outlines of this theory were drawn in the early 1970s, its viability and fine points are still under debate today.

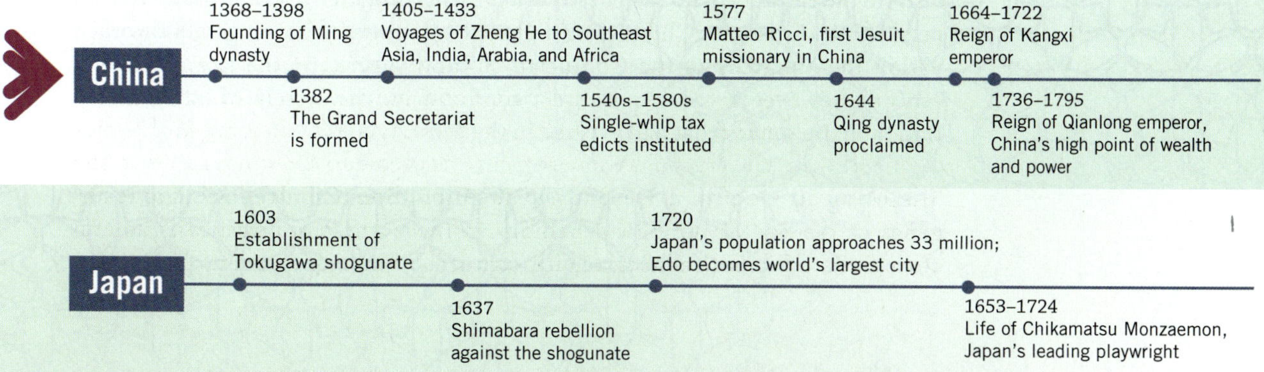

MAP 21.2 **World Trade Networks, ca. 1770**

China and the World Commercial Transformation China's rapid recovery placed the late Ming and Qing Empires in the center of an increasingly complex worldwide commercial transformation (see "Patterns Up Close"). The competition for markets among the emerging maritime Atlantic states of Europe pushed them to develop trade networks in the Indian and Pacific Oceans, along the African coast, and in the Americas. In all of these regions (except the Americas) they faced competition from local traders, particularly in the Indian Ocean, and among the many ports of what is now Indonesia.

Among the European states, commercial, political, and religious competition resulted in policies of mercantilism. Similarly, China and Japan sought to tightly control imports, regulate the export trade, and keep potentially subversive foreign influences in check. China's production of luxury goods, the seclusion policies of Japan and Korea, and the demand for porcelain, tea, silk, paper, and cotton textiles made the Chinese empire the world's dominant economic engine until the nineteenth century (see Map 21.2).

In the midst of this growth, the government simplified land taxation. Corvée labor was effectively abolished. Land was assessed and classified according to its use and relative productivity. Land taxes were then combined into a single bill, payable in silver by installments over the course of the year: the so-called single-whip tax system. The system reduced the need for peasants to borrow at high rates from moneylenders at crucial times of the yearly cycle. The requirement that the payments be in silver played a role in the increasing monetization of the economy. This was aided considerably by the increasing amounts of silver entering the Chinese economy by means of the Manila trade. Merchants from south China exchanged spices and Chinese luxury goods in Manila in the Spanish-controlled Philippines for Spanish silver from the Americas. Spanish silver from Mexico and Peru continued to be used by Chinese merchants for centuries.

Regulating the Outer Barbarians By the late fifteenth century, Ming China had made progress toward establishing peace and stability. The view of the empire cultivated by China's elites placed it at the center of a world order defined by Neo-Confucian philosophy and supported by a host of Chinese cultural assumptions. Hence, successive rulers placed restrictions on maritime trade and conceived of diplomatic relations primarily in commercial terms. Emissaries from Korea, Vietnam, the Ryukyu Islands, and occasionally Japan traveled to pay ceremonial visits to the emperor, who then bestowed presents on the envoys and granted them permission to trade in China. This diplomatic-commercial arrangement worked within the hierarchy of the Confucian cultural sphere. By the late eighteenth century, however, it came into direct conflict with the system of international trade and diplomacy that had evolved in the West.

The Ming in Decline Despite the attention directed at the Mongol resurgence of the 1440s, periodic rebellions in the north and northwest punctuated the late fifteenth and sixteenth centuries. The commitment of Chinese troops in Korea against the forces of the Japanese leader Hideyoshi from 1592 to 1598 weakened the dynasty further during a period that saw the rise of another regional power: the Manchus. By the turn of the seventeenth century, the Manchus, a nomadic people related to the Jurchens inhabiting the northeastern section of the Ming domain, had become the prime military force of the area, and dissident Chinese sought them as allies. In 1642, in the midst of factional warfare among the Ming, the Chinese general Wu Sangui invited the Manchu leader Dorgon to cross the Great Wall. The Manchus seized the opportunity and occupied Beijing in 1644. There they declared the founding of a new regime, the Qing, or "pure," dynasty.

The Spring and Summer of Power: The Qing to 1750

The Manchus now found themselves in the position of having to rule. Preparation for this had already taken place within the state they had created for themselves in south Manchuria. Long exposure to Chinese culture and Confucian administrative practices provided models that soon proved adaptable by Manchu leaders within the larger environment of China proper.

The Banner System The **banner system**, under which the Manchus were organized for military and tax purposes, was expanded under the Qing to provide for segregated Manchu elites and garrisons in major cities and towns. Under the banner system, the Manchu state consisted of eight military and ethnic divisions, each represented by a distinctive banner. The system eventually became the chief administrative tool of the Manchu leadership in China.

Banner system: The organizational system of the Manchus for military and taxation purposes; there were eight banners under which all military houses were arranged, and each was further divided into blocks of families required to furnish units of 300 soldiers to the Manchu government.

Minority Rule As a ruling minority in China, the Manchus, like the Mongols before them, walked a fine line between administrative and cultural adaptation and complete assimilation. Chinese and Manchus were recruited in equal numbers for high administrative posts, Manchu quotas in the examination system were instituted, edicts were issued in both Chinese and Manchu, Qing emperors sought to control the empire's high culture, and Manchu "bannermen" had their own special quarters. In addition, the Manchu conqueror Dorgon instituted the infamous "queue edict" in 1645: all males, regardless of ethnicity, were required on pain of death to adopt the Manchu hairstyle of shaved forehead and long pigtail in the back—the queue—as the sign of loyalty to the new order.

The results, however, were bloody and long-lasting. The queue edict provoked revolts in several cities, and the casualties caused by suppression of these revolts may have numbered in the hundreds of thousands. For the remainder of the Qing era, rebels and protestors routinely cut their queues.

As the Manchus consolidated their rule, however, their conception of their empire grew far more expansive. That is, while the Han Chinese were by far the largest ethnic group, the Manchus conceived of their state as embodying in a more or less egalitarian sense all of the peoples within it. By the time of the Kangxi, Yongzheng, and Qianlong emperors, Qing concepts of the state had become remarkably inclusive, embracing nearly all of the minorities recognized by the People's Republic today. While rebellions were put down ruthlessly, and conquest of western lands proceeded apace, the incorporated peoples were seen as partners in a world empire.

Patterns Up Close

The "China" Trade

Ming and Qing China are at the heart of two innovations of enormous importance to the patterns of world history. The first is in the development of ceramics, culminating in the creation of true porcelain during the Song period (960–1279). The early Ming period saw the elaboration of the use of kaolin white clays with minerals, metals, and compounds that can be used to form durable glazes and striking artistic features. The Song and Yuan periods were characterized by pure white and celadon green wares, while by the Ming period, highly distinctive blue and white ware set the world standard for elegance.

The artistic excellence of Chinese porcelain spawned imitations throughout the Chinese periphery. By 1500, porcelain works in Korea, Japan, and Vietnam supplied a burgeoning market both at home and throughout East and Southeast Asia. Thus, there was already a highly developed regional market for what was, at the time, arguably the world's most highly developed technology.

Porcelain Vase, Ming Period. Porcelain ware of the Song and Ming periods is among the most coveted Chinese art objects even today. Here we have a Ming vase showing characteristically vibrant colors and a degree of technical perfection indicative of the best Chinese pottery works, such as Jingdezhen. The motif of the grass carp on the vase is symbolic of endurance and perseverance, and thus associated with the god of literature and scholarship.

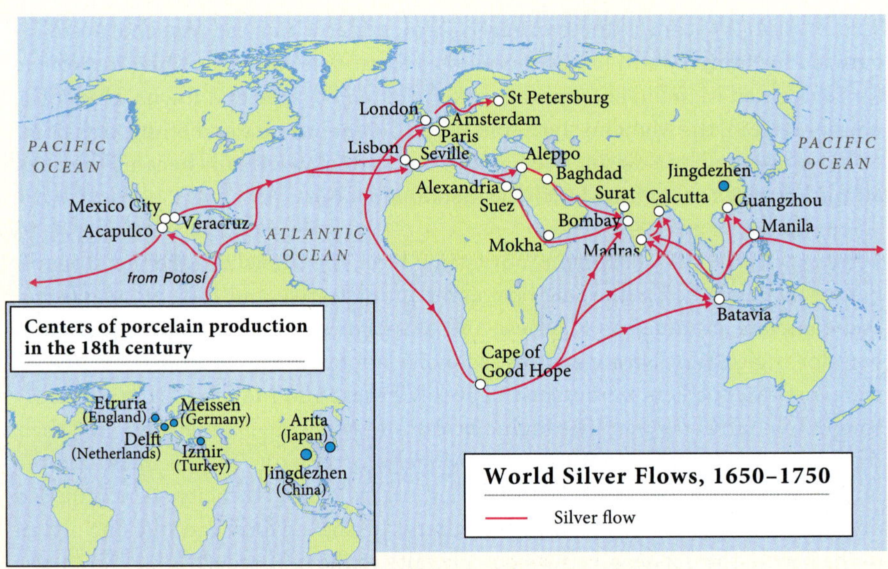

MAP 21.3 Silver Flows and Centers of Porcelain Production

Creating the New Order Though the Qing kept the centralized imperial system of the Ming largely intact, they made one significant addition to the uppermost level of the bureaucracy. While retaining the Ming Grand Secretariat, the emperor Kangxi's successor, Yongzheng, set up an inner advisory body called the Grand Council in 1733. Over the succeeding decades, the Grand Council became the supreme inner advisory group to the emperor, while the Grand Secretariat was relegated to handling less crucial "outer" matters.

The second great innovation was the world market for porcelain. China's wares had found customers for centuries in Eurasia and North and East Africa. Shipwrecks have been found in the Straits of Malacca laden with Ming porcelain; traders in the Swahili cities along the East African coast were avid collectors, while Africans farther inland decorated their graves with Chinese bowls.

Before the sixteenth century, a trickle of Ming porcelain also made its way to Europe. With the establishment of the first European trade empires, however, the demand for porcelain skyrocketed. From 1500 to 1800 it was arguably the single most important commodity in the unfolding world commercial revolution. Such was the prominence of this "export porcelain" in the furnishings of period homes that scarcely any family of means was without it (see Map 21.3).

Export Porcelain Tureen. By the early 1700s, luxury exports fom China, such as porcelain, lacquerware, and of course, tea, had become important staples of European maritime trade. Export porcelain—either items made to order by Chinese porcelain works for overseas buyers or generic ones made to suit European and colonial tastes—had become such a big business that cheaper pieces were sometimes actually used as ship's ballast on the homeward voyage. Shown here is a soup tureen made for the European market ca. 1735–1795. The color scheme is typical of Qing Dynasty ware.

With the rise of mercantilist theory and protectionism toward home markets during the seventeenth and eighteenth centuries, foreign manufacturers sought to break the Chinese monopoly. During Tokugawa times, the Japanese, for example, forced a group of Korean potters to labor at the famous Arita works to turn out Sino–Korean designs; the Dutch marketed delftware as an attempt to copy Chinese "blue willow" porcelain. It was not until German experimenters in Saxony happened upon a workable formula for hard-paste porcelain that their facility at Meissen began to produce true porcelain in 1710. Josiah Wedgwood set up his own porcelain factory in 1759 in England. But Chinese manufacturers would still drive the market until the end of the nineteenth century, and fine porcelain would continue to carry the generic name of "china," regardless of its origins.

Questions

- How does the development of porcelain serve as an example of Chinese leadership in technical innovation during the premodern and early modern periods?
- How did the emergence of a global trading network after 1500 affect both the demand for porcelain and its impact on consumer tastes?

As had been the case in past dynasties, the Qing sought to safeguard the borders of the empire by bringing peoples on the periphery into the imperial system. This meant a final reckoning with the Mongols in the 1720s, and the intervention of the Qing in religious disputes regarding Tibetan Buddhism, which had also been adopted by a number of Mongols. Toward this end, the Qing established a protectorate over Tibet in 1727, with the Dalai Lama as the approved temporal and religious leader.

The Qianlong Emperor The reign of the Qianlong [chi-en-lung] emperor, from 1736 to 1795, marked both the high point and the beginning of the decline of the Qing dynasty—and of imperial China itself.

The Qing army was many times larger than that of any potential competitor, and Qianlong wielded this power successfully, with expeditions against pirates and rebels on Taiwan and in punitive campaigns against Vietnam, Nepal, and Burma between 1766 and 1792 (see Map 21.4). Under his direction, the state also sponsored monumental literary enterprises. Based on the information on the Qing empire circulating around Europe, it seemed to some that the Chinese had solved many of the essential problems of good government and might provide models of statecraft for Europeans to emulate.

MAP 21.4 **China during the Reign of Qianlong**

Early European Contacts Just as China was abandoning its oceanic expeditions, Portugal surmounted its first big hurdle in pursuit of a worldwide maritime trade empire. By the 1440s, Portuguese navigators had opened commercial relations with the coastal kingdoms of West Africa. Scarcely a decade after Vasco da Gama arrived in Calicut in 1498, the first Portuguese ships appeared in Chinese waters. By 1557, the Portuguese had wrested the first European colony from the Chinese at Macau. From this point on, through merchants and missionaries, the contacts would frequently be profitable—and sometimes disastrous.

Matteo Ricci and Li Paul. The cross-cultural possibilities of sixteenth- and seventeenth-century Sino–Western contact were perhaps best exemplified by the activities of the Jesuit Matteo Ricci (1552–1610). Ricci predicated his mission in China on a respectful study of the language and the classical canon of the empire coupled with a thorough knowledge of the new mathematics and astronomy of the West. Here, he is pictured with one of his most prominent converts, a literatus and veteran of the war against the Japanese in Korea, Li Yingshi. Upon his conversion in 1602, Li took the Christian name of Paul.

Missionaries The arrival of the first European merchants in East Asia was followed shortly by that of the first Catholic missionaries, who were quick to realize the vast potential for religious conversions in China and Japan. Franciscan, Dominican, and Jesuit missionary orders set up headquarters in Malacca, and in 1549 the Franciscan Francis Xavier landed in Japan.

In China, the Ming at first refused entry to missionaries. Once admitted, the Franciscans and Dominicans, with their limited training in Chinese language and culture, made little headway. The Jesuits, led by Matteo Ricci (1552–1610), tried a different strategy. They immersed themselves in the classical language and high culture of the empire and gained recognition through their expertise in mathematics, astronomy, military science, and other European learning sought by the imperial court.

The papacy, however, had long considered Jesuit adaptations to local sensibilities problematic. In the case of China, the Jesuits' acquiescence to ancestor veneration and the use of tea and rice in the Eucharist, instead of bread and wine, was a particular concern. After several decades of intermittent negotiation concerning this "Rites Controversy," Kangxi's successor, Yongzheng, banned the order's activities in China in 1724. Christianity and missionary activity were thus driven underground.

The Canton Trade While China's commerce with the maritime Atlantic states grew rapidly in the eighteenth century, the Europeans had not yet been fully incorporated into the Qing hierarchical diplomatic system of ritual visits and trade permits from the emperor.

The British East India Company, having established its base at Calcutta in 1690, soon sought to expand its operations to China. At the same time, the Qing sought

Canton Factories, ca. 1800. Under the "Canton system" begun in 1699, all maritime trade with the Europeans was tightly controlled and conducted through the single port of Canton, or Guangzhou. Foreign merchants were not allowed to reside within the walled city, so they constructed their own facilities along the Pearl River waterfront. Though it kept profits high for the concerned parties, the restrictiveness of the system caused nineteenth-century merchants and diplomats to push the Chinese to open more ports to trade, which proved to be a major sticking point in Sino–Western relations.

to control contact with foreign and overseas Chinese traders as much as possible, while keeping their lucrative export trade at a sustainable level. Their solution, implemented in 1699, was to permit overseas trade only at the southern port of Guangzhou [GWAHNG-joe], known to Europeans as Canton. The local merchants' guild, or *cohong,* was granted a monopoly on the trade and was supervised by a special official from the imperial Board of Revenue. The Qing permitted only a small number of foreigners, mostly traders from the English, French, and Dutch East India Companies, to reside at the port. They were confined to a small compound of foreign "**factories,**" were not permitted inside the city walls, and could not bring their families along. Violations of the regulations could result in a suspension of trading privileges, and all infractions and disputes were judged according to Chinese law. Finally, since foreign affairs under these circumstances were considered a dimension of trade, all diplomatic issues were settled by local officials in Canton.

Factory: Here, the place where various "factors" (merchants, agents, etc.) gathered to conduct business.

The eighteenth century proved to be a boom time for all involved in the Canton trade. After 1784, the United States joined the trade; but despite the growing American presence, it was the British East India Company that dominated the Canton factories. Both the cohong and foreign-chartered companies carefully guarded their respective monopolies, and the system kept competition low and profits high on all sides.

Village and Family Life

Just as the effort toward greater centralization was visible in the government and economy of China during the Ming and Qing, it also reverberated within Chinese village life. While local custom among the peasants still revolved around family, clan, and lineage, institutions perfected under the Ming and Qing had a lasting impact.

Organizing the Countryside During the sixteenth century, the consolidation of the tax system into the single-whip arrangement led to the creation of the *lijia* system. All households were placed into officially designated villages for tax purposes; 10 households made up a *jia*, and 100 households composed a *li*, whose headmen, appointed by the magistrate, were responsible for keeping tax records and labor dues.

While the lijia system was geared primarily toward more efficient tax collection and record keeping, the *baojia* (see Chapter 12) system functioned as a more far-reaching means of government surveillance and control. The baojia system required families to register all members and be organized into units of 10 families, with one family in each unit assuming responsibility for the other nine. Each of these responsible families was arranged in groups of 10, and a member of each was selected to be responsible for that group of 100 households, and so on up to the *bao*, or 1,000-household, level. Baojia representatives at each level were to be chosen by the families in the group. These representatives were to report to the magistrate on the doings of their respective groups and held accountable for the group's behavior.

Glimpses of Rural Life Both the scholar-gentry and, starting in the seventeenth century, Westerners traveling in China wrote about peasant life. Based on these accounts, some generalizations can be made about rural and family life in Ming and Qing times.

First, while the introduction of new crops led to cultivation of more land, population increase, and the commercialization of agriculture, as in most agrarian societies, the overall rhythms of peasant life changed little over the centuries.

Second, some early signs of economic stress were already present toward the end of Qianlong's reign. Chief among these was the problem of absentee landlordism. This would grow increasingly acute as the gentry were drawn away from the countryside by urban opportunities and amenities.

Third, pressures on patterns of village life tended to be magnified in the lives of women and girls. Elite women were routinely educated to be as marriageable as possible. Women were expected to be modest and obedient and were usually separated from and subordinate to men. The custom of foot binding had long since become institutionalized, and the sale of infant girls—and, in extreme cases, female infanticide—rose markedly in rural areas during times of social stresses. While the dominance of women over the "inner realm" of the family remained largely complete, this realm was never considered equal in importance to the outer sphere of men's activities.

Science, Culture, and Intellectual Life

The Ming dynasty marked the high point as well as the beginning of the decline of China's preeminent place as a world technological innovator. One area in which this became evident by the eighteenth and nineteenth centuries was in military matters.

Superpower The Ming at their height have been described by some Chinese scholars as a military superpower. By the mid-fifteenth century the Ming arsenal was producing thousands of cannon, handguns, and "fire lances" every year;

in 1450 over half of the Ming frontier military units had cannon and one-third of all troops carried firearms. As early as the 1390s, large shipborne cannon were already being installed in naval vessels. Court historians of the late Ming credited nearly all the military successes of the dynasty to their firearms. By the Qing period, however, continual improvement of arms was seen as both too costly and unnecessary.

Chinese Commercial Enterprises. The growing volume and profits of the export trade encouraged further development and specialization of long-standing Chinese domestic industries during the eighteenth and nineteenth centuries. Moneychangers, known as *shroffs* (*a*), were involved in testing the quality of silver taken from foreign concerns in exchange for Chinese goods. A worker and overseer demonstrate the operation of a silk reeling machine (*b*). Women work to sort tea; in this photograph (*c*), packing chests for tea are stacked behind the sorters. The hairstyle of the men in these photos—shaved foreheads with a long braid called a queue—was mandatory for all Chinese males as a sign of submission to the Qing.

Science and Literature In geography, mathematics, and astronomy, a fruitful exchange was inaugurated between European Jesuit missionaries and Chinese officials in the seventeenth and eighteenth centuries. The most lasting legacy of this meeting was the observatory in Beijing and new maps of the world based on sixteenth- and seventeenth-century explorations.

The centralizing tendency of the government of China led to control in the cultural realm through patronage, monopoly, and licensing. The Kangxi, Yongzheng, and Qianlong emperors set the tone in matters of aesthetics and used cultural projects (such as dictionaries and encyclopedias) to direct the energies of scholars into approved areas. At the same time, they sought to quash unorthodox views through lack of support and, more directly, through literary inquisitions.

Neo-Confucian Philosophy In the sixteenth century new directions in Neo-Confucianism were being explored by Wang Yangming (1472–1529). While Wang's school remained popular, his intuitive approach to enlightenment placed his more radical followers increasingly on the fringes of intellectual life. In addition, the Qing victory ushered in an era of soul-searching among Chinese literati and a questioning of the systems that had failed in the face of foreign conquest.

Two of the most important later figures in Qing philosophy were Huang Zongxi [hwang zung-shee] (1610–1695) and Gu Yanwu [goo yen-woo] (1613–1682). Both men's lives spanned the Qing conquest, and both concluded that the collapse of the old order was in part due to a retreat from practical politics and too much indulgence in the excesses of the radicals of the Wang Yangming school. With a group of like-minded scholars, they devoted themselves to reconstituting an activist Confucianism based on rigorous self-cultivation and on remonstrating with officials and even the court. One outgrowth of this development was the so-called Han learning movement, which sought to recover the original meaning of classic Confucian works. Though on the fringe of approved official activities, the movement saw continued refinement of textual criticism and successfully uncovered a number of fraudulent works.

The Arts and Popular Culture Official patronage ensured that approved schools and genres of art would be maintained. The Qianlong emperor, motivated by a lifelong quest to master the fine arts, collected thousands of paintings, rare manuscripts, jade, porcelain, lacquerware, and other objets d'art. Because the force of imperial patronage was directed at conserving past models rather than creating new ones, the period is not noteworthy for stylistic innovation.

Local Custom and Religion Chinese villages often featured storytellers, street-corner poets, spirit mediums, diviners, and other entertainers. Popular village culture was also dominated by Daoism, Buddhism, and older traditions of local worship, including beliefs in ancestral spirits, "hungry ghosts" (roaming spirits of those not properly cared for in death), fairies, and demons. These beliefs were enhanced over the centuries by tales of Daoist adepts and "immortals," Buddhist bodhisattvas, and underworld demons.

A glimpse into local society comes from Pu Songling's (1640–1715) *Strange Tales from the Make-Do Studio.* Pu traveled extensively, collecting folktales, accounts of local curiosities, and especially stories of the supernatural. His grandson published the stories in 1740. In Pu's world, "fox-fairies" appear as beautiful women, men are transformed into tigers, the young are duped into degenerate behavior, and crooked mediums and storytellers take advantage of the unwary.

The Long War and Longer Peace: Japan, 1450–1750

Toyotomi Hideyoshi (1536–1598). Portraits of Japanese daimyo and shoguns tend to position them in similar ways, looking to the front left, with stiff, heavily starched official robes that reflect their austerity and dignity. In this 1601 portrait, done several years after his death, Hideyoshi is shown in a typical pose, with the signs of his adopted family and imperial crests around the canopy to denote his role of imperial guardian.

In 1185, struggles by court factions in Japan's capital of Heian-Kyo (Kyoto) resulted in the creation of the office of the shogun, the chief military officer of the realm. By the fourteenth century, the emperor had become the puppet of his first officer. When Emperor Go-Daigo attempted to reassert his prerogatives in 1333, his one-time supporter Ashikaga Takauji expelled him and set up his own headquarters in the capital. A debilitating civil war would ravage the capital and countryside until it ended with Japan's unification.

The price of unification, however, was high. The first of Japan's unifiers, Oda Nobunaga, was assassinated; the invasions of Korea undertaken by his successor Hideyoshi resulted in massive loss of life. The final custodians of Japanese unification, the Tokugawa family, created a system that they hoped would preserve Japan in a state of unity and seclusion. Yet over the two and a half centuries of the Tokugawa peace, forces were building that would allow Japan to vault into the modern world with unprecedented speed.

The Struggle for Unification

The instability of the Ashikaga regime led to battles for the shogun's office among the daimyo, or regional warlords. In 1467, these factional conflicts erupted into a civil war that would last for more than a century. The opening phase of this struggle devastated the city of Kyoto. With no real center of power, a bitter struggle among the daimyos continued into the 1570s.

Oda Nobunaga and Toyotomi Hideyoshi By the mid-sixteenth century, some daimyo began to consolidate their power and secure allies. A factor in deciding the outcome of these wars was intrusion from the outside. By the 1540s, the first Portuguese and Spanish merchants and missionaries had arrived in southern Japan. One daimyo, Oda Nobunga, was quick to use the newcomers and their improved small arms to his advantage. Oda employed newly converted Christian musketeers to secure the area around Kyoto and had largely succeeded in unifying the country when he was assassinated in 1582. His second in command, Hideyoshi, systematically brought the remaining daimyo under his sway over the next nine years.

Hideyoshi viewed a foreign adventure as a way to cement the loyalties of the daimyo. In addition, the army he had put together might prove dangerous to disband. Hence, as early as 1586 he announced his plans to conquer China itself. In

1592 he set out with a massive expeditionary force for Korea. The Japanese made good progress up the peninsula until massive Chinese counterattacks slowly eroded their gains and decimated large stretches of Korea.

Hideyoshi turned homeward to Japan with the remnants of his army in 1596. His stature kept his coalition of daimyo together until his death during his troubled second Korean campaign in 1598. The coalition then broke in two, and a civil war began between Tokugawa Ieyasu, the leader of the eastern coalition of daimyos, and their western counterparts. After a decisive Tokugawa victory, Ieyasu, who claimed to be a descendant of the original shoguns, was officially invested with the office in 1603. His accession marked the beginning of Japan's most peaceful, most secluded, and perhaps most thoroughly regulated and policed interval in its history until World War II. The Tokugawas would create a hereditary shogunate, organized along Chinese Neo-Confucian models of morality and government, which would last until 1867 (see Map 21.5).

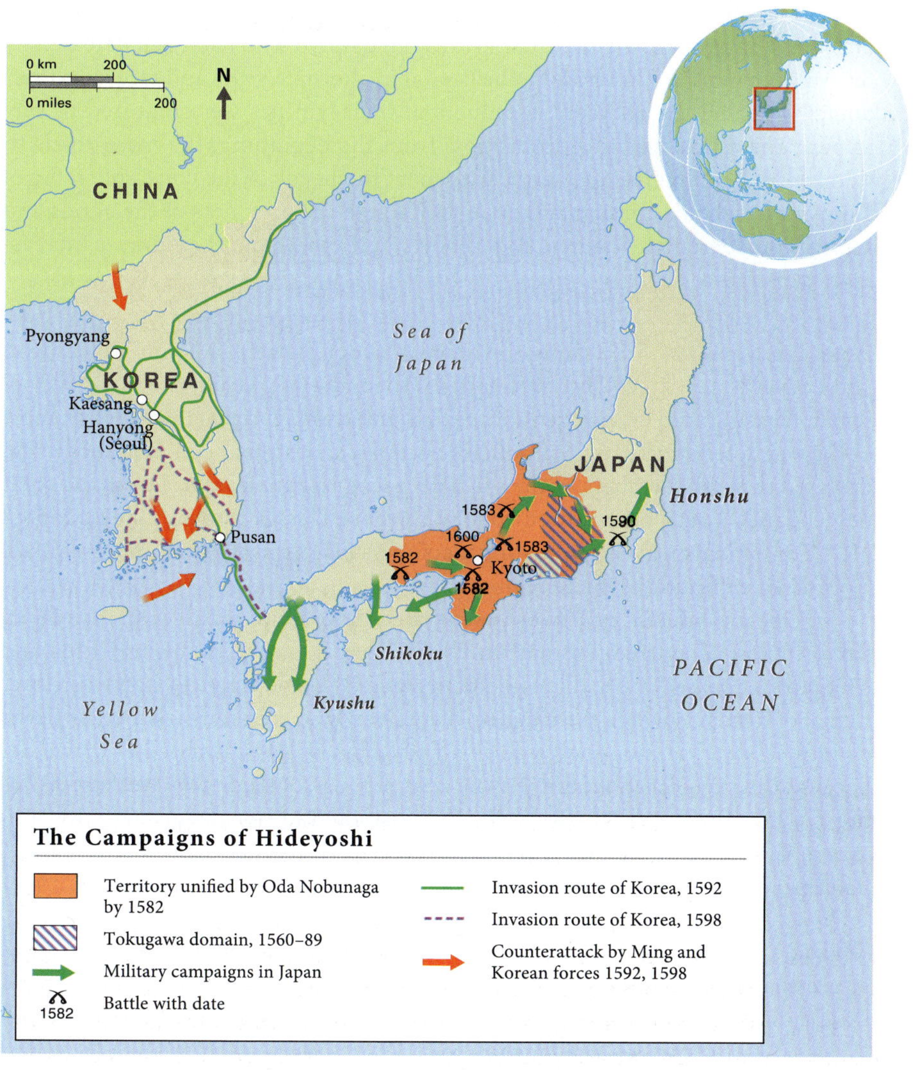

MAP 21.5 The Campaigns of Hideyoshi

The Tokugawa *Bakufu* to 1750

The realm that Tokugawa Ieyasu (1542–1616) now led had been scarred by warfare and social disruption. The daimyo and samurai employed advanced military technology, but their depredations had broken old alliances. The intrusion of European missionaries and merchants contributed to the social ferment.

Ieyasu's assumption of the shogunate in 1603 began a process of centralization and stabilization in Japan that would last more than two centuries. Initially, however, seclusion did not figure among its principles. The immediate priority was to erect a system for the daimyo that would reward the loyal and keep an eye on the defeated.

"Tent Government" The system devised under the Tokugawa *bakufu* ("tent government," referring to the shogun's official status as the emperor's mobile deputy) was called *sankin kotai,* the "rule of alternate attendance." The shogunate placed its new headquarters in the Tokugawa castle in Edo (the future city of Tokyo). In order to ensure their loyalty, all daimyo who had been defeated by Ieyasu were required to reside in the capital in alternate years and return to their domains during the off years. Members of their families were required to stay as permanent hostages in Edo. Almost from the beginning, the main roads to Edo spurred commerce and services to meet the needs of the constant traffic of daimyo households coming and going. Although the providers of the goods and services prospered, the daimyo found both their power and their purses increasingly depleted.

Freezing Society In turning the office of shogun over to his son Hidetada in 1605, Ieyasu made it legally hereditary for the first time. Given the possibility of revolt, Ieyasu stayed on as regent. Under his grandson Iemitsu (1604–1651), most of the characteristic Tokugawa policies became institutionalized. The shogunate declared that the members of the officially recognized classes in Japan and their descendants would be required to stay in those classes forever. They adopted Neo-Confucianism as the governing ideology, thus joining the commonwealth of Confucian civilizations in the region.

Significant differences, however, separated the practice of this system in Japan from similar, concurrent systems in China, Korea, and Vietnam. In China and Vietnam, a civil service had long been in place. The situation in Japan was closer to that of Korea, in which the yangban were already a hereditary aristocracy in the countryside and so monopolized the official classes. Japan differed even further because the samurai and daimyo were now not just a hereditary class of officials but a military aristocracy as well. The low position traditionally given to the military in Chinese Confucianism was totally reversed, and the daimyo and samurai had absolute power of life and death over commoners.

Giving Up the Gun The government required the samurai class to practice swordsmanship, archery, and other forms of individual martial arts. But the rapid development of firearms remained a threat to any class whose skills were built entirely around hand-to-hand combat. Thus, the Tokugawa gave up the gun. Tokugawa police confiscated and destroyed almost the entire stock of the nation's firearms. A few pieces, like the cannon in some Tokugawa seaside forts, were kept as curiosities. Thus, weapons cast in the 1600s were the ones that confronted the first foreign ships nearly 250 years later in 1853.

As the shogunate strove to impose peace on the daimyo and bring stability to the populace, it became increasingly anxious to weed out disruptive influences. They began to restrict the movements of foreigners, particularly missionaries. The influence of the missionaries on the growing numbers of Japanese Christians was worrisome to those intent on firmly establishing Neo-Confucian beliefs and rituals among the commoners. Moreover, the duel between Catholic and Protestant missionaries and merchants carried its own set of problems for social stability.

Tokugawa Seclusion Ultimately, therefore, missionaries were ordered to leave the country, followed by their merchants. The English and Spanish withdrew in the 1620s, while the Portuguese stayed until 1639. Only the Dutch, Koreans, and Chinese were allowed to remain, in small numbers and at the pleasure of the shogunate. Further, in 1635 it was ruled that Japanese subjects would be forbidden to leave the islands and that no oceangoing ships were to be built. Foreign merchants would be permitted only in designated areas in port cities and could not bring their families with them. The Dutch were restricted to a tiny artificial island in Nagasaki harbor. In return for the privilege, they were required to make yearly reports to the shogun's ministers on world events. This "Dutch learning" eventually found a small readership among educated Japanese, and along with the accounts of Chinese and Korean observers formed the basis of the Japanese view of the outside world for over two centuries. Though foreign ships would occasionally attempt to call at Japanese ports, by the eighteenth century Europeans generally steered clear of the islands.

Trampling the Crucifix Much less tolerance was shown to Japan's Christian community. Dissatisfaction with the new Tokugawa strictures provoked a rebellion in 1637 by Christian converts and disaffected samurai. As the revolt was suppressed, those who were captured were roasted to death inside a ring of fire. Subsequently, remaining missionaries were sometimes crucified upside down, while suspected converts were given an opportunity to "trample the crucifix" to show they had discarded the new faith. However, thousands continued to practice in secret until Christianity was declared legal again during the reign of Emperor Meiji (r. 1867–1912).

Growth and Stagnation: Economy and Society

By 1750, Japan had become the most urbanized society on earth. Edo had a population of one million, making it arguably the world's largest city, and as much as 10 percent of Japan's population lived in cities with populations above 10,000 (see Map 21.6). The law of alternate attendance ensured growing traffic in and out of the major cities along the major routes into Edo. Services required to support that traffic aided urban and suburban growth and spread the wealth.

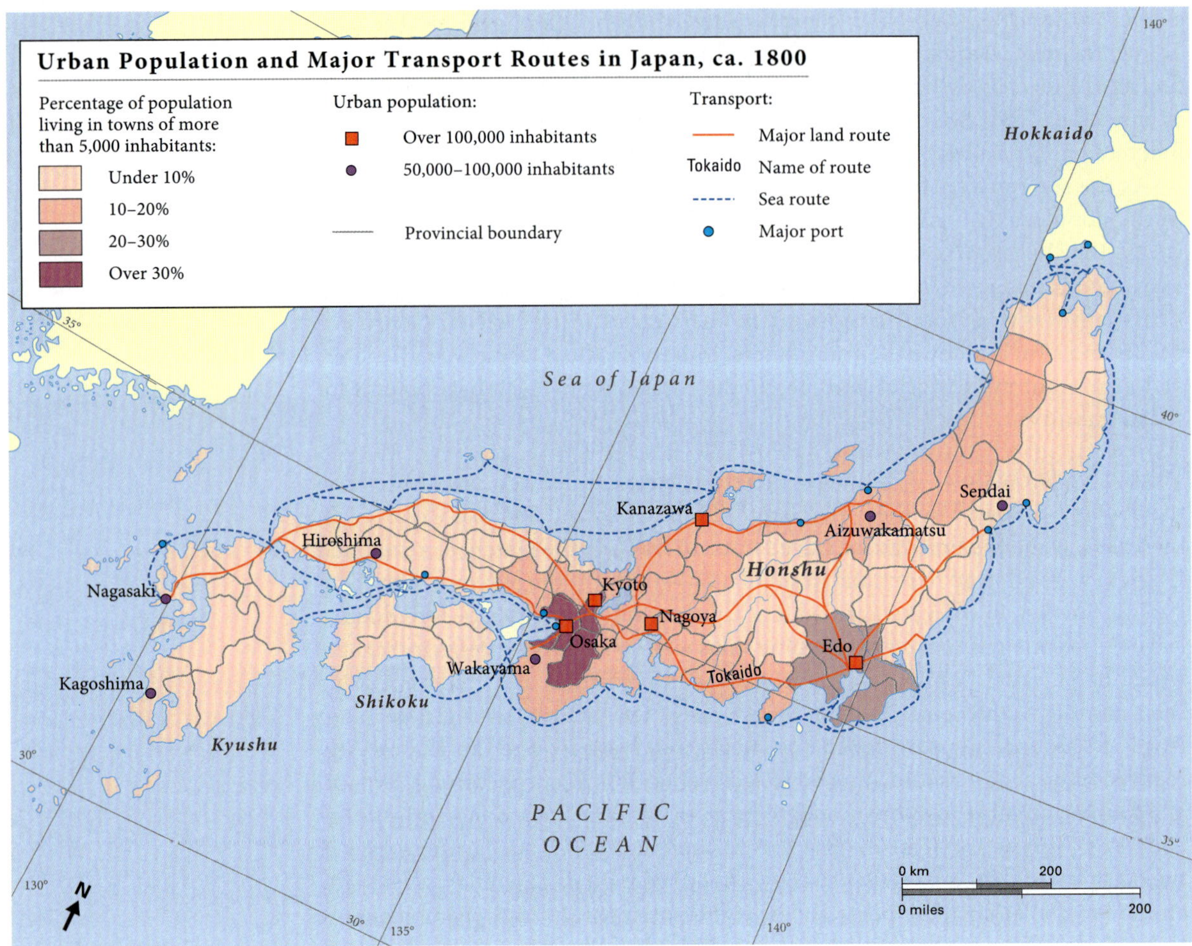

MAP 21.6 **Urban Population and Major Transport Routes in Japan, ca. 1800**

Population, Food, and Commerce One cause of this urbanization was the growth of the population as a whole. The efficiency of small-scale, intensive rice and vegetable farming, aided by simple machines, made Japanese agriculture the most efficient in the preindustrial world.

Tokugawa policies aimed at stabilizing the country had the unanticipated effect of spurring the economy. The Tokugawa tax structure set quotas of rice for each village and left the individual daimyos responsible for remitting these to the capital. Thus, traffic in bulk rice spurred the carrying trade. In addition to guaranteeing provisions for the cities, the need to convert rice to cash for the treasury contributed to a banking and credit infrastructure.

The tastes of the three largest cities—Edo, with its high concentration of the wealthy and well-connected; Kyoto, with its large retinue of the imperial household; and Osaka, the chief port—created a demand for sophisticated consumer goods and services. Such enterprises as sake brewing, wholesaling dried and prepared foods, running bathhouses, and managing large studios of artisans all became booming businesses. Books, porcelains, lacquerware, and objets d'art were exchanged for Japanese hard currency, and what was once the province of the elite was now widely available to anyone who had the money and interest to afford it.

Woodblock Print of the Fish Market at the East Side of Nihonbashi (The Bridge of Japan). The Tokugawa period, with its long interlude of peace and prosperity, was Japan's first great age of urban life. The constant traffic of daimyo progressions along the main roads and the large coasting trade along the Inland Sea ensured a growing middle class of artisans, tradespeople, and merchants. The capital, Edo, had ballooned to over a million people, and the bustle of the city is illustrated in this panel depicting a famous fish market.

Rural Transformations Life in rural areas also changed. As they had with the military houses, the Tokugawa promulgated Neo-Confucian rules for village families and their individual members. Buddhist temples kept registers of the villagers in their districts. Weddings, funerals, travel, rents, taxes, and so forth were subject to official permission through either the village headman or the samurai holding a position equivalent to a magistrate. Within these strictures, however, and subject to the hereditary occupation laws, families, clans, and villages were relatively autonomous.

This was especially true of rural families, in which families commonly worked together on their plots. While the "inner domain," so central to Neo-Confucian thought as the strict province of women, retained a good deal of that character, Japanese women were not entirely secluded, and men routinely helped with child-rearing. Women in cities and larger villages ran businesses, especially those involved in entertainment, such as geisha houses, bathhouses, taverns, restaurants, and retail establishments. By the eighteenth century, merchants utilized the spinning and weaving talents of rural women in parceling out textile manufacturing—a Japanese version of the English "putting-out system."

The Samurai in Peacetime The samurai's position evolved as his role as an official and Neo-Confucian role model became paramount. Samurai were not necessarily prosperous, and indeed their fixed incomes declined in value over time. By the later eighteenth century, many samurai lived in genteel poverty. In many rural areas, they founded village academies in the local temples for the teaching of literacy and correct moral behavior, which would result, by the mid-nineteenth century, in what was probably the world's highest level of functional literacy.

By the middle of the eighteenth century, there were signs of tension among the aims of the government in ensuring peace and stability, the dynamism of the internal economy, and the boom in population. Signs of rural impoverishment and

Monochrome: Single-color; in East Asian painting, a very austere style popular in the fourteenth and fifteenth centuries, particularly among Zen-influenced artists.

social unrest were often noted by commentators. Inflation in commodity prices outpaced efforts to increase domain revenues, squeezing those on fixed incomes and stipends. Efforts to keep rural families small enough to subsist on their plots led to an increasing frequency of infanticide. Famines in 1782 and 1830 compounded these problems. By the early nineteenth century, the government was gradually losing its ability to care for the populace.

Hothousing "Japaneseness": Culture, Science, and Intellectual Life

Two Courtesans. The new genre of *ukiyo-e*, "pictures of the floating world," developed in the late seventeenth century and remained popular through the nineteenth century. Finely wrought woodblock prints in both monochrome and color, they take their name from the pleasure districts whose people and scenes were favorite subjects. This work is from a series by the noted artist Kitagawa Utamaro (ca. 1753–1806) on famous courtesans of the "Southern District," part of the Shinagawa section of Edo.

Painting, poetry, and calligraphy flourished among the daimyo and samurai, while attracting the new middle classes. Zen-influenced **monochrome** painting, the ideals of the tea ceremony, the austere Noh theater, and principles of interior design and landscape gardening were becoming distinctly "Japanese."

New Theater Traditions Traditional cultural elements coexisted with new forms, such as Bunraku, the puppet theater still popular in Japan today. The facile movements and facial expressions of Bunraku puppets proved effective in popularizing the older, highly abstract, Noh plays. But renowned playwrights soon wrote special works for these theaters as well. The most revered was Chikamatsu Monzaemon [chick-ah-MAT-soo mon-ZAE-mon] (1653–1724), who skillfully transferred the tragically noble sentiments of the best Noh works into contemporary themes. One of his works, *Goban Taiheiki* (1706), is based on an incident in which a daimyo attacked a court official and was forced to commit suicide, leaving his samurai as *ronin*—masterless; 47 of these ronin killed the daimyo's assassin out of loyalty to their leader, knowing they would pay for the deed with their own lives. Originally written for the Bunraku theater, it was adapted a few decades later for Kabuki, the other great mass entertainment art of Tokugawa Japan, as the much better-known play *Chushingura* (1748; often known as *The Forty-Seven Ronin*). Often raucous, and occasionally risqué, Kabuki remained by far the most popular Japanese mass entertainment, and *Chushingura* remained the most frequently performed play throughout the Tokugawa period.

The era also marked the golden age of the poetic form of haiku, the most famous practitioner of which was Matsuo Basho (1644–1694). As a poet he used a dozen pen names; he took "Basho" from the banana plant he especially liked in his yard. Even more minimalist than the 31-syllable *tanka* poetry, haiku compressed emotion and release into a mere 17 syllables in a way that has made it a treasured form in Japan.

In the visual arts, fine woodblock printing allowed popular works to be widely duplicated. The new genre was called *ukiyo-e*, "pictures of the floating world," a reference to the pleasure quarters on the edge of the cities that furnished many of its subjects. During Tokugawa times, one of the most famous practitioners of the art was Kitagawa Utamaro (1753–1806), whose studies of women became forever associated with Japanese perceptions of female beauty. These and other such works formed many of the first popular images that nineteenth-century Westerners had of Japan.

Putting It All Together

During the late Ming and early Qing periods, imperial China achieved social and political stability and developed the world's largest economy. Yet by the second part of the eighteenth century, internal problems emerged that would erupt in succeeding decades. In the following century, these problems would have a profound impact on China's fortunes.

The arrival of foreign traders who brought with them the new technologies of the first scientific–industrial societies, combined with China's self-confidence in its own culture and institutions, added more pressure to an already volatile internal situation and ultimately created an unprecedented challenge for China. Over the coming decades, Chinese expectations of being able to assimilate all comers would dissolve, along with the hope that a renewed faithfulness to Confucian fundamentals would produce the leaders necessary to navigate such perilous times. But at the halfway mark of the eighteenth century, the Chinese still expected that they would successfully regulate the "inner" and "outer" domains of their empire and keep pernicious foreign influences at arm's length.

Ravaged by a century of warfare and foreign intrusion, Japan also sought to regulate its inner and outer domains and minimize outside influences. As in China, however, the stability of the seventeenth and eighteenth centuries would be threatened in the nineteenth by the commercial power of the Europeans and Americans. Before the nineteenth century was finished, China would be rent by civil war, while Japan would emerge from its own civil war to install a unified government under an emperor for the first time since the twelfth century. In the final years of the nineteenth century, Japan would once again invade Korea to attack China—this time with very different results. In the process, the historical relationship of more than two millennia between the two countries would be altered forever.

Review and Relate

Thinking Through Patterns

Examine the ways historians approach the big questions of this chapter.

Why did late Ming and early Qing China look inward after such a successful period of overseas exploration?

While the commercial prospects for China's fleets grew in prominence, maritime trade was simply not essential to the Chinese economy at that point. Moreover, urgent defense preparations were needed in the overland north against the resurgent

Mongols. Although the discontinuing of the fleets seems like a mistake in hindsight, because of what happened to China hundreds of years later due to a lack of adequate naval defenses, these measures seemed both rational and appropriate to the Chinese and outside observers at the time.

➤ How do the goals of social stability drive the policies of agrarian states? How does the history of China and Japan in this period show these policies in action?

One almost universal pattern of world history among agrarian states is that their governments adopt policies aimed at promoting social stability. This is because nearly everything depends on having reliable harvests. Given the agricultural techniques and technology of preindustrial societies, the majority of the population must be engaged in food production to ensure sufficient surpluses. If such a society places a premium on change and social mobility, it risks chronic manpower shortages and insufficient harvests. Thus, social classes are carefully delineated, and the state directs its policies toward eliminating social upheaval.

➤ In what ways did contact with the maritime states of Europe alter the patterns of trade and politics in eastern Asia?

In both China and Japan, these connections resulted in severe restrictions on maritime trade: the Canton system in China and the seclusion policies of the Tokugawa in Japan. Earlier, the Chinese emperor had welcomed Jesuit missionaries and even considered conversion to Catholicism. But the backlash against "subversive" influence induced the Qing to drive Christianity underground. In Japan such contact had earlier injected European influences into Japan's civil wars, and the reaction against this was Tokugawa seclusion.

➤ How did Neo-Confucianism in China differ from that of Tokugawa Japan?

The fundamental difference was that Japan was a military society, which adopted the forms and structures of Neo-Confucianism to make the daimyo and samurai into officials. They therefore were expected to maintain this civil role as bureaucrats but also to stand ready to fight. The low esteem in which the military was held in China was just the inverse of that of the martial elites of Japan. Another key difference was that officials in China were selected on the basis of competitive examinations, thus creating some social mobility. In Japan, the social classes were frozen, and no exams were offered for potential officials.

Against the Grain

Consider this as a counterpoint to the main patterns examined in this chapter.

Seclusion's Exceptions

- While the attempts by China, Korea, and Japan to keep out foreign influences may strike

Despite Japan's policies of seclusion during the Tokugawa era, the country was more porous than is popularly supposed. Chinese and Korean merchants continued to do business in Japan. Formal relations with Korea were maintained by the Tokugawa through the lord of the Tsushima feudal domain, who also maintained a trading post in the Korean port of Pusan. Korean vessels, like those of the Chinese, were permitted to put in at Nagasaki, and the shogunate's attempts to curtail silver exports were generally waived for Korean trade. More than a dozen Korean trade missions traveled to the shogun's court during the Tokugawa period.

No official exchanges with Chinese representatives took place, since neither side wanted to be seen as the junior partner in the Neo-Confucian hierarchy of diplomacy conducted under the so-called tribute mission system. In addition to the predominance of Chinese ships at Nagasaki, however, both Chinese and Japanese merchants took advantage of a loophole in the sovereignty of the Ryukyu Islands to trade there. China and Japan both insisted that the islands were under their protection, though the Japanese domain of Satsuma had captured Okinawa in 1609. The leaders in Okinawa, however, sent trade and tribute missions to both China and Japan in order to safeguard their freedom of action, thus keeping the conduit for trade semiofficially open for both sides.

The Dutch established an exclusive relationship with Japan. Warning the Tokugawa about the sinister religious intentions of their Iberian competitors, they suggested that the Dutch alone should handle Japan's European trade. Though their power in European markets ebbed during the eighteenth and early nineteenth centuries, their influence among the small but vital circle of Japanese leaders engaged in "Dutch learning" remained strong right up to the time of the coming of Perry's "Black Ships" in 1853.

us as impractical, many nations today still seek to limit foreign influences, particularly in the realm of culture. What are the advantages and disadvantages of such policies? Are they inevitably self-defeating?

- Were the policies of turning inward among these agrarian–urban societies part of larger historical patterns at work during this time? Why or why not?

Key Terms

Banner system 503
Factory 508
Monochrome 518

Learn more with this chapter's digital tools, including the Oxford Insight Study Guide, at http://www.oup.com/he/vonsivers4e. Please see the Further Resources section at the back of the book for additional readings and suggested websites.

PATTERNS OF EVIDENCE |

Sources for Chapter 21

SOURCE 21.1

Matteo Ricci, *China in the Sixteenth Century*

ca. 1600

When European Christian missionaries first came to Ming China, they made very little progress in converting the Chinese, in large part due to their limited training in Chinese language and culture. When he arrived in China in 1583, the Jesuit Matteo Ricci (1552–1610) encouraged his followers to immerse themselves in the language and to become conversant with the rich traditions of Chinese literature. He also came to be respected by, and especially helpful to, the emperor, as he offered his expertise in the sciences and mathematics to the imperial court. With a European Jesuit (Adam Schall von Bell) as the official court astronomer to the Kangxi emperor (1654–1722), there were reports that the emperor himself considered converting to Catholicism. Nevertheless, not every encounter between Chinese and Europeans went so smoothly, as the following anecdote from Ricci's diary reveals.

Of late they [the Chinese] had become quite disturbed by the coming of the Portuguese, and particularly so because they can do nothing about it, due to the great profit reaped from Portuguese traders by the public treasury and by certain influential merchants. Without referring to the public treasury or to the merchants who come from every other province, they complain that the foreign commerce raises the price of all commodities and that outsiders are the only ones to profit from it. As an expression of their contempt for Europeans, when the Portuguese first arrived they were called foreign devils, and this name is still in common use among the Cantonese.

The citizens of Sciauquin have their own particular reasons for hating the strangers. They are afraid that the Portuguese merchants will get into the interior of the realm with the missionaries, and their fears are not without some foundation. The frequent visits of the Fathers to the town of Macao and their growing intimacy with the Governor have already aroused their antipathy. There is nothing that stirs them up like a wide-spreading slander, and they had a good one in the story that the tower which had been

---

Source: Matthew Ricci, *China in the Sixteenth Century*, trans. Louis Gallagher (New York: Random House, 1953), 161–165.

built at such great expense, and with so much labor, was erected at the request of the foreign priests. This probably had its origin in the fact that the tower was completed while the Fathers were building their mission houses. This false rumor had such an effect that the people called it the Tower of the Foreigners instead of The Flowery Tower, as it was named. As a result of the animosity which grew out of this incident, when they realized that they could not drive out the Mission, as they wanted to, they took to insulting the missionaries whenever an occasion occurred or they could trump up a reason for doing so. It was quite annoying and dangerous to be made a continual target for stones hurled from the tower, when people came there every day to play games, the purpose for which these towers are built. Not a stone was thrown at the Mission House from the high tower nearby that missed its roof as a target. These showers of stones were heaviest when they knew that there were only one or two of the servants at home. Another silly reason for their taking offense was that the doors of our house, which were kept open for inspection while it was being built, were now kept closed according to the rule of our Society. What they wanted to do was to use the house as they did their temples of idols, which are always left wide open and are often the scenes of uncouth frivolity.

It happened one day, when their insolence became really unbearable, that one of our servants ran out and seized a boy, who had been throwing stones at the house, and dragging him inside threatened to bring him to court. Attracted by the shrieking of the boy, several men, who were known in the neighborhood, ran into the house to intercede for the culprit, and Father Ricci ordered that he be allowed to depart without further ado. Here was a good pretext for a major calumny, and two of the neighbors who disliked the Fathers went into conference with a bogus relative of the boy, who knew something about court procedure. Then they trumped up a story that the boy had been seized by the Fathers and hidden in their house for three days, that he had been given a certain drug, well known to the Chinese, which prevented him from crying out, and that the purpose of it all was to smuggle him back to Macao, where they could sell him into slavery. The two men were to be called in as witnesses.

. . .

[A trial takes place before the Governor, and he hears the "witnesses" to the crime.]

. . .

Finally, in order to save the Father present from any embarrassment, he [the Governor] declared him [Ricci] wholly innocent and. . . his next move was to summon the three members of the building commission, who were at the tower on the day the incident occurred. The plaintiff requested that he call in the neighbors also, the real authors of the charge, who had a full knowledge of all its details. The Governor dismissed the multitude and, as he was leaving, he forbade the Father to leave the court. In the meantime, and in deep humiliation, the Father betook himself to prayer, commending his cause and its solution to God, to the Blessed Mother and to the Saints.

. . .

Then he [the Governor] told the missionary and his interpreter and the three Commissioners that he had heard enough of this affair, and that they might return to their homes and their business.

. . .

On the following day the Governor sent a solemn document to be posted at the main entrance of the Mission House. This notice, after explaining that the foreigners were living here with permission of the Viceroy, stated that certain unprincipled persons, contrary to right and reason, were known to have molested the strangers living herein, wherefore: he, the Governor, strictly forbade under severest penalty that anyone from now on should dare to cause them further molestation.

Working with Sources

1. **What seems to have been Ricci's attitude toward Chinese customs and religious practices?**
2. **To what extent did trade rights and religious goals intersect in this setting? What was in the immediate and long-term interests of the Chinese "hosts" of the mission?**

SOURCE 21.2

Macartney's observations on China and possibilities for British commerce (excerpts)

The very different views taken by the first British envoy to China, Lord George Macartney, about the situation of the Qing Dynasty in China and the possibilities of trade and political representation (21.2) and by the Qianlong emperor (21.3) are spelled out in bold relief in this exchange. The Qing court's position did not change on these issues until forced to do so by the Treaty of Nanking (Nanjing) in 1842, following the First Opium War.

For it would now seem that the policy and vanity of the Court equally concurred in endeavouring to keep out of sight whatever can manifest our preeminence, which they undoubtedly feel, but have not yet learned to make the proper use of. It is, however, in vain to attempt arresting the progress of human knowledge. I am, indeed, very much mistaken if all the authority and address of the Tartar Government will be able much longer to stifle the energies of their Chinese subjects. Scarcely a year now passes without an insurrection in some of their provinces. It is true they are soon suppressed, but their frequency

Source: Wikiquote, https://en.wikiquote.org/wiki/George_Macartney

is a strong symptom of the fever within. The paroxysm is repelled, but the disease is not cured.

The Empire of China is an old, crazy, first-rate Man of War, which a fortunate succession of able and vigilant officers have contrived to keep afloat for these hundred and fifty years past, and to overawe their neighbours merely by her bulk and appearance. But whenever an insufficient man happens to have the command on deck, adieu to the discipline and safety of the ship. She may, perhaps, not sink outright; she may drift some time as a wreck, and will then be dashed to pieces on the shore; but she can never be rebuilt on the old bottom.

The breaking-up of the power of China (no very improbable event) would occasion a complete subversion of the commerce, not only of Asia, but a very sensible change in the other quarters of the world. The industry and the ingenuity of the Chinese would be checked and enfeebled, but they would not be annihilated. Her ports would no longer be barricaded; they would be attempted by all the adventures of all trading nations, who would search every channel, creek, and cranny of China for a market, and for some time be the cause of much rivalry and disorder. Nevertheless, as Great Britain, from the weight of her riches and the genius and spirits of her people, is become the first political, marine, and commercial Power on the globe, it is reasonable to think that she would prove the greatest gainer by such a revolution as I have alluded to, and rise superior over every competitor.

It should be never absent from our recollection that there are now two distinct nations in China—the Chinese and the Tartars—whose characters essentially differ, notwithstanding their external appearance be nearly the same. They are both subject to the most absolute authority that can be vested in a Prince (Qianlong), but with this distinction—that to the Chinese it is a foreign tyranny, to the Tartar a domestic despotism. The latter consider themselves as in some degree partakers of their Sovereign's dominions over the former, and that imagination may, perhaps, somewhat console them under the pressure of his power upon themselves—like the house servants and house negroes belonging to a great landlord in Livonia or planter in Jamaica, who, though serfs themselves, look down upon the peasantry and field negroes as much their inferiors.

The Government, as it stands, is properly the tyranny of a handful of Tartars over more than three hundred millions of Chinese.

Yet it cannot be concealed that the nation in general is far from being contented. The frequent insurrections in the distant provinces are ambiguous oracles of the real sentiments of the people. The predominance of the Tartars and the Emperors's partiality for them are the common subjects of conversation among the Chinese whenever they meet together in private. There are certain mysterious societies in every province, who, though narrowly watched by the Government, find means to elude its vigilance, and often hold secret assemblies, where they revive the memory of ancient independence, brood over recent injuries, and meditate revenge.

▸ Working with Sources

1. **Given Qianlong's reply to the letter Macartney presented to him from King George III, how realistic do Macartney's observations seem?**
2. **On what does Macartney appear to base his political assessment of the position of the Qing with respect to the people of the empire?**

SOURCE 21.3

Emperor Qianlong's Imperial Edict to King George III

1793

The reign of the Qianlong Emperor (r. 1736–1795) marked both the high point and the beginning of the decline of the Qing dynasty. Several European nations, driven by their desire to corner the market on the lucrative Chinese trade, sent representatives to Qianlong's court. In 1793, Great Britain dispatched Lord Macartney, its first envoy to China, to obtain safe and favorable trade relations for his country. In response, Qianlong composed a letter to King George III (r. 1760–1820) detailing his objections and conditions, which Macartney conveyed back to Britain. The terms of this letter underscore Qianlong's subtle understanding of global economic conditions and the maintenance of a balance between the interests of various nations.

You, O King, live beyond the confines of many seas, nevertheless, impelled by your humble desire to partake of the benefits of our civilisation, you have dispatched a mission respectfully bearing your memorial. Your Envoy has crossed the seas and paid his respects at my Court on the anniversary of my birthday. To show your devotion, you have also sent offerings of your country's produce.

I have perused your memorial: the earnest terms in which it is couched reveal a respectful humility on your part, which is highly praiseworthy. In consideration of the fact that your Ambassador and his deputy have come a long

Source: Sir Edmond Backhouse and John O. Bland, *Annals and Memoirs of the Court of Peking* (Boston: Houghton Mifflin, 1914), 322–331.

way with your memorial and tribute, I have shown them high favour and have allowed them to be introduced into my presence. To manifest my indulgence, I have entertained them at a banquet and made them numerous gifts. I have also caused presents to be forwarded to the Naval Commander and six hundred of his officers and men, although they did not come to Peking, so that they too may share in my all-embracing kindness.

As to your entreaty to send one of your nationals to be accredited to my Celestial Court and to be in control of your country's trade with China, this request is contrary to all usage of my dynasty and cannot possibly be entertained. It is true that Europeans, in the service of the dynasty, have been permitted to live at Peking, but they are compelled to adopt Chinese dress, they are strictly confined to their own precincts and are never permitted to return home. You are presumably familiar with our dynastic regulations. Your proposed Envoy to my Court could not be placed in a position similar to that of European officials in Peking who are forbidden to leave China, nor could he, on the other hand, be allowed liberty of movement and the privilege of corresponding with his own country; so that you would gain nothing by his residence in our midst.

Moreover, our Celestial dynasty possesses vast territories, and tribute missions from the dependencies are provided for by the Department for Tributary States, which ministers to their wants and exercises strict control over their movements. It would be quite impossible to leave them to their own devices. Supposing that your Envoy should come to our Court, his language and national dress differ from that of our people, and there would be no place in which to bestow him. It may be suggested that he might imitate the Europeans permanently resident in Peking and adopt the dress and customs of China, but, it has never been our dynasty's wish to force people to do things unseemly and inconvenient. Besides, supposing I sent an Ambassador to reside in your country, how could you possibly make for him the requisite arrangements? Europe consists of many other nations besides your own: if each and all demanded to be represented at our Court, how could we possibly consent? The thing is utterly impracticable. How can our dynasty alter its whole procedure and system of etiquette, established for more than a century, in order to meet your individual views? If it be said that your object is to exercise control over your country's trade, your nationals have had full liberty to trade at Canton for many a year, and have received the greatest consideration at our hands. Missions have been sent by Portugal and Italy, preferring similar requests. The Throne appreciated their sincerity and loaded them with favours, besides authorising measures to facilitate their trade with China. You are no doubt aware that, when my Canton merchant, Wu Chao-ping, who was in debt to foreign ships, I made the Viceroy advance the monies due, out of the provincial treasury, and ordered him to punish the culprit severely. Why then should foreign nations advance this utterly unreasonable request to be represented at my Court? Peking is nearly two thousand miles from Canton, and at such a distance what possible control could any British representative exercise?

. . .

Yesterday your Ambassador petitioned my Ministers to memorialise me regarding your trade with China, but his proposal is not consistent with our dynastic usage and cannot be entertained. Hitherto, all European nations, including your own country's barbarian merchants, have carried on their trade with our Celestial Empire at Canton. Such has been the procedure for many years, although our Celestial Empire possesses all things in prolific abundance and lacks no product within its own borders. There was therefore no need to import the manufactures of outside barbarians in exchange for our own produce. But as the tea, silk and porcelain which the Celestial Empire produces, are absolute necessities to European nations and to yourselves, we have permitted, as a signal mark of favour, that foreign hongs [merchant firms] should be established at Canton, so that your wants might be supplied and your country thus participate in our beneficence. But your Ambassador has now put forward new requests which completely fail to recognise the Throne's principle to "treat strangers from afar with indulgence," and to exercise a pacifying control over barbarian tribes, the world over. Moreover, our dynasty, swaying the myriad races of the globe, extends the same benevolence towards all. Your England is not the only nation trading at Canton. If other nations, following your bad example, wrongfully importune my ear with further impossible requests, how will it be possible for me to treat them with easy indulgence? Nevertheless, I do not forget the lonely remoteness of your island, cut off from the world by intervening wastes of sea, nor do I overlook your excusable ignorance of the usages of our Celestial Empire. I have consequently commanded my Ministers to enlighten your Ambassador on the subject, and have ordered the departure of the mission. But I have doubts that, after your Envoy's return he may fail to acquaint you with my view in detail or that he may be lacking in lucidity, so that I shall now proceed . . . to issue my mandate on each question separately. In this way you will, I trust, comprehend my meaning. . . .

. . .

(7) Regarding your nation's worship of the Lord of Heaven, it is the same religion as that of other European nations. Ever since the beginning of history, sage Emperors and wise rulers have bestowed on China a moral system and inculcated a code, which from time immemorial has been religiously observed by the myriads of my subjects. There has been no hankering after heterodox doctrines. Even the European (missionary) officials in my capital are forbidden to hold intercourse with Chinese subjects; they are restricted within the limits of their appointed residences, and may not go about propagating their religion. The distinction between Chinese and barbarian is most strict, and your Ambassador's request that barbarians shall be given full liberty to disseminate their religion is utterly unreasonable.

It may be, O King, that the above proposals have been wantonly made by your Ambassador on his own responsibility, or peradventure you yourself are ignorant of our dynastic regulations and had no intention of transgressing them when you expressed these wild ideas and hopes. . . . If, after the receipt of this explicit decree, you lightly give ear to the representations of your subordinates and allow your barbarian merchants to proceed to Chêkiang and Tientsin, with the object of landing and trading there, the ordinances of my Celestial Empire are strict in the extreme, and the local officials, both civil and military, are bound reverently to obey the law of the land. Should your vessels touch the shore, your merchants will assuredly never be permitted to land or to reside there, but will be subject to instant expulsion. In that event your barbarian merchants will have had a long journey for nothing.

Working with Sources

1. **How did Qianlong attempt to keep China and Great Britain on an equal footing, and in what specific regards?**
2. **How effectively does the emperor balance courtesy and warning in his letter?**

SOURCE 21.4

Honda Toshiaki, "Secret Plan for Managing the Country"

1798

Drawing on the conclusions of his "Western" education, Japanese economist Honda Toshiaki (1749–1821) advocated a three-pronged plan of action to level the playing field between the Tokugawa shogunate and European powers. Having studied mathematics as a young man, Honda learned the Dutch language and studied Dutch medicine, astronomy, and military science. Dutch was the only choice available, since these were the only Europeans permitted to remain in Japan after 1639. Fortunately, it was the prowess of these particular Europeans in shipping and trade, dependent on a scientific and mathematical knowledge of navigation, that most interested Honda. This section of his "Secret Plan" addresses the need for the emperor to control ships and shipping in order to ensure Japanese prosperity.

Source: Ryusaku Tsunoda, William Theodore de Bary, and Donald Keene, eds., *Sources of Japanese Tradition* (New York: Columbia University Press, 1964), vol. 2, 51–53.

As long as there are no government-owned ships and the merchants have complete control over transport and trade, the economic conditions of the samurai and farmers grow steadily worse. In years when the harvest is bad and people die of starvation, the farmers perish in greater numbers than any other class. Fields are abandoned and food production is still further reduced. There is then insufficient food for the nation and much suffering. Then the people will grow restive and numerous criminals will have to be punished. In this way citizens will be lost to the state. Since its citizens are a country's most important possession, it cannot afford to lose even one, and it is therefore most unfortunate that any should be sentenced to death. It is entirely the fault of the ruler if the life of even a single subject is thereby lost.

. . .

Some daimyo have now ceased to pay their retainers their basic stipends. These men have had half their property confiscated by the daimyo as well, and hate them so much that they find it impossible to contain their ever accumulating resentment. They finally leave their clan and become bandits. They wander lawlessly over the entire country, plotting with the natives who live on the shore, and thus entering a career of piracy. As they become ever more entrenched in their banditry one sees growing a tendency to revert to olden times.

It is because of the danger of such occurrences that in Europe a king governs his subjects with solicitude. It is considered to be the appointed duty of a king to save his people from hunger and cold by shipping and trading. This is the reason why there are no bandits in Europe. Such measures are especially applicable to Japan, which is a maritime nation, and it is obvious that transport and trade are essential functions of the government.

Ships which are at present engaged in transport do not leave coastal waters and put out to sea. They always have to skirt along the shore, and can navigate only by using as landmarks mountains or islands within visible range. Sometimes, as it inevitably happens, they are blown out to sea by a storm and lose their way. Then, when they are so far away from their familiar landmarks that they can no longer discern them, they drift about with no knowledge of their location. This is because they are ignorant of astronomy and mathematics, and because they do not possess the rules of navigation. Countless ships are thereby lost every year. Not only does this represent an enormous annual waste of produce, but valuable subjects also perish. If the methods of navigation were developed, the loss at sea of rice and other food products would be reduced, thus effecting a great saving. This would not only increase the wealth of the nation, but would help stabilize the prices of rice and other produce throughout Japan. The people, finding that they are treated equally irrespective of occupation and that the methods of government are fair, would no longer harbor any resentment, but would raise their voices in unison to pray for the prosperity of the rulers. By saving the lives of those subjects who would otherwise be lost at sea every year, we shall also be able to make up for our past shame, and will keep foreign nations from learning about weak spots in the institutions of Japan from Japanese sailors shipwrecked on their shores. Because of these and numerous other benefits to be derived from shipping, I have termed it the third imperative need.

▸ Working with Sources

1. **How does Toshiaki use comparisons to European practices to solidify his case regarding imperial control of shipping?**
2. **How does he envision the ideal relationship between the emperor and his people? What should be the emperor's central principle in ruling?**

World Period Five

The Origins of Modernity, 1750–1900

The twin novel events of constitutional and industrial revolutions, first in the Americas and western Europe and later in Japan, dramatically changed the course of world history.

- People rose to end the divine right of kings and replace their rule with popular sovereignty, constitutions, and elections.
- Machines began to replace animal power in the manufacture of textiles, means of transportation, chemicals, and urban amenities.

As a result, 10,000-year-old traditional customs and habits formed by life in agriculture gave way to what we call "modernity," that is, nontraditional new ways of life in the "machine age," characterized by such new phenomena as nation-states, social classes, megacities, colonialism, and above all, vastly increased global interactions.

Chapter 22

Patterns of Nation-States and Culture in the Atlantic World

1750–1871

CHAPTER TWENTY-TWO PATTERNS

Origins, Interactions, Adaptations The roots of the scientific–industrial modernity that characterized the Atlantic World beginning around 1750 were set two centuries earlier with the New Science and Enlightenment. It took two centuries for the right conditions to emerge. Among these conditions were a general population increase resulting from the consolidation of the nation-state, the wealth accumulated due to overseas colonies, and the application of the New Science to politics via constitutionalism and the theory of the social contract. Increased urban populations in France and British North America, with limited opportunities to participate in the political process, rose in revolutions that legitimized constitutionalism. Such was the power of revolutionary ideas that even slaves joined with their own revolution in Haiti.

Uniqueness and Similarities While the Glorious Revolution in England provided inspiration, the political revolutions in North America, France, and Haiti were unique in the sense that they produced for the first time full popular sovereignty and republican governments. France had two aftershocks after its revolution. In Germany and Italy, the monarchs who returned to power after the Napoleonic Wars repressed any revolutionary effort, but nevertheless they created unitary nation-states. Both the Enlightenment and the revolutions released an extraordinary outburst of cultural creativity in the first half of the 1800s.

When the French Revolution broke out in 1789, a young Caribbean mulatto named Vincent Ogé (ca.1755–1791) was in France on business. His extended family of free light-skinned blacks owned a coffee plantation and a commercial business with black slaves in Saint-Domingue [SAN-doh-MANG (hard g)] (modern Haiti). Caught up in the excitement, Ogé became an adherent of French constitutionalism. He joined the anti-slavery Society of the Friends of Blacks in Paris and demanded that French constitutionalism be extended to Saint-Domingue.

The society's efforts soon appeared to bear fruit. In March 1790, the National Assembly granted self-administration to the colonies, and Ogé returned to Saint-Domingue full of hope that he would be able to participate as a free citizen in the island's governance. But the French governor refused to admit mulattoes as citizens. In response, Ogé and a group of freedmen took up arms to carve out a stronghold for themselves by arresting plantation owners and occupying their properties. One plantation owner later testified that Ogé was a man of honor who treated his prisoners fairly and even left him in possession of his personal arms.

After a few weeks of fighting, government troops pushed the rebels into the Spanish part of the island. Ogé and his followers surrendered after being guaranteed their safety. But the Spanish governor betrayed his prisoners, turning them over to the French. After a trial for insurrection in February 1791, Ogé and 19 followers were condemned to death. The execution of Ogé was particularly barbaric. He was "broken on the wheel": Executioners strapped him spread-eagle on a wagon wheel and systematically broke his bones with an iron bar until he was dead.

CHAPTER OUTLINE

Origins of the Nation-State, 1750–1815

Enlightenment Culture: Radicalism and Moderation

The Other Enlightenment: The Ideology of Ethnic Nationalism

The Growth of the Nation-State, 1815–1871

Romanticism and Realism: Philosophical and Artistic Expression to 1850

Putting It All Together

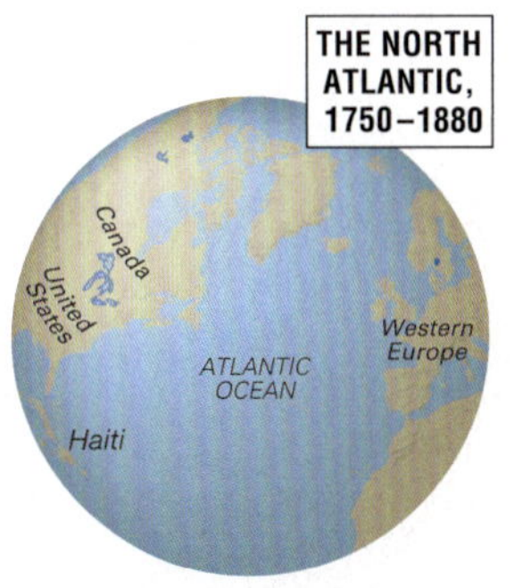

ABOVE: Haitian rebels combat Napoleonic forces in 1802, as depicted here in *Battle on Santo Domingo* by Polish painter January Suchodolski (1797–1875)

Seeing Patterns

> How did the pattern of constitutionalism, emerging from the American and French Revolutions, affect the course of events in the Western world during the first half of the nineteenth century?

> In what ways did ethnic nationalism differ from constitutionalism, and what was its influence on the formation of nation-states in the second half of the nineteenth century?

> What were the reactions among thinkers and artists to the developing pattern of nation-state formation? How did they define the intellectual–artistic movements of romanticism and realism?

The Ogé insurrection was a prelude to the Haitian Revolution, which began in August 1791 and culminated with the achievement of independence under a black government in 1804. It was the third of the great constitutional-nationalist revolutions—after the American and French Revolutions—that inaugurated, with the Industrial Revolution, the modern period of world history.

The events which led to the three constitutional revolutions were parts of a larger cultural ferment called the Enlightenment. The rising urban middle classes embraced the New Sciences and their philosophical interpretations, which provided both the intellectual ammunition for the revolutions and the inspiration for the creative movements of romanticism and realism.

Origins of the Nation-State, 1750–1815

One outcome of the Glorious Revolution of 1688 in England (Great Britain after 1707) was that the traditional divine rights of a monarch were curbed. A century later, the idea of *subjects* becoming *citizens* with constitutionally guaranteed rights and duties and of Parliament representing the citizens spread from Great Britain to North America, France, and Haiti. The American, French, and Haitian Revolutions were radical in that they rejected the British compromise of royal and parliamentary power and led to republican, middle-class, or liberated slave nation-states without traditional divine-right monarchies.

The American, French, and Haitian Revolutions

The American and French Revolutions were, in part, consequences of the Seven Years' War, which left both Great Britain and France deeply in debt. They owed this debt to their wealthy subjects, who formed the ruling class. To pay back the debt, the kings had to raise taxes on all of their subjects. The inequity of this tax burden led many to agitate for political reform and, ultimately, revolution. Once the revolutions were under way, the American and French revolutionary principles of freedom and equality had repercussions in the wider Atlantic world.

Conditions for Revolution in North America

When Britain won the Seven Years' War, it took over French possessions in Canada and the Ohio–Mississippi River valley, and France retreated entirely from the continent of North America. But the British were hugely in debt; the payment of the interest alone devoured most of the country's annual budget. Taxes had to be raised domestically as well as overseas, and in order to do so the government had to strengthen its administrative hand in its empire.

By 1763, the 13 North American colonies had experienced rapid growth. Opening lands beyond the Appalachian Mountains into the Ohio valley would relieve some of the pressure of a growing population. But the occupation of new land increased the administrative challenges for the British, who had to employ standing troops to protect settlers and Native Americans from aggression toward each other. The ongoing postwar economic slump created additional hardships (see Map 22.1).

MAP 22.1 **British North America in 1763**

The British government failed to devise a clear plan for strengthening its administration in the North American colonies and was particularly inept with the imposition of new taxes. In 1765, it introduced the Stamp Act, forcing everyone to pay a tax on the use of paper for any purpose. The tax was to be used for the upkeep of the standing troops, many of which were quartered in the colonies for the enforcement of the increased taxes.

Countdown to War Protest against the Stamp Act broke out among the urban lower-middle ranks, who organized themselves in groups such as the Daughters of Liberty and Sons of Liberty. The Daughters boycotted British goods and promoted homespun textiles. The British Parliament withdrew the Stamp Act in 1766 when exports fell but replaced it with indirect taxes on other commodities. These taxes were still levied without the colonies' consent.

One such indirect tax was on tea. This tax was a subsidy to keep the near-bankrupt East India Company afloat and had nothing to do with either America or Britain's debt. In 1773 the colonists protested the tax with the dumping of a cargo of tea into Boston Harbor. In response to this "Boston Tea Party," Britain closed the harbor, demanded restitution, and passed the so-called Coercive Acts (called the "Intolerable Acts" in the colonies), which put Massachusetts into bankruptcy. Both sides now moved toward a showdown.

The War of Independence During the Continental Association of 1774–1776, the colonial assemblies decided on an economic boycott of Britain. In an effort to isolate Massachusetts from the Association, in April 1775 British troops attempted to seize arms and ammunition in Concord. A militia of farmers—"minutemen"—stopped the British. War broke out in earnest, and delegates of the colonies appointed George Washington, a former officer from Virginia, as commander of the colonists' troops. A year later, delegates of the colonies issued the Declaration of Independence. This declaration, steeped in Enlightenment thought, was written by the university-educated Virginian plantation owner Thomas Jefferson. The great majority of the delegates who signed were also educated men of means.

Central to the declaration was the idea that the equality of all "men" was "self-evident." As such, all men are entitled to "life, liberty, and the pursuit of happiness"—citizen rights which included Hobbes's right to life but not Locke's right to property. Tacitly excluded were the one-fifth of Americans who were black slaves, the one-half who were women, and all Native Americans. When the colonists eventually won the War of Independence in 1783, the founders created a revolutionary federal republic with a Congress that represented a large proportion of the population, though it also excluded many inhabitants.

The Early United States The new republic's initial years were fraught with organizational difficulties. The governing document, the Articles of Confederation, granted extraordinary power to the individual states. In 1787, a constitutional convention created a more effective federal constitution. Careful to add checks and balances in the form of a bicameral legislature and separation of powers into legislative, executive, and judicial branches, the new constitution embodied Enlightenment ideals—although it sidestepped the issue of slavery. In 1789, under the new system, George Washington was elected the first president of the United States.

The new republic's abolition of the divine right of monarchical rule and its replacement by the sovereignty of the people was a previously unimaginable reversal of the natural order of things. In this respect, the American and French Revolutions illustrate a new pattern of state formation and the advent of modernity.

Enlightenment: European intellectual movement of the eighteenth century growing out of the New Sciences and based largely on Descartes's concept of reality consisting of the two separate substances of matter and mind.

Conditions for the French Revolution The American, French, and Haitian Revolutions were embedded in the culture of the **Enlightenment** (ca. 1700–1800). King Louis XVI (r. 1774–1792) and the French government had hoped the American War of Independence would provide an opportunity to avenge the kingdom's defeat

in the Seven Years' War. France supplied the Americans with money, arms, and officers, and in 1778–1779, in alliance with Spain, waged war on Great Britain. The French–Spanish entry into the war forced Britain into an impossible defense of its colonial empire, and Britain conceded defeat in 1783. However, the French government now had to begin exorbitant payments on the interest for the loans to carry out the war. This crippling debt was one of the preconditions of the French Revolution.

As in America, the French population had increased sharply during the 1700s. Food production could barely keep up, and inflation increased. The rural economy responded to the rising demand, and colonial trade with the Caribbean colonies boomed. Had it not been for the debt, the government would have been well financed; it collected direct taxes as well as monies from compulsory loans and the sale of titles and offices to ordinary people of means. Although claiming to be the absolute authority, the king in reality shared power with a ruling class of old and new aristocrats as well as ordinary (if wealthy) urban people.

In 1781, suspicions arose about the solvency of the regime. But the government continued to borrow, especially when bad weather leading to poor harvests in 1786–1787 diminished tax revenues. Without reserves in grain and animals, the peasants suffered severe famine. Government imports intended to help ended up in the hands of profiteers and hoarders.

By 1788, the government was nearly bankrupt, and a reform of the tax system became unavoidable. When a first attempt at reform failed, the king held elections for a general assembly, called the Estates-General, to meet in Versailles. Voters met in constituent meetings in their districts across France, according to their "estate" as clergy, aristocrats, or commoners. Peasants met in the "third estate," or commoner meetings, but the deputies they elected were overwhelmingly middle- and upper-class. At the request of the king, the deputies listed their grievances to form the basis for the reform legislation.

Amid widespread unrest among peasants in rural France and workers in Paris, the third estate now outmaneuvered the other estates and the king. In June 1789 it seceded from the Estates-General and declared itself the National Assembly. Pressured by the pro-aristocracy faction, the king issued a veiled threat: If the Assembly would not accept his reform proposals, he said, "I alone should consider myself their [the people's] representative." The king then reinforced his troops in and around Paris and Versailles. Parisians, afraid of an imminent military occupation of the city, swarmed through the streets on July 14, 1789. They provisioned themselves with arms and gunpowder and stormed the Bastille, the royal fortress and prison inside Paris.

Three Phases of the Revolution The French Revolution went through the three phases: constitutional monarchy (1789–1792), radical republicanism (1792–1795), and military consolidation (1795–1799). The first phase began with near anarchy during July and August 1789. People in the provinces, mostly peasants, chased aristocratic and commoner landlords from their estates. In October, thousands of working women marched from Paris to Versailles, forcing the king to move to Paris. The National Assembly issued the Declaration of the Rights of Man and of the Citizen (1789), subjected the Catholic Church to French civil law (1790), established a constitutional monarchy (1791), and issued laws ending the unequal taxes of the Old Regime (1792).

The French Revolution. After the storming of the Bastille (top left), the French Revolution gained momentum when Parisian women marched to Versailles, demanding that the king reside in Paris and end the famine there (top right). The inevitability of a republic became clear when the king and queen were captured after they attempted to flee (bottom right).

The second phase, radical republicanism, began as the revolutionaries were unable to establish a stable constitutional regime. After the king tried unsuccessfully in 1791 to flee Paris with his Austrian-born wife, Marie-Antoinette, Austria and Prussia threatened to intervene if the king and queen were harmed. Patriotic feelings were aroused, and in April 1792 the government declared war on its eastern neighbors.

Republicans deposed the king and held elections for a new assembly, the National Convention, to draw up a constitution. In the following year, the republicans executed the royal couple and created a conscript army. A Committee of Public Safety executed some 30,000 real and suspected "reactionaries" during its "Reign of Terror."

The Revolution entered its third phase (1795–1799) after the army had succeeded in securing the borders at the end of 1793. A growing revulsion at the Reign of Terror led to the replacement of the Committee of Public Safety by the Directory in November 1795. A new constitution and bicameral legislature were created, but political and financial stability remained elusive. The Directory depended increasingly on the army, by now the only stable institution in France, to survive.

Within the army, a brigadier general named Napoleon Bonaparte (1769–1821), of Corsican descent, was the most promising commander. From 1796 to 1798 Napoleon scored major victories against the Austrians in northern Italy and invaded Egypt. Thwarted by a pursuing British fleet, he returned to France and overthrew the ineffective Directory in November 1799, thus ending the Revolution.

Revival of Empire Napoleon embarked on domestic reforms that restored stability in France. His reform of the French legal system, promulgated in the Civil Code of 1804, established the equality of all male citizens before the law in theory, but in reality it imposed restrictions on many revolutionary freedoms. In 1804 Napoleon crowned himself emperor of the French and began a campaign of conquest in Europe. By 1810, his military victories resulted in the French domination of most of Continental Europe.

Napoleon's goal was the construction of an Enlightenment-influenced but newly aristocratic European empire (see Map 22.2). The failure of Napoleon's Russian campaign in 1812, however, marked the beginning of the end of his grand scheme. An alliance of Great Britain, Austria, Prussia, and Russia ended Napoleon's empire in 1815 and inaugurated the restoration of the pre–French Revolution regimes in Europe.

Conditions for the Haitian Revolution French Saint-Domingue was one of the richest European colonies. It had been a Spanish possession, but as Spain's power slipped during the seventeenth and eighteenth centuries, France established its colony on the western part of the island. In the following century, settlers enjoyed French mercantilist protectionism as they profited from their slave plantations.

In the second half of the 1700s, some 30,000 white settlers, 28,000 mulattos (holding about one-third of the slaves), and about 500,000 black slaves formed an extremely unequal colonial society. When France tightened colonial controls, the French administrators in Haiti were afraid that the white and mulatto plantation

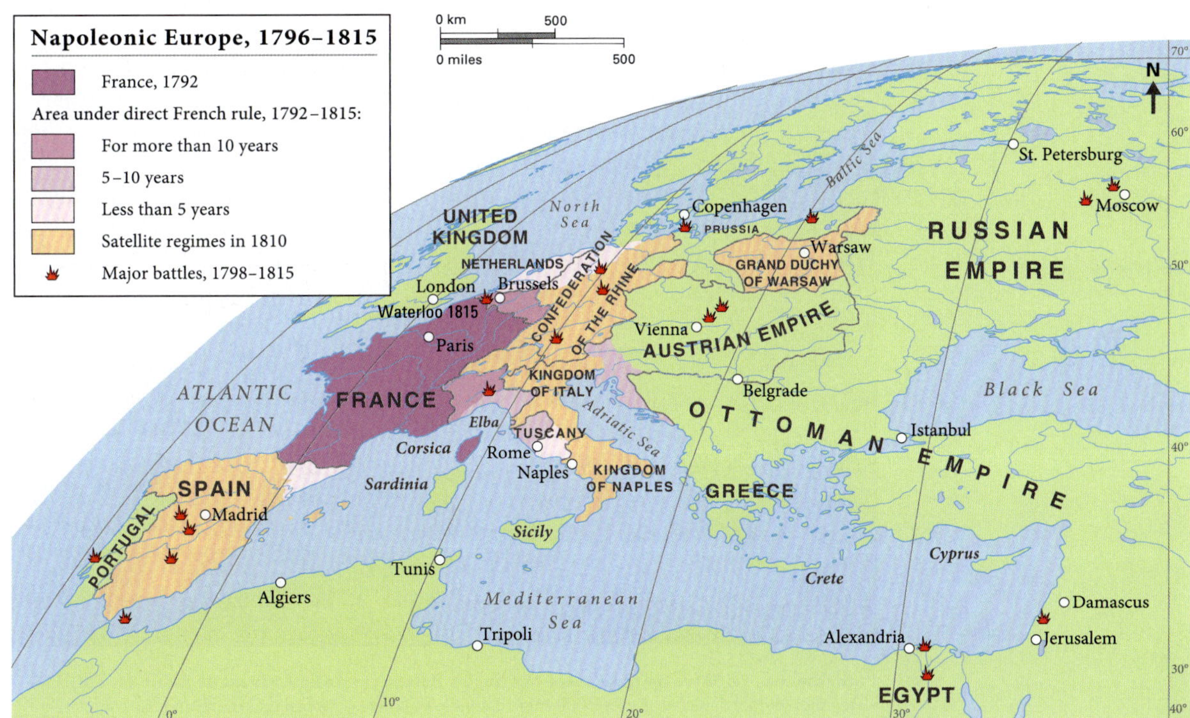

MAP 22.2 Napoleonic Europe, 1796–1815

Patterns Up Close

The Guillotine

During the period of the Terror (June 1793–July 1794), the guillotine was responsible for thousands of executions in Paris and across France. While it is popularly believed that this iconic symbol of public executions was invented by one Dr. Guillotin to speed up the rate of executions during the Reign of Terror, the actual story is far more compelling—and ironic.

The first known model of a "decapitation machine" is probably the Halifax Gibbet, in use in England from around 1300 until 1650. Another model, the Scottish Maiden, was derived from the Halifax Gibbet and used from 1565 until 1708. It was turned over to a museum in Edinburgh in 1797 and may have served as a model for the French machine.

When and how did the instrument first appear in France? Ironically, it came as an indirect result of efforts to end the death penalty. During the early days of the Revolution, the National Assembly pondered the abolition of the death penalty in France. On October 10, 1789, the Assembly was addressed by Dr. Joseph-Ignace Guillotin (1738–1814), founder of the French Academy of Medicine and an opponent of capital punishment, who urged the assembly to at least find "a machine that beheads painlessly," if they could not agree to stop executions altogether. Guillotin presented sketches of the kind of machine he had in mind, but his designs were rejected. In 1791 the Assembly finally agreed to retain the death penalty. But instead of adopting Dr. Guillotin's design, the Assembly accepted a model designed by Dr. Antoine Louis, secretary of the Academy of Surgery; Dr. Louis then turned to

Punishment of a Slave on the Estate of Charles Balthazar Julien Févret de Saint-Mémin. This watercolor vividly depicts the vast differences between the slave strapped to a frame and the completely unconcerned estate owner on horseback. During the uprising of 1791, slaves occupied the great majority of estates, ended slavery, and drove their owners into exile. Saint-Mémin, whose mother was Creole, waited for a decade in the United States for the return of his estate before giving up and returning to France.

a German engineer, Tobias Schmidt, who constructed the first version of the "painless" decapitation machine. It was not until April 25, 1792, that the guillotine, nicknamed "Louisette" after Dr. Louis, claimed its first victim. It is not clear when the name was changed to "guillotine" (the final "e" was added later), but Dr. Guillotin's early advocacy of painless executions may have been a factor. As for Dr. Guillotin himself, after fighting a losing battle with the government to change the name of the machine because of embarrassment to his family, he changed his own name.

The Execution of Louis XVI. During the radical republican period of the French Revolution, the Committee of Public Safety had Louis condemned to death for treason after a show trial. He was executed on January 21, 1793.

Questions

- Can the guillotine be viewed as a practical adaptation of Enlightenment ideas? If so, how?
- Why do societies debate the means they use to execute prisoners? What are the criteria by which one form of execution is considered more humane than others?

owners would form a united resistance. In order to split the two, they introduced increasingly racist measures to deprive the mulattos of their privileges. It was this split that created the conditions for the slave rebellion once the French Revolution itself was under way.

Revolt of the Slaves After the failure of Ogé's uprising, resentment continued to simmer among the mulattoes in the south as well as the black slaves in the north of Haiti. The white settler Provincial Assembly refused any concessions even though the French revolutionary National Constituent Assembly in May 1791 granted citizen rights to mulattoes whose parents were free. Aware of the hostility between the mulattoes and whites, slaves seized the opportunity for their own rebellion in August 1791. Almost simultaneously, the mulattoes of the south rose in rebellion as well. Within weeks, the slave and mulatto rebellion encompassed the entire northern and southern provinces of the colony. The overwhelmed settlers suffered heavy losses.

The Assembly in Paris sent commissioners and troops in November 1791 and April 1792 to reestablish order. Neither commission made much headway, largely because of the unrelenting hostility of the whites. In their desperation to gain support, even from the blacks, the second commission abolished slavery in August 1793. This decision, however, failed to rally the black military leaders who had allied themselves with the Spanish, rulers of the eastern half of the island, Santo Domingo. Revolutionary France had been embroiled in war against Spain and Britain since early 1793, and the latter had invaded the French-held part in the summer of 1793. Spain and Britain looked like inevitable victors, and the commissioners' emancipation declaration appeared to have been too late.

Both invasions stalled, however. The Assembly in Paris confirmed the emancipation declaration in February 1794, and the French position on the island began to improve. In May 1794, a black rebel leader from the north, François-Dominique Toussaint Louverture (ca. 1743–1803), and his troops abandoned the Spanish and joined the French. Toussaint, who according to one tradition was the grandson of the heir of the king of Allada in West Africa, had obtained his freedom in the 1770s. Upon his return to the French, he joined the mulatto faction of the rebellion in the south. The northern blacks and southern mulattoes transformed the rebellion into a full-fledged revolution.

Nation-State Building During the violence of 1791–1794, many plantation owners had fled the colony. Former slaves on deserted plantations grew subsistence crops for their own families. Toussaint remained committed to the plantation system, however, in order to supply revenues for his state-building ambitions. His officers attempted to force former slaves to resume production, with moderate success. In 1801, Toussaint assumed the governorship of Saint-Domingue from the French officials and proclaimed a constitution that incorporated the basic principles of French constitutionalism.

But Toussaint still had to reckon with Atlantic politics. Napoleon Bonaparte, in control of France since 1799, was at that time determined to rebuild the French overseas empire. In the Americas, he purchased Louisiana from Spain in 1800. In 1802, Napoleon dispatched troops to Saint-Domingue to add the colony to Louisiana and revive the French Atlantic empire. Toussaint was prepared for the invasion, but when the French landed, several of his officers surrendered without a fight. As the French advanced into the island against declining resistance, one general, Jean-Jacques Dessalines, betrayed Toussaint. Toussaint was arrested and sent to France, where he died in April 1803. The revolution seemed to be finished.

Jean-Jacques Dessalines (r. 1802–1806) was a former slave from northern Haiti. Seemingly obedient to the French, Dessalines waited for yellow fever to take its toll among the invaders. When more than two-thirds of the French forces were dead by the summer of 1802, Napoleon sold Louisiana to the United States in April 1803 and withdrew from Saint-Domingue in November 1803. On January 1, 1804, Dessalines assumed power and declared the colony's independence.

Subsequently, he made himself emperor, to counter Napoleon, and renamed the country Haiti, its supposed original Taíno name. When he changed the constitution in favor of autocratic rule, he provoked a conspiracy and was assassinated in 1806. The state split into an autocratically ruled black north with a state-run plantation economy and a more democratic mulatto south with a privatized economy of small farms (1806–1821).

Of the three revolutions resulting in the new form of the republican nation-state based on a constitution, that of Haiti realized the Enlightenment principles of liberty, equality, and fraternity most fully. By demonstrating the power of the new ideology of constitutionalism, it participated in the inauguration of a new pattern of state formation in world history not only among the new white and mixed-race urban middle classes but also among the uprooted black African underclass of slaves.

Enlightenment Culture: Radicalism and Moderation

The origins of this culture lay in the new mathematized sciences, which inspired a number of thinkers, such as Descartes, Spinoza, Hobbes, and Locke, to create new philosophical interpretations (see Chapter 17). The radical interpretation was **materialism**, according to which all of reality consisted of matter and Descartes's separate substance of mind or reason could either be dispensed with or be explained as a by-product of matter. Moderates held on to Descartes's mind or reason as a separate substance, struggling to explain its presence in reality. The radical Enlightenment tradition evolved primarily in France, while the moderate tradition found adherents in Germany.

Materialism: The philosophical doctrine that holds that nothing exists except matter.

The Enlightenment and Its Many Expressions

Writers popularized the new, science-derived philosophy in eighteenth-century France, Holland, England, and Germany. Adherents were still a minority, even among the growing middle class, but their voices as radical or moderate "progressives" opposing tradition-bound ministers, aristocrats, and clergy became measurably louder.

It was the late-eighteenth-century generation of this minority that was central to the revolutions in America, France, and Haiti. They translated their New Sciences–derived conception of reality into such "self-evident" ideals as life, liberty, equality, social contract, property, representation, nation, popular sovereignty, and the need for a constitution. In the wider culture of the Enlightenment, they fashioned new forms of expression in the arts.

Denis Diderot and the *Encyclopédie*

The idea to bring all knowledge together in an alphabetically organized encyclopedia appeared first in England in 1728. A French publisher decided in 1751 to have this encyclopedia translated. But under the editorship of, for the most part, Denis Diderot (1713–1784) it became a massively expanded work in its own right. Many entries dealt with provocative subjects, such as science, industry, commerce, freedom of thought, slavery, and religious tolerance. The Catholic Church and the French crown banned the project as subversive. But the twenty-eighth and last volume was finally published in 1772.

Philosophy and Morality

Jean-Jacques Rousseau (1712–1778) was a firm believer in the religious morality of the masses. To the consternation of the radicals in France, he argued in his *Social Contract* (1762) that humans had suffered a steady decline from their "natural" state ever since civilization imposed its own arbitrary authority. The radicals held that even though humans had lost their natural state of freedom and equality and had come under arbitrary authority, they were experiencing a steady progress toward freedom and equality. Rousseau, unlike the radicals, had little faith in popular sovereignty, elections, and electoral reforms. Instead, he believed that people, rallying in a nation, should express their unity directly through a sort of direct democracy.

Philosophy and the Categorical Imperative The philosopher Immanuel Kant (1724–1804) was a believer in the progress of civilization and history, as expressed in his *Perpetual Peace* (1795). Like all Enlightenment thinkers, Kant took Descartes as his point of departure. But he rejected both the two-substance theory of Descartes and the materialist turn of the radical French Enlightenment. Even though he admitted that sensory or bodily experience was primary, he insisted that this experience could be understood only through the categories of the mind or reason that were not found in experience. Reason conditioned experience, but it was not its own substance.

In contrast to Rousseau with his traditional Christian ethics, Kant sought to build morality on reason. He concluded that this morality had to be based on the *categorical imperative*: to act in such a way that the principle of your action can be a principle for anyone's action. This abstract principle later entered modern thought as the basis for concrete human rights, with their claim to universality, as in the Charter of the United Nations (1945).

Laissez-faire economics: An economic system in which markets are self-regulating and largely free of governmental regulations.

Economic Liberalism The Enlightenment also saw the birth of the academic discipline of economics. French and British thinkers who were appalled by the inefficient administration of finances, taxes, and trade by the regimes in their countries found the official pursuit of mercantilism wanting. Those opposed to mercantilist state control in France argued that the state should reduce taxes and other means of control to a minimum so that entrepreneurism in the general population could flourish. It should adopt a policy of *laissez-faire* [les-say-FAIR]—that is, "hands-off."

The Scottish economist Adam Smith (1723–1790) developed a British version of **laissez-faire economics**. In his *Inquiry into the Nature and Causes of the Wealth of Nations* (1776), Smith argued that if the market were largely left to its own devices it would regulate itself through the forces of supply and demand. It would then move in the direction of increasing efficiency as if guided by "an unseen hand." Smith became the founding father of modern economics.

Wolfgang Amadeus Mozart. Along with Joseph Haydn (1732–1809), Mozart, who composed his first symphony at the age of nine, is among the most prominent composers of "Classical" music, a product of the Enlightenment era. This portrait painted by Joseph Lange (1751–1831) in 1782 when Mozart was 26, is considered the most accurate of his portraits.

Literature and Music The Enlightenment also inspired writers and composers. Noteworthy among them were Johann Wolfgang von Goethe (1749–1832) and Wolfgang Amadeus Mozart (1756–1791), sons of a lawyer and a court musician, respectively. Among Goethe's numerous poems, novels, plays, and scientific works was his drama *Faust* about an ambitious scientific experimenter who sells his soul to the devil to acquire mastery of nature. Mozart was a former child prodigy who composed symphonies, operas, and chamber music pieces. One of his best-known operas, *The Magic Flute*, displays the influence of the Freemasons, a fraternal association popular in Enlightenment Europe devoted to "liberty, fraternity, and equality"—principles the French Revolution borrowed as its motto.

The imperial turn of the French Revolution under Napoleon effectively ended the Enlightenment. A few years later, with the fall of Napoleon and the restoration of monarchies, the Enlightenment constitutionalists went either silent or underground.

The Other Enlightenment: The Ideology of Ethnic Nationalism

In the revolutions of America, France, and Haiti, ethnic descent and linguistic affiliations were not significant factors. After 1815, however, these connections began to play increasingly important roles.

Constitutionalism versus Ethnic Nationalism In Great Britain's North American colonies prior to the Revolution, the great majority of the constitutionalists were "British," which meant that they were primarily Englishmen, with minorities from among the Irish, Welsh, and Scots.

In France, the Parisians, who expressed the constitutionalism of the French Revolution in their grammatically complex "high" French, assumed that constitutionalism would nevertheless be easily understood and accepted by provincials. Yet nearly half the population in the provinces spoke dialects that were often incomprehensible to the Parisians. The other half spoke no French at all and was ethnically either Celtic or German. But no provincials or ethnic Celts and Germans drew support for expressing their separate ethnic identities in the 1700s, nor—in contrast to Britain—even in the 1800s. It was Parisian Frenchness that eventually became the identity of what we call the French nation, and it did so on the basis of the constitutional program of the French Revolution.

Haiti presents the case of a rebellion in favor of French metropolitan constitutionalism. After the Haitians achieved their independence, they elevated their West/Central African ethnic heritage and spoken language, Kreyòl, into their national identity, deemphasizing their French constitutional heritage.

German Cultural Nationalism In contrast to Great Britain and France, the German nation was politically fragmented during the 1700s. In addition, many Germans in eastern Europe were widely dispersed among people with different linguistic, cultural, and even religious heritages. Educated Germans shared a common culture wherever they lived, but in the absence of a strong central state, this culture was largely nonpolitical.

A central figure in shaping this shared culture into a unifying ideology was Johann Gottfried Herder (1744–1803). At college, Herder became familiar with Pietism, a Lutheran version of the medieval Catholic mystical tradition. Employed first as a preacher and then as an administrator at assorted courts in central Germany, he was on close terms with Goethe and other German Enlightenment figures. In his writings, Herder sought to meld the diffuse cultural heritage into a coherent ideology of Germanness combined with the Enlightenment. This ideology, he hoped, would be preached not only to the educated but to the people in general.

The Herder-inspired ethnic version of the Enlightenment received a major boost during the French Revolution, as some Germans decided that adoption of French constitutionalism made sense only in a politically united Germany. Before any unification plan could mature, however, Napoleon ended the French Revolution, declared himself emperor, and proceeded to defeat Prussia and Austria. With this, he aroused patriotic passions for liberation from French rule and hopes for a unified Germany under a constitutional government.

Ethnic nationalism: A form of nationalism in which the nation is defined by a common language, a common faith, and a common ethnic ancestry.

The figure who decisively advanced in his writings from Herder's cultural Germanness to a fully developed political Germanness was Johann Gottlieb Fichte (1762–1814), a philosophy professor appalled by Napoleon's imperial conquests in Europe. The time seemed ripe for the realization of German political unification on the basis of a marriage of constitutionalism and **ethnic nationalism**. Instead, the eventual failure of Napoleon's conquests opened the door for a restoration of the pre-1789 monarchies.

The Growth of the Nation-State, 1815–1871

After Napoleon's defeat in Russia in 1812 and the Congress in Vienna of 1815, monarchies and aristocracies reappeared throughout the continent, and only minimal popular representation in parliaments was allowed. By contrast, in Anglo-America, the supremacy of constitutionalism was unchallenged during the 1800s. Here, a pattern of citizen participation in the constitutional process emerged, although its challenges culminated in the American Civil War.

Restoration Monarchies, 1815–1848

As monarchists in Europe sought to return to the politics of absolutism, repression and political manipulation were employed to keep the middle class out of meaningful political participation. A "Concert of Europe" emerged in which rulers avoided intervention in the domestic politics of fellow monarchs, except in cases of internal unrest.

The Congress of Vienna European leaders met in 1815 at Vienna after the fall of Napoleon in an effort to restore order to a war-torn continent. The driving principle at the session was monarchical conservatism, articulated mainly by Prince Klemens von Metternich (1773–1859), Austria's prime minister. An opponent of constitutionalism, Metternich regarded the still-struggling middle classes outside France with contempt.

To accomplish his objective of reinstituting kings and emperors ruling by divine right, Metternich had the Congress hammer out two principles: legitimacy and balance of power. The principle of legitimacy both recognized exclusive monarchical rule in Europe and reestablished the borders of France as they were in 1789. The principle of the balance of power prevented any one state from rising to dominance over any other. Members agreed to convene at regular intervals in the future in what they called the "Concert" (i.e., agreement), so as to ensure peace and tranquility in Europe. With minor exceptions, this policy of the balance of power remained intact for more than half a century (see Map 22.3).

As successful as the implementation of these two principles was, the solution devised for the German territories was less satisfactory. The Congress of

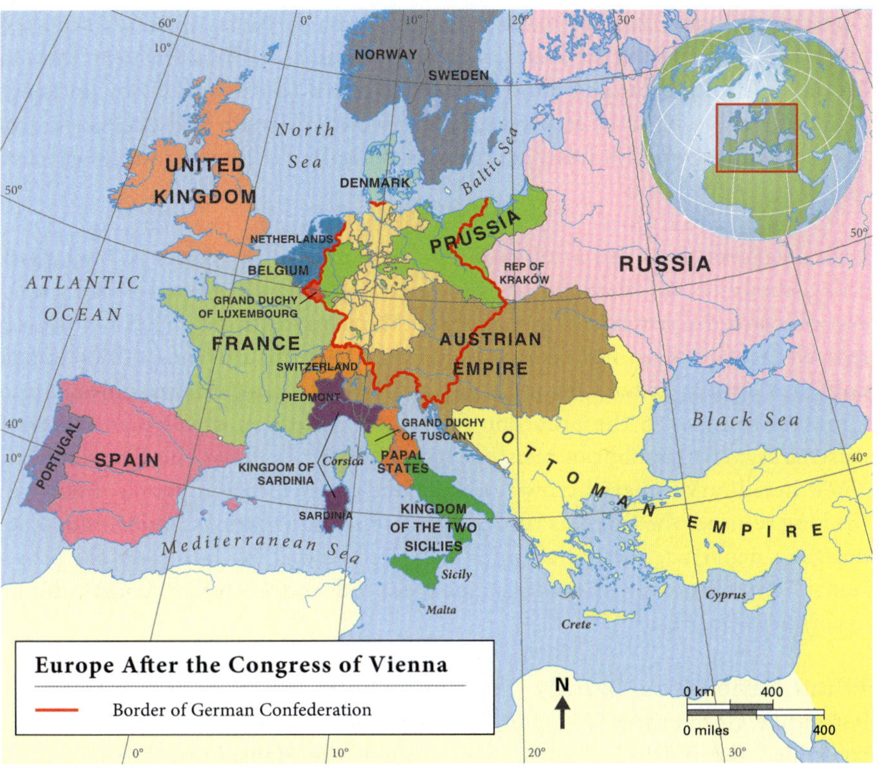

MAP 22.3 **Europe after the Congress of Vienna**

Vienna created a weak confederation of 39 German states, including the empire of Austria and the kingdoms of Prussia, Denmark, and the Netherlands. Prussia and Austria struggled over dominance in the confederation. Constitutionalist and republican Germans disliked the confederation as well, since they had no meaningful voice in it.

Further Revolutions in France The Congress restored the French Bourbon monarchy with the coronation of King Louis XVIII (r. 1814–1824), a brother of Louis XVI. When Louis died in 1824, the conservatives put Charles X (1824–1830), a second brother of Louis XVI, on the throne. Charles restored the property of the aristocracy lost during the revolution and reestablished the crown's ties to the Catholic Church.

Republican reaction to Charles's restoration policy was swift. In two elections, the republicans won a majority and overthrew the king. But they stopped short of abolishing the monarchy and elevated Louis-Philippe (r. 1830–1848), son of a pro-republican duke. Under this "bourgeois king," however, rising income gaps in the middle class as well as difficult living conditions among the industrial working class led to new tensions. In the ensuing revolution of 1848, in which thousands of workers perished, the adherents of restoration and republicanism attempted a compromise: Louis-Philippe went into exile, and the parliament elected Louis-Napoleon Bonaparte (r. 1848–1852; self-declared emperor 1852–1870), a nephew of the former emperor, as president.

Uprisings across Europe After the revolution in Paris, uprisings occurred in the spring of 1848 in cities across Europe as well as in three Irish counties. In Prussia, the king promised constitutional reforms. In Austria, hit by uprisings in multiple cities, both the emperor and Metternich resigned. The successors, with Russian help, regained military control over the Italians, Czechs, and Hungarians, as well as the Austrians.

In the German Confederation, also hit by uprisings, moderate and republican delegates convened a constitutional assembly in Frankfurt in May 1848. This assembly established the basis for a new, unified state for German speakers and elected a provisional government. The new Austrian emperor, however, refused to let go of his non-German subjects. Therefore, the constitution joined only the German Federation and Prussia (also with non-German subjects) into a unitary state, with the provision for a future addition of German-speaking Austria. Against republican resistance, the delegates offered the Prussian king a new hereditary imperial crown in the name of the German people. But when the king refused, the tide was turned against the Frankfurt Assembly. Moderate delegates departed, and radical ones instigated revolts. By July 1849, the provisional Frankfurt government had come to an end, and Germany's constitutional experiment was over.

Ethnic Nationalism in Italy Italy was as fragmented politically as Germany, but unlike Germany, a large part of it was under foreign domination. Austria controlled the north and the center through the Habsburgs. The monarchy

Rebellion. Following the successful revolution of 1848 that ended the monarchy of Louis-Philippe in France, similar uprisings broke out across Europe. This image shows the Berlin Alexander Square barricades of March 1848.

of Piedmont in the northwest, the Papal States in the center, and the kingdom of Naples and Sicily were independent but weak. After the Metternich restoration, the Italian dynasties had made concessions to constitutionalists, but Austria repressed uprisings in 1820–1821 and 1831–1832 without granting liberties. After the republican Carbonari were defeated in 1831, the remnants formed the Young Italy movement.

Realistic second-generation politicians of the Restoration recognized in the 1860s that by remobilizing the forces of ethnic nationalism, they would be able to make Italy and Germany serious players in the European Concert. Their pursuit of realpolitik—exploitation of political opportunities—resulted in 1870–1871 in the transformations of the Italian kingdom of Piedmont and the German kingdom of Prussia into the ethnic nation-states of Italy and Germany.

The Italian politician who did the most to realize Italy's unification was the prime minister of Piedmont-Sardinia, Count Camillo di Cavour (1810–1861). A constitutionalist and supporter of Adam Smith's liberal trade economics, he imported South American guano fertilizer and grew cash crops, like sugar beets, on his estate. As prime minister he was the driving force behind the development of railroads and thereby laid the foundations for the industrialization of northwest Italy.

Bismarck. Bismarck, a Prussian from the aristocratic Junker [YOONK-er] class, was known for his stern, formidable, shrewd, and calculating character and personality; thus, he was nicknamed the "Iron Chancellor." As a consummate practitioner of realpolitik, Bismarck skillfully combined diplomacy with war in order to achieve the unification of Germany in 1871.

With the backing of his similarly liberal-minded king, Victor Emanuel II (r. 1849–1878), Cavour began the Italian unification process. With the help of an alliance with France, he was able to provoke Austria, ruler of much of northern Italy, into a war in spring 1859. The allied forces defeated Austria, although not decisively, and in a compromise settlement, Piedmont gained adjoining Lombardy and five regions in north-central Italy. A year later Cavour occupied the Papal States and accepted the offer of Giuseppe Garibaldi (1807–1882) to add adjoining Naples and Sicily to a now largely unified Italy. Garibaldi, a Carbonaro and Young Italy republican nationalist, was an inspiring figure who attracted large numbers of volunteers wherever he went to fight. Cavour died shortly afterward and did not live to see Piedmont transform itself into Italy.

In the years from 1866 to 1870, the expanded Piedmont exploited the Prussian-Austrian war of 1866 to annex Venetia and then took advantage of the Franco-Prussian war of 1870 for the occupation of Rome. (Because of the Prussian threat, Napoleon III recalled his French garrison in Rome, which he had sent there against the threat of a campaign by the republican Garibaldi.) Thus, Italy was unified by a king and his aristocratic prime minister, both moderate constitutionalists (though not republicans). As realistic politicians, they tapped into a rising Italian ethnic nationalism to bring about unification.

Bismarck and Germany In contrast to Italy, neither King Wilhelm I (r. 1861–1888) nor his chancellor Otto von Bismarck (in office 1862–1890) in Prussia had sympathies for the constitutionalists. By forming a coalition, however, they succeeded in keeping the latter in the Prussian parliament in check. But they realized that they could make use of the ethnic nationalism that had emerged in 1848 for their version of realpolitik.

Bismarck, who was experienced in the diplomacy of the European Concert, realized that Prussia (a weak player in the Concert) would have greater influence only if the kingdom could absorb the German Federation. For Prussia to do so, Bismarck argued, it had to progress from talk about unification to military action. He maneuvered Prussia into an internationally favorable position for the coup that would eventually bring unification: war with France.

First, he exploited a succession crisis in Denmark for a combined Prussian–Austrian campaign to annex Denmark's southern province of Schleswig-Holstein in 1865. Then, when Austria objected to the terms of annexation, he declared war on Austria (1866). After Prussia won, Bismarck dissolved the German Confederation and annexed several German principalities. In France, Louis-Napoleon Bonaparte was greatly concerned about the rising power of Prussia. In a coup d'état in 1852, he ended the Second Republic and, in imitation of his uncle, declared himself emperor. A distraction on his eastern flank was not what Emperor Napoleon III wanted.

But he carelessly undermined his own position. First, he prevented a relative of King Wilhelm from succeeding to the vacant throne of Spain. But when he demanded that Prussia not put forward candidates for any other thrones in the future, Bismarck advised King Wilhelm to refuse the demand. The French, insulted by the refusal, declared war on Prussia but were defeated (1870).

Now Bismarck had the upper hand. He annexed Alsace-Lorraine from the French, carried out the final unification of Germany, and elevated the new state to the status of empire in April 1871 (see Map 22.4). In the meantime, French Republicans had proclaimed the Third Republic (September 1870) and deposed Napoleon III (March 1871). While the so-called Second German Empire was consolidated from the start, the French Republic struggled until 1875 to find its republican constitutional order (on this struggle, see "Against the Grain").

Nation-State Building in Anglo-America, 1783–1900

After the independence of the United States in 1783, both the United States and Great Britain pursued their versions of constitutional state development. While the growth of the United States in the 1800s followed its own trajectory, there is no question that the underlying pattern of modern state formation was not unlike that of the other two constitutionally governed countries, France and Great Britain, neither of which was much affected by ethnic nationalism.

The United States During the first half of the nineteenth century, the newly independent North American states began a rapid westward expansion. As this process unfolded, sectional differences developed. Whereas the North developed an industrial and market-driven agricultural economy, the South remained

MAP 22.4 **Europe in 1871**

primarily agrarian, relying upon the production of cotton for its economic vitality. Even more, the South relied upon slaves to work the cotton plantations. Cotton not only defined the wealth of the plantation owners but led them to see chattel slavery as the only viable way to remain prosperous. In defense of its stance, the South increasingly relied upon the notion of states' rights in opposition to federal control. With the acquisition of new territory extending to the Pacific coast after the war with Mexico from 1846 to 1848 and the push of settlement beyond the Mississippi, the question of which of the new territories would become "free states" and which would be "slave states" resulted in increasing tensions between North and South.

The result was an attempt by southern states to secede and form a new union, the Confederate States of America. When the new administration of President Abraham Lincoln attempted to suppress this movement, the American Civil War (1861–1865) ensued. Resulting in an enormous loss of life, the Civil War finally ended with a northern victory in 1865, mainly thanks to the North's greater industrial potential, agricultural diversity, and naval power. There were several major consequences to the conflict. First, Lincoln's concept of the primacy of national government over individual assertions of states' rights was now guaranteed. Second, slavery was abolished and slaves were granted full citizenship. Third, the rebuilding of the country and opening of the west resulted in a period of

MAP 22.5 **The Expanding United States in 1900**

remarkable growth, facilitated especially by the expansion of a national network of railroads (see Map 22.5).

The price of reintegrating the old South into the new order was the reversion to an imposition of de facto peonage on its black citizens. Between 1877 and 1914, state legislatures in the South stripped African Americans of voting rights and imposed formal and informal segregation. These were enforced by law and all too often by lynchings and other forms of violence. Most northern policy and opinion makers backed away from the views espoused by champions of racial equality and acquiesced to Southern efforts to maintain white hegemony. The drive for full civil rights would occupy American domestic policy debates throughout the twentieth century and beyond.

Native Americans Native Americans suffered unmitigated disasters during the 1800s. When the Louisiana Purchase in 1803 nearly doubled the size of the United States, politicians devised strategies to move Native Americans from their eastern homelands to the new territories. For their part, some Native Americans decided that only unification would help them to stay put, especially in the South and the Midwest, where white settler encroachment was strong.

In the Midwest, Tecumseh (1768–1812) and his brother Tenskwatawa (1775–1836) worked toward unification. Tecumseh traveled between the Midwest and South, seeking to forge a Native American resistance federation. Tenskwatawa, claiming his authority from visions of the Master of Life, preached that Native

Americans needed to reject white culture and return to traditional life. At the battle of Tippecanoe in Indiana, thousands of followers from a variety of nations came together but suffered a severe defeat at the hands of US troops (1811). The defeat ended the dream of Native American unity.

In the South, discriminatory legislation and brutal assaults made it difficult for Native American nations to survive on their lands. With the declared intention of helping these nations against the southern states, in 1830 the federal government issued the Indian Removal Act. In fact, however, this act only deepened the sufferings of the Native Americans east of the Mississippi: a quarter died on the "Trail of Tears" to their designated new homeland in Oklahoma. There, the survivors attempted to reconstruct their agriculture, schools, and councils while constantly accommodating the regular arrival of newly displaced Native Americans.

Two Girls of the Hopi Nation with Their Characteristic Hairstyles and Blankets. The Hopi live in the American Southwest, today's Arizona. They are best known as sophisticated farmers who live in adobe pueblos, some of which were built into the rock walls of canyons. In 1680, the Hopi rebelled for a dozen years against Spanish missionaries and colonists in their midst, achieving a degree of autonomy as a result. The United States organized the nation in 1882 into the Hopi Reservation.

Destruction of the Buffalo Herds By mid-century, white ranchers and miners were settling farther west of the Mississippi. Again, the federal government passed a law supposedly protecting the Native Americans of the Plains by creating "reservations" (1851). The obligation to stay on reservations rather than to hunt freely was a first aggravation. Further affronts came through the Homestead Act (1862), the construction of the transcontinental railroad (1863–1869), and the construction of towns and cities along the railroad corridors. One of the worst injuries was the destruction of the buffalo (bison), the hunting of which formed the principal livelihood of the Native Americans on the Plains. Within two decades (1865–1884), the herds had been decimated; fewer than 1,000 animals remained.

In the American Indian Wars (1862–1890), the Native Americans defended their homelands tenaciously but in vain. Visionaries sought to unify the various groups through the Ghost Dance, enacting a prophecy of the return of the buffalo herds and the disappearance of the whites. The Native Americans' last stand was at Wounded Knee Creek, South Dakota, in December 1890. Defeated and demoralized by 1900, the remaining indigenous people found themselves on 310 reservations.

Reform Measures Rapid industrialization that produced social and labor unrest in the United States led to the reforming initiatives of the Progressive era (1890–1914). By the 1900s, just a few hundred firms controlled two-fifths of all American manufacturing. The "trust buster" president, Theodore Roosevelt (in office 1901–1909), and Congress ended the monopolies of many such firms. A new Department of Commerce and Labor (1903) and the Pure Food and Drug and Meat Inspection Acts (1906) helped both workers and consumers. With the Federal Reserve Act (1913) and the Federal Trade Commission Act (1914), Congress created an overall framework for the supervision of the financial and business sectors.

Great Britain The pattern of constitutional nation-state construction that Britain followed in the eighteenth and nineteenth centuries was uninterrupted by wars. Challenges to this pattern came from the rise of linguistic nationalisms outside the English core. An outburst of Irish nationalism, based not only in ethnic and linguistic but also in religious traditions, appeared after the Great Famine of 1845–1849. Rural production and land issues were the main points of contention, leading to demands for home rule or even independence. A Protestant landlord class still controlled most of the land, which was farmed by Catholic tenants. During the worldwide Long Depression of 1873–1896, Irish farmers received low prices for their crops but no reductions in rent. A "land war" (mass protests against tenant evictions) ensued which the British Army sought to quell. This eventually led in 1898 to local government for the Irish and in 1903–1909 to land reform.

Scotland also developed an ethnolinguistic sense of its identity. The development began with the revival of traditional Scottish dress and music. More serious issues came to the fore in 1853 when the Scots, who felt that the British government paid more attention to Ireland, founded an association for the vindication of Scottish rights. But they had to wait until 1885, when the British government appointed the first Secretary for Scotland.

Welsh nationalism arose in the context of industrialization and the development of a Welsh working class, which organized uprisings in the 1830s. Religious issues, mostly related to opposition to the Church of England among nonconformists (e.g., Methodists, Quakers, and Presbyterians), and education issues added to the unrest. It was not until 1925, with the foundation of the Party of Wales, that Welsh nationalism became a force of its own.

During the 1800s, Parliament, the guardian of British constitutionalism, undertook major legal reforms of its constitutional order in recognition of the growing middle and working classes. The Great Reform Bill of 1832 shifted seats from southern districts to the more populated and industrialized center and north. The repeal of the Corn Laws in 1846 liberated imports and made grain cheaper, and the Second Reform Act of 1867 extended the franchise to larger numbers of working-class voters. The end result was not only that Britain escaped the revolutions of 1848 but also that the British electorate was largely united during the Victorian period (1837–1901) in its support for British imperialism around the globe.

Romanticism and Realism: Philosophical and Artistic Expression to 1850

Parallel to the evolution of the patterns of constitutionalism and ethnolinguistic nationalism, the two movements of romanticism and realism patterned the evolution of culture on both sides of the Atlantic.

Romanticism: Intellectual and artistic movement that emphasized the power of creative genius over matter and sought the sublime in nature.

Romanticism

Inspired by the Enlightenment and the revolutions, many philosophers, writers, composers, and painters of the period of **romanticism** in the early 1800s concluded that humans were free to remake themselves. To them, the mind was entirely independent, creating new aesthetic categories out of its own powers. Indeed, the stereotype of the bohemian creative "genius" crossing new imaginative thresholds became firmly implanted in the public imagination during this time.

Philosophers and Artists Building on Kant, the philosopher Georg Wilhelm Friedrich Hegel (1770–1831) postulated the freedom of mind or spirit. Hegel asserted that all thought proceeded dialectically from the "transcendental ego" to its opposite, matter, and from there to the spiritualized synthesis of nature. This **dialectic** permeates his entire system of philosophy.

Dialectic: The investigation of truth by discussion; in Hegel's thought, the belief that a higher truth is comprehended by a continuous unification of opposites.

Even more than philosophy, music became a major medium for expressing creative genius. The German Ludwig van Beethoven (1770–1827) and the Frenchman Hector Berlioz (1803–1869) pioneered the new genre of program music, with the *Pastoral Symphony* (Sixth Symphony) and the *Symphonie fantastique*, respectively, emphasizing passion and emotional intensity and the freedom of the musical spirit over traditional form. From among the emerging middle class, eager to play chamber music at home, a veritable explosion of composers erupted during the first half of the 1800s. These composers were also virtuosi on the violin or piano, playing their own new musical forms and playing concerts across Europe.

The medium of painting also lent itself to the expression of romantic feelings of passion and imagination. The common feature of these painters was that they departed from the established academic practices and styles.

Romanticism in literature appears in heroines or heroes and their passions and sentiments. In the novels of the British author Jane Austen (1775–1817), educated urbane society shapes the character and sensibilities of young women and prepares them for marriage. Also in Britain, the novels of the three Brontë sisters, Charlotte (1816–1855), Emily (1818–1848), and Anne (1820–1849), placed much greater emphasis on romantic passion, flawed characters, and social ills. The American Edgar Allan Poe (1809–1849) used these themes more explicitly in his Gothic stories and tales, such as "The Fall of the House of Usher" (1839).

Realism

Toward the middle of the 1800s, many artists and writers shifted their focus from the romanticism of the self to the **realism** of the middle classes. In philosophy, thinkers identified stages leading progressively to the rise of middle classes and industrialism. And in literature, the complex relationships that characterized the plots of the romantics were now set in the more prosaic urban world of factories and working classes.

Realism: The belief that material reality exists independently of the people who observe it.

Philosophy of History The French thinker Auguste Comte (1798–1857) published *The Course of Positive Philosophy* (1830–1842), in which he arranged world history into the three successive stages of the theological, metaphysical, and scientific. In his view, the advances of the sciences had all but eclipsed the metaphysical stage and had ushered in the last, scientific era. For Comte this was a sign of Europe's progress and a "positive" stage. His philosophy, labeled **positivism**, exerted a major influence in Europe as well as in Latin America.

Positivism: A philosophy advocated by Auguste Comte that favors the careful empirical observation of natural phenomena and human behavior over metaphysics.

Realism. The documentary power of photography spurred the new impulses of realism that emerged around 1850. The photograph here shows a reenactment of the execution of six hostages by the government of the Commune of Paris on May 24, 1871. This chilling scene was staged several weeks after the collapse of the Commune on May 28 by the photographer Eugène Appert to serve the provisional French government in Versailles in its efforts to expose the crimes of the Commune.

Prose Literature Realistic writers of fiction moved away from personal sentiments to explore middle-class society. In England, William Makepeace Thackeray (1811–1863) was a supreme satirist, whose novel *Vanity Fair* examines the foibles of the bourgeoisie. Charles Dickens (1812–1870) focused on working- and lower-middle-class characters in his many novels. George Eliot, born Mary Ann Evans (1819–1880), was politically oriented, placing small-town social relations within the context of concrete political events in Great Britain. In France, Gustave Flaubert (1821–1880) featured precise and unadorned descriptions of objects and situations in novels like *Madame Bovary* (1857). And Henry James (1843–1916), an American living in Britain, in his novel *The Ambassadors* (1903) explored the psychological complexities of individuals whose lives encompassed both sides of the Atlantic. In the end, realism, with its individuals firmly anchored in the new class society of the 1800s, moved far from the freedom and exuberance celebrated by the romantics.

Putting It All Together

Though the pattern of nation-state building in Europe and North America was relatively slow, it has become the dominant mode of political organization in the world today. The aftermath of World War I and the decolonization movement following World War II spurred the process of nation-state formation. The legacy of European colonialism both planted the idea of nationalism among the colonized and, through Enlightenment ideas of revolution, provided the ideological means of achieving their own liberation from foreign rule. In both cases, the aspirations of peoples to nationhood followed older European models as the colonies were either granted independence or fought to gain it from declining empires.

For example, although the United States achieved world economic leadership by 1914, it had faced an early constitutional crisis, endured a prolonged sectional struggle over slavery, fought a civil war that very nearly destroyed it, and remained united in part by enforcing segregation and discrimination against the 10 percent of its population that was of African descent. France adopted constitutional nationalism in 1789, but the monarchy bounced back three times. And in Germany, linguistic nationalism diluted the straightforward enthusiasm for the constitution and the symbols accompanying it.

In retrospect, it is impossible to say which of the speed bumps on the way toward the nation-state—slavery/racism, residual monarchism, or the twentieth-century experiments of communism and supremacist nationalism—were responsible for the longest delay.

Review and Relate

Thinking Through Patterns

Constitutionalism emerged as a result of the success of American and French revolutionaries in overthrowing absolute rule. The constitutional revolutionaries replaced the loyalty of subjects to a monarch with that of free and equal citizens to the national constitution. This form of republican constitutionalism called for unity among the citizens regardless of ethnic, linguistic, or religious identity. In the United States, this republicanism had to overcome the adherence to slavery in the South before it gained general recognition after the end of the Civil War. In France, republican constitutionalists battled conservative monarchists for nearly a century before they were able to finally defeat them in the Third Republic.

➤ How did the pattern of constitutionalism, emerging from the American and French Revolutions, affect the course of events in the Western world during the first half of the nineteenth century?

Constitutionalists emphasized the principles of freedom, equality, constitution, rule of law, elections, and representative assembly regardless of ethnicity, language, or religion. By contrast, ethnic nationalists in areas of Europe lacking centralized monarchies sought to first unify dispersed members of their nation through ideologies that emphasized common origin, collective history, and shared cultural traditions. In these ethnic (and sometimes also religious) ideologies, constitutional

➤ In what ways did ethnic nationalism differ from constitutionalism, and what was its influence on the formation of nation-states in the second half of the nineteenth century?

➢ What were the reactions among thinkers and artists to the developing pattern of nation-state formation? How did they define the intellectual–artistic movements of romanticism and realism?

principles were secondary. Only once unification in a nation-state was achieved would the form of government—monarchist, constitutional-monarchist, or republican—then be chosen.

Philosophers and artists in the romantic period emphasized individual creativity. By the 1850s, with the rise of the middle class, individual creativity gave way to a greater awareness, called "realism," of the social and political environment with its class structures and industrial characteristics.

Against the Grain

Defying the Third Republic

Consider this as a counterpoint to the main patterns examined in this chapter.

- Did the members of the Commune of Paris opponents run counter to the pattern of nation-state formation in the nineteenth century, and if so, how did they want to replace it?
- Did the ideas of small communities and opposition to centralized national governments retain their attraction in the twentieth and twenty-first centuries? If yes, which examples come to mind and for which reasons?

Socialist Parisians despised the government and parliament of the new conservative Third Republic of France (February 1871), headquartered in Versailles and dominated by two monarchist factions. They considered it defeatist against the Prussians who had been victorious in the war of 1870. After two failed protests, the final trigger for an outright revolution was the government's attempt in March 1871 to collect some 400 guns left over from the war and under the command of the Parisian National Guard. The attempt turned into a fiasco. The number of horses sent from Versailles to pull the cannons away was insufficient, and the government troops fraternized with the Parisian crowds. In the melee, however, several soldiers and two generals were killed (the latter probably by army deserters in Paris, not guardsmen). Seizing the opportunity, the central committee of the National Guard declared its independence and held elections for a communal council on March 26 (Commune of Paris: March 18–May 28, 1871).

The council of workers, craftsmen, and professionals issued a flurry of new laws. All deputies were under binding mandates and could be recalled anytime. As a commune of a desired universal republic, Paris considered all foreigners as equals. France itself was to become a federation of communes. Abandoned factories and workshops were to be directed by workers' councils. Church properties were confiscated, and the separation of church and state was declared. Under the auspices of the women-run Union of Women for the Defense of Paris and the Care of the Injured, measures for equal pay and pensions for retired survivors, regardless of marital status, were envisaged. The official symbol of the Commune was the red flag of the radical French Revolution of 1792, not the republican tricolor. The Commune pushed equality much further than the American and French revolutions had ever done, frightening the middle classes to their core.

The Commune had no chance of survival against the superior troops of the Third Republic, and it was bloodily repressed. The symbolical significance of the Commune, however, was immense: socialists and communists made it the mythical dawn of world revolution, working-class dictatorship, and the eventual withering away of the (national) state in the utopia of a classless society.

Key Terms

Dialectic 545
Enlightenment 526
Ethnic nationalism 536
Laissez-faire economics 534
Materialism 533
Positivism 545
Realism 545
Romanticism 544

Learn more with this chapter's digital tools, including the Oxford Insight Study Guide, at http://www.oup.com/he/vonsivers4e. Please see the Further Resources section at the back of the book for additional readings and suggested websites.

PATTERNS OF EVIDENCE |

Sources for Chapter 22

SOURCE 22.1

Declaration of the Rights of Man and of the Citizen

August 26, 1789

When the Third Estate declared itself the National Assembly in June 1789, among the first measures it considered was a universal declaration of the rights and duties of individual French citizens. A proposal was made by the Marquis de Lafayette to this effect in July, but swift-moving events in Paris, such as the fall of the Bastille on July 14, moved the Revolution in new directions. Undaunted, a subcommittee continued to debate the document, editing a draft proposal of 24 articles down to 17. Like the Declaration of Independence in the American colonies (1776), this document was a compromise statement, drawn up and edited by committee; and yet, like the American Declaration, it is a stirring statement of Enlightenment principles concerning both the individual's role in the state and the ultimate source of all government.

The representatives of the French people, constituted as a National Assembly, and considering that ignorance, neglect, or contempt of the rights of man are the sole causes of public misfortunes and governmental corruption, have resolved to set forth in a solemn declaration the natural, inalienable, and sacred rights of man: so that by being constantly present to all the members of the social body this declaration may always remind them of their rights and duties; so that by being liable at every moment to comparison with the aim of any and all political institutions the acts of the legislative and executive powers may be the more fully respected; and so that by being founded henceforward on simple and incontestable principles the demands of the citizens may always tend toward maintaining the constitution and the general welfare.

In consequence, the National Assembly recognizes and declares, in the presence and under the auspices of the Supreme Being, the following rights of man and the citizen:

1. Men are born and remain free and equal in rights. Social distinctions may be based only on common utility.

Source: Lynn Hunt, ed. and trans., *The French Revolution and Human Rights: A Brief Documentary History* (Boston: Bedford St. Martin's, 1996), 77–79.

2. The purpose of all political association is the preservation of the natural and imprescriptible rights of man. These rights are liberty, property, security, and resistance to oppression.

3. The principle of all sovereignty rests essentially in the nation. No body and no individual may exercise authority which does not emanate expressly from the nation.

4. Liberty consists in the ability to do whatever does not harm another; hence the exercise of the natural rights of each man has no other limits than those which assure to other members of society the enjoyment of the same rights. These limits can only be determined by the law.

5. The law only has the right to prohibit those actions which are injurious to society. No hindrance should be put in the way of anything not prohibited by the law, nor may any one be forced to do what the law does not require.

6. The law is the expression of the general will. All citizens have the right to take part, in person or by their representatives, in its formation. It must be the same for everyone whether it protects or penalizes. All citizens being equal in its eyes are equally admissible to all public dignities, offices, and employments, according to their ability, and with no other distinction than that of their virtues and talents.

. . .

11. The free communication of thoughts and opinions is one of the most precious of the rights of man. Every citizen may therefore speak, write, and print freely, if he accepts his own responsibility for any abuse of this liberty in the cases set by the law.

12. The safeguard of the rights of man and the citizen requires public powers. These powers are therefore instituted for the advantage of all, and not for the private benefit of those to whom they are entrusted.

13. For maintenance of public authority and for expenses of administration, common taxation is indispensable. It should be apportioned equally among all the citizens according to their capacity to pay.

14. All citizens have the right, by themselves or through their representatives, to have demonstrated to them the necessity of public taxes, to consent to them freely, to follow the use made of the proceeds, and to determine the means of apportionment, assessment, and collection, and the duration of them.

. . .

17. Property being an inviolable and sacred right, no one may be deprived of it except when public necessity, certified by law, obviously requires it, and on the condition of a just compensation in advance.

▸ Working with Sources

1. **To what extent does the declaration mix specific provisions and general principles of human rights?**
2. **How does the document aim to uphold the "common utility"? How is the "public necessity" to be determined?**

SOURCE 22.2

Olympe de Gouges, *The Declaration of the Rights of Woman*

September 1791

Women were not included among the new officeholders of revolutionary France, nor were they members of the National Assembly, which supposedly represented all members of the country's Third Estate. An immediate question arose concerning the extent to which the benefits of the Revolution should be extended to females (as well as to slaves throughout France's global empire). Some men did advocate the extension of these rights and privileges, but women also took action in their own cause. Among these was the Cercle Social (Social Circle), a group of female activists who coordinated their publishing activities on behalf of women and their own goals in the developing Revolution.

One of the leaders of this group was Marie Gouze (1748–1793), who, under her pen name "Olympe de Gouges," attacked both the institution of slavery and the oppression of women in 1791. A playwright, pamphleteer, and political activist, de Gouges published this thoughtful meditation on what the National Assembly should declare concerning "the rights of woman" (as opposed merely to "the rights of man"). Members of the Social Circle were arrested as the Revolution entered its radical phase, and Olympe de Gouges was executed by guillotine in November 1793.

To be decreed by the National Assembly in its last sessions or by the next legislature.

Preamble

Mothers, daughters, sisters, female representatives of the nation ask to be constituted as a national assembly. Considering that ignorance, neglect, or contempt for the rights of woman are the sole causes of public misfortunes and governmental corruption, they have resolved to set forth in a solemn declaration the natural, inalienable, and sacred rights of woman: so that by being constantly present to all the members of the social body this declaration may always remind them of their rights and duties; so that by being liable at every moment to comparison with the aim of any and all political institutions the acts of women's and men's powers may be the more fully respected; and so that by being founded henceforward on simple and incontestable principles the demands of the citizenesses may always tend toward maintaining the constitution, good morals, and the general welfare.

In consequence, the sex that is superior in beauty as in courage, needed in maternal sufferings, recognizes and declares, in the presence and under

---

Source: Lynn Hunt, ed. and trans., *The French Revolution and Human Rights: A Brief Documentary History* (Boston: Bedford St. Martin's, 1996), 124–126.

the auspices of the Supreme Being, the following rights of woman and the citizeness.

1. Woman is born free and remains equal to man in rights. Social distinctions may be based only on common utility.

2. The purpose of all political association is the preservation of the natural and imprescriptible rights of woman and man. These rights are liberty, property, security, and especially resistance to oppression.

3. The principle of all sovereignty rests essentially in the nation, which is but the reuniting of woman and man. No body and no individual may exercise authority which does not emanate expressly from the nation.

4. Liberty and justice consist in restoring all that belongs to another; hence the exercise of the natural rights of woman has no other limits than those that the perpetual tyranny of man opposes to them; these limits must be reformed according to the laws of nature and reason.

5. The laws of nature and reason prohibit all actions which are injurious to society. No hindrance should be put in the way of anything not prohibited by these wise and divine laws, nor may anyone be forced to do what they do not require.

6. The law should be the expression of the general will. All citizenesses and citizens should take part, in person or by their representatives, in its formation. It must be the same for everyone. All citizenesses and citizens, being equal in its eyes, should be equally admissible to all public dignities, offices, and employments, according to their ability, and with no other distinction than that of their virtues and talents.

. . .

11. The free communication of thoughts and opinions is one of the most precious of the rights of woman, since this liberty assures the recognition of children by their fathers. Every citizeness may therefore say freely, I am the mother of your child; a barbarous prejudice [against unmarried women having children] should not force her to hide the truth, so long as responsibility is accepted for any abuse of this liberty in cases determined by the law [women are not allowed to lie about the paternity of their children].

12. The safeguard of the rights of woman and citizeness requires public powers. These powers are instituted for the advantage of all and not for the private benefit of those to whom they are entrusted.

13. For maintenance of public authority and for expenses of administration, taxation of women and men is equal; she takes part in all forced labor service, in all painful tasks; she must therefore have the same proportion in the distribution of places, employments, offices, dignities, and in industry.

14. The citizenesses and citizens have the right, by themselves or through their representatives, to have demonstrated to them the necessity of public taxes. The citizenesses can only agree to them upon admission of an equal division, not only in wealth, but also in the public administration, and to determine the means of apportionment, assessment, and collection, and the duration of the taxes.

. . .

17. Property belongs to both sexes whether united or separated; it is for each of them an inviolable and sacred right, and no one may be deprived of it as a true patrimony of nature, except when public necessity, certified by law, obviously requires it, and then on condition of a just compensation in advance.

▶ Working with Sources

1. **What does de Gouges consider woman's "natural and reasonable" share in the "common" life of a society?**
2. **To what extent does biology determine the particular roles and sufferings of women? Are women (in de Gouges's context) to be considered the superior element of human society as a result?**

SOURCE 22.3

Voltaire, "Torture," from the *Philosophical Dictionary*

1769

Voltaire (the pen name of François-Marie Arouet) epitomized the Enlightenment. His *Dictionnaire philosophique* (*Philosophical Dictionary*), the first edition of which appeared in 1764, distilled his thought on philosophical matters in what he self-deprecatingly called an "alphabetical abomination." Voltaire invariably found ways to deploy humor in the pursuit of serious moral, religious, and ethical truths, as the continued popularity of his "contes philosophiques" (philosophical tales), including *Candide*, *Zadig*, and *Micromégas*, attests.

In this "dictionary," arranged alphabetically according to the entry's title (in French), Voltaire tackled matters like atheism, fanaticism, the soul, superstition, and tolerance. His tone is always light and witty, despite the weightiness of (and the violence associated with) the subject matter. Inspired by ongoing court cases and interrogation methods, Voltaire added the following miraculous little essay on the use (and, in some countries, disuse) of torture as a legal instrument to the 1769 version of the *Dictionary*. His satirical approach resonates today, as issues of what constitutes torture and how it ought to be applied continue to be a part of our political discourse.

Although there are few articles on jurisprudence in these respectable alphabetical reflections, a word must nevertheless be said about torture, otherwise named the question. It is a strange way to question one. Yet it was not invented by the merely curious. It would appear that this part of our legislation owes its first origin to a highwayman. Most of these gentlemen are still in the habit of

Source: Voltaire, *Philosophical Dictionary*, ed. and trans. Theodore Besterman (Harmondsworth, UK: Penguin, 1972), 394–396.

squeezing thumbs, burning the feet of those who refuse to tell them where they have put their money, and questioning them by means of other torments.

The conquerors, having succeeded these thieves, found this invention of the greatest utility. They put it into practice when they suspected that some vile plot was being hatched against them, as, for instance, that of being free, a crime of divine and human lèse-majesté. The accomplices had to be known; and to arrive at this knowledge those who were suspected were made to suffer a thousand deaths, because according to the jurisprudence of these first heroes anyone suspected of having had so much as a disrespectful thought about them was worthy of death. And once a man has thus deserved death it matters little whether appalling torments are added for a few days or even several weeks. All this even had something of the divine about it. Providence sometimes tortures us by means of the stone, gravel, gout, scurvy, leprosy, pox great and small, griping of the bowels, nervous convulsions, and other executants of the vengeance of providence.

Now since the first despots were images of divinity, as all their courtiers freely admitted, they imitated it so far as they could.

. . .

The grave magistrate who has bought for a little money the right to conduct these experiments on his fellow creatures tells his wife at dinner what happened during the morning. The first time her ladyship is revolted, the second time she acquires a taste for it, for after all women are curious, and then the first thing she says to him when he comes home in his robes is: "My angel, did you give anyone the question today?"

The French, who are considered to be a very humane people, I do not know why, are astonished that the English, who have had the inhumanity to take the whole of Canada from us [in 1760 and ratified in 1763, as a result of the Seven Years' War], have renounced the pleasure of applying the question.

. . .

In 1700 the Russians were regarded as barbarians. We are now only in 1769, and an **empress** has just given this vast state laws that would have done honour to Minor, to Numa, and to Solon if they had had enough intelligence to compose them. The most remarkable of them is universal toleration, the second is the abolition of torture. Justice and humanity guided her pen, she has reformed everything. Woe to a nation which, long civilized, is still led by atrocious ancient practices! "Why should we change our jurisprudence?" it asks. "Europe uses our cooks, our tailors, our wig-makers; therefore our laws are good."

Empress: Catherine the Great.

▸ Working with Sources

1. **Does Voltaire make a convincing case that the use of torture results from excessive curiosity and a warped desire to inflict suffering?**
2. **How does he ridicule the continuation of "ancient" practices into modern times, and how does this essay reflect the values of the philosophical Enlightenment?**

SOURCE 22.4

Edmund Burke, *Reflections on the Revolution in France*

1790

Born in Dublin to a Protestant father and a Catholic mother, Edmund Burke (1729–1797) struggled to build a political career in Georgian England. Having established a reputation for brilliant thinking and speaking, he entered Parliament in 1766. One of his principal causes in the 1760s and 1770s was the defense of the American colonists in their conflict with the mother country. Burke opposed the English government's position that England was sovereign over the colonies and could tax the colonists as she saw fit. By contrast, Burke insisted that a "right" was not an abstract principle and that policy should be guided by actual circumstances. When the French Revolution began in 1789, Burke surprised some of his political allies by speaking against it, mainly because he believed that "reason" and "rights" were not absolute principles that justified violent change. His statement against the extremes of revolution, published in November 1790, became one basis for a form of political ideology known as conservatism.

It is no wonder, therefore, that with these ideas of everything in their constitution and government at home, either in church or state, as illegitimate and usurped, or at best as a vain mockery, they look abroad with an eager and passionate enthusiasm. Whilst they are possessed by these notions, it is vain to talk to them of the practice of their ancestors, the fundamental laws of their country, the fixed form of a constitution whose merits are confirmed by the solid test of long experience and an increasing public strength and national prosperity. They despise experience as the wisdom of unlettered men; and as for the rest, they have wrought underground a mine that will blow up, at one grand explosion, all examples of antiquity, all precedents, charters, and acts of parliament. They have "the rights of men." Against these there can be no prescription, against these no agreement is binding; these admit no temperament and no compromise; anything withheld from their full demand is so much of fraud and injustice. Against these their rights of men let no government look for security in the length of its continuance, or in the justice and lenity of its administration.

. . .

Government is not made in virtue of natural rights, which may and do exist in total independence of it, and exist in much greater clearness and in a much greater degree of abstract perfection; but their abstract perfection is their practical defect. By having a right to everything they want everything. Government is a contrivance of human wisdom to provide for human wants. Men have a right that these wants should be provided for by this wisdom. Among these

---

Source: Edmund Burke, *Reflections on the Revolution in France*, ed. Thomas H. D. Mahoney (Indianapolis, IN: Liberal Arts, 1955), 66, 68–69, 70–71, 73–74.

wants is to be reckoned the want, out of civil society, of a sufficient restraint upon their passions. Society requires not only that the passions of individuals should be subjected, but that even in the mass and body, as well as in the individuals, the inclinations of men should frequently be thwarted, their will controlled, and their passions brought into subjection. This can only be done *by a power out of themselves*, and not, in the exercise of its function, subject to that will and to those passions which it is its office to bridle and subdue. In this sense the restraints on men, as well as their liberties, are to be reckoned among their rights. But as the liberties and the restrictions vary with times and circumstances and admit to infinite modifications, they cannot be settled upon any abstract rule; and nothing is so foolish as to discuss them upon that principle.

. . .

The pretended rights of these theorists are all extremes; and in proportion as they are metaphysically true, they are morally and politically false. The rights of men are in a sort of *middle*, incapable of definition, but not impossible to be discerned. The rights of men in governments are their advantages; and these are often in balances between differences of good, in compromises sometimes between good and evil, and sometimes between evil and evil. Political reason is a computing principle: adding, subtracting, multiplying, and dividing, morally and not metaphysically, or mathematically, true moral denominations.

. . .

In France, you are now in the crisis of a revolution and in the transit from one form of government to another—you cannot see that character of men exactly in the same situation in which we see it in this country. With us it is militant; with you it is triumphant; and you know how it can act when its power is commensurate to its will. I would not be supposed to confine these observations to any description of men or to comprehend all men of any description within them—No! far from it. I am as incapable of that injustice as I am of keeping terms with those who profess principles of extremities and who, under the name of religion, teach little else than wild and dangerous politics. The worst of these politics of revolution is this: they temper and harden the breast in order to prepare it for the desperate strokes which are sometimes used in extreme occasions. But as these occasions may never arrive, the mind receives a gratuitous taint; and the moral sentiments suffer not a little when no political purpose is served by the depravation. This sort of people are so taken up with their theories about the rights of man that they have totally forgotten his nature. Without opening one new avenue to the understanding, they have succeeded in stopping up those that lead to the heart. They have perverted in themselves, and in those that attend to them, all the well-placed sympathies of the human breast.

▸ Working with Sources

1. **Is Burke's protest against the Revolution merely the result of his estimation of its "extremist" nature?**
2. **Is Burke justified in drawing a connection between metaphysical theorizing and physical violence? Did he provide an accurate prediction of "the Terror," still to come?**

SOURCE 22.5

Thomas Paine, *Rights of Man*

1791

As a young man in England, Thomas Paine worked a series of low-paying, menial jobs, most of which he was quickly fired from, being perceived as an uncooperative troublemaker. In 1774, at the age of 37, seeming to be a total failure in every profession he had attempted, he hired passage on a ship to the American colonies. Fortunately, Paine possessed a letter of recommendation from Benjamin Franklin, whom he had met after a scientific lecture in London. On the strength of this letter, Paine found employment as a printer and writer in Philadelphia, and soon became the editor of a journal called the *Pennsylvania Magazine*. Incensed by the abuses to which the colonists were subject, he encouraged his fellow Americans to make a formal break with Britain. He also wrote and published a series of editorials protesting the American institution of slavery, castigating those who were agitating for their own liberty while denying it so cruelly to others.

Paine published his thoughts on independence in pamphlet form in January 1776 under the title *Common Sense*. So popular was the document that General Washington ordered that it be read aloud to his troops as they were freezing along the Delaware River on Christmas Eve, 1776. Declaring "These are the times that try men's souls," Paine continued to offer encouragement to the soldiers in pamphlets later published as *The American Crisis*, and his efforts on behalf of the American cause were recognized by many of the founding fathers of the country during the Revolution.

When he heard about the storming of the Bastille in Paris in July 1789, Paine rushed to France to be a part of this new revolution. Soon afterward, he had the honor of delivering the key to the Bastille from the Marquis de Lafayette to Washington, at which time, he declared, his heart "leaped with joy." When Burke's *Reflections* on the Revolution were published in 1790, Paine felt he had been betrayed by his former friend, with whom he had had many conversations and a meeting of minds in the American cause. As a result, he published *The Rights of Man*, a strong rebuke of Burke's philosophy and commentary, in February 1791. The work was dedicated to the first president of the United States, George Washington.

The three first articles [of the Declaration of the Rights of Man and of the Citizen] are the basis of liberty, as well individual as national; nor can any country be called free, whose government does not take its beginning from the principles they contain, and continue to preserve them pure; and the whole of the Declaration of Rights is of more value to the world, and will do more good, than all the laws and statutes that have yet been promulgated.

Source: Philip S. Foner, ed., *The Life and Major Writings of Thomas Paine* (New York: Citadel, 1945), 316–317, 340–341.

In the declaratory exordium which prefaces the Declaration of Rights, we see the solemn and majestic spectacle of a nation opening its commission, under the auspices of its Creator, to establish a Government; a scene so new, and so transcendently unequalled by any thing in the European world, that the name of a revolution is diminutive of its character, and it rises into a regeneration of man.

What are the present governments of Europe, but a scene of iniquity and oppression? What is that of England? Do not its own inhabitants say, It is a market where every man has his price, and where corruption is common traffic, at the expense of a deluded people? No wonder, then, that the French Revolution is traduced.

Had it confined itself merely to the destruction of flagrant despotism, perhaps Mr. Burke and some others had been silent. Their cry now is, "It is gone too far": that is, it has gone too far for them. It stares corruption in the face, and the venal tribe are all alarmed. Their fear discovers itself in their outrage, and they are but publishing the groans of a wounded vice.

But from such opposition, the French Revolution, instead of suffering, receives an homage. The more it is struck, the more sparks it will emit; and the fear is, it will not be struck enough. It has nothing to dread from attacks: Truth has given it an establishment; and Time will record it with a name as lasting as its own.

Having now traced the progress of the French Revolution through most of its principal stages, from its commencement, to the taking of the Bastille, and its establishment by the Declaration of Rights, I will close the subject with the energetic apostrophe of M. de Lafayette—May this great monument, raised to Liberty, serve as a lesson to the oppressor, and an example to the oppressed!

. . .

From the Revolutions of America and France, and the symptoms that have appeared in other countries, it is evident that the opinion of the world is changed with respect to systems of government, and that revolutions are not within the compass of political calculations. The progress of time and circumstances, which men assign to the accomplishment of great changes, is too mechanical to measure the force of the mind, and the rapidity of reflection, by which revolutions are generated. All the old governments have received a shock from those that already appear, and which were once more improbable, and are a greater subject of wonder, than a general revolution in Europe would be now.

When we survey the wretched condition of man under the monarchical and hereditary systems of government, dragged from his home by one power, or driven by another, and impoverished by taxes more than by enemies, it becomes evident that those systems are bad, and that a general revolution in the principle and construction of governments is necessary.

What is government more than the management of the affairs of a nation? It is not, and from its nature cannot be, the property of any particular man or family, but of the whole community, at whose expense it is supported; and though by force or contrivance it has been usurped into an inheritance, the usurpation cannot alter the right of things. Sovereignty, as a matter of right, appertains to the nation only, and not to any individual; and a nation has at all times an inherent indefeasible right to abolish any form of government it finds inconvenient, and establish such as accords with its interest, disposition, and happiness. The romantic and barbarous distinction of [making] men into kings and subjects, though it may suit the condition of courtiers, cannot that of citizens; and is exploded by the principle upon which governments are now founded. Every citizen is a member of the sovereignty, and, as such, can acknowledge no personal subjection; and his obedience can be only to the laws.

Working with Sources

1. **How does Paine defend the Revolution against the charge of extremism, as levied by Burke and others?**
2. **Why does Paine think it dangerous to romanticize kings and queens?**

SOURCE 22.6

Clemens von Metternich, Secret Memorandum to Tsar Alexander I

1820

After the defeat of Napoleon the leaders of the Quadruple Alliance, Great Britain, Austria, Prussia, and Russia, convened the Congress of Vienna in 1815 in order to restore peace and order throughout Europe. The Congress was led by the Austrian Prime Minister, Klemens von Metternich (1773–1859), determined to institute the principle of legitimacy, or the restoration of conservative monarchical rule. Another objective of the Congress was to establish a balance of power by orchestrating a "Concert of Europe," designed to restore the borders of France and to prevent one country from dominating any other. In his letter to Tsar Alexander I, Metternich expresses his intention to curtail the rising influence of the middle classes.

"Europe today," a celebrated writer has recently said, *"evokes pity in the man of spirit and horror in the man of virtue."*

It would be difficult to comprise in a few words a more exact picture of the situation at the time we are writing these lines!

Kings have to calculate the chances of their very existence in the immediate future; passions are let loose, and league together to overthrow everything which society respects as the basis of its existence; religion, public morality, laws, customs, rights, and duties, all are attacked, confounded, overthrown, or called in question. The great mass of the people are tranquil spectators of these attacks and revolutions, and of the absolute want of all means of defense. A few are carried off by the torrent, but the wishes of the immense majority are to maintain a repose which exists no longer, and of which even the first elements seem to be lost....

Having now thrown a rapid glance over the first causes of the present state of society, it is necessary to point out in a more particular manner the evil which threatens to deprive it, at one blow, of the real blessings, the fruits of genuine civilisation, and to disturb it in the midst of its enjoyments. This evil may be described in one word–presumption; the natural effect of the rapid progression of the human mind towards the perfecting of so many things. This

---

Source: Dennis Sherman, ed., *Western Civilization: Sources, Images, Interpretations, from the Renaissance to the Present* (New York: McGraw Hill, 1995). https://www.age-of-the-sage.org/history/metternich_memorandum.html

it is which at the present day leads so many individuals astray, for it has become an almost universal sentiment.

Religion, morality, legislation, economy, politics, administration, all have become common and accessible to everyone. Knowledge seems to come by inspiration; experience has no value for the presumptuous man; faith is nothing to him; he substitutes for it a pretended individual conviction, and to arrive at this conviction dispenses with all inquiry and with all study; for these means appear too trivial to a mind which believes itself strong enough to embrace at one glance all questions and all facts. Laws have no value for him, because he has not contributed to make them, and it would be beneath a man of his parts to recognise the limits traced by rude and ignorant generations. Power resides in himself; why should he submit himself to that which was only useful for the man deprived of light and knowledge? That which, according to him, was required in an age of weakness cannot be suitable in an age of reason and vigour amounting to universal perfection, which the German innovators designate by the idea, absurd in itself, of the Emancipation of the People! Morality itself he does not attack openly, for without it he could not be sure for a single instant of his own existence; but he interprets its essence after his own fashion, and allows every other person to do so likewise, provided that other person neither kills nor robs him.

In thus tracing the character of the presumptuous man, we believe we have traced that of the society of the day, composed of like elements, if the denomination of society is applicable to an order of things which only tends in principle towards individualising all the elements of which society is composed. Presumption makes every man the guide of his own belief, the arbiter of laws according to which he is pleased to govern himself, or to allow some one else to govern him and his neighbours; it makes him, in short, the sole judge of his own faith, his own actions, and the principles according to which he guides them. . . .

The Governments, having lost their balance, are frightened, intimidated, and thrown into confusion by the cries of the intermediary class of society, which, placed between the Kings and their subjects, breaks the sceptre of the monarch, and usurps the cry of the people—the class so often disowned by the people, and nevertheless too much listened to, caressed and feared by those who could with one word reduce it again to nothingness.

We see this intermediary class abandon itself with a blind fury and animosity which proves much more its own fears than any confidence in the success of its enterprises, to all the means which seem proper to assuage its thirst for power, applying itself to the task of persuading Kings that their rights are confined to sitting upon a throne, while those of the people are to govern, and to attack all that centuries have bequeathed as holy and worthy of man's respect—denying, in fact, the value of the past, and declaring themselves the masters of the future. We see this class take all sorts of disguises, uniting and subdividing as occasion offers, helping each other in the hour of danger, and the next day depriving each other of all their conquests. It takes possession of the press, and employs it to promote impiety, disobedience to the laws of religion and the State, and goes so far as to preach murder as a duty for those who desire what is good.

▶ Working with Sources

1. **In what ways does Metternich justify his intention to restore rule by royalty?**
2. **How does Metternich describe the middle classes?**

World Period Five

The Origins of Modernity, 1750–1900

The twin novel events of constitutional and industrial revolutions, first in the Americas and western Europe and later in Japan, dramatically changed the course of world history.

- People rose to end the divine right of kings and replace their rule with popular sovereignty, constitutions, and elections.
- Machines began to replace animal power in the manufacture of textiles, means of transportation, chemicals, and urban amenities.

As a result, 10,000-year-old traditional customs and habits formed by life in agriculture gave way to what we call "modernity," that is, nontraditional new ways of life in the "machine age," characterized by such new phenomena as nation-states, social classes, megacities, colonialism, and above all, vastly increased global interactions.

Chapter 23

Creoles and Caudillos

Latin America in the Nineteenth Century, 1790–1917

CHAPTER TWENTY-THREE PATTERNS

Origins, Interactions, Adaptations Spain's colonies broke free in the constitutional revolutions that spread throughout Latin America between 1810 and 1826, but tensions between democratic and authoritarian tendencies persisted after the colonies had achieved independence. Given the opposition of the Catholic Church, the impact of the New Science and Enlightenment was limited at first.. Brazil became independent in 1822 as a kingdom under the rule of a royal family that had fled Napoleon. It was not until 1889 that it became an authoritarian (though decentralized) republic.

Uniqueness and Similarities Even though they shared many characteristics, each Latin American country evolved along its own geographical, social, and political path. Depending on their location, countries favored either ranching or plantation agriculture. There was also great diversity in the populations of Latin American countries, with some having large numbers of Amerindians and/or Africans, and others very few. Some remained mired in authoritarianism, while others were able to strengthen their constitutional politics. Despite these internal differences, Latin America fit comfortably into the liberal world economy dominated by Great Britain. With close ties to Europe, they provided agricultural commodities and minerals to industrializing Britain and Germany.

Among the leaders of the Latin American wars of independence (1810–1826) from Spain, a woman named Juana Azurduy de Padilla (1781–1862) stands out for her bravery. Azurduy [asoor-DOO-ee] was a mestiza military commander in what are today the countries of Bolivia and Argentina. With her husband, Manuel Ascencio Padilla, she joined the cause of independence in 1810, creating a mini republic (*republiquita*) in the mountains.

Azurduy, who was adored by the locals as "Mother Earth" (*pachamama*), had learned swordsmanship, firearms handling, and logistics for fighting guerilla wars. Well versed in Quechua and Aymara, Azurduy and Ascencio recruited some 6,000 locals, armed with the traditional Inca arms of clubs and slings. In 1813, Azurduy and Ascencio and their men joined a force of independence fighters from Buenos Aires. This force suffered defeat, however, at the hands of Spanish royal troops sent by the vice-regent of Peru. In an effort to recover, Azurduy drilled what she called her "Loyal Battalion" for ambushes and quick retreats. But pressured by the viceregal troops, the battalion suffered a constant loss of men—including Ascencio—in 1816. Azurduy retreated to what is today northwestern Argentina, where she was incorporated as a lieutenant colonel in the regular independence army, in recognition of her bravery.

In 1824 Upper Peru gained its independence under the name of Bolivia (in honor of the Venezuelan independence leader Simón Bolívar). Azurduy returned from Argentina to retire. She died in 1862, and in the early 1900s Bolivians named a town near her birthplace after her.

CHAPTER OUTLINE

Independence, Constitutionalism, and Landed Elites

Latin American Society and Economy in the Nineteenth Century

Putting It All Together

The story of Juana Azurduy illustrates the important role of Amerindians, mestizos, black freedmen, and black slaves in the wars of independence in Latin America. The fact that a woman was able to overcome patriarchal conventions in the early 1800s demonstrates the power of the revolutionary ideas of liberty and of the republican and constitutional nation-state (see Chapter 22).

ABOVE: Carts loaded high with sugarcane arrive at a sugar mill in Cuba, late nineteenth century.

Seeing Patterns

➤ Which factors in the complex ethnic and social structures of Latin America were responsible for the emergence of authoritarian politicians, or caudillos?

➤ After achieving independence, why did Latin American countries opt for a continuation of mineral and agricultural commodity exports?

➤ How do the social and economic structures of this period continue to affect the course of Latin America today?

Southern Cone: Geographical term denoting the southern half of South America, comprising the countries of Brazil, Paraguay, Uruguay, and Argentina.

Independence, Constitutionalism, and Landed Elites

In the absence of a long tradition of Enlightenment thought, especially its concepts of popular sovereignty and constitutionalism, the catalyst for the demand for independence in Latin America came from the consequences of Napoleon's occupation of the Iberian peninsula (1807–1814). This occupation confronted the Spanish-speaking American Creoles with the choice of continued loyalty to the deposed Bourbon dynasty, recognition of Napoleon, or full independence. In the end, when Napoleon's regime proved to be short-lived and the restored Bourbon king refused constitutional reforms, the choice was clear: Spanish Latin America fought for its full independence. Brazil, by contrast, at first continued under its Portuguese dynasty, relocated to the colony after fleeing Napoleon from Portugal, before eventually becoming independent.

Independence in the Southern Cone: State Formation in Argentina

Independence movements in the viceroyalty of the Río de la Plata formed in June 1810. Under the guise of loyalty to the deposed Fernando VII of Spain, Creoles in the capital, Buenos Aires, established a junta [HOON-ta] rejecting the viceregal Spanish authorities. Outright independence from Spain was declared in 1816. Even though by this time Spanish loyalists in the south had been defeated, their brethren in the far northwest were still strong. Efforts by troops from Buenos Aires to defeat the loyalists of Upper Peru, part of the viceroyalty of Río de la Plata, had failed. The figure who finally broke the logjam was one of the heroes of Latin American independence, José de San Martín (1778–1850).

Independence in Argentina The viceroyalty of La Plata, comprising the modern countries of Argentina, Uruguay, Paraguay, and Bolivia, was the youngest of Spain's colonial units. La Plata, with the port of Buenos Aires as its capital, had grown through contraband trade with Great Britain, and the Bourbon reformers wanted to redirect its trade to Spain.

In 1810, when the first independence movements formed, there was a clear distinction between the Creoles of Buenos Aires, or *porteños*, who favored independence, and the Creoles of the pampas (grasslands of the interior of Argentina and Uruguay) and the subtropical plains and hills of Paraguay, who favored continued colonialism.

Uruguay, furthermore, was initially claimed by Brazil and eventually achieved its own independence only in 1828. Upper Peru, or modern Bolivia, was heavily defended by royalist colonial and Spanish troops. Given these circumstances, the porteño independence fighters achieved only a standstill during the initial period of 1810–1816.

The breakthrough for independence eventually came via an experienced military figure, José de San Martín. San Martín was a Creole from northeastern Argentina. He began service in the porteño independence movement in 1812, where he distinguished himself in the Argentine struggle for independence.

During his service, San Martín realized that success in the struggle for independence in the south would require the liberation of the viceroyalty of Peru. Accordingly, he trained the Army of the Andes, which included mulatto and black volunteers. With this army, he crossed the mountains to Chile in 1818, liberating the country from royalist forces. With the help of a newly established navy, he conquered Lima in Peru. However, San Martín was defied by the local Creoles when he sought to introduce social reforms. When he was also unable to dislodge Spanish troops from Upper Peru and come to terms about the future of Latin America with Simón Bolívar, the liberation hero of central Latin America, he resigned from the army in 1822, to live in Belgium and France for the remainder of his life.

Slow State Formation After independence, the ruling junta in Buenos Aires solidified into an oligarchy of the city's landowning Creole elite. In the interior, the largely undeveloped areas of the pampas with their small populations of Amerindians and Creole gauchos, or cowboys, remained largely outside the new state. But even the core provinces and the port city of Buenos Aires were unable to come to terms. The provinces cherished their autonomy and resented the city's economic superiority and pretensions to political dominance. Uruguay, one of the provinces of the former Spanish viceroyalty of La Plata, strove for independence from the start, but was thwarted by both Argentina, the self-declared heir of the viceroyalty's territories, and Brazil, which claimed it for itself on the grounds of its sizable Portuguese-speaking minority. The independence of Uruguay was recognized by its neighbors in 1828, but even then, meddling in its internal affairs continued.

Political Instability in the Southern Cone An Argentine constituent assembly finally drew up a definitive federal constitution in 1853, but state formation and territorial consolidation remained in flux. Buenos Aires refused to subscribe to the constitution until 1861. While the constitutional order was settled at this time, the process of territorial consolidation was not and contributed to continued tensions among Paraguay, Uruguay, Argentina, and Brazil.

Tensions among the four countries reached their height during the Paraguayan War of 1864–1870, which proved to be the most devastating in the history of nineteenth-century Latin America. In this war, Paraguay was pitted against a triple alliance among Brazil, Argentina, and Uruguay. The Paraguayan president Francisco Solano López (r. 1862–1870) miscalculated that Argentina would support his idea of a "third force," formed by an alliance between Paraguay and

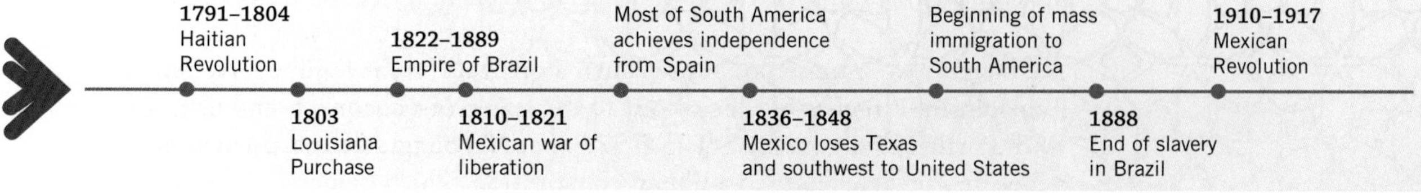

Fiercely Independent Gauchos, around 1900. Gauchos, shown here sharpening their long knives (*facones*), were recognizable by their ponchos or wool blankets, which doubled as winter coats and saddlecloths. As with cowboys in North America, they were expert riders, calf ropers, and—with their dogs, shown in front—cattle herders.

Uruguay, to block Brazil's territorial ambitions. But in spite of their diverging interests, Argentina and Brazil agreed to maintain the traditional policy of keeping Paraguay and Uruguay weak. Paraguay lost the war and suffered terrible destruction.

The War of Paraguay contributed to the industrialization and professionalization of modern warfare. In particular, it greatly strengthened the political role of the Brazilian military, which culminated in the army's overthrow of the monarchy (1889). About the only positive outcome was that it finally settled the state formation and territorial consolidation process of Argentina.

Argentine Demographic Growth In the years after 1870, the pampas of Argentina were transformed. The land was opened to settlement by European immigrants, driving the gauchos from their independent existence into becoming hired hands. The railroad spurred settlement, and the remaining Amerindians were driven south to Patagonia or exterminated. The pampas were divided up into huge estates (*estancias*) as the old system of rounding up livestock and driving it to market now gave way to ranching. As in other areas of South America, the new landed Creole elite dominated politics and the economy long into the twentieth century.

While landed interests continued to prevail, the urban center of Buenos Aires grew restless under the rotating presidency that characterized the period of 1880–1900. Spurred by the development of radical politics in Europe, two urban opposition parties took shape: the Radical Party and the Socialists. As the influence of these parties grew, electoral reforms were forced on an unwilling landed oligarchy.

Brazil: From Kingdom to Republic

During the late colonial period, Brazil underwent the same centralizing reforms as the Spanish possessions. Although the Brazilian planters and urban Creoles resented these reforms, their fear of rebellion by the huge population of black slaves restrained them from openly demanding independence. As it happened, independence arrived through the relocation of the monarchy from Portugal to Brazil in the wake of Napoleon's invasion of Iberia in 1807. Brazil became a monarchically governed empire, striving for expansion into Spanish-speaking territories. When Brazil, under pressure from Britain, finally abolished slavery in 1888, the plantation oligarchy and allied military avenged itself by deposing the emperor, switching to a republican regime under the military in 1889. The regime became solidly federal, making it difficult for authoritarian rulers in the center to succeed.

Relocation of the Dynasty When Portugal's royal family took refuge in Brazil in 1807, it elevated the colony to the status of a coequal kingdom in union with Portugal but governed from Brazil after Napoleon's defeat in 1815. In 1820, rebels in Portugal adopted a liberal constitution, which demanded the return of

Brazil to colonial status as well as the transfer of the dynasty back to Portugal. The reigning king went back but left his son, Pedro I (r. 1822–1831), behind in Brazil. In 1822 Pedro proclaimed Brazil an independent state.

Pedro I's Authoritarianism Like the restoration monarchs of Europe in the early 1800s, Pedro adhered to his belief in divine right, which was incompatible with constitutionalism. Rejecting an attempt by the landed oligarchy to limit monarchical rule, he promulgated instead his own constitution in 1823, which concentrated most powers in his hands.

In reaction, in 1824 six northeastern provinces attempted to secede. They proclaimed the republican Federation of the Equator and demanded more central government support for the traditional northern sugar and cotton plantations, as British attempts to suppress the slave trade had increased the price for slaves, and the sugar planters could ill afford the higher prices. Given the close ties between Britain and Brazil, Pedro found it difficult to resist the British demands for the abolition of slavery. As a result, early signs of alienation between the Crown and the Creole planter elite crept in.

Ultimately, a succession crisis in Portugal in 1830 led to a conservative revolt against Pedro. In 1831 he abdicated, sailing back to Portugal. He left the throne to his five-year-old son, Pedro II (r. 1831–1889), who required a regent. The landowning elite exploited the opportunity of the temporarily weak monarchy by renewing its demands for federalism.

The Federalist Interlude In 1834 the government granted the provinces their own legislative assemblies, strengthening the provincial landholding elites with their various regional interests. It also abolished the council of state but created a national guard to suppress slave revolts and urban mobs. Some provinces revolted against these reforms, most dangerously in 1835 in Rio Grande do Sul, a southern province dominated by cattle owners who did not own many slaves and commanded military forces composed of gauchos. These owners established an independent republic that attracted many who were opposed to slavery and offered refuge to runaway slaves. In reaction to the coexistence of a weakened monarchy and an anti-slavery republic, the centralists reasserted themselves. In 1840 they proclaimed the 14-year-old Pedro II emperor and curbed the powers of the provincial assemblies. In 1845 they negotiated a return of Rio Grande do Sul to Brazil.

The End of Slavery During the 1830s and 1840s, Brazil made the transition from sugar to coffee as a major export commodity. Both crops required slave labor to be profitable, and when the British in 1849 authorized warships to enter Brazilian waters to intercept slave ships, the importation of slaves virtually ceased. Sugar, coffee, and cotton plantation owners began to think of ridding themselves of a monarchy that was unable to maintain the flow of slaves from overseas.

In the 1860s and 1870s, anti-slavery agitation grew as Brazilians became sensitive to their country being isolated in the world on the issue. While the government introduced a few changes, it fell to the provinces to take more serious steps. Planters encouraged their provinces to increase the flow of foreign immigrants, to be employed as wage labor on the coffee plantations. Finally, in 1888 the central government ended slavery.

The Coffee Boom Little changed in social relations after the abolition of slavery. The coffee growers, enjoying high international coffee prices and the benefits of infrastructure improvements, could afford low-wage hired labor. Although freed, blacks received no land, education, or urban jobs, scraping by with low wages on the coffee and sugar plantations. Economically, however, Brazil expanded its economy in the five years following 1888 as much as in the 70 years of slavery since independence.

The monarchy had been thoroughly discredited among the landowners and their military offshoot, the officer corps. During the War of Paraguay (1865–1870) the military had transformed itself into a professional body with its own sense of mission. By the 1880s, officers subscribed to the ideology of positivism coming from France (see Chapter 22). Positivists were liberal and republican in political orientation. In 1889, a revolt in the military supported by the Creole plantation oligarchy resulted in the abolition of the monarchy and the proclamation of a republic.

Two political tendencies emerged in the constituent assembly after the proclamation of the republic. The coffee interests favored federalism, with the right of the provinces to collect export taxes and maintain militias. The urban professional and intellectual interests supported a strong presidency with control over tariffs and import taxes as well as powers to use the federal military against provinces in cases of national emergency. At the end of the 1800s, the two tendencies resulted in a compromise, which produced provincial authoritarian rulers on the one hand but also regularly elected democratic-leaning presidents on the other.

At this time the government was strongly supportive of agricultural commodity exports, which yielded high profits and taxes until 1896, when overproduction of coffee resulted in diminishing returns. The state of São Paulo then regulated the sale of coffee on the world market through a state purchase scheme, which brought some stabilization to coffee production. At the same time, immigrants and foreign investors laid the foundation for **import-substitution industrialization**, beginning with textile and food-processing factories.

Import-substitution industrialization: The practice by which countries protect their economies by setting high tariffs and construct factories for the production of consumer goods (textiles, furniture, shoes, followed later by appliances, automobiles, electronics) and/or capital goods (steel, chemicals, machinery).

Independence and State Formation in Western and Northern South America

Compared to the viceroyalty of La Plata in the south, the Spanish viceroyalty of New Granada in northern South America had far fewer Creoles. For its struggle for independence to succeed, leaders had to seek support from the *pardos*, as the majority population of free black and mulatto craftspeople in the cities of Cartagena, Bogotá, and Caracas was called. Independence eventually came through the building of armies from Creole and pardo elements. The Amerindian population (half of the total of New Granada), consisting of farming villagers in the highlands and hunter-gatherer groups in the rainforest, remained largely apart. After independence, the Creoles dissolved their coalitions with the pardos and embraced the **caudillo** [caw-DEE-yoh] politics that were practiced in other parts of South America.

Caudillo: Term derived from Latin *capitellum* (little head); refers to authoritarian Latin American rulers who disregarded the constitutional limits to their powers. Authoritarianism was most pronounced in northern South America.

Bolívar the Liberator The hero of the independence struggle of northern South America from Spanish rule was Simón Bolívar (1783–1830), scion of a wealthy Creole plantation family in what is today Venezuela. After training in Spain as a military officer, he became part of the junta of Caracas in Venezuela. The junta was one of several others which declared their independence in 1811 under the name of United Provinces of Granada.

After several years of a futile civil war with Spanish loyalists, Bolívar had no choice in 1816 but to go into exile in Haiti. The loyalists had been reinforced in 1815 by an expeditionary force which the restored Spanish king Fernando VII (1813–1829) had sent. But eventually, Bolívar proved to be stronger, in part because of military contingents from Haiti's president in return for the promise of an end to slavery. In 1818, Bolívar was victorious, freed all slaves two years later, and in 1822 assumed the presidency of the republic of Gran Colombia, the successor state of the United Provinces of Granada comprising the later countries of Colombia, Venezuela, Ecuador, and Panama.

Liberation of the Slaves in Colombia. As a Creole growing up on his father's cacao plantation, worked by slaves, Bolívar was intimately familiar with slavery. During Bolívar's exile in the Republic of Haiti (1815–1816) President Alexandre Pétion gave him troops under the condition of emancipating the slaves of northern South America.

The Bolívar–San Martín Encounter After their defeat in Gran Colombia, Spanish troops continued to hold Upper Peru in the Andes. The Argentinean liberator José de San Martín and Bolívar met in 1822 to deliberate on how to drive the Spanish from Peru and to shape the future of an independent Latin America.

The content of their discussion never became public. San Martín, bitterly disappointed by endless disputes among different groups, apparently favored monarchical rule to bring stability to Latin America. Bolívar, it is believed, preferred republicanism and Creole oligarchical rule. Apart from their awareness of the need for ethnic and racial integration, there was not much common ground between the two independence leaders.

San Martín soon resigned from politics, having perhaps realized that the chances for a South American monarchy were slim. Bolívar more realistically envisioned the future of Latin America as that of relatively small independent republics, held together by strong, lifelong presidencies and hereditary senates. He implemented this vision in the 1825 constitution of independent Upper Peru, renamed Bolivia after him.

Ironically, in his own country of Gran Colombia, Bolívar was denied the role of strong president. Although he made himself a caudillo, he was unable to coax recalcitrant politicians into an agreement on a constitution for Gran Colombia similar to that of Bolivia. Bolívar died in 1830, and in 1831 Gran Colombia divided into its component parts of Colombia, Venezuela, Ecuador, and (later) Panama.

Caudillo Rule Independent Venezuela became the politically most turbulent Latin American republic. In Caracas, the capital, caudillos from the landowning Creole families displaced each other at a rapid rate. The main issue that kept rival factions at odds was federalism versus tighter central control, with at least one all-out war being fought over the issue during the 1860s.

Venezuela's neighboring countries followed a similar pattern of caudillo politics. Though enjoying longer periods of stability, Colombia—the name adopted in 1861 to replace that of New Granada—also saw a continuing struggle between federalists and centralizers. Panamanian rebels took advantage of the tumult to establish an independent state of Panama in 1903, supported by the United States. After independence, the administration of Theodore Roosevelt (1901–1909) concluded a treaty with the new country granting the United States control of land for the completion of the Panama Canal.

The Andean States As with the other new states in South America, it took decades for Peru, Bolivia, and Chile to work out territorial conflicts and complete their respective patterns of state formation. One of these conflicts was the War of the Pacific from 1879 to 1884, resulting in a victorious Chile annexing Peruvian and Bolivian lands. Most devastating for Peru was the destruction that Chilean troops wrought in southern Peru.

Political stability for several decades returned to Peru under the presidency of Nicolás de Piérola, who introduced a few reforms during his terms (1879–1881 and 1895–1899). The two most important were the stabilization of the monetary system and the professionalization of the army. As the presidency from this time until the 1920s was held by men from the upper landowning Creole class, this Peruvian period is often called the period of the "Aristocratic Republic."

Independence and Political Development in the North: Mexico

In contrast to the central Spanish colony of New Granada, the viceroyalty of New Spain (Mexico and Mesoamerica) had few inhabitants of African descent and large numbers of indigenous Americans. Therefore, mestizos and Amerindians had prominent roles in the political development of the nineteenth century. As in the other viceroyalties, however, conservative landowning Creoles were dominant in the political process. Only toward the end of the 1800s did urban white, mestizo, and Amerindian residents acquire a voice. Landless rural laborers entered the political stage in the early twentieth century, during the Mexican Revolution.

The Mexican Uprising In 1810, Miguel Hidalgo y Costilla (1753–1811), the son of a Creole hacienda estate administrator and his Creole wife, declared his loyalty to the deposed king of Spain, Fernando VII, and launched a movement in opposition to the viceroyalty and its colonial military. A churchman since his youth, Hidalgo was broadly educated, well versed in Enlightenment literature, conversant in Nahuatl, and on the margins of strict Catholicism. As a young adult, he became a parish priest and devoted himself to creating employment opportunities for Amerindians in a province southeast of Mexico City.

Under the leadership of Hidalgo, thousands of poor Creoles, mestizos, and Amerindians marched on Guanajuato (in south-central Mexico). Initially, they were successful in defeating the Spanish troops marching against them, but they were indiscriminate in their looting and killing of both Spaniards and Creoles. Hidalgo, shocked by the violence, called off an attack on Mexico City, and the rebellion was eventually defeated in 1811. Colonial Spanish forces ultimately captured and executed Hidalgo.

Land and Liberty. This enormous mural by Diego Rivera (1886–1957), in the National Palace in Mexico City, shows Father Hidalgo above the Mexican eagle, flanked by other independence fighters. Above them are Emiliano Zapata, Pancho Villa, and other heroes of the Revolution of 1910. The other parts of the mural show historical scenes from the Spanish conquest to the twentieth century.

War of Independence After the defeat, associates of Hidalgo failed to make a comeback in the heartland around Mexico City. Here, royalists intent on preserving the union between Spain and Mexico after the return of Fernando VII to power in 1813 remained supreme. In 1813, Hidalgist nationalist rebels adopted a program for independence that envisioned a constitutional government, abolished slavery, and declared all native-born inhabitants of New Spain "Americans." A year later they promulgated a constitution providing for a strong legislature and a weak executive. Both program and constitution, however, still awaited the conclusion of the civil war between nationalists and royalists for their implementation.

The war ended in 1821 with Mexico's independence, based on a compromise between the nationalist Vicente Guerrero (1782–1831) and the royalist Agustín de Iturbide (1783–1824). According to the compromise, Mexico was to become an independent constitutional "empire" (in view of New Spain extending to Mesoamerica), give full citizenship rights to all inhabitants regardless of race and ethnicity, and adhere to Catholicism.

Iturbide became Mexico's first ruler, with the title "emperor," but abdicated in 1823 after a military uprising. By that time, Mexico was no longer an empire, having lost its Mesoamerican provinces. With a new constitution in 1824, Mexico became a republic. As in other parts of Latin America during the period of early independence, politics remained unstable, pitting federalists and centralists against each other. Centralists eventually triumphed and, for a long period under the caudillo Antonio López de Santa Anna (in office 1833–1836 and 1839–1845), maintained authoritarian rule (See Map 23.1).

Northern Mexico and the Comanches The nominal northern territories of Mexico—Texas, New Mexico, and California—were inhabited by numerous Native American peoples, among whom the Comanches were the most powerful. They had acquired horses during the Pueblo Revolt (1680) against Spain, and as migrants, adapted more readily to horse-breeding and contraband firearms than other, more settled Native American peoples.

In the course of the mid-1700s, the Comanches built an empire from the Arkansas River to just north of San Antonio. They raided into New Mexico and maintained a flourishing trade of horses, cattle, bison hides, and enslaved war captives, including blacks, on their borders. In the last decades of Spanish

Revolutionary Women. Women, such as these *soldaderas* taking rifle practice, played many significant roles in the Mexican Revolution, 1910–1920.

rule, colonial reformers dispatched troops to check the Comanche expansion. But during the war of Mexican independence, Comanche raids resumed and wiped out the recent gains.

Northern Immigration To make the northern borderlands more secure against the Comanches, beginning in the early 1820s Mexico supported immigration from the United States. At the same time, the United States entered a period of growth. Settlement of the formerly French Ohio and Mississippi valleys moved quickly. Demand

MAP 23.1 **The New Nation-States of Latin America and the Caribbean, 1831**

for American cotton in British and American factories drove expansion into Alabama, Mississippi, Louisiana, and Arkansas. Cotton exhausted the soil, and the availability of cheap land made it more efficient to abandon depleted lands and push the realm of "King Cotton" ever westward.

Many US citizens emigrated to Mexico, especially the Mexican province of Texas, to take advantage of its generous land policy and autonomy. While Mexico had outlawed slavery, most slave owners who migrated to Texas ignored these restrictions. The violation of the antislavery laws and the swelling numbers of immigrants to Texas alarmed the Mexican national government by the 1830s.

The US–Mexico War In 1836, the Mexican president Antonio López de Santa Anna led some 4,000 troops against the militias maintained by the Texans. At first, these troops were successful, decimating Texan militiamen and US volunteers defending the Alamo, a fort near San Antonio. But then Texan forces defeated Santa Anna, and the state declared its independence (1836). Mexico refused to recognize Texas, and nine years later Texas opted for the security of union with the United States. It settled with the Comanches in 1844 for an end to the raiding.

The other northern territories of Mexico had also suffered debilitating devastations from Comanche raids. As a result, the government found it impossible to defend itself effectively in 1846 when the United States declared war on Mexico over a Texas border dispute. Within two years, Santa Anna's troops were defeated, and Mexico was forced to give up over half of its territory (see Map 23.2).

The French Interlude in Mexico Santa Anna fell from power, and in 1857 liberals introduced a new constitution that reaffirmed federalism, guaranteed individual liberties, and separated church and state. The conservatives in Mexico detested this new constitution and waged the "Reform War" (1857–1861) to abolish it. They lost, and the liberals elected Benito Juárez (1861–1864) president, the first Amerindian to accede to the office.

Juárez soon discovered that Mexico's financial reserves were depleted, obliging him to suspend payment on the state debt. International reaction was swift, with British, Spanish, and French forces seizing the customs house in the port city of Veracruz in 1861, making a mockery of the US Monroe Doctrine of 1823, according to which no foreign intervention would be tolerated in the Americas. Not wishing to violate the pan-American opposition to European intervention with a prolonged occupation, Britain and Spain withdrew their forces quickly.

MAP 23.2 Mexico's Loss of Territory to the United States, 1824–1854

The French, however, stayed. Louis-Napoleon III Bonaparte, the self-declared emperor, seized on the debt issue and set in motion an ambitious plan of imposing a pliable ruler in the country. In 1862, taking advantage of the American Civil War, he provided military backing to the Austrian prince Maximilian, who installed himself as the emperor of Mexico (1864–1867).

With the defeat of the Confederate states in the US Civil War in April 1865, however, Maximilian's position became precarious. In 1866, aided by the US government, an uprising broke out in Mexico. Maximilian was cut off from any hope of quick support from France. The liberal forces defeated and executed him by firing squad in 1867.

Díaz's Long Peace Peace arrived with the withdrawal of most US government troops from Texas and the rise of Mexico's next caudillo, Porfirio Díaz (in office 1876–1880 and 1884–1911). This period also coincided with the defeat of the last Amerindians north of the border and the settlement and development of the American West.

Like his contemporary, President Jose Balmeceda of Chile, Díaz favored infrastructural and industrial development. Rail, telegraph, and telephone systems were laid; textile factories and heavy industries were set up; oil was produced in quantity; and agricultural improvements were made. Overall, the economy expanded by 6 percent annually during the Porfiriato, as the period of Díaz's government was called.

Much of Díaz's conservative stability was built on the faction of Creole landowners through whom Díaz had come to power. This faction had grown through the addition of groups of technocrat administrators (*científicos*), financiers, land

The Execution of Emperor Maximilian of Mexico, June 19, 1867. Édouard Manet has been characterized as the "inventor of modernity," not only for his technique but for the way he portrayed events, even significant political events, in a calm and composed manner. The soldiers who dispatch the hapless emperor come across as cool and professional—what they are doing is all in a day's work.

speculators, and industrialists. The Porfiriato regime was marked by corruption: officials sought self-enrichment while disregarding the law and even resorting to physical violence.

The number of critics among the urban and professional classes rose steadily, however, as they found themselves excluded from economic or even political participation. They demanded a return to the constitution of 1857, but they were arrested, beaten, and exiled as the Porfiriato became increasingly repressive.

Critics also arose among the working classes, who were prohibited from forming trade unions and carrying out strikes. In the early 1900s, an aging Díaz faced an increasingly restless urban population.

The countryside, where the large majority of Mexicans still lived and worked, was just as restless. Ever since colonial times, there had been a profound division between Creole estate (*hacienda*) owners and mestizo and Amerindian rural dwellers. For most of the 1800s, the economy of the countryside had been typified by self-sufficiency: nearly everything was produced and consumed there, because transportation costs were prohibitive.

But with the construction of the railroad system under Díaz, transportation costs plummeted. Hacienda landlords could now produce crops for the market, and they appropriated farmland from Amerindian villagers who could not show legal title to the land.

The Early Mexican Revolution Although the elections of 1910 had once more been manipulated in favor of Díaz, the president had declared in 1908 that he would like to have an opposition party in Mexico. Liberals, encouraged, had found a candidate.

This candidate was Francisco Madero (1873–1913), who was committed to the social justice proclaimed in the 1857 constitution. Madero refused to recognize the election and called on the middle classes, working classes, and peasants to rise up against Díaz. By mentioning the right of workers to organize in trade unions and of peasants to receive their own plots of land, he opened the floodgates for revolution.

Among the first to respond was Francisco "Pancho" Villa (1878–1923), a muleteer-cum-cattle rustler who led a rebellion in the northern state of Chihuahua. Another rebel leader was Emiliano Zapata (1879–1919), head of a village in the state of Morelos in south-central Mexico, who had begun with his *campesinos* (tenant farmers, laborers, and village peasants) to occupy sugar plantations and distribute plantation land to them. Victories of Villa and Zapata against federal troops persuaded Díaz to step down in May 1911 and leave for exile in France.

Madero was sworn in as the new president, but it was soon evident that his vision for a constitutional revolution was incompatible with the economic revolution pursued by Zapata. Madero was driven into the arms of Porfiriato officers who, supported by the US government, were nervous about the events in Mexico. The officers, however, deposed and executed him in February 1913.

The Later Revolution Power in Mexico was now disputed between the Porfiriato reactionaries in Mexico City and the Constitutionalists (those faithful to the liberal constitution of 1857) in the wealthy states along the US border. Constitutionalists were opposed to land distribution, but they needed more troops to overthrow the reactionaries. The Constitutionalists, Pancho Villa, and

Emiliano Zapata and Fellow Revolutionaries in Mexico City, June 4, 1911. Shortly after the fall of Díaz, his opponents Madero, Villa, and Zapata (seated, second from left) entered Mexico City in triumph, to celebrate the end of his regime. But already by June 8, Zapata and Madero disagreed on the issue of land reform. The moderate Madero wanted to halt it; Zapata wanted to continue it in his state of Morelos. This disagreement, among other internal rifts in the revolutionary camp, was responsible for the revolution dragging on to 1920.

Emiliano Zapata, therefore, forged an alliance that made Venustiano Carranza (1859–1920), from a wealthy but liberal Creole family, their leader. Together, they ended the reactionary regime in Mexico City in July 1914.

Once in power, the Constitutionalists dissolved the reactionary federal army but then broke apart over the issue of land reform. Villa and Zapata, at the head of the pro-reform majority, entered Mexico City but failed to form a functional central government. The working classes and their union representatives threw their support to Álvaro Obregón (1880–1928), a rising commander among the Constitutionalists who had been opposed to Díaz. After the departure of Villa and Zapata for their home states, Obregón entered Mexico City in February 1915.

The Constitutionalists remained deeply divided between a policy of a constitutional revolution under a strong central government with a modest land and labor reform program and a policy of agrarian revolutions in autonomous states. The supporters of the constitutional revolution gained the initiative when Obregón succeeded in driving Villa from power. Carranza followed up by having Zapata eliminated.

Carranza, in office as president of Mexico from 1915 to 1920, removed agrarian revolutionaries from their states and villages and ended all land distributions. But Obregón, more sympathetic to labor and land reform, challenged Carranza for the presidency in the next elections. With the support of the Constitutional army he forced Carranza to surrender and ended the Mexican Revolution late in 1920.

The Mexican Revolution expanded the constitutional process to the urban middle class, workers, farmers, and villagers by bringing about real social and economic gains for men and women other than the landowners. All this happened at tremendous human cost, but by 1920 the Mexican nation was much more cohesive than it had been a century earlier.

Latin American Society and Economy in the Nineteenth Century

Independence meant both disruptions and continuities in the economy as well as in politics. In Spanish and Portuguese America, five colonial regions eventually became 21 independent republics, organized around the pattern of constitutionalism. Deep divisions persisted between the small landowning elites and the urban masses, and the Creole landowning elite made participation of the urban classes in the constitutional process increasingly difficult. When trade with Europe resumed, this elite was primarily interested in the export of mineral and agricultural commodities, from which it reaped the most benefits (see Map 23.3).

MAP 23.3 **The Economy of Latin America and the Caribbean, ca. 1900**

Rebuilding Societies and Economies

Reconstruction in the independent Spanish-speaking republics and the Brazilian monarchy took several decades. It was only by mid-century that Latin America had overcome the aftereffects of the wars of independence.

Patterns Up Close

Slave Rebellions in Cuba and Brazil

Blacks had gained little from the American and French Revolutions, and the pattern of brutal exploitation continued in the Americas. Not surprisingly, therefore, blacks sought to emulate the example of Haiti's successful slave revolt during the first half of the 1800s. However, none of those subsequent revolts were any more successful than previous revolts had been in the 1700s, as a look at rebellions in Cuba and Brazil during the first half of the nineteenth century shows.

In Cuba, the decline of sugar production in Haiti during the revolution encouraged the expansion of plantations and the importation of African slaves. As previously in Haiti, a diversified eighteenth-century society of whites, free mulattoes, and blacks, as well as urban and rural black slaves, was transformed into a heavily

Slave Revolt Aboard Ship. Rebellions aboard ship, such as the famous 1839 mutiny aboard the *Amistad* shown here, were common occurrences. The *Amistad* was engaged in intra-American slave trafficking, and the slaves overpowered the crew shortly after embarkation in Cuba. After protracted legal negotiations, the slaves were eventually freed and returned to Africa.

After Independence The achievement of independence in the 1820s brought an end to Spain's mercantilist monopoly, weak as it had been. The Latin American republics were free to buy or sell and to borrow money anywhere in the world. Initially, however, for Latin Americans the freedom to trade was more hope than reality. Capital had fled the continent and left behind uncultivated estates and flooded mines. The Catholic Church held huge, uncollectable debts. In many areas taxes could not be collected. Troops helped themselves to payment through plunder. On average, it took until around 1850 for Latin America to fully recover.

Constitutional Nationalism and Society The Creoles were in many countries the leaders in the wars of independence, and the most powerful among them were large landowners. Independence did not produce much change in agrarian relations; landowners of self-sufficient estates and plantations continued to employ tenant farmers and slaves. Their interpretation of constitutionalism tended toward *caudillismo*—that is, the same kind of authoritarian and paternalistic form of action that they practiced on their estates.

The majority of the Creoles, however, were not landowners but people who made their money in the cities. They were urban administrators, professionals, craftspeople, and laborers. Their leaders, ardent constitutional nationalists,

African-born plantation slave society. The black freedman José Antonio Aponte (ca. 1756–1812), a militiaman and head of the Yoruba confraternity in Havana, led an abortive revolt in 1812 that drew support from both sectors. In the subsequent revolts of 1825, 1835, and 1843, the urban element was less evident. Authorities and planters unleashed a campaign of sweeping arrests of free blacks and mulattoes that cut the urban–rural link once and for all.

Brazil, like Cuba, also benefited from the collapse of sugar production on Haiti. It expanded its plantation sector and imported slaves from Africa. But here distrust divided those born in Africa from Brazilian-born slaves, freedmen, and mulattoes. Many freedmen and mulattoes served in the militias that the authorities used to suppress the revolts. Furthermore, in contrast to the island of Cuba, plantation slaves could run away more easily to independent settlements in the Brazilian interior, from where revolts were more easily organized than in cities or on plantations.

Two urban revolts of the period were remarkable for their exceptional mix of insurgents. The first was the Tailor's Rebellion of 1798 in Salvador, Bahia's capital. Freedmen, mulattoes, and white craftspeople cooperated against the Creole oligarchy. The second was the Muslim uprising of 1835, organized by African-born freedmen as well as slaves who had been educated as Islamic clerics in West Africa before their enslavement.

Questions

- Do the slave rebellions in Cuba and Brazil in the early nineteenth century confirm or complicate the pattern of slave revolutions that was manifested first in Haiti?
- What role did geography play in the success or failure of a revolution?

tended toward political and economic liberalism. In many countries they were joined by mestizos, mulattoes, and black freedmen. The main issue dividing the conservatives and liberals in the early years of independence was the extent of voting rights: conservatives sought to limit the vote to a minority of males through literacy and property requirements, while liberals wanted to extend it to all males. No influential group considered extending voting rights to women.

Political Divisions Once independence was won, distrust between the two groups set in, and the political consensus fell apart. Accordingly, landed constitutional conservatives restricted voting rights, to the detriment of the urban constitutional liberals. Nevertheless, the expansion of constitutionalism from the landowning oligarchy to larger segments of the population remained a goal for many, especially urban intellectuals and political activists.

Split over State–Church Relations Conservatives and liberals were especially divided over the relationship between state and church. Initially, Catholicism remained the national religion for all, and education and extensive property remained under church control, as guaranteed by the constitutions.

Nevertheless, the new republics ended the powers of the Inquisition and claimed the right to name bishops. At the behest of Spain, however, the pope left bishoprics empty rather than agreeing to this new form of lay investiture. In fact, Rome would not even recognize the independence of the Latin American nations until the mid-1830s. The conflict was aggravated by the church's focus on its institutional rather than pastoral role.

This hostility of the church was thus one of the factors that in the mid-1800s contributed to a swing back to liberalism, beginning with Colombia in 1849. Many countries adopted a formal separation between church and state and introduced secular educational systems. But the state–church issue remained bitter, especially in Mexico, Guatemala, Ecuador, and Venezuela, where it was often at the center of political shifts between liberals and conservatives.

Economic Recovery Given the shifts of leadership between conservatives and liberals during the period of recovery after independence (ca. 1820–1850), the reconstruction of a coherent fiscal system to support the governments was difficult to accomplish. For example, governments often resorted to taxation of trade, even if this interfered with declared policies of free trade.

This maneuvering had little effect on the domestic economy, which represented the great bulk of economic activities in Latin America. Grain production on large estates and small farms had escaped the turbulence of the independence war and recovery periods. The distribution of marketable surpluses declined, however, given the new internal borders in Latin America with their accompanying tariffs and export taxes. Self-sufficiency agriculture, and the local economies relying on it, thus remained largely unchanged throughout the 1800s.

The crafts workshops, especially for textiles, suffered from the arrival of cheap British factory-produced cottons. Their impact, however, remained relatively limited to coastal areas. Although there was an awareness in most countries of the benefits of factories, using domestic resources, and linking the agricultural sector to modern industrial development, the economic necessity of developing a manufacturing industry was not demonstrated until later in the nineteenth century.

Export-Led Growth

The pursuit of a policy of commodity exports—export-led growth—from about 1850 led to rises in the standard of living for many Latin Americans. The industrializing countries in Europe and North America were consumers of Latin American minerals as well as its tropical agricultural products. Productivity was limited, however, by a chronic labor shortage.

Raw Materials and Cash Crops Mining and agricultural cash crop production recovered gradually, so that by the 1850s nearly all Latin American governments had adopted export-led economic growth as their basic policy. Mexican and Peruvian silver production became strong again, although the British adoption of the gold standard in 1821 imposed limits on silver exports. Peru found a partial replacement for silver with guano, which was used as an organic fertilizer and as a source of nitrates for explosives. Chile benefited from guano, nitrate, and copper exports, of crucial importance during the second Industrial Revolution in Germany and the United States.

In other Latin American countries, tropical and subtropical cash crops defined export-led economic growth during the mid-1800s. In Brazil, Colombia, and Costa Rica, coffee growing redefined the agricultural sector. In Argentina, the production of jerked (dried) beef refashioned the ranching economy. Cuba, which remained a Spanish colony until 1898, profited from the relocation of sugarcane plantations from the mainland and Caribbean islands after the British outlawing of the slave trade (1807) and slavery itself (1834) as well as the Latin American wars of independence (1810–1826).

However, cane sugar had a limited future, given the rise of beet sugar production in Europe. While minerals and cash crops were excellent for export-led economic growth, competition on the world market increased during the 1800s, and thus there was ultimately a ceiling, which was reached in the 1890s.

Broadening of Exports With a focus on mineral and agricultural exports, Latin American governments responded quickly to the increased market opportunities resulting from the Industrial Revolution in Great Britain, the European continent, and the United States. Luxuries from tropical Latin America joined sugar after 1850 in becoming affordable mass consumer items in the industrialized countries. This commodity diversification met not only the broadened demand of the second Industrial Revolution but also the demand for consumer goods among the newly affluent middle classes.

Since the choice among minerals and crops was limited, however, most nations remained wedded to one commodity only. Only two, Argentina and Peru, were able to diversify. They were more successful at distributing their exports over the four main industrial markets of Great Britain, Germany, France, and the United States. Given its own endowments and under the conditions of world trade in the second half of the nineteenth century, the continent's trade was relatively well diversified.

The prices of all Latin American commodities fluctuated substantially during the second half of the nineteenth century, in contrast to imported manufactured goods, which became cheaper over time. In fact, Brazil's government was so concerned about fluctuating coffee prices in the 1890s that it regulated the amount of coffee offered on the world market, carefully adjusting production to keep market prices relatively stable.

Rising Living Standards In the period from the middle of the 1800s to the eve of World War I, Latin American governments were successful with their choice of export-led growth as their consensus policy. Living standards rose, as measured in gross domestic product (GDP). At various times during 1850–1900, between five and eight Latin American countries kept pace with living standards in the industrialized countries. Thus, although many politicians were aware that at some point their countries would have to industrialize in addition to relying on commodity export growth, they kept their faith in exports as the engine for improved living standards right up to World War I.

Labor and Immigrants As in the industrialized countries, the profitability of exports was achieved by keeping wages low. Latin America experienced high population increases during the 1800s, although the population remained small in comparison to the populations of Europe, Africa, and Asia. The increases were not large enough to alter the land–person ratio, and the high demand for labor continued during the 1800s. This demand was the reason why the institution of forced labor—revolving labor duties (*mit'a*) among Amerindians in the Andes and slavery—had come into existence in the first place.

Mit'a and slavery continued during the 1800s, liberal constitutionalism notwithstanding, in a number of countries. Even where forced labor was abolished, low wages continued. One would have expected wages to rise rapidly, given the continuing conditions of labor shortage and land availability. Mine operators and landowners, however, were reluctant to raise wages because they feared for the competitiveness of their commodities on the world market. Labor shortages were so severe that governments resorted to measures of selective mass immigration in order to enlarge the labor pool.

Typical examples of selective immigration were coolies (from Urdu *kuli*, hireling)—that is, indentured laborers recruited from India and China. During 1847–1874, nearly half a million Indians traveled to various European colonies in the Caribbean. Similarly, 235,000 Chinese came to Peru, Cuba, and Costa Rica, working in guano pits and silver mines, on sugar and cotton plantations, and later on railroads. Only about 10 percent of the coolies returned home. Coolie migration to Latin America was a part of the pattern of massive migration streams across the world that typified the nineteenth century (see Map 23.4).

Immigration to Latin America from Europe was more regular, and on a much bigger scale. In Argentina, Uruguay, Brazil, and Chile, Italians and Spaniards settled in large numbers from around 1870 on. Most immigrants settled in cities, and Buenos Aires became the first city on the continent with more than a million people. Only here did a semiregular labor market develop, with rising urban and rural wages prior to World War I. Elsewhere in Latin America, governments, beholden to large landowners, feared the rise of cities with immigrant laborers who did not share their interests. Therefore, they opposed mass immigration.

Self-Sufficiency Agriculture Except for Argentina, Chile, and Uruguay, the levels of commodity exports did not rise sufficiently to reduce the size of the rural

Dining Hall for Recently Arrived Immigrants, Buenos Aires. Immigrants, all male, and more than likely all Spanish and Italian, rub shoulders sometime around 1900 in a dining hall in Buenos Aires set up for newly arrived immigrants. By 1914, 20 percent of the population of Argentina had been born in Spain and another 20 percent in Italy.

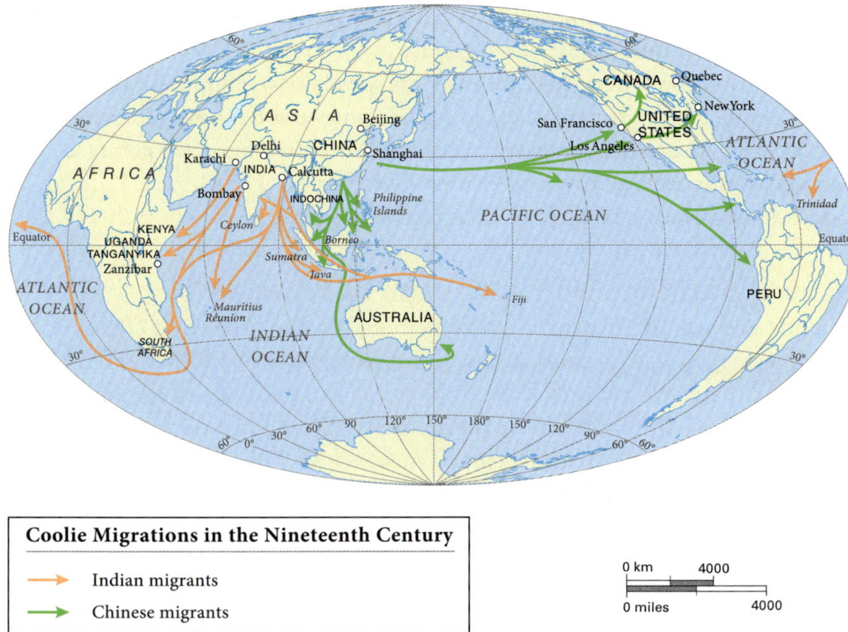

MAP 23.4 Non-Western Migrations in the Nineteenth Century

labor force engaged in self-sufficiency farming—a major condition for improved living standards. On the eve of World War I, between two-thirds and half of the laborers in most Latin American countries were still employed as tenant farmers or farmhands on large estates. Export-led growth—even though it looked like an effective economic driver—did not have much of a transformative effect on the rural masses in most countries.

Governments paid greater attention to the improvement of rural infrastructures from about 1870 onward, with the development of railroads. Almost everywhere, they looked to direct foreign investment. The foreign investors or consortiums built these railroads primarily for the transportation of commodities to ports. Many self-sufficiency farmers and even landlords, therefore, received little encouragement to produce more food staples for urban markets inland. Overall, the Latin American railroad network represented only about one-fifth to one-third of that in other Western developing settler countries.

Factories Until about 1870, the handicrafts sector met the demands of the rural and low-earning urban populations. This sector failed in most parts of the world during the 1800s and 1900s to mechanize itself and establish a modern factory system. Latin America was no exception. Most crafts shops were based on family labor, unconnected to the landowning elite and deemed too small by lending banks. There was no path from workshops to factories.

However, even entrepreneurial investors interested in building factories were hampered in their efforts. They had little chance of success prior to the appearance of public utilities in the 1880s, providing water during the dry season and electricity as an energy source, in the absence of high-quality coal in most parts of Latin America. Even then, the risk of engaging in manufacturing, requiring long-term strategies with no or low profits, was so great that the typical founders of factories were not Creoles but European immigrants.

In Argentina and Chile, these immigrants saved the start-up capital necessary to launch small but modern textile, food-processing, and beverage factories. Prior to World War I, the only country that took the step from consumer goods to capital goods (goods for building and equipping factories) was Mexico. Full capital goods industrialization had to await the postwar period.

Culture, Family, and the Status of Women

Economic growth and urbanization contributed to the growth of constitutionalist modernity in Latin America. But the absence of industrialization until the end of the nineteenth century slowed the transformation of society and its cultural institutions. The influence of the Catholic Church remained pervasive. In the second half of the nineteenth century, however, with the diversification of the urban population, the idea of separating church and state gained adherents, with legal consequences for social institutions.

Role of the Church In most countries, repeated attempts by governments after independence to reduce the role of the Catholic Church in society remained unsuccessful. In a number of civil codes, women's rights in inheritance and property control improved, but overall, husbands retained their patriarchal rights over their families. Typically, they were entitled to control the family budget, contractual engagements, choice of husbands for their daughters, and the residence of their unmarried daughters. Only after the middle of the nineteenth century did the influence of the Catholic Church diminish sufficiently to allow legislation for secular marriages and divorce in a number of countries.

Family Relations In Mexico and South America, despite the long-standing proverb *El hombre en la calle, la mujer en la casa* ("Men in the street, women in the home"), it was often the case that the two spheres were intermingled. In urban areas, women frequently ran shops, managed markets, were proprietors of cantinas, and performed skilled and unskilled jobs, particularly in the textile and food trades. In rural areas, farm work was often shared by men and women.

As in Europe and North America, there was a remarkably high level of widowhood and spinsterhood. In areas where the predominant form of employment was dangerous—mining, for example—the incidence of widowhood was very high. Widows often could not or chose not to remarry, especially if they had relatives to fall back on or were left an income. Many middle-class women chose not to marry at all.

Both of these conditions were common enough that by one estimate, one-third of all the households in Mexico City in the early nineteenth century were headed by women. Widows were entitled to their dowries and half of the community property, while boys and girls received equal portions of the inheritance. Thus, despite society's pressures to marry and raise children, many women did not marry or, after becoming widowed, remained single. In this sense, they achieved a considerable degree of autonomy in a male-dominated society.

The Visual and Literary Arts The trend in nineteenth-century culture under the aegis of Spanish and Portuguese influences after independence was toward "indigenization," an attempt to break away from European art and literary influences. Along with attempts to form national and regional styles of their own, many countries also engaged in art as a nation-building exercise, celebrating new national heroes or famous historic events through portraiture and landscape painting. Finally, there were periodic engagements with popular or folk arts in celebration of regional uniqueness.

In literature, an indigenous style developed, called *criollo* for its inception and popularity in the Creole class. Literature often turned to themes befitting countries trying to establish themselves as nations with distinct historic pasts and great future potential. In some cases, critique of the present was the order of the day.

Putting It All Together

Today, although political stability is much greater, many parts of Latin America are still poor and under-industrialized. Were Latin American elites, therefore, wrong to engage in a pattern of export-led growth through mineral and agricultural commodities? And did they collude with elites in the industrial countries to maneuver the continent into permanent dependence on the latter? Indeed, most scholars in the twentieth century answered the question in the affirmative and wrote the history of the 1800s in condemnatory tones. They called their analysis "dependency theory."

Many contemporary historians, however, compare Latin America not with the United States or western Europe but with the settler colonies of South Africa, Australia, and New Zealand or the old empires of the Middle East and Asia. In these comparisons, Latin America does not appear to have been any more dependent on the industrializing countries than the latter were on Latin America.

Dependence increased only at the very end of the 1800s, when industrial countries like the United States and Britain began to make significant capital investments. It was then that foreign companies, such as those that owned railroads in Nicaragua and Honduras, succeeded in exploiting and controlling production and export. The question we may need to ask, then, is not why Latin America failed to industrialize in the 1800s but rather whether Latin America made the right decision when it opted for export-led growth up to about 1890. Did such a choice represent a "third way" toward economic growth, separate from industrial capitalism and attempts to keep economies closed off from the vagaries of world trade? Perhaps it did.

Review and Relate

Thinking Through Patterns

Examine the ways historians approach the big questions of this chapter.

> Which factors in the complex ethnic and social structures of Latin America were responsible for the emergence of authoritarian politicians?

Like the revolutions of the United States and France in the late 1700s and early 1800s, Latin America's independence movements (1810–1824) did not extend the constitutional revolutions beyond a small number of elite property owners. The dominant class of large landlords and plantation owners was conservative and did not favor land reform for the benefit of small farmers. Urban professionals and craftspeople, divided in many places by ethnicity, did not share interests that allowed them to provide an effective opposition to the landed class. Landowning and plantation interests thus protected themselves through authoritarian caudillo politics and sought to keep the opposition weak.

➤ Why did Latin American countries, after achieving independence, opt for a continuation of mineral and agricultural commodity exports?

➤ How do the social and economic structures of this period continue to affect the course of Latin America today?

In colonial times, Latin America sent its mineral and agricultural commodities to Europe. When it acquired its independence and Europe industrialized during the 1800s, these commodities became even more important, and the continent opted for a pattern of export-led development. This meant the systematic increase of mineral and agricultural commodity exports, with rising living standards not only for those who profited directly from the exports but also for many in the urban centers. But even with rising living standards, it became clear by the turn of the century that a supplementary policy of industrialization had to be pursued.

Many countries in Latin America are barely richer than they were in the 1800s. Even though industry, mineral and commodity exports, and services expanded in urban centers in the early part of the twentieth century, poor farmers with low incomes continued to be a drag on development. This phenomenon still characterizes many parts of Latin America today.

Against the Grain

Consider this as a counterpoint to the main patterns examined in this chapter.

Resistance in Brazil's Backcountry

- What does Canudos demonstrate to us today, a century later in the march of modernity, where traditional apocalypticism is still with us (in the form of the Islamic State or ISIS) and where modernity is facing its own apocalypse (in the form of global warming)?
- Is there a perspective from which to justify the annihilation of Canudos? And if not, why not?

Not long after ending the monarchy and adopting a republican constitution, Brazil was shaken by an extraordinary display of military incompetence. Four campaigns were necessary in 1896 and 1897 to come to terms with the perceived insurrection of the 35,000 inhabitants of the town of Canudos [kan-OO-dos], in the arid backcountry (*sertão*) of Bahia in the northeast. The town had been recently founded on the land of an abandoned ranch (*fazenda*), along a river that carried enough water for some modest self-sufficiency agriculture. In spite of its limitations, Canudos rose to be the second most populous population center after the capital of Salvador.

The founder of Canudos was Antônio Vicente Mendes Maciel (1830-1897) a *pardo* (mixed blood) native of the sertão. His father was a self-made small businessman from a family of cattle herders. Maciel received a good primary education, but at home things went badly: His mother died when he was six and his remarried father succumbed to drink. When his father died, Maciel was forced to liquidate the family business.

Unable to find regular employment and unhappily married twice, Maciel became a traveling peddler making the rounds of weekly markets. Here he met priests and self-appointed preachers. By the 1870s he was a preacher himself—austere, emaciated, hiring himself out for church and cemetery repairs. Maciel's spellbinding sermons were fiery invectives against sin, immorality, depravity, and ostentatious living under the threat of God's Final Judgment soon to come. They were mainstream Catholic in content, to judge from the prayer book and sermon manual he used, even if the imminence of Judgment Day was not central to Brazilian Catholicism.

The Church, constantly short of priests, who preferred the comforts of the coast over the hardships in the interior, was not necessarily opposed to wandering "blessed ones" (*beatos*). But since they often trailed considerable crowds of followers, the coastal hierarchy watched them with some suspicion, as did the archbishop of Bahia, who already in 1882 issued a circular warning against Maciel, now called by his followers "the Counselor" (*o Conseilhero*). Similarly, politicians in Bahia—plantation owners who had to reorganize their patronage flocks after the declaration of the republic—divided into pragmatic and distrustful camps vis-à-vis Maciel with his large following.

The distrustful camp gained the upper hand in 1893 when the Counselor held a bonfire of bulletin boards announcing new municipal taxes. The police opened fire on the crowd and some armed followers of the Counselor returned the fire. After retreating to Canudos, where he was well-protected by the surrounding terrain, the Counselor devoted himself to the building of his community of resolute believers awaiting the end of the world. Three years later, when a businessman belonging to the hostile camp refused to release a prepaid consignment of timber to Canudos and the Counselor sent armed followers to collect it, open war ensued. The war ended with the near complete annihilation of the town and its inhabitants.

From the national perspective in Rio de Janeiro, which was republican, progressive, and transactional, Maciel and his followers were backward religious fanatics holding up the march of modernity. From the provincial perspective of Salvador, they were rustic rebels interfering with traditional patronage politics. Brazilians are still today divided over this traumatic event.

Key Terms

Caudillo 556

Import-substitution industrialization 556

Southern Cone 552

Learn more with this chapter's digital tools, including the Oxford Insight Study Guide, at http://www.oup.com/he/vonsivers4e. Please see the Further Resources section at the back of the book for additional readings and suggested websites.

PATTERNS OF EVIDENCE | Sources for Chapter 23

SOURCE 23.1

Josefina Bachellery, "The Education of Women"

1842

The document below belongs to the epistolary genre and appears as a letter addressed by the French headmistress of a boarding school, Josefina Bachellery, and a young Mexican woman, Angélica. Bachellery wrote extensively on women's education in France during the mid-nineteenth century, demanding the establishment of secondary schools and teachers' colleges for women. When the ideology of liberalism rose in Mexico after its defeat in the Mexican-American War (1846–1848), female secondary education, as well teachers' training, became critical social issues.

Letter to Angélica

As you have known for some time, my dear Angélica, I have developed the project of bringing together my ideas on the education of the fair sex, and regarding an issue as serious as it is fruitful, I have thought long and hard, both for pleasure and out of obligation, with the desire to publish some new reflections.

I have taken account of the immensity of such a large undertaking, and if I have decided to confront the subject, it has been to leave my daughters and yours the results of a long career in teaching, in which so many times you have said to me that a special vocation had been given me.

. . .

Until now, and you have seen it, Angélica, the education of women has not been considered for its own merit, but only from the limited and incomplete perspective of private life, and Madams Neh'er, Guizot and so many other women writers have reduced their smart exhortations and their well-informed advice to the influence of the family, to the care and vigilance of mothers; to this end, they have directed their careful and judicious observations. . . .

Source: Adapted from Nora E. Jaffary, Edward W. Osowski, and Susie Porter, eds., *Mexican History: A Primary Source Reader* (Denver, CO: Westview Press, 2010), 219–221.

There exists another fairly strong objection to the best books that we have to date on the education of women, and that is that they are written for the upper classes, and not for middle class families.

Young women without a dowry and of a middling condition, that today are called upon to make their own future, like men, in seeking true instruction that leads to talent and decides their fortune, infrequently find in these studies the lessons that would stimulate and aid them. This advice, based on contemplation, in which everything occurs in orderly and measured fashion, is still not relevant to those of adventurous professions, including those of the industrialist, artist, professor, worker, or the laborer who hope for days of prosperity and well-being for their children, and who leave no other patrimony to them than those of work and patience . . . .

Without pausing to consider theories, and taking the facts as they are, it is incontrovertible that society today advances on new paths that admire the thoughtful and observant. Everything around us is freed-up, a strange and mysterious impulse pulls us to a fast and disordered movement. Everyone runs, each hurrying: great concern for well-being concerns everyone; however, it is concern for material well-being. One would expect to see the immense mixture of the people of God persecuted by the oppressive arm of the Pharaoh . . . . And would it be out of the ordinary that such perturbation would have made it indispensable to make important modifications in the education of women?

The same need, the same lack of foresight, the same mania for luxury and for equality that exhibits itself in those poor young people in silk dresses like those of the rich classes, also demands an appropriate adornment for their souls. Everywhere, the instruction of women spreads in the same way, without discernment or concern for the future. No one knows what firm hand will establish harmony in the midst of this chaos. Without a doubt, though we speak in the name of the morality of our parents, the language needed to make oneself heard is no longer the same.

Before, the great art of women's education was to limit them to private life in a situation that prohibited them from moving or thinking, and everything was reduced to infinite precautions and to an excessive vigilance. Above all else, care was taken to uphold to grandparents the pure and unstained name of the family. Woman had no other function than that of wife and mother, and without intelligence, was never allowed to leave the domestic realm. Today, out of necessity or fortune, she needs to be open to rivaling men in education.

I do not know if we should applaud ourselves, because I believe there is more poison than happiness in the heavy branches of the tree of science. Be that as it may, in this peaceful time of labor and industry, in which women have long participated in the dangerous and agitated life of men, a great number of them go it alone, free and mistresses of their own destiny, without there having been an educated and friendly voice to teach them knowledge and strength in the midst of that liberty; not that negative knowledge that consists of sequestering oneself away from the world, but rather one that would allow them to carry the burden that they bear.

▶ Working with Sources

1. **The document is the work of a female author who lived in the early years of modernity. How does she characterize the role of women in the mid-nineteenth century?**
2. **Modernity has evolved dramatically since the mid-nineteenth century. Which characteristics of women in the document would be considered to be antiquated today?**

SOURCE 23.2

Domingo Faustino Sarmiento, *Travels in the United States in 1847*

1849

The journalist and eventual Argentine president Sarmiento (1811–1888) is most famous today for his novel *Facundo: Civilization and Barbarism* (1845), a sharp and daring satire of the caudillo Juán Manuel de Rosas. His indictment of Rosas, thinly disguised as the biography of another brutal dictator (called Juán Facundo Quiroga), was written while Sarmiento was an exile from the regime. Representing the government of Chile, Sarmiento traveled throughout Europe, North Africa, and North America, observing local political and social conditions closely and comparing them with what he knew of Argentine society. The result is a fascinating travelogue of his impressions of and reactions to the people of the United States, with vivid descriptions of many of its man-made and natural wonders. Nevertheless, his hopes for his native Argentina were never very far from the foreground, as this excerpt reveals.

The fatal error of the Spanish colonization of South America, the deep wound which has condemned present generations to inertia and backwardness, was in the system of land distribution. In Chile, great concessions of land, measuring from one hill to another and from the side of a river to the banks of an arroyo, were given to the conquistadors. The captains established earldoms for themselves, while their soldiers, fathers of the sharecropper, that worker without land who multiplies without increasing the number of his buildings, sheltered themselves in the shade of their improvised roofs. The passion to occupy lands in the name of the king drove men to dominion over entire districts, which put great distances

Source: Domingo Faustino Sarmiento, *Travels in the United States in 1847*, trans. Michael Aaron Rockland (Princeton, NJ: Princeton University Press, 1970), 164–166.

between landowners so that after three centuries the intervening land still has not been cleared. The city, for this reason, has been suppressed in this vast design, and the few villages which have been created since the conquest have been *decreed* by presidents. I know of at least five villages which were created in Chile in this official and contrived manner. But see how the American, recently called in the nineteenth century to conquer his piece of the world, does it. There the government has been careful to set aside land for all the coming generations. The young men aspiring to property each year crowd around the auction rooms in which public lands are sold, and, with the numbers of their lots in hand, they leave to take possession of their property, expecting to receive their titles later on from the offices in Washington. The most energetic Yankees, the misanthropes, the rustics, the SQUATTERS, in short, work in a manner which is more romantic, more poetic, and more primitive. Armed with their rifles, they immerse themselves in the virgin wilderness. For a pastime they kill the squirrels that unceasingly romp among the branches of the trees. A well-aimed bullet heads up into the sky to connect with an eagle which soars with majestic wings over the dark green surface formed by the boughs of the trees. The axe is the faithful companion of such a man, though he uses it for nothing more than to flex his muscles by throwing cedars and oaks to the ground. During his vagabond excursions this independent farmer looks for fertile land, a picturesque spot, something beside a navigable river; and when he has made up his mind, as in the most primitive times in the world's history, he says, "This is mine!" and without further ado takes possession of the land in name of the kings of the world: Work and Good Will. If one day the surveyor of the state's lands should arrive at the border of the land which he has laid out as his own, the auction will only serve to tell him what he owes for the land he has under cultivation, which will be the same sum as the adjacent uncultivated lands are going for. It is not unusual for this indomitable and unsociable character, overtaken by populations advancing through the wilderness, to sell his place and move away with his family, his oxen, and his horses searching for the desired solitude of the forests. The Yankee is a born proprietor. If he does not have anything and never has had anything he does not say that he is poor but that he is poor right now, or that he has been unlucky, or that times are bad. And then, in his imagination he sees the primitive, dark, solitary, isolated forests and in the midst of them the mansion he means to have on the bank of some unknown river, with smoke rising from the chimney and oxen returning home with slow step to his property as the sun goes down. From that moment he talks of nothing else but going out to occupy and settle new lands. His evenings are spent over the map, computing the stages of the journey, tracing a route for his wagon. And in the newspaper he does not look for anything except announcements of sales of state lands, or word of the new city that is being built on the shores of Lake Superior.

Alexander the Great, upon destroying Tyre, had to give world commerce a new distribution center for the spices of the Orient, one from which they could be sent at once to the Mediterranean coasts. The founding of Alexandria was an example of Alexander's renowned cleverness, even though the commercial routes were known and the Isthmus of Suez the indispensable trading ground between the waters of the India, Europe, and Africa of those days. This work is accomplished every day by American Alexanders, who wander through the wilds looking for points that a profound study of the future indicates will be centers of commerce.

▶ Working with Sources

1. **In what respects, and with what degree of conviction, does Sarmiento compare the acquisition of land in Latin America with land ownership in the United States?**
2. **Is Sarmiento convinced that this degree of cultivation and building of commerce cannot happen in Argentina? Why or why not?**

SOURCE 23.3

Amulet containing passages from the Qur'an, worn by Muslim slaves who rioted in Bahia, Brazil

1835

Although slavery was not abolished in Brazil until 1888, slave revolts were frequent and remarkable for their ambitions, success, and diversity of participating elements. Two urban revolts of the nineteenth century were especially significant. First, the Tailor's Rebellion of 1798, in Salvador, the capital of the Brazilian state of Bahia, drew on the assistance of freedmen, people of mixed race, and even craftspeople of Portuguese descent. The second was a Muslim-inspired and Muslim-directed uprising of slaves in Bahia in 1835, organized by African-born freedmen and slaves who had attained an Islamic education in West Africa before enslavement. This Muslim revolt is particularly fascinating because of the role of written documents, here deployed as protective amulets, among the members of the slave resistance. This excerpt from a book by a Brazilian scholar demonstrates the role of the written word in this rebellion, illustrating another, and less frequently recognized, "power" within historical documents.

Source: João José Reis, *Slave Rebellion in Brazil: The Muslim Uprising of 1835 in Bahia*, trans. Arthur Brakel (Baltimore: Johns Hopkins University Press, 1993), 99–103.

The written word, which the Malês used, had a great seductive power over Africans whose roots belonged in oral cultures. The amulets consisted of pieces of paper containing passages from the *Quran* and powerful prayers. The paper was carefully folded in an operation that had its own magical dimension. It was then placed in a small leather pouch, which was sewn shut. In many cases, besides the paper, other ingredients appeared in those charms. A police scribe described the contents of one amulet as follows:

> Little bundles or leather pouches were opened at this time by cutting them at the seams with a penknife. Inside were found several pieces of insignificant things such as cotton wrapped in a little powder [*sic*], others with tiny scraps of garbage, and little sacks with some seashells inside. Inside one of the leather pouches was a piece of paper with Arabic letters written on it.

The "insignificant" substances referred to here likely included sand moistened beforehand in some sort of holy water, perhaps water used by some renowned and pious alufá or water used to wash the tablets on which Malês wrote their religious texts. In the latter case, this water could also be drunk, since the ink was made of burnt rice; such a drink was believed to seal the body against outside harm. Some of the amulets were made of West African fabric; leather was used more often, since it provided better protection for both the sacred words and the other charms. There is a remarkable similarity between the Bahian Malê talismans and those still in use in black Africa, although the Bahian amulet seems to have had more "pagan" ingredients. According to Vincent Monteil, "In general the Islamic Talisman is a leather case, sewn together and containing a piece of stiff cardboard . . . and inside this is a folded piece of paper on which are written phrases in praise of God and cabalistic symbols—that is, Arabic letters, pentacles, and the like." Kabbalistic drawings such as the ones mentioned here were found in several amulets confiscated in 1835.

The Magrebian Arabic in the Malê amulets found on the bodies of dead rebels or in Muslims' houses has been studied and translated by Vincent Monteil and Rolf Reichert. Reichert took stock of twelve amulets, some of which contained kabbalistic shapes. . . .

The magic in the Islamic texts and drawings worked as protection against various threats. The Africans arrested in 1835 said little about their magic, and when they did say something, they avoided linking it to the revolt. However, besides their obvious political function, these amulets were especially designed to control daily life. A freedman named Silvestre José Antônio, a merchant, was arrested with five amulets in his case. He declared they "were prayers to save [him] from any unfortunate happenstance in his travels through the Recôncavo." Whether in Africa or in Brazil, a good Muslim merchant never traveled without a considerable number of protecting charms. A booklet of Islamic prayers could also work to protect its holder against evil spells. It was for that reason that a freedman named Pedro Pinto asked a literate Malê to make one for him, so he could "be free from wagging tongues." Pedro, by the way, was not a Malê.

. . .

Even so, one Malê fisherman made a good living from amulet making. According to one witness, Antônio, a Hausa slave residing in Itapagipe, "wrote prayers in his language and sold them to his partners making 4 *patacas* [1,280 réis] a day doing that." When he was arrested, a writing quill was found in his room: "Asked . . . by the justice [of the peace] why he kept such a quill, the same slave answered that he kept it so as to write things having to do with his Nation. He was then asked to write and he made a few scribbles with the phoney quill and the justice asked . . . what he had written. He answered that what he had written was the name of the 'Hail Mary.'" This Islamic-Christian melding does not seem to have impressed the justice of the peace. Antônio calmly went on telling his questioners that "when he was a young boy in his homeland, he went to school," and there he had learned Arabic so as to write "prayers according to the schism of his homeland."

Working with Sources

1. **How did the Malês use the written word to resist authority, and why did they use the Arabic language?**
2. **What do the documents created by the slaveholders and their supporting institutions reveal about the power of written sources as well?**

SOURCE 23.4

Photograph of a Chinese coolie, Peru

1881

Chinese migration to Latin America was a major part of the pattern of mass migration streams across the world that typified the nineteenth century. "Coolies" (from the Urdu word *kuli* "hireling") were indentured laborers recruited from India and China on 5- or 10-year contracts, who were forced to work to pay off the cost of their transportation. Roughly 235,000 Chinese came to Peru, Cuba, and Costa Rica, working in guano pits and silver mines, on sugar and cotton plantations, and later on railroads. Such work contracts were little better than slavery, and oftentimes were accompanied by institutions familiar from enslavement itself. This photograph, published in a Chilean army newspaper, depicts a Chinese coolie who is being liberated by an invading Chilean army in 1881 during the War of the Pacific.

Working with Sources

1. **Look closely at the man's feet and ankles. What might have been attached to him, and why?**
2. **How might this image have been deployed for propaganda purposes by the invading Chilean army?**

Source: http://commons.wikimedia.org/wiki/File:Enslaved_Chinese_coolie_in_Peru_1881.jpg

World Period Five

The Origins of Modernity, 1750–1900

The twin novel events of constitutional and industrial revolutions, first in the Americas and western Europe and later in Japan, dramatically changed the course of world history.

- People rose to end the divine right of kings and replace their rule with popular sovereignty, constitutions, and elections.
- Machines began to replace animal power in the manufacture of textiles, means of transportation, chemicals, and urban amenities.

As a result, 10,000-year-old traditional customs and habits formed by life in agriculture gave way to what we call "modernity," that is, nontraditional new ways of life in the "machine age," characterized by such new phenomena as nation-states, social classes, megacities, colonialism, and above all, vastly increased global interactions

Chapter 24

The Challenge of Modernity

EAST ASIA, 1750– 1900

CHAPTER TWENTY-FOUR PATTERNS

Origins, Interactions and Adaptations In 1750, China, Japan, and Korea were mature agrarian–urban civilizations. The impact of newly powerful Western trading nations on these three countries between 1750 and 1910 is difficult to overestimate. For China, wars with Western powers and internal rebellion brought the Qing Dynasty to the brink of collapse. Japan, confronted by similar forces, remade itself along Western models and became a formidable imperial power. Korea, divided by Chinese and Japanese power struggles, was annexed by Japan in 1910. Thus, the interactions among China, Japan, and Korea were intense during this period, as were their relative adaptations to each other and to foreign imperialism.

Uniqueness and Similarities For millennia, China saw itself as the center of a world civilization. Its rulers initially saw the intrusions of the modernizing Western maritime powers as temporary setbacks. By the late nineteenth century, however, China's continued weakness, Japan's rising power, and tensions over Korea forced belated and ultimately unsuccessful reform efforts. Moreover, it prompted a role reversal in which Japan would now be the model for East Asian reform and modernization.

In the broadest sense, the vast expansion of Western power posed similar challenges to all of the old agrarian civilizations. In this sense, China's belated attempts at reform while struggling to retain its territorial integrity sound a familiar refrain

> In Asia, our two countries, China and Japan, are the closest neighbors, and moreover have the same [written] language. How could we be enemies? Now for the time being we are fighting each other, but eventually we should work for permanent friendship . . . so that our Asiatic yellow race will not be encroached upon by the white race of Europe.

CHAPTER OUTLINE

China and Japan in the Age of Imperialism

Economy and Society in Late Qing China

Zaibatsu and Political Parties: Economy and Society in Meiji Japan

Putting It All Together

So commented the Chinese statesman Li Hongzhang to his Japanese counterpart, Ito Hirobumi, as they discussed terms to end the Sino–Japanese War in the Japanese town of Shimonoseki in the spring of 1895. Li was China's most powerful advocate of *self-strengthening*—using new foreign technologies and concepts to preserve China's Confucian society in the face of European and American intrusion. Now he was forced to go to Japan to sue for peace as Japanese troops occupied Korea and southern Manchuria.

For Ito, one of the architects of Japan's rise to power, the victory over China was tinged with sadness. He responded: "Ten years ago when I was at Tientsin [Tianjin], I talked about reform with [you]. . . . Why is it that up to now not a single thing has been changed or reformed? This I deeply regret." This feeling was shared by Li, whose reply betrays a weary bitterness at China's deteriorating position: "At that time when I heard you . . . I was overcome with admiration . . . [at] your having vigorously changed your customs in Japan so as to reach the present stage. Affairs in my country have been so confined by tradition that I could not accomplish what I desired. . . . I am ashamed of having excessive wishes and lacking the power to fulfill them."

The new Treaty of Shimonoseki imposed a crippling indemnity on the Qing, reduced Korea to a client state, and annexed the island of Taiwan. It also called for the occupation by Japan of Manchuria's Liaodong Peninsula, which guarded the approaches to Beijing. For the Chinese, this marked the most dramatic and humiliating role reversal of the past 1,500 years. China had always viewed Japan in Confucian terms as a younger brother. Like Korea and Vietnam, Japan was considered to be on the cultural periphery of the

ABOVE: A print depicting Japanese soldiers crushing Chinese troops during the Sino-Japanese War (1894–1895), which completely changed the relationship between these two empires.

Seeing Patterns

> What was the impact of Western imperialism on the "regulated societies" of China and Japan?

> Why did European empire building in Asia have such dramatically different effects on China and Japan?

> How have historians seen the nature of these outside forces and their influences in East Asia?

Chinese world, acculturating to Chinese institutions and following Chinese examples in those things considered "civilized." Now, after barely a generation of exposure to Euro-American influence, Japan had eclipsed China as a military power and threatened to extend its sway throughout the region.

The new order in East Asia brought about by the Sino–Japanese War underscores the larger effects of one of the most momentous patterns of world history: the phenomenon of imperialism growing from the innovations that created scientific–industrial society. In less than a century, European countries and their offshoots—and now Japan—expanded their power so rapidly that on the eve of World War I in 1914 more than 85 percent of the world's people were under their control or influence. How were countries like Japan able to resist and adapt to the broad forces of modernity, while China struggled to cope with its effects through most of the nineteenth and twentieth centuries?

China and Japan in the Age of Imperialism

The end of the reign of the Qing emperor Qianlong (r. 1736–1795) marked the period in which the first hints appeared of trouble to come. Soon after Qianlong stepped down from the throne in 1795, a Buddhist sect called the White Lotus sparked a rebellion that took years to suppress. Less obvious, but perhaps more debilitating for the agrarian urban imperial order as a whole, were the new directions in economics. China's efforts to retain close control over its export trade in luxury goods coupled with efforts to eradicate the lucrative but illegal opium trade created a crisis with Great Britain in the summer of 1839. This crisis led to the First Opium War, China's first military encounter with the industrializing West.

China and Maritime Trade, 1750–1839

The British government sought to establish diplomatic relations with the Qing in the 1790s. In the summer of 1793, they dispatched Lord George Macartney, an experienced diplomat and colonial governor, to Beijing. He sought to persuade the Qianlong emperor to allow the stationing of diplomatic personnel in the Chinese capital and create a system for the separate handling of ordinary commercial matters and diplomacy. Qianlong, however, rebuffed Macartney's attempts to establish a British embassy. China's diplomacy revolved around trade with Confucian-based surrounding states, and Qianlong saw no need to adapt the empire to the Western norms of international relations. A second British mission in 1816 met with similar results.

The Imbalance of Trade? Europeans and Americans were anxious to bring the Chinese into their diplomatic system in part because of the perception that China was benefiting from a huge trade imbalance. Merchants and political economists, convinced that China's control of trade functioned in the same way as European mercantilism, believed that the money paid to Chinese merchants essentially stayed in the "closed" economy of the Qing Empire. However, European merchants offered little that the Chinese needed or wanted.

Thus, by the end of the eighteenth century, European and American traders had become increasingly anxious to find something that Chinese merchants would buy. By the beginning of the nineteenth century, a growing number of merchants were clandestinely turning to a lucrative new commodity, with tragic consequences: opium.

Smugglers and Pirates By the end of the eighteenth century, the British East India Company's territory in Bengal included a center of medicinal opium production. While company traders were strictly prohibited from carrying opium to China as contraband, some noncompany merchants discovered that they could circumvent Chinese regulations and sell small quantities of the drug for a tidy profit. With success came increased demand, and by the early decades of the nineteenth century, an illicit system of delivery had been set up along the south China coast. Armed ships unloaded their cargoes of opium on sparsely inhabited offshore islands, from which Chinese middlemen picked up the drug and made their rounds on the mainland (see Map 24.1). The profits from this illegal enterprise encouraged piracy along the coast, and the opium trade soon became a major irritant in relations between China and the West.

The relationship that the British East India Company and the government-licensed Chinese merchant guild had developed—the "Canton System"—was increasingly undermined by the new commerce. Moreover, free-trade agitation in England put an end to the East India Company's monopoly on the China trade in 1833. With the monopoly lifted, the number of entrepreneurs seeking quick riches in the opium trade exploded. In the foreign trading establishments in Canton (Guangzhou), newcomers engaged in the opium trade vied for prestige with older firms involved in legitimate goods.

The push for legitimacy among the opium merchants coincided with an attempt by Westerners to force China to open additional trading ports for legal items. Chinese authorities, however, viewed this Western assertiveness as driven primarily by opium and Christian evangelism. Far worse, however, were the effects on the ordinary inhabitants of south China as opium usage surged to catastrophic levels. Its addictive properties created a health crisis for tens of thousands, made infinitely worse by the drug's notoriously difficult withdrawal symptoms.

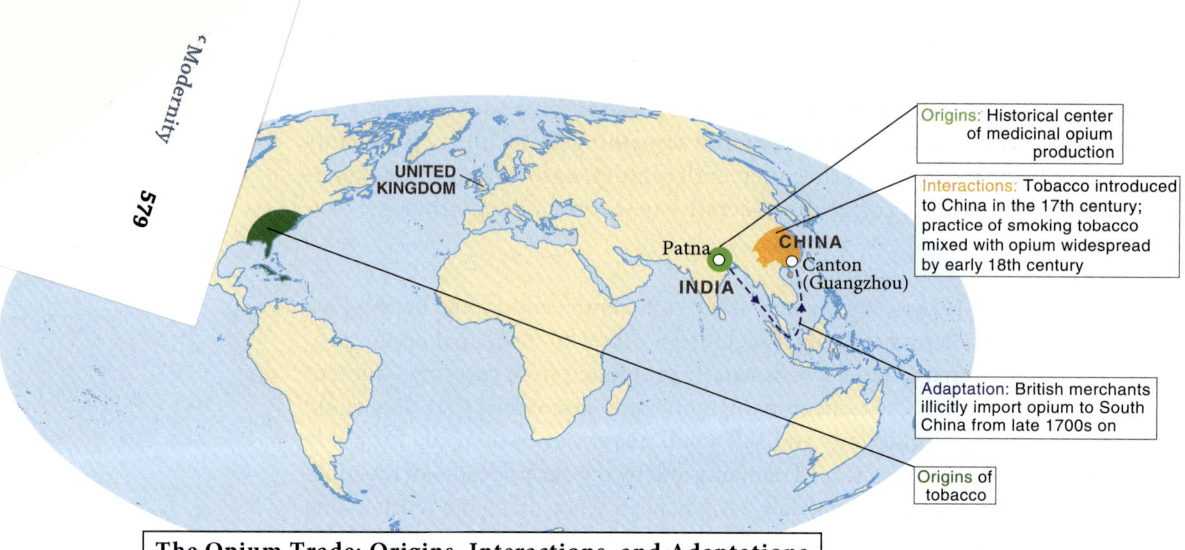

MAP 24.1 **The Opium Trade: Origins, Interactions, Adaptations**

Commissioner Lin Zexu In the spring of 1839 the emperor sent Lin Zexu (1785–1850), a widely respected official, to Canton as an imperial commissioner. Lin, charged with cutting off the opium trade at its source, was given wide-ranging powers to deal with both Chinese and foreign traffickers. In addition to setting up facilities for the recovery of addicts, he demanded that all foreign merchants surrender their opium stocks and sign a pledge that they would not, under penalty of death, deal in the drug anymore.

When the foreign community balked, Lin blockaded the port and withdrew all Chinese personnel from Western firms. The dealers eventually surrendered 20,000 chests of opium, with most also signing the pledge. Following Lin's actions, however, the dealers appealed to the British government for compensation.

In a show of force, the British sent a fleet of warships to Canton to demand reparations for the destroyed opium, pressure the Qing to establish diplomatic relations, and open more ports. When negotiations broke down, a small Chinese squadron sailed out to confront the British men-of-war, which easily scattered the Chinese ships. Such inauspicious circumstances marked the beginning of the First Opium War (1839–1842) and, with it, a century of foreign intrusion, domination, and ultimately revolution for China.

The Opium Wars and the Treaty Port Era

The hostilities that began in the fall of 1839 between China and Great Britain exposed the growing gap between the military capabilities of industrializing countries and those, like China, whose armed forces had fallen into disuse.

Over the next two years, the British attacked and occupied ports along the Chinese coast from Canton to Shanghai at the mouth of the Yangzi River. As the British planned to move north to put pressure on Beijing, Chinese officials opened negotiations in August 1842. The resulting Treaty of Nanjing (Nanking) marked the first of the century's "unequal treaties" that would be imposed throughout East Asia by European powers.

The Treaty of Nanjing In the Treaty of Nanjing, which ended the First Opium War, the British claimed the island of Hong Kong; levied an indemnity on the Chinese to pay the costs of the war; and forced the Chinese to open the ports of Shanghai, Ningbo, Fuzhou, and Xiamen (Amoy), in addition to Canton. The British also insisted on **nontariff autonomy**: By treaty, the Chinese could now charge no more than a 5 percent tariff on British goods. The British also imposed the policy of **extraterritoriality** in the newly open ports: British subjects who violated Chinese laws would be tried and punished by British consuls.

Similar treaties with France and the United States followed, together with a supplementary treaty with Britain. An important element in these later treaties was the most-favored-nation clause: any new concessions granted to one country automatically reverted to those who by treaty were "most favored nations" (see Map 24.2).

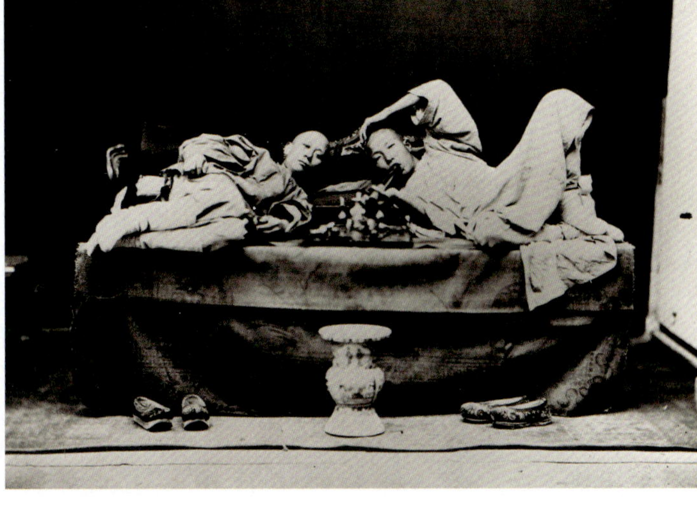

Chinese Opium Smokers. This photograph, taken in the early 1870s, shows the pervasiveness of the opium habit among ordinary Chinese. These men are smoking in the back room of a restaurant, a common practice even in British-controlled Hong Kong.

Nontariff autonomy: The loss by a country of its right to set its own tariffs.

Extraterritoriality: The immunity of a country's nationals from the laws of their host country.

Steam Power Comes to China. The new technologies of the Industrial Revolution were on painful display in China in 1840 as the British gunboat HMS *Nemesis* took on provincial warships down the river from Canton. The *Nemesis* featured a shallow draft armored hull put together in detachable sections, steam-powered paddle-wheel propulsion for river fighting, and two large pivot guns to take on shore batteries. Its power and versatility convinced Lin Zexu and a growing number of Chinese officials over the coming decades that China needed, at the very least, the same kinds of "strong ships and effective cannon" if they were to defend their coasts and rivers. By the 1860s the first attempts at such craft were finally under way.

MAP 24.2 Treaty Ports and Foreign Spheres of Influence in China, 1842–1907

The Taiping Movement, 1851–1864 In addition to the spread of the opium trade to the newly opened ports, long-established trade routes for other items shifted from Guangzhou (Canton) to more convenient outlets. Coastal trade also increased. The economic dislocation that accompanied these changes, along with discontent at the inability of the Qing government to resist foreign demands, made south China particularly volatile. In 1851 the region exploded in rebellion. This largest civil war in world history and its related conflicts would claim as many as 30 million lives.

The catalyst for revolt embodied the diverse cultural influences penetrating the area. A candidate for the local Confucian examinations, Hong Xiuquan [hung

SHI-OO-chwehn] (1813–1864), read some Christian missionary tracts passed on by a colleague. Not long after, he failed the examination for the third time and suffered a nervous breakdown. When he eventually recovered, Hong came to believe in the dreams he had during his illness in which the Christian God had revealed to him that he must now work to bring about the Heavenly Kingdom of Great Peace (*taiping tianguo*) on earth. The movement thus became known as the **Taiping Rebellion** (sometimes called "War," "Civil War," or "Revolution") and lasted from 1851 until 1864.

Taiping Rebellion: Massive rebellion or civil war that was waged in China from 1851 to 1864 between the Qing dynasty and the Taipings. With a death toll of at least 20 million people, the Taiping rebellion was one of the bloodiest wars in human history.

Hong moved into a mountain stronghold and attracted followers from the disillusioned and unemployed, anti-Manchu elements, religious dissidents, and fellow members of south China's Hakka minority. The Hakkas had originally been northerners who migrated south at several points during the turmoil of dynastic changes. They retained their native dialects, did not practice foot binding, often worked marginal farmland, and frequently fortified their villages against attacks by their local southern neighbors. By 1851 Hong and his followers had created a society based on Protestant Christian theology and pre-Confucian Chinese traditions. As a sign that they were no longer loyal to the Qing, the men cut their queues and let the hair grow in on their foreheads, prompting the Qing to refer to them as "the long-haired rebels." The rebels targeted the scholar-gentry in their land seizures and executions, as well as Manchus, Buddhists, Daoists, and other groups they considered heterodox.

By the winter of 1853, the Taipings were narrowly thwarted from driving the Qing from Beijing and were pushed back to central China by imperial forces. For the next decade, however, Hong's movement would remain in control of the Chinese heartland, with their capital at Nanjing, and the long contest to subdue them would devastate dozens of major cities and thousands of towns and villages.

Foreign missionaries and diplomats in China were unsure about the movement's aims. Although Hong talked about instituting Western-style administrative reforms and building a modern industrial base, a powerful Taiping China might throw the new trade arrangements into disarray. Thus, the foreign powers in the end grudgingly elected to continue recognizing the Qing as China's legitimate rulers (see Map 24.3).

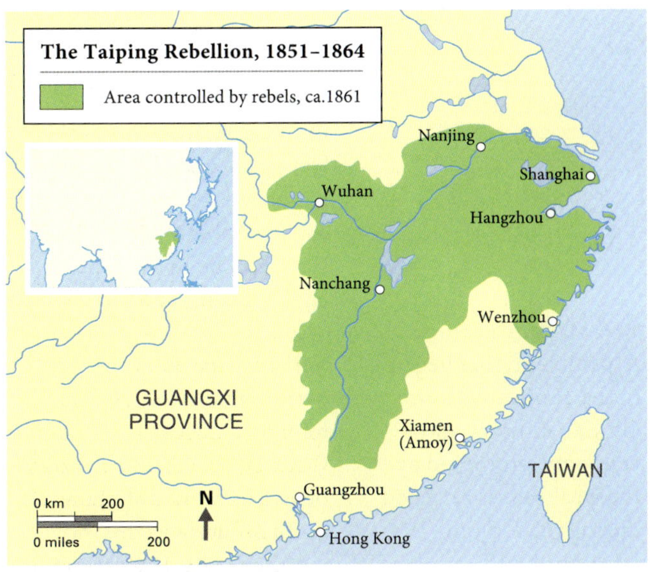

MAP 24.3 **The Taiping Rebellion, 1851–1864**

The Second Opium War, 1856–1860

At the height of the rebellion in 1856, a new dispute arose between the Qing and the British and French. Britain, France, and the United States all felt by the mid-1850s that the vastly expanded trade in China—and now Japan—called for the opening of still more ports, an end to Qing prohibitions on missionary activity, and diplomatic relations along Western lines. In the wake of an alleged insult to the British flag, hostilities commenced, with the French allied with the British to push the missionary issue.

Patterns Up Close | Interaction and Adaptation: "Self-Strengthening" and "Western Science and Eastern Ethics"

Most of the important technical innovations taking place in China and Japan during the late eighteenth and most of the nineteenth centuries came from outside East Asia. Confronted by the newly industrialized countries of Europe and America, their possible adaptive responses were reaction, reform, and revolution. Perhaps most interesting is the middle path of reform, taken by both countries in attempting to create a synthesis of Confucian social structures and the best of the new technologies and institutions.

As we saw with Neo-Confucianism in Chapter 12, Chinese philosophical concepts tended toward the desire for correlation and the reconciliation of opposites. In this tradition, *ti* and *yong*, or "essence" and "function/application," became the two key terms in the popular self-strengthening formulation *zhongxue wei ti; xixue wei yong* ("Chinese studies for the essence; Western studies for the practical application"). Thus, Chinese thinkers were able to acknowledge new foreign technologies using historically and

Interaction and Adaptation in China and Japan. Weapons on display at the Nanjing Arsenal in 1868 include an early Gatling-type rotary machine gun and a pyramid of round explosive shells (a). An 1890 lithograph of a Japanese seamstress (b) shows the delicate balance between "essence" and "function" that Japan has tried to maintain since the middle of the nineteenth century. The woman is attired in Western dress, and she works a Western-style sewing machine. Has the "function" degraded the "essence" of what she is doing? It is a question that many in Japan still ask today.

The war itself was fought in a localized fashion. In 1858 the Qing court refused a draft treaty. Returning in 1860 with a large expeditionary force, British and French troops advanced to Beijing and drove the emperor from the city. The final treaty stipulated that a dozen ports be opened to foreign trade, that opium be recognized as a legal commodity, that extraterritoriality be expanded, and that foreign embassies be set up in the capital. A newly created Chinese board was to handle Qing foreign relations, and the Chinese were invited to send their own ambassadors abroad.

Self-strengthening: A campaign that began in the 1860s to reform China's military and economy, prompted by the weaknesses revealed during the Opium Wars and the Taiping Rebellion.

Self-Strengthening

Although Chinese officials were desperate to roll back the foreign threat and suppress the Taipings, few advocated simply fighting the foreigners. Most felt that over time these new peoples would be assimilated to Chinese norms, like invaders of the past. In the meantime, however, they should be pacified, but not unconditionally.

In order to do this, however, China needed to be able to halt further encroachments by the Western powers. Toward this end, officials advocated a policy called **self-strengthening** (see "Patterns Up Close"). During the 1860s, the two philosophically acceptable terminology. The Japanese were able to justify their own transformation by means of the balanced formula they called "Western science and Eastern ethics."

However, the two sides of the concept were not evenly balanced. As with many Neo-Confucian formulae, the "essence" and "ethics" elements were considered to be primary and the method of implementation—"function"—secondary. Thus, their proponents could argue that their aim was to preserve Confucian society while remaining flexible about the appropriate means of attaining their goals. Opponents, however, argued that the formula could—and eventually would—be reversed: that "function" would eventually degrade the "essence."

Yet in both China and Japan, one can argue that this has remained a favored approach. The Japanese have made foreign technologies and institutions their own, while retaining Shinto and Buddhist practices alongside social customs still tinged with Neo-Confucianism. Similarly, in China, coupling technological and institutional modernization with an effort to rediscover and preserve what is considered to be the best of traditional Chinese civilization has been the dominant approach. Thus, the present regime pursues a policy of "socialism with Chinese characteristics" in the service of creating what the Communist Party calls "the harmonious society."

Questions

- How were the Chinese and Japanese adaptations to Western innovations similar? How were they different? What do these similarities and differences say about the cultures of these two countries?
- Do you believe that, over the course of time, the "function" of foreign innovations has degraded the "essence" in China and Japan?

most prominent were Li Hongzhang (1823–1901) and his senior colleague Zeng Guofan (1811–1872). Renowned scholars as well as militia leaders, Li and Zeng were also distinguished by the flexibility of their thinking and their growing familiarity with the weapons brought to China by foreign forces. By the end of the rebellion, they had begun to move toward a strategy of what a later slogan called "Chinese studies for the essence; Western studies for practical application."

Toward Revolution: Reform and Reaction to 1900

While China's efforts at self-strengthening seemed promising, signs of their underlying weakness were already emerging. With the ascension of the infant Guangxu emperor in 1874 came the regency of Empress Dowager Cixi (tsuh-shee). Desperate to preserve Manchu power, Cixi manipulated factions at court and among the high officials to avoid concentration of power in any particular area. Such maneuverings hampered the long-term health of many self-strengthening measures. In addition, the new programs were costly, usually required foreign experts, and China's finances were continually strained.

China and Imperialism in Southeast Asia and Korea By the 1880s foreign tensions exposed more problems. France had been steadily encroaching upon Southeast Asia since the late 1850s and completed its conquest of Vietnam in 1885 (Chapter 27). By the early 1890s rising tensions surrounding the Korean court and intrigues by Japanese and Chinese agents there threatened war. By the fall of 1894, both sides were sending troops and naval forces to Korea, and a full-scale war over the fate of Korea and northeastern Asia was under way.

The Sino–Japanese War The war between China and Japan over control of Korea dramatically exposed the problems of China's self-strengthening efforts. The

(a)

(b)

Scenes from the Sino–Japanese War. News accounts of the Sino–Japanese War aroused great interest and an unprecedented wave of nationalism in Japan. They also marked the last extensive use of *ukiyo-e* woodblock printing in the news media, as the technology of reproducing photos in newspapers was introduced to Japan shortly after the conflict. Because few of the artists actually traveled with the troops, the great majority of these works came from reporters' dispatches and the artists' imaginations. In these representative samples from the assault on Pyongyang showing the use of the new technology of the electric searchlight to illuminate an enemy fort (a), the pride in Japan's modernization and the disdain for China's "backwardness" are all too evident. Note the almost demon-like faces and garish uniforms of the Chinese, invariably depicted as being killed or cowering before the Japanese; note, too, the modern, Western uniforms and beards and mustaches of the Japanese (b).

Japanese navy soundly defeated the new Chinese armored steam fleet. While many of the land battles were hotly contested, superior organization and morale enabled the Japanese to drive steadily through Korea. A second force landed in southern Manchuria to secure the territory around the approaches to Beijing, while Japanese naval forces reduced the fortress across from it at Weihaiwei. In spring 1895, Li made his humiliating trip to Shimonoseki and was forced to agree to Japan's terms, as we saw at the beginning of this chapter. The severity of the provisions signaled to the Western powers in East Asia that China was now weak enough to have to acquiesce to massive economic and territorial demands.

A "race for concessions" began, in which France demanded economic and territorial rights in south China adjacent to Indochina, Great Britain in the Yangzi River valley, and Russia and Japan in Manchuria. A newcomer, Germany, demanded naval bases and rights at Qingdao [ching-dow] (Tsingtao) on the Shandong Peninsula. China's total dismemberment was avoided in 1899 when John Hay, the US secretary of state, circulated a note with British backing suggesting that all powers maintain an "open door" for all to trade in China.

Dismembering China. The weakness of the Qing during the final years of the nineteenth century prompted the so-called race for concessions among the imperial powers in East Asia. In this French cartoon, China is depicted as a cake around which caricatures of the monarchs and national symbols of the various powers sit with their knives poised, arguing over who should get the best pieces. A desperate Chinese official—perhaps Li Hongzhang himself—with his long fingernails and flapping queue, holds up his hands imploring them to stop.

The Hundred Days of Reform Amid this growing foreign crisis, the aftermath of the war produced a domestic crisis as well. The terms of the Shimonoseki treaty had prompted patriotic demonstrations in Beijing and prompted urgent discussion about reform. A group of younger officials headed by Kang Youwei (1858–1927) petitioned Emperor Guangxu to implement widespread reforms, many modeled on those recently enacted in Japan. Guangxu issued a flurry of edicts from June through September 1898, attempting to revamp China's government and many of its institutions. Resistance to this "hundred days' reform" program, however, was extensive, and centered on the emperor's aunt, the empress dowager. With support from her inner circle at court, she had the young emperor placed under house arrest and rounded up and executed many of Kang's supporters. Kang and his junior colleague, the writer and political theorist Liang Qichao [lee-ahng chee-chow] (1873–1929), managed to escape. For the next decade they traveled to overseas Chinese communities attempting to gather support for their Constitutional Monarchy Party.

The Boxer Rebellion and War The turmoil set off by the "race for concessions" was particularly intense in north China, where the ambitions of Russia, Japan, and Germany clashed. The activity of German missionaries on the Shandong Peninsula sparked anti-foreign sentiment, increasingly perpetrated by a Chinese group calling itself the Society of the Harmonious Fists. This group was initially anti-Qing as well as anti-foreign, and the foreign community referred to them as the "Boxers."

In the spring of 1900, the German ambassador was assassinated by one of his Manchu bodyguards. The Germans demanded that the Qing crush the Boxers and suppress all anti-foreign elements, pay a huge indemnity, and erect a statue to their ambassador. In the midst of this crisis, the empress dowager, who had been negotiating in secret with the Boxers, declared war on all the foreign powers in China and openly threw the court's support behind the movement. The result was civil war across northern China.

The foreign governments assembled a multinational relief force led by the Germans and British and largely manned by the Japanese. By August they had fought their way to the capital and chased the imperial court nearly to Xi'an. With Qing power utterly routed, the foreign governments were able to impose the most severe "unequal treaty" yet: They extracted the right to post troops in major Chinese cities, demanded the total suppression of any anti-foreign movements, and received such a huge indemnity that China had to borrow money from foreign banks in order to service the interest on the loan.

In Search of Security through Empire: Japan in the Meiji Era

At the close of the nineteenth century, Japan and China faced similar pressures. How, then, was Japan, with only a fraction of China's population and resources, able not only to survive in the face of foreign pressure but also to join the imperial powers itself?

Visions of the Barbarians. Commodore Matthew C. Perry's expeditions to Japan were thoroughly documented by a number of Japanese artists. Some of the depictions were demonic sketches emphasizing the Americans' outlandish dress and facial hair. Others, like the portrait of Perry above from the series done in 1854 by Hibata Osuke (1813–1870), were truer to life and reflect the aesthetic sensibilities of the *ukiyo-e* tradition. The Japanese calligraphy says "Envoy Perry."

The Decline of Tokugawa Seclusion

During the eighteenth century, Europeans generally honored Japan's seclusion policies. By the first decades of the nineteenth century, however, the expanded trade with China increased the volume of shipping close to Japanese waters. Moreover, the whaling industry in the northern Pacific brought European and American ships into waters adjacent to Japan.

By the 1840s, the pressure to establish relations with the Tokugawa shogunate became even more intense for the Western powers with interests in China. The treaty ports created in the wake of the First Opium War included Shanghai, which was becoming East Asia's chief commercial enclave, and major shipping routes to Shanghai ran directly adjacent to southern Japan. Moreover, the Mexican-American War (1846–1848) (see Chapter 23) brought the Pacific coast of North America under the control of the United States, while the discovery of gold in California made San Francisco the premier port for all American transpacific trade. Plans to open steamship service from San Francisco to Shanghai now threatened to place Japan squarely in the path of maritime traffic.

The Coming of the "Black Ships"

The Tokugawa were well aware of the humiliation of the Qing at the hands of the British in 1842, and as pressure increased on Japan to open its ports, divided counsels plagued the shogunate. While some advocated a military response to any attempt at opening the country, others looking at the situation in China felt that negotiation was the only way for Japan to avoid invasion.

An American fleet of new and powerful warships under the command of Matthew C. Perry arrived in Japan in July 1853. To impress the Japanese with American technology, he brought along a telegraph set and a model railroad, both of which proved immediately popular with the Japanese. When Perry returned in 1854 with even more of the "black ships," as the Japanese dubbed them, the Treaty of Kanagawa was signed, Japan's first with an outside power. Like China, Japan had now entered the treaty port era.

"Honor the Emperor and Expel the Barbarian!" The treaty with the Americans and the rapid conclusion of treaties with other Western powers reinforced anti-foreignism among many of Japan's warrior elite while emphasizing the weakness of the Tokugawa. Many samurai felt that dramatic gestures were called for to rouse the country to action. Like the Boxers in China, they attacked foreigners and assassinated Tokugawa officials in an effort to precipitate anti-foreign conflict. By 1863, a movement aimed at driving out the Tokugawa and restoring imperial rule had coalesced. Taking the slogan *Sonno joi* ("Honor the emperor, expel the barbarian") this movement challenged the shogunate and fought a Restoration War, which by the end of 1867 forced the Tokugawa to capitulate. The new regime moved to the Tokugawa capital of Edo and renamed it Tokyo (Eastern Capital).

The new emperor, 15-year-old Mutsuhito, took the reign name of Meiji (Enlightened Rule). As proof that the new regime would adopt progressive measures, in April 1868 the throne issued a "charter oath" renouncing the restrictive measures of the past. A preliminary constitution was also promulgated, which detailed how the new government was to be set up.

Creating a Nation-State While the Tokugawa had created a warrior bureaucracy based on Neo-Confucianism, Japan was still dominated by regional loyalties and fealty to the daimyo of one's feudal domain. The foreign threat and restoration of the emperor provided the opportunity for national unification. Thus, during the 1870s the new government replaced the feudal domains with a centralized provincial structure; the daimyo were replaced by governors, and the samurai were disbanded. In their place, an army modeled after that of Germany was created, and a navy modeled on Great Britain's was established. The new order was reinforced by a national system of compulsory education in which loyalty to the emperor and state was carefully nurtured.

Government-managed social experimentation flourished. Like the Chinese "self-strengtheners," Japanese senior advisors to the emperor, or *genro* [GHEN-roe, with a hard *g*], sought to use new foreign technologies and institutions to strengthen the state against further foreign intrusion. Japan's proclaimed goals of using "Western science and Eastern ethics" in the service of "civilization and enlightenment" were seen as the primary tools in reaching eventual equality with the Western imperial powers and rolling back Japan's unequal treaties.

Creating an Empire Japan's successful showing in the Sino-Japanese war surprised and alarmed the Western powers in the region. They staged the Triple Intervention, in which Russia, Germany, and France forced Japan to return the Liaodong Peninsula to China, only to have the Chinese lease it to Russia the following year. Not surprisingly, this put the Russian empire on a collision course with Japanese aspirations on the Asian mainland. Already in control of Korea, Japan was intensely interested in acquiring concessions in adjacent Manchuria. For Russia, it was vital to build rail links from the Trans-Siberian Railway to their new outposts of Port Arthur and Dairen (Dalian) in Liaodong and to extend the line across Manchuria to Vladivostok on the Pacific. Japan and Russia would shortly fight a war in 1904–1905 that would secure Japan's dominant position in northeast Asia and begin a sequence of events that would end in revolution for Russia (see Map 24.4).

MAP 24.4 Japanese Territorial Expansion, 1870–1905

Economy and Society in Late Qing China

By 1900, China's treasury was bankrupt; its finances increasingly were controlled by foreign concerns, its export trade was outstripped by European and Japanese competitors, its domestic markets were turning to factory-produced foreign commodities, and its land was growing less and less capable of sustaining its society.

The Seeds of Modernity and the New Economic Order

The economic policies of late imperial China were increasingly at odds with those of the West. For Chinese thinkers, this was considered sound in both ideological and economic terms. Confucianism held that agriculture was China's primary concern and that the values of the merchant were in direct opposition to stable agrarian values. As the nineteenth century advanced, the opium trade proved to Confucian officials the correctness of this stance.

Increasing pressure on China to lower its barriers to legitimate trade and the steps taken by those countries exerting the pressure to safeguard their own markets had equally severe long-term effects. The unequal treaties imposed artificially low tariff rates on the empire, making it increasingly difficult to protect its markets; at the same time, trading nations in the West increased tariffs on their own imports.

Self-Strengthening and Economics

Two economic forces had a profound effect on China's later economic development. The first was that in the treaty ports the economic climate created by the Western powers exposed much of China's urban population to industrial and commercial modernity. A class of Chinese people developed who made a living mediating between Westerners and Chinese interests.

The other force was the popularity of European, Japanese, and American consumer goods. While foreign curiosities had been popular with Chinese elites since the eighteenth century, by the end of the nineteenth century, large foreign concerns, including the Standard Oil Company and the British–American Tobacco Company, had established their products in the empire. With the Qing finally committed to railroad and telegraph construction and modern mining, the seeds of economic modernity had been planted.

Rural Economy and Society

While China's population remained overwhelmingly rural, the old structures of the empire's peasant-based society were slowly crumbling. Landlordism, especially the growing incidence of absentee landlordism, exacerbated these tensions. Living on the edge of poverty in many areas, many peasants saw in the Taiping Rebellion, the Nian Rebellion of 1851–1868 in northern China, and assorted local rebellions a way to change their situations. But in many places, poverty increased due to the destruction caused by rebel clashes, and the radical ideologies and ruthlessness of the rebels disillusioned the majority of the peasantry. As a result, by the beginning of the twentieth century, absentee landlordism had become an increasingly acute problem.

Social Trends While changes were certainly noticeable in the family, the durability of long-standing traditions is probably more striking. The family endured as the central Chinese institution. Within it, the father continued to be the most powerful figure, and the Confucian ideal of hierarchical relationships between husband and wife, father and son, and elder brother and younger brother remained in force. Daughters, considered a drain on family resources because they would marry outside the family, were educated only to foster the skills the family of their husbands-to-be would consider valuable. The daughters of the wealthy were kept secluded in the home, and most—with the exception of the Manchus and certain minorities like south China's Hakkas—continued the practice of foot binding.

Culture, Arts, and Science

The late Qing period begins with one of China's great literary masterpieces and ends with China's first modern writers pointing toward a vernacular-language "literary renaissance" starting around 1915. Reversing the trend of thousands of years, the most significant Chinese developments in science and technology were those arriving from the West as products of the Industrial Revolution.

The Dream of the Red Chamber Though the novel was not considered high literature by Chinese scholars during Ming and Qing times, the form proved immensely popular. During the mid-eighteenth century, what many consider to be China's greatest novel, *Hong Lou Meng* (*The Dream of the Red Chamber*), was written by Cao Xueqin [TSOW shway-CHEEN] (ca. 1715–ca. 1764). The novel, which chronicles the decline and fall of a powerful family, has been so closely studied that in China there is an entire field called "red studies" or "redology" (*hong xue*) devoted to examination of the work.

Poetry, Travel Accounts, and Newspapers China's need to understand new threats as well as opportunities prompted the publication of atlases, gazetteers of foreign lands, and eyewitness travel accounts. The most significant of these were the *Illustrated Gazetteer of the Maritime Countries* of 1844 by Wei Yuan (1794–1856) and the *Record of the World* of 1848 by Xu Jiyu (1795–1873). These accounts, especially Xu's, shaped what Chinese officials knew about the outside world until the first eyewitness accounts of travelers and diplomats arrived in the late 1860s. Officials and diplomats who visited foreign countries were required to keep journals of their experiences for use by the government and/or for publication.

The popular newspaper also emerged in most Chinese cities during this time. For centuries, newsletters tracking official doings at the capital had been circulated among the elites. However, the 1860s saw the first popular Chinese-language papers, the most prominent of which was *Shenbao*. Such publications and the growing numbers of journals and popular magazines were vitally important in the transfer of ideas between Chinese and foreigners.

Science and Technology The most pressing need for China during the early and mid-nineteenth century was military technology. During the period between the two Opium Wars, Chinese officials purchased guns and cannon from European and American manufacturers to bolster their coastal defenses. The self-strengtheners realized that China must begin to manufacture such weapons on its own. Moreover, this would require both infrastructure and such supporting industries as mining, railroads, and telegraphy.

Despite the general animosity directed against them by Chinese officials, missionaries were key players in transfers of science and technology. Protestant missionaries in the nineteenth century directed their efforts at ordinary Chinese, but often did so by attracting them with the new advantages of science. Medical missionaries set up clinics and used their presence in the community to foster conversion. The missionary community also popularized Western science and technology through journals like the *Globe Magazine*. By the latter part of the century, Chinese scholars were studying foreign subjects, going abroad for education, and translating Western works into Chinese.

Thus, while China had not yet completed its move to the new scientific–industrial society, momentum had already begun to build among the empire's intellectual leaders.

Zaibatsu and Political Parties: Economy and Society in Meiji Japan

The commercial environment developing through the Tokugawa period was well suited to the nurturing of capitalism and industrialism in the nineteenth century. The law of alternate attendance (see Chapter 21) had created a great deal of traffic to and from Edo as daimyo processions made their biannual trips to the capital. This traffic supported all the commercial establishments necessary to maintain the travelers in safety and comfort. The infrastructure of the major roads also required constant improvement, as did the port facilities for coastal shipping and fishing industries. Finally, commercial credit establishments, craft guilds, and large-scale industries had already regularized many of the institutions characteristic of the development of a modern economy.

Commerce and Cartels

Following Perry's visits, the Japanese were quick to go abroad to study the industrially advanced countries of Europe and the United States. Even during the last days of the Tokugawa regime, Japanese entrepreneurs were already experimenting with Western steamships and production techniques.

Cooperation and Capitalism When the Meiji government began its economic reforms, its overall strategy included two key elements. The first was to make sure that ownership, insofar as possible, would remain in Japanese hands. The second was that Japan would develop its exports to the utmost while attempting to keep imports to a minimum. Japanese entrepreneurship also received an enormous boost from the cashing out of the samurai, as some took to heart the government's injunction that starting economic enterprises was a patriotic duty.

Japan's expanding industrial needs meant that by the turn of the century, Japan needed to import much of its raw material.

Families with long-standing connections to capital swiftly moved to unite their enterprises to gain market share. The encouragement of the government and the cooperation of social networks among elites in finance and industry led to the creation of a number of **cartels** called *zaibatsu*. By the end of the nineteenth century, the zaibatsu would control nearly all major Japanese industries.

Cartel: A group of domestic or international businesses that form a group to control or monopolize an industry.

The Transportation and Communications Revolutions The rapid development of railroads and telegraphs was one of the most stunning transformations of the Meiji era. By the mid-1870s Japan had in place a trunk railroad line along the main coastal road and several branches to major cities in the interior. Similarly, telegraph—and, by the end of the century, telephone—lines were swiftly strung between the major cities and towns, followed by undersea cables to the Asian mainland and North America. By 1895, Japan was estimated to have over 2,000 miles of private and government railroads in operation (see Map 24.5).

The Meiji Constitution and Political Life While the charter oath and constitution of 1868 were successful, a debate began among the genro concerning the liberalization of representative government in Japan. In 1881 the emperor approved a plan whereby Prime Minister Ito Hirobumi (1841–1909) and several senior colleagues would study the constitutional governments of the United States, Great Britain, France, Germany, and other countries, to see what aspects of them might be suitable for Japan's needs. The Meiji Constitution, as it came to be called, was promulgated in 1889 and remained in force until after World War II.

Visions of the New Railroads. The marvels of the new systems of railroads and telegraphs springing up in Japan provided practitioners of *ukiyo-e* woodblock art a host of new subjects to depict in the 1870s and 1880s. Here is a view of one of the new stations, Ueno on the Ueno–Nakasendo–Tokyo Railway, with small commuter trains arriving and departing.

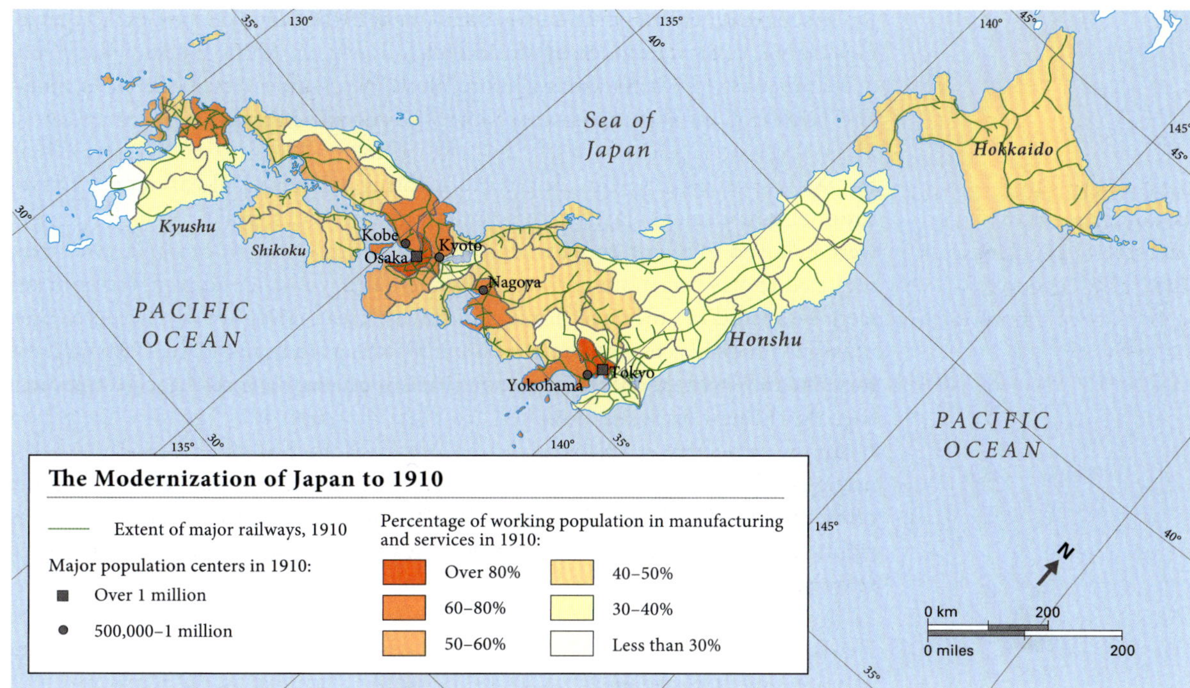

MAP 24.5 The Modernization of Japan to 1910

Ito's constitution drew from US, German, and British models. Much of it was also aimed at preserving the traditions of Japan's Confucian society that Ito and the genro most valued. Chief among these was the concept of *kokutai*, the "national polity." In this view, Japan was unique among nations because of its unbroken line of emperors and the singular familial and spiritual relationship between the emperor and his people. There was also a bicameral parliamentary body called the Diet (after the English name of the *Reichstag* of Prussia and Germany, from medieval Latin *dieta* "assembly"), with an upper House of Peers and a lower House of Representatives. Japan's House of Peers consisted of members of the nobility; the representatives were elected by the people.

As for the people themselves, 15 articles spelled out "the rights and duties of subjects." All of these, however, are qualified by such phrases as "unless provided by law," allowing the government to invoke extraordinary powers during national emergencies.

Political Parties As constitutional government began to be implemented in the 1890s, the factional debates among senior advisors began to attract followers among the Diet members and their supporters. Two major parties came to the fore by the turn of the century. The Kenseito [ken-say-toe], or Liberal Party, split into factions at the turn of the century but was later reestablished as the Minseito.

The more powerful party during this time was the Seiyukai, or Constitutional Government Party, founded by Ito and his followers in 1900. The Seiyukai dominated Japanese politics in the era before World War I; after World War II, its adherents coalesced into Japan's present Liberal Democratic Party.

Social Experiments In addition to creating an industrial base and a constitutional government, Japan's rulers attempted to curb practices in Japan that were believed to offend foreign sensibilities. Bathhouses, for example, were now required to have separate entrances for men and women, and pleasure quarters were restricted in areas near foreign enclaves; meat eating was even encouraged in largely Buddhist Japan. The government attempted to mandate Western dress for men and women, but widespread criticism ultimately forced the government to make the new dress optional.

In the same vein, traditional restrictions on women were altered. Though the home remained their primary domain, women were now seen in public far more often than they had been in the past. Concubines were now accorded the same rights as wives. Courtesans and prostitutes were no longer legally considered servants. More far-reaching, however, was the role of the new education system. With the introduction of compulsory public education, literacy would become nearly universal, and specialized women's education created entire new avenues of employment for women.

This same trend toward emancipation was evident among the rural population. The formal class barriers between peasants and samurai were eliminated, though informal deference to elites continued. During the latter part of the nineteenth century, Japan became the most intensely farmed nation in the world. The result was that although Japan's population increased to 40 million by 1890, it was a net exporter of food until the turn of the century.

"Civilization and Enlightenment": Science, Culture, and the Arts

While the Tokugawa sought seclusion, they were not cut off entirely from developments in other nations. Of particular importance in this regard was the requirement imposed on the Dutch to report to the shogun on the state of the world. By the time of Commodore Perry's visit, the accumulated amount of "Dutch learning" was impressive.

Engaging "Western Science" Nevertheless, at the time of their initial contact with the Western powers, the Tokugawa were stunned at the degree to which the accelerating technologies of the Industrial Revolution had armed their adversaries. The Japanese were immediately engaged with the notion of the railroad; just as quickly they sought to create oceangoing steamships. By 1860, they had built and manned steamers and insisted that their initial embassy to the United States travel aboard a ship the Japanese had built themselves.

The demand for industrial and military technology encouraged large numbers of Japanese to seek technical education. During the initial stages of the Meiji era, Japanese students studied in Europe and the United States, and the Japanese government and private concerns hired foreign advisors to aid in science and technical training. By the 1880s a university system was offering courses in medicine, physics, chemistry, engineering, and geology. On the whole, however, the bulk of the nation's efforts went into the practical application of science to technology and agriculture.

Culture and the Arts Japanese intellectuals read works of the Western Enlightenment and followed more recent philosophical and social science developments. Journalism played a dominant role in disseminating information to the public.

As with nearly all the arts in late nineteenth-century Japan, the novel was influenced by Western examples. The culmination of this trend was *Kokoro*, by Natsume Soseki (1867–1916), published in 1914. Soseki utilizes the wrenching changes in Meiji Japan set against traditional values to create the novel's tension.

More traditional arts such as Noh and Kabuki theater and *ukiyo-e* printing survived, but often in a somewhat altered state. Updated Kabuki variations now featured contemporary themes. As for *ukiyo-e*, it remained the most popular outlet for depictions of contemporary events until the development of newspaper photography. Especially telling in this regard are *ukiyo-e* artists' interpretations of the Sino–Japanese War.

Putting It All Together

Scholars of China and Japan have long debated the reasons for the apparent success of Japan and failure of China in their modernizing efforts of the nineteenth century. One school of thought sees the fundamental reasons growing from the respective cultural outlooks of the two countries. China, it is argued, assumed that outsiders would simply be won over to Confucian norms and modes of behavior, because this is what China's historical experience had been for the last 2,000 years. When it became apparent that defensive measures were necessary, it was still assumed that China's superior culture would win out. Japan, on the other hand, because of its long history of cultural borrowing and its much smaller size, assumed a defensive posture. In addition, the Japanese had the advantage of watching events unfold in China before the danger reached their own shores. This allowed them to act in a more pragmatic fashion to the Western threat.

Some historians, however, disagree with this analysis. They argue instead that the cultural differences between China and Japan were secondary in the face of the foreign threat. According to this school of thought, the primary cause of the radically different outcomes for China and Japan was that China was victimized by foreign imperialism much earlier and much more thoroughly than Japan. Once Japanese modernization efforts were under way, the Japanese won for themselves a breathing spell with which to keep imperialism at bay and ultimately fought their way into the great power club themselves.

Review and Relate

Thinking Through Patterns

Examine the ways historians approach the big questions of this chapter.

What was the impact of Western imperialism on the "regulated societies" of China and Japan?

The impact of the intrusion of Great Britain, France, the United States, and later Germany and Russia forced both China and Japan into defensive postures. Both countries had sought to keep out foreign influences after an earlier period of exposure to Western traders and missionaries. But the expansion of trade in both legitimate goods and opium and the need of the British for regularization of diplomatic practices pushed Britain and China into a cycle of war and "unequal treaties" under which China was at an increasing disadvantage. Japan, suddenly thrust into international commerce and diplomacy by the young United States, now sought to protect its borders without pushing the Western powers into seizing any of its territory.

Why did European empire building in Asia have such dramatically different effects on China and Japan?

China's long history of absorbing and acculturating outside invaders to Confucian norms encouraged its leaders to assume that the Westerners would be no different. Attempts at reform were often undercut by political infighting at court and in the bureaucracy. The Taiping Rebellion further depleted China's strength and resources. As time went on, increasing Western control of China's ports and tariffs, absentee landlordism, and declining agricultural productivity also played a role.

For Japan, after a decade of indecision about how to handle the foreign intrusion, a civil war ended in the dismantling of the shogunate and the unification of the country under Emperor Meiji. Japan embarked upon a reform program aimed at remaking the country along Western lines. The focus and consistency displayed by Meiji and his advisors avoided many of the problems China experienced, and Japan's late Tokugawa economics had predisposed the country toward a smoother transition into scientific–industrial society.

How have historians seen the nature of these outside forces and their influences in East Asia?

Historians have long debated the relative weight that should be assigned to cultural and material reasons for the differing paths of China and Japan. China's long history as the region's cultural leader, some have argued, made it difficult for the empire to remake itself to face the Western challenge; Japan, on the other hand, has a long history of cultural borrowing and thus found it easier to borrow from the Euro-American world. Some historians have argued that China's earlier experience with imperialism hobbled the modernizing tendencies within the empire and kept it from responding; they argue that Japan had the advantage of being "opened" later and so could respond more effectively. Others have argued that Japan's tradition of military prowess played a role, and still others contend that China's more complete incorporation into the modern "world system" hampered its ability to respond more independently.

Against the Grain

Consider this as a counterpoint to the main patterns examined in this chapter.

Reacting to Modernity

One of the enduring patterns of world history has been the complexity of acculturation to innovation from outside. As scientific and industrial society expanded its influence into the old agrarian–urban empires in the nineteenth century, the clashes were particularly fierce, especially in societies (like those of China or Japan) that felt themselves to be culturally superior to the invaders.

Not surprisingly, many people in different parts of the world chose what we might term a "culturally fundamentalist" approach. That is, faced with a threat that seemed insurmountable, they chose to take radical action by harkening back to a time when the virtues that first made their societies great prevailed. In almost every case this involved invented nostalgia and often a charismatic messiah figure. The Taipings and Boxers in China are examples of this phenomenon. In the end, however, all of these movements were ultimately crushed by the modern or modernizing forces arrayed against them. Yet the courage of their stands is often celebrated today—ironically by the representatives of the very societies that they sought to turn back.

- Are there current movements you can think of that seem to fit this phenomenon? What stresses in their societies do you think are provoking such movements?
- What factors make people turn to solutions during times of extreme stress that they wouldn't consider otherwise? Can you think of other instances in history where this phenomenon has taken place?

Key Terms

Cartel 594
Extraterritoriality 581
Nontariff autonomy 581
Self-strengthening 584
Taiping Rebellion 583

Learn more with this chapter's digital tools, including the Oxford Insight Study Guide, at http://www.oup.com/he/vonsivers4e. Please see the Further Resources section at the back of the book for additional readings and suggested websites.

PATTERNS OF EVIDENCE |
Sources for Chapter 24

SOURCE 24.1

Lin Zexu's letter to Queen Victoria of Great Britain

August 27, 1839

In March 1839, the Daoguang emperor sent Lin Zexu (1785–1850), a widely respected official with a reputation for courage and honesty, to Canton as an imperial commissioner, charged with the task of cutting off the opium trade—a trade which had proved extremely lucrative to British traders in the region. Lin confiscated vast opium stocks, ordered them destroyed, and made merchants sign an agreement that they would no longer sell the drug, on pain of death. British merchants appealed to their government for compensation—and for military action against Lin's agents. This effort led to the First Opium War (1839–1842). In the midst of his anti-opium efforts, however, Lin also attempted to shame Queen Victoria (whom he believed was at the center of governmental policy in Great Britain) into cutting off the opium trade that was causing so much damage to the Chinese people, even though it generated profits for the British.

His Majesty the Emperor comforts and cherishes foreigners as well as Chinese: he loves all the people in the world without discrimination. Whenever profit is found, he wishes to share it with all men; whenever harm appears, he likewise will eliminate it on behalf of all of mankind. His heart is in fact the heart of the whole universe.

Generally speaking, the succeeding rulers of your honorable country have been respectful and obedient. Time and again they have sent petitions to China, saying: "We are grateful to His Majesty the Emperor for the impartial and favorable treatment he has granted to the citizens of my country who have come to China to trade," etc. I am pleased to learn that you, as the ruler of your honorable country, are thoroughly familiar with the principle of righteousness and are grateful for the favor that His Majesty the Emperor has bestowed upon your subjects. Because of this fact, the Celestial Empire, following its traditional policy of treating foreigners with kindness, has been doubly considerate

Source: *Chinese Repository*, Vol. 8 (February 1840), pp. 497–503; reprinted in William H. McNeil and Mitsuko Iriye, eds., *Modern Asia and Africa*, Readings in World History, (New York: Oxford University Press, 1971), vol. 9, pp. 111–118.

towards the people from England. You have traded in China for almost 200 years, and as a result, your country has become wealthy and prosperous.

As this trade has lasted for a long time, there are bound to be unscrupulous as well as honest traders. Among the unscrupulous are those who bring opium to China to harm the Chinese; they succeed so well that this poison has spread far and wide in all the provinces. You, I hope, will certainly agree that people who pursue material gains to the great detriment of the welfare of others can be neither tolerated by Heaven nor endured by men. . . .

***Li*: Roughly 1/3 mile**

Your country is more than 60,000 ***li*** from China. The purpose of your ships in coming to China is to realize a large profit. Since this profit is realized in China and is in fact taken away from the Chinese people, how can foreigners return injury for the benefit they have received by sending this poison to harm their benefactors? They may not intend to harm others on purpose, but the fact remains that they are so obsessed with material gain that they have no concern whatever for the harm they can cause to others. Have they no conscience? I have heard that you strictly prohibit opium in your own country, indicating unmistakably that you know how harmful opium is. You do not wish opium to harm your own country, but you choose to bring that harm to other countries such as China. Why?

. . .

I have heard that the areas under your direct jurisdiction such as London, Scotland, and Ireland do not produce opium; it is produced instead in your Indian possessions such as Bengal, Madras, Bombay, Patna, and Malwa. In these possessions the English people not only plant opium poppies that stretch from one mountain to another but also open factories to manufacture this terrible drug. As months accumulate and years pass by, the poison they have produced increases in its wicked intensity, and its repugnant odor reaches as high as the sky. Heaven is furious with anger, and all the gods are moaning with pain! It is hereby suggested that you destroy and plow under all of these opium plants and grow food crops instead, while issuing an order to punish severely anyone who dares to plant opium poppies again. If you adopt this policy of love so as to produce good and exterminate evil, Heaven will protect you, and gods will bring you good fortune. Moreover, you will enjoy a long life and be rewarded with a multitude of children and grandchildren! In short, by taking this one measure, you can bring great happiness to others as well as yourself. Why do you not do it?

▶ Working with Sources

1. **How does Lin contrast honorable with dishonorable trade? Is this "honor" bound up in the product itself?**
2. **What does Lin see as the responsibility of a monarch to his/her own subjects, as well as to the subjects of other monarchs?**

SOURCE 24.2

Suppression of the Opium Trade

While opium trading and smuggling had grown to be enormously lucrative enterprises, the political, social, and ethical consequences had grown increasingly grave and, along with questions of diplomatic representation and judicial responsibility, had produced war between Great Britain and China from 1839 to 1842. While the ethical aspects of the trade were perhaps argued most plaintively by Lin Zexu, there was also considerable opposition to the trade and the war in England and particularly in Parliament, as in this excerpt from a postwar parliamentary debate.

§ Lord Ashley said, that he had three petitions to present on the subject of the opium trade with China. The first was from the committee of the Wesleyan Missionary Society, praying that the House would adopt effectual measures for the abolition of the opium trade between the British possessions in India and China. The two other petitions were of a similar nature, and were from the committee of the Baptist Missionary Society, and the directors of the London Missionary Society.

The petitions having been laid on the Table, Lord Ashley spoke as follows:

Sir, the House will, perhaps, accept as an apology from me for venturing to obtrude on them the consideration of this subject, that, although I have long felt and deplored the iniquities of the system which 1 shall now endeavour to exhibit, I should not have presumed to introduce it to their notice, had I not been pressed in such a manner as to make me prefer the charge of arrogance to that of indifference. I have no ends or purposes to serve; I have no connection, political or commercial, with the matter before us; nor are my constituents concerned in the cause beyond the interest they all must entertain as common subjects of this great empire.

But what is the position in which we now find ourselves? We are arrived at the conclusion of a sad war, of the origin of which I shall now say nothing; we are arrived at the conclusion of this war, and are most desirous of commencing the relations of peace, and of entering on an honourable and lucrative commerce. It is necessary to do all that lies in our power to avoid a recurrence of hostilities; and yet this is our condition: the causes of the war are not removed, on the contrary they are more ripe than ever; every exasperating motive is at work; audacity on the one side, and resistance on the other seem mightily increased; what has occurred once, may occur again; and will occur again, unless we hasten, while there is yet time, to be not only prudent, but generous and just.

Sir, this cause is too important for mere rhetorical declamation, and too strong for argument only; it consists of simple, hard, and indisputable facts;

Source: Commons and Lord Hansard, the Official Report of Debates in Parliament, HC Deb 04 April 1843 vol 68 cc362–469, https://api.parliament.uk/historic-hansard/commons/1843/apr/04/suppression-of-the-opium-trade if these can be disproved, the whole case falls at once to the ground; if otherwise, there is no alternative but to affirm the resolution which I shall have the honour to propose.

Now, Sir, I have but two grounds of apprehension: the one, that I may be accused of presumption in undertaking to handle so weighty a matter; the other, that I may appear as acting in a hostile feeling towards the Court of Directors of the East India Company. Of such a feeling, I can truly say, that I am utterly unconscious: I entertain the strongest esteem privately for the character of several of that body, and publicly for many parts of their administration; I am convinced that they have conferred very great benefits on the empire they are appointed to govern; and, if there be any guilt in the system which I shall develope, the guilt is not theirs, at least theirs exclusively: it is shared by the Legislature and the whole nation; it is shared by the Members of this House, which, in the year 1832, sanctioned by a law, the revenue derived from the opium trade, commending the production of the drug, and actually approving its destination.

Now, Sir, I will first assert, and then I will endeavour to prove that, so long as this traffic shall continue on its present footing, all our interests, commercial and political, must be left in perpetual hazard of interruption; and that there can, under such a state of things, be no well-grounded hope of pacific and honourable relations with the celestial empire.

Now what has occurred once, in all probability may occur again. Everything that has been said by experienced and observant men previously to the late war will hold equally good at the present moment. All the warnings which were given before the war took place, are warnings at the present time; and every syllable which I can quote of that testimony, is as valuable as though it were delivered at this very hour. I will now proceed to refer to the language of those practical men who pointed out in earlier days the fearful consequences of our nefarious practice; and which no one can gainsay as applied to our actual position.

The first authority I shall refer to is a gentleman well known to many in this House, who had long experience with the subject, having resided for seventeen years at Canton, in the service of the East India Company. I mean Mr. Majoribanks, who said, in 1830,— One of the greatest changes that has taken place, and which, in my own opinion, will, sooner or later, affect the security of our trade, is the enormous extent of the smuggling trade now carried on in China; I do not imagine they possess the means of putting it down, at least by any marine force which they have. Again, Captain Alsager, who had made nine voyages in the company's service to China, said an increase in the smuggling trade— Would lead to riot and disturbance, which would put a stop to the trade altogether. This was equally seen by intelligent foreigners residing on the spot. In confirmation of this I will refer to a work by an American gentleman of the name of King, who had long been a merchant residing at Canton. The work is entitled the "Opium Crisis," a letter addressed to the chief superintendent of the British trade with China, and written in 1839. He says,— I have been present at several of the collisions, which have taken place in our day, between the residents and Chinese; and have remarked, that the sympathies of this people have always been ranged on the side of their rulers, and against the foreigners. I have heard of late some outbursts of the native sense of injustice, at the impunity of the foreigner, under regulations which punish the Chinese opium-dealer with cruel severity. I was an eye-witness of the riot of December 12th, when the populace turned upon us, at an idle blow and but for the interposition of the city-guard, would have forced and rifled the factories. The allusion of the commissioner to "popular indignation," is to me full of meaning; yet I am concerned, not so much because he made it, as because I see the introduction of opium has lost us the affections of the good, has made us panders to the appetites of the bad; and we nay well fear lest we one day safer by the outbreaking of passions, to whose excitement we ourselves have ministered . . .

Working with Sources

1. **What are the main arguments against the trade raised in the document above?**
2. **How do the points stressed by the English opponents of the trade compare with those raised in the letter from Lin Zexu to Queen Victoria?**

SOURCE 24.3

The Meiji Constitution of the Empire of Japan

1889

The Tokugawa were forced to capitulate to the samurai of two southern domains by the end of 1867, and the new regime moved to the Tokugawa capital of Edo, renaming it Tokyo (Eastern Capital). The new emperor, 15-year-old Mutsuhito, took the name Meiji (Enlightened Rule) and quickly moved to make good on that name. The throne issued a charter oath in April 1868 and promulgated edicts that spelled out how the new government would be set up. Throughout the 1870s and 1880s, Japan experienced a flourishing of government-managed social experimentation. The proclaimed goals of using "Western science and Eastern ethics" in the service of "civilization and enlightenment" were designed to put Japan on

---

Source: Hirobumi Ito, *Commentaries on the Constitution of the Empire of Japan*, trans. Miyoji Ito (Tokyo: Igirisu-horitsu gakko, 1889), available online at the Hanover Historical Texts Project, https://history.hanover.edu/texts/1889con.html

an equal footing with Western powers. The constitution itself, composed after a painstaking study of the constitutional governments of many Western countries, reflects this drive to "Westernize." Nonetheless, the document also contained various escape clauses, in case the power of the emperor was questioned too openly.

Imperial Oath Sworn in the Sanctuary in the Imperial Palace (Tsuge-bumi)

We, the Successor to the prosperous Throne of Our Predecessors, do humbly and solemnly swear to the Imperial Founder of Our House and to Our other Imperial Ancestors that, in pursuance of a great policy co-extensive with the Heavens and with the Earth, We shall maintain and secure from decline the ancient form of government.

In consideration of the progressive tendency of the course of human affairs and in parallel with the advance of civilization, We deem it expedient, in order to give clearness and distinctness to the instructions bequeathed by the Imperial Founder of Our House and by Our other Imperial Ancestors, to establish fundamental laws formulated into express provisions of law, so that, on the one hand, Our Imperial posterity may possess an express guide for the course they are to follow, and that, on the other, Our subjects shall thereby be enabled to enjoy a wider range of action in giving Us their support, and that the observance of Our laws shall continue to the remotest ages of time. We will thereby to give greater firmness to the stability of Our country and to promote the welfare of all the people within the boundaries of Our dominions; and We now establish the Imperial House Law and the Constitution.

. . .

CHAPTER I. THE EMPEROR

Article 1. The Empire of Japan shall be reigned over and governed by a line of Emperors unbroken for ages eternal.

Article 2. The Imperial Throne shall be succeeded to by Imperial male descendants, according to the provisions of the Imperial House Law.

Article 3. The Emperor is sacred and inviolable.

Article 4. The Emperor is the head of the Empire, combining in Himself the rights of sovereignty, and exercises them, according to the provisions of the present Constitution.

Article 5. The Emperor exercises the legislative power with the consent of the Imperial Diet.

Article 6. The Emperor gives sanction to laws, and orders them to be promulgated and executed.

. . .

CHAPTER II. RIGHTS AND DUTIES OF SUBJECTS

Article 18. The conditions necessary for being a Japanese subject shall be determined by law.

Article 19. Japanese subjects may, according to qualifications determined in laws or ordinances, be appointed to civil or military or any other public offices equally.

Article 20. Japanese subjects are amenable to service in the Army or Navy, according to the provisions of law.

Article 21. Japanese subjects are amenable to the duty of paying taxes, according to the provisions of law.

Article 22. Japanese subjects shall have the liberty of abode and of changing the same within the limits of the law.

Article 23. No Japanese subject shall be arrested, detained, tried or punished, unless according to law.

Article 24. No Japanese subject shall be deprived of his right of being tried by the judges determined by law.

Article 25. Except in the cases provided for in the law, the house of no Japanese subject shall be entered or searched without his consent.

Article 26. Except in the cases mentioned in the law, the secrecy of the letters of every Japanese subject shall remain inviolate.

Article 27. The right of property of every Japanese subject shall remain inviolate. (2) Measures necessary to be taken for the public benefit shall be any provided for by law.

Article 28. Japanese subjects shall, within limits not prejudicial to peace and order, and not antagonistic to their duties as subjects, enjoy freedom of religious belief.

Article 29. Japanese subjects shall, within the limits of law, enjoy the liberty of speech, writing, publication, public meetings and associations.

Article 30. Japanese subjects may present petitions, by observing the proper forms of respect, and by complying with the rules specially provided for the same.

Article 31. The provisions contained in the present Chapter shall not affect the exercises of the powers appertaining to the Emperor, in times of war or in cases of a national emergency.

Working with Sources

1. What was the source of the emperor's power, according to this document?

2. To what extent could military considerations limit the rights and freedoms of Japanese citizens? Were these merely potential limitations?

SOURCE 24.4 Natsume Soseki, *Kokoro*

1914

Like nearly all the arts in late-nineteenth-century Japan, the novel was also heavily influenced by Western examples. The culmination of this trend, in Meiji society generally, was *Kokoro*, published by Natsume Soseki (1867–1916) in 1914. Soseki, a lecturer in English literature at the Imperial University in Tokyo, depicts the wrenching changes in Meiji Japan and their effect on traditional and generational values, leading ultimately to the tragic end of the central character in the novel. *Kokoro* (the word means, roughly, "the heart of things") was Soseki's best-known novel, and appeared two years after the death of Emperor Meiji. The following excerpts also touch on the real-life suicide of General Nogi, a hero of the Russo–Japanese War (1904–1905) who killed himself immediately after the death of the Meiji in 1912. The sense of honor that accompanied Nogi to his grave is thus at the heart of the novel, and Soseki's main theme may have been the ongoing interaction between Western-style reforms and traditional Japanese culture.

My father was the first to see the news of General Nogi's death in the paper.

"What a terrible thing!" he said. "What a terrible thing!"

We, who had not yet read the news, were startled by these exclamations.

"I really did think he had finally gone mad," said my brother later.

"I must say I was surprised too," agreed my brother-in-law.

About that time, the papers were so full of unusual news that we in the country waited impatiently for their arrival. I would read the news by my father's bedside, taking care not to disturb him, or, if I could not do this, I would quietly retire into my own room, and there read the paper from beginning to end. For a long time, the image of General Nogi in his uniform, and that of his wife dressed like a court lady, stayed with me.

The tragic news touched us like the bitter wind which awakens the trees and the grass sleeping in the remotest corners of the countryside. The incident was still fresh in our minds when, to my surprise, a telegram arrived from Sensei. In a place where dogs barked at the sight of a Western-style suit, the arrival of a telegram was a great event. My mother, to whom the telegram had been given, seemed to think it necessary to call me to a deserted part of the house before handing it to me. Needless to say, she looked quite startled.

"What is it?" she said, standing by while I opened it.

It was a simple message, saying that he would like to see me if possible, and would I come up? I cocked my head in puzzlement. My mother offered an explanation. "I am sure he wants to see you about a job," she said.

Source: Natsume Soseki, *Kokoro*, trans. Edwin McClellan (Washington, DC: Regnery, 1957), 108–110, 117–118, 120–122.

I thought that perhaps my mother was right. On the other hand, I could not quite believe that Sensei wanted to see me for that reason. At any rate, I, who had sent for my brother and brother-in-law, could hardly abandon my sick father and go to Tokyo. My mother and I decided that I should send Sensei a telegram saying that I could not come. I explained as briefly as possible that my father's condition was becoming more and more critical. I felt, however, that I owed him a fuller explanation. That same day, I wrote him a letter giving him the details. My mother, who was firmly convinced that Sensei had some post in mind for me, said in a tone filled with regret, "What a pity that this should have happened at such a time."

. . .

My father began to talk deliriously.

"Will General Nogi ever forgive me?" he would say. "How can I ever face him without shame? Yes, General, I will be with you very soon."

When he said such things, my mother would become a little frightened, and would ask us to gather around the bed. My father too, when he came out of his delirium, seemed to want everybody by his side so as not to feel lonely. He would want my mother most of all. He would look around the room and, if she was not there, he would be sure to ask, "Where is Omitsu?" Even when he did not say so, his eyes would ask the question. Often, I had to get up and find her. She would then leave her work, and enter the sickroom saying, "Is there anything you wish?" There were times when he would say nothing, and simply look at her. There were also times when he would say something quite unexpectedly gentle, such as: "I've given you a lot of trouble, haven't I, Omitsu?" And my mother's eyes would suddenly fill with tears. Afterwards, she would remember how different he used to be in the old days, and say, "Of course, he sounds rather helpless now, but he used to be quite frightening, I can tell you."

. . .

Almost violently, I tore open the tough paper which contained the letter. The letter had the appearance of a manuscript, with the characters neatly written between vertically ruled lines. I smoothed out the sheets which had been folded over twice for easier handling in the post.

I could not but wonder what it was that Sensei had written at such great length. I was, however, too much on edge to read the whole letter properly. My mind kept wandering back to the sickroom. I had the feeling that something would happen to my father before I could finish reading the letter. At least, I was sure that I would soon be called away by my brother, or my mother, or my uncle. In this unsettled state, I read the first page.

"You asked me once to tell you of my past. I did not have the courage then to do so. But now, I believe I am free of the bonds that prevented me from telling you the truth about myself. The freedom that I now have, however, is no more than an earthly, physical kind of freedom, which will not last forever. Unless I take advantage of it while I can, I shall never again have the opportunity of passing on to you what I have learned from my own experience, and my promise to you will have been broken. Circumstances having prevented me from telling you my story in person, I have decided to write it out for you."

I read thus far, and realized why it was that the letter was so long. That Sensei would not bother to write about my future career, I had more or less known from the very beginning. What really worried me was that Sensei, who hated to write at all, had taken the trouble to write such a long epistle. Why had he not waited, I asked myself, until I was once more in Tokyo?

I said to myself repeatedly, "He is free now, but he will never be free again," and tried desperately to understand what the words meant; then all of a sudden I became uneasy. I tried to read on further but, before I could do so, I heard my brother's voice calling me from the sickroom. Frightened, I stood up, and hurried along the corridor to where the others were gathered. I was prepared to learn that the end had come for my father.

▶ Working with Sources

1. **In what specific ways does this excerpt reflect the incorporation of Western ideas and items into traditional Japanese society?**
2. **How does Soseki use the dying father and the teacher as metaphors for a young man's life in the Meiji period?**

World Period Five

The Origins of Modernity, 1750–1900

The twin novel events of constitutional and industrial revolutions, first in the Americas and western Europe and later in Japan, dramatically changed the course of world history.

- People rose to end the divine right of kings and replace their rule with popular sovereignty, constitutions, and elections.
- Machines began to replace animal power in the manufacture of textiles, means of transportation, chemicals, and urban amenities.

As a result, 10,000-year-old traditional customs and habits formed by life in agriculture gave way to what we call "modernity," that is, nontraditional new ways of life in the "machine age," characterized by such new phenomena as nation-states, social classes, megacities, colonialism, and above all, vastly increased global interactions

Chapter 25

Adaptation and Resistance

The Ottoman and Russian Empires, 1683–1908

CHAPTER TWENTY-FIVE PATTERNS

Origins, Interactions, Adaptations By 1700 the Ottoman Empire found itself in financial straits. In order to pay the bills, it granted fiscal rights to provincial lords, but in the long term, these grants led to decentralization. Faced with a rapidly expanding Russian Empire, this decentralization proved disastrous. By the middle of the 1800s, however, both the Ottomans and Russians had to face the challenges of political and industrial modernity that were emanating from western Europe. In their scramble to adapt, each empire achieved only limited success, either losing territory (the Ottomans in North Africa and the Balkans) or failing with constitutional reforms (Russia).

Uniqueness and Similarities After constitutional and industrial revolutions transformed Britain, France, and the United States, adaptation was a question of survival for most other countries. Northern Europe struggled to adapt, while southern Europe tarried. For the rest of the world, adaptation was particularly difficult, in part because Britain and France had already made commercial inroads, and in part because a sense of cultural superiority kept modernity at arm's length. This was true for the Ottoman Empire, with its half-hearted constitutionalism and late-nineteenth-century industrialization. But even Russia, with its Europeanized rulers and ruling class, did not make determined efforts at constitutional reform and industrialization until the end of the 1800s.

On October 13, 1824, Aleksandr Nikitenko, born into **serfdom**, received his freedom from his lord, a landowning count. Nikitenko went on to earn a university degree. He would become a professor of literature at St. Petersburg University, a member of the Academy of Sciences, and a censor in the Ministry of Education.

From the age of 14, Nikitenko kept a diary that provides insights into the role of serfdom in the Russian Empire. He wrote that errant serfs were punished in the form of flogging with birch rods. Nikitenko's lot in life, Russian serfdom, was scarcely different from plantation slavery in the Americas or from untouchability in the Indian caste system. Slavery was also common in the Ottoman Empire, where, though limited to households, it was no less demeaning. The end of serfdom in Russia would not come until 1861 and the end of slavery in the Ottoman Empire not until 1890.

During the nineteenth and early twentieth centuries, the Russian and Ottoman Empires were bitter enemies. Because both empires became members of the Concert of Europe, however, their conflict involved the other European powers as well. The partially non-Western identity of the Russian and Ottoman Empires is important to keep in mind. As forcefully as Russia asserted itself in the European Concert in the early years after 1815 and again at the end of the nineteenth century, with its Asian hinterland it was little more "European" than the Muslim Ottoman Empire with its Middle Eastern provinces. Indeed, both empires had more in common with each other than they did with the evolving nation-states of western Europe. Therefore, we consider them together here as parallel case studies in the overall patterns of constitutionalism, nation-state formation, and the challenge of modernity.

CHAPTER OUTLINE

Decentralization and Reforms in the Ottoman Empire

Westernization, Reforms, and Industrialization in Russia

Putting It All Together

ABOVE: ***Auction of Serfs*** **(1910), a painting by Klavdiy Vasilievich Lebedev (1852–1916), shows a wealthy Russian family auctioning off its valuables—and its serfs.**

Seeing Patterns

> **Which new models did the Ottomans adopt during the nineteenth century to adapt themselves to the Western challenge?**

> **How did the agrarian Ottoman and Russian Empires, both with large landholding ruling classes, respond to the western European industrial challenge during the 1800s?**

> **Why did large, well-established empires like the Russian and the Ottoman Empires struggle with the forces of modernity, while a small, secluded island nation like Japan seemed to adapt so quickly and successfully?**

Serfdom: Legal and cultural institution in which peasants are bound to the land.

Life lease (*malikane*): Lifelong tax farm, awarded to a wealthy member of the ruling class, in return for advances to the central imperial treasury on the taxes to be collected from village farmers.

Decentralization and Reforms in the Ottoman Empire

Prior to the Russian–Ottoman rivalry in the 1800s, the traditional enemies of the Ottomans were the Austrian Habsburgs. In the 1700s the Habsburgs were increasingly sidelined by the rise of Russia as a new, Orthodox Christian empire. After consolidating itself in northeast Europe, Russia expanded eastward and southward, clashing with the Muslim Ottomans, conquerors of Constantinople. Soon Russia became the patron of nationalist movements among the Slavic populations in the European provinces of the Ottoman Empire, and the Ottomans were no match for the combined Russian–southern Slavic aggression. At the end of the Second Balkan War of 1913, the Ottomans had lost nearly the entire European part of their empire to ethnic–nationalist liberation movements and were barely able to hang on to Constantinople (today Istanbul, the official name since 1923) (see Map 25.1).

Ottoman Imperialism in the 1600s and 1700s

In the period from 1500 to 1700, the Ottoman Empire was the dominant political power in the Middle East and North Africa. At that time, the main enemy of the Ottomans was the Habsburg Empire. The two powers were fighting each other on dual fronts, the Balkans in the east and North Africa in the western Mediterranean, eventually establishing a more or less stable disengagement. It was during this disengagement period that Russia began its expansion southward at the increasing expense of the Ottomans.

From Conquests to Retreats At the end of the 1500s, the Ottoman and Habsburg militaries were overextended. Therefore, in 1606 they concluded a peace to gain time for recovery, during which the Ottomans recognized the Habsburgs for the first time as a Christian power. The peace lasted until the end of the 1600s. The Ottoman recovery was based on a shift in emphasis from their cavalry to their Janissary infantry and artillery as the main fighting force (Chapter 16).

In 1683 the Ottomans renewed their competition with the Habsburgs and laid siege to Vienna, the capital of the Austrian Habsburgs. But a Polish relief army allied with the Habsburgs arrived just in time to drive the besiegers into a retreat. The Habsburgs followed up on this retreat by seizing Hungary, Transylvania, and northern Serbia. In the peace of 1699, the Ottomans and Habsburgs finally agreed to recognize each other fully in the territories they possessed.

Renewed Reforms During the war years of the later 1600s, fiscal shortfalls meant that many Janissaries went unpaid and were forced to earn a living as craftspeople. Reforms were clearly necessary. In the early 1700s, the reformers introduced the institution of the lifetime tax farm, or **life lease**, for agricultural rents from village farmers. The idea was to diminish the short-term temptation for tax farmers to squeeze farmers dry, forcing them to flee from the countryside to the cities. Wealthy and high-ranking courtiers, officers, administrators, and Islamic clerics in Istanbul bought these life leases from the Central Treasury. Thus, here in the early 1700s was the beginning of a development parallel to similar developments in France and England, with efforts to organize a rudimentary capital market. As a result of the reforms, in 1720, for the first time in a century and a half, the central budget was balanced again.

Decentralization The transformation of cavalry-held lands into tax farms started a pattern of political decentralization in the Ottoman Empire. Agents responsible for the collection of taxes withheld increasing amounts from the treasury in Istanbul. By the mid-1700s, these agents were in positions of provincial power as "notables" in the Balkans or "valley lords" in western Anatolia. Starved for funds, the sultan and central administration were no longer able to support a large standing army of infantry and cavalry in the capital.

In 1768–1774 the notables and valley lords played a role not only in financing war against Russia but also in recruiting troops. This war was the first in which the Russian tsars exploited Ottoman decentralization for a systematic expansion southward. When the sultan lost the war, he was at the mercy of these notables and lords in the provinces.

The Western Challenge and Ottoman Responses

Soon after this Ottoman–Russian war, the Ottoman Empire faced the challenge of Western modernity. This challenge entailed severe territorial losses for the empire. But after initial humiliations, the ruling class was able to develop a pattern of responses to the Western challenge, by reducing the power of the provincial magnates, modernizing the army, introducing constitutional reforms, and transforming the manufacturing sector.

External and Internal Blows During the period 1774–1808, the Ottoman central government suffered a series of humiliations. Russia gained the north coast of the Black Sea and Georgia in the Caucasus. Napoleon invaded Egypt and destroyed the local regime of Ottoman military vassals in 1798. Napoleon's imperialist venture produced a deep shock in the Middle East: For the first time, a Western ruler had penetrated deep into the Ottoman Empire, effectively cutting it in half.

Internally, the lessening of central control in the second half of the 1700s left the provinces virtually independent. Most notables and lords were satisfied with local autonomy, but a few became warlords, engaging in campaigns to become regional leaders. In other cases, especially in Egypt, Syria, and Iraq, Mamluks—military slaves from the northern Caucasus whom Ottoman governors had previously employed as auxiliaries in the military—seized power. None of these ambitious leaders, however, renounced allegiance to the sultan, who at least remained a figurehead.

To reclaim power, the sultan and his viziers sought again to reform the empire. In 1792, they proclaimed a "new order," defined by a reorganization of the army

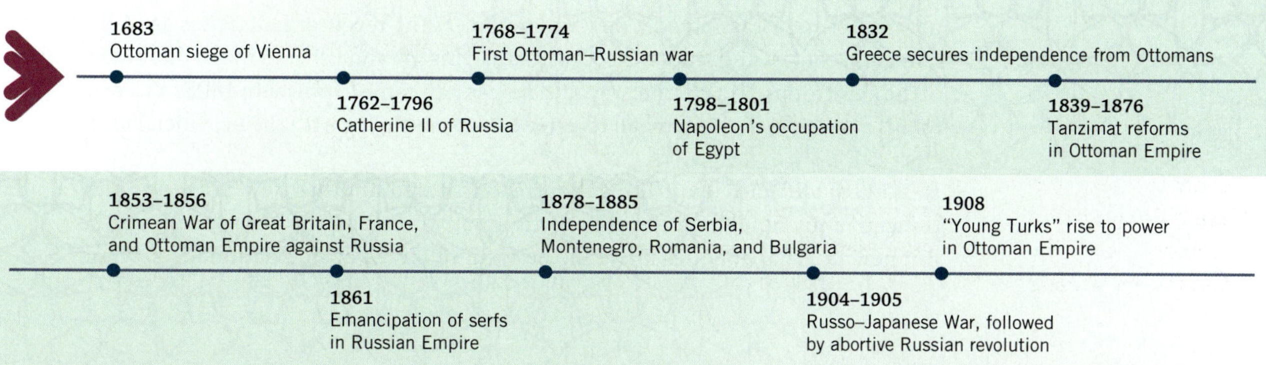

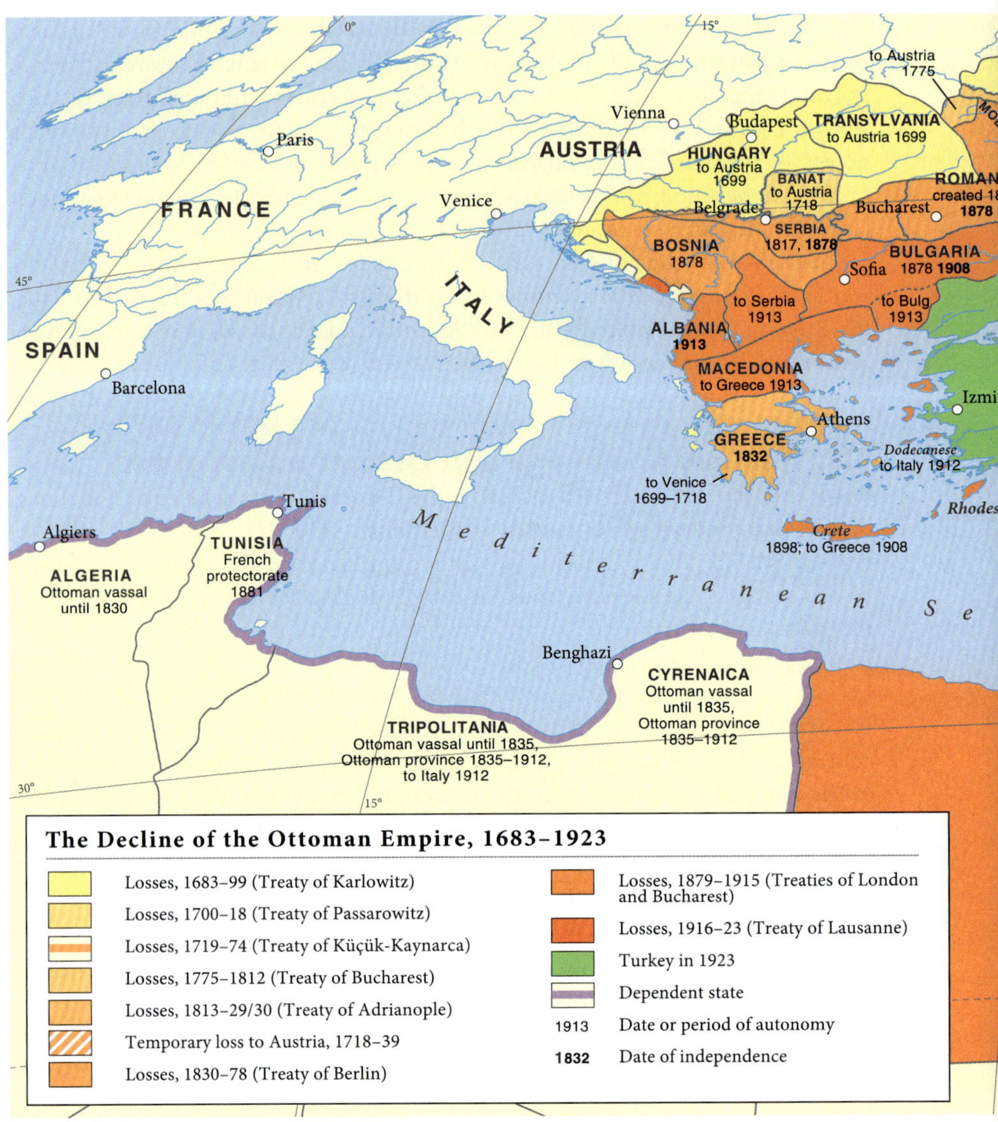

MAP 25.1 The Decline of the Ottoman Empire, 1683–1923

with the creation of a new, separate artillery and flintlock musket corps alongside the Janissaries. The ad hoc financing of the new order, however, came to haunt the reformers. During a severe fiscal crisis in 1807, auxiliary Janissaries, refusing to wear new uniforms, assassinated a new-order officer. The revolt of Janissaries as well as religious scholars and students cost the sultan his life and ushered in the dissolution of the new troops. In a counter-revolt, a new sultan came to power in 1808. As a price for his accession, the sultan had to agree to power sharing with the provincial lords.

Renewed Difficulties The sultan reconstituted another new army and neutralized many notables and valley lords, finally crushing the Janissaries in 1826. But new internal enemies arose in the form of Greek ethnic nationalists, whom

the Ottomans would have defeated had it not been for the military intervention of the European powers. As a result, Greece became independent in a war of liberation (1821–1832). Russia, providing support for its fellow Orthodox Christian Greeks, acquired new territories from the Ottomans around the Black Sea, and several Balkan provinces achieved administrative autonomy.

In 1831, the new Ottoman vassal in Egypt, Muhammad Ali (r. 1805–1848), rose in rebellion. After occupying Syria (1831–1840), he would have conquered Constantinople had he not been stopped by Russian, British, and French intervention. Without the diplomacy of Great Britain, which sought to balance the European powers after the end of the Napoleonic empire, the Ottoman Empire would not have survived the 1830s.

Tanzimat: Ottoman reforms inspired by constitutional nationalism in Europe, including the adoption of basic rights, a legal reform, and a land code.

Life, Honor, and Property Ottoman administrators realized that only recentralization would save the empire. In 1839, with a change of sultans, the government issued the Rose Garden Edict, the first of several reform edicts collectively known as **Tanzimat** ("Reorganizations"). In the Rose Garden Edict, the government bound itself to three basic principles: the guarantee of life, honor, and property of all subjects regardless of religion; the replacement of tax farms and life leases with an equitable tax system with state-employed tax collectors; and the introduction of a military conscription system, all in accordance with the Sharia, the compendium of Islamic morality and law. The edict avoided a definition of the position of the Christians and Jews in the empire, offering them the rights of life, honor, and property while maintaining their inequality vis-à-vis Muslims, as proclaimed in Islamic law.

The edict's enumeration of basic human rights was inspired by the American Declaration of Independence and the French Declaration of the Rights of Man. Here we can see a first adaptation of the Ottoman Empire to the Western challenge: The Ottoman Empire adapted, at least in a partial way, to constitutionalism, the outgrowth of Enlightenment thought.

Further Reforms As these reforms were being implemented, a new European political initiative challenged the Ottoman Empire. Napoleon III (president 1848–1852, emperor 1852–1870), self-declared emperor of France, challenged the Russian tsar's claim to be the protector of the Christian holy places in Palestine, a claim to which the Ottoman sultan had acceded after his defeat by Russia in 1774. While the French and Russian diplomats each sought to influence the sultan, the political situation turned increasingly tense. Ottoman diplomats forged a coalition with Great Britain and France. In the Crimean War of 1853–1856, this coalition was victorious against an isolated Russia. It forced Russia in the subsequent peace to recognize the Ottoman Empire's right to full integrity, provided the latter would continue the reforms announced in 1839.

Accordingly, the sultan promulgated the "Fortunate Edict" of 1856, in which he clarified the question of equality left open in the earlier edict: Regardless of religion, all subjects now had the right to education, employment, and the administration of justice. Law courts were established for the application of new commercial, maritime, and criminal legal codes, based on European models. A system of secular schools, initially for males, was introduced, but a lack of funds delayed its construction.

A measure that worked out differently from what was intended was the Land Code of 1858. Theoretically, the code subjected all users of the sultan's land—family farmers as well as landowners—to taxation, although the family farmers were now guaranteed the perpetual right to farm. But in practice the central administration had no money to appoint tax collectors. It still could not do without tax farmers, who still collected what they could get and transmitted to the government as little as they were able to get away with. Highly uneven forms of landownership and tenant farming thus developed. Overall, tax yields remained low, improving only toward the end of the nineteenth century. The much-needed land reform remained incomplete.

Constitution and War In the context of nineteenth-century constitutionalism, the decrees of the Tanzimat appeared like autocratic dictates from above, lacking popular approval. In the 1860s, younger bureaucrats and journalists, meeting in Istanbul and Paris under the name of "Young Ottomans," became advocates for the introduction of a constitution to end the autocracy of the sultan.

Muhammad Ali. Muhammad Ali transformed the province of Egypt during the first half of the nineteenth century more thoroughly than the Ottoman overlord sultan could in his far-flung empire. He astutely realized that long-staple cotton, bred first in Egypt, could make Egypt a wealthy state in the beginning industrial transformation of the world.

The idea of a constitution became reality in the midst of a crisis that embroiled the empire from 1873 to 1878. The crisis began when the Ottoman government defaulted on its foreign loans. In order to service the renegotiated loans, it had to increase taxes. This increase triggered ethnic–nationalist uprisings in Herzegovina, Bosnia, and Bulgaria in the Balkans in 1875 and 1876. The repression of these uprisings resulted in a political crisis, with a palace coup d'état by the Young Ottomans, during which a new sultan, Abdülhamit II (r. 1876–1909), ascended the throne and a constitution was adopted. The Russians exploited the perceived political weakness of the new constitutional Ottoman regime for a new Russo–Ottoman war, declared in April 1877.

Given the multiple uprisings in the Balkans but also a number of mistakes by an overly defensive Ottoman army, Abdülhamit and the new parliament were unable to prevent Russia from advancing deeply into the empire. In January and February 1878, as the Russians were practically on the doorsteps of Constantinople, dramatic events shook the city. First, a greatly alarmed Great Britain, concerned about a shift in the balance of power in Europe, threatened a naval intervention and imposed an armistice. Then, on February 14, Abdülhamit shrewdly exploited the armistice to dissolve Parliament, which had criticized him for the war effort. After a little over one year the constitutional period came to its end.

At the Congress of Berlin three months later, Abdülhamit had to accept the loss of two-thirds of the empire's European provinces. Montenegro, Serbia, Romania, and Bulgaria gained their independence. Bosnia-Herzegovina and Cyprus, although still Ottoman, received an Austrian administration and a British administration, respectively. By now it was clear that the greatly reduced Ottoman Empire was able to survive only thanks to British support.

Autocracy After ridding himself of Parliament, Sultan Abdülhamit surrounded himself with Tanzimat bureaucrats who did not have the constitutionalist leanings of the Young Ottomans. He had very little financial leeway, since the Public Debt Administration, imposed by the European powers in 1881, collected about one-third of the empire's income to pay for its accumulated foreign debt. Furthermore, the European price depression in the second half of the nineteenth century (1873–1896) was not favorable to foreign investments in the empire except for some limited improvements in communications. Once the depression was over, foreign investors enabled the government to build railroads across Anatolia. By the early 1900s, at least a basic communication infrastructure was in place in the Ottoman Empire.

Ottoman Parliament. The constitutional reforms (Tanzimat) of the Ottoman Empire culminated in elections for a parliament and two sessions, uniting deputies from a multiplicity of ethnic backgrounds (1876–1878). It met during the Russian–Ottoman War of 1877–1878, which the Ottomans lost. The newly installed Sultan Abdülhamit used the end of the war as an excuse for ending constitutional rule and governing by decree.

Given his fiscal limits, the sultan was an active propagandist, burnishing his credentials as the pan-Islamic caliph of Muslims in Eurasia. He sensed that the Balkan wars and subsequent Congress of Berlin had been a watershed in European politics. The Concert of Europe was being replaced by an imperial rivalry between Germany and Great Britain. France, Austria-Hungary, and Russia played their own imperial roles. Since France and Great Britain, furthermore, directed some of their imperialism against the Ottoman Empire, with the conquests of Tunisia in 1881 and Egypt in 1882, respectively, Abdülhamit was particularly affected. His pan-Islamism was therefore an attempt to instill the fear of jihad in European politicians and their publics.

Although most of the Ottoman Balkan provinces had become independent nations by 1878, three ethnic–nationalist movements were still left inside the empire. Abdülhamit brutally repressed them. The first movement consisted of Serbian, Bulgarian, Vlach, and Greek nationalists agitating in Macedonia during 1893–1895. (The Vlachs, who speak a language close to Romanian and are widespread in the Balkans, traditionally lived as mountain herdsmen). Without outside support, none of these feuding groups could impose itself on the province, and Ottoman troops defeated them.

Next were the Armenians, who formed sizable minorities in the six eastern provinces of Anatolia. The sultan armed Kurdish tribal units, which massacred thousands of Anatolian Armenian villagers from 1894 to 1896. Finally, when the Ottomans crushed a pro-Greek revolt in Crete in 1897 and followed up with a full-blown war against Greece, the European powers decided to step in. They forced the Ottomans to withdraw their forces from the island and settled the Cretan issue with the creation of an autonomous territory under an international force and a Greek high commissioner.

In his later years, Abdülhamit failed to stem dissatisfaction with the lack of political freedom among the graduates of the elite administrative and military academies. Improved economic conditions in the empire after the end of the worldwide depression of 1873–1896, stoked political ambitions, and oppositional circles among Ottoman intellectuals abroad merged with secret junior officer groups in Macedonia and Thrace in 1907. The officers launched a coup d'état in 1908, forcing the sultan to reinstate the constitution of 1876 and, after elections, accept a new parliament.

The final regime Emboldened by their success, leaders of the coup formed the Committee of Union and Progress (CUP), commonly referred to as the "Young Turks," and in 1909 they forcibly deposed Abdülhamit. The CUP then embarked on a policy of self-strengthening and modernization in order to create a new, Turkish national identity for the Ottoman Empire.

Unanticipated reactions to what was perceived as a reassertion of Ottoman power in the Balkans threatened to undermine the CUP and to bring down the empire. Austria-Hungary and Bulgaria formally annexed Bosnia-Herzegovina and northern Rumelia, respectively, in 1908. Albania revolted in 1910, and Italy invaded Tripolitania in 1911. In the following year Serbia, Montenegro, Bulgaria, and Greece collaborated in the First Balkan War, forcing Ottoman forces to retreat back toward Constantinople. Fortunately for the CUP, the four victorious Balkan states were unable to agree on the division of the spoils and fought a second war among themselves. The Ottomans exploited the disagreements and succeeded in a new peace settlement to push the imperial border westward into Thrace. Nevertheless, the Ottoman Empire had now been driven out of most of Europe, ending more than half a millennium of rule in the Balkans.

Economic Development While the empire was disintegrating politically, the economic situation improved. The main factor was the end of the depression of 1873–1896 and a renewed interest among European investors in creating industrial enterprises in the Middle East, Asia, and South America. When Abdülhamit II was at the peak of his reign in the 1890s and early 1900s, investors perceived the Ottoman Empire as sufficiently stable for the creation of industrial enterprises.

The traditional crafts-based textile industry of the Ottoman Empire initially suffered under the invasion of cheap industrially produced English cottons in the period 1820–1850. This invasion was facilitated further by the regime of "capitulations," that is, favorable import taxes (among other privileges) granted to Europeans in previous centuries. A recovery took place in the second half of the 1800s, however, both in the crafts sector and in a newly mechanized small factory sector of textile manufacturing. This recovery was driven largely by domestic demand and investments. Operating with low wages, domestic small-scale manufacturing was able to hold foreign factory-produced goods at bay.

The recovery of domestic textile production demonstrates that the Ottomans did not succumb completely to the British free market system. When foreign investments resumed in the 1890s and early 1900s, there was a base on which industrialization could build.

Iran's Effort to Cope with the Western Challenge

Iran had risen in the 1500s as the Shiite alternative to the Sunni Ottomans. The two dynasties of kings (shahs) who ruled Iran, the Safavids (1501–1722) and Qajars (1795–1925), nurtured a hierarchy of Shiite clerics who formed an autonomous religious institution in their state. While the Ottoman sultans controlled their Sunni religious leaders, the Iranian rulers had to respect a balance of power with their Shiite leaders. Therefore, when Iran in the 1800s faced the Western challenges, reformers had to establish an alliance with the Shiite clerics to bring about constitutional reforms.

Safavid and Qajar Kings The Safavid Empire was a less powerful state than that of the Ottomans. It comprised Shiite Iran, much of the Caucasus, Sunni Afghanistan, and parts of Sunni Central Asia. The Safavid kings

Patterns Up Close

Sunni and Shiite Islam

Like all revealed religions, Islam followed the pattern of splitting into multiple denominations. Revelation is centered on God, whose covenant with humans includes the idea of providence. God's providence is contained in his promise of salvation in the future, on the Day of Judgment. How quickly and under whom this providential future prior to the Judgment unfolds, however, was a major source of conflict among Muslims. This conflict led to the foundation of the two major branches of Islam, Sunnism and Shiism.

Husayn, Comforting His Dying Son Ali Akbar. In the early stage of the battle of Karbala, the Umayyad soldiers killed Ali Akbar, before Husayn himself was martyred. Processions and performances in remembrance of Karbala during the month of Muharram passed frequently by Shiite shrines which were embellished by local painters with frescoes showing imagined scenes of Karbala. This image, painted in 1905, is from the Imamzadeh Shah Zayd shrine in Isfahan, Iran.

During the formative period of Islam in the 800s and 900s, Muslims were deeply divided over the question of providential leadership. Was the leader of the Muslim community until the Day of Judgment a caliph (or representative) of the Prophet Muhammad and descended from the Quraysh, the dominant lineage of Mecca? Sunnis answered this question in the affirmative and regarded the caliphate as an institution guaranteeing the future of Islam until the Judgment in the distant future.

Shiites denied this answer and saw the future of Islam in a community led by the Imam (or leader), who was a descendant of Fatima and Ali, the daughter and cousin of Muhammad, respectively. The eldest son in each generation was entitled to lead the Muslims until 874, when the last Imam was believed to have entered "occultation"—that is, a state of concealment from where he would return as the Mahdi ("rightly guided leader") at the end of time, just before God's Judgment. The Shiite Imam was believed to be sinless and infallible, enabling him to pronounce authoritative interpretations of the Quran and Islamic Tradition. No Sunni caliph ever claimed inspiration, sinlessness, or infallibility.

Just before 900, a conflict broke out among the Shiites over the imminence of the Imam's return. A minority, the Ismailis, believed that the seventh Imam (in the line of descent from Fatima and Ali) would emerge from hiding already in the early 900s. When he indeed emerged at that time, he founded the Ismaili, or Fatimid, Empire in Tunisia, Egypt, and Syria. The majority, the Twelver Shiites, however, adhered to the belief that it would be the twelfth Imam who would return from occultation at a later time. They were the founders of the Buyid dynasty of emirs in Iran

could not afford a firearm infantry to match the Janissaries. As a result, the Ottomans kept the Safavid rivalry at a manageable level, especially from the mid-1600s onward.

At this time, the Safavids ruled Iran from their capital of Isfahan in the center of the country. Safavid Iran was a major exporter of silk yarn and cloth and supplemented its limited agrarian revenues with an international trade in silk.

and Iraq (934–1055) and, much later, of the Safavid dynasty in Iran (1501–1722). Both dynasties created a body of traditions and legal interpretations as guides for everyday life.

The legal school that came to dominate in Twelver Shiism was Usulism. It emerged in the second half of the 1700s and is still dominant in contemporary Iran. It emphasizes the special status of senior legal scholars (ayatollahs ["signs of God"], today about half a dozen in number) who collectively interpret theology and law in an authoritative manner, binding for all in their daily lives, even in the absence of the Hidden Imam. Among Sunnis, anyone can acquire learning and practice interpretation, although traditionally theological schools also award diplomas to specialists.

In a further interpretation, Ayatollah Ruhollah Khomeini (1902–1989), leader of the Islamic Revolution of Iran in 1979, expanded the religious guardianship of the Shiite clerics (with himself at the head) to include that of political rulership. Accordingly, Iran is a partially elective Islamic theocracy, governed by certified pious Shiites and the Shiite hierarchy of clerics. Sunnis do not have such a hierarchy or clerical establishment.

In the history of Islamic civilization, Shiites have always been a minority; today they account for about 10–20 percent of Muslims worldwide. Even in places where they could live under their own authorities, however, they developed customs that celebrate their minority status, making Shiism a religion of suffering. Shiites annually reenact the martyrdom of two of Imam Ali's sons, Husayn and Abbas, who perished in 680 at Karbala, Iraq, in an uprising against the Sunni caliph. Participants in these processions often flagellate themselves in their fervor for suffering. Today, the two mausoleums for Husayn and Abbas are important pilgrimage sites for Shiites, together with those of the other nine Imams.

Shiites today are a majority in Iran and pluralities in Iraq and Lebanon, making them important political actors in the Middle East. In present times relations between Sunnis and Shiites are shifting from the relative mutual tolerance of the 1800s and 1900s to increasing tension.

Questions

- Which other revealed religions split into denominations, and over which issues?
- Which questions do rulers face when they declare themselves the returned Imam and Mahdi, as in the case of the founders of the Fatimid Empire in the early tenth century CE and the Safavid Empire in 1501?

The Safavids were vulnerable not only to their Ottoman neighbors to the west but also to tribal federations in the Sunni provinces to the east. In 1722, a Pashtun federation in Afghanistan conquered Iran and ended Safavid rule. The Afghanis, however, were unable to establish a stable new regime. Instead, provincial Iranian rulers reunified and even expanded the empire during the 1700s. Stabilization finally occurred in 1796, with the accession of the new Qajar dynasty.

Isfahan, Naqsh-i Jahan Square. At the southeastern end of the square is the majestic Shah (today Imam) Mosque (1611–1629), a major example of the Iranian and Central Asian open courtyard mosque style.

The Qajars had been among the founding Shiite Turkic tribal federation of the Safavids, but they had no Shiite aspirations of their own. Instead, they paid respect to the clerical hierarchy that had become powerful in the aftermath of the Afghani conquest in the 1700s. The clerics supported themselves through their own independent revenues, and the Qajars were not powerful enough to interfere.

During the 1800s, two developments dominated Iran's historical evolution. First, Iran was subject to oscillating periods of decentralization and recentralization, following the decline or rise of tax revenues from the countryside. Second, the increasingly hierarchical and theologically rigid Shiite clerics were challenged by the popular, theologically less tradition-bound Babi movement. However, Qajar troops and clerically organized mobs suppressed this movement, which subsequently evolved into the Baha'i faith.

Like the Ottomans, the Qajars suffered from Russian imperialism. The Russian goal of liberating Constantinople implied the conquest of the Central Asian Turkic sultanates as well as the north face of the Caucasus Mountains. Accordingly, Russian armies sought to drive the Qajars from their Caucasus provinces. In response, the Qajar kings embarked on centralizing military and administrative reforms. In 1879 they hired Russian officers to train a small corps of new troops, the Cossack Brigade. (The tsar, although bent on expanding into the Caucasus, did not want Iran to collapse and cease being a counterweight to the Ottomans.) Swedish advisors trained the police force, and British subjects acquired economic concessions. British foreign influence aroused the ire of the conservative clerical hierarchy, however, and the kings had to withdraw the concessions.

Perceptive Iranian constitutional nationalists from among the educated younger ruling class founded a tactical alliance toward the end of the 1800s with conservative clerics and merchants. In 1906, this alliance mounted a successful constitutional revolution, imposing parliamentary limits on the Qajar regime. The constitutional–nationalist alliance with the clerics was unstable, however, and parliamentary rule failed to become a reality. As World War I drew near, Iran reverted to autocratic rule by the shahs.

Westernization, Reforms, and Industrialization in Russia

The Russian Empire that expanded during the 1800s southward at the expense of the Qajar and Ottoman Empires had begun in 1547 as a tsardom in Moscow, succeeding the Byzantine eastern Christian "caesars" (from which the Russian term "tsar," or "czar," is derived) in Constantinople. Given its geographical location at the eastern edge of Europe and outside western Christian civilization, Russia developed along an uneven pattern of relations with western Europe. Western culture became a force in Russian culture only around 1700, when the tsar Peter the Great (r. 1682–1725) was its advocate.

The idea of constitutionalism arrived in the wake of the French Revolution and Napoleon's failed invasion of Russia (1812). But it remained weak and was diluted by pan-Slavic ethnic nationalism. Small political groups rose amid the social dislocations that followed the Russian industrialization effort at the end of the nineteenth century, but none was able to take over leadership in the revolution following the defeat at the hands of Japan in 1905. Although this revolution produced a Russian parliament, the Duma, the autocratic tsarist regime lasted until World War I.

Russia and Westernization

The states of western Europe were aware of the empire to their east but did not consider it fully European. Tsar Peter the Great had begun a reform and urbanization process, against considerable resistance from both the ruling class and the population at large, to bring Russia more in line with the western European norms. His legacy included the new capital of St. Petersburg, extensive military reorganization, and efforts to rein in the power of Russia's high nobility.

Following Peter, the country entered a period of sustained rural and urban growth (1725–1800) during which the average national income per person doubled, reaching a level equal to that of England and nearly equal to that of France. Rural growth was most pronounced in the Russian heartland centered on Moscow, where it was primarily the result of an expansion of farmland. Villagers diversified their crops and increased their cottage industry of construction, textiles, and household goods. Rural-urban integration remained very limited, however, with a mere 3 percent of the agricultural production being traded into urban areas.

Catherine II's Reforms At the end of the 1700s, Russia was again governed by an outstanding ruler, Catherine, "the Great" (r. 1762–1796). She was also steeped in the Enlightenment ideas which had been spreading among the European courts—she exchanged letters with Voltaire and entertained Diderot at St. Petersburg. Her Enlightenment outlook moved Catherine far ahead of the Russian aristocracy, not to mention the small urban educated upper strata, both of which were still much beholden to eastern Christian traditions.

As much an activist as Peter the Great but more subtle, Catherine pushed through a number of major reforms. She strengthened the grip of the administration with the creation of peasant courts and a provincial reform in 1775. With a reform of the educational system in 1782, the government set up a free, mostly clergy-staffed educational system. A town reform in 1785 allowed local nonaristocratic participation. Also in 1785, Catherine strengthened the rights of the aristocracy with a charter that exempted its members from the poll tax and made them the private owners of their estates. After the aristocracy had been freed in 1762 from compulsory government service, the tsarina was concerned to provide it with new opportunities on their estates.

The unfortunate victims of the 1785 reform were the peasants who lived in villages belonging to noble estates, because they were now equivalent to private property. (These peasants comprised about half of the farmers overall; the other half lived in villages under direct government administration where the limits on their freedoms where less severe.) In theory, if not in practice, the estate peasant's status as serf—that is, as an unfree person (*krepostnoi krestyanin*) bound for life to his village—deteriorated into that of a human chattel (see the Vignette on Nikitenko at the beginning of this chapter).

Foreign Expansion In foreign affairs, Catherine continued the expansionism of Peter the Great. She undertook the dismemberment of the Kingdom of Poland, accomplished together with Prussia and the Austrian Habsburgs in three stages, from 1772 to 1795. In two wars with the Ottoman Empire (1768–1792), Catherine expanded Russian power over the Muslim Tatars, a Turkic-speaking population in Crimea and adjacent northern Black Sea lands. In the first war, Russia gained access to the Black Sea, ending the Tatar–Ottoman alliance and gaining free access for Russian ships to the Mediterranean. In the second war, Russia absorbed the Tatars within its imperial borders, which now advanced to the northern coast of the Black Sea.

Russia in the Early Nineteenth Century

The ideas of the French Revolution first emerged in Russia in the form of the Decembrist Revolt by liberal army officers in 1825. But since in the pattern of traditional empire formation the personality of the ruler counted more than the continuity of the administration, the autocratic reign of Nicholas I checked whatever the Decembrists had set in motion (see Map 25.2).

Russia and Napoleon's Invasion Catherine's grandson, Alexander I (r. 1801–1825), was educated in Enlightenment ideas. He initially showed inclinations toward constitutionalism, but Napoleon's imperial designs interrupted any idea of implementation.

Russia emerged as a key power in efforts to undo Napoleon's takeover of Europe. In 1805 it joined Britain and Austria in the Third Coalition against France. After a long war, Russia defeated Napoleon during his disastrous winter invasion of 1812. At the Congress of Vienna in 1815, Alexander advocated a "holy alliance" of monarchs to be its guarantors. As a result, Napoleon's Duchy of Warsaw became the Kingdom of Poland, with the Russian tsar as its king. In contrast to his monarchical colleagues in Europe, however, Alexander remained open to Enlightenment reforms, initiating the liberation of serfs in Russia's Baltic provinces, pursuing constitutional reform in Finland and Poland, and mapping out a new status for eastern Christianity.

Orthodoxy, Autocracy, and Nationality When Nicholas I (1825–1855) ascended the throne in December 1825, a revolt broke out, led by Russian officers who had been exposed to the ideas of constitutionalism. Known as the Decembrist Revolt, the uprising was quickly suppressed, and its leaders were hanged. Despite its relative lack of impact, the revolt represented the first anti-tsarist, constitutional-revolutionary movement and became a harbinger of things to come.

Determined to preclude any future constitutional revolts, in 1833 Nicholas implemented the doctrine known as "official nationality," according to which three concepts would guide the government: *orthodoxy*, reaffirming the adherence to eastern Christianity and rejection of secularist notions; *autocracy*, meaning the

MAP 25.2 The Territorial Expansion of the Russian Empire, 1795–1914

absolute authority of the tsar; and *nationality*, or the "spirit" of Russian identity. Nicholas created a secret police agency known as the Third Section, which vigorously suppressed dissidence from the government.

Nicholas joined other conservative European rulers in suppressing constitutional revolts. When a revolt in Poland in 1830 threatened to topple the viceroy, Nicholas abolished the country's autonomy. Then, during the widespread revolutionary constitutional movements across Europe in 1848, Nicholas supported the Austrian emperor in suppressing the Hungarian nationalists.

Hospital Ward, Scutari, Ottoman Empire, 1856. This airy, uncluttered, warm hospital room shows injured and recovering soldiers. Florence Nightingale is depicted in the middle ground, in conversation with an officer.

Nicholas was also determined to continue Russia's drive toward Constantinople, the former eastern Christian capital whose primacy the tsars claimed to have inherited. In the Russo–Ottoman War of 1828–1829, Russia helped the Greeks achieve independence. With Russian help, Serbia attained autonomy, while Moldavia and Wallachia—technically still within the Ottoman Empire—became protectorates of Russia. However, when Napoleon III of France in 1853 demanded recognition as protector of the Christians in Palestine under Ottoman rule, Russia did not fare as well. After Nicholas insisted that the Ottoman sultans honor their agreement with the Russian tsars as the actual protectors, the diplomatic wrangling ended in the outbreak of the Crimean War (1853–1856) between Britain, France, and the Ottoman Empire on one side and Russia on the other.

Both sides in the Crimean War were plagued by poor planning, missed opportunities, language barriers, and a lack of coordination between soldiers and officers. The Ottomans, still in the initial stages of their military reforms, suffered from a weak officer corps and the absence of noncommissioned officers. They would have been defeated had it not been for allied participation. The Russians did not perform well either, except for their navy, with its superior shells. The Russian army suffered from overextending its battle lines on too many fronts, the rudimentary railway network was useless for the war, communications were poor, and the bureaucracy was riddled with corruption. Thus, for both the Russian and Ottoman Empires, the war was a setback in their effort to meet the challenges of the West. However, their exposure to state-of-the-art military technology and usage would mark reform efforts of both empires in the coming decades.

The Great Reforms

The Russian defeat in the Crimean War convinced the newly enthroned Alexander II (r. 1855–1881) of the need for reforms. Russia, so he believed, lost the war because of a technologically inferior army, a lack of infrastructure, and the reluctance of the serf-owning aristocracy to shift from subsistence to market agriculture. He implemented major reforms, but with many people frustrated, the empire entered a time of social destabilization, balanced only by military successes against the Ottoman Empire.

Black Earth: A belt of highly fertile soil extending across the Eurasian steppe from the plain of the lower Danube, Moldova, and Ukraine to Siberia, narrowing from west to east. A similar belt extends from the prairies of Central Canada to the US Great Plains as far south as Kansas. The soil is rich in humus, up to six feet deep, and nutrients.

Agricultural Recession The expansion of agriculture in northern Russia during much of the 1700s, followed by the addition of the fertile **black earth** land in the south conquered from the Tatars and Ottomans in the late 1700s, ended in the early 1800s. Much of the soil was exhausted and less favorable climatic conditions during ca. 1800–1850 made farming less productive. Partial compensation was found by invading pastures and cutting down forests. Nevertheless, some 20 percent of the rural population, including serfs, left the villages and moved to towns. The average national income gains made since Peter the Great were wiped out.

In 1850, given the still modestly developed transportation network and urban grid, manufactures and commerce were dominated by preindustrial manual and animal labor. Nevertheless, the completion of the Volga-Baltic canal system in 1852 and the export of grain from ports on the Black Sea, notably Odessa, stimulated urban growth in at least some parts of Russia. One city, Ivanovo, northeast of Moscow, even grew into a factory town, with factories for the industrial production of linen and chintz. In general, however, the cities were ill-equipped to handle their growth in the first half of the 1800s.

Under powerful provincial governors, these cities possessed inadequate six-member councils to which the collectivities of merchants and manufacturers, artisans and craftsmen, and the petty bourgeoisie of laborers and peddlers elected representatives. But electoral participation remained anemic and municipal budgets too meagre to support the construction of any municipal services, such as paving, lighting, and water or sewage lines. Overall, the record of Russia in 1800–1850 was mixed: while the population grew, agriculture regressed and the urban economy stagnated.

Starving Russian Peasants. Severe weather in 1890–1891 resulted in poor harvests, which in turn led to a period of famine during the 1890s. Russian peasants were especially hard hit by grain shortages and by the government's policy of exporting surpluses in order to boost the Russian economy. Here, peasants beg food from a horse-mounted soldier in St. Petersburg.

The Emancipation of Serfs In contrast to his father, Alexander II was more liberal-minded, and given that the lost Crimean War and agricultural recession pointed to some serious deficiencies in the empire, the new tsar embarked on a reform program. A first step, in 1861, was to issue the Emancipation Edict, in which peasants were ostensibly freed from their bondage to their villages and their dues and services to the Russian landowning aristocracy. However, the edict fell short of liberating the peasantry for three key reasons. First, the decree of emancipation took two years to be fully enacted. Second, peasants were not given land titles directly. Finally, serfs had to redeem their holdings by making annual payments to the state, the proceeds from which were then used to compensate the landowning nobility. Tens of millions of farmers remained mired in poverty-stricken agricultural self-sufficiency.

Following Western models, Alexander II enacted further reforms. In 1864 the administration of government at the local level was reorganized by the establishment of regional councils known as *zemstvos*. Each zemstvo was controlled by the local aristocracy, although peasants had a say in their election. Then, in 1874, reforms aimed at modernizing the military and bringing it closer to Western standards were introduced. Planned infrastructural reforms, however, remained limited by lack of funds.

Pan-Slavism and Balkan Affairs In the 1870s, conservative intellectuals broadened Tsar Nicholas I's earlier concept of the Russian nationality into the ideology of **pan-Slavism**. Two issues contributed to Russian pan-Slavic engagement, to be extended especially into the Balkans. First, during the earlier nineteenth century a so-called cultural awakening had taken place among the Serbs, Bulgarians,

Pan-Slavism: Ideology that espoused the brotherhood of all Slavic peoples and gave Russia the mission to aid Slavs in the Balkans suffering from alleged Ottoman misrule.

and Bosnians and had led among the Serbs to a political revolution and the establishment of an autonomous kingdom (1804–1817). Second, the increasingly popular appeal of ethnolinguistic nationalism in Europe as a whole strengthened the assertiveness of the Balkan nationalities. In 1875 Bosnia-Herzegovina revolted against the Ottomans, and the rebellion then spread to Bulgaria and Montenegro. Thus, the Balkans became an area of increasing attention for the leading powers, while at the same time resembling a powder keg ready to ignite.

The Russo–Ottoman War Encouraged by Russian popular support for pan-Slavism and sensing an opportunity to exploit rising anti-Ottoman sentiments among ethnic national movements in the Balkans, the tsar declared war on the Ottomans in July 1877. The pretext was the Ottoman repression of uprisings in Bosnia-Herzegovina and Bulgaria, which had led to a declaration of war by neighboring Montenegro and Serbia in June 1876 and a call for Russian military aid. The Russians invaded, and by December had crossed the Balkan Mountains. Serbia, claiming complete independence, and Bulgaria, under Russian tutelage, were now poised to gain control of Constantinople. The other European powers stood by, anxiously waiting to see whether Russia would occupy the Ottoman capital.

In 1878, alarmed over a possible Russian occupation of Constantinople, Austria and Britain persuaded Germany to convene the Congress of Berlin. In order to defuse rising tensions over this "eastern question," the congress decided to amputate from the Ottoman Empire most of its European provinces. Russia agreed to give up its designs on Constantinople in return for maintaining control over lands in the Caucasus and acquiring the region of Kars in eastern Asia Minor. Serbia, Romania, and Montenegro became independent states. Austria acquired the right to "occupy and administer" the provinces of Bosnia and Herzegovina. There things stood for the rest of the nineteenth century.

Russian Industrialization

Alexander II was assassinated in 1881 by a leftist terrorist organization. The next Romanov tsars reaffirmed autocratic authority and exercised tight political control. These tsarist policies provoked renewed calls for constitutional reforms and generated new movements opposed to the autocracy of the regime. In the 1890s, the country enjoyed a surge in industrialization, aggravating political and social contradictions.

The Reassertion of Tsarist Authority In the face of demands by constitutionalists and social reformers, Alexander III (r. 1881–1894) unleashed "counterreforms" in order to shore up autocratic control over the country. These actions turned Russia into a police state; revolutionaries, terrorists, and opponents among the intelligentsia were targeted for intimidation, exile, or even death. Outside Russia, Alexander insisted on a program of Russification, or forced assimilation to Russian culture, for Poles, Ukrainians, and the Muslim populations of central Asia.

Nicholas II (r. 1894–1917) followed in his father's footsteps. He felt a special contempt for revolutionary groups and individuals, who increasingly called for the overthrow of the tsarist government. In addition to continuing the repressive policies of his father, Nicholas II distrusted Russian Jews as unpatriotic, and gave tacit support to a series of pogroms that climaxed in 1903–1906. These pogroms triggered mass emigrations as Russian Jews sought to escape.

Aristocratic Splendor. This oil painting of the coronation of Nicholas II and Alexandra in 1896, by the Danish painter Laurits Regner Tuxen (1853–1927), shows the rich glory of the Eastern Christian Church and the empire in ascendancy in its representation of the couple's iconic art, ermine furs, veiled ladies in waiting, and decorated officers.

Industrialization The driving force in Russia's belated push for industrialization was the minister of finance, Sergei Witte (1849–1915). He was in office during 1892–1903—a time which allowed him to take advantage of the end of the worldwide Long Depression of 1873–1896, which freed investment capital from western Europe (Britain, France, and Germany). His "Witte system" included heavy borrowing from abroad, an acceleration of heavy industrial output, the establishment of import tariffs, increased taxes on the peasantry, and conversion to the gold standard in order to stabilize the currency. Witte's crowning achievement was the Trans-Siberian Railroad, built during 1891–1905, connecting Moscow with Vladivostok on the Pacific coast. Witte's objective was not only to make Russia more competitive but also to extend Russia's reach into Siberia with its rich agricultural and mineral resources, while at the same time extending Russia's influence in East Asia.

Social Change Adjustments similar to those experienced in industrialized cities in the west inevitably had to occur also in Russian industrial centers. The populations of Moscow and St. Petersburg in the second half of the nineteenth century soared. And, like their western counterparts, industrialized urban centers consisted of overcrowded and unhealthy slums adjacent to factories. Labor conditions in factories and mines were oppressive. Calls for reforms throughout the later nineteenth century led to the formation of protest and socialist groups, all of whom contributed to the increasing pressures that would explode in the 1905 Revolution.

A striking difference between the Russian and western industrial experiences was that in Russia the numbers of wealthy factory owners, entrepreneurs, and merchants paled in comparison with the numbers of their counterparts in the West. Many Russian manufacturing plants were controlled by agents of western European investors, and those that were not were under the supervision of the Russian government. A sizable urban middle class had yet to develop, and the industrial proletariat was still small.

The Russo-Japanese War Apart from concerns about the social consequences of industrialization, the tsar and his government had to reckon also with Japan's imperial ambitions in the Far East. In the Sino–Japanese War (1894–1895), Japan occupied Taiwan and the Liaodong Peninsula of Manchuria. Japan defeated China and replaced it as the protector of Korea, but the European powers forced Japan in the Triple Intervention (1895) to give up the Liaodong Peninsula, which was leased to Russia the following year (see Chapter 24). In 1897 Witte completed the construction of a railway spur from the Trans-Siberian Railroad through Manchuria to the city of Port Arthur and proceeded to fortify the warm water port Russia ardently desired on the southern tip of Liaodong.

The construction of this spur was the final straw for Japan, whose imperial goals were threatened by Russia's action. Although it had been forced to give up Liaodong, it was determined to regain it. In early 1904, Japanese naval forces attacked the Russian fleet moored at Port Arthur. The Russian Baltic fleet, sent for relief, not only arrived too late to prevent the fall of Port Arthur but was destroyed in May 1905 by Japan when it tried to reach Vladivostok. In the peace settlement, Japan gained control of the Liaodong Peninsula and southern Manchuria, as well as increased influence over Korea, which it finally annexed in 1910.

The Abortive Russian Revolution of 1905

In addition to Russia's mauling by the Japanese in the war of 1904–1905, other factors in the early 1900s sparked the first revolution against tsarist rule. One of these was a rising discontent among the peasantry. Another was the demand by factory workers for reform of working conditions. Although the government had allowed the formation of labor unions, their grievances fell on deaf ears. In response, workers in major manufacturing centers across the country mounted protests and strikes.

Revolutionary Parties Calls for reforms resulted in the creation of new political parties. One of these was the Social Democratic Labor Party, formed in 1898 by a group of delegates who were quickly arrested; before the second congress in 1903, it was joined by Vladimir Ilyich Ulyanov, known as Lenin (1870–1924), a staunch adherent of Marxism (see Chapter 26). This group sought support from workers, whom they urged to overthrow the bourgeois capitalist tsarist government.

Mensheviks: Faction of the Russian socialist movement that supported an evolutionary transition from capitalism to communism.

Bolsheviks: Faction of the Russian socialist movement that called for revolution in the near-term.

During its second congress in London in 1903, the Social Democratic Labor Party developed two competing factions. The more moderate group, the **Mensheviks** ("minority," though they were actually numerically in the majority), was willing to follow classical Marxism, which allowed for an evolutionary process from capitalism to social revolution and then on to the eventual overthrow of tsarist rule and capitalism. The more radical faction, known as **Bolsheviks** ("majority"), led by Lenin, was unwilling to wait for the evolutionary process to unfold and instead called for revolution in the near term. Even after the split in the Social Democratic Labor Party, however, the Bolsheviks were still a long way away from the kind of elite "vanguard of the revolution" party Lenin envisaged.

The Revolution of 1905 Amid calls for political and economic reforms during the early 1900s, two concurrent events in 1904 shook the government to its foundations. First, reports of the humiliating defeats during the ongoing Russo–Japanese War began to filter to the home front. Second, on January 22, 1905, 100,000 workers gathered in St. Petersburg to present a petition of grievances to the tsar. Russian troops opened fire, killing over a hundred protestors and wounding hundreds more. The event has been remembered ever since as "Bloody Sunday," and it was regarded by Lenin as "the beginning of the Russian Revolution."

Then, from September to October, workers staged a general strike. Finally forced to make concessions, Nicholas II issued the "October Manifesto," in which he promised to establish a constitutional government, including the creation of a representative assembly, the Duma. During 1905–1907, however, Nicholas repudiated the concessions granted in the manifesto, especially an independent Duma, which remained a rubber-stamp parliament until Nicholas abdicated in 1917. Its momentum sapped, the revolution withered.

The main reason for the failure of the revolution was the absence of a broadly-based demand for constitutionalism. The small parties that existed lacked popular backing and bickered with each other. This failure of unification made the formation of broader reformist coalitions impossible. The tsarist regime still had enough military resources to wear down the small groups of reformers, revolutionaries, and demonstrators. Without sympathizers in the army, a determined tsarist regime was impossible to bring down. It was now felt that nothing short of changing the system would be effective.

Vladimir Yegorovich Makovsky (1846–1920), *Death in the Snow* (1905). This dramatic oil painting of the crowd protesting against the tsarist regime during the abortive revolution of 1905 is one of the greatest Russian realist paintings. Makovsky was one of the founders of the Moscow Art School and continued to paint after the Russian Revolution of 1917.

Putting It All Together

Both the Ottoman and Russian Empires faced the initial Western military and constitutional challenges directly on their doorsteps. The Ottoman Empire, as a mature empire struggling to regain its traditional centralism, fought largely defensive wars. Russia, still a young empire, expanded aggressively against the defensive Ottomans and its weaker Asian neighbors (except Japan) but suffered occasional military and diplomatic setbacks.

Western constitutional nationalism was another powerful and corrosive pattern. The transformation of kingdoms or colonies into nations in which subjects would become citizens entitled to vote was difficult enough in Europe. In the Ottoman Empire, a wide gap existed between constitutional theory and practice, especially as far as religion was concerned. Russia, plagued by the reluctance of its aristocracy to give up serfdom even after emancipation, left its constitutionalists out in the cold. Sultans, emperors, and kings knew well that none of their constitutions would fully satisfy the demands for liberty, equality, and fraternity.

To complicate matters for both the Ottoman and Russian Empires, in the second half of the 1800s, many members of the rising educated urban middle class deserted constitutionalism and turned to ethnic nationalism (in the Ottoman Empire) or pan-Slavism and Marxism (in the Russian Empire). By contrast, both the Ottoman and Russian Empires met the Western industrial challenge without completely surrendering their markets. Once they were able to attract foreign capital for the construction of expensive railroads and factories at the end of the 1800s, they even started on their own paths to industrialization. In spite of wrenching transformations, the two were still empires in control of themselves when World War I broke out. Neither would survive the war, however. Instead, they would be transformed by the forces that had beset them throughout the nineteenth century.

Review and Relate

Thinking Through Patterns

Examine the ways historians approach the big questions of this chapter.

➤ Which new models did the Ottomans adopt during the nineteenth century to adapt themselves to the Western challenge?

The traditional model for reform in the Ottoman Empire was based on the Islamic concept of the divinely sanctioned, absolute authority of the sultan; officials could be appointed or dismissed at will. The later history of the Ottoman Empire is significant in world history because it shows the *adaptation pattern* to the Western challenge—this time, the borrowing of constitutional nationalism and modern military technology from Europe.

➤ How did the agrarian Ottoman and Russian Empires, both with large landholding ruling classes, respond to the western European industrial challenge during the 1800s?

As agrarian polities with large landowning classes collecting rents from tenant farmers or serfs, the Ottoman and Russian Empires found it difficult to respond to the European industrial challenge. Large foreign investments were necessary for the building of steelworks, factories, and railroads. Given the long economic recession of the last quarter of the 1800s, these investments—coming from France, Great Britain, and Germany—went to an expanding Russia, more than the shrinking Ottoman Empire, as the safer bet.

➤ Why did large, well-established empires like the Russian and Ottoman Empires struggle with the forces of modernity, while a small, secluded island nation like Japan seemed to adapt so quickly and successfully?

One avenue of inquiry is cultural: How receptive were the Russians and Ottomans—or the Qing, for that matter—to the ideas of the Enlightenment? The short answer must be "Not very." Even the most willing leaders in these empires risked alienating entrenched interests by attempting reforms. The cautious reforms that resulted disrupted traditional routines but left few effective alternatives. In addition, such large multiethnic empires as those of Russia and the Ottomans found it difficult to rally subjects around a distinct "nationality," since they encompassed so many divergent ones. In contrast, the Meiji reformers had the advantage of a unity derived from outside pressures. Moreover, the new regime immediately began creating an ideology of Japaneseness—a form of ethnic nationalism—and institutionalized it in education and national policy. Japan's legacy of cultural borrowing may also have been an advantage, as well as a nascent capitalist system developing in the late Tokugawa era.

Against the Grain

Consider this as a counterpoint to the main patterns examined in this chapter.

A Precursor to Lenin

The Emancipation Edict issued in 1861 by Alexander II was touted as making vast improvements in the lives of Russia's peasantry. When it soon became apparent that reform measures fell far short of the mark, radical political factions demanded more far-reaching reforms. In the vanguard was a group of Russian intelligentsia who circulated their ideas in pamphlets and literary journals.

Of these activists, one of the most notable was Nikolai Chernyshevsky (1828–1889), who defied conventional approaches to Russia's problems. As editor of the radical journal *Contemporary*, and inspired by western intellectuals like Hegel, Chernyshevsky wrote critiques of moderate reforms, especially those advocated by liberals and intelligentsia. The only way to resolve the current status quo, according to Chernyshevsky, was through revolution, with the Russian peasantry as driver of meaningful reforms. To this end Chernyshevsky advocated the formation of social collectives, or communes, based on utopian models.

- In what ways does Chernyshevsky epitomize radical socialist ideas?
- How does Chernyshevsky compare to earlier contrarians like Thomas Paine and Joseph Sieyès?

Chernyshevsky's writing resulted in his imprisonment in 1862. During this time, he wrote the inflammatory novel *What Is to Be Done?*, frequently referred to as a "handbook of radicalism." In it, Chernyshevsky called for actions and policies informed by socialist ideals, including women's liberation, and programs of social justice. The book inspired radical activists and terrorists during the 1870s and 1880s, and Chernyshevsky was acknowledged as the first revolutionary socialist as well as the forerunner of the 1905 revolution. Lenin was so impressed by Chernyshevsky's novel that he not only referred to it as one of the most influential books he had ever read—including those of Marx—but he also entitled his own manual of revolution *What Is to Be Done?*

Key Terms

Black earth 616
Bolsheviks 620
Life lease 602
Mensheviks 620
Pan-Slavism 617
Serfdom 602
Tanzimat 606

Learn more with this chapter's digital tools, including the Oxford Insight Study Guide, at http://www.oup.com/he/vonsivers4e. Please see the Further Resources section at the back of the book for additional readings and suggested websites.

PATTERNS OF EVIDENCE | Sources for Chapter 25

SOURCE 25.1 Lady Mary Wortley Montagu, *Letters from the Levant*

April 1, 1717

Mary Wortley Montagu (1689–1762), who was born into the British aristocracy, sought out acquaintances with the leading literary and scientific figures of her day and traveled with her husband to Constantinople while he was ambassador to the Ottoman emperor. Although her husband was recalled to England within a year, Lady Mary endeavored to learn as much as possible about Turkish customs and behavior, especially those concerning women and children. She frequently had paintings made of herself (and her son) dressed in Turkish costume, and she considered it patriotic to import Turkish customs that she thought could benefit her fellow Englishmen. Her introduction of the Turkish practice of inoculation against smallpox drew the great admiration of Voltaire, who praised her intelligence and her willingness to learn from others in his *Letters Concerning the English Nation* (1733).

To the Countess of Mar [her sister], Adrianople, April 1, 1717.

. . .

Pray let me into more particulars, and I will try to awaken your gratitude, by giving you a full and true relation of the novelties of this place, none of which would surprise you more than a sight of my person, as I am now in my Turkish habit, though I believe you would be of my opinion, that is admirably becoming. I intend to send you my picture; in the mean time accept of it here.

The first part of my dress is a pair of drawers, very full, that reach to my shoes, and conceal the legs more modestly than your petticoats. They are of a thin rose-coloured damask, brocaded with silver flowers. My shoes are of white kid leather, embroidered with gold. Over this hangs my smock, of a fine white silk gauze, edged with embroidery. This smock has wide sleeves, hanging half-way down the arm, and is closed at the neck with a diamond button; but the shape and colour of the bosom are very well to be distinguished through it.

. . .

Source: Mary Wortley Montagu, *Letters from the Levant during the Embassy to Constantinople*, 1716–1718 (New York: Arno, 1971), 124, 128–129, 146–148.

Upon the whole, I look upon the Turkish women as the only free people in the empire; the very divan pays respect to them, and the grand signior himself, when a pasha is executed, never violates the privileges of the *harém*, (or women's apartment,) which remains untouched and entire to the widow. They are queens of their slaves, whom the husband has no permission so much as to look upon, except it be an old woman or two that his lady chooses. It is true their law permits them four wives; but there is no instance of a man of quality that makes use of this liberty, or of a woman of rank that would suffer it. When a husband happens to be inconstant, (as those things will happen,) he keeps his mistress in a house apart, and visits her as privately as he can, just as it is with you. Amongst all the great men here, I only know the *tefterdar*, (i.e. treasurer) that keeps a number of she slaves for his own use (that is, on his own side of the house; for a slave once given to serve a lady is entirely at her disposal,) and he is spoken of as a libertine, or what we should call a rake, and his wife will not see him, though she continues to live in his house.

Thus you see, dear sister, the manners of mankind do not differ so widely as our voyage writers would make us believe. Perhaps it would be more entertaining to add a few surprising customs of my own invention; but nothing seems to me so agreeable as truth, and I believe nothing so acceptable to you.

. . .

Letter to Mrs. S. C—— [Sarah Chiswell], Adrianople, April 1 [1717].

. . .

A propos of distempers: I am going to tell you a thing that will make you wish yourself here. The small-pox, so fatal and so general amongst us, is here entirely harmless by the invention of *ingrafting*, which is the term they give it. There is a set of old women who make it their business to perform the operation every autumn, in the month of September, when the great heat is abated. People send to one another to know if any of their family has a mind to have the small-pox: they make parties for this purpose, and when they are met (commonly fifteen or sixteen together,) the old woman comes with a nutshell full of the matter of the best sort of small-pox, and asks what vein you please to have opened. She immediately rips open that you offer to her with a large needle (which gives you no more pain than a common scratch,) and puts into the vein as much matter as can lie upon the head of her needle, and after that binds up the little wound with a hollow bit of shell; and in this manner opens four or five veins. The Grecians have commonly the superstition of opening one in the middle of the forehead, one in each arm and one on the breast, to mark the sign of the cross; but this has a very ill effect, all these wounds leaving little scars, and is not done by those that are not superstitious, who choose to have them in the legs, or that part of the arm that is concealed. The children or young patients play together all the rest of the day, and are in perfect health to the eighth. Then the fever begins to seize them, and they keep their beds two days, very seldom three. They have very rarely above twenty or thirty in their faces, which never mark; and in eight days' time they are as well as before their illness. Where they are wounded, there remain running sores during the distemper, which I do not doubt is a great relief to it. Every year thousands undergo this operation; and the French ambassador says pleasantly, that they take the small-pox here by way of diversion, as they take the waters in other countries. There is no example of any one that has died in it; and you may believe I am well satisfied of the safety of this experiment, since I intend to try it on my dear little son.

I am patriot enough to take pains to bring this useful invention into fashion in England; and I should not fail to write to some of our doctors very particularly about it, if I knew any one of them that I thought had virtue enough to destroy such a considerable branch of their revenue for the good of mankind. But that distemper is too beneficial to them, not to expose to all their resentment the hardy wight that should undertake to put an end to it.

Working with Sources

1. **Was Montagu naïve about the role of women in Turkish society? Is she using the experiences of Turkish women principally as a foil for those of English women?**
2. **How does Montagu contrast "superstition" with "reasonable" behavior, and why?**

SOURCE 25.2

Imperial Edict of the Rose Garden

November 3, 1839

With a change of Ottoman sultans in 1839, the government issued the Rose Garden Edict, the first of three reform edicts which are collectively known as the Tanzimat (reorganizations). With this edict, the government bound itself to basic principles with respect to relations between it and its subjects, and it carefully avoided a definition of the position of religious minorities in the empire. The document also enumerates basic human rights, drawing on ideas from the American and French revolutionary declarations of the eighteenth century. Accordingly, it reflects the adaptability of the Ottoman Empire to Western ideas, at least in the general context of the Tanzimat reforms.

The Hatti-Sherif of Gülhane

All the world knows that in the first days of the Ottoman monarchy, the glorious precepts of the Qur'an and the laws of the Empire were always honored.

The Empire in consequence increased in strength and greatness, and all its subjects, without exception, had acquired the highest degree of ease and prosperity. In the last one hundred and fifty years a succession of accidents

---

Source: Herbert J. Liebesny, *The Law of the Near and Middle East: Readings, Cases, and Materials* (Albany: State University of New York Press, 1975), 46–49.

and divers causes have brought about a disregard for the sacred code of laws and the regulations flowing therefrom, and the former strength and prosperity have changed into weakness and poverty; an empire in fact loses all its stability as soon as it ceases to observe its laws.

These considerations are ever present in our mind and, from the day of our advent to the throne the thought of the public weal, of the improvement of the state of the provinces, and of relief to the [subject] peoples has not ceased wholly to engage it. If, therefore, the geographical position of the Ottoman provinces, the fertility of the soil, the aptitude and intelligence of the inhabitants are considered, the conviction will remain that by striving to find efficacious means, the result, which with the help of God we hope to attain, can be obtained within a few years. Full of confidence, therefore, in the help of the Most High and supported by the intercession of our Prophet, we deem it right to seek through new institutions to provide the provinces composing the Ottoman Empire with the benefit of a good administration.

These institutions must be principally carried out under three heads which are:

1. Guarantees insuring to our subjects perfect security of life, honor, and fortune.
2. A regular system of assessing and levying taxes.
3. An equally regular system for the levying of troops and the duration of their service.

. . .

From henceforth, therefore, the cause of every accused person shall be judged publicly, as our divine law requires, after inquiry and examination, and so long as a regular judgment shall not have been pronounced, no one can secretly or publicly put another to death by poison or in any other manner.

No one shall be allowed to attack the honor of any person whatever.

Each person shall possess his property of every kind and shall dispose of it in all freedom, without let or hindrance from any person whatever; thus, for example, the innocent heirs of a criminal shall not be deprived of their legal rights, and the property of the criminal shall not be confiscated. These imperial grants shall extend to all our subjects, of whatever religion or sect they may be; they shall enjoy them without exception. Perfect security is thus given to the inhabitants of our Empire in their lives, their honor, and their fortunes, as they are secured to them by the sacred text of our law.

As for the other points, as they must be settled with the assistance of enlightened opinions, our council of justice (increased by new members as shall be found necessary), to whom shall be joined, on certain days which we shall determine, our ministers and the notables of the Empire, shall assemble in order to frame laws regulating these matters concerning the security of life and fortune and the assessment of taxes. Each one in these assemblies shall freely express his ideas and give his advice.

. . .

As the object of these institutions is solely to revivify religion, government, the nation, and the Empire, we engage not to do anything which is contrary thereto.

In testimony of our promise we will, after having deposited these presents in the hall containing the glorious mantle of the Prophet, in the presence of all the "*ulama*" and the grandees of the Empire, make oath thereto in the name of God, and shall afterwards cause the oath to be taken by the "*ulama*" and grandees of the Empire.

Working with Sources

1. **How are Islamic religious principles used to substantiate and reinforce the force of law in the Tanzimat era? Would this be applied to the adherents of *all* religions in the empire?**
2. **Were the declarations in this edict too vague to be workable? Are they deliberately vague?**

SOURCE 25.3

Tsar Alexander II's abolition of serfdom

February 19, 1861

The defeat of Russia in the Crimean War (1853–1856) convinced the newly enthroned Alexander II (r. 1855–1881) of the need for fundamental reforms in his country. The first institution he tackled was serfdom, and his Emancipation Edict (1861) ostensibly freed peasants from their bondage to the landowning aristocracy. Although the edict affected some 50 million serfs, it was not fully implemented. Peasants were not given land titles per se; the land was turned over to the control of local communities (*mirs*), which then allocated parcels to individual serfs. Moreover, they were forced to make annual payments to the government in the form of loans that would compensate the former landowners; the loan amounts were often higher than the dues aristocrats had demanded before emancipation.

By the Grace of God WE, Alexander II, Emperor and Autocrat of All Russia, King of Poland, Grand Duke of Finland, etc., make known to all OUR faithful subjects: Called by Divine Providence and by the sacred right of inheritance to the Russian throne of OUR ancestors, WE vowed in OUR heart to respond to the mission which is entrusted to Us and to surround with OUR affection and OUR Imperial solicitude all OUR faithful subjects of every rank and condition, from the soldier who nobly defends the country to the humble artisan who works in industry; from the career official of the state to the plowman who tills the soil.

Source: Alexander II, Emancipation Manifesto, 1861, in *Documents in Russian History*, http://academic.shu.edu/russianhistory/index.php/Alexander_II,_Emancipation_Manifesto,_1861

Examining the condition of classes and professions comprising the state, WE became convinced that the present state legislation favors the upper and middle classes, defines their obligations, rights, and privileges, but does not equally favor the serfs, so designated because in part from old laws and in part from custom they have been hereditarily subjected to the authority of landowners, who in turn were obligated to provide for their well being. Rights of nobles have been hitherto very broad and legally ill defined, because they stem from tradition, custom, and the good will of the noblemen. In most cases this has led to the establishment of good patriarchal relations based on the sincere, just concern and benevolence on the part of the nobles, and on affectionate submission on the part of the peasants. Because of the decline of the simplicity of morals, because of an increase in the diversity of relations, because of the weakening of the direct paternal relationship of nobles toward the peasants, and because noble rights fell sometimes into the hands of people exclusively concerned with their personal interests, good relations weakened. The way was opened for an arbitrariness burdensome for the peasants and detrimental to their welfare, causing them to be indifferent to the improvement of their own existence.

. . .

Having invoked Divine assistance, WE have resolved to execute this task.

On the basis of the above-mentioned new arrangements, the serfs will receive in time the full rights of free rural inhabitants.

The nobles, while retaining their property rights to all the lands belonging to them, grant the peasants perpetual use of their household plots in return for a specified obligation; and, to assure their livelihood as well as to guarantee fulfillment of their obligations toward the government, [the nobles] grant them a portion of arable land fixed by the said arrangements as well as other property.

While enjoying these land allotments, the peasants are obliged, in return, to fulfill obligations to the noblemen fixed by the same arrangements. In this status, which is temporary, the peasants are temporarily bound.

At the same time, they are granted the right to purchase their household plots, and, with the consent of the nobles, they may acquire in full ownership the arable lands and other properties which are allotted them for permanent use. Following such acquisition of full ownership of land, the peasants will be freed from their obligations to the nobles for the land thus purchased and will become free peasant landowners.

WE also rely upon the zealous devotion of OUR nobility, to whom WE express OUR gratitude and that of the entire country as well, for the unselfish support it has given to the realization of OUR designs. Russia will not forget that the nobility, motivated by its respect for the dignity of man and its Christian love of its neighbor, has voluntarily renounced serfdom, and has laid the foundation of a new economic future for the peasants. WE also expect that it will continue to express further concern for the realization of the new arrangement in a spirit of peace and benevolence, and that each nobleman will bring to fruition on his estate the great civic act of the entire group by organizing the lives of his peasants and his household serfs on mutually advantageous terms, thereby setting for the rural population a good example of a punctual and conscientious execution of the state's requirements.

The examples of the generous concern of the nobles for the welfare of peasants, amid the gratitude of the latter for that concern, give Us the hope that a mutual understanding will solve most of the difficulties, which in some cases will be inevitable during the application of general rules to the diverse conditions on some estates, and that thereby the transition from the old order to the new will be facilitated, and that in the future mutual confidence will be strengthened, and a good understanding and a unanimous tendency towards the general good will evolve.

. . .

And now WE confidently expect that the freed serfs, on the eve of a new future which is opening to them, will appreciate and recognize the considerable sacrifices which the nobility has made on their behalf.

They should understand that by acquiring property and greater freedom to dispose of their possessions, they have an obligation to society and to themselves to live up to the letter of the new law by a loyal and judicious use of the rights which are now granted to them. However beneficial a law may be, it cannot make people happy if they do not themselves organize their happiness under protection of the law. Abundance is acquired only through hard work, wise use of strength and resources, strict economy, and above all, through an honest God-fearing life.

Working with Sources

1. **How does the "Tsar Liberator" attempt to use religion and morality to persuade nobles to benefit their peasants?**
2. **To what extent does the document limit peasants' rights? Why?**

SOURCE 25.4

Female workers' strike at the Gal'pern matchbox factory in Pinsk

1901–1902

Since accelerated industrialization in Imperial Russia began in the 1890s, an impoverished working class grew under appalling conditions. As in Great Britain in the early half of the 1800s, wages were minimal, hours were long, and employment was insecure. Jewish workers, as well as Jewish employers, suffered additional discrimination under the reactionary rule of Tsar Nicholas II (1894–1917).

Source: Abbreviated and adapted from ChaeRan Y. Freeze and Jay M. Harris, eds., *Everyday Jewish Life in Imperial Russia: Select Documents, 1772–1914* (Waltham, MA: Brandeis University Press, 2013), 488–494.

Secret Report of the Assistant Chief of the Minsk Gendarme Administration (5 April 1901)

On the night of 1–2 April 1901, a mimeographed appeal to cabinetmakers to join the struggle against the owners was disseminated in the town of Pinsk. It was signed by the Pinsk Social-Democratic Committee of the Jewish Workers' Union in Russia and Poland and was dated April 1901. On the night of 3 April, the same Committee distributed appeals to workers of the plywood factory demanding an increase in wages and reduction in the workday. The appeal concluded: "Put an end to the domination of capital! Long live the workers' movement!"

On 2 April at the Gal'pern matchbox factory, before the start of the evening shift, the workers of the packing division informed the owner that they would not work and demanded an increase in pay given that the owner had reduced the thickness of the matches, making their work more difficult and slightly reducing their [piece-rate] wages. Four girls presented the demands to the owner: Ginda Vorona [Gleiberman], Reizla Iuzik, Shosha Segalevich, and Sora Breitbord. When the owner proposed to deal summarily with the latter [that is, fire them], they declared that they would leave the factory—not alone, but with all the girls.

On 3 April, more than one hundred young women and adolescents in the packing department did not show up to work. Moreover, the owner was informed that the four girls named above (with the assistance of several youths) did not allow the girls into the factory and threatened to beat them if they disobeyed.

After I and the chief of police arrived at the factory that day, the owner [Iosif] Gal'pern told me that he had known about the strike earlier: the previous day the girls had assembled in one of the courtyards, where they gave speeches and offered fifteen kopecks to anyone who wished to strike. In addition, in early March he received a mimeographed appeal (signed by the Pinsk Social-Democratic Committee) to the workers in his factory. He did not report this appeal to anyone but kept it to himself. Nevertheless, he was targeted by the workers: in January or February, a mimeographed newspaper of the same Committee, *The Pinsk Workers* (number 3) said that in view of the accumulated facts about the oppression of the workers in the plywood and matchbox factories, separate sheets would be released about the factories in the near future. The newspaper advised workers to unite and go to the owner. When I asked why Gal'pern kept this newspaper and appeal to himself and did not forward it to me or the chief of police, he replied that such are police and gendarme matters, but he is absolutely a private person. When I demanded the newspaper, he replied that he had given it to his manager to read and would get it by evening. Further investigation showed that the strike did ensue and included the participation of the "Pinsk Committee," which distributed strike money on the first day of the strike.

On 4 April, at 11:00 a.m. almost all the girls came to work. With the assistance of the police, I took measures to discover the local meetings and chief activists of the "Pinsk Committee."

On the night of 5 April, they produced and distributed mimeographed appeals urging girls who had not yet come to the meetings not to accede to the owner, to continue the strike, and to give worker-informers the treatment they deserved.

Here is my assessment of the strike: (1) Gal'pern himself is at fault because he changed the size of the matches in an untimely manner, even without the permission of the factory inspector; (2) his manager, Rom, who promised to increase the packers' piece-rate wages after the holidays [Passover], exploited this "Pinsk Committee" and the March appeal (which urged workers to demand a supplement for their piece-wages from the owner Gal'pern once work resumed after the holidays and to strike if he refused). The appeal worked, and on the first workday after the Jewish holidays (2 April) they submitted the demand for a supplement; he refused, with the strike as a consequence.

Based on the circular of the Department of Police (2 August, number 7587), I initiated a formal inquiry [. . .]; I propose to combine it with my investigation of the "Pinsk Committee" (see my report of 18 December 1900, number 1028). To identify the other members of the Committee, I have taken the most energetic measures. I have placed the above-named girls under arrest until the facts of the case are clear.

Deposition of Iosif Avraamov Gal'pern (4 April 1901)

My name is Gal'pern, Iosif Abraamov. I am fifty-five years old, of the Jewish confession. My rank is first-guild merchant. I live in the town of Pinsk, district 2, in a private house.

Here is my response to the questions directed to me: On the occasion of the Jewish holiday of Passover, work ended on 20 March at my factory and resumed again on 1 April; however, as it was the first day after a break, work proceeded at a slow pace. On 2 April work began properly, with the usual energy. A little later, the foreman of the packing division noticed that two girls, Gleiberman (that is, Vorona) and Segalevich, were somewhat excited and, fearing some kind of prank on their part, informed them that in fourteen days he would dismiss them and make the appropriate note in their labor books. That same day, around 2:00 p.m. (during the lunch break), twenty girls gathered in the corridor of the office. Hearing the ruckus, I opened the door; When I asked "What is going on?" the two girls, holding up their labor books, told me that their foreman had fired them because they had asked for a raise in wages. I told them that anyone who is dissatisfied with the factory could leave their jobs, and I would even free them from the fourteen-day [notice] period. In response the girl Leberkes, who was also standing there, asked me to note in her booklet that she was unwilling to continue working. Another girl, Breitbord, began to beckon to girls gathered in the courtyard. As I collected the labor books from these girls, I proposed that those wishing to work, return to the [packing] division and that those who did not, give me their books for notation. The four girls cited above began to demand that the other girls stop working, but except for these four, they all of course went back to work.

At my request, the police chief for the first district came to remove Gleiberman, Segalevich, Leberkes, and Breitbord, but when they declared that they wished to remain and resume work, he left them at the factory.

Seeing that the workers had calmed down, I went home. Within a half-hour of my departure, however, all the girls in the packing division suddenly stopped working and went into the factory courtyard. The factory administrator announced that she would make a list of all those who did not wish to work and advised them to go back into the [packing] division and get down to work. Eighty girls went in immediately, and the rest after a while. Work continued until the end of the evening. On the evening of that same day, I was informed that the girls from my factory gathered at a meeting in the courtyard of some house on Goncharnaia Street. An unidentified speaker persuaded the girls not to work the next day. Some young people at the assembly promised to give them strike money. I did not manage to learn the details about the site of the assembly, which probably ended quickly because of a fire that broke out on the same street.

On 3 April work in all the sections of the factory proceeded as usual. However, only 25 girls showed up at the packing department (which always had up to 160 girls). I learned that many of the girls (including Segalevich, Gleiberman, Leberkes, and Breitbord) stood on the corner of the street to my factory and prevented others from coming to work by threatening to beat them. In the course of the day a few more girls appeared to work, but about 80 girls were absent. Some of those who were present at the factory office yesterday came with tears in their eyes, saying that the [strikers] had not allowed them into the factory under different pretexts, as you yourself have seen.

Moreover, I suggest that the cause of the strike was the mimeographed appeal that the Pinsk Committee disseminated in March about my factory workers. I see no other reason for the strike, because I did not offend the workers. I did reduce the size of the matchsticks, but the girls' wages did not decrease—because the size of the matchboxes was reduced proportionately. However, if it did seem that wages were reduced because of this, then of course I would have supplemented the wages. On 4 April, before 11:00 a.m. up to one hundred girls gathered in the packing division and resumed the order of work. According to rumors, the agitators and members of the Pinsk Committee may consist of Ovsei Gurin and Borushok (the son of the barrister for legal matters, Faivel Borushok). Not all the girls packed [the boxes] with the new matchsticks; only part of them did, because I introduced the new matchsticks only for a trial but did not establish them definitely. . . .

[. . . The state dropped its investigation of the female workers, who thus were not punished for the strike. However, the state did arrest and imprison two political activists, Ovsei Gurin and Iuda Borushok. Significantly, the police blamed the factory disorder on the owner's decision to change the terms of work and wages.]

▶ Working with Sources

1. **The owner of the matchbox factory clearly knew what he was risking when he changed the size of the matches and matchboxes. How did he attempt to excuse his actions?**
2. **What was the importance of the Pinsk Social-Democratic Committee in the labor strike?**

World Period Five

The Origins of Modernity, 1750–1900

The twin novel events of constitutional and industrial revolutions, first in the Americas and western Europe and later in Japan, dramatically changed the course of world history.

- People rose to end the divine right of kings and replace their rule with popular sovereignty, constitutions, and elections.
- Machines began to replace animal power in the manufacture of textiles, means of transportation, chemicals, and urban amenities.

As a result, 10,000-year-old traditional customs and habits formed by life in agriculture gave way to what we call "modernity," that is, nontraditional new ways of life in the "machine age," characterized by such new phenomena as nation-states, social classes, megacities, colonialism, and above all, vastly increased global interactions.

Chapter 26

Industrialization and Its Discontents

1750–1914

CHAPTER TWENTY-SIX PATTERNS

Origins, Interactions, Adaptations Although the Netherlands possessed commercial farming, a large textile industry, a skilled workforce, and colonies from which it derived much wealth, neighboring Great Britain was the first country to industrialize. Britain had all of the above endowments, but its workers received high wages that stimulated owners to search for labor-saving machines. In a first wave of industrialization, steam engines drove textile-weaving frames, and later on, railroads and ships. Germany, Belgium, and the United States quickly adapted to these interactions, and a second wave of industrialization followed.

Uniqueness and Similarities Science as well as industry transformed European and North American societies in largely similar ways. This transformation brought much pain, creating a working class living in appalling conditions and a wealthy middle class of entrepreneurs and capitalists. Uncontrolled and repeated booms and busts created massive insecurity and prompted a search for reform through social legislation or revolution led by the working class. Cultural responses were also diverse, ranging from accommodation in the middle class to rejection of traditional values by intellectuals and the adoption of radically new styles in the visual arts and music. In retrospect, the arrival of scientific-industrial modernity was as profoundly transformative as the agrarian-urban transition was at the end of the Neolithic.

In 1845, Mary Paul, age 15, made a life-altering decision. Given her limited prospects in rural Vermont, she decided to head for Massachusetts and a job in the newly expanding textile industry.

In letters she wrote to her widowed father, Bela, Mary reveals that the reason behind her decision was to earn steady wages rather than rely on the uncertainties of farm work. On September 13, 1845, Mary wrote asking for her father's consent to seek employment in the booming mill town of Lowell, Massachusetts. On November 20, Mary wrote that she had already "found a place in a spinning room and the next morning I went to work." She continued, "I like very well [*sic*] have 50cts first payment increasing every payment as I get along in work." Shortly before Christmas, Mary reported that her wages had increased: "Last Tuesday we were paid. In all I had six dollars and sixty cents paid $4.68 for board. With the rest I got me a pair of rubbers and a pair of 50.cts shoes. Next payment I am to have a dollar a week beside my board." She described her daily routine in the mill: "At 5 o'clock in the morning the bell rings for the folks to get up and get breakfast. At half past six it rings for the girls to get up and at seven they are called into the mill. At half past 12 we have dinner are called back again at one and stay till half past seven." Mary concludes, "I think that the factory is the best place for me and if any girl wants employment I advise them to come to Lowell."

CHAPTER OUTLINE

Origins and Growth of Industrialism, 1750–1914

The Social and Economic Impact of Industrialism, 1750–1914

Intellectual and Cultural Responses to Industrialism

Putting It All Together

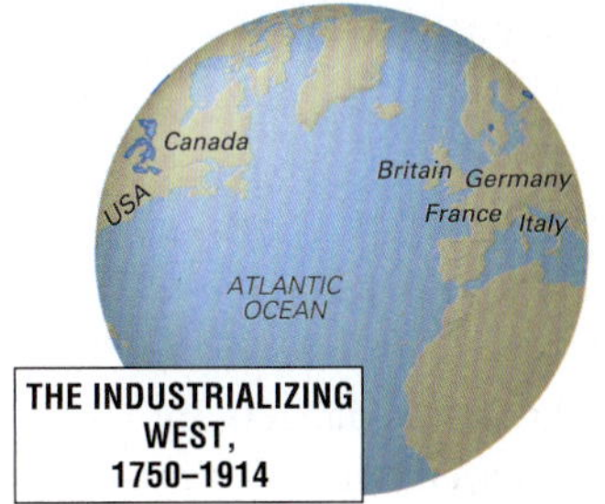

Origins and Growth of Industrialism, 1750–1914

Like the agricultural revolution of the Neolithic age, the Industrial Revolution altered lives around the globe. The process of industrialization originated in Britain in the eighteenth century, spreading to the European continent and North

ABOVE: Although rather idealized, this illustration depicts the role of women in textile mills, such as this one in Lowell, Massachusetts.

Seeing Patterns

> Where and when did the Industrial Revolution originate?

> What were some effects of industrialization on Western society? How did social patterns change?

> In what ways did industrialization contribute to innovations in technology? How did these technological advances contribute to Western imperialism in the late nineteenth century?

> What new directions in science, philosophy, religion, and the arts did industrialism generate? What kind of responses did it provoke?

America in the nineteenth century and subsequently around the globe. The transition from manual labor and natural sources of power to the implementation of mechanical forms of power and machine-driven production resulted in a vast increase in the production of goods, new modes of transportation, and new economic policies and business procedures.

Early Industrialism, 1750–1870

The industrialization of western Europe began in Britain. As with all transformative events in history, however, a number of important questions arise. Why did the industrial movement begin in Britain in the eighteenth century? Was this process "inevitable," as some have claimed, or was it contingent on interactions that we are still struggling to comprehend?

Preconditions Europe in general and Britain in particular enjoyed two distinct advantages compared to other civilizations: a prosperous and largely independent middle class, and an early scientific revolution.

Three additional factors made Britain especially suitable for launching the industrial movement. First, Britain benefited from reserves of coal and iron ore, combined with overseas colonies and subsequent global trading networks. This provided a foundation for commercial expansion, which in turn created capital to fund new enterprises. Second, a thriving merchant class supported legislation that promoted economic development. Finally, Britain developed a flourishing banking system (the Bank of England was founded in 1694) that provided funds to entrepreneurs.

Thanks to agricultural improvements, Britain experienced a surge in population, nearly doubling between1600 and 1700. At the same time, a demographic shift in which displaced tenant farmers migrated to towns and cities created greater demand for food and consumer goods. The impact of these changes was especially notable in the textile industry. Although woolen cloth had long been the staple of the British textile industry, new fabrics from Asia, such as silk and cotton, gained in popularity. At first, the demand for finished cloth goods was satisfied by weavers working at home, a system known as **cottage industry**. Owing to concern for the woolen industry, Parliament in 1700 and 1720 moved to prohibit the importation of cotton goods from India. But as this legislation led to increased domestic demand for English-made cotton textiles, it soon was apparent that production needed to be sped up.

Cottage industry: Small-scale business or industrial activity carried out in the home by family members.

British Resources The use of machines was more practical and cost-efficient in Britain than elsewhere for several reasons. Since wages for workers in rural industries were high, the use of labor-saving machinery helped firms to be profitable. At the same time, Britain's vast reserves of coal resulted in cheap energy. Moreover, Britain was singularly fortunate in its social and cultural capital. The majority of British inventors had interests in and ties to societies aligned with scientific aspects of the Enlightenment, which served as centers of exchange between scientists, inventors, experimenters, and mechanics.

New Technologies and Sources of Power These factors produced an explosion of technological innovation in Britain. From 1700 to 1800 over 1,000 inventions were developed, most of which were related to the textile industry. In addition to the steam engine (see "Patterns Up Close"), among the most prominent were the flying shuttle (1733), the spinning jenny (1764), the water frame (1769), and the spinning mule (1779). Each of these devices increased the speed and quality of spinning or weaving. The power loom (1787), which gradually replaced manually operated looms, resulted in hardship for hand weavers, whose livelihoods were now threatened. In desperation, handicrafters of all sorts mounted a campaign to sabotage the use of machines in textile factories (see "Against the Grain").

Even these improvements were not enough, however, to supply both the domestic and colonial markets with textiles. What was needed in order to speed up production was reliable power to drive the looms. The solution was provided by the development of the steam engine.

The Factory System The growing dependence on large machinery, the necessity of transporting fuel and raw materials to centers of production, and the need to house many machines under one roof necessitated the construction of large manufacturing buildings. These facilities were initially located near sources of running water in order to provide the power to run mechanical looms. The implementation of steam power to drive machinery allowed entrepreneurs to move factories away from water sources in rural areas to urban settings, where there were large pools of cheap labor and easier access to transportation. These factories drew increasing numbers of workers, which contributed to urban population surges, particularly in the north and Midlands of England. By the 1830s, close to 25 percent of Britain's industrial production came from factories (see Map 26.1).

Global Commerce The application of machines to textile production resulted in Britain's role in the development of intercontinental trade and commerce. Prior to the Industrial Revolution, India and China had dominated global trade in textiles. But thanks to its holdings in America and Asia, combined with mercantilist policies, Britain had ready-made markets for the distribution and sale of its goods. Britain also benefited from slave labor in its former colonies, which kept the price of commodities like American cotton low. One result was growing demand among colonial markets for textile products, which stimulated the necessity to step up production. Increased production led to lower prices, making British textiles more competitive in global markets.

Transportation While steam-powered factories were important to the Industrial Revolution, it was the steam railroad that captivated the public's imagination. Between 1840 and 1870, Great Britain counted a ninefold increase in miles of rail. Railroads improved the shipping of coal and other bulk commodities and enhanced the sale and distribution of manufactures. The railroad itself developed into a self-sustaining industry, employing thousands and spurring further entrepreneurial investment.

The application of steam to ships had far-reaching ramifications as well. Credit for the first practical steam-powered riverboat goes to the American engineer and inventor Robert Fulton (1765–1815), whose *Clermont*, constructed in 1807, plied the Hudson River in New York. English engineers were quick to copy Fulton's lead;

by 1815 there were 10 steamboats hauling coal across the Clyde River in Scotland. During the 1820s and 1830s, steamboats were in regular use on Europe's principal rivers. Steamboats opened the Great Lakes and the Ohio and Mississippi Rivers to commerce in the United States. By the 1830s and 1840s, the British East India Company used iron-hulled steamers to facilitate maritime trade with its markets in India. Military uses soon followed.

The Spread of Early Industrialism

By the 1830s, in Belgium, northern France, and the northern German states—all of which had coal reserves—conditions had grown more suitable for industrialization. Population increases contributed to higher consumer demand, and urban areas provided pools of available workers for factories. Roads, canals, and railways facilitated the movement of both raw materials to industrial centers and manufactured goods to markets. In addition, governmental involvement enhanced the investment climate, as protective **tariffs** for manufactures and the removal of internal toll restrictions opened up the trading industry.

Tariff: A tax on imported goods, which gives domestic manufactures an advantage.

The United States In 1793, Samuel Slater (1768–1835), a British engineer, established the first water-powered textile factory in America in Rhode Island. By 1825 factories in the American northeast were producing textile goods on mechanically powered looms.

After a brief interruption during the American Civil War, industrialization in America resumed at an accelerated pace. By 1870 America was producing far more spindles of cotton than Great Britain, and its production of iron ingots was swiftly catching up to that of British and European producers. By 1914 the United States had become the world's single largest industrial economy.

In addition to manufacturing, trade and commerce across the American continent were facilitated by the railroads, which took over the carrying trade from the canal networks created in the early nineteenth century. By the conclusion of the Civil War, the United States had more miles of rail than the rest of the world combined. In 1869 the first transcontinental railroad was completed with a final golden spike at Promontory Point, Utah.

Later Industrialism, 1871–1914

The next stage of industrialism, often referred to as "the second Industrial Revolution," introduced high-technology innovations that, taken together,

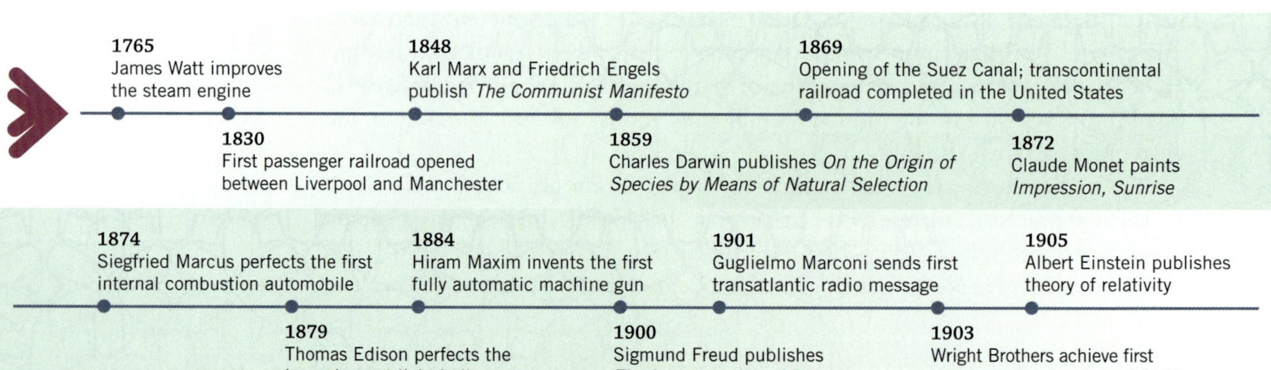

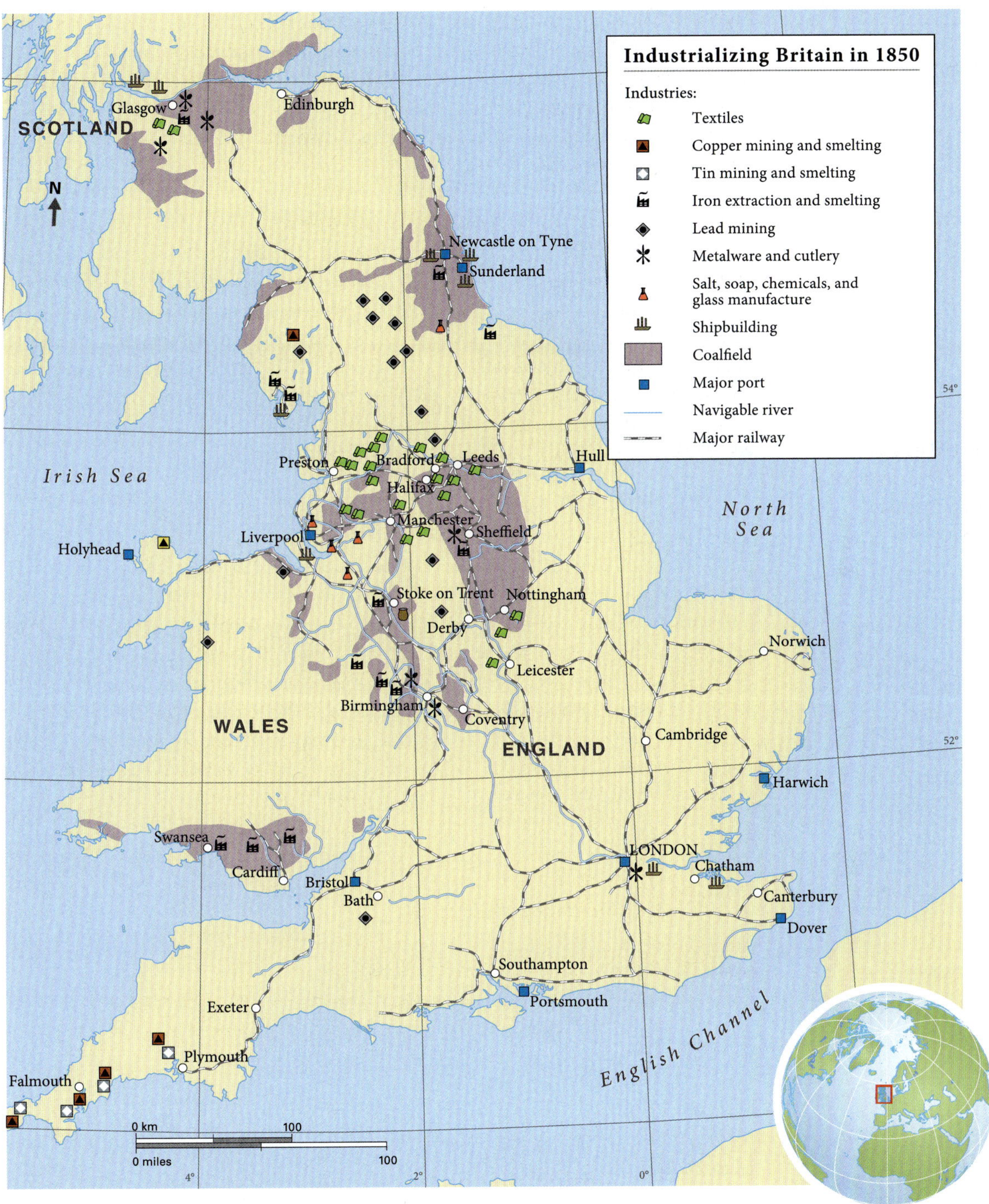

MAP 26.1 Industrializing Britain in 1850

MAP 26.2 **The Industrialization of Europe by 1914**

altered the course not only of the Industrial Revolution but also of world history. Among the most significant were steel, electricity, and chemicals (see Map 26.2).

New Materials: Steel The second Industrial Revolution saw increasing use of steel instead of iron. Refined techniques for making steel had for centuries been the province of skilled craftspeople, but new technical advances now made it possible to produce large quantities of high-grade yet inexpensive steel. Subsequent improvements in production in the 1860s and 1870s included the blast furnace and the open-hearth smelting method.

Following the conclusion of the Franco–Prussian war, Germany's annexation of the ore-rich regions of Alsace-Lorraine led to a dramatic increase in industrial production. Germany had had almost no measurable steel production in the 1870s, but by 1914 the country's annual tonnage of steel was more than twice that of Britain. Germany modeled its new industrial facilities on those of its most modern competitors, saving substantial time and investment capital and resulting in newer and more efficient equipment and business methods. Another advantage was Germany's development of sophisticated scientific research capabilities at universities.

Industrialization spread farther afield during the second half of the nineteenth century. Aware of the growing influence of western European industrial powers, both Russia and Japan implemented economic reforms to compete with the West. One factor in Russia's decision to convert from an agrarian to an industrial economy was its defeat by French and British forces in the Crimean War (1853–1856). Following the emancipation of the serfs in 1861, Russia embarked on industrialization. Following the 1853 arrival of Commodore Matthew Perry, which led to the Meiji Restoration in 1868, Japan also adapted its economy to industrialism in order to keep pace with the West.

The advantages of steel over iron were that it was lighter, harder, and more durable. Thus, it provided better rails for railroads and, increasingly, girders for the construction of high-rise buildings. The switch from iron to steel construction of ships marked a significant advance in steamship technology during the third quarter of the nineteenth century. By 1900, 95 percent of all commercial ocean liners were being constructed of steel. Steel liners were stronger, faster, and roomier than iron ones—and steel warships proved far more durable in battle.

Chemicals Advances were also made in the use of chemicals. In 1856 the first synthetic dye was created, which initiated the synthetic dyestuffs industry. New chemical compounds led to the refinement of wood-pulp products, ranging from cheaper paper to artificial silk, known as rayon. The synthesizing of ammonia and its conversion to nitrate for use in fertilizers and explosives were to have far-reaching effects during World War I. The invention of dynamite by the Swedish chemist and engineer Alfred Bernhard Nobel (1833–1896) provided the means to blast through rock formations, resulting in massive excavation projects like the Panama Canal (1914). In yet another chemical advance, Charles Goodyear (1800–1860) invented a process in 1839 that produced vulcanized rubber. Celluloid—the first synthetic plastic—was developed in 1869. Other innovations in chemistry, ranging from pharmaceuticals to soap products, contributed to improved health. By the early part of the twentieth century, these developments had led to a "hygiene revolution" among the industrialized countries.

New Energies: Electricity and the Internal Combustion Engine The development and application of electricity were greatly advanced after 1850, especially in the generation of electrical power. The first step came with Michael Faraday (1791–1867) patenting the electromagnetic generator in 1861. But large-scale electrical generation would require further innovation before it became a reality. Perhaps the most important devices in this regard were developed by engineer Nikola Tesla (1856–1943). Among Tesla's inventions were the alternating

Patterns Up Close

"The Age of Steam"

The origins of the steam age lie in an environmental crisis. A shortage of wood for fuel and charcoal making in Britain in the early 1700s—in spite of imports from North America—forced manufacturers to turn to another fuel source: coal. Britain was blessed with vast amounts of coal, but getting to it was difficult because of a high water table. Mineshafts often flooded and had to be abandoned. Early methods of water extraction featured pumps operated by either human or animal power, but these were inefficient, expensive, and limited in power.

The first steam-driven piston engine, based on experimentation with vacuum chambers and condensing steam, came from the French Huguenot Denis Papin (1647–ca. 1712), who spent his later career in England. Thomas Savery (ca. 1650–1715), taking up the idea of condensing steam and vacuum power, built a system of pipes employing the suction produced by this process dubbed the "Miner's Friend." Savery's system was able to extract water from shallow shafts but was useless for the deeper mines of rural Britain.

Although this drawback was partially addressed by Thomas Newcomen (1663–1729), who in 1712 improved the efficiency of Papin's piston-and-cylinder design, the "Newcomen engines" were still slow and energy-inefficient. It remained for James Watt (1736–1819), a Scottish engineer, to create the prototype for fast engines sufficiently efficient and versatile to drive factory machinery. His newly refined model, completed in 1765 and patented in 1769, was five times as efficient as Newcomen's engine and used 75 percent less coal.

Watt introduced a further improved model in 1783 that incorporated more advances. First, by injecting steam into both the top and the bottom of the piston cylinder, its motion was converted to double action, making it more powerful and efficient. Second, through a system of "planetary gearing"—in which the piston shaft was connected by a circular gear to the hub of a flywheel—the back-and-forth

current (AC) and the Tesla Coil (1891) for the more efficient transmission of electricity. In 1888 the introduction of Tesla's "electric induction engine" led to the adoption of electricity-generating power plants throughout industrialized Europe.

Another key source of energy was the internal combustion engine. When oil, or liquid petroleum, was commercially developed in the 1860s and 1870s, it was at first refined into kerosene and used for illumination. A by-product of this process, gasoline, soon revealed its potential as a new fuel source. The first experimental internal combustion engines utilizing the new fuel appeared in the 1860s. They were significantly lighter in weight than steam engines of comparable size and power, and the first practical attempts to use them in powering vehicles came along in the next decade.

The first true automobile was invented by the Austrian mechanic Siegfried Marcus (1831–1898). Marcus developed the carburetor, the magneto ignition system, various gears, the clutch, a steering mechanism, and a braking system. He included all of these inventions in a combustion-engine automobile that he drove in Vienna in 1874.

rhythm of the piston was converted to smooth, rotary motion, suitable for driving machines in factories and mills. Watt's steam engines proved so popular that by 1790 they had replaced all of the Newcomen engines; by 1800, nearly 500 Watt engines were in operation in mines and factories.

Within a few decades, adaptations of this design were being used not just for stationary engines to run machinery but also to move vehicles along tracks—the first railroad engines—and to turn paddle wheels and screw propellers on boats—the first steamships. Both of these innovations enhanced commerce and empire building among the newly industrializing nations. Although societies seeking to protect themselves from outside influence saw the railroad and steamer as forces of chaos, the web of railroad lines grew denser on every inhabited continent, and the continents themselves were connected by shipping lines. Steam may indeed be said to be the power behind the creation of modern global society.

Corliss Steam Engine. A tribute to the new power of the steam engine was this huge power plant in the Machinery Hall of the American Centennial Exposition in 1876. The Corliss engine pictured here produced over 1,400 horsepower and drove nearly all the machines in the exhibition hall—with the distinct exception of those in the British display. Along with the arm of the Statue of Liberty, also on exhibition there, it became the most recognized symbol of America's first world's fair.

Questions

- How is the innovation of steam power the culmination of a pattern that began with the rise of the New Sciences in western Europe in the sixteenth and seventeenth centuries?
- Do you agree that "steam may indeed be said to be the power that behind the creation of modern global society"? If yes, why? If not, which other adaptations in the period 1750–1914 better qualify for this distinction?

Internal combustion engines were also applied to early attempts at sustained flight. In 1900 Ferdinand von Zeppelin (1838–1917) constructed a rigid airship—a dirigible—consisting of a fabric-covered aluminum frame that was kept aloft by bags filled with hydrogen gas and powered by two 16-horsepower engines. The marriage of the gasoline engine to the glider created the first airplanes. The Wright brothers are credited with the first sustained engine-powered flight in Kitty Hawk, North Carolina, in 1903. By 1909, the first flight across the English Channel had been completed; in 1911 the first transcontinental airplane flight across the United States (with many stops) took place. The potential of both the automobile and the airplane were to be starkly revealed within a few years during the Great War.

The Communications Revolution Although electric telegraph messages were transmitted as early as the 1840s with the advent of the devices and code devised by Samuel F. B. Morse (1791–1872), it was only in the 1860s and 1870s that major continental landmasses were linked by submarine transoceanic cables. By the latter part of the nineteenth century, telegraphic communication was a worldwide phenomenon. The telephone, invented by Alexander Graham Bell (1847–1922) in 1876, made voice communication possible by wire.

Perhaps most revolutionary of all was the advent of wireless communication. The theoretical groundwork for this had been laid in part by Heinrich Rudolf Hertz (1857–1894), who in 1885 discovered that electromagnetic radiation produces unseen waves that emanate through the universe. In the 1890s, Guglielmo Marconi (1874–1937) developed a device using these radio waves generated by electric sparks controlled by a telegraph key to send and receive messages over several miles. By 1903 Marconi had enhanced the power and range of the device enough to send the first transatlantic radio message. The "wireless telegraph" was quickly adopted by ships for reliable communication at sea. Subsequent improvements, such as the development of the vacuum tube amplifier and oscillator, soon resulted in greater range and power, as well as the ability to transmit sound wirelessly.

Breech-loading: A firearm that is loaded from the rear portion of the barrel, making reloading much more efficient.

The Weapons Revolution The advances in chemistry and explosives, metallurgy, and machine tooling during the second half of the nineteenth century contributed to a vastly enhanced lethality among weapons. Earlier advances from the 1830s to the early 1860s (including the percussion cap, the conical bullet, the revolver, and the rifled musket) provided the base for the development of more sophisticated firearms. **Breech-loading** weapons rapidly came of age with the advent of the brass cartridge. By 1865 manufacturers were marketing repeating rifles, such as the famous Winchester lever-action models. Rifles designed by the German firms of Krupp and Mauser pioneered the bolt-action, magazine, and clip-fed rifles that remained the staple of infantry weapons through two world wars.

Artillery underwent a similar transformation. Breech-loading artillery, made possible by precision machining of breech blocks and the introduction of metallic cartridges for artillery shells, made loading and firing large guns far more efficient. By the early 1880s, the invention of the recoil cylinder meant that field artillery could be anchored, aimed, and fired continuously with enhanced accuracy. The first effective "rapid-fire" artillery piece, the "canon de 75 mm modèle 1897"—more widely known as "the French 75"—was developed in France in 1897. Its effectiveness was enhanced further by the use of new explosives like guncotton, dynamite, and later TNT in its shells. Cordite, or smokeless powder, eliminated much of the battlefield smoke generated by black powder and was three times more powerful as a propellant. Thus, the range and accuracy of small arms and artillery were pushed even further. So much so, in fact, that artillery fire was by far the most lethal of all weaponry utilized during World War I.

Another advance in weaponry during the later nineteenth century was the invention of the machine gun. Though many quick-firing weapons had been developed during these years—the most famous being the Gatling gun (1861)—the first fully automatic machine gun was conceived by Hiram Maxim (1840–1916), an American inventor.

By the outbreak of World War I, every major army in the world was equipping itself with Maxim's guns. In his memoirs, Maxim notes somewhat ruefully that he was applauded more highly for inventing his "killing machine" than for inventing a steam inhaler for those suffering from bronchitis.

Hiram Maxim. In this 1900 photo, the proud inventor of the machine gun looks on with self-satisfied pride as Albert Edward, Prince of Wales (the future King Edward VII), experiences for himself the awesome firepower of Maxim's "little daisy of a gun." In 1885 Maxim put on a similar demonstration for Lord Wolseley, commander in chief of the British Army. The British War Office adopted the gun three years later. The lethal power of the machine gun was first put to use in Africa at the Battle of Omdurman in 1898, where 20,000 Sudanese cavalrymen were slaughtered in fruitless charges against a line of 20 Maxim guns.

The Social and Economic Impact of Industrialism, 1750–1914

All of these changes in modes of production transformed the daily lives of millions around the globe. Along with new networks of transportation and communication, new materials, and new sources of energy, the industrialized nations underwent significant changes in how they viewed politics, social institutions, and economic relationships.

Demographic Changes

Changes in the demography of industrialized nations followed the development of new industries. The populations of these countries grew at unprecedented rates and became increasingly urbanized, and Great Britain became the first country to have more urban dwellers than rural inhabitants. This trend would continue among the industrialized nations through the twentieth century.

Population Surge and Urbanization Between 1700 and 1914, the industrialized nations experienced a population explosion (see Map 26.3). Advances in industrial production, the expansion of factories, and improved agriculture during the first Industrial Revolution combined to produce increasing opportunities for jobs as well as more plentiful and nutritious food. In the second Industrial Revolution, scientific advances in medicine, along with improved sanitation, contributed to a declining mortality rate. The population of Britain grew from around 9 million in 1700 to around 20 million in 1850. From 1871 to 1914, Britain's

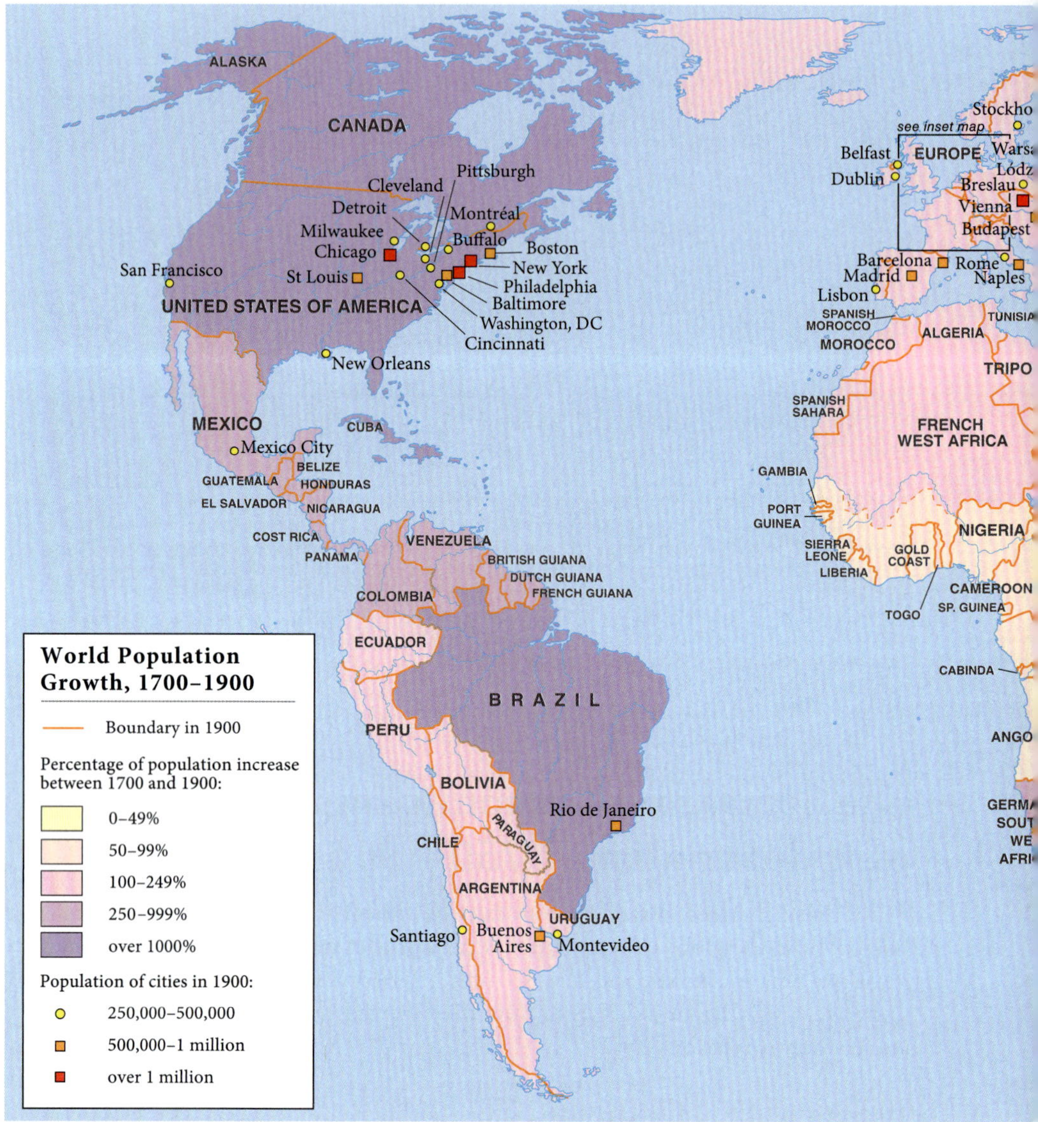

MAP 26.3 **World Population Growth, 1700–1900**

population soared from 31 million to nearly 50 million. In Germany, the population grew from around 41 million in 1871 to 58 million in 1914.

More revealing than overall population figures is the shift of populations from rural to urban areas. For example, in 1800, around 60 percent of the population of Great Britain lived in rural areas. By 1850, however, about 50 percent of the population lived in cities, including the new industrial and commercial centers of Manchester, Liverpool, Birmingham, and Glasgow. Older capital cities of Europe, such as Paris, Berlin, and St. Petersburg, also saw vast increases in population.

European Migrations Another social change during the industrial era concerns overseas emigrations of Europeans. While this movement was sparked by the dramatic rise in population in industrialized Europe, another factor was the

desire to escape the poverty of underdeveloped regions of Europe for better opportunities in America. Advances in transportation made it easier for Europeans to emigrate. In all, some 60 million Europeans left for other parts of the world between 1800 and 1914. Of these, the majority emigrated to the United States and Canada (see Map 26.4).

Industrial Society

Industrialization led to significant changes in the hierarchy of social ranks. Although the elites continued to enjoy their privileged status, the increasing importance of capitalism and commerce, and with it the accumulation of significant wealth, now enhanced the status of the upper echelons of the middle class, or **bourgeoisie**. No longer were status and power determined solely by aristocratic

Bourgeoisie: Social class that owns and controls the means of production.

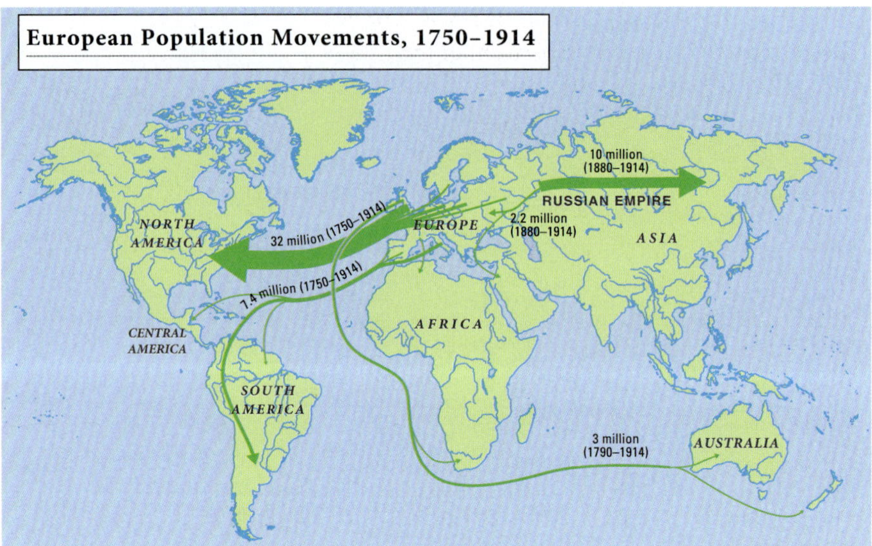

MAP 26.4 European Population Movements, 1750–1914

birth or privilege. The principal alteration in the social hierarchy, however, was the appearance of a new group: the working class. The advent of industrialism created the concept of "class consciousness," or growing awareness of social standing determined by occupation and income.

The Upper Classes At the top of the European social scene were members of the landed aristocracy, sometimes referred to as the "old money" elite. They were joined by the new urban elite, known as "nouveau riche" (or the "new money" crowd). This elite was composed of the extremely rich factory owners, bankers, and merchants who had made personal fortunes from investments, or who had married into the landed aristocracy. Together, they constituted only 5 percent of the total population. Although a tiny minority, they managed to control almost 40 percent of Europe's wealth.

The Middle Classes A notch down from the upper classes were the middle classes, who constituted around 15 percent of Europe's total population. Distinguished from the landed aristocracy above them and from the working classes below, they enjoyed comfortable lifestyles in terms of education, fine homes, and the conspicuous consumption of luxury goods. But the middle classes were themselves divided into an upper and a lower tier by a sense of class consciousness. The former included professionals (lawyers, physicians), high-ranking government officials, and prosperous businessmen and merchants. The latter was comprised of small business owners and shopkeepers, along with foremen and supervisors in factories, mines, and other places.

It was the upper middle class that set the cultural and moral tone for the second half of the nineteenth century. It set itself apart from those above their social status—and especially from those below it—by emphasizing what it considered its respectability, frugality, and industry.

The Working Class Urban factory workers were distinguished by the regulation of their daily routine by the factory time clock and by selling their labor in return for cash wages. In the working class, divisions existed between skilled and unskilled workers, largely determined by their degree of familiarity with industrial machinery and its maintenance.

Woman and Children Coal Putters, Mid and East Lothian, Scotland ca. 1848. Women and children (some as young as five or six years old) worked long hours in terrible conditions in underground mines. Here, a woman and two children, known as "putters," struggle to push a wagon of coal to the surface. Other children, called "trappers," maintained airflow in the tunnels by operating ventilation doors.

Working conditions in British textile mills in the early 1800s were deplorable. Without traditional protective guilds or associations, workers were at the mercy of factory owners. The factory clock and the pace of factory machinery determined the day's work, which was repetitive, dirty, and dangerous. Even young children worked in factories. In fact, until the 1840s in Britain, the majority of "hands," or factory workers, were women and children, who, by virtue of their inexperience and expendability, could be paid less than their male counterparts.

Conditions were often even worse in the mines. Children began work in mines most often as "trappers," responsible for opening and shutting ventilation doors in mineshafts. Because of their small size, children were put to work lugging newly dug coal along low underground passageways for conveyance to the surface. Girls were especially victimized in underground mines, where they were frequently sexually abused by their supervisors.

Factory Towns Because industrial cities expanded close to factories and mills, conditions there were as grim as within the factories themselves. The working classes lived in crowded, shoddily built tenements in narrow, dark streets. Clouds of coal smoke blackened buildings, acidified the rain and soil, and caused respiratory ailments. Piles of coal ash, pungent waste materials from coking or from gas works, and outpourings from tanneries and dye works combined with household waste, sewage, and horse manure. Waste disposal was rudimentary, access to clean water was limited, and diseases were rampant in the exploding population.

Adding to the miseries of the inhabitants of factory towns were their wretched living conditions. The working classes lived in crowded, shoddily built tenements in narrow, dark streets. One social activist, Friedrich Engels (1820–1895), the son of a wealthy mill owner and later collaborator with Karl Marx, was determined to call attention to such abysmal conditions.

Critics of Industrialism

It was not long before Engels and other socially conscious observers began to call for reform of working conditions. Efforts to improve these sordid conditions were launched in Great Britain in the 1820s and 1830s and carried over into the 1870s.

Socialists The plight of the working classes inspired many social activists to take up the fight for reform. Henri de Saint-Simon (1760–1825) argued that private property should be more equally distributed—"from each according to his abilities, to each according to his works." Louis Blanc (1811–1882) criticized the capitalist system in his *The Organization of Work* (1839), urging workers to agitate for voting rights and espousing radical ideas like the right to work. He reconfigured Saint-Simon's phrase to read "from each according to his abilities, to

Working-Class Tenements in English Industrial Cities. In this engraving, entitled *Over London by Rail*, the celebrated engraver Gustave Doré (1832–1883) depicts the overcrowded and squalid living conditions in working-class tenements during the early years of the Industrial Revolution. Notice the long rows of houses separated by walls and arranged in back-to-back fashion. Notice also the stretched lines for drying clothes, as well as the large number of occupants in each outdoor area.

each according to his needs." Charles Fourier (1772–1837) advocated the founding of self-sustaining model communities in which jobs were apportioned according to ability and interest, with those doing the most dangerous or unattractive jobs receiving the highest wages.

Robert Owen (1771–1858), a factory owner in the north of England, established a model community in Scotland called New Lanark, where more humane living and working conditions for workers resulted in greater profits. After campaigning for the formation of workers' unions, Owen left for America, where he set up a model socialist community in Indiana called New Harmony, which eventually dissolved amid internal quarrels.

Another reform movement in Britain, **Chartism**, was primarily intent on political reforms. Formed by the London Working Men's Association, its primary goal, among others, was universal male suffrage. Millions of workers signed petitions that were presented to Parliament in 1839 and 1842; these were rejected and the leaders jailed. Nevertheless, the chartist movement served as a model for future attempts at labor reform.

Chartism: A workers' movement in Britain that sought, in the 1830s and 1840s, to enact the "People's Charter" designed to achieve electoral reform.

Dialectical materialism: A Marxist theory that reinterprets Hegel's dialectical method from a materialist position to explain change in the world of human history and society in terms of the conflict of material forces.

Karl Marx By far the most famous of the social reformers was Karl Marx (1818–1883). The son of a prosperous German attorney, Marx earned a PhD in philosophy. During a visit to Manchester, where he befriended Friedrich Engels, Marx observed both the miserable lives of factory workers and the inequities of industrialism. From this experience, Marx developed his theory, which he termed "scientific socialism," that all of history involved class struggles. Borrowing the dialectical schema of the German philosopher Georg Wilhelm Friedrich Hegel (1770–1831), Marx replaced its idealism with his own materialist concept based on economic class struggle: **dialectical materialism**. Marx saw revolution as the means by which the industrial working class would topple the capitalist order.

Marx and Engels joined the nascent communist party in London. In preparation for a meeting in 1848, the two collaborators wrote *The Communist Manifesto* (1848), propaganda designed to rally support among the working class, or proletariat, and to encourage it to rise up and overthrow the capitalist factory owners, or bourgeoisie. The *Manifesto* reflects Marx's vision that "the history of all hitherto existing society is the history of class struggle" and that the time had come for the working classes to overthrow the capitalists: "The proletarians have nothing to lose but their chains. They have a world to win. *Working men of all countries, unite!*"

Inquiries and Reforms Critics of industrialism and even some factory owners called for governments to reform working conditions. In 1832 Parliament launched an inquiry into abuses within factories, resulting in the Sadler Report, which pointed out abuses related to child labor. In 1833 the Factory Act was passed, which set a minimum age of 9 for child employees and limited the workday to 8 hours for children between the ages of 9 and 13 and to 12 hours for those aged 13–18. Further reforms in 1847 and 1848 limited women and children to a maximum of 58 hours a week (the Ten Hours Act). Similar inquiries concerning working conditions within mines resulted in the Mines Act of 1842, which forbade the underground employment of all girls and women.

Improved Standards of Living

By the end of the nineteenth century, conditions in factories and mines were substantially better than at the beginning of the century. In addition, wage levels increased across the nineteenth century for industrial workers.

New Jobs for Women

As a result of the second Industrial Revolution, many women fared better in terms of employment. In overall terms, women represented around one-third of the workers in late-nineteenth-century industrial jobs. But factory work in textile mills was not the only avenue open to women as the industrial era unfolded. Inventions like the typewriter (perfected in the 1870s), the telephone, and calculating machines (in use in the 1890s), increasingly used in businesses and industries, created a wide array of white-collar jobs. As a result, women became particularly prominent in secretarial office jobs. Business firms created countless jobs for secretaries, while department stores opened up jobs for women as clerks.

Suffragettes: Women who organized to demand the right to vote. In 1893 New Zealand was the first self-governing country that granted women the right to vote.

Women's Suffrage Movement

Although women were afforded new workplace and professional opportunities, they remained in many ways second-class citizens. Women in both the United States and Europe did not begin to gain the right to own property or to sue for divorce until the third quarter of the nineteenth century.

More urgent for many female reformers was the right to vote. Throughout Europe during the late nineteenth and early twentieth centuries, women formed political groups to press for the vote. The most active of these groups was in Britain, where in 1867 the National Society for Women's Suffrage was founded. The most radical of British political feminists was Emmeline Pankhurst (1858–1928), who together with her daughters formed the Women's Social and Political Union in 1903. They and their supporters, known as **suffragettes**, resorted to civil disobedience in order to call attention to their cause.

Emmeline Pankhurst. Pankhurst was arrested numerous times for her militancy and aggressive actions against the British government and its refusal to extend the suffrage to women. In this photo, taken on May 21, 1914, Pankhurst is shown being arrested outside Buckingham Palace after attempting to present a petition to King George V.

Political feminists were also active on the Continent. The French League of Women's Rights was founded in the 1870s, and the Union of German Women's Organizations was formed in 1894; in neither country was the right to vote granted women until after World War I. In the United States, after decades of lobbying, women's suffrage was finally granted by constitutional amendment in 1920.

Improved Urban Living

Urban living conditions in industrialized nations improved significantly during the late nineteenth and early twentieth centuries. Largely as a result of the application of new technologies, the lives of urban dwellers were improved in the second half of the nineteenth century.

Sanitation and Urban Renewal

Beginning in the 1860s and 1870s, large cities in Britain and Europe established public water services and began to construct underground sewage systems to carry waste from houses, outfitted with running water, to locations beyond urban areas. By the latter part of the nineteenth century, gas lamps began to give way to electrical varieties. Thomas Edison (1847–1931) perfected the incandescent light bulb in 1879, making the lighting of homes and business interiors more affordable and practical.

Paris represents a good example of the implementation of these reforms. In the 1850s and 1860s, Napoleon III (r. 1852–1870) appointed the urban planner Georges-Eugène Haussmann (1809–1891) to begin a massive reconstruction of the city. Haussmann tore down close-packed tenements in order to construct modernized buildings and wide boulevards. Like most cities of the industrialized West, by the turn of the twentieth century Paris featured lighted and paved streets, public water systems, parks, hospitals, and police. A dramatic symbol of both the newly redesigned city of Paris and the triumph of industry and science during the second Industrial Revolution was the Eiffel Tower, designed by Alexandre Gustave Eiffel (1832–1923) for the Paris Exposition of 1889.

Leisure and Sports Another advance in urban life was an increase in leisure and sporting activities. The later nineteenth century saw the emergence of sporting organizations and clubs, along with the establishment of rules for play. Games played by professional teams provided recreation for working-class men. In Britain, for example, rules for playing soccer were established in 1863 by the Football Association, and in 1888 the English Football League was established. In the 1870s and 1880s, British cricket teams took the game to the colonies, and in 1901 the championship game of the British Football Association (FA) Cup competition drew over 100,000 spectators.

Nor was this trend confined to Britain. In 1896 the first modern Olympic Games took place in Athens, Greece. In 1903 the first Tour de France was run through the French countryside. In 1904 the game of soccer was given international rules. And by the early 1880s, the game of baseball in America had been formalized into two leagues.

Big Business

As urban planning increased toward the end of the nineteenth century, business flourished. As manufacturing, transportation, and financing matured, businessmen became concerned about competition and falling profits. Since governments generally pursued hands-off liberalism in the economy (except for protective tariffs), entrepreneurs sought to establish cartels and monopolies, creating big business enterprises in the process.

Large Firms As Britain industrialized, it shifted from a closed mercantilist economy to a liberal free-trade policy (see Chapter 22). Britain's competitors, especially Germany and the United States, by contrast, erected high tariff walls in order to help their fledgling industries. After the second wave of steel, chemical, and electrical industrialization, the scale of industrial investments rose exponentially. On domestic markets, governments did not interfere with business organization and practice, except for labor protection in Europe. As a result, big businesses emerged that protected their profit rates through cartels (market-sharing agreements) or strove for outright monopolies.

Large firms developed in Germany and the United States, the leaders of the second wave of industrialization. By the 1890s, corporations like the Krupp steelworks in Germany and Standard Oil Company in the United States

The Assembly Line. The American System of interchangeable parts for muskets of the early nineteenth century had evolved into the assembly line by the early twentieth. Here, Ford Model T automobiles are moved along a conveyor to different stations, where workers assemble them in simple, repetitive steps, resulting in production efficiency and low prices for the cars.

controlled large shares of their markets. Standard Oil at its height, for example, produced over 90 percent of the country's petroleum. The United States Steel Corporation, founded in 1901 by Andrew Carnegie (1835–1919), dominated the production of American steel.

New Management Styles New technologies that offered more efficient means of production led to significant changes in production processes during the second phase of European industrialism. One example is the implementation of the so-called **American System**, incorporating the use of interchangeable parts, which greatly enhanced mass production. A related development was the appearance of "continuous-flow production," wherein workers performed specialized tasks at stationary positions along an assembly line. In addition, new "scientific management" tactics were employed in mass-production assembly plants. Since no more than basic skills were required on many assembly lines, labor costs could be kept low. The resulting escalation in the speed of production contributed to an increase in the production of goods for daily consumption and, therefore, in the development of a consumer market at the turn of the twentieth century.

American System of Manufacturing: Manufacturing system which made extensive use of interchangeable parts and mechanization for production.

Intellectual and Cultural Responses to Industrialism

The advent of modernity was initially celebrated as an age of progress in science, industry, and the development of a mass culture. Nevertheless, there was a growing sense of unease concerning these advances, especially among intellectuals and artists. Alternative and startlingly innovative modes of cultural expression were upsetting traditional forms. The vibrant but chaotic intellectual and cultural scene in Europe was thus marked by anxiety and uncertainty on the eve of the Great War.

Scientific and Intellectual Developments

The latter half of the nineteenth century saw advances in both theoretical and empirical sciences that laid the basis for many of the findings of the twentieth century. Among the most far-reaching were atomic physics and relativity theory, Darwinism and evolution, and the foundations of modern psychology.

New Theories of Matter Researchers made important discoveries in the 1890s that would have far-reaching consequences in the development of atomic physics and the theory of relativity. In 1892 the physicist Hendrik Lorentz (1853–1928) demonstrated that the atom contained smaller particles, which he named "corpuscles"; these were later renamed electrons. A few years later, Wilhelm Roentgen (1845–1923) discovered a form of emission he called X-rays. The ability to generate these rays would shortly lead to the development of the X-ray machine. The following year, 1896, saw the first experiments in assessing radioactivity in uranium and radium by Antoine Becquerel (1852–1908) and Marie Curie (1867–1934).

As a result of these experimental findings, theoretical physics advanced new theories on the nature of light and energy. In 1900 Max Planck (1858–1947) proposed that instead of the accepted notion that energy is emitted in steady streams or waves, it is issued in bursts, or what he termed "quanta." This idea, later developed into quantum theory, suggested that matter and energy might be interchangeable. Ernest Rutherford (1871–1937), interested in this interchangeability, demonstrated in 1911 that radioactive atoms release a form of energy in the process of their disintegration. Thus, centuries of speculation about atoms as the building blocks of nature led to experimentally verified theories of subatomic particles.

Special theory of relativity: Theory put forth by Albert Einstein that maintains that all measurements of space and time are relative.

Albert Einstein Perhaps the most sensational of the turn-of-the-century scientific theories was the **special theory of relativity** of Albert Einstein (1879–1955). Einstein destroyed the Newtonian notion of a mechanical universe that can be based on the concepts of absolute space and time. He argued that these are relative to each other and depend on the position of the observer.

Moreover, Einstein demonstrated that Newton was incorrect in thinking that matter and energy were separate entities; they were, in fact, equivalent, and he developed the corresponding mathematical formula. In his equation $E = mc^2$, Einstein theorized that the atom contains an amount of energy equal to its mass multiplied by the square of the speed of light. In other words, relatively small amounts of matter could be converted into massive amounts of energy. This discovery, developed further in the twentieth century, provided the foundation for a better understanding of the forces among subatomic particles and the construction of nuclear weapons.

Charles Darwin The basis of modern theories of evolution was first proposed by Charles Darwin (1809–1882). Darwin's *On the Origin of Species by Means of Natural Selection* (1859) argued that species gradually evolved from lower to higher forms. Further, only those species equipped with the tools to survive in their environments would win out; those without these characteristics would become extinct. The most controversial part of the Darwinian theory of evolution was the notion that characteristics are passed on by means of "natural selection." In other words, there is no intelligence or plan in the universe—only random chance and the process of organisms struggling to survive and reproduce.

Although the *Origin* said nothing about the theory of evolution as applied to humankind—this appeared later in his *The Descent of Man* (1871)—there were those who quickly applied it to society and nations. The English philosopher Herbert Spencer (1820–1903) proposed a theory that came to be called "social Darwinism," which sought to apply ideas of natural selection to races, ethnicities, and peoples. Spencer's ideas were frequently used to support imperial ventures aimed at the conquest and sometimes the "uplift" of non-European or American peoples as well as to justify increasingly virulent nationalism in the years leading to World War I.

Sigmund Freud The best-known of the early psychologists was Sigmund Freud (1856–1939), an Austrian physician. Freud specialized in treating patients suffering from what was then called "hysteria," which he treated using a technique he labeled "psychoanalysis." In *The Interpretation of Dreams* (1900), Freud drew connections between dreams and the unconscious in humans. Freudian psychological theories suggest that humans are in fact irrational creatures, driven by subconscious, and not conscious, urges. Today, although Freud's ideas no longer dominate the field of psychology, his influence still survives in the form of therapeutic counseling and behavior modification.

Charles Darwin as Ape. Darwin's theories about the evolution of humankind aroused enormous scorn. In this scathing 1861 cartoon, Darwin, with the body of a monkey, holds a mirror to a simian-looking creature. The original caption quoted a line from Shakespeare's *Love's Labour's Lost:* "This is the ape of form."

The Meaning of the New Scientific Discoveries Physics, biology, and psychology—as well as advances in medicine—contributed to the emergence of scientific–industrial society at the end of the nineteenth century. With the arrival of the theories of relativity, Darwinian selection, and the psychological unconscious, however, the transition toward the scientific–industrial age began to provoke deep philosophical and religious confusion.

In previous centuries, religious skepticism had never been more convincing than religious faith for most people. The atheism of the Enlightenment and secular concepts such as the Hobbesian embodied mind and the "war of all against all" were considered to be merely unproven speculations. Now, the specter of a meaningless universe inhabited by beings devoid of free will and driven by biological forces over which they have no control seemed to be inescapable. Thus, the new era suggested a disturbing paradox: The same sciences that had eased many burdens of human life had also taken away the sense of purpose that made life worth living. It was left to philosophers, religious leaders, intellectuals, and artists to wrestle with the implications of this central problem of scientific–industrial society.

Toward Modernity in Philosophy and Religion

Despite the achievements of Western industrialized society during the late nineteenth century, detractors—mostly in the intellectual community of western Europe—decried the boastful claims of a "superior" scientific civilization. These voices ridiculed Western bourgeois values and advocated alternative approaches to personal fulfillment.

Friedrich Nietzsche The most celebrated of these detractors was the German philosopher Friedrich Nietzsche (1844–1900), who railed against the conventions of Western civilization and criticized the perceived decadence of modern culture. One object of derision for Nietzsche was the notion of scientific, rational thought as the best path toward intellectual truth. For Nietzsche, rational thought will not improve either the individual or the welfare of humankind; only recourse to "will" instead of intellect—what Nietzsche called the "will to power"—will suffice. The individual who follows this path will become a "superman" and will lead others toward truth. Another target of Nietzsche's wrath was Christianity, which in his eyes led its believers into a "slave morality"; he infamously declared that "God is dead."

Toward Modernity in Literature and the Arts

The creation of scientific–industrial society—modernity—was a slow and traumatic process. The social realities of the new order were evident in the postromantic period of realism in the arts and literature, and the succeeding decades yielded an even grimmer and more disjointed perspective.

Literature Literary expression was generally negative toward the "soulless" science and the materialism of the second half of the industrial revolution. Thomas Hardy (1840–1928), for example, in his *Far from the Madding Crowd* (1874) emphasized the despair resulting from the futility of fighting against the grinding forces of modernity. The plays of George Bernard Shaw (1856–1950) reflect the influence of Darwin and Nietzsche, mocking the pretension of urban, bourgeois society. In the mid-1880s two new movements in literature, decadence and symbolism, appeared. The decadents rejected prevailing bourgeois conventions, while the symbolists preferred to revert to a form of the earlier romantic era that emphasized the ideal and the beautiful.

Modernism: Various movements in philosophy and the arts between roughly 1860 and 1950, characterized by a deliberate break with classical or traditional forms of thought or expression.

Modernism in Art Artistic expression in the period 1871–1914, often collectively labeled **modernism**, consisted of a variety of movements skeptical of accepted middle-class conventions and truths. The impressionists, whose style dominated from the 1870s until around 1890, took their name from a painting by Claude Monet (1840–1926) entitled *Impression, Sunrise* (1874). By around 1890 the impressionist school had been superseded by more freewheeling styles.

Perhaps the best known of these styles, cubism, is represented in the early works of Pablo Picasso (1881–1973). In such works as *Les Demoiselles d'Avignon* (1907), often considered the first of the cubist paintings, Picasso reveals his interest in African masks as an alternative to conventional European motifs.

Modernism in Music In the second half of the nineteenth century, after the death of the first wave of Romantic musicians, composers added new forms to classical music, such as the symphonic poem and the integrated poetic drama-opera to the Romantic repertory. Richard Wagner (1813-1883), the proponent of the drama-opera, made much use of chromaticism, that is, the full 12 tones of the octave (produced by the white and black keys of the piano). Later composers pushed chromaticism further, so that the tonic key of the composition became more and more invisible. Arnold Schoenberg (1874–1954) eventually, in 1919, relinquished the tonic altogether that had sustained all music since the Renaissance and made the 12 tones equal to each other—creating modern "twelve-tone music."

Modernism in Art. Pablo Picasso's *Les Demoiselles d'Avignon* was unveiled in Paris in 1907. Its distorted and broken forms set in a fractured and flattened space mark a conscious break with the Western artistic tradition. The painting's borrowing from "primitivist" African and ancient Iberian sources, and its forceful and unsettling depiction of *demoiselles*, a euphemism for prostitutes, unsettle the viewer.

Putting It All Together

The dramatic changes associated with the Industrial Revolution had profound implications for both the industrializing countries and the non-industrialized world. Thanks to new technologies and facilitated by advances in transportation and communication, the period from 1871 to 1914 saw world trade networks and empires dominated by the newly industrialized nations.

The Industrial Revolution began in Britain in the early eighteenth century and eventually spread to Europe and North America during the nineteenth century. Britain began the revolution when it employed steam engines in the production of textiles. The development of the factory system along with more efficient transportation systems expanded British manufacturing. Not everyone benefited, however, from the emergence of the factory system, which led to social unrest and calls for reform.

The second Industrial Revolution in the later nineteenth century expanded the industrial economies of highly industrialized countries beyond Britain, including those of America and Germany. The daily lives of most citizens in industrialized nations were also improved by advances in transportation, communication, and sanitation.

These same advances also contributed to an expansion of European imperialism. The growth of industry and commerce, aided by new technologies and inventions, resulted in a quest among highly industrialized nations for raw materials, cheap labor, and new markets. Moreover, Western industrial nations discovered that new needs required the importation of not only raw materials but also foodstuffs. By the 1880s, faster ships powered by steam engines further enabled this expansion, while submarine cables provided for more efficient overseas communications. After 1871, the world's economy was increasingly divided into those who produced the world's manufactured products and those who both supplied the requisite raw materials and made up the growing pool of consumers.

As the basis for many of the patterns of twentieth-century modernity was being laid, World War I and its aftermath would soon reveal the divisions created by modernity and its scientific–technological underpinnings. Yet modern societies would continue their interaction and adaptation with older forms. Today, it is India and China, the successors to the agrarian–urban religious civilizations that resisted the new order most tenaciously, whose economies set the pace for twenty-first-century industrial development. It is to the story of the impact of modernity on these societies and others around the globe that we now turn.

Review and Relate

Thinking Through Patterns

Examine the ways historians approach the big questions of this chapter.

Where and when did the Industrial Revolution originate?

The Industrial Revolution began in Britain in the early eighteenth century. Britain had an earlier political revolution that empowered the merchant classes over the landed aristocracy, a prior agricultural revolution, and abundance of raw materials like coal.

What were some effects of industrialization on Western society? How did social patterns change?

Industrialization resulted in several social changes and adjustments. The capitalist middle classes were enriched and empowered by the growth of industrialism, as were the working classes, which did not exist as a group prior to industrialism. The benefits of industrialism were not evenly distributed across social strata; factory and mine workers were frequently exploited.

In what ways did industrialization contribute to innovations in technology? How did these technological advances contribute to Western imperialism in the late nineteenth century?

With the steam engine, capitalist entrepreneurs were able to substitute mechanical power for natural power and thus to develop the factory system. The factory system spread to the Continent and America as middle-class capitalism eclipsed mercantilism. Further advances contributed to a second Industrial Revolution beginning around 1850 based on steel, chemistry, and electricity.

Progress in industrial technology during the second Industrial Revolution led to practical inventions as well as advances in communication and transportation. These tools facilitated the expansion of Western imperialism in Africa and Asia during the closing years of the nineteenth century.

What new directions in science, philosophy, religion, and the arts did industrialism generate? What kind of responses did it provoke?

The new society that industrialism was creating spawned new directions in science, philosophy, religion, and the arts. Yet there was also a profound disquiet among scientists, intellectuals, and artists as traditions were abandoned. This disquiet would emerge in the immediate years after World War I.

Against the Grain

- Why did the British government react with such urgency to suppress the Luddite movement?
- How does the Luddite revolt compare with other protest movements against modernity in the later nineteenth century?

Consider this as a counterpoint to the main patterns examined in this chapter.

The Luddites

Although the mechanization of the textile industry was welcomed by some as providing new opportunities and by others as an indication of technological progress, still others were hardline opponents of the new industrial movement. One group of workers in early-nineteenth-century Britain, known as "Luddites," fiercely opposed the application of machines in the textile industry.

While the term "Luddite" now refers to those who oppose new technologies of any kind, the original Luddites feared the widespread use of new machinery that lowered their wages and threatened their livelihoods. Composed primarily of skilled artisans in the knitting and hosiery trades, Luddites mounted violent protests against the use of mechanical knitting frames and steam-powered looms. Referring to themselves as soldiers in the army of General Ludd, a mythical figure, Luddites began their assaults on the night of November 4, 1811. Breaking into the home of a weaver, they smashed several power looms. During 1812 and 1813, Luddites expanded their assaults, and in a span of 14 months Luddite "armies" smashed and destroyed around 1,000 machines.

The British government dispatched troops to suppress the Luddite movement, and in February of 1812 Parliament passed the Frame Breaking Act, which made attacks on textile machinery punishable by death. This was followed by the trial and hanging of eight Luddites later in the year. After a quick show trial in January of 1813, another 14 Luddites were executed. This effectively ended the movement, although occasional outbreaks of Luddism lingered on.

Even though the Luddite movement was relatively short-lived, it successfully called attention to inequalities inherent in early industrialism. This in turn prompted parliamentary reforms in the 1830s and 1840s, which improved working conditions for workers in factories, mines, and other occupations.

Key Terms

American System of Manufacturing 643
Bourgeoisie 637
Breech-loading 634
Chartism 640
Cottage industry 626
Chartism 640
Dialectical materialism 640
Modernism 644
Special theory of relativity 646
Suffragettes 641
Tariff 628

Learn more with this chapter's digital tools, including the Oxford Insight Study Guide, at http://www.oup.com/he/vonsivers4e. Please see the Further Resources section at the back of the book for additional readings and suggested websites.

PATTERNS OF EVIDENCE | Sources for Chapter 26

SOURCE 26.1

Charles Dickens, *Hard Times*

1854

Although his novels are beloved as works of fiction today, Charles Dickens (1812–1870) was also an acute observer of the ways in which industrialization fundamentally transformed economic conditions in England. Fully aware of the costs of economic dislocation (as a boy, Dickens had been confined in a debtors' prison with his family), the novelist described the residents of a fictional "Coketown" in one of his lesser-known works, *Hard Times*, published in 1854. The main industry in this town is a factory, owned and operated by the blowhard (and, it is ultimately revealed, self-created) Josiah Bounderby, and the people who work in the "manufactory" are the "Hands." The novel opens in a schoolroom, where children are being drilled in the acquisition of "facts, facts, facts." Their teacher is Mr. "M'Choakumchild" (Dickens was never very subtle in his nomenclature), and the director of the school is Mr. Gradgrind. The Gradgrind method will ultimately be proved a failure within Gradgrind's own family, but *Hard Times* reveals the actual "hardness" of conditions for so many in industrial Britain.

Chapter 5: The Key-note

Coketown, to which Messrs Bounderby and Gradgrind now walked, was a triumph of fact; it had no greater taint of fancy in it than Mrs Gradgrind herself. Let us strike the key-note, Coketown, before pursuing our tune.

It was a town of red brick, or of brick that would have been red if the smoke and ashes had allowed it; but, as matters stood it was a town of unnatural red and black like the painted face of a savage. It was a town of machinery and tall chimneys, out of which interminable serpents of smoke trailed themselves for ever and ever, and never got uncoiled. It had a black canal in it, and a river that ran purple with ill-smelling dye, and vast piles of buildings full of windows where there was a rattling and a trembling all day long, and where the piston of the steam-engine worked monotonously up and down, like the head of an elephant in a state of melancholy madness. It contained several large streets all very like one another, and many small streets still more like one another, inhabited by people equally like one another, who all went in and out at the

Source: Charles Dickens, *Hard Times, for These Times*, ed. David Craig (New York: Penguin, 1969), 65–66.

same hours, with the same sound upon the same pavements, to do the same work, and to whom every day was the same as yesterday and tomorrow, and every year the counterpart of the last and the next.

These attributes of Coketown were in the main inseparable from the work by which it was sustained; against them were to be set off, comforts of life which found their way all over the world, and elegancies of life which made, we will not ask how much of the fine lady, who could scarcely bear to hear the place mentioned. The rest of its features were voluntary, and they were these.

You saw nothing in Coketown but what was severely workful. If the members of a religious persuasion built a chapel there—as the members of eighteen religious persuasions had done—they made it a pious warehouse of red brick, with sometimes (but this is only in highly ornamented examples) a bell in a bird-cage on the top of it. The solitary exception was the New Church; a stuccoed edifice with a square steeple over the door, terminating in four short pinnacles like florid wooden legs. All the public inscriptions in the town were painted alike, in severe characters of black and white. The jail might have been the infirmary, the infirmary might have been the jail, the town-hall might have been either, or both, or anything else, for anything that appeared to the contrary in the graces of their construction. Fact, fact, fact, everywhere in the material aspect of the town; fact, fact, fact, everywhere in the immaterial. The M'Choakumchild school was all fact, and the school of design was all fact, and the relations between master and man were all fact, and everything was fact between the lying-in hospital and the cemetery, and what you couldn't state in figures, or show to be purchaseable in the cheapest market and saleable in the dearest, was not, and never should be, world without end, Amen.

▸ Working with Sources

1. **How does Dickens deploy imagery from the natural world to describe something as "unnatural" as Coketown?**
2. **In what specific ways is Coketown a "triumph of fact" over "fancy," and does he paint a convincing portrait of a typical town in a rapidly industrializing Britain?**

SOURCE 26.2

The death of William Huskisson, first casualty of a railroad accident

September 15, 1830

Although William Huskisson (1770–1830) was a prominent member of the British Parliament and a cabinet member in several governments, he is more famous for the circumstances of his death in a rapidly industrializing Great Britain. While attending the opening of the Liverpool and Manchester

Source: Letter from Thomas Creevey to Miss Ord, available online at *The Victorian Web*, http://www.victorianweb.org/history/accident.html

Railway in northern England on September 15, 1830, Huskisson rode in a carriage with the Duke of Wellington, a political figure and venerated hero of the Napoleonic Wars. Exiting the train during a stop, he was attempting to shake hands with the duke when he failed to notice another locomotive, George Stephenson's *Rocket*, traveling down an adjacent track. Huskisson attempted to swing into the carriage but fell on the tracks in front of the *Rocket*. With his leg horribly mangled by the train, Huskisson was rushed to a hospital (in a train driven by George Stephenson), but he died of his injuries a few hours later. He is, therefore, the world's first reported railway casualty.

Bangor, 19 September 1830

Jack Calcraft has been at the opening of the Liverpool rail road, and was an eye witness of Huskisson's horrible death. About nine or ten of the passengers in the Duke's car had got out to look about them, whilst the car stopt. Calcraft was one, Huskisson another, Esterhazy, Bill Holmes, Birch and others. When the other locomotive was seen coming up to pass them, there was a general shout from those within the Duke's car to those without it, to get in. Both Holmes and Birch were unable to get up in time, but they stuck fast to its sides, and the other engine did not touch them. Esterhazy being light, was pulled in by force. Huskisson was feeble in his legs, and appears to have lost his head, as he did his life. Calcraft tells me that Huskisson's long confinement in St George's Chapel at the king's funeral brought on a complaint that Taylor is so afraid of, and that made some severe surgical operation necessary, the effect of which had been, according to what he told Calcraft, to paralyse, as it were one leg and thigh. This, no doubt, must have increased, if it did not create, his danger and [caused him to] lose his life. He had written to say his health would not let him come, and his arrival was unexpected. Calcraft saw the meeting between him and the Duke, and saw them shake hands a very short time before Huskisson's death. The latter event must be followed by important political consequences. The Canning faction has lost its corner stone and the Duke's government one of its most formidable opponents. Huskisson, too, once out of the way, Palmerston, Melbourne, the Grants & Co. may make it up with the Beau [Wellington].

▸ Working with Sources

1. **What kind of commentary does Huskisson's death offer on the consequences of industrialization? Does this incident reveal another side of the history of industrialization?**
2. **Why does the author of this letter seem more interested in the political rather than the socioeconomic consequences of Huskisson's death?**

SOURCE 26.3

Young miners testify to the Ashley Commission

1842

The British Parliament took on a series of initiatives to investigate the lives of women and children in the mid-nineteenth century, and the resulting testimonies presented by workers to the various parliamentary commissions make for fascinating—and uniquely visceral—reading. The lives of working children are rarely detailed in historical sources from any era, but these testimonies had a direct impact, if not a fully humane one, on the lives of British laborers. These documents were collected for Lord Ashley's Mines Commission of 1842, and the shocking testimony resulted in the Mines Act of 1842, which prohibited the employment in the mines of all females and of boys under 13 years of age.

No. 116.—Sarah Gooder, aged 8 years

I'm a trapper in the Gawber pit. It does not tire me, but I have to trap without a light and I'm scared. I go at four and sometimes half past three in the morning, and come out at five and half past. I never go to sleep. Sometimes I sing when I've light, but not in the dark; I dare not sing then. I don't like being in the pit.

I am very sleepy when I go sometimes in the morning. I go to Sunday-schools and read Reading made Easy. (She knows her letters, and can read little words.) They teach me to pray. (She repeated the Lord's Prayer, not very perfectly, and ran on with the following addition:—"God bless my father and mother, and sister and brother, uncles and aunts and cousins, and everybody else, and God bless me and make me a good servant. Amen.") I have heard tell of Jesus many a time. I don't know why he came on earth, I'm sure, and I don't know why he died, but he had stones for his head to rest on. I would like to be at school far better than in the pit.

No. 14—Isabella Read, 12 years old, coal-bearer

Works on mother's account, as father has been dead two years. Mother bides at home, she is troubled with bad breath, and is sair weak in her body from early labour. I am wrought with sister and brother, it is very sore work; cannot say how many rakes or journeys I make from pit's bottom to wall face and back, thinks about 30 or 25 on the average; the distance varies from 100 to 250 fathom.

I carry about 1 cwt. and a quarter on my back; have to stoop much and creep through water, which is frequently up to the calves of my legs. When first down fell frequently asleep while waiting for coal from heat and fatigue.

Source: http://www.victorianweb.org/history/ashley.html, from *Readings in European History Since 1814*, ed. Jonathan F. Scott and Alexander Baltzly (New York: Appleton-Century-Crofts, 1930), drawing on *Parliamentary Papers*, 1842, vols. 25–27, Appendix 1, 252, 258, 439, 461; Appendix 2, 107, 122, 205.

I do not like the work, nor do the lassies, but they are made to like it. When the weather is warm there is difficulty in breathing, and frequently the lights go out.

No. 26.—Patience Kershaw, aged 17, May 15

My father has been dead about a year; my mother is living and has ten children, five lads and five lasses; the oldest is about thirty, the youngest is four; three lasses go to mill; all the lads are colliers, two getters and three hurriers; one lives at home and does nothing; mother does nought but look after home.

All my sisters have been hurriers, but three went to the mill. Alice went because her legs swelled from hurrying in cold water when she was hot. I never went to day-school; I go to Sunday-school, but I cannot read or write; I go to pit at five o'clock in the morning and come out at five in the evening; I get my breakfast of porridge and milk first; I take my dinner with me, a cake, and eat it as I go; I do not stop or rest any time for the purpose; I get nothing else until I get home, and then have potatoes and meat, not every day meat. I hurry in the clothes I have now got on, trousers and ragged jacket; the bald place upon my head is made by thrusting the corves; my legs have never swelled, but sisters' did when they went to mill; I hurry the corves a mile and more under ground and back; they weigh 300 cwt.; I hurry 11 a-day; I wear a belt and chain at the workings, to get the corves out; the getters that I work for are naked except their caps; they pull off all their clothes; I see them at work when I go up; sometimes they beat me, if I am not quick enough, with their hands; they strike me upon my back; the boys take liberties with me sometimes they pull me about; I am the only girl in the pit; there are about 20 boys and 15 men; all the men are naked; I would rather work in mill than in coal-pit.

This girl is an ignorant, filthy, ragged, and deplorable-looking object, and such an one as the uncivilized natives of the prairies would be shocked to look upon.

No. 72—Mary Barrett, aged 14, June 15

I have worked down in pit five years; father is working in next pit; I have 12 brothers and sisters—all of them but one live at home; they weave, and wind, and hurry, and one is a counter, one of them can read, none of the rest can, or write; they never went to day-school, but three of them go to Sunday-school; I hurry for my brother John, and come down at seven o'clock about; I go up at six, sometimes seven; I do not like working in pit, but I am obliged to get a living; I work always without stockings, or shoes, or trousers; I wear nothing but my chemise; I have to go up to the headings with the men; they are all naked there; I am got well used to that, and don't care now much about it; I was afraid at first, and did not like it; they never behave rudely to me; I cannot read or write.

▸ Working with Sources

1. **Do the employers of these workers seem to have taken into account the unique conditions of their age and gender?**
2. **How does the recorder of these interviews interject his own reactions to these narratives? Why does he do this?**

SOURCE 26.4

Karl Marx, "Wage Labour and Capital"

1847

Karl Marx (1818–1883) and Friedrich Engels (1820–1895) are best known for their collaborative work *The Communist Manifesto* (1848). However, the two had been observing the real consequences of industrialization for factory workers, particularly in Manchester, England, for some years before this. Working in his father's cotton factory in England, Engels had witnessed the inequities imposed by industrial systems, and he composed a scathing attack on these systems in his *Condition of the Working-Class in England* (1845). When Marx befriended Engels in Manchester, he too came to see how local conditions could lead to wide-ranging theories about labor, wages, and the measurement of "costs." In this lecture, delivered in December 1847, Marx took his audience through the most basic elements of the philosophy that would culminate in *Das Kapital* (vol. 1, 1867).

If several workmen were to be asked: "How much wages do you get?", one would reply, "I get two shillings a day," and so on. According to the different branches of industry in which they are employed, they would mention different sums of money that they receive from their respective employers for the completion of a certain task; for example, for weaving a yard of linen, or for setting a page of type. Despite the variety of their statements, they would all agree upon one point: that wages are the amount of money which the capitalist pays for a certain period of work or for a certain amount of work.

Consequently, it appears that the capitalist buys their labour with money, and that for money they sell him their labour. But this is merely an illusion. What they actually sell to the capitalist for money is their labour-power. This labour-power the capitalist buys for a day, a week, a month, etc. And after he has bought it, he uses it up by letting the worker labour during the stipulated time. With the same amount of money with which the capitalist has bought their labour-power (for example, with two shillings) he could have bought a certain amount of sugar or of any other commodity. The two shillings with which he bought 20 pounds of sugar is the price of the 20 pounds of sugar. The two shillings with which he bought 12 hours' use of labour-power, is the price of 12 hours' labour. Labour-power, then, is a commodity, no more, no less so than is the sugar. The first is measured by the clock, the other by the scales.

Their commodity, labour-power, the workers exchange for the commodity of the capitalist, for money, and, moreover, this exchange takes place at a certain ratio. So much money for so long a use of labour-power. For 12 hours' weaving, two shillings. And these two shillings, do they not represent all the other commodities which I can buy for two shillings? Therefore, actually, the worker has exchanged his commodity, labour-power, for commodities of all

Source: http://www.marxists.org/archive/marx/works/1847/wage-labour/, first published in German in the *Neue Rheinische Zeitung* (April 5–8, 11, 1849), and edited and translated by Friedrich Engels for an 1891 pamphlet kinds, and, moreover, at a certain ratio. By giving him two shillings, the capitalist has given him so much meat, so much clothing, so much wood, light, etc., in exchange for his day's work. The two shillings therefore express the relation in which labour-power is exchanged for other commodities, the exchange-value of labour-power.

The exchange value of a commodity estimated in money is called its price. Wages therefore are only a special name for the price of labour-power, and are usually called the price of labour; it is the special name for the price of this peculiar commodity, which has no other repository than human flesh and blood.

Let us take any worker; for example, a weaver. The capitalist supplies him with the loom and yarn. The weaver applies himself to work, and the yarn is turned into cloth. The capitalist takes possession of the cloth and sells it for 20 shillings, for example. Now are the wages of the weaver a share of the cloth, of the 20 shillings, of the product of the work? By no means. Long before the cloth is sold, perhaps long before it is fully woven, the weaver has received his wages. The capitalist, then, does not pay his wages out of the money which he will obtain from the cloth, but out of money already on hand. Just as little as loom and yarn are the product of the weaver to whom they are supplied by the employer, just so little are the commodities which he receives in exchange for his commodity—labour-power—his product. It is possible that the employer found no purchasers at all for the cloth. It is possible that he did not get even the amount of the wages by its sale. It is possible that he sells it very profitably in proportion to the weaver's wages. But all that does not concern the weaver. With a part of his existing wealth, of his capital, the capitalist buys the labour-power of the weaver in exactly the same manner as, with another part of his wealth, he has bought the raw material—the yarn—and the instrument of labour—the loom. After he has made these purchases, and among them belongs the labour-power necessary to the production of the cloth he produces only with raw materials and instruments of labour belonging to him. For our good weaver, too, is one of the instruments of labour, and being in this respect on a par with the loom, he has no more share in the product (the cloth), or in the price of the product, than the loom itself has.

Wages, therefore, are not a share of the worker in the commodities produced by himself. Wages are that part of already existing commodities with which the capitalist buys a certain amount of productive labour-power.

. . .

The free labourer, on the other hand, sells his very self, and that by fractions. He auctions off eight, 10, 12, 15 hours of his life, one day like the next, to the highest bidder, to the owner of raw materials, tools, and the means of life—i.e., to the capitalist. The labourer belongs neither to an owner nor to the soil, but eight, 10, 12, 15 hours of his daily life belong to whomsoever buys them. The worker leaves the capitalist, to whom he has sold himself, as often as he chooses, and the capitalist discharges him as often as he sees fit, as soon as he no longer gets any use, or not the required use, out of him. But the worker, whose only source of income is the sale of his labour-power, cannot leave the whole class of buyers, i.e., the capitalist class, unless he gives up his own existence. He does not belong to this or that capitalist, but to the capitalist class; and it is for him to find his man—i.e., to find a buyer in this capitalist class.

▸ Working with Sources

1. **How does Marx describe wages as a commodity price, equivalent to other sorts of "prices" in the marketplace?**
2. **How does he contrast larger economic forces with the lived realities of workers in a factory?**

SOURCE 26.5

Charles Darwin, *On the Origin of Species*

1859

The name of Charles Darwin (1809–1882) is inextricably linked to the earth-shattering and (even today) controversial theory he proposed in 1859. However, it is also important to remember that he was a writer of exceptional skill and a best-selling author, even though many of his observations and conclusions were certainly too difficult for nonspecialists to appreciate. The 200th anniversary of his birth—and the 150th anniversary of the appearance of *On the Origin of Species*—in 2009 resulted in a series of commemorative events around the world, a brief sample of which can be viewed online at http://darwin-online.org.uk/2009.html. Among the most famous elements of the book is the tangled-riverbank image introduced in the long book's final paragraph, and Darwin's stimulating view of the "grandeur in this view of life."

As this whole volume is one long argument, it may be convenient to the reader to have the leading facts and inferences briefly recapitulated.

That many and serious objections may be advanced against the theory of descent with modification through variation and natural selection, I do not deny. I have endeavoured to give to them their full force. Nothing at first can appear more difficult to believe than that the more complex organs and instincts have been perfected, not by means superior to, though analogous with, human reason, but by the accumulation of innumerable slight variations, each good for the individual possessor. Nevertheless, this difficulty, though appearing to our imagination insuperably great, cannot be considered real if we admit the following propositions, namely, that all parts of the organisation and instincts offer, at least individual differences—that there is a struggle for existence leading to the preservation of profitable deviations of structure or

---

Source: Charles Darwin, *The Origin of Species by Means of Natural Selection, or the Preservation of Favored Races in the Struggle for Life and The Descent of Man, and Selection in Relation to Sex* (New York: Modern Library, 1936), 353, 372, 373–374.

instinct—and, lastly, that gradations in the state of perfection of each organ may have existed, each good of its kind. The truth of these propositions cannot, I think, be disputed.

It is, no doubt, extremely difficult even to conjecture by what gradations many structures have been perfected, more especially among broken and failing groups of organic beings, which have suffered much extinction; but we see so many strange gradations in nature, that we ought to be extremely cautious in saying that any organ or instinct, or any whole structure, could not have arrived at its present state by many graduated steps. There are, it must be admitted, cases of special difficulty opposed to the theory of natural selection; and one of the most curious of these is the existence in the same community of two or three defined castes of workers or sterile female ants; but I have attempted to show how these difficulties can be mastered.

. . .

A grand and almost untrodden field of inquiry will be opened, on the causes and laws of variation, on correlation, on the effects of use and disuse, on the direct action of external conditions, and so forth. The study of domestic productions will rise immensely in value. A new variety raised by man will be a far more important and interesting subject for study than one more species added to the infinitude of already recorded species. Our classifications will come to be, as far as they can be so made, genealogies; and will then truly give what may be called the plan of creation. The rules for classifying will no doubt become simpler when we have a definite object in view. We possess no pedigrees or armorial bearings; and we have to discover and trace the many diverging lines of descent in our natural genealogies, by characters of any kind which have long been inherited. Rudimentary organs will speak infallibly with respect to the nature of long-lost structures. Species and groups of species which are called aberrant, and which may fancifully be called living fossils, will aid us in forming a picture of the ancient forms of life. Embryology will often reveal to us the structure, in some degree obscured, of the prototypes of each great class.

When we can feel assured that all the individuals of the same species, and all the closely allied species of most genera, have, within a not very remote period descended from one parent, and have migrated from some one birth-place; and when we better know the many means of migration, then, by the light which geology now throws, and will continue to throw, on former changes of climate and of the level of the land, we shall surely be enabled to trace in an admirable manner the former migrations of the inhabitants of the whole world. Even at present, by comparing the differences between the inhabitants of the sea on the opposite sides of a continent, and the nature of the various inhabitants of that continent in relation to their apparent means of immigration, some light can be thrown on ancient geography.

. . .

It is interesting to contemplate a tangled bank, clothed with many plants of many kinds, with birds singing on the bushes, with various insects flitting about, and with worms crawling through the damp earth, and to reflect that these elaborately constructed forms, so different from each other, and dependent upon each other in so complex a manner, have all been produced by laws acting around us. These laws, taken in the largest sense, being Growth with

Reproduction; Inheritance which is almost implied by reproduction; Variability from the indirect and direct action of the conditions of life, and from use and disuse; a Ratio of Increase so high as to lead to a Struggle for Life, and as a consequence to Natural Selection, entailing Divergence of Character and the Extinction of less-improved forms. Thus, from the war of nature, from famine and death, the most exalted object which we are capable of conceiving, namely, the production of the higher animals, directly follows. There is grandeur in this view of life, with its several powers, having been originally breathed by the Creator into a few forms or into one; and that, whilst this planet has gone cycling on according to the fixed law of gravity, from so simple a beginning endless forms most beautiful and most wonderful have been, and are being evolved.

Working with Sources

1. **How does Darwin manage to convey the excitement that he feels for this new scientific field and the possibilities for applying his theory to other disciplines?**
2. **How does his quest for common ancestors underscore the interconnected nature of all species on our planet?**

SOURCE 26.6

Emmeline Pankhurst, *My Own Story*

During the later nineteenth century a series of reforms extended the franchise for men in France, Germany, and Britain, but women were denied equal voting rights. As a consequence, women's associations, led by feminist activists, were created for the purpose of attaining equal rights, particularly for the right to vote. In Britain, the National Society for Women's Suffrage was formed in 1867, followed 30 years later by the National Union of Women's Suffrage Society. When it became apparent that traditional, constitutional methods were unsuccessful, in 1903 Emmeline Pankhurst (1858–1928) formed the more aggressive Women's Social and Political Union, whose members were labeled "suffragettes." Frustrated and exasperated by their inability to convince political parties, these activists resorted to violence, civil disobedience, marches, hunger strikes, and other demonstrations; Pankhurst herself was arrested at Buckingham Palace in 1911. In her memoir, *My Own Story*, Pankhurst reveals her path to militancy.

Source: Emmeline Pankhurst, *My Own Story* (London: Eveleigh Nash, 1914), 9-15.

Book I. The Making of a Militant

Those men and women are fortunate who are born at a time when a great struggle for human freedom is in progress. It is an added good fortune to have parents who take a personal part in the great movements of their time. I am glad and thankful that this was my case.

One of my earliest recollections is of a great bazaar which was held in my native city of Manchester, the object of the bazaar being to raise money to relieve the poverty of the newly emancipated negro slaves in the United States. My mother took an active part in this effort, and I, as a small child, was entrusted with a lucky bag by means of which I helped to collect money.

Young as I was—I could not have been older than five years—I knew perfectly well the meaning of the words slavery and emancipation. From infancy I had been accustomed to hear pro and con discussions of slavery and the American Civil War. Although the British government finally decided not to recognise the Confederacy, public opinion in England was sharply divided on the questions both of slavery and of secession. Broadly speaking, the propertied classes were pro-slavery, but there were many exceptions to the rule. Most of those who formed the circle of our family friends were opposed to slavery, and my father, Robert Goulden, was always a most ardent abolitionist. He was prominent enough in the movement to be appointed on a committee to meet and welcome Henry Ward Beecher when he arrived in England for a lecture tour. Mrs. Harriet Beecher Stowe's novel, "Uncle Tom's Cabin," was so great a favourite with my mother that she used it continually as a source of bedtime stories for our fascinated ears. Those stories, told almost fifty years ago, are as fresh in my mind to-day as events detailed in the morning's papers. Indeed they are more vivid, because they made a much deeper impression on my consciousness. I can still definitely recall the thrill I experienced every time my mother related the tale of Eliza's race for freedom over the broken ice of the Ohio River, the agonizing pursuit, and the final rescue at the hands of the determined old Quaker...

These stories, with the bazaars and the relief funds and subscriptions of which I heard so much talk, I am sure made a permanent impression on my brain and my character. They awakened in me the two sets of sensations to which all my life I have most readily responded: first, admiration for that spirit of fighting and heroic sacrifice by which alone the soul of civilisation is saved; and next after that, appreciation of the gentler spirit which is moved to mend and repair the ravages of war...

Manchester is a city which has witnessed a great many stirring episodes, especially of a political character. . .In the late sixties there occurred in Manchester one of those dreadful events that prove an exception to the rule. . .A man fired a pistol. . .a policeman fell, mortally wounded, and several men were arrested and were charged with murder. . .The rest of the story reveals one of those ghastly blunders which justice not infrequently makes. Although the shooting was done without any intent to kill, the men were tried for murder and three of them were found guilty and hanged. . . A certain Saturday afternoon stands out in my memory, as on my way home from school I passed the prison where I knew the men had been confined. I saw that a part of the prison wall had been torn away, and in the great gap that remained were evidences of a gallows recently removed. I was transfixed with horror, and over me there swept the sudden conviction that hanging was a mistake—worse, a crime. It was my awakening to one of the most terrible facts of life—that justice and judgment lie often a world apart.

I relate this incident of my formative years to illustrate the fact that the impressions of childhood often have more to do with character and future conduct than heredity or education. I tell it also to show that my development into an advocate of militancy was largely a sympathetic process. I have not personally suffered from the deprivations, the bitterness and sorrow which bring so many men and women to a realisation of social injustice. My childhood was protected by love and a comfortable home. Yet, while still a very young child, I began instinctively to feel that there was something lacking, even in my own home, some false conception of family relations, some incomplete ideal.

This vague feeling of mine began to shape itself into conviction about the time my brothers and I were sent to school. The education of the English boy, then as now, was considered a much more serious matter than the education of the English boy's sister. My parents, especially my father, discussed the question of my brothers' education as a matter of real importance. My education and that of my sister were scarcely discussed at all. Of course we went to a carefully selected girls' school, but beyond the facts that the headmistress was a gentlewoman and that all the pupils were girls of my own class, nobody seemed concerned. A girl's education at that time seemed to have for its prime object the art of "making home attractive"—presumably to migratory male relatives. It used to puzzle me to understand why I was under such a particular obligation to make home attractive to my brothers. We were on excellent terms of friendship, but it was never suggested to them as a duty that they make home attractive to me. Why not? Nobody seemed to know.

The answer to these puzzling questions came to me unexpectedly one night when I lay in my little bed waiting for sleep to overtake me. It was a custom of my father and mother to make the round of our bedrooms every night before going themselves to bed. When they entered my room that night I was still awake, but for some reason I chose to feign slumber. My father bent over me, shielding the candle flame with his big hand. I cannot know exactly what thought was in his mind as he gazed down at me, but I heard him say, somewhat sadly, "What a pity she wasn't born a lad."

My first hot impulse was to sit up in bed and protest that I didn't want to be a boy, but I lay still and heard my parents' footsteps pass on toward the next child's bed. I thought about my father's remark for many days afterward, but I think I never decided that I regretted my sex. However, it was made quite clear that men considered themselves superior to women, and that women apparently acquiesced in that belief. . .I suppose I had always been an unconscious suffragist.

▸ Working with Sources

1. **How does Pankhurst trace her path to militancy?**
2. **What were Pankhurst's principal interpretations of social justice?**

World Period Five

The Origins of Modernity, 1750–1900

The twin novel events of constitutional and industrial revolutions, first in the Americas and western Europe and later in Japan, dramatically changed the course of world history.

- People rose to end the divine right of kings and replace their rule with popular sovereignty, constitutions, and elections.
- Machines began to replace animal power in the manufacture of textiles, means of transportation, chemicals, and urban amenities.

As a result, 10,000-year-old traditional customs and habits formed by life in agriculture gave way to what we call "modernity," that is, nontraditional new ways of life in the "machine age," characterized by such new phenomena as nation-states, social classes, megacities, colonialism, and above all, vastly increased global interactions.

Chapter 27

The New Imperialism in the Nineteenth Century

1750–1914

CHAPTER TWENTY-SEVEN PATTERNS

Origins, Interactions, Adaptations Innovations based on coal, iron, steam, and steel—combined with Enlightenment ideas—enabled Great Britain, France, and the United States to expand territorial and overseas holdings at an unprecedented rate. The old agrarian empires of the Ottomans and the Qing faced mounting pressures, while the Mughals ceded control of India to the British. The Second Industrial Revolution triggered intensified competition for commodities in Africa, Asia, and the Pacific. Along with the search for markets in which to sell finished products, these forces pushed empire building to new heights. At the same time, theories of human development placed "modern" societies at the apex of a hierarchy of peoples and races.

Uniqueness and Similarities This vast expansion of power and its effects, though sharing broad similarities, had a number of unique characteristics. British imperialism and colonialism focused on trade concessions in Asia, resource extraction in Africa, and "settler colonies" in Australia, New Zealand, and South Africa. The French, for their part, settled colonists in North Africa but also saw their colonial endeavors in Africa and Asia as a "civilizing mission." For those under imperial and colonial rule, the challenges of resistance or collaboration, while broadly similar, varied from place to place. Though they attempted to catch up with the leading industrial powers, the older agrarian empires could not build up the necessary infrastructure to adapt and compete.

CHAPTER OUTLINE

The British Colonies of India and Australia

European Imperialism in the Middle East and Africa

Western Imperialism and Colonialism in Southeast Asia

Putting It All Together

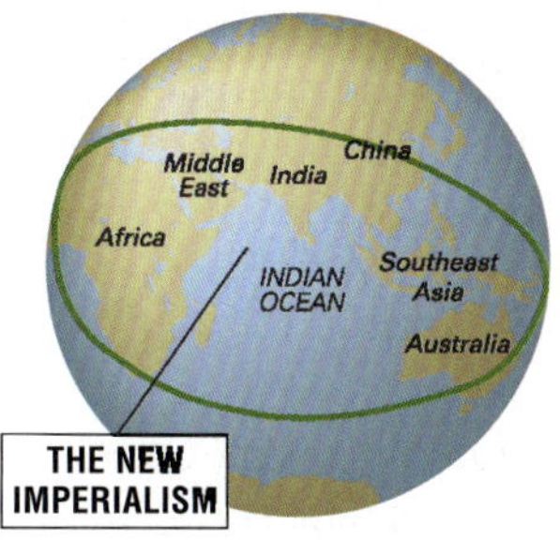

At the end of the Muslim month-long observance of Ramadan in 1827, Hussein Dey (r. 1815–1830), the ruler of the autonomous Ottoman province of Algeria in North Africa, held a celebratory reception for the diplomatic corps of consuls at his palace in the port city of Algiers. When he saw the French consul, Pierre Deval, Hussein publicly accused the consul of defrauding him of a large sum of money owed by France and demanded immediate payment of the debt. To emphasize his demand, Hussein struck Deval with his fan and declared him persona non grata, which, in terms of diplomatic protocol, meant that he had to leave the country immediately.

France's restored Bourbon king, Charles X (r. 1824–1830), found this insult to an appointee of the French court intolerable. He dispatched a naval detachment to Algiers in 1828 to demand that Hussein apologize, declare the debt liquidated, and pay reparations for piracy raids of preceding years. When Hussein rejected the demands, the French mounted a blockade of the port. In 1830, a French expeditionary force conquered Algiers, deposed Hussein, and sent him into exile. Less than two decades later, Algeria became a colony of France.

The incident illustrates the changing fortunes of those countries that were the beneficiaries of the new forces of modernity—in this case, France—and those that largely were not, like the Ottoman Empire and its territories in Algeria. In this chapter we will study the victims of conquest and occupation in south and Southeast Asia, the Middle East, Africa, and the Pacific Ocean that most clearly make visible the underlying patterns of imperialism and colonialism.

Two new patterns characterized European politics outside western and central Europe in the period 1750–1900. The first was the pursuit of a renewed imperialism by western European countries against the decentralizing Ottoman Empire, under assault by the Russian Empire since the eighteenth century. The Europeans first protected the Ottomans from Russia, only later to

ABOVE: This cartoon of a jubilant Cecil Rhodes holding aloft telegraph cables that span from Capetown to Cairo captures the power and aggressiveness of the New Imperialism.

help themselves to Ottoman provinces, beginning with the capture of Algeria by France.

The second was a shift from coastal trade forts under chartered companies to the **new imperialism** of government takeover, territorial conquest, and often **colonialism**. Of course, in the Americas the old trade-fort imperialism had given way to full-fledged Spanish and Portuguese territorial imperialism, followed by conquest and colonialism, already in the early1500s, when conquest there proved easier than in more densely settled Africa and Asia. Between 1750 and 1900, the western and central European countries of Great Britain, France, Germany, and Italy competed with each other for the establishment of colonial empires in the Middle East, Africa, Asia, and Pacific Ocean.

Seeing Patterns

- **What new patterns emerged in the transition from trade-fort imperialism to the new imperialism?**
- **How did European colonizers develop their colonies economically, given that they were industrializing themselves at the same time?**
- **What were the experiences of the indigenous people under the new imperialism? How did they adapt to colonialism? How did they resist?**

The British Colonies of India and Australia

The transition from European trade-fort activities to colonialism in India coincided with the decline of the Mughal dynasty (see Chapter 20). As a result, Britain became a colonial power in the Eastern Hemisphere, with India as its center. Australia and New Zealand began as British settler colonies, the former as a penal colony and the latter against fierce indigenous resistance.

The British East India Company

An important factor in the rise of British power in India was the Seven Years' War, during which fighting took place in Europe, in the Americas, and in India. It was the war in India, along with the political difficulties of the Mughals, that enabled the rise of the British to supremacy on the subcontinent.

New imperialism: The intensified domination that modernizing states exercised worldwide in the second half of the nineteenth century.

Colonialism: Establishment of a more or less elaborate administrative system by a European country in the conquered overseas territory, accompanied by economic exploitation. In a number of overseas territories, settlers from Europe practiced colonialism by establishing themselves as farmers, planters, and craftsmen.

The Seven Years' War By the early eighteenth century, Britain had established trading posts in provincial cities that would over time be transformed into India's greatest metropolises: Madras (Chennai), Bombay (Mumbai), and Calcutta (Kolkata). By 1750 their chief commercial competitors were the French, who were aggressively building up both trade and political power from a base in Pondicherry in southern India.

For the British East India Company, its evolution into a kind of shadow government in the area around Calcutta in Bengal would now bear dividends. The decline of Mughal central power meant that regional leaders were being enlisted as French or British allies. The more powerful sought to use the sepoy (Indian troops; from Persian *sipahi* [see-pa-HEE], "soldier") armies of the European companies as support in their own struggles. Out of this confused political and military situation, the East India Company leader, Robert Clive (1725–1774), won a victory over the Indian French allies at Plassey in 1757 and soon eliminated the French from power on the subcontinent. The East India Company ended up in 1763 as the sole European power of consequence in India, and Clive set about consolidating his position from Calcutta.

Going Native: The Nabobs The East India Company began to expand its holdings across northern India, extorting funds from local princes. The company men, however, had no interest in reforming Indian institutions. Indeed, many became great admirers of Indian culture. Some went so far as to "go native": They took Indian wives, dressed as Indian princes, and on occasion wielded power as local magnates, or **nabobs** (from Urdu *nawwab* [naw-WAHB], "deputy," "viceroy").

Nabob: A person who acquired a large fortune in India during the period of British rule.

The vast distances separating the company's London directors from operations in India made its local activities virtually autonomous. Its power, organization, and army influenced local disputes across northern India; its policy of paying low wages while turning a blind eye to employees trading locally for their private benefit led to corruption.

By 1800, British possessions extended across most of northern India (see Map 27.1). This extension prompted a shift in trading from spices to cotton goods—and, increasingly, to raw cotton—as the most lucrative commodity, due to Britain's mechanized textile revolution.

The Perils of Reform During the nineteenth century, India and China were still the primary economic engines of Eurasia. As the Industrial Revolution developed, however, Britain's share of the world's output increased, while India's declined (see Figure 27.1).

As Britain's share of India's economy grew, the British sought to create markets for their own goods there and to divert Indian exports exclusively into the British domestic market. In addition, officials of the East India Company arbitrated disputes among Indian rulers, taking over their lands as payment for loans, and strong-arming many into becoming wards of the British. Because of this attrition, by the end of the Napoleonic Wars, the Mughal emperor's lands had been reduced to the region immediately surrounding Delhi and Agra.

While many in India chafed at company rule, its policy of noninterference with Indian customs and institutions softened the blow of the conquest somewhat. The period following the Napoleonic Wars, however, brought the British government into a more direct role.

Clashes between factory owners and labor and the drive for political reform in Britain during this period

Perceptions of Empire. The British East India Company's real ascent to power in India began with Robert Clive's victory at Plassey in 1757, the symbolism of which is depicted here. Note the deference with which the assorted Indian princes treat the conqueror.

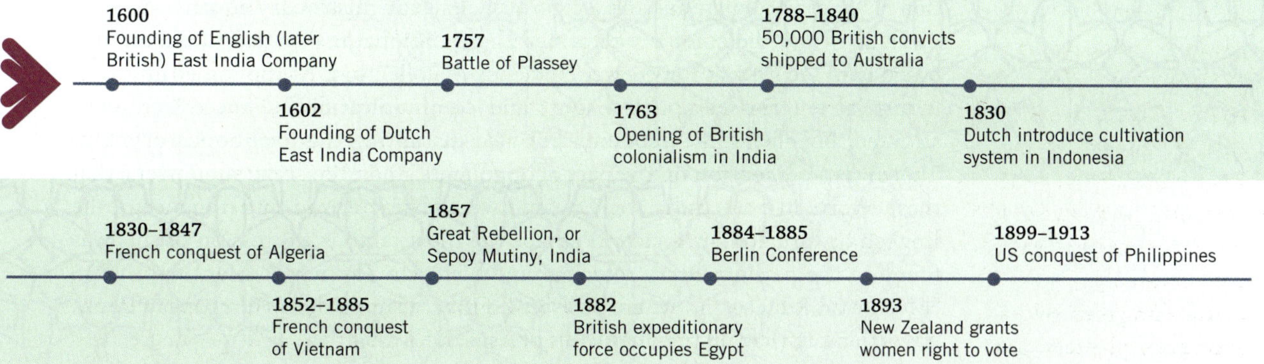

MAP 27.1 The Expansion of British Power in India, 1756–1805

found echoes in British policy toward India. From the opening decades of the century, many Protestant missionaries active in mission-based reform in India had also been involved with movements for the abolition of slavery, industrial workers' rights, and electoral reform in Britain. By 1830 they asserted that India should be similarly reformed: better working conditions for the poor, free trade, the abolition of "barbaric" customs, and a vigorous Christian missionary effort.

In addition, the company reformed the traditional tax system into a money-based land fee system for greater efficiency of collection. At the same time, new industrial enterprises and transport and communication advances were constructed, benefiting the economy but also disrupting the livelihoods of many. There was a perception on the part of opponents, and even some supporters, that these efforts in both India and England were characterized by arrogance of the English toward Indian society. Perhaps the most famous expression of this was found in the parliamentary reformer and historian Thomas B. Macaulay's 1835 "Minute on Education," where he asserted that "a single shelf of European books is worth more than all the literatures of Asia and Arabia."

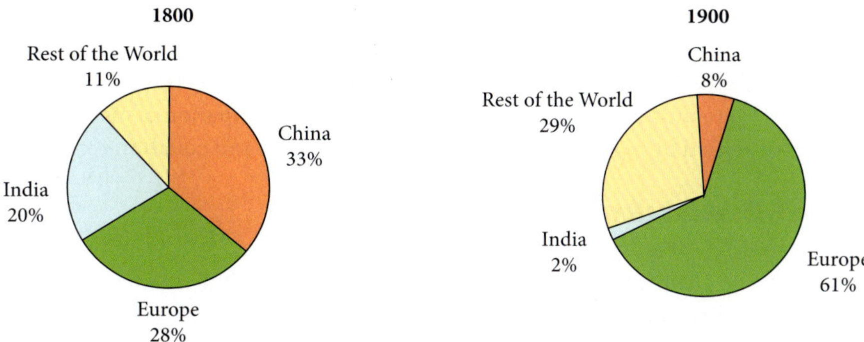

Figure 27.1 Share of World Manufacturing Output, 1800 and 1900

Execution of Indian Rebels. After British troops and loyalist Indian sepoys had restored order in northern India, retribution was unleashed on the rebels. Here, the most spectacular mode of execution is being carried out. Mutineers are tied across the mouths of cannons and blown to pieces while the troops stand in formation and are forced to watch.

India's First War of Independence Disillusionment with the rapid pace of change and fears that British missionaries were attempting, with government connivance, to Christianize India came to a head among the company's sepoy troops in 1857. With the introduction of the new Enfield rifle, which required its operator to bite the end off a greased paper cartridge full of gunpowder, a rumor started that the grease was concocted of cow and pig fat. Since this would violate the dietary restrictions of both Hindus and Muslims, the troops saw this as a plot to leave the followers of both religions ritually unclean and thus open to conversion to Christianity. Though the rumors proved untrue, the revolt became a wholesale rebellion aimed at throwing the British out of India and restoring the Mughal emperor to full power. The perceived insults to Indian religions and culture pushed the troops and their allies to frightful atrocities.

The First War of Independence (as it is commonly referred to in India, along with the Great Rebellion; it is known by the British as the Sepoy Mutiny or Great Mutiny) became a civil war as pro- and anti-British Indian forces clashed. Although the British were ultimately able to reassert control, the occupation of many towns was accompanied by mass executions of suspected rebels and collaborators.

Direct British Rule

After assuming direct rule (Hindi *raj*, hence the term "Raj" for the colonial government), the British sought to limit their apparatus of civilian administrators while maintaining an army large enough to avoid a repeat of 1857. The Raj functioned by exploiting divisions in Indian society, which prevented the Indians from uniting to challenge British rule.

Creation of the Civil Service The British government enacted sweeping reforms in 1858. The East India Company was dismantled, and the British government itself took up the task of governing India. An Indian civil service was created for British and Indians alike to administer the subcontinent's affairs. India had now become, it was said, the "jewel in the crown" of the empire (see Map 27.2).

In 1885, Indians first convened the Indian National Congress, the ancestor of India's present Congress Party. The congress's mission was to win greater autonomy for India within the structure of the British Empire and, by the opening decades of the twentieth century, to push for Indian independence.

Divide and Rule The Indian civil service was intended as a showpiece of British incorruptibility, in contrast to the perception of endemic graft customary among the Indian princes. For officials, the heavy workload demanded a sophisticated understanding of local conditions and sensibilities. The numbers of civil service members increased markedly in the twentieth century as Britain began to implement a gradual devolution to a kind of federated Indian autonomy.

How did such a small government apparatus control such a large country? In many respects it was done by bluff and artifice. The Indian Army of Great Britain was small and well trained, but made up mostly of Indians. The British officers and noncommissioned officers included many Scots and Irish, themselves minorities often subject to discrimination at home. British divide-and-rule tactics made large-scale organization across caste, religious, ethnic, and linguistic lines extremely difficult. Most importantly, advances in weaponry during the late nineteenth century—machine guns, rapid-fire artillery, repeating rifles—heavily discouraged thoughts of rebellion.

Though the bureaucracy of British India served to unite the country for administrative purposes, the British secured their rule locally and regionally by divide-and-rule tactics. A key divide they utilized was the obvious one between Hindus and Muslims. British policy had encouraged Muslims to see the British as their protectors, while also often leaning in their favor in disputes with the Hindus. Thus, Muslims often felt they had a stake in the Raj, particularly when the alternative that presented itself was a Hindu-controlled India, should independence from Britain ever come. Other divides exploited differences among the Hindus.

MAP 27.2 The British Empire in India, 1858–1914

For example, in order to undermine the power bases of Brahmans, lower castes were sometimes given favorable treatment. Different regions might be given preferential treatment as well. The British also exploited the sense of grandeur of the Indian elites with *durbars* (elaborate, formal public celebrations) at the Raj's showpiece capital of New Delhi. Such occasions reinforced traditional notions of deference and hierarchy.

By identifying British rule with India's historic past, it was hoped that the perception of legitimacy would be enhanced. This effort to co-opt local rulers into upholding the British government as the historically destined status quo placed the local rulers in a **subaltern** relationship with their colonial governors. Yet a growing elite of Western-educated Indian leaders began to use the arguments of empire against their occupiers.

Subaltern: A person or thing considered subordinate to another.

Patterns Up Close | Military Transformations and the New Imperialism

Ethiopian Forces Defeating an Italian Army at Adowa, 1896. A hundred years after Napoleon's victory, the tables were turned when an Ethiopian army equipped with repeating rifles, machine guns, and cannon routed an Italian invasion force. In response to the defeat, the *Times* of London complained that "the prestige of European arms as a whole is considerably impaired."

Between 1450 and 1750, firearm-equipped infantries rose to prominence throughout Eurasia. Scholars have debated the significance of the differences among infantries—and military organizations more generally—during this age of empire.

Historians long believed that superior firearms, cannons, and cannon-equipped ships enabled Europeans to achieve imperial conquest and colonization of the Middle East, Africa, and Southeast Asia. However, most scholars now agree that, beginning in the late seventeenth century, it was only the flintlock muskets, bayonets, and line drill that distinguished western European infantries from other armies in Asia and Africa and gave Europeans an advantage. These advantages were manifested in the Ottoman–Russian War of 1768–1774 and in Napoleon's invasion of Egypt in 1798.

The Mughals in India and the Qing in China did not have to worry about flintlock, bayonet, and line infantry attacks in the eighteenth century, either from their neighbors or from the faraway Europeans. Like the Ottomans, who continued to maintain large cavalry forces against their nomadic neighbors in the Middle East and Central

British Settler Colonies: Australia

British occupation of Australia and New Zealand began with the conquest of small and weak indigenous forager or agrarian populations, followed by the expropriation of indigenous lands and the establishment of settler colonies. In contrast to their modus operandi in India, the British also encouraged large-scale immigration of European settlers to these regions.

White Settlement in Australia Dutch navigators discovered the western coast of Australia in 1606 but did not pursue any further contacts or construct trade forts. The British navigator James Cook (1728–1779), during one of his many exploratory journeys in the Pacific, landed in 1770 on the Australian east coast and claimed it for Great Britain. After America won its independence in 1783, the British government looked to Australia as the next place to which it could ship convicts. Between 1788 and 1840, some 50,000 British convicts were sentenced to "transport" to the Australian penal colony.

Immigration by free British subjects, begun a decade before the end of convict shipments, led to a pastoral and agricultural boom. Settlers pioneered agriculture in southern Australia, where rainfall was reliable and provided the population with most of its cereal needs. Sugar and rice cultivation, introduced to the tropical northeast in the 1860s, was performed with indentured labor recruited from

Asia, the Mughals and Qing privileged their cavalries. However, once British East India Company officers elevated indigenous infantry soldiers to the privileged ranks of the sepoy regiments, their efficiency ultimately lent itself to such problems for the company as the Great Rebellion that the British Crown had to take over the governance of India in 1858.

When European innovators introduced workable breech-loading rifles and artillery in the late 1850s, the technological balance shifted decisively toward Europe. The addition of rapid-firing mechanisms in the second half of the 1800s to these improved weapons further cemented Europe's technological superiority.

Thus, in this shift from an initially slight to an eventually pronounced superiority of European arms during this period, the new imperialism and the Industrial Revolution were parallel developments engendered by the same modernity that also saw the rise of constitutionalism and the formation of a new type of polity, the nation-state. Certainly, industrially produced weapons in the later nineteenth century greatly enhanced Europe's ability to dominate much of the Middle East, Africa, and Asia.

Question

- Does the painting of Ethiopian forces defeating an Italian army in 1896 show that indigenous peoples could adapt Western innovations to their own purposes? If so, how?

Pacific islands. Even during penal colony times, sheep ranching in the east and the exportation of wool developed into a thriving business. The mining of gold and silver began in the east in 1851 and spread to nearly all parts of the continent. Although a colony, commodity-rich Australia sought its wealth through export-led growth.

Mining generated several gold-rush immigration waves, not only from Britain but also from China, as well as internal migrations from mining towns to cities when the gold rushes ended. The indigenous population of Aboriginals, who had inhabited the continent for over 50,000 years (see Chapter 1), shrank during the same time, mostly as a result of diseases but also after confrontations with ranchers intruding on their hunting and gathering lands. As in North America, whites were relentless in taking possession of the continent.

The Difficult Turn of the Century During the last quarter of the nineteenth century, the economies of the three leading industrial countries of the world—Great Britain, the United States, and Germany—slowed, first with a financial depression in the United States and Europe in 1873–1879 and later with the worldwide depression of 1890–1896. Australia had survived the first depression, mainly thanks to continuing gold finds. But in the 1890s, construction as well as banking collapsed and factories closed. Labor unrest followed; although widespread strikes failed, the newly founded Labor Party (1891) immediately became a major political force. The country adopted labor reforms, an old-age pension, fiscal reforms, and a white-only immigration policy. The discovery of huge gold deposits in western Australia in 1892–1894 helped to redress labor criticism. In 1900, Australia adopted a federal constitution, which made the country the second fully autonomous British "dominion," after Canada (1867).

European Imperialism in the Middle East and Africa

The British in the Middle East during the eighteenth and early nineteenth centuries functioned as merchants, diplomats, or military advisors in an Ottoman Empire with a long tradition of conquering European lands. The situation changed at the end of the eighteenth century when Russia attempted to drive the Ottomans back into Asia Minor, take Constantinople, and convert it back into an eastern Christian capital. The other European powers sought to slow the Russian advances, with Great Britain assuming the lead role in protecting the Ottomans. This policy of containment ultimately failed. Under Russian pressure, Ottoman territory shrank, the Europeans joined Russia in dismembering the Ottoman Empire, and an imperialist competition for carving up other parts of the world ensued.

The Rising Appeal of Imperialism in the West

The Russian Empire sought not only to replace the Ottoman Empire as the dominant eastern European power but also to become the leading Asian power. Its ambition helped spur France, Great Britain, Belgium, Germany, and Italy to embark on competitive imperialism in other parts of the world (see Map 27.3).

The Ottoman, Russian, and British Empires After the failure of Napoleon's imperial schemes in 1815, Great Britain was the undisputed leading empire in the world. On the European continent, Britain worked to restore the monarchies of France, Austria, Prussia, and Russia so that they would balance each other as "great powers" in a **Concert of Europe**. Britain would not tolerate any renewed European imperialism of the kind that Napoleon had pursued.

Concert of Europe: International political system that dominated Europe from 1815 to 1871, which advocated a balance of power among states; "concert" here means "agreement."

The Concert of Europe, however, was less successful at curbing the imperial ambitions of its members outside of western Europe. Russia did not hide its goal of throwing the Ottoman Empire (admitted to the Concert in 1856) back into "Asia"—that is, Asia Minor, or Anatolia. Great Britain, although it made itself the protector of the integrity of the Ottoman Empire, could only slow the ambitions of Russia.

The French Conquest of Algeria The French, unable to embark again on imperialism in Europe, cast their eyes across the Mediterranean to Ottoman North Africa. The conquest of Algeria was the crucial first incidence of a western European power—in this instance France—using a diplomatic incident (see beginning of this chapter) to remove the local rulers. At first, the French stayed on a small coastal strip, encouraging the rise of indigenous leaders to take over from the Ottoman corsairs

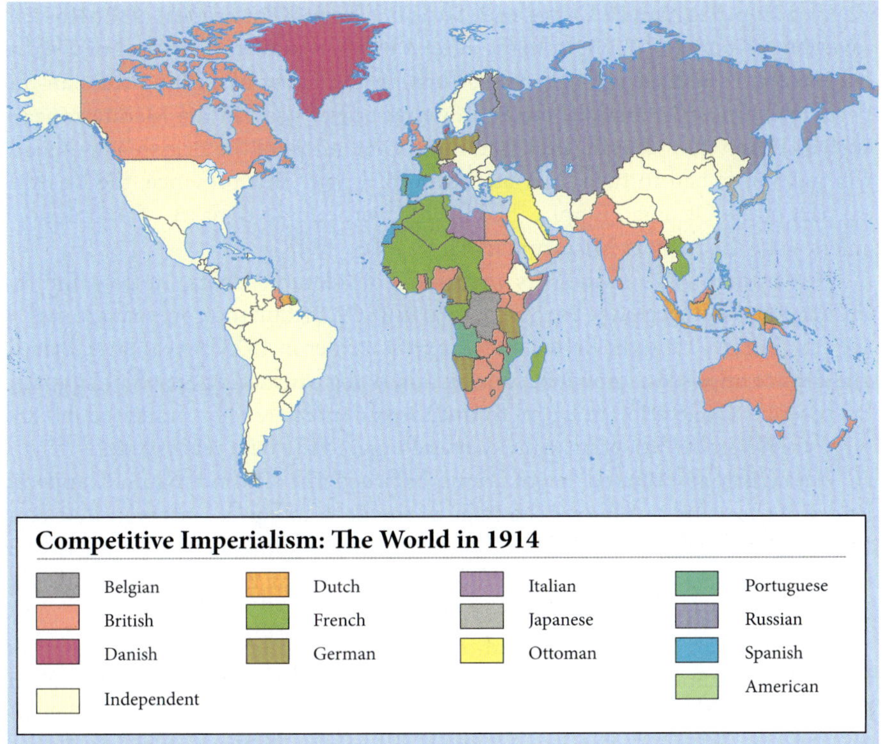

MAP 27.3 **Competitive Imperialism: The World in 1914**

and Janissaries and share the country with the French. The British discreetly supported Algerian leaders with weapons to be used against the French.

In the end, however, coexistence proved impossible, and the French military undertook an all-out conquest. The civilian colonial administration after 1870 encouraged immigration of French and Spanish farmers as well as French corporate investments in vineyards and citrus plantations on the coast. The indigenous population of Arabs and Berbers, decimated by cholera epidemics in the 1860s, found itself largely relegated to less fertile lands in the interior.

Britain's Containment Policy Great Britain sought to limit Russian ambitions in Central Asia, inaugurating what was called the **Great Game** against Russia in Asia with the first Anglo–Afghan war in 1838. Although Great Britain failed to occupy Afghanistan, it eventually succeeded in turning Afghanistan into a buffer state, keeping Russia away from India. A little later, in 1853–1856, Britain and France teamed up in the Crimean War to stop Russia from renewing its drive for Constantinople. This defeat chastened Russia for the next two decades.

The Great Game: Competition between Great Britain and Russia for conquest or control of Asian countries north of India and south of Russia, principally Afghanistan.

In the second half of the nineteenth century, the Franco–Prussian War destroyed the balance of the European Concert. Germany was now the dominant power in western Europe. Russia exploited the new imbalance in Europe during anti-Ottoman uprisings in the Balkans in 1876, breaking through Ottoman lines of defense and marching within a few miles of Constantinople. However, Great Britain still had enough clout to force Russia into retreating.

British Imperialism in Egypt and Sudan To prevent a repeat of the Russian invasion, Britain and the Ottomans agreed in 1878 to turn the island of Cyprus over to the British as a protectorate. Thus, in the name of curbing Russian imperialism, Great Britain became an imperial power itself in the Mediterranean. Instead of watching Russia, however, the commanders of the British navy squadron in Cyprus had to turn their attention to Egypt. This province, the wealthiest part of the Ottoman Empire, had been governed by a dynasty of autonomous rulers since the reign of Muhammad Ali (r. 1805–1848).

Muhammad Ali's successors incurred considerable debts, in part for the French-led construction of the Suez Canal in 1869. Britain took over a large part of the canal shares from the debt-ridden Egyptian ruler in 1875. A year later, Britain and France imposed a joint debt commission that garnished a portion of Egyptian tax revenue. Opposition in Egypt to this foreign interference culminated in 1881 with a revolt in the Egyptian army that endangered the debt repayments.

When British-initiated negotiations between the Ottoman sultan and the leader of the army revolt over the issue of the debt collapsed, interventionists in London, fearing for their bonds and the supply of Egyptian cotton for the British textile industry, gained the upper hand. Overcoming the Egyptian army, a British expeditionary force occupied Egypt in 1882.

The Ottoman sultan acquiesced to the occupation because it was supposed to be only temporary. Costly campaigns by British-led Egyptian troops in Sudan during 1883–1885, however, derailed any early departure plans. Egypt's financial troubles kept the British focused on Egypt. On one hand, the British wanted to put Egyptian finances on a sound footing, but on the other hand, they wanted to avoid responsibility for the country's governance. As a compromise, they proposed a conditional departure, with the right of return at times of internal unrest or external danger. The Ottoman sultan, however, refused to sign this compromise. In the end, Britain stayed for almost 75 years, running Egypt as an undeclared colony for the first 40 years. Without a clear plan, Britain had nonetheless transplanted the new pattern of imperialism–colonialism into the Middle East.

Scottish Troops at the Sphinx, 1882. The British occupied Egypt as a means to secure the Suez Canal and guarantee the repayment of Egyptian debts. Subsequent negotiations with the Ottoman sultan for the status of Egypt failed, and the province became an unofficial protectorate of Britain. Although granted internal independence in 1922, Egypt remained in a semi-colonial relationship with Britain until 1956.

France's Tunisian Protectorate Like Algeria and Egypt, Tunisia was an autonomous Ottoman province, ruled by its own dynasty of beys. Fertile northern Tunisia provided limited but fairly reliable tax revenues; annual tax expeditions to the south among the semi-nomadic sheep and camel tribes served mostly to demonstrate the dynasty's sovereignty.

Tunisian leaders were the first in the Muslim Middle East and North Africa to modernize their military and adopt a constitution (1857). With their more limited revenues, they hit the debt ceiling in 1869, and had to accept a British–French–Italian debt commission

for the reorganization of the country's revenues. When the French to
1881, anxious to take their share of the Middle East and North Africa i
tition with Great Britain, they faced the same task of balancing the bu
the British had in Egypt. Only later did they benefit from the French ar
settlers they invited to the protectorate to intensify agriculture and tran
colonialism.

World Period Five
664

Canary Islands

The Scramble for Africa

Competitive European imperialism intensified in 1884 as Germany clai
first protectorates in Africa. German chancellor Otto von Bismarck (in
offices 1862–1890) called a conference in Berlin, which met from late 1
early 1885. The conference agenda was how the 14 invited European countries and the United States should "define the conditions under which future territorial annexations in Africa might be recognized." Bismarck's proposed main condition was "effective occupation," with the creation of spheres of influence around the occupied places. The **Scramble for Africa** was on (see Map 27.4).

Scramble for Africa: Competition among European powers from 1885 to 1912 to conquer land in Africa and establish colonies.

Explorers, Missionaries, and the Civilizing Mission Sub-Saharan Africa was still little known by most Europeans in the 1800s. Some explorers had gained access to the interior via trade routes and caravans, long in use by Africans. David Livingstone (1813–1873), a Scottish missionary and opponent of slavery, was among the pioneers who explored much of south central Africa. Livingstone's goals were not only to terminate trafficking in slaves but also to "civilize" Africans by preaching both Christianity and commerce. The generation of explorers after Livingstone was better equipped, led larger expeditions, and composed more precise accounts of their activities. Still, in spite of extensive explorations, at the end of the century, European politicians had only the vaguest idea of the geography of the "dark continent."

European Christian missionaries were at the forefront of the **civilizing mission**, the belief that western Europeans had a duty to extend the benefits of civilization (that is, Western civilization) to the "backward" people they ruled.

Civilizing mission: Belief that Europeans had a duty to extend what they believed were the benefits of European civilization to "backward" peoples; originally French *mission civilisatrice.*

In the early 1800s, malaria and yellow fever still confined missionaries to the coasts of Africa, where they trained indigenous missionaries for the conversion of Africans in the interior. When treatment for malaria became available in the middle of the 1800s, missionaries were able to follow their indigenous colleagues into the interior—which led to tensions. While African converts preached the gospel in the spirit of Christian equality, many Western missionaries considered African Christianity to be contaminated by "superstitions" and did not accept Africans as their equals.

Conquest and Resistance in West Africa Conquest and imperialism on the coast of West Africa after 1885 were an outgrowth of the trade-fort system. Ghana, the modern name for the land of the Ashante kingdom, is a particularly instructive example of the pattern of conquest and resistance. During the time of the Songhay (Chapter 19), the Ashante mined the gold of the Akan fields that caravans carried across the Sahara. When gold declined in importance, the kingdom turned to the Atlantic slave trade. After the 1807 British prohibition of slavery, Ashante merchants switched to commodities (especially palm oil) that were

MAP 27.4 The Scramble for Africa

in demand in industrializing Europe. But the Ashante and British traders clashed over the terms of trade in the forts. Only in 1896, when the British sent regular troops to put down the Ashante, was the kingdom finally turned into a protectorate called initially the British Gold Coast.

French officers after 1850 carried out expeditions into the West African interior for alliances and trade purposes. In 1857 they came into conflict with al-Hajj Umar (ca. 1791–1864), an Islamic reformer in the interior savanna who was building a state in what is today Guinea, Senegal, and Mali. For decades, the French could advance no farther. Once the scramble was on, however, the West African

Islamic state was doomed. In 1891, despite Islamist resistance, the French began to carve a new colony in West Africa.

Al-Hajj Umar was one of several West African Muslim religious scholars who became holy warriors (jihadis) seeking to rejuvenate Islam through a return to the Islamic sources. These reformers forcibly converted black traditional spiritualists to Islam. In contrast to earlier Islamic kings and emperors, who made little or no effort to proselytize, the jihadists of the 1800s succeeded in making Islam the dominant religion of West Africa.

Conquest and Resistance in East Africa The new imperialism and colonialism in East Africa were similar to those in West Africa. Here, in the sixteenth century, the Portuguese had established trade forts. When Swahili patricians in the city-states farther north resisted, the Portuguese responded with piracy and the construction of coastal forts in their midst. But the arrival of the Dutch in the 1630s forced the Portuguese to curtail their East African engagement.

An Omani Arab expeditionary force exploited the reduced Portuguese presence in 1698 by conquering the Swahili city-state of Mombasa. Oman seized the opportunity to expand its limited domestic agricultural base on the Arabian Peninsula, developing a plantation system on the coastal islands of East Africa with slaves imported from the African interior. In the 1820s, the Omanis—by now under their separate sultan residing on the island of Zanzibar—became the main exporters of cloves on the world market. Thanks to the Omanis, the Swahili coast was prosperous again.

In 1885 Germany landed on the East African mainland opposite Zanzibar, against the protest of the island's Omani sultan, who had also claimed the nearby region on the mainland. Ignoring the sultan, by 1886 the Germans had established their colony of East Africa, comprising what are today Tanzania, Burundi, and Rwanda. In an understanding with Germany, Great Britain declared its sphere of influence over what are today Kenya (also claimed by Zanzibar) and Burundi, and in 1888 chartered a private company to exploit the territory's resources. The company failed and, in order to coordinate its scramble, Britain turned both Zanzibar and the mainland into protectorates (1890 and 1895). The lion's share of land, today's Democratic Republic of the Congo in the center of Africa, went officially in 1885 to King Leopold II (r. 1865–1909) of Belgium. The king had already established a private company several years earlier that explored Congo for its resources under the leadership of Henry Morton Stanley. Thus, the land grab in East Africa proceeded in more or less amicable fashion among the European nations.

Atrocities and Genocides Germany's colonial regime in East Africa, however, was exceedingly brutal. Its administrators decided to grow cotton for Germany's domestic textile industry, using forced labor to keep costs low. When the Maji-Maji rebellion against these labor conditions broke out among the indigenous population, German troops used their superior firepower to systematically kill some 200,000 people, amounting to one-third of the population (1905–1907). In the colony of German Southwest Africa (today's Namibia), occupied in 1884, German settlers displaced the indigenous Herero and Nama in such large numbers that they eventually provoked an uprising. Again, German troops engaged in a massive campaign of genocidal repression, nearly wiping out the Herero and Nama (1904–1907).

North of Namibia, King Leopold II turned his personal colony of the Congo into a forced-labor camp for the production of rubber. Leopold sadistically exploited the native workforce, using beatings and mutilations if collection quotas were not filled. It has been estimated that 10 million Congolese were either killed or starved to death. By the early 1900s, the violence committed in the Congo had become so notorious that the Belgian government ended Leopold II's personal regime and made it a national colony (see "Against the Grain"). As a result, the worst abuses ended, to be replaced by more subtle forms of business privileges, segregation, and racism.

Africa Carved Up The scramble for Africa was not limited to the major European powers of Great Britain, France, and Germany. Portugal, the first European country in the fifteenth century to have engaged in overseas trade-fort expansion, used the Berlin conference of 1884–1885 to expand its coastal footholds into the territorial colonies of Guinea in West Africa, Angola in southwest Africa, and Mozambique in southeast Africa. Subsequently, the country encouraged Portuguese businesses and settlers to take up residence in the colonies. Similarly, Spain acquired the desert territory of Rio de Oro (now Western Sahara, split between Mauritania and Morocco) in the northwest in 1884–1885, without, however, investing much beyond a bare-bones administration.

Italy, concentrating on its domestic industrialization, initially entered the scramble modestly, acquiring territory in East African Somalia and Eritrea (1889–1890). Bigger imperialist dreams of conquering Ethiopia in East Africa were stymied, however, by a defeat at the battle of Adowa in 1896 (see "Patterns Up Close"). Thanks to its long tradition as a relatively large, unified kingdom, Ethiopia emerged from the scramble for Africa as the only unconquered state on the continent.

To overcome its humiliation in East Africa, Italy tried its hand at imperialism again in 1911 against the Ottoman province of Tripolitania (today western Libya), just opposite its southern Mediterranean coast. Here, the small Ottoman garrison put up a fierce resistance and surrendered only in 1912. But the outbreak of World War I in July 1914 necessitated the withdrawal of Italian troops. When the Ottoman Empire entered the war in October of that year, a strong indigenous Islamic resistance emerged under the leadership of the Quran teacher Umar Mukhtar (1858–1931). He turned out to be a charismatic and skilled guerrilla leader who had support from members of the reformist Sanusiyya Brotherhood. He forced the Italians back to a few coastal enclaves and resisted the postwar return of the Italians until 1931, when they captured and hanged him.

By the end of the nineteenth century, Great Britain and France had become the dominant colonial powers in Africa. Two strategic obsessions divided them: the influential British imperialist businessman and colonial politician Cecil Rhodes (1853–1902) dreamed of a railroad from the Cape of Good Hope to Cairo, and French imperialist military officers had illusions of conquering a contiguous territory from Senegal in the west to Djibouti on the Red Sea. Troops of both countries met in 1898 at Fashoda on the White Nile in Sudan (today Kodok in South Sudan) and nearly came to blows. Under strong British pressure, the French gave up their dream of a west-east African empire, at the center of which they wished to control the waters of the White Nile. But British colonialists also had to give up their obsession with the Cape-to-Cairo railway for lack of money during the Great Depression (1929–1939).

Subsequently, in the face of Germany's rising power in Europe, France and Britain came to an agreement in the Entente Cordiale of 1904, a treaty of "friendly understanding." One key chapter of the agreement stipulated Britain's support for France's goal of beating Germany in its race for a protectorate over the Muslim Sultanate of Morocco in northwest Africa. When France eventually succeeded in occupying Morocco in 1912, the Scramble for Africa ended with all of Africa, except for Ethiopia, Libya, and Liberia, carved up among the European colonial powers. There was a price, however, for France to pay: Germany's defeat in the scramble for Morocco was one of the factors that would contribute to its grievances at the outbreak of World War I in 1914.

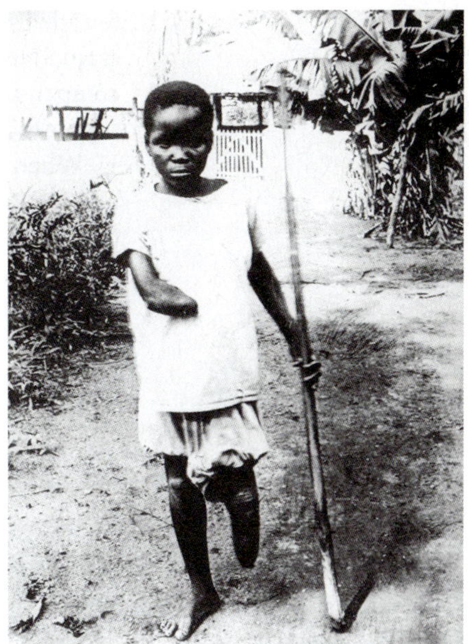

Colonial Brutality in the Congo. A young African boy whose hand and foot were severed by sentries after his village failed to meet its rubber quota. The Belgian Congo under King Leopold II employed mass forced labor of the indigenous population to extract rubber from the jungle. As the demand for rubber grew, King Leopold's private army of 16,000 mercenaries was given leave to use any method to coerce the population into meeting quotas, including random killing, mutilation, village burning, starvation, and hostage taking.

Western Imperialism and Colonialism in Southeast Asia

The new imperialism appeared also in Southeast Asia, specifically Indonesia, the Philippines, Vietnam, Cambodia, and Laos. While the new imperialism in Southeast Asia was an outgrowth of the earlier trade-fort presence of Portugal, Spain, and the Netherlands, it also included the return of France to imperial glory.

The Dutch in Indonesia

After liberating itself from Habsburg–Spanish rule, the Netherlands displaced Portugal from its dominant position as a spice importer to Europe. From 1650 to 1750, the Netherlands was the leading naval power in the world before being supplanted by Britain. After 1750, it shifted from the trade of spices in their trade forts in Indonesia to the planting of cash crops on land outside the forts. The aim of the full colonization of Indonesia during the nineteenth century was to profit from European industrial demand for agricultural and mineral commodities.

Portuguese and Dutch Trade Forts Portuguese sailors arrived in the strategic Strait of Malacca in 1511. They defeated the local sultanate and established a fort in the Malaysian capital, Malacca. Pushing onward to the spice-producing Maluku Islands (known in English as the Moluccas) in eastern Indonesia (between Sulawesi and New Guinea), they established a trade fort in 1522. From there, the Portuguese moved on to China and finally Japan, where they arrived in the mid-1500s. Overall, however, their role in the Indonesian spice trade remained small, and indigenous Islamic merchants maintained their dominance.

After declaring their independence from Spain in 1581, the northern provinces of the Netherlands formed the Republic of the United Netherlands and pushed for their own overseas network of trade forts. In 1602, the Dutch government chartered the Dutch United East India Company (VOC), which spearheaded the expansion of Dutch possessions in India and Southeast Asia. The company founded Batavia (today Jakarta) in the mid-1600s, with the island of Java as its main Southeast Asian center. The VOC was the largest and wealthiest commercial company in the world during the seventeenth century, with its merchant ships supported by large naval and land forces.

When the Dutch governor of the Netherlands, William of Orange (1650–1702), became king of England after the English Glorious Revolution (see Chapter 17), the Dutch and English overseas trade interests were pooled. Great Britain (as the country was known after England's union with Scotland in 1707) deepened its Indian interests through the British East India Company, and the Dutch VOC pursued its engagements in Indonesia, becoming after 1755 the de facto government on the island of Java over a set of pacified Islamic protectorates.

But governing and maintaining troops was expensive, and VOC employees often paid their expenses out of their own pockets. In the late eighteenth century, the inability of the VOC to shift from spices to commodities, which required costly investments in plantations and accompanying transportation infrastructures, led in 1799 to the liquidation of the VOC. As the British government would later do in India, the government of the Netherlands stepped in as the ruler of Indonesian possessions that had grown from trade forts into small colonies, surrounded by dependent indigenous principalities as well as independent sultanates.

Dutch Colonialism The Dutch government took the decisive step toward agricultural investments in 1830 when Belgium separated from the Dutch kingdom to form an independent Catholic monarchy. Faced with budgetary constraints and cut off from industrializing Belgium, the Dutch government adopted the **cultivation system** in Indonesia. According to this system, indigenous Indonesian subsistence farmers were forced to either grow government crops on 20 percent of their land or work for 60 days on Dutch plantations. Overnight, the Dutch and collaborating Indonesian ruling classes turned into landowners. They reaped huge profits while Indonesian subsistence farmers suffered. In the course of the nineteenth century, Indonesia became a major—or even the largest—exporter of sugar, tea, coffee, palm oil, coconut products, tropical hardwoods, rubber, quinine, and pepper to the industrial nations.

Cultivation system: Dutch colonial scheme of compulsory labor and planting of crops imposed on indigenous Indonesian self-sufficiency farmers.

To keep pace with demand, the Dutch pursued a program of systematic conquest and colonization. They conquered the Indonesian archipelago, finally subduing the most stubborn opponents, the Muslim guerillas of Aceh (AH-chay), in 1903 (see Map 27.5). Conquered lands were turned over to private investors, who established plantations. To deflect criticism at home and abroad, the Dutch also introduced reform measures. Severe underfunding, however, kept these reforms largely unimplemented, and it was clear that the profits from colonialism were more important than investments in the welfare of indigenous people.

Spain in the Philippines

In the Philippines, the Spanish built their first trade fort of Manila as a port from which to trade Mexican silver with China for luxury manufactures. Manila suffered from raids by indigenous highlanders in the interior, Islamic rulers from the southern islands, and Dutch interlopers. Imperial conquest had to await the later eighteenth century, and colonization followed in the middle of the nineteenth century with the introduction of sugarcane.

MAP 27.5 **Western Imperialism in Southeast Asia, 1870–1914**

Galleons and Trade with China Spain expanded from the Americas farther west in order to prevent Portugal from claiming the lucrative spice islands of Indonesia. A Portuguese explorer in Spanish service, Ferdinand Magellan (ca. 1480–1521), had successfully crossed the sea channels at the southern tip of South America in 1520 and discovered what later became known as the Philippines, named in honor of King Phillip II of Spain. It took another half century, however, before Spain could construct a trade fort and small colony. This fort, Manila, became the base for subsequent biannual silver fleets from Mexico. Spanish merchants based in Mexico, from which Manila was administered, benefited from the trade of silver for Chinese silk, porcelain, and lacquerware. Thus, Manila began as a small subcolony of the large Spanish colony of Mexico, or New Spain.

As the Spanish gradually expanded their hold outside Manila on Luzon and Visaya (where the local king had converted to Christianity), they established estates, thus advancing from trade-fort imperialism to the beginnings of territorial expansion. Like the Dutch in Indonesia, the Spanish settlers planted warm-weather cash crops on their estates.

Incipient Colonialism Indigenous farmers on the Philippine estates were obliged to deliver rents to ensure the food supply for inhabitants of Manila, mostly merchants of Spanish, Chinese, and Japanese origin. Warrior chieftains outside Spanish lands who converted to Catholicism transformed themselves into a Hispanicized landowner class. By the early eighteenth century, the Spanish were able to establish a regular administration for fiscal and juridical matters. The beginnings of colonialism in the Philippines had emerged.

However, fiscal revenue did not yield surpluses, and villagers produced only small quantities of exportable ginger, cinnamon, and gold. Much money had to be invested in defending the Spanish-controlled territory from attacks by independent Filipinos who resisted conquest and conversion. Even more vexing were raids supported by Islamic sultanates that had formed on the southern islands.

Full Colonialism Major reforms instituted by the Spanish in the early 1800s, motivated by the loss of Mexico to independence, resulted in the liberalization of trade and the beginnings of agricultural commodities for export. Ports were opened to ships from all countries, discrimination against Chinese settlements ended, and Spanish administrators and churchmen lost their trade privileges. Foreign entrepreneurs cleared rain forests and exported hardwoods, growing cash crops on the new land. Large-scale rice farms replaced many small-scale village self-sufficiency plots, and thus commercialization usurped subsistence agriculture.

Resistance by landowners against a reform of the land regime and tax system until the very end of the nineteenth century, however, ensured that Spain did not benefit much from the liberalization of trade. Additionally, Philippine society stratified into a wealthy minority and a large mass of landless rural workers and urban day laborers. This stratification differed from that in the Americas in that there was no real Creole class—that is, a Spanish–Philippine upper stratum of landowners and urban people. Agitation for independence and constitutionalism was largely limited to urban intellectuals. The Philippines remained a colony, producing no revenue and still demanding costly administrative reforms and infrastructural investments, both of which Spain was unable to afford.

The first stirrings of Filipino nationalism, primarily among Hispanicized Filipinos of mixed Spanish and indigenous or Chinese descent, emerged in the second half of the nineteenth century. The principal spokesman was novelist José Rizal (1861–1896). Colonial authorities arrested Rizal and banished him to Hong Kong, but he returned to Manila in 1892, inspiring both overt and underground resistance groups. One of the underground groups, Katipunan ("association"), advocated Filipino independence through armed struggle. In 1896 the government executed hundreds of revolutionaries, including Rizal, before firing squads. But it was unable to destroy Katipunan in the provinces, and the two sides agreed in 1897 to a truce that included the end of armed revolt in return for exile of the leadership to Hong Kong.

Philippine–American War Although it appeared that the colonial government had successfully repressed the Filipino revolt, events took a dramatic turn when the Spanish–American War broke out in 1898. The two sides fought their

American Soldiers in the Philippines. The US decision to annex the Philippines after the victory of the United States over Spain in 1898 was the first attempt to create an American overseas empire. Resistance was immediate, and a brutal war against Philippine fighters lasted from 1902 until 1913, with isolated outbreaks continuing until Philippine independence in 1946. Here, American troops dig in and fortify an outpost in Luzon.

first battle in Manila Bay, where the United States routed a Spanish squadron. An American ship fetched the exiled Filipino rebel Emilio Aguinaldo (1869–1964) from Hong Kong, and he quickly defeated the Spanish and declared independence. Over four centuries of Spanish colonialism in the Pacific had come to an end.

The United States and Spain made peace at the end of 1898, ignoring the independent Philippine government in their agreement. US forces took possession of Manila in 1899 and defeated the troops of the protesting Filipino government under the elected president, Emilio Aguinaldo. The Filipinos shifted to guerilla war, but US troops captured Aguinaldo in 1901. The United States declared the war over in 1902 but had to fight remnants of the guerillas as well as southern rebels until 1913. Thus, the United States had joined the European contest for imperial and colonial control of the non-Western world.

The French in Vietnam

Indochina, the peninsula on which Vietnam is located, also includes Cambodia, Laos, Burma (now Myanmar), and Thailand. French imperial and colonial involvement began in 1858. At first focusing on the southeast of Indochina, France gradually expanded northward, establishing protectorates over the Nguyen (pronunciation "win") royal dynasty, which ruled the last of a succession of kingdoms that had begun in the third century CE.

French Interests in Vietnam French efforts in the seventeenth and early eighteenth centuries to sponsor Catholic missions and trading companies had been largely unsuccessful and ended altogether after their defeat in the Seven Years' War. With the help of French clergy and mercenaries, however, the new Vietnamese emperor, Gia Long, defeated his competitors in the north and restored the Nguyen Dynasty in 1801, reuniting the country after a three-hundred-year division.

In the first decades of the new century the increasing perception on the part of the Nguyen rulers that French missionaries and Vietnamese Christians were subversive forces resulted in the expulsion of the former and persecution of the latter. By the 1840s, French merchants and diplomats were routinely rebuffed by the Vietnamese, who shared Chinese concerns about the Western challenge. Both China and Vietnam thus adopted a policy of isolationism as their first answer to Western patterns of challenge.

The French, under Napoleon's nephew Napoleon III (r. 1848–1870), were not deterred. Taking as a pretext the torture and execution of French missionaries and Vietnamese converts, they dispatched a squadron that occupied the sparsely inhabited Mekong River delta in 1858–1862, annexing it as the protectorate of French Cochinchina ("Cochinchina" was an old name for the southern part of Vietnam).

Conquest and Colonialism Cambodia, caught between its more powerful neighbors Vietnam and Thailand and fearing the expansive British Empire, which had already engulfed most of Burma, allied itself with the French in their conquest of Cochinchina, and in 1867 its king, Norodom (r. 1860–1904), agreed to the establishment of a French protectorate over his country. After Napoleon III fell from power in 1870, politicians were ambivalent about renewing French overseas imperialism. But a year after pro-imperialists came to power in 1883, the French defeated China in a war for the control of northern Vietnam (Annam), and they quickly occupied the center (Tonkin) as well. In contrast to the thinly settled south, the Red River estuary in the north with the capital of the Vietnamese kingdom, Hanoi, was densely populated. The French conquerors united the three parts of Vietnam and the protectorate of Cambodia into the colony of French Indochina (1887). Laos also came under French control in 1884 and became part of French Indochina in 1899. Two members of the deposed Vietnamese royal dynasty waged a guerilla war against the occupation, but by the early twentieth century the French had captured both and were in full control.

The French government and French entrepreneurs invested substantial sums in the Mekong delta, establishing plantations for the production of coffee, tea, and rubber. Indigenous rice farmers had to deliver 40 percent of their crops to the colonial government. Hanoi was made the seat of the colonial administration in 1902, and the port of Haiphong, downriver from Hanoi, became the main entry point for ships to load agricultural commodities for export. France derived major financial benefits from the agriculture of its eastern colonies. By the time of World War I, only Siam (today's Thailand) had been able to ward off colonization, mostly as a result of several strong kings deftly playing off French and British efforts at occupation.

Early Nationalism Anti-foreign Vietnamese patriotism was reasserted by Phan Boi Chau (1867–1940), who witnessed the crushing by the French of a protest by Confucian scholars in 1885. Phan's activities inspired anti-tax demonstrations and a provincial uprising in Vietnam in 1908–1909, which the French suppressed harshly. By 1912, a newly formed nationalist grouping, the Vietnam Restoration League, favored the expulsion of the French and the formation of a Vietnamese democratic republic.

Putting It All Together

Ever since Vladimir Lenin, the founder of the Soviet Union, declared in 1916 that imperialism was "the highest stage of capitalism," scholars have debated whether or not the capitalist industrialization process in Europe, North America, and Japan needed colonies to sustain its growth. Most recent historians have concluded that imperialism and colonialism were not needed for capitalism to flourish and that all the commodities crucial for industrialization could have been bought from independent countries on the world market. Great Britain, of course, had transformed its activity in India from trade-fort imperialism to territorial imperialism just prior to its industrialization and used Indian cotton as raw material for its textile factories. But this raises the reverse question: would industrialization have happened had Great Britain not conquered India?

Perhaps a better approach to the question is to think of trade-fort and territorial imperialism as world-historical patterns of long standing. By contrast, industrialization was a much later phenomenon, appearing around 1800. Thus, inherited patterns of imperialism persisted during the rise of the new pattern of industrialization. These patterns were amplified by the new power that industrialization gave the European countries. Therefore, the new imperialism of the nineteenth century, and the colonialism that followed in its wake, can be seen as phenomena in which old patterns continued but were enlarged by new patterns of industrial power.

Review and Relate

Thinking Through Patterns

Examine the ways historians approach the big questions of this chapter.

What new patterns emerged in the transition from trade-fort imperialism to the new imperialism?

During the early modern period, European monarchs commissioned merchant marine companies, such as the British East India Company and the Dutch United East India Company, in order to avoid military expeditions of their own but still receive a share of the profits of trade. The mariner-merchants built coastal forts, granted to them by the local rulers with whom they traded. In the seventeenth and eighteenth centuries, much larger trading companies were formed, and large numbers of mariner-merchants now served in dozens of trade forts overseas. In India and Indonesia, these companies needed their governments in England and the Netherlands to rescue them. In responding, governments became imperialist colonizers.

➤ How did European colonizers develop their colonies economically, given that they were industrializing themselves at the same time?

Great Britain was the pioneer in the development of exportable agricultural and mineral commodities in its colonies for the support of its expanding industries. By the middle of the nineteenth century, other industrializing countries either embarked on imperial conquests or shifted to full colonialism in order to obtain necessary commodities. Because labor for the production of these commodities was scarce, workers were forcibly recruited and paid low wages.

➤ What were the experiences of the indigenous people under the new imperialism? How did they adapt to colonialism? How did they resist?

Imperial conquests involved campaigns that claimed many indigenous victims. If the colonizers pursued commodity production, the indigenous population was recruited, often forcibly and with low wages. Resistance to European colonialism manifested itself in ethnic nationalism. In Australia and New Zealand and other colonies where European settlement was encouraged, colonial governments or settlers ousted the indigenous population from the most fertile lands, despite fierce resistance.

Against the Grain

Consider this as a counterpoint to the main patterns examined in this chapter.

An Anti-Imperial Perspective

- In what ways is Morel a good example of nonconformity with European imperialism in Africa?
- How would you compare Morel's actions with current protest movements around the world?

During the heyday of Western imperialism in the later nineteenth century, many European writers justified the conquest of foreign lands and the exploitation of native peoples by expressing attitudes reflected in social Darwinism. Seen from this perspective, Europeans were pursuing a "civilizing mission," thus exposing "lesser breeds" to the benefits of Christianity and commerce. For proponents of imperialism, it was fitting to pursue a policy of civilizing the "inferior races." Perhaps the best known of these condescending works was Rudyard Kipling's "The White Man's Burden," published in 1899 in response to America's takeover of the Philippines after their victory in the Spanish–American war of 1898.

Many Europeans, however, expressed views contrary to the majority opinion. Among the most outspoken critics of European imperialism was a contemporary of Kipling, the British journalist Edward D. Morel (1873–1924). In 1900, Morel published a series of scathing denunciations that revealed the atrocities of African slave labor on Belgian rubber plantations.

Forced to leave his job, Morel continued his activist campaign by launching a newspaper, the *West African Mail*, in 1903, followed by his foundation of the Congo Reform Association in 1904. By far the most famous of Morel's indictments, however, was *The Black Man's Burden* (1920), a condemnation of the evils of European capitalism and industrialism: "Its destructive effects are . . . permanent. . . . It kills not the body merely, but the soul. It breaks the spirit." For his pacifist activities Morel was sentenced to prison in 1917, but subsequently went on to win a seat in Parliament in 1922. Although he played only a minor role in Parliament, Morel is often considered the father of international activism on behalf of human rights.

Key Terms

Civilizing mission 663
Colonialism 652
Concert of Europe 660
Cultivation system 668
Nabob 653
New Imperialism 652
Scramble for Africa 663
Subaltern 657
The Great Game 661

Learn more with this chapter's digital tools, including the Oxford Insight Study Guide, at http://www.oup.com/he/vonsivers4e. Please see the Further Resources section at the back of the book for additional readings and suggested websites.

PATTERNS OF EVIDENCE |

Sources for Chapter 27

SOURCE 27.1

The Indian Revolt

The Great Revolt—called variously by the British "The Great Mutiny" and "The Sepoy Mutiny," and sometimes by Indians "The First War for Independence"—took the British by surprise, though as reflected in this *Atlantic* article, the signs were there for those who chose to read them. When the insurgents were defeated and the retributions ebbed, the shock was such that the British dismantled the East India Company and initiated direct rule in the subcontinent, which would last another 90 years.

For the first time in the history of the English dominion in India, its power has been shaken from within its own possessions, and by its own subjects. Whatever attacks have been made upon it heretofore have been from without, and its career of conquest has been the result to which they have led. But now no external enemy threatens it, and the English in India have found themselves suddenly and unexpectedly engaged in a hand-to-hand struggle with a portion of their subjects, not so much for dominion as for life. There had been signs and warnings, indeed, of the coming storm; but the feeling of security in possession and the confidence of moral strength were so strong, that the signs had been neglected and the warnings disregarded.

No one in our time has played the part of Cassandra with more foresight and vehemence than the late Sir Charles Napier... He saw the quarter in which the storm was gathering, and he affirmed that it was at hand. In 1850, after a short period of service as commander-in-chief of the forces in India, he resigned his place, owing to a difference between himself and the government, and immediately afterwards prepared a memoir in justification of his course, accompanied with remarks upon the general administration of affairs in that country... with the title of "Defects, Civil and Military, of the Indian Government."... On the third page is a sentence which read now is of terrible import: "Mutiny with [among?] the Sepoys is the *most* formidable danger menacing our Indian empire." And a few pages farther on occurs the following striking passage: "The ablest and most experienced civil and military servants of the East India Company consider mutiny as one of the greatest, if not *the* greatest danger threatening India,—a danger also that may come unexpectedly, and, if the first symptoms be not carefully treated, with a power to shake Leadenhall."

Source: Charles Creighton Hazewell, "The Indian Revolt," *Atlantic Monthly*, December 1857, available at https://www.theatlantic.com/magazine/archive/1857/12/the-indian-revolt/531186/

The anticipated mutiny has now come, its first symptoms were treated with utter want of judgment, and its power is shaking the whole fabric of the English rule in India.

One day toward the end of January last, a workman employed in the magazine at Barrackpore, an important station about seventeen miles from Calcutta, stopped to ask a Sepoy for some water from his drinking-vessel. Being refused, because he was of low caste, and his touch would defile the vessel, he said, with a sneer, "What caste are you of, who bite pig's grease and cow's fat on your cartridges?" Practice with the new Enfield rifle had just been introduced, and the cartridges were greased for use in order not to foul the gun. The rumor spread among the Sepoys that there was a trick played upon them,—that this was but a device to pollute them and destroy their caste, and the first step toward a general and forcible conversion of the soldiers to Christianity. The groundlessness of the idea upon which this alarm was founded afforded no hindrance to its ready reception, nor was the absurdity of the design attributed to the ruling powers apparent to the obscured and timid intellect of the Sepoys. The consequences of loss of caste are so feared,—and are in reality of so trying a nature,—that upon this point the sensitiveness of the Sepoy is always extreme, and his suspicions are easily aroused. Their superstitious and religious customs "interfere in many strange ways with their military duties."

"The brave men of the 35th Native Infantry," says Sir Charles Napier, "lost caste because they did their duty at Jelalabad; that is, they fought like soldiers, and ate what could be had to sustain their strength for battle." But they are under a double rule, of religious and of military discipline,—and if the two come into conflict, the latter is likely to give way.

The discontent at Barrackpore soon manifested itself in ways not to be mistaken. There were incendiary fires within the lines. It was discovered that messengers had been sent to regiments at other stations, with incitements to insubordination. The officer in command at Barrackpore, General Hearsay, addressed the troops on parade, explained to them that the cartridges were not prepared with the obnoxious materials supposed, and set forth the groundlessness of their suspicions. The address was well received at first, but had no permanent effect. The ill-feeling spread to other troops and other stations. The government seems to have taken no measure of precaution in view of the impending trouble, and contented itself with despatching telegraphic messages to the more distant stations, where the new rifle practice was being introduced, ordering that the native troops were "to have no practice ammunition served out to them, but only to watch the firing of the Europeans." On the 26th of February, the 19th regiment, then stationed at Berhampore, refused to receive the cartridges that were served out, and were prevented from open violence only by the presence of a superior English force. After great delay, it was determined that this regiment should be disbanded. The authorities were not even yet alarmed; they were uneasy, but even their uneasiness does not seem to have been shared by the majority of the English residents in India. It was not until the 3d of April that the sentence passed upon the 19th regiment was executed. The affair was dallied with, and inefficiency and dilatoriness prevailed everywhere.

But meanwhile the disaffection was spreading. The order for confining the use of the new cartridges to the Europeans seems to have been looked upon by the native regiments as a confirmation of their suspicions with regard to them. The more daring and evil-disposed of the soldiers stimulated the alarm, and roused the prejudices of their more timid and unreasoning companions. No general plan of revolt seems to have been formed, but the materials of discontent were gradually being concentrated; the inflammable spirits of the Sepoys were ready to burst into a blaze. Strong and judicious measures, promptly put into action, might even now have allayed the excitement and dissipated the danger. But the imbecile commander-in-chief was enjoying himself and shirking care in the mountains; and Lord Canning and his advisers at Calcutta seem to have preferred to allow the troops to take the initiative in their own way. Generally throughout Northern India the common routine of affairs went on at the different stations, and the ill-feeling and insubordination among the Sepoys scarcely disturbed the established quiet and monotony of Anglo-Indian life. But the storm was rising,—and the following extracts from a letter, hitherto unpublished, written on the 30th of May, by an officer of great distinction, and now in high command before Delhi, will show the manner of its breaking.

"A fortnight ago no community in the world could have been living in greater security of life and property than ours. Clouds there were that indicated to thoughtful minds a coming storm, and in the most dangerous quarter; but the actual outbreak was a matter of an hour, and has fallen on us like a judgment from Heaven,—sudden, irresistible as yet, terrible in its effects, and still spreading from place to place. I dare say you may have observed among the Indian news of late months, that here and there throughout the country mutinies of native regiments had been taking place. They had, however, been isolated cases, and the government thought it did enough to check the spirit of disaffection by disbanding the corps involved. The failure of the remedy was, however, complete, and, instead of having to deal now with mutinies of separate regiments, we stand face to face with a general mutiny of the Sepoy army of Bengal. To those who have thought most deeply of the perils of the English empire in India this has always seemed the monster one. It was thought to have been guarded against by the strong ties of mercenary interest that bound the army to the state, and there was, probably, but one class of feelings that would have been strong enough to have broken these ties,—those, namely, of religious sympathy or prejudice. The overt ground of the general mutiny was offence to caste feelings, given by the introduction into the army of certain cartridges said to have been prepared with hog's lard and cow's fat. The men must bite off the ends of these cartridges; so the Mahometans are defiled by the unclean animal, and the Hindoos by the contact of the dead cow. Of course the cartridges are *not* prepared as stated, and they form the mere handle for designing men to work with. They are, I believe, equally innocent of lard and fat; but that a general dread of being Christianized has by some means or other been created is without doubt, though there is still much that is mysterious in the process by which it has been instilled into the Sepoy mind, and I question if the government itself has any accurate information on the subject.

Working with Sources

1. **According to the article, why did the rumor of the greased cartridges persist despite being repeatedly shown to be false?**
2. **What might have been some underlying causes of the suddenness and fury of the revolt that the military mutiny brought to the surface?**

SOURCE 27.2

Ismail ibn 'Abd al-Qadir, *The Life of the Sudanese Mahdi*

ca. 1884

The religiously inspired uprising against the British in Sudan during the 1880s is associated with the figure of the self-styled Mahdi. However, the primary motivation of Muhammad Ahmad Ibn Abdallah (1844–1885), who took on the title Mahdi ("rightly guided" or "messiah"), was to reform Islam from within. Similar to other early modern Islamic reformers, beginning with 'Abd al-Wahhab in eighteenth-century Arabia, the Mahdi aimed to eliminate Sufi brotherhoods and remove the (to his mind) abominable medieval aberrations from Islam. The Mahdi's anti-imperialist stance against the British was thus incidental: the British happened to occupy Egypt and to be moving on the Sudan in the midst of his anti-Sufism campaigns. The British focused on the siege of Khartoum in 1884–1885, but this contemporary biographer of the Mahdi focuses on the renovation of Islam.

1. The Mahdi's Propaganda (*Di 'aya*)

When God bestowed the Mahdiship on the Mahdi, he secretly commenced to call the people to God. He called them to arise and save Islam and to abandon the innovations and the reprehensible characteristics of the people of the time particularly those who belonged to Sufi *tariqas* (*al-muntamun ila al-diyana*). Such characteristics are the love of honour, authority, flattery and the use, as hunters' nets for ensnaring the temporal world, of the ways which would lead to God. The Mahdi also urged them to the *jihad* and to make the *hijra* to him. He persistently called on the people, despite the troubles inflicted by some people on him and on his veteran Companions. These he bore with patience and perseverance, since the Mahdiship involves burdens which only one endowed by God with the Prophetic heritage can bear.

Source: Haim Shaked, *The Life of the Sudanese Mahdi: A Historical Study of 'Kitab Sa'adat al-Mustahdi bi-Sirat al-Imam al-Mahdi' (The Book of the Bliss of Him Who Seeks Guidance by the Life of the Imam al-Mahdi)* (New Brunswick, NJ: Transaction, 1978), 66–68.

When the Mahdi was ordered to manifest his call (*da'wa*) and announce his Mahdiship he arose publicly, calling the people to God, to revive the religion, rectify the Custom of the Prophet, support the Truth, resist the innovators and make them repent. This is the pure religion of the Prophet and all his Companions, and it is in accordance with the Book and the Custom. The Mahdi proceeded with his call to the people until God guided the Community through him, and his Companions attained closeness to the Companions of the Prophet. The author remarks that it is impossible to give an exhaustive account of the Mahdi's propaganda.

2. The Mahdi's Correspondence

Since communication by correspondence was a custom of the Prophet and as the Mahdi was his representative (*khalifa*) and followed in his footsteps, he dispatched letters to the people of Islam, in which he called them to God and to revive the Custom of the Prophet. These letters are numerous and some of them will be mentioned in the Sira so as to enjoy a blessing (*'ala wajh al-tabarruk*).

. .

The Mahdi's correspondence can be studied by reference to the collection of proclamations (*Jami' al-manshurat*). His correspondence to the Community—thereby saving them from grief—derives from the Custom of God with the essence of His creation. Its source is the announcement of good tidings (*tabshir*), warning (*indhar*), and a call for the revival of the principles of the Community which God enacted. All the Mahdi's actions and utterances are sustained by the Book and by the Custom, for he is infallible (*dhu al-'isma*). The author remarks that he will incorporate the Mahdi's correspondence to the kings and commanders wherever it is appropriate in the course of the Sira. The Mahdi's letters, like the Prophet's, are written in a manner which should enable their recipients to understand them, for the Mahdi is the Successor of the Prophet and follows in his footsteps. An informant told the author that the Mahdi had said: "Verily, the Prophet. . . speaks with us now in the speech (*kalam*) of the people of our time." The author interprets this as the language and the terms with which people are acquainted at present, so that they would easily understand the meaning and come to God in the shortest time.

▸ Working with Sources

1. **How does the document reveal that the Mahdi's primary concern was the challenge posed by Sufism?**
2. **How and why is the Mahdi strongly identified with the Prophet Muhammad?**

SOURCE 27.3

Rudyard Kipling, "The White Man's Burden"

1899

The phrase "the white man's burden" and its association with the British writer Rudyard Kipling (1865–1936) is well known today, but few realize that this exhortation was addressed to the American people, who had taken possession of the Philippines in 1899 as a result of the Spanish–American War (1898). Ignoring the independent Philippine government when signing a peace treaty with Spain, the United States occupied Manila and within a year defeated the troops of that government under its elected president Emilio Aguinaldo. US troops captured Aguinaldo in 1901, but a full-scale guerilla war continued—and tactics like the "waterboarding" of captured insurgents were introduced—until 1913. Kipling, however, consistently advocated the position that, as he claimed for the British in India, "East is East and West is West, and never the twain shall meet."

Take up the White Man's burden—
Send forth the best ye breed—
Go bind your sons to exile
To serve your captives' need;
To wait in heavy harness,
On fluttered folk and wild—
Your new-caught, sullen peoples,
Half-devil and half-child.

Take up the White Man's burden—
In patience to abide,
To veil the threat of terror
And check the show of pride;
By open speech and simple,
An hundred times made plain
To seek another's profit,
And work another's gain.

Take up the White Man's burden—
The savage wars of peace—
Fill full the mouth of Famine

Source: http://www.fordham.edu/halsall/mod/kipling.asp.

And bid the sickness cease;
And when your goal is nearest
The end for others sought,
Watch sloth and heathen Folly
Bring all your hopes to nought.

Take up the White Man's burden—
No tawdry rule of kings,
But toil of serf and sweeper—
The tale of common things.
The ports ye shall not enter,
The roads ye shall not tread,
Go mark them with your living,
And mark them with your dead.

Take up the White Man's burden—
And reap his old reward:
The blame of those ye better,
The hate of those ye guard—
The cry of hosts ye humour
(Ah, slowly!) toward the light:—
"Why brought he us from bondage,
Our loved Egyptian night?"

Take up the White Man's burden—
Ye dare not stoop to less—
Nor call too loud on Freedom
To cloke your weariness;
By all ye cry or whisper,
By all ye leave or do,
The silent, sullen peoples
Shall weigh your gods and you.

Take up the White Man's burden—
Have done with childish days—
The lightly proferred laurel,
The easy, ungrudged praise.
Comes now, to search your manhood
Through all the thankless years
Cold, edged with dear-bought wisdom,
The judgment of your peers!

▶ Working with Sources

1. Why, in Kipling's estimation, should the Americans expect to encounter "sullen" reactions among the Filipinos if they go out of their way to provide "aid"?
2. Why does Kipling consider the "civilizing" of Filipinos to be a burden and a duty, and not merely an opportunity to exploit the native people?

SOURCE 27.4

Mark Twain, "To the Person Sitting in Darkness"

1901

To some extent, Kipling was wrong that "East is East and West is West, and never the twain shall meet," since the preeminent American man of letters Mark Twain (1835–1910) did meet the challenge posed by the poem "The White Man's Burden." Incensed by the blatant racism of Kipling's exhortation—as well as the role of racism in sparking the Civil War in his own United States—Twain lashed out with a brilliant satire of imperialist attitudes. This essay is emblematic of Twain's final years, during which he became increasingly embittered and pessimistic about the chances of "civilization" to overcome barbarism. It is posed in the form of a preacher's address to an American audience. The voice of the huckster-preacher conveys what to him seems the perfect alignment of financial and moral considerations; to his mind, it is just a matter of public relations to obtain the willing incorporation of the Filipinos into this (fraudulent) "Blessings-of-Civilization Trust."

Extending the Blessings of Civilization to our Brother who Sits in Darkness has been a good trade and has paid well, on the whole; and there is money in it yet, if carefully worked—but not enough, in my judgment, to make any considerable risk advisable. The People that Sit in Darkness are getting to be too scarce—too scarce and too shy. And such darkness as is now left is really of but an indifferent quality, and not dark enough for the game. The most of those People that Sit in Darkness have been furnished with more light than was good for them or profitable for us. We have been injudicious.

The Blessings-of-Civilization Trust, wisely and cautiously administered, is a Daisy. There is more money in it, more territory, more sovereignty, and other kinds of emolument, than there is in any other game that is played. But Christendom has been playing it badly of late years, and must certainly suffer by it, in my opinion. She has been so eager to get every stake that appeared on the green cloth, that the People who Sit in Darkness have noticed it—they have noticed it, and have begun to show alarm. They have become suspicious of the Blessings of Civilization. More—they have begun to examine them. This

---

Source: Mark Twain, *The Family Mark Twain* (New York: Harper & Brothers, 1935), 1390–1391, 1394–1395, 1397, 1398.

is not well. The Blessings of Civilization are all right, and a good commercial property; there could not be a better, in a dim light. In the right kind of a light, and at a proper distance, with the goods a little out of focus, they furnish this desirable exhibit to the Gentlemen who Sit in Darkness:

LOVE,
JUSTICE,
GENTLENESS,
CHRISTIANITY,
PROTECTION TO THE WEAK,
TEMPERANCE,
LAW AND ORDER,
LIBERTY,
EQUALITY,
HONORABLE DEALING,
MERCY,
EDUCATION,

—and so on.

There. Is it good? Sir, it is pie. It will bring into camp any idiot that sits in darkness anywhere. But not if we adulterate it. It is proper to be emphatic upon that point. This brand is strictly for Export—apparently. *Apparently.* Privately and confidentially, it is nothing of the kind. Privately and confidentially, it is merely an outside cover, gay and pretty and attractive, displaying the special patterns of our Civilization which we reserve for Home Consumption, while inside the bale is the Actual Thing that the Customer Sitting in Darkness buys with his blood and tears and land and liberty. That Actual Thing is, indeed, Civilization, but it is only for Export. Is there a difference between the two brands? In some of the details, yes.

. . .

The more we examine the mistake, the more clearly we perceive that it is going to be bad for the Business. The Person Sitting in Darkness is almost sure to say: "There is something curious about this—curious and unaccountable. There must be two Americas: one that sets the captive free, and one that takes a once-captive's new freedom away from him, and picks a quarrel with him with nothing to found it on; then kills him to get his land."

The truth is, the Person Sitting in Darkness is saying things like that; and for the sake of the Business we must persuade him to look at the Philippine matter in another and healthier way. We must arrange his opinions for him. I believe it can be done; for Mr. Chamberlain has arranged England's opinion of the South African matter, and done it most cleverly and successfully. He presented the facts—some of the facts—and showed those confiding people what the facts meant. He did it statistically, which is a good way. He used the formula: "Twice 2 are 14, and 2 from 9 leaves 35." Figures are effective; figures will convince the elect.

. . .

We must bring him to, and coax him and coddle him, and assure him that the ways of Providence are best, and that it would not become us to find fault with them; and then, to show him that we are only imitators, not originators, we must read the following passage from the letter of an American soldier-lad in the Philippines to his mother, published in Public Opinion, of Decorah, Iowa, describing the finish of a victorious battle:

"WE NEVER LEFT ONE ALIVE. IF ONE WAS WOUNDED, WE WOULD RUN OUR BAYONETS THROUGH HIM."

. . .

Now then, that will convince the Person. You will see. It will restore the Business. Also, it will elect the Master of the Game to the vacant place in the Trinity of our national gods; and there on their high thrones the Three will sit, age after age, in the people's sight, each bearing the Emblem of his service: Washington, the Sword of the Liberator; Lincoln, the Slave's Broken Chains; the Master, the Chains Repaired.

. . .

[And as for a flag for the Philippine Province], it is easily managed. We can have a special one—our states do it: we can have just our usual flag, with the white stripes painted black and the stars replaced by the skull and crossbones.

▸ Working with Sources

1. **How does Twain incorporate the language of the marketplace into this oration, and why?**
2. **Is Twain justified in seeing the conquest of the Philippines as a betrayal of American values and historical development?**

World Period Six

From Three Modernities to One

Modern scientific–industrial society underwent dramatic transformations after World War I (1914–1918). Three competing models for modernity—capitalist democracy, communism, and supremacist nationalism—shrank to one in the course of the twentieth century. German and Japanese supremacist nationalism collapsed in 1945 as a result of their overextended military aggression. Soviet and Eastern European communism collapsed in 1989–1991 due to a top-heavy central command economy. Western capitalist democracy survived but did so only after enduring decolonization and regulating its economy. After 1991, it expanded its global dominance, buttressed by the computer revolution, but questions have arisen whether its model of modernity is sustainable. Under current conditions, the natural environment will not be able to support the exploitative framework of capitalist democracy much longer. The grave threat posed by COVID-19 has further undermined its credibility.

Chapter 28

World Wars and Competing Visions of Modernity

1900–1945

CHAPTER TWENTY-EIGHT PATTERNS

Origins, Interactions, Adaptations World War I pitted two alliance systems in Europe against one another, each composed of rising industrial nation-states (with overseas colonies) and aging continental multiethnic empires. The pressures of incipient nationalism within the empires and intense nationalism among them proved to be powerful forces in leading to war. As the first truly industrial and total war, it killed and wounded vast numbers of men and women. Unfortunately, the victors neglected to bind themselves or the loser Germany to a strong supranational mediating organization that would prevent future conflicts.

Uniqueness and similarities Serious doubts arose during and after World War I as to whether the form of capitalism that had been at the heart of the industrialization process in most nations during the nineteenth century was really the best form of modernity. The Bolsheviks in the Russian Revolution of 1917 declared Soviet communism to be the better system, not merely for the economy but also for society. Supremacist nationalism became a third choice taken up by Japan, Germany, and other countries. The three mutually incompatible versions of modernity made a second world war almost inevitable. This second total and industrial world war resulted in immense numbers of dead and wounded, as well as the industrial annihilation of 5.8 million Jews by Germany in the name of the country's racial purity.

For 30 years, Minobe Tatsukichi (1873–1948) had been Japan's leading jurist and constitutional theorist. He had received a noble rank and occupied an honored place in Japan's House of Peers, the upper chamber of its Diet, or parliament. An erudite, self-confident man, he was not accustomed to having his legal constructs challenged.

But today was different, and only later would Minobe realize what a dramatic turning point it was. On this February day in 1934, his fellow peer Baron Takeo Kikuchi publicly denounced Minobe's most famous legal theory, which posited that the relationship of the emperor to the constitution was one in which the emperor was an organ of the state. More than a generation of Japanese lawyers and scholars had practiced law according to Minobe's "organ theory." But now, the baron had accused Minobe of belittling the emperor's role in Japan's unique *kokutai*, or "national polity/essence." This concept played a key role in Japanese supremacist nationalism during the 1930s.

Though Minobe skillfully defended his position, the damage had been done. Following more attacks in the Diet, he resigned from his position, narrowly escaped being tried for his views, and was nearly assassinated in 1936. Already, however, in their drive to "clarify" the meaning of the "national essence," the cabinet had banned Minobe's works from study or circulation. Minobe's experience thus personalizes a struggle to come to grips with new visions of modernity not only in Japan but in much of the world as well.

CHAPTER OUTLINE

The Great War and Its Aftermath

New Variations on Modernity: The Soviet Union and Communism

New Variations on Modernity: Supremacist Nationalism in Italy, Germany, and Japan

Putting It All Together

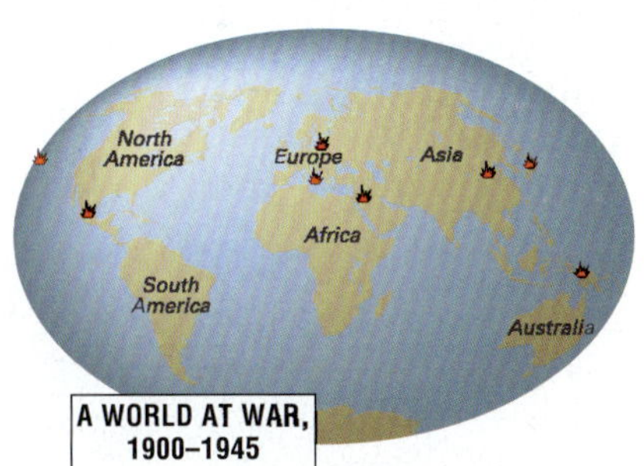

ABOVE: Shown here are the "Big Four," who negotiated the Treaty of Versailles: David Lloyd George, British prime minister, Vittorio Orlando, Italian prime minister, Georges Clemenceau, French prime minister, and US president Woodrow Wilson.

By the 1930s, the liberal principles of modernity—constitutionalism, capitalism, science, and industry—were severely tested by the Great Depression. In Japan, these values gave way to "supremacist nationalism,"

Seeing Patterns

➤ Which three patterns of modernity emerged after World War I? How and why did these patterns form?

➤ What were the strengths and flaws of each of the three visions of modernity?

➤ Why did supremacist nationalism disappear in the ashes of World War II?

similar to the ideologies of fascism in Italy and Nazism in Germany. In Russia, communism represented another new pattern of modernity. Other nations—Spain, Portugal, and China, for example—struggled with variations of these competing ideologies.

The Great War and Its Aftermath

In early 1914, the nations on the brink of World War I represented different conditions on their way to modernity. Some, like Great Britain, Germany, and France, were, along with the United States, among the world leaders in the development of scientific–industrial society. Others, like Austria-Hungary, the Ottoman Empire, the Balkan nations, Russia, and Japan, were at various stages of industrialization. In terms of political modernity, all of these initial members of what would shortly be known as the Allies and Central Powers—with the exception of France—were monarchies, though a number had become modified with the addition of constitutions and legislative assemblies. The larger powers were also imperial powers that had reduced much of Asia and Africa to the status of colonies. Over the next four years, this picture would change completely.

A Savage War and a Flawed Peace

Imperial competition, tempered by the need for a balance of power among the major states, dominated Europe during the century following the Napoleonic Wars. This intersected with two trends of nineteenth-century modernity: the political patterns of constitutionalism and ethnic nationalism, and the pattern of industrialization. The rise of the new imperialism in the nineteenth century disrupted the efforts of statesmen to adjust the balance of power to ever-shifting political conditions.

Total War. By 1918, large swaths of northern France and Belgium resembled moonscapes from four years of destruction and carnage. One of the unluckiest places was the Belgian city of Ypres, which suffered three battles and was all but completely obliterated by war's end.

Empires and Nations in the Balkans

German aspirations for expansion into Eastern Europe were one reason for its support of Austria against Serbia in 1914. For its part, France had sought revenge for Germany's annexing of Alsace and Lorraine in 1871. In the first decade of the twentieth century, however, the key to the preservation of peace in Europe was seen as maintaining the balance among the three empires that met in the Balkans.

The shrinking Ottoman Empire, beset by continuing demands from ethnic-nationalist minorities for independence, struggled to survive. The expanding Russian Empire, despite having suffered a defeat at the hands of Japan and an abortive revolution in 1904–1905, was rapidly recovering its military strength. And the Habsburg Empire of Austria-Hungary opposed Russian expansionism but also sought to benefit from Ottoman weakness. Germany had replaced Great Britain as the protector of the Ottomans and assisted the latter in strengthening their army. Though it had taken Mediterranean territories from the Ottomans, Britain still had a stake in preserving the rest of the Ottoman Empire, as did the other powers, all of whom feared a territorial scramble if the Ottoman Empire collapsed. Hence, there was a rough community of interest aimed at strengthening the Ottoman Empire, whose leaders were seeking to improve their military posture.

One unresolved ethnic-nationalist issue was Bosnia-Herzegovina. After the Balkan war of 1878, Austria-Hungary had become the territory's administrator—but not sovereign—as a compromise with the Ottomans, who were unable to keep Serbs, Croats, and Muslims apart. When Russia renewed its support for Serb ethnic nationalism in the Balkans after 1905, Austria-Hungary assumed sovereignty of Bosnia-Herzegovina in a protective move in 1908. Russia, committed to the policy of pan-Slavism, reacted to Austria-Hungary's move by stirring up Serb nationalists in Bosnia-Herzegovina who sought to join their province to the neighboring Kingdom of Serbia. On June 28, 1914, members of a Bosnian Serb nationalist group assassinated the Austrian heir to the throne, Franz Ferdinand, and his wife in the Bosnian city of Sarajevo. This assassination began the slide of Europe into World War I.

The Early Course of the War This war was comprehensive from the start: **total war**. The combatants relied on precise timing and speedy mobilization of their forces. For example, in order to avoid a two-front war, Germany, with its allies Austria-Hungary and, later, the Ottoman Empire and Bulgaria (who as a group were called the Central Powers), had to defeat France before Russia's massive army was fully mobilized (France, Russia, and Great Britain formed the Allied powers). The German Schlieffen Plan therefore called for a massive assault on northern France through Belgium, while trapping and isolating the French armies seeking to invade Alsace and Lorraine.

Total war: A type of warfare in which all the resources of the nation—including all or most of the civilian population—are marshaled for the war effort. As total war unfolded, all segments of society were increasingly seen as legitimate targets for the combatants.

The German plan ultimately failed after the French–British victory in the first Battle of the Marne in September 1914, a more rapid Russian mobilization than expected, and a poor showing by the Austrians against Russia. After months of fighting along the lines of the initial German advance into France, the Germans and the French and British dug in. By 1915 the two sides were forced into trench warfare in northeastern France and Belgium and an initially inconclusive war in the east against Russia.

The Germans were able to halt the Russian advances and to begin inflicting heavy losses on their troops. For its part, the Ottoman Empire suffered a crushing Russian invasion in the Caucasus, prompting it to massacre its Armenian minority, which was alleged to have helped in the invasion. This planned genocidal massacre, which may have killed a million Armenians, still requires a full accounting today.

As the war dragged on, both camps sought to recruit supporters to their sides. The Allies recruited volunteers from their dominions and colonies. Italy, Greece, and Romania entered on the Allied side with the hope of gaining territory from Austria-Hungary and the Ottomans; Bulgaria joined the Central Powers in the service of its own territorial ambitions. Japan declared war on Germany in 1914 as part of a previous alliance with Britain but used its occupation of German colonies in the Pacific and concessions in China as a step toward expanding its own empire. With the entrance of China in 1917 and the pivotal entrance of the United States that same year, the war now involved every major state in the world.

The Turning Point: 1917 In March 1917, the toll of the war contributed to the collapse of tsarist Russia. The February Revolution (actually in March, so called because it took place during February in the old-style Julian calendar still in use in Russia) forced Tsar Nicholas II to abdicate and created a provisional government. The new social-democratic government committed itself to carrying on the war, which grew even more unpopular. The communist Bolshevik Party of Vladimir Lenin (1870–1924) campaigned against continuing the war, and in early November (October in the Julian calendar), armed workers, sailors, and soldiers launched a takeover of the government in the capital of Petrograd (as St. Petersburg had been renamed).

After seizing power, the Bolsheviks began negotiations with the Germans, which resulted in the disastrous Treaty of Brest-Litovsk in March 1918. Roughly one-third of the Russian Empire's population, territory, and resources were handed over to the Germans in return for Russia's withdrawal from the war. The Germans had now come close to achieving their secret war goal: the creation of *Lebensraum* (living space) for Germany in the industrialized European part of Russia.

The United States had declared neutrality at the outset of the war, but the course of the war had shifted US opinion toward the Allied side. The German torpedoing and sinking of the British liner *Lusitania* on May 7, 1915, which cost the lives of more than 100 Americans, brought the United States to the brink of war. Germany discontinued unrestricted submarine warfare but, in early 1917, resumed it in a bid to isolate Great Britain. Wilson asked Congress to declare war, which it did on April 6, 1917.

The entrance of the United States added the critical resources needed by the Allies to ultimately win the war. Wilson's war aims (the Fourteen Points) called for freedom of the seas, the rights of neutral powers, self-determination for all peoples, and peace "without annexations or indemnities." These clauses represented not only American goals but now were presented as the Allies' war aims as well.

In early 1918, American troops began to land in France in appreciable numbers. This coincided with a spring offensive mounted by Germany, with support of troops moved from Russia to France. The new American troops in France, however, gave the Allies the advantage they needed to stop the German effort, which soon collapsed. Faced with these new conditions and reeling from the Allies' September counteroffensive, which now threatened to advance into Germany, the Germans agreed to an armistice on November 11, 1918.

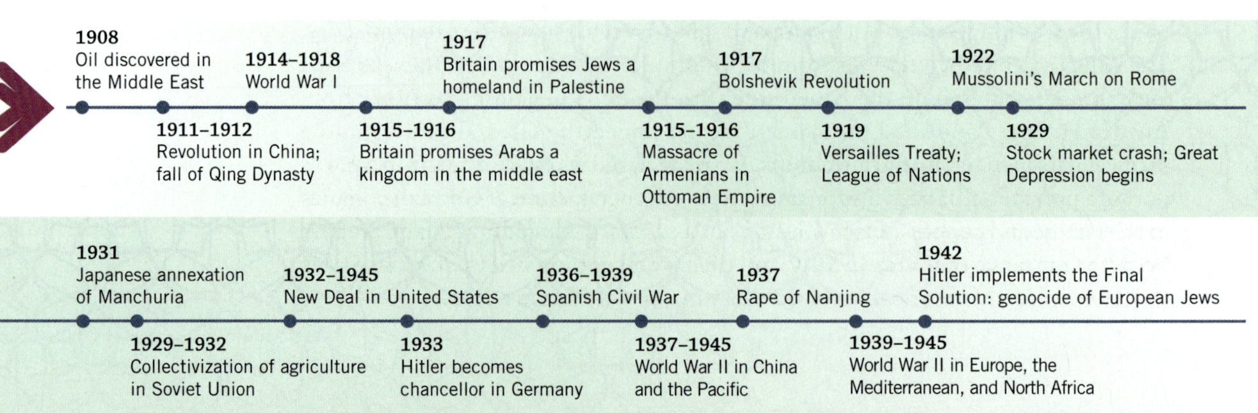

The Versailles Peace The toll of the war was staggering. About 20 million soldiers and civilians were dead, and 21 million were wounded. Many more (between 20 and 50 million) perished in a global influenza pandemic, abetted by the transportation of goods and soldiers at war's end. The pandemic began in Spring 1918, grew worse in Fall, and lingered well into 1919. The combattants of WWI censored early reports about it while Spain, neutral during the war, reported it freely. As a result, people called the disease the "Spanish Flu," even though the place of origin was never identified satisfactorily.

The peace settlement was signed at Versailles on June 28, 1919—the fifth anniversary of the assassination of Franz Ferdinand. The German, Austro-Hungarian, and Ottoman Empires were all dismantled, and new nation-states were created. Germany lost its overseas colonies as well as Alsace-Lorraine. The Allies declared Germany responsible for the war and subjected it to military restrictions and reparation payments. France acquired temporary custody of the German Saar province with its coal reserves and steel factories as a guarantee for the payment of war reparations. While historians long considered the Allied-imposed reparations excessive, recent research has concluded that Germany, which was not destroyed by war, had the industrial-financial capacity to pay.

A new supranational **League of Nations** was entrusted with the maintenance of peace. But since one of its clauses required collective military action in case of aggression, the US Senate refused ratification, rejecting this infringement on American sovereignty. Altogether, the Versailles peace was deeply flawed. Instead of binding Germany into a common western European framework, the Allies actually encouraged it to go it alone by flanking it in the east with weak countries that could be dominated in the future (see Map 28.1).

League of Nations: An international body of 58 states, created as part of the Versailles Treaty and functioning between 1919 and 1946, that sought to ensure world peace.

America First: The Beginnings of a Consumer Culture and the Great Depression

The United States emerged from the war as the strongest among the Allied democracies. It had turned from a debtor country into a creditor country, a majority of Americans now lived in nonrural environments, and the war economy shifted initially into a sustained peacetime expansion.

Modernity Unfolding in the United States Increased mechanization in many industries spurred the economic expansion. Americans aspired to move from countryside to city and to own a house, a car, and appliances. During the Roaring Twenties, as the 1920s came to be called, Americans wanted to be entertained. A flourishing of popular culture accompanied the rising urban prosperity. The film industry of Hollywood and a recording industry came into being, churning out hits for the entertainment of the new consumers. And the rapid development of the radio allowed news and entertainment to enter every household that could afford a set.

The New Woman The Nineteenth Amendment of 1920 gave American women the right to vote. In addition to winning political rights, American women heightened their social profile. Many colleges and universities went co-ed, and women became teachers, secretaries, and nurses. Similarly, women swiftly dominated the new occupation of telephone operator as the new century advanced.

MAP 28.1 Europe, the Middle East, and North America in 1914 and 1923

For people of color, however, the situation was far different. Black women, if they were not agricultural laborers, often worked as domestic servants or laundry workers in the growing urban economy. In larger segregated areas with more diversified economies, some black women found jobs similar to those of white women, but for the most part, their opportunities were far more limited. Hence, although emancipation was expanding for white women, it remained gendered, while the situation for black women continued to be hampered by racism.

High Artistic Creativity American intellectuals, writers, and artists viewed consumer and pop culture modernity with mixed feelings. While they hailed what they viewed as the progress of liberal values, they were uneasy about what they perceived as an increasing superficiality and materialism. After World War I, the ambiguities of modernity engendered tremendous creativity in American culture.

A cohort of artists and intellectuals viewed themselves as belonging to a "lost generation,"—a generation that had lost its best years of life, or even life altogether, to the war. The Harlem Renaissance featured leading African American innovators in jazz and literature (see "Patterns Up Close"). Modernist writers experimented with the inner emotional tensions of a "stream of consciousness" style, or offered counter-models of spirituality, naturalness, Greek classicism, or Chinese monism. The United States set the pace for mass culture, providing many of the literary tools readers needed to grapple with modernity.

Business and Labor Just as much energy characterized American business. Presidents Harding, Coolidge, and Hoover, along with Congress, exercised a minimum of political control, illustrated by Harding's campaign slogan "Less government in business and more business in government." While business boomed, trade and industrial unions stagnated. The American Federation of Labor (AFL), the largest trade union pushing for improved labor conditions, was hampered by the fact that its members were unskilled workers of many diverse ethnic backgrounds and were therefore difficult to organize. Business easily quashed widespread strikes for the right to unionize in 1919. An anti-immigration and anti-radical hysteria followed, with laws that cut immigration by half and the famous murder trial of immigrant anarchists Nicola Sacco and Bartolomeo Vanzetti.

The Backlash Anti-foreigner and anti-communist hysteria was part of a larger unease with modernity. Fundamentalist religion, intolerance toward Catholics and Jews, and fear and violence directed at African Americans rose visibly. The Ku Klux Klan was at the center of repeated waves of lynchings in the South and attempts to control the local politics of many states. The Klan remained a powerful force in the South and Midwest until World War II.

The most startling offenses against the modern principles of liberty and equality, however, came from ideologues wrapping themselves in the mantle of modern science. Researchers at the leading private universities lent respectability to the pseudoscience of **eugenics**, conceptualizing an ideal of a "Nordic" race. Foundations such as the Carnegie Endowment and businessmen such as

Eugenics: The discredited idea of the hereditary breeding of better human beings by genetic control.

Great Depression: The global economic crisis that followed the crash of the New York Stock Exchange on October 29, 1929, and resulted in massive unemployment and economic misery worldwide.

Henry Ford financed research on how to prevent the reproduction of genetically "inferior" races. California and other states passed laws that allowed for the sterilization of thousands of women. Ironically, some of the practices that would inspire Hitler and the Nazis were already in place during the 1920s in the United States, where they were regarded by some as progressive, and during the 1930s in Scandinavia—particularly in Sweden—which initiated sterilization for women.

The Great Depression By 1929, saturation of the market for consumer goods behind high tariff walls led to falling profit rates in businesses. Many of the wealthy had begun to shift their money from investments in manufacturing to speculation on the stock market. In addition, ordinary investors participated in the stock market, many buying shares on high margins (i.e., borrowing much of the money from a broker). As long as the market boomed, investors made money, but if stocks went down, investors could be bankrupted as their margins were called in.

Down and Out in Wales. The 1930s' prosperity was largely limited to southern England. Most of the rest of the British Isles, such as this family in Wales, were largely left out. George Orwell (1903–1950) published his investigations of British poverty in *The Road to Wigan Pier* (1937), a widely read essay in which he castigated the Conservatives for their lack of a job-creating policy. A strong advocate for social democracy, he became well known after World War II for his opposition to antidemocratic regimes, expressed in his novels *Animal Farm* (1945) and *Nineteen Eighty-Four* (1949).

A slowdown in production shifted attention to unsustainable debt levels. Farmers were deep in debt, having borrowed to mechanize while speculating wrongly on a continuation of high prices for commodities. In October 1929, the speculators panicked, selling their stock for pennies on the dollar. The panic rippled through both the finance and manufacturing sectors. As banks began calling in loans at home and abroad, the panic became a worldwide crisis: the **Great Depression** of 1929–1933. Harrowing levels of unemployment and poverty put the American system of capitalist democratic modernity to a severe test.

Americans largely blamed their president, Herbert Hoover (in office 1929–1933), for failing to manage the crisis, and in 1932 they elected Franklin D. Roosevelt (in office 1933–1945). Hoover's approach had been one that previous administrations had turned to in times of economic crisis: cut government spending, raise tariffs to protect US industries, and let market forces correct themselves. But such measures now only made things worse, while the record high Smoot-Hawley Tariff of 1930 encouraged retaliatory tariffs in other countries and discouraged world commerce, thus contributing to a worldwide economic collapse.

Under Roosevelt's prodding, Congress enacted what he called the "New Deal," in which the government engaged in deficit spending to help the unemployed and revive business and agriculture. One showpiece of the New Deal was the Tennessee Valley Authority, a government-owned corporation for the economic development of large parts of the southeastern United States particularly hard hit by the Depression. In addition, a social safety net was created, which included retirement benefits through the Social Security Act as well as unemployment benefits. Finally, the Securities and Exchange Commission (SEC) was enacted in 1934 to enforce regulations governing the stock market in order to prevent practices that had led to the collapse of 1929.

In 1937, however, a Congress frightened by the deficit slackened efforts to reduce unemployment, while the Supreme Court declared several of the New Deal programs unconstitutional. The result was a new slump, from which the economy finally recovered only with America's entry into World War II.

Great Britain and France: Slow Recovery and Troubled Empires

In the aftermath of World War I, Britain and France suffered severely. A lack of finances hampered the recovery, as did the enormous debt both countries took on during the war. Although socialist politicians gained in importance, they did not succeed in improving working-class conditions or the safety net. The demands of the League of Nations mandate system, whereby the colonies were to be prepared for future independence, were not pursued vigorously by either France or Britain.

Weak British Recovery

The British-dominated free trade global economy ended in 1918. Many countries had been forced to be on their own during the war and now pursued policies of **autarky**. A 25 percent loss of exports was compounded by a militant labor force, seeking to protect its wartime gains. In addition, Britain owed a war debt of $4.3 billion to the United States. Since much of Britain's ability to repay these debts rested upon Germany's ability to pay its reparations, the entire European economic system remained fragile throughout the 1920s.

Autarky: The condition of economic independence and self-sufficiency as state policy.

With the restructuring of Germany's debts in 1924, some stability finally came to the international capital markets. Still, close to half of the annual British budgets in the interwar period went to paying off the war debt. In this situation, industrial investments were low and unemployment was high. In response, business lowered wages, causing labor to respond with a massive general strike in 1926.

The dominant conservatives in the government could not bring themselves in the 1930s to accept deficit spending. At a minimum, however, they went off the gold standard and devalued the currency to make exports competitive again. World trade had declined, but by lowering tariffs within the empire, Britain created the equivalent of the autarky that Nazi Germany and militaristic Japan were dreaming of with their planned conquests. A semblance of prosperity returned to the country after the Great Depression in the 1930s.

France: Moderate Recovery

France suffered devastating human losses and destruction of property during the war. Alsace-Lorraine, the most important industrial region and the territory that France had desperately wanted to recover from the Germans, was now a wasteland. The war had been fought with war materiel borrowed from the United States and Great Britain, to be paid for after the war. The money for the reconstruction of industry and housing came from increased taxes, German reparations, and taxes from German provinces occupied after the war. But reconstruction could be completed only in 1926–1929, when taxes were once more increased and Germany finally made full reparation payments.

Patterns Up Close | The Harlem Renaissance and the African Diaspora

The modern period saw some of the largest migrations in human history. Such diasporas—a term originally used to describe the scattering of the Jews around Europe, the Middle East, and North Africa—not only threw those affected into new and sometimes hostile environments but over time also created complex cultural conditions in which new generations forged their identities. In the case of African Americans in the 1920s, a new and vital cultural touchstone was the Harlem Renaissance.

Growing—though still limited—educational opportunities, an increase in urbanization stemming from the "Great Migration" of rural southern African Americans seeking work in northern factory cities during World War I, and a new political assertiveness all contributed to a cultural explosion. As the largest African American enclave in America's largest city, New York, Harlem became the most vital black cultural center. Jazz and its offshoots came to dominate popular tastes; young people of all ethnicities sought to take up the latest dances from "uptown"; and writers such as Claude McKay (1889–1948), Langston Hughes (1902–1967), James Weldon Johnson (1871–1938), Zora Neale Hurston (1891–1960), and many others achieved national and international recognition.

Though relatively few writers (among them Langston Hughes) actually visited Africa, its resonance was powerful. To be African in this sense was to be beyond the history of slavery and oppression and to be part of a larger and richer collective history extending to the first human beings. This solidarity was expressed in the Pan-African movement of which the educator, activist, and cofounder of the NAACP, W. E. B. DuBois (1868–1963) was a prominent popularizer. During the 1920s the

French governments were dependent on coalitions among parties, and labor was more often than not represented. France did not suffer a traumatic general strike as Britain did, and even though it returned like Great Britain to the gold standard (1928–1936), it avoided the British mistake of returning to prewar parity, thereby making the comparatively low wages for its workers a bit more bearable.

Thanks to its successful reconstruction, France weathered the Depression until 1931. Even then, its politicians found the idea of deficit spending as a way to get out of the Depression too counterintuitive. As in Great Britain and the United States, they slashed government spending and refused to devalue the currency. By 1933–1934, unrest in the population and rapidly changing governments made supremacist nationalism an attractive model, especially for business, which was afraid of labor strife. When fascist–communist street fighting broke out in Paris, the Communist Party initiated the formation of a Popular Front coalition with the Socialist Party and others (1936–1938). Although this coalition checked supremacist nationalism, it was too short-lived to allow the centrist middle-class core to broaden, with disastrous consequences for France's ability to resist Hitler in World War II.

most popular mass movement among African Americans was the Universal Negro Improvement Association led by the Jamaican Marcus Garvey (1887–1940), which sought to help those of the African diaspora repatriate to the continent with a view to creating a prosperous Africa for the Africans.

For its part, the Harlem Renaissance also had a profound effect on people of African descent in places far removed from the United States. African expatriates in Paris in the 1930s championed a cultural movement called Négritude, which called for a new pride in African history, culture, and "blackness" itself. Influenced by such writers as Aimé Césaire (1913–2008) and Léopold Senghor (1906–2001), the movement was powerfully influential in French-speaking Africa. Senghor himself became Senegal's first president and served for two decades.

Langston Hughes. The noted poet and writer Langston Hughes first emerged on the literary scene during the Harlem Renaissance and went on to influence the shaping of African and African American literary identity for decades afterward.

Questions

- What were some of the factors that led to the Harlem Renaissance emerging in the 1920s, instead of some other time?
- Why were the questions these writers raised about identity so important to them? Why was this especially so in the new "modern" age?

Colonies and Mandates After World War I, the British Empire grew by 2 million square miles to 14 million, or one-quarter of the earth's surface, encompassing one-quarter of the world's population. The French Empire at the same time measured 5 million square miles, with a population of 113 million. Although the wisdom of maintaining expensive empires was debated in the interwar period, conservatives clung to the prestige that square mileage was presumed to bestow on its holders. Defense of these empires dominated the policies of Britain and France toward their dependencies and mandates during the interwar period (see Map 28.2).

The most important area, strategically, for both the British and the French after World War I was the Middle East. Under the postwar peace terms, the British and French had received the Arab provinces of the former Ottoman Empire (other than Egypt and Sudan, acquired already in 1881) as **mandates**—that is, as territories to be prepared for independence. Because of the discovery of oil in southwestern Iran, however, neither Britain nor France was in a hurry to guide its mandates to independent nationhood.

Mandates: Quasi-colonies created by the League of Nations, which mandated key territories of the defunct Ottoman Empire to Britain and France.

Twice-Promised Lands Arab leaders were strongly opposed to the British and French mandates. During World War I, a British agent, T. E. Lawrence

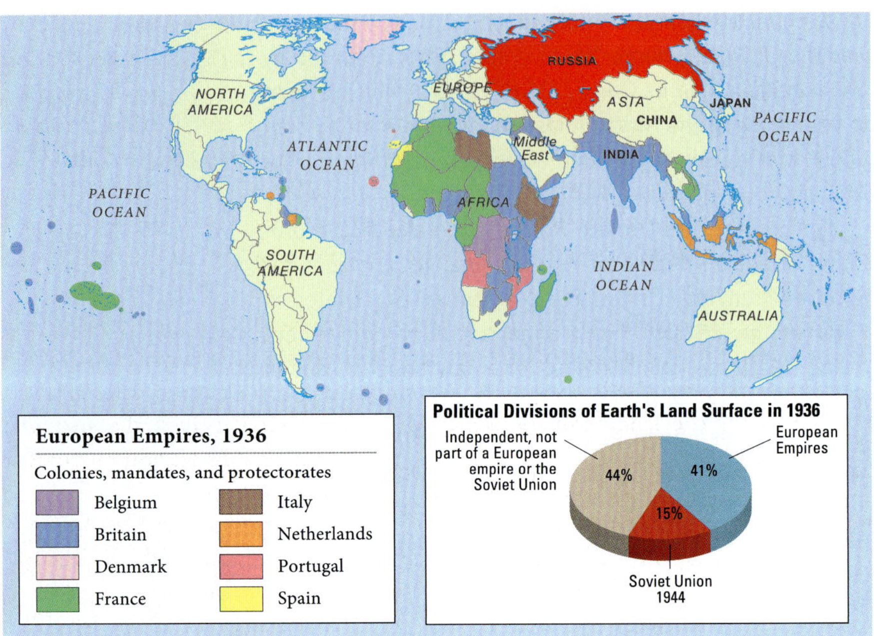

MAP 28.2 European Empires, 1936

(1888–1935), the famous "Lawrence of Arabia," helped the members of a prominent family, the Hashemites from Mecca in western Arabia, to assume leadership of the Arabs for a promised national kingdom in Syria and Palestine in the so-called McMahon–Hussein correspondence of 1915–1916.

Since the British, seeking Jewish support for World War I, also promised the Jews a "national home" in Palestine in the Balfour Declaration of 1917, Arab nationalism was stymied even before it could unfold. The British moved the Hashemites into their mandates of Iraq and Transjordan in 1921, in accordance with the Sykes–Picot agreement (1916) concerning the imperial division of the Middle East between the Allies. As Iraq was divided by majority Shiites and minority Sunnis, the British inaugurated a policy of divide and rule in this Middle Eastern mandate.

Zionism: The belief, based on the writings of Theodor Herzl, that European Jews—and by extension all Jews everywhere—were entitled to a national homeland corresponding to the territory of ancient Israel. It grew into a form of ethno-religious nationalism and ultimately led to the formation of the state of Israel in 1948.

In Palestine, the contradiction between the promises to Arabs and Jews during the war forced Britain to build a direct administration under a high commissioner. Many religious Jews had arrived in Palestine as refugees from anti-Semitic riots, or pogroms, in Russia and Eastern Europe. When the Austrian Jewish journalist Theodor Herzl (1860–1904) made ethnic nationalism the ideology for secular Jews, early pioneers of **Zionism**, as secular Jewish nationalism was called, began to arrive as well. Jewish settlers purchased land from willing Palestinian absentee landlords and evicted the landlords' Palestinian tenant farmers. These evictions were the root cause of two Palestinian–Arab nationalist uprisings, in 1929 and 1936–1939, for which the British had no real answer except force and belated efforts in 1939 to limit Jewish immigration.

Egypt and Turkey As the Suez Canal was vitally important for the British in India, relinquishing it was unthinkable. They rejected a demand in 1919 by a delegation of Egyptian nationalists for independence out of hand and exiled its leader, Saad Zaghlul (ca. 1859–1927). After deadly riots, the British relented and invited Zaghlul to peace negotiations. But the independence the British granted in 1923 withheld both military defense and control of the Suez Canal from Egypt. A year later, Zaghlul and the Wafd Party won the first independent elections. The land-owning Egyptian ruling class was largely uninterested in industrial development. Thus, at the onset of World War II, Egypt still depended on agricultural production and exports, while its strategic position was absolutely vital to the British Empire.

Swaraj: Literally, "self-rule" [swah-RAHJ]. Gandhi interpreted this term as meaning "direct democracy," while the Congress Party identified it with complete independence from Great Britain.

The severe punishment of the Ottoman Empire by the Allies (besides removing the Arab provinces, they had carved out large "zones of influence" within Anatolia itself) provoked the rise of grassroots resistance groups in Anatolia. These groups merged under the leadership of General Mustafa Kemal (given the surname Atatürk, "Father of the Turks,"1881–1938) into a national liberation movement that drove out the Greeks from western Anatolia, occupied one-half of Armenia, and ended the Ottoman sultanate/caliphate (1921–1924). Atatürk, who had earned renown during World War I for his defense of Gallipoli against the British, was the driving force behind the creation of a modern, secular Turkey that could stand up against the European powers.

Secularizing Turkey. Atatürk was a committed educational reformer who sought to create a "public culture." He was advised by the famous American philosopher of education John Dewey (1859–1952). Here, in 1928, dressed in a Western-style suit and necktie, he gives a lesson on the new Turkish alphabet, a variant of the Latin alphabet, whose use was mandated throughout the republic.

Although authoritarian, Atatürk kept the new Turkish parliament open to pluralism. Parliament adopted the French model of separation of state and religion, European family law, the Latin alphabet, the Western calendar, metric weights and measures, modern clothing, and women's suffrage. During the Depression, Atatürk's economic advisors launched etatism a state-controlled version of economic development. Both modernism and étatism showed only modest successes by 1939, and the rural masses in Anatolia remained mired in small-scale self-sufficiency farming and religious tradition. But the foundation was laid in Turkey for both a Westernized ruling class and an urbanized middle class.

Indian Demands for Independence In India in April 1919, frustrated by a British crackdown on political protest, a crowd gathered in the Sikhs' sacred city of Amritsar. On orders of a British general, at least 379 protesters were slaughtered by an elite unit of Gurkha troops. As the international furor over this "Amritsar Massacre" raged, the British offered token reforms to the Indian Legislative Assembly. The Indian National Congress was infuriated by this minimal improvement and called for full self-rule (Hindi ***swaraj***), urging nonviolent noncooperation.

Inevitably, civil disturbances accompanied the Congress's push for self-rule. In a change of tactics, Mohandas "Mahatma" (Great Soul) Gandhi (1869–1948), the most prominent advocate of nonviolence, suspended the push in 1921. Party leaders exited the cities and, with the help of party workers, preached nonviolent civil disobedience in the countryside. It was during this time that the National Congress transformed itself from a small, urban Westernized elite into a mass party.

In 1929, the new Labour government in Britain explored the possibility of giving India dominion status, but there was strong opposition from the other parties. When Labour could not deliver, Gandhi demanded complete independence and, on March 12, 1930, embarked on the 24-day Salt March to the sea with his followers to pan salt, which the government had refused to free from taxation. Disturbances accompanied the marches, and in a massive crackdown, the British government succeeded in repressing the National Congress.

The British government in 1935 passed the Government of India Act, which devolved all political functions except defense and foreign affairs to India. The members of the National Congress were unhappy, however, because of the decentralized structure of the reformed Indian government and particularly because the act recognized the Muslim League of Muhammad Ali Jinnah (1876–1948), not the Congress, as the representative of the Muslims. As in Egypt and Iraq, there was a profound reluctance by the Western powers to relinquish colonialism.

Latin America: Independent Democracies and Authoritarian Regimes

Latin America remained faithful to its constitutionalist heritage throughout the nineteenth century, though with a preference for authoritarian rule. A pattern of elite rule had evolved in which large estate owners controlled the politics of their countries and, through the military, kept rural black and indigenous peoples, as well as the mixed urban populations, in check. Politicians in some countries realized the voting potential of the urban populations after World War I and pursued a new type of autocratic politics, called populism, in conjunction with industrialization. Estate-owner politics and populism, together with industrialization programs, characterized Latin America during the interwar period.

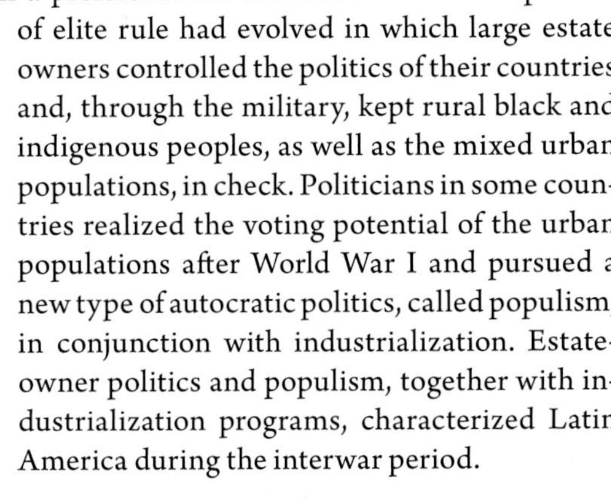

Gandhi Leading the Salt March. Perhaps the most famous act of civil disobedience in Gandhi's career was the Salt March in 1930 to protest the British salt monopoly in India. It was a perfect embodiment of Gandhi's belief in nonviolent civil disobedience, which he called *satyagraha*, "soul-" or "truth-force." Though it failed to win major concessions from the British, it focused worldwide attention on the Indian independence movement.

The Years of Depression In Mexico, rapid urbanization continued during the interwar period. Immigration from overseas as well as rural–urban migration fueled this process. In 1929 the new Institutional Revolutionary Party (Partido Revolucionario Institucional, PRI) brought the revolution of 1910–1917 to an end. A now strong government moved to complete land distribution to poor farmers, expand education, and begin social legislation. The PRI weathered the Depression with some difficulty, but thanks to increased state control of economic investments, it maintained its footing until European and East Asian war preparations increased demand for commodities.

The South American countries with the largest internal markets, such as Argentina and Brazil, rode out the Depression more successfully than others. Nevertheless, overall the impact was substantial, with a reduction of commodity exports by over 50 percent. The Depression resulted in urban unrest, especially in countries with newly expanded mines or oil wells, such as Chile, Peru, and Venezuela, or expanded administrative bureaucracies, such as Brazil.

An important shift away from landed oligarchies, however, began to appear among the ruling classes. A new generation of military officers, with urban backgrounds and no ties to the traditional oligarchy, appeared. They offered populist authoritarian programs that mixed elements from the prevailing European ideologies.

New Variations on Modernity: The Soviet Union and Communism

Communism was the second pattern of modernity that arose out of the ashes of World War I. Following their coup in November 1917, the Bolsheviks under Lenin triumphed in a debilitating civil war and established the Union of Soviet Socialist Republics. Lenin's successor, Joseph Stalin (1879–1953), built the Communist Party into a powerful apparatus that shifted resources from agriculture into industry and dealt ruthlessly with opposition. By World War II, the Soviet Union had joined the ranks of the industrialized powers.

The Communist Party and Regime in the Soviet Union

Karl Marx, the founder of communism, did not think that the Russian Empire would be ready for a communist revolution for a long time to come. It was the achievement of Vladimir Lenin to adapt Marxism to Russian circumstances. For him, the party was not the mass movement envisioned by Marx but rather a disciplined, armed vanguard that ruled with monopoly power and instilled the ideology of communism in an expanding working class after the revolution.

The Bolshevik Regime Lenin was from a middle-class family; his father had been given a patent of nobility, and Lenin himself had a degree in law. The execution of his brother by the tsarist government for alleged complicity in the assassination of Tsar Alexander II (1881) imbued him with hatred for Russian autocracy.

The fall of the tsar's government in the spring of 1917 allowed Lenin and his fellow Bolsheviks to return from political exile. These included Leon Trotsky 1879–1940), the son of an affluent Ukrainian Jewish family, and Joseph Stalin, the son of an impoverished Georgian cobbler. By the summer of 1917, the Bolsheviks were mounting massive demonstrations. The collapse of a disastrous Russian summer offensive emboldened the Bolsheviks, who controlled the Petrograd Soviet (council of workers and soldiers that helped maintain order), to make a bid for power. In early November 1917, the Bolsheviks staged a successful coup d'état in Petrograd.

Civil War and Reconstruction The takeover of Russia by a radical minority unleashed a storm of competing factions. For the Bolsheviks, the first necessity was building an army. From his armored train, flying the new "hammer and sickle" red flag, Trotsky rallied his "Red" forces against the more numerous but disunited "White" (antirevolutionary) armies. From 1918 to 1921, Georgia, Armenia, Azerbaijan and the Ukraine were each forced back into the new Bolshevik state.

The price for communist victory in the civil war was a complete collapse of the economy, amid a coincidental harvest failure. Lenin's policy of "war communism" sent the Red Army into the countryside to requisition food, often with brutality. Peasants fought back, and by 1922 a second civil war threatened. Only then did Lenin relent by inaugurating the temporary New Economic Policy (NEP), with a mixture of private and state investment in factories and small-scale food marketing by peasants. By 1928, a successful NEP had helped the Soviet Union to return to prewar levels of industrial production.

The Collectivization of Agriculture and Industrialization

Lenin died in 1924. His successor, Joseph Stalin, took his place as the general secretary of the Communist Party. Stalin fought for six years against potential and imagined rivals, a struggle that left him deeply suspicious. His chief victim was Trotsky, whom he forced into exile and ultimately had assassinated in Mexico in1940.

"Liquidation of the Kulaks as a Class" Stalin decided that industrialization through the NEP was advancing too slowly. Funds to finance industrialization came from the sale of grain and oil on the world market, but farmers had lost all trust in the communist regime after the forcible requisitions during the civil war, and they hoarded their grain. In November 1929, the party decreed the collectivization of agriculture as the necessary step for an accelerated industrialization. Over the next two years, 3–5 percent of the farmers on grain-producing lands, called kulaks (from the Russian for "fist," indicating the tightfistedness of wealthier peasants vis-à-vis poor indebted ones), were "liquidated"—selected for execution, removal to labor camps, or resettlement on inferior soils. Their properties were confiscated, and the remaining peasants were regrouped as employees either of state farms or of poorer collective farms. Between 6 and 14 million farmers were forcibly removed, with the majority killed outright or worked and starved to death.

Stalinism The impact on agriculture was devastating. Production plummeted, food requisitions were resumed, bread was rationed, and wages sank. This one-time transfer of confiscated wealth from the kulaks to industry was substantial. Income from renewed grain exports and from accelerated oil exports in the 1930s was poured into factory construction. By 1939, industrialization had been accomplished, though at an unparalleled human cost.

The industrial and urban modernity that the Soviet Union reached was one of enforced solidarity without private enterprises and markets. The communist prestige objects were huge plant complexes producing industrial basics. Little investment was left over for consumer goods and household articles, and people had to make do with shoddy goods, delivered irregularly to government outlets and requiring patient waiting in long lines.

The disaster of collectivization made Stalin even more concerned about potential resistance. Regular party and army purges decimated the top echelons of the communist ruling apparatus. Considering the enormity of Stalin's policies, scholars have since wondered about the viability of this communist–socialist attempt at accelerated modernity.

New Variations on Modernity: Supremacist Nationalism in Italy, Germany, and Japan

The third vision of modernity was an ideology of supremacist nationalism. Fascism became a persuasive alternative to democracy and communism in Italy after World War I. The much more brutal German Nazi and Japanese militarist ideologies became acceptable only after the Depression appeared to reveal capitalist democracy to be incapable of weathering the crisis.

From Fascism in Italy to Nazism in the Third Reich

Benito Mussolini (1883–1945) worked as a journalist at various socialist newspapers. His support for the war as an instrument of radical change brought him into conflict with the majority of socialists, who opposed the war. Disillusioned with Marxism, he founded the *Fasci Italiani di Combattimento* (Italian Combat Squad) in 1919. War veterans, dressed in black shirts and organized in paramilitary units, broke up communist rallies and strikes. The symbol of the movement was the *fasces* [FAS-sees], derived from the old Roman emblem of solidarity in the form of a bundle of sticks and an ax, tied with a ribbon, and taken over from radical Sicilian workers' groups of the 1890s called *fasci dei lavoratori*.

"Comrade, Come Join Us at the Collective Farm!" This is the call with which the woman on this wildly optimistic poster of 1930 is seen. In reality, Russian peasants experienced the collectivization program of 1929–1940 as a second serfdom, especially in the Ukraine, where private rather than collective village farming was widespread. They resisted it both passively and actively, through arson, theft, and especially the slaughtering of livestock.

With their street brawls, the fascist "Blackshirts" contributed to the impression of a breakdown of law and order, which the democratic government could not control. Anticommunism thus was accompanied by denunciations of democracy as incapable of decisive action. Although Mussolini's party was still behind other parties in the parliament, he demanded the premiership by threatening a march on Rome by 10,000 Blackshirts. This turned into a victory parade, with the king acquiescing to the fascists.

In 1923 Mussolini led his coalition government in the passing of a law that gave two-thirds of the seats in parliament to the party that garnered the most votes. A year later, Il Duce ("the Leader"), as he now styled himself, won his two-thirds and began to implement his fascist **corporate state**.

By 1926, elections were abolished, the press was censored, and the secret police monitored the population. Fascist party officials, provincial governorships, and mayors were appointed from above, and labor unions were closed down. In the Ministry of Corporations, industrialists and bureaucrats representing labor, met and sharply curtailed wages and labor regulations. Catholicism was made the Italian state religion in return for full support by the Vatican for the fascists.

Corporate state: Sometimes called an "organic state"; based on a philosophy of government that sees all sectors of society contributing in a systematic, orderly, and hierarchical fashion to the health of the state, the way that the parts of the body do to a human being.

Depression and Conquests Italy weathered the Depression through deficit spending and state investments. In 1933, Mussolini formed the Industrial Reconstruction Institute, which took over the industrial and commercial holdings of the banks that had failed earlier. This institute was crucial in efforts to revive the Italian industrial sector. Only in the mid-1930s did the urban population, concentrated mostly in the north, come to outnumber its rural counterpart. The fascists had no solution for southern Italy, a region that remained overwhelmingly rural and poor.

Italy's military industry allowed Mussolini to proclaim a policy of autarky with the help of overseas territories. First, the conquest of formerly Ottoman Libya (see Chapter 27) was brutally completed in 1931. The other major colony was Ethiopia, conquered by Italy in 1935–1936 and merged with Italian Eritrea and Somalia into Italian East Africa. Eager to avenge Italy's defeat by the Ethiopians forty years before, Mussolini's forces crushed Ethiopian resistance and then pacified the new colony with the settlement of 200,000 Italians.

The Ethiopian conquest prompted protests by the League of Nations. Although these were ineffective, Mussolini felt sufficiently isolated that he sought closer relations with Adolf Hitler and the Nazis, whom he found to be a counterweight against international isolation. An increasingly close cooperation began between the two dictators, who formed the nucleus of the Axis powers, joined in 1941 by Japan.

The Founding of the Weimar Republic In September 1918, the German Supreme Army Command (OHL) concluded that Germany had lost World War I. Soon after, unrest broke out in the military and among workers, spreading gradually across the country. The climax was reached in early November when the war government forced Emperor William II to abdicate, turned power over to the opposition party in parliament, and resigned. This party, the Social Democratic Party of Germany (SPD), had supported the war even though it was officially devoted to a program of proletarian revolution. Communists, including dissidents from the SPD, were agitating for the revolution to be carried out, but the new government, backed by the OHL, sued the Allies for an armistice (November 11, 1918) and defeated the revolutionaries. Three months later a new parliament met in the central German city of Weimar and ratified a republican constitution.

In the peace negotiations at Versailles in France, the French would have liked to have Germany divided into individual states again, as it was before 1871. The British and the Americans, however, were opposed to such a drastic settlement. Germany was let off with what historians now see in retrospect as relatively moderate reparations for civilian casualties, along with a reduction of the army and the loss of land, although it was also forced to accept responsibility for beginning the war. The settlement satisfied no one. France's security remained uncertain, German conservatives and nationalists screamed defiance, and the democrats of Weimar who accepted the settlement were embittered by its consequence: devastating inflation.

As in all countries with the onset of peace, pent-up consumer demand caused inflation to rise. But Germany, forced by the Allies to make reparation payments immediately, was faced with hyperinflation. The German mark became virtually worthless and Germany had to suspend payments. France and Belgium responded by occupying the industrial Ruhr province in 1923. German workers in the Ruhr retaliated with passive resistance, and a deadlock was the result.

The eventual solution was the American-crafted Dawes Plan of 1924. US banks advanced credits to European banks to refinance the resumed German but significantly reduced reparation payments. France and Belgium withdrew from the Ruhr, inflation was curtailed, and the currency stabilized. The newly solvent and recovering Weimar Republic entered into its version of the roaring twenties.

The Rise of the Nazis After only five years, all exuberance evaporated after the US stock market crash of 1929. American banks, desperate for cash, began to recall their loans made to Europe. European banks began to fail, and as world trade shrank, exporting nations like Germany were hit particularly hard. Unemployment soared to 30 percent of the workforce. The number of people voting for extremist opponents of democracy—communists and supremacist nationalists—rose to more than half of the electorate by July 1932, and the National Socialist German Workers' Party (NSDAP, or Nazi Party) became the largest party in parliament.

The Nazi leader, Adolf Hitler (1889–1945), had led a failed uprising in 1923 and done time for it in prison. In *Mein Kampf* (*My Struggle*), published in 1925, he advocated ridding Germany of its Jews, whom he blamed for World War I, and communists, whom he blamed for the Central Powers losing the war. He further supported the German conquest of a "living space" (*Lebensraum*) in Russia and Eastern Europe for the "superior" "Aryan" (German) race, with the "inferior" Slavs reduced to forced labor. No one who followed politics in Germany during the 1920s could be in doubt about Hitler's unrestrained and violent supremacist nationalism. Throughout the decade, however, he remained marginalized.

Play Money. German children in 1923 playing with bundles of money in the streets. Hyperinflation had made money in the early Weimar Republic worthless: At the height of the inflation, in November 1923, 1 trillion "paper marks" was worth $0.24 US. To overcome the hyperinflation, the German Central Bank cut the "trillions" off the mark and created the "Reichsmark." This currency was tied again to the gold standard and was in circulation until 1948.

The Nazis in Power When the Nazis won a plurality in parliament in 1932, Hitler demanded the chancellorship. President Paul von Hindenburg (in office 1925–1934) nominated Hitler to the post in January 1933, in an effort to neutralize Nazism and keep Hitler under control. Hitler, however, wasted no time in escaping all restraints.

Following a fire in the Reichstag (German parliament) building in February 1933, which Hitler blamed on the communists, the president allowed his new chancellor the right to declare martial law for a limited time. Two months later, the Nazi Party in parliament passed the Enabling Act with the votes of the mostly Catholic Centrist Party; its leaders calculated that they could control Hitler and also reach a much-desired agreement between the Vatican and Germany parallel to the one of Mussolini. According to the constitution, Hitler now had the power to rule by emergency decree for four years.

Taking their cue from Mussolini's policies, the Nazis abolished the federalist structure of the Weimar Republic, purged the civil service of Jews, closed down all parties except the NSDAP, enacted censorship laws, and sent communists to newly constructed concentration camps. Other inmates of these camps were Roma (Gypsies), homosexuals, and religious minorities. In order to gain the support of Germany's professional army, Hitler replaced his *Sturmabteilung* (SA) militias with the *Schutzstaffel* (SS). A new secret police force (abbreviated *Gestapo*) established a pervasive surveillance system in what was now called the Third Empire (*Reich*), following that of the Holy Roman Empire and Germany after its unification in 1871.

Hitler gained enthusiastic support among the population. Aided by a recovery of the economy, within a year of coming to power he lowered unemployment to 10 percent. Economists advised him to reduce unemployment through deficit spending and build a mixed economy of state-subsidized private industrial cartels. Hitler denounced the "decadence" of modern art and pushed his planners to create monumental buildings in older neoclassical or contemporary Art Deco styles. In his appeal to their patriotic and economic aspirations, Hitler made himself a genuinely popular leader (*Führer*) among the great majority of Germans.

German rearmament became public knowledge after 1935 with the introduction of the draft and the repudiation of the peace settlement cap on troop numbers. France, realizing the danger this rearmament signified for its security, signed a treaty of mutual military assistance with the Soviet Union, which Hitler took as a pretext for the remilitarization of the Rhineland (one of the German provinces temporarily occupied by France after World War I) in 1936.

This first step of German military assertion was followed with unofficial support for General Francisco Franco (1892–1975), who rose against the legitimate republican government in the Spanish Civil War (1936–1939), and the incorporation of Austria into Nazi Germany in 1938. Now alarmed at Germany's appetite for expansion and committed by treaty to defend the Eastern European states created after the war, the heads of state of Britain and France met with Hitler and Mussolini in Munich in the summer of 1938 to hammer out an agreement on limiting German and Italian territorial claims. The British prime minister, Neville Chamberlain (in office 1937–1940), claimed that this "Munich Agreement," which allowed Germany to annex part of Czechoslovakia, was no appeasement and promised "peace in our time." Hitler went to war, however, in little more than a year.

World War II in Poland and France In 1939 Hitler decided that the German armed forces were ready to begin his quest for *Lebensraum* in Eastern Europe. Because Poland needed to be taken first, Stalin had to be convinced that it was in the best interests of the Soviet Union and Germany to share in the division of Eastern Europe. Stalin needed more time to rebuild his army after earlier purges and found the idea of a Russian-dominated Polish buffer against Germany appealing. Accordingly, the two signed a nonaggression pact on August 23, 1939, and German troops invaded Poland on September 1, triggering declarations of war by Poland's allies Britain and France two days later. World War II had begun in Europe.

Having removed the two-front problem that had plagued Germany in World War I, Hitler had to eliminate Britain and France before turning to the next phase in the east. This he did by attacking France on May 10, 1940. The German army in Poland had pioneered a new kind of warfare: *Blitzkrieg*, or "lightning war," which turned warfare from the stagnant defensive posture of World War I into a fast, highly mobile conflict. The French, bled dry of manpower in WWI, had since relied on the fixed defenses of their Maginot Line. Now, the German troops simply went around these fortifications and broke through the Ardennes Forest in southern Belgium. To the great surprise of the French and British, the German troops then turned northward, driving the Allies toward the Atlantic coast. The encircled French and British troops escaped across the English Channel to Britain as the Germans regrouped for their final thrust.

France surrendered and agreed to an armistice. Hitler divided the country into a German-occupied part, consisting of Paris and the Atlantic coast, and a smaller unoccupied territory under German control, with its capital in Vichy. The German attempt of an invasion of Britain failed when the air force, having suffered more losses than anticipated in the invasion of France, was unable to deliver the final blow. During the period of the worst air raids, the Conservative politician Winston Churchill (in office 1940–1945) replaced Neville Chamberlain as prime minister. Churchill's unbending will during the aerial Battle of Britain proved to be a turning point in rallying the Allied cause.

The Eastern Front Hitler launched an invasion of the Soviet Union on June 22, 1941, to the surprise of an unprepared Stalin. Although the Soviet forces were initially severely beaten, they did not disintegrate, thanks in part to a force of superior T-34 tanks that were four times more numerous than the Germans expected, and the offensive bogged down due to supply problems and the harsh Russian winter, for which German troops were unprepared. Neither side made much progress until the Soviets succeeded in trapping a large force of Germans in Stalingrad. The Soviet victory on February 2, 1943, became the turning point in the European war. Thereafter, it was an almost relentless and increasingly desperate retreat for the Germans, particularly after the western Allies invaded the European continent in Italy and France.

Mass Murder As Hitler's *Mein Kampf* foretold, the war in the east became an ideological war of annihilation: Either the supremacist or the communist vision of modernity would prevail. The Soviets massacred nearly 22,000 Polish officers and intellectuals in 1940 at Katyn and subsequently condemned hundreds of thousands of Eastern Europeans to death in labor camps. The German SS and army, driven by their racism against Slavs, murdered millions of civilians and soldiers alike, and German businesses worked their Slavic slave laborers to death.

The so-called **Final Solution,** the genocide of the European Jews, was the horrendous culmination of this war. After Poland and the western Soviet Union were conquered, the number of Jews under German authority increased by several millions. The Final Solution, set in motion in January 1942, entailed transporting Jews to extermination camps to be murdered. In its technological sophistication in creating a kind of assembly line of death and the calm, bureaucratic efficiency with which its operators went about their business, the Holocaust marks a milestone in twentieth-century inhumanity.

Final Solution: German supremacist-nationalist plan formulated in 1942 by Adolf Hitler and leading Nazis to annihilate Jews through factory-style mass extermination in concentration camps, resulting in the death of about 6 million Jews, or roughly two-thirds of European Jewry.

The Turn of the Tide in the West The first counteroffensives of the Allies in the west after their defeat in 1940 came in November 1942. After fighting a desperate rearguard action, British forces in Egypt and American forces landing in occupied French North Africa launched a combined offensive, driving German forces there to capitulate six months later. But it took another 2.5 years to grind down the forces of the Axis powers. Here, advantages in manpower as well as the industrial capacity of the United States proved to be the determining factors. Finally, the natural barriers of the Atlantic and Pacific Oceans and American naval power protected America against invasion, while the lack of a long-range strategic bombing force prevented Axis air attacks on North America.

Starting in 1943, the US Army Air Force and Britain's Royal Air Force began around-the-clock bombing of military and civilian targets in Germany. Despite heavy Allied losses in planes and men, by war's end there was scarcely a German city or industrial center that had not been reduced to rubble by air attack. With the landing of troops in Sicily in July 1943, on the Italian Peninsula in early September, and in Normandy in June 1944, along with the steady advance of Soviet forces in the east, the eventual unconditional German surrender on May 8, 1945 (VE, or "Victory in Europe" Day) was inevitable (see Map 28.3).

Japan's "Greater East Asia Co-Prosperity Sphere" and China's Struggle for Unity

Genocide. The specters of the Holocaust that haunt us usually involve the infamous extermination camps—Auschwitz, Treblinka, Majdanek, Sobibor—but millions of Jews and other "undesirables"—Slavs, Gypsies (Roma), and homosexuals—were shot, such as this man calmly waiting for the bullet to penetrate his brain while SS executioners look on.

The Japanese ruling class that implemented the Meiji industrialization consisted of lower-ranking samurai "oligarchs." After World War I, this generation retired, and for the first time, commoners entered politics. They formed two unstable conservative party coalitions, representing small-business and landowner interests, respectively, but were financed by big-business cartels, the *zaibatsus* (see Chapter 24). By the mid-1920s Japan's interwar liberalizing era had reached a high point. Thereafter, the military increased its power and ended the liberalizing era.

Liberalism and Military Assertion In the midst of the middle-class ferment of "Taisho Democracy," as Japan's politics during the reign of Emperor Taisho (r. 1912–1926) was known, the government not only broadened suffrage but also enacted the first of many security laws. Worried about communist influence, the Peace Preservation Law of 1925 drew a line against frequent labor strikes and general leftist agitation. Anyone violating the "national essence" (*kokutai*) in thought or action could be arrested. A branch of the secret services, the *Tokko*, made some 70,000 mostly arbitrary arrests between 1925 and 1945. The law was the turning point when Western-inspired liberalism began to swing toward militarism.

Military officers of modest rural origin were unable or unwilling to comprehend the democracy, cultural transformation, and labor strikes of the 1920s. Supremacist nationalism, especially the absolutism of the emperor and the right of junior officers to refuse to execute parliamentary laws, were decisive for actions through which the military achieved dominance over parliament in the 1930s.

MAP 28.3 World War II in Europe, 1939–1945

The Republican Revolution in China The Qing dynasty had failed to develop a sustained effort at reform in response to the Western challenge during the 1800s. Following the Boxer Rebellion in 1900, radical groups, aided by overseas Chinese, began to work for the overthrow of the Qing. The most important figure among these groups was Sun Yat-sen (1866–1925), with his Revolutionary Alliance of 1905.

On October 10, 1911, an explosion in a Wuhan barracks signaled a takeover of the base. The movement quickly spread, and by the end of the year three groups of Qing opponents—provincial warlords, scholar-gentry, and nationalists—staged uprisings that reduced the Qing to a small territory in the north. The Qing commander, Yuan Shikai (1859–1916), struck a deal with the insurgents whereby he came over to them in return for the presidency of the new republic, formed upon the abdication of the Qing in February 1912. Sun was thus elbowed aside by the revolution he had done so much to begin. With Yuan's death in 1916, the remaining warlords feuded with each other for control of the country, which remained divided.

Militaristic Expansion The early 1930s saw the end of a period of diplomacy by which Japan sought to consolidate its gains in international prestige. The growth of the power of the Chinese Nationalist Party (Guomindang, GMD) altered the fragile balance of power among the contending warlord regimes that Japan had exploited in order to expand its influence. The junior officers who chafed at the liberalization of Japan and hearkened back to samurai values increasingly found opportunity in the colonial armies of Manchuria.

The first step in this new direction was taken in 1928 when the Japanese Kwantung Army (Japan's force in Manchuria) blew up the train of the Chinese warlord Zhang Zuolin because of his leanings toward the GMD. This was followed by the Mukden Incident of 1931, in which the Japanese military engineered another railroad bombing, which was blamed on local warlords and used as the pretext for the annexation of Manchuria. Civilian politicians in Tokyo, cowed by the aggressiveness of supremacist nationalist officers, acquiesced. By way of making it a puppet state, these officers had the last Manchu Qing Chinese emperor, (Henry) Pu-Yi (r. 1908–1912 and 1932–1945), installed. (He had been deposed as a six-year-old boy in the Chinese Republican Revolution of 1911–1912.) Over the next several years, the Japanese army in Manchuria moved into northern China. In July 1937, after a clash between Chinese and Japanese forces near the Marco Polo Bridge outside Beijing, Japan launched an invasion of China.

Reemergence of Nationalism Sun Yat-sen, however, remained an inspirational figure for Chinese nationalists, even though he was exiled in the Western treaty port of Guangzhou (Canton). Meanwhile, the decision announced in May 1919 by the Allies at Versailles to allow Japan to keep the German territory in China it had seized at the beginning of the war set off mass demonstrations and a boycott of foreign businesses. This May Fourth Movement, as it came to be called, is often cited as the modern beginning of Chinese nationalism. Shortly thereafter, inspired by the Bolshevik Revolution in Russia, the Chinese Communist Party (CCP) was founded (1921).

By 1923, Sun's Nationalist Party was being reorganized and supplied with Soviet help through the Third Communist International (Comintern), in return for which the party agreed to allow members of the CCP to join with it to form what became known as the First United Front (1924–1927). Sun died in 1925, and a year later Chiang K'ai-shek (1887–1975) ascended to the leadership of the party. Chiang was a military officer trained in the Nationalist Party academy and in Moscow and deeply committed to the unification of China. The two parties mobilized an army, and the so-called Northern Expedition of 1926–1927 successfully brought about the unification of southern China as far north as the Yangzi River.

In the middle of the campaign, however, the bonds between the GMD and the CCP ruptured. The socialist wing of the GMD and the CCP had taken the important industrial centers of Wuhan and Shanghai in the Yangtze Delta from warlords, setting the stage for a showdown with the nationalist wing. Chiang had grown suspicious of Comintern and CCP goals and thus launched a preemptive purge of communists in nationalist-held areas.

Though Chiang was able to eliminate much of the communist opposition, a remnant under Mao Zedong (1893–1976) fled to the remote province of Jiangxi to regroup and create its own socialist state. Mao, an inspiring rural organizer, set about developing his ideas of Marxist revolution with the heretical idea of having peasants in the vanguard. Mao replaced the capitalists with the landlords as the class enemy and promised a much-needed land reform to the peasants. Moreover, the peasants would be the leading participants in the "People's War"—a three-stage guerrilla conflict involving the entire populace.

Believing the communist threat to be effectively eliminated, Chiang resumed his Northern Expedition in 1928, subjugating Beijing but failing to eliminate the strongest northern warlords. Nevertheless, China was now at least nominally unified, with the capital in Nanjing, the National Party Congress functioning as a parliament, and Chiang as president. Chiang made substantial progress with railroad and road construction as well as cotton and silk textile exports. Thanks to the silver standard of its money, rather than the fatally overvalued gold standard of many other countries, the financial consequences of the Depression of 1929–1933 remained relatively mild. Chiang made little headway, however, with land reform. Furthermore, the volatile relations with the remaining warlords made the government vulnerable to border violence and corruption. Hovering above all after 1931 was the Japanese annexation of Manchuria and encroachment on northern China.

The Long March and the Rape of Nanjing In the early 1930s, Chiang was aware of the need to completely eliminate his internal opponents. He resolved to eliminate the remaining threat from Mao's "Jiangxi Soviet" by mounting "bandit extermination" campaigns from 1931 to 1934. Each campaign, however, was defeated by Mao's growing People's Liberation Army. With the help of German advisors, Chiang turned to encircling the CCP areas to limit the mobility of his opponents. By the fall of 1934 he had tightened the noose around the communists and almost succeeded in destroying their army.

But Mao and about 100,000 soldiers broke out in October 1934, thanks to the inaction of a treacherous warlord. Once free, the majority of the Red Army embarked on a **Long March** of 6,000 miles, from the south through the far west and then northeast toward Beijing. Along the way, harassment by nationalist troops, warlords, and local people as well as other hardships decimated the marchers. In the fall of 1935 some 10,000 communists eventually straggled into Yan'an out of Chiang's reach.

Long March: Military retreat undertaken by the Red Army in 1934–1935 of the Communist Party of China to evade the pursuit of the Guomindang (GMD) army. The Long March solidified the power of Mao Zedong, whose leadership during the retreat gained him the support of the members of the Communist party.

The communists had seized upon Japan's aggression as a valuable propaganda tool and declared war against Japan in 1932. Chiang's obsession with eliminating his internal enemies increasingly made him subject to criticism of appeasement toward Japan. In 1936, a group of dissident nationalist generals arrested Chiang and brought him to CCP headquarters at Yan'an. After weeks of negotiations, Chiang was released as the leader of a China now brought together under a Second United Front, this time against Japan.

Seeing their prospects for gradual encroachment quickly fading, Japan seized on the so-called Marco Polo Bridge Incident in July 1937, a battle that followed an earlier Japanese border crossing, and launched an all-out assault on China. Though Chinese resistance was stiff in the opening months, the Japanese were able to use their superior mobility and airpower to flank the Chinese forces and take the capital of Nanjing (Nanking) by December 1937. Realizing the need to

Rape of Nanjing: Mass murder and mass rape committed by Japanese soldiers against the residents of Nanjing during the Second Sino-Japanese War.

defeat China as quickly as possible, the Japanese military subjected the capital to the first major atrocity of World War II: the **Rape of Nanjing.** It is estimated that between 200,000 and 300,000 people were slaughtered in deliberately gruesome ways. Rape was systematically used as a means of terror and subjugation.

The message of this brutality was that other Chinese cities could expect similar treatment if surrender was not swiftly forthcoming. However, the destruction only stiffened the will of the Chinese to resist. Continually harassed as they retreated from Nanjing, the Chinese adopted the strategy of trading space for time to regroup. In an epic mass migration, Chinese soldiers and civilians moved to the region around the remote city of Chongqing (Chungking), which became the wartime capital of China until 1945. Thereafter, both nationalists and communists used the vast interior as a base for hit-and-run tactics, effectively limiting Japan to the northeast and coastal urban centers but remaining incapable of mounting large offensives themselves.

World War II in the Pacific While Japan had used its control of Manchuria, Korea, and Taiwan in its quest for autarky in the 1930s, it portrayed its imperial bid in the Pacific as the construction of a "Greater East Asia Co-Prosperity Sphere." This expansion was considered essential because raw materials were still imported from the United States and the Dutch and British possessions in Southeast Asia. After Hitler defeated the Netherlands and France in 1940, the opportunity arrived for the Japanese to remove the United States from the Pacific. Moreover, the stalemate in China was increasingly bleeding Japan of resources, while mounting tensions with the United States over China were already resulting in economic sanctions.

Accordingly, in the summer of 1941, the Japanese government decided on extending the empire into the Dutch East Indies and Southeast Asia, even if this meant war with the United States. Under the premiership of General Tojo Hideki (in office 1941–1944), Japan attacked Pearl Harbor in Hawaii, the Philippines, and Dutch and British territories on December 7–8, 1941. Within a few months, the Japanese completed the occupation of all important Southeast Asian and Pacific territories (see Map 28.4).

However, within six months, in the naval and air battle around Midway Atoll in June 1942, American forces gained the initiative. The Japanese now exploited the populations of their new territories in extracting their raw materials with increasing urgency. Using an "island hopping" strategy of bypassing Japanese strongholds, American forces came within bombing range of the Japanese home islands by late 1944. Starting in March 1945, they subjected Japan to devastating firebomb attacks. Finally, President Harry S Truman (in office 1945–1953) had two experimental atomic bombs dropped on Hiroshima and Nagasaki (August 6 and 9, 1945). With the Soviets declaring war against Japan on August 8 and advancing into Manchuria, the Japanese were finally convinced that the war was lost. They surrendered on August 14, 1945.

Putting It All Together

The patterns of constitutionalism and industrialization were most visible in Great Britain, the United States, and France. Two further patterns complicated the evolution of nations engaging in the pursuit of modernity: ethnic nationalism and the rise of the industrial working class. All of these patterns collided in

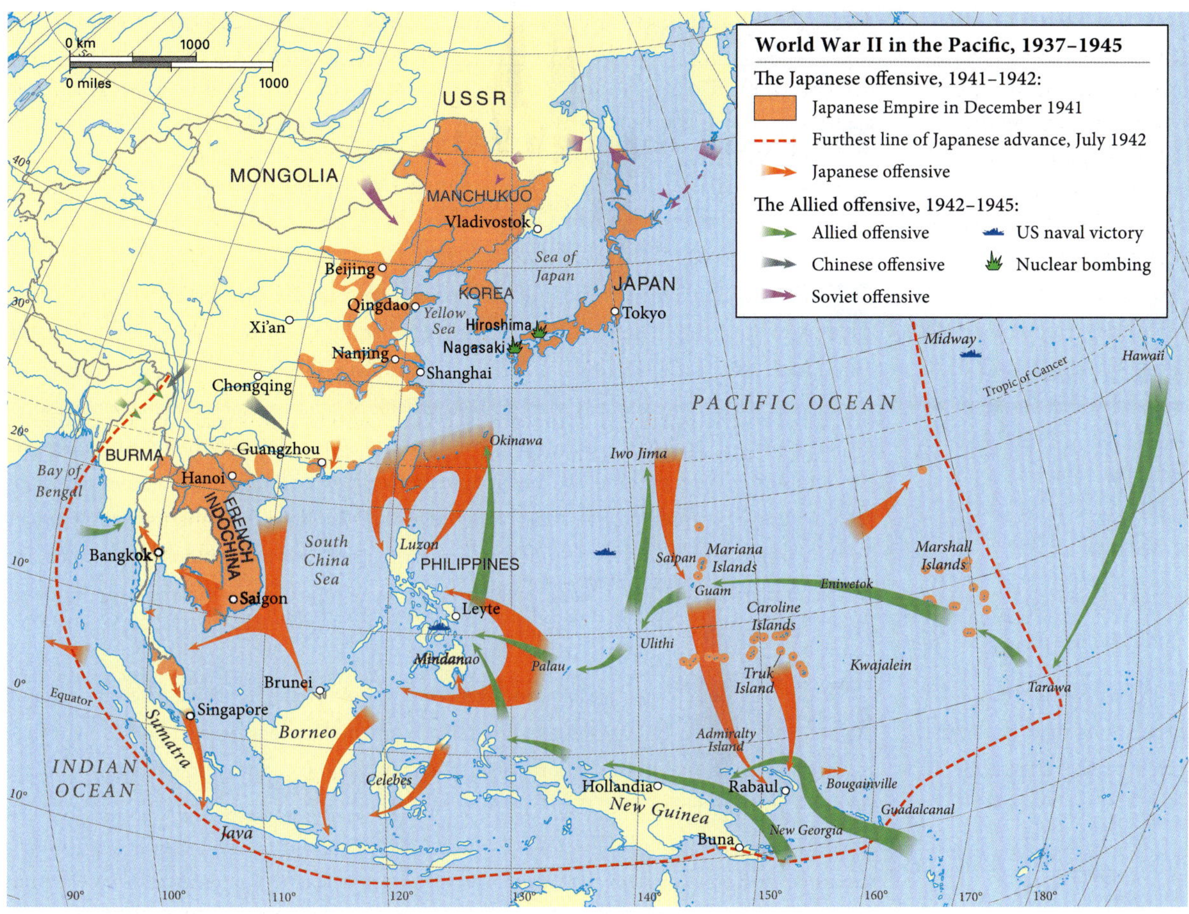

MAP 28.4 World War II in the Pacific, 1937–1945

World War I. After the war, they recombined into the three ideologies of modernity analyzed in this chapter: capitalist democracy, communism, and supremacist nationalism.

By most, only democracy and communism are considered to be genuine ideologies of modernity, in the sense of being based on relatively coherent programs. More recent historians, however, argue that supremacist nationalism was a genuine variety of modernity as well. The adherents of the three modernities bitterly denounced each other. All three considered themselves to be "progressive" or modern.

It may be difficult to understand how anyone could be an ardent ethnic nationalist, have little faith in constitutional liberties, find the conquest of a large and completely self-sufficient empire perfectly logical, and think of all this as the ideal of modernity. Yet, as we have seen so often, innovations frequently cause their opposition to take new and often unexpected forms. The "modern" notion of ethnic nationalism thus created ways of opposing other modern innovations such as constitutionalism by insisting on a purer, more mystical bond for the modern nation-state that, ironically, harkened back to a simpler, reimagined past. But Mussolini, Hitler, and the Japanese generals all aspired to the same scientific–industrial future as Roosevelt, Churchill, Stalin, Chiang K'ai-shek, and Mao Zedong.

Review and Relate

Thinking Through Patterns

Examine the ways historians approach the big questions of this chapter.

Which three patterns of modernity emerged after World War I? How and why did these patterns form?

Ethnic nationalism was difficult to accommodate in the nineteenth century, which began with the more inclusive constitutionalism of Great Britain, the United States, and France. New nations like Italy, Germany, and Japan, formed on the basis of ethnic nationalisms, were not necessarily inspired by the ideals of equality embodied in constitutional nation-states. After World War I, Germany, Italy, and Japan elevated their ethnic nationalism into supremacist nationalism and adopted imperialism, all under the banner of modernity. In Russia, communists used the turmoil of World War I to turn a constitutionally as well as industrially underdeveloped empire into a communist, one-party industrial empire. The United States, Britain, and France, each based on variations of constitutionalism, industry, and smaller or larger empires, became advocates of a capitalist democratic modernity.

What were the strengths and flaws of each of the three visions of modernity?

Capitalist democracy was a modernity that upheld free enterprise, the market, and consumerism. It suffered a major setback in the Depression and had to be reined in through tightened political controls. It also withheld freedom and equality from minorities and the colonized. Communism succeeded in industrializing an underdeveloped empire and providing the bare necessities for modern life; it did so with untold human sacrifices. Supremacist nationalism was attractive to nationalists who were not workers and therefore afraid of communism. Supremacist nationalists held democracies in disdain because they considered constitutions meaningless.

Why did supremacist nationalism disappear after World War II?

Supremacist nationalism was a modernity that failed because the conquest of new, self-sufficient empires proved to be impossible. The advocates of democratic capitalist and communist modernity—most notably the United States, Great Britain, France, and the Soviet Union—felt dangerously threatened by Germany, Italy, and Japan and came together to destroy these supremacist-nationalist countries.

Against the Grain

Consider this as a counterpoint to the main patterns examined in this chapter.

- Faced with a situation similar to that of Irena Sendler, what would you do?
- Can you think of other twentieth-century mass atrocities in which people like Irena Sendler desperately tried to save innocent lives?

Righteous among the Nations

Thousands of men and women defied the Nazi regime (1932–1945) and saved Jews from arrest, deportation, and the gas chamber. Their acts of defiance are proof that ordinary citizens in Germany and the countries conquered by Germany during

World War II did not all cower before the Gestapo, nor did they all attempt to claim helplessness or ignorance regarding what was happening around them. Although many of the saviors were martyred at the hands of Nazi authorities, they acted as they did because they considered it their human calling.

Thousands of the saviors of Jews were Poles, Dutch, French, Ukrainians, and Belgians, all under German occupation during the war. By contrast, only 563 and 525 Italians and Germans, respectively, have been recognized as helping Jews to survive. The contrast in numbers illustrates the feelings of hatred among many in the conquered territories for the Germans on one hand and the pervasiveness of the supremacist-nationalist fascist and Nazi ideologies in the populations of Italy and Germany on the other. Even if it had not been as difficult to help Jews in Nazi Germany as many Germans pretended after the war, their anti-Semitism prevented them from feeling any pangs of conscience.

Today, Israel recognizes 24,811 saviors of Jews as "Righteous among the Nations" and honors them in the Yad Vashem Holocaust memorial museum in Jerusalem. One of them, Irena Sendler (1910–2008), was a health worker, the daughter of a Polish physician who treated Jewish patients. When the Germans invaded she was an administrator for the Warsaw Social Welfare Department. During the time of the Warsaw Ghetto (1940–1943), she smuggled some 2,500 Jewish children out of the country, hiding them under loads of goods, in potato sacks or even in coffins. She provided them with false identities and had them taken to hiding places with Christian families. When the Nazis finally discovered her activities in 1943, they arrested and tortured her. But after members of the Polish resistance succeeded in bribing her would-be executioners, Sandler escaped and went into hiding until the end of the war. Yad Vashem honored Irena Sendler in 1965 as a righteous person and planted a tree in her name at the entrance of the Avenue of the Righteous among Nations.

Key Terms

Autarky 685
Corporate state 693
Eugenics 683
Final Solution 697
Great Depression 684
League of Nations 681
Long March 701
Mandates 687
Rape of Nanjing 702
Swaraj 689
Total war 679
Zionism 688

Learn more with this chapter's digital tools, including the Oxford Insight Study Guide, at http://www.oup.com/he/vonsivers4e. Please see the Further Resources section at the back of the book for additional readings and suggested websites.

Sources for Chapter 28

SOURCE 28.1 ANZAC troops at Gallipoli

August 1915

In the aftermath of the Great War, the Allied nations compiled both regimental and general histories of the conflict. In these narratives, the experiences of the soldiers and their commanders are filtered through the ultimate outcomes—and attendant sufferings—inflicted by the war. The errors of judgment and planning made by commanders are preserved in these records, and are particularly significant to our understanding today of battles whose brutality and massive death tolls are still shocking. The contribution of ANZAC (the acronym for Australian and New Zealand Army Corps) troops to the campaigns at Gallipoli and the Dardanelles (April 1915–January 1916) against the Ottoman Turks is marked in the ANZAC countries as a solemn day of remembrance. In this excerpt from a multivolume narrative of the campaigns compiled by C. E. W. Bean, the casualty figures, and Bean's reactions to the deployment of soldiers and the possible waste of war, are striking.

Perceiving the difficulty of advancing under such an enfilade, Major Powles directed the next platoons to swing to the left and advance northwards or north-eastwards in order to subdue the fire from that direction. This attempt was quickly shattered. A part of the third company, under Major Lane, advancing towards Goodsell's left, succeeded in reaching the same trench and pushed along it towards the east. These later lines, however, only reached the trench in fragments, and the situation of the left flank was desperate. From a point of vantage in a cross-trench the Turks were flinging bombs with impunity among the Australians. An unauthorised order to retire had been given to some of Lane's men, and in withdrawing over the open they had lost heavily. At 7 o'clock the battalion was urged by a message from Russell to push on and seize the summit, but such an attempt would have been hopeless. Goodsell's left gradually withdrew southward along the trench. With such parts of the later lines as reached him he had extended farther to his right along the same sap and, finding there some of the Hampshire, discovered that he was actually in the trench which had

Source: C. E. W. Bean, *The Story of ANZAC from 4 May, 1915, to the Evacuation of the Gallipoli Peninsula*, 11th ed. (Sydney: Angus & Robertson, 1941), 743–745, 761–762.

been captured by the New Zealanders, and which encircled the lower slope of the hill. By 10 o'clock the remnant of Goodsell's men had retired along it until they reached the flank of the New Zealanders, where they remained, stubbornly holding fifty yards of the trench.

The attempt to round off the capture of Hill 60 by setting a raw battalion, without reconnaissance, to rush the main part of a position on which the experienced troops of Anzac had only succeeded in obtaining a slight foothold, ended in failure. Its initiation was due to the fact that Russell and his brigade-major, Powles, both careful and capable officers, lacked the realisation—which came to many commanders only after sharp experience—that the attack upon such a position required minute preparation, and that the unskillfulness of raw troops, however brave, was likely to involve them in heavy losses for the sake of results too small to justify the expense. Within a few hours the 18th Battalion, which appears to have marched out 750 strong, had lost 11 officers and 372 men, of whom half had been killed. The action had been a severe one for all the troops engaged, the losses of the comparatively small force which attacked from Anzac amounting to over 1,300. The flank had been brought up to Susak Kuyu, and a lodgment had been obtained in the enemy's strongly entrenched position at Hill 60. Slight though it was, this gain was the only one achieved on the whole battle-front. In the Suvla area the position at first secured by the 29th Division on the crest of Scimitar Hill was untenable, a brave advance by the reserve—the 2nd Mounted Division—availing nothing. On the plain the 11th Division was unable to maintain its unconnected line in the first Turkish trench. A barricade built across the Asmak creek-bed was blown down by the enemy, and the British flank was forced back to Kazlar Chair, from which it had started, 1,000 yards in rear of the Gurkha post at Susak Kuyu, the Turks still intervening near the "poplars." To fill this dangerous space, the 19th Battalion of the new Australian brigade was marched to the left and stationed near the gap. Cox reported that he believed the new line could be held, although the position on Hill 60 "cannot be considered satisfactory."

If the Battle of Sari Bair was the climax of the Gallipoli campaign, that of Scimitar Hill was its anti-climax. With it the great offensive ended. In the words of Kitchener's message received by Hamilton on July 11th: ". . . When the surprise ceases to be operative, in so far that the advance is checked and the enemy begin to collect from all sides to oppose the attackers, then perseverance becomes merely a useless waste of life." The attempt to prolong the offensive by driving through the flank of the enemy's now established trench-line had utterly failed; and Hamilton had not the troops, nor had all the troops the morale, necessary for a fresh attack. Birdwood, however, in agreement with his subordinate commanders, desired to strengthen his flank by capturing the summit of Hill 60, and he obtained leave to renew this effort on August 27th.

. . .

Thus ended the action at Hill 60. Birdwood believed that the actual knoll had been captured, and so reported to Hamilton, who wrote: "Knoll 60, now ours throughout, commands the Biyuk Anafarta valley with view and fire—a big tactical scoop." As a matter of fact half the summit—or possibly rather more—was still in possession of the Turks. The fighting of August 27th,

28th, and 29th had, however, given the troops on the left of Anzac a position astride the spur from which a fairly satisfactory view could be had over the plain to the "W" Hills. The cost was over 1,100 casualties. The burden of the work had been sustained by war-worn troops. The magnificent brigade of New Zealand Mounted Rifles, which was responsible for the main advances, had been worked until it was almost entirely consumed, its four regiments at the end numbering only 365 all told. The 4th Australian Infantry Brigade which, through defective co-ordination with the artillery, had been twice thrown against a difficult objective without a chance of success, was reduced to 968. General Russell and his brigade-major, Powles, had worked untiringly, the latter personally guiding almost every attacking party to its starting point in the dangerous maze of trenches. It was not their fault that at this stage of the war both staff and commanders were only learning the science of trench-warfare. Had the experience and the instruments of later years been available, the action at Hill 60 would doubtless have been fought differently.

Working with Sources

1. **What factors, in Bean's estimation, led to the very high casualty figures among the Allied troops in this campaign?**
2. **Does Bean consider the loss of these troops a "useless waste of life"? Were the leaders of the effort incompetent?**

SOURCE 28.2

Vera Brittain, *Testament of Youth*

1933

Born in 1893 into an upper-class family at a time when society expected neither intellectual nor professional achievement from such women, Vera Brittain obtained a scholarship to Somerville College at Oxford University in 1914. When the war began in August 1914, her brother, Edward, and his best friend, Roland Leighton, enlisted. Brittain left college the following year to study nursing, and she joined a VAD (Voluntary Aid Detachment) unit. Having become engaged to Leighton while he was home on leave in August 1915, Brittain learned in December of that year that he had been killed in action on the Western Front. Continuing her nursing work, Brittain experienced the loss of numerous other friends and relatives, including her brother, over the course of the war. After the war, she returned to Oxford and developed an important literary career in her own right, publishing her beautifully written and compelling wartime memoir *Testament of Youth* in 1933. Throughout the 1930s, she advocated international peace and women's rights, insisting that the shattering experiences of her youth should not be reinflicted on contemporary young people.

Source: Vera Brittain, *Testament of Youth* (New York: Seaview, 1980), 239–241.

Perhaps . . .
To R. A. L.

Perhaps some day the sun will shine again,
And I shall see that still the skies are blue,
And feel once more I do not live in vain,
Although bereft of You.

Perhaps the golden meadows at my feet
Will make the sunny hours of spring seem gay,
And I shall find the white May-blossoms sweet,
Though You have passed away.

Perhaps the summer woods will shimmer bright,
And crimson roses once again be fair,
And autumn harvest fields a rich delight,
Although You are not there.

But though kind Time may many joys renew,
There is one greatest joy I shall not know
Again, because my heart for loss of You
Was broken, long ago.
V. B. 1916.

—From *Verses of a V.A.D.*

Whenever I think of the weeks that followed the news of Roland's death, a series of pictures, disconnected but crystal clear, unroll themselves like a kaleidoscope through my mind.

A solitary cup of coffee stands before me on a hotel breakfast-table; I try to drink it, but fail ignominiously.

Outside, in front of the promenade, dismal grey waves tumble angrily over one another on the windy Brighton shore, and, like a slaughtered animal that still twists after life has been extinguished, I go on mechanically worrying because his channel-crossing must have been so rough.

In an omnibus, going to Keymer, I look fixedly at the sky; suddenly the pale light of a watery sun streams out between the dark, swollen clouds, and I think for one crazy moment that I have seen the heavens opened. . . .

At Keymer a fierce gale is blowing and I am out alone on the brown winter ploughlands, where I have been driven by a desperate desire to escape from the others. Shivering violently, and convinced that I am going to be sick, I take refuge behind a wet bank of grass from the icy sea-wind that rushes, screaming, across the sodden fields.

It is late afternoon; at the organ of the small village church, Edward is improvising a haunting memorial hymn for Roland, and the words: "God walked in the garden in the cool of the evening," flash irrelevantly into my mind.

I am back on night-duty at Camberwell after my leave; in the chapel, as the evening voluntary is played, I stare with swimming eyes at the lettered wall, and remember reading the words: "I am the Resurrection and the Life," at the early morning communion service before going to Brighton.

I am buying some small accessories for my uniform in a big Victoria Street store, when I stop, petrified, before a vase of the tall pink roses that Roland gave me on the way to *David Copperfield*; in the warm room their melting sweetness brings back the memory of that New Year's Eve, and suddenly, to the perturbation of the shop-assistants, I burst into uncontrollable tears, and find myself, helpless and humiliated, unable to stop crying in the tram all the way back to the hospital.

It is Sunday, and I am out for a solitary walk through the dreary streets of Camberwell before going to bed after the night's work. In front of me on the frozen pavement a long red worm wriggles slimily. I remember that, after our death, worms destroy this body—however lovely, however beloved—and I run from the obscene thing in horror.

It is Wednesday, and I am walking up the Brixton Road on a mild, fresh morning of early spring. Half-consciously I am repeating a line from Rupert Brooke:

"The deep night, and birds singing, and clouds flying. . ."

For a moment I have become conscious of the old joy in rainwashed skies and scuttling, fleecy clouds, when suddenly I remember—Roland is dead and I am not keeping faith with him; it is mean and cruel, even for a second, to feel glad to be alive.

Working with Sources

1. **How did Brittain cope with the grief of losing her fiancé?**
2. **Did the Great War impose unique burdens on women? In what respects?**

SOURCE 28.3

Benito Mussolini and Giovanni Gentile, "Foundations and Doctrine of Fascism"

1932

Through a series of small demonstrations and gatherings in 1919, Benito Mussolini (1883–1945) created, at least in his own estimation, a completely new political ideology. He named this philosophy for a symbol used in the ancient Roman Empire and more recently by radical Sicilian workers in the 1890s: the fasces, which was a bundle of rods together with an ax and carried by lictors as a representation of power. Mussolini was installed as Italy's leader, or "Duce," in October 1922. He published an explanation of what he had achieved as well as a statement of his political beliefs in the *Enciclopedia Italiana* in June 1932. Reflecting on the decade of rule following his seizure of "totalitarian" power (the word itself was coined by this regime, and specifically with the collaboration of Mussolini's court philosopher, Giovanni Gentile), Mussolini justified the violence inflicted by his regime and emphasized its fundamentally "moral" basis.

Anti-individualistic, the fascist conception of life stresses the importance of the state. It affirms the value of the individual only insofar as his interests coincide with those of the state, which stands for the conscience and the universal will of man in history. It opposes classical liberalism, which arose as a revolt against absolutism and exhausted its historical function when the state became the expression of the conscience and will of the people. Liberalism denied the state in the name of the individual; fascism reasserts the state as the true reality of the individual. And if liberty is to be the attribute of living men and not of the sort of abstract dummies invented by individualistic liberalism, then fascism stands for liberty. Fascism stands for the only liberty worth possessing: the liberty of the state and of the individual within the state. The fascist conception of the state is all-embracing. Outside of it no human or spiritual values can exist, much less have value. Thus understood, fascism is totalitarian, and the fascist state—in which all values are synthesized and united—interprets, develops, and heightens the life of the people.

No individuals outside the state; no groups (political parties, associations, trade unions, social classes) outside the state. This is why fascism is opposed to socialism, which sees in history nothing but class struggle and neglects the possibility of achieving unity within the state (which effects the fusion of classes into a single economic and moral reality). This is also why fascism is opposed to trade unionism as a class weapon. But when brought within the orbit of the state, fascism recognizes the real needs that gave rise to socialism and trade unionism, giving them due weight in the corporative system in which divergent interests are harmonized within the unity that is the state.

Source: Jeffrey T. Schnapp, ed., *A Primer of Italian Fascism*, trans. Jeffrey T. Schnapp, Olivia E. Sears, and Maria G. Stampino (Lincoln: University of Nebraska Press, 2000), 48–50.

Grouped according to their interests, individuals make up classes. They make up trade unions when organized according to their economic activities. But, first and foremost, they make up the state, which is no mere matter of numbers, or simply the sum of the individuals forming the majority. Accordingly, fascism is opposed to that form of democracy that equates a nation with the majority, reducing it to the lowest common denominator. But fascism represents the purest form of democracy if the nation is considered—as it should be—from the standpoint of quality rather than quantity. This means considering the nation as an idea, the mightiest because the most ethical, the most coherent, the truest; an idea actualizing itself in a people as the conscience and will of the few, if not of One; an idea tending to actualize itself in the conscience and the will of the mass, of the collective ethnically molded by natural and historical conditions into a single nation that moves with a single conscience and will along a uniform line of development and spiritual formation. Not a race or a geographically delimited region but a people, perpetuating itself in history, a multitude unified by an idea and imbued with the will to live, with the will to power, with a self-consciousness and a personality.

To the degree that it is embodied in a state, this higher personality becomes a nation. It is not the nation that generates the state (an antiquated naturalistic concept that afforded the basis for nineteenth-century propaganda in favor of national governments); rather, it is the state that creates the nation, granting volition and therefore real existence to a people that has become aware of its moral unity.

. . .

A higher, more powerful expression of personality, the fascist state embodies a spiritual force encompassing all manifestations of the moral and intellectual life of man. Its functions cannot be limited to those of maintaining order and keeping the peace, as liberal doctrine would have it. The fascist state is no mere mechanical device for delimiting the sphere within which individuals may exercise their supposed rights. It represents an inwardly accepted standard and rule of conduct. A discipline of the whole person, it permeates the will no less than the intellect. It is the very principle, the soul of souls [*anima dell'anima*], that inspires every man who is a member of a civilized society, penetrating deep into his personality and dwelling within the heart of the man of action and the thinker, the artist, and the man of science.

Fascism, in short, is not only a law giver and a founder of institutions but also an educator and a promoter of spiritual life. It aims to refashion not only the forms of life but also their content: man, his character, his faith. To this end it champions discipline and authority; authority that infuses the soul and rules with undisputed sway. Accordingly, its chosen emblem is the lictor's fasces: symbol of unity, strength, and justice.

▸ Working with Sources

1. **How does Mussolini contrast fascism with "liberalism"? Is his contrast merely empty rhetoric?**
2. **Why does Mussolini pay so much attention to the "spiritual" elements that animate fascism? Why does he avoid attributing historical development to materialist causes?**

SOURCE 28.4 Adolf Hitler, *Mein Kampf*

1925

As a result of the failure of his Beer Hall Putsch in Munich in November 1923, Adolf Hitler (1889–1945) was sent to a minimum security prison at Landsberg. However, he was paroled, four years before the completion of his sentence, in December 1924. Having met with the respect of his judges during his trial in February 1924 and with the approval of the Bavarian Supreme Court, although against the advice of state prosecutors, he had his sentence—after his conviction for a treasonable attempt to take over the state—commuted. Nevertheless, there were some restrictions, both in Bavaria and elsewhere in Germany, on Hitler's speaking and freedom of movement. In spite of these restrictions, he emerged from prison with the manuscript of a new political statement of his life and philosophy, a document he titled *Mein Kampf* (*My Struggle*). As recently discovered documents reveal, Hitler hoped to use the proceeds from the sale of this book for a new car as well as to fund his political movement. The party growing out of this movement would be labeled the National Socialist German Workers' Party, and he would be installed as its unquestioned *Führer* (leader) by 1925. The following excerpt from *Mein Kampf* reveals what he had learned about rhetoric and political action in his nascent career.

I have already stated in the first volume that all great, world-shaking events have been brought about, not by written matter, but by the spoken word. This led to a lengthy discussion in a part of the press, where, of course, such an assertion was sharply attacked, particularly by our bourgeois wiseacres. But the very reason why this occurred confutes the doubters. For the bourgeois intelligentsia protest against such a view only because they themselves obviously lack the power and ability to influence the masses by the spoken word, since they have thrown themselves more and more into purely literary activity and renounced the real agitational activity of the spoken word. Such habits necessarily lead in time to what distinguishes our bourgeoisie today; that is, to the loss of the psychological instinct for *mass effect and mass influence.*

While the speaker gets a continuous correction of his speech from the crowd he is addressing, since he can always see in the faces of his listeners to what extent they can follow his arguments with understanding and whether the impression and the effect of his words lead to the desired goal—the writer does not know his readers at all. Therefore, to begin with, he will not aim at a definite mass before his eyes, but will keep his arguments entirely general. By this to a certain degree he loses psychological subtlety and in consequence suppleness. And so, by and large, a brilliant speaker will be able

---

Source: Adolf Hitler, *Mein Kampf*, trans. Ralph Mannheim (Boston: Houghton Mifflin, 1998), 469–471.

to write better than a brilliant writer can speak, unless he continuously practices this art. On top of this there is the fact that the mass of people as such is lazy; that they remain inertly in the spirit of their old habits and, left to themselves, will take up a piece of written matter only reluctantly if it is not in agreement with what they themselves believe and does not bring them what they had hoped for. Therefore, an article with a definite tendency is for the most part read only by people who can already be reckoned to this tendency. At most a leaflet or a poster can, by its brevity, count on getting a moment's attention from someone who thinks differently. The picture in all its forms up to the film has greater possibilities. Here a man needs to use his brains even less; it suffices to look, or at most to read extremely brief texts, and thus many will more readily accept a *pictorial presentation* than *read* an *article* of any *length*. The picture brings them in a much briefer time, I might almost say at one stroke, the enlightenment which they obtain from written matter only after arduous reading.

The essential point, however, is that a piece of literature never knows into what hands it will fall, and yet must retain its definite form. In general the effect will be the greater, the more this form corresponds to the intellectual level and nature of those very people who will be its readers. A book that is destined for the broad masses must, therefore, attempt from the very beginning to have an effect, both in style and elevation, different from a work intended for higher intellectual classes.

Only by this kind of adaptability does written matter approach the spoken word. To my mind, the speaker can treat the same theme as the book; he will, if he is a brilliant popular orator, not be likely to repeat the same reproach and the same substance twice in the same form. He will always let himself be borne by the great masses in such a way that instinctively the very words come to his lips that he needs to speak to the hearts of his audience. And if he errs, even in the slightest, he has the living correction before him. As I have said, he can read from the facial expression of his audience whether, firstly, they *understand* what he is saying, whether, secondly, they can *follow the speech as a whole*, and to what extent, thirdly, he has *convinced* them of the *soundness* of what he has said. If—firstly—he sees that they do not understand him, he will become so primitive and clear in his explanations that even the last member of his audience has to understand him; if he feels—secondly—that they cannot follow him, he will construct his ideas so cautiously and slowly that even the weakest member of the audience is not left behind, and he will—thirdly—if he suspects that they do not seem convinced of the soundness of his argument, repeat it over and over in constantly new examples. He himself will utter their objections, which he senses though unspoken, and go on confuting them and exploding them, until at length even the last group of an opposition, by its very bearing and facial expression, enables him to recognize its capitulation to his arguments.

Here again it is not seldom a question of overcoming prejudices which are not based on reason, but, for the most part unconsciously, are supported only by sentiment. To overcome this barrier of instinctive aversion, of emotional hatred, of prejudiced rejection, is a thousand times harder than to correct a faulty or erroneous scientific opinion. False concepts and poor knowledge can be eliminated by instruction, the resistance of the emotions never. Here only an appeal to these mysterious powers themselves can be effective; and the writer can hardly ever accomplish this, but almost exclusively the orator.

▸ Working with Sources

1. **What advantages does the orator have over the writer, in Hitler's assessment? Is he convincing on this point?**
2. **How does a skillful speaker manipulate an audience? Does the substance of the speech matter at all, according to Hitler's description of the process of public speaking?**

SOURCE 28.5

Franklin D. Roosevelt, undelivered address planned for Jefferson Day

April 13, 1945

During his first inaugural address as the president of the United States in March 1933, Franklin D. Roosevelt had warned his fellow Americans, "The only thing we have to fear is fear itself." Through a series of radio broadcasts called "fireside chats," the president continued to reassure the American public during the darkest days of the Depression. He would go on, in January 1941, to enumerate the "four freedoms" to which every American, and perhaps every person around the globe, was entitled. These were freedom of speech, freedom of worship, freedom from want, and, perhaps most important, freedom from fear.

Suffering from debilitating illness in the final years of the war, Roosevelt persisted in envisioning a world in which those four freedoms could be guaranteed—and in which the unprecedented and horrific suffering of World War II could be transformed into a new period of human development. As Thomas Paine had argued about the American Revolution, there was now a chance "to begin the world over again." Roosevelt prepared an oration on the subject to be delivered on the occasion of Thomas Jefferson's birthday. The war was drawing to its close in Europe, and would end several months later in Asia—but Roosevelt did not live to see the achievement of peace.

Source: Gerhard Peters and John T. Woolley, the American Presidency Project, http://www.presidency.ucsb.edu/ws/?pid=16602

Although he died on April 12, 1945, the day before he was to deliver this address, the prepared speech demonstrates the tenor of Roosevelt's thought at this point in his life.

Today this Nation which Jefferson helped so greatly to build is playing a tremendous part in the battle for the rights of man all over the world.

Today we are part of the vast Allied force—a force composed of flesh and blood and steel and spirit—which is today destroying the makers of war, the breeders of hatred, in Europe and in Asia.

In Jefferson's time our Navy consisted of only a handful of frigates headed by the gallant U.S.S. Constitution—Old Ironsides—but that tiny Navy taught Nations across the Atlantic that piracy in the Mediterranean—acts of aggression against peaceful commerce and the enslavement of their crews—was one of those things which, among neighbors, simply was not done.

Today we have learned in the agony of war that great power involves great responsibility. Today we can no more escape the consequences of German and Japanese aggression than could we avoid the consequences of attacks by the Barbary Corsairs a century and a half before.

We, as Americans, do not choose to deny our responsibility.

Nor do we intend to abandon our determination that, within the lives of our children and our children's children, there will not be a third world war.

We seek peace—enduring peace. More than an end to war, we want an end to the beginnings of all wars—yes, an end to this brutal, inhuman, and thoroughly impractical method of settling the differences between governments.

The once powerful, malignant Nazi state is crumbling. The Japanese war lords are receiving, in their own homeland, the retribution for which they asked when they attacked Pearl Harbor.

But the mere conquest of our enemies is not enough.

We must go on to do all in our power to conquer the doubts and the fears, the ignorance and the greed, which made this horror possible.

Thomas Jefferson, himself a distinguished scientist, once spoke of "the brotherly spirit of Science, which unites into one family all its votaries of whatever grade, and however widely dispersed throughout the different quarters of the globe."

Today, science has brought all the different quarters of the globe so close together that it is impossible to isolate them one from another.

Today we are faced with the preeminent fact that, if civilization is to survive, we must cultivate the science of human relationships—the ability of all peoples, of all kinds, to live together and work together, in the same world, at peace.

Let me assure you that my hand is the steadier for the work that is to be done, that I move more firmly into the task, knowing that you—millions and millions of you—are joined with me in the resolve to make this work endure.

The work, my friends, is peace. More than an end of this war—an end to the beginnings of all wars. Yes, an end, forever, to this impractical, unrealistic settlement of the differences between governments by the mass killing of peoples.

Today, as we move against the terrible scourge of war—as we go forward toward the greatest contribution that any generation of human beings can make in this world—the contribution of lasting peace, I ask you to keep up your faith. I measure the sound, solid achievement that can be made at this time by the straight edge of your own confidence and your resolve. And to you, and to all Americans who dedicate themselves with us to the making of an abiding peace, I say:

The only limit to our realization of tomorrow will be our doubts of today. Let us move forward with strong and active faith.

Working with Sources

1. **What did Roosevelt consider the root and ultimate causes of war?**
2. **How, in his belief, would a lasting peace be achieved and a "third world war" avoided?**

SOURCE 28.6

Hiroshima Diary

Hiroshima Diary, written by Dr. Michihiko Hachiya (1903–1980), Director of the Hiroshima Community Hospital, presents an eyewitness and emotional account of the gruesome horrors and chaos caused by the dropping of an atomic bomb, equal to 20,000 tons of TNT, on the city on August 6, 1945. Dr. Hachiya lived approximately one mile from the center of the massive explosion, which obliterated over 50 percent of the city. Far from a homiletic rant expressing rage and hatred for America, Dr. Hachiya presents a poignant and emotional account of how he and others, horribly injured, struggled for their lives.

6 August 1945

The hour was early; the morning still, warm, and beautiful. Shimmering leaves, reflecting sunlight from a cloudless sky, made a pleasant contrast with shadows in my garden as I gazed absently through wide-flung doors opening to the south.

Clad in drawers and undershirt, I was sprawled on the living room floor exhausted because I had just spent a sleepless night on duty as an air warden in my hospital.

Suddenly, a strong flash of light startled me—and then another. So well does one recall little things that I remember vividly how a stone lantern in the garden became brilliantly lit and I debated whether this light was caused by a magnesium flare or sparks from a passing trolley.

Garden shadows disappeared. The view where a moment before all had been so bright and sunny was now dark and hazy. Through swirling dust I

Source: Michihiko Hachiya, *Hiroshima Diary: The Journal of a Japanese Physician, August 6–September 30 1945*, trans. and ed. Warner Wells (Chapel Hill: University of North Carolina Press, 1995).

could barely discern a wooden column that had supported one corner of my house. It was leaning crazily and the roof sagged dangerously.

Moving instinctively, I tried to escape, but rubble and fallen timbers barred the way. By picking my way cautiously I managed to reach the *roka* and stepped down into my garden. A profound weakness overcame me, so I stopped to regain my strength. To my surprise I discovered that I was completely naked. How odd! Where were my drawers and undershirt?

What had happened?

All over the right side of my body I was cut and bleeding. A large splinter was protruding from a mangled wound in my thigh, and something warm trickled into my mouth. My cheek was torn, I discovered as I felt it gingerly, with the lower lip laid wide open. Embedded in my neck was a sizable fragment of glass which I matter-of-factly dislodged, and with the detachment of one stunned and shocked I studied it and my blood-stained hand.

Where was my wife?

Suddenly thoroughly alarmed, I began to yell for her: "Yaekosan! Yaekosan! Where are you?"

Blood began to spurt. Had my carotid artery been cut? Would I bleed to death? Frightened and irrational, I called out again: "It's a five-hundred-ton bomb! Yaeko-san, where are you? A five-hundred-ton bomb has fallen!"

Yaeko-san, pale and frightened, her clothes torn and bloodstained, emerged from the ruins of our house holding her elbow. Seeing her, I was reassured. My own panic assuaged, I tried to reassure her.

"We'll be all right," I exclaimed. "Only let's get out of here as fast as we can."

She nodded, and I motioned for her to follow me.

The shortest path to the street lay through the house next door so through the house we went—running, stumbling, falling, and then running again until in headlong flight we tripped over something and fell sprawling into the street. Getting to my feet, I discovered that I had tripped over a man's head.

"Excuse me! Excuse me, please!" I cried hysterically.

There was no answer. The man was dead. The head had belonged to a young officer whose body was crushed beneath a massive gate.

We stood in the street, uncertain and afraid, until a house across from us began to sway and then with a rending motion fell almost at our feet. Our own house began to sway, and in a minute it, too, collapsed in a cloud of dust. Other buildings caved in or toppled. Fires sprang up and whipped by a vicious wind began to spread.

It finally dawned on us that we could not stay there in the street so we turned our steps towards the hospital* Our home was gone; we were wounded and needed treatment; and after all, it was my duty to be with my staff. This latter was an irrational thought—what good could I be to anyone, hurt as I was.

We started out, but after twenty or thirty steps I had to stop. My breath became short, my heart pounded, and my legs gave way under me. An overpowering thirst seized me and I begged Yaekosan to find me some water. But there was no water to be found. After a little my strength somewhat returned and we were able to go on.

I was still naked, and although I did not feel the least bit of shame, I was disturbed to realize that modesty had deserted me. On rounding a corner we came upon a soldier standing idly in the street. He had a towel draped across his shoulder, and I asked if he would give it to me to cover my nakedness. The soldier surrendered the towel quite willingly but said not a word. A little later I lost the towel, and Yaeko-san took off her apron and tied it around my loins.

Our progress towards the hospital was interminably slow, until finally, my legs, stiff from drying blood, refused to carry me farther. The strength, even the will, to go on deserted me, so I told my wife, who was almost as badly hurt as I, to go on alone. This she objected to, but there was no choice. She had to go ahead and try to find someone to come back for me.

Yaeko-san looked into my face for a moment, and then, without saying a word, turned away and began running towards the hospital. Once, she looked back and waved and in a moment she was swallowed up in the gloom. It was quite dark now, and with my wife gone, a feeling of dreadful loneliness overcame me.

I must have gone out of my head lying there in the road because the next thing I recall was discovering that the clot on my thigh had been dislodged and blood was again spurting from the wound. I pressed my hand to the bleeding area and after a while the bleeding stopped and I felt better.

Could I go on?

I tried. It was all a nightmare—my wounds, the darkness, the road ahead. My movements were ever so slow; only my mind was running at top speed.

In time I came to an open space where the houses had been removed to make a fire lane. Through the dim light I could make out ahead of me the hazy outlines of the Communications Bureau's big concrete building, and beyond it the hospital. My spirits rose because I knew that now someone would find me; and if I should die, at least my body would be found.

I paused to rest. Gradually things around me came into focus. There were the shadowy forms of people, some of whom looked like walking ghosts. Others moved as though in pain, like scarecrows, their arms held out from their bodies with forearms and hands dangling. These people puzzled me until I suddenly realized that they had been burned and were holding their arms out to prevent the painful friction of raw surfaces rubbing together. A naked woman carrying a naked baby came into view. I averted my gaze. Perhaps they had been in the bath. But then I saw a naked man, and it occurred to me that, like myself, some strange thing had deprived them of their clothes. An old woman lay near me with an expression of suffering on her face; but she made no sound. Indeed, one thing was common to everyone I saw—complete silence.

▸ Working with Sources

1. **What were Dr. Hachiya's first reactions following the explosion of the atomic bomb?**
2. **How did he and his accomplices manage to survive during the first hours after the blast?**

World Period Six

From Three Modernities to One

Modern scientific–industrial society underwent dramatic transformations after World War I (1914–1918). Three competing models for modernity—capitalist democracy, communism, and supremacist nationalism—shrank to one in the course of the twentieth century. German and Japanese supremacist nationalism collapsed in 1945 as a result of their overextended military aggression. Soviet and Eastern European communism collapsed in 1989–1991 due to a top-heavy central command economy. Western capitalist democracy survived but did so only after enduring decolonization and regulating its economy. After 1991, it expanded its global dominance, buttressed by the computer revolution, but questions have arisen whether its model of modernity is sustainable. Under current conditions, the natural environment will not be able to support the exploitative framework of capitalist democracy much longer. The grave threat posed by COVID-19 has further undermined its credibility.

Chapter 29

Reconstruction, Cold War, and Decolonization

1945–1962

CHAPTER TWENTY-NINE PATTERNS

Origins, Interactions, Adaptations The defeat of Japan and Germany in World War II ended the supremacist-nationalist strand of modernity. In the ensuing competition between the two remaining models for modernity—capitalist democracy and communism—the United States assumed the leading role. It spearheaded the creation of the United Nations, abandoned its prewar isolationism, and assumed hegemony over the "Free World." In a parallel move, the Soviet Union, initiated a "Cold War" to export the communist model of modernity. It became the hegemon of the "East Bloc" in central and eastern Europe. The Cold War between the two superpowers dominated the entire period 1945–1962.

Uniqueness and similarities A "Third World" of nations emerged in two waves after World War II when it became apparent that Great Britain and France were financially too exhausted to hold on to their colonies. A special case was China, liberated from Japan and under communist rule. All newly independent nations were similar to each other in their aspiration to industrial modernity, but since they lacked financial resources, they joined either the capitalist or the communist bloc for loans or grants. A number of more ambitious new nations forged a "nonaligned" path. Most new nations were multiethnic societies and struggled to establish democratic institutions. Meanwhile, a majority of western European countries formed the European Economic Union and foreswore any future return to excessive nationalism.

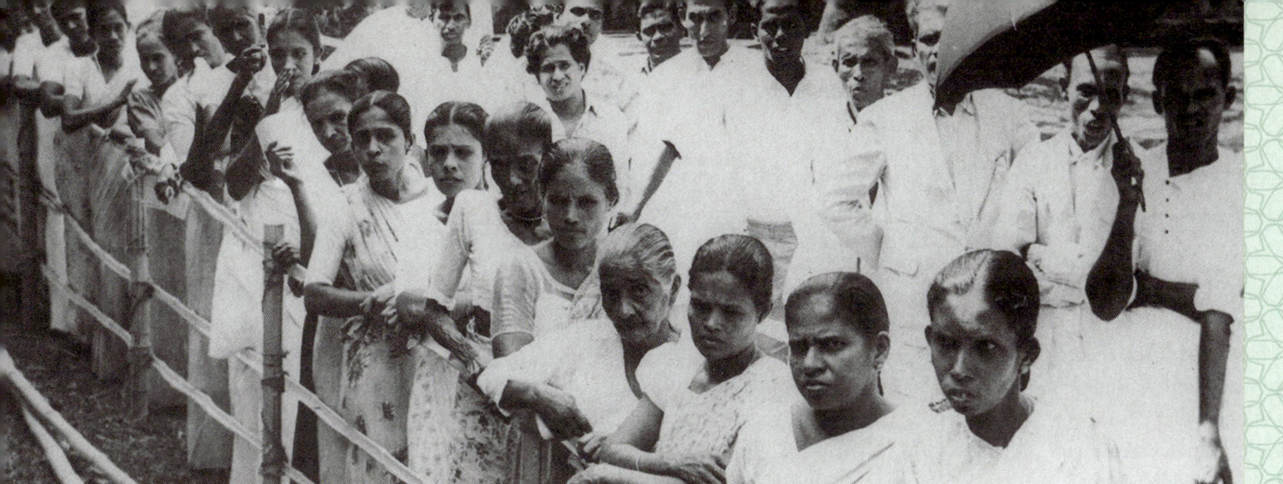

The 1960 election of the world's first female prime minister, Sirimavo Bandaranaike (1916–2000), of what was then called Ceylon (renamed Sri Lanka in 1972), seemed symbolic of a new pattern, one in which the emerging nonaligned nations would set the pace of world history.

Bandaranaike believed in her country as an independent nation beholden to neither West nor East. As a socialist, she undertook the nationalization of the banking, insurance, and petroleum sectors; ordered the state to take over all Catholic schools; and joined the Non-Aligned Movement in 1961. The movement sought to bring India, Egypt, Yugoslavia, Indonesia, and other states together as a bloc to retain their independence from the Cold War superpowers—the United States and the Soviet Union—and their allies. Her commitment to a Sinhalese-only language policy, however, aroused resistance from the Tamil minority in the north. Only two years into Bandaranaike's tenure, the country was gripped by a Tamil civil disobedience campaign and Ceylon entered a time of political turbulence. Ultimately, anti-Tamil discrimination led to the brutal Tamil Tiger liberation war (1976–2009). Bandaranaike's legacy, therefore, is mixed: On one hand she was a paradigmatic first-generation non-Western nationalist leader, but on the other, her failure to balance constitutional and ethnic principles led inevitably to civil war.

CHAPTER OUTLINE

Superpower Confrontation: Capitalist Democracy and Communism

Populism and Industrialization in Latin America

The End of Colonialism and the Rise of New Nations

Putting It All Together

The pattern of newly independent former colonies banding together and seeking economic development along a common socialist path in the Non-Aligned Movement comprised Bandaranaike and her fellow female prime ministers Benazir Bhutto in Pakistan and Indira Gandhi in India as well as Jawaharlal Nehru of India, Sukarno of Indonesia, and Gamal Abdel Nasser of Egypt. As much as it strove to pursue this path, the Non-Aligned Movement found itself subordinated to what evolved into the dominant dynamics of the post 1945 period, the confrontation between the United States and the Soviet Union called the "Cold War." It is this dynamics, together with the newly independent countries, which dominated the years of 1945–1962.

ABOVE: Voters line up to cast their ballots in Ceylon (now Sri Lanka) on March 22, 1960. Sirimavo Bandaranaike was elected the world's first woman prime minister.

Seeing Patterns

> Why did the pattern of unfolding modernity, which offered three choices after World War I, shrink to just capitalist democracy and socialism–communism in 1945? How did each of these two patterns evolve between 1945 and 1962?

> What are the cultural premises of modernity?

> How did the newly independent countries of the Middle East, Asia, and Africa adapt to the divided world of the Cold War?

United Nations: Successor of the League of Nations, founded in 1945 and today comprising 193 countries, with a Secretary General, a General Assembly meeting annually, and a standing Security Council composed of permanent members (United States, China, Russia, the United Kingdom, and France) as well as five rotating temporary members.

First Phase of the Cold War: While it may be impossible to establish an exact event marking the beginning of the **Cold War**, we can point to certain mileposts in its development.

Superpower Confrontation: Capitalist Democracy and Communism

World War II was the most destructive war in human history. The total loss of life is estimated at over 50 million, more than double that of World War I. Most ominous was the use of the first atomic weapons. Yet in the aftermath, the foundations of a new world organization—the **United Nations (UN)**—to overcome the excesses of nationalist supremacism were being laid. Within a few years, the world's remaining patterns of modernity—capitalism–democracy and socialism–communism—would reemerge from the ruins stronger than ever.

The Cold War Era, 1945–1962

As the world rebuilt, the United States and the Soviet Union promoted their contrasting visions of modernity. While each on occasion engaged in brinkmanship, both sought to avoid direct confrontation. Instead, they pursued their aims of expansion and consolidation in a conflict dubbed the "**Cold War**" through ideological struggle and proxy states. During the first phase of the Cold War (1945–1956), the Soviet Union continued to pursue Stalin's prewar policy of "socialism in one country," which in his definition included the conquered countries of Eastern Europe. During the second phase (1956–1962), Stalin's successor, Nikita Khrushchev (1894–1971, in office 1953–1964), reformulated the policy to include spreading aid and influence to new nationalist regimes in Asia and Africa that had won their independence from Western colonialism (see Map 29.1).

A first milepost was established in the spring of 1945, when the Soviet Red Army occupied German-held territories in Eastern Europe and communist guerillas advanced in the Balkans. In a secret deal between British prime minister Churchill and Soviet leader Stalin in May 1944, Greece became part of the British sphere, in return for Romania and Bulgaria being apportioned to the Soviets for occupation at war's end.

Another milestone was reached in March 1946 when it became increasingly clear that Stalin was determined to maintain a communist presence in Eastern Europe. At that time, Churchill warned in a speech at Westminster College in Fulton, Missouri, of an "iron curtain" descending across Europe "from Stettin in the Baltic to Trieste in the Adriatic." Accordingly, the United States formulated a policy known as **containment** to thwart Soviet expansion. The proposed policy served as the foundation for the administration's effort to confront communist expansion.

Confrontations, 1947–1949

The apportionment of spheres of interest in the Balkans did not work out well. In Yugoslavia, Josip Broz Tito (1892–1980) took over the government in November 1945 with the help of Soviet advisors. He then provided Greek communists with aid to overthrow the royal government that had returned to rule with British support in 1946. The United States stepped in with supplies for the Greek government in 1947. Under the **Truman Doctrine**, the United States announced its support of all "free peoples who are resisting attempted subjugation by armed minorities or by outside pressures."

Destruction and Despair in the Nuclear Age. World War II was the most destructive human conflict in history, far exceeding the damage of what had only a short time before been considered to be "the war to end all wars"—World War I. Nowhere was the damage more complete than in Japan, where an aerial campaign of firebombing Japanese cities by American B-29s had destroyed nearly every major Japanese center. The Japanese cities of Hiroshima and Nagasaki were bombed in August 1945 in the first—and, to date, last—use of nuclear weapons in warfare. Here, a mother and child who survived the nuclear destruction of Hiroshima sit amid the utter devastation of their city in December 1945.

A two-year proxy civil war in Greece ended in a split between Tito and Stalin. In 1948, Tito claimed his right to regional communism, against Stalin's insistence on unity in the Communist bloc. Although Stalin had never supported the Greek communists directly, a surprising majority of the Greeks opted for Stalin. Tito withdrew his support for the pro-Stalin Greek communists, and the bid for communism in Greece collapsed in 1949.

In keeping with his doctrine, Truman announced the **Marshall Plan** of aid to Europe for the recovery of the continent from the ruins of the war. Stalin rejected American aid and forbade Hungary, Czechoslovakia, and Poland to ask for it. In addition to the political reasons behind Stalin's injunction, the Marshall Plan's requirement of free markets and convertible currencies contradicted the communist ideology of a central command economy. Stalin instead engineered communist governments in Eastern Europe and the Balkans, transforming them into the Communist bloc and integrating their economies with the Soviet Union. This integration was formalized in 1949 as the Council for Mutual Economic Assistance (COMECON).

The American Marshall Plan proved to be a success, irritating Stalin because it made the Western sectors of Germany and Berlin magnets for Eastern Europeans fleeing to the West. In 1948, therefore, the Soviets took the provocative step of setting up a highway and rail blockade of food and supplies to Berlin. The United States and Britain responded with the "Berlin Airlift," a demonstration of technological prowess as well as humanitarian compassion. For nearly a year, food, fuel, and other supplies required by this large city were flown in until Stalin finally gave up the blockade.

So far, the Cold War in Europe had been confined to political maneuvering between Washington and Moscow. The confrontation soon assumed military dimensions, however, as the Soviets accelerated their efforts to build a nuclear bomb. In 1949, they detonated their first device four years earlier than anticipated.

Cold War: Ideological struggle between the United States and its allies, and the Soviet Union and its allies that lasted from 1945 to 1989.

Containment: US foreign policy doctrine formulated in 1946 to limit as much as possible the spread of communism.

Truman Doctrine: Policy formulated in 1947, initially to outline steps directed at preventing Greece and Turkey from becoming communist, primarily through military and economic aid.

Marshall Plan: Financial program of $13 billion to support the reconstruction of the economies of 17 European countries during 1948–1952, with most of the aid going to France, Germany, Italy, and the Netherlands.

MAP 29.1 The Cold War, 1947–1991

Now, with its advantage in nuclear weapons eliminated and concern increasing over the possibility of a communist takeover in Western Europe, the United States formed a defensive alliance known as the North Atlantic Treaty Organization (NATO) in 1949. In response, the Soviet Union formed the Warsaw Pact among the states of the Eastern Bloc (1955).

The Central Intelligence Agency In addition to political and military initiatives to contain the spread of communism, the United States used covert means to overthrow left-leaning and socialist movements and governments around the globe. For these purposes the government relied primarily on the Central Intelligence Agency (CIA), an offshoot of the Office of Strategic Services (OSS) developed during World War II. To carry out its mission the CIA employed a variety of covert operations, including spy missions, electronic eavesdropping, photographs obtained by high-flying aircraft, and even outright assassination plots. CIA involvement in regime changes spanned the globe.

Hot War in Korea In June 1950, the Cold War turned hot as North Korean communist troops invaded South Korea in an attempt at forcible unification. South Korean troops fought a desperate rearguard action at the southern end of the peninsula. Under US pressure and despite a Soviet boycott, the UN Security Council branded North Korea as the aggressor, entitling South Korea to UN intervention. By October, US troops, augmented by troops from a number of UN members, had fought their way into North Korea, occupied the capital (Pyongyang), and advanced to the Chinese border.

In the meantime, the United States had sent a fleet to the remnant of the Chinese nationalists who had formed the Republic of China on the southern island of Taiwan, to protect it from a threatened invasion by a newly communist China. Thwarted in the south at Taiwan, Mao Zedong seemingly took the pronouncements of General Douglas MacArthur, the commander of the UN forces in Korea, about raiding Chinese supply bases on the North Korean border seriously. With Stalin's approval, communist Chinese troops launched a massive surprise offensive into the peninsula in October 1950, pushing the UN forces back deep into South Korea. Unwilling to expand the war further or use nuclear weapons,

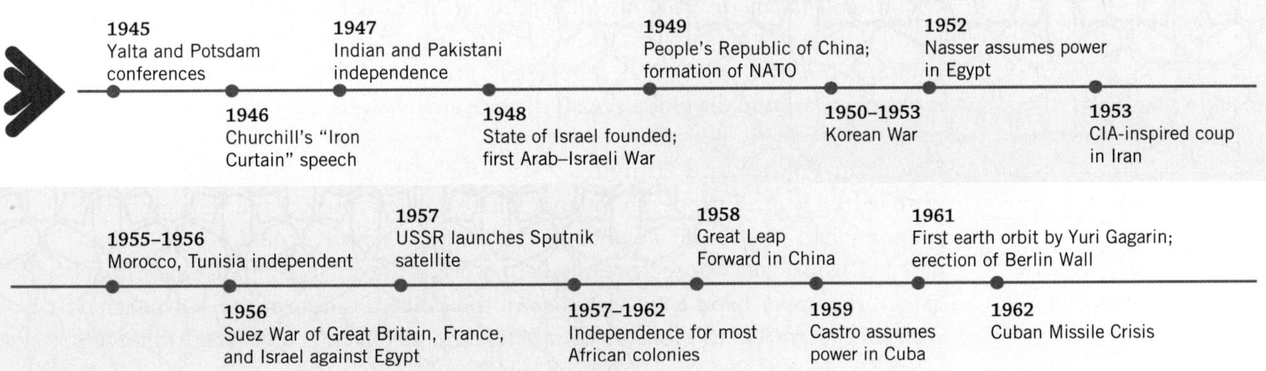

the new Eisenhower administration agreed to an armistice in 1953. No official peace treaty was ever signed, and the border between the two Koreas remains a volatile line of separation.

McCarthyism in the United States The war in Korea had a troubling domestic impact in the increasingly anticommunist United States. Joseph McCarthy (1908–1957), a Republican senator from Wisconsin, sensationally announced in 1950 that he had a list of members of the Communist Party employed by the State Department. Though he never produced the list, his smear tactics, together with the inquisitorial hearings of the House Un-American Activities Committee, ruined the careers of hundreds of government employees, celebrities, and private persons. After four years of anticommunist hysteria, enough voices of reason arose in the Senate to censure McCarthy. The legacy of bitterness engendered by the "McCarthy era" generated abundant political accusations on both sides.

Uprising in East Germany Stalin died suddenly from a stroke in March 1953. His death was profoundly unsettling for the governments of the Eastern Bloc, especially in the German Democratic Republic (East Germany). The East German government, nervous about defections to the Federal Republic (West Germany), had sealed off the border with fences and watchtowers. But Berlin—divided into East and West sectors—was still a gaping hole. The population was seething over rising production quotas, shortages resulting from the shipment of industrial goods to the Soviet Union (in the name of reparations), and the beginnings of a West German economic boom in which it could not share.

In June 1953, a strike among East Berlin workers quickly grew into a general uprising. East German police and Soviet troops, stunned at first, quickly moved to suppress the revolt. The Politburo (the Communist Party's Central Committee Political Bureau) in Moscow refused any concessions, and the German Stalinist government obediently complied by brutally suppressing the uprising.

Khrushchev and Anticolonialism After a power struggle, Nikita Khrushchev emerged in September 1953 as the new secretary of the Politburo. He consolidated his position by making substantial investments in agriculture, housing, and consumer goods. In a February 1956 speech, he denounced Stalin's "excesses" during collectivization and the purges of the 1930s. In the Communist bloc, Khrushchev replaced Stalinists with new faces willing to improve general living conditions. To balance the new flexibility within the Soviet Bloc, Khrushchev maintained toughness toward the West. He alarmed leaders of the West when he announced a new policy that supported anticolonial nationalist independence movements around the globe even if the movements were not communist.

Revolt in Poland and Hungary Khrushchev's reforms awakened hopes for change in Eastern Europe. In Poland, where collectivization and the command economy had progressed slowly and the Catholic Church could not be intimidated, Khrushchev's speech resulted in worker unrest. Nationalist reformists gained the upper hand over Stalinists in the Polish Politburo, and Khrushchev realized that he had to avoid another Tito-style secession at all costs. After a few tense days in mid-October, Poland received limited autonomy.

Unrest in the Soviet Bloc. In the Hungarian uprising from October to November 1956, some 2,500 Hungarians and 700 Soviet troops were killed, while 200,000 fled to neighboring Austria and elsewhere in the West. Here, a young boy and older man walk by while a Soviet tank rumbles through an intersection with barricades set up by Hungarian "freedom fighters."

In Hungary, the Politburo was similarly divided between reformers and Stalinists. People in Budapest and other cities, inspired by events in Poland, took to the streets. The Politburo lost control, and the man appointed to lead the country to a national communist solution similar to that of Poland, Imre Nagy [noj] (1896–1958), announced a multiparty system and the withdrawal of Hungary from the Warsaw Pact. This was too much for Khrushchev, who unleashed the Soviet troops stationed in Hungary to repress what had become a grassroots revolution. Aware that the British, French, and Americans were preoccupied with the Suez Crisis (see below), the Soviets crushed the uprising in November 1956. The new pro-Moscow government arrested Nagy and executed him in 1958.

ICBMs and Sputniks Advances in weapons technologies, including missiles and space flight, put a powerful military punch behind Soviet repression. In 1957 the Soviet Union developed the world's first intercontinental ballistic missile (ICBM), with a range capable of reaching America's East Coast. In the same year, the Soviet Union launched the world's first orbiting satellite, named Sputnik ("traveling companion" or "satellite"), into space. Then, in 1961, Russian scientists sent the world's first cosmonaut, Yuri Gagarin (1934–1968), into space.

As the implications of nuclear weapons descending from space with no practicable defense against them began to set in, Americans became frightened. The US Congress accelerated its missile and space program even at the risk of deepening the Cold War with the Soviet Union. In 1958 the United States successfully launched its first satellite, Explorer 1, and in the following year its first ICBM, the Atlas. The space and missile races were now fully under way.

Communism in Cuba In 1959, Fidel Castro (1926–2016), a nationalist guerilla fighter opposed to the influence of American companies over a government generally perceived as corrupt, seized power in Cuba. About six months after the coup, Cuba became the symbol of the Khrushchev government's openness toward national liberation movements, lavishing huge sums on the development of the island's economy. Khrushchev's instincts were proven right when Castro openly embraced communism in 1960.

To counter Khrushchev's overtures to national liberation movements, President Eisenhower and the head of the CIA, Allen Dulles (1893–1969), secretly supported and trained anticommunist dissidents in Latin America, the Middle East, and Africa. In the case of Latin America, a group of Cuban anticommunists trained in Guatemala for an invasion and overthrow of Castro in Cuba. The so-called Bay of Pigs invasion in April 1961 (named for the small bay in southern Cuba where the anticommunist invasion began) was easily defeated by Castro's forces, to the great embarrassment of Kennedy (in office 1961–1963), who had secretly sanctioned it, though without military support.

The Berlin Wall East Germany, which retained its Stalinist leadership, pressured Khrushchev in 1961 to close the last opening in Berlin through which its citizens could escape to West Germany. Between 1953 and 1961, nearly one-fifth of the East German population had defected. The East German Stalinists, allied with a few remaining Stalinists in the Politburo, prevailed over Khrushchev's

Aiming for the Stars. As this commemorative postcard reveals, the connection between the technological achievement of Sputnik and Russian popular interest in space travel was strong. The legend reads in Russian: "4 October, the USSR launched Earth's first artificial satellite; 3 November, the USSR launched Earth's second artificial satellite."

opposition and built the Berlin Wall in 1961, effectively turning the German Democratic Republic into a prison.

The Cuban Missile Crisis The climax of the Cold War came in October 1962 with a direct confrontation between the United States and USSR. US spy planes discovered the presence of missile launching pads as well as missiles in Cuba. President Kennedy demanded their immediate destruction and then followed up with a naval quarantine. In defiance, Khrushchev dispatched Russian ships to Cuba. When it was discovered that they were bearing more missiles, President Kennedy demanded that Khrushchev recall the ships. The world held its breath as the Soviet ships continued to head for Cuba (see Map 29.2).

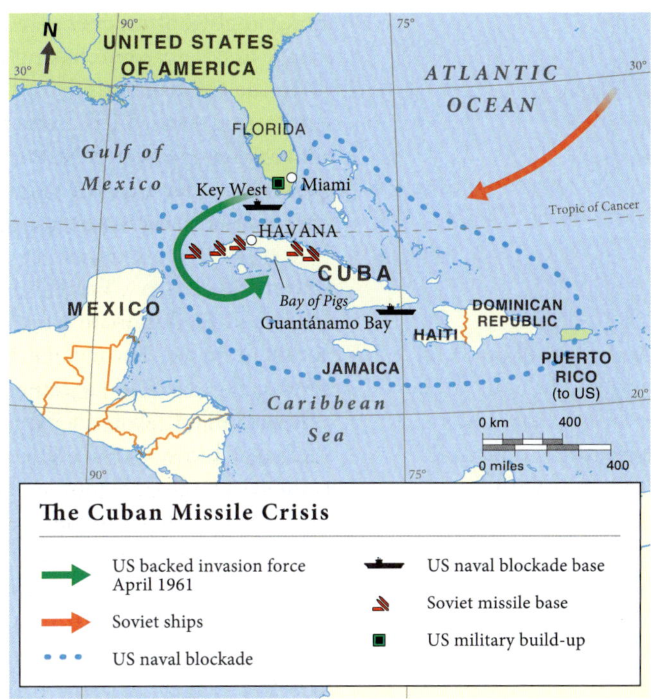

MAP 29.2 The Cuban Missile Crisis

In the end, Khrushchev recalled the ships at the last minute, while Kennedy secretly agreed to remove American missiles from Turkey. The two signed the Nuclear Test Ban Treaty in 1963, an agreement banning the aboveground testing of nuclear weapons. The treaty also sought to prevent the spread of these technologies to other countries. Thus the first phase of the Cold War ended with a decision of the two superpowers to de-escalate the often dangerous tensions of the past two decades.

Society and Culture in Postwar North America, Europe, and Japan

In the years after World War II, veterans pursued civilian lives of normalcy and comfort. Intellectuals and artists cast a critical eye on modern culture, as the previous generation had after World War I. Among the emerging nations, artists and intellectuals forged new paths, often combining indigenous culture and socialist and democratic ideas.

Mass Consumption Culture After WWII, soldiers returned to civilian life and started families, launching the so-called baby-boom generation (1945–1961). The growing population triggered increased consumer demand for basics as well as consumer durables that increased the comfort of living, such as appliances, televisions, and cars. In the United States, the GI Bill supported housing and university studies for veterans that led to better-paying jobs. Americans

Homeward Bound. This photo illustrates prevailing concepts of the ideal American family in postwar America during the 1950s and 1960s: husbands worked downtown from 9:00 to 5:00 and expected to be served dinner by the woman of the household when they returned home.

increasingly took on debt to move into middle-class lives, while Europeans tended to save first before purchasing consumer goods.

In the idealized family of the 1950s and early 1960s, gender roles and spatial segregation—in which men tended to commute to work while women ran the households—were highly structured, corresponding to the yearning of the middle classes for order after the years of economic depression and war. These yearnings were similar to each other in all leading industrial countries of the West.

Existentialism: A form of thought built on the premise that modern scientific–industrial society is without intrinsic meaning unless an answer to the question of what constitutes authentic existence is found.

Artistic Culture Enlightenment ideas of materialism and the social contract continued to dominate the Anglo-American cultural sphere and also became dominant in the European arts. They were reflected in new forms of modernism in thought, writing, theater, painting, music, and film, such as neorealism, **existentialism**, abstract expressionism (see the images below), and serialism. After two world wars, intellectuals and artists remained strongly committed to modernism, yet were more sensitive to its contradictions.

Thinkers and artists reflecting on modernity versus tradition provided for rich artistic post–World War II cultures in Western countries. As culture-specific as many artists were, by not merely dwelling on the inevitability of modernity but rather confronting it with their inherited premodern traditions, they created works that could be understood across cultures.

Abstract Expressionism. (a) Hans Hofmann (1880–1966), *Delight*, 1947. (b) Willem de Kooning (1904–1997), *Montauk Highway*, 1958. Abstract expressionism was a New York–centered artistic movement that combined the strong colors of World War I German expressionism with the abstract art pioneered by the Russian-born Wassily Kandinsky and the artists of the Bauhaus school. Before and during the Nazi period, many European artists had flocked to New York, including Hofmann and de Kooning. The movement caught the public eye when Jackson Pollock, following the surrealists, made the creation of a work of art—the process of painting a large canvas on the floor through the dripping of paint—an art in itself.

Populism and Industrialization in Latin America

Western political and cultural modernity was also a part of the Latin American experience. But the region's Amerindians and blacks participated only marginally, as many were mired in rural subsistence. Since these populations increased rapidly after World War II, Latin America began to resemble Asia and Africa, which also had massive rural populations, small middle classes, and limited industrial sectors. Populist leaders relying on the urban poor thus sought to steer their countries toward industrialization.

Slow Social Change

Latin America had stayed out of World War II. The postwar aftermath therefore neither disrupted established patterns nor offered new opportunities to its patterns of social and economic development. The region had suffered from the disappearance of commodity export markets during the Depression of the 1930s, and politicians realized that import-substitution industrialization, replacing imported manufactures with domestically produced ones, had to be adopted with greater energy. However, landowners opposed industrialization and the great majority of rural and urban Latin Americans were too poor to become consumers.

Rural and Urban Society Prior to 1945, the rural population still composed about two-thirds of the total population. But during 1945–1962, the pace of urbanization picked up, with the proportions nearly reversing (see Map 29.3). While overall population growth during this period accelerated, poverty rates remained the same or even increased, making Latin America the world region with the greatest income disparities. Cuba's land reform (1959) and the threat of local peasant revolutions made the issue of land reform urgent, and agrarian reforms picked up in the 1960s.

Much of the landless population migrated to the cities, settling in sprawling shantytowns with no urban services. While some migrants found employment in the expanding industrial sector, more worked in the so-called informal sector, a new phenomenon of peddling, repairing, and recycling. In contrast to the villages, rural–urban migrants had some access to the health and education benefits that populist politicians introduced. The industrial labor force grew to about one-quarter of the total labor force, a rate that reflected the hesitant attitude of politicians toward industrialization in view of rebounding commodity exports in the 1960s.

At the end of World War II, industrialism was still confined mainly to food processing and textile manufacturing. In the later 1940s and early 1950s, the larger Latin American countries moved to capital goods and consumer durables. As a result, expanded production of manufactures reduced dependence on foreign imports. Unfortunately, limited private capital was available on the domestic market for risky industrialization ventures, requiring the state to allocate the necessary funds. Smaller countries that overextended themselves with industrial import substitution had to return in the early 1950s to prioritizing commodity exports.

MAP 29.3 Urbanization and Population Growth in Latin America and the Caribbean, ca. 1950

Populist-Guided Democracy

During the period 1945–1962, democracy and communism were the main political and ideological choices. The attraction of democracy in its constitutional North American and European forms in Latin America, however, was limited, since the United States, in the grip of the Cold War, was primarily interested in the professed loyalty of autocratic rulers in its Latin American backyard. Communism was initially also of limited appeal, and flourished only once Khrushchev supported national liberation movements, as in Cuba. **Populism** was an intermediate form of governance between democracy and autocracy that found strong support in Latin America from 1945–1962.

Populism: Type of governance in which rulers seek support directly from the population, through organizing mass rallies, manipulating elections, and intimidating or bypassing representative bodies.

The Populist Wave Democracy in Latin America was represented by Venezuela (1958), Colombia (1953–1964), and Costa Rica (1953). Democratic politicians, however, were unable to put Venezuela's oil to productive use or bring about land reform in Colombia, resulting in the formation of a communist guerilla underground in the latter country in 1964. By contrast, eight Latin American countries had populist regimes from the mid-1940s onward: Guatemala (1944–1954), Argentina (1946–1955), Brazil (1946–1954), Venezuela (1945–1948), Peru (1945–1948), Chile (1946–1952), Costa Rica (1948–1953), and Ecuador (1948–1961).

Peronism is the best-known example of the populist phase in Latin America. Colonel Juan Perón (1895–1974) was a member of a group of urban-born officers who staged a coup in 1943 against the traditional landowners and their conservative military allies. As minister of labor, Perón entered into an alliance with labor unions and improved wages, set a minimum wage, and increased pensions. At a fundraiser after an earthquake, Perón met Eva Duarte (1919–1952), a popular movie actress. They were married and became the symbols of Peronism. In elections in 1946, at the head of a fractious coalition of nationalists, socialists, and communists, Perón gained a legitimate mandate as president.

Peronism: Argentinian political movement that aims to mediate tensions between the classes of society, with the state responsible for negotiating compromise in conflicts between business and workers.

After the elections, he started a five-year plan of nationalization and industrialization—the characteristic form of state socialism pursued also in Asia and Africa. A year later, construction of plants for the production of primary and intermediate industrial goods got under way. During Perón's tenure, the economy expanded by 40 percent. The factories, however, had to be equipped with imported machinery. Initially, Perón paid for these imports with reserves accumulated from commodity exports during World War II. But soon the costs exceeded the internal reserves and revenues of Argentina, leading to inflation and strikes. Plagued by chronic deficits and unable to pay its foreign debts, the Perón government was overthrown by a conservative-led coup in 1955.

The End of Colonialism and the Rise of New Nations

Like Latin America, Asia and Africa experienced rapid population growth and urbanization in the period 1945–1962. But in contrast to the politically independent American continent, colonialism was still dominant in Asia and Africa. The governments of Great Britain and France had no inclination to relinquish their empires, but both were too exhausted to hold them completely. Thus, in a first wave after the end of the war, a few independence movements succeeded. A major shift in attitudes toward colonialism had to take place, however, before Britain and France were eventually willing to loosen their grip in Africa.

"China Has Stood Up"

After World War II, China was still fundamentally a peasant-based economy with scant industrial resources. Mao's reinterpretation of Marxism opened up fresh possibilities of development, leading eventually to an abortive attempt at decentralized village industrialization. During the Stalin years, China depended on Soviet material aid and advisors. Under Khrushchev, estrangement set in, culminating in the Soviet Union's withdrawal of all advisors from China in 1960.

Victory of the Communists China emerged from World War II severely battered. Moreover, the wartime alliance between the communists under Mao Zedong and the nationalists under Chiang K'ai-shek unraveled in the ensuing civil war. The communists, entrenched in the countryside, were at a strategic advantage in China's rural society. Despite the nationalists' material superiority, resulting partly from American support, the communists systematically strangled the cities, causing hyperinflation in Shanghai and other urban centers in 1947.

By 1948 the size of the two armies had reached parity, but Mao's People's Liberation Army had popular momentum, and the United States cut back on its aid to Chiang. By 1949, Chiang had fled to Taiwan, Mao's forces took Beijing, and the new People's Republic of China began implementing the Maoist vision of the communist pattern of collectivist modernity. For millions of Chinese, Mao's pronouncement that "China has stood up" against imperialism was a source of enormous pride.

Land Reform During the 1950s, a central aspect of Maoism was that Chinese peasants were the vanguard of the revolution. With China lacking an industrial and transportation base, the early Maoist years were marked by repeated mass mobilization campaigns, the most important of which was the national effort at land reform. Party cadres expropriated rural land, dividing it among the local peasants. Landlords who resisted were punished and sometimes executed by local "people's tribunals." By some estimates, land reform between 1950 and 1955 took as many as 2 million lives. As hoped, however, increased peasant landownership caused agricultural productivity to increase.

When party leaders decided to take the next step toward socialized agriculture, Mao sought to avoid the chaos of Soviet collectivization of agriculture in 1930–1932. The party leadership felt that by going slowly they could greatly ease the transition. Thus, in 1953 peasants were encouraged to form "agricultural producers' cooperatives" in which villages would share resources. Those who joined were given incentives. By 1956, agricultural production was registering impressive gains.

"Let a Hundred Flowers Bloom" By 1957, Mao was ready to evaluate the commitment of the nation's intellectuals to the revolution. Adopting a slogan from China's late Zhou period, "Let a hundred flowers bloom, let a hundred schools of thought contend," the party invited intellectuals to submit public criticism of the party's record, assuring the intellectuals that offering their critique was patriotic.

But in mid-1957, when some critics suggested forming an opposition party, Mao acted swiftly. The "Hundred Flowers" campaign was terminated and the "Anti-Rightist" campaign was launched. Calls for an opposition party were denounced as opposed to the "correct" left-wing thinking of the monopoly Communist Party. Those accused of rightism were subjected to "re-education." In addition to being imprisoned, many intellectuals were sentenced to "reform through labor" in remote peasant villages.

The Great Leap Forward Mao, growing impatient with the pace of Chinese agricultural collectivization, prodded the Communist Party into its most colossal mass mobilization project yet: the **Great Leap Forward** (1958–1961). The entire population of the country was to be pushed into a campaign to communalize agriculture into self-sustaining units that would function like factories in the fields. Men and women would work and live on enormous collective farms. Peasants were to surrender all their iron implements to be melted down and made into steel to build the new infrastructure of these communes. The most recognizable symbol of the campaign was the backyard steel furnace, which commune members were to build and run for their own needs. Technical problems were to be solved by the "wisdom of the masses" through "red" (revolutionary) thinking as opposed to those who emphasized technical skills ("experts").

Great Leap Forward: Mobilization project led by Mao Zedong that aimed to rapidly transform China from an agrarian economy into a socialist society through rapid industrialization and collectivization.

Predictably, the Great Leap was the most catastrophic policy failure in the history of the People's Republic. Peasants began to actively resist the seizure of their land and implements. So many were forced into building the communal structures and making unusable steel that by 1959 agricultural production in China had plummeted and the country experienced its worst famine in modern times. By 1961 an estimated 30 million people had died.

During 1959 conditions in China became so bleak that Mao stepped down from his party chairmanship in favor of "expert" Liu Shaoqi (1898–1969) and retreated into semiretirement. Liu, along with Deng Xiaoping (1904–1997), moved to rebuild the shattered economy and political structures. They had to do so without Soviet help, however. For the Soviet leader Nikita Khrushchev, Mao's Great Leap Forward was the kind of relapse into the Stalinism that he sought to leave behind. In 1960 the Soviets withdrew their aid and technical personnel in what became known as the "Sino-Soviet Split." The return to something like normalcy in 1961 was such a relief in China that even without Soviet aid the country achieved impressive gains in the technical, health, and education sectors.

Decolonization, Israel, and Arab Nationalism in the Middle East

After World War II, independence movements arose in the Middle East and North Africa against the British and French colonial regimes. Here, countries achieved their independence in two waves, the first following World War II and the second during 1956–1970 (see Map 29.4). The first wave was the result of local pressures, while the second had to await the realization by the British and French governments that they could no longer maintain their empires in a world dominated by the United States and the Soviet Union.

Palestine and Israel

As World War II ended, Britain found itself in a tight spot in Palestine. After the suppression of the uprising of 1936–1939, Zionist guerrilla action protesting the restrictions on Jewish immigration and land acquisitions had begun. Sooner or later, some form of transition to self-rule had to be offered, but British leaders were determined to hold on to the empire's strategic interests (oil and the Suez Canal), especially once the Cold War began. Unable to overcome the Palestinian–Zionist impasse, in February 1947 Britain turned the question of Palestinian independence over to the United Nations. Accordingly,

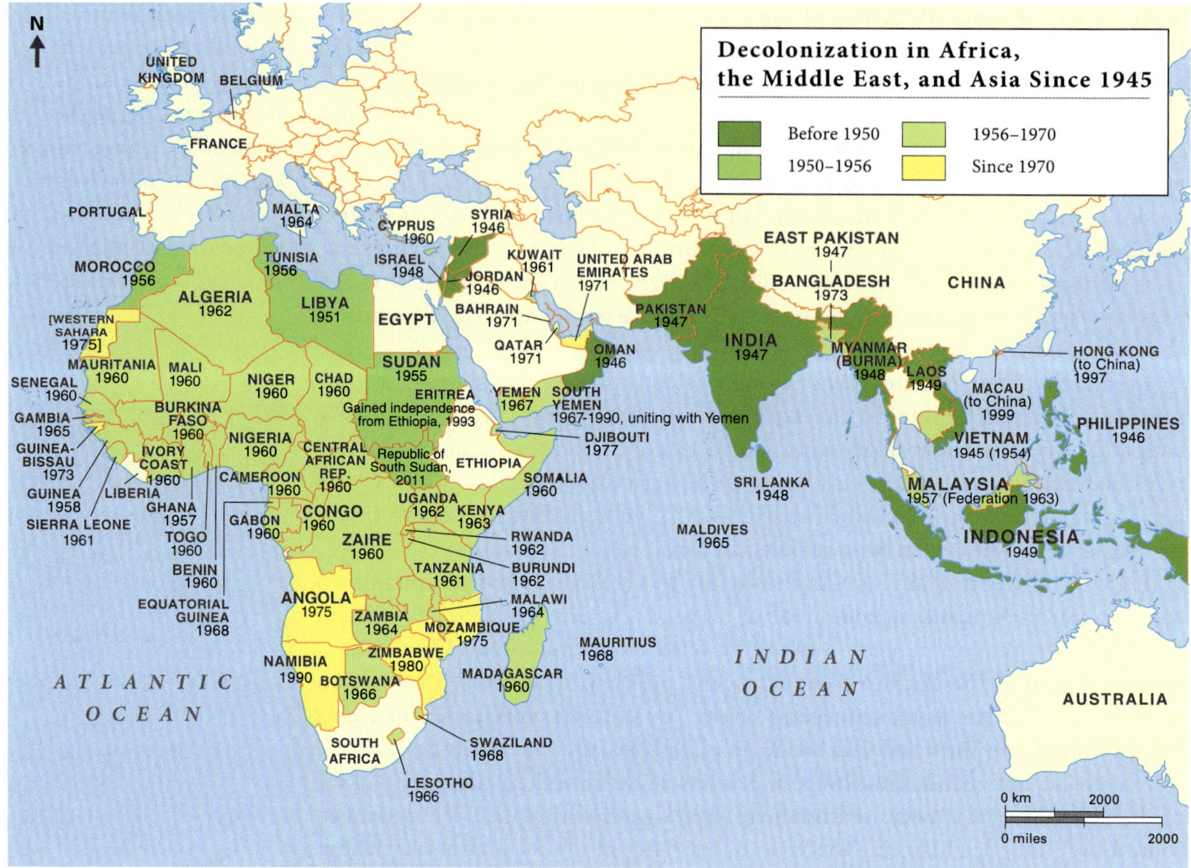

MAP 29.4 Decolonization in Africa, the Middle East, and Asia since 1945

the United Nations adopted a partition plan worked out with American assistance in November. Israel declared its independence unilateraly on May 14, 1948 (see Map 29.5).

The Soviet Union backed up its Cold War–motivated support for Israel by releasing 200,000 Jewish emigrants from the Soviet Bloc and having Czechoslovakia deliver weapons to Israel. Israel was victorious against the Arab armies that invaded from surrounding countries, which were unable to obtain weapons as the result of British and American embargoes. Only Jordan was partly successful, conquering the West Bank and the Old City of Jerusalem. Between November 1947 and the end of fighting in January 1949, some three-quarters of a million Palestinians were either forced from their villages or fled, leaving only 150,000 in an Israeli territory now substantially larger than that of the original partition plan.

In response, the Arab countries expelled about half a million Jews from their countries during the next decade. In the end, the Soviet Union's Cold War tactics were a miscalculation; Israel became a staunch Western ally. But the Western camp did not fare much better: among the Palestinian Arabs, liberal landowning nationalists were replaced by militant hard-liners of refugee background determined to end Western colonialism—which now, in their eyes, included the state of Israel.

The Officer Coup in Egypt One Egyptian officer in the Arab war against Israel was Colonel Gamal Abdel Nasser (1918–1970), the eldest son of a postal clerk from southern Egypt. He was bitter toward the Egyptian royalty and the landowners who supported them; neither had done much to support the country in the 1947–1949 war. In the middle of a declining internal security situation, the secret "Free Officers," with Nasser at the center, assumed power in a coup in July 1952. They closed down parliament and sent the king into exile. The coup was bloodless, and there was little reaction in the streets.

MAP 29.5 **The Palestine Conflict, 1947–1949**

To break the power of the landowners, the Free Officers in 1952 initiated a land reform that eliminated large estates. A rival for power was the Muslim Brotherhood, a militant organization founded in 1928 by the preacher Hasan al-Banna (1906–1949), who advocated the establishment of an Islamic regime. Accusing the Brotherhood of an assassination attempt, Nasser outlawed it in 1954. In a plebiscite in 1956, Nasser made himself president.

Once in power, Nasser espoused the Arab nationalist cause. Palestinian Arab "freedom fighters" raided Israel from refugee camps in the Arab countries, which provoked Israeli reprisals. After the first raid and reprisal involving Egypt in February 1955, Nasser realized that the Egyptian military needed urgent improvements. Khrushchev, pursuing his strategy of supporting anticolonial nationalists, stepped up. After its failure in Israel, the Soviet Union was in the Middle Eastern Cold War struggle again.

Nasser also planned infrastructural improvements in Egypt and asked the World Bank for a loan to finance the Aswan High Dam. Initially, the United States and Britain, the main underwriters of the World Bank, were in support. But they withdrew this support in spring 1956 when Nasser pressured Jordan into dismissing the British commander of its troops, the Arab Legion. Nasser responded with the nationalization of the Suez Canal and closure of the Strait of Tiran (used by Israel for Indian Ocean shipping) in July 1956. Without the necessary loans, Nasser had to suspend construction of the High Dam.

Israel considered the closure of the Strait of Tiran an act of war and, with French participation, prepared for a campaign to reopen the straits. France persuaded Britain to join in the plan, which would be initiated with an attack on Egypt by Israel. If Nasser closed the Suez Canal, France and Britain would occupy it, reestablishing Western control. The plan unraveled badly when Israel ended its canal campaign victoriously on November 2, but the British and French troops were unable to complete their own occupation of the Canal Zone before November 4, the day of the ceasefire called by the UN General Assembly and the United States. Although defeated militarily, Nasser scored a diplomatic victory, effectively ending the last remnants of British and French imperialism in the Middle East.

After the Suez War, monarchical regimes in the Middle East were on the defensive and maintained themselves only due to the United States, heir to the strategic oil interests of Britain after the demise of the latter's empire. Although unification with Syria as the United Arab Republic (1958–1961) did not work out, Egypt succeeded in establishing an ideological hegemony from North Africa to Yemen. The relationship with the Soviet Union deepened: Thanks to the Soviets, the Aswan Dam was completed, Soviet military and technical support grew, and Egyptian students received advanced educations in the Eastern Bloc. In 1961, the regime cofounded the **Non-Aligned Movement**, together with Indonesia's Sukarno, India's Nehru, Yugoslavia's Tito, and Ceylon's Bandaranaike. In the same year, Nasser announced his first five-year plan, which embraced industrial modernity but under the aegis of state investments similar to what Stalin had pioneered in 1930. Nasser called this "Arab socialism."

Non-Aligned Movement: An international, anticolonialist movement of state leaders that promoted the interests of countries not aligned with the superpowers.

Decolonization and Cold War in Asia

Nationalist forces arose also in South and Southeast Asia as a consequence of World War II. The war had diminished or destroyed the colonial holdings of Great Britain, France, the Netherlands, and Japan in Asia. In several colonies, independence movements established nationalist governments or fought against the attempted reimposition of European rule. In quick succession, India and Pakistan (1947), Burma (1948), Malaysia (1957), Ceylon (1948), Indonesia (1949), and Vietnam (1954) achieved independence from the British and French.

Independence and Partition on the Subcontinent India, Pakistan, and Bangladesh illustrate the tribulations of colonial populations just prior to and during the achievement of independence. In 1943, the British Raj requisitioned so much grain from northeastern India to fight the Japanese in Burma, without reallocating available food stocks from elsewhere in India, that the ensuing "Bengal Famine" ravaged some 3 million victims. During World War II, the all-volunteer Indian troops of some 2.5 million soldiers contributed heavily to the Allied victory, mourning some 90,000 deaths at war's end.

In view of these sacrifices, the Indian nationalists renewed their "Quit India" protests of 1942 and demanded full independence at the end of World War II. Gandhi, Nehru, and the majority of the Indian National Congress envisaged an Indian nation on the entire subcontinent in which a constitution, patterned after that of Britain, would trump any ethnic, linguistic, and/or religious identities. The Muslim minority, however, had drifted increasingly toward religious nationalism since the 1930s, and demanded a separate state for themselves in regions where they formed a majority. There was also a small minority of Hindu religious nationalists who advocated independence under the banner of "Hindu-ness" (*hindutva*). To the dismay of the Indian National Congress, the British negotiators listened to the Islamic religious nationalists and prevailed on Gandhi and Nehru to accept independence with partition.

When, on August 15, 1947, the two nations of India and Pakistan became independent, the jubilation of freedom was immediately mixed with the horrors of a massive population exchange. Desperate to save themselves from their Hindu or Muslim neighbors, millions of people fled from their homes to reach their new respective countries. More than 300,000 Indians died in the accompanying communal violence. Gandhi himself fell victim five months later to an assassin from the *hindutva* religious-nationalist minority.

While India settled into federal parliamentary democracy, Pakistan shifted uneasily back and forth between democracy and military rule. As it came into existence, the country was composed of diverse groups of refugees from India held together only by Sunni Islam and a dozen or so regional ethnic-linguistic peoples (to think only of the largest ones). Both civilian and military politicians found it very hard to balance the issues of religion and ethnicity, hence the phenomena of periodic drifts toward unsustainable religious extremism on one hand and paralyzing provincial divisions on the other.

Given the instability of Pakistani politics in 1947–1962, there was no surprise that the two separate parts of the country of 1947 grew more and more alienated from each other and eventually split into (West) Pakistan and Bangladesh in 1971. Pakistan also failed miserably in its efforts to capture Kashmir, the one province where religion and ethnicity happened to coincide. In 1947, the majority Muslim population of the province demanded to join Pakistan, while its Hindu prince opted for India. In two wars against India (1947–1948 and 1965) the Pakistani army was unable to wrest Kashmir away. Not surprisingly after these defeats, Pakistan inaugurated a nuclear bomb program in 1972, two years before India did the same.

Independent India India's first prime minister, Jawaharlal Nehru (in office 1947–1964), worked to tie the subcontinent's disparate constituencies together into a united government. Local princes now had to surrender their realms to the national government, but the array of castes and systemic social inequalities still posed a powerful obstacle to unity. In the end, the British parliamentary and court systems were adopted and the old civil service was retained, while the economy of the new government would officially be a modified, nonrevolutionary kind of socialism. Nehru's admiration for Soviet successes persuaded him to adopt the five-year-plan system of development, and India's first five-year plan (1951–1955) was similarly geared toward raising agricultural productivity as a precondition for industrial development.

The most formidable problem was poverty. Though the cities were rapidly expanding, India was still fundamentally rural. The strains upon the land and reliance on the sometimes irregular monsoon cycle meant a constant risk of famine. In the 1950s, India launched a family planning program, but cooperation from villagers was difficult to achieve as long as urbanization and industrialization were in their initial stages. For poor families, children were important laborers as soon as they were old enough to work.

Patterns Up Close | Bandung and the Origins of the Non-Aligned Movement (NAM)

One of the most momentous events of the post–World War II period was the dismantling of the colonial empires of the Western powers and Japan and the emergence from them of new nation-states. While nationalist movements in these empires had long predated the war, the complete defeat of Japan accompanied by the exhaustion of Great Britain, France, and the Netherlands and the emergence of the Cold War proved powerful catalysts for independence—as had Allied propaganda during the war and the newly created United Nations after 1945.

As these new nations arrived on the scene, they faced unprecedented problems, including poverty, developmental gaps, and ethnic and religious conflicts. Looming over all of these emerging nations was the intensifying struggle during the Cold War between the United States and its allies in the capitalist camp and the Soviet Union and the Communist bloc. As a result, many leaders of these new nations saw themselves as natural colleagues. They shared a common colonial experience, and many had also been fighters for national independence. Now, they also had to contend with (and could take advantage of) both Cold War rivals attempting to enlist their support. Thus, led by the dynamic Indonesian president Sukarno and India's Prime Minister Nehru, Indonesia, India, Burma (Myanmar), Pakistan, and Ceylon (Sri Lanka) convened a conference in April 1955 attended by 25 countries at the Indonesian town of Bandung.

Although the Bandung Conference established the base on which the Non-Aligned Movement was founded, politics proved a corrosive force in its interactions. Delegates agreed on the principle of Afro-Asian solidarity and cooperation and were unanimous in their opposition to colonialism by any country. They were much less agreed, however, on exactly what constituted colonialism. Some equated the Soviet position in Eastern Europe with colonialism and worried about China's emergent predominance in East Asia. Others, friendlier toward Marxist developmental approaches and eager for aid from socialist countries, dismissed such ideas as Western propaganda. The United States refused to attend, at least in part because of its policy of not recognizing the People's Republic, though American congressman Adam Clayton Powell and the writer Richard Wright—both African American—did attend in unofficial capacities. In the end, the conference unanimously adopted a 10-point declaration of "world peace and cooperation," very much in keeping with the tenets of the UN Charter.

Political and Economic Nonalignment Nehru and the Congress Party argued that the pressing rural poverty could be overcome only through rapid industrialization undertaken by the state and its financial power. A hybrid regime of capitalist–democratic constitutionalism with private property and guided "socialist" state investments emerged, which was officially aligned with neither the West

Though regional rivalries and competing political aims, as well as the circumstances of the Cold War, never allowed the development of the kind of solidarity championed at Bandung, successive conferences in Cairo and Belgrade led to the official creation of the Non-Aligned Movement in 1961. The movement marked the maturation of an important pattern that helped to regulate the behavior of the Cold War players. The search for a third way beyond capitalism and Soviet communism spurred economic and developmental experimentation and encouraged both Cold War camps to woo nonaligned members into their respective ideological orbits. New nations seeing security in a coalition opposed to superpower domination made the movement a genuine power of its own.

Bandung Conference. (L-R) Dr. Ali Sastroamidjojo (premier of Indonesia), Sir John Kotelawala (premier of Sri Lanka), Chaudry Mohammed Ali (premier of Pakistan) Jawaharlal Nehru (premier of India), and U Nu (premier of Burma, today Myanmar) at the Bandung Conference, April 1, 1955.

The pattern of resistance to superpower dominance continues today, decades after the end of the Cold War. The Non-Aligned Movement still casts itself as the champion of the developing "global south" in opposition to the economic power of the wealthy "north." Accordingly, it pushes the United Nations toward greater attention to the inequalities in the world economic order. Although the NAM boasts a membership of 120 countries and 17 observer nations, at present it is increasingly fighting for relevance. The Tehran summit of 2012 was attended by more than 30 heads of state, but the Venezuela summit of 2016 assembled only 12, with the notable absence of Norendra Modi, Prime Minister of India. Muhammadu Buhari, President of Nigeria was in attendance and demanded a restructuring of NAM, without, however, submitting details. Venezuela's chairmanship of the NAM elicited protests and led in 2019 to Colombia and Peru suspending their membership. Thus, the future of the movement seems to be uncertain.

Questions

- How does the Non-Aligned Movement reflect the pattern of postwar developments regarding the trend toward anticolonialism?
- Will the revival of the Russia–United States rivalry allow NAM to regain relevance? If yes, how?

nor the East. This nonalignment became the official policy of India and under its initiative also the founding principle of the Non-Aligned Movement, formally inaugurated in 1961 (see "Patterns Up Close"). The Non-Aligned Movement, still in existence today, sought to maintain neutrality in the Cold War and was successful in maintaining its own course independent from the Western and Soviet blocs.

The Strains of Nonalignment. India's determined stance to navigate its own course between the superpowers was a difficult one, especially during the height of the Cold War. Here, however, a degree of diplomatic warmth appears to pervade the proceedings in Geneva, Switzerland, as the foreign minister of the People's Republic of China, Chen Yi (left), toasts his Indian colleague, defense minister V. K. Krishna Menon (right), and the Soviet foreign minister, Andrei Gromyko (center background), smiles at them both. The date of this conference, however, formally convened to discuss issues between the Soviet and American sides over influence in the Southeast Asian nation of Laos in July 1962, also coincided with rising border tensions between India and China. This photo was specifically released to show that both sides were still on friendly terms. Within a few months, however, they were shooting at each other.

Indian state socialism began with the state's second five-year plan (1956–1961), which focused on state investments in heavy industry. Planners hoped that private Indian investors would buy the heavy industrial goods to construct housing and build factories for the production of basic consumer goods. The giant domestic market of India was to become fully self-sufficient and independent of imports.

Though begun with much hope at a time of prosperity, the second plan failed to reach its goals. The government debt grew astronomically. Tax collection was notoriously difficult and unproductive, and chronic budget deficits drove up inflation. Bad monsoon seasons caused food shortages. In democratic India it was not possible to use the draconian dictatorial powers that Stalin had employed.

Southeast Asia In contrast to the British in India, the French under Charles de Gaulle (1890–1970) in 1944–1946 were determined to reconstitute their empire. De Gaulle found it inconceivable that the new postwar Fourth Republic would be anything less than the imperially glorious Third Republic. However, French military efforts to hold on to Lebanon and Syria failed against discreet British support for independence and the unilateral establishment of national governments by the Lebanese and Syrians in 1943–1944. After these losses, the French were determined not to lose more colonies.

Unfortunately for the French, however, when they returned to Indochina (composed of Vietnam, Laos, and Cambodia) in the fall of 1945, the prewar communist independence movement had already taken over. With covert American assistance, the communist Vietminh had fought the Japanese occupiers in a guerrilla war, and on September 2, 1945, the day of Japan's surrender to the United States, Ho Chi Minh, the leader, declared Vietnamese independence.

Following a stalemate in negotiations between Ho and the French, the Vietminh relaunched their guerilla war. Because of the rapid escalation of the Cold War, the French persuaded the American administration that a Vietminh victory meant an expansion of communism. By the early 1950s, the United States was providing much of the funding, and the French and allied Vietnamese troops did the actual fighting. In May 1954, however, the Vietminh defeated the French decisively at Dien Bien Phu. During negotiations later that year, the French surrender resulted in a division of Vietnam into north and south, pending national elections, and the creation of the new nations of Laos and Cambodia.

The elections, however, never took place. Instead President Ngo Dinh Diem [no deen ziem] (in office 1955–1963), a politician who envisioned a republican Vietnam but had a limited power base, emerged in the south. President Dwight D. Eisenhower (in office 1953–1961) initially took a dim view of Diem's staying power. But when Diem was able in 1955 to eliminate his strongest opponents and legitimize his rule through a (fraudulent) plebiscite, the United States renewed its aid for Vietnam, previously given to France. Sharing Diem's vision of nation building, the United States granted the Vietnamese president more than $2 billion in military and economic aid during 1955–1961. As a result of this aid, Diem's military was able by 1957 to drive the South Vietnamese communist guerillas, the Vietcong, into the mountains. The unification of the South Vietnamese population appeared to be making progress. John F. Kennedy, who had a high regard for Diem, continued the aid and increased the US troop strength to 16,000. But in 1959–1960, after Ho Chi Minh had gained the support of both the Soviet Union and China (by now fierce rivals, see above, p. 721), the Vietcong rebuilt their insurgency in South Vietnam. President Kennedy was increasingly forced to subordinate nation-building in South Vietnam to less lofty Cold War considerations. The Diem government, beset by major Vietcong gains, eventually hastened its own demise when it alienated the Buddhist majority of South Vietnam in May–August 1963 by having its special armed forces and combat police suppress unarmed protests and raid several temples. But it took several months of plotting and counter-plotting in Saigon before Kennedy decided to drop Diem and support a generals' coup on November 1–2. Once the generals were firmly in power, in the name of the Cold War the United States committed itself fully to the war against the Vietcong, with half a million troops by1967.

Decolonization and Cold War in Africa

On November 1, 1954, the French faced a declaration of a war for independence by the Algerian Front of National Liberation. Algeria, a French colony of 10 million Muslim Arabs and Berbers, had a European settler population of nearly 1 million. France hung on to Algeria and was even able to largely repress the liberation war by the later 1950s. But in the long run, Algerian independence (in 1962) could not be prevented. France's colonial interests were too costly to be maintained, and the United States took over the West's strategic interests in the world.

While some European governments began to liquidate their African empires beginning in 1957, Portugal and Spain (governed by national-supremacist dictators) maintained their colonies of Angola, Mozambique, and Rio de Oro. South Africa introduced its apartheid regime (1948–1994), designed to segregate the white ruling class from the black majority. As the British, French, and Belgians decolonized, however, they ensured that the newly independent African countries would remain their loyal subalterns. For them, African independence would be an exchange for support in the Cold War and continued economic dependence.

The Legacy of Colonialism Between 1918 and 1957, vast changes had occurred in sub-Saharan Africa. The population had more than doubled, urbanization was accelerating, economies were relying too heavily on commodity exports, and an emerging middle class was becoming restless. Heavy investments were required in mining and agriculture as well as in social services. Faced with this financial burden, most of the colonial powers decided to grant independence rather than divert investments badly needed at home.

Ghana, the African Pioneer Once Britain had decided to decolonize, the governmental strategy toward African independence was to support nationalist groups that adopted British-inspired constitutions, guaranteed existing British economic interests, and abided by the rules of the British Commonwealth of Nations. The first to fit these criteria was Ghana in 1957. Its leader, Kwame Nkrumah (1909–1972), son of an Ashante goldsmith, held a master's degree in education from the University of Pennsylvania and appeared to be a sound choice.

Ghana was the pioneer of sub-Saharan independence and development. It had a healthy economy, and its middle class was perhaps the most vital of any African colony. Nkrumah was an activist for African independence and a leading advocate of pan-African unity. Although he had been jailed during the 1950s for his activism, the British nevertheless realized that Nkrumah wielded genuine authority among a majority of politically inexperienced Ghanaians.

Only two years into his rule, however, Nkrumah discarded the independence constitution. Exploiting ethnic tensions among Ashante groups, where an emerging opposition to his rule was concentrated, he promulgated a new republican constitution, removing the country from the British Commonwealth. A year later, he turned to socialist state planning.

The construction of a hydroelectric dam on the Volta River, begun in 1961, was supposed to be the starting point of a heavy industrialization program. But the country soon ran into financing problems, since prices for cocoa, the main export commodity, were declining and large foreign loans were required to continue the program. On the political front, Nkrumah in 1964 amended the constitution again, making Ghana a one-party state with Nkrumah himself as leader for life. An unmanageable foreign debt eventually stalled development, and an army coup, supported by the CIA, ousted Nkrumah in 1966.

Resistance to Independence in Kenya In Kenya, decolonization was not achieved as easily as in Ghana. Efforts to terminate British colonialism were advanced by Jomo Kenyatta (1894–1978), who founded the Kenya African National Union. Kenyatta's movement was met with resistance by British settlers who were reluctant to relinquish control of their economic and political interests. In the face of British opposition, the African nationalists formed the Mau Mau movement, which resorted to terrorist attacks on British estates. Finally, independence was granted Kenya in 1963, and in the following year Kenyatta was named as the first president of the newly created republic.

The Struggle for the Congo's Independence The Belgian Congo, like Vietnam, became a battleground of the Cold War. It had been under the authority of the Belgian government since the beginning of the twentieth century, when it took over from the king (see Chapter 27). During the interwar period, concession companies invested in mining, especially in the southern and central provinces of Katanga and Kasai. Little money went into human development until after World War II. The urban and mine workforce expanded considerably, but no commercial or professional middle classes existed.

Serious demands for independence arose in the Congo only after Ghana became independent in 1957. Groups of nationalists, some advocating a federation and others a centralized state, competed with each other. The urban and mine worker–based National Congolese Movement (*Mouvement National Congolais*, MNC), founded in 1958 by Patrice Lumumba (1925–1961), was the most popular group, favoring a centralized constitutional nationalism that transcended ethnicity, language, and religion. After riots in 1959 and the arrest of Lumumba, Belgian authorities decided to act quickly; they needed compliant nationalists who would continue existing economic arrangements. A Brussels conference with all nationalists—including Lumumba, freed from prison—decided to hold local and national elections in early 1960. To the dismay of Belgium, the centralists, led by Lumumba, won. On June 30, 1960, the Congo became independent, with Lumumba as prime minister and the federalist Joseph Kasa-Vubu (ca. 1910–1969) from the province of Katanga as president.

Lumumba's first political act was the announcement of a general pay raise for state employees, which the Belgian army commander undermined by spreading a rumor that the Congolese foot soldiers would be left out. Outraged, the soldiers mutinied, and amid a general breakdown of public order, Katanga declared its independence. Lumumba fired the Belgian officers, but to restore order he turned to the United Nations. Order was indeed restored by the United Nations, although Belgium made sure that Katanga did not rejoin the Congo. To force Katanga to rejoin, Lumumba turned for support to the Soviet Union. The Cold War had arrived in Africa.

At that time, the Belgian and American governments were convinced that Lumumba was another Castro in the making, a nationalist who would soon become a communist, influenced by Khrushchev. In the Cold War, the fierce but inexperienced Lumumba was given no chance by the Belgian and American governments, acting with mutual consultation. At all costs, the Congo had to remain in the Western camp as a strategic, mineral-rich linchpin in central Africa.

Kasa-Vubu and Lumumba dismissed each other from the government on September 5, giving the new Congolese army chief, Mobutu Sese Seko (1930–1997), the opportunity to seize power on September 14. Mobutu was a member of the MNC whom Lumumba had appointed as army chief, even though it was general knowledge that he was in the pay of the Belgians and the CIA. (Mobutu went on to become the dictator of the Congo, renamed Zaire, and was a close ally of the United States during the period he held power, 1965–1996.) He promptly had Lumumba arrested. Eventually, Belgian agents took Lumumba to Katanga, where they murdered him on January 17, 1961.

During the 1960s, some 35 sub-Saharan colonies achieved their independence through a mostly peaceful transfer of power from their British, French, Belgian, Italian, and Spanish colonial masters. Only Portugal dragged its feet, holding on to its large settler colonies until its own "Carnation Revolution" of 1974 that ended the authoritarian Salazar regime established in 1933. The majority of the newly independent states fell under the sway of authoritarian rulers paying scant attention to their constitutions and favoring their ethnic relatives over the myriads of other ethnic groups. The tension between constitutionalism and ethnicity continues to be a major factor in African politics today.

Putting It All Together

Rapid, breathtaking change characterized the pattern of modernity in the middle of the twentieth century as an intense Cold War competition between the proponents of the ideologies of capitalist democracy and communism unfolded. Imperialism and colonialism collapsed, and nearly 200 nations came to share the globe in the United Nations. Compared to the slow pace of change in the agrarian–urban period of world history, the speed of development during just 145 years of scientific–industrial modernity was dizzying.

Perhaps the most noteworthy events characterizing the early and intense Cold War between capitalist democracy and communism in 1945–1962 was the sad fate of many countries as they emerged into independence or struggled to accommodate themselves in the Western camp, the Eastern Bloc, or the Non-Aligned Movement. As we have seen, US and Soviet leaders were ruthless wherever they perceived communist or capitalist influence in their ranks. But even when new nations pursued a policy of nonalignment, there were subtler ways through which both West and East could apply financial pressures with devastating consequences: Egypt lost its original finances for the Aswan Dam, and China lost its Soviet advisors during the Great Leap Forward.

Not that capitalist democracy and communism were on the same plane; the former provided greater political participation than the latter, which paid only lip service to its notions of equality, as became obvious in 1989–1991, when it collapsed. But the period of the early, active Cold War and decolonization from 1945 to 1962 was far less brutal than the preceding interwar period.

Review and Relate

Thinking Through Patterns

Examine the ways historians approach the big questions of this chapter.

Why did the pattern of unfolding modernity, which offered three choices after World War I, shrink to just capitalist democracy and socialism–communism in 1945? How did each of these two patterns evolve between 1945 and 1962?

The pattern of modernity evolved in the nineteenth century with four major ingredients: constitutional nationalism, ethnic–linguistic–religious nationalism, industrialism, and communism. However, traditional institutions such as monarchies and empires from times prior to 1800 continued to flourish. World War I wiped out most monarchies, capitalist democracy continued, communism came into its own in the Soviet Union, imperialism and colonialism survived, and supremacist nationalism attracted those who found democracy and communism wanting. World War II eliminated supremacist nationalism and, eventually, also imperialism and colonialism. The remaining choices of capitalist democracy and communism were divided between two power blocs, which during the early Cold War period of 1945–1962 shared the world almost evenly.

What are the cultural premises of modernity?

Modernity's roots are in the New Sciences of the 1600s, with its assumptions of materialism and the social contract. It evolved into scientific–industrial modernity, with profound cultural consequences. Successive waves of increasingly modern artistic movements were insufficient to address the basic materialist flaw of modernity, which in each generation gave rise to the question of the meaning of it all.

How did the newly independent countries of the Middle East, Asia, and Africa adapt to the divided world of the Cold War?

After 1945 the number of nations on earth rose to the total of 196 today. The new nations, emerging from colonialism, were largely agrarian, putting industrialism beyond reach. With great hope, the ruling elites in many new nations embraced a mixed capitalist–democratic and socialist regime, with heavy state investments in basic industries. However, in contrast to Stalin, who introduced these types of investments under the label of state-guided socialism, none of the elites in the new nations had the will to collect the money for these investments from their rural population. Instead, they borrowed heavily from the capitalist–democratic countries. True independence remained elusive.

Against the Grain

Consider this as a counterpoint to the main patterns examined in this chapter.

Postwar Counterculture

- What did the Beat Generation find so offensive and alienating about America during the postwar era of the 1950s?
- How does the Beat countercultural movement following World War II compare with expressions of the Lost Generation in the aftermath of World War I?

Postwar Europe and North America during the 1950s embarked on programs of reconstruction, reflecting a yearning for normalcy following years of hardship. Central to this agenda was a mood of traditionalism. In America, however, fear of socialism and communism amid Cold War tensions generated a new element of suspicion. Crackdowns on groups by the House Un-American Activities Committee promoted a prevailing trend toward conformity with traditional Western values.

Not everyone fell in line with this trend. The early 1950s witnessed the emergence of a countercultural movement known as the "Beat Generation," initiated by a group of writers and students affiliated with Columbia University. Finding prevailing conformity stultifying, Jack Kerouac, Allen Ginsberg, William Burroughs, and others sought new avenues of nonconformist expression, including experimentation with drugs, alternative sexuality, and a fascination with Eastern religions—especially Buddhism—and music. Ginsberg's *Howl and Other Poems* (1956), an indictment of traditional norms, represents the earliest expression of the Beat ethic. *Howl* was followed by Kerouac's *On the Road* (1957); drawn from a series of road trips around America, the work expresses the emptiness of current culture.

Beats roamed the globe in quest of non-Western intellectual inspiration. In turn, Beat culture transcended American borders, and was assimilated into countercultural movements in Europe and Asia. Among the more telling instances of Beat influence abroad was John Lennon's meeting with a teenaged British Beat poet in 1960, which resulted in his changing the spelling of the name of the famous rock group from "Beetles" to "Beatles."

The Beat Generation nurtured later countercultures, including the hippies of the 1960s. Whereas the Beats simply explored alternative lifestyles, later exemplars were more motivated by, and interested in, political expressions. Their reach even extended to musical expressions of the 1960s; Bob Dylan, Jim Morrison, and the Beatles are among their many devotees.

Key Terms

Cold War 708
Containment 708
Existentialism 716
Great Leap Forward 721
Marshall Plan 709
Non-Aligned Movement 724
Peronism 719
Populism 718
Truman Doctrine 708
United Nations 708

Learn more with this chapter's digital tools, including the Oxford Insight Study Guide, at http://www.oup.com/he/vonsivers4e. Please see the Further Resources section at the back of the book for additional readings and suggested websites.

PATTERNS OF EVIDENCE |

Sources for Chapter 29

SOURCE 29.1

The Universal Declaration of Human Rights

December 10, 1948

The Universal Declaration of Human Rights, adopted by the United Nations General Assembly on December 10, 1948, was one of the most significant and lasting results of World War II. The League of Nations, created after the World War I, had failed to prevent the beginning of another, even more catastrophic and costly conflict. The United Nations was planned throughout the war as a substitute mechanism for global peace and security, but world leaders also believed that a document was necessary to affirm the rights of individuals throughout the entire world. A formal drafting committee, consisting of members from eight countries, was charged with the task. The committee chair was Eleanor Roosevelt, the widow of President Franklin D. Roosevelt and a strong advocate for human rights in her own right. By its resolution 217 A (III), the General Assembly, meeting in Paris, adopted the Universal Declaration of Human Rights. Eight nations abstained from the vote, but none dissented.

PREAMBLE

Whereas recognition of the inherent dignity and of the equal and inalienable rights of all members of the human family is the foundation of freedom, justice and peace in the world,

Whereas disregard and contempt for human rights have resulted in barbarous acts which have outraged the conscience of mankind, and the advent of a world in which human beings shall enjoy freedom of speech and belief and freedom from fear and want has been proclaimed as the highest aspiration of the common people,

Whereas it is essential, if man is not to be compelled to have recourse, as a last resort, to rebellion against tyranny and oppression, that human rights should be protected by the rule of law,

Whereas it is essential to promote the development of friendly relations between nations,

---

Source: http://www.un.org/en/documents/udhr/

Whereas the peoples of the United Nations have in the Charter reaffirmed their faith in fundamental human rights, in the dignity and worth of the human person and in the equal rights of men and women and have determined to promote social progress and better standards of life in larger freedom,

Whereas Member States have pledged themselves to achieve, in cooperation with the United Nations, the promotion of universal respect for and observance of human rights and fundamental freedoms,

Whereas a common understanding of these rights and freedoms is of the greatest importance for the full realization of this pledge,

Now, Therefore THE GENERAL ASSEMBLY proclaims THIS UNIVERSAL DECLARATION OF HUMAN RIGHTS as a common standard of achievement for all peoples and all nations, to the end that every individual and every organ of society, keeping this Declaration constantly in mind, shall strive by teaching and education to promote respect for these rights and freedoms and by progressive measures, national and international, to secure their universal and effective recognition and observance, both among the peoples of Member States themselves and among the peoples of territories under their jurisdiction.

Article 1.

All human beings are born free and equal in dignity and rights. They are endowed with reason and conscience and should act towards one another in a spirit of brotherhood.

Article 2.

Everyone is entitled to all the rights and freedoms set forth in this Declaration, without distinction of any kind, such as race, colour, sex, language, religion, political or other opinion, national or social origin, property, birth or other status. Furthermore, no distinction shall be made on the basis of the political, jurisdictional or international status of the country or territory to which a person belongs, whether it be independent, trust, non-self-governing or under any other limitation of sovereignty.

Article 3.

Everyone has the right to life, liberty and security of person.

Article 4.

No one shall be held in slavery or servitude; slavery and the slave trade shall be prohibited in all their forms.

Article 5.

No one shall be subjected to torture or to cruel, inhuman or degrading treatment or punishment.

Article 6.

Everyone has the right to recognition everywhere as a person before the law.

. . .

Article 15.

(1) Everyone has the right to a nationality.

(2) No one shall be arbitrarily deprived of his nationality nor denied the right to change his nationality.

Article 16.

(1) Men and women of full age, without any limitation due to race, nationality or religion, have the right to marry and to found a family. They are entitled to equal rights as to marriage, during marriage and at its dissolution.

(2) Marriage shall be entered into only with the free and full consent of the intending spouses.
(3) The family is the natural and fundamental group unit of society and is entitled to protection by society and the State.

Article 17.

(1) Everyone has the right to own property alone as well as in association with others.
(2) No one shall be arbitrarily deprived of his property.

Article 18.

Everyone has the right to freedom of thought, conscience and religion; this right includes freedom to change his religion or belief, and freedom, either alone or in community with others and in public or private, to manifest his religion or belief in teaching, practice, worship and observance.

Article 19.

Everyone has the right to freedom of opinion and expression; this right includes freedom to hold opinions without interference and to seek, receive and impart information and ideas through any media and regardless of frontiers.

. . .

Article 23.

(1) Everyone has the right to work, to free choice of employment, to just and favorable conditions of work and to protection against unemployment.
(2) Everyone, without any discrimination, has the right to equal pay for equal work.
(3) Everyone who works has the right to just and favorable remuneration ensuring for himself and his family an existence worthy of human dignity, and supplemented, if necessary, by other means of social protection.
(4) Everyone has the right to form and to join trade unions for the protection of his interests.

Article 24.

Everyone has the right to rest and leisure, including reasonable limitation of working hours and periodic holidays with pay.

Article 25.

(1) Everyone has the right to a standard of living adequate for the health and well-being of himself and of his family, including food, clothing, housing and medical care and necessary social services, and the right to security in the event of unemployment, sickness, disability, widowhood, old age or other lack of livelihood in circumstances beyond his control.
(2) Motherhood and childhood are entitled to special care and assistance. All children, whether born in or out of wedlock, shall enjoy the same social protection.

Article 26.

(1) Everyone has the right to education. Education shall be free, at least in the elementary and fundamental stages. Elementary education shall be compulsory. Technical and professional education shall be made generally available and higher education shall be equally accessible to all on the basis of merit.
(2) Education shall be directed to the full development of the human personality and to the strengthening of respect for human rights and fundamental freedoms. It shall promote understanding, tolerance and friendship among all

nations, racial or religious groups, and shall further the activities of the United Nations for the maintenance of peace.
(3) Parents have a prior right to choose the kind of education that shall be given to their children.

▸ Working with Sources

1. **According to the Universal Declaration of Human Rights, what would be the practical benefits of guaranteeing human rights for the entire human family?**
2. **How likely were these goals to be applied globally in 1948? Which articles remained to be fulfilled at that point—and perhaps even today?**

SOURCE 29.2

Winston Churchill, "The Iron Curtain Speech"

March 5, 1946

Throughout the 1930s, Churchill had opposed the policy of "appeasement" advocated by Prime Minister Neville Chamberlain and his allies in the British Parliament. His rise to the highest political office was facilitated by Chamberlain's failure to deliver on the "peace in our time" he had promised after the Munich Agreement in September 1938. However, it was not until May 1940 that Churchill got his chance. Having calmed, encouraged, and directed the British people—and others—throughout the war years, Churchill was himself removed from power in 1945. Nevertheless, at this famous address delivered at Westminster College in Missouri in 1946, Churchill warned of a new regime that also could not, and should not, be appeased. It is considered one of the first salvos in the developing Cold War between the West and the Soviet bloc.

The safety of the world, ladies and gentlemen, requires a unity in Europe, from which no nation should be permanently outcast. It is from the quarrels of the strong parent races in Europe that the world wars we have witnessed, or which occurred in former times, have sprung. Twice the United States has had to send several millions of its young men across the Atlantic to fight the wars.

Source: http://www.fordham.edu/halsall/mod/churchill-iron.asp

But now we all can find any nation, wherever it may dwell, between dusk and dawn. Surely we should work with conscious purpose for a grand pacification of Europe within the structure of the United Nations and in accordance with our Charter. In a great number of countries, far from the Russian frontiers and throughout the world, Communist fifth columns are established and work in complete unity and absolute obedience to the directions they receive from the Communist center. Except in the British Commonwealth and in the United States where Communism is in its infancy, the Communist parties or fifth columns constitute a growing challenge and peril to Christian civilization. The outlook is also anxious in the Far East and especially in Manchuria. The agreement which was made at Yalta, to which I was a party, was extremely favorable to Soviet Russia, but it was made at a time when no one could say that the German war might not extend all through the summer and autumn of 1945 and when the Japanese war was expected by the best judges to last for a further eighteen months from the end of the German war. I repulse the idea that a new war is inevitable—still more that it is imminent. It is because I am sure that our fortunes are still in our own hands and that we hold the power to save the future, that I feel the duty to speak out now that I have the occasion and the opportunity to do so. I do not believe that Soviet Russia desires war. What they desire is the fruits of war and the indefinite expansion of their power and doctrines. But what we have to consider here today while time remains, is the permanent prevention of war and the establishment of conditions of freedom and democracy as rapidly as possible in all countries. Our difficulties and dangers will not be removed by closing our eyes to them. They will not be removed by mere waiting to see what happens; nor will they be removed by a policy of appeasement. What is needed is a settlement, and the longer this is delayed, the more difficult it will be and the greater our dangers will become. From what I have seen of our Russian friends and allies during the war, I am convinced that there is nothing they admire so much as strength, and there is nothing for which they have less respect than for weakness, especially military weakness. For that reason the old doctrine of a balance of power is unsound. We cannot afford, if we can help it, to work on narrow margins, offering temptations to a trial of strength.

. . .

If the population of the English-speaking Commonwealth be added to that of the United States, with all that such cooperation implies in the air, on the sea, all over the globe, and in science and in industry, and in moral force, there will be no quivering, precarious balance of power to offer its temptation to ambition or adventure. On the contrary there will be an overwhelming assurance of security. If we adhere faithfully to the Charter of the United Nations and walk forward in sedate and sober strength, seeking no one's land or treasure, seeking to lay no arbitrary control upon the thoughts of men, if all British moral and material forces and convictions are joined with your own in fraternal association, the high roads of the future will be clear, not only for us but for all, not only for our time but for a century to come.

Working with Sources

1. What does this speech reveal about changing commitments and alliances after the end of the war in 1945? What factors caused a change in policy in Western countries toward the Soviet Union?
2. Why was Churchill commenting on the dangers of appeasement with regard to Soviet foreign policy?

SOURCE 29.3

Letters on the Cuban Missile Crisis between Fidel Castro and Nikita Khrushchev

October 28 and 30, 1962

The Cuban Missile Crisis of October 1962 marked the climax, and the most dangerous point, of the Cold War between the United States and the Soviet Union. When US spy planes discovered the presence of missiles and launching pads in Cuba, President John F. Kennedy demanded their immediate destruction and followed up this demand with a naval blockade of the island—and continued reconnaissance missions in Cuban airspace—to prevent the arrival of Russian reinforcements. The world held its breath for several days as Soviet ships, bearing more nuclear missiles, sailed steadily for Cuba. The globe teetered on the brink of nuclear annihilation, and this exchange of letters reveals, from the Soviet and Cuban side, how very close to that brink the world actually came.

Letter to Nikita Khrushchev from Fidel Castro regarding defending Cuban air space

October 28, 1962

Dear Comrade Khrushchev:

I have just received your letter.

The position of our Government regarding your statement can be found in the text of the declaration announced today, with which you are surely familiar.

I must clarify a point relating to the anti-aircraft measures which we adopted. You said: "Yesterday you shot down one of them, yet previously you did not when they flew over your territory."

Previously, there were isolated violations with no particular military purpose, and they did not result in real danger.

This is no longer the case. There was the danger of a surprise attack on certain military sites. We decided that we could not remain idle because of the

Source: http://cubanet.org/htdocs/ref/dis/10110201.htm

danger of a surprise attack. With our warning radars turned off, the potential attackers could fly with impunity over the sites and totally destroy them. We did not believe that we should allow this, given the cost and effort which we have expended, and because an attack would have gravely weakened our morals and military capability. Because of this, Cuban forces mobilized fifty anti-aircraft batteries, our entire reserves, on October 24 in order to support the positions of the Soviet forces. If we wanted to prevent the risk of a surprise attack, the crews had to have orders to shoot. The Soviet Forces Command can give you further details on what happened with the plane that was shot down.

In the past, violations of our airspace were de facto and were conducted furtively. Yesterday the American Government tried to make official the privilege of violating our air space at any time, day and night. This we could not accept because it would mean renouncing our sovereign prerogative. Nevertheless, we agree to avoid an incident at this moment that could gravely harm the negotiations. We will instruct the Cuban batteries to hold their fire while the negotiations last, without reversing the decision we announced yesterday to defend our air space. We must consider the dangers of possible incidents in the present conditions of high tension.

I also wish to inform you that we are opposed, by principle, to inspections on our territory.

I appreciate the enormous efforts which you have made to maintain the peace, and we totally agree with the necessity to fight for this aim. If we achieve it in a just, solid, and permanent way it will be an enormous service to humanity.

Fraternally,
Fidel Castro

Letter to Fidel Castro from Nikita Khrushchev stating Khrushchev will help to defend Cuba

October 30, 1962

Dear Comrade Fidel Castro:

We have received your letter of October 28, along with the reports of the conversations that you and President Dorticos had with our ambassador.

We understand your situation and are taking into account your difficulties in this first stage following the elimination of the maximum tension that resulted from the threat of an attack by American imperialists which you expected at any moment.

We understand that for you certain difficulties may have emerged as a consequence of the promises we made to the United States to withdraw the missile bases from Cuba in exchange for their promise to abandon their plans to invade Cuba and to prevent their allies in the Western hemisphere from doing so, to end their so-called "quarantine"—their blockade of Cuba. This commitment has led to an end to the conflict in the Caribbean, a conflict which implied, as you can well understand, a superpower confrontation and its transformation into a world war where the missiles and thermonuclear weapons would have been used. According to our ambassador, certain Cubans feel that the

Cuban people would prefer a different kind of statement, one that would not deal with the withdrawal of the missiles. It is possible that such feelings exist among the people. But we, politicians and heads of state, are the people's leaders and the people do not know everything. This is why we must march at the head of the people. Then they will follow and respect us.

If, by giving in to popular sentiment, we had allowed ourselves to be swept up by the more inflamed sectors of the populace, and if we had refused to reach a reasonable agreement with the government of the USA, war would have probably broken out, resulting in millions of deaths. Those who survived would have blamed the leaders for not having taken the measures that would have avoided this war of extermination.

The prevention of war and of an attack on Cuba did not depend only on the measures taken by our governments, but also on the analysis and examination of the enemy's actions near your territory. In short, the situation had to be considered as a whole.

Some people say that we did not consult sufficiently with each other before taking the decision of which you know.

In fact, we consider that consultations did take place, dear Comrade Fidel Castro, since we received your cables, one more alarming than the other, and finally your cable of October 27 where you said that you were almost certain that an attack against Cuba was imminent. According to you it was only a matter of time: 24 or 72 hours.

Having received this very alarming cable from you, and knowing of your courage, we believed the alert to be totally justified.

Wasn't that consultation on your part? We interpreted that cable as a sign of maximum alert. But if we had carried on with our consultations in such conditions, knowing that the bellicose and unbridled militarists of the United States wanted to seize the occasion to attack Cuba, we would have been wasting our time and the strike could have taken place.

We think that the presence of our strategic missiles in Cuba has polarized the attention of the imperialists. They were afraid that they would be used, which is why they risked wanting to eliminate them, either by bombing them or by invading Cuba. And we must recognize that they had the capability to put them out of action. This is why, I repeat, your sense of alarm was totally justified.

In your cable of October 27 you proposed that we be the first to carry out a nuclear strike against the enemy's territory. Naturally you understand where that would lead us. It would not be a simple strike, but the start of a thermonuclear world war.

Dear Comrade Fidel Castro, I find your proposal to be wrong, even though I understand your reasons.

We have lived through a very grave moment, a global thermonuclear war could have broken out. Of course the United States would have suffered enormous losses, but the Soviet Union and the whole socialist bloc would have also suffered greatly. It is even difficult to say how things would have ended for the Cuban people. First of all, Cuba would have burned in the fires of war. Without a doubt the Cuban people would have fought courageously but, also without a doubt, the Cuban people would have perished heroically. We struggle against imperialism, not in order to die, but to draw on all of our potential, to lose as little as possible, and later to win more, so as to be a victor and make communism triumph.

The measures which we have adopted have allowed us to reach the goal which we had set when we decided to send the missiles to Cuba. We have extracted from the United States the commitment not to invade Cuba and not to allow their Latin American allies to do so. We have accomplished all of this without a nuclear war.

Working with Sources

1. **Why was Castro so insistent in drawing Khrushchev's attention to violations of Cuba's sovereignty by the United States?**
2. **How did Khrushchev attempt to calm Castro down? Why did he do so, and what does the document reveal about his intentions during this crisis?**

SOURCE 29.4

Ho Chi Minh, "The Path Which Led Me to Leninism"

April 1960

On September 2, 1945, the day of Japan's surrender to the United States, the leader of the communist resistance in Indochina, Ho Chi Minh, read a Vietnamese declaration of independence to half a million people in Hanoi. Newly liberated from occupation by Nazi Germany, France hoped to reassert its power in the region it had colonized in the previous century, but the communist Vietminh refused to budge from their demands for independence. The French persuaded the United States that this colonial conflict was an outgrowth of the larger Cold War between the West and the Soviet Union, and the American administrations of Presidents Truman and Eisenhower (1945–1961) provided financial and moral support to the French as they clashed with Vietnamese insurgents. The French surrendered in 1954, but Vietnam was divided. The United States continued its involvement in South Vietnam—soon to be accelerated with the dispatch

Source: Ho Chi Minh, *Selected Works*, vol. 4 (Hanoi: Foreign Languages Publishing House, 1962), available online at http://www.marxists.org/reference/archive/ho-chi-minh/works/1960/04/x01.htm

of military advisors and military personnel by Presidents Eisenhower and Kennedy (1961–1963). Published in April 1960 in a Soviet journal titled *Problems of the East*, this statement by Ho Chi Minh encapsulates his thinking on the example of Vladimir Lenin in his own struggle against Western imperialism.

After World War I, I made my living in Paris, now as a retoucher at a photographer's, now as painter of "Chinese antiquities" (made in France!). I would distribute leaflets denouncing the crimes committed by the French colonialists in Viet Nam.

At that time, I supported the October Revolution only instinctively, not yet grasping all its historic importance. I loved and admired Lenin because he was a great patriot who liberated his compatriots; until then, I had read none of his books.

The reason for my joining the French Socialist Party was that these "ladies and gentlemen"—as I called my comrades at that moment—had shown their sympathy towards me, towards the struggle of the oppressed peoples. But I understood neither what was a party, a trade-union, nor what was socialism nor communism.

Heated discussions were then taking place in the branches of the Socialist Party, about the question whether the Socialist Party should remain in the Second International, should a Second and a half International be founded or should the Socialist Party join Lenin's Third International? I attended the meetings regularly, twice or thrice a week and attentively listened to the discussion. First, I could not understand thoroughly. Why were the discussions so heated? Either with the Second, Second and a half or Third International, the revolution could be waged. What was the use of arguing then? As for the First International, what had become of it?

What I wanted most to know—and this precisely was not debated in the meetings—was: which International sides with the peoples of colonial countries?

I raised this question—the most important in my opinion—in a meeting. Some comrades answered: It is the Third, not the Second International. And a comrade gave me Lenin's "Thesis on the national and colonial questions" published by l'Humanité to read.

There were political terms difficult to understand in this thesis. But by dint of reading it again and again, finally I could grasp the main part of it. What emotion, enthusiasm, clear-sightedness and confidence it instilled into me! I was overjoyed to tears. Though sitting alone in my room, I shouted out aloud as if addressing large crowds: "Dear martyr compatriots! This is what we need, this is the path to our liberation!"

After then, I had entire confidence in Lenin, in the Third International.

Formerly, during the meetings of the Party branch, I only listened to the discussion; I had a vague belief that all were logical, and could not differentiate as to who were right and who were wrong. But from then on, I also plunged into the debates and discussed with fervour. Though I was still lacking French words to express all my thoughts, I smashed the allegations attacking Lenin and the Third International with no less vigour. My only argument was: "If you do not condemn colonialism, if you do not side with the colonial people, what kind of revolution are you waging?"

. . .

At first, patriotism, not yet communism, led me to have confidence in Lenin, in the Third International. Step by step, along the struggle, by studying Marxism-Leninism parallel with participation in practical activities, I gradually came upon the fact that only socialism and communism can liberate the oppressed nations and the working people throughout the world from slavery.

Working with Sources

1. **What did Ho make of the inner divisions among socialists? How did these divisions affect the interests of the Vietnamese, as he saw them?**
2. **In what respects did Ho see Lenin as a liberator of all "colonized" peoples? Was he justified in this conclusion?**

SOURCE 29.5

Indira Gandhi, "What Educated Women Can Do"

November 23, 1974

The only child of Jawaharlal Nehru, the first prime minister of India, Indira Gandhi served in turn as prime minister between 1966 and 1977 and again from 1980 until her assassination in 1984. She was the third of the country's prime ministers and the first female to hold the position. Gandhi pursued many of the same policies as her father, supported the Non-Aligned Movement, and was especially concerned to promote the interests of the women and girls of her nation and of the world. This speech, delivered to students in a women's college, reveals her concern to combine women's rights with India's drive for modernization.

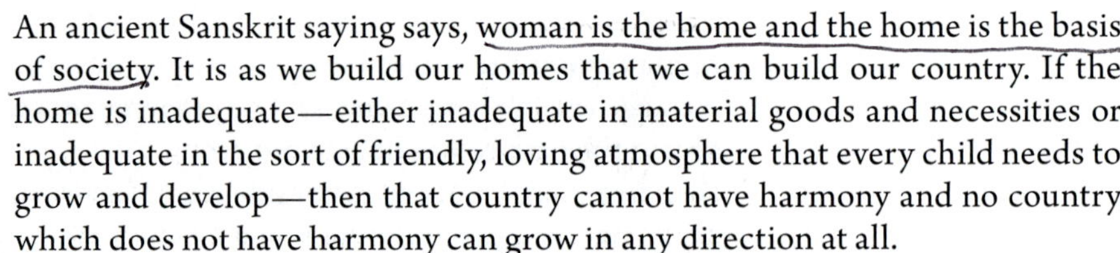

An ancient Sanskrit saying says, woman is the home and the home is the basis of society. It is as we build our homes that we can build our country. If the home is inadequate—either inadequate in material goods and necessities or inadequate in the sort of friendly, loving atmosphere that every child needs to grow and develop—then that country cannot have harmony and no country which does not have harmony can grow in any direction at all.

Source: http://www.edchange.org/multicultural/speeches/indira_gandhi_educated.html

That is why women's education is almost more important than the education of boys and men. We—and by "we" I do not mean only we in India but all the world—have neglected women's education. It is fairly recent. Of course, not to you but when I was a child, the story of the early days of women's education in England, for instance, was very current. Everybody remembered what had happened in the early days.

Doli: A covered litter.

I remember what used to happen here. I still remember the days when living in old Delhi even as a small child of seven or eight. I had to go out in a **doli** if I left the house. We just did not walk. Girls did not walk in the streets. First, you had your sari with which you covered your head, then you had another shawl or something with which you covered your hand and all the body, then you had a white shawl, with which every thing was covered again although your face was open fortunately. Then you were in the doli, which again was covered by another cloth. And this was in a family or community which did not observe **purdah** of any kind at all. In fact, all our social functions always were mixed functions but this was the atmosphere of the city and of the country.

Purdah: Ritual seclusion of females.

Now, we have got education and there is a debate all over the country whether this education is adequate to the needs of society or the needs of our young people. I am one of those who always believe that education needs a thorough overhauling. But at the same time, I think that everything in our education is not bad, that even the present education has produced very fine men and women, especially scientists and experts in different fields, who are in great demand all over the world and even in the most affluent countries. Many of our young people leave us and go abroad because they get higher salaries, they get better conditions of work.

. . .

Sometimes, I am very sad that even people who do science are quite unscientific in their thinking and in their other actions—not what they are doing in the laboratories but how they live at home or their attitudes towards other people. Now, for India to become what we want it to become with a modern, rational society and firmly based on what is good in our ancient tradition and in our soil, for this we have to have a thinking public, thinking young women who are not content to accept what comes from any part of the world but are willing to listen to it, to analyse it and to decide whether it is to be accepted or whether it is to be thrown out and this is the sort of education which we want, which enables our young people to adjust to this changing world and to be able to contribute to it.

Some people think that only by taking up very high jobs, you are doing something important or you are doing national service. But we all know that the most complex machinery will be ineffective if one small screw is not working as it should and that screw is just as important as any big part. It is the same in national life. There is no job that is too small; there is no person who is too small. Everybody has something to do. And if he or she does it well, then the country will run well.

In our superstition, we have thought that some work is dirty work. For instance, sweeping has been regarded as dirty. Only some people can do it;

others should not do it. Now we find that manure is the most valuable thing that the world has today and many of the world's economies are shaking because there is not enough fertilizer—and not just the chemical fertilizer but the ordinary manure, night-soil and all that sort of thing, things which were considered dirty.

Now it shows how beautifully balanced the world was with everything fitted in with something else. Everything, whether dirty or small, had a purpose. We, with our science and technology, have tried to—not purposely, but somehow, we have created an imbalance and that is what is troubling, on a big scale, the economies of the world and also people and individuals. They are feeling alienated from their societies, not only in India but almost in every country in the world, except in places where the whole purpose of education and government has to be to make the people conform to just one idea. We are told that people there are very happy in whatever they are doing. If they are told to clean the streets, well, if he is a professor he has to clean the streets, if he is a scientist he has to do it, and we were told that they are happy doing it. Well, if they are happy, it is alright.

But I do not think in India we can have that kind of society where people are forced to do things because we think that they can be forced maybe for 25 years, maybe for 50 years, but sometime or the other there will be an explosion. In our society, we allow lots of smaller explosions because we think that that will guard the basic stability and progress of society and prevent it from having the kind of chaotic explosion which can retard our progress and harmony in the country.

So, I hope that all of you who have this great advantage of education will not only do whatever work you are doing keeping the national interests in view, but you will make your own contribution to creating peace and harmony, to bringing beauty in the lives of our people and our country. I think this is the special responsibility of the women of India. We want to do a great deal for our country, but we have never regarded India as isolated from the rest of the world. What we want to do is to make a better world. So, we have to see India's problems in the perspective of the larger world problems.

▶ Working with Sources

1. **What were the parameters of the "modern, rational society" that Gandhi envisioned?**
2. **In what terms did she contrast ancient superstitions and modern science, and how did she relate this dichotomy to Indian history and cultural identity?**

SOURCE 29.6

Kwame Nkrumah, "I Speak of Freedom"

1961

In his early years Kwame Nkrumah (1909–1972) studied in America and Britain, earning several degrees in economics, education, and philosophy while at the same time involved in assorted activist associations calling for the independence of African states from colonial rule. After returning to his native Africa in 1947, Nkrumah rose to power as the leader of the Convention People's Party, which protested existing conditions under British rule. After the CCP's victory in 1951 elections, Nkrumah continued to strive for the Gold Coast's independence, which was finally granted in 1957. As prime minister of the newly renamed country of Ghana, Nkrumah's governing policies devolved into a dictatorship, which was overthrown by military forces in 1966. Nevertheless, Nkrumah is remembered for his advocacy of pan-Africanism, which he pronounced in a speech delivered in 1961.

For centuries, Europeans dominated the African continent. The white man arrogated to himself the right to rule and to be obeyed by the non-white; his mission, he claimed, was to "civilise" Africa. Under this cloak, the Europeans robbed the continent of vast riches and inflicted unimaginable suffering on the African people. All this makes a sad story, but now we must be prepared to bury the past with its unpleasant memories and look to the future. All we ask of the former colonial powers is their goodwill and co-operation to remedy past mistakes and injustices and to grant independence to the colonies in Africa.

It is clear that we must find an African solution to our problems, and that this can only be found in African unity. Divided we are weak; united, Africa could become one of the greatest forces for good in the world.

Although most Africans are poor, our continent is potentially extremely rich. Our mineral resources, which are being exploited with foreign capital only to enrich foreign investors, range from gold and diamonds to uranium and petroleum. Our forests contain some of the finest woods to be grown anywhere. Our cash crops include cocoa, coffee, rubber, tobacco and cotton. As for power, which is an important factor in any economic development, Africa contains over 40% of the potential water power of the world, as compared with about 10% in Europe and 13% in North America. Yet so far, less than 1% has been developed. This is one of the reasons why we have in Africa the paradox of poverty in the midst of plenty, and scarcity in the midst of abundance.

Never before have a people had within their grasp so great an opportunity for developing a continent endowed with so much wealth. Individually, the independent states of Africa, some of them potentially rich,

---

Source: Kwame Nkrumah, *I Speak of Freedom: A Statement of African Ideology* (London: William Heinemann Ltd., 1961), xi–xiv.

others poor, can do little for their people. Together, by mutual help, they can achieve much. But the economic development of the continent must be planned and pursued as a whole. A loose confederation designed only for economic co-operation would not provide the necessary unity of purpose. Only a strong political union can bring about full and effective development of our natural resources for the benefit of our people.

The political situation in Africa today is heartening and at the same time disturbing. It is heartening to see so many new flags hoisted in place of the old; it is disturbing to see so many countries of varying sizes and at different levels of development, weak and, in some cases, almost helpless. If this terrible state of fragmentation is allowed to continue it may well be disastrous for us all.

There are at present some 28 states in Africa, excluding the Union of South Africa, and those countries not yet free. No less than nine of these states have a population of less than three million. Can we seriously believe that the colonial powers meant these countries to be independent, viable states? The example of South America, which has as much wealth, if not more than North America, and yet remains weak and dependent on outside interests, is one which every African would do well to study.

Critics of African unity often refer to the wide differences in culture, language and ideas in various parts of Africa. This is true, but the essential fact remains that we are all Africans, and have a common interest in the independence of Africa. The difficulties presented by questions of language, culture and different political systems are not insuperable. If the need for political union is agreed by us all, then the will to create it is born; and where there's a will there's a way.

The present leaders of Africa have already shown a remarkable willingness to consult and seek advice among themselves. Africans have, indeed, begun to think continentally. They realise that they have much in common, both in their past history, in their present problems and in their future hopes. To suggest that the time is not yet ripe for considering a political union of Africa is to evade the facts and ignore realities in Africa today.

The greatest contribution that Africa can make to the peace of the world is to avoid all the dangers inherent in disunity, by creating a political union which will also by its success, stand as an example to a divided world. A Union of African states will project more effectively the African personality. It will command respect from a world that has regard only for size and influence. The scant attention paid to African opposition to the French atomic tests in the Sahara, and the ignominious spectacle of the U.N.in the Congo quibbling about constitutional niceties while the Republic was tottering into anarchy, are evidence of the callous disregard of African Independence by the Great Powers.

We have to prove that greatness is not to be measured in stockpiles of atom bombs. I believe strongly and sincerely that with the deep-rooted wisdom and dignity, the innate respect for human lives, the intense humanity that is our heritage, the African race, united under one federal government, will emerge not as just another world bloc to flaunt its wealth and strength, but as a Great Power whose greatness is indestructible because it is built not on fear, envy and suspicion, nor won at the expense of others, but founded on hope, trust, friendship and directed to the good of all mankind.

The emergence of such a mighty stabilising force in this strife-worn world should be regarded not as the shadowy dream of a visionary, but as a practical proposition, which the peoples of Africa can, and should, translate into reality. There is a tide in the affairs of every people when the moment strikes for political action. Such was the moment in the history of the United States of America when the Founding Fathers saw beyond the petty wranglings of the separate states and created a Union. This is our chance. We must act now. Tomorrow may be too late and the opportunity will have passed, and with it the hope of free Africa's survival.

Working with Sources

1. **How does Nkrumah describe the indigenous strengths of Africa?**
2. **What future does Nkrumah foresee for a united Africa?**

World Period Six

From Three Modernities to One

Modern scientific–industrial society underwent dramatic transformations after World War I (1914–1918). Three competing models for modernity—capitalist democracy, communism, and supremacist nationalism—shrank to one in the course of the twentieth century. German and Japanese supremacist nationalism collapsed in 1945 as a result of their overextended military aggression. Soviet and Eastern European communism collapsed in 1989–1991 due to a top-heavy central command economy. Western capitalist democracy survived but did so only after enduring decolonization and regulating its economy. After 1991, it expanded its global dominance, buttressed by the computer revolution, but questions have arisen whether its model of modernity is sustainable. Under current conditions, the natural environment will not be able to support the exploitative framework of capitalist democracy much longer. The grave threat posed by COVID-19 has further undermined its credibility.

Chapter 30

The End of the Cold War, Western Social Transformation, and the Developing World

1963–1991

CHAPTER THIRTY PATTERNS

Origins, Interactions, Adaptations The question of which of the two patterns of modernity would define the future—democratic capitalism or communism—dominated the latter part of the twentieth century. The communist bloc shrank when the Soviet Union and China split in the early 1960s. But it grew again when the Soviet Union began supporting national liberation movements and engaged itself in the Middle East and Latin America. In this way, Cuba became communist and promptly prepared to acquire Soviet missiles that threatened the United States. In a dramatic showdown in 1962, the United States forced a Soviet retreat. Both sides then agreed to more peaceful interactions.

Uniqueness and Similarities One exception was the Vietnam War. The perceived role of the United States as an undemocratic superpower in the Free World became the flashpoint for the rise of the unique social phenomenon of the "1968 Rebellion," a generational revolt against parental authority. This revolt, similar in all Western democracies, engendered a thoroughgoing relaxation of values in gender, family, and school. It even reached the Eastern Bloc, where the Soviets at first directly or indirectly crushed uprisings but later allowed for some reforms. The communist command economy, however, resisted all efforts of reform and collapsed in 1989–1991. Thus ended the second of the three models of modernity, leaving just democratic capitalism.

CHAPTER OUTLINE

The Climax of the Cold War

Transforming the West

From "Underdeveloped" to "Developing" World, 1963–1991

Putting It All Together

As the helicopter approached, the fighter on the ground recognized it immediately: *Shaitan Arba,* "Satan's Chariot," the Soviet Mi-24 (known in the West by the NATO code name "Hind"), a heavily armed and armored gunship that had proven largely impervious to the rifle and small arms fire of the Afghan Islamic guerilla fighters (*mujahideen*). In this fight in the Afghan high country, the Soviets, it appeared, had acquired a technological edge as they sought to eliminate resistance to the client regime they had installed in the capital of Kabul in 1979.

But just before the soldier took cover, the helicopter exploded in a fireball. A vapor trail marked a spot from where it appeared a rocket had been fired. A group of men shouted, "God is great!" as they cheered their victory.

The weapon that had downed the helicopter was a new American "Stinger" shoulder-fired missile, which the United States was clandestinely supplying to the Afghan Muslim fighters attempting to expel the Soviet occupying forces. The Stinger went far to neutralize the Soviet advantage in airpower and enable the mujahideen to push the Soviets out of Afghanistan in this last contest of the Cold War. In fact, the immense cost of the Soviet–Afghan War, combined with the price of trying to match the American effort to create a missile defense system against intercontinental ballistic missiles (ICBMs), contributed to the collapse of the Soviet economy by the end of the 1980s and led to the end of the Eastern Bloc and the Soviet Union itself. The West and its version of modernity—capitalist democracy—had won both the physical and ideological contests of the Cold War.

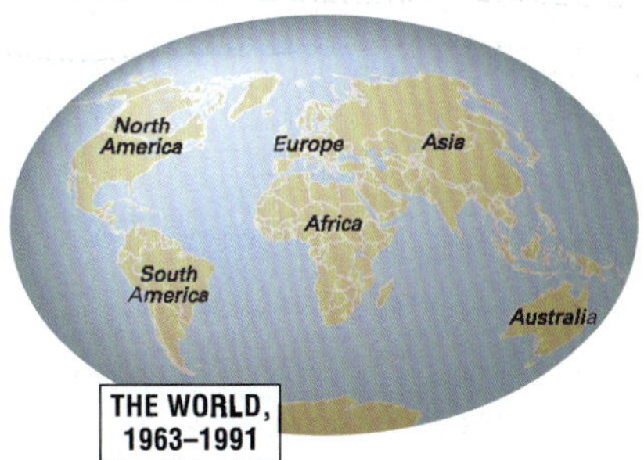

Although the end result of the Cold War was an apparent victory for democracy and capitalism, the contest in the developing world was still active. From the triumph of Muslim resistance in Afghanistan would emerge a new global movement of resistance to the secular West and democratic capitalism: al-Qaeda and its affiliates.

ABOVE: Afghan Mujahideen soldiers, battling the Soviet invasion, celebrate the downing of a Russian helicopter in January 1980.

Seeing Patterns

> How did the political landscape of the Cold War change from 1963 to 1991?

> Why did such radically different lifestyles emerge in the United States and the West during the 1960s and 1970s? What is their legacy today?

> Why did some nations that had emerged from colonialism and war make great strides in their development while others seemed to stagnate?

The Climax of the Cold War

The Cold War continued into the 1980s with its third phase, during which the power of the Soviet Union began to ebb. In the 1960s, despite the enactment of the Nuclear Test Ban Treaty, the United States and the Soviet Union remained bitter ideological enemies, with both sides upgrading and expanding their nuclear arsenals. The late 1960s and early 1970s, however, witnessed an era of détente: a downplaying of overt aggression and the pursuit of competition through diplomatic, social, and cultural means.

The Soviet Superpower in Slow Decline

In 1963, only a few months after the Cuban Missile Crisis, it appeared that the Soviet Union was an adversary more or less equal to the United States. But in less than 30 years, the Soviet Union would fall apart. What set this course of events in motion?

From the Brink of War to Détente The initial success of Nikita S. Khrushchev in rolling back some of the worst abuses of Stalinism were subsequently overshadowed by three failures during the early 1960s. The first was the Sino–Soviet split of 1960, which became a complete break. Second, Khrushchev's building of the Berlin Wall in 1961 had been a propaganda failure. But Khrushchev's key blunder had been in appearing to back down during the Cuban Missile Crisis in October 1962, which meant the dismantling of Soviet bases in Cuba. Though the United States also agreed to dismantle its own medium-range missiles in Turkey, the Soviet Politburo ousted Khrushchev, who resigned in October 1964.

The years of Leonid Brezhnev (in office 1964–1982) were marked by actions demonstrating just how shaken the Soviet Union and United States had been by the Cuban Missile Crisis. One way that this danger had been partially defused was by the Nuclear Test Ban Treaty, signed in October 1963. Nonnuclear nations were discouraged from developing their own weapons in subsequent "nonproliferation" treaties. Additional safeguards were built into the detection and early warning systems both sides used as part of missile defense. Finally, a direct telephone link between the White House and the Kremlin was created, so that American and Soviet leaders could alert each other if an accident or false attack signal was in progress. Nonetheless, the mood of the 1960s remained one of nuclear tension on both sides.

By the late 1960s, the United States and the Soviet Union had entered into a period often referred to by historians as "détente," from the French term for "release of tension." However, for the Soviets, tensions were mounting with the People's Republic of China over borders along the Amur River and the chaos of the Cultural Revolution. At several points, military engagements took place, and at least once, the Americans were approached by the Soviets about the possibility of a preemptive nuclear strike against China.

The era of détente ended in the fall of 1973 with the Egyptian and Syrian surprise attack on Israel, which sparked the largest Arab–Israeli conflict to date. The Soviets actively supported the boycott by the largely Arab Organization of the Petroleum Exporting Countries (OPEC) of oil shipments to the United States during the mid-1970s and resumed support for North Vietnam's final drive to conquer South Vietnam after the American withdrawal in 1973.

Détente. In the wake of the Arab–Israeli War, President Lyndon B. Johnson (in office 1963–1969) and Soviet Minister of Foreign Affairs Andrei Gromyko (in office 1957–1985) met in the beginning of June 1967, at Glassboro State College (now Rowan University) in New Jersey. The talks centered on the US position in Vietnam and the possibility of opening talks on lessening nuclear tensions. Here President Johnson and Premier Gromyko are engaged in a frank discussion.

Prague Spring in Czechoslovakia and Solidarity in Poland The Brezhnev years were marked by increasing dissent, both in the Soviet Union and in its Eastern European client states (see Map 30.1). In Hungary, for example, government efforts to stifle dissent threatened to stir up nationalistic feelings. One result was what came to be called "goulash communism": a relatively relaxed attitude toward criticism of the regime, the introduction of limited market reforms, some attention to consumer demands, and limited trade with the West.

In 1968, dissent took a more direct course in Czechoslovakia, in what came to be called the "Prague Spring." With the rise to power of Alexander Dubček [DOOB-check] (in office 1968–1969) in January 1968, there were calls for a new decentralized administrative structure, relaxation of censorship, and opposition political parties. Brezhnev's government entered into negotiations in

MAP 30.1 **Communist Eastern Europe, 1945–1989**

order to bring the country back into line. By August, however, as the push for reform became more persistent, the Soviets sent Warsaw Pact forces into Czechoslovakia, where they ousted Dubček, installed Gustáv Husák (1913–1991), and dismantled the reforms. The Soviet move demonstrated the "Brezhnev Doctrine"—the right of the Soviets and the Warsaw Pact to forcibly restrain any member country attempting to abandon its alliance with the Soviet Union.

With the shadow cast by the Brezhnev Doctrine, dissent went underground. In 1980, however, it reemerged in Poland with a strike by electrical workers at the Lenin Shipyard in Gdańsk. A new labor union called "Solidarity," led by an electrician named Lech Wałęsa [lekh va-WEN-sa] (1943–), called for an end to censorship, the lifting of economic restrictions, and the right of workers to organize outside of the Communist Party. Despite arrests, by the end of 1980, 80 percent of Poland's workers had joined the movement.

The Polish government declared martial law in an attempt to stave off a Soviet invocation of the Brezhnev Doctrine (1981–1983), but the installation of Mikhail Gorbachev as the new Soviet leader in 1985 and his liberalizing policies of glasnost and perestroika ensured the future of Solidarity as a political movement. When communist rule ended, Wałęsa was elected president of Poland and served from 1991 to 1995.

Afghanistan and "Star Wars" Despite the tensions following the collapse of détente and the Brezhnev Doctrine, progress on strategic arms limitation was achieved between the superpowers. During the SALT II talks from 1977 to 1979, a historic agreement was reached in 1979 that would, for the first time, require the United States and the Soviet Union to limit certain types of nuclear weapons and begin a process of actually reducing them—a process that would later be known as START (Strategic Arms Reduction Talks/Treaty).

Much of the sense of progress achieved by this breakthrough was checked, however, by the Soviet invasion of Afghanistan in December 1979. Fearful of a weak, nominally communist Afghan government on its flank since 1978, adjacent to pro-American Pakistan and a China that appeared to have shifted toward the United States, the Soviets launched a coup in Afghanistan. They installed a communist leader with a massive military force to back him up.

Given these actions in Afghanistan, the new administration of President Ronald Reagan (in office 1981–1989) in the United States sought a more assertive policy toward the Soviet Union. Technological breakthroughs in computers and satellite communications had made it theoretically possible for the United States to create an antiballistic missile system. Such a system was in violation of the antiballistic missile provisions of the 1969 SALT I accords, but its advantages appeared overwhelming to American defense planners. Thus, the United States began to develop its Strategic Defense Initiative (SDI), nicknamed "Star Wars" after the popular movie of the same name. The Soviets protested but now began to develop their version of the system. Ironically, neither system was ever put in place.

From the mid-1980s, both superpowers thus undertook an enormously expensive strategic arms development race. For the Soviets, however, the drain of this new arms race, combined with the increasingly costly war in Afghanistan, was unsustainable.

Glasnost and Perestroika

The death of Leonid Brezhnev in 1982 ushered in two short-lived successors before Mikhail Gorbachev (b. 1931) took office as general secretary in the Politburo in 1985. Faced with growing dissent in Eastern Bloc countries, an increasingly inefficient economy, the endless war in Afghanistan, and now the arms race with the United States, Gorbachev called for large-scale structural reforms.

Up until the 1980s, the Soviet economy had functioned as a giant economic command pyramid. An army of ministerial bureaucrats oversaw every detail of the production and distribution process, but both workers and managers had every incentive to overreport production figures and to manufacture shoddy consumer goods as cheaply as possible. Periodic shortages were the inevitable result.

By the mid-1980s, Soviet planners realized that their command system was delivering diminishing returns. Several factors were responsible for the decline: fewer people were working in factories and more people were in the service sector, a lack of investment in new technologies meant that factories were becoming less productive, and the percentage of people over 60 years of age had doubled between World War II and the mid-1980s, requiring the labor force to support more and more retirees.

Two years after becoming secretary of the Politburo in 1985, Gorbachev launched two economic and political programs, "restructuring" (**perestroika**) and "openness" (**glasnost**), which were intended to revitalize communism. Restructuring entailed the partial dismantling of the command economy. Freed somewhat from the planners' oversight, managers could sell part of what their factories produced on the market instead of delivering everything to the state. Citizens were free to establish "cooperatives," the communist euphemism for private business enterprises. Gorbachev promoted the new mixed command and market economy as a "socialist" or "regulated" system.

Perestroika: "Restructuring" of the Soviet bureaucracy and economic structure in an attempt to make it more efficient and responsive to market demand.

Glasnost: "Openness"; an attempt to loosen restrictions on media in the Soviet Union with an aim at more accurate reporting of events and the creation of "socialist pluralism."

In practice, perestroika did not work out as intended. Market production rose by a meager 5 percent of total production, and many managers were stuck with the manufacture of unprofitable goods. Consumers still complained about shortages. Some who established small businesses charged outrageous prices and evaded payment of taxes. Practical support structures for the co-ops were lacking. Gorbachev's measures, therefore, inadvertently encouraged the rise of wild "carpetbagger" capitalism.

Gorbachev also introduced political "openness," or glasnost. The catalyst for glasnost was the nuclear accident at Chernobyl in Ukraine in April 1986, about which reporting in the media was remarkably frank (after an initial suppression of the facts). However, while Gorbachev's glasnost was supposed to produce a "socialist pluralism," the unintended result was a more individualist pluralism, reducing communism to just one of many competing ideologies.

Transformations in the Soviet Bloc The countries of the Soviet Bloc had borrowed heavily from the West in the 1970s and early 1980s for oil imports and industrial renewal. Others borrowed to build oil and gas pipelines from Russia via their territories to Western Europe. But the oil price collapse of 1985–1986 (due to reductions of oil consumption following the price increases of 1973) forced all Soviet bloc countries to reschedule their debts and cut their budgets. Protests against these cuts in 1989 and 1990 in Poland, Hungary, and Czechoslovakia were accompanied by demands for power sharing.

Yielding to pressure, in 1989 the Communist Party in Poland permitted the first free elections in over 40 years, in which Solidarity won a landslide victory. When no reprisals from Moscow were forthcoming, Lech Wałęsa was elected Poland's president in 1990. In Czechoslovakia, demonstrations toppled the ruling communist regime of President Husák in 1989 without bloodshed (the so-called Velvet Revolution). In its place, a coalition government consisting of the Communist Party and members of the noncommunist Civic Forum was established, and in 1990 Václav Havel (1936–2011), a writer and dissident, was named president.

In the German Democratic Republic (GDR, East Germany), a particularly dramatic shift occurred. Massive demonstrations led to the fall first of the communist government and then of the Berlin Wall on the night of November 9, 1989. A year later, with Gorbachev's blessing, the two Germanys united, ending nearly a half century of division.

Communist governments now collapsed in other Soviet bloc countries, as well (see Map 30.2). The governments of the Baltic states of Estonia, Latvia, and Lithuania, as well as that of Bulgaria, gave way to democracy. Albania followed suit in 1992. The only exception was Romania, where Nicolae Ceauşescu [tshow-SHES-koo] (in office 1974–1989) had built a strong personality cult. Following a mass demonstration in Bucharest in November 1989, portions of the army defected and arrested Ceauşescu and his wife, Elena. Army elements assembled a tribunal, sentenced the two to death, and executed them on December 25, 1989. Subsequently, the army and the Communist Party reconciled, and the country returned to a dictatorship. It was not until 1996 that Romania adopted a democratic system.

In 1990, most of the 15 states making up the Soviet Union declared their sovereignty or independence. Gorbachev agreed with the state presidents to a new federal union treaty for the Soviet Union in spring 1991. This treaty triggered an abortive plot in late August by eight communist hardliners who briefly succeeded in arresting Gorbachev. In a tense showdown with troops sent to occupy the Russian parliament, a crowd of Muscovites forced the hardliners to relent. Officially, the Soviet Union ended on Christmas Day, 1991, replaced by the Commonwealth of Independent States; Boris Yeltsin was the president of the new Russian Federation (1991–1999), while Gorbachev became a private citizen.

MAP 30.2 The Fall of Communism in Eastern Europe and the Soviet Union

Transforming the West

While North America and Western Europe enjoyed growth and social change from the late 1940s through the early 1960s, the period from 1963 through the early 1970s was particularly dynamic. Social movements involving peaceful protests and civil disobedience rose in prominence. Other movements, however, advocated violent confrontation.

Civil Rights Movements

The massive mobilization of Americans during World War II accelerated civil rights efforts. Recognition of African American participation in the armed forces, along with repugnance toward Nazi racial policies, made segregation in the military increasingly untenable. In 1947, therefore, President Truman desegregated the American armed forces. In 1954, the Supreme Court reversed its earlier stand on segregation in education in the *Brown v. Board of Education* ruling. Overturning the 1896 *Plessy v. Ferguson* decision that "separate but equal" facilities were constitutional, the court now ruled that the separate facilities were by definition not equal. This met with resistance in many communities; in 1957, President Dwight D. Eisenhower (in office 1953–1961) was compelled to deploy US Army troops to Little Rock, Arkansas, to enforce the ruling. By the early 1960s there was a dramatic movement under way for civil rights and equal treatment for African Americans in the American south.

The Postwar Drive for Civil Rights The movement for desegregation was prompted by international conditions, as well. Postwar anticolonialism, particularly in Africa, had a powerful influence on the American civil rights movement. The Cold War also played a role, as Soviet propaganda had exploited the discrepancies between American claims of equality and its treatment of African Americans. Guaranteeing civil rights would render that Soviet argument obsolete. Finally, when participants in civil rights marches were attacked in some cities in the early 1960s, President John F. Kennedy reacted by sponsoring civil rights legislation.

After Kennedy was assassinated in 1963, his successor, Lyndon B. Johnson, secured the passage of the Civil Rights Act of 1964, followed by the 1965 Voting Rights Act. With legal remedies now in place for past discrimination, civil rights leaders increasingly turned their attention to economic and social justice.

The Civil Rights Struggle. The career of the charismatic minister Dr. Martin Luther King, Jr., was launched during the 1955 Montgomery, Alabama, bus boycott. By the early 1960s he had emerged as America's preeminent civil rights leader. Here he is shown at the peak of his influence, delivering his famous "I Have a Dream" speech on the Mall in Washington, DC, in August 1963.

Civil Rights for Native Americans Native American activists in the 1960s and 1970s also campaigned to rectify previous abuses, including past treaty violations. The American Indian Movement (AIM) initiated actions in 1968 to end police mistreatment and harassment and advocate for better housing and other issues. In 1973 armed AIM members laid siege to Wounded Knee, South Dakota, to commemorate the massacre of hundreds of Native Americans there in 1890. After a standoff with federal troops, several AIM leaders were charged with violations of federal laws; a negotiated settlement was eventually reached when these charges were dismissed. The end result was improved conditions for Native Americans.

Women's Rights and the Sexual Revolution While the suffragist movement during World War I had led to voting rights for women in both Great Britain and the United States, the more sweeping social changes brought on by World

War II and the Cold War advanced the movement for equality in gender relations further. European and American women demanded an end to restrictions placed upon their reproductive and sexual freedoms. Laws prohibiting contraception and abortion were overturned in several Western countries during the 1960s and 1970s, and the 1973 US Supreme Court decision *Roe v. Wade* protected a woman's right to have an abortion. By the late 1960s, the "women's liberation" movement worked toward equal pay for equal work and more social freedom for women to pursue careers outside the home.

Stonewall Inn. Venerated by gays and lesbians, the Stonewall Inn in New York City was the site of the Stonewall riots. On June 28, 1970, the first annual gay pride (or simply "pride") parade was organized by gay rights activists to commemorate the first demonstration of resistance to harassment and intimidation by New York City Police. Here, unidentified revelers line up along the parade route at the Stonewall Inn on June 26, 2011.

Gay Rights Movement Gay and lesbian Americans also fought for their civil rights during this era. The so-called Stonewall Riot is considered the flashpoint of the contemporary gay rights movement. On the night of June 28, 1969, New York City police raided the Stonewall Inn, a gay bar in Greenwich Village. Patrons fought back, shouting "Gay power!" Gay activists and protesters converged on the scene in subsequent days, demanding an end to discrimination against gays and lesbians.

In the months that followed, gay and lesbian activists launched the Gay Liberation Front (GLF), and the movement spread around the globe. In subsequent years, greater social and legal equality for LGBTQ (Lesbian, Gay, Bisexual, Transgender, and Queer) people, including same-sex marriages, has emerged.

The Global Youth Movement A new global generation, known as "baby boomers" (those born during the postwar "baby boom" between 1945 and 1964), emerged during the postwar era. United by common bonds expressed in terms of dress, pop music, and shared ideologies, this new generation of "hippies" repudiated the rigidity of their parents by growing their hair long; wearing jeans, T-shirts, and "workers'" clothing; dabbling in Asian philosophies; taking drugs; and engaging in sexual experimentation.

The early center for the hippie movement was San Francisco, where the "summer of love" was proclaimed in 1967. Musical groups espousing hippie values—often colloquially summed up as "sex, drugs, and rock and roll"—dominated much of the popular music scene during this time. Perhaps the peak of this movement came in August 1969, when the Woodstock Festival in New York State drew an estimated 300,000–500,000 attendees. Though the hippie movement as a force for liberation from confining mainstream values had largely spent itself by the early 1970s, its influence in fashion, sexual attitudes, music, and drug use continues to some extent even today.

Student Demonstrations in the 1960s In protest against what they perceived as the excessive materialism, conformism, and sexual prudishness of the previous generation, student activists in the 1960s and 1970s held protests in the United States, Japan, and European and South American countries. Even developing countries like Cuba and China, as well as Eastern Bloc countries,

Patterns Up Close | From Women's Liberation to Feminism

The 1960s and 1970s are considered to mark the beginning of "second-wave feminism," a renewal of the push that had crested with "first-wave" feminism's achievement of suffrage (see Map 30.3). During this second period, women seeking change had the examples of the African American civil rights and antiwar movements on which to draw.

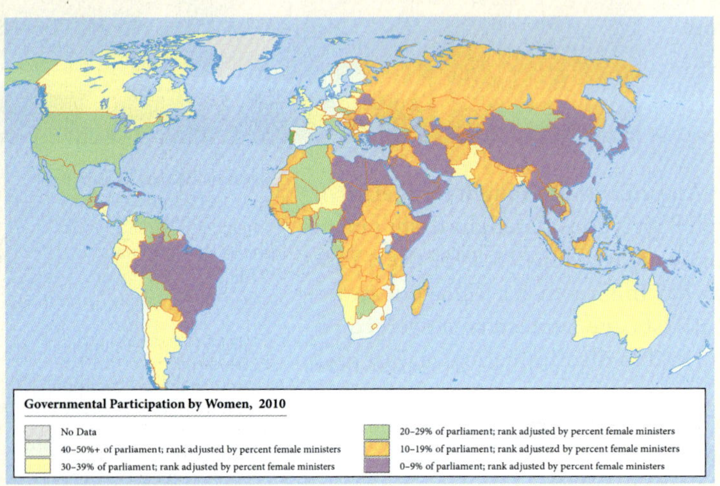

MAP 30.3 Governmental Participation by Women

By the mid-1960s, American women were becoming dissatisfied with what they perceived as the sexism of other progressive organizations. In response, they founded the National Organization for Women (NOW) in 1966. The term "women's liberation" began to appear and was popularized in the media. At first, leaders of the movement agitated for equity in the workplace, women's studies in higher education, and the use of forms of address (like "Ms.") that did not indicate marital status. Previously personal matters, such as birth control and abortion, became political issues as well.

Then, in 1971–1972, the US Congress passed the Equal Rights Amendment (ERA) to the Constitution, which guaranteed

experienced similar protests. In each instance, student activists shared similar ideologies and goals.

For many of the thousands of idealistic students who had taken part in civil rights demonstrations in the early 1960s, the antiwar movement seemed to be a natural transition. By 1965, the American war in Vietnam sparked protests, particularly from young people of draft age. From the United States, the antiwar movement spread abroad and became an anti-US protest movement in the world.

In 1968, the assassinations of civil rights leader Martin Luther King, Jr., and the antiwar presidential candidate Robert Kennedy increased tensions. Outside the United States, the most serious protest occurred in Paris, where students at the University of Paris took to the streets in a rebel movement that spread beyond the students to the labor sector and eventually brought down the French government. Many around the world now called for revolutionary violence directed against governments and programs funded by the military.

In Italy and West Germany, violent revolutionary organizations such as the Red Brigades and the Baader-Meinhof Gang emerged. With the end of American involvement in Vietnam and the draft in the early 1970s, however, these groups disbanded, went fully underground, or were dismantled by the authorities.

equal rights to all American citizens regardless of sex and required the approval of 38 states for ratification by 1979. A highly controversial approval and deadline extension process followed, with the ratification remaining out of reach. Thanks to the rise of the Me Too movement after 2006, to expose sexual transgressions by men, interest in the ERA revived and in January 2020 Virginia became the 38th state to approve the amendment. The legal questions involving the approval process are still awaiting their final resolution.

Cross-cultural interactions have enhanced worldwide movements to advance women's rights. In 1977 the UN General Assembly declared the first annual International Women's Day. Feminist authors and activists found audiences in countries around the world—among them, Ding Ling in China, Huda Sha'arawi and Nawal El-Sa'adawi in Egypt, Madhu Kishwar in India, and Fatima Mernissi in Morocco. As an indication of women's increasing importance in global politics, many countries have had female prime ministers and presidents.

Women's Liberation in India. Members of the National Federation of Dalit Women demonstrate in support of rights for women of the dalit ("untouchable") caste in New Delhi, India, in 2008. While discrimination against dalits is proscribed by law in India, bias against dalit women is still widespread.

Questions

- How does the women's liberation movement demonstrate many of the characteristics of evolving modernity?
- Why does feminism promise to be the great emancipation movement of the twenty-first century?

Economy and Politics in the 1970s and 1980s A sudden economic downturn in the early 1970s initiated a prolonged period of economic stagnation. One cause was the ramping down of the Vietnam War effort, which had driven the US defense industry. Another cause stemmed from renewed hostilities between the Arabs and Israelis in 1973. In retaliation for American support of Israel in the so-called Yom Kippur or Ramadan War of this year (see Ch. 29), the newly formed OPEC, led by Arab states, dramatically increased the price of oil for export to America. The consequences of these economic downturns were at first inflation and then, by the late 1970s, **stagflation**. At the same time, the emergence of developing economies in Asia and South America began to lure American manufacturers to relocate to these countries in order to take advantage of lower labor costs. The manufacturing sector began to shrink and the importance of the service sector began to rise.

Stagflation: Increased prices and record high interest rates but a stagnant economy overall.

These economic circumstances caused corresponding realignments in politics in the 1970s and 1980s. In some Western countries, the trend shifted toward the adoption of more conservative policies, most notably those of the American president Ronald Reagan and Britain's prime minister Margaret Thatcher (in office 1979–1990). Both leaders orchestrated cutbacks in governmental spending for social services and welfare programs. In both countries industrial strikes and the power of labor unions were restricted and the nationalization of major industries was replaced by privatization.

From “Underdeveloped” to “Developing” World, 1963–1991

From the 1960s through the 1980s, the drive for economic development, national prestige, and national power continued to grow among newly independent nations. The period marked the height of the contest among the nonaligned nations for preeminence between the two competing modernisms: market capitalism with democratic governments and variants of communism. Successful development allowed a number of countries to move from the category of “underdeveloped” to the more optimistic one of “developing.”

China: Cultural Revolution to Four Modernizations

The People’s Republic of China experienced wrenching policy changes during the period 1963–1991. The death of Mao in 1976, for example, ushered in a complete reversal of economic course. In 1978, the new Chinese leader Deng Xiaoping [dung shiao-PING] called for opening the country and creating a market economy—that is, introducing capitalism. To this day, China’s economic policy is officially called “socialism with Chinese characteristics.”

China’s “Thermidorean Reaction,” 1960–1966 The turbulence of the first round of the Maoist years calmed under the leadership of Liu Shaoqi. Some scholars, seeing in this retreat from radicalism a movement akin to France’s end of the Reign of Terror during the month of Thermidor (July–August) in 1794, have dubbed the Liu Shaoqi period as China’s “Thermidorean Reaction.” The decade began, however, with the Sino–Soviet split, in which mutual distrust between Mao and Khrushchev led to a withdrawal of Soviet aid in 1960.

In the early 1960s, China made important technological advances with military implications: the detonation of China’s first nuclear device in October 1964, the testing of a thermonuclear (hydrogen) device in 1966, and advances in missile technology that led to the first Chinese satellites. In addition, Liu’s regime engaged in a more assertive policy of border “rectification,” most notably with India in 1962. This kind of display of force would be seen later in China’s attack on Vietnam in 1979.

The Cultural Revolution As China’s Communist Party and government assumed a more Soviet-style approach, Mao Zedong grew uneasy about the party’s seeming lack of interest in pushing the revolution toward pure communism. Mao’s position was in direct opposition to the increasingly technocratic stance he saw in Liu Shaoqi’s policies. He plotted his comeback, publishing his famous “little red book,” *Quotations from Chairman Mao Zedong*, in 1964. His ideological ally, Lin Biao, vice premier and head of the People’s Liberation Army (in office 1954–1971), made it required reading for the troops and helped Mao establish a power base.

In the spring of 1966, Mao called on the nation's youth to rededicate itself to "continuous revolution." He announced the Great Proletarian **Cultural Revolution**, the purpose of which was to stamp out the last vestiges of "bourgeois" and "feudal" Chinese society. Students formed squads of Red Guards and attacked their teachers, bosses, and elders. By August, millions of Red Guards converged on Beijing, where Mao addressed them in Tiananmen Square.

Cultural Revolution: Sociopolitical movement (1966–1969) set in motion by Mao Zedong that purged remnants of capitalist and traditional elements from Chinese society and reimposed Maoist thought as the dominant ideology within the Communist Party.

From 1966 until 1969, when the Cultural Revolution was officially declared over, millions of people were persecuted or murdered by Red Guards and their allies. China's official ideology was now listed as "Marxism–Leninism–Mao Zedong Thought." By 1968 the country was in complete chaos as pro– and anti–Cultural Revolution factions battled each other, causing Mao to implicitly concede defeat and declare the Cultural Revolution over the following year.

"To Get Rich Is Glorious": China's Four Modernizations

Despite the Sino–Soviet split, the People's Republic had maintained a strong anti-American posture. This was matched by American Cold War antipathy toward "Red China" as a linchpin of the Communist bloc. By the early 1970s, however, with Soviet–Chinese tensions still high, President Richard Nixon made a bold visit to the People's Republic, which resulted in the Shanghai Communiqué of 1972. In this document, the United States and the People's Republic of China announced plans to initiate formal diplomatic and cultural relations, the United States pledged to no longer block the People's Republic's bid for a seat in the United Nations, and the United States agreed to downgrade its diplomatic presence in Taiwan.

Tiananmen Square Demonstrations. At their peak in May 1989, the demonstrations by students seeking greater government accountability and a more open political system were joined by workers and people from all walks of life. This memorable image of the suppression of the demonstration shows a lone figure, known to the world afterward only as "Tank Man," confronting a Chinese armored column. The driver of the tank tried to get around the man and eventually stopped, together with the other tanks. At that point, demonstrators pulled the man back to safety. His subsequent fate remains unknown. Both images were widely broadcast throughout the world.

The death of Mao Zedong in September 1976 led to a repudiation of the Cultural Revolution and an entirely different direction in strategy for China. Deng Xiaoping (in office 1978–1992) emerged in 1978 as the new leader. The pragmatic Deng implemented the fundamental policies that remain in force in China, the Four Modernizations. Deng's strategy relied on upgrading the quality of agriculture, industry, defense, and science and technology. China would pursue a new "open-door" policy with regard to foreign expertise from the West, it would allow Chinese students to study abroad, and it would allow the market forces of capitalism to encourage innovation in all sectors of the economy. A popular slogan appearing on t-shirts now proclaimed: "To get rich is glorious!"

The "responsibility system," as it was called, was introduced in a special economic zone set up in south China at Shenzhen. The experiments in capitalism would then be expanded to the country at large once any flaws had been corrected. Peasants were among the first beneficiaries as the communes were disbanded, individual plots assigned, and market incentives introduced. By the mid-1980s, China was rapidly approaching self-sufficiency in food production; by the 1990s, it would register surpluses. With the privatization and modernization of Chinese industry, the 1990s saw the People's Republic's GDP register annual double-digit rises. By 2010 it had surpassed Japan as the second-largest economy in the world, after the United States.

Another, more controversial, innovation was the one-child policy. Population pressures were a powerful brake on China's development. Thus, a policy was inaugurated in 1979 mandating that most families were to have only one child. Despite the problems in enforcing such a policy, and its severe cultural impact on the male-centered traditional Chinese family structure, China's population has remained remarkably stable since the 1980s at around 1.3–1.5 billion. The policy has, however, abetted problems of selective female abortion, the giving up of girl babies for adoption, and even female infanticide. There is also a significant gender imbalance: at the turn of the twenty-first century, China had 117 male births for every 100 female births. Because of this imbalance and the fear that a reduced working population would not be able to support the expanding number of retirees, the one-child policy was effectively discontinued in 2015.

Tiananmen Square Massacre Pro-democracy protests began taking place in Beijing following the death of the popular moderate leader Hu Yaobang in 1989. The gatherings grew as the seventieth anniversary of the May Fourth nationalist movement grew closer. The Politburo debated how to deal with the protests. When they prepared a declaration of martial law, a number of high-ranking army officers expressed doubts; they argued that the People's Army could not possibly shoot its own people. The most prominent figure refusing any order to shoot was Major General Xu Qinxian [shoo chin-shee-yen] (1935–), according to documents publicized by the *New York Times* at the occasion of the twenty-fifth anniversary of the Tiananmen Massacre in 2014. But the Politburo prevailed, and during June 2–4, soldiers crushed what to many among the leaders seemed to be an incipient rebellion. To this day, the number of killed is unknown. General Xu was court-martialed and imprisoned for four years, living thereafter in a military sanatorium in northern China.

Vietnam and Cambodia: War and Communist Rule

In a US-supported coup in Vietnam, a group of generals overthrew President Ngo Dinh Diem [no-din-YIEM] shortly after the climax of the Cold War, the Cuban Missile Crisis, in November 1963. Neither the generals nor the new constitutional government under the now civilian President Nguyen Van Thieu ([win-van-TEE-YO] in office 1965–1975), however, were able to stem the advances of the Communist Vietcong that had begun in 1959–1960 under the direction of the North Vietnamese communists. In spite of massive American support until 1973, the Thieu government, plagued by accusations of corruption, failed to gain popular support and eventually fell to the communists in 1975.

The American War in Vietnam In the summer of 1964, a US-supported South Vietnamese naval raid on two North Vietnamese islands provoked a North Vietnamese retaliation with torpedo boats against American ships in the Gulf of Tonkin. (Documents declassified in 2005–2006 reveal that there was indeed such a retaliation but that a reported massive follow-up two days later never took place.)

The American Secretary of Defense, Robert McNamara (in office 1961–1968), failing to reveal the US-supported raid and asserting the truth of the North Vietnamese follow-up attack, persuaded President Johnson to ask and receive from Congress the so-called Gulf of Tonkin Resolution. This resolution empowered Johnson to conduct full conventional warfare in Southeast Asia, including against North Vietnam.

Accordingly, by 1965 tens of thousands of American combat troops had been sent to support the South Vietnamese against the Vietcong. But the US action was plagued by murky goals and the impatience of a domestic American public hoping for quick, decisive results. Was this war a necessary part of the Cold War—pushing back against Soviet Communism—or was it a war against a Southeast Asian communist national liberation movement? Should young Americans, at that time subject to the draft, serve in this war? The task of "winning the hearts and minds of the people" of South Vietnam against the Vietcong, in addition, was tortuous at best and hampered by the increasing presence of the foreign US military, which reached a high of over a half-million troops by 1967 (see Map 30.4).

In February 1968, on the Vietnamese lunar new year (Tet), the Vietcong, supported by North Vietnamese forces, attacked the South Vietnamese capital of Saigon and other cities. American and South Vietnamese forces counterattacked, destroying the Vietcong as an effective fighting force. In the United States, however, the magnitude of the Tet Offensive, as it came to be called, was seen as evidence that US strategy had not been effective and was thus considered by many as an American defeat. In the wake of massive protests against the war, President Johnson announced he would not seek reelection, and the way was clear for the United States to begin negotiations to end the war by political means. With the election of Richard Nixon

MAP 30.4 The Vietnam War

The Arab–Israeli War of June 1967. The stunning victory of Israel over the combined armies of Syria and Egypt generated admiration in the West and consternation in the Arab world and the Soviet bloc. The Israelis' preemptive use of air power against Egyptian and Syrian air forces and tank and troop concentrations and their expert use of armor proved the deciding factors in the conflict. Here, Egyptian prisoners (in white underclothes in the truck to the right) are being transferred to holding camps (*top*). The war also led to a dramatic rise in the popularity of the Palestinian cause in the Arab and communist spheres. Here, Yasir Arafat marches with members of Fatah in 1970 (*bottom*).

in 1968, a combination of massive bombings of North Vietnam and Cambodian supply lines for North Vietnamese forces and peace talks in Paris eventually brought America's role in the war to an end. Though South Vietnam survived the peace treaty in 1973, the American withdrawal spelled its demise within two years. The country was now finally united under Communism.

The Khmer Rouge Much of Vietnam, Cambodia, and Laos lay devastated from fighting and bombing. Over the next two years, a Cambodian revolutionary group, the Khmer Rouge ("Red Khmers," that is, the Communists in the dominant ethnic group of Khmers), launched a radical program of urban depopulation, forced labor, and mass killing against religious and political opponents. Perhaps one-third of the country's population (equal to 1.3 million dead) was killed as a result. The genocidal ideas and practices of the Khmer Rouge leader, Pol Pot (1925–1998), were so radical and brutal that in 1977 Vietnam invaded Cambodia and initiated his overthrow in favor of a more moderate and pliable candidate. In response, China invaded Vietnam in 1979 but was soon repulsed by Vietnamese forces—an invasion that was the last and least successful of the many Chinese attempts launched over two millennia.

The Middle East

One of the most troubled areas of the world during the twentieth century was the Middle East. Since 1945, the area encompassing the Arabian Peninsula, Iran, Iraq, and the eastern shores of the Mediterranean has seen a number of major wars and minor conflicts, as well as attacks directed against the religious symbols of Judaism, Christianity, and Islam.

Israeli and Arab Conflict By far the most contentious issue in the Middle East has been the presence of the Jewish state of Israel. During the 1950s and 1960s, Israel was largely seen in the West as fighting democracy's battles against authoritarian Arab states supported by the Soviet Union. Immigrants in the postwar decades helped the new state to build an efficient agriculture—often through the socialist device of the communal farm, or kibbutz—and a sophisticated manufacturing sector. West German reparations, compensating for Jewish losses during the Third Reich, helped financially. Mandatory military service and American support also contributed to the creation of superior armed forces.

The "Six-Day War" For the Palestinian Arabs and their allies, the rise of Israel was the *Nakba* ("disaster"). Hundreds of thousands displaced since 1948 waited for decades hoping to return. In the Cold War climate, the Arab states viewed Israel as a new Western imperial outpost in what was rightfully Arab territory. Consequently, attempts at Arab unity were premised on war with Israel. While Arab nationalism was largely secular, and often socialist-leaning with Soviet support, Muslim fundamentalist groups such as Egypt's Muslim Brotherhood gained adherents despite government repression.

In 1964, Yasir Arafat (1929–2004) formed the Palestine Liberation Organization (PLO), whose militant wing, Fatah, began a guerilla war against Israel. Matters came to a head on May 22, 1967, when Egypt closed the Gulf of Aqaba to Israeli shipping, preventing the importation of oil. President Gamal Abdel Nasser (in office 1956–1970) relied on faulty Soviet secret service information of an Israeli mobilization. Following an Egyptian military buildup along the Sinai border and the expulsion of UN forces there, Iraq sent troops to Jordan at its invitation, and local Muslim leaders began to call for holy war against Israel. On June 5 the Israelis launched an air assault to neutralize the Egyptian and Syrian air forces. With an overwhelming advantage in numbers and quality of aircraft, Israel took out the Arab armor and ground troops. The Six-Day War, as it came to be called, enlarged the state of Israel by its conquest of the West Bank, the Golan Heights, the Gaza Strip, and the Sinai Peninsula—territories belonging to Jordan, Syria, and Egypt, respectively. To many observers in the Middle East, it appeared that Israel was now a state bent on expansion.

The Yom Kippur/Ramadan War In early October 1973, Egypt, Syria, and a coalition of Arab states launched a massive attack during the Jewish holy day of Yom Kippur, which in 1973 coincided with the Muslim holy month of Ramadan. This time, with Israel, the United States, and the Soviet Union caught unawares, Egyptian tanks crossed the Suez Canal and attacked Israeli forces (see Map 30.5). After initially conceding ground, however, the Israelis managed to ultimately defeat the Arabs once again.

A ceasefire was brokered by the United Nations, but the intensity of the fighting and the resupply efforts by the United States

MAP 30.5 The Arab–Israeli Wars, 1967 and 1973

and Soviet Union moved both superpowers dangerously close to direct confrontation. For their part, the Arab oil producers and Iran launched an oil embargo against the United States. Stringent measures and sharply higher gasoline prices drove home to Americans how dependent they had become on foreign oil and encouraged new interests in alternative forms of energy.

For Egypt, the defeat resulted in a transformation of its hitherto futile policy toward Israel. President Anwar el-Sadat (in office 1970–1981) took the initiative in undertaking peace talks by visiting Israel in 1977. In 1979, with the backing of the American president Jimmy Carter, Egypt and Israel signed the first treaty between an Arab country and the Jewish state. Egypt and Jordan are the only Arab states to date to maintain diplomatic and cultural relations with Israel. Syria remained hostile, while the PLO continued its efforts from Jordan. Profound resentment of Sadat for signing the treaty festered among many Egyptians. Despite some concessions to increasingly vocal fundamentalist Muslim groups, Sadat was assassinated in 1981.

The Lebanese Civil War Lebanon's war of 1975–1989 had its roots in the transfer of the PLO's power base from Jordan to Lebanon in the aftermath of the 1967 war. Jordan's existence was built on a precarious balance between the Palestinian refugees of 1948 and the indigenous Jordanian Arab population. After Jordan lost the West Bank to Israel, Arafat moved the PLO to the east bank and intended to build up a state within the state of Jordan from which to continue to attack Israel. But in the "Black September" of 1970, the Jordanian army expelled the PLO to protect the integrity of its state.

After transferring to Lebanon, the PLO upset the precarious balance among the different religious and political factions of this Arab country. The Maronites (eastern Christians in communion with Catholicism) were politically dominant, though numerically inferior to the Muslims, who were divided into a Shiite majority and a Sunni minority. By taking over command in the Palestinian refugee camps (12 percent of Lebanon's population), Arafat again built a Palestinian base, this time within the state of Lebanon, from which the PLO and other Palestinian groups launched attacks on Israel.

The Maronites, taking a dim view of the growing strength of the PLO, expanded their paramilitary militias, which existed parallel to the national army. Since the government refused to have the national army intervene in the Christian–PLO conflict in favor of one or the other side, the Christian militias took matters into their own hands in April 1975. In a number of clashes, they inflicted severe losses on the PLO and allied Muslims. The army dissolved and its constituent elements joined the various militias. The Christian–PLO confrontation evolved into a general Christian–Muslim civil war, which the Christians were losing.

Syria entered the war in 1976 and Israel in 1982, complicating the civil war further. On one hand, Syria ended the worst fighting, but on the other, its entry on the Christian side meant that the sectarian lines were frozen, with each group establishing its predominance in a part of the country. The PLO, for its part, became the dominant faction in the Shiite south, from where it launched raids into Israeli territory. Israel responded first with the erection of a security zone in southern Lebanon in 1976 and then, in 1982, with a three-month invasion of the country, in order to drive the PLO from Lebanon.

The PLO was forced to relocate to Tunisia, far from Israel. Syria remained the dominant power in Lebanon, but in the face of its unrestrained manipulation of Lebanese politics, which included disappearances and assassinations, the Arab League eventually stepped in and in 1989 brokered the so-called Taif Agreement, which established an uneasy peace. In 2005 the UN eventually forced Syria to withdraw, but Lebanon found it difficult to return a unified government to power.

The Iranian Islamic Revolution Massive urban unrest drove Shah Muhammad Reza Pahlavi (r. 1941–1979) into exile in November–December 1979. Moderately Islamist opposition leaders took over the government but were soon outmaneuvered by Ayatollah Ruhollah Khomeini (1902–1989), who returned triumphantly from his French exile on February 1, 1980. Using a small book entitled *Islamic Government*, based on lectures he had given in Iraq and published in 1970, as his blueprint, Khomeini proclaimed an Islamic revolution in the country and systematically revamped all Iranian institutions according to this blueprint. For the execution of the revolution, he relied on a half-dozen militant and paramilitary groups that bypassed the Iranian army with its many royal sympathizers.

The overthrow of the Pahlavi monarchy was possible because the shah, an indecisive but at times also ambitious ruler, lost his nerve in the course of urban demonstrations in 1978. He had introduced the so-called White Revolution in 1964 with which he wanted to bring about an agrarian reform and industrial revolution that would propel Iran within a short time into the ranks of the industrial powers. While in principle such a revolution made sense, the shah was not ruthless enough—nor could he count on enough dedicated supporters—to see his White Revolution to its end. Among the losers in the White Revolution was the Shiite clergy, which had to give up a great deal of the agricultural property associated with the shrines and seminaries—hence Khomeini's bitter opposition and exile beginning in 1964.

The Islamic Republic created by Khomeini is a theocracy ruled by the Quran and the Islamic tradition as defined by Shiite Islamic religious scholars and additionally defined by Khomeini. Accordingly, Iranian women have to follow a dress code, men and women are gender-segregated, and candidates for office are vetted for their faith. This utopian return to a premodern Islamic past is modernized by a constitution that allows for elections and a parliament and president.

But ultimate authority lies with a Spiritual Guide, who appoints a Guardian Council to assist him. The Guardian Council vets the 80-member Assembly of Experts, voted for by the general public and responsible for appointing or deposing the Spiritual Guide. Until the return of the Twelfth Imam at the end of time (see Chapter 10), the Spiritual Guide rules on both spiritual and worldly matters.

While the Iranian revolution was still unfolding, the president of neighboring Iraq, Saddam Hussein (in office 1979–2003) decided in September 1980 to invade the fledgling theocracy and occupy the oil-rich province of Khuzistan. But after some initial successes, his army got bogged down, and a ferocious war of position ensued, in which the initially militarily inferior Iranians sent wave after wave of young men into the artillery fire of the Iraqis.

During the war, one of Khomeini's militant groups, the "Muslim Student Followers of the Imam's Line," sought to keep the Shiite revolutionary fervor at a high pitch by taking 52 US embassy personnel hostage in November 1980, in retaliation for the United States granting the Shah medical asylum. The hostage crisis, lasting 444 days, was eventually resolved by President Carter in January 1981, and the Iran–Iraq War was eventually settled with UN intervention in 1988, largely in favor of Iran.

Africa: From Independence to Development

During the period 1963–1991, the main struggles in Africa moved from ones mainly concerned with completing the pattern of decolonization and independence to ones involving development. As in other parts of the postcolonial world, vigorous internal debates were conducted about strategies for economic development. But in nearly all cases, the economies of the newly independent states were problematic. In most cases they were tied to their former colonial regimes by means of the same raw materials that had been exploited under colonialism. Moreover, they were competing in the markets for these products with other former colonies.

Nigeria: Troubled Legacies and Civil War Nigeria's independence had a promising start; it entered the postcolonial era as a republic with a British parliamentary system, Commonwealth membership, and a federal-style constitution. Like many African former colonies, however, Nigeria was saddled with ethnic and religious conflicts as a legacy of the colonial divisions of the continent. Thus, its growing pains were marked by clashes between its established system of constitutionalism and the desires of its major constituent groups for their own ethnic nation-states.

The three major antagonistic groups, the Hausa, Igbo, and Yoruba, were divided by history, culture, religion, and language. The largest, the Hausa, were Muslims from the northern region. The Igbo, living mostly in the eastern region where valuable oil deposits had been recently discovered, were predominantly Christian or African-spiritual. The Yoruba in the west, who controlled most of the national offices, were predominantly Muslim, although there were also Christian Yoruba.

Starting in 1966, under strongman Yakubu Gowon (in office 1966–1975), the central government authorized raids to bring Igbo areas under greater control. In response in 1967, the eastern Igbo region declared itself independent as the state of Biafra. What followed was perhaps the bloodiest civil war of the era. More than 1 million Biafrans died before the province surrendered in early 1970. From then until 1991, Nigeria was ruled by a series of military strongmen. By 1991, the future that had seemed so promising in 1960 seemed impossible.

Zimbabwe and Angola: The Revolution Continued Some of the former European colonies in Africa came to independence with substantial populations of white settlers who were opposed to independence. When independence arrived, they sought guarantees from the new governments against expropriation of land, discrimination, and reprisals.

Threatened by the independence of nearby black African nations (such as Northern Rhodesia becoming Zambia in 1964) and confident of support from apartheid-based South Africa, the white leaders of the territory that had been Southern Rhodesia but now calling itself simply Rhodesia declared unilateral independence in 1965 and set up a government under Ian Smith (in office 1965–1970). Distressed at this move, Britain refused to recognize the new government and expelled Rhodesia from the Commonwealth. Few countries outside of South Africa recognized the regime, which now faced guerilla movements from within.

Two rival groups in Rhodesia, the Zimbabwe African National Union (ZANU) under Robert Mugabe (1924–2019) and the Zimbabwe African People's Union (ZAPU) led by Joshua Nkomo (1917–1999), struggled to bring Smith's regime down and create a majority-rule state. The war lasted throughout the 1960s and 1970s, until Mugabe and ZANU finally triumphed and rebaptized the country under the name of "Zimbabwe" in 1980. Mugabe's regime pledged fairness to the remaining white settlers and set about creating a socialist state. In the 1990s, however, vigilante seizures of white lands by "revolutionary veterans" became a regular occurrence. By the early 2000s, the chaotic agricultural sector combined with repression of opposition to ZANU one-party rule had plunged the country into a serious economic crisis. Mugabe steadfastly refused any meaningful reforms and was eventually deposed by the military in 2017. He died in 2019 amidst continuing economic chaos.

Angola also suffered an extended civil war following its independence from Portugal in 1975. This war exemplified yet another of the so-called Cold War "proxy wars" between Soviet-backed forces on one hand and forces backed by the United States (later by South-Africa) on the other: MPLA (People's Movement for the Liberation of Angola) and UNITA (National Union for the Total Independence of Angola). When the civil war finally ended in 2002, Angola had yet to benefit from rich oil deposits discovered in 1955.

South Africa: From Apartheid to "Rainbow Nation" South Africa, the richest of the continent's countries, had the most complex and restrictive racial relations. It had been founded by the Dutch (see Chapter 19), but when the British assumed rule in 1806, the Dutch-descended Boers moved inland, pushing out the local blacks. The expansion of the Zulu kingdom further inland, however, forced the Boers and the British into protracted wars which ended only in 1879.

By the end of the nineteenth century, the discovery of vast mineral wealth led to both the expansion of the British colony's holdings and an influx of immigrants, including Chinese and Indians. After 1910, immigration restrictions on Asians went into effect along with laws governing relations between whites and Africans. This trend culminated in the institution of **apartheid** (Afrikaans, "apartness") in 1948. Black South Africans were relegated to a legalized second-class status.

Apartheid: System of social and legal segregation by race enforced by the government of South Africa from 1948 until 1994.

Through the 1950s, South Africa faced international criticism for its policies. Moreover, as newly independent black majority countries completed the pattern of decolonization, the white government felt itself increasingly besieged. It pointed out that a few of these emerging states were Marxist (such

Black Commuters in South Africa. The regime of apartheid (the strict separation of the races) that had been inaugurated by the white minority government in South Africa in 1948 obliged all black citizens, such as these workers congregating in a Johannesburg train station in the late 1950s, to carry "passbooks" that specified what areas they were permitted to enter. Resentment at the passbook requirement prompted mass demonstrations that resulted in the Sharpeville Massacre of March 21, 1960, which in turn sparked widespread protests against the apartheid system.

as Ethiopia and Mozambique) and thus claimed that it was fighting against the expansion of the Soviet bloc in Africa. South Africa withdrew from the British Commonwealth in 1961 and a number of black political organizations—most prominently the African National Congress (ANC)—began to campaign against apartheid. This campaign was accentuated by a particularly ugly incident, the so-called Soweto uprising in 1976, when thousands of South African black students marched in protest against the Afrikaans Medium Decree, which stipulated that only Afrikaners would be appointed as teachers in black schools. Armed police brutally put down the revolt, resulting in the death of hundreds of protesters.

International boycotts of South Africa gained momentum at the same time, and the ANC, through a political and guerilla campaign, was making gradual gains. Finally, amid the collapse of communism in the Soviet bloc, the newly elected president, Frederik Willem de Klerk (b. 1936), began reforms aimed ultimately at dismantling apartheid. The ANC was legalized and became South Africa's largest political party; its leader, Nelson Mandela (1918–2013), who had been imprisoned for nearly three decades, was released; in 1991 all apartheid laws were repealed; and finally, in 1992 white voters amended the constitution to mandate racial equality among all citizens. By 1994, the first multiracial elections were held, and Mandela became president of the new South Africa.

Latin America: Proxy Wars

The 1960s in Latin American politics were marked by the forces contending for dominance against the backdrop of the Cold War. Here, however, because the countries in question had long since achieved their independence, the issues were largely ideological and economic, and centered around revolutionary politics.

By the 1970s, dissatisfaction with the authoritarian regimes of the region, particularly in Central America, resulted in revolutionary efforts, the most notable being in Nicaragua and El Salvador. Since the mid-1930s, the United States had supported the family of the authoritarian Nicaraguan strongman Anastasio Somoza García (collectively in office from 1936 to 1979). From the early 1960s a guerilla insurgency called the Sandinista National Liberation Front (FSLN) had sought to overthrow the Somozas and mount a socialist land-reform scheme. The Somoza regime fell in 1979, and Daniel Ortega (in office 1979–1990; 2007–) took the head of a new Sandinista government.

The socialist revolution of the new regime, which included a land distribution and literacy campaign, prompted the American administration to cut off aid to Nicaragua. It began a covert operation to destabilize Ortega through the funding and arming of opposition groups known collectively as the Contras, and end trade with the regime. With US support for the Contras increasing and aid from Cuba and the Soviet Bloc fading in the late 1980s, the two sides agreed to elections in 1990. These resulted in the presidency of the conservative Violeta Chamorro (in office 1990–1997). Ortega lost three more elections but was returned in 2007 to the presidency. This time he introduced again a series of social and economic reforms and returned to authoritarianism, silencing criticism from politicians and the media as well as securing his continued hold on power. But protests, initially against tax increases and social security in 2018, snowballed throughout 2019, efforts at violent repression notwithstanding.

The commitment of the United States to opposing any groups espousing Marxist or communist beliefs in Latin America also revealed itself in covert policy toward governments recognized as legitimate. One such action was directed at Chilean President Salvador Allende (in office 1970–1973) in 1973. Allende had led a political coalition to a plurality win in 1970. Many of his policies met opposition within Chile, while his ideology and nationalization of American interests in Chile's mines pushed the Nixon administration to back his opposition.

With CIA help, Allende was overthrown, and the repressive regime of General Augusto Pinochet (in office 1973–1990) installed. Determined to suppress leftist groups, Pinochet launched Operation Colombo in 1975, resulting in the disappearance of activists and others perceived as threats to the government's plan to restore a capitalist economy. Throughout Pinochet's 16 years in power, his rule remained repressive, but Chile also became economically vibrant and began to move toward a more democratic government. In 1998 Pinochet was arrested in London on charges of human rights violations and torture. After a court battle, he was ultimately released and returned to Chile, where he died in 2006.

The Dirty War" and the "Disappeared" One of the most tragic and internationally condemned episodes of this period was the "Dirty War" initiated by the military junta that overthrew the authoritarian regime of the Peróns (Juan and his third wife, Isabel) in Argentina. During the brutal regime of this junta, tens of thousands of real and alleged leftist Argentinians were kidnapped, imprisoned, and killed. These victims became known as the "disappeared." Their fate was poignantly brought to light by the Mothers of the Plaza de Mayo (a large square in front of the presidential palace), a group of women who kept vigil for lost friends and relatives in that plaza in Buenos Aires during 1977–2006.

In 1983, having provoked and lost the Falklands War with Great Britain, the junta stepped down, elections were held, and a National Commission on the Disappearance of Persons (CONADEP) was established in December. The progress of the commission and its findings of torture, killing, and indefinite incarceration caused an international sensation. Today, most of the surviving military and political leaders held responsible are in prison or have already served lengthy terms.

The Brazilian Economic Miracle Brazil experienced a right-wing military coup and regime during almost the same time (1964–1985) as Argentina. The military came to power during a period of import substitution industrialization, when the government made far-reaching plans for the nationalization of businesses and agrarian reform, both considered by the military to be communist-inspired. As in Argentina, the military hunted down dissidents, whether they were professed communists or not, and tortured them in prison. Small leftist guerilla movements operated in a few urban centers as well as in the rain forest, but their numbers were too small to withstand determined government action to wipe them out. Brazil coordinated its anti-leftist measures closely with the other southern cone countries, including Argentina.

The military leaders were astute enough to entrust the Brazilian economy to technocrats who continued the policy of import substitution. Easy foreign loans allowed for further investments in basic industries, infrastructure, nuclear research, and oil exploration. The results of the import substitution policy were impressive: society became mostly urban (67 percent), and industrial exports grew from 20 percent in 1968 to 57 percent in 1979. The two massive oil price increases of 1973 and 1979, however, threw Brazil's foreign-debt-heavy economy into a deep crisis, severely damaging the popularity of the military regime. After years of economic crisis, the officers resigned themselves to retreating from politics and initiating a transition toward democracy with elections in 1985 and an amended constitution in 1988.

Putting It All Together

During the years 1962 to 1991, the Cold War contest between capitalist democracy and various types of communism and socialism reached its climax. In the end, the wealth and power of the West, particularly the United States, ultimately wore the Soviet bloc down. Along the way, China abruptly changed from extreme radical leftist programs during its Cultural Revolution to a capitalist style of market economics by 1991. Many other countries were now looking for some mixture of the two systems or a third way between the two. As the period drew to a close, it was, ironically, the two iconic communist regimes, the Soviet Union and the People's Republic of China, that were pioneering the way out of Marxist socialism. The Chinese sought to do this by retaining a powerful authoritarian government while embracing market economics. The former Soviet Union adopted democratic political values and guardedly introduced capitalism.

Review and Relate

Thinking Through Patterns

Examine the ways historians approach the big questions of this chapter.

How did the political landscape of the Cold War change from 1963 to 1991?

Perhaps the biggest changes came in the 1980s. Though the United States had been defeated in Vietnam and was facing a recession at home, it still was the world's largest economy and could weather a protracted arms race. The Soviet Union was far more economically fragile—which ultimately made it ideologically fragile as well. The strains of Polish dissent, the Afghan War, and a renewed arms race with the United States wore the Soviet state down.

Why did such radically different lifestyles emerge in the United States and the West during the 1960s and 1970s? What is their legacy today?

The prosperity of the United States and the West allowed younger people to experiment with new ideas of living and indulge their desires for new experiences. The idealism of the era also played a role, as did the threats of the military draft and nuclear war. The materialism of the age repelled many and made them long for a simpler existence.

Why did some nations that had emerged from colonialism and war make great strides in their development while others seemed to stagnate?

The nations that prospered had already achieved self-sufficiency in agriculture, had a transportation and communications infrastructure, and maximized their labor force. China, under Deng Xiaoping, followed a modified version of this strategy and was already growing at record levels by 1991. In the following decades, nearly all Asian countries would follow suit, with India moving into the top ranks of development and growth. Many Latin American countries—in particular, Brazil—also made great strides.

In all cases, culture and ideology played a powerful role in encouraging citizens to believe that progress was possible. Peace and stability also played an important role. The many internal conflicts that plagued Latin America and Africa held back development during this period.

Against the Grain

The African National Congress

Consider this as a counterpoint to the main patterns examined in this chapter.

In the early 1900s, the Union of South Africa adopted laws that formed the backbone of what in 1948 was to become apartheid, an official program of racial segregation. According to these laws, blacks were to be removed to reservations and trust lands, called "Bantustans," in the less-fertile eastern part of the country.

In protest against segregation and demanding equal rights, in 1912 a few black professionals organized what was to become the African National Congress (ANC). Their demands set the beginnings of the pattern of decolonization in the twentieth century. It required another generation, however, and the leadership of the law partners Oliver Tambo (1917–1993) and Nelson Mandela (1918–2013), before the ANC was able to become a mass movement. Tambo and Mandela formulated demands for land distribution, labor organization, and mass education.

- How do the ANC's support for racial integration and acceptance of differing political views contrast with other nationalist and liberation movements from this period?
- Compare and contrast South African apartheid and segregation in the United States between 1918 and 1964. What are the similarities? What are the differences?

After the Afrikaner nationalists came to power in 1948 and established outright apartheid, black South Africans were increasingly driven to join the ANC. During the 1950s, the government introduced race-marked passports, outlawed interracial marriages and sexual relations, demolished black shantytowns, resettled blacks, banned communism, and decreed segregated parks, beaches, buses, hospitals, schools, and universities. Determined to enforce apartheid, the government built up a massive bureaucracy, including an effective secret service.

Even though the events of the 1950s made the ANC a true representative of South African blacks, it held fast to its original program of multiracial and ideologically varied integration. Its mass protests and acts of sabotage through a newly created armed wing in 1961–1964 were met by the government with brutal repression. In the so-called Rivonia trial, the arrested ANC leadership, including Mandela, was condemned to imprisonment on Robben Island.

Courageous protests by student and labor organizations, churches, and white liberals continued, as did government brutality in response. The ANC, driven underground, also operated from abroad, where it helped in the creation, by the 1980s, of a coalition of Western states and organizations that sought to force South Africa to abolish apartheid. Ultimately, the ANC prevailed because of the collapse of the Soviet Bloc in

1989–1991; the apartheid regime could no longer claim that it was the final bulwark against world communism. In 1994, South Africa became a black-governed nation under the rule of the ANC.

Key Terms

Apartheid 757
Cultural Revolution 749
Glasnost 741
Perestroika 741
Stagflation 747

Learn more with this chapter's digital tools, including the Oxford Insight Study Guide, at http://www.oup.com/he/vonsivers4e. Please see the Further Resources section at the back of the book for additional readings and suggested websites.

PATTERNS OF EVIDENCE |

Sources for Chapter 30

SOURCE 30.1

Mikhail Gorbachev, *Perestroika: New Thinking for Our Country and the World*

1987

Two years after becoming first secretary of the Soviet Politburo in 1985, Mikhail Gorbachev (b. 1931) launched his two trademark economic and political programs, perestroika ("restructuring") and glasnost ("openness"). Hoping to revitalize communism, he restructured and partially dismantled the command economy that had dominated the Soviet Union since the Bolshevik Revolution. While perestroika did not work out as intended, glasnost, which permitted frank commentary and the exposure of incompetence and cover-ups by the Soviet leadership, had more wide-ranging consequences for the Soviet Union, which finally collapsed in 1991. Gorbachev summarized his attitude toward domestic politics for Western readers in a book published in English in 1987. However, a significant portion of the book also deals with Cold War tensions, as he was negotiating with President Reagan (1981–1989) of the United States, especially over the destruction of nuclear weapons.

Who Needs the Arms Race and Why?

Pondering the question of what stands in the way of good Soviet-American relations, one arrives at the conclusion that, for the most part, it is the arms race. I am not going to describe its history. Let me just note once again that at almost all its stages the Soviet Union has been the party catching up. By the beginning of the seventies we had reached approximate military-strategic parity, but on a level that is really frightening. Both the Soviet Union and the United States now have the capacity to destroy each other many times over.

It would seem logical, in the face of a strategic stalemate, to halt the arms race and get down to disarmament. But the reality is different. Armories already overflowing continue to be filled with sophisticated new types of weapons, and new areas of military technology are being developed. The US sets the tone in this dangerous, if not fatal pursuit.

Source: Mikhail Gorbachev, *Perestroika: New Thinking for Our Country and the World* (New York: Harper & Row, 1987), 218–221.

I shall not disclose any secret if I tell you that the Soviet Union is doing all that is necessary to maintain up-to-date and reliable defenses. This is our duty to our own people and our allies. At the same time I wish to say quite definitely that this is not our choice. It has been imposed upon us.

All kinds of doubts are being spread among Americans about Soviet intentions in the field of disarmament. But history shows that we can keep the word we gave and that we honor the obligations assumed. Unfortunately, this cannot be said of the United States. The administration is conditioning public opinion, intimidating it with a Soviet threat, and does so with particular stubbornness when a new military budget has to be passed through Congress. We have to ask ourselves why all this is being done and what aim the US pursues.

It is crystal clear that in the world we live in, the world of nuclear weapons, any attempt to use them to solve Soviet-American problems would spell suicide. This is a fact. I do not think that US politicians are unaware of it. Moreover, a truly paradoxical situation has now developed. Even if one country engages in a steady arms build up while the other does nothing, the side that arms itself will all the same gain nothing. The weak side may simply explode all its nuclear charges, even on its own territory, and that would mean suicide for it and a slow death for the enemy. This is why any striving for military superiority means chasing one's own tail. It can't be used in real politics.

Nor is the US in any hurry to part with another illusion. I mean its immoral intention to bleed the Soviet Union white economically, to prevent us from carrying out our plans of construction by dragging us ever deeper into the quagmire of the arms race.

. . .

We sincerely advise Americans: try to get rid of such an approach to our country. Hopes of using any advantages in technology or advanced equipment so as to gain superiority over our country are futile. To act on the assumption that the Soviet Union is in a "hopeless position" and that it is necessary just to press it harder to squeeze out everything the US wants is to err profoundly. Nothing will come of these plans. In real politics there can be no wishful thinking. If the Soviet Union, when it was much weaker than now, was in a position to meet all the challenges that it faced, then indeed only a blind person would be unable to see that our capacity to maintain strong defenses and simultaneously resolve social and other tasks has enormously increased.

I shall repeat that as far as the United States foreign policy is concerned, it is based on at least two delusions. The first is the belief that the economic system of the Soviet Union is about to crumble and that the USSR will not succeed in restructuring. The second is calculated on Western superiority in equipment and technology and, eventually, in the military field. These illusions nourish a policy geared toward exhausting socialism through the arms race, so as to dictate terms later. Such is the scheme; it is naïve.

Current Western policies aren't responsible enough, and lack the new mode of thinking. I am outspoken about this. If we don't stop now and start practical disarmament, we may all find ourselves on the edge of a precipice. Today, as never before, the Soviet Union and the United States need responsible policies. Both countries have their political, social and economic problems: a vast field for activities. Meanwhile, many brain trusts work at strategic plans and juggle millions of lives. Their recommendations boil down to this: the Soviet Union is the most horrible threat for the United States and the world. I repeat: it is high time this caveman mentality was given up. Of course, many political leaders and diplomats have engaged in just such policies based on just such a mentality for decades. But their time is past. A new outlook is necessary in a nuclear age. The United States and the Soviet Union need it most in their bilateral relations.

We are realists. So we take into consideration the fact that in a foreign policy all countries, even the smallest, have their own interests. It is high time great powers realized that they can no longer reshape the world according to their own patterns. That era has receded or, at least, is receding into the past.

Working with Sources

1. **Why does Gorbachev describe American foreign policy as being dictated by "illusions" and "delusions"? Was he being disingenuous or hypocritical in this assertion?**
2. **In what ways was Gorbachev advocating a global position on the problems of the world? Was he also guided by "delusions" in this advocacy?**

SOURCE 30.2 Martin Luther King, Jr., "I Have a Dream"

August 28, 1963

Under the accelerating pressure of the American civil rights movement—and with images of African Americans being attacked and beaten as they demanded equality beaming across television screens—President Kennedy introduced civil rights legislation during his administration. Realizing that advocacy of this position might endanger the position of his Democratic Party, particularly in the South, in the elections of 1964, Kennedy continued to find ways to shape American public opinion while also cajoling Congress to implement this legislation. Civil rights advocates, spearheaded by the Reverend Dr. Martin Luther King, Jr. (1929–1968), convened in a march on Washington, DC, in August 1963. Marchers explicitly demanded "jobs and freedom." While the electrifying speech King gave on that day is more remembered for its stirring conclusion about his "dream" and about letting "freedom ring," the prepared remarks at the beginning of the speech reveal even more of King's brilliance and the depth of his political thought.

Source: Reprinted by arrangement with The Heirs to the Estate of Martin Luther King Jr., c/o Writers House as agent for the proprietor New York, NY.

I am happy to join with you today in what will go down in history as the greatest demonstration for freedom in the history of our nation.

Five score years ago, a great American, in whose symbolic shadow we stand today, signed the Emancipation Proclamation. This momentous decree came as a great beacon light of hope to millions of Negro slaves who had been seared in the flames of withering injustice. It came as a joyous daybreak to end the long night of their captivity.

But one hundred years later, the Negro still is not free. One hundred years later, the life of the Negro is still sadly crippled by the manacles of segregation and the chains of discrimination. One hundred years later, the Negro lives on a lonely island of poverty in the midst of a vast ocean of material prosperity. One hundred years later, the Negro is still languished in the corners of American society and finds himself an exile in his own land. And so we've come here today to dramatize a shameful condition.

In a sense we've come to our nation's capital to cash a check. When the architects of our republic wrote the magnificent words of the Constitution and the Declaration of Independence, they were signing a promissory note to which every American was to fall heir. This note was a promise that all men, yes, black men as well as white men, would be guaranteed the "unalienable Rights" of "Life, Liberty and the pursuit of Happiness." It is obvious today that America has defaulted on this promissory note, insofar as her citizens of color are concerned. Instead of honoring this sacred obligation, America has given the Negro people a bad check, a check which has come back marked "insufficient funds."

But we refuse to believe that the bank of justice is bankrupt. We refuse to believe that there are insufficient funds in the great vaults of opportunity of this nation. And so, we've come to cash this check, a check that will give us upon demand the riches of freedom and the security of justice.

We have also come to this hallowed spot to remind America of the fierce urgency of Now. This is no time to engage in the luxury of cooling off or to take the tranquilizing drug of gradualism. Now is the time to make real the promises of democracy. Now is the time to rise from the dark and desolate valley of segregation to the sunlit path of racial justice. Now is the time to lift our nation from the quicksands of racial injustice to the solid rock of brotherhood. Now is the time to make justice a reality for all of God's children.

It would be fatal for the nation to overlook the urgency of the moment. This sweltering summer of the Negro's legitimate discontent will not pass until there is an invigorating autumn of freedom and equality. Nineteen sixty-three is not an end, but a beginning. And those who hope that the Negro needed to blow off steam and will now be content will have a rude awakening if the nation returns to business as usual. And there will be neither rest nor tranquility in America until the Negro is granted his citizenship rights. The whirlwinds of revolt will continue to shake the foundations of our nation until the bright day of justice emerges.

But there is something that I must say to my people, who stand on the warm threshold which leads into the palace of justice: In the process of gaining our rightful place, we must not be guilty of wrongful deeds. Let us not seek to satisfy our thirst for freedom by drinking from the cup of bitterness and hatred. We must forever conduct our struggle on the high plane of dignity and discipline. We must not allow our creative protest to degenerate into physical violence. Again and again, we must rise to the majestic heights of meeting physical force with soul force.

The marvelous new militancy which has engulfed the Negro community must not lead us to a distrust of all white people, for many of our white brothers, as evidenced by their presence here today, have come to realize that their destiny is tied up with our destiny. And they have come to realize that their freedom is inextricably bound to our freedom.

We cannot walk alone.

And as we walk, we must make the pledge that we shall always march ahead.

We cannot turn back.

There are those who are asking the devotees of civil rights, "When will you be satisfied?" We can never be satisfied as long as the Negro is the victim of the unspeakable horrors of police brutality. We can never be satisfied as long as our bodies, heavy with the fatigue of travel, cannot gain lodging in the motels of the highways and the hotels of the cities. We cannot be satisfied as long as the Negro's basic mobility is from a smaller ghetto to a larger one. We can never be satisfied as long as our children are stripped of their self-hood and robbed of their dignity by signs stating: "For Whites Only." We cannot be satisfied as long as a Negro in Mississippi cannot vote and a Negro in New York believes he has nothing for which to vote. No, no, we are not satisfied, and we will not be satisfied until "justice rolls down like waters, and righteousness like a mighty stream."

▸ Working with Sources

1. **How and why did King use financial metaphors to describe the position of African Americans a century after their supposed "emancipation"?**
2. **How did he describe the rights and equality of African Americans as being in the interests of *all* Americans?**

SOURCE 30.3

Simone de Beauvoir, *The Second Sex*

1949

Encouraged by the successful strategy and tactics of the civil rights and antiwar movements, a new assertiveness marked the drive for women's rights after the conclusion of World War II. One important voice in the movement for women's freedoms was that of a leading French philosopher and intellectual, Simone de Beauvoir (1908–1986). Her lengthy, detailed, and

Source: Simone de Beauvoir, *The Second Sex*, trans. Constance Borde and Shelia Malovany-Chevallier (New York: Vintage Books, 2011), 346–347.

compelling study *The Second Sex*, published in 1949, challenged women to take action on their own behalf in order to gain full equality with their male counterparts. Her analysis traced the origins of sexism and a sense of women's inferiority to the unique circumstances of girlhood and to society's instilling of "feminine" characteristics in young women. Only by breaking the barriers of societal expectations for "well-bred young girls," she argued, could women achieve the goal of true and complete equality with men.

Housework or everyday chores that the mother does not hesitate to impose on the girl student or trainee completely exhaust her. During the war I saw my students in Sèvres worn out by family tasks added on top of their schoolwork: one developed Pott's disease, the other meningitis. Mothers—we will see—are blindly hostile to freeing their daughters and, more or less deliberately, work at bullying them even more; for the adolescent boy, his effort to become a man is respected, and he is already granted great freedom. The girl is required to stay home; her outside activities are watched over: she is never encouraged to organize her own fun and pleasure. It is rare to see women organize a long hike on their own, a walking or biking trip, or take part in games such as billiards and bowling. Beyond a lack of initiative that comes from their education, customs make their independence difficult. If they wander the streets, they are stared at, accosted. I know some girls, far from shy, who get no enjoyment strolling through Paris alone because, incessantly bothered, they are incessantly on their guard: all their pleasure is ruined. If girl students run through the streets in happy groups as boys do, they attract attention; striding along, singing, talking, and laughing loudly or eating an apple are provocations, and they will be insulted or followed or approached. Lightheartedness immediately becomes a lack of decorum. This self-control imposed on the woman becomes second nature for "the well-bred girl" and kills spontaneity; lively exuberance is crushed. The result is tension and boredom. This boredom is contagious: girls tire of each other quickly; being in the same prison does not create solidarity among them, and this is one of the reasons the company of boys becomes so necessary. This inability to be self-sufficient brings on a shyness that extends over their whole lives and even marks their work. They think that brilliant triumphs are reserved for men; they do not dare aim too high. It has already been observed that fifteen-year-old girls, comparing themselves with boys, declare, "Boys are better." This conviction is debilitating. It encourages laziness and mediocrity. A girl—who had no particular deference for the stronger sex— reproached a man for his cowardice; when she was told that she herself was a coward, she complacently declared: "Oh! It's not the same thing for a woman."

The fundamental reason for this defeatism is that the adolescent girl does not consider herself responsible for her future; she judges it useless to demand much of herself since her lot in the end will not depend on her. Far from destining herself into man because she thinks she is inferior to him, it is because she is destined for him that, in accepting the idea of her inferiority, she constitutes it.

In fact, she will gain value in the eyes of males not by increasing her human worth but by modeling herself on their dreams. When she is inexperienced, she is not always aware of this. She sometimes acts as aggressively as boys; she tries to conquer them with a brusque authority, a proud frankness: this attitude is almost surely doomed to failure, From the most servile to the haughtiest, girls all learn that to please, they must give in to them. Their mothers urge them not to treat boys like companions, not to make advances to them, to assume a passive role. If they want to flirt or initiate a friendship, they should carefully avoid giving the impression they are taking the initiative; men do not like tomboys, nor bluestockings, nor thinking women; too much audacity, culture, intelligence, or character frightens them. In most novels, as George Eliot observes, it is the dumb, blond heroine who outshines the virile brunette; and in *The Mill on the Floss*, Maggie tries in vain to reverse the roles; in the end she dies and it is the blond Lucy who marries Stephen. In *The Last of the Mohicans*, vapid Alice wins the hero's heart and not valiant Cora; in *Little Women* kindly Jo is only a childhood friend for Laurie; he vows his love to curly-haired and insipid Amy.

▸ Working with Sources

1. **How, in de Beauvoir's estimation, do young women internalize feelings of inferiority and carry these ideas with them into adulthood?**
2. **What role do the practical, daily experiences of women in the wider world play in the development of "feminine" expectations? Can these be overcome?**

SOURCE 30.4

Coverage of the Tiananmen Square protests

1989

In May 1989, a protest movement gathered strength in Tiananmen Square in Beijing, as students convened and constructed a large statue called the Goddess of Democracy. By the beginning of June, the movement had turned into a generalized protest by workers and ordinary citizens in addition to the students. When they refused to disperse, the government sent in the army on June 4 to crush what, to many in the Communist Party, had become an incipient rebellion. The image of a lone man attempting to face down an approaching tank became the instant icon of the movement,

Source: http://news.bbc.co.uk/2/hi/asia-pacific/3775907.stm

but there are many other arresting narratives of the events that occurred during this protest. On the fifteenth anniversary of the suppression of these protests, the British Broadcasting Corporation interviewed survivors and eyewitnesses, gathering their testimonies into the report subsequently excerpted.

Witnessing Tiananmen: Clearing the Square

The BBC's Chinese Service has interviewed some of those who witnessed the protests and subsequent bloodshed.

Zhang Boli was deputy director of the students' hunger strike at Tiananmen Square. He then spent two years on the run before fleeing to the United States, where he now lives.

While we were making preparations news came from all sides saying that the troops had started to open fire.

I remember many students ran to the square with blood running down their faces.

In some places, troops were shooting and in some places there were clashes. Zhang Huajie had actually been beaten up. When he ran to the square his face was full of blood.

He grabbed the microphone and spoke into it: "Fellow students, they have really opened fire now. They are really shooting! They are using their guns and using real bullets!"

I couldn't believe it. We at the square at the time could not really believe it.

There was a speaker's platform under the statue of the Goddess of Democracy. It was at the time when Yan Jiaqi and I had just started to speak, the troops arrived. And they were moving into Tiananmen Square.

Under the floodlight I could see all those dark helmets moving like waves into the square towards us. I felt that the final moment must have come.

So I spoke to the students, telling them that we should still behave in the spirit we had adopted all along: "We will not fight back even if we are beaten up, and we will not talk back even if we are cursed upon."

We decided to retreat to the Monument of Heroes to wait there for instructions from our command centre. Finally we reached the Monument.

Later, Zhou Duo and Hou Dejian removed their white vests and, using them as white flags, they walked over to the troops to negotiate. After all, Hou Dejian was a famous singer of some influence. He couldn't be cast as an anti-revolutionary rebel.

When Zhou Duo returned he told the students: "They say over there 'We'll give you only half an hour to leave, to evacuate. If you don't, you will have to bear the consequences.'"

So a very important decision was to be made at the time. What are we going to do with the several thousand students here? To leave, to evacuate, or not? Actually it was quite obvious at the time that it was time that we should leave. So when Feng Congde took over the microphone he knew that a heavy burden of history was handed to him.

Finally, the lights (at the square) were switched off. When the lights were out the students thought the troops would start shooting. So, many students huddled together. When the lights were out the microphone was also cut off.

Feng Congde then used a loud-speaker to speak to the students: "Fellow students, we have two opinions here. One says we should leave now. Another says we should stay put. As I can't see you, please speak aloud to respond. I will first say "WE WILL NOT LEAVE." If you agree, please say aloud WE AGREE. Then I will say "WE WILL LEAVE." If you agree, please say "AGREE." I'll see which response is louder."

Actually it was not easy to tell which response from the crowd was louder.

Feng Congde quickly made a wise decision: "I am standing here. This is the highest place. I could hear the response for us TO LEAVE was louder. So the command centre have now decided WE SHOULD LEAVE."

After it was decided that we should leave, they left only a very small gap for us to leave—just about as wide as this room. But nobody dared to move first.

. . .

The guns of the People's Army were pointing at [us] and they were loaded. They were holding machine guns. With one pull of the finger they could fire on us.

Hou Dejian went over to say: "Would it be OK for you people to raise your guns a bit higher and point at the sky?"

It was quite a painful experience. But we came out of the Square. And they didn't fire on us. I think that was because they also had to consider the opinions of the people of the nation and of the whole world.

If they were rash enough to decide to finish the lot of us on the spot, they could, but it would not do them any good at all. So it was still quite peaceful when we left Tiananmen Square.

But when we reached Liulukou suddenly there was trouble.

It was already dawn. A speeding tank came upon us like a gust of wind trying to cut through the lines of people. It was not just trying to run over people, it was also throwing out tear gas.

I remember we were all choking and couldn't open our eyes. We just heard the loud rumblings of the tanks.

About a dozen metres behind me people were crying in hysteria. I think more than 12, or 20-odd people were in a mess of blood and flesh.

It was said later that 11 people were killed there."

Working with Sources

1. **What did the Goddess of Democracy mean to the students, and how did they envision their protest?**
2. **What do the varying reactions of the soldiers sent to quell the protests suggest about the prodemocracy movement in China at that time?**

SOURCE 30.5

Salvador Allende, "Last Words to the Nation"

September 11, 1973

Salvador Allende led a coalition of socialists, communists, and liberal Christian democrats to a plurality win as president of Chile in 1970. Many of his policies met opposition within Chile, while his ideology and nationalization of American interests in the country's mines prompted the administration of US President Nixon (1969–1974) to back Allende's opposition. With American blessings and CIA help, Allende was overthrown and (according to the official 2011 autopsy report) committed suicide. He would be replaced with the repressive but friendlier (to the United States) regime of General Augusto Pinochet, who remained in office and repeatedly violated the human rights of Chileans until 1990. Nevertheless, the coup that toppled Allende ended with a riveting address by the deposed leader to his people.

My friends,

Surely this will be the last opportunity for me to address you. The Air Force has bombed the towers of Radio Portales and Radio Corporación.

My words do not have bitterness but disappointment. May they be a moral punishment for those who have betrayed their oath: soldiers of Chile, titular commanders in chief, Admiral Merino, who has designated himself Commander of the Navy, and Mr. Mendoza, the despicable general who only yesterday pledged his fidelity and loyalty to the Government, and who also has appointed himself Chief of the Carabineros [national police].

Given these facts, the only thing left for me is to say to workers: I am not going to resign!

Placed in a historic transition, I will pay for loyalty to the people with my life. And I say to them that I am certain that the seed which we have planted in the good conscience of thousands and thousands of Chileans will not be shriveled forever.

They have strength and will be able to dominate us, but social processes can be arrested neither by crime nor force. History is ours, and people make history.

Workers of my country: I want to thank you for the loyalty that you always had, the confidence that you deposited in a man who was only an interpreter of great yearnings for justice, who gave his word that he would respect the

Source: https://www.marxists.org/archive/allende/1973/september/11.htm

Constitution and the law and did just that. At this definitive moment, the last moment when I can address you, I wish you to take advantage of the lesson: foreign capital, imperialism, together with the reaction, created the climate in which the Armed Forces broke their tradition, the tradition taught by General Schneider and reaffirmed by Commander Araya, victims of the same social sector which will today be in their homes hoping, with foreign assistance, to retake power to continue defending their profits and their privileges.

I address, above all, the modest woman of our land, the campesina who believed in us, the worker who labored more, the mother who knew our concern for children. I address professionals of Chile, patriotic professionals, those who days ago continued working against the sedition sponsored by professional associations, class-based associations that also defended the advantages which a capitalist society grants to a few.

I address the youth, those who sang and gave us their joy and their spirit of struggle. I address the man of Chile, the worker, the farmer, the intellectual, those who will be persecuted, because in our country fascism has been already present for many hours—in terrorist attacks, blowing up the bridges, cutting the railroad tracks, destroying the oil and gas pipelines, in the face of the silence of those who had the obligation to protect them. They were committed. History will judge them.

. . .

Workers of my country, I have faith in Chile and its destiny. Other men will overcome this dark and bitter moment when treason seeks to prevail. Go forward knowing that, sooner rather than later, the great avenues will open again where free men will walk to build a better society.

Long live Chile! Long live the people! Long live the workers!

These are my last words, and I am certain that my sacrifice will not be in vain, I am certain that, at the very least, it will be a moral lesson that will punish felony, cowardice, and treason.

Working with Sources

1. **How did Allende combine the notions of "patriotism" and resistance to "foreign capital"?**
2. **What forces and institutions were most guilty, in his assessment, of betraying the economic and political interests of ordinary Chileans?**

SOURCE 30.6

Nelson Mandela's inauguration speech

NELSON MANDELA'S ADDRESS TO THE PEOPLE OF CAPE TOWN, GRAND PARADE, ON THE OCCASION OF HIS INAUGURATION AS STATE PRESIDENT

Born in British South Africa, Nelson Mandela (1918-2013), a universally renowned advocate of social justice and peace, joined the African National Congress (ANC) in 1943 and quickly became engaged in anticolonial and antiracist politics. During the 1950s, Mandela emerged as a prominent figure among black South African activists who were determined to adopt more violent measures against apartheid policies consisting of protests and other civil disobedience actions than those supported by the ANC. Placed on trial for sabotage and treason in 1963, Mandela was subsequently imprisoned for 27 years. Following F. W. de Klerk's election as president of South Africa in 1989, Mandela was released from prison in 1990. Mandela and de Klerk then cooperated in creating an anti-apartheid government devoted to multiracial policies, for which they were jointly awarded the Nobel Peace Prize in 1993. After South Africa's first multiracial elections in 1994, Mandela and the ANC emerged as winners. In his carefully and eloquently constructed inauguration address presented at Cape Town on May 9th, 1994, Mandela called for the unification of all South Africans.

Mr Master of Ceremonies,
Your Excellencies,
Members of the Diplomatic Corps,
My Fellow South Africans:

Today we are entering a new era for our country and its people. Today we celebrate not the victory of a party, but a victory for all the people of South Africa.

Our country has arrived at a decision. Among all the parties that contested the elections, the overwhelming majority of South Africans have mandated the African National Congress to lead our country into the future. The South Africa we have struggled for, in which all our people, be they African, Coloured, Indian or White, regard themselves as citizens of one nation is at hand.

Perhaps it was history that ordained that it be here, at the Cape of Good Hope that we should lay the foundation stone of our new nation. For it was here at this Cape, over three centuries ago, that there began the fateful convergence of the peoples of Africa, Europe and Asia on these shores.

It was to this peninsula that the patriots, among them many princes and scholars, of Indonesia were dragged in chains. It was on the sandy plains of this peninsula that first battles of the epic wars of resistance were fought.

Source: https://www.southafrica.to/people/Quotes/NelsonMandela/Nelson-Mandela-inauguration.htm

When we look out across Table Bay, the horizon is dominated by Robben Island, whose infamy as a dungeon built to stifle the spirit of freedom is as old as colonialism in South Africa. For three centuries that island was seen as a place to which outcasts can be banished. The names of those who were incarcerated on Robben Island is a roll call of resistance fighters and democrats spanning over three centuries. If indeed this is a Cape of Good Hope, that hope owes much to the spirit of that legion of fighters and others of their calibre.

We have fought for a democratic constitution since the 1880s. Ours has been a quest for a constitution freely adopted by the people of South Africa, reflecting their wishes and their aspirations. The struggle for democracy has never been a matter pursued by one race, class, religious community or gender among South Africans. In honouring those who fought to see this day arrive, we honour the best sons and daughters of all our people. We can count amongst them Africans, Coloureds, Whites, Indians, Muslims, Christians, Hindus, Jews—all of them united by a common vision of a better life for the people of this country.

It was that vision that inspired us in 1923 when we adopted the first ever Bill of Rights in this country. That same vision spurred us to put forward the African Claims in 1946. It is also the founding principle of the Freedom Charter we adopted as policy in 1955, which in its very first lines, places before South Africa an inclusive basis for citizenship.

In 1980s the African National Congress was still setting the pace, being the first major political formation in South Africa to commit itself firmly to a Bill of Rights, which we published in November 1990. These milestones give concrete expression to what South Africa can become. They speak of a constitutional, democratic, political order in which, regardless of colour, gender, religion, political opinion or sexual orientation, the law will provide for the equal protection of all citizens.

They project a democracy in which the government, whomever that government may be, will be bound by a higher set of rules, embodied in a constitution, and will not be able to govern the country as it pleases.

Democracy is based on the majority principle. This is especially true in a country such as ours where the vast majority have been systematically denied their rights. At the same time, democracy also requires that the rights of political and other minorities be safeguarded.

In the political order we have established there will be regular, open and free elections, at all levels of government—central, provincial and municipal. There shall also be a social order which respects completely the culture, language and religious rights of all sections of our society and the fundamental rights of the individual.

The task at hand will not be easy. But you have mandated us to change South Africa from a country in which the majority lived with little hope, to one in which they can live and work with dignity, with a sense of self-esteem and confidence in the future. The cornerstone of building a better life of opportunity, freedom and prosperity is the Reconstruction and Development Programme.

This needs unity of purpose. It needs action. It requires us all to work together to bring an end to division, an end to suspicion and build a nation united in our diversity.

The people of South Africa have spoken in these elections. They want change! And change is what they will get. Our plan is to create jobs, promote peace and reconciliation, and to guarantee freedom for all South Africans. We will tackle the widespread poverty so pervasive among the majority of our people. By encouraging investors and the democratic state to support job creating projects in which manufacturing will play a central role we will try to change our country from a net exporter of raw materials to one that exports finished products through beneficiation.

The government will devise policies that encourage and reward productive enterprise among the disadvantaged communities—African, Coloured and Indian. By easing credit conditions we can assist them to make inroads into the productive and manufacturing spheres and break out of the small-scale distribution to which they are presently confined.

To raise our country and its people from the morass of racism and apartheid will require determination and effort. As a government, the ANC will create a legal framework that will assist, rather than impede, the awesome task of reconstruction and development of our battered society.

While we are and shall remain fully committed to the spirit of a government of national unity, we are determined to initiate and bring about the change that our mandate from the people demands.

We place our vision of a new constitutional order for South Africa on the table not as conquerors, prescribing to the conquered. We speak as fellow citizens to heal the wounds of the past with the intent of constructing a new order based on justice for all.

This is the challenge that faces all South Africans today, and it is one to which I am certain we will all rise.

Working with Sources

1. **How does Mandela describe the quest for democracy in South Africa?**
2. **In what ways does Mandela propose to improve the lives of all South Africans?**

World Period Six

From Three Modernities to One

Modern scientific–industrial society underwent dramatic transformations after World War I (1914–1918). Three competing models for modernity—capitalist democracy, communism, and supremacist nationalism—shrank to one in the course of the twentieth century. German and Japanese supremacist nationalism collapsed in 1945 as a result of their overextended military aggression. Soviet and Eastern European communism collapsed in 1989–1991 due to a top-heavy central command economy. Western capitalist democracy survived but did so only after enduring decolonization and regulating its economy. After 1991, it expanded its global dominance, buttressed by the computer revolution, but questions have arisen whether its model of modernity is sustainable. Under current conditions, the natural environment will not be able to support the exploitative framework of capitalist democracy much longer. The grave threat posed by COVID-19 has further undermined its credibility.

Chapter 31

A Fragile Capitalist-Democratic World Order

1991–2020

CHAPTER THIRTY-ONE PATTERNS

Origins, Interactions, Adaptations After the collapse of communism as an alternative path to modernity, capitalist democracy triumphed during the next quarter century. Aided by the latest round of scientific-industrial innovation, the IT revolution, North America, the European Union, and Japan pioneered a new pattern of financial deregulation, investment globalization, world consumerism, and democratization. Interacting with this pattern, large, newly industrialized countries such as China, India, Brazil, and Turkey successfully adapted to the new pattern. Known as the "Washington Consensus," this pattern also benefited developing countries by the imposition of fiscal discipline and the rule of law for their political processes, resulting in a substantial reduction of poverty.

Uniqueness and Similarities Unfortunately, during the 2010s it became increasingly clear that the new pattern left many people behind in various parts of the world, increasing the numbers of terrorists, asylum seekers, migrants, and refugees. While surges in the inequality of income, wealth, education, and environmental degradation have been fairly similar across the world, expressions of protest, as well as governmental responses, have been highly diverse, depending on regional cultures and traditions.

During the winter and spring months of 2010–2011, crowds across the Arab world gathered to remonstrate with authoritarian governments over a wide range of issues. The governments challenged by these movements had long been propped up by brutal security services. Further, even if rulers pretended to have liberalized the economies of their countries, in fact "crony capitalism" benefited their relatives and followers. Chronic unemployment left both the poor and the middle classes in despair over their future. While some unemployed youth had found solace in an Islamism whose preachers promised the solution for all ills, these preachers were no more able than the rulers to improve the daily lives of the people.

By mid-spring 2011, the massive protests had toppled the governments of Tunisia and Egypt. Syria and Bahrain sought to suppress the democracy movements, while in Libya, Yemen, and Syria, civil wars tore the populations apart. Remarkably, in conservative and male-dominated Yemen, the movement was led by a woman. Tawakkol Karman, 32, the leader of Women Journalists Without Chains, harangued mostly male crowds with calls for revolution. "We are in need of heroes," said one Yemeni observer. "She manages to do what most men cannot do in a society that is highly prejudiced against women." The Norwegian Nobel Committee made Tawakkol Karman a co-winner of the Peace Prize in 2013.

Unfortunately, the Yemeni political process did not stabilize. The country slid into a civil war after 2012, in which the Shiite minority of the Houthis sought to dominate the Sunni majority. The civil war turned into a proxy war between Shiite Iran and Sunni Saudi Arabia, the two dominant Middle Eastern powers. Unhappily, the civil war, which continues as of this writing, pushed Tawakkol Karman and her hope for a democratic Yemen completely to the sidelines.

CHAPTER OUTLINE

Capitalist Democracy: The Dominant Pattern of Modernity

The Environmental Limits of Modernity

Putting It All Together

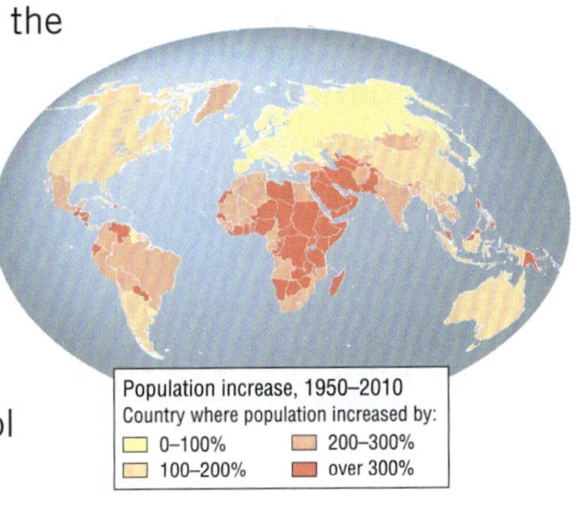

ABOVE: Traumatized inhabitants lining up for humanitarian aid in the besieged eastern part of Aleppo, Syria, 2016, just prior to its fall.

Seeing Patterns

> How did the United States demonstrate its dominant economic position toward the end of the twentieth century? How did it accelerate the pattern of globalization?

> What made capitalist democracy so attractive toward the end of the twentieth century that it became a generic model for many countries around the world to strive for?

> Which policies did China and India pursue so that they became the fastest-industrializing countries in the early twenty-first century?

> How have information technology and social networking altered cultural, political, and economic interactions around the world?

> What is climate change, and why is it a source of grave concern for the future?

Postmodernism and postcolonialism: Cultural movements influential across the world from ca. 1970 to 2010 which centered on "critical theory," according to which reality is constructed through discourse and the will to power determines society's institutions.

Achieving modernity through urbanization, science, industrialization, the accumulation of capital, and grassroots participation in political pluralism was until about 2010 the near universal goal in the world. At this time, the sudden rise of populists with their polemics against urbanism, expertise, international finance, globalization, and democracy shook the optimism of many in the future of modernity. With the blow of the COVID-19 pandemic the future became even less predictable. The story of how the pattern of modernity became nearly universal, yet could also within a short period of time begin to fray at its margins, is the focus of this chapter.

Capitalist Democracy: The Dominant Pattern of Modernity

With the demise of communism, the struggle among the three ideologies of modernity that had characterized much of the twentieth century was now over. One influential study asserted that, in the absence of genuine ideological competition, the world was seeing "the end of history." Another posited the opening of a new kind of "clash of civilizations." Some viewers argued that modernity had ended and we were at the beginning of a new age of **postmodernism** and **postcolonialism**. Less triumphant observers realized that democracy would not spread as long as countries remained poor and stuck in inherited forms of authoritarianism or even autocracy.

A Decade of Global Expansion: The United States and the World in the 1990s

In the aftermath of the collapse of communism, the United States was the most economically and politically powerful country on earth. Two characteristics made the United States the sole superpower. First, the US dollar functioned as the currency for all oil sales and purchases. Second, with its giant consumer economy, the United States functioned as the world's favored destination for manufactured goods. The leverage the United States gained from these two economic functions was bolstered by its possession of overwhelming military force.

A Hierarchy of Nations During the 1990s, the sovereign countries of the world formed a three-tier hierarchy. At the top of the first tier was the United States. Below the United States, the fully industrialized democracies in Europe and North America, Japan, and Australia occupied the rest of the first tier. In the course of the 1990s, four "newly industrialized countries" joined this tier: Taiwan, South Korea, Hong Kong, and Singapore. In the early 2000s, the so-called BRIC countries—Brazil, Russia, India, and China—as well as Turkey and Mexico, were added. In 2010 China surpassed Japan to have the second largest economy by nominal GDP (Gross Domestic Product).

In the second tier of the world hierarchy were "middle-income countries," according to the United Nations's definition. They were either industrializing states in the Middle East, south Asia, East Asia, and Latin America or reindustrializing states in the former Communist bloc. In the broad bottom tier were countries defined as "low-income" or "poor," located for the most part in sub-Saharan Africa and Southeast Asia (see Map 31.1).

In 2000 about one-fifth of the world's population of 6 billion lived in fully industrialized countries, two-thirds in middle-income countries, and 15 percent in poor countries. Only two centuries after the beginnings of capitalist modernity, 90 percent of the world population was more or less integrated into the pattern characterized by market exchange and consumerism.

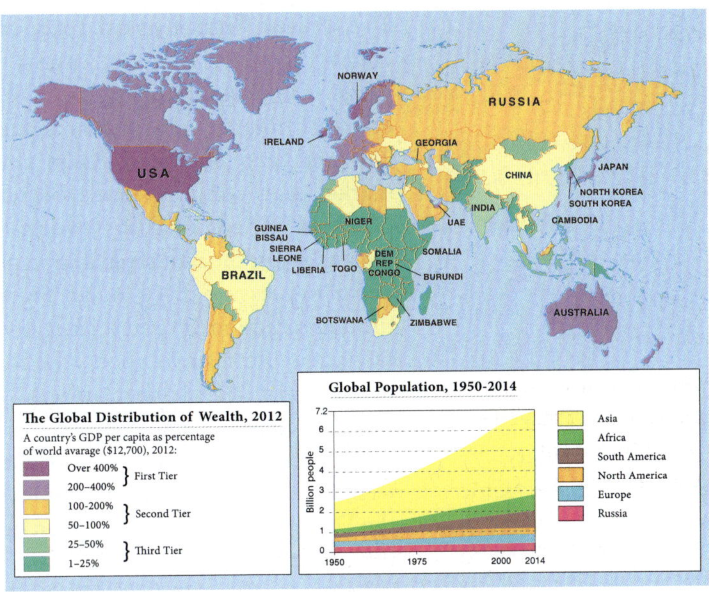

MAP 31.1 **The Global Distribution of Wealth, 2012**

The Dollar Regime The United States stood at the top of the world hierarchy, thanks largely to the power of its financial system. The beginnings of this system date to the years following 1971, when President Richard Nixon took the dollar off the gold standard. Two years later, Nixon persuaded the Middle East–dominated Organization of the Petroleum Exporting Countries (OPEC) to accept only dollars as payment for oil. OPEC, anxious to remain in the good graces of the United States as its largest buyer, agreed. As a result of the Nixon–OPEC deal, the dollar replaced gold as the acknowledged international standard of exchange.

Dollar regime: A system maintained by the United States whereby dollars are the sole currency in which the price of oil and most other commodities and goods in the world are denominated; the regime forces most countries to maintain two currencies, with consequent financial constraints.

Under the **dollar regime**, all oil-importing countries except the United States had to manage two currencies. One, denominated in dollars, was for energy purchases; the other, in domestic currencies, was for the internal market of oil consumption. There were repeated grumblings among the non–oil producers of the world, both developed and developing, about being cheated by the dollar regime. But the US–OPEC deal endured, backed up by a gigantic American financial system that emerged as a result of the dollar regime.

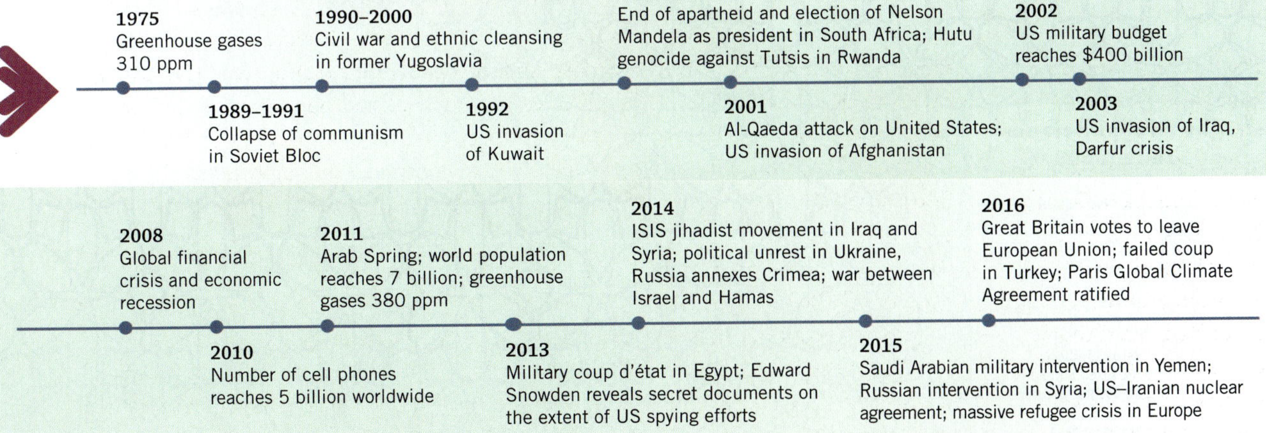

The United States as an Import Sinkhole The United States became the country to which everyone wanted to export. Building this relationship was particularly important in East Asia. During the Cold War, the United States had encouraged import substitution industrialization in Korea, Taiwan, Hong Kong, Thailand, and Southeast Asian countries on the Japanese model, which had marked that country's remarkable recovery after World War II. By becoming prosperous, it was assumed, these countries would be less susceptible to communism. By the 1990s, the industrialization process reached levels where the United States began to pressure these "Asian Tigers" along with Japan to reduce import substitution protectionism and replace it with free trade. In return for the United States buying their industrial goods, the countries of East Asia agreed to give free access to American financial institutions.

After communism collapsed, China, pushing its own import substitution industrialization, began to export cheap industrial goods to the United States as well. In the 1990s, these goods undercut those produced by the Asian Tigers, and the United States became an even deeper "sinkhole," this time for products made in the People's Republic of China. The United States in effect underwrote China's industrialization, binding the country's economic interests closely to its own financial interests within the dollar regime (see Map 31.2).

Information technology: The array of computers, information, electronic services, entertainment, and storage available to business and consumers, with information increasingly stored in the "cloud"—that is, online storage centers rather than individual computer hard drives.

US Technological Renewal and Globalization Electronics was one of those periodic new technologies with which capitalism, always threatened by falling profit rates in maturing industries, became more profitable again. An entirely new branch of industry, **information technology (IT)**, put personal computers, cell

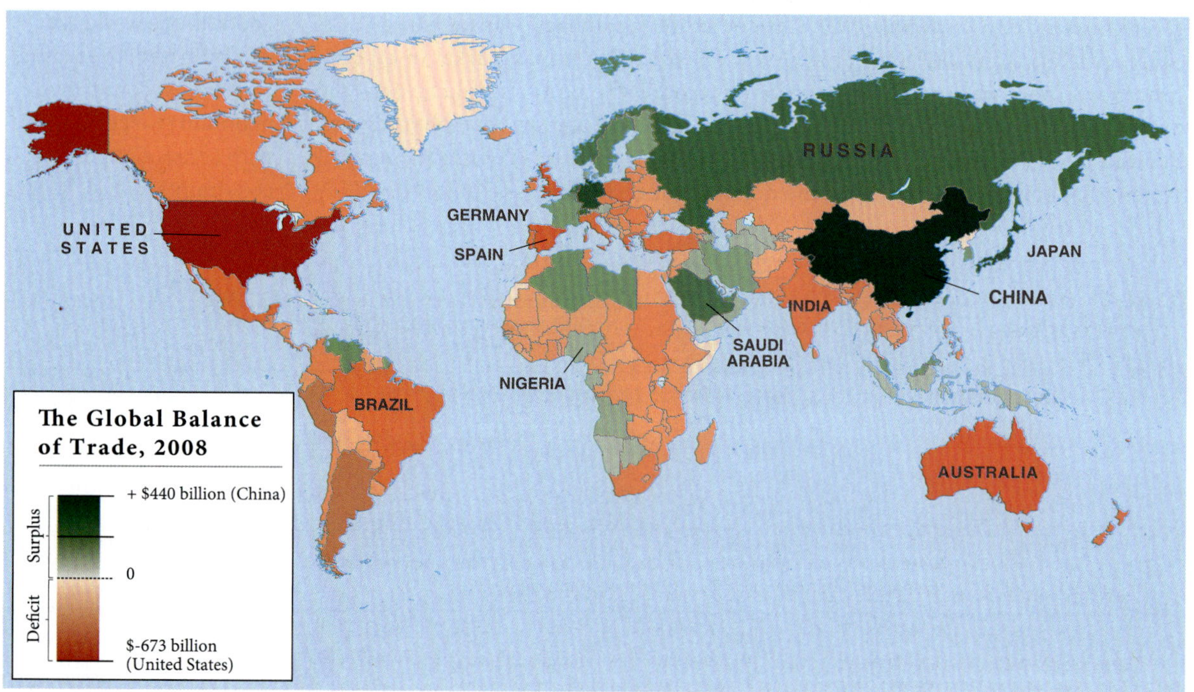

MAP 31.2 **The Global Balance of Trade, 2008**

phones, online delivery of music and entertainment, and a host of other services into the hands of consumers.

During the 1990s, America became the leader in the "high-tech industries" of electronics, biotechnology, and pharmacology. Worldwide, the volume of trade goods doubled and the volume of capital flows quadrupled. The only blemishes in this **globalization** process, from an American perspective, were continued protectionism and low consumption in many Asian countries. The closest economic advisors of President Bill Clinton (in office 1993–2001) were bankers and investors who had greatly expanded the size and influence of the financial services sector. The US globalization offensive in the 1990s was thus in large part an effort to open protected foreign markets to American financial institutions.

Globalization: The ongoing process of integrating the norms of market economies throughout the world and binding the economies of the world into a single uniform system.

The dollar- and import-sinkhole regimes attracted critics from the entire political spectrum. Conservative critics were appalled that the United States no longer adhered to the gold standard. They further bemoaned the disappearance of the traditional manufacturing sector and its replacement by financial institutions and Internet start-ups that produced nothing tangible. Progressive critics accused the United States of using its arrangements with OPEC and the East Asian countries to exclude poorer countries. In their opinion, the United States upheld an imperialist capitalist system that limited wealth to a minority and refused to share it with the have-nots.

US Military Dominance By the year 2002, the US military budget had risen to $400 billion. This astronomical sum was considerably smaller than during the Cold War but still larger than the defense budgets of the next eight countries combined. On the basis of this military machine, President Bill Clinton operated from a position of de facto world dominance.

His successor, President George W. Bush (in office 2001–2009), articulated this dominance eventually in a formal doctrine, the National Security Strategy of 2002. American might became highly visible in all parts of the world in part as a byproduct of the "War on Terror" brought on by the attacks on New York's World Trade Center and Washington DC's Pentagon on September 11, 2001. This also had the effect, however, of generating resentment among those for whom the combined economic–military power of the United States amounted to a new kind of world dominance. After 2009, however, President Barack Obama (in office 2009–2017) sought to reduce the American military posture by withdrawing troops from Iraq and Afghanistan and reducing the now-unsustainable military budget. In spite of these reductions, American predominance remained undiminished (see Map 31.3).

Intervention in Iraq The national security strategy sought to prevent countries from establishing dominance in a region and to destroy terrorist organizations bent on destruction in the United States. The first policy was enacted after Iraq's Saddam Hussein (1937–2006) occupied Kuwait (1990–1991). President George H. W. Bush (in office 1989–1993) intervened when it became clear that Hussein, by invading Kuwait, sought dominance over Middle Eastern oil exports. At the head of a coalition force and with UN backing in 1992, US troops drove the Iraqi occupiers from Kuwait.

In the following decade, the United States and the United Nations subjected Iraq to a stringent military inspection regimen to end Saddam Hussein's efforts to acquire nuclear and chemical weapons. The inspectors were successful in destroying these weapons, but Hussein, anxious to project his power among the Arabs, did his best to pretend that he still possessed them. This pretense touched off an intense debate among the members of the UN Security Council. In the end, in March 2003, President George W. Bush ordered a preemptive invasion without Security Council backing, arguing that Iraq had once more become a regional threat. To the surprise of many, Saddam Hussein's regime put up little resistance and fell after just three weeks to the US armed forces. Afterward, no weapons of mass destruction were discovered.

Intervention in Afghanistan The second US principle announced in President George W. Bush's national security strategy was a response to the rise of Islamic terrorism. In 1992, al-Qaeda ("the Base") under the leadership of Osama bin Laden (1957–2011) had emerged as the principal international terrorist organization.

Day of Infamy. Smoke billowing from the south tower of the World Trade Center in New York City on September 11, 2001. The north tower had already collapsed. Nearly 2,600 people died in the inferno, in which the heat of the exploding commercial airplanes in the interior of the high rises melted the steel girders supporting the buildings.

Al-Qaeda's campaign of terrorism climaxed on September 11, 2001, when suicide commandos hijacked four commercial airliners and crashed them into the World Trade Center's Twin Towers in New York City, the Pentagon outside Washington, DC, and a field near Shanksville, Pennsylvania. Nearly 3,000 people died in the disasters. In response, US troops invaded Afghanistan on October 7, 2001, in an effort to eliminate bin Laden, who was protected by the Islamist Taliban regime in power. They destroyed the regime and drove the al-Qaeda terrorists to western Pakistan. It took another decade for the United States to track down and assassinate bin Laden (May 2011), and even then, it failed to come to grips with the resurgent Taliban terrorists in its ongoing war in Afghanistan. In the course of 2017, this resurgence made considerable progress, ineffectively dealt with by the fledgling Afghan army and a residual US military, a situation that continued to the end of the decade.

The United Nations and Regional Peace During the 1990s and early 2000s, the United Nations fulfilled vital, if not always successful, peace missions in regional conflicts. A tragic failure in this regard was the Rwandan civil war of 1994, in which peacekeeping troops serving under UN auspices stood by as the Hutu ethnic majority massacred the Tutsi ethnic minority.

On the other hand, despite the bloodshed on both sides, the crisis in the Sudan saw the United Nations fare somewhat better. Two civil wars raged—one between Arab Muslims in northern Sudan and Christian and African-spiritual populations in southern Sudan (1983–2005), and the other within the non-Arab Muslim region of Darfur in western Sudan (2003–present). After UN mediation, the two sides in the first conflict agreed to the secession of South Sudan as an independent country in 2011. The Darfur conflict continued to smolder, with the United Nations pursuing criminal charges against the president of Sudan and an African Union force seeking to protect the refugees from Arab-inspired attacks. Unfortunately, after two years of independence in South Sudan, a desperate ethnic civil war followed, precariously settled by early 2020.

American Finances Go Global: Crisis and Recovery The world economy dominated by the dollar regime expanded during the late 1900s and early 2000s. In the so-called Washington Consensus (1989–2002), Western economists and foreign aid officers preached the motto "Stabilize, Privatize, and Liberalize" to emerging nations. To receive investments, foreign aid, or emergency loans to overcome recurrent economic crises, recipient countries had to submit to stringent rules concerning balanced budgets, the privatization of state firms, and the opening of protected branches of the economy.

Spurred by the Consensus in the 1990s, private US investors had nearly tripled the value of their assets abroad. The now more accessible financial systems in many newly industrialized and developing countries, however, often could not respond adequately. A series of financial crises gripped Mexico and most Southeast Asian countries. Here, either the state finances were in disarray (Mexico) or overcommitted banks with nonperforming portfolios (Southeast Asia) proved so vulnerable that the US Congress or the International Monetary Fund (IMF) had to step in with loans. (The IMF is an international bank, with the US government as the largest shareholder, that provides emergency loans to countries in sudden financial distress.) In return, these countries had to tighten credit, close unprofitable banks and factories, tolerate higher unemployment, and promote increased exporting. Newly industrialized South Korea was relatively successful with its reforms and quickly cranked up its exports again.

Russia's Crisis and Recovery Russia defaulted in 1998 on its internal bonds and from 1999 to 2001 on several of its external loans. These defaults were a culmination of the disastrous post-communist economic free fall. In the decade after 1991, Russia's gross domestic product (GDP) dropped by nearly half, a decline far worse than that experienced by the United States during the Great Depression of the 1930s. Fortunately, higher oil prices after 2001 eased the debt situation of Russia somewhat.

The oil and gas revenues from state firms available directly to the government, however, strengthened its autocratic tendencies. The former KGB officer Vladimir Putin, president of Russia 2000–2008 and again after 2012, was the principal engineer of this autocracy. Given the small size of the private sector in the early 2000s, the country was still years away from subjecting its state enterprises to market rules and creating a comprehensive market economy.

In addition, Putin sharply curtailed civil rights, restricted press freedom, and made it difficult for non-governmental organizations (NGOs) and human rights organizations to operate in Russia. In his desire to restore the country to its former imperial greatness, he promoted an agenda of Russian hegemony over neighbors. In August 2008, Putin provoked the former Soviet republic of Georgia, which was on track for admission into NATO, into a conflict that resulted in Russian control over one-fifth of its territory. The biggest prize in Putin's imperial land grab

MAP 31.3 US Security Commitments since 1945

was Crimea, part of Ukraine since 1954. When the pro-Russian Ukrainian president Viktor Yanukovych was overthrown in 2014, Putin used this opportunity to invade and seize Crimea. A separatist, pro-Russian rebellion in eastern Ukraine continued thereafter to tie down Ukraine's weak army.

Globalization and Poor Countries The mixed record of development in the middle-income countries was mirrored in the bottom tier of poor

countries, whose governments relied on the export of mineral or agricultural commodities to finance development. Some 50 poor states depended on three or fewer commodities for over half of their export earnings. As a result of overproduction on the world market, commodity prices were depressed through most of the 1990s. The price depression imposed severe budget cutbacks on many poor countries, with consequent unemployment and middle-class shrinkage.

Generally, however, the developing world benefited from the globalization of the 1990s. Poverty declined up until the recession of 2008, although this decline was unevenly distributed. The number of people in absolute poverty actually increased in sub-Saharan Africa, Southeast Asia (except Vietnam), Russia and Central Asia, and Latin America. Thus, while globalization benefited an absolute majority of humans, its uneven geographical distribution made the benefits look substantially smaller in many regions.

Two Communist Holdouts: China and Vietnam

Communism or socialism as an official ideology survived in North Korea, China, Vietnam, and Cuba. China and Vietnam opened their command economies to the market but maintained many large state firms and single-party control. In both cases, the parties remained communist in name but became in fact autocracies presiding over capitalist economies.

The Chinese Economic Boom After 1989, the new Chinese middle class, benefiting from the economic reforms of the Open Door and Four Modernizations, had to accommodate itself to a monopoly party that was communist in name but authoritarian in practice. Socially conservative migrants from the provinces to the cities found unskilled jobs in the early 1980s. They acquired skills and earned enough to send their children to school. From around 2005, the children, now with college degrees, took jobs as managers, technicians, professionals, and entrepreneurs in state companies, private firms, and Chinese branches of foreign firms. They began to flex their muscles as consumers.

To keep the middle class from demanding political participation outside the Communist Party, the government pursued accelerated annual GDP growth. Instead of spending its earnings, however, the middle class saved at rates double those in Japan or Europe prior to the recession of 2008–2011. The only partially subsidized new health care and education systems consumed many of those savings. In addition, urban real estate and rental apartments became increasingly unaffordable in many Chinese cities during the early 2000s.

Youth of the People's Republic. Despite attempts to regulate its rate, China's economic acceleration continued at a torrid pace. In 2010, its GDP surpassed that of Japan to become second only to that of the United States. The new prosperity created startling contrasts and a growing diversity of lifestyles in the People's Republic. In the image above, young Chinese hipsters sport T-shirts harkening back with deliberate irony to revolutionary leaders—China's Mao Zedong and Cuba's Che Guevara

Under the slogan of the "harmonious society"—in which all segments of the populace worked together, with no toleration for "disruptive elements"—the government and party staked their continued legitimacy to ongoing economic progress. For how long this progress can be maintained is unclear; the economic growth rate—about 6.7 percent in 2015–2016—was still strong in comparison to that of Europe and the United States, but the legitimacy of the Communist Party was increasingly called into question by a middle class opposed to corruption and less afraid of censorship. The economy was disrupted further by the trade war of increasing tariff barriers with the United States since 2018. China's estimated economic growth rate for 2019 was 6 percent, but could no longer be maintained in 2020, after the outbreak of the COVID-19 pandemic (expected to hit a mortality rate of 3.4 percent in the world population).

Vietnam Taking Off With double-digit growth rates in the 1990s, Vietnam outpaced other poor Asian neighbors, such as Cambodia and Bangladesh, by diversifying its manufacturing sector. Companies in Hong Kong, Taiwan, and Korea showed a strong preference for investment in Vietnam, because it had a high literacy rate and a low wage rate. A major new export sector from the later 1990s onward was aquaculture—the farming of shrimp, catfish, and tilapia. Vietnam moved in 2010 from the poor to the intermediate countries on the world list of nations.

Pluralist Democracy under Strain

In the first and early second decade of the 2000s, there was a palpable swing toward pessimism in the West. Two recessions, the demise of the Washington Consensus, and the problematic postwar settlements in Afghanistan and Iraq demonstrated the limits of US power. Syria fared even worse, with a continuing civil war that killed by one estimate 570,000 and forced 5.7 million to flee abroad by the end of 2019. Peace continued to elude the Palestinians, and Turkey lost its political and economic stability after the renewal of terrorism by Kurdish militants and a failed military coup. The only ray of hope in this region was the US–Iran agreement of 2016, according to which Iran would not build a nuclear bomb during the next 15 years. This agreement was, however, later abrogated by the United States as inadequate.

The future in the other parts of the world looked a bit less grim. China and India, with robust economic growth rates, expanded their educated and entrepreneurial middle classes. Africa and Latin America, except for Venezuela, benefiting from the demand for oil and minerals in China and India, experienced similarly strong growth. But by the second decade of the 2000s, all world regions were struggling to overcome the effects of the recession of 2008–2011.

Unease in the West Two recessions in the first decade of the 2000s in the United States sapped enthusiasm about the future of modernity. The first recession, of 2001–2003, was the so-called dot-com crisis, which had its origins in uncontrolled speculation about the expansion of the Internet. The second—much more severe—recession of 2008–2011 began with the collapse of the housing market, a result of the overly risky granting of real-estate mortgages to buyers with insufficient funds. The mortgage crisis snowballed into a general credit crisis, reducing consumer demand. Manufacturers became insolvent, and mass unemployment deepened the recession. The unemployment rate reached 9.6 percent in 2010, compared to half that rate in 2000–2008.

The crisis of 2001–2003 hit the African American and Hispanic working class particularly hard; in the following recession of 2008–2011, many white workers lost their jobs. By contrast, a majority of employees in the financial sector and the information technology industry, as well as the upper management of large corporations, survived the recession relatively unscathed. The American public became increasingly aware of the gap that separated the top one percent of income earners and asset owners from the middle and working classes, whose incomes stagnated.

In addition to the unease about economic inequalities, unhappiness about political and social issues grew, especially among white, working-class, older, and evangelical voters. The Tea Party movement of 2009, named for the Boston Tea Party of 1773 (see Chapter 22; some protesters later used TEA as an acronym for "Taxed Enough Already") introduced radically populist anti-establishment and anti-foreigner agendas into the political debate. This movement opted to work inside the Republican Party, pushing the party to the right and polarizing American politics.

At first, the presidential campaign of Barack Obama (in office 2009–2017), the first African American president, gave many Americans a boost of optimism to emerge from the recession. The president's deficit spending helped to steady the economy, and the nation finally drew even with the other industrialized countries by making health care insurance available to all citizens through the Affordable Care Act (ACA). But Tea Party activists and conservatives unleashed a storm of criticism over the ACA (passed without Republican votes and derided as "Obamacare"), unemployment, government spending, illegal immigration, and abortion and questioned the reality of climate change.

In midterm elections, the Republicans regained the House (2010) and Senate (2014). The Republican majority brought the country twice (2011 and 2013) to a standstill over the national debt ceiling and the ACA. Last-minute compromises patched differences over, but the relationship between President Obama (re-elected 2012) and the Democrats on one side and the Republican Party (more and more beholden to its hard-line populists) on the other became embittered.

Out of this stalemate came the unlikely election of the Republican real-estate developer and reality-television show host Donald Trump (b. 1946) as president in the 2016 election, over former First Lady and Secretary of State Hillary Clinton. Trump advocated building a wall along the US–Mexican border to curtail illegal immigration, abandoning a number of existing and proposed international trade agreements, and "bringing back" American manufacturing jobs. His brash persona and often coarse speech appealed to many voters who considered him "authentic" and who felt the "system" was rigged against them. Yet he also alienated many women, who considered him sexist, and the vast majority of people of color. He actively courted the National Rifle Association and various pro-life/anti-abortion groups and evangelicals, as well as the so-called "Alt-Right," whose supporters include white supremacists, anti-immigration activists, and anti-government militias. In one of the most hard-fought campaigns in American history, Ms. Clinton won the popular vote, but Mr. Trump won the electoral college and thereby the presidency. His election, closely following the United Kingdom's decision to exit from the European Union (called "Brexit") and strong nationalist, isolationist, anti-globalization movements in various European countries, appeared to signal a major retreat from post–Cold War internationalist political, economic, and diplomatic trends.

Europe saw a similar trend of rising income disparities, although this was mitigated by a stronger manufacturing sector (around 20 percent of GDP versus 11 percent in the United States in 2010) and a more generous social safety net. But the costs of this net seriously imperiled the future not only of Greece, Portugal,

Spain, and Ireland (all of which fell into near-bankruptcy during the recession of 2008–2011), but also of the European Union itself. Questions arose whether the euro, which had been launched with great fanfare in 1999, could be maintained as the common currency.

Since the unemployed were entitled to long-term support in most European countries, the angry populist debate was more muted during the early stages of the recession. But the rigorous policy of budget-cutting and public savings in the countries of the European Union, largely imposed by Germany, slowed the recovery to a crawl in 2011. After several years of political and economic immobility in the European Union (EU), elections in Hungary (2014) and Poland (2015) brought nationalist parties to power that voiced frustration with the bureaucratic policies of the EU, which remained largely unchanged.

A Bloody Civil War in Yugoslavia Like Russia and the other former Soviet republics, Eastern Europe and the Balkans went through an economic collapse and political restructuring during the 1990s. This collapse and restructuring was mostly peaceful except in Yugoslavia, where a civil war raged from 1990 to 1995. Until the 1980s, communism was the main ideology in Yugoslavia, through which the country's ethnic nationalisms of the Orthodox Christian Serbs, Catholic Croats, Muslim Bosnians, Catholic Slovenes, and mostly Muslim Kosovar Albanians were subsumed under a federal constitution granting these ethnic groups a degree of autonomy. The main enforcer of communist unity was President Josip Tito (1892–1980), a Croat. After Tito's death, however, the Serb president Slobodan Milošević [mee-LOH-sheh-vich] (1941–2006) exploited the demographic superiority of his ethnic community for the establishment of political dominance while retaining communism.

Yugoslavia had borrowed heavily from Western countries to keep its industries from collapsing during the oil price slump of 1985–1986. At the end of the 1980s, it was practically bankrupt. This disappointment exploded in 1990 into religious-nationalist hatred, led by the smaller ethnic groups against Serbs in their territories. The Serb supremacist-nationalist backlash, with an effort to "cleanse" minorities from "greater Serbian" territory, was no less explosive. It took more than a decade for the European Union and the United States to stop the Orthodox Serbs from murdering Muslim Bosnians and Albanians and to enforce a semblance of peace in the Balkans.

Since then, the five successor states of Yugoslavia have struggled to adapt to capitalism and democracy. Serb supremacist nationalism survived the longest and only gradually began to subside when the democratically elected pro-European government decided to arrest the main perpetrators of ethnic cleansing. With these arrests and much relief, the Serbian government began to steer a course between friendship with Putin's Russia and economic ties with the EU.

The Middle East: Paralysis, Liberation, and Islamism The momentum generated after the collapse of communism largely dissipated in the Middle East and North Africa during the early 2000s. With the exception of Turkey, a pall of economic and political paralysis hung over the region. The republics in the 1990s and early 2000s (e.g., Egypt, Syria, Algeria, Tunisia, and Yemen) inched toward privatization of state-run businesses but not at all toward democratization.

Monarchies (Saudi Arabia, Jordan, Oman, and the Gulf sheikhdoms) encouraged private investment but were extremely cautious, if not altogether hostile, toward democratic reforms. The "rejection front" of autocratic regimes in Iran and Syria, as well as the guerilla terrorist organizations Hezbollah in southern Lebanon and Hamas in the Gaza Strip, rejected the Washington Consensus and globalization out of hand. Syria did, however, cautiously open its state-controlled economy to privatization in the early 2000s.

Islamism: Religious-nationalist ideology in which the reformed Sunni or Shiite Islam of the twentieth century is used to define all institutions of the state and society.

Fear of **Islamism** accounted for the immobility of "republican autocrats" as well as monarchs. While Islam was less visible in the region in the twentieth century when the political elites consisted of secular liberals and nationalists, it had not receded at all from the villages and poor city quarters, where it remained as vital as ever.

The rise of Islamism was rooted in the acceleration of rural–urban migration in the Middle East in the late 1990s and early 2000s. When Middle Eastern and North African governments built the first large state-run manufacturing plants in their cities in the 1960s, the workers were largely peasants who encountered militant preachers for the first time in the cities. These preachers represented a reformed, standardized, urban Sunni Islam. The children of these workers learned a standardized Islam in the schools, intended to buttress Arab nationalism, in which the Prophet Muhammad was the first nationalist. Standard Islam and militant urban Islamism gradually produced offshoots of Islamist terrorism, such as al-Qaeda, the Taliban, and the Salafists.

In the 1990s and early 2000s, Middle Eastern governments essentially barricaded themselves behind their secret services and armies against the onslaughts of these Islamists. Under the threat of Islamist terrorism, Middle Eastern and North African governments found it impossible to pursue bold new initiatives of the kind that China or India advanced.

The Growth of Hezbollah One area where Islamists achieved a breakthrough was in Lebanon. Hezbollah ("Party of God"), an Islamist guerilla organization recruiting from among the Shiite majority of Lebanese Muslims, waged an underground war against Israel. It succeeded in driving Israel from southern Lebanon in 2000, after an 18-year occupation that had begun with Israel expelling the Palestine Liberation Organization (PLO) from the country (see Chapter 30). By the second decade of the 2000s, Hezbollah had evolved into the most formidable enemy of Israel.

In 2013, Hezbollah even grew into the role of a regional, quasi-state actor. Not only did it come to dominate the Lebanese administration after the end of the civil war in 1989, it became a decisive force strengthening Syrian President Bashar al-Assad (b. 1965) in his civil war against his Arab Spring challengers. Increasingly, Sunni terrorist groups were elbowing the challengers aside, seeking to turn the Syrian civil war into a sectarian conflict. Hezbollah and its patron, Iran, were determined to assert the role of Shiism in the contemporary Middle East.

Israel and Gaza In 1994 Israel was officially at peace with two Arab neighbors, Egypt and Jordan. But it continued to face a hostile Arab Middle East in general and restless Palestinians in the occupied territories in the West Bank and Gaza in particular. To protect its citizens from guerilla attacks, the Israeli government built a border fence in 2002–2013 inside the entire length of the occupied West Bank. In a parallel move, it withdrew from the fenced-in Gaza Strip in 2005. Suicide attacks were fewer, but cross-border rocket attacks from Gaza increased.

After 2006, Israel slid into an even worse trap. In the first-ever Palestinian elections, the victory in Gaza went to the Islamic guerilla organization Hamas, founded in 1988, over the older, secular, ethnic-nationalist PLO. The PLO refused to recognize the elections, and a civil war broke out in which Hamas was victorious, forcing the PLO to retreat to the West Bank. Israel imposed a complete embargo on Hamas-ruled Gaza in an attempt to bring the organization down.

For those in Israel who wished to renew the peace process, the PLO–Hamas split was a disaster, since it threw the entire idea of a two-state solution into doubt. Hamas deepened this doubt in the following years by launching rockets against Israel. In retaliation, Israel invaded Gaza in December–January 2008–2009, causing unmitigated misery for the Palestinian population of Gaza, but was not able to defeat Hamas. Efforts at healing the split between PLO and Hamas produced no results. Likewise, the hostility between Israel and Hamas continued unabated.

Israel's Predicament and Iranian Ambitions The failure of the Lebanon invasion in 2009 brought a conservative government into power in Israel. The government renewed Israeli settlement construction in the West Bank while tightening the embargo on Gaza. But neither building more Jewish settlements in the West Bank nor punishing Israel's neighbors Hezbollah and Hamas with invasions and embargoes brought the country closer to peace. The formation of a PLO–Hamas unity government of technocrats in 2014 was greeted by Israel with further settlement plans. Israel's long dominance over its neighbors appeared to have reached its limits.

Hezbollah and Hamas used Iranian-supplied rockets against Israel. Iran, a leader of the rejectionist front against Israel, had experienced a "pragmatic" period of reform after the death of its spiritual guide, Ruhollah Khomeini, in 1989. But the reformers were timid, and the still-powerful clerics systematically undermined attempts at democratic and cultural reforms.

Any remaining hopes for reform were dashed when Mahmoud Ahmadinejad (b. 1956) was elected president. He renewed the anti-Western crusade and adopted a policy of populism. Under his leadership, the Revolutionary Guard became not only the most effective military organization but also a huge patronage machine.

The precipitous decline of revenues from oil exports during the recession of 2008–2011, however, seriously reduced Ahmadinejad's populist appeal. Hence, he needed the Revolutionary Guard commanders to falsify the elections of 2009 to stay in power. Suspected Iranian ambitions for acquiring a nuclear bomb, coupled with North Korea's already existing nuclear arsenal, created global concerns about the possibility of nuclear war by "rogue" nations. Put under a severe economic sanctions regime by the United Nations, Iran elected a less populist and more pragmatic president, Hasan Rouhani (b. 1948), in 2013 (reelected 2017), with a mandate to improve the stagnating economy. After two years of negotiations with the United States, the UN Security Council nations, and Germany, Iran agreed in 2015 to sign a nuclear deal in which it gave up on building nuclear bombs for 15 years in return for an end to the sanctions. As noted above, however, the Trump administration repudiated the nuclear agreement and imposed crippling sanctions on Iran which, as of 2020, were still in place.

The Ascent of Turkey Turkey largely escaped Islamist militancy to become one of the most dynamic newly industrialized countries in the world. In contrast to other regimes in the Middle East, Turkish Muslims enjoyed a well-established and functioning multiparty system. A right-of-center party with a strong contingent of Islamists in 1983 not only captured the premiership of the country but simultaneously implemented new initiatives of economic privatization and industrial export orientation. Benefiting from these initiatives, a middle class of socially conservative but economically liberal businesspeople arose.

In a second wave of Islamist middle-class expansion after 2003, under Prime Minister Recep Tayyip Erdoğan [RE-jep TAY-ip ER-doh-ahn] (b. 1954), Turkey's GDP grew to become the world's fifteenth largest. Elections in June 2011 enabled Erdoğan's party, the AKP, to garner slightly more than half of the vote. On the basis of this vote, it enacted constitutional reforms that rescinded the military's power in politics. The party's electoral strength, however, led Erdoğan to believe that he could on occasion ignore the democratic process, as in 2013 when he took unilateral action to suppress popular demonstrations in Istanbul and in 2014 when he ignored a court injunction to stop constructing his massive new government palace.

After the election of 2014, Erdoğan changed the president's ceremonial office into an executive one, similar to that of Iran, with a vision to transform Turkey from a secular into an Islamic republic. Although two parliamentary elections in 2015 denied his party the supermajority necessary for this constitutional change, he made himself into an executive president anyway. In both elections, for the first time in the Republic's history, a Kurdish party won seats in parliament. But the arrival of this party in parliament meant not only that it stood in the way for the AKP's efforts at changing the constitution but also resulted in the end of a truce with the Kurdish guerilla organization PKK. The renewed Kurdish guerilla war in southeastern Turkey weighed heavily on Turkish resources, as did 2.7 million refugees from the civil war in Syria.

The mounting problems for Turkey climaxed with a military coup attempt in July 2016. Erdoğan, however, was able to evade arrest and call for the citizenry to stage mass rallies the next day. In the face of these rallies, the coup collapsed, and in waves of unprecedented retaliatory purges, the government dismissed 200,000 military officials, police officers, judges, governors, civil servants, university administrators, and professors (2 percent of state employees) from their positions. It declared the Gülen religious and educational movement to be responsible for the coup attempt and demanded the extradition of its founder, Fethullah Gülen (b. 1941), from his self-imposed exile in the United States. As the dust began to settle at the end of 2016, President Erdoğan was the undisputed autocrat in a by now constitutionally hollowed-out republic.

The Arab Spring of 2011 Prior to the failed coup of July 2016, Turkey was the most frequently cited model for the compatibility of Islam and democracy in the Middle East. In spring 2011, however, Tunisia and Egypt each underwent

Turkish Citizen with His Daughter. A Turkish father and daughter during mass demonstrations in support of President Recep Erdoğan after the failed military coup of July 15, 2016. A referendum in April 2017 gave the presidency sweeping new executive powers, allowing Erdoğan to consolidate his position.

constitutional revolutions which demonstrated that democracy could sprout in Arab countries as well. On December 17, 2010, 26-year-old Mohamed Bouazizi set himself ablaze in an act of despair brought about by the humiliations he had suffered at the hands of a Tunisian policewoman and thereby unleashed massive demands for democracy across the Middle East.

Bouazizi's death touched off the mostly peaceful democratic revolutions dubbed the "Arab Spring." Beginning in Tunisia, they spread into Egypt, Libya, Bahrain, Yemen, and Syria in the course of early 2011. In Tunisia and Egypt, they ousted longtime and aging autocrats. After months of fighting, Libya's Muammar el-Qaddafi (r. 1969–2011) was toppled in September 2011 and killed a month later. Autocratic rulers in other Arab countries held on with unrestrained brutality. The demonstrators—for the most part young, urban, and Internet-savvy—documented the events online and revealed police violence for the world to see. As these revolutions developed, however, they raised the question of how closely the young demonstrators were integrated into the rest of the population, which included urban and rural traditional Muslims as well as Islamists.

Unfortunately, the Arab Spring activists could not translate their newfound power into electoral victories among the masses. In both Tunisia and Egypt, elections brought Islamist parties to power. These parties sought to Islamize Tunisia and Egypt, even though they had not participated much in the Arab Spring demonstrations. Renewed demonstrations in 2013, this time against the Islamization measures, became unmanageable, and in Egypt the military stepped in. In a coup d'état, the military ended both the tenure of President Muhammad Morsi (r. 2012–2013) and the Arab Spring. The outcome was an

Democracy's Martyr. This monument in Sidi Bouzid, Tunisia, was erected in December 2011 in honor of Mohamed Bouazizi, a street vendor selling fruits and vegetables. After months of harassment by the police, he set himself afire in despair on December 17, 2010. His example galvanized young, educated, and social network–savvy Tunisians into their peaceful "Arab Spring" revolution during December 2010–January 2011, which culminated with the resignation of the Tunisian president.

autocratic regime under President Abdel Fattah Sisi (b. 1954). In Tunisia, the political process also broke down in 2013, but the opponents were able to resolve the breakdown through negotiations and eventually established a coalition government in 2020.

In Syria, the hopes for an Arab Spring were dashed almost immediately. The first pro-democracy protests began in March 2011, but the president, Bashar al-Assad, brutally suppressed them. By early June, the protests turned into an armed rebellion. Assad was the heir of the secular Arab-socialist regime of the Baath Party, in which members of the Shiite sect of the Alawites held the key army and secret service positions. Baath bureaucrats pursued a policy of state capitalism as late as 1991, when first concessions to economic liberalization were finally granted.

Although a large majority of Sunni Arabs, Sunni Kurds, and Christian Arabs benefited from the Baath's policies, income disparities grew during the period of economic liberalization in the 1990s and early 2000s. Although Syria was led by a young president, it did not differ much from the old-men regimes of Tunisia and Egypt in early 2011.

During the summer of 2011, the Arab Spring uprising became a civil war. The rebels were joined in 2012 by Sunni jihadists with battle experience from Afghanistan, Iraq, Yemen, and the Russian Caucasus. At the same time, Assad released Islamists from his own prisons to the rebels in order to discourage the United States and Europe from arming the secular wing of the opposition, for fear of their weapons falling into the hands of the jihadists. The brutality with which Assad battled his opponents caused a mass exodus of refugees to neighboring countries. Until the end of 2013 Assad was on the defensive, but thanks to unwavering support from Russia and Iran, as well as soldiers from Iran and the Lebanese Hezbollah, he regained the initiative and reestablished his hold over the main west-Syrian population centers.

In the northeast, Assad discreetly gave some of the most radical jihadists free rein. The organization "Islamic State in Iraq and al-Sham" [historical Syria], or ISIS, took advantage of the opportunity. Aiming for the reconstruction of the seventh-century caliphate allegedly based on the pristine Islam of the Quran and Sunna (including the apocalyptic end-time vision of conquering Constantinople, Rome, and Washington, DC), ISIS developed forms of brutality that alienated it from the other anti-Assad jihadist groups in northern Syria. Led by the former Iraqi al-Qaeda operative Abu Bakr al-Baghdadi (1971–2019), ISIS built a state in northeastern Syria.

In early 2014, ISIS units crossed into Iraq. The troops of the Iraqi government fled with hardly a shot fired. The result of this unexpected turn of events was not only the de facto division of Iraq into a triad of Kurdish, Sunni, and Shiite polities but also the evaporation of the minimal achievements of the US war in Iraq during 2003–2011. An intensive US air campaign during 2015–2016, with support from Kurdish fighters on the ground, weakened ISIS and reduced its territory by nearly half, but suspected donors in the Persian Gulf and Saudi Arabia were still keeping it functional. By the fall of 2019, however, ISIS territory, which had been reduced to a small area in Syria, was retaken. Baghdadi himself was killed that October in a raid by US Special Operations forces.

The New Middle Class in India During the 1990s and early 2000s, India saw the rise of a religiously conservative Hindu middle class of shopkeepers, traders, merchants, and small manufacturers. The secular Congress Party enjoyed the trust of the new middle class. But an economic slowdown in 2013 and the perception of bureaucratic immobility and corruption returned the religiously oriented Bharatiya Janata Party to power in the 2014 elections.

The rapid expansion of Indian urban centers contributed to the decline of the traditional caste divisions in Hinduism. Since a person's ancestry could be hidden in the cities, even the untouchable (*dalit*) caste began to enter the new middle class. Widespread protests in 2006 and again in 2016, however, indicated continuing tensions among the castes. Other areas of tension arose in 2019 when the ruling party, devoted to Hindu nationalism, revoked Kashmir's special status and issued a controversial citizen law that discriminated against Muslims. Later in the year, the parliament passed the Citizen Amendment Bill, which allowed members of religious groups, except Muslims, fleeing Pakistan, Bangladesh, and Afghanistan for India prior to 1954 to apply for citizenship. The bill met with widespread and violent protests and illustrates how far Prime Minister Narendra Modi (in office since 2014) is willing to play the Hindu populist card.

The success of the middle class in India must be measured against conditions in the countryside, much of which is still largely outside the market economy. In the 1990s, an overwhelming majority of villagers continued to live in extreme poverty (less than $1.25 per day), existing completely outside the market circuit and depending on handouts. This majority declined in the first decade of

Driving Toward Prosperity. The Bajaj scooter was the early status symbol of the emerging Indian middle class. On account of their size, the Indian and Chinese middle classes, numbering in the hundreds of millions, are powerful groups, representing a huge reservoir of ever-more-demanding consumers. This picture is from 2010, when the Indian middle class had come of age.

the 2000s, perhaps by one-quarter, helped by a sinking birthrate. A major factor in the persistence of poverty was an incomplete land reform. Landlordism and tenancy continued to encompass nearly half of the rural population. As a major voting bloc in the Congress Party, the landlords were successful in resisting further land reform.

African Transformations The half-decade between the oil price slump and the debt crisis (1985) and the disappearance of Communism (1991) was challenging for sub-Saharan Africa. The continent's GDP in the early 1990s was down by almost half from what it had been in 1975, when all main social and economic indicators had been at their peak. Many countries now expended more hard currency on their debt services than on education. With a doubling of the population at the absolute poverty level, sub-Saharan Africa became by far the poorest region in the world.

During this time, the urban population of sub-Saharan Africa increased to almost one-third of the total population. The urbanization process was an important factor for the political consequences of the crisis: students, civil servants, and journalists demanded political reforms. Up until the early 1990s, almost everywhere state structures were patronage hierarchies; the civilian or military rulers provided cushy government jobs for the ethnic groups from which they hailed. Urban dwellers, however, were less tied to ethnicity and more committed to constitutionalism. They felt little sympathy for autocratic rulers and their kin who were running the states into financial ruin and pushed for democratic reforms in the late 1990s and early 2000s.

This push for reforms had mixed results. Autocratic incumbents still won elections more often than not, and honest elections were rare. Yet some regime changes were truly thrilling, notably the end of apartheid and the election of Nelson Mandela (1918–2013, president 1994–1999) in the Republic of South Africa; four cycles (2004–2016) of clean multiparty elections in Ghana; the first election of a female African president, the Harvard-trained economist Ellen Johnson Sirleaf (b. 1938, elected 2006 and reelected 2011) in Liberia; the relatively clean Nigerian presidential elections of 2007, 2011, and 2015, and the much delayed but eventually peaceful election in the Democratic Republic of Congo in 2018.

As in the Middle East, Islamism became a major factor in a number of countries with Muslim populations, such as Nigeria. In Northern Nigeria, the government proved to be completely incompetent against the Islamist movement Boko Haram ("Western education is sin"). Founded in 2002, this jihadist organization intent on introducing Sharia law staged daring raids, culminating in 2014 with the abduction of over 276 Christian schoolgirls (82 released in May 2017, in exchange for five Boko Haram leaders). In Somalia, the jihadist movement Shabab [sha-BAB, "Youth"] became increasingly powerful (beginning 2009) in the country's ongoing civil war and in several West African countries jihadists began campaigns of terror in 2016. African as well

Freedom, Justice, and Dignity. The end of apartheid in 1994 and the election of Nelson Mandela (1918–2013), seen here visiting his former prison cell, were inspiring events in Africa and the rest of the world. South Africa is the richest and most industrialized country of Africa, with large mineral and agricultural resources. Nearly 80 percent of the population are black, speaking their own languages, including isiZulu and isiXhosa. But Afrikaans (a Dutch-originated language) remained the dominant media language, with English being only the fifth most spoken language. In spite of South Africa's relative wealth, years of apartheid have resulted in vast income disparities.

Patterns Up Close

Social Networking

The movements of the Arab Spring were organized and carried out by means of social networking sites (SNSs) like Twitter, Facebook, and YouTube, supported by cell phones and other modern communication technologies. But what are the origins of these devices, and how have they developed into such important tools of political and social revolution?

SNSs can be traced back to the origins of the Internet and the World Wide Web. The Internet is a product of the Cold War. In 1969 the US government initiated the Advanced Research Projects Agency (ARPA), which created a system linking computers at major universities into a network (ARPANET) that allowed them to share information. This fledgling Internet expanded during the 1990s into a global computer network. The World Wide Web was conceived in 1989 and launched two years later as a part of the Internet.

SNSs sprang up in the 1990s when it was recognized that the Internet allowed social groups to communicate with each other and to share information. By the 2000s, social networking sites revolutionized the nature of communication.

as foreign observers noted the rise in sectarian conflicts on the continent with growing concern.

The African economy picked up in the early 2000s, mostly because of rising commodity prices. The main oil exporters benefited from higher oil prices, as did the mining countries. Agricultural products also regained significance in the early 2000s. The global recessions of 2001 and 2008 did not have a major impact, largely because of the arrival of China on the scene as a major buyer and investor. Optimism about a sustained recovery and modernity within reach was clearly visible on the continent, even if tempered by continuing ethnic and Islamist conflicts.

Latin American Expansion Elections after the financial meltdowns of the 1990s produced more fiscally restrained, socially engaged governments in the large Latin American countries during the early 2000s. Democratic transitions in Mexico, Brazil, Argentina, and Chile demonstrated that the unhappy years of military dictatorships in the 1980s had been left behind. In Mexico the long rule of the Institutional Revolutionary Party (PRI) was interrupted from

An early example of the power of SNSs to effect change was the so-called Twitter Revolution in Iran in 2009, during which anti-government activists used SNSs in an ultimately futile effort to overthrow the Iranian regime. Following the success of the Tunisian revolution, however, an even more spectacular display of the power of SNSs erupted in Egypt on January 25, 2011, when thousands of protesters took to the streets to demand the ouster of the authoritarian president Hosni Mubarak. This "Facebook Revolution" was launched by the April 6 Youth Movement, a Facebook group composed of social and political activists.

For all their success in facilitating uprisings against authoritarian governments, however, SNSs are used with equal effectiveness by terrorist groups. Al-Qaeda and the Taliban take advantage of Facebook and Twitter to broadcast their calls for global jihad. Moreover, SNSs serve as effective recruitment tools. It is ironic that Internet websites originally intended for exchanges among friends have been transformed into tools to spread revolution, violence, and terrorism.

Questions

- How do SNSs show that an innovation can be adapted for purposes wholly different from the original purposes for which they were intended?
- Do you believe SNSs have allowed young people around the world to make their wishes and aspirations more powerfully felt? If so, what does this say about the connection between technology and youth?

2000 to 2012, with an orderly transition to less socially engaged Christian Democratic presidents. Only in 2012 did a markedly rejuvenated PRI return to power. It continued the pattern of economic liberalization begun at the beginning of the century.

In Colombia, a Marxist guerilla war of more than half a century came to an end with a truce in 2016, followed—after some complications—by an uneasy peace. In neighboring Venezuela, President Hugo Chávez (in office 2002–2013), a former officer from a working-class background, used the country's vast oil revenues to construct an ambitious state-socialist system. After his death, however, when the world oil price slump of 2014–2016 deprived the government of revenue, state socialism fell apart, with the population being unable to buy even the most basic staples. Nevertheless, with Russian help, authoritarianism continued to survive in Venezuela.

Industrialization, largely through foreign investments but increasingly also through internal financing, stimulated state-run firms to become competitive and even to privatize in several large Latin American countries. In some cases, Latin American countries have become world competitors. All four large economies—Brazil, Mexico, Argentina, and Chile—exported more manufactured goods than commodities by 2008. These countries clearly displayed the features of scientific–industrial modernity by the second decade of the 2000s, even though corruption (in Brazil and Mexico) and foreign debt woes (in Argentina), as well as a highly unequal income distribution still weigh heavily on economic and social development.

The Environmental Limits of Modernity

Systems of capitalism, consumerism, and democracy embodied by the United States, Canada, Western Europe, and Australia have increasingly become the ones to emulate. All new nations in the world are either industrializing or seeking to do so. The principal obstacle for these nations is the debilitating poverty of the great majority of their inhabitants, who are still mired in either subsistence farming or marginal work in the cities. The poorest are unskilled and uneducated and still view large families as a necessity. Improved public health care is helping to lengthen life spans for the poorest people, but the combination of modern medicine and the desire for large families has caused a startling increase in the world population.

Sustainability and Global Warming In 1800, there was only one country (Great Britain) embarking on industrialization; today, about two-thirds of the 193 independent countries of the world are either industrialized or on the way toward full industrialization. We are beginning to grasp the environmental consequences of this move to scientific–industrial modernity. Between the start of the industrial revolution and the last quarter of the twentieth century, the carbon footprint of these countries had risen from 280 parts per million (ppm) of atmospheric carbon dioxide and other chemical compounds—commonly called "greenhouse gases"—to 330 ppm. Between 1975 and 2010 the concentration of greenhouse gases in the atmosphere climbed to 380 ppm, and in September 2016 it reached the record of 400 ppm for an entire month. According to climate scientists, this milestone means that the atmosphere can never be restored to the "safe" level of ca. 350 ppm.

While there has been considerable debate on the nature and degree of global warming—whether it is a natural cyclical phenomenon or human-produced, or even if it exists at all—there is a general scientific consensus that greenhouse gases are the main contributors to temperature increases on earth. Scientists generally assume that at current rates of greenhouse gas production, the earth will reach a "tipping point" of 450 ppm, with irreversible consequences for the planet's climate, before the middle of this century.

What will happen when this tipping point is reached? If projections hold true, the polar ice caps and high mountain glaciers will melt completely. Ocean levels, rising from the melted ice, will submerge islands and make inroads on the coasts of all continents. Widespread droughts and violent storms will erode by wind and flood what had been fertile land. Forests, already reduced from timber harvesting and agricultural expansion, may well be wiped out, removing

A Smoggy Future. China, the world's worst emitter of greenhouse gases, has large numbers of coal-fed power plants and factories that continue to belch out carbon dioxide as well as toxic substances into the air, with little scrubbing or other devices to clean the emissions before they reach the atmosphere. Here, a power plant on the outskirts of Linfen in Shanxi Province southwest of Beijing fouls the environment in 2009. China's latest Five-Year Plan (2016) calls for stringent efforts to cut back air pollution by 2021, though whether these goals are feasible is the subject of considerable debate.

the most important agents for cleaning the atmosphere of greenhouse gases. Pollution and overfishing will leave little of the world's marine life. Biodiversity will be dramatically reduced. The consequence of these grim developments will likely be a severe reduction of the earth's arable land and fisheries needed for the production of food.

The ultimate outcome of this prospective climate transformation will be much worse for the new countries than for the older ones that industrialized early and have the resources to adjust. The irony of such projections, therefore, is that the nations that viewed their adaptation to modernity as their salvation may well find themselves among the first to be doomed.

Scientific and Political Debate There is an overwhelming consensus among scientists that the warming trend in the world from greenhouse gases is real. Very few scientists still hold a skeptical view. Vocal minorities still vociferously denounce climate warming as a hoax or conspiracy. So far, political responses have been tepid and largely divided.

By 2013, nine UN conferences had been convened since the 1997 Kyoto Protocol that established benchmarks for the reduction of greenhouse gases in the European Union and 38 industrialized countries. But only the European Union was on track to meet its provision, mandating an annual reduction of 5.2 percent. The remaining countries were substantially off the mark. The 2013 Warsaw conference saw bitter conflicts over the inclusion of newly

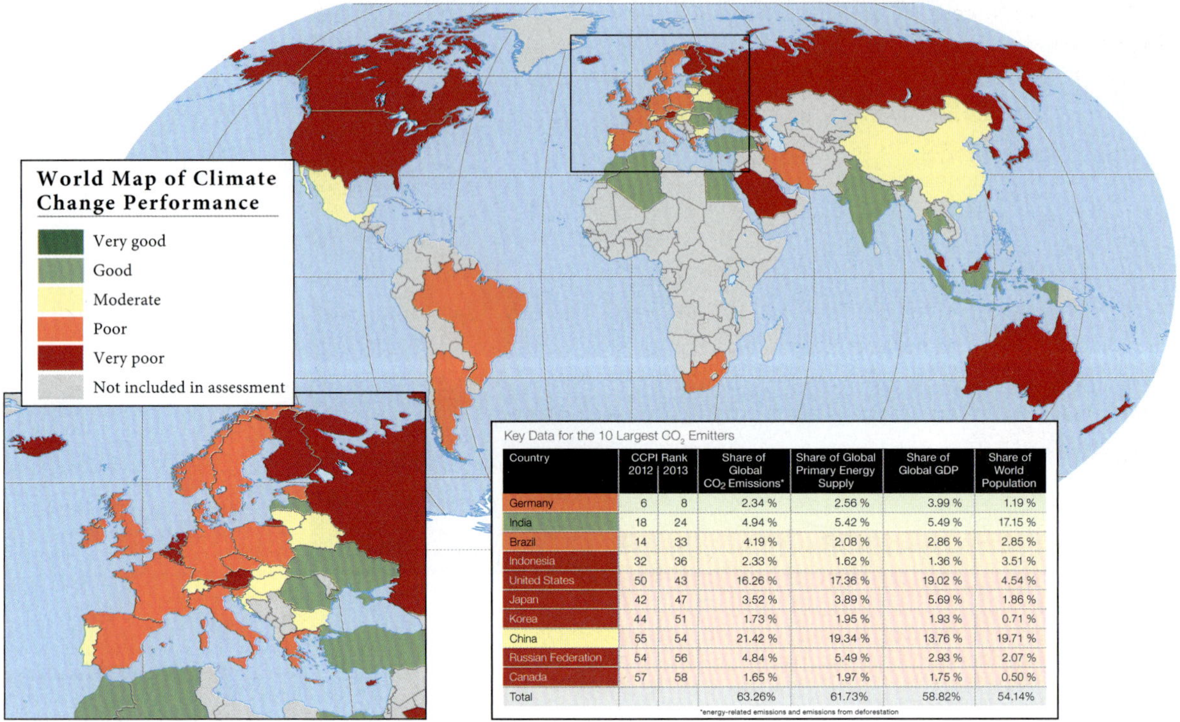

Key Data for the 10 Largest CO_2 Emitters

Country	CCPI Rank 2012	CCPI Rank 2013	Share of Global CO_2 Emissions*	Share of Global Primary Energy Supply	Share of Global GDP	Share of World Population
Germany	6	8	2.34 %	2.56 %	3.99 %	1.19 %
India	18	24	4.94 %	5.42 %	5.49 %	17.15 %
Brazil	14	33	4.19 %	2.08 %	2.86 %	2.85 %
Indonesia	32	36	2.33 %	1.62 %	1.36 %	3.51 %
United States	50	43	16.26 %	17.36 %	19.02 %	4.54 %
Japan	42	47	3.52 %	3.89 %	5.69 %	1.86 %
Korea	44	51	1.73 %	1.95 %	1.93 %	0.71 %
China	55	54	21.42 %	19.34 %	13.76 %	19.71 %
Russian Federation	54	56	4.84 %	5.49 %	2.93 %	2.07 %
Canada	57	58	1.65 %	1.97 %	1.75 %	0.50 %
Total			63.26%	61.73%	58.82%	54.14%

*energy-related emissions and emissions from deforestation

MAP 31.4 World Map of Climate Change Performance

industrialized countries into the Kyoto Protocol and financial compensation demanded by developing countries for damages suffered from extreme weather. In the Paris conference of 2015, new targets for curbs were proclaimed, but the follow-up conference in Madrid 2019 was unable to translate them into practical measures.

At present, the consensus is that if the European 5.2 percent reduction rate were to continue after 2013 and everyone were to sign on to this rate, the temperature by the middle of the twenty-first century would be 0.2 degrees Fahrenheit below the current average temperature. But President Trump's decision in 2017 to withdraw from the Paris Agreement might instead lead to an increase of 3–4 degrees Fahrenheit, enough to make climate change irreversible—unless collective efforts can still be maintained. The 2019 transatlantic voyage of sixteen-year-old Greta Thunberg, and her public addresses—including one to the United Nations—have once again underscored this mounting crisis.

Putting It All Together

The first decade of the twenty-first century witnessed the final transformation of the world from the agrarian–urban pattern of life to a new scientific–industrial pattern. Everywhere in the world, people have been adapting to a new role as individuals with well-defined human rights, who aspire to be educated, find fulfilling jobs, become consumers, and achieve a materially secure life—in short, they are becoming modern.

The twentieth century also saw the original pattern of modernity split into three. The first modernity sought to create competitive, capitalist, democratic societies; the second modernity sought equality in socialist–communist societies; and in the third modernity, supremacist-nationalist societies sought to impose the will of allegedly superior races or ethnic groups through conquest (if not complete elimination) of "inferior" ones. Tremendous destruction accompanied the struggle among the proponents of these visions of modernity, and capitalist democracy was the form that ultimately survived.

With regard to the future of the environment, the devil's bargain of materialism that accompanied the evolution of modernity continues to haunt us: on one hand, it gave us the expectation of a decent existence in material security; on the other hand, the means of achieving that security through exploitation of the earth's material resources has given us the nightmare prospect of an irreversibly damaged planet.

Review and Relate

Thinking Through Patterns

Examine the ways historians approach the big questions of this chapter.

> How did the United States demonstrate its dominant economic position toward the end of the twentieth century? How did it accelerate the pattern of globalization?

The United States demonstrated its dominant economic position through the dollar regime and by becoming a sinkhole for industrial exports from developing countries. In compensation for the latter, it expanded the reach of its financial system worldwide. The result was the globalization of the world economy.

> What made capitalist democracy so attractive toward the end of the twentieth century that it became a generic model for many countries around the world to strive for?

Capitalist democracy became the universal model of modernity in part because growing middle classes in cities demanded liberalized markets where they could develop personal initiative and accumulate capital. Socially conservative new middle classes empowered successful industrialization processes throughout Asia, Latin America, and Africa.

> Which policies did China and India pursue so that they became the fastest-industrializing countries in the early twenty-first century?

China and India accelerated their industrialization by encouraging the expansion of their middle classes as the engines of investment and innovation. China, however, did not allow the development of a multiparty system, fearing the chaos of popular agitation. India, by contrast, possessed constitutional traditions that included constraints against populism and allowed for peaceful democratic competition. The communications revolution has reshaped the way humans interact with each other. Because of this connectedness, politics, culture, and economic activity now mutate more rapidly—and with more volatility—than ever before.

➤ How have information technology and social networking altered cultural, political, and economic interactions around the world? What is climate change, and why is it a source of grave concern for the future?

Climate change—sometimes referred to as "global warming" is caused by carbon dioxide and other gases that accumulate in the upper atmosphere and trap the sun's heat in the lower atmosphere. Warming and cooling trends have occurred periodically since the end of the last ice age, and for a long time scientists labored to distinguish clearly between a temporary trend toward warmer temperatures and a permanent, greenhouse gas–caused trend that will permanently alter nature. Today, there is an overwhelming scientific consensus concerning the reality of global warming. But politicians and the general public are not yet entirely convinced that the efforts reached with the Paris Agreement of 2015 should be translated into serious action.

Against the Grain

Consider this as a counterpoint to the main patterns examined in this chapter.

North Korea: Lone Holdout against the World

- Which factors explain the spectacular agricultural collapse in North Korea during the 1990s?
- Why is North Korea so steadfastly devoted to its military program? Why is this military program so worrisome for the world?

In the second decade of the 2000s, North Korea was among the few countries that remained committed to socialism. Although it formally abandoned the ideologies of Marxism-Leninism and communism in its constitutions of 1972 and 2009, respectively, as unfulfillable, it retained its commitment to socialism, self-sufficiency, isolation, and militarism.

The disappearance of Soviet bloc aid in 1991, in combination with harvest failures during the 1990s, led to mass starvation on a scale similar to famines earlier in the century in the Soviet Union and China. Chinese, South Korean, and international food aid brought only minimal relief. The constitutional principle of food self-sufficiency was a cruel joke.

In 2002 the regime enacted the first small steps of economic reform, recognizing the existence of an informal sector of private garden plots, mechanical workshops, and neighborhood markets. An economic free zone with South Korean factories was established near the border, and some foreign investment was allowed. Collective farmers were entitled to their own produce, in return for a steep 15 percent "rent" on their state-owned lands. After Kim Jong-un's succession to his father's position of supreme leader in 2013, reforms accelerated, and North Korean businesses began to export cheap consumer products.

But sanctions imposed by the UN after the country's nuclear tests in 2006 significantly slowed its small arms and missile exports to developing countries, which had provided revenue for keeping the regime and its outsized military program in power. Yet it continued doggedly with its nuclear and missile testing programs, evidently still pursuing the elusive dream of a limited nuclear war in Korea leading to its reunification with South Korea. With the country ranking lowest in the democracy index, and number 29 in military expenditures among the 196 nations in the world, North Korea is the most extreme example of a nation going against the grain of the twenty-first century.

Key Terms

Dollar regime 767
Globalization 769
Information technology 768
Islamism 778
Postmodernism and Postcolonialism 766

Learn more with this chapter's digital tools, including the Oxford Insight Study Guide, at http://www.oup.com/he/vonsivers4e. Please see the Further Resources section at the back of the book for additional readings and suggested websites.

PATTERNS OF EVIDENCE |

Sources for Chapter 31

SOURCE 31.1

Osama bin Laden, "Declaration of War against the Americans Occupying the Land of the Two Holy Places"

August 23, 1996

In 1992, al-Qaeda ("the base") under the leadership of Osama bin Laden (1957–2011) emerged as a significant terrorist organization operating on an international scale. Bin Laden, the multimillionaire son of a Yemeni-born Saudi Arabian contractor, had fought the Soviet occupation of Afghanistan (1979–1989). He now turned his attention to the United States (which had covertly funded the "mujahid" Afghan resistance in the interest of its own Cold War ambitions). In bin Laden's eyes, America was a godless country without moral principles, bent on a Western crusade to destroy Muslim independence. The al-Qaeda campaign of terrorism climaxed on September 11, 2001, but bin Laden had already ordered bombings and terrorist attacks in several parts of the world in the 1990s. This fatwa (an opinion or ruling based on Islamic law) was issued by bin Laden against the "Zionist-Crusader alliance" in 1996.

It should not be hidden from you that the people of Islam had suffered from aggression, iniquity and injustice imposed on them by the Zionist-Crusaders alliance and their collaborators; to the extent that the Muslims' blood became the cheapest and their wealth as loot in the hands of the enemies. Their blood was spilled in Palestine and Iraq. The horrifying pictures of the massacre of Qana, in Lebanon are still fresh in our memory. Massacres in Tajikistan, Burma, Kashmir, Assam, the Philippines, Fatani, Ogaden, Somalia, Eritrea, Chechnya and in Bosnia-Herzegovina took place, massacres that send shivers in the body and shake the conscience. All of this and the world watch and hear, and not only didn't respond to these atrocities, but also with a clear conspiracy between the USA and its allies and under the cover of the iniquitous United Nations, the dispossessed people were even prevented from obtaining arms to defend themselves.

Source: https://ctc.usma.edu/wp-content/uploads/2013/10/Declaration-of-Jihad-against-the-Americans-Occupying-the-Land-of-the-Two-Holiest-Sites-Translation.pdf

The people of Islam awakened and realised that they are the main target for the aggression of the Zionist-Crusaders alliance. All false claims and propaganda about "Human Rights" were hammered down and exposed by the massacres that took place against the Muslims in every part of the world.

. . .

Utmost effort should be made to prepare and instigate the Ummah against the enemy, the American-Israeli alliance—occupying the country of the two Holy Places [Saudi Arabia] and the route of the Apostle (Allah's Blessings and Salutations may be on him) to the Furthest Mosque (Al-Aqsa Mosque). Also to remind the Muslims not to be engaged in an internal war among themselves, as that will have grave consequences namely:

1-Consumption of the Muslims' human resources as most casualties and fatalities will be among the Muslim people.

2-Exhaustion of the economic and financial resources.

3-Destruction of the country infrastructures.

4-Dissociation of the society.

5-Destruction of the oil industries. The presence of the USA Crusader military forces on land, sea and air of the states of the Islamic Gulf is the greatest danger threatening the largest oil reserve in the world. The existence of these forces in the area will provoke the people of the country and induces aggression on their religion, feelings and pride and push them to take up armed struggle against the invaders occupying the land; therefore spread of the fighting in the region will expose the oil wealth to the danger of being burned up. The economic interests of the States of the Gulf and the land of the two Holy Places will be damaged and even greater damage will be caused to the economy of the world. I would like here to alert my brothers, the Mujahideen, the sons of the nation, to protect this (oil) wealth and not to include it in the battle as it is a great Islamic wealth and a large economic power essential for the soon to be established Islamic state, by Allah's Permission and Grace. We also warn the aggressors, the USA, against burning this Islamic wealth (a crime which they may commit in order to prevent it, at the end of the war, from falling in the hands of its legitimate owners and to cause economic damages to the competitors of the USA in Europe or the Far East, particularly Japan which is the major consumer of the oil of the region).

6-Division of the land of the two Holy Places, and annexing of the northerly part of it by Israel. Dividing the land of the two Holy Places is an essential demand of the Zionist-Crusader alliance. The existence of such a large country with its huge resources under the leadership of the forthcoming Islamic State, by Allah's Grace, represent a serious danger to the very existence of the Zionist state in Palestine. The Nobel Ka'ba,—the Qiblah of all Muslims—makes the land of the two Holy Places a symbol for the unity of the Islamic world. Moreover, the presence of the world largest oil reserve makes the land of the two Holy Places an important economical power in the Islamic world. The sons of the two Holy Places are directly related to the life style (Seerah) of their forefathers, the companions, may Allah be pleased with them. They consider the Seerah of their forefathers as a source and an example for re-establishing the greatness of this Ummah and to raise the word of Allah again. Furthermore the presence of a population of fighters in the south of Yemen, fighting in the cause of Allah, is a strategic threat to the Zionist-Crusader alliance in the area. The Prophet (ALLAH'S BLESSING AND SALUTATIONS ON HIM) said: (around twelve thousands will emerge from Aden/Abian helping—the cause of—Allah and His messenger, they are the best, in the time, between me and them) narrated by Ahmad with a correct trustworthy reference.

7-An internal war is a great mistake, no matter what reasons there are for it. The presence of the occupier—the USA—forces will control the outcome of the battle for the benefit of the international **Kufr**.

Kufr: Unbelief

. . .

Our Lord, guide this Ummah, and make the right conditions (by which) the people of your obedience will be in dignity and the people of disobedience in humiliation, and by which the good deeds are enjoined and the bad deeds are forebode.

Our Lord, bless Muhammad, Your slave and messenger, his family and descendants, and companions and salute him with a (becoming) salutation.

And our last supplication is: All praise is due to Allah.

Working with Sources

1. **How did bin Laden conflate oil interests with the goals of religious regeneration?**
2. **How and why did he address the Israeli–Palestinian conflict in this document?**

SOURCE 31.2

Vladimir Putin, Address to the Duma concerning the annexation of Crimea

March 19, 2014

Vladimir Putin, the former KGB officer who has dominated Russian political life since 2000, delivered this remarkable oration after annexing the Crimea region from the nation of Ukraine in March 2014. This move came after a protest movement had driven the pro-Russian president of Ukraine out of office, and as tensions between ethnic Ukrainians and ethnic Russians in the country had erupted into violence in several Ukrainian cities. Once a referendum was held in the Crimean peninsula about whether to

Source: http://rt.com/politics/official-word/vladimir-putin-crimea-address-658/

remain within Ukraine or to be united to Russia, Putin, believing that "the numbers speak for themselves," authorized the annexation of the region as Russian territory. In this speech, justifying his country's move against a fellow former Soviet Socialist Republic, Putin appealed to both recent and distant history—and, perhaps, signaled his further intentions for the future.

Dear friends, we have gathered here today in connection with an issue that is of vital, historic significance to all of us. A referendum was held in Crimea on March 16 in full compliance with democratic procedures and international norms.

More than 82 percent of the electorate took part in the vote. Over 96 percent of them spoke out in favour of reuniting with Russia. These numbers speak for themselves.

To understand the reason behind such a choice it is enough to know the history of Crimea and what Russia and Crimea have always meant for each other.

Everything in Crimea speaks of our shared history and pride. This is the location of ancient Khersones, where Prince Vladimir was baptised. His spiritual feat of adopting Orthodoxy predetermined the overall basis of the culture, civilisation and human values that unite the peoples of Russia, Ukraine and Belarus. The graves of Russian soldiers whose bravery brought Crimea into the Russian empire are also in Crimea. This is also Sevastopol—a legendary city with an outstanding history, a fortress that serves as the birthplace of Russia's Black Sea Fleet. Crimea is Balaklava and Kerch, Malakhov Kurgan and Sapun Ridge. Each one of these places is dear to our hearts, symbolising Russian military glory and outstanding valour.

Crimea is a unique blend of different peoples' cultures and traditions. This makes it similar to Russia as a whole, where not a single ethnic group has been lost over the centuries. Russians and Ukrainians, Crimean Tatars and people of other ethnic groups have lived side by side in Crimea, retaining their own identity, traditions, languages and faith.

. . .

In people's hearts and minds, Crimea has always been an inseparable part of Russia. This firm conviction is based on truth and justice and was passed from generation to generation, over time, under any circumstances, despite all the dramatic changes our country went through during the entire 20th century.

After the revolution, the Bolsheviks, for a number of reasons—may God judge them—added large sections of the historical South of Russia to the Republic of Ukraine. This was done with no consideration for the ethnic make-up of the population, and today these areas form the southeast of Ukraine. Then, in 1954, a decision was made to transfer Crimean Region to Ukraine, along with Sevastopol, despite the fact that it was a city of union subordination. This was the personal initiative of the Communist Party head Nikita Khrushchev. What stood behind this decision of his—a desire to win the support of the Ukrainian political establishment or to atone for the mass repressions of the 1930's in Ukraine—is for historians to figure out.

What matters now is that this decision was made in clear violation of the constitutional norms that were in place even then. The decision was made behind the scenes. Naturally, in a totalitarian state nobody bothered to ask the citizens of Crimea and Sevastopol. They were faced with the fact. People, of course, wondered why all of a sudden Crimea became part of Ukraine. But on the whole—and we must state this clearly, we all know it—this decision was treated as a formality of sorts because the territory was transferred within the boundaries of a single state. Back then, it was impossible to imagine that Ukraine and Russia may split up and become two separate states. However, this has happened.

Unfortunately, what seemed impossible became a reality. The USSR fell apart. Things developed so swiftly that few people realised how truly dramatic those events and their consequences would be. Many people both in Russia and in Ukraine, as well as in other republics hoped that the Commonwealth of Independent States that was created at the time would become the new common form of statehood. They were told that there would be a single currency, a single economic space, joint armed forces; however, all this remained empty promises, while the big country was gone. It was only when Crimea ended up as part of a different country that Russia realised that it was not simply robbed, it was plundered.

At the same time, we have to admit that by launching the sovereignty parade Russia itself aided in the collapse of the Soviet Union. And as this collapse was legalised, everyone forgot about Crimea and Sevastopol—the main base of the Black Sea Fleet. Millions of people went to bed in one country and awoke in different ones, overnight becoming ethnic minorities in former Union republics, while the Russian nation became one of the biggest, if not the biggest ethnic group in the world to be divided by borders.

Now, many years later, I heard residents of Crimea say that back in 1991 they were handed over like a sack of potatoes. . . .

Like a mirror, the situation in Ukraine reflects what is going on and what has been happening in the world over the past several decades. After the dissolution of bipolarity on the planet, we no longer have stability. Key international institutions are not getting any stronger; on the contrary, in many cases, they are sadly degrading. Our western partners, led by the United States of America, prefer not to be guided by international law in their practical policies, but by the rule of the gun. They have come to believe in their exclusivity and exceptionalism, that they can decide the destinies of the world, that only they can ever be right. They act as they please: here and there, they use force against sovereign states, building coalitions based on the principle "*If you are not with us, you are against us.*" To make this aggression look legitimate, they force the necessary resolutions from international organisations, and if for some reason this does not work, they simply ignore the UN Security Council and the UN overall.

This happened in Yugoslavia; we remember 1999 very well. It was hard to believe, even seeing it with my own eyes, that at the end of the 20th century, one of Europe's capitals, Belgrade, was under missile attack for several weeks, and then came the real intervention. Was there a UN Security Council resolution on this matter, allowing for these actions? Nothing of the sort. And then, they hit Afghanistan, Iraq, and frankly violated the UN Security Council resolution on Libya, when instead of imposing the so-called no-fly zone over it they started bombing it too.

. . .

Let me say one other thing too. Millions of Russians and Russian-speaking people live in Ukraine and will continue to do so. Russia will always defend their interests using political, diplomatic and legal means. But it should be above all in Ukraine's own interest to ensure that these people's rights and interests are fully protected. This is the guarantee of Ukraine's state stability and territorial integrity.

We want to be friends with Ukraine and we want Ukraine to be a strong, sovereign and self-sufficient country. Ukraine is one of our biggest partners after all. We have many joint projects and I believe in their success no matter what the current difficulties. Most importantly, we want peace and harmony to reign in Ukraine, and we are ready to work together with other countries to do everything possible to facilitate and support this. But as I said, only Ukraine's own people can put their own house in order.

▶ Working with Sources

1. **In what specific ways, and for what purpose, did Putin appeal to the historical past?**
2. **What does he believe will be the consequences of the end of "bipolarity" in global politics—and of the belief in American "exceptionalism" demonstrated by US military action since 1999?**

SOURCE 31.3 Remarks by President Obama in Address to European Youth, March 26, 2014

Barely a week after Vladimir Putin's address to the Duma, US President Obama outlined America's position on Russia's annexation of Crimea from Ukraine in this speech in Brussels. Citing the struggles of Europe over the centuries to build representative government and overcome nationalist rivalries, he placed Russia's act as a dangerous renewal of the forces that had led to so much bloodshed and destruction and pledged the United States and NATO to oppose any such forcible seizures of territories.

Source: https://www.defenseone.com/ideas/2014/03/full-text-obamas-contest-ideas-speech-nato/81322/

March 26, 2014
REMARKS BY PRESIDENT OBAMA
IN ADDRESS TO EUROPEAN YOUTH
Palais des Beaux Arts
Brussels, Belgium
6:16 P.M. EDT

Leaders and dignitaries of the European Union; representatives of our NATO Alliance; distinguished guests: We meet here at a moment of testing for Europe and the United States, and for the international order that we have worked for generations to build.

Throughout human history, societies have grappled with fundamental questions of how to organize themselves, the proper relationship between the individual and the state, the best means to resolve inevitable conflicts between states. And it was here in Europe, through centuries of struggle—through war and Enlightenment, repression and revolution—that a particular set of ideals began to emerge: The belief that through conscience and free will, each of us has the right to live as we choose. The belief that power is derived from the consent of the governed, and that laws and institutions should be established to protect that understanding. And those ideas eventually inspired a band of colonialists across an ocean, and they wrote them into the founding documents that still guide America today, including the simple truth that all men—and women—are created equal.

But those ideals have also been tested—here in Europe and around the world. Those ideals have often been threatened by an older, more traditional view of power. This alternative vision argues that ordinary men and women are too small-minded to govern their own affairs, that order and progress can only come when individuals surrender their rights to an all-powerful sovereign. Often, this alternative vision roots itself in the notion that by virtue of race or faith or ethnicity, some are inherently superior to others, and that individual identity must be defined by "us" versus "them," or that national greatness must flow not by what a people stand for, but by what they are against. . .

This morning at Flanders Field, I was reminded of how war between peoples sent a generation to their deaths in the trenches and gas of the First World War. And just two decades later, extreme nationalism plunged this continent into war once again—with populations enslaved, and great cities reduced to rubble, and tens of millions slaughtered, including those lost in the Holocaust.

It is in response to this tragic history that, in the aftermath of World War II, America joined with Europe to reject the darker forces of the past and build a new architecture of peace. Workers and engineers gave life to the Marshall Plan. Sentinels stood vigilant in a NATO Alliance that would become the strongest the world has ever known. And across the Atlantic, we embraced a shared vision of Europe—a vision based on representative democracy, individual rights, and a belief that nations can meet the interests of their citizens through trade and open markets; a social safety net and respect for those of different faiths and backgrounds. . .

Today, what would have seemed impossible in the trenches of Flanders, the rubble of Berlin, or a dissident's prison cell—that reality is taken for granted. A Germany unified. The nations of Central and Eastern Europe welcomed into the family of democracies. Here in this country, once the battleground of Europe, we meet in the hub of a Union that brings together age-old adversaries in peace and cooperation. The people of Europe, hundreds of millions of citizens—east, west, north, south—are more secure and more prosperous because we stood together for the ideals we share. . .

While technology has opened up vast opportunities for trade and innovation and cultural understanding, it's also allowed terrorists to kill on a horrifying scale. Around the world, sectarian warfare and ethnic conflicts continue to claim thousands of lives. And once again, we are confronted with the belief among some that bigger nations can bully smaller ones to get their way—that recycled maxim that might somehow makes right.

So I come here today to insist that we must never take for granted the progress that has been won here in Europe and advanced around the world, because the contest of ideas continues for your generation. And that's what's at stake in Ukraine today. Russia's leadership is challenging truths that only a few weeks ago seemed self-evident—that in the 21st century, the borders of Europe cannot be redrawn with force, that international law matters, that people and nations can make their own decisions about their future. . .

And the consequences that would arise from complacency are not abstractions. The impact that they have on the lives of real people—men and women just like us—have to enter into our imaginations. Just look at the young people of Ukraine who were determined to take back their future from a government rotted by corruption—the portraits of the fallen shot by snipers, the visitors who pay their respects at the Maidan. There was the university student, wrapped in the Ukrainian flag, expressing her hope that "every country should live by the law." A postgraduate student, speaking of her fellow protestors, saying, "I want these people who are here to have dignity." Imagine that you are the young woman who said, "there are some things that fear, police sticks and tear gas cannot destroy."

We've never met these people, but we know them. Their voices echo calls for human dignity that rang out in European streets and squares for generations. Their voices echo those around the world who at this very moment fight for their dignity. These Ukrainians rejected a government that was stealing from the people instead of serving them, and are reaching for the same ideals that allow us to be here today. . .

Yes, we believe in democracy—with elections that are free and fair; and independent judiciaries and opposition parties; civil society and uncensored information so that individuals can make their own choices. Yes, we believe in open economies based on free markets and innovation, and individual initiative and entrepreneurship, and trade and investment that creates a broader prosperity. And, yes, we believe in human dignity—that every person is created equal, no matter who you are, or what you look like, or who you love, or where you come from. That is what we believe. That's what makes us strong.

And our enduring strength is also reflected in our respect for an international system that protects the rights of both nations and people—a United

Nations and a Universal Declaration of Human Rights; international law and the means to enforce those laws. But we also know that those rules are not self-executing; they depend on people and nations of goodwill continually affirming them. And that's why Russia's violation of international law—its assault on Ukraine's sovereignty and territorial integrity—must be met with condemnation. Not because we're trying to keep Russia down, but because the principles that have meant so much to Europe and the world must be lifted up. . .

Of course, Ukraine is not a member of NATO—in part because of its close and complex history with Russia. Nor will Russia be dislodged from Crimea or deterred from further escalation by military force. But with time, so long as we remain united, the Russian people will recognize that they cannot achieve security, prosperity and the status that they seek through brute force. And that's why, throughout this crisis, we will combine our substantial pressure on Russia with an open door for diplomacy. I believe that for both Ukraine and Russia, a stable peace will come through de-escalation—direct dialogue between Russia and the government of Ukraine and the international community; monitors who can ensure that the rights of all Ukrainians are protected; a process of constitutional reform within Ukraine; and free and fair elections this spring. . .

Of course, neither the United States nor Europe are perfect in adherence to our ideals, nor do we claim to be the sole arbiter of what is right or wrong in the world. We are human, after all, and we face difficult choices about how to exercise our power. But part of what makes us different is that we welcome criticism, just as we welcome the responsibilities that come with global leadership. . .

So our approach stands in stark contrast to the arguments coming out of Russia these days. It is absurd to suggest—as a steady drumbeat of Russian voices do—that America is somehow conspiring with fascists inside of Ukraine or failing to respect the Russian people. My grandfather served in Patton's Army, just as many of your fathers and grandfathers fought against fascism. We Americans remember well the unimaginable sacrifices made by the Russian people in World War II, and we have honored those sacrifices. . .

So America, and the world and Europe, has an interest in a strong and responsible Russia, not a weak one. We want the Russian people to live in security, prosperity and dignity like everyone else—proud of their own history. But that does not mean that Russia can run roughshod over its neighbors. Just because Russia has a deep history with Ukraine does not mean it should be able to dictate Ukraine's future. No amount of propaganda can make right something that the world knows is wrong. . .

For the young people here today, I know it may seem easy to see these events as removed from our lives, remote from our daily routines, distant from concerns closer to home. I recognize that both in the United States and in much of Europe there's more than enough to worry about in the affairs of our own countries. There will always be voices who say that what happens in the wider world is not our concern, nor our responsibility. But we must never forget that we are heirs to a struggle for freedom.

Our democracy, our individual opportunity only exists because those who came before us had the wisdom and the courage to recognize that our ideals will only endure if we see our self-interest in the success of other peoples and other nations. . .

And it is you, the young people of Europe. . .who will help decide which way the currents of our history will flow. Do not think for a moment that your own freedom, your own prosperity, that your own moral imagination is bound by the limits of your community, your ethnicity, or even your country. You're bigger than that. You can help us to choose a better history. That's what Europe tells us. That's what the American experience is all about. . .

And just as we meet our responsibilities as individuals, we must be prepared to meet them as nations. Because we live in a world in which our ideals are going to be challenged again and again by forces that would drag us back into conflict or corruption. We can't count on others to rise to meet those tests. The policies of your government, the principles of your European Union, will make a critical difference in whether or not the international order that so many generations before you have strived to create continues to move forward, or whether it retreats.

And that's the question we all must answer—what kind of Europe, what kind of America, what kind of world will we leave behind. And I believe that if we hold firm to our principles, and are willing to back our beliefs with courage and resolve, then hope will ultimately overcome fear, and freedom will continue to triumph over tyranny—because that is what forever stirs in the human heart.

▸ Working with Sources

1. **How does President Obama counter President Putin's arguments justifying annexation of Ukraine?**
2. **Which speech do you think has the most persuasive argument? Why?**

SOURCE 31.4

United Nations Framework Convention on Climate Change, Paris

2015

While there has been considerable debate over the last several decades on the nature and degree of global warming, there is general scientific consensus that greenhouse gases are the main contributors to temperature increases on earth. Scientists assume that at current rates of greenhouse gas production the earth will reach a "tipping point" of 450 parts per million, with catastrophic consequences for the planet's climate, before the middle of this century. Although 169 nations joined the 2005 Kyoto Protocol to reduce greenhouse emissions, the United States refused to sign the agreement because of the nonparticipation of important developing countries in the Protocol. Under President Obama, the United States in 2015 did eventually sign on, together in Paris with 194 other nations, to an international agreement regarding climate change and the reduction of its global threat. But in 2017 President Trump withdrew from the Agreement.

Paris Agreement: Essential elements

The Paris Agreement builds upon the Convention and—for the first time—brings all nations into a common cause to undertake ambitious efforts to combat climate change and adapt to its effects, with enhanced support to assist developing countries to do so. As such, it charts a new course in the global climate effort.

The Paris Agreement's central aim is to strengthen the global response to the threat of climate change by keeping a global temperature rise this century well below 2 degrees Celsius above pre-industrial levels and to pursue efforts to limit the temperature increase even further to 1.5 degrees Celsius. Additionally, the agreement aims to strengthen the ability of countries to deal with the impacts of climate change. To reach these ambitious goals, appropriate financial flows, a new technology framework and an enhanced capacity building framework will be put in place, thus supporting action by developing countries and the most vulnerable countries, in line with their own national objectives. The Agreement also provides for enhanced transparency of action and support through a more robust transparency framework. . . .

Nationally determined contributions

The Paris Agreement requires all Parties to put forward their best efforts through "nationally determined contributions" (NDCs) and to strengthen

Source: http://unfccc.int/paris_agreement/items/9485.php

these efforts in the years ahead. This includes requirements that all Parties report regularly on their emissions and on their implementation efforts.

In 2018, Parties will take stock of the collective efforts in relation to progress towards the goal set in the Paris Agreement and to inform the preparation of NDCs.

There will also be a global stocktake every 5 years to assess the collective progress towards achieving the purpose of the Agreement and to inform further individual actions by Parties.

81 Parties of 197 Parties ratified the Convention

On 5 October 2016, the threshold for entry into force of the Paris Agreement was achieved. The Paris Agreement entered into force on 4 November 2016.

Working with Sources

1. **What is the meaning of the "tipping point" in climate change?**
2. **Why is it important that developed as well as developing countries decided to participate in signing the Paris Agreement?**

Further Resources

Chapter 1

Burroughs, William J. *Climate Change in Prehistory: The End of the Reign of Chaos*. Cambridge: Cambridge University Press, 2005. Very well-researched and up-to-date discussion of climate and human evolution.

Condemi, Silvana, and François Savatier. *A Pocket History of Human Evolution: How We Became Sapiens*. Paris: Flammarion, 2019. A short, up-to-date introduction to the ever-changing story of human evolution by a prominent paleoanthropologist and a science journalist. Includes new research on the Neanderthals and the discovery of the Denisovans.

Finlayson, Clive. *The Smart Neanderthal: Bird Catching, Cave Art, and the Cognitive Revolution*. Oxford and New York: Oxford University Press, 2019. The author is a foremost authority on the rise and disappearance of the Neanderthals and is emphatic on their contributions to emerging human culture in Europe.

Flood, Josephine. *The Original Australians: The Story of the Aboriginal People*. Crows Nest, Australia: Allen and Unwin, 2019. A summary of the research carried out for more than half a century by one of the leading Australian archaeologists on Aboriginal culture.

Johanson, Donald, and Kate Wong. *Lucy: The Quest for Human Origins*. New York: Three Rivers, 2009. Bestseller that made Lucy famous and provided the inspiration for the vignette at the beginning of Chapter 1.

McBrearty, Sally. *Companion to Human Evolution*. San Diego, CA: Cognella, 2014. The author carried out pioneering work, emphasizing the African origins of *H. sapiens* not only as an anatomically but also intellectually modern human being before ever migrating to the rest of the world.

Pääbo, Svante. *Neanderthal Man: In Search of the Lost Genomes*. New York: Basic Books, 2014. Pääbo is the first paleogeneticist to sequence the full genome of a Neanderthal fossil as well as that of a new species of hominin, Dinoseva, discovered in Siberia in 2010.

Tattersall, Ian. *Masters of the Planet: The Search for Human Origins*. New York: Palgrave Macmillan, 2012. A scholarly, well-founded overview for the general reader by one of the leading senior paleoanthropologists.

Von Petzinger, Genevieve. *First Signs: Unlocking the Mysteries of the World's Oldest Symbols*. New York: Atria Books, 2016. Very little is known about the meaning of the prehistoric cave paintings found across the world. Von Petzinger focuses on a set of similar symbols found in many of these caves and attempts to interpret them as predecessors of the much later early writing systems.

WEBSITES

Bradshaw Foundation, http://www.bradshawfoundation.com/. The Bradshaw Foundation has a large website on human evolution and rock art, with many images, and a link to Stephen Oppenheimer's website Journey of Mankind: The Peopling of the World, an important overview of *Homo sapiens* migrations.

Institute of Human Origins, Arizona State University, http://iho.asu.edu/. Arizona State University's Institute of Human Origins runs the popular but scholarly website Becoming Human (http://www.becominghuman.org/).

Chapter 2

Alcock, Susan E., John Bodel, and Richard J. A. Talbert, eds. *Highways, Byways, and Road Systems in the Pre-Modern World*. Chichester: John Wiley & Sons, 2012. Fascinating global survey of methods of transport and communication.

Assmann, Jan. *The Search for God in Ancient Egypt*. Ithaca, NY: Cornell University Press, 2001. Reflective investigation of the dimensions of Egyptian polytheism by a leading Egyptologist.

Bottéro, Jean. *Mesopotamia: Writing, Reasoning, and the Gods*. Chicago: University of Chicago Press, 1992. Classic intellectual history of ancient Mesopotamia.

Cline, Eric H. *1177 B.C.: The Year Civilization Collapsed*. Princeton, NJ: Princeton University Press, 2014. Revisionist study by a scholar of classics and anthropology attempting to understand the sudden irruption of the mysterious "Sea People" into the Near East, conventionally assumed to mark the end of the Bronze Age and the beginning of the Iron Age. This authoritative study replaces Robert Drews, 1993.

Finkelstein, Israel, and Neil Asher Silberman, *The Bible Unearthed: Archaeology's New Vision of Ancient Israel and the Origin of Its Sacred Texts*. New York, London, Toronto, Sydney: The Free Press, 2001. The two authors are the leading archaeologists of Israel. Their research revolutionized our understanding of the ancient Israelites.

Kramer, Samuel Noah. *The Sumerians: Their History, Culture, and Character*. Chicago: University of Chicago Press, 2010. An expanded version of Kramer's earlier work, *History Begins at Sumer* (1988), this is a fascinating presentation of the many "firsts" originating in the world's earliest urban civilization, written by a leading Sumerologist.

Mithen, Steven. *After the Ice: A Global Human History, 20,000–5000 B.C.* Cambridge, MA: Harvard University Press, 2003. Engagingly written story of humans settling, becoming farmers, and founding villages and towns, as seen through the eyes of a modern time traveler.

Svärd, Saana, and Agnès Garcia-Ventura. *Studying Gender in the Ancient Near East*. University Park, PA: Eisenbrauns, 2018. A new book that brings together established and emerging scholars of gender for the exploration of case studies as well as current theories of gender applicable to the ancient Near East.

Van de Mieroop, Marc. *The Ancient Mesopotamian City*. Oxford: Clarendon, 1997. Full examination of Mesopotamian urban institutions, including city assemblies.

WEBSITES

British Museum, *Ancient Egypt*, http://www.ancientegypt.co.uk/menu.html. Pictorial introduction, with short texts.

Livius.org, "Mesopotamia," http://www.livius.org/babylonia.html. A large collection of translated texts and references to philological articles, with portals on Mesopotamia, Egypt, Anatolia, and Greece.

Oriental Institute, University of Chicago. Ancient Mesopotamia, http://mesopotamia.lib.uchicago.edu/. A user-friendly portal to the world-renowned Mesopotamia collection of the Oriental Institute.

Chapter 3

Avari, Burjor. *India: The Ancient Past*. 2nd ed. New York: Routledge, 2016. Recent, accessible scholarship on the subcontinent from pre-Harappan times to the Turco-Afghan invasions. Particularly useful on the transition from the Harappan to the Vedic period and the latest work on the role of Indo-Europeans.

Bryant, Edwin. *The Quest for the Origins of Vedic Culture: The Indo-Aryan Migration Debate*. Oxford and New York: Oxford University Press, 2001. A scholarly yet readable attempt to address the linguistic and archaeological evidence surrounding the thesis of Aryan migration versus the more recent theory of indigenous Vedic development.

Embree, Ainslee T., ed. *Sources of Indian Tradition*, vol. 1, 2nd ed. New York: Columbia University Press, 1988. Though the language is dated in places, this is still the most comprehensive sourcebook of Indian thought available. Recent additions on women and gender make it even more so. Sophisticated yet readable introductions, glosses, and commentary.

Eraly, Abraham. *Gem in the Lotus: The Seeding of Indian Civilization*. London: Weidenfeld & Nicholson, 2004. Readable, comprehensive survey of recent scholarship from prehistory to the reign of Ashoka during the Mauryan dynasty of the fourth and third centuries BCE. Emphasis on transitional period of sixth-century religious innovations, particularly Buddhism.

Kenoyer, Jonathan Mark. *Ancient Cities of the Indus Valley Civilization*. Oxford and New York: Oxford University Press, 1998. Comprehensive work by team leader of Harappan Research Project. Particularly good on Lothal.

Klostermaier, Klaus. *A Survey of Hinduism*, 3rd ed. Albany, NY: SUNY Press, 2007. Comprehensive thematic treatment of major themes of Hinduism from the Vedas to Hinduism's relationship to modern science.

Possehl, Gregory L., ed. *Harappan Civilization: A Recent Perspective*, 2nd ed. New Delhi: Oxford University Press, 1993. Sound and extensive treatment of recent work and issues in Indus Valley archaeology by one of the leading on-site researchers and a former student of Walter Fairservis. Used to best advantage by experienced students.

Singh, Upinder. *A History of Ancient and Early Medieval India: From the Stone Age to the 12th Century*. New Delhi: Pearson, 2008. Sweeping text by a longtime instructor of Indian history at the University of Delhi. Suitable for undergraduates and current on the latest debates on ancient origins.

Wolpert, Stanley. *A New History of India*, 5th ed. Oxford and New York: Oxford University Press, 2004. Another extremely useful, readable, one-volume history from Neolithic times to the present. Excellent first work for serious students.

WEBSITES

Columbia University Libraries. South and Southeast Asian Studies, www.columbia.edu/cu/lweb/indiv/southasia/cuvl/history.html. Run by Columbia University, this site contains links to "WWWVirtual Library: Indian History," "Regnal Chronologies," "Internet Indian History Sourcebook," and "Medical History of British India."

Harappa, http://www.harappa.com. Contains a wealth of images of artifacts and other archaeological treasures from the Indus Valley.

Chapter 4

Chang, Kwang-chih. *The Archaeology of Ancient China*, 4th ed. New Haven, CT: Yale University Press, 1986. Sophisticated treatment of archaeology of Shang China. Prime exponent of the view of overlapping periods and territories for the Three Dynasties (Sandai) period. Erudite, yet accessible for experienced students.

Keightly, David N., ed. *The Origins of Chinese Civilization*. Berkeley and Los Angeles: University of California Press, 1983. Symposium volume on a variety of Three Dynasties topics by leading scholars. Some exposure to early Chinese history and archaeology is necessary in order to best appreciate these essays.

Linduff, Katheryn M., and Yan Sun, eds. *Gender and Chinese Archaeology*. Walnut Creek, CA: Altamira, 2004. Re-examines the role of gender in ancient China in the context of a critique of the general lack of gendered research in archaeology as a whole.

Liu, Xiang. *Exemplary Women of Early China: The Lienu zhuan of Liu Xiang*. Edited and translated by Anne Behnke Kinney. New York: Columbia University Press, 2014. One of the few accounts we have of the lives of women during the Three Dynasties period; covers 120 short biographies of Zhou women.

Lowe, Michael, and Edward L. Shaughnessy, eds. *The Cambridge History of Ancient China: From the Origins of Civilization to 221 B.C.* Cambridge, UK: Cambridge University Press, 1999. The opening volume of the Cambridge History of China series, this is the most complete multi-essay collection on all aspects of recent Chinese ancient historical and archaeological work. The place to start for the serious student contemplating in-depth research.

Szonyi, Michael, ed. *A Companion to Chinese History*. Hoboken, NJ: Wiley Blackwell, 2017. Part of "Wiley Blackwell Companions to World History," this work is ideally suited to world history instructors interested in sampling the latest scholarship from American, European, Chinese, and Japanese authors.

Thorp, Robert L. *China in the Early Bronze Age: Shang Civilization*. Philadelphia: University of Pennsylvania Press, 2006. Comprehensive yet accessible survey of recent archaeological work on the period 2070–1046 BCE, including traditional Xia and Shang periods under the heading of China's "bronze age."

Wang, Aihe. *Cosmology and Political Culture in Early China*. Cambridge, UK: Cambridge University Press, 2000. Part of the Cambridge Studies in Chinese History, Literature, and Institutions series. Wang argues that control of cosmology—how the world and universe operate—was a vital key to the wielding of power by the Shang and Zhou rulers. Recommended for serious students.

Wang, Robin. *Images of Women in Chinese Thought and Culture: Writings from the Pre-Qin Period Through the Song Dynasty*. Indianapolis, IN: Hackett Publishing, 2003. Excerpts from classical and more obscure texts on the role and treatment of women in early China. A large and useful section on pre-Confucian texts.

Watson, Burton, trans. *The Tso Chuan: Selections from China's Oldest Narrative History*. New York: Columbia University Press, 1989. Elegant translation by one of the most prolific of scholars working today. Excellent introduction to Zhou period and politics. Appropriate for beginning students, though more useful for those with some prior introduction to the period.

WEBSITES

http://lucian.uchicago.edu/blogs/earlychina/ssec/. This is the site of the journal *Early China*, published by the Society for the Study of Early China. Accessible only to members.

British Museum. Ancient China, http://www.ancientchina.co.uk. This site provides access to the British Museum's ancient Chinese collections and is highly useful for students seeking illustrations of assorted artifacts in a user-friendly environment.

Chapter 5

The Americas

Bellwood, Peter. *First Migrants: Ancient Migration in Global Perspective*. Chichester, UK: John Wiley & Sons, 2013. An intriguing study of prehistoric migration and its role in shaping the emergence of civilization.

Bruhns, Karen Olsen, and Karen E. Stothert. *Women in Ancient America*. Norman: University of Oklahoma Press, 2nd ed. 2014. A comprehensive account of women's roles in daily life, religion, politics, and war in foraging and farming as well as urban societies in the Americas.

Grove, David C. *Discovering the Olmecs: An Unconventional History*. Austin, TX: University of Texas Press, 2014. During his long career, the author became one of the foremost authorities on the Olmecs. His history is "unconventional" because it includes extensive discussions of the personalities of scholars and their excavations of Olmec sites.

Quilter, Jeffrey. *The Ancient Central Andes*. Milton Park and New York: Routledge, 2014. Comprehensive overview of Andean history by an anthropologist with many years of research on South America. The book brings together the results of much of the work done in recent years.

Solis, Ruth Shady, Haas, Jonathan, and Creamer, Winifred. "Dating Caral, a Preceramic Site in the Supe Valley on the Central Coast of Peru," *Science* 292:5517 (2001): 723–726. Pathbreaking early report of early scientific work on Caral Supe and the oldest American cities.

Suarez, Rafael, and Ciprian F. Ardelean, eds. *People and Culture in Ice Age Americas: New Dimensions in Paleoamerican Archaeology*. Salt Lake City, UT: University of Utah Press, 2019. Collection of articles by leading scholars discussing the most recent results (to 2014) of prehistoric American archaeology.

von Hagen, Adriana, and Craig Morris. *The Cities of the Ancient Andes*. New York: Thames & Hudson, 1999. While more geared to later periods, still a useful overview, with illustrations, by specialists on Andean cultures.

Oceania

Carson, Mike T., *First Settlement of Remote Oceania: Earliest Sites in the Mariana Islands*. Heidelberg, Germany: Springer-Verlag, 2014. Study based on new archaeological research by a specialist on Pacific research.

Hunt, Terry, and Carl Lipo. *The Statues that Walked: Unraveling the Mystery of Easter Island*. New York, London, Toronto, Sydney: The Free Press, 2014. Revisionist book by two anthropologists who challenge the societal collapse theory of Easter Island (Rapa Nui) society and offer fascinating new views on the precolonial history of the island.

Kirch, Patrick V. *A Shark Going Inland Is My Chief: The Island Civilization of Ancient Hawai'i*. Berkeley and Los Angeles: University of California Press, 2019. Book on the precolonial civilization of Hawaii by one of the most published specialists on Oceania. Written for nonspecialists wishing to find an introduction to the precolonial Pacific world.

Matsuda, Matt K. *Pacific Worlds: A History of Seas, Peoples, and Cultures*. Cambridge, UK: Cambridge University Press, 2012. General history of the Pacific with an emphasis on the early modern period.

WEBSITES

Foundation for the Advancement of Mesoamerican Studies (FAMSI), http://www.famsi.org/. Collaborates with the Los Angeles County Museum of Art and runs a wide range of scholarly, funding, and educational outreach programs aimed at advancing studies of Mesoamerica.

Britannica. http://www.britannica.com/EBchecked/topic/468832/Polynesian-culture. Good link leading to an 8,000-word essay on leading topics concerning Polynesia and Oceania. In order to access the complete essay the reader must apply for a free trial of the online *Encyclopedia Britannica*.

Chapter 6

Sub-Saharan Africa

Chami, Félix. *The Unity of African Ancient History: 3000 BC to 500 AD*. Dar es Salaam: E&D, 2006. General overview by one of the leading archaeologists of East Africa.

Insoll, Timothy, ed. *Material Explorations in African Archaeology*. Oxford and New York: Oxford University Press, 2015. The first book of its kind to explore the ethnographic and archaeological record of Africa for human and material evidence dealing with topics such as ancestry, monuments, animals, shrines, landscapes, healing, and divination.

McIntosh, Roderick J. *Ancient Middle Niger: Urbanism and the Self-Organizing Landscape*. Cambridge, UK: Cambridge University Press, 2005. Important revisionist work on the origins of urbanism and kingship in West Africa.

Mitchell, Peter, and Paul Lane. *The Oxford Handbook of African Archaeology*. Oxford: Oxford University Press, 2013. A total of 70 essays by specialists on all aspects of human culture in Africa, with an emphasis on foragers, agriculturalists, and early urbanists.

Vansina, Jan. *Paths in the Rainforests: Toward a History of Political Tradition in Equatorial Africa*. Madison: University of Wisconsin Press, 1990. Magisterial presentation of the Bantu dispersal and village life in the rain forest.

Mesoamerica and the Andes

Braswell, Geoffrey E., ed. *The Ancient Maya of Mexico: Reinterpreting the Past of the Northern Lowlands*. Milton Park, UK, and New York: Routledge, 2014. Contains articles on the origins of the ballgame and the Mayan "collapse."

Evans, Susan Tobey. *Ancient Mexico and Central America: Archaeology and Culture History*. London: Thames & Hudson, 2004. Densely but clearly written and detailed, with many sidebars on special topics.

Grube, Nikolai, ed. *Maya: Divine Kings of the Rain Forest*. Cologne, Germany: Könemann, 2001. Lavishly illustrated book with short contributions by many hands.

Martin, Simon. *Ancient Maya Politics: A Political Anthropology of the Classic Period, 150–900 CE*. Cambridge, UK: Cambridge University Press, 2020. Making use of newly deciphered Mayan glyptic inscriptions, Martin explains the coexistence of many Mayan polities without leading to the eventual establishment of an empire; that is, why no Mayan kingdom ever succeeded in forcibly uniting the many coexisting Maya kingdoms into a single unit.

Schele, Linda, and David Freidel. *A Forest of Kings: The Untold Story of the Ancient Maya*. New York: Quill-William Morrow, 1990. Classic study summarizing the results of the decipherment of Maya glyphs, by two pioneers.

Stuart, David. *The Order of Days: Unlocking the Secrets of the Ancient Maya*. New York: Three Rivers Press, 2011. Magisterial summary of our current knowledge of Maya culture.

WEBSITES

Stanford University Libraries, Africa South of the Sahara, https://library.stanford.edu/areas/african-collections: A large, resource-filled website based at Stanford University.

Ancient Wisdom, http://www.ancient-wisdom.com/americaprecolumbian.htm: Basic essays on pre-Columbian peoples and civilizations.

Chapter 7

Boyce, Mary. *A History of Zoroastrianism*. Vol. 1, *The Early Period*, rev. ed. Handbuch der Orientalistik. Leiden, the Netherlands: E. J. Brill, 1989. Standard work by the leading scholar on the subject.

Briant, Pierre. *From Cyrus to Alexander: A History of the Persian Empire*. Winona Lake, IN: Eisenbrauns, 2000. Monumental work; the most detailed and authoritative study of the topic to date.

Dignas, Beate, and Engelbert Winter. *Rome and Persia in Late Antiquity: Neighbours and Rivals*. Cambridge, UK: Cambridge University Press, 2007. Detailed historical investigation of the rivalry between Rome and Persia.

Freeman, Phillip. *Alexander the Great*. New York: Simon & Schuster, 2011. Illuminating study of Alexander the Great intended for a general audience.

Harper, Kyle. *The Fate of Rome: Climate, Disease, and the End of an Empire*. Princeton, NJ: Princeton University Press, 2017. Describes how a combination of climatic changes and the spread of epidemic diseases contributed to the fall of Rome.

Hubbard, Thomas K., ed. *A Companion to Greek and Roman Sexualities*. Chichester, UK: John Wiley & Sons, 2014. Far-ranging and informative collection of essays on all aspects of sexuality in ancient Greece and Rome.

Karanika, Andromache. *Voices at Work: Women, Performance, and Labor in Ancient Greece*. Baltimore: Johns Hopkins University Press, 2014. An analysis of ancient Greek work songs, primarily those of women, and how they were incorporated in assorted literary genres.

Lehoux, Daryn. *What Did the Romans Know? An Inquiry into Science and Worldmaking*. Chicago: University of Chicago Press, 2012. Sophisticated analysis of Roman science in both its derivative and unique aspects.

Mathisen, Ralph. *Ancient Mediterranean Civilizations: From Prehistory to 640 CE*, 2nd ed. Oxford and New York: Oxford University Press, 2014. Revised overview with special emphasis on ethnicity, gender, and slavery.

Shaked, Shaul. *Dualism in Transformation: Varieties of Religion in Sasanian Iran*. London: School of Oriental and African Studies, 1994. Short history of the different religions in Sasanid Persia.

Smith, Mark S. *The Early History of God: Yahweh and the Other Deities in Ancient Israel.* San Francisco: Harper & Row, 1990. Very readable introduction to the problem of early monotheism among Israelites.

WEBSITES

British Museum. Ancient Greece, http://www.ancientgreece.co.uk/menu.html. Open the door to the compelling world of Ancient Greece. The British Museum has compiled a collection of images and information on various aspects of Greek history such as the Acropolis, Athens, daily life, festivals and games, Sparta, war, and gods.

Harvard University. Digital Atlas of Roman and Medieval Civilizations, http://darmc.harvard.edu/icb/icb.do?keyword=k40248&pageid=icb.page188868. Harvard University allows students to tailor searches in order to access specific geopolitical and spatial cartographical representations of the Roman and medieval worlds.

Perseus Digital Library, http://www.perseus.tufts.edu/hopper/. Probably the largest website on Greece and Rome, with immense resources, hosted by Tufts University.

Chapter 8

Auboyer, Jeannine. *Daily Life in Ancient India.* London: Phoenix, 2002. Overview consisting of sections on social structures/religious principles, individual/collective existence, and royal and administrative existence. Multidisciplinary approach appropriate for most undergraduates.

Chakravarti, Uma. *The Social Dimensions of Early Buddhism.* New Delhi: Oxford University Press, 1987. Thorough analysis, with extensive glossary, of the influence of the north Indian economic transition to peasant market farming on the social milieu of early Buddhism.

Diem-Lane, Andrea. *Ahimsa: A Brief Guide to Jainism.* Walnut, CA: MSAC Philosophy Group, 2016. Short, student-friendly guide to Jain concepts, history, and Jainism today.

Doniger, Wendy. *The Hindus: An Alternative History.* New York: Penguin, 2009. Vivid but controversial new interpretation of the history of Hinduism by one of the leading scholars of Indian history. The book's portrayals of Hindu history, particularly in the area between myth and history, have prompted a lawsuit in India, which resulted in the withdrawal of the book there by the publisher in early 2014.

Embree, Ainslee T. *Sources of Indian Tradition,* 2 vols. 2nd ed. New York: Columbia University Press, 1988. The latest edition contains a number of new selections useful for the study of social relations in addition to the older religious material. As with all of the works in this series, the level of writing is sophisticated, though accessible; the overviews are masterly; and the works are ably translated.

Keay, John. *India: A History.* New York: Grove, 2000. Lively, highly detailed narrative history, with a number of useful charts and genealogies of ruling houses. Sympathetic treatment of controversial matters.

Knott, Kim. *Hinduism: A Very Short Introduction.* Oxford and New York: Oxford University Press, 1998. Sound, brief discussion of modern Hinduism and its formative influences. Asks provocative questions such as "What is a religion?" and "Is Hinduism something more than the Western conception of religion?"

Nikam, N. A., and Richard McKeon, eds. and trans. *The Edicts of Asoka.* Chicago: University of Chicago Press, 1959. Slim but useful volume for those interested in reading the entire collection of Ashoka's Pillar, Cave, and Rock Edicts. Short, accessible introduction.

Padoux, Andre. *The Hindu Tantric World: An Overview.* Chicago: University of Chicago Press, 2017. Erudite but accessible entre into the complex and often misunderstood field of Tantric studies. Padoux deals with definitions, ritual, sacred literature and its history down to the present. Best for undergraduates with some grounding in Hinduism.

Willis, Michael. *The Archaeology of Hindu Ritual.* Cambridge, UK: Cambridge University Press, 2009. Best utilized by experienced students, this book uses site archaeology, Sanskrit documents, and studies of ancient astronomy to plot the development of Hinduism under the Guptas and their use of it in statecraft as they created their vision of a universal empire.

Wolpert, Stanley. *A New History of India,* 6th ed. Oxford and New York: Oxford University Press, 2000. The standard introductory work to the long sweep of Indian history. Evenly divided between the period up to and including the Mughals and the modern era. Good coverage of geography and environment, as well as social and gender issues. Good select bibliography arranged by chapter; highly useful glossary of Indian terms.

WEBSITE

Digital Library of India, http://www.dli.ernet.in. This online resource, hosted by the Indian Institute of Science, Bangalore, contains primary and secondary sources not only for history but also for culture, economics, literature, and a host of other subjects.

Chapter 9

Henricks, Robert C., trans. *Lao-Tzu, Te-Tao Ching. A New Translation Based on the Recently Discovered Ma-wang-tui Texts.* New York: Ballantine Books, 1989. Some of the initial work done on the earliest extant Daoist texts, reinterpreting our understanding of philosophical Daoism.

Hinsch, Bret. *Women in Early Imperial China.* Lanham, MD: Rowman & Littlefield, 2002. Broad examination of the place of women, and transition of the place of women, during the crucial early Chinese dynasties.

Huang, Ray. *China: A Macro History.* Armonk, NY: M. E. Sharpe, 1997. Readable, entertaining, and highly useful one-volume history. Particularly good on the complex politics of the post-Han and Song–Yuan periods.

Keay, John. *China: A History*. New York: Basic Books, 2009. Adventurous and well-written general history of China from prehistory to the present. Especially good for students with some previous grounding in the essentials of Chinese history.

Lewis, Mark Edward. *The Early Chinese Empires: Qin and Han*. Cambridge, MA: Harvard University Press, 2007. Detailed exploration of the rise and adaptations of China's initial empires. Better for advanced students.

Qian, Sima. *Records of the Grand Historian*. Translated by Burton Watson. 3 vols., rev. ed. New York: Columbia University Press, 1993. Powerful translation of China's supreme historical work by one of its best interpreters. Includes material from the Qin and Han dynasties. Invaluable source for serious students.

Whitfield, Susan. *Silk, Slaves, and Stupas: Material Culture of the Silk Road*. Oakland: University of California Press, 2018. A work covering the latest scholarship on the people, objects, modes of travel, and societies along the various tracks that made up what later came to be called "The Silk Road."

Yao Xinzhong. *An Introduction to Confucianism*. Cambridge, UK: Cambridge University Press, 2000. Overview of the tradition of the *ru* as it evolved and its status today.

WEBSITES

Asian Topics for Asian Educators. "Defining 'Daoism': A Complex History," http://afe.easia.columbia.edu/cosmos/ort/daoism.htm. Looks at Daoism as a term, its use, and its practice in terms of morality, society, nature, and the self.

Chapter 10

The Arabian Nights. Translated by Husain Haddawy. New York: Norton, 1990. Based on the critical edition by Muhsin Mahdi, which reconstitutes the original thirteenth-century text.

Barry, Michael. *Figurative Art in Medieval Islam and the Riddle of Bihazâd of Herât (1465–1535)*. Paris: Flammarion, 2004.

Chaudhuri, K. N. *Trade and Civilization in the Indian Ocean*. Cambridge, UK: Cambridge University Press, 1985. Discusses the historical evolution of the trade and its various aspects (sea routes, ships, commodities, and capital investments).

Decker, Michael J. *The Byzantine Dark Ages*. London and New York: Bloomsbury Academic, 2016. The period of 600–900 CE is the least documented period in Byzantine history. This wide-ranging new study takes a fresh look at the urban, rural, and economic situation during this period on the basis of the available documentation, from written sources and numismatics to archaeological sites and ceramics.

Fryde, Edmund. *The Early Palaeologan Renaissance (1261–c. 1360)*. Leiden, the Netherlands: E. J. Brill, 2000. Detailed presentation of the main philosophical and scientific figures of Byzantium after the recovery from the Latin interruption.

Herrin, Judith. *Unrivalled Influence: Women and Empire in Byzantium*. Princeton, NJ: Princeton University Press, 2013. Detailed investigation by a leading Byzantine historian and engaged feminist.

Hoyland, Robert. *In God's Path: The Arab Conquests and the Creation of an Islamic Empire*. Oxford and New York: Oxford University Press, 2014. A new history of Islamic origins, seeking to combine Christian and Islamic sources.

Khalili, Jim al-. *The House of Wisdom: How Arabic Science Saved Ancient Knowledge and Gave Us the Renaissance*. New York: Penguin, 2010. In spite of the somewhat overwrought title, an expertly written introduction to the golden age of Arabic science by a scientist.

Laiou, Angeliki E., and Cécile Morrisson. *The Byzantine Economy*. Cambridge, UK: Cambridge University Press, 2007. Comprehensive and well-researched study of ups and downs in the demography, productive capacity, and long-distance trade of Byzantium.

Lapidus, Ira. *Muslim Cities in the Later Middle Ages*. Cambridge, UK: Cambridge University Press, 1984. Seminal work and still the only study of Muslim urban society, although it should be supplemented by Shlomo D. Goitein's monumental study of Jews, *A Mediterranean Society* (1967–1993).

Rippin, Andrew. *Muslims: Their Religious Beliefs and Practices*, 5th ed. London: Routledge, 2018. One of the best and most accessible introductions to the basic beliefs and practices of Islam, based on the re-evaluation of Islamic origins also presented in this chapter.

Tyerman, Christopher. *God's War: A New History of the Crusades*. Cambridge, MA: Belknap, 2006. Persuasive revisionist history by a leading Crusade historian.

WEBSITES

BBC—Religion: Islam. http://www.bbc.co.uk/religion/religions/islam/. A very basic overview of Islamic civilization. Most websites on Islam and Islamic civilization are apologetic (pro-Muslim or pro-Christian), and earlier scholarly websites are no longer available.

Islamic Awareness. http://www.islamic-awareness.org/. This website, even though Islam-apologetic, is a fountain of early documents relevant for Islamic history.

Chapter 11

Berend, Norma, Przemyslaw Urbanczlyk, and Przemyslaw Wiszewski. *Central Europe in the High Middle Ages: Bohemia, Hungary and Poland, ca. 900–ca. 1300*. New York: Cambridge University Press, 2013. Learned and insightful study that explores frequently overlooked aspects of medieval Europe.

Brown, Peter. *The Rise of Western Christendom: Triumph and Diversity, A.D. 200–1000*, Tenth Anniversary Revised Edition. Chichester, UK: John Wiley & Sons, Inc., 2013. Traces the development of Christian Europe from the perspective of the church.

Grant, Edward. *The Foundation of Modern Science in the Middle Ages*. Cambridge, UK: Cambridge University Press, 1996. Seminal study of the contributions of medieval science to the scientific revolution of the seventeenth century.

Jambroziak, Emilia. *The Cistercian Order in Medieval Europe, 1090–1520.* New York: Routledge, 2013. Presents new perspectives regarding the spread of Cistercians across Europe, with emphasis on their unique administrative policies.

König, Daniel G. *Arabic-Islamic Views of the Latin West: Tracing the Emergence of Medieval Europe.* New York: Oxford University Press, 2015. Challenges the traditional view of Bernard Lewis that Muslims considered Europe a backward and infantile culture.

Lawrence, C. H. *Medieval Monasticism: Forms of Religious Life in Western Europe in the Middle Ages,* 2nd ed. New York: Longman, 1984. Thorough survey of the development of the Western monastic tradition.

McKitterick, Rosamond. *Charlemagne: The Formation of a European Identity.* Cambridge, UK: Cambridge University Press, 2008. An examination of how Charlemagne's policies contributed to the idea of Europe.

Platt, Colin. *King Death: The Black Death and Its Aftermath in Late-Medieval England.* Toronto: University of Toronto Press, 1997. Riveting analysis of the effects of the Black Death on all aspects of society.

Riley-Smith, Jonathan, ed. *The Oxford Illustrated History of the Crusades.* Oxford and New York: Oxford University Press, 1995. A very useful and readable history of the crusading movement.

Turner, Denys. *Thomas Aquinas: A Portrait.* New Haven, CT: Yale University Press, 2013. Up-to-date biography of one of the greatest figures in medieval philosophy.

Wickham, Chris. *Medieval Europe.* New Haven, CT: Yale University Press, 2016. A scintillating and innovative study that presents new interpretations of important turning points in the development of medieval European civilization.

WEBSITES

British Library. Treasures in Full: Magna Carta, http://www.bl.uk/treasures/magnacarta/virtual_curator/vc9.html. An excellent website that makes available a digitized version of Magna Carta. Audio files answer many FAQs about the manuscript and its significance.

Chapter 12

Asif, Manan Ahmed. *A Book of Conquest: The Chachnama and Muslim Origins in South Asia.* Cambridge, MA: Harvard University Press, 2016. Comprehensive study of the pivotal story of deceit and conquest and the contentious legacy surrounding the initial Muslim forays into India.

Chiu-Duke, Josephine. *To Rebuild the Empire: Lu Chih's Confucian Pragmatist Approach to the Mid-Tang Predicament.* Albany, NY: SUNY Press, 2000. Political and philosophical study of one of the Tang era's most important prime ministers and his attempts to retrieve Tang fortunes and actions in the beginning of the period's Confucian revival.

De Bary, William T., and Irene Bloom, eds. *Sources of Chinese Tradition,* 2nd ed., vol. 1. New York: Columbia University Press, 1999. Excellent introduction to major Chinese philosophical schools. Extensive coverage of Buddhism and Neo-Confucianism with accessible, highly informative introductions to the documents themselves.

Ebrey, Patricia Buckley, ed. *The Inner Quarters.* Berkeley and Los Angeles: University of California Press, 1993. Perhaps the best scholarly exploration of the roles of women in Song China.

Hansen, Valerie. *The Open Empire: A History of China to 1600.* New York: W. W. Norton, 2000. A fresh and accessible synthesis of premodern Chinese history.

Lane, George. *A Short History of the Mongols.* London: I.B. Tauris, 2018. An introductory text as part of Tauris' Short Histories, this provides an excellent overview of the latest scholarship on the role of the Mongols in Asian and world history, while challenging commonly held views of the Mongols as simply ruthless conquerors.

Levathes, Louise.. *When China Ruled the Seas: The Treasure Fleet of the Dragon Throne 1405–1433.* New York: Simon & Schuster, 1994. Delightful coverage of the voyages of Zheng He from 1405 to 1433. Particularly good on the aftermath of the voyages.

Robinson, Francis. *Islam and Muslim History in South Asia.* Oxford and New York: Oxford University Press, 2004. Compendium of essays and reviews by the author on a variety of subjects concerning the history and status of Islam in the subcontinent. Of particular interest is his response to Samuel Huntington's famous "clash of civilizations" thesis.

Singh, Patwant. *The Sikhs.* London: John Murray, 1999. Readable popular history of the Sikh experience to the present by an adherent. Especially useful on the years from Guru Nanak to the changes of the early eighteenth century and the transition to a more militant faith.

WEBSITES

Asian Topics in World History. "The Mongols in World History," http://afe.easia.columbia.edu/mongols/. With a timeline spanning 1000–1500, "The Mongols in World History" delivers a concise and colorful history of the Mongols' impact on global history.

Fordham University. Internet Indian History Sourcebook, http://www.fordham.edu/halsall/india/indiasbook.asp. One of the series of online "sourcebooks" by Fordham containing links to important documents, secondary literature, and assorted other web resources.

Fordham University. Internet East Asian History Sourcebook, http://www.fordham.edu/halsall/eastasia/eastasiasbook.asp. As with its counterpart above, this is one in the series of useful online sources and links put together by Fordham, in this case about East Asia, with particular emphasis on the role of China as a center of cultural diffusion.

Chapter 13

General

Holcombe, Charles. *A History of East Asia, From the Origins of Civilization to the Twenty-First Century.* Cambridge, UK: Cambridge University Press, 2011. A top one-volume history of China, Korea, and Japan, with an emphasis on the region's shared past.

Mann, Susan. *East Asia (China, Korea, Japan)*. Washington, DC: American Historical Association, 1999. The second volume in the Women's and Gender History in Global Perspective series. Short, informative work with historiographic overviews and cross-cultural comparisons among the three countries named in the title. Critical annotated bibliographies on the use of standard texts in integrating women and gender into Asian studies.

Neuman, W. Lawrence. *East Asian Societies*. Ann Arbor, MI: Association For Asian Studies, 2014. Part of the AAS's "Key Issues in Asian Studies," this provides a short, accessible introduction to the region for beginning students.

Ramusack, Barbara N., and Sharon Sievers. *Women in Asia*. Bloomington: Indiana University Press, 1999. Part of the series Restoring Women to History. Far-ranging book divided into two parts, "Women in South and Southeast Asia" and "Women in East Asia." Coverage of individual countries, extensive chronologies, valuable bibliographies. Most useful for advanced undergraduates.

Korea

De Bary, William T., ed. *Sources of Korean Tradition*, vol. 1. Introduction to Asian Civilizations. New York: Columbia University Press, 1997. Part of the renowned Columbia series on the great traditions of East Asia. Perhaps the most complete body of accessible sources for undergraduates.

Korean Overseas Information Service. *A Handbook of Korea*. Seoul: KOIS, 1993. Wonderfully complete history, geography, guidebook, and sociology text. Excellent source, but students should keep in mind its provenance and treat some of its historical claims to uniqueness accordingly.

Seth, Michael J. *A Concise History of Korea*. 2nd ed. Lanham, MD: Rowman and Littlefield, 2016. Well-researched and comprehensive history of the Korean peninsula from Neolithic times to 2016. Covers both North and South Korea, though the South comes in for the most detailed treatment.

Japan

De Bary, William T., ed. *Sources of Japanese Tradition*, vol. 1. *Introduction to Asian Civilizations*. 2nd ed. New York: Columbia University Press, 2002. Like the volume above on Korea and the others in this series on India and China, the sources are well selected, the glossaries are sound, and the overviews of the material are masterful. As with the other East Asia volumes, the complexities of the various Buddhist schools are especially well drawn. Students with some previous experience will derive the most benefit from this excellent volume.

Murasaki Shikibu. *The Tale of Genji*. Dennis Washburn, trans. New York: W. W. Norton, 2015. The latest of only four complete translations of this classic into English, it is notable for its clarity, accessibility, literal accuracy to the source material, and literary quality.

Totman, Conrad. *A History of Japan*. Oxford, UK: Blackwell, 2000. Part of Blackwell's History of the World series. A large, well-balanced, and comprehensive history. More than half of the material is on the pre-1867 period, with extensive coverage of social history and demographics.

Vietnam

Steinberg, Joel David, ed. *In Search of Southeast Asia*, rev. ed. Honolulu: University of Hawaii Press, 1987. Extensive coverage of Vietnam within the context of an area study of Southeast Asia. Though weighted toward the modern period, very good coverage of agricultural and religious life in the opening chapters.

Taylor, Keith W. *The Birth of Vietnam*. Berkeley and Los Angeles: University of California Press, 1983. Comprehensive, magisterial volume on early Vietnamese history and historical identity amid the long Chinese occupation. Best for students with some background in Southeast Asian and Chinese history.

WEBSITES

https://www.britishmuseum.org/collection/search?keyword=asian&keyword=studies Department of Prints and Drawings, British Museum,. A comprehensive source for all manner of interests related to Asian studies.

Public Broadcasting Service, Hidden Korea, http://www.pbs.org/hiddenkorea/history.htm. Sound introduction to the geography, people, history and culture of Korea, with links to additional source material.

Chapter 14

Berzock, Kathleen, ed. *Caravans of Gold, Fragments in Time: Art, Culture, and Exchange Across Medieval Saharan Africa*. Princeton, NJ: Princeton University Press, 2019. Richly illustrated catalogue of an exhibit by the Block Museum of Art, Northwestern University, with wide-ranging articles by international scholars.

Birmingham, David, and Phyllis M. Martin, eds. *History of Central Africa*, vol. 1. London: Longman, 1983. The first chapter, by Birmingham, provides an excellent summary of the history of Luba prior to 1450.

Collins, Robert O., and James M. Burns. *A History of Subsaharan Africa*, 2nd ed. Cambridge: Cambridge University Press, 2014. Authoritative history by two well-known Africanists, updated by Burns after the death of Collins.

Crummey, David. *Land and Society in the Christian Kingdom of Ethiopia: From the Thirteenth to the Twentieth Century*. Urbana: University of Illinois Press, 2000. The first book in which the rich land records of the church have been used for a reconstruction of agriculture and land tenure.

Gomez, Michael A. *African Dominion: A New History of Empire in Early and Medieval West Africa*. Princeton, NJ: Princeton University Press, 2018. A detailed new history of West Africa during its imperial period, based on new documents from archives in Timbuktu and Jenné as well as the traditional written sources. The author sets new standards following the previous work by Nehemia Levtzion.

Horton, Mark, and John Middleton. *The Swahili: The Social Landscape of a Mercantile Society*. Oxford, UK: Blackwell, 2000. A study that gives full attention to the larger context of East Africa in which the Swahilis flourished. Middleton is the author of another important study, *The World of the Swahili: An African Mercantile Civilization* (Yale University Press, 1992).

Huffman, Thomas. *Palaces of Stone: Uncovering Ancient Southern African Kingdoms*. Capetown and Johannesburg: Penguin Random House South Africa, 2020. Definitive study of the precolonial southern African kingdoms by their foremost archaeologist.

Ruffini, Giovanni. *Medieval Nubia: A Social and Economic History*. Oxford and New York: Oxford University Press, 2012. Revisionist history based on new sources, arguing for the existence of a sophisticated money economy.

WEBSITES

Heilbrunn Timeline of Art History, Ife (from ca. 350 B.C.): http://www.metmuseum.org/toah/hd/ife/hd_ife.htm. An excellent introductory website hosted by the Metropolitan Museum of Art. It contains many links and presents clear overviews.

Ancient History Encyclopedia, https://www.ancient.eu/article/1383/the-gold-trade-of-ancient--medieval-west-africa/. Focuses on the gold trade, with excellent summaries on the kingdoms and empires.

Chapter 15

Bruhns, Karen Olsen, and Karen E. Stothert. *Women in Ancient America*. Norman: University of Oklahoma Press, 2nd ed. 2014. Comprehensive account of women's role in daily life, religion, politics, and war in forager and agrarian–urban societies.

Carrasco, Davíd. *The Aztecs: A Very Short Introduction*. Oxford and New York: Oxford University Press, 2012. Clear, compressed account by a specialist, containing all essential information.

D'Altroy, Terence. *The Incas*. 2nd ed. Hoboken, NJ: John Wiley and Sons, 2014. Well-organized and comprehensive overview by a leading anthropologist.

Hassig, Ross. *War and Society in Ancient Mesoamerica*. Berkeley and Los Angeles: University of California Press, 1992. Best study of the rising importance of militarism in Mesoamerican city-states, up to the Aztec Empire.

Kelly, John, and James A. Brown. *Cahokia: City of the Cosmos*. Cowley Road, UK, and Casemate Books, Haverton, PA: Oxbow Books Limited, 2020. Archaeological and anthropological study of this important early North American site, assembling the most recent research.

Malpass, Michael A. *Daily Life in the Inca Empire*, 2nd ed. Westport, CT: Greenwood, 2009. Clear, straightforward, and readable account of ordinary people's lives by a specialist.

Smith, Michael E., *The Aztecs*, 3rd ed. Hoboken, NJ: Wiley, 2013. Up-to-date, extensive account of all aspects of Inca history and civilization.

Townsend, Camilla. *Fifth Sun: A New History of the Aztecs*. Oxford and New York: Oxford University Press, 2019. This revisionist study makes full use of the so-called yearly accounts, or annals, composed by Aztecs in Nahuatl in an effort to overcome the one-sided perspective of the Spanish conquerors.

WEBSITE

Aztec history: *Aztec-History*, http://www.aztec-history.com/. Introductory website, easily navigable, with links.

Inca history: *Ancient History Encyclopedia*, https://www.ancient.eu/Inca_Civilization. Informed, well-written summaries.

Chapter 16

Ágoston, Gábor. *Guns for the Sultan: Military Power and the Weapons Industry in the Ottoman Empire*. Cambridge, UK: Cambridge University Press, 2005. Thorough study, which is based on newly accessible Ottoman archival materials and emphasizes the technological prowess of Ottoman gunsmiths.

Casale, Giancarlo. *The Ottoman Age of Exploration*. Oxford and New York: Oxford University Press, 2010. Detailed correction, based on Ottoman and Portuguese archives, of the traditional characterization of the Ottoman Empire as a land-oriented power.

Casey, James. *Early Modern Spain: A Social History*. London: Routledge, 1999. Detailed, well-documented analysis of rural–urban and king–nobility tensions.

Elliott, John Huxtable. *Spain, Europe, and the Wider World: 1500–1800*. New Haven, CT: Yale University Press, 2009. A comprehensive overview, particularly strong on culture during the 1500s.

Fichtner, Paula Sutter. *Terror and Tolerations: The Habsburg Empire Confronts Islam, 1526–1850*. London: Reaktion, 2008. A revisionist perspective of relationships between Habsburgs and Ottomans.

Glete, Jan. *War and the State in Early Modern Europe: Spain, the Dutch Republic, and Sweden as Fiscal–Military States, 1500–1660*. London: Routledge, 2002. A complex but persuasive construction of the forerunner to the absolute state. Unfortunately leaves out the Ottoman Empire.

Murphey, Rhoads. *Ottoman Warfare, 1500–1700*. New Brunswick, NJ: Rutgers University Press, 1999. Author presents a vivid picture of the Janissaries, their discipline, organization, campaigns, and voracious demands for salary increases.

Pamuk, Sevket. *A Monetary History of the Ottoman Empire*. Cambridge, UK: Cambridge University Press, 2000. Superb analysis of Ottoman archival resources on the role and function of American silver in the money economy of the Ottomans.

Phillips, William D., Jr., and Carla Rhan Phillips. *The Worlds of Christopher Columbus*. New York: Cambridge University

Press, 1992. A biographical study of Columbus, emphasizing the establishment of global interconnections resulting from his voyages

Ruiz, Teofilo R. *Spanish Society, 1400–1600.* London: Longman, 2001. Richly detailed social studies rewarding anyone interested in changing class structures, rural–urban movement, and extension of the money market into the countryside.

Subrahmanyam, Sanjay. *The Career and Legend of Vasco da Gama.* Cambridge, UK: Cambridge University Press, 1997. Focuses on the religious motivations of Vasco da Gama and the commercial impact of his journey to India.

WEBSITES

Frontline, "Apocalypse! The Evolution of Apocalyptic Belief and How It Shaped the Western World," *PBS*, 1995, http://www.pbs.org/wgbh/pages/frontline/shows/apocalypse/. The contribution by Bernard McGinn, University of Chicago, under the heading of "Apocalypticism Explained: Joachim of Fiore," is of particular relevance for the understanding of Christopher Columbus viewing himself as a precursor of Christ's Second Coming.

Islam: Empire of Faith: Timeline, http://www.pbs.org/empires/islam/timeline.html. Comprehensive and informative, this PBS website on the Ottoman Empire examines various facets of this Islamic culture, such as scientific innovations, faith, and leaders.

Chapter 17

Biro, Jacquelin. *On Earth as in Heaven: Cosmography and the Shape of the Earth from Copernicus to Descartes.* Saarbrücken, Germany: VDM Verlag Dr. Müller, 2009. Short study establishing the connection between geography and cosmology in Copernicus. Uses the pathbreaking articles by Thomas Goldberg.

Black, Jeremy. *Kings, Nobles, and Commoners: States and Societies in Early Modern Europe—A Revisionist History.* London: I. B. Tauris, 2004. Available also electronically on ebrary; persuasive thesis, largely accepted by scholars, of a continuity of institutional practices in Europe across the sixteenth and seventeenth centuries, casting doubt on absolutism as being more than a theory.

Cañizares-Esguerra, Jorge. *Nature, Empire, and Nation: Explorations of the History of Science in the Iberian World.* Stanford, CA: Stanford University Press, 2006. A collection of essays that provides new perspectives on the history of science in early modern Iberia.

Geanakoplos, Deno John. *Constantinople and the West: Essays on the Late Byzantine (Palaeologan) and Italian Renaissances and the Byzantine and Roman Churches.* Madison: University of Wisconsin Press, 1989. Fundamental discussion of the extensive transfer of texts and scholars during the 1400s.

Jacob, Margaret C. and Larry Stewart. *Practical Matter: Newton's Science in the Service of Industry and Empire, 1687–1851.* Cambridge, MA: Harvard University Press, 2004. An interesting and important description of interconnections between Newtonian sciences and eighteenth-century industrial developments.

Margolis, Howard. *It Started with Copernicus: How Turning the World Inside Out Led to the Scientific Revolution.* New York: McGraw-Hill, 2002. Important scholarly study of the connection between the discovery of the Americas and Copernicus's formulation of a sun-centered planetary system.

Nexon, Daniel H. *The Struggle for Power in Early Modern Europe: Religious Conflict, Dynastic Empires and International Change.* Princeton, NJ: Princeton University Press, 2009. Charles Tilly–inspired re-evaluation of the changes occurring in sixteenth- and seventeenth-century Europe.

Park, Katharine, and Lorraine Daston, eds. *The Cambridge History of Science. Vol. 3, Early Modern Science.* Cambridge, UK: Cambridge University Press, 2006. Voluminous coverage of all aspects of science, under the currently paradigmatic thesis that there was no dramatic scientific revolution in Western Christian civilization.

Roper, Lyndal. *Martin Luther: Renegade and Prophet.* New York: Random House, 2017. A brilliant study of Luther's multifaceted and coarse character and personality.

Schiebinger, Londa. *The Mind Has No Sex? Women in the Origins of Modern Science.* Cambridge, MA: Harvard University Press, 1989. A pioneering study presenting biographies and summaries of scientific contributions made by women. Discusses the importance of Maria Cunitz.

Wiesner-Hanks, Merry E. *Early Modern Europe, 1450–1789.* 2nd ed. Cambridge, UK: Cambridge University Press, 2013. Textbook in the Cambridge History of Europe series with a broad coverage of topics.

WEBSITES

Ames Research Center. "Johannes Kepler: His Life, His Laws and Times," http://kepler.nasa.gov/Mission/JohannesKepler/. This NASA website looks at the life and views of Johannes Kepler. It examines his discoveries, his contemporaries, and the events that shaped modern science.

Howard, Sharon. "Early Modern Resources," http://sharonhoward. org/earlymodern.html. Website with many links on the full range of institutional and cultural change.

Chapter 18

Alchon, Suzanne A. *A Pest in the Land: New World Epidemics in a Global Perspective.* Albuquerque: University of New Mexico Press, 2003. A broad overview, making medical history comprehensible.

Behringer, Wolfgang. *Witches and Witch-Hunts: A Global History.* Cambridge, UK: Polity, 2004. A well-grounded overview of the phenomenon of the fear of witches, summarizing the scholarship of the past decades.

Bulmer-Thomas, Victor, John S. Coatsworth, and Roberto Cortés Conde, eds. *The Cambridge Economic History of Latin America. Vol. 1, The Colonial Era and the Short*

Nineteenth Century. Cambridge, UK: Cambridge University Press, 2006. Collection of specialized summary articles on aspects of Iberian colonialism.

Eastman, Scott, *Preaching Spanish Nationalism across the Hispanic Atlantic, 1759–1823*. Baton Rouge: Louisiana State University Press, 2012. Close look at the national reform debates in the Iberian Atlantic world at the close of colonialism.

Ekberg, Carl J. *French Roots in the Illinois Country: The Mississippi Frontier in Colonial Times*. Urbana: University of Illinois Press, 1998. Detailed, deeply researched historical account.

Peloso, Vincent. *Race and Ethnicity in Latin America*. Milton Park and New York: Routledge, 2014. Excellent presentation of the publicly enshrined, complex racial and ethnic identities during colonialism and since independence.

Restall, Matthew, and Kris Lane. *Latin America in Colonial Times*, 2nd ed. Cambridge, UK: Cambridge University Press, 2018. This study offers a new social and cultural focus not only of the European settlers but also of the conquered Amerindian population. Clear and engagingly written narrative.

Richter, Daniel K. *Facing East from Indian Country: A Native History of Early America*. Cambridge, MA: Harvard University Press, 2003. One of the few, and still unsurpassed, scholarly books that seeks to understand early modern North American history from the Native American perspective.

Socolow, Susan M. *The Women of Latin America*. Cambridge, UK: Cambridge University Press, 2nd ed. 2015. Surveys the patriarchal order and the function of women within it.

Stein, Stanley J., and Barbara H. Stein. *Silver, Trade, and War: Spain and America in the Making of Early Modern Europe*. Baltimore: Johns Hopkins University Press, 2000. Covers the significance of American silver reaching as far as China.

Taylor, Alan. *American Colonies*. London: Penguin, 2001. History of the English colonies in New England, written from a broad Atlantic perspective.

WEBSITE

Conquistadors, http://www.pbs.org/conquistadors/. Interactive website that allows you to track the journeys made by the Conquistadors such as Cortés, Pizarro, Orellana, and Cabeza de Vaca. Learn more about their conquests in the Americas and the legacy they left behind them.

Chapter 19

Carney, Judith A. *Black Rice: The African Origins of Rice Cultivation in the Americas*. Cambridge, MA: Harvard University Press, 2001. Study which goes a long way toward correcting the stereotype that black slaves were unskilled laborers, and carefully documents the transfer of rice-growing culture from West Africa to the Americas.

Dubois, Laurent, and Julius S. Scott, eds. *Origins of the Black Atlantic: Rewriting Histories*. New York: Routledge, 2010. Book that focuses on African slaves in the Americas as they had to arrange themselves in their new lives.

Gray, Richard, and David Birmingham, eds. *Pre-Colonial African Trade*. London and New York: Oxford University Press, 1970. Collective work in which contributors emphasize the growth and intensification of trade in the centuries of 1500–1800.

Hall, Gwendolyn Midlo. *Slavery and African Ethnicities in the Americas: Restoring the Links*. Chapel Hill: University of North Carolina Press, 2005. Study that focuses on slaves in the Americas according to their regions of origin in Africa.

Heywood, Linda M., and John K. Thornton. *Central Africans, Atlantic Creoles, and the Foundation of the Americas*. Cambridge, UK: Cambridge University Press, 2007. Pathbreaking investigation of the creation and role of Creole culture in Africa and the Americas.

Iliffe, John. *Africans: The History of a Continent*. 3rd ed. Cambridge, UK: Cambridge University Press, 2015. Standard historical summary by an established African historian.

Kriger, Colleen E. *Cloth in West African History*. Lanham, MD: Altamira, 2006. Detailed investigation of the sophisticated indigenous West African cloth industry.

LaGamma, Alisa. *Kongo: Power and Majesty*. New York: Metropolitan Museum of Art, 2015. Superbly illustrated exhibition catalogue, with articles by leading Africanists.

Lovejoy, Paul E. *Slavery in the Global Diaspora of Africa*. London and New York: Routledge, 2019. Discussion of the impact of the slave trade on migration, social structures, women and children from a West African perspective. The author is one of the foremost authorities on black slavery in Africa and the Americas.

Oliver, Roland, and Anthony Atmore. *Medieval Africa, 1250–1800*. Cambridge, UK: Cambridge University Press, 2001. Revised and updated historical overview, divided into regions and providing detailed regional histories on the emerging kingdoms.

Stapleton, Timothy J. *A Military History of Africa. Vol. 1, The Precolonial Period: From Ancient Egypt to the Zulu Kingdom (Earliest Times to ca. 1870)*. Santa Barbara, CA: Praeger, 2013. Summary of the historical evolution of West, East, Central, and South Africa.

Thornton, John. *The Kongolese Saint Anthony: Dona Beatriz Kimpa Vita and the Antonian Movement, 1684–1706*. Cambridge, UK: Cambridge University Press, 1998. Detailed biography of Dona Beatriz, from which the vignette at the beginning of the chapter is borrowed; includes a general overview of the history of Kongo during the civil war.

WEBSITE

Early modern African history: *South African History Online*, https://www.sahistory.org.za/. Website with a broad range of topics.

Chapter 20

Bernier, François. *Travels in the Mogul Empire, A.D. 1656–1668*. Translated by Archibald Constable. Delhi: S. Chand, 1968.

One of many fascinating travel accounts by European diplomats, merchants, and missionaries.

Eaton, Richard M. *Essays on Islam and Indian History*. Oxford and New York: Oxford University Press, 2002. A compendium of the new scholarly consensus on, among other things, the differences between the clerical view of Islamic observance and its actual impact in rural India. Contains both historiography and material on civilizational and cultural issues.

Gommans, J. J. L. *Mughal Warfare: Indian Frontiers and Highroads to Empire 1500–1700*. New York: Routledge, 2002. Sound examination of the Mughal Empire as a centralizing state increasingly reliant on a strong military for border defense and extending its sway. Examination of the structure of Mughal forces and the organization and weapons of the military.

Hunt, Margaret R., and Philip J. Stern, eds. *The English East India Company at the Height of Mughal Expansion: A Soldier's Diary of the 1689 Siege of Bombay with Related Documents*. Boston and New York: Bedford/St. Martin's, 2016. Illuminating look at the interplay of Mughal and European actors during the reign of Aurangzeb through the eyes of James Hilton, an English East India Company soldier, whose diary had previously been unpublished.

Nizami, Khaliq A. *Akbar and Religion*. Delhi: IAD, 1989. Extensive treatment of Akbar's evolving move toward devising his *din-i ilahi* movement, by a leading scholar of Indian religious and intellectual history.

Palat, Ravi. *The Making of an Indian Ocean World-Economy, 1250–1650*. New York: Palgrave Macmillan, 2015. This work seeks to break out of proto-capitalist perspectives of noncapitalist countries and instead sees much of the Indian Ocean system growing from the "paddy fields and bazaars" named in the subtitle, which provided a rich agricultural environment that stimulated "commercialization without capitalism."

Richards, John F. *The Mughal Empire*. Cambridge, UK: Cambridge University Press, 1993. Comprehensive volume in the New Cambridge History of India series. Sophisticated treatment; best suited to advanced students. Extensive glossary and useful bibliographic essay.

Sen, Siddhartha. *Colonizing, Decolonizing, and Globalizing Kolkata: From a Colonial to a Post-Marxist City*. Amsterdam: Amsterdam University Press, 2017. Centered on the urban history of Kolkata (Calcutta) as the nexus of British imperial rule and since independence, it examines areas of contested identity, particularly in the city's architecture and material culture.

Schimmel, Annemarie. *The Empire of the Great Mughals: History, Art, and Culture*. London: Reaktion, 2004. Revised edition of a volume published in German in 2000. Lavish illustrations, wonderfully drawn portraits of key individuals, and extensive treatment of social, family, and gender relations at the Mughal court.

WEBSITE

Association for Asian Studies, http://www. asian-studies.org/ As with other Asian topics, one of the most reliable websites is sponsored by the Association for Asian Studies, the largest professional organization for scholars of Asia.

Chapter 21

China

Crossley, Pamela K. *A Translucent Mirror: History and Identity in Qing Imperial Ideology*. Los Angeles: University of California Press, 1999. Pioneering study of the transformation of Qing self-image to one of leading a universal, multicultural empire.

De Bary, William T., and Irene Bloom, comps. *Sources of Chinese Tradition*, 2 vols., 2nd ed. New York: Columbia University Press, 1999. Thoroughgoing update of the classic sourcebook for Chinese literature and philosophy, with a considerable amount of social, family, and women's works now included.

Mungello, D. E. *The Great Encounter of China and West*. Lanham, MD: Rowman & Littlefield, 1999. Sound historical overview of the period marking the first European maritime expeditions into East Asia and extending to the height of the Canton trade and the beginnings of the opium era.

Pomeranz, Kenneth. *The Great Divergence: China, Europe, and the Making of the Modern World Economy*. Princeton, NJ: Princeton University Press, 2001. Pathbreaking work mounting the strongest argument yet in favor of the balance of economic power remaining in East Asia until the Industrial Revolution was well under way.

Shuo Wang. "Manchu Women in Transition: Gender Relations and Sexuality," in Stephen A. Wadley and Carsten Naeher, eds. *Proceedings of the First North American Conference on Manchu Studies*. Wiesbaden, Germany: Otto Harrassowitz, 2006: 105–130. Pathbreaking study of the role of Manchu women in Qing China in resistance to assimilation and preserving cultural identity.

Spence, Jonathan. *The Memory Palace of Matteo Ricci*. New York: Penguin, 1984. Highly original treatment of Ricci and the beginning of the Jesuit interlude in late Ming and early Qing China that attempts to penetrate Ricci's world through the missionary's own memory techniques.

Japan

De Bary, William T., ed. *Sources of Japanese Tradition*, 2 vols. New York: Columbia University Press, 1964. The Tokugawa era spans volumes 1 and 2, with its inception and political and philosophical foundations thoroughly covered in volume 1 and the Shinto revival of national learning, the later Mito school, and various partisans of national unity in the face of foreign intrusion covered in the beginning of volume 2.

Gordon, Andrew. *A Modern History of Japan from Tokugawa Times to the Present*. Oxford and New York: Oxford University Press, 2009. One of the few treatments of Japanese history that spans both the Tokugawa and the modern eras, rather than making the usual break in either 1853 or 1867/1868. Both the continuity of the past and the novelty of the new era are therefore juxtaposed and highlighted. Most useful for students with a background at least equivalent to that supplied by this text.

Lippit, Yukio, ed. *The Artist in Edo*. Washington, DC: National Gallery of Art and New Haven: Yale University Press, 2018. Compendium volume of essays by Japanese and Western scholars on contemporary issues surrounding the role of art, politics, and aesthetics in Tokugawa Japan. Useful for students with some grounding in the era.

WEBSITE

Zheng He. https://exploration.marinersmuseum.org/subject/zheng-he/. Good capsule history of the Chinese mariner with sources.

Chapter 22

Hardman, John. *Louis XVI*. New Haven: Yale University Press. 1993. An insightful analysis of Louis XVI from the perspective of his inner self—his strange preoccupation with minutiae rather than the impending revolution.

Herb, Guntram H. *Nations and Nationalism: A Global Historical Overview*. Santa Barbara, CA: ABC-Clio, 2008. Contains a large number of articles on the varieties of ethnic nationalism and culture and the proliferation of nationalism in Europe and Latin America.

Israel, Jonathan I. *A Revolution of the Mind: Radical Enlightenment and the Origins of Modern Democracy*. Princeton, NJ: Princeton University Press, 2010. Israel is a pioneer of the contemporary renewal of intellectual history, and his investigations of the Enlightenment tradition are pathbreaking.

Kaiser, Thomas E., and Dale K. Van Kley, eds. *From Deficit to Deluge: The Origins of the French Revolution*. Stanford, CA: Stanford University Press, 2011. Thoughtful re-evaluation of the scholarly field that takes into account the latest interpretations.

Kitchen, Martin. *A History of Modern Germany: 1800 to the Present*. Hoboken, NJ: Wiley-Blackwell, 2011. A broadly conceived historical overview, ranging from politics and economics to culture.

Osterhammel, Jürgen. *The Transformation of the World: A Global History of the Nineteenth Century*. Princeton, NJ: 2015. Celebrated evaluation of the myriads of changes and transformations characterizing the nineteenth century.

Rakove, Jack. *Revolutionaries: A New History of the Invention of America*. Boston: Houghton Mifflin, 2010. A new narrative history focusing on the principal figures in the revolution.

Riall, Lucy. *Risorgimento: The History of Italy from Napoleon to Nation-State*. New York: Palgrave Macmillan, 2009. Historical summary, incorporating the research of the past half-century, presented in a clear overview.

Suchet, John. *Beethoven: The Man Revealed*. New York: Atlantic Monthly Press, 2012. A fascinating biographical study of Beethoven's personal struggles.

West, Elliott. *The Last Indian War: The Nez Perce Story*. Oxford and New York: Oxford University Press, 2009. Vivid story of the end of the US wars for the subjugation of the Native Americans.

Wood, Gordon S. *The American Revolution: A History*. New York: Modern Library, 2002. A short, readable summary reflective of many decades of revisionism in the discussion of the American Revolution.

WEBSITES

Liberty, Equality, Fraternity: Exploring the French Revolution, http://chnm.gmu.edu/revolution/. This website boasts 250 images, 350 text documents, 13 songs, 13 maps, and a timeline all focused on the French Revolution.

Nationalism Project, http://www.nationalismproject.org/. A large website with links to bibliographies, essays, new books, and book reviews.

Chapter 23

Adelman, Jeremy. *Sovereignty and Revolution in the Iberian Atlantic*, Princeton, NJ: Princeton University Press, 2006. A leading study in a group of recent works on the transatlantic character of colonial and postcolonial Latin America.

Bulmer-Thomas, Victor. *The Economic History of Latin America since Independence*, 2nd ed. Cambridge, UK: Cambridge University Press, 2003. A highly analytical and sympathetic investigation of the Latin American export and self-sufficiency economies, calling into question the long-dominant dependency theories of Latin America.

Burkholder, Mark, and Lyman Johnson. *Colonial Latin America*, 6th ed. New York: Oxford University Press, 2008. Overview, with focus on social and cultural history.

Dawson, Alexander. *Latin America since Independence: A History with Primary Sources*. New York: Routledge, 2011. Selection of topics with documentary base; for the nineteenth century, covers the topics of the nation-state, caudillo politics, race, and the policy of growth through commodity exports.

Drake, Paul W. *Between Tyranny and Anarchy: A History of Democracy in Latin America*. Stanford, CA: Stanford University Press, 2009. The author traces the concepts of constitutionalism, autocracy, and voting rights since independence in clear and persuasive strokes.

Dupuy, Alex. *Rethinking the Haitian Revolution: Slavery, Independence, and the Struggle for Recognition*. Lanham, MD, Boulder, CO, New York, and London: Rowman and Littlefield, 2019. Ambitious effort by a sociologist to view the Haitian Revolution within the framework of early modern capitalism and the European, Hegelian-inspired ideology of races.

Girard, Philippe. *Toussaint Louverture: A Revolutionary Life*. New York: Basic Books, 2016. The most recent biography of the pioneer of Haiti's independence, written by the leading biographer of Toussaint.

Hämäläinen, Pekka. *The Comanche Empire*. New Haven, CT: Yale University Press, 2008. A revisionist account that puts the extraordinary importance of the Comanche empire for the history of Mexico and the United States in the nineteenth century into the proper perspective.

Moya, Jose C., ed. *The Oxford Handbook of Latin American History*. Oxford and New York: Oxford University Press, 2011. Important collection of political, social, economic, and cultural essays by leading specialists on nineteenth-century Latin America.

Sabato, Hilda. *Republics of the New World: The Revolutionary Political Experiment in Nineteenth-Century Latin America*. Princeton, NJ: Princeton University Press, 2018. Explores the specifically Latin American conditions for the development of a republican tradition.

Sanders, James E. *Vanguard of the Atlantic World: Creating Modernity, Nation, and Democracy in Nineteenth-Century Latin America*. Durham, NC: Duke University Press, 2014. Ambitious effort to evaluate the Latin American contributions to the creation of the modern state.

Sater, William F. *Andean Tragedy: Fighting the War of the Pacific, 1879–1884*. Lincoln: University of Nebraska Press, 2007. Close examination of this destructive war on the South American west coast.

Skidmore, Thomas. *Brazil: Five Centuries of Change*, 2nd ed. Oxford and New York: Oxford University Press, 2010. Short but magisterial text on the history of Brazil, with a detailed chapter on Brazil's path toward independence in the nineteenth century.

Wright, Thomas C. *Latin America since Independence: Two Centuries of Continuity and Change*. Lanham, MD, Boulder, CO, New York, and London: Rowman and Littlefield, 2017. A clearly written text on the five legacies of authoritarianism, social hierarchy, Catholicism, economic dependency, and landownership.

WEBSITE

Latin American Independence: *Macro History: World History*, http://www.fsmitha.com/h3/h36-2gr.html. Essays on independence from Spain and Portugal.

Chapter 24

China

Cohen, Paul. *Discovering History in China*. New York: Columbia University Press, 1984. Pivotal work on the historiography of American writers on China. Critiques their collective ethnocentrism in attempting to fit Chinese history into Western perspectives and approaches.

Fairbank, John K., and Su-yu Teng. *China's Response to the West*. Cambridge, MA: Harvard University Press, 1954. Though dated in approach, still a vitally important collection of sources in translation for the period from the late eighteenth century till 1923.

Meyer-Fong, Tobie. *What Remains: Coming to Terms with Civil War in 19th Century China*. Stanford, CA: Stanford University Press, 2013. Extensive treatment of individual experiences during the world's bloodiest civil war, the Taiping Rebellion.

Platt, Stephen R. *Autumn in the Heavenly Kingdom*. New York: Knopf, 2012. Reinterpretation of the Taiping era as global political and economic phenomena involving the curtailing of US cotton exports during its civil war, the effects on the British textile industry, and the loss of Chinese markets during the Taiping Rebellion.

Shan, Patrick Fuliang. *Yuan Shikai: A Reappraisal*. Vancouver: University of British Columbia Press, 2018. While Yuan is best remembered for his failed presidency of the Chinese Republic and last-minute attempt to revive the imperial government, Shan's study gives us a far more nuanced picture of his role as diplomat and military reformer.

Spence, Jonathan D. *The Search for Modern China*. New York: Norton, 1990. Extensive, far-reaching interpretation of the period from China's nineteenth-century decline in the face of Western imperialism, through its revolutionary era, and finally to its recent bid for global preeminence.

Japan

Keene, Donald. *Emperor of Japan: Meiji and His World, 1852–1912*. New York: Columbia University Press, 2002. Masterly treatment of Japan's modernizing emperor and his vast influence on Japan and Asia, by one of the twentieth century's finest translators and scholars of Japan.

Reischauer, Edwin O., and Albert M. Craig. *Japan: Tradition and Transformation*. Boston: Houghton Mifflin, 1989. Somewhat dated but still highly useful introductory text by two of the twentieth century's leading scholars of Japanese history.

Totman, Conrad. *Politics in the Tokugawa Bakufu, 1600–1843*. Berkeley: University of California Press, 1988. Updated edition of Totman's breakthrough 1967 work. It remains one of the few highly detailed and deeply sourced monographs on the inner workings of the Tokugawa shogunate.

Walthall, Anne, and M. William Steele, *Politics and Society in Japan's Meiji Restoration: A Brief History with Documents*. New York: Bedford/St. Martin's, 2016. As with others in this series, a sound introduction for students with little or no background in the subject, accompanied by well-chosen documents.

WEBSITES

Association for Asian Studies, http://www.asian-studies.org/. This website of the Association for Asian Studies has links to sources more suited to advanced term papers and seminar projects.

Education about Asia, http://www.asian-studies.org/eaa/. This site provides the best online sources for modern Chinese and Japanese history.

Sino-Japanese War 1894–5, http://sinojapanesewar.com/. Packed with maps, photographs and movies depicting the conflict between Japan and China at the end of the nineteenth century; students can learn more about causes and consequences of the Sino–Japanese War.

Chapter 25

Brisku, Adrian. *Political Reform in the Ottoman and Russian Empires: A Comparative Approach*. London, Oxford,

New York, New Delhi, and Sydney: Bloomsbury Academic, 2019. Both empires faced the same challenges, that is, to undertake constitutional reforms without undermining the traditional hierarchical order. A clear exposition of these challenges and the efforts made to respond to them.

Gaudin, Corinne. *Ruling Peasants: Village and State in Later Imperial Russia*. DeKalb: Northern Illinois University Press, 2007. A close and sympathetic analysis of rural Russia.

Inalcik, Halil, and Donald Quataert, eds. *An Economic and Social History of the Ottoman Empire. Vol. 2, 1600–1914*. Cambridge, UK: Cambridge University Press, 1994. A pioneering work with contributions by leading Ottoman historians on rural structures, monetary developments, and industrialization efforts.

Kasaba, Resat, ed. *The Cambridge History of Turkey. Vol. 5, Turkey in the Modern World*. Cambridge, UK: Cambridge University Press, 2008. An ambitious effort to assemble the leading authorities on the Ottoman Empire and provide a comprehensive overview.

Lapavitsas, Costas, and Pinar Cakiroglu. *Capitalism in the Ottoman Balkans: Industrialisation and Modernity in Macedonia*. London: I. B. Tauris, 2019. Based on archival sources, this study reveals for the first time the dynamic push toward urbanization and industrial development in this European province of the Ottoman Empire, beginning at the end of the nineteenth century.

Massie, Robert K. *Catherine the Great: Portrait of a Woman*. New York: Random House, 2012. A comprehensive and insightful biography of one of the most fascinating women in history, whose policies, reforms, and personal life changed the course of Russian history.

Nikitenko, Aleksandr. *Up from Serfdom: My Childhood and Youth in Russia, 1804–1824*. Translated by Helen Saltz Jacobson. New Haven, CT: Yale University Press, 2001. Touching autobiography summarized at the beginning of the chapter.

Pamuk, Şevket. *Uneven Centuries: Economic Development of Turkey since 1820*. Princeton, NJ: Princeton University Press, 2018. Study by the leading economic historian of the Ottoman Empire which, for the first time, looks at the larger picture of economic and social change in this important multiethnic empire facing the challenges of Western modernity.

Poe, Marshall T. *Russia's Moment in World History*. Princeton, NJ: Princeton University Press, 2003. A superb scholarly overview of Russian history, written from a broad perspective and taking into account a good number of Western stereotypes about Russia, especially in the nineteenth century.

Rieber, Alfred J. *The Imperial Russian Project: Autocratic Politics, Economic Development, and Social Fragmentation*. Toronto, Buffalo, London: University of Toronto Press, 2018. Essays by the author on three interwoven subjects: the autocratic system of governance, the impact of economic change on the empire, and the fragmentation of society in the nineteenth century.

Uyar, Mesut, and Edward J. Erickson. *A Military History of the Ottomans: From Osman to Atatürk*. Santa Barbara, CA: Praeger Security International, 2009. A detailed, well-documented history of the Ottoman Empire from the perspective of its imperial designs and military forces, by two military officers in academic positions.

Zurcher, Erik J. *The Young Turk Legacy and Nation Building: From the Ottoman Empire to Atatürk's Turkey*. London: I. B. Tauris, 2010. Detailed yet readable account of how the Young Turk movement laid the foundation for Kemal Atatürk's Republic of Turkey.

WEBSITE

Russian Legacy. "Russian Empire (1689–1825)," http://www.russianlegacy.com/en/go_to/history/russian_empire.htm. A website devoted to the Russian Empire, organized as a timeline with links.

Chapter 26

Allen, Robert C. *The British Industrial Revolution in Global Perspective*. Cambridge, UK: Cambridge University Press, 2009. An in-depth analysis, well supported by economic data, not only of why the Industrial Revolution occurred first in Britain but also of how new British technologies carried industrialism around the world.

Dublin, Thomas, ed. *Farm to Factory: Women's Letters, 1830–1860*. New York: Columbia University Press, 1981. A fascinating collection of correspondence written by women who describe their experiences in moving from rural areas of New England to urban centers in search of work in textile factories.

Griffin, Emma. *Liberty's Dawn: A People's History of the Industrial Revolution*. New Haven, CT: Yale University Press, 2013. Riveting study of the impact of the Industrial Revolution on the lives of working men and women in Britain, as told in autobiographies and memoirs.

Headrick, Daniel R. *The Tools of Empire: Technology and European Imperialism in the Nineteenth Century*. Oxford and New York: Oxford University Press, 1981. A fascinating and clearly written analysis of the connections between the development of new technologies and their role in European imperialism.

Hobsbawm, Eric. *The Age of Revolution: 1789–1848*. London: Vintage, 1996. A sophisticated analysis of the Industrial Revolution (one element of the "twin revolution," the other being the French Revolution) that examines the effects of industrialism on social and cultural developments from a Marxist perspective.

Landers, Jane G. *Atlantic Creoles in the Age of Revolutions*. Cambridge: Harvard University Press, 2010. A fastidiously researched presentation of several black men (e.g., Big Prince Whitten) who carved out comfortable lives amid revolution in the Atlantic world.

Lynch, John. *Simón Bolívar: A Life*. New Haven: Yale University Press, 2006. A fresh look at the life and times of the Liberator, particularly his determination to enact reformist measures.

Rosen, William. *The Most Powerful Idea in the World: A Story of Steam, Industry, and Innovation.* Chicago: University of Chicago Press, 2012. Absorbing history of the importance of steam technologies in the development of industrialism.

Roudinesco, Elisabeth, and Catherine Porter. *Freud: In His Time and Ours.* Cambridge, MA: Harvard University Press, 2016. A bold, comprehensive, and innovative analysis of one of the most influential—and complex—figures at the turn of the twentieth century.

Sperber, Jonathan. *Karl Marx: A Nineteenth-Century Life.* New York: W. W. Norton, 2013. A carefully researched biography that contextualizes Marx vis-à-vis the age of early industrialism and in comparison with other luminaries in the turbulent nineteenth century.

WEBSITES

Claude Monet: Life and Paintings, http://www.monetpainting.net/. A visually beautiful website which reproduces many of Monet's masterpieces, it also includes an extensive biographical account of the famous painter's life and works as well as information about his wife Camille, his gardens at Giverny, and a chronology.

Darwin Online, http://darwin-online.org.uk/. This website has reproduced, in full, the works of Charles Darwin. In addition to providing digitized facsimiles of his works, private papers, and manuscripts, it has also added a concise biographical account and numerous images of Darwin throughout his life.

Einstein Archives Online, http://www.alberteinstein.info/. Fantastic and informative website that houses digitized manuscripts of Einstein's work. Also includes a gallery of images.

ThomasEdison.org, http://www.thomasedison.org/. Remarkable website that explores Thomas Edison's impact on modernity through his innovations and inventions. This site also reproduces all of Edison's scientific sketches, which are available to download as PDF files.

Chapter 27

Belich, James. *Replenishing the Earth: The Settler Revolution and the Rise of the Anglo-World, 1783–1939.* Oxford and New York: Oxford University Press, 2009. Important study by an Australian historian, focusing on the British settler colonies.

Chamberlain, M. E. *The Scramble for Africa.* New York: Routledge, 2013. Insightful account of the European colonization of Africa during the period 1870 to 1914.

Ferguson, Niall. *Empire: The Rise and Demise of the British World Order and the Lessons for Global Power.* New York: Perseus, 2002. Controversial but widely acknowledged analysis of the question of whether imperialism deserves its negative reputation or not.

Hobsbawm, Eric. *The Age of Empire, 1875–1914.* New York: Vintage, 1989. Immensely well-informed investigation of the climactic period of the new imperialism at the end of the nineteenth century.

Hochschild, Adam. *King Leopold's Ghost: A Story of Greed, Terror, and Heroism in Colonial Africa.* New York: Houghton Mifflin, 1998. A gripping exposé of Leopold II's brutal tactics in seizing territory and exploiting African labor in the Congo.

Jefferies, Matthew. *Contesting the German Empire, 1871–1918.* Malden, MA: Blackwell, 2008. Up-to-date summary of the German historical debate on the colonial period.

Kiernan, Ben. *Viet Nam: A History from Earliest Times to the Present.* Oxford: Oxford University Press, 2017. Extensive, scholarly, yet accessible to undergraduates, this is currently the most complete history of Vietnam to date. Welcome emphasis on environmental factors as well as French archival and newly declassified American materials.

Vickers, Adrian. *A History of Modern Indonesia*, 2nd ed. Cambridge, UK: Cambridge University Press, 2013. Well-written account of Indonesia growing from heteregenous Dutch colonial islands into a modern nation state.

Singer, Barnett, and John Langdon. *Cultured Force: Makers and Defenders of the French Colonial Empire.* Madison: University of Wisconsin Press, 2004. Study of the principal military figures who helped create the French nineteenth-century empire.

Streets-Salter, Heather, and Trevor R. Getz, *Empires and Colonies in the World: A Global Perspective.* Oxford and New York: Oxford University Press, 2015. Particularly illuminative chapters on the new imperialism in the nineteenth century.

WEBSITES

The Colonization of Africa, http://exhibitions.nypl.org/africanaage/essay-colonization-of-africa.html. An academically based summary with further essays on African topics.

South Asian History—Colonial India, http://www.lib.berkeley.edu/SSEAL/SouthAsia/india_colonial.html. Very detailed website with primary documents and subtopics of nineteenth-century British India.

Chapter 28

Clark, Christopher. *The Sleepwalkers: How Europe Went to War in 1914.* New York: Harper Perennial, 2014. One of a slew of new investigations into the origins of the war published to mark its centennial; emphasizes the Austrian–Serbian roots of the war.

Cohen, Adam. *Imbeciles: The Supreme Court, American Eugenics, and the Sterilization of Carrie Buck.* New York: Penguin, 2016.

Fritzsche, Peter. *Life and Death in the Third Reich.* Cambridge, MA: Harvard University Press, 2008. Book that seeks to understand the German nation's choice of adapting itself to Nazi rule.

Gelvin, James L. *The Modern Middle East: A History*, 4th ed. Oxford and New York: Oxford University Press, 2015. Contains chapters on Arab nationalism, British and French colonialism, and Turkey and Iran in the interwar period.

Gordon, Andrew. *A Modern History of Japan: From Tokugawa Times to the Present*, 2nd ed. Oxford and New York: Oxford

University Press, 2009. Detailed overview of Japan's interwar period in the middle chapters.

Grasso, June M., J. P. Corrin, and Michael Kort. *Modernization and Revolution in Modern China: From the Opium Wars to the Olympics*, 4th ed. Armonk, NY: M. E. Sharpe, 2009. General overview with a focus on modernization in relation to the strong survival of tradition.

Hung, Chang-Tai. *Mao's New World: Political Culture in the Early People's Republic*. Ithaca, NY: Cornell University Press, 2011. A broad collection of cultural expressions, ranging from dancing to cartoons, utilized to enhance loyalty to the CCP.

Martel, Gordon, ed. *A Companion to Europe 1900–1945*. Malden, MA: Wiley-Blackwell, 2010. Collective work covering a large variety of cultural, social, and political European topics in the interwar period.

Meade, Teresa A. *A History of Modern Latin America: 1800 to the Present*. Malden, MA: Wiley-Routledge, 2010. Topical discussion of the major issues in Latin American history, with chapters on the first half of the twentieth century.

Neiberg, Michael S. *The Treaty of Versailles: A Concise Study*. Oxford and New York: Oxford University Press, 2017. An assessment of the complexities attending the settlement of World War I, along with the consequences of its many flaws and failures.

Service, Robert. *Lenin: A Biography*. Cambridge, MA: Harvard University Press, 2000. An interesting portrait of Lenin's character and personality, highlighting his idiosyncrasies.

Snyder, Timothy. *Bloodlands: Europe between Hitler and Stalin*. New York: Basic Books, 2010. Book that chronicles the horrific destruction left behind by these two dictators.

Wilson, Mark R. *Destructive Creation: American Business and the Winning of World War II*. Philadelphia: University of Pennsylvania Press, 2016. A thoroughly researched revisionist interpretation of the strained relationship between big business and the federal government as America mobilized for, and engaged in, World War II.

WEBSITES

BBC. World War One, http://www.bbc.co.uk/ww1, and World War Two (archived), http://www.bbc.co.uk/history/worldwars/wwtwo/. The BBC's treatment of the causes, course, and consequences of both WWI and WWII from an Allied position.

Marxists Internet Archive. "The Bolsheviks," http://www.marxists.org/subject/bolsheviks/index.htm. A complete review of the Bolshevik party members, including biographies and links to archives which contain their works.

1937 Nanking Massacre, http://www.nanking-massacre.com/Home.html. A disturbing collection of pictures and articles tell the gruesome history of the Rape of Nanjing.

United States Holocaust Memorial Museum. Holocaust Encyclopedia, http://www.ushmm.org/wlc/en/article.php? ModuleId=10005151. The US Holocaust Memorial Museum looks back on one of the darkest times in Western history.

U.S. History, http://www.ushistory.org/us/. Maintained by Independence Hall Association in Philadelphia, this website contains many links to topics discussed in this chapter.

Chapter 29

Baret, Roby Carol. *The Greater Middle East and the Cold War: US Foreign Policy under Eisenhower and Kennedy*. London: I.B. Tauris, 2007. Thoroughly researched analysis of American policies in the Middle East, North Africa, and South Asia.

Birmingham, David. *Kwame Nkrumah: Father of African Nationalism*. Athens: University of Ohio Press, 1998. Short biography by a leading modern African historian.

Conniff, Michael L. *Populism in Latin America*. Tuscaloosa: University of Alabama Press, 1999. The author is a well-published scholar on modern Latin America.

Damrosch, David, David Lawrence Pike, Djelal Kadir, and Ursula K. Heise, eds. *The Longman Anthology of World Literature. Vol. F, The Twentieth Century*. New York: Longman/Pearson, 2008. A rich, diverse selection of texts. Alternatively, Norton published a similar, somewhat larger anthology of world literature in 2003.

De Witte, Ludo. *The Assassination of Lumumba*. Translated by Ann Wright and Renée Fenby. London: Verso, 2002. An admirably researched study of the machinations of the Belgian government in protecting its mining interests, with the connivance of CIA director Allen Dulles and President Dwight D. Eisenhower.

Guha, Ramachandra. *India after Gandhi: A History of the World's Largest Democracy*. New York: Harper Collins 2007. Highly readable, popular history with well-sketched biographical treatments of leading individuals, more obscure cultural figures, and ordinary people. Accessible to even beginning students.

Hasegawa, Tsuyoshi. *The Cold War in East Asia, 1945–1991*. Stanford, CA: Stanford University Press, 2011. A new summary, based on archival research by a leading Japanese historian teaching in the United States. New insights on the Soviet entry into World War II against Japan.

Herman, Arthur. *Joseph McCarthy: Reexamining the Life and Legacy of America's Most Hated Senator*. New York: Free Press, 2000. A fascinating study of the Wisconsin senator whose virulent campaign against communism launched decades of fear and reprisals in America during the Cold War era.

Jansen, Jan C., and Jürgen Osterhammel. *Decolonization: A Short History*. Princeton, NJ: Princeton University Press, 2017. Superb, analytical well-grounded summary of the decolonization process and its aftermath in the second half of the twentieth century.

Jankowski, James. *Nasser's Egypt, Arab Nationalism, and the United Arab Republic*. Boulder, CO: Lynne Rienner, 2002. A carefully researched account of the origin, evolution, and eventual collapse of the United Arab Republic.

Meredith, Martin. *The Fate of Africa: A History of the Continent since Independence*. Philadelphia: Perseus, 2011. A revised and up-to-date study of a fundamental analysis of Africa during the modern era.

Wang, Juoyue. *In Sputnik's Shadow: The President's Science Advisory Committee and Cold War in America*. New Brunswick, NJ: Rutgers University Press, 2008. Traces the evolution of the President's Science Advisory Committee following new directions after Russia's successful launching of Sputnik in 1957.

WEBSITES

Economist. "The Suez Crisis: An Affair to Remember," http://www.economist.com/node/7218678. The *Economist* magazine looks back on the Suez Crisis.

NASA. "Yuri Gagarin: First Man in Space," http://www.nasa.gov/mission_pages/shuttle/sts1/gagarin_anniversary.html. In addition to information and video footage regarding Yuri Gagarin's orbit of the earth, students will also find information on America's space history.

The History.com website has a detailed, illustrated subsection on the Berlin Wall: https://www.history.com/topics/cold-war/berlin-wall.

Chapter 30

Ash, Timothy Garton. *The Magic Lantern: The Revolution of '89 Witnessed in Warsaw, Budapest, Berlin, and Prague*. New York: Random House, 1999. A gripping first-hand account of the wave of anticommunist revolutions that rocked Eastern Europe after 1989.

Cooper, James. *Margaret Thatcher and Ronald Reagan: A Very Political Special Relationship*. New York: Palgrave Macmillan, 2012. Insightful observations regarding conjoined policies of Reagan and Thatcher, particularly their economic policies during the 1980s.

Emery, Christian. *US Foreign Policy and the Iranian Revolution: The Cold War Dynamics of Engagement and Strategic Alliance*. New York: Palgrave Macmillan, 2013. Discusses the 1979 Iranian revolution with emphasis on the Carter administration's mishandling of critical developments, resulting in the radicals' overtaking of the Iranian Revolution.

Fanon, Frantz. *The Wretched of the Earth*. New York: Grove, 1961. One of the most provocative and influential treatments of theoretical and practical issues surrounding decolonization. Fanon champions violence as an essential part of the decolonization process and advocates a modified Marxist approach that takes into consideration the nuances of race and the legacies of colonialism.

Frieden, Jeffrey. *Global Capitalism: Its Fall and Rise in the Twentieth Century*. New York: W. W. Norton, 2006. Despite the title, a comprehensive history of global networks from the days of mercantilism to the twenty-first century. Predominant emphasis on twentieth century; highly readable, though the material is best suited for more advanced students.

Gaddis, John Lewis. *The Cold War: A New History*. New York: Penguin, 2005. Though criticized by some scholars for his pro-American positions, America's foremost historian of the Cold War produces here a vivid, at times counterintuitive, view of the Cold War and its global impact. Readable even for beginning students.

Gitlin, Todd. *The Sixties: Years of Hope, Days of Rage*, rev. ed. New York: Bantam, 1993. Lively, provocative account of this pivotal decade by the former radical, now a sociologist. Especially effective at depicting the personalities of the pivotal period 1967–1969.

Goodwin, Doris Kearns. *Lyndon Johnson and the American Dream*. New York: St. Martin's Press, 1991. Insightful and probing study of President Johnson's character and personality, from his early years through his extensive political career.

Harmer, Tanya. *Allende's Chile and the Inter-American Cold War*. Chapel Hill, NC: *University of North Carolina Press*, 2014. A reinterpretation of American determination to overturn Allende's leftist government and its subsequent results.

Liang Heng and Judith Shapiro. *After the Nightmare: A Survivor of the Cultural Revolution Reports on China Today*. New York: Knopf, 1986. Highly readable, poignant first-person accounts of people's experiences during the trauma of China's Cultural Revolution by a former husband-and-wife team. Especially interesting because China was at the beginning of its Four Modernizations when this was written, and the wounds of the Cultural Revolution were still fresh.

Raleigh, Donald J. *Soviet Baby Boomers: An Oral History of Russia's Cold War Generation*. Oxford and New York: Oxford University Press, 2012. A revealing and entertaining account of new social and cultural trends among Russia's youth, as told in a series of interviews.

Smith, Bonnie, ed. *Global Feminisms since 1945*. London: Routledge, 2000. Part of the Rewriting Histories series, this work brings together under the editorship of Smith a host of essays by writers such as Sara Evans, Mary Ann Tetreault, and Miriam Ching Yoon Louie on feminism in Asia, Africa, and Latin America, as well as Europe and the United States. Sections are thematically arranged under such headings as "Nation-Building," "Sources of Activism," "Women's Liberation," and "New Waves in the 1980s and 1990s." Comprehensive and readable, though some background in women's history is recommended.

WEBSITES

Cold War International History Project, https://www.wilsoncenter.org/program/cold-war-international-history-project. Run by the Woodrow Wilson International Center for Scholars. Rich archival materials, including collections on the end of the Cold War, the Soviet invasion of Afghanistan, the Cuban Missile Crisis, and Chinese foreign policy documents.

The "Office of the Historian," a semi-official website of the State Department and associated foreign policy historians offers studies on a variety of 20th-century topics: https://history.state.gov/about.

The United Nations has a detailed website on decolonization: https://www.un.org/en/sections/issues-depth/decolonization/index.html.

Chapter 31

Daniels, Robert V. *The Rise and Fall of Communism in the Soviet Union*. New Haven, CT: Yale University Press, 2010. A magisterial summary of the communist period by a specialist.

Dillon, Michael. *Contemporary China: An Introduction*. New York: Routledge, 2009. Concise yet specific overview of the economy, society, and politics of the country.

Eichengreen, Barry. *Exorbitant Privilege: The Rise and Fall of the Dollar and the Future of the Monetary System*. Oxford and New York: Oxford University Press, 2011. The author is an academic specialist on US monetary policies, writing in an accessible style and presenting a fascinating picture of the role of something as prosaic as greenbacks.

Faust, Aaron M. *The Ba'thification of Iraq: Saddam Hussein's Totalitarianism*. Austin, TX: University of Texas Press, 2015. Based on meticulous research among Ba'th Party documents, this study reveals how Saddam Hussein developed a totalitarian regime in Iraq and why his dictatorship succeeded in gaining the loyalty of millions of Iraqis for nearly 25 years.

Gelvin, James L. *The Arab Uprisings: What Everyone Needs to Know*. Oxford and New York: Oxford University Press, 2012. Concise overview of the Arab Spring events with carefully selected background information.

Houghton, John. *Global Warming: The Complete Briefing*. 5th ed. Cambridge, UK: Cambridge University Press, 2015. One of the most authoritative summaries of all aspects of global warming.

Jacka, Tamara, Andrew Kipnis, and Sally Sargeson. *Contemporary China: Society and Social Change*. Cambridge, UK: Cambridge University Press, 2013. Ambitious sociological–historical study focusing on the many differences within Chinese society and the forces that drive change in contemporary China.

Luong, Hy V. *Postwar Vietnam: Dynamics of a Transforming Society*. Lanham, MD: Institute of Southeast Asian Studies and Rowman & Littlefield, 2003. Important study of reforms geared toward opening up Vietnam's economy and its effects on society, among them a growing divide between urban and rural areas.

Meade, Teresa A. *A History of Modern Latin America: 1800 to the Present*. 2nd ed. Malden, MA: Wiley-Blackwell, 2016. The book is an excellent, comprehensive analysis and has a strong final chapter on recent Latin America.

Saxonberg, Steven. *The Fall: A Comparative Study of the End of Communism in Czechoslovakia, East Germany, Hungary, and Poland*. Amsterdam, The Netherlands: Harwood Academic, 2001. A well-informed overview of the different trajectories by an academic teaching in Prague.

Swanimathan, Jayshankar M. *Indian Economic Superpower: Fact or Fiction?* Singapore: World Scientific Publishing, 2009. A thoughtful evaluation of the pros and cons of economic growth in India, in concise overviews.

WEBSITES

Wikiwand has a website on contemporary history with many tabs on recent events and topics: https://www.wikiwand.com/en/Contemporary_history.

BBC. Nelson Mandela's Life and Times, http://www.bbc.co.uk/news/world-africa-12305154. The BBC News looks back at the life and career of Nelson Mandela.

Sierra Club, http://sierraclub.org/. Balanced and informative environmental websites.

Credits

Chapter 1: Bettman/Getty Images, p. 5; Reprinted with permission from Macmillan Publishers Ltd: Nature 521, 310-315 (21 May 2015), copyright 2015, p. 7; © Kenneth Garrett Photography, p. 10; CC-by-SA-2.0 Bradshaw Art, TimJN1, p. 13; Walter Geiersperger/Getty Images, p. 15; Philippe Psaila/Science Source, p. 16

Chapter 2: The Trustees of the British Museum/Art Resource, NY, p. 27; Erich Lessing/Art Resource, NY, p. 34; Réunion des Musées Nationaux/Art Resource, NY, p. 37; pius/iStock photo, p. 39; SOTK2011/Alamy Stock Photo, p. 43; Ivy Close Images/Alamy Stock Photo, p. 48

Chapter 3: Mukul Banerjee, p. 55; Mukul Banerjee, p. 61; © Doranne Jacobson/International Images, p. 63; bpk, Berlin/ Museum fuer Asiatische Kunst, Staatliche Museen/Iris Papadopoulos/Art Resource, NY, p. 67; © Doranne Jacobson/ International Images, p. 72 (top and bottom)

Chapter 4: Metropolitan Museum of Art, p. 77; Liu Liquin/ ChinaStock, p. 81; Martha Avery/Getty Images, p. 82; V&A Images, London/Art Resource, NY, p. 84; TAO Images Limited/Alamy Stock Photo, p. 86; AP Photo/Chris Carlson, p. 94; © Laomacz | Dreamstime.com, p. 94; Martha Avery, Getty Images, p. 95

Chapter 5: ERNESTO BENAVIDES/AFP/Getty Images, p. 101; The Witte Museum, p. 107; Insights/UIG via Getty Images, p. 111; © Sean Sprague/The Image Works, p. 112; akg/Bildarchiv Steffens, p. 114; Caroline Penn/Alamy Stock Photo, p. 118

Chapter 6: Kazuyoshi Nomachi/Getty Images, p. 125; Werner Forman/Art Resource, NY, p. 129; The Metropolitan Museum of Art, New York. Purchase, Buckeye Trust and Mr. and Mrs. Milton F. Rosenthal Gifts, Joseph Pulitzer Bequest and Harris Brisbane Dick and Rogers Funds, 1981, p. 130; Werner Forman, Art Resource, NY, p. 133; Gardel Bertrand/ Hemis/Alamy Stock Photo, p. 136; Photograph K2803© Justin Kerr, p. 138; bpk, Berlin/Ethnologisches Museum, Staatliche Museen/Art Resource, NY, p. 140; DEA/G. DAGLI ORTI/Getty Images, p. 143

Chapter 7: Vanni/Art Resource, NY, p. 149; 205 Louis and Nancy Hatch Dupree Collection, Williams Afghan Media Project Archive, p. 155; Vanni/Art Resource, NY, p. 158; Wolfgang Kaehler/Getty Images, p. 164; Mido Semsem/ Shutterstock Images, p. 165; © Zev Radovan/Bridgeman Images, p. 167; akg-images/Gerard Degeorge, p. 169; MS Vat. Lat. 3867 (Romanus), folio 106 recto (15th c CE) p. 171

Chapter 8: Metropolitan Museum of Art, p. 175; Boromeo/ Art Resource, NY, p. 179; Jeremy Richards/iStock Photo, p. 183 (top); Roland and Sabrina Michaud/akg-images/A.F. Kersting, p. 186; © The Trustees of the British Museum, p. 190

Chapter 9: © The Trustees of the British Museum/Art Resource, NY, p. 197; photo by Gary Lee Todd, p. 206; mauritius images GmbH/Alamy Stock Photo, p. 208; Courtesy of ChinaStock, p. 210; Photograph © 2014 Museum of Fine Arts, Boston, p. 214; SSPL/Getty Images, p. 215

Chapter 10: John Hicks/Getty Images, p. 230; Album/Art Resource, NY, p. 233; Paris, Bibliotheque Nat., p. 235; © British Library Board. All Rights Reserved/Bridgeman Images, p. 239; Scala/White Images/Art Resource, NY, p. 240; bpk, Berlin/ Bibliotheque National/Gérard Le Gall/Art Resource, NY, p. 243

Chapter 11: Metropolitan Museum of Art, p. 253; bpk, Berlin/Cathedral (Palatine Chapel), Aachen, Germany/ Stefan Diller/Art Resource, NY, p. 257; World History Archive / Alamy Stock Photo, p. 258; © Santa Sabina, Rome Italy, Alinari/Bridgeman Images, p. 265; Jorge Royan/Alamy Stock Photo, p. 268; akg-images/VISIOARS, p. 273

Chapter 12: Wikimedia Commons, p. 281; Ivan Vdovin/ Alamy Stock Photo, p. 273; akg-images/Gerard DeGeorge, p. 287; Martha Avery/Getty Images, p. 289; © British Library Board/Robana/Art Resource, NY, p. 290; RMN-Grand Palais/Art Resource, NY, p. 300

Chapter 13: Photo © AISA/Bridgeman Images, p. 305; Images copyright © The Metropolitan Museum of Art/Art Resource, NY, p. 315; Image copyright © The Metropolitan Museum of Art/Art Resource, NY, p. 305; Image copyright © The Metropolitan Museum of Art/Art Resource, NY, p. 320

Chapter 14: © Bibliotheque Nationale, Paris, France/ Bridgeman Images, p. 329; © Franck Guizou/Hemis/Getty Images, p. 334; Werner Forman/Art Resource, NY, p. 339 (top); Mapungubwe Museum, Department of UP Arts, at the University of Pretoria, p. 339 (bottom); Desmond Kwande/ Getty Images, p. 340; akg-images/André Held, p. 344; Image courtesy of The Minneapolis Institute of Arts, p. 345; Werner Forman/Art Resource, NY, p. 346

Chapter 15: Granger Historical Archive/Alamy Stock Photo, p. 351; Album/Art Resource, NY, p. 355; DEA/M. Seemuller/Getty Images, p. 356; Bpk/Ibero-Amerikanisches Institut Stiftung Pressischer Kulturbesitz, Berlin, Germany, 360; © Gianni Dagli Orti/The Art Archive at Art Resource, NY,

p. 362; RICKEY ROGERS/Reuters, p. 363; © Ellisphotos/Alamy Stock Photo, p. 364; Bettmann/Getty Images, p. 366

Chapter 16: Courtesy of the Library of Congress, p. 371; WGBH Stock Sales/Scala, Florence, p. 375; (a) (c) DeA Picture Library/Art Resource, NY; (b) ART Collection/Alamy Stock Photo; (c) (c) John Warburton-Lee Photography/Alamy Stock Photo, p. 378; (d) AP Photo/Thomas Haentzschel; (e) North Wind Picture Archives/Alamy Stock Photo, p. 365; Cameraphoto Arte, Venice/Art Resource, NY, p. 384; Topkapi Palace Museum, Istanbul, Turkey/The Bridgeman Art Library, p. 386; Bridgeman-Giraudon/Art Resource, NY, p. 387; Kerry Whitworth/Alamy Stock Photo, p. 388; Erich Lessing/Art Resource, NY, p. 390

Chapter 17: Courtesy of the Library of Congress, p. 395; (a) Alinari, Art Resource, NY; (b) Reunion des Musees Nationaux/Art Resource, NY, p. 399; Courtesy of the Library of Congress, p. 400; akg-images/Guericke/Magdeburg Hemispheres, p. 403; Wikimedia Commons, p. 407; akg-images, p. 418

Chapter 18: Courtesy of the Library of Congress, p. 423; Archives Charmet/Bridgeman Images, p. 425; bpk, Berlin/Athnologisches Museum/Dietrich Graf/Art Resource, NY, p. 426; Scala/White Images/Art Resource, NY, p. 429; DEA/G. DAGLI ORTI/Getty Images, p. 433; Courtesy of the Hispanic Society of America, New York, p. 439; Granger Historical Archive/Alamy Stock Photo, p. 444; The Stapleton Collection/Bridgeman Images, p. 427

Chapter 19: Werner Forman/Art Resource, NY, p. 457; Werner Forman/Art Resource, NY, p. 458; Image copyright © The Metropolitan Museum of Art. Image source: Art Resource, NY, p. 459; Art Resource/Art Resource, NY, p. 465; © Robert Holmes/CORBIS/VCG/Getty Images, p. 468; Collection of Herbert M. and Shelley Cole. Photo by Don Cole, p. 469; Abby Aldrich Rockefeller Ford Art Museum, The Colonial Williamsburg Foundation, Williamsburg, VA, p. 471

Chapter 20: © travelib prime/Alamy Stock Photo, p. 477; V&A Images/The Art Archive at Art Resource, NY, p. 480; RobMeador.com/Shutterstock Images, p. 482; © The Metropolitan Museum of Art/Art Resource, NY, p. 483 (top); Joana Kruse/Alamy Stock Photo, p. 483 (bottom); Akbar and the Jesuits, The Book of Akbar (In 03.363), © The Trustees of the Chester Beatty Library, Dublin, p. 484; Digital Image © 2009 Museum Associates/LACMA. Licensed by Art Resource, NY, p. 491; Erich Lessing/Art Resource, NY, p. 494

Chapter 21: Wikimedia Commons, p. 499; The Metropolitan Museum of Art, p. 504; Bettmann/Getty Images, p. 507; Roy Miles Fine Paintings/Bridgeman Images, p. 508; © The Granger Collection, New York, p. 512; akg-images, p. 517; V&A Images, London/Art Resource, NY, p. 518

Chapter 22: HIP/Art Resource, NY, p. 523; (a) (top left) (c) Bettmann/Getty Images; (b) (bottom left) Classic Images/Alamy Stock Photo; (c) (right) Niday Picture Library/Alamy Stock Photo, p. 528; (c) RMN-Grand Palais/Art Resource, NY, p. 530; Print Collection/Getty Images, p. 531; Culture Club/Getty Images, p. 538; Artokoloro Quint Lox Limited/Alamy Stock Photo, p. 543; Hulton-Deusch Collection/Getty Images, p. 546

Chapter 23: Courtesy of Library of Congress, p. 551; Library of Congress Reproduction Number: LC-USZ62-99485, p. 554; Gianni Dagli Orti/Topkapi Museum Istanbul/The Art Archive/Art Resource, NY, p. 557; Schalkwijk/Art Resource, NY. © 2017 Blanco de Mexico Diego Rivera Frida Kahlo Museums Trust, Mexico, D.F./Artists Rights Society (ARS), New York, p. 559; Library of Congress/Getty Image, p. 560; Erich Lessing/Art Resource, NY, p. 562; Library of Congress reproduction number LC-USZ62-73425, p. 564; The Granger Collection, New York, p. 566; Courtesy of the Library of Congress, p. 570

Chapter 24: Collection of Museum of Fine Arts, Boston via Wikimedia Commons, p. 577; The Art Archive at Art Resource, NY, p. 581; (a) akg-images/British Library; (b) Peter NEWark Pictures/Bridgeman Images, p. 584; Heritage Images/Getty Images, p. 587; Courtesy of the Library of Congress, p. 594

Chapter 25: Bettmann/Getty Images, p. 607; Bettmann/Getty Images, p. 608; SEF/Art Resource, NY, p. 610; dbimages/Alamy Stock Photo, p. 612; Print Collector/Getty Images, p. 616; North Wind Picture Archives/Alamy Stock Photo, p. 617; RussiaSputnik/Bettman Images, p. 621

Chapter 26: SSPL/Science Museum/Art Resource, NY, p. 625; Science & Society Picture Library/Getty Images, p. 633; Robert Hunt Library/Chronicle/Alamy Stock Photo, p. 635; The Print Collector/Alamy Stock Photo, p. 639; Stapleton Collection/Bridgeman Images, p. 640; Chronicle/Alamy Stock Photo, p. 641; Peter NEWark Pictures/Bridgeman Images, p. 643; Natural History Museum, London, UK/The Bridgeman Art Library International, p. 645

Chapter 27: Sarin Images/GRANGER, p. 651; Peter Horree/Alamy Stock Photo, p. 653; Bettmann/Getty Images, p. 655; Reunion des Musees Nationaux/Art Resource, NY, p. 658; © Hulton-Deutsch Collection/Getty Images, p. 662; Panos Pictures ASL00010DRC, p. 667; Courtesy of the Library of Congress, p. 671

Chapter 28: © Hulton-Deutsch Collection/Getty Images, p. 678; GRANGER, p. 684; Library of Congress LC-USW3-001543-D, p. 687; Fotosearch/Getty Images, p. 689; Bettmann/Getty Images, p. 690; Heritage Partnership Ltd/Alamy

Stock Photo, p. 693; World History Archive/Alamy Stock Photo, p. 695; Courtesy of the Library of Congress, p. 698

Chapter 29: Keystone/Getty Images, p. 707; Getty Images, p. 709; © Bettmann/Getty Images, p. 713; Rykoff Collection/Getty Images, p. 714; George Marks/Getty Images, p. 715; (a) (c) The Museum of Modern Art/Licensed by SCALA/Art Resource, NY. With permission of the Renate, Hans & Maria Hofmann Trust/Artists Rights Society (ARS), New York; (b) (c) 2009 Museum Associates/LACMA/Art Resource, NY. (c) 2017 The Willem de Kooning Foundation/Artists Rights Society (ARS), New York, p. 716; Lisa Larsen/Getty Images, p. 727; Courtesy of the Library of Congress, p. 728

Chapter 30: © Alain DeJean/Sygma/Getty Images, p. 737; Historical/Getty Images, p. 739; © Bettmann/Getty Images, p. 744; Mark Lenniham/Associated Press, p. 745; India Today Group/Getty Images, p. 747; Bettman/Getty Images, p. 749; CHAUVEL/Getty Images, p. 752; Courtesy of the Library of Congress, p. 758

Chapter 31: Getty Images, p. 770; str/Associated Press, p. 774; Ali Atmaca/Anadolu Agency/Getty Images, p. 781; Fred Dufour/Getty Images, p. 782; Manish Swarup/Associated Press, p. 784; Louise Gubb/Getty Images, p. 785; Mazuffar Salman/Associated Press, p. 786; Peter Parks/Getty Images, p. 789

Source Index

Page numbers of the form S8-7–S8-8 indicate, in this case, a source document in chapter 8 on pages 7–8 in the source documents at the end of chapter 8. If the page number for the source document is followed by (d) this indicates a text source document. If the page number for the source document is followed by (v) this indicates a visual source document.

'Abd al-'Azīz al-Bakrī: on West Africa, S14-7–S14-8 (d)
Abelard, Peter: *The Story of My Misfortunes* by, S11-7–S11-8 (d)
Adelard of Bath: *Questiones naturales* by, S11-3–S11-5 (d)
Admonitions for Women (Nüjie) (Ban Zhao), S9-6–S9-7 (d)
Afonso I (Nzinga Mbemba) of Kongo: letter to King of Portugal, S19-3–S19-5 (d)
Africa: 'Abd al-'Azīz al-Bakrī on, S14-7–S14-8 (d); bananas from, S6-2–S6-3 (d); Ibn Battuta's journey to the East African coast, S14-4–S14-6 (d)
Ahuitzotl: eighth king of Aztec Empire, S15-3–S15-4 (d)
Alexander II: abolition of serfdom by, S25-6–S25-8 (d)
Alexander I: Metternich's secret memorandum to, S22-12–S22-13 (d)
Álfaro, José de: in scandal at the church, S18-2–S18-4 (d)
Allende, Salvador: "Last Words to the Nation" by, S30-11–S30-12 (d)
amulet containing passages from Qur'an worn by Muslim slaves who rioted in Bahia, Brazil, S23-6–S23-8 (d)
Analects (Lunyu) (Confucius), S9-2–S9-3 (d)
ANZAC. *See* Australian and New Zealand Army Corps
Ashley Commission: miners' testimony at, S26-5–S26-6 (d)
Ashoka: Seven Pillar Edicts of, S8-2–S8-4 (d)
Aten: great hymn to, S2-8–S2-9 (d)
Aurangzeb, edicts of, S20-5–S20-6 (d)
Australian and New Zealand Army Corps (ANZAC) at Galliopi, S28-2–S28-4 (d)
Avalokiteshvara: copper head of, Vietnam, S13-9 (v)
Aztec Empire: Ahuitzotl eighth king of, S15-3–S15-4 (d)

Babur, Zahiruddin Muhammad: *The Baburnama* by, S20-2–S20-3 (d)
The Baburnama (Babur), S20-2–S20-3 (d)
Bachellery, Josefina: "The Education of Women" by, S23-2–S23-4 (d)
Bahia, Brazil: amulet containing passages from Qur'an worn by Muslim slaves who rioted in, S23-6–S23-8 (d)
Al-Bakrī, 'Abd al-'Azīz: *Kitāb al-masālik wa-'l-mamālik* by, S14-7–S14-8 (d)
bananas: Africa's earliest, S6-2–S6-3 (d)
Ban Zaho: *Admonitions for Women* by, S9-6–S9-7 (d)
Bhagavad Gita, S3-2–S3-4 (d)
bin Laden, Osama: "Declaration of War against the Americans Occupying the Land of Two Holy Places," S31-2–S31-4 (d)
Black Death: flagellants attempt to ward off in Germany and England, S11-10–S11-11 (d)
Boccaccio, Giovanni: *The Decameron* "Putting the Devil Back in Hell" by, S11-8–S11-10 (d)
Bodhisattva Avalokiteshvara: copper head of, Vietnam, S13-9 (v)
The Book of Lord Shang (Shangjun Shu), S4-5–S4-6 (d)
Book of Mencius (Mengzi) (Mencius), S9-3–S9-4 (d)
The Book of Odes (Shijing), S4-2–S4-3 (d)
The Book of Prophecies (Columbus), S16-5–S16-6 (d)
The Book of Routes and Realms (*Kitāb al-masālik wa-'l-mamālik*) (al-Bakrī), S14-7–S14-8 (d)
Botswana, Rhino Cave in: python–Shaped ornamented rock from, S1-3 (v)
Bravo, Doña Theresa: in scandal at the church, S18-2–S18-4 (d)
Brazil: amulet containing passages from Qur'an worn by Muslim slaves who rioted in, S23-6–S23-8 (d)
Brihadaranyaka Upanishad, S3-6–S3-7 (d)
Brittain, Vera: *Testament of Youth* by, S28-4–S28-6 (d)
Buddhism, in Korea: *Haedong kosŭng chŏn* on, S13-6–S13-8 (d)
Burke, Edmund: *Reflections on the Revolution in France* by, S22-8–S22-9 (d)

Cadena, Joséfa: in scandal at the church, S18-2–S18-4 (d)
Caral–Supe culture, Peru: quipu from, S5-2 (v)
casta paintings: in Mexico, S19-10–S10-11 (v)
Castellio, Sebastian: *Concerning Whether Heretics Should Be Persecuted* by, S17-7–S17-9 (d)
Castro, Fidel: letters between Nikita Khrushchev and on Cuban Missile Crisis, S29-7–S29-10 (d)
Çelebi, Evliya: "A Procession of Artisans at Istanbul" by, S16-9–S16-11 (d)
The Chachnamah, S12-2–S12-3 (d)
Châtelet, Emilie du: *Discourse on Happiness* by, S17-4–S17-7 (d)
Chavin de Huántar, Peru: textile fragment from, S5-3 (v)
China in the Sixteenth Century (Ricci), S21-2–S21-4 (d)
China: Mccartney on possibilities of British commerce, S21-4–S21-6 (d)
Chinese coolie photograph: Peru, S23-9 (v)
Christian Topography (Cosmas Indicopleustes), S6-8–S6-9 (d)
Chronicles of Japan (Nihongi), S13-4–S13-6 (d)
Churchill, Winston: "The Iron Curtain Speech" by, S29-5–S29-7 (d)
Cieza de León, Pedro: on Incan roads, S15-6–S15-7 (d)
climate change: United Nations framework convention on, S31-12–S31-13 (d)
The Cloud Messenger (Kalidasa), S8-9–S8-11 (d)
Code of Manu, S3-8–S3-9 (d)
Columbus, Christopher: *The Book of Prophecies* by, S16-5–S16-6 (d); reports on his first voyage, 1493, S16-2–S16-4 (d)
Concerning Whether Heretics Should Be Persecuted (Castellio), S17-7–S17-9 (d)
Confucius: *Analects* of, S9-2–S9-3 (d)
The Conquest of New Spain (Díaz), S15–S15-6 (d)
Constantinople: "The Fall of Constantinople" on, S16-7–S16-8 (d)
Cosmas Indicopleustes (Cosmas the India-Voyager): *Christian Topography* by, S6-8–S6-9 (d)
"The Court of Suleiman the Magnificent" (Ghiselin de Busbecq), S16-11–S16-12 (d)
Crimea annexation: Vladimir Putin address to Duma concerning, S31-04–S31-7 (d)
Cuban Missile Crisis: letters between Fidel Castro and Nikita Khrushchev, S29-7–S29-10 (d)
Cyrus Cylinder, S7-2–S7-3 (d)

"The Daily Habits of Louis XIV at Versailles" (duc de Saint-Simon), S17-9–S17-11 (d)
Darwin, Charles: *The Origin of Species* by, S26-9–S26-11 (d)
de Beauvoir, Simone: *The Second Sex* by, S30-6–S30-8 (d)

The Decameron "Putting the Devil Back in Hell" (Boccaccio), S11-8–S11-10 (d)
Declaration of the Rights of Man and of the Citizen: France, S22-2–S22-3 (d)
The Declaration of the Rights of Woman (de Gouges), S22-4–S22-6 (d)
"Declaration of War against the Americans Occupying the Land of Two Holy Places" (bin Laden), S31-2–S31-4 (d)
de Gouges, Olympe: *The Declaration of the Rights of Woman,* S22-4–S22-6 (d)
de' Medici, Christina: Galileo Galilei: letter to, S17-13–S17-15 (d)
Díaz, Bernal: *The Conquest of New Spain* by, S15–S15-6 (d)
Dickens, Charles: *Hard Times* by, S26-2–S26-3 (d)
Diplovatatzes, Joshua: "The Fall of Constantinople" by, S16-7–S16-8 (d)
Discourse on Happiness (Châtelet), S17-4–S17-7 (d)
Dzudzuana Cave, Republic of Georgia, Caucasus Mountains: flax fibers from, S1-7 (v)

East African coast: Ibn Battuta's journey to, S14-4–S14-6 (d)
East Asia: pottery's origins in, S1-4–S1-6 (v)
edicts: of Aurangzeb, S20-5–S20-6 (d); from Qianlong Emperor to King George III, S21-6–S21-9 (d); Rose Garden, S25-4–S25-6 (d)
"The Education of Women" (Bachellery), S23-2–S23-4 (d)
Edwin Smith Papyrus: three spinal injury cases in, S2-4–S2-5 (d)
Egypt, Middle Kingdom, Twelfth Dynasty: advice from a royal scribe to his apprentice, S2-6–S2-7 (d)
Einhard: *Life of Charlemagne* by, S11-2–S11-3 (d)
El Castio de Huarmey, Peru: skeletons in Wari royal tomb site, S15-2–S15-3 (v)
emerald box: Mughal, S20-7 (v)
England: flagellants attempt to ward off Black Death in, S11-10–S11-11 (d)
Equiano, Olaudah: *The Interesting Narrative of the Life of Olaudah Equiano* by, S19-8–S19-10 (d)
Eredo, Sungbo's Eredo, walls and moats, Nigeria, S14-8–S14-9 (d)
Ethiopia: *The Fetha Nagast* from, S14-2–S14-4 (d)
examination of Lady Jane Grey, London, S17-2–S17-4 (d)

"The Fall of Constantinople" (Thomas the Eparch and Diplovatatzes), S16-7–S16-8 (d)
The Fetha Nagast: Ethiopia, S14-2–S14-4 (d)
feudal contracts and the swearing of fealty, S11-5–S11-6 (d)
flagellants attempt to ward off Black Death in Germany and England, S11-10–S11-11 (d)
flax fibers: Dzudzuana Cave, Republic of Georgia, Caucasus Mountains, S1-7 (v)
"Foundations and Doctrine of Fascism" (Mussolini and Gentile), S28-7–S28-8 (d)
France: *Declaration of the Rights of Man and of the Citizen,* S22-2–S22-3 (d); *Reflections on the Revolution in France* on, S22-8–S22-9 (d)
French North America: *The Jesuit Relations,* S18-9–S18-11 (d)
Fustat: Jewish engagement contract from, S10-8–S10-9 (d)

Galileo Galilei: letter to the Grand Duchess Christina de' Medici, S17-13–S17-15 (d)
Gallipoli: ANZAC troops at, S28-2–S28-4 (d)
Gal'pern Matchbox Factory female workers' strike: Pinsk, S25-8–S25-11 (d)
Gandhi, Indira: "What Educated Women Can Do" by, S29-12–S29-14 (d)
Genghis Khan strikes West, S12-7–S12-9 (d)
Gentile, Giovanni: "Foundations and Doctrine of Fascism" by, S28-7–S28-8 (d)
George III: Qianlong Emperor's edicts to, S21-6–S21-9 (d)
Germany: flagellants attempt to ward off Black Death in, S11-10–S11-11 (d)
Ghiselin de Busbecq, Ogier: "The Court of Suleiman the Magnificent" by, S16-11–S16-12 (d)
Gorbachev, Mikhail: *Perestroika: New Thinking for Our Country and the World* by, S30-2–S30-4 (d)
Great Britain: Lin Zexu's letter to Queen Victoria, S24-2–S24-3 (d); miners' testimony at Ashley Commission, S26-5–S26-6 (d)
Great Hymn to the Aten, S2-8–S2-9 (d)
Great Revolt: in India, S27-2–S27-5 (d)
Grey, Lady Jane; examination of, S17-2–S17-4 (d)
Grotte des Pigeons, Taforalt, Morocco: shell bead jewelry from, S1-2 (v)

Hachiya, Michihiko: *Hiroshima Diary* by, S28-13–S28-15 (d)
Haedong kosŭng chŏn (The Lives of Eminent Korean Monks): on Buddhism in Korea, S13-6–S13-8 (d)
Hammurabi: Law Code of, S2-2–S2-3 (d)
Hard Times (Dickens), S26-2–S26-3 (d)
Henan Museum, Guo state, Sanmenxia city: iron sword with jade handle, earliest cast-iron object, S4-6–S4-7 (v)
Hippocrates: *On The Sacred Disease* by, S7-5–S7-8 (d)
Hiroshima Diary (Hachiya), S28-13–S28-15 (d)
Histories (Herodotus), S7-3–S-75 (d)
Hitler, Adolf: *Mein Kampf* by, S28-9–S28-11 (d)
Ho Chi Minh: "The Path Which Led Me to Leninism" by, S29-10–S29-12 (d)
Huskisson, William: death as first casualty of railroad accident, S26-3–S26-4 (d)
Hypatia, Alexandria, Egypt: murder of, S7-13–S7-15 (d)

Ibn 'Abd al-Qadir, Ismail: *The Life of the Sudanese Mahdi* by, S27-5–S27-6 (d)
Ibn Battuta: journey to the East African coast, S14-4–S14-6 (d)
Ibn Munqidh, Usama: *Memoirs of Usama Ibn Munqidh* by, S10-6–S10-8 (d)
iconoclasm controversy: documents related to, S10-4–S10-6 (d)
"I Have a Dream" (King), S30-4–S30-6 (d)
Incan roads: Cieza de León on, S15-6–S15-7 (d)
India: Great Revolt in, S27-2–S27-5 (d)
Inland Niger Delta, S6-4–S6-6 (v)
Inquisition: confessions of Marina de San Miguel before, S18-4–S18-6 (d)
"The Iron Curtain Speech" (Churchill), S29-5–S29-7 (d)
iron sword with jade handle: Henan Museum, Guo state, Sanmenxia city, S4-6–S4-7 (v)
Islamic mystic's highest meditative state, S10-10–S10-11 (d)
Istanbul: "A Procession of Artisans at Istanbul" on, S16-9–S16-11 (d)

Al-Jahiz: "The Story of the Judge and the Fly" by, S10-2–S10-3 (d)
Janissary musket, S16-12–S16-13 (v)
Japan: Meiji Constitution of, S24-6–S24-8 (d); *Nihongi* of, S13-4–S13-6 (d); "Secret Plan for Managing the Country" on, S21-9–S21-11 (d)
Jefferson Day: Roosevelt's undelivered address planned for, S28-11–S28-13 (d)
The Jesuit Relations: French North America, S18-9–S18-11 (d)
Jewish engagement contract from Fustat, S10-8–S10-9 (d)

Kalidasa *(The Cloud Messenger),* S8-9–S8-11 (d)
K'atun, Lady: queen of Piedras Negras, S6-6–S6-8 (v)
Kennewick Man: DNA results showing him as Native American, S5-4–S5-6 (v)
Khrushchev, Nikita: letters between Fidel Castro on Cuban Missile Crisis, S29-7–S29-10 (d)
King, Martin Luther, Jr.: "I Have a Dream" by, S30-4–S30-6 (d)

Kipling, Rudyard: "The White Man's Burden" by, S27-7–S27-9 (d)
Kitāb al-masālik wa-'l-mamālik (The Book of Routes and Realms) (al-Bakrī), S14-7–S14-8 (d)
Knossos, Minoan Crete: sketch of palace complex at, S2-7–S2-8 (v)
Kokoro (Soseki), S24-9–S24-11 (d)
Kongo, Afonso I of: letter to King of Portugal, S19-3–S19-5 (d)
Korea, Buddhism in: *Haedong kosŭng chŏn* on, S13-6–S13-8 (d)

"Last Words to the Nation" (Allende), S30-11–S30-12 (d)
Law Code of Hammurabi, S2-2–S2-3 (d)
Letters from the Levant (Montagu), S25-2–S25-4 (d)
Life of Charlemagne (Vita Caroli Magni) (Einhard), S11-2–S11-3 (d)
The Life of Michelangelo Buonarroti (Vasari), S17-11–S17-13 (d)
The Life of the Sudanese Mahdi (Ibn 'Abd al-Qadir), S27-5–S27-6 (d)
Lin Zexu's letter to Queen Victoria of Great Britain, S24-2–S24-3 (d)
Li Si: "Memorial on the Burning of Books" by, S9-4–S9-5 (d)
The Lives of Eminent Korean Monks (Haedong kosŭng chŏn): on Buddhism in Korea, S13-6–S13-8 (d)
London, examination of Lady Jane Grey in, S17-2–S17-4 (d)
Louis XIV: "The Daily Habits of Louis XIV at Versailles" on, S17-9–S17-11 (d)

Maccabees, S7-8–S7-10 (d)
Mandela, Nelson: inauguration speech of, S30-13–S30-15 (d)
Marx, Karl: "Wage Labour and Capital" by, S26-7–S26-9 (d)
Mccartney, George: on China and possibilities of British commerce, S21-4–S21-6 (d)
Meiji Constitution of Empire of Japan, S24-6–S24-8 (d)
Mein Kampf (Hitler), S28-9–S28-11 (d)
Memoirs of Usama Ibn Munqidh (Ibn Munqidh), S10-6–S10-8 (d)
"Memorial on the Burning of Books" (Li Si), S9-4–S9-5 (d)
Mencius: *Book of Mencius* by, S9-3–S9-4 (d)
Meroë, Sudan: relief sculpture from, S6-3–S6-4 (v)
Metternich, Clemens von: secret memorandum to Tsar Alexander I, S22-12–S22-13 (d)
Mexico: casta painting of, S19-10–S10-11 (v); Nahuatl land sale documents in, S18-7–S18-8 (d); scandal at the church: José de Álfaro accuses Doña Theresa Bravo and others of insulting and beating his Castiza wife, Joséfa Cadena in, S18-2–S18-4 (d)
Mexico City: confessions before the Inquisition in, S18-4-18-6 (d)
Michelangelo Buonarroti: *The Life of Michelangelo Buonarroti* on, S17-11–S17-13 (d)
Middle Kingdom Egypt, Twelfth Dynasty: advice from a royal scribe to his apprentice, S2-6–S2-7 (d)
The The Milindapanha (Questions of King Milinda), S8-4–S8-7 (d)
miners' testimony: Ashley Commission, S26-5–S26-6 (d)
Ming Dynasty: model of ship in flotilla of Zheng He, S12-6–S12-7 (v)
The Mingling of Two Oceans (Shikuh), S20-3–S20-5 (d)
Montagu, Mary Wortley: *Letters from the Levant* by, S25-2–S25-4 (d)
Mughal emerald box, S20-7 (v)
musket: of Janissaries, S16-12–S16-13 (v)
Mussolini, Benito: "Foundations and Doctrine of Fascism" by, S28-7–S28-8 (d)
My Own Story (Pankhurst), S26-11–S26-13 (d)

Nahuatl land sale documents: Mexico, S18-7–S18-8 (d)
Nigeria, Sungbo's Eredo, walls and moats, S14-8–S14-9 (d)
Nihongi (Chronicles of Japan), S13-4–S13-6 (d)
Nkrumah, Kwame, "I Speak of Freedom" by, S29-15–S29-17 (d)
Nüjie (Admonitions for Women) (Ban Zhao), S9-6–S9-7 (d)
Nzinga Mbemba (Afonso I) of Kongo: letter to King of Portugal, S19-3–S19-5 (d)

Obama, Barack: address to American youth, S31-7–S31-11 (d)
On The Sacred Disease (Hippocrates), S7-5–S7-8 (d)
opium trade suppression, S24-4–S24-6 (d)
The Origin of Species (Darwin), S26-9–S26-11 (d)
Ottoman Empire: Rose Garden Edict, S25-4–S25-6 (d)

Paine, Thomas: *Rights of Man* by, S22-10–S22-12 (d)
Pankhurst, Emmeline: *My Own Story* by, S26-11–S26-13 (d)
Paris: United Nations framework convention on climate change in, S31-12–S31-13 (d)
"The Path Which Led Me to Leninism" (Ho Chi Minh), S29-10–S29-12 (d)
Perestroika: New Thinking for Our Country and the World (Gorbachev), S30-2–S30-4 (d)
Peru: Caral–Supe culture: quipu from, S5-2 (v); Chavin de Huántar in: textile fragment from, S5-3 (v); Chinese coolie photograph, S23-9 (v); El Castio de Huarmey in: skeletons in Wari royal tomb site, S15-2–S15-3 (v)
Piedras Negras: Lady K'atun of, S6-6–S6-8 (v)
Pinsk, Russia: Gal'pern Matchbox Factory female workers' strike, S25-8–S25-11 (d)
poetry of Tang Dynasty, S12-4–S12-6 (d)
Pompeii: graffiti from walls of (anon.), S7-11–S7-12 (d)
Portugal, King of: letter from Afonso I of Kongo, S19-3–S19-5 (d)
"A Procession of Artisans at Istanbul" (Çelebi), S16-9–S16-11 (d)
Putin, Vladimir: address to Duma concerning annexation of Crimea, S31-04–S31-7 (d)

Qianlong Emperor: edicts to King George III of, S21-6–S21-9 (d)
Questiones naturales (Adelard of Bath), S11-3–S11-5 (d)
The Questions of King Milinda (The Milindapanha), S8-4–S8-7 (d)
Qur'an: amulet containing passages from worn by Muslim slaves who rioted in Bahia, Brazil, S23-6–S23-8 (d)

railroad: William Huskisson as first casualty of accident, S26-3–S26-4 (d)
A Record of Buddhistic Kingdoms: excerpts from, S8-8–S8-9 (d)
Reflections on the Revolution in France (Burke), S22-8–S22-9 (d)
Republic of Georgia, Dzudzuana Cave in: flax fibers from, S1-7 (v)
Rhino Cave, Botswana: python–Shaped ornamented rock from, S1-3 (v)
Rhode Island: documents on slave ship *Sally*, S19-5–S19-8 (v)
Ricci, Matteo: *China in the Sixteenth Century* by, S21-2–S21-4 (d)
Rights of Man (Paine), S22-10–S22-12 (d)
Roosevelt, Franklin D.: undelivered address planned for Jefferson Day, S28-11–S28-13 (d)
Rose Garden Edict, S25-4–S25-6 (d)
Russia: Alexander II's abolition of serfdom, S25-6–S25-8 (d); Metternich's secret memorandum to Alexander I, S22-12–S22-13 (d); Pinsk in: Gal'pern Matchbox Factory female workers' strike, S25-8–S25-11 (d)

Al–Saadi, Abd al-Rahman: on scholars of Timbuktu, S19-2–S19-3 (d)
Saint–Simon, duc de: "The Daily Habits of Louis XIV at Versailles" by, S17-9–S17-11 (d)

Sally slave ship: documents concerning, Rhode Island, S19-5–S19-8 (v)
San Miguel, Marina de: confessions before the Inquisition, Mexico City, of, S18-4–S18-6 (d)
Sarmiento, Domingo Faustino: *Travels in the United States in 1847* by, S23-4–S23-6 (d)
scandal at the church: José de Álfaro accuses Doña Theresa Bravo and others of insulting and beating his Castiza wife, Joséfa Cadena, S18-2–S18-4 (d)
The Second Sex (de Beauvoir), S30-6–S30-8 (d)
"Secret Plan for Managing the Country" (Toshiaki), S21-9–S21-11 (d)
serfdom abolition: by Alexander II, S25-6–S25-8 (d)
Seven Pillar Edits of King Ashoka, S8-2–S8-4 (d)
The Shangjun Shu (Book of Lord Shang), S4-5–S4-6 (d)
Shao, Duke of: announcement of, S4-3–S4-5 (d)
Shiji: "Memorial on the Burning of Books" from, S9-4–S9-5 (d)
Shijing (The Book of Odes), S4-2–S4-3 (d)
Shikibu, Murasaki: *The Tale of Genji* by, S13-2–S13-3 (d)
Shikuh, Muhammad Dara: *The Mingling of Two Oceans* by, S20-3–S20-5 (d)
slave ship *Sally:* documents concerning, Rhode Island, S19-5–S19-8 (v)
Smith, Edwin, Papyrus, three spinal injury cases in, S2-4–S2-5 (d)
Soseki, Natsume: *Kokoro* by, S24-9–S24-11 (d)
The Story of My Misfortunes (Abelard), S11-7–S11-8 (d)
"The Story of the Judge and the Fly" (Al-Jahiz), S10-2–S10-3 (d)
Sudan: *The Life of the Sudanese Mahdi* (Ibn 'Abd al-Qadir), S27-5–S27-6 (d); Meroë in: relief sculpture from, S6-3–S6-4 (v)
Suleiman the Magnificent: "The Court of Suleiman the Magnificent" on, S16-11–S16-12 (d)
Sungbo's Eredo: walls and moats, Nigeria, S14-8–S14-9 (d)

The Tale of Genji (Shikibu), S13-2–S13-3 (d)
Tang Dynasty: poetry of, S12-4–S12-6 (d)
Testament of Youth (Brittain), S28-4–S28-6 (d)
Thomas the Eparch: "The Fall of Constantinople" by, S16-7–S16-8 (d)
Tiananmen Square protests: coverage of, S30-8–S30-10 (d)
Timbuktu scholars: al–Saadi on, S19-2–S19-3 (d)
"Torture" from *Philosophical Dictionary* (Voltaire), S22-6–S22-7 (d)
Toshiaki, Honda: "Secret Plan for Managing the Country" by, S21-9–S21-11 (d)
"To the Person Sitting in Darkness" (Twain), S27-9–S27-11 (d)
Travels in the United States in 1847 (Sarmiento), S23-4–S23-6 (d)
Twain, Mark: "To the Person Sitting in Darkness" by, S27-9–S27-11 (d)

United Nations: framework convention on climate change of, S31-12–S31-13 (d); Universal Declaration of Human Rights of, S29-2–S29-5 (d)
United States: *Travels in the United States in 1847* on, S23-4–S23-6 (d)
Universal Declaration of Human Rights: of United Nations, S29-2–S29-5 (d)

Vanuatu, western Pacific: Lapita pot shards from, S5-7 (v)
Varuna: prayer to, S3-5 (d)
Vasari, Giorgio: *The Life of Michelangelo Buonarroti* by, S17-11–S17-13 (d)
Victoria (Queen): Lin Zexu's letter to, S24-2–S24-3 (d)
Vietnam: Bodhisattva Avalokiteshvara copper head from, S13-9 (v)
Vita Caroli Magni (Life of Charlemagne) (Einhard), S11-2–S11-3 (d)
Voltaire: "Torture" from *Philosophical Dictionary* by, S22-6–S22-7 (d)

"Wage Labour and Capital" (Marx), S26-7–S26-9 (d)
Wari royal tomb site: at El Castio de Huarmey, Peru, S15-2–S15-3 (v)
West Africa: 'Abd al-'Azīz al-Bakrī: on, S14-7–S14-8 (d)
"What Educated Women Can Do" (Gandhi), S29-12–S29-14 (d)
"The White Man's Burden" (Kipling), S27-7–S27-9 (d)

Zheng He: Ming Dynasty model of ship in flotilla of, S12-6–S12-7 (v)

Subject Index

Page numbers followed by *f* denote a figure, page numbers followed by *m* denote a map, and page numbers in italics denote a picture.

Abbasids, 261; Byzantium and, 229; Nubia and, 331; Shiite Islam and, 228; in Syria, 225; Umayyads and, 224
Abd al-Malik, 223, 226
Abdülhamit II, 607–8
Abelard, Peter, 268–69
Abhidharma, 185
Abolition of slavery: in Brazil, 555; by Great Britain, 663; in Latin America, 569–70; in US, 541
Aboriginals: of Japan, 313; of Taiwan, 118. *See also* Australian Aboriginals
Abortion, 745; with China's one-child policy, 750
Absolutism: in France, 415–16; Locke and, 405
Abstract expressionism, *716*
Abzu, 49
AC. *See* Alternating current
ACA. *See* Affordable Care Act
Academy of Florence, 248
Academy of Medicine (France), 530
Academy of Sciences (Paris), 401
Aceh, 382, 668
Achaemenids: empire of, 150–52, 151*m*; government of, 152; Greece and, 154–55; Judaism and, 163, 165–66; military of, 151; polytheism of, 152; as Zoroastrians, 152
Acheulian tools, 7, *7*
Acropolis, 154, 155
Adal, 456
Adelard of Bath, 270
Adena, 115, 116*m*
Admonitions for Women (Ban Zhao), 214
Adriatic Sea, Ottoman Empire and, 376–77
Advanced Research Projects Agency (ARPA), 786
The Aeneid (Virgil), 170, 171, *171*
Aeschylus, 170
Aesthetics, in China, 215
Affordable Care Act (ACA), 776
Afghanistan: Achaemenids and, 151; Great Britain and, 661; Mughals in, 479, 482; Soviet Union and, 737, *737*, 740–41; Sunni Islam in, 379; US and, 770
AFL. *See* American Federation of Labor
Africa: agriculture of, 125–31, 786; Americas and, 134; chiefdoms of, 126; China and, 786; Christianity in, 663; city-states of, 126–28; civilizing mission in, 663; Cold War in, 730–32; colonialism in, 663–67, 663–67*m*, 730; constitutionalism in, 732; economy of, 786; empires in, 473; fossils from, 3; France and, 666–67; Great Britain and, 666–67; history of, 134; Islam in, 785–86; kingdoms of, 125–30, 128*m*, 473; migrations from, 10, 11*m*; nation-states in, 722*m*, 730–32; origins of humanity in, 2–25, *6*; population growth in, 784–85; railroads in, 666–67; rain forests in, 17, 130–31; religion in, 451–52; rock art in, 47; savanna of, 130–31; sculptures in, 344–45, *345*; slaves from, 440, 461*m*, 473; state formation in, 328–49; transformations in, 784–86; witchcraft in, 451. *See also* East Africa; Northeast Africa; Southern Africa; Sub-Saharan Africa; West Africa; *specific countries*
African Americans: Harlem Renaissance of, 683, 686–87; lynchings of, 542; voting rights of, 542
African diaspora, 686–87; culture of, 468–71
African National Congress (ANC), 758, 762–63
African spirituality, 133, 330; in ancient Ghana, 342
Afrikaans Medium Decree, 758
Afrikaners, 459
Afro-Eurasian world commercial system, trade in, 241–42, 242*m*
Agrarian–urban centers (society): in Americas, 108–12; in China, 76–99; in East Africa, 131–34; in eastern Mediterranean, 26–53; in Egypt, 31–41, 32*m*; in Fertile Crescent, 27–31; gender relations in, 9; of *Homo sapiens*, 9; in India, 54–75; in Mesopotamia, 31–41, 32*m*; in Middle East, 26–53; in southern Africa, 131–34; in sub-Saharan Africa, 130–31, 132*m*; in Vietnam, 321–22
Agricultural estates (*haciendas*), 439, 563
Agriculture: in Africa, 125–31, 786; in Aksum, 128; in Amazon, 369; in Americas, 107–17; in China, 720–21; in East Africa, 132–33; in eastern Mediterranean, 29*m*; in Egypt, 39; in Europe, 260–61; in Fertile Crescent, 23, 27, 28–31; in Han dynasty, *210*, 210–11; in India, 66, 725; industrialization and, 626; of Islam, 261; in Japan, 314, 318; in Korea, 306; in Latin America, 568–69; in Middle East, 29*m*, 41; in Ming dynasty, 500–501, 509; of Mughals, 488; in Neolithic Age, 47; in Nubia, 331; in Papua New Guinea, *118*; in Philippines, 670; revolution in, 260–61; in Russia, 616–17; of Sasanids, 228; in Shang dynasty, 89; in Soviet Union, 693, *693*; of Tiwanaku, 355–56; in Vietnam, 323–24, 672; Yellow River and, 96; in Zhou dynasty, 90. *See also* Animal domestication; Plant domestication; *specific crops*
Agrippina the Younger, 159
Aguinaldo, Emilio, 671
Ahadith, 226
Ahimsa (nonviolence), 178, 183–84
Ahmadinejad, Mahmoud, 779
Ahoms, 483
Ahura Mazda, 152, 164
AIM. *See* American Indian Movement
Ainu, 313
Airplanes: invention of, 633; in September 11, 2011 terrorist attack, *770*
Akbar, Jalal ud-Din, 480–81, 481*m*, *483*, 484–85
Akhenaten, 48, *48*, 52–53
Akkad, 26, 35, 35*m*
Aksum, 128*m*, 128–30, *129*; silk and, 211
Alamo, 561
Alaouite dynasty, in Morocco, 377
Alaska, 10, 18, 19, 105
Albania, 609, 742, 777
Albigensians, 278–79
Alexander I, 614
Alexander II, 617, 623, 691
Alexander the Great, 67, 155, 157*m*; in Babylonia, 175; in India, 175, 176–77
Alexander V, 274
Alexius I Comnenus, 234–36
Algebra, 50, 168, 193, 244
Algeria, France and, 651, 660–61, 730
Alhambra of Granada, 245
Ali, Muhammad, 605, *607*, 662
Allah, 223, 301, 477
Allegory, 477
Allende, Salvador, 759
Alpaca, 108, 111, 142, 356
Alphabet: of Meroë, 127; of Phoenicians, 44, *44*
Altaics, 86, 306; Japan and, 313
Alternating current (AC), 631–33
Alt-Right, 776
Altruism, in Buddhism, 184
Amazon, rain forests of, 116, 369
The Ambassadors (James), 546
Amda Seyon, 335
Amenemhet III, 39
Amenhotep IV, 53
American Civil War, 541, 562
American Federation of Labor (AFL), 683
American Indian Movement (AIM), 744

American Indian Wars, 543
American Philosophical Society, 445
American Revolution, 524–26; constitutionalism and, 547
American System, 643, *643*
Americas, 100–117; Africa and, 134; agrarian-urban centers of, 108–12; agriculture of, 107–17; animal domestication in, 108, *108*; asteroids in, 106; caste system in, 440–43; Catholicism in, 443–44; cattle in, 439; climate change in, 106; colonialism in, 424–37, 428*m*; empires in, 350–69, 353*m*; environment of, 102–5, 104*m*; European culture and, 443–46; foraging in, 105–7; gravesites in, 107; iron in, 146; migrations to, 17–23, 22*m*; in Neolithic Age, 108–9; ocean currents of, 103–5; plantation slavery in, 439–40, 459–68; pyramids of, 101, 109; rock art in, 107, *107*; separate evolution of, 120–21; silver in, 438–39, *439*; slavery in, 463*m*; social classes in, 109, 440–43; spears (points) in, 105–6, 107; sub-Saharan Africa and, 145; wheat in, 439; women in, 441. *See also* Central America; Mesoamerica; North America; South America; *specific countries*
Amerindians. *See* Native Americans
Amida (Buddha of the Pure Land), 215, *320*
Amistad, *566*
Amitabha (Heavenly Buddha of the Western Paradise), 185
Ammonia, 631
Amun-Re, 52
Analects (*Lunyu*) (Confucius), 198, 299
Anales deTula, 444
Anatolia, 42; Achaemenids and, 151; Arabs in, 229; Byzantium and, 226, 229, 231; fire temples of, 165; Greece and, 689; polytheism in, 47–48
Anaximander, 165
ANC. *See* African National Congress
Ancestral worship, in Ming dynasty, 511
Ancient Ghana, 341–42
Andes, 102; chiefdoms of, 141–44, 144*m*; cities in, 109–12, 110*m*; foraging in, 115; human sacrifice in, *366*, 366–67; mummies of, 366–67; roads in, 108; Tiwanaku of, 355–56, *356*, 357*m*, 368; trade in, 110; Wari of, 357*m*, 357–58, 368. *See also* Inca
Anglican Church, 412–13
Anglo-Saxons, 253
Angola, 666; civil war in, 757
Aniconism, 245–46
Animal domestication: in Americas, 108, *108*; in Fertile Crescent, 51–52; in Harappa, 60, *61*; in India, 65; in Middle East, 41; in Oceania, 119; in Shang dynasty, 89. *See also* Cattle
Animal Farm (Orwell), *684*
An Lushan, 289
Anne of Bohemia, 274
Anselm, Saint, 268
Anthony of Padua, Saint, 451
Antigonids, 156–57
Antinomian group, 445
Antioch, siege of, 236
Anti-Semitism, Black Death and, 271
Anzick-1 fossil, 20
Apaches, 435
Apartheid, in South Africa, 757–58, *758*, 762–63, 785
Aphorisms of Love (*Kama Sutra*) (Vatsyayana), 69–70, 192
Apocalypse: of Christianity, 166, 373–74; of Zoroastrians, 164
Apocalypticism, 228
Aponte, José Antonio, 567
Appeasement: of Japan, 701; of Nazi Germany, 696
Aquinas, Thomas, Saint, 265, 269, 276
Arabian Nights, 245
Arab-Israeli Wars, *752*, 752–54, 753*m*
Arab League, 755
Arabs, 45; in Anatolia, 229; Christianity of, 222; conquests of, 223–24, 224*m*–25*m*; in East Africa, 335; in Egypt, 222; in India, 281; nationalism of, 778; Nubia and, 330, 331; oil embargo of, 754; OPEC of, 738; Sasanids and, 222; in Syria, 222; Zionism and, 688
Arab Spring, 778, 780–83; SNSs in, 786
Arafat, Yasir, 753, 754
Aragon, 372, 374
Archimedes, 168, 399
Architecture: of Harappa, 61; of Islam, 245; of Japan, 314; of Mughals, 494; of Ottoman Empire, 387–89, *388*; of Roman Empire, 171; of Sasanids, 169
Ardashir, 159
Ardi species, 5
Argentina, 551; cattle in, 569; colonialism of, 438; Creoles in, 552–54; Dirty War in, 760; exports of, 788; as nation-state, 552–54; populism in, 719
Aripithecus kaddaba, 4
Aristocratic landlords: in Byzantium, 239–41; of centralizing states, 387; in feudalism, 258; in Japan, 591; in Korea, 311; in Latin America, 552–64
Aristocratic Republic, 558
Aristophanes, 170
Aristotle, 165, *165*, 267; challenges to, 270; Machiavelli and, 397; scholasticism and, 268
Arjuna, 67
Ark of the Covenant, 334
Armenia: Ottoman Empire and, 608; Soviet Union and, 691; Turkey and, 689
Army of the Andes, 553
Arouet, François-Marie, 402
ARPA. *See* Advanced Research Projects Agency
Art Deco, 696
Artha, 69
Arthashastra (Kautilya), 67, 176
Articles of Confederation, 526
Artillery. *See* Cannons
Art of War (Sun Zi), 67
Arts: in Byzantium, 245–47; of Greece, 169–70; of India, 192–93; Islam and, 244; in Japan, 597; of Latin America, 572–73; in Ming dynasty, 511; modernity in, 646–47, *647*, 716; of Mughals, 493–94; of Persia, 168–69; of Renaissance, 396–98, *399*; of Roman Empire, 170–71; of romanticism, 545. *See also* Rock art; *specific topics*
Aryans, 695; Harappa and, 63; Indo-Europeans and, 64–65
Asceticism: in Hinduism, 72, *72*; in Jainism, 182–83
Asháninka, 429
Ashante, 663–64
Ashoka, 178*m*, 178–79, *179*, 194
Asia: in Cold War, 724–29; migrations to Australia, 10–14; migrations to Europe from, 14–16; monsoons in, 57; nation-states in, 722*m*, 724–29. *See also* East Asia; Southeast Asia; *specific countries*
Al-Assad, Bashar, 782–83
Assemblies, in Mesopotamia, 32
Assembly line, 643, *643*; for Holocaust, 697
Assur, 43
Assyrians: in Egypt, 126; empire of, 43; Greece and, 170
Asteroids, in Americas, 106
Astrolabe, 406
Astronomy, 168; in China, 215–16; of Mughals, 491–92; in Renaissance, 395, 398–400
Aswan High Dam, 723
Atahualpa, *426*, 426–28
Atatürk (Mustafa Kemal), 689, *689*
Atheism, of Jainism, 184
Athens, 46, 152–54; democracy in, 153, 154, 173; women in, 173
Atlantic system, for slave trade, 466, 466*m*
Atlatl, 107
Atman (self), 72
Atomic bombs, at Hiroshima and Nagasaki, 702, *709*
Atomic physics, 644
Atum, 49
Augustine, 167, 253
Augustus, *158*, 158–59
Aurangzeb, 485–86
Austen, Jane, 545
Australia: geography of, 11–12; Great Britain and, 658–60; human adaptations from Africa in, 7–16; Ice Age in, 12,

17; migration from South Asia, 10–14; migrations to, 658–59; rain forests in, 17; rock art in, 47
Australian Aboriginals, 659; culture of, 12–13; Dreamtime of, 13; foraging by, 12; gender relations of, 12; rock art of, 2, *13*, 13–14; women of, 12
Australopiths (*Australopithecus*), 5
Austria: Habsburgs and, 382; Nazi Germany and, 696; Ottoman Empire and, 382; uprising in, 538
Austria-Hungary, 608; Treaty of Versailles and, 681
Austronesian language, 81
Autarky, 685
Auto-da-fé, 389, *390*
Automobile: assembly line for, *643*; invention of, 632
Avatars, 186–87
Averroes (Ibn Rushd), 244
Avesta, 164
Avicenna (Ibn Sina), 244, 270
Ayllu, 361–62
Azerbaijan, Soviet Union and, 691
Aztec, 145, 351, 358–60, *359m*, *360*, *362*, 364–65, *365m*; *Anales de Tula* of, 444; Spain and, 359, 424–26
Azurduy de Padilla, Juana, 551

Baath Party, 782
Babi movement, 612
Babur, Zahir ud-Din Muhammad, 479, *480*, *480m*
Baby-boom generation, 715, 745
Babylonia, 35, *35m*; Achaemenids and, 151; Alexander the Great in, 175; Assyrians and, 43; Judaism and, 163; laws of, 36–37. *See also* Neo-Babylonia
Babylonian captivity, 45
Bach, Johann Sebastian, 398
Bacon, Roger, 270
Bactria-Margiana Archaeological Complex (BMAC), 60, 61, 65
Badshahi Mosque, 494
Al-Baghdadi, Abu Bakr, 783
Baha'i faith, 612
Bahrain, 781
Bajondillo Cave, 21
Bakufu (tent government), 514
Balban, 284
Balfour Declaration, 688
Balkans: Byzantium and, 229; Islam in, 375–84; Ottoman Empire and, 609; Soviet Union and, 708; in World War I, 678–79
Balmeceda, José, 562
Baltic states, 742
Baluchistan, 58
Bambuk, 342
Bana, 282
Banana, 134
Ban Biao, 214
Bandaranaike, Sirimavo, 707, 724
Bandeirantes, 432
Bandung Conference, 726–27, *727*
Bangladesh, 56; as nation-state, 724
Ban Gu, 214
Banjo, 470
Bank of England, 626
Banks: China and, 588; in Dawes Plan, 695; in Europe, 275; factories and, 571; Great Depression and, 684; in Mexico, 771
Al-Banna, Hasan, 723
Banner system, of Manchus, 503
Banpo Village, 80–81, *81*
Bantus, 131, 132–33, 134
Bantustans, 762
Banu, Nadira, 494
Ban Zhao, 211, 214
Baojia, 298, 509
Barbados, 462, 464
Barometer, 402–3
Baron, 260
Baroque arts, 397–98
Barrel vaults, 169, 268
Baseball, 642
Basho, Matsuo, 518
Basilica, *265*, 268
Ba states, in Zhou dynasty, 88
Bathhouses, in Japan, 516, 517, 596
Battle of Adowa, 666
Battle of Agincourt, 273
Battle of Chaldiran, 378
Battle of Crécy, 273
Battle of Hastings, 259
Battle of Manzikert, 234, *235*
Battle of Poitiers, 273
Battle of the Marne, 679
Battle of Tippecanoe, 543
Battle of Tours, 224, 255
Bautista de Toledo, Juan, 389
Bay of Pigs, 714
Beat Generation, 734–35
The Beatles, 734
Beatriz, Dona, 451–52
Becquerel, Antoine, 644
Beethoven, Ludwig van, 545
Being, 165
Belgium: Congo and, 666, *667*, 674–75, 731–32; industrialization in, 628
Bell, Alexander Graham, 634
Benedict, Saint, 255
Benedictines, 255, 264
Benin, 458, *458*
Berbers, 223–24; in ancient Ghana, 342
Beringia Land Bridge, 18
Beringia Standstill, 19
Berlin Airlift, 709
Berlin Wall, 714–15, 742
Berlioz, Hector, 545
Bhagavad Gita, 67, 69, 186
Bharat, 67
Biafra, 756
Bible: in Germany, 409; translation of, 274. *See also* Hebrew Bible; New Testament
Big business: industrialization and, 642–43; in Japan, 698
Bilal, 329
Bin Laden, Osama, 770
Bipedalism, of hominins, 4
Birth of a Nation, 471
Al-Biruni, 406
Bismarck, Otto von, *539*, 539–40
Bismarck Archipelago, 118
Black Death (plague), 271–72, *272m*, 273; centralized kingdoms and, 405; in China, 243, 294, 500
Black earth, 616
The Black Man's Burden (Morel), 675
Black pepper, *190*, 190–91
Black Sea: Black Death and, 243; Catherine I "The Great" and, 614; Eastern Christianity and, 232; Ottoman Empire and, 603
Blackshirts, 693
Blanc, Louis, 639–40
Blitzkrieg (lightning war), 696
Blombos Cave, 10, *10m*
Bloody Sunday, 620
Bluefish Caves, 19
BMAC. *See* Bactria-Margiana Archaeological Complex
Board of Overseers, of Sparta, 154
Boccaccio, Giovanni, 276
Bodhisattva, *214*, 215, *320*; sculpture of, *192*
Bodhisattva, 185
Boers, 459, 757
Bohemia, 382
Bolan Pass, 56
Bolívar, Simón, 556–57
Bolivia, 551; as nation-state, 552–54, 556–57; silver in, 429
Bolshevik Revolution, 700
Bolsheviks, 620, 680, 691
Bonaparte, Louis-Napoleon. *See* Napoleon III
Bonaparte, Napoleon. *See* Napoleon Bonaparte
Boniface, Saint, 253
Boniface VIII, 273
Book of Hamza (*Hamzanama*), 493, *494*
Book of History. See Shujing
Book of Kings (*Shahname*) (Firdosi), 168, 245
Book of Mencius (*Mengzi*) (Mencius), 199, 299
The Book of Odes. See Shijing
Book of Sentences (Lombard), 270
The Book of Songs. See Shijing
Borana lunar calendar, 125, 133

Bosnia-Herzegovina: Bulgaria and, 608; Congress of Berlin and, 607; ethnic nationalism in, 679
Boston, 433
Boston Tea Party, 526
Bouazizi, Mohamed, 781, *782*
Bourbons, 431–32
Bourgeoisie, 263, 637
Boxer Rebellion, 587–88, 699
Bradshaw paintings (Gwion Gwion), *13*, 13–14
Brahe, Sophie, 401
Brahe, Tycho, 401
Brahma, 186
Brahman, 72, 182
Brahmans, 70
Brazil: abolition of slavery in, 555; Canudos in, 574–75; Catholicism in, 575; coffee in, 556, 569; economy of, 760; exports of, 788; federalism in, 555; gold in, 432–33, *433*, 439; maps of, *429*; as nation-state, 554–56; plantation slavery in, 439, 462; populism in, 719; Portugal and, 428, 432–33, 554–55; slave revolts in, 566–67; Uruguay and, 554
Brazil, Russia, India, and China (BRIC), 766
Breech-loading weapons, 634
Brexit, 776
Brezhnev, Leonid, 738, 739–40
Brezhnev Doctrine, 740
BRIC. *See* Brazil, Russia, India, and China
Bride-price, 322
British East India Company, 507–8, *653*; in India, 652–56; opium and, 579; Stamp Act and, 525–26
Brontë, Anne, 545
Brontë, Charlotte, 545
Brontë, Emily, 545
Bronze Age, 33–34; Achaemenids in, 150; in China, 96–97; collapse, 42, 43; India in, 65; in Japan, 314
Bronzes: in Jenné-jeno, 130; of Neolithic China, 81; of Shang dynasty, 77, 86, 93; of Xia dynasty, 83
Brunelleschi, Filippo, 397, *399*
Bubonic plague. *See* Black Death
Buddha of the Pure Land (Amida), 215
Buddhism, *186*; Ashoka and, 178–79; caste system and, 190; in China, 214–15; of counterculture, 734; of East Asia, 215; Four Noble Truths of, 184–85; Hinduism and, 180; in India, 189, 194, 281–82; Islam and, 226; in Japan, 315, 319–20, 327; in Korea, 308, *309*, 312–13; Middle Way of, 184; in Ming dynasty, 511; Neo-Confucianism and, 298, 299, 302; *nirvana* and, 184–85; Noble Eightfold Path of, 184–85; spread of, 187*m*; in Tang dynasty, 206–7, 287–90, 302; texts of, 185; in Vietnam, 321–22, 324–25; Zen, 215, 320, 327
Buffalo, 543
Buhari, Muhammadu, 727
Bulgaria: Bosnia-Herzegovina and, 608; Congress of Berlin and, 607; democracy in, 742; Ottoman Empire in, 608; in World War I, 679
Bulgars, 229, 231
Bullfights, 389
Bunraku, 518
Bunyoro kingdom, 455
Bureaucracy: of British India, 656–57; of China, 200; of Egypt, 38–39; of France, 416; of Harappa, 61; of Korea, 308; of Ming dynasty, 296; of Mughals, 478, 487–88; of Ottoman Empire, 386; of Song dynasty, 290; of Spanish colonialism, 429–31; of Tang dynasty, 289; of Vietnam, 323; of Zhou dynasty, 90–91
Burial sites. *See* Gravesites
Burma, 672; as nation-state, 724
Burroughs, William, 734
Burundi, 665
Bush, George H. W., 770
Bush, George W., 769, 770
Bushido (Way of the Warrior), 317, 327
Buyids, 336
Bye industries, 263
Byzantium, 231*m*; Anatolia and, 226, 229, 231; aristocratic landlords in, 239–41; arts in, 245–47; Balkans and, 229; Charlemagne and, 257; commonwealth of, *230*, 230–32; Eastern Christianity of, 223, 229–37; Egypt and, 223; iconoclasm in, 229–30; icons of, 246–47, *247*; Manzikert and, 234–35, *235*; military of, 232–33; Ottoman Empire and, 376; philosophy in, 247–48; provincial and central organization of, 239–40, *240*; recentralization of, 241; Renaissance in, 248; Roman Empire as, 223; Seljuk Turks and, 233–34; Zoroastrianism in, 278

Cahokia, 134
Cahuachi, 143
Calakmul, 135, 136
Calculus, 400, 491
Calendar: in Africa, 133; Borana lunar calendar, 125, 133; of Maya, 137; in Mexico, 125; of Mughals, 492; Nazca geoglyphs as, 146; in Russia, 680
Calicoes, 490
Caliphates, 227; Kanem-Bornu as, 454–55
Caliphs, 223, 227
Calligraphy: of China, 94, *95*, 215; of Japan, 316, 317, 518; Zen Buddhism and, 327
Calvin, John, 409
Calvinism, 409–12; in New England, 444–45
Cambodia, 672; Khmer Rouge in, 752
Camel, 32, 106, 222
Canaanites (Phoenicians), 44; alphabet of, *44*
Canada, France and, 435
Canadian Shield, 103
Canary Islands, 372
Cannons (artillery): breech-loading, 634; in colonialism, 658–59; in Iran-Iraq War, 755; of Ming dynasty, 509–10; of Ottoman Empire, 385
Canoes, 17
Canon law, 270
Canon of Medicine (Avicenna), 270
Canterbury Tales (Chaucer), 276
Canton system, of Ming dynasty, 507–8, *508*
Canudos, 574–75
Cao Xueqin, 592
Capet, Hugh, 259
Capetians, 259
Capitalism: in China, 748, 749; colonialism as, 673; critics of, 639; in Europe, 263; in Japan, 593–94; in Russia, 620
Capitalist democracy: Great Depression and, 684; modernity of, 766–74; of US, 766–74
Caral-Supe, 101, 109, 134
Caravel, 379
Carbon footprint, 788
Carburetor, 632
Caribbean: climate of, 103; Columbus to, 375; economy of, 565*m*; foraging in, 116–17; plantation slavery in, 460–62; population growth in, 718*m*; Spain in, 424; sugarcane in, 569; urbanization in, 718*m*
Caribs, 424
Carnation Revolution, 732
Carnegie, Andrew, 643
Carnegie Endowment, 683–84
Carolingians, 255, 277
Carranza, Venustiano, 564
Cartels: of big business, 642; in Japan, 593–94, 698
Carter, Jimmy, 754, 756
Carthage, 156–57
Cascajal stone, 115
Caste system: in Americas, 440–43; of Bunyoro Kingdom, 455; of India, 69, 70–71, 189–90, 286, 783
Castile, 372, 374
Castro, Fidel, 714
Çatal Hüyük, 47
Cataphracts, 151, 156
Catastrophe (Diamond), 122
Categorical imperative, 534
Cathars, 278–79
Catherine II "The Great," 613–14
Catholicism, 167; in Americas, 443–44; in Brazil, 575; in China, 507; in France, 537; French Revolution and, 527; Galileo and, 399–400; in Italy, 693; in Kongo, 459; Ku Klux Klan and, 683; in Latin America, 567–68, 572; in Mexico, 559; Nazi Germany and, 695; in Poland, 712; saints in, 444;

Thirty Years' War and, 413–15; in Vietnam, 672. *See also* Papacy
Catholic Reformation, 411; Baroque arts and, 397; education and, 444; New Sciences and, 401
Cattle: in Americas, 439; in Argentina, 569; in central Africa, 455
Cattle lords, 455
Caudillismo, 566
Caudillo, 556; in Mexico, 559; in Venezuela, 557–58
Cave painting. *See* Rock art
Caves: hominins in, 6–7; *Homo sapiens* in, 8; Neanderthals in, 14–15
Cavour, Camillo di, 539
Ceauşescu, Nicolae, 742
Celibacy, 232
Celluloid, 631
Celts, 253; ships of, 378
Central Africa, 455; chiefdoms and kingdoms of, 340–41; Livingstone in, 663
Central America: colonialism in, 430*m*; proxy wars in, 759. *See also* Mesoamerica
Central Intelligence Agency (CIA), 711; in Chile, 759; in Congo, 732; in Ghana, 731
Centralized kingdoms, 405–7
Centralizing states: in Europe, 386–87, 392, 420; in Middle East, 392
Cervantes, Miguel de, 390–91, 392–93
Césaire, Aimé, 687
Cesspits, 60
Ceuta, 374
Ceylon. *See* Sri Lanka
Chagatai, 292, 478, 493
Chalcedon (Chalcedonian church), 149–50
Chalcolithic Age (Copper Age), 33
Chalukyas, 180, 283
Chamberlain, Neville, 696, 697
Chan Buddhism. *See* Zen Buddhism
Chandragupta I, 180
Chandragupta Maurya, 175, 176–78, 183
Chaos, 170
Charaka Samhita, 193
Chariots: of Hittites, 42; in India, 65; in Middle East and eastern Mediterranean, 41; in Shang dynasty, 84–85, 86
Charlemagne, empires of, 254, 256*m*, 256–57, *257*; Germany and, 260
Charles I, 420
Charles IV, 272
Charles V, 371, 380–82, 386–87; Protestant Reformation and, 409
Charles VII, 273
Charles X, 537, 651
Chartism, 640
Châtelet, Émilie du, 402
Chattel, slaves as, 460
Chaucer, Geoffrey, 276
Chauvet Cave, 15
Chávez, Hugo, 787
Chavín de Huántar, 110–12, *111*, 134
Chemicals, 631
Cheng (First Emperor), *202*, 202–3, 217
Chernobyl nuclear accident, 742
Chernyshevsky, Nikolai, 623
Cheyenne, 435
Chiang K'ai-shek, 700–701, 720
Chiapas, 254
Chichén Itzá, 354–55, *355*
Chiefdoms: of Africa, 126; of Andes, 141–44, 144*m*; of central Africa, 340–41; of Mesoamerica, 134–41; in Mexican Basin, 352; of sub-Saharan Africa, 146
Childebert II, 255
Child labor, 640–41; in coal mines, 639, *639*
Chile: copper in, 568; exports of, 788; gold in, 429; as nation-state, 558; populism in, 719; proxy war in, 759
China: aesthetics in, 215; Africa and, 786; agrarian society in, 76–99; agriculture of, 720–21; astronomy in, 215–16; Black Death in, 243, 294, 500; in BRIC, 766; Bronze Age in, 96–97; Buddhism in, 185, 214–15; bureaucracy in, 200; calligraphy of, 94, *95*, 215; capitalism in, 748, 749; Catholicism in, 507; climate of, 78–80, 79*m*, 97; colonialism by, 586–87; communism in, 774–75; Communist Party in, 700, 720–21; Confucianism in, 198–200; coolies from, 570; cotton in, 502; Cultural Revolution in, 738, 748–50; culture of, 82, 96; Daoism in, 200–201; deserts of, 78, 80; economy of, 766, *774*, 774–75; empires in, 198–207; environment of, 97; Europe and, 507; exports of, 290; feudalism in, 295; Four Modernizations in, 749–50, 774; France and, 587; geography of, 78–80, 79*m*; Great Leap Forward in, 720–21; Great Wall of, 2–5, 202, 216, 296; greenhouse gases in, 789; imperial unification of, 196–218; import-substitution industrialization in, 768; India and, 748; Industrial Revolution in, 500; irrigation in, 202; Japan and, 326, 512–13, 513*m*, 515, 584–85, *586*, 586–87, 700, 701; Korea and, 307–9, 315, 326, 711–12; land reform in, 720; languages in, 81; literature in, 300; migrations from, 571*m*; modernism in, 577; Mongols in, 275; nationalism in, 700–701; Neo-Confucianism in, 520; in Neolithic Age, 80–82, 97; nomads in, 203–4; nuclear weapons of, 748; one-child policy in, 750; porcelain in, 208, 216, 502, 505, *505*; Portugal and, 507; printing in, 216; Protestantism in, 593; responsibility system of, 749; rice in, 82; roads in, 202; science and technology in, 584–85; ships of, 262, 378; silk in, 80–81, 208, 502; Silk Road in, 203, 210–11; social classes in, 203; social stratification in, 84; South Africa and, 757; Soviet Union and, 719, 721, 738, 748; steam engine in, *581*; stirrups in, *206*, 206–7; tea from, 290, 317, 320, 502; textile industry in, 627; Thermidorean Reaction by, 748; Three Kingdoms period in, 205; trade by, 502, 502*m*; treaty ports in, 582*m*; in UN, 749; Vietnam and, 729, 748, 752; women in, 98–99, 217–18; women's rights in, 747; in World War I, 679; writing in, 202, 204; Yellow River in, 78–83. *See also* Han dynasty; Mandate of Heaven; Ming dynasty; Qin dynasty; Qing dynasty; Shang dynasty; Song dynasty; Tang dynasty; Xia dynasty; Yuan dynasty; Zhou dynasty
Chinampas, 364–65
Chishti, Salim, 482, *483*
Cholas, 180, 283
Choson, 307
Christianity: in Africa, 663; in Aksum, 129; apocalypse of, 166, 373–74; of Arabs, 222; church of, 166–67; in Ethiopia, 333–35, 456; in Granada, 374–75; in Iberia, 372–75; in India, 654, 655; in Indian Ocean, 382; Islam and, 226, 372–84, 391; in Japan, 515; in Kongo, 458–59, *459*; in Mesopotamia, 149–50; of Native Americans, 432, 435; Nietzsche on, 646; in Nigeria, 756; in northeast Africa, 330–35, 347; origins of, 166; in Ottoman Empire, 606; paganism to, 255; in Persia, 160; in Roman Empire, 159–61; as state religions, 249; Sufism and, 243. *See also* Catholicism; Coptic Christianity; Eastern Christianity; Protestantism; Western Christianity
Chromaticism, 647
Chronicles of Japan (Nihongi), 321
Chungin, 312
Chu nom (southern characters), 325
Church Fathers, 167, 708
Churchill, Winston, 697
Chushingura (The Forty-Seven Ronin) (Monzaemon), 518
CIA. *See* Central Intelligence Agency
Circumcision, 388
Cistercians, 264
Cities, city-states: of Africa, 126–28; of Andes, 109–12, 110*m*; of East Africa, 133–34, 335–37; of Greece, 46, 152–55, 153*m*; of Harappa, 59*m*, 59–60; of Inca, 362; of Italy, 156; of Mesoamerica, 112–16; of Mesopotamia, 4, 33–34; of Ming dynasty, 297; of Oceania, 121; of Phoenicians, 44; of Sicily, 156; of sub-Saharan Africa, 146; of Swahili, 134, 336, 338*m*, 665
Citizen Amendment Bill, in India, 783
The City of God (Augustine), 167
"City of Victory" (Vijayanagar), 283
Civil Code, in France, 529

Civilizing mission, in Africa, 663
Civil Rights, Act of 1964, 744
Civil rights movement: student demonstrations for, 745–46; in US, 744–45
Civil service (India), 656
Civil wars: American Civil War, 541, 562; in Angola, 757; from Arab Spring, 782–82; in England, 412–13, 420–21; in France, 411–12; in Lebanon, 754–55; in Nigeria, 756; in Rwanda, 770; in Somalia, 785; in Soviet Union, 692–93; in Spain, 696; in Sudan, 771; in Syria, 778; in Yemen, 765; in Yugoslavia, 777
Cixi (Empress Dowager), 290, 303, 585
Clans: in African diaspora, 469; of Andes, 357; of Australian Aboriginals, 13; of Aztec, 365; in India, 69, 70–71; in Japan, 314, 315; in Vietnam, 322, 324; in Xia dynasty, 83
Clarified butter (ghee), 65
Classic of Documents. See Shujing
Classic of Filial Piety (*Xiaojing*), 214
Classic of the Way and Virtue (*Daode Jing*), 200
Claudius Ptolemy, 168
Cleisthenes, 153
Clement V, 273
Clement VII, 274
Clermont (steam ship), 627
Client states, of Shang dynasty, 85
Climate: of Caribbean, 103; of China, 78–80, 79*m*, 97; of Japan, 313, 314*m*; of Korea, 306, 308*m*; of Mesoamerica, 103; of North America, 103; of South America, 103
Climate change, 790*m*; in Americas, 106; global warming and, 788–90; Harappa and, 62; hominins and, 4; Neanderthals and, 20; in Teotihuacán, 141. *See also* Ice Age
Clinton, Bill, 769
Clinton, Hillary, 776
Clive, Robert, 652, *653*
Cloves, 283
Clovis (Frankish king), 254
Clovis-first debates, 106
Clovis points, 19, 105–6
Coal mines, 626, 639, 640–41
Cochinchina, 672
Code of Manu, 69
Codex Justinianus, 162
Coercive Acts (Intolerable Acts), 526
Coffee: in Brazil, 556, 569; in Latin America, 569; New Sciences and, 401; Ottoman Empire and, 382; in Vietnam, 672
Cold War, 708–33, 710*m*; in Africa, 730–32; Asia in, 724–29; containment in, 708; Cuban Missile Crisis in, 715, 738, 750; Egypt in, 723–24; end of, 736–63; Hungary in, 713, *713*; Korea in, 711–12; NAM in, 707, 724, 726–27; nation-states in, 719–32; Palestine and, 721–23; Poland in, 712; weapons in, 713–14; Yugoslavia in, 708–9
College of Cardinals, 264, 273, 274
Colombia: democracy in, 718; land reform in, 719; Marxism in, 787; in NAM, 727; slave revolts in, 471
Colonialism: in Africa, 663–67, 663–67*m*, 730; in Americas, 424–37, 428*m*; as capitalism, 673; in Central America, 430*m*; by China, 586–87; competition in, 661*m*; in Cuba, 438; in East Africa, 665–66; by England, 435–36, 524–25, 525*m*; in Korea, 586–87; in Middle East, 660–63; in North America, 433–46, 435*m*, 524–25, 525*m*; in Polynesia, 119; by Portugal, 432–33; 1750-1914, 650–75; social Darwinism and, 645; in South America, 430*m*; in Southeast Asia, 586–87, 667–73, 669*m*; by Spain, 428–32; in West Africa, 663–65
Columbian Exchange, 436–37, 437*m*, 438; China and, 500
Columbus, Christopher, 375, *375*
Comanches, 435; Mexico and, 559–60
COMECON. *See* Council for Mutual Economic Assistance
Commanderies, in China, 203
Commedia dell'arte, 397
Committee of Public Safety, in French Revolution, 528
Committee of Union and Progress (CUP), 608–9
Commonwealth of Independent States, 742
Commune, 548–49
Communism: in China, 774–75; in Congo, 732; in Cuba, 714; in Greece, 708–9; Hitler and, 695; Marx and Engels in, 640; McCarthy and, 712; in sub-Saharan Africa, 784; in Vietnam, 750–52, 775; in Yugoslavia, 777. *See also* Soviet Union
The Communist Manifesto (Marx and Engels), 640
Communist Party: in China, 700, 720–21; in France, 686; in Poland, 742; in Soviet Union, 691–92
Companion to Urania (*Urania propitia*) (Cunitz), 395
Compass, 262, 406
Comte, Auguste, 545
CONADEP. *See* National Commission on the Disappearance of Persons
Concert of Europe, 660
Concordat of Worms, 264
Confessions (Augustine), 167
Confucianism: in China, 198–200; in Han dynasty, 212–14; Islam and, 226; in Korea, 308; Legalism and, 200; in Ming dynasty, 297; in Qin dynasty, 203; in Vietnam, 323. *See also* Neo-Confucianism
Confucius, 96, 97, 198, 217
Congo (Zaire): Belgium and, 666, *667*, 674–75, 731–32; as nation-state, 731–32. *See also* Democratic Republic of the Congo
Congo Reform Association, 675
Congress of Berlin, 607
Congress of Vienna, 536–37, 537*m*, 614
Conrad III, 267
Constance of Sicily, 260
Constantine I the Great, 159–60, 171
Constantine XI, 377
Constantinople, 232; Jerusalem and, 236, 237; Ottoman Empire and, 376–77; Russia and, 616, 618; Western Christianity in, 234, 270–76
Constitutionalism: in Africa, 732; American Revolution and, 547; in England, 418–19; ethnic nationalism and, 535, 547–48; in France, 523; French Revolution and, 547; in Haiti, 535; in Latin America, 552–64, 566–67, 690; Locke and, 405; in Mexico, 563–64; in Nigeria, 756; in Ottoman Empire, 606–7; in Russia, 613
Constitutional monarchy, in France, 527
Consumerism: in US, 681–83; after World War II, 715–16
Containment, in Cold War, 708
Continental Association, 526
Continuous-flow production, 643, *643*
Contraception, 745
Cook, James, 658
Coolidge, Calvin, 683
Coolies, 570
Cooper's Ferry, 19, 102
Copernicus, Nicolaus, 168, 398
Copper: in Africa, 130; in Chile, 568; of Hopewell, 101, *101*; of Neolithic China, 81; in Tichitt and Oualata, 126; of Toltec, 352
Copper Age (Chalcolithic Age), 33
Coptic Christianity, 167; in Aksum, 129; in Ethiopia, 456; in Nubia, 330, 331, 333
Cordilleran ice sheet, 17, 19
Cordilleras, 102
Cordite, 634
Coricancha, 365
Corn, 108, *112*, 112–13, 113*m*, 146; in central Africa, 455; in Ming dynasty, 500
Corn Laws, of England, 544
Coronation, 255
Corporate state, 693–94
Corpus Iuris Civilis (Justinian), 269–70
Corsairs, 371
Cortés, Hernán, *425*, 425–26
Corvée, 324
Costa Rica: coolies in, 570; democracy in, 718; populism in, 719
Cottage industries, 626
Cotton: calicoes of, 490; in China, 502; coolies and, 570; in East Africa, 665; from India, 490, 626; in Nubia, 331
Council for Mutual Economic Assistance (COMECON), 709
Council of Constance, 275
Council of Elders, of Sparta, 153–54

Council of Nicaea, 160
Council of Trent, 411
Counterculture, 734–35
The Course of Positive Philosophy (Comte), 545
COVID-19, 681, 766; China and, 775
Creation myths, 49, 170; of Inca, 360
Creed, 232
Creole Christianity, 435
Creoles, 428, 431, 440, 550–75; from African diaspora, 468–70; in Argentina, 552–54; in Kongo, 459; literature of, 573; in Mexico, 558–59, 562–63
Crete, 39–41
Crimea: Catherine II "The Great" and, 614; Russia and, 772
Crimean War, 616, 631, 661
Cro-Magnon, 2
Cromwell, Oliver, 413
Crucifixion, of Jesus of Nazareth, 264–65, *265*
Crusades, 235–37, 236*m*, 266–67; Egypt and, 237; First, 234, 266*m*; Fourth, 234, 237, 248; Jerusalem in, 267; Second, 236; Third, 237, 267
Ctesiphon, 156, 169, *169*
Cuauhtémoc, 426
Cuba: colonialism in, 438; communism in, 714; coolies in, 570; Cortés and, 425; land reform in, 717; slave revolts in, 566–67
Cuban Missile Crisis, 715, 738, 750
Cubism, 646, *647*
Cultivation system, in Indonesia, 668
Cultural nationalism, of Germany, 535–36
Cultural Revolution, in China, 738, 748–50
Culture: of African diaspora, 468–71; of Australian Aboriginals, 12–13; in China, 82, 96; of Enlightenment, 533–35; of Europe, Americas and, 443–46; of Greece, 169–70; of Habsburgs, 392; of Harappa, 60–61; Hellenism, 155, 165; in High Middle Ages, 267–70; of *Homo sapiens*, 3–4; in India, 68–73; of Islam, 243–45, 249; in Japan, 320–21, 597; in Korea, 312–13; of Latin America, 572–73; of Meroë, 127–28; in Middle East, 47–50; in Ming dynasty, 511; of Ottoman Empire, 392; of Persia, 168–69; of Qing dynasty, 592–93; of Renaissance, 394–421; of slaves, *471*; of Song dynasty, 290; of Vietnam, 323; after World War II, 715–16. *See also* Arts; Enlightenment; *specific topics*
Cuneiform writing, 34, *34*
Cunitz, Maria, 395, 401
Cunningham, Alexander, 55
CUP. *See* Committee of Union and Progress
Curie, Marie, 644
Cuzco, 144, 360–61, 365, 368, 428
Cyprus: Great Britain and, 662; Minoan kingdoms of, 39–41
Cyrus II the Great, 150–51
Czar (tsar), 416; collapse of, 680
Czechoslovakia: Marshall Plan and, 709; Nazi Germany and, 696; Prague Spring in, 739–40

Da Gama, Vasco, 375, 486, 507
Daimyo, 317, *318*, 320, 327, 514
Dai Viet (Great Viet), 323
Dalai Lama, 505
Dalits, 70
Dante Alighieri, 276
Dao (Way), 198, 299
Daode Jing (*Classic of the Way and Virtue*), 200
Daoism, 200–201; Han dynasty and, 205; Islam and, 226; in Ming dynasty, 511; Neo-Confucianism and, 298, 299, 302
Daoxue, 299
Dapenkeng, 81
Darwin, Charles, 644–45, *645*
Dasas, 63, 70
Daughters of Liberty, 525
Da Vinci, Leonardo, 397
Dawes Plan (US), 695
Death in the Snow (Makovsky), *621*
Decameron (Boccaccio), 276
Deccan Plateau, 56
Decembrist Revolt, 614
Decimal system, of Harappa, 60
Declaration of Independence, 526, 606
Declaration of the Rights of Man and of the Citizen, 527, 606
Decolonization. *See* Nation-states
Decretum (Gratian), 270
De Gaulle, Charles, 728
De Klerk, Frederik Willem, 758
De la Cruz, Juana Inés, 448
Demesne, 259
Democracy, 47; in Athens, 153, 154, 173; in Bulgaria, 742; in India, 725; in Latin America, 718–19. *See also* Capitalist democracy
Democratic Republic of the Congo, 665, 785
Les Demoiselles d'Avignon (Picasso), 646, *647*
Deng Xiaoping, 721, 748, 749
Denisovans, 14
Denmark, Protestant Revolution in, 409, 540
Department of Commerce and Labor, US, 543
Descartes, René, 404, 534
The Descent of Man (Darwin), 645
Description of Africa (al-Wazzan), 371
Deserts: of China, 78, 80; in Ghana, 341; of India, 57; Kalahari, 17, 133
Dessalines, Jean-Jacques, 532
Détente, 738, 739
Deutero-Isaiah (Second Isaiah), 163–64
Deval, Pierre, 651
Devotion, in Hinduism, 180, 185–87
Devşirme, 385, *386*
Dharma: in Buddhism, 178–79; in Vedas, 67, 69; wheel of, 192
Di, 94
Dialectic, 545
Dialectical materialism, 640
Diamond, Jared, 122
Díaz, Porfirio, 562–63
Dickens, Charles, 546
Diderot, Denis, 533; Catherine I the Great and, 613
Diggers, in England, 420–21
Dihar, 281
Dinh Bo Linh, 323
Diocletian, 159
Dionysiac cult, 170
Dionysius Exiguus, 265
Dirigibles, 633
Dirty War, in Argentina, 760
Disease burdens, Neanderthals and, 21
The Divine Comedy (Dante), 276
Divine wind (*kamikaze*), 316
Dmanisi Cave, 6–7
Doctrine of the Mean, 299
Dollar regime, of US, 767, 771
Dome of the Rock, 223
Dominic, Saint, 265
Dominicans, 265; in China, 507
Donatello, 397
Donation of Constantine, 233
Don Quixote (Cervantes), 390–91, 392–93
Dorgon, 503
The Dream of the Red Chamber (*Hong Lou Meng*) (Cao Xueqin), 592
Dreamtime, 13
Duarte, Eva, 719
Dubček, Alexander, 739–40
DuBois, W. E. B., 686–87
Du Fu, 290
Dulles, Allen, 714
Duma, 621
Dura-Europos, *167*
Durga, 187
Dutch learning, 515, 521
Dutch United East India Company (VOC), 667–68
Dutch West India Company, 459
Dynamite, 634

Early Classic Period, of Maya, 136
Early Dynastic Period, of Egypt, 26, 38
Early humans. *See* Agrarian–urban centers; Neolithic Age; Paleolithic Age
Earthquake detector, *215*, 216
East Africa: agrarian–urban centers of, 131–34; agriculture of, 132–33; city-states in, 133–34, 335–37; colonialism in, 665–66; foraging in, 132; Indonesia and, 133; Islam in, 348; kingdoms in, 335–37; trade by, 242
East Asia: Buddhism of, 215; printing in, 310–11. *See also* China; Japan
Easter, 265
Easter Island (Rapa Nui), 118, 119, *122*, 122–23

Eastern Christianity: Black Sea and, 232; of Bulgars, 231; of Byzantium, 223, 229–37; evolution of, 249–50; height of civilization, 237–43; iconoclasm of, 229–30; Western Christianity and, 233
Eastern Mediterranean: agrarian–urban centers in, 26–53; agriculture of, 29*m*; chariots in, 41
Eastern Syriac Church, 167
East Germany (German Democratic Republic): Berlin Wall and, 714–15, 742; uprising in, 712
East India Railway, 55
Economy: of Africa, 786; of Brazil, 760; of Caribbean, 565*m*; of China, 766, 774, 774–75; of Enlightenment, 534; of Europe, 776–77; of Han dynasty, 208–11, 209*m*; of India, 188–89, 286; of Japan, 318, 515–18, 516*m*; of Latin America, 564–72, 565*m*, 574; money, 385; of Mughals, 488–90; of Nazi Germany, 696; of 1970s and 1980s, 747–48; of Ottoman Empire, 609; of Qing dynasty, 591–92; of Russia, 771–72; of Shang dynasty, 89–90; of US, 771, 776–77; of Vietnam, 323–24; of Zhou dynasty, 90–91
Ecuador, 719
Edict of Nantes, 412
Edison, Thomas, 642
Education: Catherine II "The Great" and, 613; Catholic Reformation and, 444
Edward I, 260
Edward III, 272–73
Edwin Smith Papyrus, 50
Egypt: Achaemenids and, 152; agrarian–urban centers in, 31–41, 32*m*; Arabs in, 222; Arab Spring in, 780–82; Assyrians in, 126; bureaucracy in, 38–39; Byzantium and, 223; in Cold War, 723–24; Coptic Christianity in, 167; creation myth of, 49; Crusades and, 237; Early Dynastic Period in, 26; Free Officers in, 723–24; Great Britain and, 662, *662*, 688–89; hieroglyphic writing in, *38*, 38–39; Hittites and, 42; India and, 74–75; irrigation in, 32; Islam in, 236, 242; Israel and, 738, 754; Judaism in, 242; kingdoms of, 38–39, 42; land reform in, 723; literature in, 48–49; Mamluks in, 233, 237, 238–39, *239*; medical science in, 50; Muslim Brotherhood in, 723, 753; in NAM, 707, 724; Napoleon Bonaparte in, 603; nomads in, 32; Nubia in, 126; Ottoman Empire and, 605, 608; paintings of, 49–50; Philistines and, 44–45; Phoenicians and, 44; polytheism in, 48; pyramids of, 38–39, *39*; religion in, 52–53; sharecroppers in, 32; in Six-Day War, 753; Sunni Islam in, 237; temples in, 33; tombs in, 33; women in, 37–38; women's rights in, 747. *See also* Nile River
Eiffel, Alexandre Gustave, 642
Einstein, Albert, 644
Eisai, 320
Eisenhower, Dwight D., 712, 714, 729
Elamo-Dravidian family, 58
El Castillo cave, 15
Electricity: for incandescent light bulb, 642; in second Industrial Revolution, 631–32
Elements (Euclid), 399
El Greco, 390
Eliot, George, 546
Elizabeth I, 412
Elmina, *457*
El Mirador, 136, *136*
El Niño, 105
El Paraíso, Peru, 109–10
El Salvador, 759
Emancipation Edict (Russia), 617, 623
Emmebaragesi of Kish, 35
Empires: in Africa, 473; in Americas, 350–69, 353*m*; in China, 198–207; in India, 174–95; of Japan, 590, 590*m*; of Persia, 155–63; World War I and, 677–81. *See also specific empires*
Empress Dowager (Cixi), 290, 303, 585
Encomiendas (land-labor grants), 424, 425
Encyclopédie (Diderot), 533
Energy: for industrialization, 626–27; in second Industrial Revolution, 631–33
Enfield rifles, 655
Engels, Friedrich, 639, 640
England: American Revolution and, 524–26; Black Death in, 271; Brexit of, 776; Calvinism in, 412–13; civil war in, 412–13, 420–21; colonialism by, 435–36, 524–25, 525*m*; constitutionalism in, 418–19; Glorious Revolution in, 524, 668; Hundred Years' War and, 272–73, 274; India and, 486–87; Jamaica and, 431; Luddites in, 649; mercantilism of, 462; military of, 413; New Sciences in, 401; opium in, 579–84, 580*m*; Plantagenet kings of, 259; political reorganization in, 274; privateers of, 465; Protestant Revolution in, 409; Scotland and, 418; in Seven Years' War, 437, 524, 526–27, 652; Three Kingdoms of, 413
Enheduanna, 27
Enlightenment, 524; Catherine II "The Great" and, 613; culture of, 533–35; economy of, 534; ethnic nationalism and, 535–36; French Revolution and, 526; in Germany, 535–36; Haiti and, 532; industrialization and, 626; Jefferson and, 526; literature of, 534; Mexico and, 558; music of, 534; Napoleon Bonaparte and, 529; philosophy of, 533–34; romanticism and, 544–45; after World War II, 716
Entente Cordiale, 667
Enuma Elish, 49, 170
Environment: of Americas, 102–5, 104*m*; of China, 97; of Fertile Crescent, 28–29, 51; of Ice Age, 17; of Korea, 306, 308*m*; of Oceania, 118–19. *See also* Climate; Climate change
Equal Rights Amendment (ERA), 746–47
Erasmus, Desiderius, 397
Erdoğan, Recep Tayyip, 780, *781*
Eritrea, 666; Italy and, 694
Erligang, 89
Erlitou, 83
El Escorial, 389
Estancias (estates), 554
Estates-General, 259, 527
Estonia, 742
Ethiopia, 130, 333–35, 335*m*, 667; Christianity in, 333; coffee in, 382; Coptic Christianity in, 456; Italy and, 666, 694; Meroë and, 129; Portugal and, 456–57; Roman Empire and, 163
Ethnic cleansing, in Yugoslavia, 777
Ethnic nationalism: in Bosnia-Herzegovina, 679; constitutionalism and, 547–48; Enlightenment and, 535–36; of Greece, 604–5; in Italy, 538–39; of Zionism, 688
Eubanks, Mary, 113
Eucalyptus, 12
Eucharist, 232, 507
Euclid, 399
Eugenics, 683–84
Eunuchs, of Ottoman Empire harems, 388
Euphrates River, 28, 31; Judaism on, *167*; Sasanids and, 228; synagogues on, *167*
Eurasia, 148–73; contrasting patterns in, 280–303; human adaptations from Africa in, 7–16; India and, 56; Meroë and, 128; rock art in, 14; Shang dynasty and, 86; trade in, 285*m*. *See also specific countries*
Euripides, 170, 173
Europe: agricultural revolution in, 260–61; banks in, 275; capitalism in, 263; centralizing states in, 386–87, 392, 420; China and, 507; colonialism by, 119, 424–37, 428*m*; culture of, Americas and, 443–46; economy of, 776–77; famine in, 271; feudalism in, 257–58, 258*f*; firearms in, 384; guilds in, 263; High Middle Ages in, 267–70; industrialization in, 625, 630*m*; Jews and Judaism in, 263; literature in, 276; migrations from Asia, 14–16; migrations in, 636–37, 638*m*; Napoleon Bonaparte and, 529*m*; nation-states in, 536–40, 537*m*, 541*m*; philosophy in, 276; privateers of, 431; rock art in, 15, *16*; ships of, 379; social classes in, 263; trade in, 261–62, 275; urbanization in, 263; World War II in, 696–98, 699*m*. *See also* Colonialism; Western Christianity; *specific countries*
European Concert, 539, 540
Evans, Mary Ann (George Eliot), 546
Evolution, theory of, 644–45
Ewuare, 458

"The Exaltation of Inanna" (Enheduanna), 27
Existentialism, 716
Explorer I, 714
Exports: from Australia, 659; from China, 290; from Latin America, 568–72, 574, 788; to US, 768; from Vietnam, 775
Extraterritoriality, 581
Ezana, 129

Factories, 639; in China, 508, *508*; industrialization and, 627; in Latin America, 571–72
Factory Act, 640
Falklands War, 760
"The Fall of the House of Usher" (Poe), 545
Family: in India, 190–91; in Japan, 318–19; in Latin America, 572; in Ming dynasty, 297–98; of Mughals, 490–91; in Qing dynasty, 508–9, 592; in Shang dynasty, 89–90
Famine: in Europe, 271; Great Famine, of Ireland, 544; in India, 725; in Japan, 518; in Russia, *617*
Faraday, Michael, 631
Far from the Madding Crowd (Hardy), 646
Fascism, in Italy, 693–94
Fashoda, 666
Fatehpur Sikri, 482
Fatimids, 228, 234, 236; Nubia and, 331
Faust (Goethe), 534
Fayyum, 31, 39
February Revolution, in Russia, 680
Federalism: in Brazil, 555; in Venezuela, 557
Federal Reserve Act, 543
Federal Trade Commission Act, 543
Female infanticide, 298
Feminism, 746*m*, 746–47
Ferdinand I, 381–82
Ferdinand II, 374, 375, 386–87; Thirty Years' War and, 413–14
Ferdinand IV, 262
Fernando VII, 557, 559
Fertile Crescent: agrarian–urban centers in, 27–31; agriculture of, 23, 27, 28–31; animal domestication in, 51–52; environment of, 28–29, 51; foraging in, 27, 28–31; hamlets in, 29–30; plant domestication in, 51–52
Fertilizers, manure, 261
Festivities: of Habsburgs, 390; of Ottoman Empire, 388
Feudalism: in China, 295; in Europe, 257–58, 258*f*; in Zhou dynasty, 88–89. *See also* Serfdom
Fichte, Johann Gottlieb, 536
Film industry: in US, 681; after World War II, 716
Final Solution, 697
Firdosi, 168, 245
Firearms, 384; breech-loading, 634; in colonialism, 658–59; Enfield rifles, 655; flintlock muskets, 406, 433, 658; in Japan, 514–15; matchlock musket, 406; of Ming dynasty, 509–10; of Mughals, 491; of Native Americans, 433, 435, 559; of Ottoman Empire, 386; revolver, 634; rifled musket, 634; samurai and, 514–15
Fire temples, 165
First Balkan War, 266*m*
First Crusade, 233, 264
First Emperor (Cheng, Qin Shi Huangdi), *202*, 202–3, 217
The First New Chronicle and Good Government (Poma de Ayala), 444
First Opium War, 580, 588
First War of Independence, in India, 655–56
Flaubert, Gustave, 546
Flemish weavers, 253, 261
Flintlock muskets, 406, 658; of Native Americans, 433, 559
Flores Island, Indonesia, 24–25
Flying buttresses, on Gothic cathedrals, 269
Flying shuttle, 627
Food: from African diaspora, 470; French Revolution and, 527; in Japan, 516
Football Association, in Great Britain, 642
Foot binding, 217, 298, 592
Foraging: in Americas, 105–7; in Andes, 115; by Australian Aboriginals, 12; in Caribbean, 116–17; in East Africa, 132; in Fertile Crescent, 27, 28–31; by *Homo sapiens*, 8; in Mesoamerica, 115
Ford, Henry, 684
Former (Western) Han, 204
Fortunate Edict, 606
The Forty-Seven Ronin (*Chushingura*) (Monzaemon), 518
Fossils, 20; from Africa, 3
Fourier, Charles, 640
Four Modernizations, in China, 749–50, 774
Four Noble Truths, of Buddhism, 184–85
Fourteen Points, of Wilson, 680
Fourth Crusade, 234, 237, 248
Frame Breaking Act (England), 649
France: absolutism in, 415–16; Africa and, 666–67; Algeria and, 651, 660–61, 730; American Revolution and, 527; Calvinism in, 409–11; Canada and, 435; Catholicism in, 537; Catholic Reformation in, 411; China and, 587; civil war in, 411–12; Communist Party in, 686; constitutionalism in, 523; in Crimean War, 616, 631, 661; Estates-General in, 259; Great Depression and, 686; Haiti and, 523–24, 529–32, *530*; Hispaniola and, 431; Hundred Years' War and, 272–73, 274; India and, 486–87; industrialization in, 628; mandates to, 687–88; mercantilism of, 462; Mexico and, 561–62; modernity in, 651; monasteries in, reform of, 264; Nazi Germany and, 696; New Sciences in, 401; Ottoman Empire and, 381, 606; political reorganization in, 274; restoration monarchy in, 537; Russia and, 614; in Seven Years' War, 437, 524, 526–27, 652; Suez Canal and, 723–24; Third Republic of, 540, 548–49; Thirty Years' War and, 413–15; Triple Intervention by, 590, 619; Tunisia and, 662–63; Vietnam and, 671–73, 729; West Africa and, 664–65; women's suffrage in, 641; World War II in, 696–97. *See also* French Revolution; Paris; World War I
Franciscans, 265, 373; in China, 507
Francis of Assisi, Saint, 265
Franco, Francisco, 696
Franco-Prussian War, 539, 661
Frankish Gaul, 254–55
Frankish inquest, 257
Franz Ferdinand, 681
Frederick I, 260
Frederick II "The Great," 417–18
Freemasons, 534
Free Officers, in Egypt, 723–24
French Revolution, 523, 526–29, *528*; constitutionalism and, 547; guillotine in, 530–31, *531*; Russia and, 614
Freud, Sigmund, 645
FSLN. *See* Sandinista National Liberation Front
Fugitive Slave Act, 471
Fu Hao, 77, 86, 91–92
Fujiwara no Kamatari, 315
Fulton, Robert, 627

Gaia, 170
Galen, 270
Galileo Galilei, 270, 399–400; Descartes and, 404
Gandhi, Indira, 497, 707
Gandhi, Mohandas "Mahatma," 689–90, *690*, 724–25
Ganges River, 56, 64, 74; Mauryas and, 176; Vedas and, 182
Gaozu (Liu Bang), 203
Garibaldi, Giuseppe, 539
Garvey, Marcus, 687
Gasoline, 632
Gatling gun, 634, *635*
Gauchos, 553
Gautama, Siddhartha, 182, 184
Gay Liberation Front (GLF), 745
Gays. *See* Homosexuals
Gaza, 778–79
Geisha, 517
Gender relations: of agrarian–urban society, 9; of Australian Aboriginals, 12; of Han dynasty, 211; of Inca, 365–66; of India, 69–70, 192; of Middle East, 35–38; of Ming dynasty, 298; of Mughals, 490–91; of Tang dynasty, 211. *See also* Women
Genesis, 49, 265
Genghis Khan, 237, 291, 294, 302; Timur and, 478–79

Genji Monagatori (*Tale of Genji*) (Murasaki Shikibu), 305, 321
Genoa, 372
Genocide: in Cambodia, 752; in East Africa, 665–66; of Jews, 697, *698*
Genro, 589
Gentleman (*junzi*), 199
Geoglyphs, of Nazca, 143–44, 146–47
Geometry, 168; Islam and, 244
Georgia (nation-state): Ottoman Empire and, 603; Russia and, 771; Soviet Union and, 691
Georgia (US state), 474–75
Gerbert of Aurillac, 267–68, 270
German Confederation, 538
German Democratic Republic. *See* East Germany
German Southwest Africa, 665
Germany: Bible in, 409; big business in, 642–43; Bismarck and, *539*, 539–40; Boxer Rebellion and, 587–88; Charlemagne empire and, 260; Congress of Vienna and, 536–37; cultural nationalism of, 535–36; East Africa and, 665; Enlightenment in, 535–36; hyperinflation in, 694–95, *695*; industrialization in, 628; Morocco and, 667; New Sciences in, 401; papal reform and, 264; Soviet Union and, 708; steel from, 631; textile industry in, 665; Thirty Years' War in, 413–15; Triple Intervention by, 590, 619; Weimar Republic in, 694–95; women's suffrage in, 641. *See also* East Germany; Nazi Germany; World War I; World War II
Gestapo, 696
Ghana, 329–30; ancient, 341–42; as nation-state, 730–31. *See also* Ancient Ghana
Ghee (clarified butter), 65
Ghettos, Jews in, 263
Ghost Dance, 543
Gibbet, Halifax, 530
Gibraltar, 262
Gilgamesh, 48–49, 170
Ginsberg, Allen, 734
Glasnost, 740, 741–42
GLF. *See* Gay Liberation Front
Globalization: poor countries and, 772–74; US and, 768–69
Global warming, 788–90
Glorious Revolution (England), 413, 524, 668
Glyphic script, of Maya, 136
Goban Taiheiki (Monzaemon), 518
Göbekli Tepe, 47
Gobi Desert, 78
Go-Daigo, 316
Goethe, Johann Wolfgang von, 534, 535
Gold: Achaemenids and, 152; in Australia, 659, 660; of Aztec, 424; in Brazil, 432–33, *433*, 439; at Chavín de Huántar, 110, 111; in Chile, 429; in East Africa, 338–40; in ancient Ghana, 342; in Iberia, 341; of Inca, 426–28; in Jenné-jeno, 130; in Mali, 342–45; Mauryans and, 179; of Neolithic China, 81; in Nubia, 126; in West Africa, 341, 374, 377, 663
Golden Horde, 292
Golden Horn, 376, 388
Gold standard: China and, 701; of Great Britain, 568; US and, 767
Goodyear, Charles, 631
Gorbachev, Mikhail, 740, 741–42
Gothic cathedrals, *267*, 267–68
Gouache, 493
Government: of Achaemenids, 152; Confucianism and, 198–99; Daoism and, 200–201; of East Africa, 337; of Harappa, 60–61; of Inca, 362; of Mughals, 487–88; of Nubia, 331; of Zhou dynasty, 90, 97. *See also* Bureaucracy
Government of India Act, 690
Gowon, Yakubu, 756
Granada: Christianity in, 374–75; Jews of, 375; Morisco of, 382, 384
Gran Colombia, 557
Grand Canal, in China, 205
Grand Secretariat, 296, 504
Grasses: in Australia, 12; teosinte, 108
Grasslands: in Ethiopia, 129; in India, 65; Neanderthals in, 20
Gratian, 270
Gravesites (tombs): in Americas, 107; in Egypt, 33; Egypt's pyramids, 38–39, *39*; in Harappa, 62; of *Homo sapiens*, 99–10; in Japan, 315; of Neanderthals, 14; of Nubia, 126; of Olmec, 114; of Qin dynasty, 202, *202*; in Shang dynasty, 91–92, 94; in Xia dynasty, 83
Gray, Tom, 3
Great Awakening, 446
Great Britain: abolition of slavery by, 663; Afghanistan and, 661; Africa and, 666–67; Australia and, 658–60; big business in, 642; coal mines in, 626; Concert of Europe and, 660; in Crimean War, 616, 631, 661; Cyprus and, 662; Egypt and, 662, *662*, 688–89; in Falklands War, 760; Football Association in, 642; gold standard of, 568; Great Depression and, 685; India and, 652–56, *654m*, *655*, *655f*, *657m*, 689–90; industrialization in, 625, 626–27, *629m*; Iraq and, 688; Israel and, 722; mandates to, 687–88; nation-states of, 544; Nazi Germany and, 696; in 1970s and 1980s, 747–48; Ottoman Empire and, 605, 662; paganism in, 253; Palestine and, 721–23; Russia and, 661; Sudan and, 662; Suez Canal and, 723–24; textile industry in, 639; Turkey and, 689, *689*; urbanism in, 636; West Africa and, 663–64; women's suffrage in, 641; in World War II, 697–98; Zionism and, 688. *See also* England; Scotland; World War I
Great Depression, *684*, 684–85; African railroads and, 667; France and, 686; Great Britain and, 685; in Italy, 694; in Latin America, 690–91
Great Enclosure, 340
Greater East Asia Co-Prosperity Sphere, 702
Great Famine (Ireland), 544
Great Game, 661
Great Indian (Thar) Desert, 57
Great Leap Forward, in China, 720–21
Great Learning, 299
Great Plains, Native Americans of, 435
Great Reform (*Taika*), 315
Great Reform Bill (England), 544
Great Viet (Dai Viet), 323
Great Wall of China, 2–5, 202, 216; Korea and, 308; in Ming dynasty, 296
Great War. *See* World War I
Great Zimbabwe, 339–40, *340*
Greece: Achaemenids and, 154–55; alphabet of, *44*; Anatolia and, 689; arts of, 169–70; city-states of, 152–55, *153m*; communism in, 708–9; culture of, 169–70; kingdoms of, 45–47; literature of, 169–70; Middle East and, 155; Ottoman Empire and, 604–5, 608; Persians and, 150–55; philosophy of, 165; political rights in, 46–47; Russia and, 616; sculpture in, 170; Sea People from, 42, 44; Sufism and, 243; women in, 154; in World War I, 679; Yugoslavia and, 708–9
Greenhouse gases, 788–89; in China, *789*
Gregory I, 253, 255
Gregory VII, 264
Gregory XI, 273–74
Gromyko, Andrei, *739*
Grosseteste, Robert, 270
Guanajuato, 438
Guanches, 372
Guanyin, *214*, 215
Guardian Council, in Iran, 755
Guatemala: populism in, 719; Toltec in, 354
Gudit, 333
Guerrero, Vicente, 559
Guilds, in Europe, 263
Guillotin, Joseph Ignace, 530–31
Guillotine, 530–31, *531*
Gülen, Fethullah, 780
Gulf of Tonkin Resolution, 750–51
Gulf Stream, 103–5
Gullah, 470
Gumbos, 470
Guncotton, 634
Gunpowder, *292*, 292–93; in second Industrial Revolution, 634
Gunpowder empires, 491
Gupta Empire, 161, 179–80, *181m*; Huns and, 281
Gustavus II Adolphus, 414
Gu Yanwu, 511

Gwion Gwion (Bradshaw paintings), *13*, 13–14
Gypsies (Roma), 696

H1N1 influenza, 681
Habsburgs: centralizing states of, 386–87; culture of, 392; festivities of, 390; in Italy, 381; Ottoman Empire and, 376–84, 602; Poland and, 614; rise of, 380; in Spain, 380; Thirty Years' War and, 413–15
Haciendas (agricultural estates), 439, 563
Hadar AL 288-1 (Lucy), 3
Hadith, 226
Haiku, 518
Haiti: constitutionalism in, 535; plantation slavery in, 529–30; slave revolts in, 523–24, 529–32, *530*
Hajj (pilgrimage), 226
Hakra-Nara River, 62
Halo, 246, *483*
Hamas, 779
Hamlets: in Chavín de Huántar, 110; in Fertile Crescent, 29–30; of Paracas, 143
Hammurabi, 35, 36–37
Hamzanama (Book of Hamza), 493, *494*
Han dynasty, in China, 88, 203–5, 204*m*; agriculture of, *210*, 210–11; Confucianism in, 212–14; economy of, 208–11, 209*m*; gender relations in, 211; historians in, 214; India and, 189; Korea and, 307; land reform in, 209; Parthians and, 156; Red Eyebrow Revolt in, 204; science and technology in, 215–16; ships of, 378; unity under, 216; Vietnam and, 323; women in, 211
Han Fei, 200, 202
Hangul, 312
Hanseatic League, 275, 406
Hanshu (*The History of the Former Han*) (Ban Biao and Ban Gu), 214
Hara-kiri (ritual suicide), 317
Harappa, 55, 56–63; animal domestication in, 60, *61*; architecture of, 61; Aryans and, 63; city-states in, 59*m*, 59–60; collapse of, 62–63, 74; culture of, 60–61; government in, 60–61; Indo-Europeans and, 63–64; origins of, 73; religion in, 62; trade by, 61; uniformity of, 59–60
Harding, Warren G., 683
Hardy, Thomas, 646
Harems, in Ottoman Empire, 388
Al-Hariri, 240, 243, 245
Harlem Renaissance, 683, 686–87
Harmonious society, in China, 774–75
Harnesses, for horses, 261
Harsha Vardhana, 282–83, 283*m*
Harvard College, 445
Hashemites, 688
Hasmonean, 166
Hausa, 756
Hausaland, 455
Haussmann, Georges-Eugène, 642
Havel, Václav, 742
Hawaii, 119
Headmen, 203
Heavenly Buddha of the Western Paradise (Amitabha), 185
Heavenly Kingdom of Great Peace (*taiping tianguo*), 583
Hebrew Bible, 45, 49; Galileo and, 399; iconoclasm and, 230
Hegel, Georg Wilhelm Friedrich, 545, 623; Marx and, 640
Hegemony, in Zhou dynasty, 88–89
Heian period (Japan), 315, 316, 316*m*
Hellenism, 155; India and, 193; Islam and, 244; in Palestine, 165
Helots, 154
Henry II, *258*, 259–60
Henry III of Navarre, 411–12
Henry IV, 264
Henry the Navigator, 374, 456
Henry VI, 260
Henry VIII, 409
Heraclitus, 165
Heraclius, 150, 222–23
Herder, Johann Gottfried, 535–36
Herero, 665
Heresy: of Cathars, 278–79; in Western Christianity, 265
Herodians, 166
Hertz, Heinrich Rudolf, 634
Herzl, Theodore, 688
Hesiod, 170
Hezbollah, 778
Hidalgo y Costilla, Miguel, 558–59
Hidden Imam (Messiah), 377
Hidden Twelfth Imam (Ismail), 377
Hideki, Tojo, 702
Hideyoshi, Toyotomi, 499, 503, *512*, 512–13, 513*m*
Hierakonopolis, 38
Hieroglyphic writing: in Egypt, *38*, 38–39; of Meroë, 127
High Middle Ages, 267–70
Himalaya Mountains, 56; China and, 78
Himyar, 129
Hindenburg, Paul von, 695
Hinduism, 70–73, 282–83; asceticism in, 72, *72*; devotion in, 180, 185–87; Great Britain and, 656–57; of Gupta Empire, 180; in India, 783; Islam and, 226, 301–2; nationalism of, 724–25, 783; property rights in, 191; Sikhism and, 286
Hippies, 745
Hippodrome, 388
Hirobumi, Ito, 577, 594
Hiroshima, 702, *709*
Hispaniola, 431
The History of the Former Han (*Hanshu*) (Ban Biao and Ban Gu), 214
Hitler, Adolf, 695–96, 697; eugenics and, 684
Hittites: Assyrians and, 43; Egypt and, 42; empire of, 41–42; Phoenicians and, 44
Hobbes, Thomas, 404–5, 526
Hobbits, of Flores Island, 24–25
Ho Chi Minh, 729
Hohenzollern, 417–18
Hohlenstein-Stadel cave, 16
Holocaust, 697
Holy Christian League, 382
Holy Roman Empire, 260; Council of Constance and, 275; Habsburgs and, 382; papacy and, 264; Thirty Years' War and, 413
Holy Rule (St. Benedict), 255
Holy war. *See Jihad*
Homer, 170
Homestead Act, 543
Hominids, 3
Hominins: bipedalism of, 4; in caves, 6–7; climate change and, 4; of Flores Island, 24–25; in savanna, 5
Homo erectus, 4, 6–7; hobbits of Flores Island and, 25
Homo floresiensis, 25
Homo neanderthalensis. *See* Neanderthals
Homo sapiens, 7–8; agrarian–urban society of, 9; in caves, 8; culture of, 3–4; foraging by, 8; migrations of, 10–14, 11*m*; rock art of, 24; symbols of, 9–10
Homosexuals: gay rights movement for, 745, *745*; Islam and, 245; Nazi Germany and, 696
Honduras, 573
Hong Lou Meng (*The Dream of the Red Chamber*) (Cao Xueqin), 592
Hongwu (Zhu Yuanzhang), 296, 297, 309
Hong Xiuquan, 582–83
Hong xue (redology), 592
Hoover, Herbert, 683, 684
Hopewell, 101, *101*, 115, 116*m*
Hoplites, 151
Horace, 170
Horses: in agricultural revolution, 261; of Comanches, 435; harnesses for, 261; in Middle East, 41; of Mongolia, 84–85; stirrups for, *206*, 206–7. *See also* Chariots
Horus, 38
Hostage crisis, in Iran, 756
Household slavery, 457
House of Commons, 274
House Un-American Activities Committee, 712
Howl and Other Poems (Ginsberg), 734
Huaca, 147
Huainan zi, 213
Huang Zongxi, 511
Hughes, Langston, 686, *687*
Huguenots, 411–12
Hui Neng, 215
Hui of Liang, 197
Huitzilpochtli, 358
Humanism, 396, 397; of Renaissance, 276

Human sacrifice: in Andes, *366*, 366–67; at Chavín de Huántar, 111; by Maya, 137, 139, 141; in Mesoamerica, *366*, 366–67; in Shang dynasty, 94
Humayun, 479–80, *482*; Shiite Islam of, 483
Hunas, 180
Hundred days of reform, of Ming dynasty, 587
Hundred Flowers campaign, in China, 720
Hundred Years' War, 272–73, 274
Hungary: in Cold War, 713, *713*; Marshall Plan and, 709; nationalism in, 713, *713*, 777; Ottoman Empire in, 377
Huns, 281
Hunt, Terry, 123
Hunting and gathering. *See* Foraging
Hurricanes, 103, 105
Hurston, Zora Neale, 686
Husák, Gustáv, 740, 742
Husayn, 227
Huss, John, 274, 275, 409
Hussein, Saddam, 755, 769–70
Hussein Dey, 651
Hutchinson, Anne, 445
Hutu, 455, 770
Hu Yaobang, 750
Hydrostatics, 168
Hygiene revolution, 631
Hyperinflation, in Germany, 694–95, *695*
Hysteria, 645

Ibangala, 459
Iberia: Christianity in, 372–75; military orders of, 372; natural sciences of, 400. *See also* Portugal; Spain
Ibn Battuta of Tangier, 294
Ibn Khaldun, 244
Ibn Qasim, Muhammad, 281
Ibn Rushd (Averroes), 244
Ibn Sina (Avicenna), 244, 270
Ibn Taymiyya, Taqi al-Din, 250–51
Ibn Tughluq, Muhammad ("Muhammad the Bloody"), 285
ICBM. *See* Intercontinental ballistic missile
Ice Age, 17–23, *18*; in Australia, 12, 17; canoes in, 17; clothing in, 17; environment of, 17; Japan and, 313; Middle East in, 28–29; Neanderthals and, 21
Iconoclasm: in Byzantium, 229–30; of Eastern Christianity, 229–30
Icons, of Byzantium, 246–47, *247*
Ieyasu, Tokugawa, 513, 514–15, 520–21, 588–89
Igbo, 756
Ijebu, 346
Iliad (Homer), 170
Ilkhans, 291–92
Illustrated Gazetteer of the Maritime Countries (Wei Yuan), 592
IMF. *See* International Monetary Fund
Immigration. *See* Migrations
Imperialism. *See* Colonialism; Empires
Import-substitution industrialization: in Brazil, 556, 760; in China, 768
Impression, Sunrise (Monet), 646
Impressionism, 646
Inca, 144, 351, 360–63, 361*m*; gender relations of, 365–66; government of, 362; quipu of, 109; roads of, 363, *363*; Spain and, 426–28, *444*
Incandescent light bulb, 642
Indentured laborers, 462, 464; in Australia, 658–59
India, 68*m*; agrarian society in, 54–75; agriculture of, 66, 725; Alexander the Great in, 175, 176–77; animal domestication in, 65; Arabs in, 281; arts of, 192–93; in BRIC, 766; British East India Company in, 652–56; in Bronze Age, 65; Buddhism in, 189, 194, 281–82; caste system of, 69, 70–71, 189–90, 286, 783; China and, 748; Christianity in, 654, 655; civil service in, 656; in Common Era, 281; coolies from, 570; cotton from, 490, 626; culture of, 68–73; da Gama to, 375; democracy in, 725; economy of, 188–89, 286; empires in, 174–95; England and, 486–87; family in, 190–91; famine in, 725; First War of Independence in, 655–56; France and, 486–87; gender relations in, 69–70, 192; grasslands in, 65; Great Britain and, 652–56, 654*m*, *655*, 655*f*, 657*m*, 689–90; Gupta Empire of, 161, 179–80, 181*m*, 281; industrialization in, 725; Islam in, 283–86, 301–2, 724, 783; kingdoms of, 67–68, 179; literature of, 192–93; Mauryans of, 176–79, 178*m*; middle class in, *784*; migrations from, 571*m*; monsoon system in, 56–57, 57*m*, 725; in NAM, 707, 724, 727; as nation-state, 724–28; Netherlands and, 486–87; nomads in, 179; pepper from, *190*, 190–91; Portugal and, 375, 486–87; power in, 66–68; railroads in, 55; religion in, 68–73; republicanism in, 194–95; rice in, 66; Sasanids and, 168; science and technology of, 192–93; self-rule for, 689–90; sexuality in, 69–70; silk in, 488; Silk Road in, 189; social classes in, 69, 70–71; South Africa and, 757; Southeast Asia and, 189; taxes in, 188, 286; textile industry in, 627; topography of, 56–57; trade by, 188–89, 489*m*, 489–90; urbanization in, 725, 783; Vedas of, 64–66; women in, 69–70; women's rights in, 747. *See also* Harappa; Hinduism; Mughals; North India; South India
Indian National Congress, 656
Indian Ocean: Christianity in, 382; East Africa and, 133; Islam in, 382; Ming dynasty and, 337; Ottoman Empire and, 383*m*; Portugal and, 383*m*
Indian Removal Act, 543
Indigo: in Ming dynasty, 500; in North America, 464–65
Individualism, 218
Indo-Aryans, 65
Indo-Europeans: Aryans and, 64–65; Harappa and, 63–64; Shang dynasty and, 84
Indonesia: East Africa and, 133; Flores Island, 24–25; NAM and, 707; as nation-state, 724; Netherlands and, 667–68
Indulgences, 408, 409, 411
Indus River (Valley): Achaemenids and, 152; Hinduism and, 71. *See also* Harappa
Industrialization, 624–49; agriculture and, 626; big business and, 642–43; critics of, 639–41; 1871-1914, 628–34; energy for, 626–27; in Europe, 625, 630*m*; factories and, 627; global warming and, 788; in Great Britain, 625, 626–27, 629*m*; in India, 725; in Japan, 631; in Latin America, 717–19, 787–88; leisure and, 642; Luddites and, 648–49; migrations and, 636–37, 638*m*; mining and, 639, *639*; modernity and, 646–47; in North America, 625–26; origins and growth of, 625–34; population growth and, 635–36, 636*m*–37*m*; in Russia, 618–20, 631; science and technology and, 644–46; 1750-1914, 635–43; sewer systems and, 641–42; social and economic impacts of, 635–43; social classes and, 637–39; socialism and, 639–40; in Soviet Union, 693; sports and, 642; in Turkey, 780; urbanism and urbanization and, 635–36; in US, 628; women and, 641. *See also* Import-substitution industrialization
Industrial Revolution, 625; in China, 500; Latin America and, 569; second, 628–34
Infanticide: female, in China, 298, 509, 750; in Japan, 518
Influenza, 681
Information technology (IT), 768–69
Inland Delta, Niger, 130
Inner Mongolia, 80
Innocent III, 265, 267; Cathars and, 279
Inquiry into the Nature and Causes of the Wealth of Nations (Smith, A.), 534
Institutionalization, of Mughals, 480
Institutional Revolutionary Party (PRI), 786–87
Intercontinental ballistic missile (ICBM), 713–14
Internal combustion engine, 632–33
International Monetary Fund (IMF), 771
The Interpretation of Dreams (Freud), 645
Interstadials, 107
Inti, 360
Intolerable Acts (Coercive Acts), 526
Inuit, 115
Investiture controversy, 264
Ionia, 154
Iran: Baha'is in, 612; fire temples of, 165; hostage crisis in, 756; Islamic Revolution in, 611, 755–56; Israel and, 779–80;

Mongols in, 237; Ottoman Empire and, 609–12; Qajars in, 609–12; Safavids in, 377, 609–12; Shiite Islam in, 227, 609. *See also* Persians
Iran-Iraq War, 755–56
Iraq: Great Britain and, 688; in Iran-Iraq War, 755–56; Mongols in, 237; Shiite Islam in, 227; US and, 769–70
Ireland, Great Famine of, 544
Iron: in Africa, 130; in Americas, 146; in Greece, 46; in Han dynasty, 208; of Hittites, 41–42; in Meroë, 128; steel and, 630–31; in Zhou dynasty, 95–96
Iron Age, 42; African spirituality in, 133
Iron curtain, 708
Iroquois, 435
Irrigation: in Americas, 109; in China, 202; in Japan, 318; in Mesopotamia and Egypt, 32; in Nazca, 143
Isabella, 374, 375, 386–87
ISIS. *See* Islamic State in Iraq and al-Sham
Islam (Muslims): in Africa, 785–86; agriculture of, 261; in ancient Ghana, 342; architecture of, 245; arts and, 244; in Balkans, 375–84; Christianity and, 372–84, 391; circumcision in, 388; commonwealth of, 228, 228*m*; culture of, 243–45, 249; duties of, 226; in East Africa, 336, 348; in Egypt, 236, 242; in Ethiopia, 334–35, 456; formation of, 222–28; height of civilization, 237–43; Hinduism and, in India, 301–2; in India, 283–86, 301–2, 724, 783; in Indian Ocean, 382; literature and, 245; in Mediterranean, 236; miniatures of, 246–47; in Nigeria, 756; in northeast Africa, 330–35; of Seljuks, 233–34; Sikhism and, 286; slavery and, 385; in Spain, 265; in sub-Saharan Africa, 454–55; Sufism and, 243; theology of, 226; of Umayyads, 223; in West Africa, 348, 664–65. *See also* Byzantium; Mughals; Ottoman Empire; Sharia Law; Shiite Islam; Sunni Islam
Islamic Government (Khomeini), 755
Islamic Revolution (Iran), 611, 755–56
Islamic State in Iraq and al-Sham (ISIS), 783
Islamism, 778
Ismail (Hidden Twelfth Imam), 377
Israel, 721–23; in Arab-Israeli Wars, *752*, 752–54, 753*m*; Egypt and, 723, 738, 754; Gaza and, 778–79; Iran and, 779–80; Jordan and, 754; Soviet Union and, 722; Syria and, 738. *See also* Jerusalem
Israelites, 44–45. *See also* Jews and Judaism
Isthmus Declaration, 156–57
IT. *See* Information technology
Italy: Byzantium and, 232; Catholicism in, 693; city-states in, 156; corporate state in, 693–94; East Africa and, 666; Ethiopia and, 694; ethnic nationalism in, 538–39; fascism in, 693–94; Genoa in, 372; Great Depression in, 694; Habsburgs in, 381; Libya and, 694; New Sciences in, 401; Norman Conquest of, 261; poetry in, 276; in World War I, 679. *See also* Roman Empire
Iturbide, Agustín de, 559
Itzcóatl, 359

Jacobite Church, 167
Jade: Maya and, 135; of Neolithic China, 81; of Olmec, 114, *114*
Jahan, Nur, 490, *491*
Jahangir, 482–83
Jainism, 177, 180; asceticism of, 182–83; caste system and, 190
Jamaica: England and, 431; Rastafarians in, 334; slave revolts in, 471
Jama Masjid, 494
Jambalya, 470
James, Henry, 546
Jamestown, 433, 464
Janapadas, 66, 70
Janissaries, 385, 602, 604
Japan, 313–21, 512–19; aboriginals of, 313; agriculture of, 314, 318; aristocratic landlords in, 591; arts in, 597; bathhouses in, 516, 517, 596; Buddhism in, 185, 315, 319–20, 327; calligraphy of, 316, 317, 518; capitalism in, 593–94; cartels in, 593–94, 698; China and, 326, 512–13, 513*m*, 515, 584–85, *586*, 586–87, 700, 701; Christianity in, 515; climate of, 313, 314*m*; culture of, 319–20, 597; economy of, 318, 515–18, 516*m*; empire of, 590, 590*m*; family in, 318–19; firearms in, 514–15; First Opium War and, 588; food in, 516; industrialization in, 631; Korea and, 326; languages of, 313; literature in, 305, 592, 597; Manchuria and, 577, 700; Meiji in, 515, 588–90, 590*m*, 593–97, 631; military of, 316–17, 698, 700; modernism in, 577; modernity and modernism in, 595*m*; navy of, 587; Neo-Confucianism in, 499, 513, 515, 517; Netherlands and, 515, 521; newspapers in, 592; novel in, 305, 592, 597; paintings in, 305, *305*, 518, *518*; political parties in, 595–96; porcelain in, 516; railroads in, 589, 594, *594*; religion in, 319–20; roads in, 593; in Russo-Japanese War, 620; science and technology in, 584–85, 596–97; seclusion of, 515, 520–21, 588; Shogun in, 316–17; in Sino-Japanese War, *586*, 586–87; Taiwan and, 619; telegraph in, 589, 594; telephone in, 594; theater in, 518, 597; Triple Intervention on, 590, 619; US and, 589; Vietnam and, 326; women in, 318–19, 517; in World War I, 679; in World War II, 702. *See also* World War II
Japan Current, 313
Jati, 69
Jazz, 683, 686
Jebel Irhoud, 7–8
Jefferson, Thomas, 526
Jenné-jeno, *130*, 130–31, 134, 341
Jerusalem, 45; Achaemenids and, 151; Constantinople and, 236, 237; in Crusades, 267; First Crusade and, 233; Henry the Navigator and, 456; Jesus in, 166; Mamluks in, 234, 335; Second Temple at, 164, 165
Jesuits: in Brazil, 432; Catholic Reformation and, 411; in China, 507; in Ethiopia, 456; Iroquois and, 435; papacy and, 507
Jesus of Nazareth, 160, 166; Crucifixion of, 264–65, *265*; divinization of, 167; iconoclasm and, 230; Jews as murderers of, 263; passion plays and, 389; as son of God, 223
Jews and Judaism, 163–64; Achaemenids and, 165–66; in Aksum, 129; in Egypt, 242; on Euphrates River, *167*; in Europe, 263; genocide of, 697, *698*; in ghettos, 263; of Granada, 375; Hitler and, 695; Holocaust of, 697; Ku Klux Klan and, 683; in Mesopotamia, 163; as murderers of Christ, 263; Nazi Germany and, 705–6; in Ottoman Empire, 606; in Palestine, 163, 165–66; in Persia, 160; saviors of, 704–5; Zionism and, 688. *See also* Israel
Ji, Lady, 92
Jihad (holy war), 226; in Arab Spring, 782; of Seljuks, 234; in Somalia, 785
Jinnah, Muhammad Ali, 690
Joan of Arc, 273
Johanson, Donald, 3, 5
John, King, 260
Johnson, James Weldon, 686
Johnson, Lyndon B., 739, 744; Vietnam War and, 750
John the Baptist, 166
Jordan, 754
Jousts, 389
Juárez, Benito, 561
Judah, 45
Judaism. *See* Jews and Judaism
Julius Caesar, 158
Junzi (gentleman), 199
Jurchens, 291
Justinian I "The Great," 162, 269–70; Plague of, 160–61; silk and, 211

Kabuki, 518, 597
Kahun Papyrus, 50
Kailsantha Temple, *183*
Kalahari Desert, 17, 133
Kali, 187
Kalinga, 178
Kama Sutra (*Aphorisms of Love*) (Vatsyayana), 69–70, 192
Kamikaze (divine wind), 316
Kana system, 321
Kanchipuram, 283
Kanem-Bornu, 454–55
Kang (heated bed), 80

Kangxi, 504, 511
Kang Youwei, 587
Kanishka, 179
Kannon, *214*, 215, *320*
Kant, Immanuel, 534
Karbala, 227
Karma, 183
Karman, Tawakkol, 765
Karma-samsara, 72–73
Kasa-Vubu, Joseph, 731–32
Kashmir, 725
Katipunan, 670
Kaudinya, 189
Kautilya, 67, 176
Kelp Highway, 19
Kemal, Mustafa. *See* Atatürk
Kennedy, John F., 714, 715, 729; assassination of, 744
Kennedy, Robert, 746
Kennewick Man, 21
Kenya, 145, 665; as nation-state, 731
Kenyatta, Jomo, 731
Kepler, Johannes, 395
Kerma, 126
Kerosene, 632
Kerouac, Jack, 734
Kharijis, 336, 342
Khartoum, 126
Khmer Rouge, 752
Khmers, 189
Khoi, 459
Khomeini, Ayatollah Ruhollah, 611, 755, 756, 779
Khosrow I, 162–63
Khosrow II, 149–50, 222, 223
Khrushchev, Nikita, 708, 713; Cuba and, 714; Cuban Missile Crisis and, 715, 738; Great Leap Forward and, 721; Mao Zedong and, 748; for nationalism, 712; Stalin and, 721, 738
Khubilai Khan, 291, 295
Khufu, 39
Khurram (Shah Jahan), 483–84
Al-Khwarizmi, Muhammad ibn Musa, 244
Khyber Pass, 56, 78
Kibbutz, 752
Kiev, 232, 234
Kikuchi, Takeo, 677
Kim Jong-un, 792
King, Martin Luther, Jr., *744*, 746
Kingdoms: in Africa, 125–30, 473; of Africa, 126–30, 128*m*; of central Africa, 340–41; centralized, 405–7; in East Africa, 335–37; of Egypt, 38–39, 42; of Greece, 45–47; of India, 67–68, 179; of Maya, 354–55, *355*; of Mesoamerica, 134–41, 352–55; of Mesopotamia, 34–38, 35*m*; of Minoans, 39–41; of Mycenaeans, 45–47; of north India, 283; in Nubia, 330–33; of Philistines and Israelites, 45; of Phoenicians, 44; in southern Africa, 337–40; of south India, 180–81; of sub-Saharan Africa, 146, 454*m*; in West Africa, 341–46, 343*m*
King List (Mesopotamia), 34
King's Peace of 386 BCE, 154–55
Kipling, Rudyard, 674
Kofun, 315
Koguryo kingdom (Korea), 308
Kojiki (*Records of Ancient Matters*), 321
Kokoro (Soseki), 597
Kokutai (national polity/essence), 677, 698
Komnenos dynasty, in Byzantium, 241
Kong, 198
Kong fuzi, 198
Kongo, 451–52; Christianity in, 458–59, *459*; slaves from, 459
Korea: agriculture of, 306; aristocratic landlords in, 311; Buddhism in, 308, *309*, 312–13; bureaucracy in, 308; China and, 307–9, 315, 326; climate of, 306, 308*m*; in Cold War, 711–12; colonialism in, 586–87; Confucianism in, 308; culture of, 312–13; environment of, 306, 308*m*; Japan and, 326, 515; land reform in, 310–11; literacy in, 312–13; literature in, 313; marriage in, 312; Neo-Confucianism in, 309–12; printing in, 312–13; Qin dynasty and, 577; religion in, 312–13; silk in, 311; social classes in, 310, 312; taxes in, 308; Three Kingdoms of, 307–8; Vietnam and, 326; women in, 312; writing in, 312; in Yuan dynasty, 292. *See also* North Korea
Koryo kingdom, 308–9, 309*m*
Kosala, 176
Krishna (god), 67, 69, 186; Krishna I (ruler), 180
Kshatriyas, 70
Ku Klux Klan, 683
Kulaks, 692
Kurds, Kurdish: ISIS and, 783; Saladin and, 237
Kuroshio current, 105
Kushans, 179
Kushites, 145
Kuwait, 770
Kyoto Protocol, 789–91

Labor assignments (*repartimiento*), 425, 429; in Mexico, 431
Lady Ji, 92
Lahori, Ustad Ahmad, 494
Laissez-faire, 534
Land bridges, 17
Land Code, of Ottoman Empire, 606
Land grants: in Hittite Empire, 42; in Korea, 310; in Ottoman Empire, 384–85; in Qin dynasty, 201
Land-labor grants (*encomiendas*), 424–25
Land reform: in China, 720; in Colombia, 719; in Cuba, 717; in Egypt, 723; in Han dynasty, 209; in Korea, 310–11
Langland, William, 276
Languages: of Akkad, 35; Austronesian, 81; in China, 81; of East Africa, 131, 132–33; of Hittites, 42; of Japan, 313; in Middle East, 26; Proto-Indo-European, 41; Sino-Tibetan, 81; of Vietnam, 325. *See also* Writing
Laos, 672
Lao Tzu, 200
Lapita, 118–19; from Taiwan, 100
Lascaux Cave, 16, *16*
Last Glacial Maximum (LGM), 18
Last Judgment, 377
Lateen sail, 262
Later (Eastern) Han, 204
Latin America, 550–75; abolition of slavery in, 569–70; agriculture of, 568–69; aristocratic landlords in, 552–64; arts of, 572–73; Catholicism in, 567–68, 572; coffee in, 569; constitutionalism in, 552–64, 566–67, 690; culture of, 572–73; democracy in, 718–19; economy of, 564–72, 565*m*, 574; expansion of, 786–88; exports from, 568–72, 574, 788; factories in, 571–72; family in, 572; Great Depression in, 690–91; industrialization in, 717–19, 787–88; Industrial Revolution and, 569; literature of, 572–73; migrations in, 569–70, *570*; nation-states of, 560*m*; population growth in, 718*m*; populism in, 718–19; proxy wars in, 759–60; urbanization in, 717, 718*m*; women in, 572. *See also* Caribbean; Central America; Mesoamerica; South America; *specific countries*
Latin Christianity, 254–55
Latvia, 742
La Venta, 114, 115
Lawrence, T. E., 687–88
Laws: of Babylonia, 36–37; canon, 270; Corn Laws, of England, 544; in High Middle Ages, 269–70; of Roman Empire, 162. *See also* Sharia Law
League of Nations, 681; Ethiopia and, 694; mandates of, 687–88
Leang Bulu' Sipong 4 cave, 15
Lebanon: civil war in, 754–55; Shiite Islam in, 227
Lebensraum (living space), 680, 695
Le dynasty, in Vietnam, 323, 325
Legalism, Confucianism and, 200, 212
Legge, James, 197
Legionaries, 156–58
Leisure, industrialization and, 642
Le Loi, 323
Lenin, Vladimir Ilyich, 620, 623, 673, 680, 691
Lennon, John, 734
Leo III, 257
Leo IX, 232
Leopold II, 665, 666
Leo Africanus, "the African" (al-Wazzan, al-Hasan Ibn Muhammad), 371
Leo X, 371

Lesbian, Gay, Bisexual, Transgender, and Queer (LGBTQ), 745
Letters of marque, 462
Levallois tools, 8
Leviathan (Hobbes), 405
LGBTQ. *See* Lesbian, Gay, Bisexual, Transgender, and Queer
LGM. *See* Last Glacial Maximum
Li (ritual), 199, 298–99
Liang Qichao, 587
Li Bai, 290
Liberia, 667, 785
Library of Alexandria, 168
Libya (Tripolitania): Arab Spring in, 781; Italy and, 666, 694
Li dynasty, in Vietnam, 323
Life lease (*malikane*), 602
Life of Harsha (Bana), 282
Light bulb, 642
Lightning war (*Blitzkrieg*), 696
Li Hongzhang, 577, 585
Lijia, 509
Lin Biao, 748
Lincoln, Abraham, 541
Linear A, 41
Linear B, 45
Lin Zexu, 580
Lipo, Carl, 123
Li Shimin, 206
Li Si, 202, 203
Literacy: in Japan, 319; in Korea, 312–13; Protestant Reformation and, 407
Literature: of China, 300; of Egypt, 48–49; of Enlightenment, 534; of Europe, 276; of Greece, 169–70; of Habsburgs, 390–91; of India, 192–93; Islam and, 245; of Japan, 305, 592, 597; of Korea, 313; of America, 572–73; of Mesopotamia, 48–49; of Ming dynasty, 511; modernity in, 646; of Mughals, 493; of realism, 546; of Renaissance, 396; of Roman Empire, 170–71; of romanticism, 545; after World War II, 716. *See also* Novel; Poetry
Lithuania, 742
Little Ice Age, 271; centralized kingdoms and, 405
Liu Bang (Gaozu), 203
Liu Shaoqi, 721, 748
Livia, 159
Living space (*Lebensraum*), 680, 695
Livingstone, David, 663
Llama, 142, 356
Locke, John, 405
Lodi, Ibrahim, 479
Lombard, Peter, 270
London Working Men's Association, 640
Long Depression, 544, 619
Long March, in China, 701–2
Longshan period, in China, 81, *82*; Xia dynasty and, 83
López, Francisco Solano, 553–54
Lord of Sipán, 142
Lord of the Rings (Tolkien), 25
Lorentz, Hendrik, 644
Lothal, 61–62, *63*
Lotus Sutra, 319
Louis, Antoine, 530–31
Louisiana Purchase, 542
Louisiane, 435
Louis-Philippe, 537
Louis the Pious, 257
Louis VII, 267
Louis XIII, 414
Louis XIV, 415–16, 435
Louis XVI, 526–27, 537; execution of, *531*
Louis XVIII, 537
Loyola, Ignatius, 411
Luba kingdom, 340*m*, 340–41
Lucy (Hadar AL 288-1), 3, *5*
Luddites, 648–49
Lumumba, Patrice, 731–32
Lunyu (*Analects*) (Confucius), 198, 299
Lusitania, 680
Luther, Martin, 409, 452
Lynchings, of African Americans, 542

MacArthur, Douglas, 711
Macaulay, Thomas B., 654
Macedonia, 155
Machiavelli, Niccolò, 397
Machine gun, 634, *635*
Maciel, Vicente Mendes, 574–75
Madame Bovary (Flaubert), 546
Madero, Francisco, 563
Magadha, 175
Magellan, Ferdinand, 669
The Magic Flute (Mozart), 534
Maginot Line, 697
Magna Carta, 260
Magnetic compass, 262
Maguey, 140
Magyars, 257
Mahabharata, 67, *67*, 186
Mahajanapadas, 66
Mahal, Mumtaz, 477
Mahapadma Nanda, 176
Maharajas, 66
Mahavira, 177, 182
Mahayana, 185; Vietnam and, 324–25
Mahendra Varman I, 180
Maize, 112–13
Maji-Maji rebellion, 665
Makovsky, Vladimir Yegorovich, *621*
Malacca, Strait of, 515
Malaria, 663
Malaysia, 724
Mali, 342–46, *346*; Songhay Empire and, 452–53
Malikane (life lease), 602
Malinche, 425, *425*
Malinke, 343–44
Maluka Islands, 667
Mami Wata, 469, *469*
Mamluks, 233; in Egypt, 237, 238–39, *239*; in Jerusalem, 335; Mongols and, 237; Nubia and, 330; Ottoman Empire and, 377; Palestine and, 372
Manchuria: Choson and, 307; Japan and, 577, 700
Manchus, 292; Qing dynasty and, 503
Mandate of Heaven, in China, 87–88, 98, 315; Confucius and, 198; Mencius and, 199
Mandates, of League of Nations, 687–88
Mandela, Nelson, 758, 762, 785, *785*
Manichaeism, 278
Manorialism, 258, 258*f*
Mansabdars, 487–88
Mansa Musa, 345
Manumission, 464
Manure fertilizers, 261
Man'yoshu (*The Ten Thousand Leaves*), 321
Manzikert, 234–35, *235*
Mao Zedong, 701, 720; death of, 748, 749; Khrushchev and, 748
Maps: of Brazil, *429*; of Renaissance, 406–7; of Waldseemüller, *400*
Mapuche, 429
Mapungubwe, 337–38
Maqamat (al-Hariri), 245
Marajó, 116
Marathas, 486
Marathon, 154
Marconi, Guglielmo, 634
Marcus, Siegfried, 632
Marduk, 49, 151
Marie-Antoinette, 528
Marius, 158
Maronites, 754
Maroons, 472
Marriage: of Australian Aboriginals, 12–13; in Japan, 319; in Korea, 312; in Mesopotamia, 37; in Mexico, 572; same-sex, 745; in Vietnam, 322
Marshall Plan, 709
Martel, Charles ("the Hammer"), 224, 255
Martial Emperor (Wudi), 156, 203–4
Martin V, 275
Marx, Karl, 623, 639, 640
Marxism, 620; in Colombia, 787; Mussolini and, 693; in Soviet Union, 691
Mary (mother of Jesus), 230
Matchlock musket, 406
Mathematical Principles of Natural Philosophy (Newton), 401
Mathematics: algebra, 50, 168, 193, 244; calculus, 400, 491; geometry, 168, 244; in High Middle Ages, 270; of Mughals, 491; in Renaissance, 399
Matriarchal clans, 314
Matrilineal clans, 314

Matrilocal clans, 322
Matrilocal marriage, 312
Mauryan Empire (India), 176–79, 178*m*
Maxim, Hiram, 634, *635*
Maximilian, 562, *562*
Maya, 354–55, *355*; ball game of, *138*, 138–39; calendar of, 137; in Caribbean, 117; collapse of, 139; glyphic script of, 136; human sacrifice by, 137, 139, 141; in Mesoamerica, 135*m*, 135–41; polytheism of, 137, 139; *Popol Vuh* of, 444; social classes of, 137–38; writing of, 136, 139, *140*; in Yucatán Peninsula, 135*m*, 135–41
Mazdak, 162
McCarthy, Joseph, 712
Mccartney, George, 578
McKay, Claude, 686
McMahon-Hussein correspondence, 688
McNamara, Robert, 750
Mean speed theorem, 270
Meat Inspection Act, 543
Mecca, 226, 377
Medea (Euripides), 173
Medes, 150–51
Medical science: in Egypt, 50; in High Middle Ages, 269–70; Islam and, 244
Medici, Giovanni Leone di, 371
Medina, 226
Mediterranean: Islam in, 236; Middle East and, 172; ships in, *378*, 378–79, *379*; trade on, 261–62, 262*m*. *See also* Eastern Mediterranean
Megasthenes, 177
Mehmet II, "The Conqueror," 376–77
Mehrgarh, 58
Meiji (Mutsuhito), in Japan, 515, 588–90, 590*m*, 593–97, 631
Mein Kampf (Hitler), 695, 697
Meluhha, 61
Menander, 179
Mencius, 197, 199, 217
Mengzi (*Book of Mencius*) (Mencius), 199, 299
Mensheviks, 620
Mercantilism: in Caribbean, 462; Navigation Acts and, 465; in Zhou dynasty, 91
Mercury, in Peru, 429
Meroë, 126, 127–29; Nubia and, 330
Merovingians, 254, 277
Mesoamerica, 353*m*; chiefdoms of, 134–41; city-states in, 112–16; climate of, 103; foraging in, 115; human sacrifice in, *366*, 366–67; kingdoms of, 134–41, 352–55; Maya in, 135*m*, 135–41, 354–55, *355*; pottery in, 109; Toltec in, 352–55. *See also* Aztec
Mesopotamia, 27, *27*; Achaemenids and, 152; agrarian–urban centers in, 31–41, 32*m*; Akkad and, 26; assemblies in, 32; Assyrians and, 43; Christianity in, 149–50; city-states of, 4, 33–34; India and, 74–75; irrigation in, 32; Judaism in, 163; kingdoms of, 34–38, 35*m*; literature in, 48–49; nomads in, 32; paintings of, 49–50; polytheism in, 48; sharecroppers in, 32; trade in, 32–33; women in, 36–37
Messiah, 223, 224, 377
Mestizos, 441, 558
Metternich, Klemens von, 536
Mexican-American War, 588
Mexican Basin: Aztec of, 358–60, 359*m*, *360*, 364–65, 365*m*; military in, 352–54; Teotihuacán in, 134, 140–41
Mexican Revolution, 559, *560*, 563–64
Mexico: banks in, 771; border wall with, 776; calendar in, 125; Catholicism in, 559; caudillo in, 559; Comanches and, 559–60; constitutionalism in, 563–64; Creoles in, 558–59, 562–63; Díaz and, 562–63; exports of, 788; France and, 561–62; independence of, 559; labor assignments in, 431; marriage in, 572; Native Americans in, 423–24; Oaxaca in, 125; PRI in, 786–87; silver in, 438, 669; Spain and, 424–26; Teotihuacán in, 352–55; uprising in, 558–59; urbanism in, 690; US and, 560–61, 561*m*, 776. *See also* Mesoamerica
Michael I Cerularius, 232–33
Michelangelo, 397
Microlith, 314
Midden, 108
Middle class: in China, 774; in France, 686; in India, 783–84, *784*; industrialization and, 638; in Turkey, 689, 780
Middle East, 777–83; agrarian society in, 29; agrarian–urban centers of, 26–53; agriculture of, 29*m*, 41; Black Death and, 243; centralizing states in, 392; chariots in, 41; colonialism in, 660–63; culture of, 47–50; firearms in, 384; gender relations in, 35–38; Greece and, 155; horses in, 41; in Ice Age, 28–29; Islamism in, 778; mandates in, 687–88; Mediterranean and, 172; migrations in, 778; monotheism in, 163–67, 172; nation-states in, 722*m*; Ottoman Empire in, 602; patriarchy in, 35–38; religion in, 47–50; science and technology in, 50; selective breeding in, 30; Seljuk Turks in, 265. *See also specific countries*
Middle Kingdom, of Egypt, 39
Middle Passage, 467
Middle Way, 184
Migrations: African diaspora, 468–71, 686–87; to Australia, 658–59; from China, 571*m*; in Europe, 636–37, 638*m*; from India, 571*m*; industrialization and, 636–37, 638*m*; in Latin America, 569–70, *570*; in Middle East, 778; in South Africa, 757; Zionism and, 688
Military: of Achaemenids, 151; of Aztecs, 360, *362*; of Byzantium, 232–33; of centralized kingdoms, 406–7; of England, 413, 418; of France, 527, 528–29; of Greece, 46; of Inca, 362–63; of Japan, 316–17, 698, 700; of Mali, 344–45; of Manchus, 503; in Mexican Basin, 352–54; of Nazi Germany, 696; of North Korea, 792–93; of Nubia, 126; of Ottoman Empire, 386; of Philistines, 45; of Prussia, *418*; of Qianlong, 506; of Qin dynasty, 202; of Roman Empire, 156–58; of Russia, 416–17; of Shang dynasty, 77, 90; of Toltecs, 353–54; of US, 769; of Zhou dynasty, 90–91
Military orders, of Iberia, 372
Millet, 134
Milošević, Slobodan, 777
Mines Act of 1842, 641
Ming dynasty, in China, 296–300, 500–510, 501*m*; agriculture of, 500–501, 509; bureaucracy in, 296; Canton system in, 507–8, *508*; cities in, 297; Confucianism in, 297; culture of, 511; decline of, 502–3; in East Africa, 337, *339*; family in, 297–98; gender relations in, 298; Grand Secretariat of, 504; Great Wall in, 296; hundred days of reform of, 587; Indian Ocean and, 337; literature in, 511; navy of, 296–97; Neo-Confucianism in, 298–99, 502, 511; religion in, 511–12; rice in, 500; science and technology in, 299, 509–11; social classes in, 297; trade in, *504*, 504*m*, 504–5, *505*; tribute system of, 309; women in, 298, 509
Miniatures, of Islamic, 246–47
Mining: in Africa, 130; in Australia, 659; coal, 626, 639, 640–41; in Egypt, 39; in Han dynasty, 208; of Hittites, 41–42; industrialization and, 639, *639*; in Latin America, 568; in Mesopotamia, 33; of Minoans, 41. *See also specific metals*
Minoans: kingdoms of, 39–41; paintings of, 49–50
Minutemen, 526
"Minute on Education" (Macaulay), 654
Mit'a, 362
Mithridates II "The Great," 156
Moche Valley, in Peru, 134, 142–43
Moctezuma II, 426
Modernity (modernism): in arts, 646–47, *647*, 716; of capitalist democracy, 766–74; in China, 576–99; in France, 651; industrialization and, 646–47; in Japan, 576–99, 595*m*; in literature, 646; in music, 647; in Ottoman Empire, 603, 622; in philosophy, 646; reactions to, 599; in religion, 646; in Russia, 622; in Soviet Union, 691–92; in US, 681; World War I and, 677–81, 704; after World War II, 716. *See also* Capitalism; Communism; Urbanization
Mo Di, 218

Modi, Narendra, 783
Mohenjo-Daro, 56, 59, 60*m*
Moksha, 182, 184
Moldboard, 261, 299
Molucca Islands, 283
Monasteries, 255; in Ethiopia, 333; in France, reform of, 264; in Japan, 316, 319
Monet, Claude, 646
Money economy, 385
Mongolia: horses of, 84–85; in Yuan dynasty, 292
Mongols, 295*m*; in China, 275; in Iran, 237; in Iraq, 237; in Japan, 316; in Korea, 308–9; Mamluks and, 237; Qing dynasty and, 505; slaves of, 309; Song dynasty and, 291; strengths of, 302; in Vietnam, 243, 323; Yuan dynasty and, 291–95, 309, 478
Monism, 165, 172; Upanishads and, 182
Monochrome painting, 518
Monogamous marriage, of Australian Aboriginals, 12–13
Monopolies: of big business, 642; in Chinese porcelain, 505; in US, 543
Monotheism: Akhenaten and, 53; in Middle East, 163–67, 172; in Roman Empire, 158–60. *See also* Christianity; Islam; Jews and Judaism; Zoroastrians
Monroe Doctrine, 561
Monsoon system: in India, 56–57, 57*m*, 725; in Japan, 313
Montenegro: Congress of Berlin and, 607; Ottoman Empire in, 608
Monzaemon, Chikamatsu, 518
Moquegua, 356
Morel, Edward D., 674–75
Morisco, 382, 384
Morocco: Germany and, 667; Ottoman Empire in, 377–79; women's rights in, 747
Morse, Samuel F. B., 633
Morsi, Muhammad, 781
Mosaics, 166
Mosques, 245; of Mughals, 494; in Ottoman Empire, 388–89
Most-favored nations, 581
Mothers of Plaza de Mayo, 760
Mound building, 115; in Tichitt and Oualata, 126
"Mourning Chen Tao" (Du Fu), 290
Mozambique, 666
Mozart, Wolfgang Amadeus, 534, *534*
Muawiya, 223
Mugabe, Robert, 757
Mughals, 476–97; agriculture of, 488; Akbar and, 480–81, 481*m*, *483*, 484–85; architecture of, 494; arts of, 493–94; Aurangzeb and, 485–86; Babur and, 479, *480*, 480*m*; bureaucracy of, 478, 487–88; decline of, 496; economy of, 488–90; family of, 490–91; gender relations of, 490–91; government of, 487–88; history and politics of, 478–87; in India, 285–86, 286*m*; literature of, 493; Marathas and, 486; mosques of, 494; in north India, 480–81, 481*m*; paintings of, 493–94; religion and, 484–85, *485*, 492–93, 495–96; Revolt of the Sons of, 482; Safavids and, 483; science and technology of, 491–92; Shah Jahan and, 483–84; Shiite Islam of, 483; Sikhism and, 486, 496–97; strengths and weaknesses of, 495; Timur and, 478–79, 479*m*; women of, 490–91
Muhammad (Prophet), 226, 610
"Muhammad The Bloody" (ibn Tughluq, Muhammad), 285
Mujahideen, 737
Mukhtar, Umar, 666
Mulattoes, 441
Mummies: of Andes, 366–67; black pepper for, 190; in Nazca, 143; of Neolithic Age, 108; in Peru, 142, 351; of Shang dynasty, 84
Munich Agreement, 696
Music: of African diaspora, 470; of Enlightenment, 534; modernity in, 647; of Renaissance, 397; of romanticism, 545; of Tang dynasty, *289*; after World War II, 716
Muslim Brotherhood, in Egypt, 723, 753
Muslim Student Followers of the Imam's Line, 756
Mussolini, Benito (Il Duce), 693–94
Mutsuhito (Meiji), in Japan, 588–90, 590*m*, 593–97, 631
Myanmar, 56
Mycenaeans, 42, 45–47; Phoenicians and, 44

NAACP, 686
Nabobs, 652–53
Nagarjuna, 192
Nagasaki, 702, *709*
Nagy, Imre, 713
Nahuatl, 352, 425, 559
Naia, 20
Nakbé, 136
NAM. *See* Non-Aligned Movement
Nama, 665
Namibia, 666
Nanak, 286
Napata, 126
Napoleon Bonaparte, 528–29, 529*m*; in Egypt, 603; Haiti and, 532; Ottoman Empire and, 603; in Russia, 613, 614
Napoleon III, 537, 539; Mexico and, 562; Ottoman Empire and, 606; Palestine and, 616; Paris and, 642; Vietnam and, 672
Naram-Sin of Akkad, 35, 43
Narasimha Varman II, 180
Nasser, Gamal Abdel, 707, 723–24
Nataputta, Nigantha, 182
National Commission on the Disappearance of Persons (CONADEP), in Argentina, 760
Nationalism: of Arabs, 778; in China, 700–701; cultural, of Germany, 535–36; of Hindus, 724–25, 783; in Hungary, 713, *713*, 777; Khrushchev for, 712; in Philippines, 670; in Poland, 712, 777; in Vietnam, 673; World War I and, 645. *See also* Ethnic nationalism; Supremacist nationalism
National Organization of Women (NOW), 746
National polity/essence (*kokutai*), 677, 698
National Rifle Association, 776
National Security Strategy of 2002, of US, 769
National Socialist German Workers' Party. *See* Nazi Germany
Nation-states: in Africa, 722*m*, 730–32; Argentina as, 552–54; in Asia, 722*m*, 724–29; Bolivia as, 552–54, 556–57; Brazil as, 554–56; Chile as, 558; in Cold War, 719–32; Congo as, 731–32; in Europe, 536–40, 537*m*, 541*m*; Ghana as, 730–31; of Great Britain, 544; of Haiti, 532–33; India as, 724–28; Japan as, 589; Kenya as, 731; of Latin America, 560*m*; in Middle East, 722*m*; Paraguay, 552–54; Peru as, 558; Poland as, 740; in Southeast Asia, 728–7729; in sub-Saharan Africa, 732; Uruguay as, 552–54; US as, 540–44, 542*m*; Vietnam as, 729
Native Americans, 21–23; Beringia Standstill and, 19; Christianity of, 432, 435; civil right movement for, 744; foraging by, 105–7; Louisiana Purchase and, 542; in Mexico, 423–24; in North America, 433–35; on reservations, 543; slavery of, 429, 432; social level of, 441–43; tobacco and, 464; in US, 542, 542–43. *See also specific tribes and empires*
NATO. *See* North Atlantic Treaty Organization
Natufians, 29–30, 47
Naturalism, 47
Natural sciences, of Habsburg Empire, 400
Natural selection, 645
Navigation Acts, 465
Navy: of Achaemenids, 151; of England, 418; of Japan, 587; of Ming dynasty, 296–97; of Ottoman Empire, 382–83; of Song dynasty, 292; of Sparta, 154
Nazca, 143–44, 146–47
Nazi Germany: Aryans and, 63; Catholicism and, 695; defiance of, 705–6; eugenics and, 684; Jews and, 705–6; in World War II, 696–98, 704–5. *See also* World War II
Ndongo, 459
Neanderthals (*Homo neanderthalensis*): disappearance of, 20–21; rock art of, 14–15, 20, *20*
Négritude, 687
Nehru, Jawaharlal, 724, 725
Neo-Assyrian Empire, 43
Neo-Babylonia, 45; Achaemenids and, 151; Judaism and, 163

Neo-Confucianism, 302; in China, 520; in Japan, 319, 499, 513, 515, 517; in Korea, 309–12; in Ming dynasty, 298–99, 502, 511; in Song dynasty, 290; tribute mission system of, 521
Neolithic Age (New Stone Age): agriculture of, 47; Americas in, 108–9; China in, 80–82, 97; in Egypt, 31; India in, 58; in Middle East, 30; in Vietnam, 321
NEP. *See* New Economic Policy
Netherlands: Calvinism in, 411, 412; India and, 486–87; Indonesia and, 667–68; Japan and, 515, 521; New Sciences in, 401; privateers of, 465; South Africa and, 459; Spain and, 412
New Amsterdam, 433
Newcomen, Thomas, 403
New Deal, 684–85
New Economic Policy (NEP), in Soviet Union, 692
New England, 443; Calvinism in, 444–45; Protestantism in, 444–46; Puritans in, 435, 444–45; witchcraft in, 445, *445*
New Harmony, 640
New Kingdom, of Egypt, 38, 42, 48
New Lanark, 640
New Model Army, 413
New Sciences (Scientific Revolution), 398–405, 419–20; Enlightenment and, 526; philosophy and, 404–5; social impact of, 401–3
Newspapers: in Japan, 592; photography for, 597
New Stone Age. *See* Neolithic Age
New Testament, 166; Erasmus on, 397; Protestant Reformation and, 409
Newton, Isaac, 400–401, 402; Einstein and, 644
New Zealand, 119
Ngangas, 451
Ngo Dinh Diem, 729, 750
NGOs. *See* Non-governmental organizations
Nguyen dynasty, in Vietnam, 671
Nguyen Van Thieu, 750
Nian Rebellion, 591
Nicaragua, 759
Nicene Creed, 160
Nichiren, 320
Nicholas I, 614–16, 617
Nicholas II, 680
Nietzsche, Friedrich, 646
Niger, 134
Nigeria, 131, 785; civil war in, 756
Nihongi (*Chronicles of Japan*), 321
Nikitenko, Aleksander, 601
Nile River (Valley), 28, 31; Akkad and, 26; Meroë on, 126, 127–29; Nubia in, 330–33
Nineteen Eighty-Four (Orwell), *684*
Nineteenth Amendment, 681
Nirvana, 184–85
Nixon, Richard, 749; dollar regime and, 767; Vietnam War and, 751–52
Nkomo, Joshua, 757
Nkrumah, Kwame, 730–31
Nobel, Alfred Bernhard, 631
Noble Eightfold Path, of Buddhism, 184–85
Nobunaga, Oda, 512–13
Noh, 518, 597
Nomads: in China, 203–4; of East Africa, 131; in India, 179; in Meroë, 129; in Mesopotamia and Egypt, 32; Roman Empire and, 161–63, 162*m*; in Tang dynasty, 291
Non-Aligned Movement (NAM), 707, 724, 726–27
Non-governmental organizations (NGOs), 771
Nonproliferation, of nuclear weapons, 738
Nontariff autonomy, 581
Nonviolence (*ahimsa*), 178, 183–84
Norman Conquest: Frankish inquest and, 257; Hundred Years' War and, 272–73; of Italy, 261; of Sicily, 261
Normans, Byzantium and, 232, 234
North Africa: Ottoman Empire in, 602; Spain in, 377
North America: climate of, 103; colonialism in, 433–46, 435*m*, 524–25, 525*m*; industrialization in, 625–26; Native Americans in, 433–35; revolutions in, 524–26; slavery in, 464–65, *465*. *See also* Canada; Mexico; United States
North Atlantic Treaty Organization (NATO), 711
Northeast Africa: Christianity in, 330–35, 347; Islam in, 330–35; trade in, 331, 332*m*
Northern Expedition, 700, 701
North India: British East India Company in, 653–54; kingdoms of, 283; Mughals in, 480–81, 481*m*
North Korea: nuclear weapons in, 779, 793; socialism in, 792–93
North Pacific current, 105
Novel: in Japan, 305, 592, 597; in Russia, 623; in Yuan dynasty, 300
NOW. *See* National Organization of Women
Nubia, 126; Arabs and, 330, 331
Nuclear Test Ban Treaty, 715, 738
Nuclear weapons: of China, 748; Cuban Missile Crisis and, 715, 738, 750; at Hiroshima and Nagasaki, 702, 709; ICBMs for, 713–14; Iran and, 779–80; nonproliferation of, 738; of North Korea, 779, 793; SALT II and, 740. *See also* Cold War

Oaxaca, 125
Obama, Barack, 769, 776
Obregón, Álvaro, 564
Obsidian, 8–9; of Maya, 135, 140; of Minoans, 41; of Toltec, 352–53
Ocean currents, of Americas, 103–5
Oceania: city-states in, 121; environment of, 118–19; migrations in, 117–19, 118*m*
Ochre, 10, 10*m*
Octavian, 157, 158
October Manifesto, 620–21
Office of Strategic Services (OSS), 711
Official nationality, in Russia, 614–15
Ogé, Vincent, 523–24, 531
Oglethorpe, James, 465, 474–75
Ohio Company of Virginia, 436
Oil: in Angola, 757; Arab embargo of, 754; for internal combustion engine, 632; in Iran, 755, 779; OPEC and, 738; price collapse of, 742; in Venezuela, 719, 787
Old Kingdom, of Egypt, 40*m*, 53; pyramids of, 38–39, *39*
Oldowan tools, 5, 7, *7*
Old Stone Age (Paleolithic Age), 6
Olmec, *113*, 113–15, 134
Olympic Games, 152–53, 642
One-child policy, in China, 750
On the Origin of Species by Means of Natural Selection (Darwin), 644–45
On the Road (Kerouac), 734
OPEC. *See* Organization of the Petroleum Exporting Countries
Operation Colombo, 759
Opium, 579–84, 580*m*, *581*; First Opium War, 580, 588; Second Opium War, 583–84; Taiping Rebellion and, 582–83, 583*m*; Treaty of Nanjing and, 580, 581
Oracle bones, 93, 93–94
Oracles, 152; women at, 154
Oral tradition, of Mali, 344
Ordos Desert, 78, 80
Organization of the Petroleum Exporting Countries (OPEC), 738; dollar regime and, 767
The Organization of Work (Blanc), 639
Orrorin femurs, 4
Ortega, Daniel, 759
Orthodox Church, 167
Ortiz, Alonso, 423–24
Orwell, George, *684*
Osman, 376
OSS. *See* Office of Strategic Studies
Otto I of Saxony, 260
Ottoman Empire, 380*m*, 602–12; Adriatic Sea and, 376–77; architecture of, 387–89, *388*; Armenia and, 608; Austria and, 382; Balkans and, 609; in Bulgaria, 608; bureaucracy of, 386; Byzantium and, 376; cannons of, 385; centralizing states of, 386–87; Christianity in, 606; coffee and, 382; colonialism by, 660; Constantinople and, 376–77; constitutionalism in, 606–7; in Crimean War, 616, 631, 661; culture of, 392; decentralization in, 603; decline of, 603–9, 604*m*–5*m*; economy of, 609; Egypt and, 605, 608; festivities of, 388;

firearms of, 386; France and, 381; Great Britain and, 605, 662; Greece and, 604–5, 608; Habsburgs and, 376–84, 602; Indian Ocean and, 383*m*; Iran and, 609–12; Jews in, 606; land-grants system of, 384–85; in Middle East, 602; military of, 386; modernity and modernism in, 603, 622; in Montenegro, 608; in Morocco, 377–79; mosques in, 388–89; Napoleon Bonaparte and, 603; Napoleon III and, 606; navy of, 382–83; in North Africa, 602; Parliament of, 607, *608*; in Persia, 377–79; Portugal and, 382; reforms in, 602, 606; Russia and, 614, 616, 618; in Russo-Ottoman War, 616, 618; Safavids and, 377, 383; in Serbia, 608; Sunni Islam of, 377; Syria and, 605; Tanzimat in, 606; tax farming by, 385–86; textile industry in, 609; theater in, 388; Treaty of Versailles and, 681; Tunisia and, 608; World War I and, 677–78
Oualata, 126–27
Owen, Robert, 640
Oxford Calculators, 270
Oyo, 346

Pääbo, Svante, 21
Pachacuti, 361, 362
Pacific Ocean: El Niño in, 105; World War II in, 702, 703*m*. *See also* Oceania
Paekche kingdom (Korea), 308
Paganism: to Christianity, 255; in Great Britain, 253
Pahlavi, Muhammad Reza, 755
Paintings: of Habsburgs, 390–91; icons, in Byzantium, 246–47; of Japan, 305, *305*, 518, *518*; of Mesopotamia, Egypt, and Minoans, 49–50; of Ming dynasty, 511; miniatures, Islamic, 146–47; monochrome, 518; of Mughals, 493–94; of Roman Empire, 171; of romanticism, 545; of Russia, *621*; after World War II, 716, *716*. *See also* Rock art
Pakistan, 56; as nation-state, 724, 725
Palace-states: of Minoans, 39–40; of Mycenaeans, 46
Palaiologos, 241
Paleolithic Age (Old Stone Age), 6; Ice Age and, 17
Palestine, 723*m*; Cold War and, 721–23; Egypt and, 723; Gaza and, 778–79; Great Britain and, 721–23; Judaism in, 163, 165–66; Mamluks and, 372; Napoleon III and, 616; Zionism and, 688
Palestine Liberation Organization (PLO), 753, 754–55, 778, 779
Pali Canon, 185
Pallavas, 180
Pamir Mountains, 78
Panama Canal, 558, 632
Pandyas, 180
Pankhurst, Emmeline, 641, *641*
Pan-Slavism, 617–18; Bosnia-Herzegovina and, 679
Pantheon, 171
Papacy: canon law of, 270; Catholic Reformation and, 411; Jesuits and, 507; Protestant Reformation and, 408; reform of, 264; in Western Christianity, 255; Western Schism of, 273–74, 274*m*. *See also specific popes*
Papal Election Decree, 264
Papal States, 539
Paper, 208, *208*; in China, 502
Papin, Denis, 403
Papua New Guinea, *118*
Paracas, 143–44
Paraguay: colonialism of, 438; as nation-state, 552–54
Pardos, 556
Pargana, 488, 490
Paris: Academy of Sciences in, 410; redesign of, 642; universities in, 267–68
Paris Agreement, 790
Parliament, 260; in England, 274, 413, 544; House of Commons in, 274; of Ottoman Empire, 607, *608*
Parthians: Han dynasty and, 156; Roman Empire and, 156–59
Pascal, Blaise, 403
Passion plays, 389
Pastoral Symphony (Beethoven), 545
Patriarchy: in Middle East, 26, 35–38; Vedas and, 65
Patricians, 336, 337
Paul, Mary, 625
Paul of Tarsus, 166
Pax Mongolica, 275
Pax romana (Roman Peace), 158
Peace of Westphalia, 414
Peace Preservation Law of 1925, in Japan, 698
Peanuts, 500
Pearl Harbor, 702
Pearl River, 78
Peasants' Revolt, 272; Protestant Revolution and, 409
Pedra Furada, 107, *107*
Pedro I, 555
Pedro II, 555
Pedro IV, 452
Pelesets (Philistines), 42, 44–45
Peloponnesian War, 154
Peloponnesus Peninsula, 153
People's Liberation Army, of China, 701
People's War, in China, 700
Pepin III, "The Short," 255, 256
Pepper, *190*, 190–91
Perestroika, 740, 741–42
Periplus of the Erythrean Sea, 189
Perón, Isabel, 760
Perón, Juan, 719, 760
Peronism, 719
Perpetual Peace (Kant), 534
Perry, Matthew C., *588*, 589, 631
Persepolis, 152
Persia: arts of, 168–69; culture of, 168–69; empires of, 155–63; Greece and, 150–55; Ottoman Empire in, 377–79; recovery of, 162–63; religion in, 160; roads of, 152; Roman Empire and, 155–63, 222–23. *See also* Achaemenids; Parthians; Safavids; Sasanids
The Persians (Aeschylus), 170
Peru: Caral-Supe in, 101, 109, 134; coolies in, 570; independence of, 551; mercury in, 429; Moche Valley in, 134, 142–43; in NAM, 727; as nation-state, 558; Nazca of, 143–44, 146–47; Paracas in, 143–44; populism in, 719; rain forests of, 429; Shining Path in, 351; Spain and, 426–28, 557; Tiwanaku of, 355–56, *356*, 357*m*, 368; Wari of, 144, 357*m*, 357–58, 368. *See also* Inca
Peter I "The Great," 416, 613
Petrarch, Francesco, 276
Petronius, 276
Phallic stones, 62
Phan Boi Chau, 673
Pharisees, 166
Philip II, 155, 382, 383, 389, 412, 444
Philip IV, 259, 273
Philippine-American War, 670–71, *671*
Philippines: East Africa and, 133; nationalism in, 670; Spain and, 668–71; in World War II, 702
Philip VI, 272
Philistines (Pelesets), 42, 44–45
Philology, 397
Philosophy: in Byzantium, 247–48; of Enlightenment, 533–34; in Europe, 276; of Greece, 165; modernity in, 646; New Sciences and, 404–5; of realism, 545; of romanticism, 544–45; of Sufism, 244
Phoenicians (Canaanites), 44; alphabet of, *44*
Photography: for newspapers, 597; for realism, *546*
Physics, 168
Phytoliths, 131
Picasso, Pablo, 646, *647*
Pictures of the floating world (*ukiyo-e*), 518–19
Piedmont, 539
Piérola, Nicolás de, 558
Piers Plowman (Langland), 276
Pietism, 535
Pilgrimage (*hajj*), 226
Pillow Talk (Shonagon), 305
Pinochet, Augusto, 759
Pitaka, 185
Pizan, Christine de, 276
Pizarro, Francisco, 426–28
Plague. *See* Black Death
Plague of Justinian, 160–61
Planck, Max, 644
Plantagenet kings, of England, 259

Plantation slavery: in Americas, 439–40, 459–68; in Brazil, 439, 462; in Caribbean, 460–62; in Haiti, 529–30; slave revolts of, 470–71, 472*m*
Plant domestication: in Africa, 131; in Americas, 108; of corn, *112*, 112–13, 113*m*; in Fertile Crescent, 51–52; of rice, 66, 82. *See also specific crops*
The Platform of the Sixth Patriarch (Hui Neng), 215
Plato, 165, 248
PLO. *See* Palestine Liberation Organization
Plow, 260–61
Plymouth, 433
Poe, Edgar Allan, 545
Poetry: Islam and, 245; in Italy, 276; in Japan, 321, 518, 592; in Tang dynasty, 290; for women, 170
Poetry Classic. See Shijing
Pointed arches, on Gothic cathedrals, 269
Poland: Catholicism in, 712; in Cold War, 712; Communist Party in, 742; Marshall Plan and, 709; nationalism in, 712, 777; as nation-state, 740; Russia and, 614, 615; World War II in, 696–97
Politics and political parties: in England, 418–19; in Germany, 694; in Greece, 46–47; of Han dynasty, 203; in India, 689–90; in Japan, 595–96; in Mexico, 690; in Polynesia, 119; in Russia, 620; in Turkey, 780; in Vietnam, 324
Polo, Marco, 294
Pol Pot, 752
Polynesia, 119
Polytheism, 47–48; of Achaemenids, 152; breakdown of, 165; challenges to, 163–65; Judaism and, 166; of Maya, 137, 139; in Roman Empire, 159
Poma de Ayala, Felipe Guamán, 444
Pompeii, 171
Pompey, 158
Poopó, Lake, 356
Pop culture, 683
Popol Vuh, 444
Popular piety, 264–65
Population growth: in Africa, 784–85; in Caribbean, 718*m*; industrialization and, 635–36, 636*m*–37*m*; in Latin America, 718*m*
Populism: in Latin America, 718–19; of Tea Party movement, 776
Porcelain: in China, 208, 216, 502, 504–5, *505*; in Europe, 505; in Japan, 516; in Song dynasty, 299, *300*
Portugal: apocalypse and, 374; Brazil and, 428, 432–33, 554–55; China and, 507; colonialism by, 432–33; East Africa and, 665; Ethiopia and, 456–57; India and, 375, 486–87; Indian Ocean and, 383*m*; Japan and, 515; Ottoman Empire and, 382; *Reconquista* in, 372, 374; ships of, 379; slaves of, 456–59, *457*; Spain and, 669; spice trade of, 486; West Africa and, 456, 507
Positivism, 545, 556
Post-colonialism, 766
Postmodernism, 766
Potatoes, 108, 146; in Ming dynasty, 500
Potosí, 438, *439*
Pottery: at Chavín de Huántar, 110; in Jenné-jeno, 130, *130*; of Maya, 136; in Mesoamerica, 109; in Nazca, 143; of Olmec, 114. *See also* Porcelain
Powell, Adam Clayton, 726
Power loom, 627
Powhatan confederacy, 433–35
Prague Spring, 739–40
Predestination, 410
Prehistory. *See* Hominins; Neolithic Age; Paleolithic Age
Presentism, 460
PRI. *See* Institutional Revolutionary Party
Priest-rulers, of Olmec, 114
The Prince (Machiavelli), 397
Printing: in China, 216; in East Asia, 310–11; in Japan, 518–19; in Korea, 312–13; Protestant Reformation and, 407–8; in Renaissance, 396
Privateers, 431, 462, 465
Progressive era, in US, 543
Property rights: in Egypt, 37; in Hinduism, 191; in Mesopotamia, 36
Proskouriakoff, Tatiana, 139
Protestantism: in China, 583 2, 593; in New England, 444–46
Protestant Reformation, 407–11, 410*m*; Baroque arts and, 397
Proto-Indo-European language, 41
Proto-Mediterraneans, 60
Proxy wars, in Latin America, 759
Prussia, 417–18; Bismarck and, 539–40; in Franco-Prussian War, 539, 661; German Federation and, 538; military of, *418*; Poland and, 614
Psychoanalysis, 645
Ptolemaic kings, 166
Ptolemy, 244
Public Debt Administration, of Ottoman Empire, 607
Pueblo, 134, 352, 435
Pueblo Revolt, 559
Pulque, 140, 365
Puquios, 147
Pure Food and Drug Act, 543
Puritans, 413; in New England, 435, 444–45
Puruchuco, 351
Purusha, 70
Pu Songling, 511–12
Putin, Vladimir, 771–72
Pu-Yi, 700
Pygmies, 132
Pyramids: of Americas, 101, 109; of Egypt, 38–39, *39*; of Tenochtitlán, 364; in Teotihuacán, 141

Qaddafi, Muammar el-, 781
Qadesh, 42
Al-Qaeda, 770, 783
Qajars, 609–12
Qi, 298–99
Qianlong, 506, 506*m*, 511
Qin dynasty, in China, 201*m*, 201–3; Confucianism in, 213; First Emperor of, *202*, 202–3; gravesites of, 202, *202*; Korea and, 307, 577; unity under, 216; Vietnam and, 322–23; Zhou dynasty and, 201–2
Qing dynasty, in China, 503–12; Boxer Rebellion and, 587–88, 699; culture of, 592–93; economy of, 591–92; family in, 508–9, 592; Manchus and, 503; Mongols and, 505; opium in, 579–84, 580*m*; race for concessions in, 587, *587*; republicanism in, 699–700; science and technology in, 592–93; trade in, 507–8, *508*, 578–80
Qin Shi Huangdi (First Emperor), *202*, 202–3, 217
Quantum Theory, 644
Que, 77
Quetzalcoatl, 141
Queue edict, 503
Quipu, 109, 362
Quotations from Chairman Mao Zedong (Mao Zedong), 748
Quran, 227; in Iran, 755; ISIS and, 783; Muhammad in, 226

Race for concessions, in Qing dynasty, 587, *587*
Racism: from slavery, 474; against Slavs, 697; of South African apartheid, 757–58, 762–63, 785
Radical republicanism, in France, 527, 528
Radioactivity, 644
Radiocarbon dating: of Borana lunar calendar, 125; at Caral-Supe, 101; of spear (points), 19
Railroads: of Africa, 666–67; coolies and, 570; of India, 55; of Industrial Revolution, 627-28, 631; of Japan, 589, 594, *594*; Trans-Siberian, 590, 619; of US, 543, 628
Rain-forest kingdoms, of West Africa, 346
Rain forests: in Africa, 17, 130–31; of Amazon, 116, 369; in Americas, 103; in Australia, 17; Maya and, 136; in Mesoamerica, 354; of Peru, 429
Raj, 656–57
Rajputs, 479
Ramadan, 226

Ramadan War, 753–54
Ramayana, 67, 186
Rapa Nui (Easter Island), 118, 119, *122*, 122–23
Rape of Nanjing, 701–2
Raphael, 397
Al-Rashid, Harun, 257
Rastafarians, 334
Rayon, 631
Raziya, 284
Reagan, Ronald, 747–48
Realism, 545–46, *546*, 548
Reciprocity, 198, 358; of Aztec, 359–60; of Inca, 361–62; of Tiwanaku, 356
Reconquista, 265; in Portugal, 372, 374
Records of Ancient Matters (*Kojiki*), 321
The Records of the Grand Historian (*Shiji*) (Sima Qian), 214, 307
Red Eyebrow Revolt, 204–5
Redology (*hong xue*), 592
Red Sea: Ethiopia and, 335, 456; Meroë and, 129; Nubia and, 331
Re-education, in China, 720
Reformation. *See* Protestant Reformation
Reform War, of Mexico, 561
Regency, 480
Reiche, Maria, 146
Reichstag fire, 695
Reign of Terror, in French Revolution, 528
Relativity Theory, 644
Religion: in Africa, 451–52; in Caribbean, 117; of counterculture, 734; in Egypt, 52–53; in Harappa, 62; of Hittites, 42; in India, 68–73; in Japan, 319–20; in Korea, 312–13; of Meroë, 127; in Mesopotamia, 48; in Middle East, 26, 47–50; in Ming dynasty, 511–12; modernity in, 646; Mughals and, 484–85, *485*, 492–93, 495–96; in Persia, 160; schism in, 183; in Shang dynasty, 92–96; of slaves, 468–69; in Tichitt and Oualata, 126; of Umayyads, 223; in Zhou dynasty, 92–96. *See also* State religions; *specific religions or religion types*
Renaissance: arts of, 396–97, *399*; in Byzantium, 248; culture of, 394–421; *Donation of Constantine* and, 233; Harlem, 683, 686–87; humanism of, 276; maps of, 406–7; music in, 397; science and technology in, 398–405, 419–20; theater in, 397; of twelfth century, 277–78
Renewed imperialism, 651–75
Repartimiento (labor assignments), 425, 429; in Mexico, 431
Republicanism, 47; of Bolívar, 557; in France, 527, 528; in India, 194–95; in Qing dynasty, 699–700; in Roman Empire, 156
Responsibility system, in China, 749
Restoration monarchies, 536–40
Revivalism, 446
Revolt of the Sons, of Mughals, 482
Revolver, 634
Rhapta, 133–34
Rhind Mathematical Papyrus, 50
Rhodes, Cecil, 666
Rhodesia, 757
Ribbed vaults, on Gothic cathedrals, 269
Ricci, Matteo, 507
Rice: in Africa, 134; in Australia, 658; in China, 82; in Eucharist, 507; in India, 66; in Japan, 314, 315; in Ming dynasty, 500; in North America, 464–65; in Vietnam, 323
Richard I, 267
Rifled musket, 634
Rig-Veda, 63, 65, 70, 74
Rikyu, Sen-no, 320
Rio de Oro, 666
Rites Controversy, 507
Ritual (*li*), 199
Ritual pollution, 189
Ritual suicide (*hara-kiri*), 317
Rivera, Diego, 559, *559*
Rizal, José, 670
Roads: of Achaemenids, 152; of Andes, 108; of China, 202; of Inca, 363, *363*; of Japan, 593; of Persia, 152; of Qin dynasty, 202
The Road to Wigan Pier (Orwell), *684*
Roaring Twenties, 681
Rock art: in Africa, 47; in Americas, 107, *107*; in Australia, 47; of Australian Aboriginals, 2, *13*, 13–14; in Blombos Cave, 10, 10*m*; of Cro-Magnon, 2; in Eurasia, 14; in Europe, 15, *16*; of *Homo sapiens*, 24; of Neanderthals, 14–15, 20, *20*; on Sulawesi, Indonesia, 15
Rocky Mountains, 102
Roentgen, Wilhelm, 644
Roe v. Wade, 745
Rojdi, 61
Roma (Gypsies), 696
Roman Empire: ancient Ghana and, 341; architecture of, 171; arts of, 170–71; Christianity in, 159–61; imperial beginnings, 156–57; India and, 189; laws of, 162; legionaries of, 156–58; literature of, 170–71; Meroë and, 128; military of, 156–58; monotheism in, 158–60; nomads and, 161–63, 162*m*; paintings of, 171; Parthians and, 156–59; Persians and, 155–63, 222–23; polytheism in, 159; recovery of, 162; republicanism in, 156; Sasanids and, 149–50, 159–63, 222; sculpture in, 170–71; ships of, 378; silk and, 211; slaves of, 157–58; triumvirate of, 158; women in, 158–59
Romania: Congress of Berlin and, 607; democracy in, 742; in World War I, 679
Roman Inquisition, 399
Romanov dynasty, in Russia, 416
Roman Peace (*pax romana*), 158
Romanticism, 544–45, 548; modernity in, 646; in music, 647
Roosevelt, Franklin D., 684–85
Roosevelt, Theodore, 558
Rose Garden Edict, 606
Rouhani, Hasan, 779
Rousseau, Jean-Jacques, 533–34
Royal Society of London, 401, 403
Rubber: in Congo, 665; slaves for, 674; in Vietnam, 672; vulcanization of, 631
Rule of alternate attendance (*sankin kotai*), 514
Rumelia, 608
Rumi, Jalal al-Din, 245
Rus, 232, 234
Russia, 612–21; agriculture of, 616–17; in BRIC, 766; colonialism by, 660; Constantinople and, 616, 618; constitutionalism in, 613; in Crimean War, 616, 631, 661; economy of, 771–72; expansion of, 416–17, 417*m*, 615*m*; famine in, *617*; February Revolution in, 680; first Revolution of, 620–21; France and, 614; French Revolution and, 614; Great Britain and, 661; Greece and, 616; industrialization in, 618–20, 631; modernity and modernism in, 622; Napoleon Bonaparte in, 613, 614; novel in, 623; official nationality in, 614–15; Ottoman Empire and, 614, 616, 618; paintings in, *621*; Poland and, 614, 615; political parties in, 620; reforms in, 616–18; Serbia and, 777; serfdom in, 601, 616–17; Triple Intervention by, 590, 619; Venezuela and, 787. *See also* Soviet Union; World War I
Russian Revolution, first, *621*
Russo-Japanese War, 620
Russo-Ottoman War, 616, 618
Rutherford, Ernest, 644
Rwanda, 665; civil war in, 770

SA. *See Sturmabteilung*
Saadids, 377
Sacco, Nicola, 683
Sacraments, 274
El-Sadat, Anwar, 754
Sadler Report, 640
Safavids: in Iran, 377, 609–12; Mughals and, 483; Ottoman Empire and, 377, 383; Shiite Islam of, 377, 378–79
Sahel, 130, 341
Saints: in Catholicism, 444. *See also specific saints*
Saint-Simon, Henri de, 639–40
Saladin (Salah al-Din), 237, 267
Salem witch trials, 445, *445*
Salons, for New Sciences, 401–2
SALT II, 740

Salt March, 690, *690*
Same-sex marriage, 745
Samudragupta, 180
Samurai, 317, *318*, 514–15; in peacetime, 517–18
Sandinista National Liberation Front (FSLN), 759
Sandrokottos, 175
Sankin kotai (rule of alternate attendance), 514
San Lorenzo, 113–14
San Martín, José de, 552–53, 557
Santa Anna, Antonio López de, 559, 561
Sappho of Lesbos, 170
Sargon of Akkad, 27, 35
Sasanids: agriculture of, 228; Aksum and, 129–30; Arabs and, 222; architecture of, 169; India and, 168, 189; Roman Empire and, 149–50, 159–63, 222; as Zoroastrians, 149–50
Satori, 320, 327
Saul, 45
Savanna: of Africa, 130–31; hominins in, 5
Savery, Thomas, 632
Savior, of Zoroastrians, 164
Schism: in religion, 183; Western Schism, 273–74, 274*m*
Schmidt, Tobias, 531
Schoenberg, Arnold, 647
Scholasticism, 268
Schutzstaffel (SS), 696
Science and technology: of China, 584–85; of Han dynasty, 215–16; of High Middle Ages, 270; of India, 192–93; industrialization and, 644–46; of Japan, 584–85, 596–97; at Library of Alexandria, 168; of Middle East, 50; of Ming dynasty, 299, 509–11; of Mughals, 491–92; of Qing dynasty, 592–93; of Renaissance, 398–405, 419–20; of Song dynasty, 290; of Zhou dynasty, 95–96. *See also* New Sciences
Scientific management, 643
Scientific Revolution. *See* New Sciences
Scientific socialism, 640
Scotland: England and, 418; as nation-state, 544; New Lanark in, 640; Protestant Revolution in, 409
Scotus, John Duns, 276
Scramble for Africa, 663–67*m*
Sculpture: in Africa, 344–45, *345*; of bodhisattva, *192*; in Greece, 170; in Roman Empire, 170–71
SDI. *See* Strategic Defense Initiative
Sea People, from Greece, 42, 44, 46
Sebastião I, 459
Second Crusade, 236
Second Industrial Revolution, 628–34
Second Isaiah (Deutero-Isaiah), 163–64
Second Opium War, 583–84
Second Reform Act (England), 544
Second Temple, 164, 165
Secret History of the Mongols, 294
Securities and Exchange Commission (SEC), 684–85
Selective breeding, 30
Seleucids: Judaism and, 166; Parthians and, 156
Seleucus Nikator, 67, 175, 177
Self (*atman*), 72
Self-rule (*swaraj*), 689–90
Self-strengthening, 577, *584*, 584–85, 591; of Ottoman Empire, 608–9
Seljuk Turks: Byzantium and, 233–34; in Middle East, 265
Senegal, 666
Senghor, Léopold, 687
Sen-no Rikyu, 320
September 11, 2001 terrorist attack, 769, *770*
Serbia: Bosnia-Herzegovina and, 679; Congress of Berlin and, 607; Ottoman Empire in, 377, 608; supremacist nationalism of, 777
Serfdom, in Russia, 601, 616–17
Seveners, 228, 234
Seven Years' War, 437, 524, 526–27; British East India Company and, 652
Sewer systems: of Harappa, 59, 60; industrialization and, 641–42; of Tenochtitlán, 364; of Teotihuacán, 141
Sexuality: in India, 69–70. *See also* Homosexuals
Sexual revolution, 744–45
Shabab, 785
Shahinshahs, 152
Shah Jahan (Khurram), 483–84
Shahname (*Book of Kings*) (Firdosi), 168, 245
Shakas, 180
Shakespeare, William, 397
Shakti, 187
Shamans, 107, *107*; in Caribbean, 117
Shan, 482–83
Shangdi, 93, 94
Shang dynasty, in China, 77, *84*, 85*m*; agriculture of, 89; animal domestication in, 89; bronzes of, 86, 93; chariots in, 84–85, *86*; client states of, 85; culture of, 96; economy of, 89–90; family in, 89–90; gravesites in, 91–92, 94; human sacrifice in, 94; religion in, 92–96; *Shujing* on, 82, 84; social classes in, 89–90; trade in, 86; women in, 91–92; writing in, 93–95, *94*; Yellow River and, 77–78
Shanghai Communiqué, 749
Shapur II, 160
Sharecroppers, in Mesopotamia and Egypt, 32
Sharia Law, 227; in India, 486; Islamism and, 785; Sufism and, 244
Shaw, George Bernard, 646
Shi, 91
Shiite Islam, 227–28, 610–11; Hidden Imam of, 377; in Iran, 609, 755; of Mughals, 483; of Safavids, 377, 378–79; Seljuks and, 234
Shiji (*The Records of the Grand Historian*) (Sima Qian), 214, 307
Shijing (*The Book of Odes, Poetry Classic, The Book of Songs*), 92, 96, 98
Shikibu, Murasaki, 305, 321
Shining Path, in Peru, 351
Shinto (way of the gods), 315, 319–20
Ships: of China, 262; in colonialism, 658–59; of Genoa, 372; in Mediterranean, 378, 378–79, *379*; of Portugal, 372; for slave trade, 467, *467*; steam engine for, 627–28; sternpost rudder on, 262. *See also* Navy
Shiraz, 336
Shirin, 149–50
Shiva, 180, 186
Shoguns, 316–17, 512
Shonagon, Sei, 305
Shotoku (Prince), 315
Shudra, 70
Shujing (*Book of History, Classic of Documents*), 82, 83, 84, 87
Shun, 82
Siam. *See* Thailand
Sicily, 236; city-states in, 156; in Holy Roman Empire, 260; Norman Conquest of, 261
Sierra Madre Mountains, 102
Sikhism, 286; Mughals and, 486, 496–97
Silk: in China, 80–81, 208, 502; in India, 488; in Korea, 311; rayon and, 631
Silk Road, 78, 212*m*–13*m*, 242, 478; agricultural revolution and, 261; Black Death and, 243; in China, 203, 210–11; in India, 189; Mongols and, 275; Mughals and, 482; Parthians and, 156; in Tang dynasty, 289, 290; Xiongnu on, 203
Silla kingdom, in Korea, 308, 315
Silver: Achaemenids and, 152; in Americas, 438–39, *439*; in Bolivia, 429; at Chavín de Huántar, 110; coolies and, 570; of Inca, 426–28; Mauryans and, 179; in Mexico, 669; tax farming and, 385
Sima Qian, 214, 307
Sima Tan, 214
Single-whip tax system, of Ming dynasty, 502
Sinicization, 203–4, 322–23
Sino-Japanese War, *586*, 586–87
Sino-Soviet Split, 721
Sino-Tibetan language group, 81
Sioux, 435
Sirleaf, Ellen Johnson, 785
Sisi, Abdel Fattah, 782
Six-Day War, 752
Slater, Samuel, 628
Slave revolts: in Brazil, 566–67; in Cuba, 566–67; in Haiti, 523–24, 529–32, *530*; of plantation slavery, 470–71, 472*m*

Slaves and slavery: from Africa, 440, 461*m*, 473; in agrarian–urban society, 9; in Americas, 463*m*; as chattel, 460; culture of, *471*; from East Africa, 336; Islam and, 385; from Kongo, 459; in Middle East, 35; of Mongols, 309; music of, 470; of Native Americans, 429, 432; in North America, 464–65, *465*; from Nubia, 331; of Portugal, 456–59, *457*; racism from, 474; religions of, 468–69; of Roman Empire, 157–58; for rubber, 674; ships for, 467, *467*; social class of, 464; from sub-Saharan Africa, 452–59; from West Africa, 663. *See also* Abolition of slavery; Plantation slavery

Slavs: Byzantium and, 376; pan-Slavism and, 617–18, 679; racism against, 697; Varangians and, 232

Sleeping sickness, 132

Smallpox, 424, 426, 431, 435, 442

Smriti, 69

Smith, Adam, 534, 539

Smith, Ian, 757

SNSs. *See* Social networking sites

Soccer, 642

Social classes: in Americas, 109, 440–43; in China, 203; in Europe, 263; in Greece, 46; in Harappa, 61; of Inca, 362; in India, 69, 70–71; industrialization and, 637–39; in Korea, 310, 312; of Maya, 137–38; in Middle East, 35–38; in Ming dynasty, 297; of Neolithic China, 81; in Shang dynasty, 89–90; of slaves, 464; Vedas and, 182; in Xia dynasty, 83; in Zhou dynasty, 91. *See also* Caste system; Middle class

Social contract, 404–5; after World War II, 716

Social Contract (Rousseau), 533–34

Social Darwinism, 645; colonialism and, 674

Socialism: in China, 701; in India, 725, 726–27; industrialization and, 639–40; in Latin American proxy wars, 759; in North Korea, 792–93; scientific, 640; in Sri Lanka, 707; in Venezuela, 787. *See also* Communism

Social networking sites (SNSs), *786*, 786–87

Social Security Act, 684

Social stratification: in China, 84; in Jenné-jeno, 130; of Maya, 136

Society of Friends of Blacks, 523

Society of the Harmonious Fists, 588

Soga clan, 315

Solidarity, in Poland, 740, 742

Solomon, 45

Solomonid dynasty, in Ethiopia, 334

Somalia, 666; civil war in, 785; Italy and, 694; *jihad* in, 785

Somoza García, Anastasio, 759

Song dynasty, in China: bureaucracy in, 290; gunpowder in, *292*, 292–93; Mongols and, 291; Neo-Confucianism in, 290; porcelain in, 216, 299, *300*; women in, 218

Songhay Empire, 452–54

Soninke, 341, 342

Sonno joi, 589

Sons of Liberty, 525

Sophocles, 170

Soseki, Natsume, 597

Sot-weed. *See* Tobacco

South Africa, 757–58, *758*, 762–63, 785; Netherlands and, 459

South America: climate of, 103; colonialism in, 430*m*. *See also* Andes; *specific countries*

South Asia, migrations to Australia, 10–14

South Carolina, 464

Southeast Asia, 322*m*; colonialism in, 586–87, 667–73, 669*m*; India and, 189; nation-states in, 728–7729; trade in, 489*m*; in World War II, 702

Southern Africa: agrarian–urban centers of, 131–34; kingdoms in, 337–40

Southern characters (*chu nom*), 325

Southern Cone, 552

South India, kingdoms of, 180–81

Soviet Union: Afghanistan and, 737, *737*, 740–41; agriculture of, 693, *693*; Angola and, 757; Balkans and, 708; China and, 719, 721, 738, 748; civil war in, 692–93; Communist Party in, 691–92; decline of, 738–42, 742*m*; Germany and, 708; industrialization in, 693; Israel and, 722; modernity in, 691–92; Prague Spring and, 739–40; Vietnam and, 729; in World War II, 697. *See also* Cold War

Spain: American Revolution and, 527; Aztec and, 359, 424–26; in Caribbean, 424; Catholic Reformation in, 411; colonialism by, 428–32, 434–28; Gibraltar and, 262; Habsburgs in, 380; Inca and, 426–28, *444*; Islam in, 265; Mexico and, 424–26; Morisco expulsion from, 384; Netherlands and, 412, 667; in North Africa, 377; Peru and, 426–28, 557; Philippines and, 668–71; Portugal and, 669; Pueblo Revolt and, 559; Rio de Oro and, 666

Spanish-American War, 670–71

Spanish Civil War, 696

"Spanish Flu," 681

Spanish Inquisition, 374

Sparta, 46, 47, 152–54

Spartacus, 158

Spears (points): in Americas, 105–6, 107; radiocarbon dating of, 19

Spencer, Herbert, 645

Spice trade, 130; for black pepper, *190*, 190–91; Netherlands and, 667; of Portugal, 486; Spain and, 669

Spinning jenny, 627

Spinning mule, 627

Spinoza, Baruch, 404

Sports, industrialization and, 642

Spring and Autumn Chronicles, 87

Sputnik, 713–14, *714*

Squinches, 169

Sri Lanka (Ceylon): Cholas in, 283; in NAM, 707, 724; as nation-state, 724

Srivijaya, 283

SS. *See Schutzstaffel*

Stagflation, 747

Stalin, Joseph, 697, 708; death of, 712; Khrushchev and, 721, 738; Marshall Plan and, 709; Tito and, 709

Stamp Act, 525–26

Standard of Ur, 27

Standard Oil Company, 642–43

Stanley, Henry Morton, 665

START. *See* Strategic Arms Reduction Talks/Treaty

Star Wars. *See* Strategic Defense Initiative

State religion, 174; in Aksum, 129; Calvinism as, 411; in China, 196, 315; Christianity as, 249; of Italy, 692; monotheism as, 159, 163; of Roman Empire, 327; of Safavids, 493; Zoroastrianism as, 249

Steam engine, 403; in China, *581*; for ships, 627–28; for textile industry, 627

Steel: big business in, 642–43; in second Industrial Revolution, 630

Sterilization, of women, 684

Sternpost rudder, 262

Stirrups, *206*, 206–7

Stoics, 166

Stonewall Inn, 745, *745*

Strait of Gibraltar, 262

Strait of Tiran, 723

Strange Tales from the Make-Do Studio (Pu Songling), 511–12

Strategic Arms Reduction Talks/Treaty (START), 740

Strategic Defense Initiative (SDI, Star Wars), 741

Stream of consciousness, 683

Striation, 306

Stuart monarchs, of England, 412–13

Sturmabteilung (SA), 696

Subaltern, 657

Subatomic particles, 644

Subconscious, 645

Sub-Saharan Africa: agrarian–urban centers of, 130–31, 132*m*; Americas and, 145; chiefdoms of, 146; city-states of, 146; communism in, 784; history of, 134; Islam in, 454–55; kingdoms of, 146, 454*m*; nation-states in, 732; slaves from, 452–59

Sudan: Great Britain and, 662; UN in, 770–71

Suez Canal, 662, 688–89, 723–24

Suffragettes, 641, *641*

Sufism, 482, 493; Sunni Islam and, 243–44, 250–51

Sugarcane: in Australia, 658; in Brazil, 462; in Canary Islands, 372; in Caribbean, 460–62, 569; coolies and, 570; in Ming dynasty, 500; in North America, 464–65

Suger, Abbot, 269

Sui, 205; Tang dynasty and, 287
Suiko, 315, 319
Sukarno, 707
Süleyman I, "The Magnificent," 377, 386
Sultanates, of north India, 286, 286*m*
Sumer, Sumerian, 34–37, *34*, 48
Summa Theologica (Aquinas), 269
Summer of love, 745
Sundiata, 344, 348–49
Sungbo's Eredo, 346
Sunna, 226, 227
Sunni Islam, 227, 610–11; in Afghanistan, 379; in Egypt, 237; ISIS and, 783; of Ottoman Empire, 377; Sufism and, 243–44, 250–51
Sun Yat-sen, 699
Sun Zi, 67
Supremacist nationalism, 693–98, 704; of Serbia, 777
Surinam, 471
Sustainability, 788–90
Swahili, city-states of, 134, 336, 338*m*, 665
Swaraj (self-rule), 689–90
Swastika, 62
Sweden: Protestant Revolution in, 409; sterilization of women in, 684; Thirty Years' War and, 414
Switzerland: Calvinism in, 409–11; Protestant Revolution in, 409
Sykes-Picot agreement, 688
Syllabary, 305, 321
Sylvester II, 267
Symbols: in Harappa, 62; of *Homo sapiens*, 9–10; modernity in, 646; of Neanderthals, 14
Symphonie fantastique (Berlioz), 545
Synagogues, 166; on Euphrates River, *167*
Syria: Abbasids in, 225; Achaemenids and, 151; Arabs in, 222; Arab Spring in, 781–83; Assyrians and, 43; civil war in, 778; Israel and, 738; Jacobite Church in, 167; Judaism in, 163; in Lebanese civil war, 754–55; Ottoman Empire and, 605; in Six-Day War, 753; Treaty of Kadesh and, 42; in United Arab Republic, 724; Syriac Orthodox Church, 149–50

Taejo, 308
Taif Agreement, 755
Taiho Code, 315
Taika (Great Reform), 315
Tailor's Rebellion, 567
Taíno, 117, 424–25
Taiping Rebellion (Qing dynasty), 582–83, 583*m*
Taiping tianguo (Heavenly Kingdom of Great Peace), 583
Taisho Democracy (Japan), 698
Taiwan: Aboriginals of, 118; Austronesian language on, 81; Japan and, 619; Lapita from, 100; Qing dynasty and, 577
Taj Mahal, 477, *477*, 494
Takauji, Ashikaga, 316–17
Taklamakan Desert, 78
Takrur, 342
Tale of Genji (*Genji Monagatori*) (Shikibu), 305, 321
Taliban, 770
Tambo, Oliver, 762
Tamerlane (Timur-i-Lang), 285, 376, 478–79, 479*m*
Tamils, 180
Tang dynasty, in China, 206–7; Buddhism in, 287–90, 302; bureaucracy in, 289; gender relations in, 211; music in, *289*; nomads in, 291; poetry in, 290; porcelain in, 216; ships of, 379; Silk Road in, 289, 290; Sui and, 287; trade in, 290; Vietnam and, 325; women in, 218
Tantra, 187
Tanzania, 134, 665
Tanzimat, 606
Tariffs, 628; in India, 188
Tatars, 614
Tatsukichi, Minobe, 677
Tawantinsuyu, 360
Taxes: of Aksum, 129; American Revolution and, 525–26; of Aztec, 365; of centralized kingdoms, 406–7; of France, 416; French Revolution and, 527; of India, 188, 286, 654; of Korea, 308; of Manchus, 503; of Mauryans, 176, 179; of Ming dynasty, 502; of Mughals, 488; of Nubia, 331; of Roman Empire, 159; of US, 776; of Zhou dynasty, 90–91. *See also* Tariffs
Tax farming, 242, 385–86
Taxila, 175, 176
Tea: ceremony, 320; from China, 290, 317, 320, 502; Stamp Act on, 525–26; in Tang dynasty, 290; in Vietnam, 672
Tea Party movement, 776
Technology. *See* Science and technology
Tecumseh, 542–43
Telegraph, 633–34; in Japan, 589, 594
Telephone, 634; in Japan, 594
Temples: in Egypt, 33; in Greece, 46; of Hinduism, 180; in Jerusalem, 151; of Maya, 136, *136*; in Mesopotamia, 48; in Moche Valley, 142; of Nubia, 126; of Roman Empire, 171; in Teotihuacán, 141, *143*; of Zoroastrians, *164*
Tenements, 639, *640*
Ten Hours Act, 641
Tennessee Valley Authority, 684
Tenochtitlán, 359, 364–65, 365*m*, 368; Cortés in, 426
Tenskwatawa, 542–43
Tent government (*bakufu*), 514
The Ten Thousand Leaves (*Man'yoshu*), 321
Teosinte, 108
Teotihuacán, 134, 140–41, *143*, 352–55
Tesla, Nikola, 631–33
Tet Offensive, 751
Texas, 561
Texcoco, Lake, 140
Textile industry: in China, 627; in Germany, 665; in Great Britain, 639; in India, 627; in Ottoman Empire, 609; steam engine for, 627; in US, 625, 628
Thackeray, William Makepeace, 546
Thailand (Siam), 672
Thales, 165
Thar (Great Indian) Desert, 57
Thatcher, Margaret, 747–48
Theater: of Habsburgs, 390–91; in Japan, 518, 597; in Ottoman Empire, 388; in Renaissance, 397; after World War II, 716
Themata, 229
Theogony (Hesiod), 170
Theory of Relativity, 644
Theravada, 185; Vietnam and, 324–25
Thermidorean Reaction, 748
Third Coalition, 614
Third Crusade, 237, 267
Third estate, 527
Third Reich, 696
Third Republic, in France, 540, 548–49
Third Section, 615
Thirty Years' War, 413–15
Three Kingdoms: of China, 205; of England, 413; of Korea, 307–8
Thunberg, Greta, 790
Tiamat, 49
Tiananmen Square, 749, *749*, 750
Tiantai, 215
Tibet: in Qing dynasty, 505; in Yuan dynasty, 292
Tichitt, 126–27
Tigris River, 28, 31; Assyrians and, 43; Sasanids and, 228
Tikal, 135, 136
Timbuktu, 345, 377; Songhay Empire and, 453
Timurids, 479, 487
Timur-i-Lang (Tamerlane), 285, 376, 478–79, 479*m*
Titicaca, Lake, 355–56
Tito, Josip Broz, 708–9, 777
Tituba, 445
Tiwanaku, 355–56, *356*, 357*m*, 368; Wari and, 357–58
Tlaxcala, 359, 425
TNT, 634
Toba, 205
Tobacco, 464; in Ming dynasty, 500
Tocharian, 84
Tokugawa. *See* Ieyasu, Tokugawa
Toledo, 236
Tolkien, J. R. R., 25
Toltec, 352–55
Tombs. *See* Gravesites
Topkapı Palace, 377, 387–88, *388*

Tories, 419
Torricelli, Evangelista, 403
Total war, in World War I, *678*, 679
Toumaï skull, 4
Tour de France, 642
Toussaint Louverture, François-Dominique, 532
Trade: in Afro-Eurasian world commercial system, 241–42, 242*m*; by Aksum, 128, 130; in Andes, 110; by Athens, 153; by China, 502, 502*m*; in Egypt, 39; in Eurasia, 285*m*; in Europe, 261–62, 275; in Ghana, 341; global balance of, 768*m*; in Greece, 46; by Harappa, 61; by India, 188–89, 489*m*, 489–90; in Mali, 342–43; on Mediterranean, 261–62, 262*m*; in Mesopotamia, 32–33; in Ming dynasty, *504*, 504*m*, 504–5, *505*; by Minoans, 41; in northeast Africa, 331, 332*m*; by Olmec, 114; by Phoenicians, 44; in Qing dynasty, 507–8, *508*, 578–80; in Shang dynasty, 86; in Southeast Asia, 489*m*; in Tang dynasty, 290; by Toltec, 354; in Vietnam, 324; in Zhou dynasty, 91. *See also* Exports; Silk Road
Trade forts: for African slave trade, 457; of Netherlands and Portugal, 667–68; of Spain, 669
Trade winds, 103–5
Trail of Tears, 543
Tran dynasty, in Vietnam, 323
Transcendence, 163, 172; in Being, 165; Buddhism and, 184; Daoism and, 200; Jainism and, 184; in Sufism, 244; in Upanishads, 182
Trans-Siberian Railroad, 590, 619
Treaty of Brest-Litovsk, 680
Treaty of Kadesh, 42
Treaty of Kanagawa, 589
Treaty of Nanjing, 580, 581
Treaty of Paris, 273
Treaty of Shimonoseki, 577
Treaty of Verdun, 257
Treaty of Versailles, 681, 694
Tres Zapotes, 114
Tribute system: of Ming dynasty, 309; of Neo-Confucianism, 521
Trinitarianism, 223
Tripitaka, 185, 312
Triple Intervention, 590, 619
Tripolitania. *See* Libya
Triumvirate, of Roman Empire, 158
Trotsky, Leon, 691
Truman, Harry S, 702
Truman Doctrine, 708–9
Trump, Donald, 776, 780, 790
Trung Nhi, 323
Trung Trac, 323
Tsar (czar), 416; collapse of, 680
Tsetse fly, 132
Tughluq, Muhammad, "The Bloody," 286
Tulans, 352
Tundra, 18
Tunisia, 156; Arab Spring in, 780–82; France and, 662–63; Ottoman Empire and, 608
Túpac Amaru, 351
Turkana steppe, 5
Turkey, *781*; Great Britain and, 689, *689*; industrialization in, 780
Turkistan, 163
Turks: Abbasids and, 228; Byzantium and, 376. *See also* Ottoman Empire; Seljuk Turks
Turner, Nat, 471
Tutankhamen, *43*, 53
Tutenkhaten, 53
Tuxen, Laurits Regner, *619*
Twelve Tablets, of Roman Empire, 156
Twelve-tone music, 647
Tzompantii, 366–67

Ubaid, 31, 48
Uji, 318
Ukiyo-e (pictures of the floating world), 518–19
Ukraine: Chernobyl nuclear accident in, 742; Russia and, 772; Soviet Union and, 691
Ulama, 227
Umar, Al-Hajj, 664–65
Umayyads, 261; Abbasids and, 224; Byzantium and, 229; religion of, 223
Umma, 226
UN. *See* United Nations
Unction, 255
Union of German Women's Organizations, 641
Union of Soviet Socialist Republics. *See* Soviet Union
United Arab Republic, 724
United Nations (UN), 708; Charter of, 534; China in, 749; Iran and, 779; Iraq and, 770; North Korea and, 792–93; Palestine and, 721–22; peacekeeping by, 770–71
United States (US): abolition of slavery in, 541; Afghanistan and, 770; big business in, 642–43; capitalist democracy of, 766–74; China and, 749; civil rights movement in, 744–45; consumerism in, 681–83; Dawes Plan of, 695; dollar regime of, 767, 771; early years of, 526; economy of, 771, 776–77; exports to, 768; globalization and, 768–69; in Great Depression, 684–85; industrialization in, 628; Iran hostage crisis and, 756; Iraq and, 769–70; ISIS and, 783; IT in, 768–69; Japan and, 589; Korea and, 711–12; in Latin American proxy wars, 759; McCarthyism in, 712; in Mexican-American War, 588; Mexico and, 560–61, 561*m*, 776; military of, 769; modernity in, 681; as nation-state, 540–44, 542*m*; Native Americans in, *542*, 542–43; in 1970s and 1980s, 747–48; Ottoman Empire and, 606; in Philippine-American War, 670–71, *671*; Progressive era in, 543; railroads in, 543, 628; security commitments of, 772*m*–73*m*; in Spanish-American War, 670–71; taxes in, 776; textile industry in, 625, 628; Vietnam and, 729; in Vietnam War, 750–52, 751*m*; women in, 681–83; women's suffrage in, 641; in World War II, 697–98, 702. *See also* Cold War; World War I
United States Steel Corporation, 643
Universal love, 218
Universal Negro Improvement Association, 687
Universities, in High Middle Ages, 267–69
Untouchables, 70
Upanishads, 72, 182
Urania propitia (*Companion to Urania*) (Cunitz), 395
Urban II, 234, 265
Urbanization (urbanism): in Caribbean, 718*m*; in East Africa, 336–37; in Europe, 263; in India, 725, 783; industrialization and, 635–36; in Latin America, 717, 718*m*; of Maya, 355; in Mexico, 690. *See also* Cities, city-states
Urban VI, 274
Uruguay, 552–54
Uruk, 33
Urukagina of Lagash, 36
US. *See* United States
Usulism, 611
Usury, 410
Utamaro, Kitagawa, 519
Utari, 313

Vacuum, 402–3, *403*
Vaishyas, 70
Valencia, 384
Vanity Fair (Thackeray), 546
Vanzetti, Bartolomeo, 683
Varangians, 231–32, *233*, 234–35; as mercenaries, 241
Varnas, 69, 70, 71
Vatsyayana, 69–70, 192
Vedanta, 72
Vedas, 64–67; Hinduism and, 70–73; reformers of, 182–87
Venezuela: caudillo in, 557–58; colonialism of, 438; democracy in, 718, 719; in NAM, 727; oil in, 719, 787; populism in, 719; socialism in, 787
Venus figurines, 15, *15*, 47
Vernacular, 276
Veronese, Paolo, *384*
Versailles Palace, 398, *414*
Versailles Treaty, 681, 694, 700
Vesuvius, Mount, 171
Vichy government, 697
Victor Emanuel II, 539

Victoria, Lake, 31, 455
Vietcong, 729, 750, 751
Vietminh, 729
Vietnam: agrarian–urban centers in, 321–22; agriculture of, 323–24; Buddhism in, 321–22, 324–25; China and, 748, 752; communism in, 750–52, 775; culture of, 323; economy of, 323–24; France and, 671–73, 729; Japan and, 326; Korea and, 326; Mongols in, 243; as nation-state, 724, 729; Neolithic Age in, 321; US and, 729; writing in, 325; in Yuan dynasty, 292
Vietnam Restoration League, 673
Vietnam War, 750–52, 751*m*
Vijayanagar ("City of Victory"), 283
Vikings, 257
Villa, Francisco "Pancho," 563–64
Vinaya, 185
Viracocha, 360
Virgil, 170, 171, *171*
Virgin Mary, 444, 494
Vishnu, 180, 186
Visigoths, 223
Vivaldi, Antonio, 398
VOC. *See* Dutch United East India Company
Volga trade route, 242
Voltaire, 402; Catherine I "The Great" and, 613
Voodoo, 115, *168*, 468–69
Voting rights: of African Americans, 542; Chartism and, 640; of women, 641, 681, 689
Voting Rights Act of 1965, 744
Vulcanization of rubber, 631

Wagner, Richard, 647
Waldseemüller, Martin, *400*
Wales, 544
Wałęsa, Lech, 740, 742
Wang Anshi, 290–91
Wang Chong, 216
Wang Mang, 204–5
Wang Yangming, 299, 511
Wari, 144, 357*m*, 357–58, 368
War on Terror, 769
Warring States period, in China, 89, 197; Confucianism in, 213; Xunzi and, 200
Warsaw Pact, 711, 713; Brezhnev Doctrine of, 740
Washington, George, 526
Washington Consensus, 771, 775
Water frame, 627
Watermills, 261
Watt, James, 632
Way (*Dao*), 198, 299
Way of the Warrior (*bushido*), 317, 327
Al-Wazzan, al-Hasan Ibn Muhammad (Leo Africanus ["the African"]), 371
Weapons: in Cold War, 713–14; in second Industrial Revolution, 634. *See also* Cannons; Firearms; Nuclear weapons
Weapons of mass destruction, in Iraq, 770
Weimar Republic, 694–95
Wei Yuan, 592
Well-field system, in Zhou dynasty, 90–91
Wells, 261
Wen Bo, 92
Wesley, Charles, 446
Wesley, John, 446
West Africa: colonialism in, 663–65; gold in, 374, 377; Islam in, 348; kingdoms in, 341–46, 343*m*; Portugal and, 456, 507
Western Christianity: adaptation of, 248, 252–79; centralized kingdoms and, 405; in Constantinople, 234, 270–76; Eastern Christianity and, 233; evolution of, 249–50; expansion of, 370–92; formation of, 254–58; heresy in, 265; papacy in, 255; popular piety in, 264–65; recovery of, 259–63; reform of, 264–67
Western Schism, 273–74, 274*m*
What Is to Be Done? (Chernyshevsky), 623; (Lenin), 623
Wheat: in Americas, 439; in Nubia, 331
Wheel, 108, 121, 146; of *dharma*, 192
Whigs, 419
Whitefield, George, 446
"The White Man's Burden" (Kipling), 674
Wilhelm I, 539
William I, 259, 264
William of Ockham, 276
William of Orange, 668
Wilson, Woodrow, 680
Windmills, 261
Winstanley, Gerrard, 420–21
Wireless telegraph, 634
Witchcraft: in Africa, 133, 451; in New England, 445, *445*
Women: in Americas, 441; in Athens, 173; of Australian Aboriginals, 12; in China, 98–99, 217–18; civil rights for, 744–45, 746*m*, 746–47; in Egypt, 37–38; Equal Rights Amendment (ERA), 746–47; in Greece, 154; in Han dynasty, 211; of Inca, 365–66; in India, 69–70; industrialization and, 641; in Japan, 318–19, 517; in Korea, 312; in Latin America, 572; in Mesopotamia, 36–37; in Ming dynasty, 298, 509; in mining, 639, *639*; of Mughals, 490–91; New Sciences and, 401–2; of Ottoman Empire harems, 388; poetry for, 170; in Roman Empire, 158–59; in Shang dynasty, 91–92; in Song dynasty, 218; sterilization of, 684; in Tang dynasty, 218; in US, 681–83; in Vietnam, 324; voting rights of, 641, 681, 689; in Zhou dynasty, 92
Women Journalists Without Chains, 765
Women's Social and Political Union, 641
Woodstock Festival, 745
Working class: industrialization and, 639, *640*; in Venezuela, 787
The Works of Mencius (Legge), 197
World Trade Center, 769, *770*
World War I: empires and, 677–81; Gatling guns in, 634; modernity and, 677–81, 704; nationalism and, 645; total war in, *678*, 679; Turkey and, 689
World War II: culture after, 715–16; in Europe, 696–98, 699*m*; in France, 696–97; Great Britain in, 697–98; Japan in, 702; Nazi Germany in, 696–98, 704–5; in Pacific Ocean, 702, 703*m*; in Poland, 696–97; Soviet Union in, 697; US in, 697–98, 702
Wounded Knee, 543, 744
Wright, Richard, 726
Wright brothers, 633
Writing: of Achaemenids, 152; in China, 202, 204; cuneiform, 34, *34*; in Harappa, 62; in Korea, 312; of Maya, 136, 139, *140*; of Minoans, 39; of Olmec, 115; of Phoenicians, 44; in Shang dynasty, 93–95, *94*; in Vietnam, 325; in Zhou dynasty, 93–95, *94*. *See also* Calligraphy; Hieroglyphic writing
Writs, 260
Wu (Empress), 290, *290*, 302–3
Wudi (Martial Emperor), 156, 203–4; Vietnam and, 323
Wu Ding, 77, 85, 93
Wu Sangui, 503
Wycliffe, John, 274

Xavier, Francis, 507
Xesspe, Toribio Mejia, 146
Xia dynasty, in China: culture of, 96; *Shujing* on, 82, 83; Yellow River and, 80
Xiang, 197
Xiaojing (*Classic of Filial Piety*), 214
Xiongnu, 179, 202, 203
X-rays, 644
Xuan Zang, 214–15, 282–83
Xunzi, 199–200
Xu Qinxian, 750

Yahweh, 163–64, 166
Yam, 470
Yamato, 314, 315
Yang, 299
Yang Jian, 205
Yangshao period, in Xia dynasty, 83
Yang Zhu, 218
Yangzi River, 78

Yanukovych, Viktor, 772
Yao, 82
Yasht, 160, 164
Yayoi period (Japan), 314
Yellow fever, 663
Yellow River, 78–83; agriculture and, 96; Shang dynasty and, 77–78
Yeltsin, Boris, 742
Yemen, 129, 133–34; Arab Spring in, 781; civil war in, 765; coffee in, 382; Persia and, 163
Yi dynasty, in Korea, 309–11
Yin, 299
Yoga, 72
Yom Kippur War, 753–54
Yongban, 312
Yongle, 296–97
Yongzheng, 504, 507, 511
Yoritomo, Minamoto, 316
Yoruba, 756
Younger Dryas, 30, 106
Young Ottomans, 607
Yu, 80, 82
Yuan dynasty, in China, 291–95; Mongols and, 309, 478; novel in, 300
Yuan Shikai, 699–700
Yucatán Peninsula: Maya in, 135*m*, 135–41, 354–55, *355*; Teotihuacán in, 352–55
Yuezhi, 179
Yugoslavia: civil war in, 777; in Cold War, 708–9; in NAM, 707, 724

Zacatecas, 438
Zacuto, Abraham, 406
Zaghlul, Saad, 689
Zagwe dynasty, in Ethiopia, 333–34
Zaibatsu (cartels), 593–94, 698
Zaire. *See* Congo
Zanzibar, 134, 665
Zapata, Emiliano, *464*, 563–64
Zemstvos, 617
Zen Buddhism, 215, 320, 327
Zeng Guofan, 585
Zengi, Imad al-Din, 236
Zeppelin, Ferdinand von, 633
Zeus, 170
Zhang Heng, 215–16
Zhang Zuolin, 700
Zheng He, 296, 337
Zhou dynasty, in China, 87*m*; agriculture of, 90; culture of, 96; economy of, 90–91; feudalism in, 88–89; government in, 90, 97; hegemony in, 88–89; iron in, 95–96; Korea and, 307; Qin dynasty and, 201–2; religion in, 92–96; science and technology of, 95–96; *Shujing* on, 82, 87; social classes in, 91; trade in, 91; Vietnam and, 321–22; western and eastern, 88; women in, 92; writing in, 93–95, *94*
Zhu Xi, 299
Zhu Yuanzhang (Hongwu), 296, 297, 309
Zimbabwe, 349–50, 756–57
Zionism, 688
Zoroastrians, *164*, 164–65; Achaemenids as, 152; in Byzantium, 278; Islam and, 226; Sasanids as, 149–50; as state religions, 249; Sufism and, 243; Yasht of, 160, 164
Zulu, 131, 757